INTERNET INFORMATION SERVICES (IIS) 6.0

The Microsoft IIS Team

PUBLISHED BY
Microsoft Press
A Division of Microsoft Corporation
One Microsoft Way
Redmond, Washington 98052-6399

Library of Congress Cataloging-in-Publication Data
    Internet Information Services (IIS) 6.0 Resource Kit / the Microsoft IIS Team.
        p. cm.
    Includes index.
    ISBN 0-7356-1420-2
    1. Microsoft Internet information server. 2. Microsoft Windows server. 3.
Internet--Computer programs. 4. Web servers. I. Microsoft IIS Team.

    TK5105.875.I57I5565   2003
    005.7'13769--dc21   2003056127

Printed and bound in the United States of America.

1 2 3 4 5 6 7 8 9   QWT   8 7 6 5 4 3

Distributed in Canada by H.B. Fenn and Company Ltd.

A CIP catalogue record for this book is available from the British Library.

Microsoft Press books are available through booksellers and distributors worldwide. For further information about international editions, contact your local Microsoft Corporation office or contact Microsoft Press International directly at fax (425) 936-7329. Visit our Web site at www.microsoft.com/mspress. Send comments to *rkinput@microsoft.com*.

Acquisitions Editor: Martin DelRe
Project Editor: Maureen Williams Zimmerman

Body Part No. X08-22441

Contents at a Glance

Contents

Acknowledgments

Microsoft would like to thank the following people for their contributions:

Part 1

Book Lead: Sharon Slade

Writers: Suzanne Girardot, John Meade, Doug Steen

Part 2

Book Lead: John Meade

Writers: Jim Brotherton, Ryan Kivett, Abe Klagsbrun, John Meade, Melissa Pearlstein, Thelma Warren

Tools

Program Manager: Alexis Eller

Development Team: Chris Adams, Faith Allington, Raymond Benedict, Tudor Baraboi, Roger Brady, Riccardo Cerchier, David Cox, Bruno K. Da Costa, Bhavesh Doshi, Cindy Du, Jaroslav Dunajsky, Pat Filoteo, Gabriele Giuseppini, Ciprian Gociman, Wade Hilmo, Rick James, Jeff Johnson, Jeff Kercher, Jihyun Kim, Uladzimir Malashanka, Ram Papatla, Sam Patton, Lubdha Puranik, Peter Schenk, Jemearl Smith, Nikolaj Stam, Ryan Steffen, David Wang, Ivo Zheglov

Writers: Jim Brotherton, John Meade, Melissa Pearlstein

Editors and Legal Reviewers: Nona Allison, Noel Anderson, Lara Ballinger, Ann Becherer, Shannan Frisbie, Chris Meyers, Janet Micka, Anika Nelson, Dee Teodoro

IIS 6.0 Resource Kit

Kit Lead: Sharon Slade

Kit Editor: Lara Ballinger

Documentation Manager: Pilar Ackerman

Writing Managers: David Mills, Louise Rudnicki

Editing Managers: Chris Clements, Laura Graham, Jay Schram, Ken Western

Editors: Nona Allison, Lara Ballinger, Ann Becherer, Jim Becker, Bonnie Birger, Dale Callison, Alexandra Coury, Laura Graham, Janet Micka, Anika Nelson, Dee Teodoro, Scott Turnbull, Thelma Warren

Lab Management: Todd Bryan-White, Brent Hatfield, David Meyer, Shaun Searcy, Robert Thingwold, Frank Zamarron

Project Managers: Clifton Hall, Paulette McKay, Neil Orint

Publishing Team: Barbara Arend, Eric Artzt, Jim Bevan, Jon Billow, Chris Blanton, Eric Camplin, Julie Geren, Marina Hayrapetyan, Jason Hershey, Heather Klauber, Richard Min, Thomas Moore, Patrick Ngo, Rochelle Parry, Mark Pengra, Steve Pyron, Ben Rangel, Gino Sega, Amy Shear, Karla van der Hoeven, Gabriel Varela, Erica Westerlund, Matt Winberry

Indexing Team: Stephanie Marr, David Pearlstein, Lee Ross, Tony Ross

Technical Reviewers: Chris Achille, Chris Adams, Bilal Alam, Faith Allington, Allen Atwood, Simon Attwell, Tudor Baraboi, Roger Brady, Brett Brewer, Jim Brotherton, Mike Brown, Riccardo Cerchier, Thomas Christmann, Dan Conley, Steve Connor, Bruno K. Da Costa, Judy Cowan, David Cox, Dean Cron, Jeff Cruzan, Andrew Cushman, Rayner D'Souza, Joseph Davies, Eric Deily, Thomas Deml, Nick Diaz, Bhavesh Doshi, Cindy Du, Jaroslav Dunajsky, Richard Edwards, Alexis Eller, Richard Ersek, Pat Filoteo, Gabriele Giuseppini, Ciprian Gociman, Susan Hill, Wade Hilmo, Chad Hilton, Raymond Ho, Rick James, Jeff Johnson, Stephen Johnson, Dan Kahler, Bill Karagounis, Shai Kariv, Jeff Kercher, Jihyun Kim, Herman King, Ryan Kivett, Emily Kruglick, Aaron Lee, Bob Lee, Wynne Leon, Yale Li, Ming Lu, James McIllece, Uladzimir Malashanka, Vikas Malhotra, Gabriel Mandala, Bradley Millington, Asim Mitra, Satish Mohanakrishnan, Chris Montgomery, Andy Morrison, David Mowers, Erik Olsen, Ram Papatla, Ivan Pashov, Sam Patton, Jim Pierson, Mike Poulson, George Reilly, Jiri Richter, Samantha Robertson, Anil Ruia, Stephane Saunier, Peter Schenk, Chad Sheffield, Jemearl Smith, Robert Solomon, Bill Staples, Eric Stenson, Jeff Stucky, Paul Thompson, Anuraag Tiwari, Ali Turkoglu, David Wang, James Webster, Chun Ye, Ivo Zheglov

Special thanks to Martin DelRe and Bill Staples for their support and sponsorship. Without their contribution, the publication of this kit would not have been possible.

Introduction

Welcome to *Internet Information Services (IIS) 6.0 Resource Kit* from Microsoft.

Microsoft® Windows® Server 2003 and Internet Information Services (IIS) 6.0 provide the services to support a secure, available, and scalable Web server on which to run your Web sites and applications. Whether you manage a single Web server or many, *Internet Information Services (IIS) 6.0 Resource Kit* will help you effectively plan, deploy, operate, and troubleshoot your IIS 6.0 solution. This comprehensive technical resource delivers an in-depth description of the new IIS 6.0 architecture, as well as reference information about IIS 6.0 features and services. It also includes practical information and tools to help you accomplish everyday administrative tasks.

Deployment scenarios in part one of this book include installing a new Web server, upgrading an existing Web server from an earlier version of IIS, and migrating existing Apache or IIS Web sites and applications to a newly installed Web server. Part two of this book includes information about running IIS 6.0 as a platform for Web applications, managing a secure IIS 6.0 solution, administering servers programmatically, and capitalizing on built-in scalability features to manage large-scale deployments. In addition, part two includes a thorough discussion of IIS 6.0 troubleshooting concepts, tools, and procedures.

Resource Kit Compact Disc

The following contents are included on the *Internet Information Services (IIS) 6.0 Resource Kit* companion CD:

- **Documentation.** Convenient online resources to help you effectively use IIS 6.0 and Windows Server 2003, including the following:

  - **Deploying Internet Information Services (IIS) 6.0.** A searchable online version of *Deploying Internet Information Services (IIS) 6.0* of the *Microsoft Windows Server 2003 Deployment Kit*.

  - **Internet Information Services (IIS) 6.0 Resource Guide.** A searchable online version of the *Internet Information Services (IIS) 6.0 Resource Guide*.

  - **IIS 6.0 Help.** The searchable Help file included with the Windows Server 2003 operating system that provides detailed step-by-step procedures for working with IIS, as well as reference information for metabase properties, the Registry, and events.

  - **Resource Kit Registry Reference for Windows Server 2003.** A searchable online reference providing detailed descriptions of the Windows Server 2003 registry, including many entries that cannot be edited by using Windows Server 2003 tools or programming interfaces.

- **IIS 6.0 Resource Kit eBook.** A searchable eBook version of *Internet Information Services (IIS) 6.0 Resource Kit*.

- **IIS 6.0 Resource Kit Tools.** A collection of tools and documentation that can help you deploy, administer, secure, and manage IIS 6.0.

- **Link to the IIS 6.0 Web Site.** A portal to online resources for IIS 6.0, such as product support information, downloads, troubleshooting tips, guidelines for writing applications, and links to IIS community forums.

- **Links to Microsoft Press.** Links to the Microsoft Press Support site, which you can search for Knowledge Base articles, and to the Microsoft Press product registration site, which you can use to register this book online.

Document Conventions

The following art symbols and text conventions are used throughout this book.

Flowchart Symbols

Use the following table of symbols as a resource for understanding the flowcharts included in this guide.

Symbol	Meaning	Symbol	Meaning
	Step or component process		Data stored to a database
	Predefined process or subroutine		Flowchart beginning or end
	Decision point	1	Intra-chart connector: Flow continues to next page
	Output to a document or input from a document	1	Intra-chart connector: Flow continues from previous page
	Data transfer to a file on disk	A	Inter-chart connector: Indicates an exit point to another flowchart
	Data transfer to a data store	B	Inter-chart connector: Indicates an entry point from another flowchart

Art Symbols

Use the following table of the art symbols as a resource for understanding the graphics included in this guide.

Symbol	Meaning	Symbol	Meaning
	Workstation		Macintosh client
	Portable computer		Tablet computer
	Terminal		Cellular phone
	Portable digital assistant (PDA)		Document

(continued)

(continued)

Symbol	Meaning	Symbol	Meaning
	File folder		E-mail
	Chart		Wireless network adapter
	Modem		Video camera
	Network adapter		Digital camera
	Facsimile		Printer
	Telephone		Scanner
	Hard disk		Tape drive
	Database		Tape
	Compact disc		Security key
	Digital certificate		Padlock
	Padlock		Uninterruptible power supply
	Access token		Hub
	Modem bank		Automated library

(continued)

(continued)

Symbol	Meaning	Symbol	Meaning
	Windows NT–based server		Generic server
	Mainframe computer		Host
	Data jack		Input/output (I/O) filter
	Shadowed router		Windows 2000–based router
	Router		Switch
	Server farm		Clustered servers
	Transceiver		Script
	Internet		An intranet
	Firewall		Tunnel

(continued)

(continued)

Symbol	Meaning	Symbol	Meaning
✕	Process or communication failure	" . "	DNS root
○	Directory tree root	○	Root
⬭	Organization	○	Organizational unit
△	Active Directory domain	👥	User group
■	Common name	◈	Generic node
Windows 2000 Domain	Windows 2000 domain		
Active Directory™	Active Directory™	⬭	Site or Windows NT 4.0 domain

Reader Alert Conventions

Reader alerts are used throughout this guide to notify you of both supplementary and essential information. The following table explains the meaning of each alert.

Reader Alert	Meaning
💡 Tip	Alerts you to supplementary information that is not essential to the completion of the task at hand.
📝 Note	Alerts you to supplementary information.
◈ Important	Alerts you to supplementary information that is essential to the completion of a task.
⚑ Caution	Alerts you to possible data loss, breaches of security, or other more serious problems.
⚠ Warning	Alerts you that failure to take or avoid a specific action might result in physical harm to you or to the hardware.

Command-line Style Conventions

The following style conventions are used in documenting scripting and command-line tasks throughout this book.

Element	Meaning
bold font	Characters that you type exactly as shown, including commands and parameters. User interface elements are also bold.
Italic font	Variables for which you supply a specific value. For example, *Filename.ext* can refer to any valid file name.
`Monospace font`	Code samples.
`Command`	Command that is typed at the command prompt.
`Syntax`	Syntax of script elements.
`Output`	Output from running a script.

Support Policy

Microsoft does not support the software supplied in the *Internet Information Services (IIS) 6.0 Resource Kit*. Microsoft does not guarantee the performance of the scripting examples, job aids, or tools, bug fixes for the tools, or response times for answering questions. However, we do provide a way for customers who purchase the *Internet Information Services (IIS) 6.0 Resource Kit* to report any problems with the software and receive feedback for such issues. You can do this by sending e-mail to rkinput@microsoft.com. This e-mail address is only for issues related to the *Internet Information Services (IIS) 6.0 Resource Kit*. For issues related to the Windows Server 2003 operating systems, please refer to the support information included with your product

PART I

Deploying Internet Information Services (IIS) 6.0

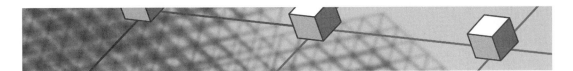

Microsoft® Windows® Server 2003 and Internet Information Services (IIS) 6.0 provide the services to support a secure, available, and scalable Web server on which to run your Web sites and applications. Part one of this book provides prescriptive, task-based, and scenario-based guidance to help you design an IIS 6.0 solution that meets the specific needs of your organization. Deployment scenarios include installing a new Web server, upgrading an existing Web server from an earlier version of IIS, and migrating existing Apache or IIS Web sites and applications to a newly installed Web server.

In This Part

C H A P T E R   1

Overview of Deploying IIS 6.0

Deploying Internet Information Services (IIS) 6.0 identifies the key design and deployment processes that you must complete for your IIS 6.0 solution. This book provides prescriptive, task-based, and scenario-based guidance to help you design an IIS 6.0 solution and then deploy that solution within your organization. After you deploy and secure your IIS 6.0 solution as a platform for your Web applications, you can then deploy your Web applications. However, because the target audience of this book is Web server administrators, modifying Web applications is considered a developer-related topic and is not covered in this book.

In This Chapter

Overview of Deploying an IIS 6.0 Web Server

Organizations and individuals use Web sites and applications every day as a way to do business on the Internet and within their intranets. Internet Information Services (IIS) 6.0 helps you meet your business needs by providing the services to support a secure, available, and scalable Web server on which to run these Web sites and applications.

This chapter describes the high-level processes that are presented in this book for deploying a new IIS 6.0 Web server in your organization's production environment. The other chapters in this book are divided into separate IIS deployment topics that target a specific area of the deployment process including server security, application availability, deploying ASP.NET applications, Web site migration, and server upgrades. For a comprehensive understanding of IIS 6.0 deployment, read all of the chapters in sequential order. For information about a specific aspect of IIS 6.0 deployment, read the individual chapter that corresponds to your area of interest.

Everyone deploying IIS 6.0 needs to decide in which application isolation mode IIS should run. This book highlights worker process isolation mode because of the security and availability improvements from earlier versions of IIS. This book also compares worker process isolation mode to IIS 5.0 isolation mode, which is provided for maximum backward compatibility with existing applications. If your existing Web applications do not possess these characteristics, you should run IIS in worker process isolation mode.

Finally, while you prepare to deploy IIS 6.0, you must verify that your existing Web sites and applications are compatible with IIS 6.0 and with the Microsoft® Windows® Server 2003, Standard Edition; Windows® Server 2003, Enterprise Edition; Windows® Server 2003, Datacenter Edition; and Windows® Server 2003, Web Edition operating systems. Verification of the Web site and application compatibility should be done on a test Web server before deploying on a production Web server.

The processes in this book have been carefully developed and tested to provide a blueprint for an easy and comprehensive deployment of IIS 6.0. Following the recommendations presented during the deployment process will help your Web servers be as secure as possible and highly available.

Process for Deploying an IIS 6.0 Web Server

The IIS 6.0 deployment process is written for Web server administrators who are responsible for installing and configuring IIS on new or existing servers. The chapters in this book can be divided into two main deployment scenarios:

- Deploying a new Web server running Windows Server 2003 with IIS 6.0

- Upgrading or migrating to a Web server running Windows Server 2003 with IIS 6.0

Figure 1.1 illustrates the chapters in this book that correspond to these scenarios. Review the flowchart in this figure and read the descriptions of each chapter to help identify the deployment tasks that you need to complete for your IIS 6.0 solution and to discover which chapters will help you complete those tasks.

Figure 1.1   IIS 6.0 Deployment Process Steps and the Corresponding Chapters

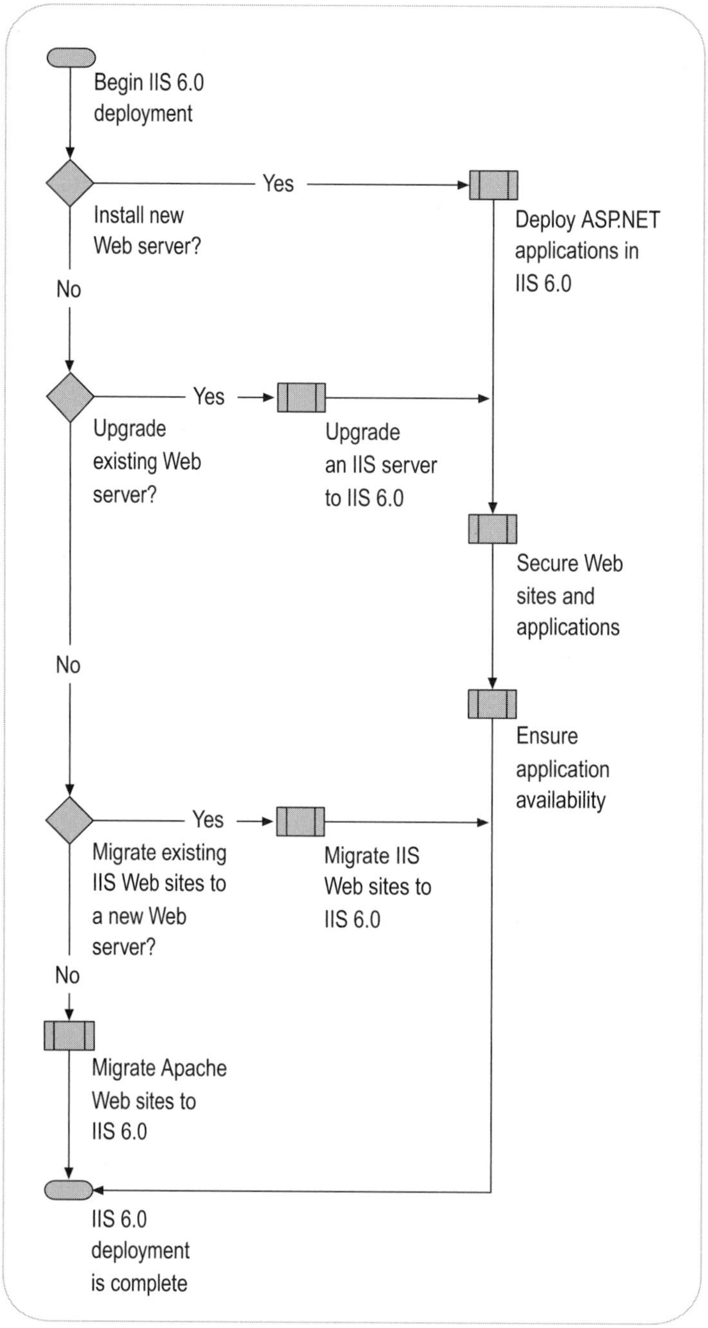

Begin IIS 6.0 deployment

Install new Web server? — Yes → Deploy ASP.NET applications in IIS 6.0

No

Upgrade existing Web server? — Yes → Upgrade an IIS server to IIS 6.0

Secure Web sites and applications

No

Ensure application availability

Migrate existing IIS Web sites to a new Web server? — Yes → Migrate IIS Web sites to IIS 6.0

No

Migrate Apache Web sites to IIS 6.0

IIS 6.0 deployment is complete

Each chapter includes a flowchart that represents the organizing principle of the chapter content. Each chapter also includes a quick-start guide to facilitate the fastest possible deployment. You can use these quick-start guides to help identify the steps of the deployment process that you need additional information to complete, and then you can skip the information with which you are already familiar.

Deploying a New IIS 6.0 Web Server

The following chapters in this book are about deploying a new server running IIS 6.0 to host your Web sites and applications:

- Chapter 2: "Deploying ASP.NET Applications in IIS 6.0"

  Read this chapter to understand specific considerations for deploying ASP.NET applications in IIS 6.0. In particular, the chapter describes how you can run multiple versions of the Microsoft .NET Framework on the same Web server and how you can configure ASP.NET applications to use the appropriate version of the .NET Framework.

  After completing the process in this chapter, you must still optimize your server for security and scalability. The remaining chapters in this book focus on topics that are applicable to all Web applications, including ASP.NET applications, noting exceptions where appropriate.

   Important

  ASP.NET is not available on the following operating systems: Microsoft® Windows® XP 64-Bit Edition; the 64-bit version of Windows® Server 2003, Enterprise Edition; and the 64-bit version of Windows® Server 2003, Datacenter Edition. For more information, see "Features unavailable on 64-bit versions of the Windows Server 2003 family" in Help and Support Center for Windows Server 2003.

- Chapter 3: "Securing Web Sites and Applications"

  Read this chapter to learn how you can further protect the Web sites and applications that are hosted on a Web server running IIS 6.0. This chapter describes how to secure a Web server and how to secure individual Web sites and applications running on IIS 6.0. In particular, this chapter describes the process for reducing the attack surface of a Web server, preventing unauthorized access to Web sites and applications, isolating Web sites and applications, configuring user authentication, encrypting confidential data exchanged with clients, and maintaining the security of Web sites and applications.

- Chapter 4: "Ensuring Application Availability"

  Read this chapter to learn how you can fully utilize the features of IIS 6.0 to enhance the availability of your Web applications. This chapter describes how you can set realistic application availability goals and then verify that you are attaining those goals. In addition, it describes how you can configure the features of worker process isolation mode for optimum application availability, depending on your business needs and the processing load on your applications. Finally, this chapter identifies common application incompatibilities with IIS 6.0, and it explains how you can test your applications for compatibility with worker process isolation mode.

Upgrading and Migrating a Server to IIS 6.0

The following chapters in this book assume that you have Web sites and applications that are hosted on an existing Web server running Apache or an earlier version of IIS. Select one of the following chapters to perform the deployment of IIS 6.0 when you have an existing server:

- Chapter 5: "Upgrading an IIS Server to IIS 6.0"

  Read this chapter when you are upgrading Web sites and applications that are hosted on a server running the Microsoft Windows NT® Server 4.0 operating system with IIS 4.0 or a server running the Microsoft® Windows® 2000 Server operating system with IIS 5.0, to a server running Windows Server 2003 with IIS 6.0. This chapter defines *upgrading* as the process of updating a Web server running IIS 4.0 or IIS 5.0 to run IIS 6.0 when the Web sites and applications hosted by that Web server are not moved to another server.

- Chapter 6: "Migrating IIS Web Sites to IIS 6.0"

  Read this chapter when you are migrating Web sites that are hosted on a server running Windows NT Server 4.0 with IIS 4.0, or a server running Windows 2000 Server with IIS 5.0, to a newly installed server running Windows Server 2003 with IIS 6.0. This chapter assumes that you are moving Web sites from an existing Web server running an earlier version of IIS, to a newly installed Web server running IIS 6.0. This chapter explains how you can use the IIS 6.0 Migration Tool to migrate your IIS Web sites to IIS 6.0. This chapter also describes a manual process for migrating IIS Web sites to IIS 6.0.

- Chapter 7: "Migrating Apache Web Sites to IIS 6.0"

  Read this chapter when you are migrating Apache Web sites that are hosted on an existing server to a server running IIS 6.0 and Windows Server 2003. This chapter assumes that you are moving applications from an existing Web server running a Linux-based operating system with Apache to a newly installed Web server running Windows Server 2003 with IIS 6.0. The process in this chapter describes how you can use the Apache to IIS 6.0 Migration Tool to migrate your Apache Web sites to IIS 6.0.

Overview of IIS 6.0

IIS 6.0 with Windows Server 2003 provides integrated, reliable, scalable, secure, and manageable Web server capabilities over an intranet or the Internet. IIS is a stable and secure platform for running dynamic network applications. Organizations of all sizes use IIS to host and manage Web sites on the Internet or on their intranets, to host and manage FTP sites, and to route news or mail by using the Network News Transfer Protocol (NNTP) and the Simple Mail Transfer Protocol (SMTP).

IIS 6.0 takes advantage of the latest Web standards like ASP.NET, XML, and Simple Object Access Protocol (SOAP) for the development, implementation, and management of Web applications. IIS 6.0 includes new features that are designed to help organizations, IT professionals, and Web administrators achieve their goals of performance, reliability, scalability, and security for potentially thousands of Web sites hosted on a single server or on multiple servers.

IIS 6.0 Benefits and Features

IIS 6.0 provides the following benefits and features:

- **Reliability.** IIS 6.0 uses a new request-processing architecture and application isolation environment that enables individual Web applications to function within a self-contained worker process. This environment prevents one application or Web site from stopping another, and it reduces the amount of time that administrators spend restarting services to correct application-related problems. The new environment also includes proactive health monitoring for application pools. For more information about application reliability in IIS 6.0, see "Ensuring Application Availability" in this book.

- **Scalability.** IIS 6.0 introduces a new kernel-mode driver for Hypertext Transfer Protocol (HTTP) parsing and caching that is specifically tuned to increase Web server throughput and scalability of multiprocessor computers. The result is an increase in the following:

  - The number of Web sites that a single IIS 6.0 server can host

  - The number of concurrently active worker processes

  - The performance for startup and shutdown times for the Web server and for individual Web sites

  - The number of simultaneous requests that a Web server can service.

Also, by configuring the startup and shutdown time limits for worker processes, IIS allocates resources to active Web sites instead of keeping resources on idle requests.

- **Security.** IIS 6.0 provides significantly improved security over IIS 5.0. For example, to reduce the attack surface of systems, IIS 6.0 is not installed by default on Windows Server 2003, Standard Edition; Windows Server 2003, Enterprise Edition; and Windows Server 2003, Datacenter Edition. After installing these products, administrators must manually install IIS 6.0. When IIS 6.0 is installed, it is locked down by default so that it can serve only static content. By using the Web Service Extensions node in IIS Manager, Web site administrators can enable or disable IIS functionality based on the individual needs of their organization.

  IIS 6.0 includes a variety of security features and technologies to help ensure the integrity of your Web and FTP site content, as well as the data that is transmitted through your sites. These security features and technologies include Advanced Digest authentication, improved access control, Secure Sockets Layer (SSL) encryption, centralized certificate storage, and detailed auditing capabilities.

  For more information about IIS security, see "Securing Web Sites and Applications" in this book; and see "Security" in IIS 6.0 Help, which is accessible from IIS Manager.

- **Manageability.** To meet the needs of a diverse set of organizations, IIS 6.0 provides a variety of manageability and administration tools. Administrators can configure an IIS 6.0 server by using IIS Manager, by running administration scripts, or by directly editing the IIS metabase. Administrators can also remotely administer IIS servers and Web sites.

- **Enhanced Development.** Compared to Windows 2000 Server, Windows Server 2003 offers an improved developer experience with ASP.NET and IIS integration. ASP.NET runs most Active Server Pages (ASP) code while providing greater functionality for building enterprise-class Web applications that can work as a part of the .NET Framework. Use ASP.NET to fully utilize the features of the common language runtime, such as type safety, inheritance, language interoperability, and versioning. IIS 6.0 also offers support for the latest Web standards including XML, SOAP, and Internet Protocol version 6 (IPv6).

  For more information about enhanced development of ASP.NET applications, see "Deploying ASP.NET Applications in IIS 6.0" in this book.

- **Application Compatibility.** According to feedback from thousands of customers and independent software vendors (ISVs), IIS 6.0 is compatible with most of their existing Web applications. Also, to ensure maximum compatibility, you can configure IIS 6.0 to run in IIS 5.0 isolation mode.

Internet and Intranet Applications on IIS 6.0

The IIS 6.0 deployment process can be applied to Web sites and applications that are hosted on the Internet or within the intranet of your organization. Throughout the deployment process, explicit references are made for deployment considerations relating to Web servers facing the Internet or within an intranet.

 Note
The deployment processes and recommendations described in this book can be used to deploy an Internet or intranet Web server, unless otherwise noted.

Determining Application Compatibility with IIS 6.0

One of the primary concerns when deploying IIS 6.0 is whether or not your existing applications are compatible with IIS 6.0. Windows Server 2003 and IIS 6.0 are designed to provide maximum application compatibility. In most cases, existing Web sites and applications will run on IIS 6.0 without modification.

The deployment process in this book provides prescriptive guidance about how to address known Web site and application compatibility issues. For a more detailed explanation of Web site and application compatibility with IIS 6.0, read the following:

- "Preparing for Upgrade" in "Upgrading an IIS Server to IIS 6.0" in this book when you are performing an upgrade of an existing Web server running an earlier version of IIS.

- "Preparing for Migration" in "Migrating IIS Web Sites to IIS 6.0" in this book when you are moving existing Web sites and applications that are hosted on a Web server running an earlier version of IIS to a newly installed Web server running IIS 6.0.

- "Preparing for Migration" in "Migrating Apache Web Sites to IIS 6.0" in this book when you are moving existing Web sites and applications that are hosted on a Web server running Apache to a newly installed Web server running IIS 6.0.

For a more detailed explanation of application compatibility with Windows Server 2003, see "Planning and Testing for Application Deployment" in *Planning, Testing, and Piloting Deployment Projects* of this kit.

Moving from IIS 5.0 Isolation Mode to Worker Process Isolation Mode

IIS 6.0 can run in one of two distinct modes of operation, which are called application isolation modes. *Application isolation* is the separation of applications by process boundaries that prevent the applications from affecting one another, and it is configured differently for each of the two IIS application isolation modes: IIS 5.0 isolation mode and worker process isolation mode.

Before you begin deployment, review the following:

- Differences between IIS 5.0 isolation mode and worker process isolation mode
- Benefits of moving from IIS 5.0 isolation mode to worker process isolation mode

 Note

This book assumes that IIS 6.0 is running in worker process isolation mode, unless otherwise noted.

Reviewing Application Isolation Modes

Worker process isolation mode uses the redesigned architecture for IIS 6.0. This isolation mode runs all application code in an isolated environment. However, unlike earlier versions of IIS, IIS 6.0 provides isolation without a performance penalty because fewer processor instructions are ran when switching from one application pool to another. Worker process isolation mode is compatible with most existing Web sites and applications. Whenever possible, run IIS 6.0 in worker process isolation mode to benefit from the enhanced performance and security in IIS 6.0.

IIS 5.0 isolation mode provides compatibility for applications that depend upon the process behavior and memory model of IIS 5.0. Run IIS in this mode only when a Web site or application cannot run in worker process isolation mode, and run it only until the compatibility issues are resolved.

 Important

IIS 6.0 cannot run both application isolation modes simultaneously on the same server. Therefore, on a single server running IIS 6.0, you cannot run some Web applications in worker process isolation mode and others in IIS 5.0 isolation mode. If you have applications that require separate modes, you must run them on separate servers.

IIS 6.0 defaults to a different application isolation mode based on the type of deployment you select. For new installations and migrations, IIS is configured to run in worker process isolation mode by default. After you perform an upgrade from an earlier version of IIS, IIS is configured to run in IIS 5.0 isolation mode by default.

Before configuring IIS 6.0 to run in worker process isolation mode, evaluate whether your Web sites and applications are compatible with worker process isolation mode. In most cases, IIS hosts your Web sites and applications in worker process isolation mode without any problems. Nevertheless, determine application compatibility in your lab before deploying your IIS solution into production.

For more information about worker process isolation mode, IIS 5.0 isolation mode, and evaluating Web site and application compatibility with worker process isolation mode, see "Determining Application Compatibility with Worker Process Isolation Mode" in "Upgrading an IIS Server to IIS 6.0" in this book.

 Note

Identifying a complete list of potential incompatibilities that applications can experience with worker process isolation mode is beyond the scope of this book. Even after following the guidelines in this chapter, you still need to verify in your lab whether your Web sites and applications are compatible with worker process isolation mode.

Benefits of Moving to Worker Process Isolation Mode

Worker process isolation mode provides higher levels of security and availability for Web sites and applications than IIS 5.0 isolation mode. Therefore, it is recommended that you configure IIS 6.0 to run in worker process isolation mode.

In IIS 5.0, applications can be pooled together out-of-process, but in only one application pool. In IIS 6.0, worker process isolation mode supports multiple application pools, where each application pool can have a different configuration, such as a unique recycling configuration. Therefore, you can prevent a single Web site or application that periodically fails from disrupting other Web sites and applications. In addition, worker process isolation mode provides the following improvements to IIS.

Security Enhancements

IIS 6.0 includes a variety of security features and technologies that help ensure the integrity of your Web site content, and of the data that is transmitted through your sites. The following security enhancement is only available when IIS 6.0 is running in worker process isolation mode.

Default process identity for Web sites and applications set to NetworkService

In IIS 5.0 isolation mode, the default process identity is LocalSystem, which enables access to, and the ability to alter, nearly all of the resources on the Web server.

Performance and Scaling Enhancements

Future growth in the utilization of your Web sites and applications requires increased performance and scalability of Web servers. By increasing the speed at which HTTP requests can be processed and by allowing more applications and sites to run on one Web server, the number of Web servers that you need to host a site is reduced. The following are a few of the performance improvements included in worker process isolation mode.

Support for processor affinity for worker processes in an application pool

You can configure all of the worker processes in an application pool to have affinity with specific processors in a multiprocessor or server. Processor affinity allows the worker processes to take advantage of more frequent processor caching (Level 1 or Level 2).

Elimination of inactive worker processes and reclamation of unused resources

You can configure application pools to have worker processes request a shutdown if they are idle for a certain amount of time. This can free unused resources for other active worker processes. New worker processes are then started only when they are needed.

Distributing client connections across multiple worker processes

You can configure an application pool to have more than one worker process servicing client connections, also known as a *Web garden*. Because there are multiple worker processes, the incoming client connections are distributed across the worker processes and throughput is not constrained by a single worker process.

Ability to isolate Web sites and applications from each other

You can isolate Web sites and applications without incurring a performance penalty.

Availability Enhancements

Because worker process boundaries isolate the applications in an application pool from the applications in other application pools, if an application fails, it does not affect the availability of other applications running on the server. Deploying applications in application pools is a primary advantage of running IIS 6.0 in worker process isolation mode.

Reduced number of server restarts that are required when administering Web sites and applications

Many of the common operation tasks do not force the restart of the server or the Web service. These tasks, such as upgrading site content or components, debugging Web applications, or dealing with faulty Web applications, can be performed without affecting service to other Web sites or applications on the server.

A fault-tolerant request-processing model for Web sites and applications

In IIS 5.0 isolation mode, each Web site or application has only one worker process. However, in worker process isolation mode, you can create a *Web garden* by configuring a number of worker processes to share the processing. The benefit of a Web garden is that if one worker process stops responding, other worker processes are available to accept and process requests.

Isolation of failed worker processes from healthy worker processes

In worker process isolation mode, IIS can determine that a worker process has failed and start a new worker process. To minimize the interruption of service, new requests are queued until the new worker process is active. In the case where a worker process has not yet failed but is considered unhealthy, IIS starts a new worker process. When the new worker process is active, IIS shuts down the unhealthy worker process. After IIS creates the new worker process, the failed worker process can be separated, or *orphaned*, from the application pool. The advantage of orphaning a worker process rather than terminating it is that debugging can be performed on the orphaned worker process.

Health monitoring of Web sites and applications

In worker process isolation mode, you can configure an application pool to monitor not only the health of the entire application pool, but also individual worker processes servicing the application pool. Monitoring the health of a worker process allows IIS to detect that a worker process is unable to serve requests and to take corrective action, such as recycling the failed worker process.

In addition, worker process isolation supports other responses when a failed worker process or application pool is detected. For example, IIS can attach a debugger to an orphaned worker process or notify an administrator that an application pool has failed due to rapid-fail protection.

Prevention of Web sites or applications that fail quickly from consuming system resources

In some instances, availability can be affected by Web sites and applications that fail very quickly, are automatically restarted, and then fail quickly again. The endless cycle of failure and restarting can consume system resources, causing other Web sites and applications to experience denial of services because of system resource shortages.

Worker process isolation mode includes *rapid-fail protection* that stops an application pool when too many of the worker processes assigned to an application pool are found to be unhealthy within a specified period of time.

Automatic restart of poorly performing Web sites and applications

Some Web sites and applications have memory leaks, are poorly coded, or have other unidentified problems. In IIS 5.0 isolation mode, these applications can force you to restart the entire Web server. The recycling feature in worker process isolation mode can periodically restart the worker processes in an application pool without affecting service availability. Worker processes can be scheduled to restart based on several options, such as elapsed time or the number of requests served.

Deploying ASP.NET Applications in IIS 6.0

Microsoft® Windows® Server 2003 includes support for ASP.NET applications and the Microsoft .NET Framework version 1.1 with the operating system installation. This chapter describes how to deploy ASP.NET applications on a newly installed server running Internet Information Services (IIS) 6.0. Version 1.1 of the .NET Framework is installed with Windows Server 2003. Most ASP.NET applications run without modification on version 1.1 of the .NET Framework.

In This Chapter

Related Information

- For information about improving the availability of your ASP.NET applications, see Ensuring Application Availability in this book.

- For information about ASP.NET-specific considerations when migrating to IIS 6.0, see Migrating IIS Web Sites to IIS 6.0 in this book.

- For information about IIS 6.0 security, see Securing Web Sites and Applications in this book.

- For information about ASP.NET-specific considerations when upgrading to IIS 6.0, see Upgrading an IIS Server to IIS 6.0 in this book.

Overview of Deploying ASP.NET Applications in IIS 6.0

ASP.NET is a unified Web application platform that provides services to help you build and deploy enterprise-class Web applications and XML-based Web services. ASP.NET is supported on the Microsoft® Windows® Server 2003, Standard Edition; Windows® Server 2003, Enterprise Edition; Windows® Server 2003, Datacenter Edition; and Windows® Server 2003, Web Edition operating systems. ASP.NET is installed with the Microsoft .NET Framework version 1.1 as a part of Windows Server 2003. However, to run ASP.NET applications, you must also install IIS 6.0.

 Important

ASP.NET is not available on the following operating systems: Microsoft® Windows® XP 64-Bit Edition; the 64-bit version of Windows® Server 2003, Enterprise Edition; and the 64-bit version of Windows® Server 2003, Datacenter Edition. For more information, see "Features unavailable on 64-bit versions of the Windows Server 2003 family" in Help and Support Center for Microsoft® Windows® Server 2003.

The deployment process presented in this chapter describes how to deploy ASP.NET applications on a newly installed IIS 6.0 Web server. Before you begin this process, complete the following steps:

- Install Windows Server 2003, which includes version 1.1 of the .NET Framework, with the default options.

- Install IIS 6.0 with the default settings in **Add or Remove Programs** in Control Panel.

If you need to install ASP.NET applications that were written for IIS 5.0 or version 1.0 of the .NET Framework on a new Web server, see "Migrating IIS Web Sites to IIS 6.0" in this book. If you want to upgrade a Web server running IIS 5.0 that is hosting existing ASP.NET applications, see "Upgrading an IIS Server to IIS 6.0" in this book.

When you configure IIS 6.0 to run in IIS 5.0 isolation mode, the settings in the **<processModel>** section of the Machine.config file are configured in the same way as they were in IIS 5.0 — in the Machine.config or Web.config files. For more information about configuring ASP.NET applications when IIS 6.0 is configured to run in IIS 5.0 isolation mode, see "ASP.NET Configuration" in IIS 6.0 Help, which is accessible from IIS Manager.

Upon completing the process described in this chapter, you will have a Web server running IIS 6.0 and hosting your ASP.NET applications. However, you can further configure the Web server to improve the security and availability of your ASP.NET applications. For more information about configuring your Web server to improve the security and availability of your ASP.NET applications, see "Securing Web Sites and Applications" and "Ensuring Application Availability" in this book.

 Note

The configuration settings discussed in this chapter are appropriate for Web sites and applications that are hosted on Web servers on an intranet and the Internet, unless specifically noted.

Process for Deploying ASP.NET Applications in IIS 6.0

The process for deploying new ASP.NET applications on a newly installed Web server requires no understanding of earlier versions of IIS or the .NET Framework. All of the ASP.NET configuration sections in the Machine.config and Web.config files are configured the same way in IIS 6.0, except for the <**processModel**> section of the Machine.config file. When IIS 6.0 is configured to run in worker process isolation mode, some of the attributes in the <**processModel**> section of the Machine.config file are now in equivalent IIS 6.0 metabase properties. For more information about how to migrate attributes in the Machine.config file to their equivalent IIS 6.0 metabase property settings, see "Migrating Machine.config Attributes to IIS 6.0 Metabase Property Settings" in "Upgrading an IIS Server to IIS 6.0" in this book.

In addition, if your ASP.NET applications need to retain session state, you must configure IIS 6.0 to use the appropriate ASP.NET application session state method. Depending on the method you select, you might need to configure the ASP.NET state service or Microsoft SQL Server™ to act as the repository for centralized state storage.

The process for deploying ASP.NET applications in IIS 6.0 is shown in Figure 2.1.

Figure 2.1 Deploying ASP.NET Applications in IIS 6.0

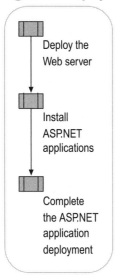

Deploy the
Web server

Install
ASP.NET
applications

Complete
the ASP.NET
application
deployment

 Note

Before deploying your ASP.NET applications on a production server, perform
the process outlined in this chapter on a test server that is configured
identically to your production server.

The following quick-start guide provides a detailed overview of the process for deploying
ASP.NET applications in IIS 6.0. You can use this guide to help identify the steps of the
ASP.NET application deployment process that you need additional information to complete, and
to skip the steps with which you are already familiar. In addition, all of the procedures that are
required to complete the ASP.NET application deployment process are documented in "IIS
Deployment Procedures" in this book.

Deploy the Web Server

1. Install Windows Server 2003.

2. Install and configure IIS 6.0.

3. Enable ASP.NET in the Web service extensions list.

Install ASP.NET Applications

1. Create Web sites and virtual directories for each ASP.NET application by doing the following:

   - Create Web sites and home directories.

   - Create virtual directories.

2. Copy ASP.NET application content to the Web server.

3. Enable common storage for ASP.NET session state by completing the following steps:

   - Select the method for maintaining and storing ASP.NET session state.

   - If you decided to maintain session state with the ASP.NET state service, configure out-of-process session state with the ASP.NET state service.

   - If you decided to maintain session state with SQL Server, configure out-of-process session state with SQL Server.

   - Configure encryption and validation keys.

   - Configure ASP.NET to the use the appropriate session state.

   - Secure the ASP.NET session state connection string.

Complete the ASP.NET Application Deployment

1. Ensure the security and availability of your ASP.NET applications.

2. Verify that the ASP.NET applications were deployed successfully.

3. Back up the Web server.

4. Enable client access to your ASP.NET applications.

Deploying the Web Server

You must install the Web server before you can install your ASP.NET applications. In addition to installing Windows Server 2003, you must install and configure IIS 6.0 on the Web server. You must also enable ASP.NET so that the Web server can run ASP.NET applications.

Figure 2.2 illustrates the process for deploying the Web server.

Figure 2.2 Deploying the Web Server

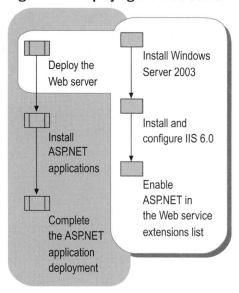

Installing Windows Server 2003

The deployment process presented here assumes that you install Windows Server 2003 with the default options. If you use other methods for installing and configuring Windows Server 2003, such as unattended setup, your configuration settings might be different.

 Note

> When you complete the installation of Windows Server 2003, Manage Your Server automatically starts. The deployment process assumes that you quit Manage Your Server, and then further configure the Web server in **Add or Remove Programs** in Control Panel.

For more information about the essential components and services you should enable in Windows Server 2003 see "Enabling Only Essential Windows Server 2003 Components and Services" in "Securing Web Sites and Applications" in this book.

Installing and Configuring IIS 6.0

Because IIS 6.0 is not installed during the default installation of Windows Server 2003, the next step in deploying the Web server is to install and configure IIS 6.0. The deployment process presented here assumes that you install IIS 6.0 with the default options in **Add or Remove Programs** in Control Panel. If you use other methods for installing and configuring Windows Server 2003, such as Manage Your Server, the default configuration settings might be different.

Install and configure IIS 6.0 by completing the following steps:

1. Install IIS 6.0 with only the essential components and services.

    As with installing Windows Server 2003, the primary concern when installing and configuring IIS 6.0 is to ensure that the security of the Web server is maintained. Enabling unnecessary components and services increases the attack surface of the Web server. You can help ensure that the Web server is secure by enabling only the essential components and services in IIS 6.0.

    For more information about how to install IIS 6.0, see "Install IIS 6.0" in "IIS Deployment Procedures" in this book. For more information about the IIS 6.0 components and services that you should enable, see "Enabling Only Essential IIS Components and Services" in "Securing Web Sites and Applications" in this book.

2. If you want to manage the Web site content by using Microsoft® FrontPage®, install FrontPage 2002 Server Extensions from Microsoft on the Web server.

    For information about how to enable FrontPage Server Extensions after installing them on the Web server, see "Configure Web Service Extensions" in "IIS Deployment Procedures" in this book.

Enabling ASP.NET in the Web Service Extensions List

After you install IIS 6.0, you need to enable ASP.NET. You can enable ASP.NET in **Add or Remove Windows Components**, which is accessible from **Add or Remove Programs** in Control Panel. When you enable ASP.NET by using this method, ASP.NET is also enabled in the Web service extensions list. If you enabled ASP.NET in this way, then you can continue to the next step in the deployment process. To continue to the next step in the deployment process, see "Installing ASP.NET Applications" later in this chapter.

For more information about enabling ASP.NET in **Add or Remove Programs** see "Enable ASP.NET" in "IIS Deployment Procedures" in this book.

ASP.NET might not be enabled in the Web service extensions list if either of the following is true:

- You installed a version, other than version 1.1, of the .NET Framework and ASP.NET from a Web download or as part of an application such as the Microsoft Visual Studio® .NET development tool.

- You disabled ASP.NET in the Web service extensions list because you were not running ASP.NET applications on an existing Web server.

If ASP.NET is not already enabled, view the Web service extensions list in IIS Manager and configure the status of the **ASP.NET v1.1.4322** Web service extension to **Allowed**. For more information about enabling ASP.NET in the Web service extensions list see "Configure Web Service Extensions" in "IIS Deployment Procedures" in this book.

Installing ASP.NET Applications

After the Web server is deployed, you can install your ASP.NET applications. First, you must create a Web site and virtual directories for each ASP.NET application. Then you need to install each ASP.NET application in the corresponding Web site and virtual directory.

When there are provisioning or setup scripts for your ASP.NET applications, use these scripts to install the ASP.NET applications on the Web server. Because the provisioning and setup scripts create the Web sites and virtual directories while installing ASP.NET applications, you do not need to perform any manual steps to install the ASP.NET applications. In this case, run the provisioning or setup scripts to install and configure the Web sites and applications, and then continue to the next step in the application deployment process. To continue to the next step in the process, see "Enabling Common Storage for ASP.NET Session State" later in this chapter.

Figure 2.3 illustrates the process for installing your ASP.NET applications.

Figure 2.3   Installing ASP.NET Applications

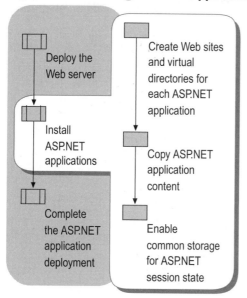

Creating Web Sites and Virtual Directories for each ASP.NET Application

For each ASP.NET application, you must create a virtual directory in a new or existing Web site. Later in the installation process, you will install your ASP.NET applications into their corresponding Web sites and virtual directories.

Create the Web sites and virtual directories for your ASP.NET applications by completing the following steps:

1.   Create Web sites and home directories.

2.   Create virtual directories.

Creating Web Sites and Home Directories

Each Web site must have one home directory. The home directory is the central location for your published Web pages. It contains a home page or index file that serves as a portal to other pages in your Web site. The home directory is mapped to the domain name of the Web site or to the name of the Web server.

Create a Web site and home directory for an ASP.NET application by completing the following steps:

1. Create the folder that will be the home directory for the Web site on the Web server.

The folder that is the home directory of the Web site contains all of the content and subdirectories for the Web site. The folder can be created on the same computer as the Web server or on a Universal Naming Convention (UNC)–shared folder on a separate server. At a minimum, create the folder on the following:

- An NTFS file system partition, which helps ensure proper security

- A disk volume other than the system volume, which reduces the potential of an attack on a Web site bringing down the entire Web server and improves performance

For more information about securing Web sites and applications, see "Securing Web Sites and Applications" in this book. For more information about creating directories for the Web sites, see "Create a Web Site" in "IIS Deployment Procedures" in this book.

2. Create the Web site on the server.

For more information about how to create a Web site, see "Create a Web Site" in "IIS Deployment Procedures" in this book.

3. If the Web site is FrontPage extended, then configure the Web site on the Web server to be FrontPage extended.

For more information about how to configure a Web site to be FrontPage extended, see "Configure a Web Site to be FrontPage Extended" in "IIS Deployment Procedures" in this book.

Creating Virtual Directories

A *virtual directory* is a folder name, used in an address, which corresponds to a physical directory on the Web server or a UNC location. This is also sometimes referred to as *URL mapping*. Virtual directories are used to publish Web content from any folder that is not contained in the home directory of the Web site. When clients access content in a virtual directory, the content appears to be in a subdirectory of the home directory, even though it is not.

For security reasons, you might want to move the Web site content to a different disk volume during the application deployment process. You can move the content to another disk volume on the Web server or to a shared folder on a separate server. You can use virtual directories to specify the UNC name for the location where the content is placed, and provide a user name and password for access rights.

For each virtual directory required by the ASP.NET application, create a corresponding virtual directory on the Web server by completing the following steps:

1.   Create the folder on the Web server to contain the virtual directory content.

     Ensure that you create the folder in a secure manner that does not compromise the security of the Web server.

     For more information about securing virtual directories, see "Preventing Unauthorized Access to Web Sites and Applications" in "Securing Web Sites and Applications" in this book.

2.   Create the virtual directory under the appropriate Web site on the server.

     For more information about how to create virtual directories, see "Create a Virtual Directory" in "IIS Deployment Procedures" in this book.

Copying ASP.NET Application Content

When no installation program or provisioning scripts exist for your ASP.NET application, you can copy the content of the ASP.NET application to the corresponding Web site and virtual directories that you created on the Web server.

You can copy the ASP.NET application content to the Web server by using one of the following methods:

- Run the **Xcopy** command to copy ASP.NET application content to the Web server on an intranet or internal network.

- Use Microsoft Windows Explorer to copy ASP.NET application content to the Web server on an intranet or internal network.

- Use the **Copy Project** command in Visual Studio .NET to copy ASP.NET application content to the Web server on an intranet or internal network, if the application has been developed by using Visual Studio .NET.

     Note

    FrontPage Server Extensions must be installed on the Web server to use the **Copy Project** command.

- Use the **Publish Web** command in FrontPage to copy ASP.NET application content to the Web server on an intranet or over the Internet, if the Web site that contains the application has been developed by using FrontPage.

    For more information about how to publish ASP.NET application content by using FrontPage, see "Publish Web Site Content with FrontPage" in "IIS Deployment Procedures" in this book.

Enabling Common Storage for ASP.NET Session State

ASP.NET session state lets you share client session data across all of the Web servers in a Web farm or across different worker processes or worker process instances on a single Web server. Clients can access different servers in the Web farm across multiple requests and still have full access to session data.

You can enable common storage for ASP.NET session state by performing the following steps:

1. Select the method for maintaining and storing ASP.NET session state.

2. If you decided to maintain session state with the ASP.NET state service, configure out-of-process session state with the ASP.NET state service.

3. If you decided to maintain session state with SQL Server, configure out-of-process session state with SQL Server.

4. Configure the encryption and validation keys.

5. Configure ASP.NET to use the session state method that you selected in Step 1.

6. Secure the ASP.NET session state connection string in the registry.

Selecting the Method for Maintaining and Storing ASP.NET Session State

You can configure the method used by ASP.NET to maintain session state. ASP.NET supports the following methods for maintaining session state:

- **In-process.** The process for maintaining session state runs in the same worker process as the ASP.NET application and approximates how Active Server Pages (ASP) applications maintain session state. If the worker process for the ASP.NET application recycles, all session state information is lost.

- **Out-of-process.** The process for maintaining session state runs in a different worker process, either on the same Web server or another server, than the worker process for the ASP.NET application. If the worker process for the ASP.NET application recycles, session state information is retained.

You can configure ASP.NET session state settings by modifying the **mode** attribute in the **<sessionState>** section of the Machine.config file for all applications or in the Web.config file for specific applications. The session state settings in the IIS 6.0 metabase only apply to ASP applications. ASP.NET and ASP applications cannot share session state.

Select one of the following methods for storing.ASP.NET session state:

- **In-process, local to the Web server.** ASP.NET session state is managed by and stored on the local Web server. This is the default mode for ASP.NET session state management and it approximates how ASP applications manage session state.

  This method allows the session state to be stored across worker process threads in a Web garden. However, the in-process mode does not allow session state to be store across servers in a Web farm. For more information about Web gardens, see "Configuring Web Gardens" in "Ensuring Application Availability" in this book.

  To use this method to store ASP.NET session state, set the session state **mode** attribute to **InProc**.

- **Out-of-process, by using the ASP.NET state service.** The ASP.NET state service (aspnet_state.exe) runs as a service on Windows Server 2003. You can run the ASP.NET state service local to a Web server to support Web gardens, or on a separate server to support Web farms.

  To use this method to store ASP.NET session state, set the session state **mode** attribute to **StateServer**.

- **Out-of-process, by using a computer running SQL Server.** ASP.NET session state can be managed by and stored in a database on a computer running Microsoft SQL Server. Like the ASP.NET state service, this out-of-process mode provides support for Web gardens or Web farms.

  To use this method to store ASP.NET session state, set the session state **mode** attribute to **SQLServer**.

Table 2.1 compares the methods for maintaining ASP.NET session state, listing the advantages and disadvantages of each method.

Table 2.1 Comparison of Methods for Maintaining ASP.NET Session State

Method	Advantages	Disadvantages
In-process	<ul><li>Requires no additional computers.</li><li>Provides faster access to session state than the out-of-process modes because state is maintained in memory and is in-process.</li></ul>	<ul><li>Does not provide centralized storage of session state for Web farms.</li><li>Provides no redundancy in the event of a Web server failure.</li><li>Does not survive application restarts or process recycles.</li></ul>
Out-of-process with the ASP.NET state service running on the local Web server	<ul><li>Provides centralized storage of session state to support Web gardens.</li><li>Requires no additional computers.</li></ul>	<ul><li>Does not have a mechanism for failover or partitioning.</li><li>Out-of-process state requires serializing data and does not perform as well as-in-process state.</li><li>Provides slower access to session state than in-process mode.</li></ul>
Out-of-process with the ASP.NET state service running on a separate server	<ul><li>Provides centralized storage of session state to support Web gardens or Web farms.</li></ul>	<ul><li>Requires an additional computer to store the session state.</li><li>Does not have a mechanism for failover or partitioning.</li><li>Does not support remote authentication, so administrators must control access to the computer with IPSEC and/or firewall rules.</li><li>Out-of-process state requires serializing data and does not perform as well as in-process state.</li><li>Provides slower access to session state than in-process mode.</li></ul>
Out-of-process with session state stored on a separate computer running SQL Server	<ul><li>Provides centralized storage of session state to support Web gardens or Web farms.</li><li>Can store session state on a computer running SQL Server that is used for other purposes and share the costs of the server.</li><li>Can cluster the computer running SQL Server to provide higher availability.</li></ul>	<ul><li>Requires an additional computer to store the session state.</li><li>Out-of-process state requires serializing data and does not perform as well as in-process state.</li><li>Provides slower access to session state than in-process mode.</li></ul>

Note

Before you can use an out-of-process state method for managing and storing session state, you must ensure that the objects defined by and used by your ASP.NET application are *serializable*. Making an object serializable is usually a matter of adding the object class with the [Serializable] attribute. Consult with the ASP.NET application developer to ensure that all of the objects stored in session state by your ASP.NET applications are serializable.

Configuring Out-of-Process Session State with the ASP.NET State Service

If you decide to manage session state by using the ASP.NET state service, you must determine whether you are going to maintain session state for a Web garden or a Web farm. Then you need to ensure that the ASP.NET state service (aspnet_state.exe) is running and, that it is configured to start automatically.

Configure out-of-process session state with the ASP.NET state service by completing one of the following tasks:

- If you are configuring session state for a Web garden, then configure the ASP.NET state service on the local Web server.

  For more information about configuring the ASP.NET state service on the local Web server, see "Configure the State Service on the ASP.NET State Server" in "IIS Deployment Procedures" in this book.

- If you are configuring session state for a Web farm, then complete the following steps:

  1. Install Windows Server 2003 on separate computer that will run the ASP.NET state service.

     The ASP.NET state service is installed as part of the .NET Framework with Windows Server 2003. Install Windows Server 2003 by using the process described in "Installing Windows Server 2003" earlier in this chapter.

  2. Configure the ASP.NET state service on the newly installed Web server.

     For more information about configuring the ASP.NET state service on the new server, see "Configure the State Service on the ASP.NET State Server" in "IIS Deployment Procedures" in this book.

Configuring Out-of-Process Session State with SQL Server

If you decide to store the session state in SQL Server, you need to create the session state database on the computer running SQL Server that is used by the ASP.NET state service. You can create the database by running the InstallSqlState.sql script on the computer running Microsoft SQL Server that is going to be storing the session data. This script creates a database called ASPState, which includes several stored procedures and adds the ASPStateTempApplications and ASPStateTempSessions tables to the TempDB database.

For more information about creating the SQL Server database for storing ASP.NET session state, see "Create a SQL Server Database for Storing ASP.NET Session State" in "IIS Deployment Procedures" in this book.

Configuring Encryption and Validation Keys

ASP.NET uses a key to help protect data so that session state data is only accessible from the Web server that created the data. In a Web garden, all of the worker processes use the same Machine.config or Web.config file, so no additional configuration is necessary. If you are configuring ASP.NET session state for a Web garden, continue to the next step in the deployment process. To continue to the next step in the ASP.NET application deployment process, see "Configuring ASP.NET Applications to Use the Appropriate Session State" later in this chapter.

In a Web farm, each Web server in the farm has a separate Machine.config or Web.config file. As a result, you need to manually configure each Web server in the farm to share the same encryption and validation keys so that they can share session state data. This allows one server to decrypt the session state data created by another server in the Web farm. You can configure the encryption and validation keys in the <**machineKey**> section of the Machine.config file.

 Tip

When you want all of the ASP.NET applications on a Web server to use the same encryption and validation keys, make the modifications in the Machine.config file. When you want to customize the encryption and validation keys for each ASP.NET application, modify the corresponding Web.config file for the application.

For each server in the Web farm, identically configure the values of the following attributes in the Machine.config or Web.config file:

- **The validationKey attribute.** This attribute contains the key that is used to validate that data tampering has not occurred. The validation algorithm, which is specified in the **validation** attribute, validates the data by using the key in the **validationKey** attribute. The **validationKey** attribute can range from 40 to 128 hexadecimal characters in length. The default value for the **validationKey** attribute is auto-generated. Configure the value for the **validationKey** attribute to be the same value for all of the servers in a Web farm.

- **The validation attribute.** This attribute is used to configure the validation algorithm used to verify the data. The validation algorithms that you can select include Message Digest 5 (MD5), Secure Hash Algorithm 1 (SHA1), or triple DES (3DES). The Web server validates the data with the key in the **validationKey** attribute and the algorithm specified by the **validation** attribute. Configure the value of the **validation** attribute to be the same value for all of the servers in a Web farm.

- **The decryptionKey attribute.** This attribute contains the key that is used to encrypt data. Valid values are 16 or 48 hexadecimal characters, which corresponds to the Data Encryption Standard (DES) or 3DES algorithm, respectively. The default value for the **decryptionKey** attribute is auto-generated. Configure the value of the **decryptionKey** attribute to be the same value for all of the servers in a Web farm.

For an example that describes how to configure the encryption and validation keys for Microsoft Content Management Server 2002, see the MSDN Online link on the Web Resources page at http://www.microsoft.com/windows/reskits/webresources, and then search for "Best Practices for Authentication for Web Farms". You can use this example to assist you in configuring the encryption and validation keys for your ASP.NET application.

Configuring ASP.NET Applications to Use the Appropriate Session State

You can configure ASP.NET session state persistence in the **<sessionState>** section of the Machine.config file for all of the ASP.NET applications on the Web server, or you can configure it in the Web.config file for each ASP.NET application. If the **<sessionState>** section of the Web.config file for an ASP.NET application is empty, the session state configuration for the application is inherited from the **<sessionState>** section of the Machine.config file.

If the **<sessionState>** section does not exist in the Machine.config file or the Web.config file, the following is the default session state behavior:

- The session time-out value for an ASP.NET session state is 20 minutes.

- The session state is maintained within all of the applications running in the same application pool.

- The session state is only maintained on the local Web server (where the session state **mode** attribute is set to **InProc**), not across multiple servers in a Web farm.

In addition to the configuration settings that are specific to the mode you selected for maintaining session state, the following attributes need to be configured:

- **The cookieless attribute.** This attribute determines whether or not the session identifier is transferred between the Web server and the client by using cookies. When the **cookieless** attribute is set to **True**, cookies are not used to convey session identifiers. When the **cookieless** attribute is set to **False**, cookies are used to convey session identifiers. The default setting is **False**.

- **The timeout attribute.** This attribute specifies the number of minutes that a session is considered valid. When the time specified in the **timeout** attribute expires, the session is disconnected. The default time-out limit is 20 minutes.

Configure the session state settings in the <**sessionState**> section for the mode that you selected.

Session state is maintained in-process

To maintain session state in-process, you can either delete the <**sessionState**> section or configure the <**sessionState**> section in the Machine.config file or the Web.config file.

The following is an example of the configuration when maintaining session state in-process:

```
<configuration>
  <system.web>
    <sessionState
        mode="InProc"
        cookieless="true"
        timeout="20"
    </sessionState>
  </system.web>
</configuration>
```

Session state is maintained out-of-process with the ASP.NET state service

To configure ASP.NET to maintain session state with the ASP.NET state service, modify the following attributes in addition to the **mode** attribute:

- **The stateConnectionString attribute.** This attribute specifies the IP address and port number where the ASP.NET state service is running. The format for this attribute is "tcpip=*server:port*", where *server* is the IP address or host name of the server, and *port* is the TCP port number that the ASP.NET state service is configured to use. The default port number is 42424.

- **The stateNetworkTimeout attribute.** This optional attribute specifies the length of time, in seconds, that the TCP/IP network connection between the Web server and the server running the ASP.NET state service can be idle before the session is abandoned. The default time-out limit is 10 seconds.

The following is an example of the configuration when maintaining session state out-of-process with the ASP.NET state service:

```
<configuration>
  <system.web>
    <sessionState
        mode="StateServer"
        cookieless="true"
        timeout="20"
        stateConnectionString="tcpip=127.0.0.1:42424"
        stateNetworkTimeout="10"
    </sessionState>
  </system.web>
</configuration>
```

Session state is maintained out-of-process with a computer running Microsoft SQL Server

To configure ASP.NET to maintain session state with a computer running SQL Server, modify the **sqlConnectionString** attribute in addition to the **mode** attribute. The **sqlConnectionString** attribute specifies the ODBC data connection string used for establishing the connection to the computer running SQL Server.

The format for the **sqlConnectionString** attribute is "data source=*odbc_connection_string*", where *odbc_connection_string* is any valid ODBC data connection string that is valid for the computer running SQL Server. For more information about creating ODBC data connection strings for Microsoft SQL Server, see the MSDN Online link on the Web Resources page at http://www.microsoft.com/windows/reskits/webresources, and then search for "How to allocate handles and connect to SQL Server (ODBC)".

The following is an example of the configuration when maintaining session state out-of-process with a computer running SQL Server:

```
<configuration>
  <system.web>
    <sessionState
        mode="SQLServer"
        cookieless="true"
        timeout="20"
        sqlConnectionString="data source=localhost;
                             Integrated Security=SSPI;
                             Initial Catalog=northwind"
    </sessionState>
  </system.web>
</configuration>
```

Securing the ASP.NET Session State Connection String

When using either of the out-of-process methods for maintaining session state — by using the ASP.NET state service or Microsoft SQL Server — the ASP.NET session state connection string is stored in the Machine.config or Web.config file in plaintext. You can further secure the ASP.NET session state connection strings by placing the session state connection strings in the registry. Then the Machine.config or Web.config files are modified to point to the corresponding registry keys.

For more information about configuring ASP.NET to store the session connection strings in the registry, see the Microsoft Knowledge Base link on the Web Resources page at http://www.microsoft.com/windows/reskits/webresources, and then search for article 329290, "HOW TO: Use the ASP.NET Utility to Encrypt Credentials and Session State Connection Strings."

 Caution

Do not edit the registry unless you have no alternative. The registry editor bypasses standard safeguards, allowing settings that can damage your system, or even require you to reinstall Windows. If you must edit the registry, back it up first and see the Registry Reference on the *Microsoft Windows Server 2003 Deployment Kit* companion CD or on the Web at http://www.microsoft.com/reskit.

Completing the ASP.NET Application Deployment

At this point in the process, your ASP.NET applications are installed on the Web server and the ASP.NET session state settings have been configured on the Web server. Now you need to ensure that the ASP.NET applications are configured to provide the appropriate levels of security and availability for your organizational needs. Then you can verify that the ASP.NET applications have been deployed successfully, capture the current configuration of the Web server, and enable client access to the ASP.NET applications on your Web server. After you complete these last steps, the deployment of your ASP.NET applications is complete.

Figure 2.4 illustrates the process for finalizing the deployment of your ASP.NET applications in IIS 6.0.

Figure 2.4   Completing the ASP.NET Application Deployment Process

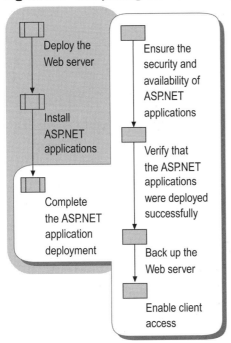

Ensuring the Security and Availability of ASP.NET Applications

At this point in the ASP.NET application deployment process, your ASP.NET applications are installed on IIS 6.0, and they are configured to run in the default application pool with the default identity of NetworkService. However, you should take further steps to help ensure that the individual ASP.NET applications are secure. In addition, you can help ensure that if any ASP.NET application fails, the remaining ASP.NET applications remain unaffected.

You can help ensure the security and availability of your ASP.NET applications by completing the following steps:

1. Follow the recommendations and process steps described in "Securing Web Sites and Applications" in this book to help ensure the security of the ASP.NET applications running on your Web server.

2. Follow the recommendations and process steps described in "Ensuring Application Availability" in this book to help ensure the availability of the ASP.NET applications running on your Web server.

Verifying That the ASP.NET Applications Were Deployed Successfully

Before deploying the Web server into a production environment, verify that the ASP.NET applications were deployed successfully by completing the following steps:

1. Review the system log in Windows Server 2003 on the Web server to determine whether any of the ASP.NET applications did not start.

   IIS 6.0 creates entries in the system log when a Web site fails to start for any reason. Search the system log on the Web server to determine whether any errors occurred. For more information about how to troubleshoot Web sites that fail to start, see "Troubleshooting" in IIS 6.0 Help, which is accessible from IIS Manager. For information about how to troubleshoot ASP.NET-specific problems, see "Troubleshooting an ASP.NET Installation" in IIS 6.0 Help, which is accessible from IIS Manager.

2. Perform functional testing of your ASP.NET applications to ensure that they behave as expected.

   You can help eliminate many obvious causes of ASP.NET application failure by reviewing the Windows logs and the application configuration settings. However, the only way to accurately assess the successful deployment of your ASP.NET applications is to perform functional testing. Functional testing is designed to ensure that the ASP.NET applications are functioning correctly for the most common usage scenarios, such as URLs and inputs. This helps ensure that the ASP.NET applications behave as designed, based on typical user interaction.

   Describing the procedures for performing functional testing of your ASP.NET applications is beyond the scope of this chapter. For more information about the general subject of testing, see the MSDN Online link on the Web Resources page at http://www.microsoft.com/windows/reskits/webresources, and then search for "testing".

Backing Up the Web Server

Before you enable client access to the Web server, perform a complete image backup. The purpose of performing this image backup is to provide a point-in-time snapshot of the Web server. If you need to restore the Web server in the event of a failure, you can use this backup to restore the Web server to a known configuration.

 Important

Do not continue unless you have a successful backup of the entire Web server. Otherwise, you can lose Web sites, applications, or data that you deployed to the Web server.

For more information about how to back up the Web server, see "Back Up and Restore the Web Server to a File or Tape" in "IIS Deployment Procedures" in this book.

Enabling Client Access

After you have deployed the ASP.NET application to the Web server, you are ready to enable client access to the ASP.NET applications. For a period of time that meets your business needs, monitor the client traffic to ensure that clients are successfully accessing the ASP.NET applications on your Web server and that the clients are experiencing expected response times.

Enable client access to the ASP.NET applications on the Web server by completing the following steps:

1. Create the appropriate DNS entries for the ASP.NET applications running on the Web server.

   For more information about how to create DNS entries for your applications, see "Managing resource records" in Help and Support Center for Windows Server 2003.

2. Monitor client traffic to determine whether clients are successfully accessing the ASP.NET applications.

   For more information about how to monitor client traffic to ASP.NET applications on the Web server, see "Monitor Active Web and FTP Connections" in "IIS Deployment Procedures" in this book.

3. Establish a monitoring period, such as a few hours or a day, to confirm that clients are accessing the ASP.NET applications on the Web server and that they are experiencing response times and application responses that meet or exceed your requirements.

Additional Resources

These resources contain additional information and tools related to this chapter.

Related Information

- "Ensuring Application Availability" in this book for information about configuring your Web server to improve the availability of your ASP.NET applications.

- "IIS Deployment Procedures" in this book for information about specific procedures for deploying ASP.NET applications in IIS 6.0.

- "Migrating Machine.config Attributes to IIS 6.0 Metabase Property Settings" in "Upgrading an IIS Server to IIS 6.0" in this book for information about how to migrate attributes in the Machine.config file to their equivalent IIS 6.0 metabase property settings.

- "Securing Web Sites and Applications" in this book for information about configuring your Web server to improve the security of your ASP.NET applications.

- The Microsoft Knowledge Base link on the Web Resources page at http://www.microsoft.com/windows/reskits/webresources, and then search for article 329290, "How To: Use the ASP.NET Utility to Encrypt Credentials and Session State Connection Strings", for information about configuring ASP.NET to store the session connection strings in the registry.

- The MSDN Online link on the Web Resources page at http://www.microsoft.com/windows/reskits/webresources, and then search for "How to allocate handles and connect to SQL Server (ODBC)", for information about creating ODBC data connection strings for Microsoft SQL Server.

- The MSDN Online link on the Web Resources page at http://www.microsoft.com/windows/reskits/webresources, and then search for "testing", for information about the general subject of testing.

Related IIS 6.0 Help Topics

- "ASP.NET Configuration" in IIS 6.0 Help, which is accessible from IIS Manager, for information about configuring ASP.NET applications when IIS 6.0 is configured to run in IIS 5.0 isolation mode.

- "Troubleshooting" in IIS 6.0 Help, which is accessible from IIS Manager, for information about how to troubleshoot Web sites that fail to start.

- "Troubleshooting an ASP.NET Installation" in IIS 6.0 Help, which is accessible from IIS Manager, for information about how to troubleshoot ASP.NET-specific problems.

Related Windows Server 2003 Help Topics

For best results in identifying Help topics by title, in Help and Support Center, under the **Search** box, click **Set search options**. Under **Help Topics**, select the **Search in title only** check box.

- "Features unavailable on 64-bit versions of the Windows Server 2003 family" in Help and Support Center for Windows Server 2003 for information about features, such as ASP.NET, that are not supported on 64-bit versions of Windows Server 2003.

- "Managing resource records" in Help and Support Center for Windows Server 2003 for information about how to create DNS entries for your applications.

CHAPTER 3

Securing Web Sites and Applications

3

Because the day-to-day operations of your organization depend on the mission-critical applications that are running on Internet Information Services (IIS) 6.0 Web servers, your Web sites and applications need the highest possible security. When you install IIS 6.0, it is installed in a highly secure and locked configuration. Depending on your Web sites and applications, you might need to configure IIS to be less restrictive so that your Web sites and applications can operate correctly. Your Web sites and applications might also need increased security configuration to authenticate users or to restrict the Web sites, applications, and data that can be accessed by users.

In This Chapter

Related Information

- For information about ASP.NET-specific deployment considerations, see "Deploying ASP.NET Applications in IIS 6.0" in this book.

- For information about balancing application security and availability, see "Ensuring Application Availability" in this book.

Overview of the Securing Web Sites and Applications Process

To provide comprehensive security for your Web sites and applications, you must ensure that the entire Web server, including each Web site and application that the server hosts, is protected from unauthorized access. Also, you might have to ensure that the Web sites and applications are protected from other Web sites and applications that are hosted on the same server. Finally, you need to initiate practices to help ensure that your Web sites and applications remain secure.

For security reasons, IIS 6.0 is not installed by default on the Microsoft® Windows® Server 2003, Standard Edition; Windows® Server 2003, Enterprise Edition; and Windows® Server 2003, Datacenter Edition operating systems. When you install IIS 6.0, it is locked down — only request handling for static Web pages is enabled, and only the World Wide Web Publishing Service (WWW service) is installed. Features such as Active Server Pages (ASP), ASP.NET, Common Gateway Interface (CGI) scripting, FrontPage® 2002 Server Extensions from Microsoft, and Web Distributed Authoring and Versioning (WebDAV) do not work by default. You can serve dynamic content and enable these features in the Web Service Extensions node in IIS Manager.

Before you begin this process, complete the following steps:

- Install Windows Server 2003 with the default options.

- Install IIS 6.0 with the default settings in **Add or Remove Programs** in Control Panel.

If you use other methods for installing and configuring Windows Server 2003, such as unattended setup, or enabling IIS 6.0 by using Manage Your Server, then the default configuration settings might not be identical.

Upon completing the process outlined in this chapter, you will have a Web server running IIS 6.0 that fulfills your security requirements. However, to maintain the security of your server, you need to implement continuing security practices such as security monitoring, detection, and response. For more information about maintaining Web server security, see "Managing a Secure IIS Solution in *Internet Information Services (IIS) 6.0 Resource Guide* of the *Microsoft® Windows® Server 2003 Resource Kit.*

 Note

The security settings described in this chapter are appropriate for Web sites and applications that are hosted on Web servers on an intranet and the Internet, unless specifically noted.

Although not the focus of this chapter, you can apply many of the security recommendations described in this chapter to enhance the security of Web servers that have been upgraded from earlier versions of IIS.

Process for Securing Web Sites and Applications

To configure security for Web sites and applications that are hosted on a newly installed Web server, you need to follow certain security practices, such as enabling only the *Web service extensions* that you need. Web service extensions provide content and features beyond serving static Web pages. Any dynamic content that is served by the Web server is done by using Web service extensions, such as content and features that are provided by ASP, ASP.NET, or CGI. In addition, each Web site and application might have specific requirements for security settings. Figure 3.1 shows the process for securing your Web sites and applications.

Figure 3.1 Securing Web Sites and Applications

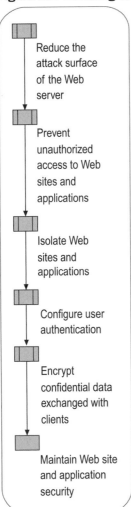

Reduce the attack surface of the Web server

Prevent unauthorized access to Web sites and applications

Isolate Web sites and applications

Configure user authentication

Encrypt confidential data exchanged with clients

Maintain Web site and application security

Securing the Web sites and applications requires that the Web server as a whole is secure. The process presented in this chapter assumes that the network infrastructure connecting the Web servers to the clients and to other servers is secure. The security of the network infrastructure is determined by the placement and configuration of the firewalls, routers, and switches in the network infrastructure.

Note

The process presented in this chapter includes all of the steps for securing your Web sites and applications in one of many possible sequences. You can complete these steps in the sequence that is recommended in this chapter, or in another sequence. Regardless of the sequence, it is recommended that you evaluate all of the steps in the process.

In addition to assuming that the network infrastructure is secure, the process presented here assumes that the server is a *dedicated Web server*. A dedicated Web server is a server that is only being used as a Web server and not for other purposes, such as a file server, print server, or database server running Microsoft SQL Server™.

For more information about securing IIS components other than Internet services, such as Simple Mail Transfer Protocol (SMTP) or Network News Transfer Protocol (NNTP), see "SMTP Administration" or "NNTP Administration" in IIS 6.0 Help, which is accessible from IIS Manager. For more information about securing other services on a multipurpose server, see "Planning a Secure Environment" in *Designing and Deploying Directory and Security Services* of the *Microsoft® Windows® Server 2003 Deployment Kit*.

Tip

To secure the Web sites and applications in a Web farm, use the process described in this chapter to configure security for each server in the Web farm.

The following quick-start guide provides a detailed overview of how to configure security for IIS 6.0. You can use this guide to help identify the steps of the security process that you need additional information to complete and skip the information with which you are already familiar. In addition, all of the procedures that are required to complete the security process are documented in "IIS Deployment Procedures in this book.

Reduce the Attack Surface of the Web Server

1. Enable only essential Windows Server 2003 components and services.
2. Enable only essential IIS 6.0 components and services.
3. Enable only essential Web service extensions.
4. Enable only essential Multipurpose Internet Mail Extensions (MIME) types.
5. Configure Windows Server 2003 security settings.

Prevent Unauthorized Access to Web Sites and Applications

1. Store content on a dedicated disk volume.
2. Set IIS Web site permissions.
3. Set IP address and domain name restrictions.
4. Set the NTFS file system permissions.

Isolate Web Sites and Applications

1. Evaluate the effects of impersonation on application compatibility:
   - Identify the impersonation behavior for ASP applications.
   - Select the impersonation behavior for ASP.NET applications.
2. Configure Web sites and applications for isolation.

Configure User Authentication

1. Configure Web site authentication.
   - Select the Web site authentication method.
   - Configure the Web site authentication method.
2. Configure File Transfer Protocol (FTP) site authentication.

Encrypt Confidential Data Exchanged with Clients

1. Use Secure Sockets Layer (SSL) to encrypt confidential data.
2. Use Internet Protocol security (IPSec) or virtual private network (VPN) with remote administration.

Maintain Web Site and Application Security

1. Obtain and apply current security patches.
2. Enable Windows Server 2003 security logs.
3. Enable file access auditing for Web site content.
4. Configure IIS logs.
5. Review security policies, processes, and procedures.

Reducing the Attack Surface of the Web Server

Immediately after installing Windows Server 2003 and IIS 6.0 with the default settings, the Web server is configured to serve only static content. If your Web sites consist of static content and you do not need any of the other IIS components, then the default configuration of IIS minimizes the attack surface of the server. When your Web sites and applications contain dynamic content, or you require one or more of the additional IIS components, you will need to enable additional features. However, you still want to ensure that you minimize the *attack surface* of the Web server. The attack surface of the Web server is the extent to which the server is exposed to a potential attacker.

However, if you reduce the attack surface of the Web server too much, you can eliminate functionality that is required by the Web sites and applications that the server hosts. You need to ensure that only the functionality that is necessary to support your Web sites and applications is enabled on the server. This ensures that the Web sites and applications will run properly on your Web server, but that the attack surface is minimized.

 Tip

In addition to new installations, you can use the information in this section to reduce the attack surface of existing Web servers.

Figure 3.2 illustrates the process for reducing the attack surface of the Web server.

Figure 3.2 Reducing the Attack Surface of the Web Server

Figure 3.2 Reducing the Attack Surface of the Web Server

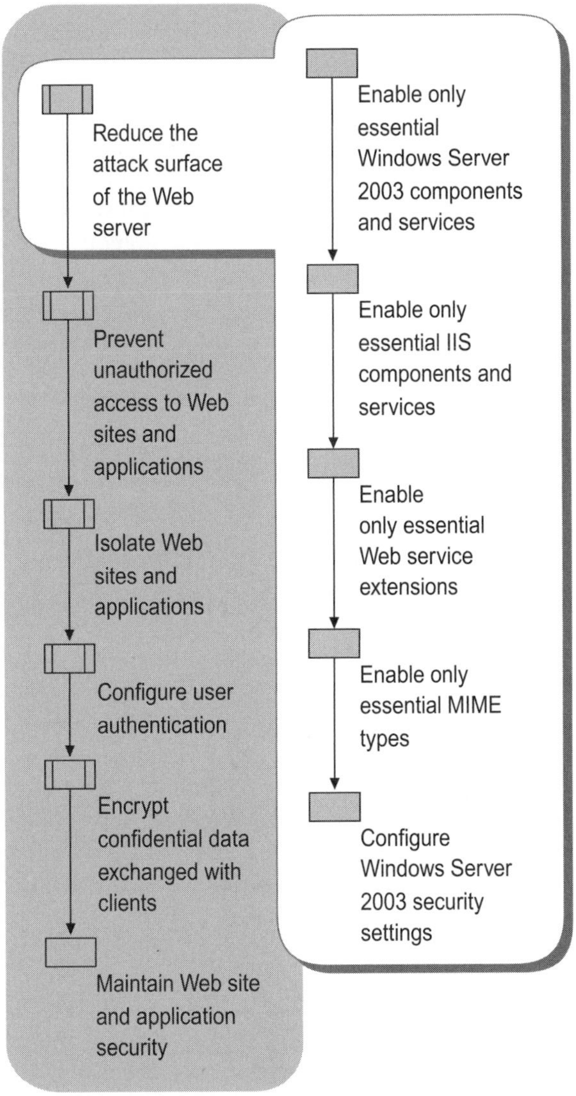

Each additional Windows Server 2003 and IIS 6.0 component is configured with the most restrictive possible security that will allow the component to still function. However, in providing any functionality, there is still an opportunity for potential attackers to exploit any weakness of the component.

For example, enabling the Domain Name System (DNS) component in Windows Server 2003 with the default configuration settings would make the server susceptible to any of the standard attacks common to DNS on Windows, UNIX, Linux, or other operating systems. Additional configuration would be required to further secure DNS, such as requiring zones that are integrated with Microsoft Active Directory® directory service.

In addition, if your primary focus is Web server administration, you might not be familiar with DNS-related security attacks. So reducing the attack surface of the server helps eliminate potential attacks that you cannot predict because of your familiarity with other Windows Server 2003 and IIS 6.0 components.

 Important

In addition to enabling only essential Windows Server 2003 and IIS 6.0 components, ensure that you configure the components to the highest possible security settings. By enabling nonessential components and services, you can increase the attack surface of your server because you have enabled these components and services without further configuring them to the most restrictive security settings.

Enabling Only Essential Windows Server 2003 Components and Services

The attack surface of the Web server is also affected by the other Windows components and services that are enabled in Windows Server 2003. When you install Windows Server 2003 as a dedicated Web server, the default components and services are configured to provide the smallest possible attack surface. In some cases, you might have installed Windows Server 2003 for other purposes, such as a file server, print server, or computer running SQL Server, so you are installing IIS 6.0 on an existing server. In this situation, you need to reevaluate the components and services that are currently running on the Web server to ensure that only the components and services that you need are enabled.

To enable and disable services, change the startup type of the service. You can configure the startup type of the service to one of the following:

- **Automatic.** The service starts automatically when the operating system starts.

- **Manual.** The service can be started by an administrator, a related operating system service, a system device driver, or an action in the user interface that is dependent on the manual service.

- **Disabled.** The service cannot be started automatically or manually; to start a disabled service, you must change the startup type to Automatic or Manual.

Table 3.1 lists the Windows Server 2003 services, as well as the default startup type, the recommended startup type, and comments about the services.

For each of the Windows Server 2003 services that are listed in Table 3.1, complete the following steps:

1. Review the recommended startup type to determine whether you need to change the default startup type.

2. Determine, based on the information provided in the comments, if the recommendation applies to your Web server.

3. Configure the startup type for the service based on the decisions made in the previous steps.

For more information about how to change the startup type of Windows Server 2003 services, see "Configure Windows Server 2003 Services" in "IIS Deployment Procedures" in this book.

Table 3.1 Recommended Service Startup Types on a Dedicated Web Server

Service Name	Default Startup Type	Recommended Startup Type	Comment
Alerter	Disabled	No change	Notifies selected users and computers of administrative alerts.
Application Layer Gateway Service	Manual	No change	Provides support for application-level plug-ins and enables network and protocol connectivity.
Application Management	Manual	See comment	Provides software installation services for applications that are deployed in **Add or Remove Programs** in Control Panel. On a dedicated Web server, this service can be disabled to prevent unauthorized installation of software.
Automatic Updates	Automatic	See comment	Provides the download and installation of critical Windows updates, such as security patches and hotfixes. This service can be disabled when automatic updates are not performed on the Web server.
Background Intelligent Transfer Service	Manual	See comment	Provides a background file-transfer mechanism and queue management, and it is used by Automatic Update to automatically download programs (such as security patches). This service can be disabled when automatic updates are not performed on the Web server.

(continued)

Table 3.1 Recommended Service Startup Types on a Dedicated Web Server *(continued)*

Service Name	Default Startup Type	Recommended Startup Type	Comment
ClipBook	Disabled	See comment	Enables the Clipbook Viewer to create and share data that can be reviewed by remote users.
COM+ Event System	Manual	No change	Provides automatic distribution of events to COM+ components.
COM+ System Application	Manual	No change	Manages the configuration and tracking of COM+-based components.
Computer Browser	Automatic	No change	Maintains the list of computers on the network, and supplies the list to programs that request the list.
Cryptographic Services	Automatic	No change	Provides three management services: Catalog Database Service, which confirms the signatures of Windows files; Protected Root Service, which adds and removes Trusted Root Certification Authority certificates from the Web server; and Key Service, which helps in enrolling certificates.
DHCP Client	Automatic	No change	Required to automatically obtain IP configuration and to dynamically update records in DNS.
Distributed File System	Automatic	Disable	Manages logical volumes that are distributed across a local area network (LAN) or wide area network (WAN). On a dedicated Web server, disable Distributed File System.
Distributed Link Tracking Client	Automatic	Disabled	Maintains links between NTFS V5 file system files within the Web server and other servers in the domain. On a dedicated Web server, disable Distributed Link Tracking.
Distributed Link Tracking Server	Manual	Disabled	Tracks information about files that are moved between NTFS V5 volumes throughout a domain. On a dedicated Web server, disable Distributed Link Tracking.

(continued)

Table 3.1   Recommended Service Startup Types on a Dedicated Web Server *(continued)*

Service Name	Default Startup Type	Recommended Startup Type	Comment
Distributed Transaction Coordinator	Automatic	No Change	Coordinates transactions that span multiple resource managers, such as databases, message queues, and file systems.
DNS Client	Automatic	No change	Allows resolution of DNS names.
Error Reporting Service	Automatic	See comment	Collects, stores, and reports unexpected application crashes to Microsoft. If this service is stopped, then Error Reporting will occur only for kernel faults. On a dedicated Web server, disable Error Reporting Service.
Event Log	Automatic	No change	Writes event log messages that are issued by Windows-based programs and components to the log files.
Fax Service	Manual	Disabled	Provides the ability to send and receive faxes through fax resources that are available on the Web server and network. On a dedicated Web server, this service can be disabled because sending and receiving faxes is not a typical function of a Web Server.
File Replication Service	Manual	No change	Enables files to be automatically copied and maintained simultaneously on multiple servers.
Help and Support	Automatic	No change	Enables Help and Support Center to run on the Web server.
HTTP SSL	Manual	No change	Implements the Secure Hypertext Transfer Protocol (HTTPS) for the HTTP service by using SSL. HTTP.sys automatically starts this service when any Web sites require SSL.
Human Interface Device Access	Disabled	No change	Enables generic input to Human Interface Devices (HIDs), which activates and maintains the use of predefined hot buttons on keyboards, remote controls, and other multimedia devices.

(continued)

Table 3.1 Recommended Service Startup Types on a Dedicated Web Server *(continued)*

Service Name	Default Startup Type	Recommended Startup Type	Comment
IMAPI CD-Burning COM Service	Disabled	No change	Manages CD recording by using the Image Mastering API (IMAPI).
Indexing Service	Manual	See comment	Indexes content and properties of files on the Web server to provide rapid access to the file through a flexible query language. On a dedicated Web server, disable this service unless Web sites or applications specifically leverage the Indexing Service for searching site content.
Internet Connection Firewall (ICF)/Internet Connection Sharing (ICS)	Disabled	No change	Provides network address translation (NAT), addressing and name resolution, and intrusion detection when connected through a dial-up or broadband connection. On a dedicated Web server, disable to prevent inadvertent enabling of NAT, which would prevent the Web server from communicating with the remainder of the network.
Intersite Messaging	Disabled	No changes	Required by Distributed File System (DFS).
IPSec Services	Automatic	No change	Provides management and coordination of Internet Protocol security (IPSec) policies with the IPSec driver.
Kerberos Key Distribution enter	Disabled	No change	Provides the ability for users to log on using the Kerberos V5 authentication protocol.
License Logging Service	Disabled	No change	Monitors and records client access licensing for portions of the operating system, such as IIS, Terminal Services, and file and print sharing, and for products that are not a part of the operating system, such as Microsoft SQL Server or Microsoft Exchange Server. On a dedicated Web server, this service can be disabled.
Logical Disk Manager	Automatic	No change	Required to ensure that dynamic disk information is up to date.

(continued)

Table 3.1   Recommended Service Startup Types on a Dedicated Web Server *(continued)*

Service Name	Default Startup Type	Recommended Startup Type	Comment
Logical Disk Manager Administrative Service	Manual	No change	Required to perform disk administration.
Messenger	Disabled	No change	Transmits net sends and Alerter service messages between clients and servers.
Microsoft Software Shadow Copy	Manual	No change	Manages software-based volume shadow copies taken by the Volume Shadow Copy service. On a dedicated Web server, this service can be disabled when volume shadow copies are not used.
Net Logon	Manual	No change	Maintains a secure channel between the domain controller, other domain controllers, member servers, and workstations in the same domain and trusted domains.
NetMeeting Remote Desktop Sharing	Manual	Disabled	Eliminates potential security threats by allowing domain-controller remote administration through NetMeeting.
Network Connections	Manual	No change	Manages objects in the Network Connections directory.
Network DDE	Disabled	No change	Provides network transport and security for Dynamic Data Exchange (DDE) for programs running on the Web server. This service can be disabled when no DDE applications are running locally on the Web server.
Network DDE DSDM	Disabled	No change	Used by Network DDE. This service can be disabled when Network DDE is disabled.
Network Location Awareness (NLA)	Manual	No change	Collects and stores network configuration and location information, and notifies applications when this information changes.
NTLM Security Support Provider	Manual	No change	Provides security to RPC programs that use transports other than named pipes, and enables users to log on using the NTLM authentication protocol.

(continued)

Table 3.1 Recommended Service Startup Types on a Dedicated Web Server *(continued)*

Service Name	Default Startup Type	Recommended Startup Type	Comment
Performance Logs and Alerts	Manual	See comment	Collects performance data for the domain controller, writes the data to a log, or generates alerts. This service can be set to automatic when you want to log performance data or generate alerts without an administrator being logged on.
Plug and Play	Automatic	No change	Required to automatically recognize and adapt to changes in the Web server hardware with little or no user input.
Portable Media Serial Number Service	Manual	No change	Retrieves the serial number of any portable media player that is connected to the computer.
Print Spooler	Automatic	See comment	Manages all local and network print queues and controls all print jobs. On a dedicated Web server, this service can be disabled when no printing is required.
Protected Storage	Automatic	No change	Protects storage of sensitive information, such as private keys, and prevents access by unauthorized services, processes, or users. This service is used on a dedicated Web server for smart-card logon.
Remote Access Auto Connection Manager	Manual	See comment	Detects unsuccessful attempts to connect to a remote network or computer and provides alternative methods for connection. On a dedicated Web server, this service can be disabled when no VPN or dial-up connections are initiated.
Remote Access Connection Manager	Manual	See comment	Manages VPN and dial-up connection from the Web server to the Internet or other remote networks. On a dedicated Web server, this service can be disabled when no VPN or dial-up connections are initiated.

(continued)

Table 3.1 Recommended Service Startup Types on a Dedicated Web Server *(continued)*

Service Name	Default Startup Type	Recommended Startup Type	Comment
Remote Desktop Help Sessions Manager	Manual	Disabled	Manages and controls Remote Assistance. On a dedicated Web server, this service can be disabled. Use Terminal Services instead.
Remote Procedure Call (RPC)	Automatic	No change	Serves as the RPC endpoint mapper for all applications and services that use RPC communications.
Remote Procedure Call (RPC) Locater	Manual	See comment	Enables RPC clients using the RpcNs* family of application programming interfaces (APIs) to locate RPC servers and manage the RPC name service database. This service can be disabled if no applications use the RpcNs* APIs.
Remote Registry Service	Automatic	No change	Enables remote users to modify registry settings on the Web server, provided the remote users have the required permissions. By default, only members of the Administrators and Backup Operators groups can access the registry remotely.
Removable Storage	Manual	See comment	Manages and catalogs removable media, and operates automated removable media devices, such as tape auto loaders or CD jukeboxes. This service can be disabled when removable media devices are directly connected to the Web server.
Resultant Set of Policy Provider	Manual	No change	Enables a user to connect to a remote computer, access the Windows Management Instrumentation (WMI) database for that Web server, and then either verify the current Group Policy settings or check the settings before they are applied.
Routing and Remote Access	Disabled	No change	Enables LAN-to-LAN, LAN-to-WAN, VPN, and NAT routing services.

(continued)

Table 3.1 Recommended Service Startup Types on a Dedicated Web Server *(continued)*

Service Name	Default Startup Type	Recommended Startup Type	Comment
Secondary Logon	Automatic	No change	Allows you to run specific tools and programs with different permissions and user rights than the default permissions and user rights of the account under which you logged on.
Security Accounts Manager	Automatic	No change	A protected subsystem that manages user and group account information.
Server	Automatic	No change	Provides RPC support, file sharing, print sharing, and named pipe sharing over the network.
Shell Hardware Detection	Automatic	No change	Provides notification for AutoPlay hardware events.
Smart Card	Manual	No change	Manages and controls access to a smart card that is inserted into a smart card reader attached to the Web server.
Special Administration Console Helper	Manual	No change	Allows administrators to remotely access a command prompt by using Emergency Management Services. This service can be disabled when Emergency Management Services is not being used to remotely manage the Web server.
System Event Notification	Automatic	No change	Monitors system events and notifies subscribers to the COM+ Event System of these events.
Task Scheduler	Automatic	No change	Provides the ability to schedule automated tasks on the Web server.
TCP/IP NetBIOS Helper Service	Automatic	No change	Provides support for the NetBIOS over TCP/IP (NetBT) service and NetBIOS name resolution for clients.
Telephony	Manual	See comment	Provides Telephony API (TAPI) support of client programs that control telephony devices and IP-based voice connections. On a dedicated Web server, this service can be disabled when TAPI is not used by applications.

(continued)

Table 3.1   Recommended Service Startup Types on a Dedicated Web Server *(continued)*

Service Name	Default Startup Type	Recommended Startup Type	Comment
Telnet	Manual	Disabled	Enables a remote user to log on and run applications from a command line on the Web server. To reduce the attack surface, disable Telnet unless it is used for remote administration of branch offices or of Web servers that have no keyboard or monitor directly attached (also known as *headless* Web servers). Because Telnet traffic is plaintext, Terminal Services is the preferred method for remote administration.
Terminal Services	Manual	See comment	Allows multiple remote users to be connected interactively to the Web server, and provides display of desktops and run applications. To reduce the attack surface, disable Terminal Services unless it is used for remote administration of branch offices or headless Web servers.
Terminal Services Session Directory	Disabled	No change	Enables a user connection request to be routed to the appropriate terminal server in a cluster.
Themes	Disabled	No change	Provides user-experience theme management.
Uninterruptible Power Supply	Automatic	No change	Manages an uninterruptible power supply (UPS) that is connected to the Web server by a serial port.

(continued)

Table 3.1 Recommended Service Startup Types on a Dedicated Web Server *(continued)*

Service Name	Default Startup Type	Recommended Startup Type	Comment
Upload Managers	Manual	See comment	Manages the synchronous and asynchronous file transfers between clients and servers on the network. Driver data is anonymously uploaded from these transfers and then used by Microsoft to help users find the drivers they need. The Driver Feedback Server asks for the permission of the client to upload the hardware profile of the Web server and then search the Internet for information about how to obtain the appropriate drivers or how to get support. To reduce the attack surface, disable this service on dedicated Web servers.
Virtual Disk Services	Manual	No change	Provides software volume and hardware volume management service.
Volume Shadow Copy	Manual	No change	Manages and implements volume shadow copies that are used for backup and other purposes. This service can be disabled when volume shadow copies are used on the Web server.
WebClient	Disabled	No change	Enables Windows-based programs to create, access, and modify Internet-based files.
Windows Audio	Disabled	No change	Manages audio devices for Windows-based programs.
Windows Image Acquisition (WIA)	Disabled	No change	Provides image acquisition services for scanners and cameras.
Windows Installer	Manual	No change	Adds, modifies, and removes applications that are provided as a Windows Installer (.msi) package.
Windows Management Instrumentation	Automatic	No change	Provides a common interface and object model to access management information about the Web server through the WMI interface.

(continued)

Table 3.1   Recommended Service Startup Types on a Dedicated Web Server *(continued)*

Service Name	Default Startup Type	Recommended Startup Type	Comment
Windows Management Instrumentation Driver Extensions	Manual	No change	Monitors all drivers and event trace providers that are configured to publish WMI or event trace information.
WinHTTP Web Proxy Auto-Discovery Service	Manual	See comment	Implements the Web Proxy Auto-Discovery (WPAD) protocol for Windows HTTP services (WinHTTP) and enables an HTTP client to automatically discover a proxy configuration. On dedicated Web servers, this service can be disabled
Wireless Configuration	Automatic	See comment	Enables automatic configuration for IEEE 802.11 adapters. On dedicated Web servers without wireless network adapters, this service can be disabled.
WMI Performance Adapter	Manual	See comment	Provides performance library information from WMI providers to clients on the network. On dedicated Web servers that do not use WMI to provide performance library information, this service can be disabled.
Workstation	Automatic	No change	Creates and maintains client network connections to remote servers.

Enabling Only Essential IIS Components and Services

IIS 6.0 includes other components and services in addition to the WWW service, such as the File Transfer Protocol Service (FTP service) and the Simple Mail Transfer Protocol (SMTP) service. You can install and enable IIS components and services by using the **Application Server** subcomponent, which is found in **Add or Remove Windows Components** in **Add or Remove Programs** in Control Panel. After installing IIS, you need to enable the IIS 6.0 components and services that are required by the Web sites and applications running on your Web server.

Enable only the essential IIS 6.0 components and services that are required by your Web sites and applications. Enabling unnecessary components and services increases the attack surface of the Web server.

When a Web site or application does not function on the Web server and you suspect that an IIS 6.0 component or service might need to be enabled, complete the following steps:

1. Enable the individual IIS 6.0 component or service that you believe will allow the Web site or application to function.

2. Test the Web site or application for proper operation.

3. If the Web site or application functions correctly, further configure the IIS 6.0 component or service to the most restrictive security settings.

4. If enabling the IIS 6.0 component or service does not allow the Web site or application to function, disable the IIS 6.0 component or service and continue troubleshooting the problem.

The Web site or application might not function properly because of issues that are not security-related. For example, an Internet Server API (ISAPI) extension that is used by an application might not be installed properly. Although it might appear that the ISAPI extension is disabled, the problem might actually be caused by a faulty installation or configuration setting for the ISAPI extension. For more information about troubleshooting problems related to Web sites and applications that are not functioning, see "Troubleshooting" in IIS 6.0 Help, which is accessible from IIS Manager.

 Important

When you are troubleshooting Web site- and application-related problems, do not enable all of the IIS 6.0 components and services. Enabling all of the IIS 6.0 components and services will unnecessarily increase the attack surface of the Web server.

For each of the subcomponents of the application server that are listed in Table 3.2 through Table 3.6, complete the following steps:

1. Review the recommended settings to determine whether you need to make changes to the default settings.

2. Determine, based on the information provided in the comments, if the recommendation applies to your server.

3. Enable or disable the component based on the decisions made in the previous steps.

   For more information about how to configure the IIS 6.0 protocols and services, see "Configure IIS Components and Services" in "IIS Deployment Procedures" in this book.

Table 3.2   Subcomponents of the Application Server

Subcomponent	Default Setting	Recommended Setting	Comment
Application Server Console	Enabled	No change	Provides an MMC snap-in that includes administration for all of the Web Application Server (WAS) components. On a dedicated Web server, this component is not required because only IIS Manager is used.
ASP.NET	Disabled	See comment	Provides support for ASP.NET applications. Enable this component when you need to run ASP.NET applications on the Web server.
Enable network COM+ access	Enabled	See comment	Allows the Web server to host COM+ components for distributed applications. Disable this component unless it is required by your applications.
Enable network DTC access	Disabled	See comment	Allows the Web server to host applications that participate in network transactions through Distributed Transaction Coordinator (DTC). Disable this component unless it is required by your applications.
Internet Information Services (IIS)	Enabled (See Table 3.3 for subcomponents)	No change	Provides basic Web and FTP services. This component is required on a dedicated Web server. Note: If this component is not enabled, then all subcomponents are not enabled.

(continued)

Table 3.2 Subcomponents of the Application Server *(continued)*

Subcomponent	Default Setting	Recommended Setting	Comment
Message Queuing	Disabled (See Table 3.4 for subcomponents)	See comment	Provides guaranteed messaging, security, and transactional support for applications that communicate through messaging services provided by Message Queuing (also known as MSMQ). This component is required when your Web sites and applications use Message Queuing. Note: If this component is not enabled, then all subcomponents are not enabled.

Table 3.3 Subcomponents of Internet Information Services (IIS)

Subcomponent	Default Setting	Recommended Setting	Comment
Background Intelligent Transfer Service (BITS) server extension	Disabled	See comment	BITS is a background file transfer mechanism used by applications such as Windows Updates and Automatic Updates. Enable this component when you have software that depends on it, such as Windows Updates or Automatic Updates to automatically apply service packs, hot fixes, or install other software on the Web server. For more information, see "Obtaining and Applying Current Security Patches" later in this chapter.
Common Files	Enabled	No change	On a dedicated Web server, these files are required by IIS and must always be enabled.

(continued)

Table 3.3   Subcomponents of Internet Information Services (IIS) *(continued)*

Subcomponent	Default Setting	Recommended Setting	Comment
File Transfer Protocol (FTP) Service	Disabled	No change	Allows the Web server to provide FTP services.
			This component is not required on a dedicated Web server. However, you might need to enable FTP on a server that is only used for posting content, to support software such as Microsoft FrontPage® 2002 without enabling FrontPage 2002 Server Extensions.
			Because the FTP credentials are always sent in plaintext, it is recommended you connect to FTP servers through a secured connection, such as those provided by IPSec or a VPN tunnel.
			For more information, see "Using IPSec or VPN with Remote Administration" later in this chapter.
FrontPage 2002 Server Extensions	Disabled	See comment	Provides FrontPage support for administering and publishing Web sites.
			On a dedicated Web server, disable when no Web sites are using FrontPage Server Extensions.
Internet Information Services Manager	Enabled	See comment	Administrative interface for IIS.
			Disable when you do not want to administer the Web server locally.
Internet Printing	Disabled	No change	Provides Web-based printer management and allows printers to be shared by using HTTP.
			This component is not required on a dedicated Web server.

(continued)

Table 3.3   Subcomponents of Internet Information Services (IIS) *(continued)*

Subcomponent	Default Setting	Recommended Setting	Comment
NNTP Service	Disabled	No change	Distributes, queries, retrieves, and posts Usenet news articles on the Internet. This component is not required on a dedicated Web server.
SMTP Service	Enabled	Disabled	Supports the transfer of electronic mail. This component is not required on a dedicated Web server.
World Wide Web Service	Table 3.6 for subcomponents)	No change	Provides Internet services, such as static and dynamic content, to clients. This component is required on a dedicated Web server. Note: If this component is not enabled, then all subcomponents are not enabled.

Table 3.4   Subcomponents of Message Queuing

Subcomponent	Default Setting	Recommended Setting	Comment
Active Directory Integration	Disabled	See comment	Provides integration with Active Directory whenever the Web server belongs to a domain.
Common	Disabled	See comment	Required by Message Queuing.
Downlevel Client Support	Disabled	See comment	Provides access to Active Directory and site recognition for clients that are not Active Directory-aware.
MSMQ HTTP Support	Disabled	See comment	Provides the sending and receiving of messages over the HTTP transport.
Routing support	Disabled	See comment	Provides store-and-forward messaging as well as efficient routing services for Message Queuing.

(continued)

Table 3.4   Subcomponents of Message Queuing *(continued)*

Subcomponent	Default Setting	Recommended Setting	Comment
Triggers	Disabled	See comment	Provides support to associate the arrival of incoming messages at a queue with functionality in a COM component or stand-alone program. This component is required when your Web sites and applications use Message Queuing and use Message Queuing triggers.

Table 3.5   Subcomponents of the Background Intelligent Transfer Service (BITS) Server Extension

Subcomponent	Default Setting	Recommended Setting	Comment
BITS management console snap-in	Disabled	No change	Installs an MMC snap-in for administering BITS. Enable this component when you enable the BITS server extension ISAPI component.
BITS server extension ISAPI	Disabled	No change	Installs the BITS ISAPI so that the Web server can transfer data by using BITS. This component is required when you want to use Windows Updates or Automatic Updates to automatically apply service packs and hot fixes to the Web server. For more information, see "Obtaining and Applying Current Security Patches" later in this chapter.

Table 3.6 Subcomponents of the World Wide Web Service

Subcomponent	Default Setting	Recommended Setting	Comment
Active Server Pages	Disabled	See comment	Provides support for Active Server Pages (ASP). Disable this component when none of the Web sites or applications on the Web server uses ASP. You can disable this component in **Add or Remove Windows Components**, which is accessible from **Add or Remove Programs** in Control Panel, or in the Web Service Extensions node in IIS Manager. For more information, see "Enabling Only Essential Web Service Extensions" later in this chapter.
Internet Data Connector	Disabled	See comment	Provides support for dynamic content provided through files with .idc extensions. Disable this component when none of the Web sites or applications on the Web server include files with .idc extensions. You can disable this component in **Add or Remove Windows Components**, which is accessible from **Add or Remove Programs** in Control Panel, or in the Web Service Extensions node in IIS Manager. For more information, see "Enabling Only Essential Web Service Extensions" later in this chapter.

(continued)

Table 3.6   Subcomponents of the World Wide Web Service *(continued)*

Subcomponent	Default Setting	Recommended Setting	Comment
Remote Administration (HTML)	Disabled	No change	Provides an HTML interface for administering IIS. Use IIS Manager instead to provide easier administration and to reduce the attack surface of the Web server. This component is not required on a dedicated Web server.
Remote Desktop Web Connection	Disabled	No change	Includes Microsoft ActiveX® controls and sample pages for hosting Terminal Services client connections. Use IIS Manager instead to provide easier administration and to reduce the attack surface of the Web server. This component is not required on a dedicated Web server.
Server-Side Includes	Disabled	See comment	Provides support for .shtm, .shtml, and .stm files. Disable this component when none of the Web sites or applications on the Web server includes files with these extensions.

(continued)

Table 3.6 Subcomponents of the World Wide Web Service *(continued)*

Subcomponent	Default Setting	Recommended Setting	Comment
WebDav Publishing	Disabled	Disabled	Web Distributed Authoring and Versioning (WebDAV) extends the HTTP/1.1 protocol to allow clients to publish, lock, and manage resources on the Web. Disable this component on a dedicated Web server. You can disable this component in **Add or Remove Windows Components**, which is accessible from **Add or Remove Programs** in Control Panel, or in the Web Service Extensions node in IIS Manager For more information, see "Enabling Only Essential Web Service Extensions" later in this chapter.
World Wide Web Service	Enabled	No change	Provides Internet services, such as static and dynamic content, to clients. This component is required on a dedicated Web server.

Enabling Only Essential Web Service Extensions

If your Web sites and applications that are hosted on IIS 6.0 have extended functionality beyond static Web pages, including the generation of dynamic content, any dynamic content served or extended features provided by the Web server are done through Web service extensions.

For security reasons, you can enable or disable individual Web service extensions in IIS 6.0. After a new installation, IIS serves only static content. You can enable dynamic content capabilities, such as ASP.NET, Server-Side Includes, WebDAV publishing, and FrontPage 2002 Server Extensions, in the Web Service Extensions node in IIS Manager.

For example, one of your applications might use a custom ISAPI extension to provide access to a proprietary database. First, you need to add the custom ISAPI extension to the Web service extensions list. Then you can set the ISAPI extension that is used by the application to **Allowed**, explicitly granting it permission to run.

Enabling all of the Web service extensions ensures the highest possible compatibility with existing applications, regardless of whether you enable each of the Web service extensions individually or change the status of **All Unknown ISAPI Extensions** to **Allowed**. However, enabling all of the Web service extensions creates a security risk because it increases the attack surface of the Web server by enabling functionality that might be unnecessary for your server.

Web service extensions allow you to enable and disable the serving of dynamic content. MIME types allow you to enable and disable the serving of static content. For more information about enabling and disabling the serving of static content, see "Enabling Only Essential MIME Types" later in this chapter.

 Tip

If the appropriate Web service extension is not enabled, the Web server returns a 404 error to the client when attempting to serve the dynamic content. When the 404 error is returned as a result of a Web service extension not being enabled, a 404.2 error entry is placed in the IIS log. For more information about troubleshooting IIS, see "Troubleshooting" in IIS 6.0 Help, which is accessible from IIS Manager.

Configure the Web service extensions by completing the following steps:

1. Enable the essential predefined Web service extensions based on the information in Table 3.1.

Table 3.7   Predefined Web Service Extensions

Web Service Extension	Description
Active Server Pages	Enable this extension when one or more of the Web sites and applications contains ASP content.
ASP.NET version 1.1.4322	Enable this extension when one or more of the Web sites and applications contains ASP.NET content.
FrontPage Server Extensions 2002	Enable this extension when one or more of the Web sites use FrontPage Server Extensions.
Internet Data Connector	Enable this extension when one or more of the Web sites and applications uses the Internet Data Connector (IDC) to display database information (content includes .idc and .idx files).
Server-Side Includes	Enable this extension when one or more of the Web sites use server-side include (SSI) directives to instruct the Web server to insert various types of content into a Web page.
WebDAV	Enable this extension when you want to support WebDAV on the Web server. This Web service extension is not recommended on a dedicated Web server.

2. For each Web service extension that is used by your Web sites and applications and that is not one of the default Web service extensions, add a new entry to the Web service extensions list and configure the status of the new entry to **Allowed**. For information about how to add a Web service extension to the list, see "Configure Web Service Extensions" in "IIS Deployment Procedures" in this book.

3. Use a Web browser on a client computer to verify that the Web sites and applications function properly on the server.

Enabling Only Essential MIME Types

IIS 6.0 serves only the static files with extensions that are registered in the Multipurpose Internet Mail Extensions (MIME) types list. IIS 6.0 is preconfigured to recognize a default set of global MIME types, which are recognized by all configured Web sites. You can define MIME types at the Web site and directory levels, independently of one another or the types defined globally. IIS also allows you to change, remove, or configure additional MIME types. For any static content file extensions used by the Web sites hosted by IIS that are not defined in the MIME types list, you must create a corresponding MIME type entry.

For example, a Web site or application might include static content with an extension that is not included in the default set of global MIME types. To allow the Web server to serve the new static content, you must add the extension to the MIME types list.

 Tip
If the appropriate MIME type entries are not created in the MIME types list, the Web server returns a 404 error to the client when attempting to serve unknown static content types. When the 404 error is returned as a result of an unknown MIME type, a 404.3 error entry is placed in the IIS log. For more information about troubleshooting IIS, see "Troubleshooting" in IIS 6.0 Help, which is accessible from IIS Manager.

Configure the MIME types by completing the following steps:

1. For each static file type used by your Web sites and applications, ensure that an entry exists in the MIME types list.

   When your application uses the standard MIME types that are included in IIS 6.0, no new entry is required in the MIME types list. For information about how to add a MIME type to the MIME types list, see "Configure MIME Types" in "IIS Deployment Procedures" in this book.

2. Use a Web browser on a client computer to verify that the Web sites and applications function properly on the server.

Configuring Windows Server 2003 Security Settings

After installing Windows Server 2003, the security settings are configured so that the server is locked down. After installing IIS 6.0, evaluate the default security settings to determine whether they are sufficient for the Web sites and applications that your Web server hosts. You might need more stringent security requirements for Web sites and applications when the following is true:

- Users on the Internet access the Web sites and applications.

- The Web sites and applications contain confidential information.

Configure Windows Server 2003 to more restrictive security settings by completing the following steps:

1. Rename the Administrator account.

The built-in account, Administrator, exists by default on every newly installed Web server. Potential attackers only have to guess the password for this well-known user account to exploit it. You can rename the Administrator user account to help protect your Web server from potential attackers. For more information about how to rename the Administrator user account, see "Secure Windows Server 2003 Built-in Accounts" in "IIS Deployment Procedures" in this book.

 Important

During the default installation of Windows Server 2003, the Guest account is disabled. Ensure that the Guest account has not been enabled since the installation.

2. Format all disk volumes with the NTFS file system.

From a security perspective, the primary reason for requiring that all disk volumes are formatted with NTFS is that NTFS is the only file system supported by Windows Server 2003 that allows you to secure files and folders. FAT or FAT32 partitions cannot be secured.

Because the Web sites and applications are stored as files and folders on the Web server, NTFS helps prevent unauthorized users from directly accessing or modifying the files and folders that make up your Web sites and applications. For more information about the benefits of formatting disk volumes as NTFS on Web servers, see "NTFS Permissions" in IIS 6.0 Help, which is accessible from IIS Manager.

If any existing disk volumes are FAT or FAT32, convert the disk volumes to NTFS. For more information about how to convert existing disk volumes to NTFS, see "Convert Existing Disk Volumes to NTFS" in "IIS Deployment Procedures" in this book.

3. Remove NTFS permissions that are granted to the Everyone group on the root folder of all disk volumes.

By default, the Everyone group is granted Read and Execute permissions on the root folder of each disk volume. The default permissions can pose a potential security threat for any newly created folders on the volumes because, unless explicitly denied, these permissions are inherited in any new folders. To help prevent this potential security problem, remove all permissions that are granted to the Everyone group on the root folder of all disk volumes.

 Important

The Administrators group still has full control on the root folder of each disk volume. In "Setting NTFS Permissions", later in this chapter, you will grant access to the Web site users by setting the appropriate NTFS permissions on the Web site content.

For more information about how to remove the permissions that are granted to the Everyone group on the root folder of each disk volume, see "Secure the Root Folder of Each Disk Volume" in "IIS Deployment Procedures" in this book.

4. Remove any compilers or development environments.

If compilers or development environments are installed on production Web servers, potential attackers can use them to upload source files to a malicious program and then use the Web server to compile the malicious program. In many instances, the source files might not be perceived as a threat, whereas an executable file would be. You can remove any compilers and development environments to help ensure that potential attackers cannot remotely compile a malicious program and then run that malicious program on the Web server.

Consult the documentation of the compiler or development environment for information about how to remove them.

5. Disable NetBIOS over TCP/IP.

To prevent attackers from executing the NetBIOS Adapter Status command on a server, and reveal the name of the user who is currently logged on, disable NetBIOS over TCP/IP on public connections of the server.

 Important

Before you disable NetBIOS over TCP/IP, make sure that it doesn't affect the management tools that you use to manage the server and other applications running on the server. You can do this by disabling NetBIOS over TCP/IP on a test server before disabling it on your production servers.

Preventing Unauthorized Access to Web Sites and Applications

Each Web site and application in IIS 6.0 and Windows Server 2003 is stored as a grouping of folders and files. Unauthorized access to, or modification of, these files and folders can present a serious breach of security. You must ensure that only authorized users can access or modify the Web sites and applications that are hosted on your Web server.

To help prevent unauthorized access to Web sites and applications on your Web server, use any combination of the steps illustrated in Figure 3.3. Based on the security requirements of your organization, you might perform a subset of the steps or all of the steps.

Figure 3.3 Preventing Unauthorized Access to Web Sites and Applications

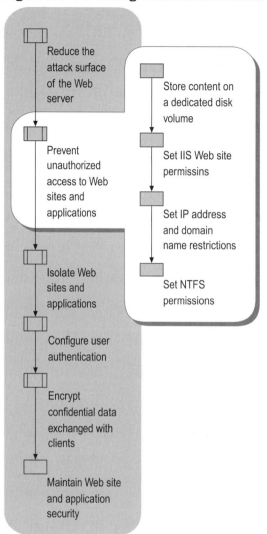

Storing Content on a Dedicated Disk Volume

Store the files and folders that comprise the content of your Web sites and applications on a dedicated disk volume that does not contain the operating system. Doing this helps prevent *directory transversal attacks*. Directory transversal attacks occur when an attacker attempts to send the Web server a request for a file that is located in another directory structure.

For example, Cmd.exe exists in the *systemroot*\System32 folder. Without the appropriate security settings, an attacker might be able to make a request to *systemroot*\System32\Cmd.exe and invoke the command prompt. If the Web site content is stored on a separate disk volume, such a directory transversal attack cannot work because Cmd.exe does not exist on the same disk volume. The default NTFS permissions for Windows Server 2003 prohibit anonymous users from executing or modifying any files in the systemroot folder and subfolders, so that only an unauthorized authenticated user can perform this type of attack.

In addition to security concerns, placing the content on a disk volume that is dedicated to Web site and application content makes administration tasks, such as backup and restore, easier. In cases where you store the content on a separate physical drive that is dedicated to the content, you will reduce the disk contention on the system volume and improve overall disk-access performance. Ensure that the dedicated disk volume is formatted as NTFS.

To help protect your Web sites and applications, store content on dedicated disk volumes by completing the following steps:

1. Create a disk volume, or designate an existing disk volume, where the Web sites and applications will be stored.

2. Configure the NTFS permissions on the root of the disk volume so that:

    ▪ The Administrators group has full control.

    ▪ All other permissions are removed.

3. Create a folder, or designate an existing folder, on the dedicated disk volume to hold the subfolders that will contain the Web sites and applications.

4. Beneath the folder that you created, or designated, in the previous step, create a subfolder for each Web site or application that will be installed on the Web server.

5. Install the Web sites and applications in the subfolders that you created in the previous step.

At this step in the deployment process, only members of the Administrators group have access to the content. You will grant access to the users who will access the Web sites and applications in "Setting NTFS Permissions" later in this chapter.

Setting IIS Web Site Permissions

In IIS 6.0, you can set Web site permissions, which allow you to control access to a Web site or virtual directory. IIS examines Web site permissions to determine which type of action can occur, such as accessing the source code of a script or browsing folders.

Use Web site permissions in conjunction with NTFS permissions, not in place of NTFS permissions. You can set Web site permissions for specific sites, directories, and files. Unlike NTFS permissions, Web site permissions affect everyone who tries to access your Web site.

 Note

If Web site permissions conflict with NTFS permissions for a directory or file, the more restrictive settings are applied.

Table 3.8 lists and describes the Web site permissions that are supported by IIS 6.0.

Table 3.8   Web Site Permissions That Are Supported by IIS 6.0

Permission	Description
Read	Users can view the content and properties of directories or files. This permission is set by default. This permission is required for Web sites that have static content. If all of your content is scripted, such as a Web site that only uses ASP content, you can remove the Read permission.
Write	Users can change content and properties of directories or files.
Script Source Access	Users can access source files. If the Read permission is set, then users can read source files; if the Write permission is set, then users can modify the content and properties of the source files. The Script Source Access permission also applies to the source code for scripts. This option is not available if both the Read and Write permissions are not set.
	Set this permission only when using WebDAV. In addition, make sure that you require authentication for this site and that your file permissions are set correctly.
	Important
	When you set the Script Source Access permission, users might be able to view sensitive information, such as a user name and password. Users might also be able to change source code that runs on your server, and seriously affect the security and performance of your server.
Directory browsing	Users can view file lists and collections.
Log visits	A log entry is created for each visit to the Web site. As an operational security practice, it is highly recommend that you enable logging.
Index this resource	Indexing Service can index this resource. This allows searches to be performed on the resource.
Execute	Users have the appropriate level of script execution:
	▪ **None.** Does not allow scripts or executables to run on the server.
	▪ **Scripts only.** Allows only scripts to run on the server.
	▪ **Scripts and Executables.** Allows both scripts and executables to run on the server.

For information about how to set Web site permissions, see "Configure Web Site Permissions" in "IIS Deployment Procedures" in this book.

Setting IP Address and Domain Name Restrictions

One method of protecting the Web sites and applications that are hosted on your server is to restrict access from specific IP addresses or domain names. You can explicitly grant or deny access to any combination of IP address ranges or domain names.

By restricting access to Web sites and applications by using IP address ranges or domain names, you can grant or deny access to a specific set of computers or to an organization. The restrictions that you specify affect the entire Web site or application and cannot be configured for individual portions of the Web site or application.

Restrict access to a specific Web site for a specific IP address range or domain name by completing the following steps:

1. Specify the default access that will be given to the majority of users accessing the application by doing one of the following:

   - To allow the majority of users to access the application, enable default access.

   - To allow a limited number of users to access the application, disable default access.

2. For each computer, or group of computers, that you want to grant or deny access, specify the IP address range or domain name for the clients that are exceptions to the default access specified in Step 1.

   Unless you are unable to identify the IP address range for the computers, you must specify the domain name. From a performance perspective, specifying the IP address range is preferred. If you specify a domain name, DNS reverse lookups must be done each time a user accesses the application and the performance of your application is degraded.

   Specify the IP address range in the form of a single IP address or a network ID with a corresponding subnet mask.

For more information about setting IP address and domain name restrictions, see "Configure IP Address and Domain Name Restrictions" in "IIS Deployment Procedures" in this book.

Setting NTFS Permissions

NTFS permissions allow you to set permissions that are observed by IIS and by other Windows Server 2003 components. Windows Server 2003 examines NTFS permissions to determine the types of access a user, or a process, has on a specific file or folder.

Use NTFS permissions in conjunction with Web site permissions, not in place of Web site permissions. NTFS permissions affect only the accounts that have been granted or denied access to the Web site and application content. Web site permissions affect all of the users who access the Web site or application.

 Note
If Web site permissions conflict with NTFS permissions for a directory or file, the more restrictive settings are applied.

You need to set NTFS permissions to allow the following situations:

- Administrators can manage the content of the Web sites and applications.

- Users can, at a minimum, read the content of the Web sites and applications.

- Application pool identities can, at a minimum, read the content of the Web sites and applications.

Web sites and applications can run under the identity of the following:

The user who is accessing the Web sites and applications

When you want to restrict access to resources, such as specific Web pages or database content that is stored in SQL Server, run your Web sites and applications under the identity of the user. For example, Basic authentication can allow Web sites and applications to pass through the identity of the user to other servers, such as a computer running SQL Server. By using this method, you can control the behavior of the Web site or application on a user-by-user basis.

The application pool identity that is used by the Web sites and applications

When you want to isolate Web sites or applications that are hosted on the same Web server from one another, run the Web sites or applications under the application pool identity. By using this method, you can prevent Web sites and applications from interfering with one another independent of the users who are accessing the Web sites and applications. For more information about isolating Web sites and applications, see "Isolating Web Sites and Applications" later in this chapter.

Regardless of the identity that is used to run the Web site or application, you need to assign the appropriate NTFS permissions to the Web site or application so that it can run under the corresponding identity. Typically, these NTFS permissions are assigned to a group to which a number of users belong. Use this group when setting the permissions on the resources.

The primary disadvantage of restricting access by user accounts and NTFS permissions is that each user must have an account and must use that account to run the Web sites and applications. For your Internet-based Web sites and applications, requiring users to have accounts might be impractical. However, for intranet Web sites and applications you can use the existing accounts of users.

Explicitly deny access to anonymous accounts on Web sites and applications when you want to prevent anonymous access. *Anonymous access* occurs when a user who has no authenticated credentials accesses system resources. Anonymous accounts include the built-in Guest account, the group Guests, and the IIS anonymous accounts.

In addition to explicitly denying access to anonymous accounts, eliminate write access permissions for all users except members of the Administrators group.

 Tip

If IIS denies access to content, you can enable object access auditing to find out the account that was used to access the content. The failed access event is recorded in the Security event log. The event log entry specifies the account that was used in the failed access. After you identify the account used in the failed access, grant the appropriate NTFS permissions to the account.

Isolating Web Sites and Applications

Although some of the Web servers that you deploy host only one Web site or application, you might also need to host multiple Web sites and applications on the same Web server. When a Web server hosts multiple Web sites and applications, each Web site and application requires a certain level of isolation.

For example, an Internet service provider (ISP) might host Web sites and applications for hundreds of organizations, each having a unique Web site. In this situation, the security requirements of each organization require a high degree of isolation between Web sites and applications.

Figure 3.4 illustrates the tasks involved in the process isolating your Web sites and applications.

Figure 3.4   Isolating Web Sites and Applications

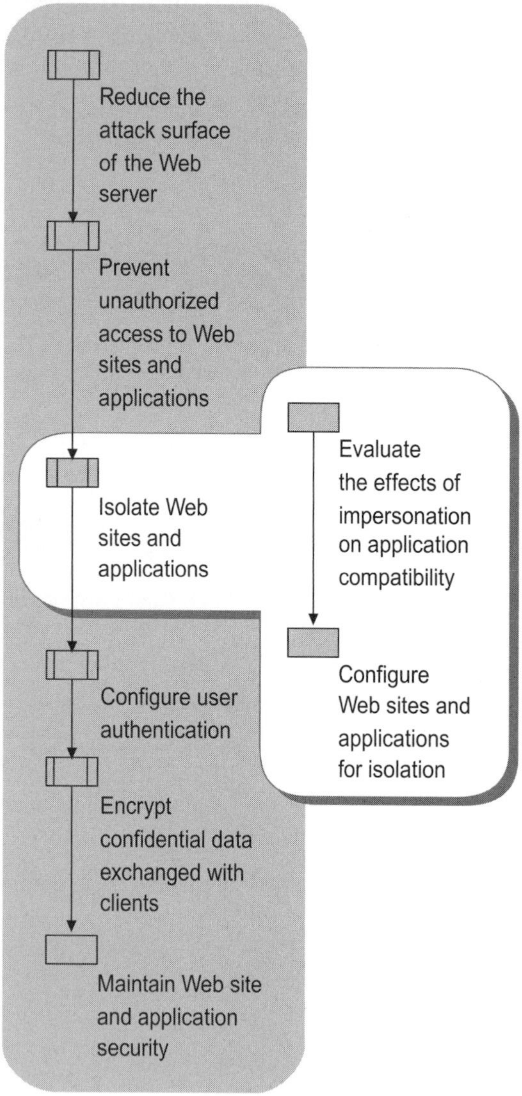

You need to prevent multiple Web sites and applications that are hosted on the same Web sever from adversely interacting with one another. When IIS 6.0 is running in worker process isolation mode, you can isolate Web sites and applications hosted on the same Web server by specifying that the Web sites and applications belong to separate *application pools*. An application pool is a grouping of Web sites or applications served by the same worker process. Application pools can be used to help prevent the Web sites and applications running in one application pool from accessing the content contained in another application pool.

For each application pool, you can specify an *application pool identity*, which is a user account that is assigned to an application pool. After specifying the application pool identity, you assign permissions (such as NTFS permissions or SQL database permissions) for each application pool identity. Because individual application pools can use different identities, you can selectively grant or deny resource access to an application pool. The Web sites and applications running in an application pool have the same user rights and resource permissions assigned to the application pool identity.

For more information about setting NTFS permissions for Web sites and applications, see "Setting NTFS Permissions" earlier in this chapter.

 Note

Web sites and applications that are running in the same application pool can affect the availability of other Web sites and applications in the same application pool. To enhance the availability of your Web sites and applications, isolate unstable Web sites and applications in a separate application pool. For more information about improving the availability of your Web server through application pools see, "Ensuring Application Availability in this book.

Evaluating the Effects of Impersonation on Application Compatibility

Securing your Web sites and applications by isolating them into separate application pools with unique identities can cause application compatibility problems when you are using anything but anonymous access. The application compatibility problems arise from the complexities of *impersonation*.

Impersonation allows a worker process to run under security credentials that are different from its base identity. Because the two are commonly confused, it is important to understand how the worker process identity that is established by the application pool identity is related to the impersonated user.

When a worker process is created by the WWW service, it is created with a process token that is associated with the application pool identity. This establishes the process identity of the worker process. By default, all of the actions taken by the worker process are completed in the context of this worker process identity account. However, when a client request is processed, the thread that processes the request uses a token associated with the client, which is also known as the *authenticated user's token*, during the duration of the request.

Before IIS serves a URL, the authenticated user's token is verified against the access control list (ACL) of the resource that is being requested. Additionally, if the request is for an ISAPI extension, such as ASP, the worker process applies the authenticated user's token as an impersonation token to the thread that calls the ISAPI extension. When the ISAPI extension begins processing the request, this impersonation token applies to the actions it takes. Consequently, the actions taken by an ISAPI extension are associated with the authenticated user, not the process identity.

Evaluate the effects of impersonation behavior on compatibility for the following:

- ASP applications
- ASP.NET applications

Identifying the Impersonation Behavior for ASP Applications

For ASP applications, the type of authentication that is used by the user automatically determines impersonation behavior. Because the impersonation behavior is automatic, no configuration is required.

The impersonation behavior in an ASP application is as follows:

- If an anonymous user makes a request, the thread token is based on the user account that is configured as the anonymous user identity (by default, this is the IUSR_*machinename* user account).
- If an authenticated user makes a request, the thread token is based on the authenticated account of the user.

Selecting the Impersonation Behavior for ASP.NET Applications

Unlike ASP applications, you need to configure the impersonation behavior for ASP.NET applications. If you enable impersonation, ASP.NET receives the security token to impersonate from IIS. By specifying a value in the Web.config file of the application, you control the impersonation setting. You have the following three options when specifying this setting.

Impersonation is disabled

This is the default setting. In this instance, the ASP.NET thread runs using the process token of the application worker process regardless of which combination of IIS and ASP.NET authentication is used. By default, the process token of the application worker process is NetworkService.

Disable impersonation by modifying the Web.config file of the application to include the following setting:

```
<identity impersonate="false" />
```

Impersonation is enabled

In this instance, ASP.NET impersonates the token passed to it by IIS, which is either an authenticated user or the anonymous user account (IUSR_*machinename*). For backward compatibility with ASP, you must enable impersonation.

Enable impersonation by modifying the Web.config file of the application to include the following setting:

```
<identity impersonate="true" />
```

Impersonation is enabled and a specific impersonation identity is specified

In this instance, ASP.NET impersonates the token that is generated using the configured identity. In this case, ASP.NET does not use the token of the authenticated client, if applicable, except when performing access checks.

Enable impersonation and specify an impersonation identity by modifying the Web.config file of the application to include the following setting:

```
<identity impersonate="true" name="domain\user" password="password" />
```

Configuring Web Sites and Applications for Isolation

Complete the following steps to identify when Web sites and applications require isolation for security reasons:

 Tip
Running worker processes under different identities can cause application compatibility problems, especially for Web sites that use user authentication. For more information, see "Web Application Isolation" in IIS 6.0 Help, which is accessible from IIS Manager.

1. Create a list of the Web sites and applications to be hosted on the Web server.

2. Group the Web sites and applications by organization (or business unit within an organization if all of the Web sites and applications hosted on the Web server are owned by one organization).

3. Subdivide each group created in the previous step into smaller groups of Web sites and applications that require the same user rights and resource access.

4. For each group created in the previous step, create a new application pool to be used by the Web sites and applications within the pool.

    For information about how to create application pools, see "Isolate Applications in Worker Process Isolation Mode" in "IIS Deployment Procedures" in this book.

5. Assign the Web sites and applications within each group to the corresponding application pool.

    For information about how to assign the Web site to the new application, see "Isolate Applications in Worker Process Isolation Mode" in "IIS Deployment Procedures" in this book.

6. For each application pool, create a service account, to be used as the application pool identity.

    In IIS, the default identity for newly created application pools is NetworkService. To ensure that you can properly assign permissions to resources, create a new *service account*. A service account is a user account that is created explicitly for the purpose of providing a security context for services running on Windows Server 2003.

    In addition, you must add the service account to the IIS_WPG group to provide the appropriate access to the IIS metabase and content. The IIS_WPG group is granted the appropriate user rights and resource permissions to allow most Web sites and applications to run properly.

    For more information about how to create a service account to be used as an identity for an application pool and how to add the account to the IIS_WPG group, see "Create a Service Account" in "IIS Deployment Procedures" in this book.

7. Assign any additional *user rights* to the application pool identities.

    User rights authorize users to perform specific actions, such as logging on to a system interactively or backing up files and directories. User rights are different from permissions because user rights apply to user accounts, whereas permissions are attached to objects.

    The user rights granted to the IIS_WPG group are sufficient for most Web sites applications. When the user rights granted to the IIS_WPG group are insufficient, grant only the user rights to the user account, which is used as the identify for the application pool, that are necessary to ensure the appropriate operation and behavior of the application. Ensure that any nonessential user rights are removed to prevent the Web sites and applications from having elevated user rights.

    For more information about how to grant the appropriate user rights for an application pool identity, see "Grant User Rights to a Service Account" in "IIS Deployment Procedures" in this book.

8. Assign the service account identity to the corresponding application pool.

   For more information about how to assign the identity to the corresponding application pool, see "Configure Application Pool Identity" in "IIS Deployment Procedures" in this book.

9. Assign the appropriate resource permissions, such as NTFS or SQL database permissions, to the application pool identities.

   Assign only the NTFS file and folder permissions that are necessary to ensure the appropriate operation and behavior of the application. By default, grant only read permissions to the application pool identity to insure that the Web sites and applications in the application pool cannot modify the Web site content or other files on the Web server. If the applications require write access to any files and folders, consult the application developers to determine if the application can be modified so that write access is not required.

Configuring User Authentication

Authenticating users early in the connection process reduces the amount of information about that can be gained regarding your IIS 6.0 solution through anonymous access. In highly-secure Web sites and applications, you need to require authentication before the user can access any of the information. For other Web sites and applications, you might require authentication only when the user is going to access portions of the Web site or application that contain confidential information.

Figure 3.5 illustrates the process for configuring user authentication.

Figure 3.5 Configuring User Authentication

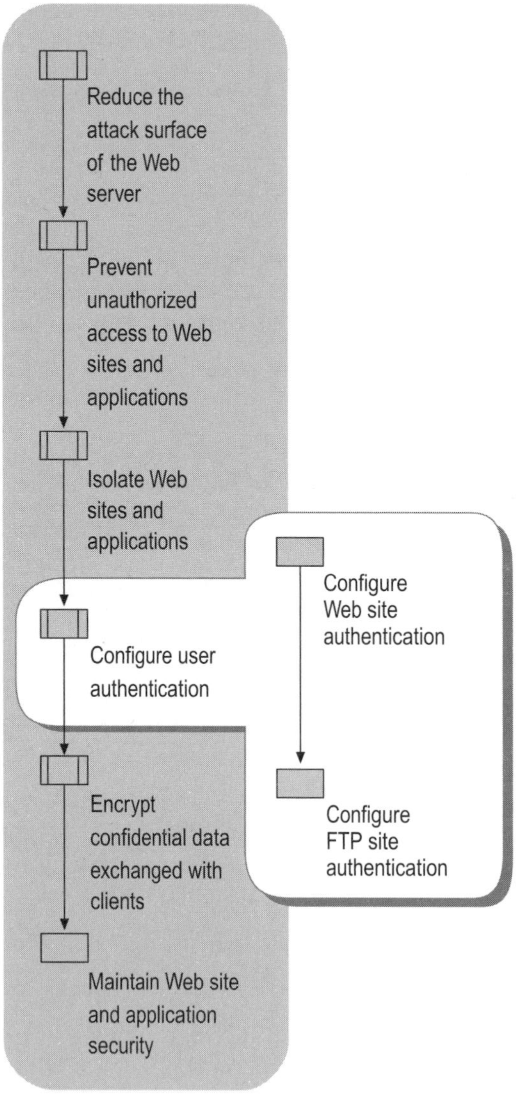

Based on the types of services provided by the Web server, you might need to provide user authentication for Web sites or FTP sites. Web sites and FTP sites support different methods for authenticating users.

Configuring Web Site Authentication

The Web site authentication methods you chose are determined by whether you deploy your Web sites and applications on an intranet or the Internet and the relation of the users accessing the Web sites and applications to your organization.

Intranet -based Web sites and applications   With intranet-based Web sites and applications, you can typically mandate the type of authentication that is used because the clients are controlled by your organization. In most instances, use Integrated Windows authentication to provide single sign on for users and the strongest possible protection of user credentials. If you are unable to use Integrated Windows authentication, then select the next strongest authentication method from the authentication methods that are described in Table 3.9 in "Selecting a Web Site Authentication Method" later in this chapter.

Internet -based Web sites and applications   With Internet-based Web sites and applications, you typically need to support a broad range of client operating systems and browsers because users outside your organization own the clients. Anonymous and Basic authentication are the most common authentication methods used for Internet-based Web sites and applications. For more information about these authentication methods, see "Selecting a Web Site Authentication Method" later in this chapter.

Configure Web site authentication by completing the following steps:

1. Select the authentication methods for each Web site.

2. Configure the authentication methods for each Web site.

Selecting a Web Site Authentication Method

The authentication method that you select varies based on the level of protection it provides for user credentials (user account and password information), and on the relationship of the user to your organization. Select the strongest authentication method possible to help ensure that the credentials of your users are protected.

Web site authentication methods can be divided into two categories:

- Methods that do not require or encrypt user credentials
- Methods that encrypt user credentials

Authentication Methods that Do Not Require or Encrypt User Credentials

For Internet-based Web sites and applications, the most commonly used authentication methods do not require or encrypt user credentials. Select one of these authentication methods when any combination of the following is true:

- Access to the Web sites and applications needs to be anonymous.
- Access to the Web sites and applications needs to be independent of the client configuration and relationship of the user to your organization.

Anonymous access

Anonymous access requires no authentication whatsoever. Anonymous access is used for intranet and Internet Web sites when you want unauthenticated users to be able to access the information provided by the Web sites and applications. The majority of Internet Web sites use anonymous access.

Authentication that is independent of the client configuration and user

Use Basic authentication when you want to require authentication to access a Web site or application, but need to use an authentication method that provides any combination of the following:

- No special configuration is required on the client. For example, the client can run any operating system or Web browser.

- The users have no close affiliation with your organization, and they are typically not employees or employees of partner organizations. As a result, you cannot require them to use an authentication method that encrypts user credentials.

- Your network infrastructure does not support encrypted authentication methods. For example, to use Windows Integrated authentication, you need the connection between requests to be maintained. Most proxy servers do not support such keep-alive connections.

Because Basic authentication does not encrypt user credentials, use a SSL-secured channel to encrypt user credentials. If you cannot encrypt Basic authentication traffic by using a SSL-secured channel, use one of the authentication methods that encrypt user credentials. These authentication methods are described in Table 3.9.

Authentication Methods That Encrypt User Credentials

Authentication methods that encrypt user credentials typically require some level of control over the client computer, and the user is usually an employee of your organization or a partner organization. Table 3.9 provides a comparison of the Web site authentication methods for Web sites and applications that encrypt user credentials.

Table 3.9 Web Site Authentication Methods That Encrypt User Credentials

Authentication Method	Advantages	Disadvantages
Digest	<ul><li>Supports authentication through firewalls and proxies.</li><li>Encrypts user credentials.</li><li>Requires Active Directory running on Microsoft Windows® 2000 Server or later.</li><li>Provides medium security.</li></ul>	<ul><li>Requires Microsoft Internet Explorer 5.0 or later.</li><li>Stores user password unencrypted in Active Directory.</li><li>Cannot be used to authenticate local accounts.</li><li>Requires the associated Application Pool identity to be configured as LocalSystem.</li></ul>

(continued)

Table 3.9 Web Site Authentication Methods That Encrypt User Credentials *(continued)*

Authentication Method	Advantages	Disadvantages
Advanced digest	▪ Supports authentication through firewalls and proxies. ▪ Encrypts user credentials. ▪ Stores hash of the user credentials in Active Directory. ▪ Provides medium security.	▪ Requires Internet Explorer 5.0 or later. ▪ Requires Active Directory running on Windows Server 2003. ▪ Cannot be used to authenticate local accounts.
Integrated Windows	▪ Encrypts user credentials. ▪ Provides high security. ▪ Requires Internet Explorer 2.0 or later.	▪ Requires Microsoft clients.
Client Certificates	▪ For server authentication (certificates stored on the server), your organization obtains certificates from a trusted certification authority. ▪ For client authentication, map certificates to users accounts stored in Active Directory running on Windows 2000 Server or later. ▪ Provides high security.	▪ For client authentication (certificates stored on the clients), your organization has, or is willing to deploy, a public key infrastructure (PKI). ▪ For client authentication, you have a method of securely distributing the certificates to the clients.
Microsoft .NET Passport	▪ Supports authentication through firewalls and proxies. ▪ Encrypts user credentials. ▪ Requires Internet Explorer 4.0 or later and Netscape Navigator 4.0 or later.	▪ Requires Active Directory when account mapping is used. ▪ Requires your organization to license the .NET Passport authentication service.

Configuring the Web Site Authentication Method

After you select the Web site authentication method for each Web site, you need to configure the Web site to use that method. For more information about how to configure Web server authentication, see "Configure Web Server Authentication" in "IIS Deployment Procedures" in this book.

Configuring FTP Site Authentication

Configure FTP site authentication for your FTP server by completing the following steps:

1. Select the FTP site authentication method that fulfills the security requirements of your organization, based on the information in Table 3.10.

    The authentication methods that you select vary, based on the ability of the method to protect user credentials (user account and password information). Select the strongest authentication method possible to help ensure that the credentials of your users are protected. Table 3.10 lists and describes these FTP site authentication methods.

Table 3.10   FTP Site Authentication Methods

Authentication Method	Description
Anonymous FTP authentication	For transferring any confidential information, avoid using Anonymous FTP authentication because no user authentication is performed with Anonymous FTP authentication, and anyone can transfer the information.
Basic FTP authentication	Basic FTP authentication sends the user name, password, and data in plaintext and can easily be discovered.

2. Configure the FTP server to use the FTP site authentication method that you selected in the previous step.

When you are transferring confidential data:

- **Within your intranet by using FTP.** IPSec is required between the client computers and the FTP server to encrypt the user name, password, and any data transferred.

- **Outside your intranet (for remote users) by using FTP.** A VPN tunnel is required between the client computers and your intranet to encrypt the user name, password, and any data transferred.

For information about how to configure FTP server authentication, see "Configure FTP Server Authentication" in "IIS Deployment Procedures" in this book.

Encrypting Confidential Data Exchanged with Clients

Your business needs might require that confidential data be exchanged between the client computers and the Web server. You can help ensure that this information is safeguarded on the network by using *encryption*. Encryption is a cryptographic process that helps prevent unauthorized users from viewing the encrypted data.

Figure 3.6 illustrates the process for encrypting confidential data that is exchanged between client computers and the Web server.

Figure 3.6   Encrypting Confidential Data Exchanged with Clients

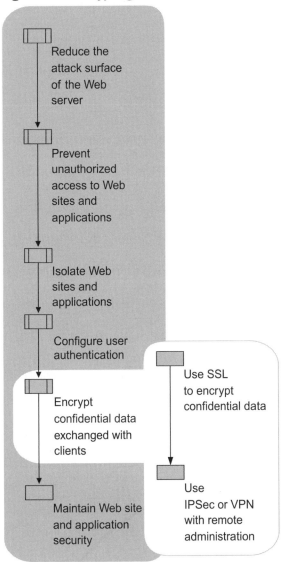

The method you select for encrypting the data exchanged between the client computers and the Web server is based on a number of factors. You can encrypt the data exchanged between clients by using:

- SSL for users accessing the Web sites and applications hosted on the Web server.

- IPSec or VPNs for administrators who remotely manage the Web sites and applications hosted on the Web server.

Using SSL to Encrypt Confidential Data

You can configure Secure Sockets Layer (SSL) security features on your Web server to encrypt network transmissions, which will help ensure the integrity of your data transmission, and to verify the identity of users. SSL can be configured to provide security for any portion of the Web sites or applications on the Web server.

 Note

The process presented here describes how to configure SSL to use *server certificates*. Server certificates are installed on the Web server and typically require no additional configuration on the clients. Server certificates allow the clients to verify the identity of the server. Alternatively, some Web sites and applications might require *client certificates*. Client certificates are installed on the client and allow the server to authenticate the clients. For more information about configuring client certificates, see "Enabling Client Certificates" in IIS 6.0 Help, which is accessible from IIS Manager.

You can configure SSL to help protect confidential data on a URL-by-URL basis (individual portions of the Web site or application). One portion of the application might require encryption of data transmissions with SSL (by specifying HTTPS in the URL), while another portion of the application might allow unencrypted data transmission (by specifying HTTP in the URL). This flexibility in security configuration allows you to provide encryption of confidential data as required, which is unlike IPSec and VPNs because they require that you encrypt all traffic between the clients and the Web server.

As an example, consider a fictitious organization called Contoso Pharmaceuticals that has an e-commerce Web site on the Internet. The Web site contains both secured and unsecured content. The URL for the unsecured home page is http://www.contoso.com. The URL for the secured e-commerce portion of the Web site is https://purchase.contoso.com. Traffic between clients and the home page is unencrypted; whereas SSL encrypts traffic between clients and the e-commerce portion of the Web site.

To use SSL, you must install a valid server certificate on the Web server for each Web site that you want to use with SSL. Certificates are usually granted to organizations through trusted certification authorities. Part of the information that is contained in a certificate is information about the organization to which the certificate was granted, such as the registered domain name. Thus, Web sites with registered domain names need their own certificate.

Client browsers perform a number of verification checks on the SSL certificate. When a client browser detects an incorrect value in the certificate, the browser displays warning messages. The client browser can verify the following:

- Digital signature of the certificate
- Expiration date of the certificate
- Registered domain name to which the certificate was issued against the URL requested

To enable SSL, complete the following steps for each Web site and application:

1. Request a server certificate for the Web site from a certification authority.

    You can use the Web Server Certificate Wizard either to generate a certificate request file (Certreq.txt, by default) that you send to a certification authority, or to generate a request for an online certification authority, such as Microsoft Certificate Services in Windows Server 2003. Depending on the level of identification assurance offered by your server certificate, you can expect to wait several days to several months for the certification authority to approve your request and send you a certificate file.

    For more information about requesting a server certificate by using the Web Server Certificate Wizard, see "Request a Server Certificate" in "IIS Deployment Procedures" in this book.

2. Install the server certificate to be used by the Web site on the Web server.

    For more information about installing the server certificate on the Web server by using the Certificate MMC snap-in, see "Install a Server Certificate" in "IIS Deployment Procedures" in this book.

3. Assign the server certificate to the Web site.

    For more information about assigning the server certificate to the Web site, see "Assign a Server Certificate to a Web Site" in "IIS Deployment Procedures" in this book.

Using IPSec or VPN with Remote Administration

You can use Internet Protocol security (IPSec) and virtual private networks (VPNs) to help secure traffic for Web server administration tasks performed over the network, such as uploading content by using FTP or managing the Web server. In addition to encrypting administrative traffic, IPSec and VPNs provide cryptographically strong authentication methods, such as computer certificates, smart cards, and strong password requirements, to provide improved *identity checking*.

Identity checking is the process of verifying the authenticity of the user credentials. Computer certificates, issued by your organization, ensure that remote administration is performed from specific computers and provides improved identity checking.

If your organization provides hosting of Web sites for other organizations, these organizations need to have a secure method for posting their Web site content to your Web servers. Because the organizations post their Web site content over the Internet, you need to encrypt the traffic and provide enhanced identity checking to help protect confidential information.

For example, you can use FTP to upload Web site content to be published on production Web servers. Because FTP exchanges content and user credentials in plaintext, you need to use IPSec or VPNs to encrypt the traffic.

For more information about designing and deploying IPSec, see "Deploying IPSec" in *Deploying Network Services* of this kit. For more information about designing and deploying VPNs, see "Deploying Dial-up and VPN Remote Access Servers" in *Deploying Network Services* of this kit.

Maintaining Web Site and Application Security

After securing the Web sites and applications on your Web server, you need to help ensure that the Web sites and applications stay secure. You need to deploy Web servers that are easy to manage and operate. As you deploy the Web server, keep in mind the operations processes that must be performed after the Web server is deployed.

Figure 3.7 illustrates the process for maintaining the security of your Web sites and applications.

Figure 3.7   Maintaining Web Site and Application Security

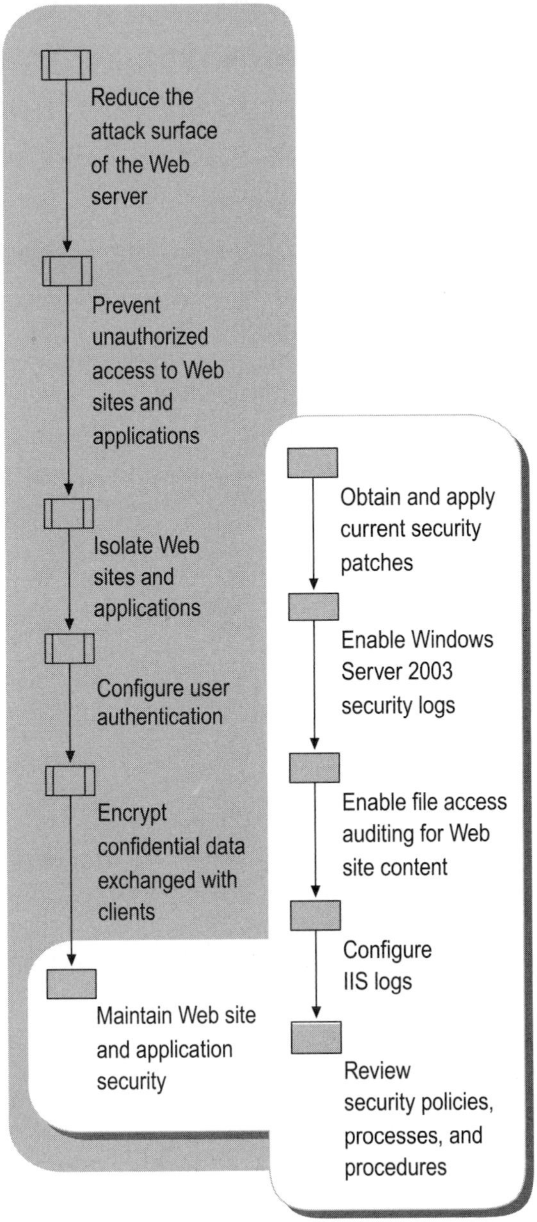

For more detailed coverage of security operations processes, see "Managing a Secure IIS Solution" in *Internet Information Services (IIS) 6.0 Resource Guide*.

Obtaining and Applying Current Security Patches

You should always evaluate and apply the latest security updates to help ensure that your Web sites and applications remain secure. These security updates are published as service packs or hotfixes. As new security vulnerabilities are discovered, Microsoft publishes updates to help mitigate any security risks they might cause. You need to apply these security updates to help ensure that your Web server is protected from the most current security risks.

Stay current with security updates by completing the following steps:

1. Obtain the current security updates by using any combination of the following:

   - **Subscribe to the Microsoft Security Notification Service newsletter.** The Microsoft Security Notification Service newsletter is a free subscription-based service that sends notification e-mails about available security updates to administrators.

     To subscribe to the Microsoft Security Notification Service newsletter, see the Microsoft.com Profile Center link on the Web Resources page at http://www.microsoft.com/windows/reskits/webresources. There is no charge for registering to receive the newsletters.

   - **Run Windows Update on a regular basis.** Windows Update is a service that runs on Windows-based computers. Windows Update scans the local computer and identifies any updates that are applicable for the software installed on the computer. Windows Update is installed on Windows Server 2003 by default. You must manually start Windows Update on the Web server from Help and Support Center for Microsoft® Windows® Server 2003.

     For more information about running Windows Update, see "Windows Update" in Help and Support Center for Windows Server 2003.

   - **Deploy Microsoft Software Update Services (SUS).** SUS is a service that acts as an intermediary between the Windows Update server on Microsoft.com and the Windows-based computers in your organization running Windows Update. By using SUS, you can download the latest updates to a server on your intranet, test the updates on test servers, select the updates that you want to deploy, and then deploy the updates to computers within your organization.

     For more information about deploying SUS, see "Deploying Software Update Services" in *Designing a Managed Environment* of this kit.

Table 3.11 lists the options for obtaining security updates, and describes the advantages and disadvantages of each option.

Table 3.11 Options to Obtain Security Updates

Option	Advantages	Disadvantages
Microsoft Security Notification Service Newsletter	<ul><li>Does not require Web servers to be directly connected to the Internet</li><li>Does not require a dedicated server</li><li>Free</li></ul>	<ul><li>Is not specific to a particular technology, such as IIS</li><li>Is not specific to a particular operating system version</li><li>Requires administrators to manually review newsletters for recommended updates</li></ul>
Windows Update	<ul><li>Provides automatic notification of available updates</li><li>Free</li></ul>	<ul><li>Requires the Web server to have Internet access.</li></ul>
SUS	<ul><li>Provides automatic notification of available updates</li></ul>	<ul><li>Requires a dedicated server to run properly</li><li>Requires the SUS server be able to access the Internet</li><li>Requires separate purchase of SUS</li></ul>

2. Test the security updates on a Web server in a test environment.

Before deploying the security updates on your production Web server, use one of the options described in Step 1 to test the security updates on a test Web server that is configured identically to your production Web server. Table 3.12 lists the methods for deploying the security updates on a Web server in a test environment.

Table 3.12 Methods for Deploying Security Updates

Method	Deployment
Microsoft Security Notification Service Newsletter	Manually download the updates and then deploy them manually or automatically by using a software distribution program, such as Microsoft System Management Server.
Windows Update	Configure Windows Update to do one of the following:<ul><li>Inform an administrator that is logged on to the Web server that updates are available and then allow the administrator to install the updates</li><li>Automatically install the updates.</li></ul>
SUS	Configure the SUS to provide updates to the Web server through an updated version of Windows Update called Automatic Updates.

You can configure Windows Update and Automatic Updates in SUS to install updates automatically, with or without confirmation, based on the security rating of the update. Table 3.13 lists the security ratings used by Windows Update and Automatic Updates, and provides a description of each rating.

Table 3.13 Security Ratings Used by Windows Update and Automatic Updates

Rating	Description
Critical	A vulnerability that, if exploited, might allow the propagation of an Internet worm without user action.
Important	A vulnerability that, if exploited, might result in a compromise of the confidentiality, integrity, or availability of users' data, or of the integrity or availability of processing resources.
Moderate	A vulnerability risk that can be mitigated by factors such as default configuration, auditing, or difficulty to exploit.
Low	A vulnerability that is extremely difficult to exploit, or that has minimal impact.

3. Deploy the security updates to your production Web server by using the same option that you tested on the test Web server.

Enabling Windows Server 2003 Security Logs

Collecting information about the security aspects of the Web server is required to help ensure that the Web server stays secure. Windows Server 2003 uses security and system logs to store collected security events. The security and system logs are repositories for all events recorded on the Web server. Many management systems, such as Microsoft Operations Manager, periodically scan these logs and can report security problems to your operations staff.

If you audit or log too many events, the log files might become unmanageable and contain superfluous data. Before enabling the system and security logs, you need to enable auditing for the system log and establish the number of events that you want recorded in the security log. You cannot change the information that is logged in the system log: These events are preprogrammed into Windows Server 2003 services and applications. You can customize system log events by configuring *auditing*. Auditing is the process that tracks the activities of users and processes by recording selected types of events in the security log of the Web server. You can enable auditing based on categories of security events. At a minimum, enable auditing on the following categories of events:

- Any changes to user account and resource permissions
- Any failed attempts for user logon
- Any failed attempts for resource access
- Any modification to the system files

You can customize which types of events are recorded in the security log. The most common security events recorded by the Web server are associated with user accounts and resource permissions.

For more information about how to enable security auditing, see "Enable Security Auditing" in "IIS Deployment Procedures" in this book.

Enabling File Access Auditing for Web Site Content

In addition to enabling Windows Server 2003 security logs, enable file access auditing for your Web site content. This is a separate step that must be completed to monitor any changes to the files and directories that contain your application and content.

You can enable auditing on a user-by-user basis for each file and directory. However, at a minimum, enable auditing for all users for any successful or failed attempts to do the following:

- Modify or delete existing content
- Create new content

 Tip

Beyond these minimal events, you can audit content for other purposes, such as forensic analysis of intruder detection.

For more information about how to enable file auditing on Web site content and files, see "Enable Web Site Content Auditing" in "IIS Deployment Procedures" in this book.

Configuring IIS Logs

In addition to the Windows Server 2003 system and security logs, you should configure IIS to log site visits. When users access your server running IIS 6.0, IIS logs the information. The logs provide valuable information that you can use to identify any unauthorized attempts to compromise your Web server.

Depending on the amount of traffic to your Web site, the size of your log file (or the number of log files) can consume valuable disk space, memory resources, and CPU cycles. You might need to balance the gathering of detailed data with the need to limit files to a manageable size and number. If you are planning to put thousands of Web sites on one Web server with high traffic volumes and disk writes, you might want to use centralized binary logging to preserve server resources. Also, consider limiting log size by changing the frequency of log file creation. For more information, see "Saving Log Files" in IIS 6.0 Help, which is accessible from IIS Manager.

The IIS logs allow you to record events for each application and Web site on the Web server. You can create separate logs for each of your applications and Web sites. Logging information in IIS 6.0 goes beyond the scope of the event logging or performance monitoring features provided by Windows. The IIS logs can include information, such as who has visited your site, what the visitor viewed, and when the information was last viewed. You can use the IIS logs to identify any attempts to gain unauthorized access to your Web server.

IIS 6.0 supports different log formats for the IIS logs that you enable. IIS 6.0 supports the following log formats.

W3C Extended log file format

World Wide Web Consortium (W3C) Extended format is a customizable ASCII format with a variety of different properties. You can log properties that are important to you, while limiting log size by omitting unwanted property fields. Properties are separated by spaces. Time is recorded as Universal Time Coordinate (UTC).

For information about customizing this format, see "Customizing W3C Extended Logging" in IIS 6.0 Help, which is accessible from IIS Manager. For more information about the W3C Extended format specification, see the W3C World Wide Web Consortium link on the Web Resources page at http://www.microsoft.com/windows/reskits/webresources.

IIS log file format

IIS log file format is a *fixed* (meaning that it cannot be customized) ASCII format. This file format records more information than other log file formats, including basic items, such as the IP address of the user, user name, request date and time, service status code, and number of bytes received. In addition, IIS log file format includes detailed items, such as the elapsed time, number of bytes sent, action (for example, a download carried out by a **GET** command), and target file. The IIS log file is an easier format to read than the other ASCII formats because the information is separated by commas, while most other ASCII log file formats use spaces for separators. Time is recorded as local time.

For more information about the IIS log file format, see "About Logging Site Activity" in IIS 6.0 Help, which is accessible from IIS Manager.

NCSA Common log file format

National Center for Supercomputing Applications (NCSA) Common log file format is a fixed ASCII format that is available for Web sites, but not for FTP sites. This log file format records basic information about user requests, such as remote host name, user name, date, time, request type, HTTP status code, and the number of bytes sent by the server. Items are separated by spaces. Time is recorded as local time.

For more information about the NCSA Common log file format, see "About Logging Site Activity" in IIS 6.0 Help, which is accessible from IIS Manager.

ODBC logging

Open Database Connectivity (ODBC) logging format is a record of a fixed set of data properties in a database that complies with ODBC, such as Microsoft Access or Microsoft SQL Server. Some of the items logged include the IP address of the user, user name, request date and time (recorded as local time), HTTP status code, bytes received, bytes sent, action carried out (for example, a download carried out by a **GET** command), and the target file. With ODBC logging, you must both specify the database to be logged to, and set up the database to receive the data.

 Note

When ODBC logging is enabled, IIS disables the kernel-mode cache. As a result, overall server performance can be degraded.

For more information about ODBC logging, see "About Logging Site Activity" in IIS 6.0 Help, which is accessible from IIS Manager.

Centralized binary logging

Centralized binary logging is the process of multiple Web sites writing binary, unformatted log data to a single log file. Each Web server running IIS creates one log file for all of the Web sites on that server. Centralized binary logging preserves valuable memory resources. Depending on your configuration, you can see dramatic performance and scalability gains with centralized binary logging.

For more information about centralized binary logging, see "Centralized Binary Logging" in IIS 6.0 Help, which is accessible from IIS Manager.

For more information about how to configure IIS logs, see "Enable Logging" in "IIS Deployment Procedures" in this book. For more information about logging Web site activity, see "Logging Site Activity" in IIS 6.0 Help. For more information about managing IIS logs, see "Analyzing Log Files" in *Internet Information Services (IIS) 6.0 Resource Guide* of the *Windows Server 2003 Resource Kit*.

Reviewing Security Policies, Processes, and Procedures

As a part of maintaining the security of your Web server, you must perform periodic reviews of the security policies, processes, and procedures in use by your organization. Review your security practices for any changes that might affect the security of the Web server. These changes in security practices can include the following:

Ensuring that any recent security risks are mitigated   As new security risks are identified, such as new viruses, you need to ensure that your security practices help mitigate these risks. If your current security practices do not address the new risks, then modify them to help mitigate the risks.

Identifying changes in Web server configuration that can compromise security

Through the course of normal administration of the Web server, configuration changes are made. During this process, security settings might have been inadvertently changed. You need to periodically review the configuration of the Web server to ensure that it complies with the security requirements of your organization.

You can categorize these Web server security practices by their function, such as operating system security, security policies, firewall security, and router security. In addition, the frequency with which these processes and procedures are completed varies. Some security practices need to be completed continuously while others might be completed monthly.

Table 3.14, Table 3.15, Table 3.16, and Table 3.17 list examples of security policies, processes, and procedures for an ISP, grouped by categories. These examples are representative of the types of security practices that are required to maintain the security of your Web server. For more information about the security policies, processes, and procedures for your Web server, see "Managing a Secure IIS Solution" in *Internet Information Services (IIS) 6.0 Resource Guide* of the *Windows Server 2003 Resource Kit.*

Table 3.14 Windows Server 2003 Operating System Security

Security Policy, Process, or Procedure	Frequency
Limit user rights to only those that are required.	Constant
Limit any windows for vulnerabilities that can be exploited when deploying new servers.	Constant
Limit Terminal Services access to only necessary accounts.	Constant
Run a two-tier DNS structure to protect the identity of internal servers.	Constant
Run an intrusion detection system.	Constant
Scan the ports in use on your server addresses and addresses assigned to remote users.	Daily
Review event and IIS logs.	Weekly
Test firewalls from inside and outside by using port scanners and other appropriate tools.	Weekly

Table 3.15 Windows Server 2003 Policy Security

Security Policy, Process, or Procedure	Frequency
Explicitly deny interactive logon user right to all nonadministrative accounts.	Constant
Explicitly deny "Allow logon through Terminal Services" user right to all nonadministrative accounts.	Constant
Enable FULL (Success/Failure) auditing on domain Group Policy objects.	Constant
Send event notification when events like "User added to Domain Administrators" occur.	Constant

(continued)

Table 3.15   Windows Server 2003 Policy Security *(continued)*

Security Policy, Process, or Procedure	Frequency
Allow only Administrators to have write permissions on all content servers.	Constant
Require strong passwords for all users.	Constant
Require smart cards for all administrators.	Constant
Allow administrators to log on only to specific workstations.	Constant
Enable account lockout policies for failed logon attempts.	Constant
Audit the domain Group Policy object.	Monthly
Audit Active Directory user rights.	Monthly
Audit all servers to determine if nonessential services are running.	Monthly

Table 3.16   Firewall and Router Security

Security Policy, Process, or Procedure	Frequency
Restrict the network segments where management traffic is allowed.	Constant
By default, deny IP traffic and log any failed attempts.	Constant

Ensure that the minimal firewall rules are enforced, including:
 	
• Explicitly deny all traffic to the following:
   • TCP and UDP ports 135-139, 455 (NetBIOS/SMB)
   • TCP and UDP ports 3389 (Terminal Services)
   • Domain controllers
   • Internal DNS servers
• Permit traffic to TCP and UDP port 53 (DNS) to external DNS servers.
	Constant

Table 3.17   Miscellaneous Security

Security Policy, Process, or Procedure	Frequency
Run virus scans on all servers.	Constant
Monitor security distribution lists and newsgroups for potential security issues.	Constant
During virus outbreaks, block any suspicious content (such as e-mail attachments).	Constant
Monitor the number of Non-Delivery mail reports generated (indicates e-mail spamming).	Weekly
Monitor SMTP relay attempts that are not valid (indicates e-mail spamming).	Weekly
Audit accounts to determine the users who are no longer employed at the organization, partner organizations, or customer organizations.	Monthly

Additional Resources

These resources contain additional information and tools related to this chapter.

Related Information

- "Deploying ASP.NET Applications in IIS 6.0" in this book for information about ASP.NET-specific deployment considerations.

- "Ensuring Application Availability" in this book for information about balancing application security and availability.

- "IIS Deployment Procedures in this book for information about specific procedures for securing Web sites and applications.

- "Deploying Dial-up and VPN Remote Access Servers" in *Deploying Network Services* of the *Microsoft® Windows® Server 2003 Deployment Kit* for information about designing and deploying VPN.

- "Deploying IPSec" in *Deploying Network Services* of this kit for information about designing and deploying IPSec.

- "Deploying Software Update Services" in *Designing a Managed Environment* of this kit for information about deploying SUS.

- "Planning a Secure Environment" in *Designing and Deploying Directory and Security Services* of this kit for information about securing other services on a multipurpose server.

- "Analyzing Log Files" in *Internet Information Services (IIS) 6.0 Resource Guide* of the *Windows Server 2003 Resource Kit* for information about managing IIS logs.

- "Managing a Secure IIS Solution in *Internet Information Services (IIS) 6.0 Resource Guide* of the *Windows Server 2003 Resource Kit* for information about maintaining Web server security.

- The Microsoft.com Profile Center.link on the Web Resources page at http://www.microsoft.com/windows/reskits/webresources for information about how to subscribe to the Microsoft Security Notification Service newsletter.

- The W3C World Wide Web Consortium link on the Web Resources page at http://www.microsoft.com/windows/reskits/webresources for information about the W3C Extended format specification.

Related IIS 6.0 Help Topics

- "About Logging Site Activity" in IIS 6.0 Help, which is accessible from IIS Manager, for information about log file formats.

- "Enabling Client Certificates" in IIS 6.0 Help, which is accessible from IIS Manager, for information about configuring client certificates.

- "NTFS Permissions" in IIS 6.0 Help, which is accessible from IIS Manager, for information about the benefits of formatting disk volumes as NTFS on Web servers.

- "Saving Log Files" in IIS 6.0 Help, which is accessible from IIS Manager, for information about balancing the gathering of detailed data with the need to limit files to a manageable size and number.

- "SMTP Administration" or "NNTP Administration" in IIS 6.0 Help, which is accessible from IIS Manager, for information about securing SMTP or NNTP.

- "Troubleshooting" in IIS 6.0 Help, which is accessible from IIS Manager, for information about troubleshooting problems related to Web sites and applications that are not functioning.

- "Web Application Isolation" in IIS 6.0 Help, which is accessible from IIS Manager, for information about potential application compatibility problems that can occur when running worker processes under different identities, especially for Web sites that use user authentication.

Related Windows Server 2003 Help topics

For best results in identifying Help topics by title, in Help and Support Center, under the **Search** box, click **Set search options**. Under **Help Topics**, select the **Search in title only** check box.

- "Windows Update" in Help and Support Center for Windows Server 2003 for information about using Windows Update.

C H A P T E R   4

Ensuring Application Availability

Application availability is the readiness of an application and the service it runs under to handle customer requests and to return timely and accurate responses. Ensuring consistently high application availability requires that you set availability goals that meet your business needs, configure your Web server to achieve those goals, and measure the compatibility and reliability of your applications. Internet Information Services (IIS) 6.0 running in worker process isolation mode provides the advanced features that you need to achieve and maintain a high degree of application availability.

In This Chapter

Related Information

- For information about migrating IIS applications, see "Migrating IIS Web Sites to IIS 6.0" in this book.

- For information about securing IIS applications, see "Securing Web Sites and Applications" in this book.

- For information about migrating Apache Web sites, see "Migrating Apache Web Sites to IIS 6.0" in this book.

Overview of the Ensuring Application Availability Process

To help ensure optimum availability of your applications to users who need them, you need to do more than ensure that the network is available and that your server is up and running. You need to set availability goals, configure IIS to meet the demands that users are placing on your applications, and test your applications for functional compatibility with IIS 6.0 worker process isolation mode.

To be certain that the level of application availability on your server meets the needs of your customers, you must first establish availability, service, and request-handling goals that accurately represent those customer needs. Next, you need to create application pools, and then configure IIS features to isolate applications and to tune and monitor your application pools. Finally, you need to assess the tradeoffs between availability and other aspects of running your applications, such as performance.

To help maintain high availability of the applications that your server hosts, you can use two kinds of testing: compatibility testing and comparison testing. Functional compatibility testing verifies that your applications will work with the IIS 6.0 worker process isolation mode features that you have enabled. Comparison testing measures the availability of your applications against your application availability goals, which reveals how closely the day-to-day availability of applications hosted on your server matches your original goals.

Before you begin this process, you must:

- Install the Microsoft® Windows® Server 2003, Standard Edition; Windows® Server 2003, Enterprise Edition; Windows® Server 2003, Datacenter Edition; or Windows® Server 2003, Web Edition operating system with the default options.

- Install IIS 6.0 with the default settings by using Add or Remove Programs in Control Panel.

If you use other methods for installing and configuring Windows Server 2003, such as unattended setup, or enabling IIS 6.0 by using Manage Your Server, then the default configuration settings might not be identical to the configuration settings described in this chapter.

When you complete the process for ensuring application availability, you will meet the basic requirements for achieving high availability for your applications. You will set and begin to measure availability goals for you applications based on your business needs. Your applications will be configured to make effective use of IIS 6.0 features. Also, you will know whether your applications are compatible with IIS 6.0 worker process isolation mode.

Process for Ensuring Application Availability

The process for ensuring application availability includes setting availability goals, configuring IIS to achieve your availability goals, and testing your applications to ensure that they meet the availability goals that you set. Ensure that your availability goals accommodate the needs of your users for high application reliability and reasonable application response times. Figure 4.1 shows the process for ensuring application availability.

Figure 4.1   Ensuring Application Availability

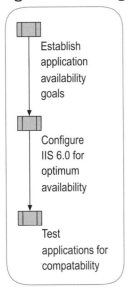

Establish application availability goals

Configure IIS 6.0 for optimum availability

Test applications for compatability

Application pools are sets of applications and the worker processes that service them. For you to create and configure application pools and make application pool assignments, IIS 6.0 must be running in worker process isolation mode. Thus, you need to evaluate the compatibility of your applications with IIS 6.0 worker process isolation mode in a test environment before deploying them in your production environment.

 Important

The application-pool functionality is only available in IIS 6.0 worker process isolation mode.

The following quick-start guide provides a detailed overview of how to help ensure the availability of your applications. You can use this guide to help identify the steps of the ensuring application availability process that you need additional information about to complete so that you can disregard the information with which you are already familiar. In addition, for the procedures that are required to complete this process, see "IIS Deployment Procedures in this book.

Establishing Application Availability Goals

1. Set service availability goals.

2. Set request-handling reliability goals.

Configuring IIS 6.0 for Optimum Availability

1. Isolate applications by completing the following steps:

   - Determine the application isolation needs of your server.

   - Create application pools and assign applications to them.

2. Recycle worker processes in one of the following ways:

   - Recycle by elapsed time.

   - Recycle by number of requests.

   - Recycle at scheduled times.

   - Recycle on a virtual-memory threshold.

   - Recycle on a used-memory threshold.

3. Tune performance by completing the following steps:

   - Configure idle time-out for worker processes.

   - Configure a request queue limit.

   - Configure Web gardens.

   - Set processor affinity on servers that include multiple CPUs.

4. Manage application pool health by completing the following steps:

   - Configure worker process pinging.

   - Configure rapid-fail protection for worker processes.

   - Configure the startup time limit for worker processes.

   - Configure the shutdown time limit for worker processes.

   - Enable debugging for application pool failures.

5. Configure application pool identity.

Testing Applications for Compatibility

1. Test applications for setup compatibility with IIS 6.0.

2. Test applications for functional compatibility with IIS 6.0.

Establishing Application Availability Goals

To set effective availability goals for your applications, you need to measure the availability of the World Wide Web Publishing service (WWW service), your Web sites, and the worker processes that service your applications. These availability measurements can be calculated as a percentage by dividing the uptime of the WWW service, Web site, or worker process by the time elapsed. In addition, a good user application availability experience depends upon successful handling of correctly formed requests, which are requests that are complete and error-free.

At times, users cannot access your applications because of these common request-handling problems:

- Correctly formed requests are sent, but they are not correctly served.

- Correctly formed requests are sent, but they are served only after a time interval that is unacceptable to the user.

To ensure that you set application availability goals that represent the needs of your users, you must first define how you will measure the successful serving of requests. Make sure that your goals address the following:

- Service availability, which includes the WWW service and individual Web sites.

- Application availability, which includes request processing reliability and the average time that is needed to process requests.

Figure 4.2 shows the process for establishing application availability goals.

Figure 4.2 Establishing Application Availability Goals

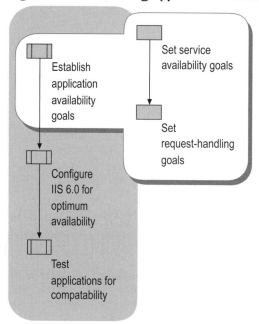

Setting Service Availability Goals

To set effective service availability goals, you need to measure the percentage of time that the WWW service and your Web sites are available to process client requests. WWW service availability is the time that the WWW service and your Web sites are up and running, expressed as a percentage of a set period of time. For example, an organization might set a goal to have a WWW service availability of 99.999 percent over a 21-day period.

You can achieve high WWW service availability when running IIS 6.0 in worker process isolation mode. This is because worker process isolation mode isolates the WWW service from the impacts of failed applications. Generally, the WWW service is unavailable only when the system is restarted and when IIS is taken offline for major service upgrades, such as the installation of a service pack. When the WWW service is available, your Web sites are available unless you deliberately take them offline.

Test service availability and compare the test results to your goals. First, run the tests in a test environment, and then run the tests periodically in your production environment.

Measuring Service Availability

You can measure WWW service availability by completing the following steps:

1. Use Performance Monitor to gather the data for WWW service uptime, which measures uptime for w3svc.exe, and uptime for each Web site on the server. The data for WWW service uptime is displayed in the Total instance of the Service Uptime counter. The data for Web site uptime is displayed in the Sites instances of the same counter. For more information about gathering uptime data for the WWW service and Web sites, see "Gather and Display WWW Service Uptime Data" in "IIS Deployment Procedures" in this book.

2. Use Service Monitor to display the data for the Service Uptime counter. The Service Monitor displays the uptime data for the WWW service and for each Web site on the server. For more information about displaying WWW service and Web site uptime data, see "Gather and Display WWW Service Uptime Data" in "IIS Deployment Procedures" in this book.

3. Calculate the availability of the WWW service by dividing the time (in seconds) for the Total instance by the elapsed time that the server was running (in seconds) during the test; multiply the result by 100 to express the figure as a percent availability.

4. Calculate the availability of each Web site by dividing the time (in seconds) for the Site instance for each site by the elapsed time (in seconds) that the server was running during the test; multiply the result by 100 to express the figure as a percent availability.

5. Compare the results to your goals.

Setting Request-Handling Goals

Request handling measures whether client requests were served correctly and the time needed for the WWW service to process client requests. There are two important measures for request handling: *request-handling reliability* and *request processing time*. Request-handling reliability measures the percentage of correctly formed requests that are returned successfully; request processing time measures the average elapsed time for IIS to process a client request.

Request-Handling Reliability

For a range of request rates that your applications receive, set goals to achieve the level of overall request handling reliability that you want. Measure only correct requests. Do not consider a request that a client composed incorrectly as a failed request.

For example, you can establish a request processing reliability goal of 99.999% for a rate of 20 correctly formed requests per second. You meet this goal when a Web server that receives requests at a rate of 20 per second successfully serves 99,999 responses out of each 100,000 requests. A response may be considered successful if the request returns the expected message, such as 200 OK, and the correct content.

When testing your applications in a test environment, you can use a request rate such as 20 requests per second. However, when testing applications in a production environment, you might need to set a range of request rates. If you estimate that 20 requests per second is a reasonable goal, you might try a range of 10-30 requests per second. Also, monitor request handling over a long period of time, such as 21 days or a month, to ensure that you cover the periods of heaviest loads on the application.

The following is an example of a full expression of a request reliability goal for a Web site or application:

- Duration: 21 days

- Load: 10-30 requests per second

- Success rate goal: 99.999 percent responses with the expected return message, such as 200 OK, measured against 100,000 requests.

Keep in mind that you must adjust your goals to accommodate your needs, taking into account client expectations, application backend processing, and caching.

Request Processing Time

When a request is processed so slowly that the user is not willing to wait for a return, the effect on the user is similar that of to a request failure. The user experiences a loss of availability.

The following is an example of a request reliability goal that accommodates request-handling execution time:

- Duration: 21 days

- Load: 10-30 requests per second

- Success rate goal: 99.999 percent responses with the expected return message, such as 200 OK, measured against 100,000 requests.

- Average response time of 5 seconds for each request

To set your own goals for request processing time, evaluate the availability requirements of your organization and the equipment and software that you are using.

Testing Request-Handling

Test request handling and compare the test results to your goals. First run tests in a test environment, and then periodically run tests in your production environment. Measure request-handling performance for an application by completing the following steps:

1. Send correctly formed requests from a remote client to the target application on the server that is hosting the application that you are testing. If you are testing an application on a production server, measure the performance of requests sent by users. If you are testing an application running on a test server, use automated load-testing software, such as WebCAT, to send client requests to the application at a rate appropriate to test it. You can use WebCAT to automate sending customized request loads to simulate a wide variety of conditions. You can use Log parser to create request schemes that WebCAT can use. For information about WebCAT and Log parser, see the *Internet Information Services (IIS) 6.0 Resource Guide* of the *Microsoft® Windows® Server 2003 Resource Kit* (or see the *Internet Information Services (IIS) 6.0 Resource Guide* on the Web at http://www.microsoft.com/reskit).

2. Measure the rate at which the correctly formed requests are being processed successfully by the target application on your test server (responses that return 200 messages and correct content).

3. Calculate the average elapsed time to process requests. One way to do this is to average the readings of the TimeTaken counter. The readings are in the IIS log.

4. Compare the results to your goals.

Configuring IIS 6.0 for Optimum Availability

Worker process isolation mode allows you to optimize the availability of applications installed on a Web server. To configure worker process isolation mode for optimum availability of your IIS 6.0 applications and Web sites, you need to determine availability requirements for each application and isolate applications into application pools based on those needs. You can then configure each application pool for recycling, health monitoring, performance, and identity to meet your availability requirements.

Figure 4.3 shows the process for configuring IIS for optimum application availability.

Figure 4.3   Configuring IIS 6.0 for Optimum Availability

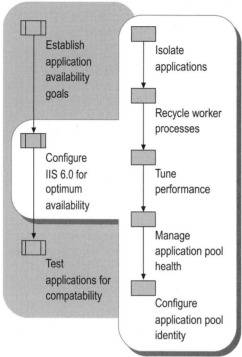

Isolating Applications

Because applications in an application pool are isolated from the applications in other application pools by worker process boundaries, if an application fails, it does not affect the availability of applications that are running in other application pools. Deploying applications in application pools is a primary advantage of running IIS 6.0 in worker process isolation mode because you can customize the application pools to achieve the degree of application isolation that you need.

Configuring application isolation involves completing the following steps:

- Categorizing applications according to their isolation profiles for initial deployment.

- Creating and naming the application pools.

- Assigning applications to the appropriate application pools.

Note

When you configure application pools for optimum availability, also consider how to configure application pools for application security. For example, you might need to create separate application pools for applications that require a high level of security, while allowing applications that require a lower level of security to share the same application pool. Also, client requests might be running identities that are different from the identities that are assigned to the applications that serve them, which can make the application unavailable to customers. For more information about securing applications by configuring applications pools, see "Securing Web Sites and Applications" in this book.

If your organization includes network configurations that require more than one server for implementation, such as Web farms, this involves clustering and load balancing. For more information about clustering and load balancing and the specific processes for setting up replication and clustering on IIS, search for "clustering" and "load balancing" in Help and Support Center for Windows Server 2003.

Determining the Application Isolation Needs of Your Server

The applications that you deploy on a server might fit into several categories, based on your assessment of their importance, demand for server resources, or history of instability. Group your applications according to the following categories, or make up your own set of application categories, before assigning your applications to application pools:

- **Typical.** The application is stable and is not subject to extremely high user demand.

- **High-demand.** The application is expected to receive a large number of requests, putting stress on your the resources of your server.

- **Mission-critical.** The application availability is mandatory for business purposes.

- **Problem.** The application must be isolated from other applications and Web sites due to known or anticipated unstable behavior. If you must run test versions of an application on the same server that runs production applications and Web sites, consider it a problem application that must be isolated from all of the other applications on the server.

- **Unique.** The application requires a configuration that is different from other applications that you have categorized as typical. For example, an application might require an identity that has access to more system resources than the default identity.

Creating Application Pools and Assigning Applications to Them

After establishing similar groups for your applications and Web sites, you can assign them to application pools according to the degree of application isolation they require.

To create application pools and assign applications to them when you are deploying a set of Web sites or applications of different types:

1. Create one application pool for all of the applications that you categorized as typical.

2. Assign all of the applications categorized as typical to the application pool that you created in Step 1.

3. Create one application pool for each high-demand, mission-critical, problem, and unique application. Name each application pool after the application that it will contain.

4. Assign each of your high-demand, mission-critical, problem, and unique applications to the corresponding application pool that you created and named in Step 3.

   You can add application pools by using IIS Manager, by using a command-line procedure, or by running Active Directory® Service Interfaces (ADSI)– or Windows Management Instrumentation (WMI)–compatible scripts. It is recommended that you use IIS Manager because IIS Manager provides clear, complete, and well-organized visibility to application pools and their properties.

For more information about how to create and name application pools, and how to assign applications to application pools through IIS Manager, see "Isolate Applications in Worker Process Isolation Mode" in "IIS Deployment Procedures" in this book. For information about how to assign applications to application pools by using the command line or scripts, see the **AppPoolId** property in the "Metabase Property Reference" in IIS 6.0 Help, which is accessible from IIS Manager.

If you create a large number of application pools running many worker processes concurrently, server performance may suffer. The key factor to consider is that large numbers of worker processes with dynamic applications (ASP or ASP.NET applications) may use up available memory.

Unless you have specific reasons for altering the settings for an application pool, deploy your application pools using the default settings. For more information about specific reasons for using non-default settings, see "Recycling Worker Processes," "Tuning Performance," "Managing Application Pool Health," and "Configuring Application Pool Identity" later in this chapter.

Recycling Worker Processes

If an application contains code that causes problems, and you cannot easily rewrite the code, it might be useful to limit the extent of the problems by periodically recycling the worker process that services the application. *Worker process recycling* is the replacing of the instance of the application in memory. IIS 6.0 can automatically recycle worker processes by restarting the worker process, or worker processes, that are assigned to an application pool. This helps keep problematic applications running smoothly, and minimizes problems such as memory leaks.

You can trigger the recycling of the worker processes assigned to an application pool by using worker process recycling methods that are based on elapsed time, the number of Hypertext Transfer Protocol (HTTP) requests, a set time of day, and two kinds of memory consumption, in addition to recycling on demand. Table 4.1 lists and describes the worker process recycling methods and when to use each.

Table 4.1 Worker Process Recycling Methods

Method	Description	Usage
Elapsed time	Recycles the worker process based on a time frame, in minutes, that is specified by the administrator.	Use this method when applications have problems running for extended time periods.
Number of requests	Recycles the worker process when the number of HTTP requests exceeds a threshold that is specified by the administrator.	Use this method when applications are failing based on the number of requests they receive.
Scheduled times	Recycles the worker process at specified times within a 24-hour period.	Use this method when conditions are similar to the conditions for elapsed time.
Virtual memory	Recycles the worker process when the worker process virtual memory reaches a threshold that is specified by the administrator.	Use this method when the memory heap becomes highly fragmented, which occurs when applications reserve memory multiple times. This is indicated by a steady increase in virtual memory.
Used memory	Recycles the worker process when the memory that is used by the W3wp.exe process reaches a threshold that is specified by the administrator.	Use this method when some of your applications have memory leaks.
On demand	Recycles the worker process when an administrator uses Microsoft Management Console (MMC) or a script to request the recycling of an entire application pool.	Use this method when an application pool is causing problems while the other sites are up and running. Consider recycling the application pool, as opposed to resetting the entire WWW service.

By setting the values for worker process recycling methods, you can schedule recycling events to manage application problems in a timely manner. Table 4.2 lists recommendations for adjusting the values of worker process recycling methods.

Table 4.2   Recommended Settings for Values of Worker Process Recycling Methods

Recycling Method	Recommended Setting
Elapsed time	Set this value to be less than the length of time elapsed before the worker process fails.
Number of requests	Set this value to be less than the number of requests processed before the application fails.
Scheduled times	Set this value to be at intervals that are frequent enough to prevent application failure.
Virtual memory	Initially, set this value to be less than 70 percent of available virtual memory. Then monitor the memory usage of the worker process, and adjust the setting if memory usage continues to increase. Calculate this value in megabytes.
Used memory	Set this value to be less than 60 percent of available physical memory. Calculate this value in megabytes.
On demand	Consider using one of the automated methods for recycling instead, because on-demand recycling is typically performed in response to a failure.

Recycling and Maintaining State

If you have an application pool with applications that depend on state data, then you must decide whether or not to recycle the worker processes that are assigned to that application pool. When you recycle a worker process, the state data for applications that is maintained in process is lost. In this case, do not use recycling.

One alternative to increasing application availability by recycling worker processes is to maintain state data external to the worker process, such as in a database. However, moving data to an external database to allow recycling can affect server performance in the following two ways:

- Performance is reduced because of the added data management that is needed to move the data between the application and the database.

- Recycling flushes any in-process data caches, so the caches need to be rebuilt.

ASP.NET gives you the option of persisting session state using a session state service or a SQL database. For more information on deploying ASP.NET applications, see "Deploying ASP.NET Applications in IIS 6.0" in this book.

Global Locks and Overlapped Recycling

Using global locks, configuring files for exclusive read, and other methods of exclusive resource ownership prevent the use of *overlapped recycling*, or the loading of an application in two application pools simultaneously. Exlcusive ownership requires the use of non-overlapped recycling and the routing of all requests for that application to the same application pool. Also, you can run only one worker process for that application pool, which means that exclusive ownership does not work in a Web garden. One way to work around this is to write multithreaded applications, or use shared reads, which might eliminate the need for exclusively owned resources.

Recycling by Elapsed Time

You can configure an application pool to recycle the worker process, or worker processes, that are assigned to it at specified intervals. By default, recycling by elapsed time is enabled in IIS 6.0, with the elapsed time set to 29 hours. This default setting fits the recycling needs of applications that are problem-free, or that have flaws that cause problems gradually. Recycling worker processes at this interval refreshes applications often enough to correct problems that build up slowly, without creating the severe overhead that can be caused by closely spaced recycling.

Reset the elapsed-time interval for recycling a worker process if your tests or log records indicate that the application that the worker process is assigned to is encountering problems after a given period of uptime. Set the elapsed time to a shorter period of time if problems are building up in less than the default time interval of 29 hours.

Microsoft does not recommend recycling ASP.NET applications by elapsed time.

For information about how to use IIS Manager to configure a worker process to be recycled after a set elapsed time, see "Configure Application Pool Recycling" in "IIS Deployment Procedures" in this book. For information about how to configure a worker process to be recycled after a set elapsed time by using a command-line procedure or scripts, see the **PeriodicRestartTime** property in the "Metabase Property Reference" in IIS 6.0 Help.

Recycling by Number of Requests

You can configure an application pool to recycle the worker process, or processes, that are assigned to it whenever the worker process handles a specified number of requests since the last recycle. By default, recycling by number of requests is disabled in IIS 6.0. When this feature is enabled, the default is 35,000 requests.

Enable recycling by number of requests if your log records or tests indicate that an application you are deploying causes significant problems on your server, or encounters significant problems, after the application handles a certain number of requests. Then, for the worker process assigned to the application pool containing the unhealthy application, set the number of requests to be handled before the worker process is recycled.

For information about how to configure a worker process to be recycled after processing a set number of requests through IIS Manager, see "Configure Application Pool Recycling" in "IIS Deployment Procedures" in this book. For information about how to configure a worker process to be recycled after processing a set number of requests by using the command-shell or scripts, see the **PeriodicRestartRequests** property in the "Metabase Property Reference" in IIS 6.0 Help.

Recycling at Scheduled Times

To avoid recycling worker processes when server demand is heaviest, you can configure an application pool to recycle the worker process, or worker processes, that are assigned to it at a specified time of day, which is based on a 24-hour format. By default, recycling at a scheduled time is disabled in IIS 6.0.

You might need to schedule some, or all, of your applications to recycle worker processes at times of the day when the server load is light. Enable recycling at a scheduled time so that worker processes are rescheduled at times that best fit the load. Be careful to stagger the recycling of your application pools because allowing them to recycle at the same time can degrade the performance of your server during the recycle period.

For information about how to use IIS Manager to configure a worker process to be recycled at scheduled times, see "Configure Application Pool Recycling" in "IIS Deployment Procedures" in this book. For information about how to configure a worker process to be recycled at scheduled times by using a command-line procedure or script, see the **PeriodicRestartSchedule** property in the "Metabase Property Reference" in IIS 6.0 Help.

Recycling on a Virtual-Memory Threshold

A problem application might periodically increase virtual memory without subsequently releasing it. In this way, virtual memory can increase indefinitely. To limit the impact of increased virtual memory, you can set an application pool to recycle the worker processes that are assigned to it whenever virtual memory reaches a specified threshold.

By default, recycling on a virtual-memory threshold is disabled in IIS 6.0. When this feature is enabled, the default virtual-memory setting is 500 megabytes (MB). Enable recycling on a virtual-memory threshold and set a virtual memory threshold that prevents unacceptable degradation. Begin with a setting of 70 percent of available virtual memory.

For information about using IIS Manager to configure a worker process to be recycled after consuming a set amount of memory, see "Configure Application Pool Recycling" in "IIS Deployment Procedures" in this book. For information about how to configure a worker process to be recycled after consuming a set amount of memory by using a command-line procedure or scripts, see the **PeriodicRestartMemory** property in the "Metabase Property Reference" in IIS 6.0 Help.

Recycling on a Used-Memory Threshold

A problem application might indefinitely increase the amount of memory that it uses without releasing the memory. This is also known as an application memory leak. You can set an application pool to recycle the worker processes that are assigned to it whenever used memory, which is also called private memory, reaches a specified threshold.

By default, recycling on a used-memory threshold is disabled in IIS 6.0. When it is turned on, the default used-memory threshold is 192 MB. To limit the impact from an application that increases used memory over time, enable recycling on a used-memory threshold and set a threshold that prevents unacceptable degradation such as a memory-bound application that is unable to process requests. Initially, try a threshold of 60 percent of available memory.

For information about using IIS Manager to configure a worker process to be recycled after consuming a set amount of memory, see "Configure Application Pool Recycling" in "IIS Deployment Procedures" in this book. For information about how to configure a worker process to be recycled after consuming a set amount of memory by using a command-line procedure or scripts, see the **PeriodicRestartPrivateMemory** property in the "Metabase Property Reference" in IIS 6.0 Help.

Tuning Performance

When IIS is running in worker process isolation mode, you can tune the performance of your applications to conserve CPU and memory resources, and to add worker processes to application pools that need them. By setting the application pool properties for idle time-out, you can optimize the time that worker processes remain idle for each application pool, removing them from memory. Another way to conserve memory is to shorten the request queue length limit property for the worker processes in each application pool.

You can increase the number of worker processes that are available to an application pool by configuring a *Web garden*, which is an application pool that is served by more than one worker process. When a worker process is engaged, another worker process can continue to process requests, enhancing server performance. Finally, on a computer with more than one CPU, you can establish affinity between worker processes and specific CPUs, ensuring that applications are tied to processors in accordance with your priorities.

Managing Isolation and Performance

To help achieve high levels of application availability, you can assign fewer applications to each application pool, as low as one application per application pool. This increases isolation, protecting applications from each other. However, configuring fewer applications per application pool increases the total number of application pools. This results in greater CPU and memory usage, degrading server performance, and resulting in reduced request-processing throughput.

The performance impact of increasing the number of application pools on a computer varies based on the number of application pools that are running worker processes. If there are a large number application pools, but few worker processes are running, the impact is relatively small; if there are a large number application pools and many worker processes are running, worker processes can impact each other as they use up memory and CPU capacity, thereby negatively impacting performance.

The degree to which increasing application isolation causes performance degradation can only be determined by testing. You can test for the optimum level of isolation by doing the following:

1. Set the highest level of isolation that your configuration can support, and test with all application pools running simultaneously. Assess the results after using Performance Monitor to record requests processed per second, CPU usage, and memory usage. If performance is satisfactory, the test is complete; if performance is not satisfactory, proceed to Step 2.

2. If the results in Step 1 are unsatisfactory, reduce the isolation level by reducing the number of application pools, and then run the test again.

3. Continue Step 2 until you achieve satisfactory performance. In addition to reducing the number of application pools, you might need to remove applications from the server.

For information about isolating applications, see "Isolate Applications in Worker Process Isolation Mode" in "IIS Deployment Procedures" in this book. For information about assigning applications to application pools by using a command-line procedure or scripts, see the **AppPoolId** property in the "Metabase Property Reference" in IIS 6.0 Help.

Configuring Idle Time-out for Worker Processes

To conserve system resources, configure the idle time-out interval of an application pool to shut down its worker process, or worker processes, after a specified period of idle time. This reduces memory consumption and CPU overhead. This also helps you manage the resources on a Web server when the processing load is heavy, when identified applications consistently fall into an idle state, or when new processing space is not available. To preserve performance, as the number application pools running simultaneously on a server increases, the idle timeout setting should be decreased.

By default, idle time-out is enabled, and the default time-out period is 20 minutes. To automatically shut down worker processes as they become idle, configure a scheduled shutdown of the idle worker process, or worker processes.

For information about how to configure idle time-out by using IIS Manager, see "Configure Application Pool Performance" in "IIS Deployment Procedures" in this book. For information about how to configure idle time-out by using a command-line procedure or scripts, see the **IdleTimeout** property in the "Metabase Property Reference" in IIS 6.0 Help.

Configuring a Request Queue Limit

When an application pool receives requests faster than it can handle them, the unprocessed requests might consume all of the memory on the server, slowing the server and preventing other application pools from processing requests. This can happen when the queue size limit for the requests is large and legitimate requests are coming in at a rapid rate, or during a denial of service attack.

To prevent requests from consuming all the memory for an application pool, limit the size of the request queue for the application pool. To monitor and manage CPU consumption, you must enable CPU monitoring, gather data on CPU usage, and reduce the request queue limit when CPU consumption exceeds the specified limit.

For example, if you have a Web server that is capable of processing 10,000 requests per minute, and you have an application that can queue up 5,000 requests within that period of time, the application consumes 50 percent of the capacity of the server. You can configure IIS 6.0 to limit the number of requests to 2,000, reducing the potential memory consumption of the application and reducing the Web server capacity used by the application to 20 percent.

By default, request queue limit is enabled in IIS 6.0, and the default value is 1,000 requests. When resetting the default value, remember that a value that is too high can prevent other applications from having an equal share of the server resources and a value that is too low can cause the server to return 503 errors, or a disruption of service for the clients.

For information about how to configure a request queue limit by using IIS Manager, see "Configure Application Pool Performance" in "IIS Deployment Procedures" in this book. For information about how to configure a request queue limit by using a command-line procedure or scripts, see the **AppPoolQueueLength** property in the "Metabase Property Reference" in IIS 6.0 Help.

Managing ASP.NET and Request Queue Limit

Recycling worker processes that are serving ASP.NET applications requires that you restart under a request processing load. Starting the new worker processes under a load might cause requests to be rejected because the queue is too full. When this occurs, either increase the queue size limit or disable recycling.

For more information about ASP.NET–specific considerations for applications, see "Deploying ASP.NET Applications in IIS 6.0" in this book.

Configuring Web Gardens

To improve availability for a Web site or application, you can increase the number of worker processes servicing the application pool by implementing a *Web garden*, an application pool that uses more than one worker process on a single computer. This might be helpful if you have already configured a single-application application pool and need to improve availability.

Creating a Web garden for an application pool enhances performance by providing the following benefits:

- **Robust processing of requests.** When a worker process in an application pool is tied up (for example, when a script engine stops responding), other worker processes can accept and process requests for the application pool.

- **Reduced contention for resources.** When a Web garden reaches a steady state, each new TCP/IP connection is assigned, according to a round-robin scheme, to a worker process in the Web garden. This helps smooth out workloads and reduce contention for resources that are bound to a worker process.

Because Web gardens enable the use of multiple processes, all processes have their own copy of application state, in-process session state, caches, and static data. Web gardens are not advantageous for applications that depend on application state. Identify the standard relative performance in a Web garden before you decide whether Web gardens are the best solution for your server.

 Note

A Web garden differs from a *Web farm*, which distributes the load across multiple Web servers. You can design Web farms to provide your applications with the highest availability. For more information about Web farms, see "Scalability" in IIS 6.0 Help.

By default, the Web garden feature is disabled in IIS 6.0, and the default number of worker processes assigned to an application pool is set to one. You can enable Web garden functionality by setting the number of worker processes assigned to an application pool to a number greater than one.

For information about how to configure a Web garden by using IIS Manager, see "Configure Application Pool Performance" in "IIS Deployment Procedures" in this book. For information about how to configure a Web garden by using a command-line procedure or scripts, the **MaxProcesses** property in the "Metabase Property Reference" in IIS 6.0 Help.

Setting Processor Affinity on Servers with Multiple CPUs

On a multi-CPU server, you can configure application pools to establish affinity between worker processes and CPUs to take advantage of more frequent CPU cache hits. By using processor affinity, you can control processors when applications place demands on system resources. Processor affinity is used in conjunction with the processor affinity mask setting to specify the CPUs.

Use processor affinity on computers with multiple processors when it is necessary to continue processing an application that is tied to a subset of the hardware in such a way that transitions from one processor to another are minimized. By default, processor affinity is disabled in IIS 6.0, and the load is distributed across all available CPUs. On a server that is supporting multiple applications, you can enable processor affinity so that a processor is dedicated to each application.

For information about how to set processor affinity, see "Set Processor Affinity" in "IIS Deployment Procedures" in this book, or see the **SMPAffinitized**, and **SMPProcessorAffinityMask** properties in the "Metabase Property Reference" in IIS 6.0 Help.

Managing Application Pool Health

IIS 6.0 health-monitoring and management features support application availability by detecting problems with worker processes that are assigned to application pools, and by taking action to manage the problems. When IIS 6.0 is running in worker process isolation mode, you can detect the health condition of a specific application pool by enabling WWW service to ping a worker process that is assigned to it. Also, you can set features to take corrective action when an unhealthy condition occurs.

Generally, a healthy worker process responds to periodic pings that are sent by WWW service. If a worker process does not respond to the pings within the time interval specified by the **PingResponseTime** property, the WWW service determines the worker process to be unhealthy and triggers other health management features.

Consider using worker process health detection for the following reasons:

- It allows IIS to determine whether each process has at least one thread available to work on requests, and then decide whether to pull new requests from HTTP.sys or to continue processing existing requests.

- It allows the worker process to request recycles when Internet Server Application Programming Interface (ISAPI) extensions such as ASP.NET and ASP are identified to be unhealthy. The health detection feature uses the ability of a worker process to respond to a ping message. The worker process responds to a ping by requesting a recycle if one or more of the ISAPI extensions it has loaded is identified to be unhealthy.

Configuring Worker Process Pinging

Application pool health detection is the ability of the WWW service to detect that a worker process assigned to the application pool is in an unhealthy state by periodically *pinging*, or sending a ping message to, the worker process.

Optimizing Ping Intervals

You can specify a value for the ping interval by examining the potential amount of system resources that can be consumed by unhealthy worker processes over the interval (the default is 30 seconds). Then determine how long you can wait for system resources that unhealthy worker processes are using to be freed so that they are available to other worker processes.

If a worker process becomes unhealthy, the client does not receive a response until another worker process is started to replace the unhealthy worker process. This leaves the unhealthy worker process active without releasing the system resources used by the process. Over a period of time, the amount of system resources used by an unhealthy worker process can accumulate and affect the overall performance of the Web server.

For example, you might have an application that causes worker processes to become unstable. Over a five-minute period of time, the amount of system resources consumed by these unstable worker processes can consume Web server resources and affect the performance of other applications that are on the same Web server. You can configure IIS 6.0 to ping worker processes in that application pool to check the health of the worker processes every 30 seconds, which ensures that the unhealthy worker processes are shut down before system resources are consumed.

Set ping intervals to avoid false failure conditions caused by healthy worker processes that do not respond within the specified response time. You can check this by testing to ensure that the WWW service does not shut down a worker process that is still running, but is too busy to return the ping in the specified response time. If your tests indicate that your worker processes are shutting down because of false failure conditions, increase the ping response time, or alter the load on the worker process.

By default, worker process pinging is enabled in IIS 6.0. The default ping interval is 30 seconds, and the default ping response time is 60 seconds.

For information about how to configure worker process pinging by using IIS Manager, see "Configure Application Pool Health" in "IIS Deployment Procedures" in this book. For information about how to configure worker process pinging by using a command-line procedure or scripts, see the **PingingEnabled**, **PingInterval**, and **PingResponseTime** properties in the "Metabase Property Reference" IIS 6.0 Help.

Configuring Rapid-Fail Protection for Worker Processes

When WWW service detects that a worker process fails more than a set maximum number of times in a specified time period, it places the application pool that the worker process is serving in a rapid-fail state. Rapid-fail protection reduces processing overhead for unhealthy applications because the requests do not enter user-mode processing. As a result, applications that are running in other application pools are protected from the unhealthy application.

By default, rapid fail protection is enabled in IIS 6.0, with a maximum of 5 failures in a 10-minute interval. You can specify the threshold for placing an application pool in rapid-fail state by setting the maximum number of worker process failures that you want to allow over a specific period of time. Specify a threshold that allows IIS 6.0 to detect that a significant number of the worker processes in an application pool are failing and prevent system resources from being consumed.

For information about how to configure rapid-fail protection by using IIS Manager, see "Configure Application Pool Health" in "IIS Deployment Procedures" in this book. For information about how to configure rapid-fail protection by using a command-line procedure or scripts, see the **RapidFailProtection**, **RapidFailProtectionMaxCrashes**, and **RapidFailProtectionInterval** properties in the "Metabase Property Reference" in IIS 6.0 Help.

Configuring the Startup Time Limit for Worker Processes

The startup time limit specifies how long IIS will wait for a worker process to start servicing requests. By default, worker process startup time limit is enabled in IIS 6.0 with a default setting of 90 seconds. If 90 seconds is not long enough to allow the application to begin processing requests, then try a longer time interval.

For information about how to configure the startup time limit for worker processes by using IIS Manager, see "Configure Application Pool Health" in "IIS Deployment Procedures" in this book. For information about how to configure the startup time limit for worker processes by using a command-line procedure or scripts, see the **StartupTimeLimit** property in the "Metabase Property Reference" in IIS 6.0 Help.

Configuring the Shutdown Time Limit for Worker Processes

When IIS 6.0 detects that a worker process is unhealthy, IIS 6.0 marks the worker process for termination. The shutdown time limit specifies how long IIS waits until forcibly terminating the worker process when the worker process does not shut down automatically.

By default, worker process shutdown time limit is enabled in IIS 6.0 with a default of 90 seconds. If you have an accurate profile of requests, specify a shutdown time limit that is long enough to allow the worker process to complete any pending requests before shutting down.

For information about how to configure the shutdown time limit for worker processes by using IIS Manager, see "Configure Application Pool Health" in "IIS Deployment Procedures" in this book. For information about how to configure the shutdown time limit for worker processes by using a command-line procedure or scripts, see the **ShutdownTimeLimit** property in the "Metabase Property Reference" in IIS 6.0 Help.

Enabling Debugging for Application Pool Failures

Debugging a specific worker process that is serving an application pool helps you build high-availability applications. By default, debugging is disabled in IIS 6.0. When you enable debugging, the WWW service stops managing worker processes that fail to respond to a ping in the specified time period. Rather than terminating the application when a process fails to respond to a ping, IIS executes an action such as a process dump or an e-mail notification to alert you to the problem. You can then review the application to identify the cause of the failure.

Note

Enable debugging on an application pool only if the application pool continues to fail to respond to pings. The unhealthy process that is left running will continue to take up system resources until the process is terminated by the administrator or until IIS causes it to self-terminate. If you enable debugging, be sure to terminate the worker process after the debugging action is finished.

For more information about how to enable debugging, see "Debug Application Pool Failures" in "IIS Deployment Procedures" in this book, or see the **OrphanWorkerProcess**, **OrphanActionExe**, and **OrphanActionParams** properties in the "Metabase Property Reference" in IIS 6.0 Help.

Configuring Application Pool Identity

Application pool identity is the user account that serves as the process identity for the worker processes that are servicing the application pool. *Process identity* is the account that a process runs under. Every Windows Server 2003 process has a process identity that is used to control access to resources on the system.

Application pool identity can be assigned to a predefined account. Predefined accounts are known as *service-user accounts* and they are created by the operating system. You can use the predefined NetworkService, LocalSystem, or LocalService accounts for the application pool identity.

In IIS 6.0 worker process isolation mode, application pools have a default identity of NetworkService. The NetworkService identity has minimal administrative credentials, which helps reduce the attack surface of your Web server. If you deploy applications that require a fixed worker process identity, you can change the application pool identity. For information about security and application pool identities, see "Configuring Application Pool Identity Settings" in "Deploying ASP.NET Applications on IIS 6.0" in this book.

For information about how to configure application pool identity by using IIS Manager, see "Configure Application Pool Identity" in "IIS Deployment Procedures" in this book. For information about how to configure application pool identity by using a command-line procedure or scripts, see the **AppPoolIdentityType** property in the "Metabase Property Reference" in IIS 6.0 Help.

Testing Applications for Compatibility

Whether you are deploying existing applications that were developed for earlier versions of IIS on a server running IIS 6.0 in worker process isolation mode, or you are deploying new applications, it is important to test the applications for compatibility with worker process isolation mode features.

Functional testing consists of installing and configuring applications on a test server, and then sending HTTP requests to the application from a client on another computer. Load testing is functional testing that consists of sending HTTP requests in rapid succession to stress the worker process and the server. In both cases, you must diagnose the results for possible incompatibilities.

Figure 4.5 shows the process for testing application compatibility with worker process isolation mode.

Figure 4.5   Testing Applications for Compatibility

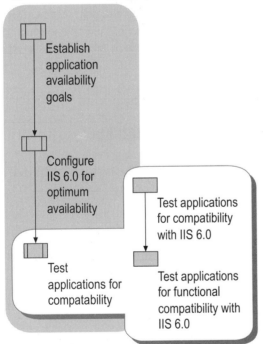

Checking for Known Conflicts with IIS 6.0

Most Web applications that run on earlier versions of IIS will run on IIS 6.0 in worker process isolation mode. However, in some cases, applications cannot run in worker process isolation mode. In other cases, you might be required to disable certain features to run an application in worker process isolation mode.

Applications that have the following characteristics are incompatible with worker process isolation mode, or must have certain features disabled to run in worker process isolation mode:

- **Require Read Raw Data Filters.** Applications that require Read Raw Data Filters are not compatible with worker process isolation mode. The Read Raw Data Filters feature is only supported in IIS 5.0 isolation mode.

- **Require Digest authentication.** You must use LocalSystem as the application pool identity for standard Digest authentication. This restriction does not apply when you are using Advanced Digest authentication.

- **Run only as a single instance.** When an application only runs as a single instance, you cannot configure Web gardens, you cannot run the application in more than one application pool, and you cannot use overlapped recycling.

- **URL length exceeds 16 kilobytes.** The default request header limit for HTTP.SYS is 16KB.

- **ASP applications that use consecutive dots in an include file.** Using two or more consecutive dots in an include file only works if parent paths are enabled. Alternatively, consider not using includes files.

- **Dependency on Inetinfo.exe.** The application requires Inetinfo.exe, but the Inetinfo.exe process does not run in worker process isolation mode. This occurs rarely, if at all.

- **Require Dllhost.exe.** The application requires Dllhost.exe, but the Dllhost.exe process is not available in worker process isolation mode. This occurs rarely, if at all.

Testing Applications for Compatibility with IIS 6.0

You can begin to test the compatibility of an application during the setup process for each application that you install on IIS 6.0.

To perform a setup test, complete the following steps:

1. Install the application by using the setup software provided.

2. Examine the IIS log (in \\Windows\System32\LogFiles\W3SVC*xxx*) for messages that indicate a WWW service failure. Also, look at the system Event log for 500-level errors.

Some common incompatibilities can be identified when you set up applications to run in IIS 6.0 worker process isolation mode. You can recognize these common incompatibilities by their symptoms, and then take the appropriate action to resolve them.

Version Detection Incompatibility

During setup, some applications fail to detect the IIS version correctly because they try to read non-standard registry keys that do not exist in IIS 6.0. The supported version information is under the following registry key: **HKLM\SOFTWARE\Microsoft\InetStp**

Symptoms

Some applications check for a 5 or a 4 in the version information, and then quit setup if the value is 6.

Non-standard registry locations where applications might look for version information include the following:

```
HKLM\SYSTEM\CurrentControlSet\Services\W3SVC\Parameters
```

```
HKLM\SOFTWARE\Microsoft\InetMGR\Parameters
```

Resolution

Add the registry keys that the application is searching for to the registry. Otherwise, you cannot run the applications until you modify them to search for an existing registry key.

Wwwroot and Scripts Retrieval Incompatibility

Some applications use a nonexistent registry key to retrieve wwwroot and scripts. When this is true, the following message appears during setup:

```
HKLM/System/CurrentControlSet/W3svc/Parameters/Virtual Roots
"/ "=REZ_SZ:<physical location of wwwroot>
"/Scripts"=REZ_SZ:<physical location of scripts>
```

Symptom

Setup shows no default value for the wwwroot and scripts directories.

Resolution

Add the registry keys that the application is searching for to the registry. Otherwise, you cannot run the applications until you modify them to search for an existing registry key.

Testing Applications for Functional Compatibility with IIS 6.0

You can test the functional compatibility of an application running in worker process isolation mode by installing the application on a test server, and then sending HTTP requests to the application from another computer. You can identify the following functional incompatibilities when you send correctly composed HTTP requests to applications that were developed for earlier versions of IIS, or to new applications yet to be tested.

ISAPIs Not Enabled in the Web Service Extensions Node

Some application setups install script maps for their script engine but do not enable the script engine, and the documentation for the application might not mention the need to set the properties (by using IIS Manager, for example).

Symptoms

If your log file (%systemroot%\system32\logfiles\w3svc*Filename*.log) returns a 404 error with suberror code 2, then your application is trying to use a disabled ISAPI or Common Gateway Interface (CGI) file.

Resolution

Use the Web Service Extensions node in IIS Manager to enable the ISAPI or CGI file. Be sure to enter the exact path entry that is in the scriptmaps setting in the path part of the entry.

MIME Types Incompatibility

Your application might use a file name extension that is not recognized by IIS 6.0.

Symptoms

If your WWW service log file, which is located in %systemroot%\system32\logfiles\w3svc*Filename*.log, returns a 404 error with suberror code 3, then a file name extension is not recognized by IIS 6.0.

Resolution

Manually add the file name extension to the computer-level properties in IIS Manager. For more information about configuring MIME types, see "Configure MIME Types" in "IIS Deployment Procedures" in this book.

Recycling Incompatibility

The configurable recycling feature in IIS 6.0 might expose some design flaws in your applications. The most common problem is that applications take too long to start up or to shut down. For example, it is not a problem in IIS 5.0 if an application receives an access violation when shutting down. However, an IIS 6.0 administrator might see error messages in the Event log indicating that the application pool is taking too long to shut down. If the application needs to warm up when it starts up, then recycling causes the application to run at low efficiency every time it starts up. If the application does not save its state data when it shuts down, it loses state data often. Test the impact of the recycling period by configuring it to a shorter time and continuing to check the log.

Symptoms

You can identify recycling incompatibility problems by testing the worker process with a short recycle period. If problems exist in the applications in the application pool that is served by the worker process, the following symptoms might occur:

- If an application is shutting down slowly, you might find error messages in the Event log, which indicate that the worker process is exceeding its shutdown time limit.

- If the application needs time to warm up when it starts, response times might be very slow at first.

Resolution

The application might require extensive modification. While running the application unmodified, you cannot use recycling. For more information about configuring the features for worker process recycling, see "Configure Application Pool Recycling" in "IIS Deployment Procedures" in this book.

Overlapped Recycling and Single Instance Application Incompatibility

If your application cannot run as multiple instances, then overlapped recycling fails. The failure occurs because the new worker process is running before the existing worker process is terminated, resulting in an attempt to run two instances of the same application.

Symptoms

The symptoms are synchronization-related, such as an access denied error that appears in the IIS log (in \\Windows\System32\LogFiles\W3SVC*xxx*).

Resolution

Do not use overlapped recycling. For more information about configuring the features for recycling worker processes, see "Configure Application Pool Recycling" in "IIS Deployment Procedures" in this book.

Subauthentication Is Not Installed

Subauthentication is not installed by default. You require subauthentication if both of the following are true:

- You are using Digest authentication on your server running IIS 6.0.

- The domain controller is running IIS 5.0.

Symptom

Digest authentication fails.

Resolution

Install subauthentication on your server. For information about how to install subauthentication, see "Install Subauthentication" in "IIS Deployment Procedures" in this book.

Additional Resources

These resources contain additional information and tools related to this chapter.

Related Information

- "Deploying ASP.NET Applications in IIS 6.0" in this book for more information about ASP.NET–specific considerations for applications.

- "Securing Web Sites and Applications" in this book for information about securing IIS applications.

- "Migrating IIS Web Sites to IIS 6.0" in this book for information about migrating IIS applications.

- "Migrating Apache Web Sites to IIS 6.0" in this book for information about migrating Apache Web sites.

- "IIS Deployment Procedures" in this book for more information about procedures for ensuring application availability.

- The MSDN Online link on the Web Resources page at http://www.microsoft.com/windows/reskits/webresources for more information about the HSE_REQ_REPORT_UNHEALTHY support function. Search for ISAPI Reference, and select Extension Reference.

Related Help Topics

- The "Metabase Property Reference" in IIS 6.0 Help, which is accessible from IIS Manager, for more information about programmatically configuring IIS for optimum availability.

- "Scalability" in IIS 6.0 Help, which is accessible from IIS Manager, for more information about Web farms.

Upgrading an IIS Server to IIS 6.0

5

You can move Web sites and applications to Internet Information Services (IIS) 6.0 in two ways. *Upgrading* is installing the Microsoft® Windows® Server 2003 operating system and IIS 6.0 on an existing server running the Windows NT® Server 4.0 operating system and IIS 4.0 or the Windows® 2000 Server operating system and IIS 5.0. *Migrating*, on the other hand, is installing Windows Server 2003 and IIS 6.0 on a new server and then moving, or reinstalling, existing Web sites and applications to that server. Both processes involve minimal outage of service to users that access the Web sites and applications, while retaining the majority of the original configuration settings and fully preserving the content of the Web sites and applications.

In This Chapter

Related Information

- For information about migrating IIS Web sites, see "Migrating IIS Web Sites to IIS 6.0" in this book.

- For information about migrating Apache Web sites, see "Migrating Apache Web Sites to IIS 6.0" in this book.

Overview of Upgrading an IIS Server to IIS 6.0

The advantages of upgrading the server that hosts your existing IIS Web sites and applications to IIS 6.0 include the following:

- **Reduces the time required to deploy IIS 6.0.** Upgrading requires minimal user interaction.

- **Reduces possible configuration errors.** Because the majority of the current operating system, IIS, and Web site configuration settings are retained during upgrade, fewer configuration errors result.

The disadvantages of upgrading the server that hosts your existing IIS Web sites and applications to IIS 6.0 include the following:

- **Retains previous versions of software.** The upgrade process upgrades only software components identified by Microsoft® Windows® Server 2003, Standard Edition; Windows® Server 2003, Enterprise Edition; and Windows® Server 2003, Web Edition. Any other installed software components, such as applications or application dynamic-link libraries (DLLs), remain unchanged.

   During the IT lifecycle of the server, you can install and subsequently remove many of these additional software components. The software removal process often leaves DLLs, other files, and folders on the system. Over time, these unused components can accumulate, consume available disk space, and potentially cause instability with existing applications.

- **Retains the previous registry configuration.** The upgrade process makes the appropriate modifications to the registry entries identified by Windows Server 2003. Registry entries are created by an application as it is installed, but are not removed when the application is removed. Cumulatively, these registry entries consume disk storage and can make troubleshooting registry-related problems more difficult because the unused registry entries can have similar naming conventions to active registry entries.

After upgrading a server to Windows Server 2003 and IIS 6.0, the server runs in *IIS 5.0 isolation mode*, which allows IIS 6.0 to emulate the memory and request processing model in IIS 5.0. However, to take advantage of the security and performance benefits of IIS 6.0, you need to configure the server to run in *worker process isolation mode*, which is the new IIS 6.0 memory and request processing model.

When upgrading existing IIS Web sites is not the best solution for your existing server, consider migrating your IIS Web sites to a newly installed server running IIS 6.0. For information about migrating your existing IIS Web sites to IIS 6.0, see "Migrating IIS Web Sites to IIS 6.0" in this book.

Process for Upgrading an IIS Server to IIS 6.0

The process for upgrading an existing IIS server hosting IIS Web sites and applications includes preparing for the upgrade, as well as performing the upgrade. Upon completing the upgrade process outlined in this chapter, you can then configure IIS 6.0 to run your applications in worker process isolation mode. Lastly, if the newly upgraded IIS 6.0 server hosts existing ASP.NET applications, you must configure IIS to use the proper version of the Microsoft .NET Framework for these applications.

Figure 5.1 illustrates the process for upgrading an existing IIS server hosting Web sites and applications to IIS 6.0.

Figure 5.1   Upgrading an Existing IIS Server to IIS 6.0

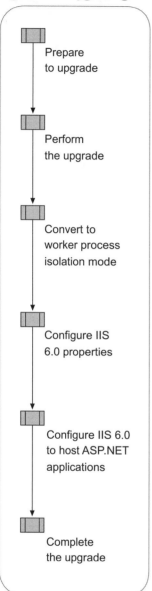

In addition to upgrading the existing operating system and IIS, the upgrade process automatically upgrades any components that are a part Windows Server 2003, such as FrontPage® Server Extensions from Microsoft. As a part of the upgrade process, you need to evaluate the compatibility of the software that is installed on your existing server, including device drivers, other Windows components, and software, before performing the upgrade of the server.

 Tip
To upgrade a Web farm, use the process described in this chapter to upgrade each server in the Web farm.

Depending on your familiarity with IIS and its upgrade process, you might require less information to complete the upgrade process. To facilitate the fastest possible upgrade, the following quick-start guide is provided. You can use this guide to help identify the steps of the upgrade process that you need additional information to complete, and then you can skip the information with which you are already familiar. In addition, all of the procedures that are required to complete the upgrade process are documented in "IIS Deployment Procedures" in this book.

Prepare to Upgrade

1. Determine compatibility with Windows Server 2003.
2. Identify and compensate for changes to IIS 6.0:
   - Ensure that the World Wide Web Publishing Service (WWW service) is enabled after upgrade.
   - Compensate for changes to IIS components.
3. Determine application compatibility with worker process isolation mode by completing the following steps:
   - Evaluate the benefits of worker process isolation mode.
   - Evaluate application changes required for worker process isolation mode.
   - Evaluate management and provisioning script changes required for worker process isolation mode.
   - Verify application compatibility with worker process isolation mode in a lab.
4. Determine application compatibility with the .NET Framework.

Perform the Upgrade

1. Back up the Web server before upgrade.
2. Verify that clients are not accessing Web sites.
3. Prevent the WWW service from being disabled.
4. Upgrade the Web server to IIS 6.0.
5. Verify that the operating system upgrade was successful.
6. Back up the IIS 6.0 metabase after upgrade.

Convert to Worker Process Isolation Mode

1. Document the current application isolation settings.

2. Configure IIS to run in worker process isolation mode.

3. Configure application isolation settings in IIS 6.0.

Configure IIS 6.0 Properties

1. Enable the WWW service.

2. Configure Web service extensions.

3. Configure Multipurpose Internet Mail Extensions (MIME) types.

4. Modify references to IIS 6.0 metabase properties that have changed or are no longer supported.

5. Upgrade FrontPage extended Web sites.

6. Determine whether to run the IIS Lockdown Tool and UrlScan.

7. Make the following security-related configuration changes:

   - Enable essential IIS components and services.

   - Remove any unnecessary IIS virtual directories.

   - Configure the anonymous user identity.

Configure IIS to Host ASP.NET Applications

1. Configure IIS to use the correct version of the .NET Framework.

2. Configure the .NET Framework.

3. Review how ASP.NET applications run in each application isolation mode.

4. Migrate Machine.config attributes to IIS 6.0 metabase property settings by completing the following steps:

   - Migrate recycling-related attributes.

   - Migrate performance-related attributes.

   - Migrate health-related attributes.

   - Migrate identity-related attributes.

Complete the Upgrade

1. Verify that the Web sites and applications run properly.

2. Back up the Web server.

3. Enable client access after upgrade is complete.

Preparing to Upgrade

Before upgrading your existing server running IIS, ensure that Windows Server 2003 supports all of the hardware devices that are on the server. You must also ensure that your Web sites and applications are compatible with IIS 6.0, Windows Server 2003, and worker process isolation mode. Lastly, you must determine whether any of your existing ASP.NET applications are compatible with version 1.1 of the .NET Framework that is installed with Windows Server 2003.

Figure 5.2 illustrates the process for preparing to upgrade an IIS server to IIS 6.0.

Figure 5.2   Preparing to Upgrade

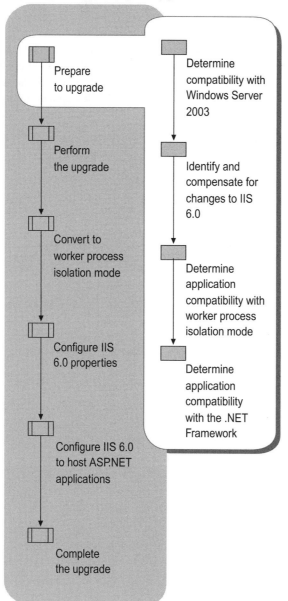

Determining Compatibility with Windows Server 2003

At a minimum, your existing system hardware and software must be compatible with Windows Server 2003 before you upgrade your existing server to IIS 6.0. The upgrade process identifies any software or hardware devices that are incompatible with Windows Server 2003 and allows you to stop the upgrade process after notifying you of any incompatible software or device drivers.

Determining the Compatibility of Existing Windows Servers with Upgrade

Your current Windows server operating system can limit which version of Windows Server 2003 that you can upgrade to. Table 5.1 lists the existing Windows server operating systems and the versions of Windows Server 2003 that are supported for upgrade.

Table 5.1   Windows Server Upgrades Supported by Windows Server 2003

Existing Windows Server	Standard	Enterprise	Web
Windows NT Server 4.0	●	●	
Windows NT Server 4.0, Enterprise Edition		●	
Windows 2000 Server	●	●	
Windows 2000 Advanced Server		●	
Windows Server 2003, Standard Edition		●	
Windows Server 2003, Web Edition			●

If you want to move from an existing Windows server operating system to a version of Windows Server 2003 that is not supported by upgrade, migrate the existing Web server to a new Web server. For more information about migrating Web sites to a new Web server running IIS 6.0, see "Migrating IIS Web Sites to IIS 6.0" in this book.

Determining the Compatibility of Existing Hardware

In most cases, your existing hardware will be compatible with Windows Server 2003. The most common hardware incompatibility is a device driver that is no longer supported. When devices are no longer supported, remove the existing devices and install an equivalent device that is supported by Windows Server 2003. It is also important that you have the latest BIOS version that is available from your computer manufacturer.

For example, the Web server might have an ISA network adapter that is no longer supported in Windows Server 2003. In this situation, you can obtain and install a new network adapter that is compatible with Windows Server 2003.

For more information about the hardware devices that are supported on Windows Server 2003, see the *Hardware Compatibility List* on the product disc or see the Hardware Driver Quality link on the Web Resources page at http://www.microsoft.com/windows/reskits/webresources.

Determining the Compatibility of Existing Software

Before upgrading, you need to consider the compatibility of your existing applications, or other software that is installed on your server, with Windows Server 2003. This includes software and tools from manufacturers other than Microsoft, as well as Microsoft server products that do not ship with the Windows operating system. Make sure that you have the latest versions of all pre-existing software or service packs that are compatible with Windows Server 2003.

The most common software incompatibilities are caused when your application depends on software from another manufacturer that does not support Windows Server 2003. Or, you might have applications that were designed to run on the Microsoft Windows NT® Server 4.0 or Windows 2000 Server operating systems, which reference application programming interfaces (APIs) that have been changed or removed in Windows Server 2003.

To help you determine the compatibility of your existing software with Windows Server 2003, use the Windows Application Compatibility Toolkit before upgrading your server. To download the latest version of the Windows Application Compatibility Toolkit, see the Windows Application Compatibility link on the Web Resources page at http://www.microsoft.com/windows/reskits/webresources.

For the latest information about application compatibility with Windows Server 2003, see the Windows Server 2003 link on the Web Resources page at http://www.microsoft.com/windows/reskits/webresources.

Identifying and Compensating for Changes to IIS 6.0

Although most of the changes to IIS that are made during the upgrade process have little affect, some of the changes can affect the Web sites and applications, as well as the administration of the Web server. Before upgrading your existing IIS server, review the changes that will be made to IIS during upgrade and determine whether these changes can affect your Web sites and applications. Otherwise, after the upgrade, applications might not function as they were originally designed to. In addition, you need to identify the changes made to IIS during upgrade so that you can properly administer and configure the Web server upon completion of the upgrade.

Identify the changes incurred during the upgrade by completing the following steps:

1. Select a method to ensure that the WWW service is enabled after upgrading a Web server running Windows 2000 Server.

2. Identify changes made to IIS components during upgrade.

Ensuring That the WWW Service is Enabled After Upgrade

For security reasons, the World Wide Web Publishing Service (WWW service) is disabled when you upgrade from Windows 2000 Server or Windows 2000 Advanced Server to Windows Server 2003 or Windows Server 2003, Enterprise Edition, respectively.. The WWW service is disabled on upgrade because IIS 5.0 was installed by default during the Windows 2000 Server installation, and, in many cases, the WWW service was not used. To decrease the attack surface of the server, IIS 6.0 is disabled by default when you upgrade from Windows 2000 Server to Windows Server 2003 unless you do one of the following:

- For manual or unattended upgrades, run the IIS Lockdown Tool on your Windows 2000 Server before starting the upgrade process.

- For manual or unattended upgrades, add the registry entry **RetainW3SVCStatus** to the registry.

- For unattended upgrades, add the entry "DisableWebServiceOnUpgrade = False" in the unattended install script.

- Continue with the upgrade and enable the WWW service after upgrade. For more information about enabling the WWW service, see "Preventing the WWW Service from Being Disabled" later in this chapter.

 Note

Because IIS 4.0 is not installed by default on computers running Windows NT Server 4.0, the Windows Server 2003 upgrade does not disable the WWW service when upgrading from IIS 4.0 to IIS 6.0.

Compensating for Changes to IIS Components

Because of increased security measures, which remove any unnecessary Web sites or configuration settings from the Web server, the upgrade process can remove or change the existing IIS configuration. The upgrade process ensures that you take the necessary steps to accommodate these changes so that your applications run as they did before the upgrade.

Table 5.2 lists the changes in the behavior, administration, and support of IIS 6.0

Table 5.2   Changes to IIS Components After Upgrade

Before Upgrade	After Upgrade
The IISAdmin virtual directory exists.	The IISAdmin virtual directory is removed and a default Web page is placed in the directory. [1]
Web service extensions are mapped to 404.dll. [2]	All extensions mapped to 404.dll are disabled. All other extensions are enabled.

(continued)

Table 5.2   Changes to IIS Components After Upgrade *(continued)*

Before Upgrade	After Upgrade
Web Distributed Authoring and Versioning (WebDAV) is disabled by using NTFS file system permissions. [3]	WebDAV permissions are changed to allow proper operation, and WebDAV is added to the Web service extensions list as *prohibited*.
Indexing Service is disabled by using NTFS permissions. [3]	Indexing Service remains disabled with the same NTFS permissions.
Web services hosted on IIS 5.0 are enabled.	Web services supported by the WWW service are disabled. [4]
FrontPage 2000 Server Extensions included lightweight server support.	FrontPage 2002 Server Extensions does not include lightweight server support.
FrontPage 2000 Server Extensions support.	FrontPage 2000 Server Extensions is not supported. Upgrade all Web sites to FrontPage 2002 Server Extensions.

1 Directory is removed if the IIS Lockdown Tool is run before upgrade.

2 The IIS Lockdown Tool maps all Web service extensions, used by IIS, to 404.dll to disable the extensions. Additional Web service extensions installed beyond the default IIS Web service extensions are not mapped to 404.dll.

3 The IIS Lockdown Tool disables WebDAV and the Indexing Service by changing the permissions.

4 If the IIS Lockdown Tool runs before upgrade or the appropriate registry modifications are made, the Web services remain enabled after upgrade. For more information about preventing the Web services from being disabled, see "Preventing the WWW service from Being Disabled" later in this chapter.

As a part of the architectural changes to IIS 6.0, many of the features that were previously implemented as Internet Server API (ISAPI) filters are now integrated into IIS directly. Table 5.3 lists the ISAPI filters that have been removed and have the functionality of the ISAPI filter implemented in IIS 6.0

Table 5.3   ISAPI Filters Removed During Upgrade

ISAPI Filter Removed	ISAPI Filter File Name	Implemention in IIS 6.0
Compression	Sspifilt.dll	Integrated into IIS 6.0 directly
SSL encryption	Compfilt.dll	Integrated into IIS 6.0 directly
Kerberos authentication	Md5filt.dll	Integrated into IIS 6.0 directly

Determining Application Compatibility with Worker Process Isolation Mode

IIS 6.0 can run in one of two distinct modes of operation, which are called application isolation modes. *Application isolation* is the separation of applications by process boundaries that prevent the applications from affecting one another, and it is configured differently for each of the two IIS application isolation modes: IIS 5.0 isolation mode and worker process isolation mode.

Worker process isolation mode uses the redesigned architecture for IIS 6.0. This application isolation mode runs all application code in an isolated environment. However, unlike earlier versions of IIS, IIS 6.0 provides isolation without a performance penalty because fewer processor instructions are run when switching from one application pool to another. Worker process isolation mode is compatible with most existing Web sites and applications. Whenever possible, run IIS 6.0 in worker process isolation mode benefit from the enhanced performance and security in IIS 6.0.

IIS 5.0 isolation mode provides compatibility for applications that depend upon the process behavior and memory model of IIS 5.0. Run IIS in this mode only when a Web site or application cannot run in worker process isolation mode, and run it only until the compatibility issues are resolved.

 Important

IIS 6.0 cannot run both application isolation modes simultaneously on the same server. Therefore, on a single server running IIS 6.0, you cannot run some Web applications in worker process isolation mode and others in IIS 5.0 isolation mode. If you have applications that require separate modes, you must run them on separate servers.

After you perform an upgrade of the operating system, IIS is configured to run in IIS 5.0 isolation mode by default. Before configuring IIS 6.0 to run in worker process isolation mode, you should evaluate whether your Web sites and applications are compatible with worker process isolation mode. Most of the compatibility issues with IIS 6.0 occur when configuring IIS 6.0 to run in worker process isolation mode.

One of the most common reasons for incompatibility with worker process isolation mode is that applications do not recognize custom ISAPI extensions or DLLs that depend on the memory and request processing models used by earlier versions of IIS. Determine application compatibility in your lab before upgrading your existing IIS server, and if you determine that your applications are not compatible with worker process isolation mode, you can run the applications in IIS 5.0 isolation mode.

 Note

Identifying a complete list of potential incompatibilities that applications can experience with worker process isolation mode is beyond the scope of this book. Even after following the guidelines in this chapter, you need to verify in a lab whether your Web sites and applications are compatible with worker process isolation mode.

Determine the compatibility of an application with worker process isolation mode by completing the following steps:

1. Evaluate the benefits of moving to worker process isolation mode.

2. Evaluate the application changes that are required so that the applications can run in worker process isolation mode.

3. Evaluate the management and provisioning script changes that are required to set up programs and provisioning scripts in worker process isolation mode.

4. Verify the compatibility of the application with worker process isolation mode in a lab.

Evaluating the Benefits of Worker Process Isolation Mode

Worker process isolation mode provides higher levels of security and availability for Web sites and applications than IIS 5.0 isolation mode. Therefore, it is recommended that you configure IIS 6.0 to run in worker process isolation mode.

Worker process isolation mode provides the following improvements to IIS 6.0.

Security Enhancements

IIS 6.0 includes a variety of security features and technologies that help ensure the integrity of your Web site content, and of the data that is transmitted through your sites. The following security enhancement is only available when IIS 6.0 is running in worker process isolation mode.

Default process identity for Web sites and applications is set to NetworkService

In IIS 5.0 isolation mode, the default process identity is LocalSystem, which enables access to, and the ability to alter, nearly all of the resources on the Web server. The potential of attacks is reduced in worker process isolation mode because Web sites and applications run under the NetworkService identity. The NetworkService identity is granted less privileges, which helps prevent an attack from compromising the Web server, which is possible with the LocalSystem identity.

Performance and Scaling Enhancements

Future growth in the utilization of your Web sites and applications requires increased performance and scalability of Web servers. By increasing the speed at which HTTP requests can be processed and by allowing more applications and sites to run on one Web server, the number of Web servers that you need to host a site is reduced. The following are a few of the performance improvements included in worker process isolation mode.

Support for processor affinity for worker processes in an application pool

You can configure all of the worker processes in an application pool to have affinity with specific processors in a multiprocessor or server. Processor affinity allows the worker processes to take advantage of more frequent processor caching (Level 1 or Level 2).

Elimination of inactive worker processes and reclamation of unused resources

You can configure application pools to have worker processes request a shutdown if they are idle for a certain amount of time. This can free unused resources for other active worker processes. New worker processes are then started only when they are needed.

Distributing client connections across multiple worker processes

You can configure an application pool to have more than one worker process servicing client connections, also known as a *Web garden*. Because there are multiple worker processes, the incoming client connections are distributed across the worker processes and throughput is not constrained by a single worker process.

Ability to Isolate Web sites and applications from each other

You can isolate applications without incurring a performance penalty.

Availability Enhancements

Because worker process boundaries isolate the applications in an application pool from the applications in other application pools, if an application fails, it does not affect the availability of other applications running on the server. Deploying applications in application pools is a primary advantage of running IIS 6.0 in worker process isolation mode.

Reduced number of Web server restarts required when administering Web sites and applications

Many of the common operation tasks do not force the restart of the server or the Web service restart. These tasks, such as upgrading site content or components, debugging Web applications, or dealing with faulty Web applications, can be performed without affecting service to other sites or applications on the server.

A fault-tolerant request processing model for Web sites and applications

In IIS 5.0 isolation mode, each Web site or application has only one worker process. However, in worker process isolation mode, you can create a *Web garden* by configuring a number of worker processes to share the processing. The benefit of a Web garden is that if one worker process stops responding, other worker processes are available to accept and process requests.

Isolation of failed worker processes from healthy worker processes

In worker process isolation mode, IIS can determine that a worker process is failing and start a new worker process to replace the failing worker process. Because a new worker process is created before the old worker process terminates, users requesting the Web site or application experience no interruption of service. After IIS creates the new worker process, the failed worker process can be separated, or *orphaned*, from the application pool. The advantage of orphaning a worker process rather than terminating it is that debugging can be performed on the orphaned worker process.

Health monitoring of Web sites and applications

In worker process isolation mode, you can configure an application pool to monitor not only the health of the entire application pool, but also individual worker processes servicing the application pool. Monitoring the health of a worker process allows IIS to detect that a worker process is unable to serve requests and to take corrective action, such as recycling the failed worker process.

In addition, worker process isolation supports other responses when a failed worker process or application pool is detected. For example, IIS can attach a debugger to an orphaned worker process or notify an administrator that an application pool has failed due to rapid-fail protection.

Prevention of Web sites or applications that fail quickly from consuming system resources

In some cases, availability can be affected by Web sites and applications that fail very quickly, are automatically restarted, and then fail quickly again. The endless cycle of failure and restarting can consume system resources, causing other Web sites and applications to experience denial of services because of system resource shortages.

Worker process isolation mode includes *rapid-fail protection* that stops an application pool when too many of the worker processes assigned to an application pool are found to be unhealthy within a specified period of time.

Automatic restart of poorly performing Web sites and applications

Some Web sites and applications have memory leaks, are poorly coded, or have other unidentified problems. In IIS 5.0 isolation mode, these applications can force you to restart the entire Web server. The recycling feature in worker process isolation mode can periodically restart the worker processes in an application pool to manage faulty applications. Worker processes can be scheduled to restart based on several options, such as elapsed time or the number of requests served.

Evaluating Application Changes Required for Worker Process Isolation Mode

In most cases, the existing Web sites and applications can be hosted in worker process isolation mode without modification. However, the following are known application issues that can create incompatibilities with worker process isolation mode and require you to run IIS 6.0 in IIS 5.0 isolation mode.

- **Requires Inetinfo.exe.** When the application must run in the same process with Inetinfo.exe, IIS must be configured to run in IIS 5.0 isolation mode because Inetinfo.exe does not process Web requests in worker process isolation mode. In worker process isolation mode, W3wp.exe processes Web requests.

- **Requires Dllhost.exe.** When the application depends on Dllhost.exe to process Web requests for the application, IIS must be configured to run in IIS 5.0 isolation mode because Dllhost.exe is not available in worker process isolation mode.

- **Requires read raw data filters.** If the application uses an ISAPI raw data filter, IIS must be configured to run in IIS 5.0 isolation mode.

- **Requires version 1.0 of the .NET Framework.** When the application requires version 1.0 of the .NET Framework, IIS must be configured to run in IIS 5.0 isolation mode because version 1.0 of the .NET Framework is only supported in IIS 5.0 isolation mode.

- **Requires ISAPI filters or extensions that are incompatible with worker process isolation mode.** When the application requires ISAPI filters or extensions that are incompatible with worker process isolation mode, IIS must be configured to run in IIS 5.0 isolation mode. ISAPI filters or extensions might be incompatible if the filter or extension has one of the following characteristics:

  - Runs in multiple instances and expects to be recycled by using the recycling provided in IIS 5.0.

  - Expects to have exclusive lock on a resource, such as a log file.

If any of the Web sites and applications running on the existing Web server has one or more of these characteristics, then do one of the following:

- Configure IIS to run in IIS 5.0 isolation mode to ensure Web site and application compatibility. If the Web sites and applications need to be hosted in IIS 5.0 isolation mode, then the upgrade process is complete.

- Modify the existing applications to remove the dependencies.

Evaluating Management and Provisioning Script Changes Required for Worker Process Isolation Mode

When management or provisioning scripts exist for your Web sites and applications, you might need to modify them so that they properly set up the Web sites and applications for the application isolation mode that is running on the Web server — IIS 5.0 isolation mode or worker process isolation mode. If you do not modify your management and provisioning scripts as required, you will be unable to use them to install and configure your Web sites and applications on IIS 6.0.

For example, you might have a provisioning script that uses Microsoft Active Directory® Service Interfaces (ADSI) to create a Web site and configure the site for High isolation in IIS 5.0 isolation mode, which does not exist in worker process isolation mode. After upgrade when the Web server is running in worker process isolation mode, you need to modify the script to create application pools instead.

Common modifications that might be necessary to your setup programs and provisioning scripts include:

- When the script installs an ISAPI extension or filter, you might need to modify the script to add an entry for the ISAPI extension or filter to the Web service extensions restriction list and set the status of the entry to **Allowed**.

  For more information about modifying your setup programs or provisioning scripts to install and enable an ISAPI extension or filter, see "Configuring Web Service Extensions" later in this chapter.

- When the script installs an application that contains dynamic content, you might need to modify the script to set the status of the appropriate Web service extensions to **Allowed**, so that IIS allows the dynamic content to run.

  For more information about modifying your setup programs or provisioning scripts to enable dynamic content, see "Configuring Web Service Extensions" later in this chapter.

- When the script installs a Web site or application that runs in High isolation in IIS 5.0, you might need to modify the script to create an application pool and configures the application pool with settings that are comparable to the original IIS 5.0 isolation settings.

  For more information about modifying your setup programs or provisioning scripts to create and configure application pools, see "Configuring Application Isolation Settings in Worker Process Isolation Mode" later in this chapter.

- When the script references metabase properties, you might need to modify the script if it references metabase properties that have changed or are no longer supported in IIS 6.0.

  For more information about modifying your setup programs or provisioning scripts to reference the proper metabase properties in IIS 6.0, see "Modifying References to IIS 6.0 Metabase Properties" later in this chapter.

Verifying Application Compatibility with Worker Process Isolation Mode in a Lab

After modifying your Web sites, applications, setup programs, and provisioning scripts to be compatible with worker process isolation mode, you need to test your modifications in a lab. Be sure to test for compatibility before performing the upgrade process on a production Web server.

Verify the compatibility of your Web sites, applications, setup programs, and provisioning scripts with worker process isolation mode in a lab by completing the following steps:

1. Make an image backup of the Web server you are going to upgrade.

2. Restore the backup to a Web server in your lab, referred to hereafter as a *test Web server*. Ensure that the test Web server is not connected to your production network to prevent any problems encountered during the upgrade from affecting your production network.

3. Perform an upgrade on the test Web server.

4. Configure the Web server to run in worker processor isolation mode.

5. Make the necessary modifications to the Web sites, applications, setup programs, and provisioning scripts so that they are compatible with worker process isolation mode.

6. Verify the Web sites, applications, setup programs, and provisioning scripts run correctly on the test Web server.

For more information about setting up a test lab, see "Designing a Test Environment" in *Planning, Testing, and Piloting Deployment Projects* of the *Microsoft® Windows® Server 2003 Deployment Kit*.

Determining Application Compatibility with the .NET Framework

For a successful upgrade to Windows Server 2003 and IIS 6.0, you need to determine whether your ASP.NET applications are dependent on specific versions of the .NET framework. Windows Server 2003 includes version 1.1 of the .NET Framework, although most of the .NET applications that were developed before the release of Windows Server 2003 were designed to run on version 1.0 of the .NET framework.

Note

Version 1.0 of the .NET Framework is only supported in IIS 5.0 isolation mode. Therefore, you can only run version 1.0 and version 1.1 of the .NET Framework on the same server when IIS 6.0 is configured to run in IIS 5.0 isolation mode. Version 1.1 of the .NET Framework is supported in IIS 5.0 isolation mode or worker process isolation mode.

Typically, ASP.NET applications running on version 1.0 of the .NET Framework are compatible with version 1.1 of the .NET Framework. However, there might be some incompatibilities, the majority of which are security related and can be corrected by configuring the .NET Framework to be less restrictive.

For example, in the .NET Framework version 1.0, the .NET Framework only examines the **SQLPermission.AllowBlankPassword** attribute if the user includes the password keyword in their connection string. If an administrator or user sets "SQLPermision.AllowBlankPassword=False", it is possible to specify a connection string like "server=(localhost);uid=sam" and succeed. In the .NET Framework version 1.1, this connection string fails.

You can use both version 1.0 and version 1.1 of the .NET Framework on the same server running IIS 6.0, also known as *side-by-side configuration*. Side-by-side configuration allows you to run a mixture of applications that require version 1.0 or version 1.1 of the .NET Framework. During your lab testing, determine the version of the .NET Framework that is required by your applications.

For a current list of possible compatibility issues when upgrading from version 1.0 to version 1.1 of the .NET Framework, see the Compatibility Considerations and Version Changes link on the Web Resources page at http://www.microsoft.com/windows/reskits/webresources. For more information about using multiple versions of the .NET Framework in side-by-side configuration, see "Configuring IIS 6.0 to Use the Correct Version of the .NET Framework" later in this chapter.

 Important

Before upgrading the script maps for your ASP.NET applications, point to version 1.0 of the .NET Framework. Upon completion of the upgrade, version 1.1 of the .NET Framework is installed and the script maps are modified to use version 1.1. When your applications require version 1.0, you need to modify the script maps to use version 1.0, rather than version 1.1. For more information about how to modify the script maps to use version 1.0 of the .NET Framework, see "Configuring IIS 6.0 to Use the Correct Version of the .NET Framework" later in this chapter.

Performing the Upgrade

Before upgrading your existing server to Windows Server 2003 and IIS 6.0, you must back up the server, verify that clients are not accessing Web sites on the server, and optionally prevent the WWW service from being disabled. Then upgrade the Web server to Windows Server 2003 and IIS 6.0. Finally, verify that the upgrade to Windows Server 2003 completed successfully.

Figure 5.3 illustrates the process for performing to upgrade an IIS server to IIS 6.0.

Figure 5.3 Performing the Upgrade

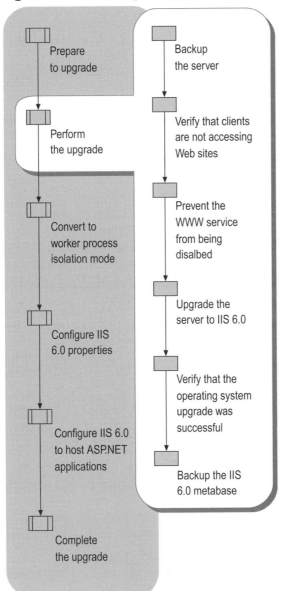

Backing Up the Server

Before you change any of the configuration settings on the existing Web server, perform a complete image backup. The purpose of this image backup is to provide a point-in-time snapshot of the Web server. If unforeseen problems occur during the upgrade, you can use this backup to restore the Web server to a known configuration.

 Important

Do not continue with the upgrade process unless you have a successful backup of the entire Web server or you have another Web server that has the same Web sites and applications. Otherwise, you can lose Web sites, applications, or data stored on the Web server.

For more information about how to back up the Web server, see "Back Up and Restore the Web Server to a File or Tape" in "IIS Deployment Procedures" in this book.

Verifying That Clients Are Not Accessing Web Sites

Before you upgrade the existing server, ensure that no active client sessions are running. Upgrading the server without doing this can result in abnormally terminated client processes and a loss of information.

Verify that clients are no longer accessing Web or File Transfer Protocol (FTP) sites by completing the following steps:

1. Prevent new clients from accessing the sites by pausing the sites.

   For more information about how to pause Web or FTP sites, see "Pause Web or FTP Sites" in "IIS Deployment Procedures" in this book.

2. Enable monitoring of active Web and FTP connections.

   For more information about how to monitor the active Web and FTP connections, see "Monitor Active Web and FTP Connections" in "IIS Deployment Procedures" in this book.

3. When the number of active Web and FTP counters is zero, disable the network adapter that clients use to access the Web server.

   For more information about how to disable the network adapter used by clients, see "Disable Network Adapters" in "IIS Deployment Procedures" in this book.

Preventing the WWW Service from Being Disabled

Earlier in the deployment process, you selected the method for enabling the WWW service after upgrading from a server running Windows 2000 Server and IIS 5.0. If you decided to prevent the WWW service from being disabled after completion of the upgrade, you must do one of the following:

- Modify the registry or unattended setup script.
- Run the IIS Lockdown Tool.

Note

If you are upgrading a Web server running Windows NT Server 4.0 and IIS 4.0, you do not need to run the IIS Lockdown Tool before upgrade.

Modifying the Registry or Unattended Setup Script

Prevent the WWW service from being disabled during upgrade by doing one of the following:

- Create the registry entry **do_not_disable** in the subkey HKLM\SYSTEM\CurrentControlSet\Services\W3SVC\RetainW3SVCStatus as data type REG_DWORD with a value of 0x1. For more information about how to configure the registry, see "Configure the Registry" in "IIS Deployment Procedures" in this book.

Caution

Do not edit the registry unless you have no alternative. The registry editor bypasses standard safeguards, allowing settings that can damage your system, or even require you to reinstall Windows. If you must edit the registry, back it up first and see the Registry Reference on the *Microsoft Windows Server 2003 Deployment Kit* companion CD or on the Web at http://www.microsoft.com/reskit.

- Include the entry "DisableWebServiceOnUpgrade = False" in the [InternetServer] section in an unattended installation script.

Running the IIS Lockdown Tool

The IIS Lockdown Tool is designed to help secure earlier versions of IIS by doing the following:

- Preventing the WWW service from being disabled after upgrade on Web servers that are currently running Windows 2000 Server and IIS 5.0. Disabling the WWW service prevents any Web sites or applications from functioning.

- Helping to secure the existing Web server by disabling or removing unnecessary features that are present in IIS 4.0 and IIS 5.0 installations. These features would otherwise remain on the Web server after upgrading, leaving it vulnerable to attacks.

The IIS Lockdown Tool works by turning off unnecessary features, thereby reducing the attack surface that is available to malicious users. To provide multiple layers of protection for an in-depth defense against potential attackers, the IIS Lockdown Tool includes UrlScan and customized security templates based on supported server roles.

 Note

The WWW service is enabled after the upgrade process is complete on servers running IIS 4.0 because IIS is installed by default in Windows 2000 Server.

Custom Server Configurations with the IIS Lockdown Tool

The IIS Lockdown Tool secures the existing IIS server by performing one or more of the following user-specified transactions:

- Enabling or disabling IIS services such as the WWW service, the FTP service, or the Simple Mail Transfer Protocol (SMTP) service

- Removing services that are disabled

- Disabling active Active Server Pages (ASP) applications on the server

- Disabling optional components, including:

  - Index Server Web interface

  - Server-side includes (SSI)

  - Internet Data Connector (IDC)

  - Internet printing

  - HTR scripting

  - WebDAV

- Disabling anonymous user access to the server by denying:

  - Execute permissions on the operating system executables and DLLs

  - Write permissions on all Web site content directories

- Removing unnecessary virtual directories, including:

    - IIS Samples

    - Scripts

    - Microsoft Data Access Components (MDAC)

    - IIS Admin

- Installing UrlScan

 Tip

The IIS Lockdown Tool helps secure IIS. However, to maintain IIS security, install all available security patches and hotfixes to help protect against known security vulnerabilities.

Server Roles in the IIS Lockdown Tool

Depending upon the applications that you are hosting and the software that you are using on the existing IIS server, select the server role that most closely corresponds to the server you are upgrading. The IIS Lockdown Tool uses the specified server role to determine the appropriate actions to configure the existing IIS server.

Regardless of the server role selected, UrlScan is not required for the purposes of upgrade. UrlScan can be installed by using the IIS Lockdown Tool or separately. For more information about determining whether you need to run UrlScan after upgrade, see "Determining Whether to Run the IIS Lockdown Tool and UrlScan" later in this chapter.

The server roles that are included in the IIS Lockdown Tool include the following:

- Small Business Server for Windows NT Server 4.0

- Small Business Server 2000

- Exchange Server 5.5

- Exchange Server 2000

- Microsoft SharePoint™ Portal Server

- FrontPage Server Extensions

- SharePoint Team Services

- BizTalk® Server 2000

- Commerce Server 2000

- Proxy Server

- Static Web server

- Dynamic Web server (ASP-enabled)

- Server that does not require IIS

- Other (a server that does not match any of the roles in this list)

Each of the server roles in the IIS Lockdown Tool secures the Web server by performing a different combination of the security configuration changes listed earlier. For example, if you select the Exchange Server 2000 (OWA, PF Management, IM, SMTP, NNTP) server role, then FTP is disabled, and SMTP and NNTP are enabled. However, if you select the SharePoint Portal Server, server role then FTP, SMTP, and NNTP are disabled. To determine the configuration performed by each server role, review the contents of the IisLockd.ini file in the same folder that contains the IIS Lockdown Tool.

After running the IIS Lockdown Tool, thoroughly test the server before upgrading to ensure that your Web sites and applications function as they did before. If you find that the configuration settings adversely affect your applications, run the IIS Lockdown Tool again to undo the changes that were made. If you are uncertain whether the IIS Lockdown Tool has been run on the server, you can run the tool again without adversely affecting the system.

 Tip

When the IIS Lockdown Tool locks down a server, it creates a log file named Oblt-log.log and saves it in the folder that contains IISLockd.exe. This file contains information about every action the IIS Lockdown Tool implemented on the system.

Administrators can run the IIS Lockdown Tool unattended, allowing consistent configuration across many servers through unattended scripts. For more information about running the IIS Lockdown Tool unattended, see RunLockdUnattended.doc, which is located in the folder that contains the files for the IIS Lockdown Tool.

To download the latest version of the IIS Lockdown Tool, see the IIS Lockdown Tool link on the Web Resources page at http://www.microsoft.com/windows/reskits/webresources.

Upgrading the Server to IIS 6.0

The upgrade process from IIS 4.0 or IIS 5.0 to IIS 6.0 completes with minimal interaction because the majority of the IIS 4.0 or IIS 5.0 settings are retained. After the upgrade is complete, the Web sites and applications typically function as they did before the upgrade.

The upgrade process runs a number of compatibility tests before actually performing the upgrade. The compatibility tests relate directly to IIS 6.0 and determine the following:

- Whether system volume for the server is formatted with the NTFS file system

- Whether the IIS Lockdown Tool has been run on the server

- Whether the existing server is currently a node in a Microsoft server cluster

A dialog in the Windows Server 2003 upgrade notifies you if any potential compatibility issues exist. After reviewing the potential compatibility issues, you can abort the upgrade process and resolve the compatibility issues, or you can continue the process. None of the compatibility issues prevent the upgrade process from completing.

Verifying That the Operating System Upgrade Was Successful

In most cases, the upgrade process completes without any difficulties. However, before continuing with the upgrade process, verify that the operating system was upgraded successful by completing the following steps:

1. Open *systemroot*\Setuperr.log in Notepad and search for "IIS" to determine if any IIS-related errors occurred.

   During the upgrade process, the Windows Server 2003 upgrade creates an error log file (Setuperr.log) for the entire Windows Server 2003 operating system that records any errors encountered during upgrade. In addition to resolving any IIS related-problems encountered during upgrade, resolve any other upgrade problems listed in Setuperr.log before continuing with the upgrade process.

2. If you find any IIS-related errors, open *systemroot*\Iis6.log in Notepad and search the log file for "fail" to determine the source of the errors.

   During the upgrade of the IIS components, the Windows Server 2003 upgrade creates an IIS-specific log file, Iis6.log in the systemroot folder that records any IIS-specific errors encountered during upgrade. Iis6.log entries with the word "fail" reflect problems encountered during the upgrade process. Review Iis6.log and resolve the problems encountered during upgrade before continuing further in the upgrade process.

   Resolve any operating system upgrade-related problems before continuing further in the upgrade process. Subsequent steps in the upgrade process, such as moving the applications to worker process isolation mode, are dependent upon these issues being resolved.

Backing Up the IIS 6.0 Metabase

Metabase backups created with IIS 4.0 or IIS 5.0 cannot be restored on IIS 6.0. As a result, you cannot use any existing metabase backups of the Web server after the upgrade. After you have verified that IIS 6.0 hosts Web sites and applications as it did before the upgrade, back up the metabase before continuing with the upgrade process.

The remaining steps in the upgrade process focus on hosting the Web sites and applications in worker process isolation mode. Before changing the IIS configuration to worker process isolation mode, verify that you have a backup of the current IIS configuration by backing up the metabase.

In the event that an unforeseen problem occurs while you are configuring IIS 6.0 to run the applications in worker process isolation mode, you can restore the applications to a known operational state. This will provide a known starting place from which to retry the configuration of the server.

For information about how to back up the IIS 6.0 metabase, see "Back Up and Restore the IIS Metabase" in "IIS Deployment Procedures" in this book.

 Note

Upon completion of the upgrade process, a backup of the IIS 6.0 metabase is automatically created. However, changes to the Web service extensions list are not reflected in that backup.

Converting to Worker Process Isolation Mode

When the upgrade process is complete, IIS 6.0 is configured to run in IIS 5.0 isolation mode. Although IIS 5.0 isolation mode provides compatibility with existing applications, it is unable to provide all the security, availability, and performance improvements in worker process isolation mode. To take full advantage of these improvements, you must configure IIS 6.0 to run in worker process isolation mode.

After upgrade, most Web sites and applications function in worker process isolation mode without modification. IIS can run in only one application isolation mode at a time — either IIS 5.0 isolation mode or worker process isolation mode. As a result, configuring IIS to run in worker process isolation mode affects all of the Web sites and applications hosted by IIS. Therefore, before configuring IIS to run in worker process isolation mode, you must determine whether your applications are compatible with this isolation mode. If the existing Web sites and applications are not compatible with worker process isolation mode, you can continue to "Configuring IIS for ASP.NET Applications" later in this chapter.

Figure 5.4 illustrates the process for converting the Web server to worker process isolation mode.

Figure 5.4   Converting to Worker Process Isolation Mode

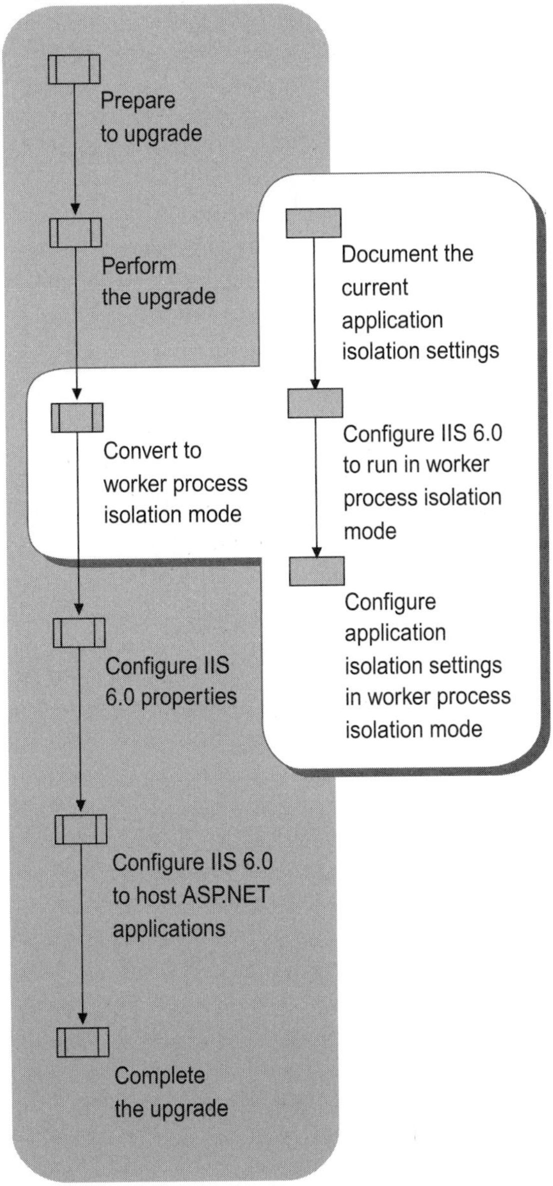

For more information about worker process isolation mode and IIS 5.0 isolation mode, see "Determining Application Compatibility with Worker Process Isolation Mode" earlier in this chapter.

Documenting the Current Application Isolation Settings

Before you configure IIS 6.0 to run in worker process isolation mode, document the existing application isolation settings of the Web sites and applications that are hosted by IIS. Later in the upgrade process, you will use this baseline configuration for configuring the application isolation mode for your Web sites and applications.

For each Web site and application currently running on the server, document the following:

Application isolation settings

Earlier versions of IIS can host Web sites and applications in pooled or isolated process configurations. For information about how to view the current application isolation mode, see "View Application Isolation Configuration" in "IIS Deployment Procedures" in this book.

If you are running IIS 4.0 on Windows NT Server 4.0, your applications are isolated in one of the following ways:

- In-process (running in-process with Inetinfo.exe)

- Isolated (running under Microsoft Transaction Server [MTS])

If you are running IIS 5.0 on Windows 2000, your applications are isolated in one of the following ways:

- In-process (running in-process with Inetinfo.exe)

- Pooled (running in a pooled COM+ package)

- Isolated (running in an isolated COM+ package)

Process identity that is used by the Web site or application

Each Web site or application configured in high isolation, or pooled isolation, uses an *identity*. An identity is a user account that provides a security context for worker process servicing the Web site or application. The identity can be used to secure content, by using NTFS permissions, or data, such as data stored in Microsoft SQL Server™. For more information about how to view the identity for each Web site or application, see "View Web Site and Application Process Identities" in "IIS Deployment Procedures" in this book.

 Note

All Web sites and applications without identities run under the security context of LocalSystem.

Configuring IIS 6.0 to Run in Worker Process Isolation Mode

As previously mentioned, configuring the IIS application isolation mode is a Web server-wide configuration setting that affects all Web sites and applications running on the Web server. The server is currently configured in IIS 5.0 isolation mode.

If you determined that one or more of your Web sites or applications are incompatible with worker process isolation mode, leave the Web server in IIS 5.0 isolation mode. Otherwise, configure IIS 6.0 to run in worker process isolation mode either in IIS Manager, or by setting the IIS metabase property **IIs5IsolationModeEnabled** to a value of **False**.

> **Note**
>
> If you configure IIS 6.0 to run in IIS 5.0 isolation mode and then decide to change the configuration back to worker process isolation mode, the original worker process isolation mode settings are retained. Similarly, if you configure IIS 6.0 to run in IIS 5.0 isolation mode, change to worker process isolation mode, and then change back to IIS 5.0 isolation mode, the IIS 5.0 isolation mode settings are retained.

For more information about how to configure IIS to run in worker process isolation mode or in IIS 5.0 isolation mode, see "Configure Application Isolation Modes" in "IIS Deployment Procedures" in this book. For more information about determining compatibility with worker process isolation mode, see "Evaluating Application Changes Required for Worker Process Isolation Mode" earlier in this chapter.

Configuring Application Isolation Settings in Worker Process Isolation Mode

Immediately after configuring IIS to run in worker process isolation mode, you need to configure the application isolation settings to closely approximate their configuration in IIS 5.0 isolation mode by assigning them to *application pools*. An application pool is a grouping of one or more Web sites or applications served by one or more worker processes. You might need to apply additional configurations so that the applications retain their original isolation settings.

After converting to worker process isolation mode, all applications run in the pre-existing application pool named "DefaultAppPool." If all of the applications run in the same process in the previous version of IIS, then they all are assigned to the default application pool.

However, if any one of the applications in the same application pool fails, the other applications can be adversely affected. For this reason it is recommended that you isolate your applications into separate application pools whenever possible.

Configure Web sites and applications to run in their own application pool by completing the following steps:

For each Web site or application configured in High isolation in IIS 5.0

1. Create a new application pool to be used by the Web site or application.

    For information about how to create application pools, see "Isolate Applications in Worker Process Isolation Mode" in "IIS Deployment Procedures" in this book.

2. If the Web site or application previously ran under an identity that is still required by the Web site or application, configure the application pool to use that same identity.

    For information about how to configure the identity for an application pool, see "Configure Application Pool Identity" in "IIS Deployment Procedures" in this book.

3. Assign the Web site or application to the new application pool.

    For information about how to assign the Web site to the new application pool, see "Isolate Applications in Worker Process Isolation Mode" in "IIS Deployment Procedures" in this book.

For each Web site or application configured in Low or Medium isolation in IIS 5.0

In earlier versions of IIS, applications ran in-process as DLLs in Inetinfo.exe (Low isolation) and the default process identity (account the application runs as) was LocalSystem. With worker process isolation mode in IIS 6.0, applications never run in Inetinfo.exe. However, any applications that are not explicitly assigned to an application pool are assigned to the default application pool, which runs under the NetworkService process identity by default. Because LocalSystem has an elevated security context, run Web sites and applications under the security context of the NetworkService account.

For each Web site or application that ran in Low or Medium isolation in IIS 5.0, do one of the following:

- When the Web site or application is able to function under the identity of the NetworkService account in the default application pool, continue to host the Web sites or applications in the default application pool, named "DefaultAppPool."

- When the Web site or application is unable to function under the identity of the NetworkService account in the default application pool, perform the following steps:

    1. Create a new application pool.

    2. Create a service account to be used as the identity for the application pool.

        For more information about how to create a service account to be used as an identity for an application pool, see "Create a Service Account" in "IIS Deployment Procedures" in this book.

3. Configure the application pool identity to use the service account.

For more information about how to configure the identity for an application pool, see "Configure Application Pool Identity" in "IIS Deployment Procedures" in this book.

4. Place the Web site or application in the new application pool.

Example: Converting to Worker Process Isolation Mode

A fictitious organization, Contoso, has an existing IIS 5.0 Web server that hosts four Web applications. The administrator plans to upgrade the Web server to IIS 6.0, and has tested the applications for compatibility with IIS 6.0 worker process isolation mode and Windows Server 2003. Table 5.4 lists the existing configuration of the Web applications before upgrading to IIS 6.0.

Table 5.4   Configuration Before Upgrade

Application Name	Request Processing Model	Identity
Application-A	Isolated	AppIdent-01
Application-B	In-process	LocalSystem
Application-C	Isolated	AppIdent-02
Application-D	In-process	LocalSystem
Application-E	In-process	LocalSystem

After the upgrade, the administrator verified that the Web applications continued to run properly in IIS 5.0 isolation mode. Then the administrator configured IIS 6.0 to run in worker process isolation mode. Table 5.5 lists the configuration of the Web applications immediately after configuring IIS to run in worker process isolation mode.

Table 5.5   Configuration After Converting to Worker Process Isolation Mode

Application Name	Application Pool	Application Pool Identity
Application-A	Default Application Pool	NetworkService
Application-B	Default Application Pool	NetworkService
Application-C	Default Application Pool	NetworkService
Application-D	Default Application Pool	NetworkService
Application-E	Default Application Pool	NetworkService

To approximate the original configuration of the Web applications in worker process isolation mode, the administrator does the following:

1. Creates a new application pool for each application that was configured for isolation.

2. Configures each application pool with the identity assigned previously to the application configured for isolation.

3. Ensures that the identity assigned to each newly created application pool is added to the IIS_WPG local user group.

4. Assigns each application to the corresponding application pool.

5. Continues hosting all other applications in the default application pool.

6. Verifies that the applications in the default application pool properly run under the NetworkService account identity.

Table 5.6   Final Configuration of Web Sites and Applications

Application Name	Application Pool	Application Pool Identity
Application-A	AppPool-01	AppIdent-01
Application-B	Default	NetworkService
Application-C	AppPool-02	AppIdent-02
Application-D	Default	NetworkService
Application-E	Default	NetworkService

Configuring IIS 6.0 Properties

Up to this point in the upgrade process, you have upgraded the operating system and all of the operating system components, including IIS 6.0, on the Web server. However, you might need to further configure the IIS 6.0 properties on the Web server so that the Web sites run as they did before the server was upgraded. In addition, you can configure your Web server to take advantage of the enhanced security and availability capabilities of IIS 6.0.

Figure 5.5 illustrates the process for configuring the IIS 6.0 properties on your Web server.

Figure 5.5   Configuring IIS 6.0 Properties

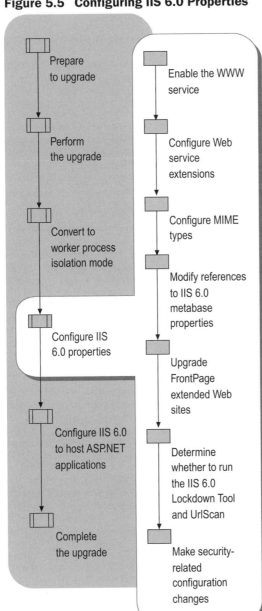

Enabling the WWW Service

When you upgrade a Web server running Windows 2000 Server and IIS 5.0, the World Wide Web Publishing Service (WWW service) is disabled unless, before upgrading, you elected to run the IIS Lockdown Tool or make the appropriate changes to the registry. However, if you did not choose either of those methods, you must now enable the WWW service.

 Note

If you are upgrading a Web server that is currently running Windows NT Server 4.0 and IIS 4.0, the WWW service is not disabled. Therefore, you can continue to the next step in the deployment process.

For more information about how to enable the WWW service after upgrade see "Enable the WWW Service After Upgrade" in "IIS Deployment Procedures" in this book.

Configuring Web Service Extensions

Many Web sites and applications hosted on IIS include dynamic content and other enhanced capabilities. Providing dynamic content and other enhanced capabilities requires executable code, such as ASP, ASP.NET, and ISAPI extensions. The handlers that extend IIS functionality beyond serving static pages are known as *Web service extensions*.

Because of the enhanced security features in IIS 6.0, you can enable or disable individual Web service extensions. After upgrade, all of the Web service extensions are enabled except for the extensions that are mapped to 404.dll by the IIS Lockdown Tool. If you did not run the IIS Lockdown Tool prior to upgrade, all of the Web service extensions are enabled.

The Windows Server 2003 upgrade creates a permission entry for Web service extensions, which enables all of the Web service extensions that are not explicitly prohibited. Enabling all of the Web service extensions ensures the highest possible compatibility with your Web sites. However, doing this creates a security risk by enabling functionality that might not be necessary for your server, which increases the attack surface of the server.

 Note

Web service extensions allow you to enable and disable the serving of dynamic content. *MIME types* allow you to enable and disable the serving of static content. For more information about enabling and disabling the serving of static content, see "Configuring MIME Types" later in this chapter.

Configure the Web service extensions after upgrade by completing the following steps:

1. Configure the Web service extensions list so that the following entries, which enable all Web service extensions, are set to **Prohibited**:

   - **All Unknown CGI Extensions**

   - **All Unknown ISAPI Extensions**

   For information about how to prohibit a Web service extension, see "Configure Web Service Extensions" in "IIS Deployment Procedures" in this book.

2. Enable the essential predefined Web service extensions based on the information in Table 5.7.

Table 5.7   Predefined Web Service Extensions

Web Service Extension	Enable When
Active Server Pages	One or more of the Web sites or applications contains ASP content.
ASP.NET version 1.1.4322	One or more of the Web sites or applications contains ASP.NET content.
FrontPage Server Extensions 2002	One or more of the Web sites are FrontPage extended.
Internet Data Connector	One or more of the Web sites or applications uses the IDC to display database information (content includes .idc and .idx files).
Server-Side Includes	One or more of the Web sites uses server-side include (SSI) directives to instruct the Web server to insert various types of content into a Web page.
WebDAV	You want to support WebDAV on the Web server. Not recommended for dedicated Web servers.

3. For each Web service extension that is used by your applications and is not a one of the default Web service extensions, add a new entry to the Web service extensions list and configure the status of the new entry to **Allowed**.

   For example, one of your applications might use an ISAPI extension to provide access to a proprietary database. Add the ISAPI extension to the Web service extensions list, and then configure the status of the ISAPI extension to **Allowed**.

   For information about how to add a Web service extension and enable the extension, see "Configure Web Service Extensions" in "IIS Deployment Procedures" in this book.

4. Use a Web browser on a client computer to verify that the Web sites and applications run on the server.

Configuring MIME Types

IIS serves only the static files with extensions that are registered in the Multipurpose Internet Mail Extensions (MIME) types list. IIS is preconfigured to recognize a default set of global MIME types, which are recognized by all configured Web sites. MIME types can also be defined at the Web site and directory levels, independent of one another or the types defined globally. IIS also allows you to change, remove, or configure additional MIME types. For any static content file extensions used by the Web sites and applications hosted by IIS that are not defined in the MIME types list, you must create a corresponding MIME type entry.

Configure the MIME types after upgrade by completing the following steps:

1. Remove the entry **.* application/octet-stream**, which enables all MIME types. Removing this entry allows you to restrict the static content served by IIS.

   For information about how to remove a MIME type from the list, see "Configure MIME Types" in "IIS Deployment Procedures" in this book.

2. For each static file type that is used by your applications, ensure that an entry exists in the MIME types list.

   When your application uses the standard MIME types included in IIS, no new MIME type entry is required. For information about how to add a MIME type, see "Configure MIME Types" in "IIS Deployment Procedures" in this book.

3. Use a Web browser on a client computer to verify that the Web sites and applications run on the server.

Modifying References to IIS 6.0 Metabase Properties

There are metabase properties that were used to configure features in earlier versions of IIS that are no longer supported in IIS 6.0. Because some features are eliminated, or implemented differently in IIS 6.0, the corresponding unused metabase properties are not referenced by any code in IIS 6.0. In cases where the feature is implemented differently in IIS 6.0, new metabase properties have been created to replace the obsolete, or unused, property.

In addition, there is one IIS 5.0 metabase property — **CPUResetInterval** — whose behavior has changed because of architectural changes made to IIS 6.0.

To determine whether any of your Web sites, applications, or setup programs reference these changed or unsupported IIS metabase properties, see "Changes to Metabase Properties in IIS 6.0" in this book. You can follow the recommendations associated with each changed metabase property to accommodate functionality changes.

Tip

The metabase properties that are no longer supported in IIS 6.0 are not available in IIS 6.0, even when IIS 6.0 is configured to run in IIS 5.0 isolation mode.

Upgrading FrontPage Extended Web Sites

When you upgrade a Web server that has FrontPage 2000 Server Extensions, the upgrade process automatically installs FrontPage 2002 Server Extensions. After upgrade, both FrontPage 2000 Server Extensions and FrontPage 2002 Server Extensions are installed. After upgrade, you must upgrade each of the FrontPage extended Web sites and configure IIS 6.0 so that FrontPage 2000 Server Extensions is prohibited.

Upgrade your FrontPage extended Web sites by completing the following steps:

1. Set the status of the **FrontPage Server Extensions 2000** entry in the Web service extensions list to **Prohibited**.

    For more information about configuring Web service extensions, see "Configure Web Service Extensions" in "IIS Deployment Procedures" in this book.

2. For each FrontPage extended Web site, upgrade the Web site to FrontPage 2002 Server Extensions.

    You can upgrade individual Web sites by using the FrontPage 2002 Server Extensions Server Administration Web page. You can also upgrade individual sites, or multiple sites in a batch, by using Owsadm.exe.

    For more information about how to upgrade FrontPage extended Web sites to FrontPage 2002 Server Extensions, see "Upgrade FrontPage Extended Web Sites" in "IIS Deployment Procedures" in this book.

Determining Whether to Run the IIS Lockdown Tool and UrlScan

UrlScan and the IIS Lockdown Tool are IIS security related programs designed for IIS 5.1 and earlier. Each tool provides different types of protection for earlier versions of IIS.

IIS Lockdown Tool

The IIS Lockdown Tool is provided to assist administrators in configuring optimal security settings for existing IIS servers. You cannot install the IIS Lockdown Tool after migration because all of the default configuration settings in IIS 6.0 meet or exceed the security configuration settings made by the IIS Lockdown Tool.

UrlScan

UrlScan is a tool that is provided to reduce the attack surface of Web servers running earlier versions of IIS. By default, IIS 6.0 has features that significantly improve security by reducing the attack surface of the Web server. UrlScan provides flexible configuration for advanced administrators, while maintaining the improved security in IIS 6.0. When you need this flexibility in configuring your Web server, you can run UrlScan on IIS 6.0.

For more information about determining whether to run UrlScan after migrating your server to IIS 6.0, see the Using UrlScan link on the Web Resources page at http://www.microsoft.com/windows/reskits/.

Making Security-Related Configuration Changes

After upgrading your server to IIS 6.0, you can make additional security-related configuration changes on the Web server. If you ran the IIS Lockdown Tool before upgrading the Web server, most of these changes are already in place. The IIS Lockdown Tool removes unnecessary IIS components, including virtual directories, to reduce the attack surface available to malicious users. Otherwise, make these security-related configuration changes to help reduce the attack surface and increase the security of the Web server.

Make the security-related configuration changes by completing the following steps:

1. Enable essential IIS components and services.

2. Remove unnecessary IIS virtual directories.

3. Configure the anonymous user identity.

Enabling Essential IIS Components and Services

IIS 6.0 includes other components and services in addition to the WWW service, such as the FTP service and SMTP service. IIS components and services are installed and enabled by means of the **Application Server** subcomponent in **Add or Remove Windows Components**. After installing IIS, you must enable the IIS 6.0 components and services required by the Web sites and applications running on the Web server.

Enable only the essential IIS 6.0 components and services required by your Web sites and applications. For more information about enabling the essential IIS protocols and services see "Enabling Only Essential IIS Components and Services" in "Securing Web Sites and Applications" in this book.

Removing Unnecessary IIS Virtual Directories

Table 5.8 lists the virtual directories that can be removed from IIS 6.0. Compare the virtual directories in IIS Manager to the virtual directories in Table 5.8, and then remove any of the virtual directories listed in Table 5.8.

Table 5.8   Virtual Directories that Can Be Removed After Upgrade

Virtual Directory	Description
IISAdmin	Provides an HTML-based administration tool. It is designed primarily for administrators who administer the Web server through a Web interface, but IIS Manger is the recommended method for Web server administration. The virtual directory is not installed as part of IIS 6.0, but it is not removed when a Web server running an earlier version of IIS is upgraded to IIS 6.0.
IISADMPWD	This virtual directory allows you to reset passwords from Windows NT Server 4.0 and Windows 2000 Server. It is designed primarily for intranet scenarios and is not installed as part of IIS 6.0, but it is not removed when a Web server running IIS 4.0 is upgraded to IIS 6.0. For more information about this functionality, see the Microsoft Knowledge Base link on the Web Resources page at http://www.microsoft.com/windows/reskits/webresources, and search for article Q184619.
IISHelp	Provides an HTML version of the IIS documentation. It is designed primarily for application developers and is not installed as part of IIS 6.0, but it is not removed when a Web server running an earlier version of IIS is upgraded to IIS 6.0.
MDAC	Contains sample applications that illustrate the use of Microsoft Data Access Components that are not required on production Web servers. It is designed primarily for application developers and is not installed as part of IIS 6.0, but it is not removed when a Web server running an earlier version of IIS is upgraded to IIS 6.0.
IISSamples	Contains sample applications that are not required on production Web servers. It is designed primarily for application developers and is not installed as part of IIS 6.0, but it is not removed when a Web server running an earlier version of IIS is upgraded to IIS 6.0.
Printers	Provides an HTML-based printer administration tool. It is designed primarily for administrators who administer printers through a Web interface, but using the Windows Server 2003 printer administration interface is the recommended method for printer administration. The virtual directory is not installed as part of IIS 6.0, but it is not removed when a Web server running an earlier version of IIS is upgraded to IIS 6.0.
Scripts	Contains scripts that are used for the sample applications in other virtual directories and is required on production Web servers. It is designed primarily for application developers and is not installed as part of IIS 6.0, but it is not removed when a Web server running an earlier version of IIS is upgraded to IIS 6.0.

For more information about how to remove unnecessary virtual directories after upgrade, see "Remove Virtual Directories" in "IIS Deployment Procedures" in this book.

Configuring the Anonymous User Identity

When the Web sites and applications running on the Web server require anonymous access, IIS is configured with a user account specifically for anonymous access. When a user connects to the Web server anonymously, IIS creates a process token for the user based on the user account that you configured in the anonymous user identity. The user account can be stored in the local account database on the Web server, or in a domain.

If, before upgrade, the anonymous user identity is configured to use a domain-based user account, after upgrade you need to configure the anonymous user account to the same domain-based user account. This is because the upgrade process automatically configures IIS to user the default anonymous account IUSR_*computername*, where *computername* is the name of the computer on which IIS is running. You can configure the anonymous user identity to the domain-based user account in IIS Manager.

For more information about how to configure the anonymous user identity, see "Configure Anonymous User Identity" in "IIS Deployment Procedures" in this book.

Configuring IIS 6.0 to Host ASP.NET Applications

If the newly upgraded IIS 6.0 server includes existing ASP.NET applications, you need to configure IIS to use the correct version of the .NET Framework, and you must configure the .NET Framework to support your applications. If IIS 6.0 is configured to run in worker process isolation mode, you need to migrate ASP.NET configuration settings from the Machine.config file to the equivalent settings in IIS 6.0.

Figure 5.6 illustrates the process for configuring IIS for ASP.NET applications

Figure 5.6   Configuring IIS for ASP.NET Applications

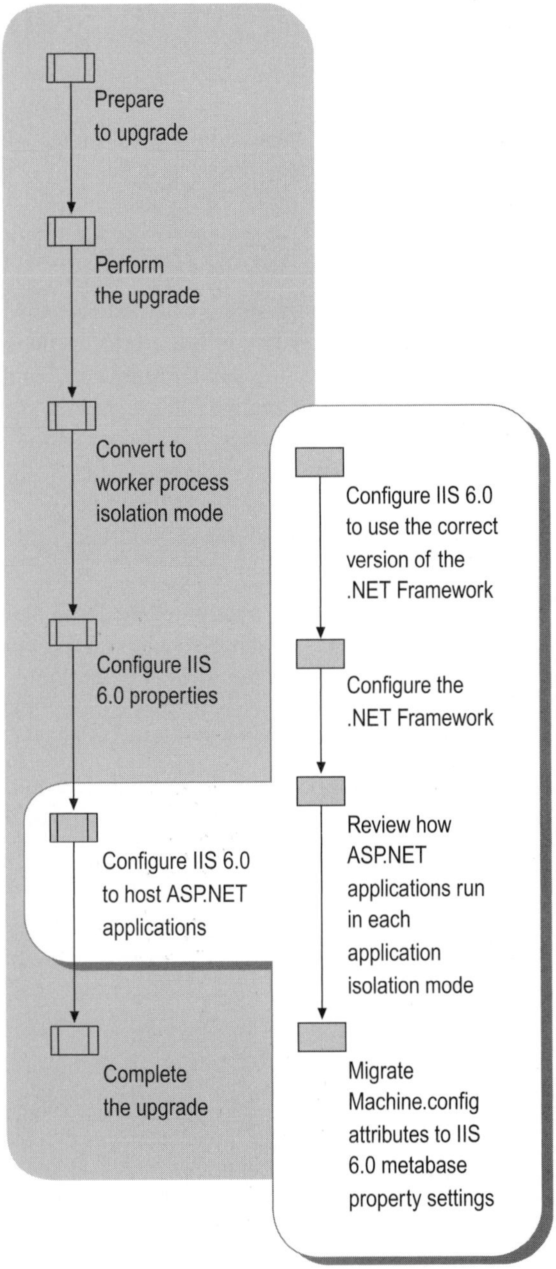

Configuring IIS 6.0 to Use the Correct Version of the .NET Framework

Before upgrading a Web server that hosts ASP.NET applications, version 1.0 of the .NET Framework is installed on the server and the applications are configured to use that version of the .NET Framework. After upgrade, version 1.1 of the .NET Framework is installed and the applications are configured to use version 1.1 of the .NET Framework. However, version 1.0 of the .NET Framework is still installed, which is referred to as side-by-side support.

Running versions 1.0 and 1.1 of the .NET Framework side-by-side is only supported when IIS is configured to run in IIS 5.0 isolation mode. If you have already configured IIS to run in worker process isolation mode, then you can only use version 1.1 of the .NET Framework. In most cases, ASP.NET applications function correctly with version 1.1 of the .NET Framework. For more information about possible application incompatibilities when upgrading from version 1.0 to version 1.1 of the .NET Framework, see "Determining Application Compatibility with the .NET Framework" earlier in this chapter. When your ASP.NET application is incompatible with version 1.1 of the .NET Framework, configure the application to use version 1.0 of the .NET Framework and configure IIS to run in IIS 5.0 isolation mode.

You can configure each ASP.NET application to use a specific version of the .NET Framework by registering a *script map* in IIS for the application. A script map associates a file name extension and HTTP verb with the appropriate ISAPI for script handling. For example, when IIS receives a request for a .aspx file, the script map for the corresponding application directs IIS to forward the requested file to the appropriate version of the ASP.NET ISAPI for processing.

The script map for each ASP.NET application can be applied directly to an application, or inherited from a parent application. However, ASP.NET supports only one version of the .NET Framework for each application pool. For more information about how to configure the script map for an ASP.NET application, see "Configure an ASP.NET Application for ASP.NET" in "IIS Deployment Procedures" in this book.

Configuring the .NET Framework

The configuration method for the .NET Framework is determined by the application isolation mode that you use to configure IIS 6.0. Table 5.9 lists the methods for configuring the .NET Framework that are associated with each IIS 6.0 application isolation mode.

Table 5.9   Methods for Configuring the .NET Framework

Application Isolation Mode	Configuration Method for the .NET Framework
IIS 5.0 isolation mode	Configured by making changes to the Machine.config file in the *systemroot*\Microsoft.NET\Framework*VersionNumber*\Config folder.
Worker process isolation mode	Configured by making changes to the IIS 6.0 metabase.

When IIS 6.0 is configured to run in IIS 5.0 isolation mode, the .NET Framework uses the processModel section of the Machine.config file (in the *systemroot*\Microsoft.NET\Framework*versionNumber*\Config folder) for its configuration and no additional steps are required.

However, if you configured IIS 6.0 to run in worker process isolation mode, the .NET Framework largely ignores the **<processModel>** section of the Machine.config file, and instead gets its process configuration from the IIS 6.0 metabase. Because the upgrade process does not migrate the existing settings in the Machine.config file, you must manually convert any settings required by the ASP.NET applications.

For information about how to convert the Machine.config attribute settings to IIS 6.0 metabase property settings, see "Migrating Machine.config Attributes to IIS 6.0 Metabase Property Settings" later in this chapter. For more information about configuring IIS 6.0 for ASP.NET applications, see "Deploying ASP.NET Applications in IIS 6.0" in this book.

Reviewing How ASP.NET Applications Run In Each Application Isolation Mode

When running in worker process isolation mode, ASP.NET applications use the W3wp.exe worker process and application pool properties, which are stored in the IIS 6.0 metabase. When you configure IIS 6.0 to run in IIS 5.0 isolation mode, ASP.NET applications use the ASP.NET request processing model, Aspnet_wp.exe, and configuration settings. These configuration settings are stored in the Machine.config file.

Behavior of ASP.NET Applications that Are Running in IIS 5.0 Isolation Mode

By default, ASP.NET applications are configured to run in worker process isolation mode. If your application can only run in the ASP.NET process model, you must configure the server to run in IIS 5.0 isolation mode to be able to run the application on IIS 6.0. When IIS 6.0 is configured to run in IIS 5.0 isolation mode, ASP.NET applications behave as follows:

- The applications run within Aspnet_wp.exe.

  Aspnet_wp.exe is a request processing model similar to worker process isolation mode and contains similar worker process management capabilities as the WWW service in IIS 6.0. Aspnet_wp.exe includes most of the IIS application management features, such as recycling, health detection, and *processor affinity* — the ability to force worker processes to run on specific microprocessors.

- The configuration settings are stored in the Machine.config file.

  When configured in IIS 5.0 isolation mode, the configuration settings for ASP.NET applications are managed by modifying the Machine.config file, not the IIS metabase file. Because there is no administrative console for the Machine.config settings, any configuration settings for ASP.NET must be made directly to the Machine.config file.

   Important

  > In IIS 5.0 isolation mode, the .NET Framework ignores any configuration changes made in the IIS metabase. Administrative consoles, such as IIS Manager, make changes to the IIS 6.0 metabase, but those changes are not read by the .NET Framework.

When IIS 6.0 is configured in IIS 5.0 isolation mode, your ASP.NET applications should behave as they did in IIS 5.0. However, incompatibilities can result when running version 1.1 of the .NET Framework. For more information about configuring IIS to support ASP.NET applications that use version 1.0 of the .NET Framework, see "Configuring IIS 6.0 to Use the Correct Version of the .NET Framework" earlier in this chapter.

Behavior of ASP.NET Applications that Are Running in Worker Process Isolation Mode

When IIS 6.0 is configured to run in worker process isolation mode, ASP.NET applications behave as follows:

- The process model within the ASP.NET ISAPI extension is disabled and ASP.NET applications run using worker process isolation mode in IIS 6.0.

  In this configuration, the ASP.NET application runs in worker process isolation mode like any other application, such as an ASP application. In addition, IIS 6.0 provides all of the management features, such as recycling, health detection, and processor affinity.

- The ASP.NET ISAPI extension is configured by a combination of configuration settings that are stored in the IIS metabase (MetaBase.xml) and configuration settings in the Machine.config file.

  When configured in worker process isolation mode, the majority of the configuration settings are stored in the IIS metabase. You can adjust these settings directly in MetaBase.xml or from administrative consoles, such as IIS Manager, or scripts.

  However, if there are existing settings in the **\<processModel\>** section of the Machine.config file, those configuration settings must be converted to the appropriate application pool settings when the Web server is configured to run in worker process isolation mode Additionally, there are other configuration settings that are still made through the Machine.config file, regardless of the application mode. For more information about converting Machine.config attributes to worker process isolation mode settings, see "Migrating Machine.config Attributes to IIS 6.0 Metabase Property Settings" later in this chapter.

When IIS 6.0 is configured in worker process isolation mode, your ASP.NET applications should behave as they did on IIS 5.0. Before deploying your ASP.NET applications on your production Web servers, test compatibility with IIS 6.0 running in worker process isolation mode and version 1.1 of the .NET Framework. For more information about determining application compatibility with IIS 6.0 running in worker process isolation mode, see "Determining Application Compatibility with Worker Process Isolation Mode" earlier in this chapter. For more information about determining compatibility with version 1.1 of the .NET Framework see "Determining Application Compatibility with the .NET Framework" earlier in this chapter.

If you determine that your ASP.NET applications are incompatible with IIS 6.0 running in worker process isolation mode, reconfigure IIS to run in IIS 5.0 isolation mode. If your ASP.NET applications are incompatible with version 1.1 of the .NET Framework, configure IIS to use version 1.0 of the .NET Framework with your ASP.NET application.

For more information about configuring IIS 6.0 to run in IIS 5.0 isolation mode, see "Configure Application Isolation Modes" in "IIS Deployment Procedures" in this book.

Migrating Machine.config Attributes to IIS 6.0 Metabase Property Settings

When you upgrade a server running IIS 5.0 and version 1.0 of the .NET Framework, the ASP.NET applications can depend on specific attribute settings in the **\<processModel\>** section of the Machine.config file. The **\<processModel\>** section configures the ASP.NET process model settings and therefore affects all ASP.NET applications running on an IIS Web server. If any of the following Machine.config attributes exist, you must migrate the attribute configuration settings to their equivalent metabase property settings in IIS 6.0.

 Note

Follow the deployment steps in this section only when IIS 6.0 is configured to run in worker process isolation mode. When IIS 6.0 is configured to run in IIS 5.0 isolation mode, IIS 6.0 reads the ASP.NET settings from the Machine.config file, and you do not need to migrate the Machine.config attribute settings. Thus, you can continue to the next step in the upgrade process.

Migrate the Machine.config attributes by adjusting the configuration settings in the Application Pools node in IIS Manager. Table 5.10 lists the Machine.config attributes and where to find more information about how to migrate the attributes.

Table 5.10   Machine.config Attributes and How To Migrate Them

Machine.config Attribute	Migrating This Attribute
cpuMask	See "Migrating Performance Related Attributes later in this chapter.
idleTimeout	See "Migrating Performance Related Attributes" later in this chapter.
memoryLimit	See "Migrating Recycling Related Attributes later in this chapter.
password	See "Migrating Identity Related Attributes later in this chapter.
pingFrequency	See "Migrating Health Related Attributes later in this chapter.
pingTimeout	See "Migrating Health Related Attributes later in this chapter.
requestLimit	See "Migrating Recycling Related Attributes later in this chapter.
restartQueueLimit	See "Migrating Performance Related Attributes later in this chapter.
shutdownTimeout	See "Migrating Health Related Attributes later in this chapter.
timeout	See "Migrating Recycling Related Attributes later in this chapter.
username	See "Migrating Identity Related Attributes later in this chapter.
webGarden	See "Migrating Performance Related Attributes later in this chapter.

The Machine.config attribute settings in Table 5.10 must be migrated to IIS 6.0 settings. However, you must still configure the following attribute settings in the Machine.config file:

- **maxWorkerThreads**
- **maxIoThreads**
- **responseDeadlockInterval**

When configured to run in worker process isolation mode, IIS 6.0 and the .NET Framework ignore any **<processModel>** section Machine.config attribute settings that are not in the previous list or in Table 5.10.

 Note

The <processModel> section of the Machine.config file configures the ASP.NET process model settings on an IIS Web server. The <processModel> section provides global configuration settings for all of the ASP.NET applications running on the server.

Migrating Recycling-Related Attributes

In worker process isolation mode, you can assign one or more Web sites or applications to an application pool. Each application pool has one or more worker processes that process client requests for the Web sites and applications in the application pool. You can configure IIS to periodically recycle worker processes assigned to an application pool, which in turn recycles the Web sites and applications running in that application pool. Recycling worker processes keeps problematic Web sites and applications running smoothly, especially when it is not feasible to modify the application code. Recycling worker processes within an application pool ensures that the Web sites and applications in the application pools remain healthy, and that system resources can be recovered.

The Machine.config attributes that affect recycling-related metabase properties include:

- **timeout**
- **requestLimit**
- **memoryLimit**

Migrating the timeout Attribute

The **timeout** Machine.config attribute, default value infinite, specifies the time limit after which ASP.NET starts a new worker process to take the place of the current one. The attribute is a string value in the format of hr:min:sec. To configure this value in IIS 6.0, you need to convert this format to time in minutes.

Configure the **Recycling Worker Processes (in minutes)** setting in IIS 6.0 to the same time value, in minutes, that is configured in the **timeout** Machine.config attribute.

For more information about how to configure the **Recycling Worker Processes (in minutes)** setting, see "Configure Application Pool Recycling" in "IIS Deployment Procedures" in this book.

Migrating the requestLimit Attribute

The **requestLimit** Machine.config attribute, default value infinite, specifies the number of requests after which ASP.NET starts a new worker process to take the place of the current one.

Configure the **Recycling Worker Processes (in requests)** setting in IIS 6.0 to the same value, in number of requests, that is configured in the **requestLimit** Machine.config attribute.

For more information about how to configure the **Recycling Worker Processes (in requests)** setting, see "Configure Application Pool Recycling" in "IIS Deployment Procedures" in this book.

Migrating the memoryLimit Attribute

The **memoryLimit** Machine.config attribute, default value 60 percent, specifies the percentage of physical memory that the worker process can consume before ASP.NET starts a new worker process to take the place of the current one.

Recycling based on memory consumption works slightly different in IIS 6.0, where worker processes can be recycled based on both virtual memory and physical memory. Also, the memory limit is not a percentage value, but is specified as a value in megabytes.

Configure the **Maximum used memory (in megabytes)** setting in IIS 6.0 to the amount of physical memory represented by the percentage specified in the **memoryLimit** Machine.config attribute.

Also, adjust the **Maximum virtual memory (in megabytes)** settings in IIS 6.0 if necessary. The **Maximum virtual memory (in megabytes)** is the maximum amount of virtual memory, which includes the used memory plus the reserved memory,

For more information about how to configure the **Maximum used memory (in megabytes)** setting, see "Configure Application Pool Recycling" in "IIS Deployment Procedures" in this book.

Migrating Performance-Related Attributes

In worker process isolation mode, IIS 6.0can be configured to optimize the performance of an application pool, allowing you optimize the performance of your Web applications. Migrating the performance-related Machine.config attributes helps ensure that your Web applications perform as they did on IIS 5.0.

Note

In addition to the configuration settings mentioned in this section, IIS 6.0 provides CPU utilization monitoring for worker processes. For more information, see "Configuring Applications Pools and Worker Processes for ASP.NET Applications" in "Deploying ASP.NET Applications in IIS. 6.0" in this book.

The Machine.config attributes that affect performance-related metabase properties include:

- **webGarden and cpuMask**
- **idleTimeout**
- **restartQueueLimit**

Migrating the webGarden and cpuMask Attributes

The combination of the **webGarden** and **cpuMask** Machine.config attributes provide configuration for ASP.NET on IIS 5.0 for *Web gardens*. Web gardens are created when there is more than one worker process servicing applications. In IIS 5.0, Web gardens are created for use by all applications running on the Web server. In IIS 6.0, Web gardens are created within each application pool.

Web gardens in IIS 5.0 allow ASP.NET to schedule a separate worker process for each microprocessor on a Web server with multiple microprocessors. In contrast, you can create a Web garden on IIS 6.0 by specifying multiple worker processes for an application pool, regardless of the number of microprocessors in the Web server. For more information about Web gardens in IIS 6.0, see "Configuring Web Gardens" in "Ensuring Application Availability" in this book.

The **webGarden** Machine.config attribute, which has a default value of **False**, controls CPU affinity when used in conjunction with the **cpuMask** attribute. When the **webGarden** attribute is set to:

- **True.** ASP.NET creates a separate worker process for each processor specified in the **cpuMask** Machine.config attribute.

- **False.** ASP.NET creates only one worker process and the **cpuMask** Machine.config attribute is ignored.

The **cpuMask** Machine.config attribute, default value 0xffffffff, specifies which microprocessors on a multiprocessor Web server are able to run worker processes initiated by ASP.NET. By default, all processors are able to run worker processes initiated by ASP.NET. The **cpuMask** attribute also contains a bitmask value that indicates the microprocessors that are able to run ASP.NET processes. When a bit in the **cpuMask** bitmask value is set to 1, the corresponding microprocessor is able to run ASP.NET processes. You need to record the number of bitmasks enabled to convert this to the correct number of application pools.

For example, if **cpuMask** is set to a value of 0x0d, the equivalent of the binary bit pattern is 1101. If your Web server has four microprocessors, the bitmask value 1101 indicates that you need three worker processes.

Configure the **Maximum number of worker processes** setting in IIS 6.0 to the number of microprocessors that are enabled in the **cpuMask** Machine.config attribute. The default value for **Maximum number of worker processes** is 1, indicating that Web gardens are not enabled.

For more information about how to configure the **Maximum number of worker processes** setting, see "Configure Application Pool Performance" in "IIS Deployment Procedures" in this book.

Migrating the restartQueueLimit Attribute

The **restartQueueLimit** Machine.config attribute, which has a default value of 10, specifies the maximum number of requests that will be queued in ASP.NET while waiting for the worker process to recycle after an abnormal termination.

Configure the **Limit the kernel request queue to** setting in IIS 6.0 to the same value that is configured in the **restartQueueLimit** Machine.config attribute.

For more information about how to configure the **Limit the kernel request queue to** setting, see "Configure Application Pool Performance" in "IIS Deployment Procedures" in this book.

 Note

When application pool queue length limits are enabled, IIS monitors the number of requests for a designated application pool queue before queuing a new request. If adding a new request to the queue causes it to exceed the queue length limit, the server rejects the request and sends a 503-error response (that cannot be customized) to the client. However, requests that are already queued remain in the queue even if the limit is changed to a value that is less than the current queue length.

Migrating the idleTimeout Attribute

The **idleTimeout** Machine.config attribute, default value infinite, specifies the maximum number of minutes that a worker process can be inactive before it is automatically shut down by ASP.NET. The attribute is a string value in the format of hr:min:sec. To configure this value in IIS 6.0, you need to convert this format to time in minutes.

Configure the **Shutdown worker processes after being idle for** setting in IIS 6.0 to the same time value, in minutes, that is configured in the **idleTimeout** Machine.config attribute.

For more information about how to configure the **Shutdown worker processes after being idle for** setting, see "Configure Application Pool Performance" in "IIS Deployment Procedures" in this book.

Migrating Health-Related Attributes

By detecting the degree of stability (or health) of an ASP.NET application, IIS determines whether corrective action is required. In IIS 5.0, ASP.NET detects an unhealthy worker process. In IIS 6.0, the WWW service detects an unhealthy worker process that has terminated abnormally if all of the available IIS threads in the worker process assigned to the application pool are blocked.

The Machine.config attributes that affect health-related metabase properties include:

- **shutdownTimeout**
- **pingFrequency** and **pingTimeout**

Migrating the shutdownTimeout Attribute

The **shutdownTimeout** Machine.config attribute, default value five seconds, specifies the maximum number of seconds allotted for a worker process to shut down before ASP.NET automatically shuts it down. The attribute is a string value in the format of hr:min:sec. To configure this value in IIS 6.0, you need to convert this format to time in seconds.

Configure the **Worker process must shutdown** setting in IIS 6.0 to the same time value, in minutes, that is configured in the **shutdownTimeout** Machine.config attribute.

For more information about how to configure the **Worker process must shutdown** setting, see "Configure Application Pool Health" in "IIS Deployment Procedures" in this book.

Migrating the pingFrequency and pingTimeout Attributes

In IIS 5.0, the combination of the **pingFrequency** and **pingTimeout** Machine.config attributes specifies whether ASP.NET should monitor the health of worker processes. If IIS 6.0 is running in worker process isolation mode, the WWW service periodically monitors the health of a worker process.

The **pingFrequency** Machine.config attribute, default value 30 seconds, specifies the interval at which ASP.NET queries the worker processes to determine if each worker process is still operating correctly. The **pingFrequency** Machine.config attribute is a string value in the format of hr:min:sec. To configure this value in IIS 6.0, you need to convert this format to time in seconds.

The **pingTimeout** Machine.config attribute, default value five seconds, specifies the interval after which ASP.NET restarts a worker process if there was no response to the most recent query. If a worker process does not respond to the "ping" within the value set by the **pingTimeout** Machine.config attribute, the worker process is restarted. The **pingTimeout** Machine.config attribute is a string value in the format of hr:min:sec. To configure this value in IIS 6.0, you need to convert this format to time in seconds.

You can configure the equivalent settings in IIS 6.0 by making changes to the equivalent IIS metabase properties, listed in Table 5.11.

Table 5.11 Equivalent IIS 6.0 Metabase Properties for pingFrequency and pingTimeout

Machine.config Attribute	Equivalent IIS Metabase Property
pingFrequency	PingInterval
pingTimeout	PingResponseTime

Note

Unless required by your ASP.NET applications, use the default settings in IIS 6.0. In IIS 6.0, the default setting for PingInterval is 30 seconds and the default setting for PingResponseTime is 90 seconds.

You can configure the **PingInterval** metabase property through the **Ping worker process** setting for application pools in IIS 6.0 Manager. For more information about how to configure the **Ping worker process** setting, see "Configure Application Pool Health" in "IIS Deployment Procedures" in this book.

You can only configure **PingResponseTime** by directly modifying the metabase or programmatically through Windows Management Instrumentation (WMI) or ADSI. For more information about directly modifying the metabase, see "Modify the IIS Metabase Directly" in "IIS Deployment Procedures" in this book.

Migrating Identity-Related Attributes

In IIS 5.0, specifying an identity allowed a worker process in ASP.NET to use a Windows identity other than that of the default *process identity*. Process identity is an operating system term used to denote the account that a process runs under. Every running process on a Windows Server 2003 has a process identity that is used to control access to resources on the Web server.

 Note

> In IIS 6.0, the application pool identity allows worker processes servicing the application pool to use an identity other than the default identity NetworkService. In IIS 5.0, the default identity is LocalSystem.

The Machine.config attributes that affect identity-related metabase properties include:

- **username**
- **password**

Migrating the username Attribute

The **username** Machine.config attribute specifies the user account used by ASP.NET as an identity for worker processes. The attribute is a string value and does not exist in Machine.config by default.

In IIS 5.0, the **username** Machine.config attribute has the following values:

- **No entry.** When the **username** attribute does not exist in the Machine.config file, this causes ASP.NET to run worker processes under the identity of LocalSystem.

- **Machine.** Causes ASP.NET to run worker processes under a user account named ASPNET that is created automatically when ASP.NET is installed. This is the default configuration.

- **System.** Causes ASP.NET to run worker processes under a user account named System that is created automatically when ASP.NET is installed and allows ASP.NET processes to have full administrative privileges. Applications running under the identity of the System account have unconstrained privileges on the Web server. Run applications under the identity of the System account only when required by your applications.

- **Configured account.** When the **username** attribute contains a service account, this causes ASP.NET to run worker processes under the identity of the service account.

Configure the equivalent settings in IIS 6.0 by selecting an IIS 6.0 configuration setting that allows the ASP.NET application to run properly while not compromising the security of the Web server. This selection is done in an order of preference, from most secure to least secure.

Configure the User name settings in IIS 6.0 by selecting one of the following in order of security preference:

- **Option 1.** Configure IIS 6.0 to use NetworkService.

- **Option 2.** Configure IIS 6.0 to use a new service account and grant the account the minimal user rights or group membership to allow the applications to run successfully.

- **Option 3.** Configure IIS 6.0 to use a new service account that belongs to the local Administrators group.

Option 1   Configure IIS 6.0 to use NetworkService

This is the default identity for IIS 6.0 and is the recommend identity. Most ASP.NET applications can run by using this configuration. Test your ASP.NET application to ensure proper operation with NetworkService as the identity.

For more information about how to configure the **username** setting, see "Configure Application Pool Identity" in "IIS Deployment Procedures" in this book.

Option 2   Configure IIS 6.0 to use a new service account and grant the account the minimal user rights or group membership to allow the applications to run successfully

Select this option when the ASP.NET application is unable to run under the NetworkService identity. You might need to do this when the **username** Machine.config attribute does not exist or is set to Machine, System, or to a configured account.

For more information about how to create an account see "Create a Service Account" in "IIS Deployment Procedures" in this book. For more information about how to grant user rights, see "Grant User Rights to a Service Account" in "IIS Deployment Procedures" in this book. For more information about how to configure the **username** setting, see "Configure Application Pool Identity" in "IIS Deployment Procedures" in this book.

Option 3   Configure IIS 6.0 to use a new service account that belongs to the local Administrators group

As a last resort, select this option when the ASP.NET application requires an identity that is a member of the local Administrators group. You might need to do this when the **username** Machine.config attribute does not exist, is set to System, or is set to a configured account that is a member of the local Administrators group.

For more information about how to create an account see "Create a Service Account" in "IIS Deployment Procedures" in this book. For more information about how to make a service account a member of the local Administrators group, see "Make a Service Account a Member of the Local Administrators Group" in "IIS Deployment Procedures" in this book. For more information about how to configure the **username** setting, see "Configure Application Pool Identity" in "IIS Deployment Procedures" in this book.

Migrating the password Attribute

The **password** Machine.config attribute specifies the password for the user account used by ASP.NET as an identity for worker processes. The attribute is a string value and does not exist in Machine.config by default, which indicates that the worker processes should run under the default identity of LocalSystem in IIS 5.0.

If you selected NetworkService for the identity for the worker processes, then no password is required. If you decided to create a service account, then configure the **Password** setting in IIS 6.0 with the password for the service account.

For more information about how to configure the **Password** setting, see "Configure Application Pool Identity" in "IIS Deployment Procedures" in this book.

Completing the Upgrade

At this point in the process, your Web sites and applications have been upgraded on the server. Also, the IIS 6.0 properties have been configured so that you are now ready to verify that the Web sites and applications are running properly. After you confirm that the Web sites and applications are running properly, you can back up the Web server and enable client access. When you complete these steps, the upgrade process is complete.

Figure 5.7 illustrates the process for completing the upgrade to IIS 6.0.

Figure 5.7   Completing the Upgrade to IIS 6.0

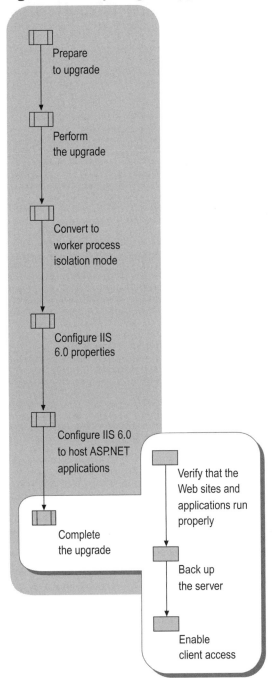

Verifying That the Web Sites and Applications Run Properly

Before deploying your server to a production environment, verify that the Web site content and application configuration information upgraded successfully.

Verify that your Web sites and applications are running properly by completing the following steps:

1. Review the system log in Windows Server 2003 on the Web server to determine if any of the Web sites did not start.

   IIS 6.0 creates entries in the system log when a Web site fails to start for any reason. Search the System log on the target server to determine if any errors occurred. For more information about how to troubleshoot Web sites that fail to start, see "Troubleshooting" in IIS 6.0 Help, which is accessible from IIS Manager.

2. Run your existing validation procedures against the Web sites and applications that run on the server.

   Because the network adapter that connects the Web server to the clients is disabled, you might need to directly connect the Web server to a client computer and enable the network adapter to validate the Web sites and applications.

   After running your existing validation procedures, disable the network adapter that connects the Web server to the clients and reconnect the Web server as it was originally.

 Tip
See "Troubleshooting" in IIS 6.0 Help, which is accessible from IIS Manager, to assist you in resolving any difficulties in running the applications.

Backing Up the Server

Before you enable client access to the Web server, perform a complete image backup. The purpose of performing this image backup is to provide a point-in-time snapshot of the Web server. If you need to restore the target Web server in the event of a failure, you can use this backup to restore the Web server to a known configuration.

 Important

Do not continue to the next step until you have a successful backup of the entire Web server. Otherwise, you can lose Web sites, applications, or data that you changed after upgrading the Web server.

For more information about how to back up the Web server, see "Back Up and Restore the Web Server to a File or Tape" in "IIS Deployment Procedures" in this book.

Enabling Client Access

After you have upgraded the Web server, you are ready to enable client access to the Web sites. During the upgrade process, you disabled the network adapter on the Web server to prevent users from accessing the Web server during the upgrade process. Now that you know the upgrade is completed successfully, you can re-enable the network adapters.

Enable client access to the Web server by completing the following steps:

1. Enable the network adapter used by clients to access the Web server.

   For more information about how to enable the network adapter used by clients, see "Enable Network Adapters" in "IIS Deployment Procedures" in this book.

2. Monitor client traffic to determine if clients are accessing the Web server.

   For more information about how to monitor client traffic to Web sites on the Web server, see "Monitor Active Web and FTP Connections" in "IIS Deployment Procedures" in this book.

3. Establish a monitoring period, such as a few hours or a day, to confirm that clients that are accessing Web sites and applications on the Web server are experiencing the response times and application responses that you expected.

Additional Resources

These resources contain additional information and tools related to this chapter.

Related Information

- "Deploying ASP.NET Applications in IIS 6.0" in this book for information about deploying ASP.NET applications in IIS.

- "Ensuring Application Availability" in this book for information about improving the availability of Web sites and applications in IIS.

- "Migrating IIS Web Sites to IIS 6.0" in this book for information about migrating Web sites to a new Web server running IIS 6.0.

- "Securing Web Sites and Applications in IIS 6.0" in this book for information about securing Web sites and applications in IIS.

- "Designing a Test Environment" in *Planning, Testing, and Piloting Deployment Projects* of the *Windows Server 2003 Deployment Kit.*

- The Compatibility Considerations and Version Changes link on the Web Resources page at http://www.microsoft.com/windows/reskits/webresources for a current list of possible compatibility issues when upgrading from version 1.0 to version 1.1 of the .NET Framework.

- The *Hardware Compatibility List* on the product disc or the Hardware Driver Quality link on the Web Resources page at http://www.microsoft.com/windows/reskits/webresources for information about the hardware devices that are supported on Windows Server 2003.

- The Using UrlScan link on the Web Resources page at http://www.microsoft.com/windows/reskits/ for information about determining whether to run UrlScan after migrating your server to IIS 6.0.

Related IIS 6.0 Help Topics

- "Troubleshooting" in IIS 6.0 Help, which is accessible from IIS Manager, for information about how to troubleshoot Web sites that fail to start.

Related Tools

- The IIS Lockdown Tool link on the Web Resources page at http://www.microsoft.com/windows/reskits/webresources to download the latest version of the IIS Lockdown Tool.

- The Windows Application Compatibility link on the Web Resources page at http://www.microsoft.com/windows/reskits/webresources to download the latest version of the Windows Application Compatibility Toolkit.

CHAPTER 6

Migrating IIS Web Sites to IIS 6.0

6

You can move Web sites and applications to Internet Information Services (IIS) 6.0 in two ways. *Migrating* is installing the Microsoft® Windows® Server 2003 operating system and IIS 6.0 on a new server and then moving, or reinstalling, existing Web sites and applications to that server. *Upgrading* is installing Windows Server 2003 and IIS 6.0 on an existing server running the Microsoft Windows NT® Server 4.0 operating system and IIS 4.0 or the Microsoft Windows® 2000 Server operating system and IIS 5.0. Both processes involve minimal outage of service to users who access the Web sites and applications, while retaining the majority of the original configuration settings and fully preserving the content of the Web sites and applications.

In This Chapter

Related Information

- For information about securing IIS Web sites, see "Securing Web Sites and Applications" in this book.

- For information about upgrading from IIS 4.0 or IIS 5.0 to IIS 6.0, see "Upgrading an IIS Server to IIS 6.0" in this book.

- For information about migrating Apache Web sites, see "Migrating Apache Web Sites to IIS 6.0" in this book.

Overview of Migrating IIS Web Sites to IIS 6.0

You begin the migration process by determining the compatibility of your existing Web sites and applications with IIS 6.0 and the Microsoft® Windows® Server 2003, Standard Edition; Windows® Server 2003, Enterprise Edition; Windows® Server 2003, Datacenter Edition; or Windows® Server 2003, Web Edition operating system. Next, you install Windows Server 2003 and IIS 6.0 on the *target server*, which is the server that will host your Web sites after migration. Then, you migrate the Web site content and configuration settings from the *source server*, which is a server running the Microsoft Windows NT® Server 4.0 operating system and IIS 4.0 or the Windows 2000 Server operating system and IIS 5.0, to the target server.

After the migration of your Web site content, you customize the configuration of IIS 6.0, based on your Web sites and applications. Finally, after you have completed the customization of IIS 6.0, you back up the target server, enable client access to the Web sites and applications on the target server, and decommission the source server.

The process in this chapter focuses on transferring the Web site content and configuration settings, and not on the details of how to make application code changes in dynamic content. If your Web sites contain only static content, you can most likely complete the migration process in a few simple steps. However, if your IIS Web sites contain dynamic content, such as Active Server Pages (ASP), ASP.NET, or Common Gateway Interface (CGI) scripts, you might need to modify the code in the dynamic content separately. In addition, any provisioning scripts or setup programs for your existing Web sites and applications might need to be modified after the migration process is complete. Ensure that you test any modifications after the migration process is complete. For more information about potential modifications, see "Preparing for Migration" later in this chapter.

Also, if the existing Web sites and applications depend on software other than the Windows operating system and IIS, the complexity of the migration process increases. For example, the process for migrating a Web server that hosts Web sites and applications that were designed to run on Windows 2000 Server and IIS 5.0 is relatively simple. On the other hand, the process for migrating a Web server that hosts Web sites, applications, and other software — such as Microsoft Commerce Server, Microsoft BizTalk® Server, monitoring software, custom applications, or other non-Microsoft software — is more difficult because all of the software must be compatible with Windows Server 2003 and IIS 6.0.

In some cases, you can simplify the Web site migration process by using the IIS 6.0 Migration Tool. For more information about using the IIS 6.0 Migration Tool, see "Preparing for Migration" later in this chapter.

Process for Migrating IIS Web Sites to IIS 6.0

The process for migrating Web sites hosted on IIS consists of preparing for and performing the migration. Before performing the migration, you need to evaluate the compatibility of the software installed on your existing Web server (including software that generates dynamic content, database connections, and any non-Microsoft software) with Windows Server 2003 and IIS 6.0. You can then perform the migration manually or with the IIS 6.0 Migration tool. After the migration is complete, you must further customize the configuration of IIS 6.0.

Figure 6.1 illustrates the process for migrating existing IIS Web sites to IIS 6.0.

Figure 6.1 Migrating IIS Web Sites to IIS 6.0

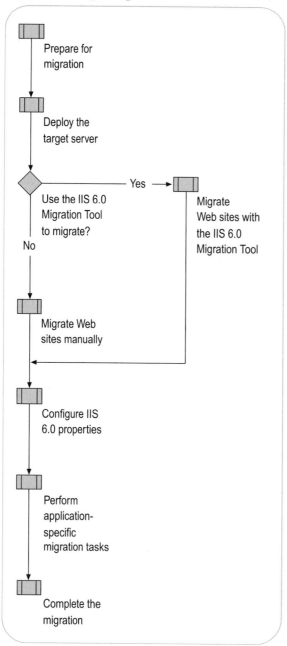

Tip

To migrate a Web farm, use the process described in this chapter to migrate Web sites from each Web server in the source Web farm. Then, use provisioning or Web site staging software to propagate the migrated content and site configuration to other Web servers in the target Web farm.

Depending on your familiarity with Windows server operating systems, IIS, and the migration process, you might require less information to complete the IIS 6.0 migration process. To facilitate the fastest possible migration, the following quick-start guide is provided. You can use this guide to help identify the steps of the IIS 6.0 migration process that you need additional information to complete, and then you can skip the information with which you are already familiar. In addition, all of the procedures that are required to complete the IIS migration process are documented in "IIS Deployment Procedures" in this book.

Prepare for Migration

1. Identify which Web site and application components to migrate.

2. Determine compatibility with Windows Server 2003.

3. Determine application compatibility with worker process isolation mode by evaluating the following:

    - The benefits of worker process isolation mode

    - The application changes that are required for worker process isolation mode

    - The management and provisioning script changes that are required for worker process isolation mode

    - The results of lab tests that were completed to verify application compatibility with worker process isolation mode

4. Determine application compatibility with the Microsoft .NET Framework on Windows Server 2003.

5. Select one of two methods for migration:

    - Using the IIS 6.0 Migration Tool

    - Completing the migration process manually

6. If you are using the IIS 6.0 Migration Tool, identify the following:

    - Tasks that are automated by the migration tool

    - Subsequent tasks that must be performed manually

Deploy the Target Sever

1. Install Windows Server 2003.

2. Install and configure IIS 6.0.

Migrate Web Sites with the IIS 6.0 Migration Tool

1. Install the IIS 6.0 Migration Tool.

2. Verify that clients are not accessing Web sites.

3. Run the migration tool.

4. Verify that the migration tool ran successfully.

5. Migrate additional Web site content that is in the following two locations:

   - Outside the home directory of the Web site

   - Inside virtual directories

6. Modify IIS metabase properties that reference the systemroot folder.

Migrate Web Sites Manually

1. Verify that clients are not accessing the Web sites.

2. Create Web sites and virtual directories.

3. Migrate Web site content to the target server.

4. Configure Web site application isolation settings by completing the following tasks, if appropriate:

   - Document the current application isolation settings on the source server.

   - Configure application isolation settings in IIS 5.0 isolation mode.

   - Configure application isolation settings in worker process isolation mode.

5. Modify IIS 6.0 metabase properties that reference the systemroot folder.

Configure IIS 6.0 Properties

1. Configure IIS 6.0 properties that reference local user accounts.

2. Configure Web service extensions.

3. Configure Multipurpose Internet Mail Extensions (MIME) types.

4. Migrate server certificates for Secure Sockets Layer (SSL).

5. Migrate Microsoft FrontPage® users and roles.

6. Configure IIS 6.0 to host ASP.NET applications by completing the following tasks:

   - Configure IIS to use the correct version of the .NET Framework.

   - Configure the .NET Framework.

   - Review how ASP.NET applications run in each application isolation mode.

   - Migrate Machine.config attributes to their equivalent IIS 6.0 metabase property settings.

7. Determine whether to run the IIS Lockdown Tool and UrlScan.

Perform Application-Specific Migration Tasks

1. Modify application code for compatibility with Windows Server 2003 and IIS 6.0 by doing the following:

   - Modify references to Windows platform components and application programming interfaces (APIs) that are no longer supported in Windows Server 2003.

   - Modify references to IIS 6.0 metabase properties that have changed or are no longer supported in IIS 6.0.

   - Modify applications to be compatible with worker process isolation mode.

2. Install additional software required by applications.

3. Migrate Microsoft Transaction Server (MTS) packages, Component Object Model (COM) objects, and COM+ applications that are required by applications.

4. Modify data source names (DSNs) and Open Database Connectivity (ODBC) connections required by applications.

5. Create IP addresses that are used by applications.

6. Create users and groups that are used by applications.

7. Create registry entries required by applications on the target server.

Complete the Migration

1. Verify that the Web sites and applications migrated successfully.

2. Back up the target server.

3. Enable client access.

Preparing for Migration

Before migrating your existing IIS Web sites, ensure that the Web sites, applications, and their components are compatible with Windows Server 2003 and IIS 6.0. If you have setup programs or provisioning scripts that you are currently using on the source server and that you intend to continue using after migration, then ensure that the setup programs and provisioning scripts are compatible with Windows Server 2003 and IIS 6.0.

In addition, determine whether the existing Web sites and applications are compatible with worker process isolation mode in IIS 6.0. In cases where the existing Web sites and applications are not compatible with worker process isolation mode, you can still migrate to IIS 6.0 and Windows Server 2003 by configuring IIS to run in IIS 5.0 isolation mode. This allows the Web sites and applications to utilize other Windows Server 2003 and IIS 6.0 improvements

Also, if you are migrating ASP.NET applications, you must ensure that the ASP.NET applications are compatible with the latest version of the .NET Framework. If your ASP.NET applications require version 1.0 of the .NET Framework, you must configure IIS to run in IIS 5.0 isolation mode.

Lastly, you must determine whether you can perform the migration with the IIS 6.0 Migration Tool or if you need to perform the migration manually. You need to be aware of the additional migration steps that you must complete manually, regardless of the migration method that you choose. This allows you to have the appropriate tools and resources available when you are ready to perform the migration.

Figure 6.2 illustrates the process for preparing to migrate Web sites to IIS 6.0.

Figure 6.2 Preparing for Migration of Web Sites to IIS 6.0

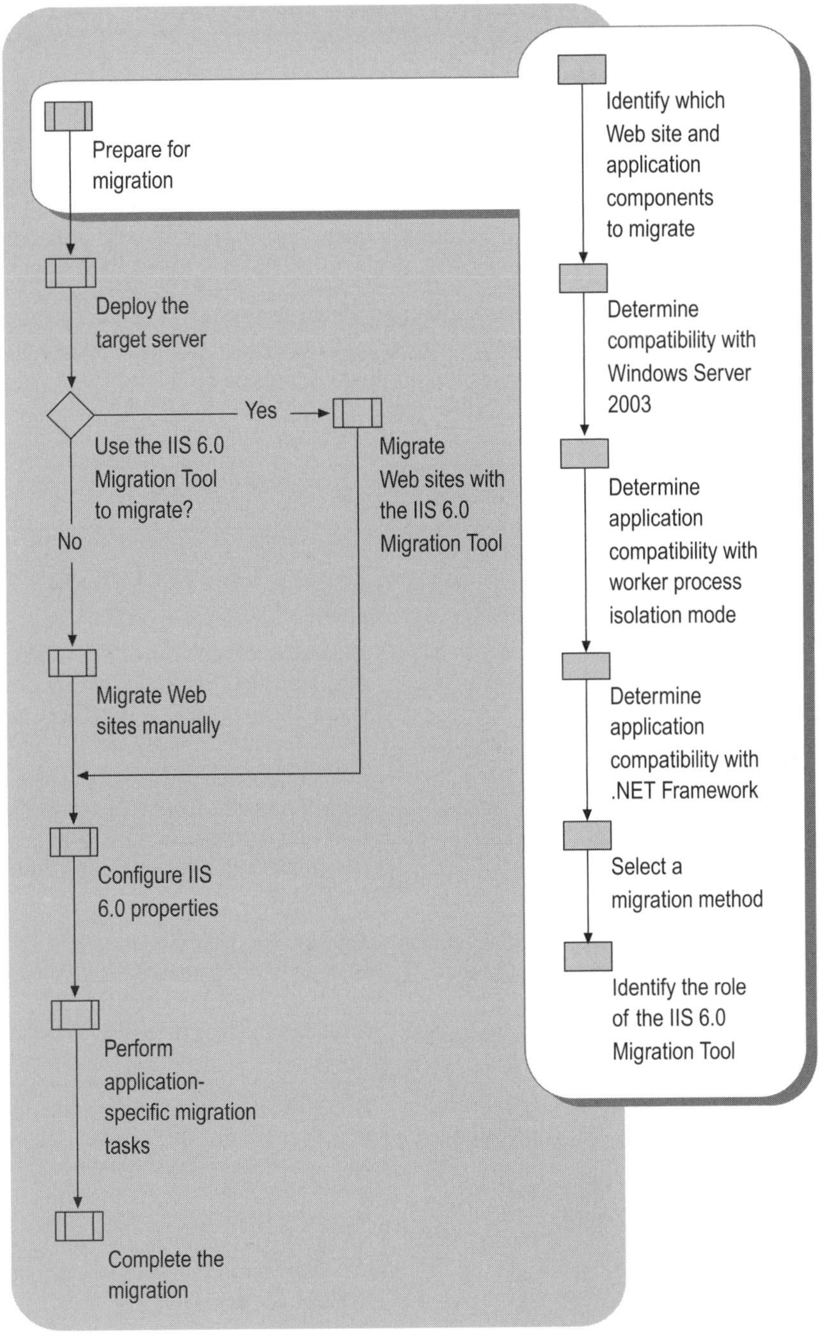

Identifying Which Web Site and Application Components to Migrate

Before you begin the migration, identify the *components* that comprise the Web sites and applications. In addition to identifying the components, you must determine if there are any special circumstances associated with migrating these components. This Web site and application component migration is in addition to the Web site content and configuration that needs to also be migrated.

If you have setup, installation, or provisioning scripts for these Web sites and applications, you can use them to help you identify the components. If no setup, installation, or provisioning scripts exist, you must identify the Web site and application components manually.

Table 6.1 illustrates common application components that require a specific action when migrating to IIS 6.0.

Table 6.1   Migration Issues Associated with IIS Web Site Components

Web Site Component	Description	Migration Issues
MTS packages, COM objects, and COM+ applications	MTS, COM, and COM+ provide object-oriented access to business logic and other data in n-tier applications.	MTS packages and COM+ applications need to be re-created in COM+ on the target server. COM objects that are registered on the source server need to be reregistered on the target server. In some cases, you might need to modify the MTS packages, COM objects, and COM+ applications, to make them compatible with Windows Server 2003 and IIS 6.0.
Registry entries	These entries are custom registry entries that are required by the application.	Applications might save custom configuration information in the Windows registry. The registry entries must be identified and then re-created on the target server.
DSN data connection strings	DSN data connection strings are used to provide connectivity to databases for IIS Web sites.	The DSNs might need to be modified on the target server for each of the Web sites and applications that access databases.
ODBC data connections	ODBC data connections are used to provide connectivity to databases for IIS Web sites.	The ODBC settings might need to be configured on the target server for each of the Web sites and applications that use ODBC to access databases.

(continued)

Table 6.1   Migration Issues Associated with IIS Web Site Components *(continued)*

Web Site Component	Description	Migration Issues
ISAPI applications	ISAPI applications are DLLs that are called by Web sites and applications. There are ISAPI applications (ISAPI extensions) that are shipped with IIS 6.0, such as the ASP.NET ISAPI extension. In addition, your Web sites and applications might rely on ISAPI applications written by your organization.	The ISAPI application must be installed on the target server and then enabled from the Web services extensions node in IIS Manager. In some cases, you might need to modify the ISAPI application to make it compatible with IIS 6.0 and Windows Server 2003.
SSL Server Certificates	SSL server certificates are installed on the server and they enable encrypted communications with clients	Certificates must be copied to, or re-created on, the target computer
Custom user and group accounts	User and group accounts that are created specifically for the Web sites and applications.	If the user and group accounts are local to the source server, the user and group accounts need to be created on the target server.
Additional software	Additional software refers to installed commercial software and applications required by the applications on your server.	This additional software must be installed on the target server. This software might require modification to be compatible with Windows Server 2003 and IIS 6.0.

Determining Compatibility with Windows Server 2003

At a minimum, your existing system hardware and software must be compatible with the Windows Server 2003 family before migrating the Web sites and applications to IIS 6.0. You must identify any software or hardware devices that are incompatible with Windows Server 2003.

Compatibility of Existing Hardware

When you select the computer that will be the target server, ensure that the computer is compatible with Windows Server 2003. The most common hardware incompatibility is a device driver that is no longer supported or is not yet supported in Windows Server 2003. When a device is no longer supported, remove the existing device and then install an equivalent device that is supported by Windows Server 2003. When a device is not supported, look for updated drivers on the device manufacturer's Web site or see the Windows Update link on the Web Resources page at http://www.microsoft.com/windows/reskits/webresources. It is also important that you have the latest BIOS version that is available from your computer manufacturer.

For example, the target server might have a network adapter that is not included with Windows Server 2003. You can review the manufacturer's Web site to obtain a driver that is compatible with Windows Server 2003.

For more information about the hardware devices supported by the Windows Server 2003 operating systems, see the *Hardware Compatibility List* on the product CD-ROM or see the Hardware Driver Quality link on the Web Resources page at http://www.microsoft.com/windows/reskits/webresources.

Compatibility of Existing Software

Before migrating, you need to consider the compatibility of your existing applications, or other software that is installed on your server, with Windows Server 2003. This includes software and tools from manufacturers other than Microsoft, as well as Microsoft server products that do not ship with the Windows operating system. Make sure that you have the latest versions of all pre-existing software or service packs that are compatible with Windows Server 2003.

The most common software incompatibilities are caused when your application depends on software from another manufacturer that does not support Windows Server 2003. Or, you might have applications that were designed to run on Windows NT Server 4.0 or Windows 2000 Server operating systems, which reference APIs that have been changed or removed in Windows Server 2003.

To help you determine the compatibility of your existing software with Windows Server 2003, use the Windows Application Compatibility Toolkit before migrating your Web sites and applications to the target server. To download the latest version of the Windows Application Compatibility Toolkit, see the Windows Application Compatibility link on the Web Resources page at http://www.microsoft.com/windows/reskits/webresources. For the latest information about compatibility with Windows Server 2003, see the Windows Server 2003 link on the Web Resources page at http://www.microsoft.com/windows/reskits/webresources.

Determining Application Compatibility with Worker Process Isolation Mode

IIS 6.0 can run in one of two distinct modes of operation, which are called application isolation modes. *Application isolation* is the separation of applications by process boundaries that prevent the applications from affecting one another, and it is configured differently for each of the two IIS application isolation modes: IIS 5.0 isolation mode and worker process isolation mode.

Worker process isolation mode uses the redesigned architecture for IIS 6.0. This application isolation mode runs all application code in an isolated environment. However, unlike earlier versions of IIS, IIS 6.0 provides isolation without a performance penalty because fewer processor instructions are run when switching from one application pool to another. Worker process isolation mode is compatible with most existing Web sites and applications. Whenever possible, run IIS 6.0 in worker process isolation mode benefit from the enhanced performance and security in IIS 6.0.

IIS 5.0 isolation mode provides compatibility for applications that depend upon the process behavior and memory model of IIS 5.0. Run IIS in this mode only when a Web site or application cannot run in worker process isolation mode, and run it only until the compatibility issues are resolved.

Important

IIS 6.0 cannot run both application isolation modes simultaneously on the same server. Therefore, on a single server running IIS 6.0, you cannot run some Web applications in worker process isolation mode and others in IIS 5.0 isolation mode. If you have applications that require separate modes, you must run them on separate servers.

During the migration process, you install Windows Server 2003 and IIS 6.0 on the target server. IIS 6.0 is configured to run in worker process isolation mode by default. Before you begin migrating your production Web sites and applications, evaluate whether your Web sites and applications are compatible with worker process isolation mode. Most of the compatibility issues with IIS 6.0 occur when configuring IIS 6.0 to run in worker process isolation mode.

One of the most common reasons for incompatibility with worker process isolation mode is that applications do not recognize custom Internet Server API (ISAPI) extensions or dynamic-link libraries (DLLs) that depend on the memory and request processing models used by earlier versions of IIS. Determine application compatibility in your lab before migrating your existing IIS Web sites and application, and if you determine that your applications are not compatible with worker process isolation mode, you can run the applications in IIS 5.0 isolation mode.

Note

Identifying a complete list of potential incompatibilities that applications can experience with worker process isolation mode is beyond the scope of this book. Even after following the guidelines in this chapter, you need to verify in a lab whether your Web sites and applications are compatible with worker process isolation mode.

Determine the compatibility of an application with worker process isolation mode by completing the following steps:

1. Evaluate the benefits of moving to worker process isolation mode.

2. Evaluate the application changes that are required so that the applications can run in worker process isolation mode.

3. Evaluate the management and provisioning script changes that are required to set up programs and provisioning scripts in worker process isolation mode.

4. Verify the compatibility of the application with worker process isolation mode in a lab.

Evaluating the Benefits of Worker Process Isolation Mode

Worker process isolation mode provides higher levels of security and availability for Web sites and applications than IIS 5.0 isolation mode. Therefore, it is recommended that you configure IIS 6.0 to run in worker process isolation mode.

Worker process isolation mode provides the following improvements to IIS 6.0.

Security Enhancements

IIS 6.0 includes a variety of security features and technologies that help ensure the integrity of your Web site content, and of the data that is transmitted through your sites. The following security enhancement is only available when IIS 6.0 is running in worker process isolation mode.

Default process identity for Web sites and applications is set to NetworkService

In IIS 5.0 isolation mode, the default process identity is LocalSystem, which enables access to, and the ability to alter, nearly all of the resources on the Web server. The potential of attacks is reduced in worker process isolation mode because Web sites and applications run under the NetworkService identity. The NetworkService identity is granted less privileges, which helps prevent an attack from compromising the Web server, which is possible with the LocalSystem identity.

Performance and Scaling Enhancements

Future growth in the utilization of your Web sites and applications requires increased performance and scalability of Web servers. By increasing the speed at which Hypertext Transfer Protocol (HTTP) requests can be processed and by allowing more applications and sites to run on one Web server, the number of Web servers that you need to host a site is reduced. The following are a few of the performance improvements included in worker process isolation mode.

Support for processor affinity for worker processes in an application pool

You can configure all of the worker processes in an application pool to have affinity with specific processors in a multiprocessor or server. Processor affinity allows the worker processes to take advantage of more frequent processor caching (Level 1 or Level 2).

Elimination of inactive worker processes and reclamation of unused resources

You can configure application pools to have worker processes request a shutdown if they are idle for a certain amount of time. This can free unused resources for other active worker processes. New worker processes are then started only when they are needed.

Distributing client connections across multiple worker processes

You can configure an application pool to have more than one worker process servicing client connections, also known as a *Web garden*. Because there are multiple worker processes, the incoming client connections are distributed across the worker processes and throughput is not constrained by a single worker process.

Ability to Isolate Web sites and applications from each other

You can isolate Web sites and applications without incurring a performance penalty. This is because the Web site and applications, and their associated ISAPI filters, run in the same process.

Availability Enhancements

Because worker process boundaries isolate the applications in an application pool from the applications in other application pools, if an application fails, it does not affect the availability of other applications running on the server. Deploying applications in application pools is a primary advantage of running IIS 6.0 in worker process isolation mode.

Reduced number of Web server restarts required when administering Web sites and applications

Many of the common operation tasks do not force the restart of the server or the Web service restart. These tasks, such as upgrading site content or components, debugging Web applications, or dealing with faulty Web applications, can be performed without affecting service to other sites or applications on the server.

A fault-tolerant request processing model for Web sites and applications

In IIS 5.0 isolation mode, each Web site or application has only one worker process. However, in worker process isolation mode, you can create a *Web garden* by configuring a number of worker processes to share the processing. The benefit of a Web garden is that if one worker process stops responding, other worker processes are available to accept and process requests.

Isolation of failed worker processes from healthy worker processes

In worker process isolation mode, IIS can determine that a worker process is failing and start a new worker process to replace the failing worker process. Because a new worker process is created before the old worker process terminates, users requesting the Web site or application experience no interruption of service. After IIS creates the new worker process, the failed worker process can be separated, or *orphaned*, from the application pool. The advantage of orphaning a worker process rather than terminating it is that debugging can be performed on the orphaned worker process.

Health monitoring of Web sites and applications

In worker process isolation mode, you can configure an application pool to monitor not only the health of the entire application pool, but also individual worker processes servicing the application pool. Monitoring the health of a worker process allows IIS to detect that a worker process is unable to serve requests and to take corrective action, such as recycling the failed worker process.

In addition, worker process isolation supports other responses when a failed worker process or application pool is detected. For example, IIS can attach a debugger to an orphaned worker process or notify an administrator that an application pool has failed due to rapid-fail protection.

Prevention of Web sites or applications that fail quickly from consuming system resources

In some cases, availability can be affected by Web sites and applications that fail very quickly, are automatically restarted, and then fail quickly again. The endless cycle of failure and restarting can consume system resources, causing other Web sites and applications to experience denial of services because of system resource shortages.

Worker process isolation mode includes *rapid-fail protection* that stops an application pool when too many of the worker processes assigned to an application pool are found to be unhealthy within a specified period of time.

Automatic restart of poorly performing Web sites and applications

Some Web sites and applications have memory leaks, are poorly coded, or have other unidentified problems. In IIS 5.0 isolation mode, these applications can force you to restart the entire Web server. The recycling feature in worker process isolation mode can periodically restart the worker processes in an application pool in order to manage faulty applications. Worker processes can be scheduled to restart based on several options, such as elapsed time or the number of requests served.

Evaluating Application Changes Required for Worker Process Isolation Mode

In most cases, the existing Web sites and applications can be hosted in worker process isolation mode without modification. However, the following are known application issues that can create incompatibilities with worker process isolation mode and require you to run IIS 6.0 in IIS 5.0 isolation mode.

- **Requires Inetinfo.exe.** When the application must run in the same process with Inetinfo.exe, IIS must be configured to run in IIS 5.0 isolation mode because Inetinfo.exe does not process Web requests in worker process isolation mode. In worker process isolation mode, W3wp.exe processes Web requests.

- **Requires Dllhost.exe.** When the application depends on Dllhost.exe to process Web requests for the application, IIS must be configured to run in IIS 5.0 isolation mode because Dllhost.exe is not available in worker process isolation mode.

- **Requires read raw data filters.** If the application uses an ISAPI raw data filter, IIS must be configured to run in IIS 5.0 isolation mode.

- **Requires version 1.0 of the .NET Framework.** When the application requires version 1.0 of the .NET Framework, IIS must be configured to run in IIS 5.0 isolation mode because version 1.0 of the .NET Framework is only supported in IIS 5.0 isolation mode.

- **Requires ISAPI filters or extensions that are incompatible with worker process isolation mode.** When the application requires ISAPI filters or extensions that are incompatible with worker process isolation mode, IIS must be configured to run in IIS 5.0 isolation mode. ISAPI filters or extensions might be incompatible if the filter or extension has one of the following characteristics:

  - Runs in multiple instances and expects to be recycled by using the recycling provided in IIS 5.0.

  - Expects to have exclusive lock on a resource, such as a log file.

If any of the Web sites and applications running on the existing Web server has one or more of these characteristics, then do one of the following:

- Configure IIS 6.0 to run in IIS 5.0 isolation mode to ensure Web site and application compatibility. If the Web sites and applications need to be hosted in IIS 5.0 isolation mode, then the migration process is complete.

- Modify the existing applications to remove the dependencies.

Evaluating Management and Provisioning Script Changes Required for Worker Process Isolation Mode

When management or provisioning scripts exist for your Web sites and applications, you might need to modify them so that they properly set up the Web sites and applications for the application isolation mode that is running on the Web server — IIS 5.0 isolation mode or worker process isolation mode. If you do not modify your management and provisioning scripts as required, you will be unable to use them to install and configure your Web sites and applications on IIS 6.0.

For example, you might have a provisioning script that uses Microsoft Active Directory® Service Interfaces (ADSI) to create a Web site and configure the site for High isolation in IIS 5.0 isolation mode, which does not exist in worker process isolation mode. After migration and when the Web server is running in worker process isolation mode, you need to modify the script to create application pools instead.

Common modifications that might be necessary to your setup programs and provisioning scripts include:

- When the script installs an ISAPI extension or filter, you might need to modify the script to add an entry for the ISAPI extension or filter to the Web service extensions restriction list and set the status of the entry to **Allowed**.

  For more information about modifying your setup programs or provisioning scripts to install and enable an ISAPI extension or filter, see "Configuring Web Service Extensions" later in this chapter.

- When the script installs an application that contains dynamic content, you might need to modify the script to set the status of the appropriate Web service extensions to **Allowed**, so that IIS allows the dynamic content to run.

  For more information about modifying your setup programs or provisioning scripts to enable dynamic content, see "Configuring Web Service Extensions" later in this chapter.

- When the script installs a Web site or application that runs in High isolation in IIS 5.0, you might need to modify the script to create an application pool and configure the application pool with settings that are comparable to the original IIS 5.0 isolation settings.

  For more information about modifying your setup programs or provisioning scripts to create and configure application pools, see "Configuring Application Isolation Settings in Worker Process Isolation Mode" later in this chapter.

- When the script references metabase properties, you might need to modify the script if it references metabase properties that have changed or are no longer supported in IIS 6.0.

  For more information about modifying your setup programs or provisioning scripts to reference the proper metabase properties in IIS 6.0, see "Modifying References to IIS 6.0 Metabase Properties" later in this chapter.

Verifying Application Compatibility with Worker Process Isolation Mode in a Lab

After modifying your Web sites, applications, setup programs, and provisioning scripts to be compatible with worker process isolation mode, you need to test your modifications in a lab. Be sure to test for compatibility before performing the migration process on a production Web server.

Verify the compatibility of your Web sites, applications, setup programs, and provisioning scripts with worker process isolation mode in a lab by completing the following steps:

1. Make an image backup of the source server.

2. Restore the backup to a Web server in your lab, referred to hereafter as a *test source server*. Ensure that the test source server is not connected to your production network, to prevent any problems encountered during the migration from affecting your production network.

3. Perform a migration from the test source server to the test target server.

4. Configure the test target server to run in worker processor isolation mode or IIS 5.0 isolation mode.

5. Make the necessary modifications to the Web sites, applications, setup programs, and provisioning scripts so that they are compatible with worker process isolation mode.

6. Verify that the Web sites, applications, setup programs, and provisioning scripts run correctly on the test target server.

For more information about setting up a test lab, see "Designing a Test Environment" in *Planning, Testing, and Piloting Deployment Projects* of the *Microsoft® Windows® Server 2003 Deployment Kit.*

Determining Application Compatibility with the .NET Framework

For a successful migration to Windows Server 2003 and IIS 6.0, you need to determine whether your ASP.NET applications are dependent on specific versions of the .NET framework. Windows Server 2003 ships with version 1.1 of the .NET Framework, while most of the .NET applications that were developed before the release of Windows Server 2003 were designed to run on version 1.0 of the .NET framework.

 Note

Version 1.0 of the .NET Framework is only supported in IIS 5.0 isolation mode. Therefore, you can only run version 1.0 and version 1.1 of the .NET Framework on the same server when IIS 6.0 is configured to run in IIS 5.0 isolation mode. Version 1.1 of the .NET Framework is supported in IIS 5.0 isolation mode or worker process isolation mode.

Typically, ASP.NET applications running on version 1.0 of the .NET Framework are compatible with version 1.1 of the .NET Framework. However, there might be some incompatibilities, the majority of which are security related and can be corrected by configuring the .NET Framework to be less restrictive.

For example, in the .NET Framework version 1.0, the .NET Framework only examines the **SQLPermission.AllowBlankPassword** attribute if the user actually includes the password keyword in their connection string. If an administrator or user sets the **SQLPermision.AllowBlankPassword** attribute to **False**, it is possible to specify a connection string like "server=(localhost);uid=sam" and succeed. In the .NET Framework version 1.1, this connection string fails.

You can use both version 1.0 and version 1.1 of the .NET Framework on the same server running IIS 6.0, which is also known as *side-by-side configuration.* Side-by-side configuration allows you to run a mixture of applications that require version 1.0 or version 1.1 of the .NET Framework. During your lab testing, determine the version of the .NET Framework that is required by your applications.

For a current list of possible compatibility issues when upgrading from version 1.0 to version 1.1 of the .NET Framework, see the Compatibility Considerations and Version Changes link on the Web Resources page at http://www.microsoft.com/windows/reskits/webresources. For more information about using multiple versions of the .NET Framework in side-by-side configuration, see "Configuring IIS to Use the Correct Version of the .NET Framework" later in this chapter.

 Important

ASP.NET is not available on the following operating systems: Microsoft® Windows® XP 64-Bit Edition; the 64-bit version of Windows® Server 2003, Enterprise Edition; and the 64-bit version of Windows® Server 2003, Datacenter Edition. For more information, see "Features unavailable on 64-bit versions of the Windows Server 2003 family" in Help and Support Center for Windows Server 2003.

Selecting a Migration Method

Before migrating your Web sites and applications to IIS 6.0, you need to determine whether to perform the migration manually or with the IIS 6.0 Migration Tool. It is recommended that you use the migration tool to begin the migration process, except when one of the following is true:

- **You have set up programs, installation scripts, or provisioning scripts for the Web sites and applications that you are migrating.** When the Web sites and applications that you are migrating have setup programs, installation scripts, or provisioning scripts, use those programs or scripts to install the Web sites and applications on the target server. Ensure that the setup programs, installation scripts, and provisioning scripts have been properly modified to install the Web sites and applications on IIS 6.0.

- **The target server is configured to run in IIS 5.0 isolation mode.** When the Web sites and applications that you are migrating require the target server to run in IIS 5.0 isolation mode, you must perform the migration manually. To determine whether your Web sites and applications are compatible with worker process isolation mode, see "Determining Application Compatibility with Worker Process Isolation Mode" earlier in this chapter.

- **The source server has a significant number of FrontPage extended Web sites.** When the FrontPage extended Web sites make extensive use of the administrative and publishing security-related settings found in FrontPage 2000 Server Extensions, perform the migration manually. To ensure that these security-related settings are migrated properly to the target server, perform the migration manually and use FrontPage publishing to transfer the Web site to the target server.

- **You want to migrate individual virtual directories.** When you want to migrate individual virtual directories, perform the migration manually. The IIS 6.0 Migration Tool only moves Web site content and configuration settings at the Web site level, which means that all of the virtual directories beneath the Web site are migrated to the target server.

If you determine that you need to perform the migration manually, then you can proceed to the next step in the migration process — Deploying the Target Server. Otherwise, you need to know which steps in the migration process are automated by the IIS 6.0 Migration Tool, and which steps you must complete manually after running the migration Tool. Knowing the role of the IIS 6.0 Migration Tool in the migration process enables you to have the appropriate tools and resources available when you are ready to begin the migration.

Identifying the Role of the IIS 6.0 Migration Tool

The IIS 6.0 Migration Tool is a command-line utility that automates some of the steps in the process for migrating Web sites and applications hosted on IIS 4.0 or IIS 5.0 to IIS 6.0. The migration tool does not provide an end-to-end migration solution, but it automates some of the time-consuming, repetitive migration tasks. Although the migration tool is conceptually similar to the IIS 5.0 Migration Tool, the IIS 6.0 Migration Tool is a completely new tool designed specifically for Windows Server 2003 and is not compatible with the previous tool.

Migration Tasks That Are Automated by the IIS 6.0 Migration Tool

The IIS 6.0 Migration Tool automates the following steps in the IIS migration process:

- **Transferring the Web site content.** All of the files and folders located in the home directory of the Web site and virtual directories (which can be located outside of the home directory of the Web site) are copied from the source server to the target server. The NTFS file system permissions assigned to the files and directories that make up the Web site content on the source server are granted to the corresponding files and directories on the target server. Any content referenced by the Web site or application that is not located in subdirectories of the home directory of the Web site or in virtual directories is not migrated.

- **Transferring the Web site configuration in the IIS metabase.** The configuration for each Web site and application, which is stored in the IIS metabase properties on the source server, is translated and then the corresponding IIS 6.0 metabase properties are appropriately configured on the target server.

- **Translating the application isolation configuration.** The target server is running in worker process isolation mode. The application isolation configuration for each Web site and application on the source server is translated into application pool configuration settings on the target server.

- **Backing up the IIS metabase configuration to the target server.** The IIS metabase configuration is backed up on the target server before migration. You can use this backup to restore the target server to a known state in the event that the migration process is not successful.

Migration Tasks That Must Be Completed Manually

The following steps in the Web site migration process must be completed after running the IIS 6.0 Migration Tool.

Migrating Additional Web Site and Application Content

The IIS 6.0 Migration Tool migrates all of the content that is located in the home directory of the Web site and in any subdirectories contained in that home directory. You can migrate any Web site and application content that is not located in these directories by completing the following steps:

- **Migrate content located outside the home directory and subdirectories of the Web site.** When the Web sites and applications reference content that is located in folders outside of the home directory of the Web site or the virtual directories beneath the home directory, you must migrate this content manually.

- **Migrate content located in a virtual directory.** When the virtual directory content on the source server is stored on a disk volume, such as F:, that does not exist on the target server, you must migrate this content manually.

Configuring Additional Web Site and Application Properties

After running the IIS 6.0 Migration Tool, the Web sites are configured comparably to how they were configured on the source server. However, depending on the configuration of the Web sites and applications on the source server, you might need to configure additional Web site and application properties, by completing the following steps:

- **Change the IIS metabase settings to reflect where Windows is installed.** If the Windows Server 2003 systemroot path does not match the Windows systemroot path on the source server, you must modify the metabase settings on the migrated Web sites to reference the correct folder on the target server. For example, if Windows was installed on C:\WINNT on the source server, the IIS metabase entries for **ScriptMaps**, and **HTTPErrors** properties might still reference these paths, and therefore need to be updated on the target server.

- **Configure IIS properties that reference local user accounts.** There are a number of Web site configuration properties on the source server that you can configure to utilize user accounts that are local to the source server. Local user and group accounts are not migrated from the source server to the target server by the IIS 6.0 Migration Tool. As a result, the migrated Web sites reference user accounts that do not exist on the target server. In these cases, you must configure the Web sites to utilize user accounts that are domain-based or local to the target server, and then re-create the file system permissions on migrated content by completing the following steps:

  - **Configure local user NTFS permissions on content.** If NTFS permissions are granted to local user accounts on the source server, you must create new user accounts, or designate existing user accounts, for use on the target server and then grant the corresponding NTFS permissions to the user accounts on the target server.

- **Configure anonymous account properties for Web sites and virtual directories.** If a Web site or virtual directory is configured to use a user account on the source server for anonymous access (other than the default IUSR_computername account), you must create a new user account, or designate an existing user account, for use on the target server.

- **Configure IIS 4.0 and IIS 5.0 application isolation identities.** If the Web sites or applications are isolated and are configured to use a local user account on the source server as the application isolation identity, you must create a new user account, or designate an existing user account, for use on the target server. Then you must configure the corresponding application pool, on the target server, to use the newly created account as the identity of the application pool.

- **Add Web service extensions for dynamic content used by the Web sites.** Any dynamic content types, including ISAPI extensions, ISAPI filters, or CGI applications, which are not automatically migrated by the IIS 6.0 Migration Tool need to be added to the Web service extensions list.

- **Add MIME types for static content used by the Web sites.** MIME types define the types of static files that are served by the Web server. You must identify the MIME types defined on the source Web server and then create the same associations of MIME types to file name extensions on the target Web server.

- **Configure SSL certificates.** You must export server certificates for Secure Sockets Layer (SSL)-enabled Web sites from the source server, and then install the certificates on the target server after the migration process is complete.

- **Configure FrontPage Server Extensions users and roles.** If FrontPage Server Extensions is configured to use a local user account on the source server as the FrontPage administrator, you must create a new user account, or designate an existing user account, for use on the target server. In addition, you must assign the user the same FrontPage role as the corresponding user had on the source server.

- **Configure IIS for ASP.NET applications.** If you migrate ASP.NET applications from the source server, you might need to migrate the attribute settings in the Machine.config file that are used to set process-model behavior. When the target server is configured for worker process isolation mode, the attribute settings in the Machine.config file need to be converted to corresponding application pool settings. This is because ASP.NET uses the IIS process model when IIS is running in worker process isolation mode. For more information, see "Migrating Machine.config Attributes to IIS 6.0 Metabase Property Settings" later in this chapter.

Performing Application-Specific Migration Tasks

In addition to the IIS 6.0 configuration changes that are required, you might need to complete any migration tasks that are specific to the applications running on the source server. The application-specific steps that you might need to perform include the following:

- **Modifying application code for compatibility with Windows Server 2003 and IIS 6.0.** When the applications on the source server are not compatible with Windows Server 2003 and IIS 6.0, you need to modify the applications. Most of these modifications are required when applications use application programming interfaces (APIs) no longer supported by Windows Server 2003 and IIS 6.0.

- **Installing additional software required by the applications.** When applications on the source server require additional software that was developed by your organization, by Microsoft, or by other organizations, you need to install that software on the target server. This software can include filters and ISAPI extensions. You must obtain a version of the software that is compatible with Windows Server 2003 and IIS 6.0.

- **Migrating MTS packages, COM objects, and COM+ applications.** When your applications include MTS packages, COM objects, or COM+ applications, you must migrate them to the target server. For MTS packages, you need to rewrite the MTS as a COM+ application.

- **Creating IP addresses that are used to uniquely identify the applications.** Web sites and applications are uniquely identified by a unique IP address, a unique combination of an IP address and a TCP port, or host headers. When Web sites and applications on the source server are uniquely identified by IP addresses, you must create corresponding IP addresses on the target server and then configure the migrated Web sites and applications to use the new IP addresses.

- **Creating users and groups that are used by the applications.** When users that access the applications on the source server have accounts that are local to the source server, you need to create new accounts on the source server and then assign the appropriate NTFS permissions on the target server to the new accounts. When the user accounts are in Active Directory, you only need to assign the appropriate NTFS permissions on the target server to the accounts in Active Directory.

- **Creating registry entries for the applications.** When your applications store configuration information in the registry, you might need to create the same registry entries for the applications on the target server.

> ☑ | **Note**
>
> The IIS 6.0 Migration Tool does not migrate the IIS logs from the source server to the target server. The migration of the IIS logs is not necessary for proper operation of the Web sites and applications on the target server. However, you might want to archive the IIS logs before decommissioning the source server for historical reference to events that occurred on the source server before migration.

For information about using the IIS 6.0 Migration Tool to perform your migration, see "Migrating Web Sites with the IIS 6.0 Migration Tool" later in this chapter.

Deploying the Target Server

You must install Windows Server 2003 on the target Web server before you can migrate the Web sites and applications. In addition to installing Windows Server 2003, you must install and configure IIS 6.0 on the target server. To follow the process described in this chapter, install Windows Server 2003 and IIS 6.0 with the default options.

You must also configure the target server to run in worker process isolation mode or in IIS 5.0 isolation mode. Run IIS in IIS 5.0 isolation mode only when a Web site or application cannot run in worker process isolation mode. If there are no incompatibilities, configure IIS to run in worker process isolation mode to utilize the benefits of IIS 6.0 features.

Figure 6.3 illustrates the process for deploying the target server.

Figure 6.4 Deploying the Target Server

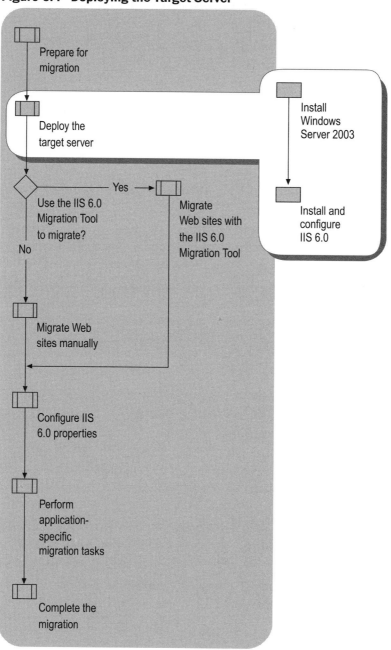

If you have already installed Windows Server 2003 on the target server, and you have already installed and configured IIS 6.0 on the target server, you can proceed to "Migrating Web Sites with the IIS 6.0 Migration Tool" or Migrating Web Sites Manually later in this chapter.

Installing Windows Server 2003

The primary concern when installing Windows Server 2003 is to ensure that the security of the target server is maintained. When you install Windows Server 2003 as a dedicated Web server, the default components and services are configured to provide the lowest possible attack surface. You can further reduce the attack surface of the target server by enabling only the essential Windows Server 2003 components and services.

The migration process presented in this chapter assumes that you install Windows Server 2003 with the default options. If you use other methods for installing and configuring Windows Server 2003, such as unattended setup, your configuration settings might be different.

 Note

When you complete the installation of Windows Server 2003, Manage Your Server automatically starts. The migration process assumes that you quit Manage Your Server and then further configure the Web server in **Add or Remove Programs** in Control Panel.

For more information about enabling the essential Windows Server 2003 components and services required by your server, see "Enabling Only Essential Windows Server 2003 Components and Services" in "Securing Web Sites and Applications" in this book.

Installing and Configuring IIS 6.0

Because IIS 6.0 is not installed during the default installation of Windows Server 2003, the next step in deploying the target server is to install and configure IIS 6.0. The migration process presented here assumes that you install IIS 6.0 with the default options in **Add or Remove Programs** in Control Panel. If you use other methods for installing and configuring Windows Server 2003, such as Manage Your Server, the default configuration settings might be different.

Install and configure IIS 6.0 by completing the following steps:

1. Install IIS 6.0 with only the essential components and services.

    As with installing Windows Server 2003, the primary concern when installing and configuring IIS 6.0 is to ensure that the security of the target server is maintained. Enabling unnecessary components and services increases the attack surface of the target server. You can help ensure the target server is secure by enabling only the essential components and services in IIS 6.0.

    For more information about how to install IIS 6.0, see "Install IIS 6.0" in "IIS Deployment Procedures" in this book. For more information about the IIS 6.0 protocols and services, see "Enabling Only Essential IIS 6.0 Components and Services" in "Securing Web Sites and Applications" in this book.

2. If the source server has Web sites with FrontPage Server Extensions, install FrontPage 2002 Server Extensions from Microsoft on the target server.

   For more information about how to enable FrontPage Server Extensions, see "Configure Web Service Extensions" in "IIS Deployment Procedures" in this book.

3. Configure IIS 6.0 to run in IIS 5.0 isolation mode.

   If you determined that one or more of your Web sites or applications are incompatible with worker process isolation mode (the target server is currently configured to run in worker process isolation mode), configure IIS 6.0 to run in IIS 5.0 isolation mode in IIS Manager, or by setting the IIS metabase property **IIs5IsolationModeEnabled** to a value of **True**.

 Note

> If you configure IIS 6.0 to run in IIS 5.0 isolation mode and then decide to change the configuration back to worker process isolation mode, the original worker process isolation mode settings are retained. Similarly, if you configure IIS 6.0 to run in IIS 5.0 isolation mode, change to worker process isolation mode, and then change back to IIS 5.0 isolation mode, the IIS 5.0 isolation mode settings are retained.

For more information about how to configure IIS 6.0 to run in worker process isolation mode or in IIS 5.0 isolation mode, see "Configure Application Isolation Modes" in "IIS Deployment Procedures" in this book. For more information about determining compatibility with worker process isolation mode, see "Evaluating Application Changes Required for Worker Process Isolation Mode" earlier in this chapter.

Migrating Web Sites with the IIS 6.0 Migration Tool

Earlier in the process, you determined whether to migrate your Web sites by using the IIS 6.0 Migration Tool or to migrate them manually. If you decided to use the IIS 6.0 Migration Tool to complete the migration process, perform the steps that are described in this section.

If you decided to complete the migration process manually, you can skip this step and proceed directly to "Migrating Web Sites Manually" later in this chapter. For more information about how to determine whether to perform the migration with the IIS 6.0 Migration Tool, see "Selecting a Migration Method" earlier in this chapter.

Figure 6.5 illustrates the process of performing the migration to IIS 6.0 with the IIS 6.0 Migration Tool.

Figure 6.5   Migrating Web Sites to IIS 6.0 with the IIS 6.0 Migration Tool

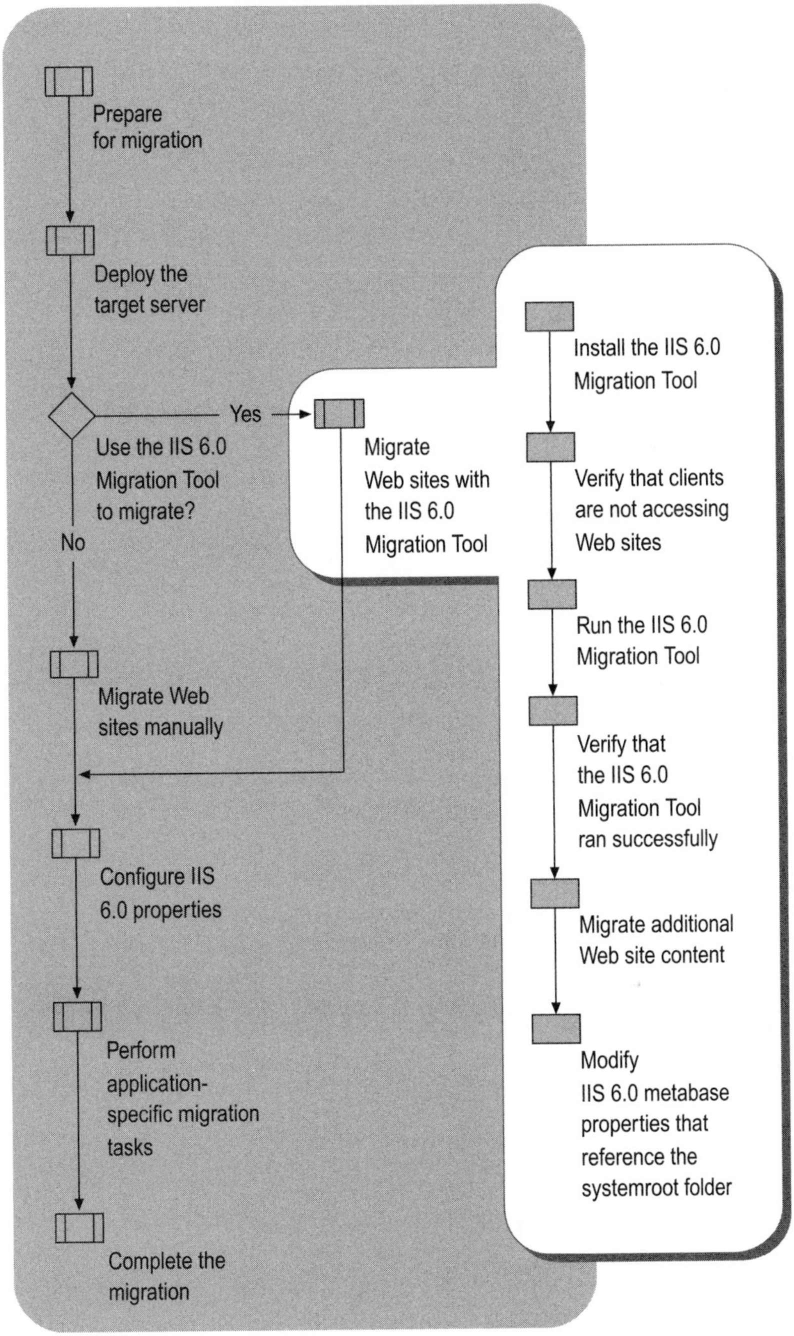

Installing the IIS 6.0 Migration Tool

The IIS 6.0 Migration Tool and its accompanying user documentation are included in the default installation of the *Windows Server 2003 Deployment Kit* companion CD and the *Internet Information Services (IIS) 6.0 Resource Kit* companion CD. There is no setup program for the migration tool; you need only copy the IIS 6.0 Migration Tool to the target server. You do not need to install any software on the source server. To avoid installing the entire contents of the companion CD onto your target server, install the companion CD on a workstation first, and then copy the migration tool to the target server.

Install the IIS 6.0 Migration Tool by completing the following steps:

1. Install the *Windows Server 2003 Deployment Kit* companion CD or the *Internet Information Services (IIS) 6.0 Resource Kit* companion CD on a computer other than the source server or target server.

2. Create a folder on the target server to contain the migration tool.

3. Copy the IIS 6.0 Migration Tool (Iismt.exe) from Program Files\IIS Resources\IIS 6.0 Migration Tool, on the computer listed in Step 1, to the folder on the target server that you created in Step 2.

4. Verify that the migration tool operates correctly by typing **iismt** at the command prompt.

   This starts the migration tool and displays Help for the tool only. The migration process does not actually begin.

Verifying That Clients Are Not Accessing Web Sites

The IIS 6.0 Migration Tool requires only read access to the Web site content and configuration settings on the source server. Therefore, the source server can remain online in your production environment. However, you might need to remove the source server from your production network and move it to a private network segment that has direct network connectivity to the target server under the following circumstances:

- The number of files and amount of configuration information being copied across the network generates a high volume of traffic and slows the production network.

- Firewalls that exist between the source and target servers prevent the migration tool from performing the migration. This often occurs because the migration tool uses DCOM ports that are blocked by the firewalls for communicating with the source and target servers.

- Security-related configuration settings on the source server need to be modified to allow the migration tool to work.

  Examples of these security-related configuration settings that can prevent the migration tool from working include the following:

  - Remote access to disk volumes through administrative shares is prohibited.

    The IIS 6.0 Migration Tool requires access to the disk volume that contains the Web site content to perform the migration. For example, if the Web site content is stored in D:\Inetpub\Wwwroot, the migration tool must access the administrative share (D$) of the disk volume. The administrative shares are often removed to help prevent unauthorized access to the Web server. In order to use the migration tool, you must re-create the appropriate administrative shares.

  - Remote access to the source server must be allowed for members of the local Administrators group on the source server.

    For security reasons, many organizations restrict the members of the local Administrators group so that they can only log on locally, not over the network. However, the migration tool must be able to remotely access the source server over the network, as a member of the local Administrators group.

Verify that clients are no longer accessing Web sites by completing the following steps:

1. Prevent new clients from accessing the sites by pausing the sites.

   For more information about how to pause Web sites, see "Pause Web or FTP Sites" in "IIS Deployment Procedures" in this book.

2. Monitor the active Web connections to determine when clients are no longer accessing the source server.

   For more information about how to monitor the active Web connections, see "Monitor Active Web and FTP Connections" in "IIS Deployment Procedures" in this book.

3. When the number of active Web counters is zero, stop the WWW service or move the source server to another network segment.

   If you elect to stop the WWW service, ensure that the IIS Admin service is running because the migration tool requires the IIS Admin service. For more information about how to stop the WWW service, see "Stop the WWW Service" in "IIS Deployment Procedures" in this book.

Running the IIS 6.0 Migration Tool

The IIS 6.0 Migration tool is a command-line utility that is designed to run on the target server. To run the migration tool, type **iismt** at the command prompt, and provide the parameters, listed in Table 6.2, that are appropriate to the Web sites and applications that you are migrating. For more information about each of the parameters and on how to perform the migration with the IIS 6.0 Migration Tool, see the "IIS 6.0 Migration Tool User Guide" on the *Windows Server 2003 Deployment Kit* companion CD or the *Internet Information Services (IIS) 6.0 Resource Kit* companion CD.

The IIS 6.0 Migration Tool uses the following syntax:

iismt.exe *Server Website* [**/user** *Username*] [**/password** *Password*] [**/path** *path*] [**/serverbindings** *ServerBindings String*] [**/siteid** *SiteID* | **Replace**] [**/configonly**] [**/fpse**] [**/verbose**] [**/overwrite**] [**/noninteractive**]

Table 6.2 lists all the command-line parameters that the migration tool accepts, although not all of the parameters listed are required.

Table 6.2   Command-Line Parameters Accepted by the IIS 6.0 Migration Tool

Parameter	Required or Optional	Description
SourceServer	Required	Identifies the source server by providing the following: ▪ DNS or NetBIOS name for the source server. ▪ IP address of the source server.
WebSite	Required	Identifies the site to be migrated by providing the following: ▪ Web site description, such as "Default Web Site." ▪ Metabase key path, such as W3SVC/1.
/user *UserName*	Optional	Specifies the user name of an account that is a member of the Administrators group on the source server. This parameter is not necessary if you log on with an account that is a member of the Administrators group on both the source server and the target server.
/password *Password*	Optional	Specifies the password that is associated with the user name.
/path *Path*	Optional	Specifies a different directory location for the home directory of the Web site on the target server. This parameter is ignored if /configonly is included.

(continued)

Table 6.2   Command-Line Parameters Accepted by the IIS 6.0 Migration Tool *(continued)*

Parameter	Required or Optional	Description
/serverbindings *ServerBindingsString*	Optional	Allows a change to the IP address, host header, or port configuration of the Web site during the migration.
/siteid *SiteID* | Replace	Optional	Specifies the site ID on the target server, which can be specified as one of the following: ■ *Site*ID- Overwrites the site ID on the target server. ■ Replace - Overwrites the site ID on the target server with the site ID from the source server.
/configonly	Optional	Migrates only the Web site configuration and not the Web site content.
/fpse	Optional	Re-applies FrontPage Server Extensions to the migrated site on the target server. This parameter is ignored if **/configonly** is included.
/verbose	Optional	Displays metabase path copy and file copy operations to the screen during the migration process.
/overwrite	Optional	Does not display messages that prompt the user to confirm the overwrite of an existing destination folder or file when content is being copied from the source server to the target server.
/noninteractive	Optional	Does not display messages that prompt the user for input. The migration tool will exit on the first error condition. This is a useful switch for invoking the migration tool from a batch file or script program to perform an unattended migration.

Verifying That the IIS 6.0 Migration Tool Ran Successfully

Before continuing with the Web site migration, verify that the IIS 6.0 Migration Tool migrated the Web site content and configuration information successfully. When you run the migration tool, the output displayed by the migration tool indicates the success or failure of the migration. If the output indicates that errors occurred, you can use the IIS 6.0 Migration Tool log file to resolve any errors.

Verify that the IIS 6.0 Migration Tool ran successfully by completing the following steps:

1. Open *systemroot*\System32\LogFiles\IISMT\iismt_*date_time*.log in a text editor and determine if any errors occurred (where *date* is the date when the tool ran and *time* is the time the tool started).

2. Review the log file and resolve any problems that occurred during migration before proceeding to the next step in the process.

Migrating Additional Web Site Content

Some Web sites and applications have content that is not located in the home directory of the Web site or in subdirectories that are inside the home directory. The IIS 6.0 Migration Tool only migrates Web site content from the following locations:

- Within the home directory and subdirectories of the Web site.

- In virtual directories whose disk volume letter exists on both the source server and the target server.

If the code in your applications directly references content that is located outside the home directory and subdirectories of the Web site, or if a virtual directory is stored on a disk volume letter that does not exist on the target server, you must migrate this Web site content manually.

Migrating Content Located Outside the Home Directory of the Web Site

A Web site or application can have content that is referenced by the Web site, but is located outside the home directory and subdirectories of the Web site. This content must be migrated manually because the IIS 6.0 Migration Tool migrates content only in the home directory and subdirectories of the Web site.

Migrate content that is located outside the home directory and subdirectories of the Web site by completing the following steps:

1. Create a folder on the target server to contain the content.

   Ensure that the folder is in the same relative location to the home directory of the Web site. For example, if a Web site on the source server is in D:\Wwwroot*WebSite* and the content to be migrated is in D:\Program Files*SiteContent*, create the same folder (D:\Program Files*SiteContent*) on the target server.

2. Copy the content from the source server to the target server.

   Use the process of your choice for copying the content as described in "Migrating Web Site Content" later in this chapter.

3. If necessary, modify any references to the content that is located in directories that are external to the home directory of the Web site on the target server.

   The target server might have a different disk configuration than the source server, or you might be migrating the content to a different disk volume letter on the target server than the source server. You need to modify any references in the Web site to content that is located outside the home directory and subdirectory of the Web site.

Migrating Content Located in Virtual Directories

Virtual directory content on the source server might be stored on a disk volume, such as F:, that does not exist on the target server. This content must be migrated manually because the IIS 6.0 Migration Tool migrates virtual directories only when the disk volume letter on which the virtual directory is located exists on both the source server and the target server.

Migrate content that is located in virtual directories, which are stored on a disk volume that does not exist on the target server, by completing the following steps:

1. Create a folder on the target server to contain the virtual directory and the content.

   Ensure that the folder is in the same relative location on the target servers as on the source server.

2. Copy the content from the source server to the target server.

   Use the process of your choice for copying the content as described in "Migrating Web Site Content" later in this chapter.

3. Create the virtual directory under the appropriate Web site on the target server that references the folder created in Step 1.

   For more information about how to create virtual directories on the target server, see "Create a Virtual Directory" in "IIS Deployment Procedures" in this book.

Modifying IIS 6.0 Metabase Properties That Reference the Systemroot Folder

The IIS 6.0 Migration Tool migrates metabase properties that reference the systemroot folder on the source server, but does not update the references to the systemroot folder on the target server. If the location of systemroot folder on the target server does not match the location of the systemroot folder on the source server, you must modify the metabase settings on the migrated Web sites to reference the correct systemroot folder on the target server. Because the default systemroot folder name changed from WINNT to Windows in Windows 2000 Server and later versions, you might need to manually modify the metabase properties that reference the systemroot folder on the target server.

These metabase properties that reference the location of the systemroot folder can include the following:

- **HttpErrors.** The **HttpErrors** metabase property specifies the custom error string sent to clients in response to HTTP 1.1 errors. Each string in the list specifies the HTTP error code and subcode, indicates whether the handler will be a URL or a file, and specifies which URL or file the client will be sent. Each string can be in either a URL or a file format. If you migrate the Default Web Site on Windows NT 4.0 or Windows 2000, you must reset the HttpErrors metabase property to contain the systemroot folder for Windows Server 2003, even if the systemroot folder exists on the same drive on both the source and target computer.

- **ScriptMaps.** The **ScriptMaps** metabase property specifies the file name extensions of applications that are used for script processor mappings. This property contains references to paths with default ISAPIs, such as C:\Windows\system32\inetsrv\asp.dll.

Compensate for the differences in the location of the systemroot folder on the target server by completing the following steps:

1. Enable the IIS 6.0 metabase edit-while-running feature.

2. Open the MetaBase.xml file in Microsoft Notepad.

3. Search for any references to the systemroot folder on the source server and replace these references with the systemroot folder path on the target server.

    For example, if the source server had been installed in C:\WINNT and the target server is installed into C:\Windows, you should replace any occurrences of "C:\WINNT" with "C:\Windows".

4. Save the MetaBase.xml file.

5. Disable the metabase edit-while-running feature.

    For more information about the edit-while-running feature, see "Metabase Edit-While-Running Feature" in IIS 6.0 Help, which is accessible from IIS Manager.

Migrating Web Sites Manually

Earlier in the process, you decided whether to migrate your Web sites with the IIS 6.0 Migration Tool or to migrate them manually. If you are unable to use the migration tool, you must migrate manually, or use existing provisioning or setup scripts. For more information about how to determine whether you can perform the migration with the IIS 6.0 Migration Tool, see "Selecting a Migration Method" earlier in this chapter.

When there are provisioning or setup scripts for your Web sites and applications, use these scripts to install the Web sites and applications on the target server. These scripts might require modification to be compatible with worker process isolation mode, which is discussed in "Evaluating Application Changes Required for Worker Process Isolation Mode" earlier in this chapter.

Because the scripts install and configure the Web sites and applications, no migration is required. In this case, run the scripts to install and configure the Web sites and applications and then proceed to "Configuring IIS 6.0 Properties" later in this chapter to continue with the process.

Figure 6.6 illustrates the process migrating Web sites manually to IIS 6.0.

Figure 6.6 Performing a Manual Migration to IIS 6.0

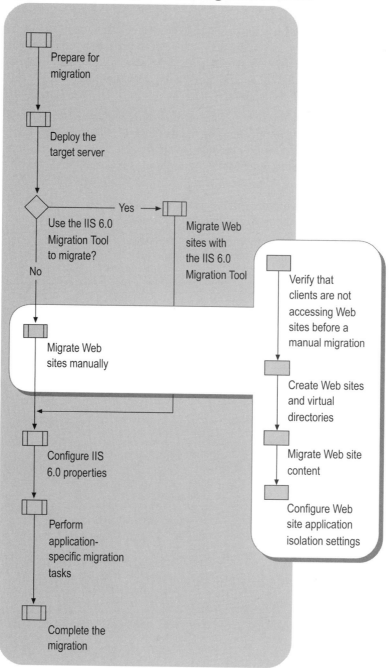

Verifying That Clients Are Not Accessing Web Sites Before a Manual Migration

Before migrating your existing Web sites and applications, ensure that no active client sessions are running. For more information about verifying that clients are not accessing Web sites, see "Verifying That Clients Are Not Accessing Web Sites" earlier in this chapter.

Creating Web Sites and Virtual Directories

For each Web site and virtual directory on the source server, you must create a corresponding Web site and virtual directory on the target server. Later in the migration process, you will copy the content into these Web sites and virtual directories.

Create the Web sites and virtual directories by completing the following steps:

1. Create the Web sites and home directories on the target server.

2. Create the virtual directories.

Creating Web Sites and Home Directories on the Target Server

Each Web site must have one home directory. The home directory is the central location for your published pages. It contains a home page or index file that welcomes visitors and contains links to other pages in your site. The home directory is mapped to the Web site's domain name or to the name of the Web server.

Create a Web site and home directory on the target server by completing the following steps:

1. Create the folder that will be the home directory for the Web site on the target server.

   The folder that is the home directory of the Web site contains all of the content and subdirectories for the Web site. The folder can be created on the Web server or on a UNC-shared folder on a separate server. At a minimum, create the folder on the following:

   - An NTFS partition, which helps ensure proper security.

   - A disk volume other than the system volume, which reduces the potential of an attack on a Web site bringing down the entire Web server, and improves performance.

   For more information about securing Web sites and applications see "Securing Web Sites and Applications" in this book. For more information about creating directories for your Web sites see "Create a Web Site" in "IIS Deployment Procedures" in this book.

2. Determine whether to generate the Web site identification number incrementally, or from the Web site name.

   Although site identification numbers were generated incrementally in IIS 5.1 and earlier, when you create a new site on IIS 6.0, a Web site identification number is randomly generated by using the name of the Web site. If you have administration scripts, setup programs, or provisioning scripts that depend upon the IIS 5.1 method of generating site identification numbers, you can force IIS 6.0 to use incremental site identification numbers by creating the **IncrementalSiteIDCreation** registry entry in the subkey HKEY_LOCAL_MACHINE\SOFTWARE\Microsoft\InetMgr\Parameters with the data type REG_DWORD and the value set to 0x1.

   For more information about configuring the Web site identification number see "Configure the Web Site Identification Number" in "IIS Deployment Procedures" in this book.

3. Create the Web site on the target server.

   Configure the Web site to have the same configuration as the corresponding Web site on the source server. For more information about how to create a Web site, see "Create a Web Site" in "IIS Deployment Procedures" in this book.

4. If the Web site on the source server is FrontPage extended, then configure the Web site on the target server to be FrontPage extended.

   For more information about how to configure a Web site to be FrontPage extended see "Configure a Web Site to be FrontPage Extended" in "IIS Deployment Procedures" in this book.

Creating Virtual Directories

For each virtual directory within each Web site on the source server, you must create a corresponding virtual directory on the target server. A *virtual directory* is a folder name, used in an address, which corresponds to a physical directory on the Web server or a Universal Naming Convention (UNC) location. This is also sometimes referred to as *URL mapping*. Virtual directories are used to publish Web content from any folder not located in the home directory of the Web site. When clients access content in a virtual directory, the content appears to be in a subdirectory of the home directory even though it is not.

For security reasons, you might want to move the Web site content to a different disk volume during the migration process. You can move the content to another disk volume on the target server or to a shared folder on a separate server. You can use virtual directories to specify the UNC name for the location where the content is placed, and provide a user name and password for access rights.

For each virtual directory in each Web site on the source server, create a corresponding virtual directory on the target server by completing the following steps:

1. Create the folder on the target server to contain the virtual directory content.

    Create the folder in the same location on the target server unless you are placing the content on a different disk volume than the source server or you are using a UNC share to store the content. Ensure that you create the folder in a secure manner that does not compromise the security of the target server.

    For more information about securing virtual directories, see "Preventing Unauthorized Access to Web Sites and Applications" in "Securing Web Sites and Applications" in this book.

2. Create the virtual directory under the appropriate Web site on the target server.

    For more information about how to create virtual directories, see "Create a Virtual Directory" in "IIS Deployment Procedures" in this book.

Migrating Web Site Content

For each Web site and virtual directory on the source server, you must migrate the content to the corresponding Web site and virtual directory on the target server. You can migrate the content from the source server to the target server by using one of the following methods:

- Run the **Xcopy** command to migrate Web site content to the target server on an intranet or internal network.

- Use Windows Explorer to migrate Web site content to the target server on an intranet or internal network.

- Use the **Copy Project** command in Microsoft Visual Studio® .NET to migrate Web site content to the target server on an intranet or internal network, if the application has been developed by using Visual Studio .NET.

   Note

  Front Page Server Extensions must be installed on the Web server to use the **Copy Project** command.

- Use the **Publish Web** command in FrontPage to migrate Web site content to the target server on an intranet or over the Internet, if the Web site has been developed using FrontPage.

  For more information about how to publish Web site content on the target server by using FrontPage, see "Publish Web Site Content with FrontPage" in "IIS Deployment Procedures" in this book.

Configuring Web Site Application Isolation Settings

Based on the application isolation mode settings of the target server, you need to configure the application isolation settings for each migrated Web site. Configure the Web site application isolation settings so that the Web sites provide the highest possible security and availability.

Configure the Web site applications isolation settings by completing the following steps for each Web site on the source server:

1. Document the current application isolation settings for each Web site on the source server.

2. When the target server is configured for IIS 5.0 isolation mode, configure the target server to use the same the isolation settings as the source server.

3. When the target server is configured for worker process isolation mode, convert the isolation settings on the source server to application pool settings on target server.

Documenting the Current Application Isolation Settings on the Source Server

Before you configure the application isolation settings, document the existing application isolation settings of the Web sites and applications that are hosted on the source server. Later in the migration process, you will use these settings for configuring the application isolation mode for your Web sites and applications.

For each Web site and application currently running on the server, document the following:

Application isolation settings

Earlier versions of IIS can host Web sites and applications in pooled or isolated process configurations. For information about how to view the current application isolation mode, see "View Application Isolation Configuration" in "IIS Deployment Procedures" in this book.

If you are running IIS 4.0 on Windows NT Server 4.0, your applications are isolated in one of the following ways:

- In-process (running in-process with Inetinfo.exe)

- Isolated (running under MTS)

If you are running IIS 5.0 on Windows 2000, your applications are isolated in one of the following ways:

- In-process (running in-process with Inetinfo.exe)

- Pooled (running in the pooled COM+ application)

- Isolated (running in an isolated COM+ application)

Process identity that is used by the Web site or application

Each Web site or application configured in High isolation, or pooled isolation, uses a configurable *identity*. An identity is a user account that provides a security context for worker process servicing the Web site or application. The identity can be used to secure content, by using NTFS permissions or data, such as data stored in Microsoft SQL Server™. For more information about how to view the identity for each Web site or application, see "View Web Site and Application Process Identities" in "IIS Deployment Procedures" in this book.

 Note

All Web sites and applications that are configured to run in the Inetinfo.exe process run under the security context of LocalSystem.

Configuring Application Isolation Settings in IIS 5.0 Isolation Mode

When the target Web server is configured to run in IIS 5.0 isolation mode, configure the application isolation settings on the target server identically to the settings on the source server. Web sites and applications on a Web server running in IIS 5.0 isolation mode can be configured with the following application isolation settings:

- Low (in-process).
- Medium (pooled).
- Low (isolated).

If the identity on the source server is an account local to the source server, you need to create a service account.

Configure the application isolation settings when IIS 6.0 is configured to run in IIS 5.0 isolation mode by completing the following steps:

1. Review the application isolation settings on the source server, documented earlier in the migration process.

    For more information about how the application isolation settings were documented, see "Documenting the Current Application Isolation Settings on the Source Server" earlier in this chapter.

2. Create any required local service accounts used for application isolation identities on the target server.

When the application pool identity is a service account that is local to the source server, you need to create a new service account, or designate an existing service account, on the target server. Create the service account in Active Directory to:

- Provide centralized administration of the account.

- Provide stronger security because the account is stored in Active Directory rather than locally on the Web server.

- Allow more than one Web server (for instance, in a Web farm) to use the same service account for the same instance of the application pool on other Web servers.

For more information about how to create a service account to be used as an identity, see "Create a Service Account" in "IIS Deployment Procedures" in this book.

3. Configure the application isolation settings for the Web sites on the target server to be identical to the settings in Step 1.

For more information about how to configure the application isolation settings for a Web site, see "Configure Application Isolation Settings for IIS 5.0 Isolation Mode" in "IIS Deployment Procedures" in this book.

4. Configure the application process identities for the Web sites on the target server to be identical to the settings in Step 1.

For more information about how to configure the application process identities for the Web site, see "Configure Application Identity for IIS 5.0 Isolation Mode" in "IIS Deployment Procedures" in this book.

Configuring Application Isolation Settings in Worker Process Isolation Mode

When the target server is configured to use worker process isolation mode, you need to configure the application isolation settings to closely approximate their configuration in IIS 5.0 isolation mode by assigning them to *application pools*. An application pool is a grouping of one or more Web sites or applications served by one or more worker processes. You might need to apply additional configurations so that the applications retain their original isolation settings.

After converting to worker process isolation mode, all applications run in the preexisting application pool named "DefaultAppPool." If all of the applications run in the same process in the previous version of IIS, then they all are assigned to the default application pool.

However, if any one of the applications in the same application pool fails, the other applications can be adversely affected. For this reason it is recommended that you isolate your applications into separate application pools whenever possible.

Configure Web sites and applications to run in their own application pool by completing the following steps:

For each Web site or application configured in High isolation in IIS 5.0

1. Create a new application pool to be used by the Web site or application.

    For information about how to create application pools, see "Isolate Applications in Worker Process Isolation Mode" in "IIS Deployment Procedures" in this book.

2. If the Web site or application previously ran under an identity that is still required by the Web site or application, configure the application pool to use that same identity.

    For information about how to configure the identity for an application pool, see "Configure Application Pool Identity" in "IIS Deployment Procedures" in this book.

3. Assign the Web site or application to the new application pool.

    For information about how to assign the Web site to the new application pool, see "Isolate Applications in Worker Process Isolation Mode" in "IIS Deployment Procedures" in this book.

For each Web site or application configured in Low or Medium isolation in IIS 5.0

In earlier versions of IIS, applications ran in-process as DLLs in Inetinfo.exe (Low isolation) and the default process identity (account that the application runs under) was LocalSystem. With worker process isolation mode in IIS 6.0, applications never run in Inetinfo.exe. However, any applications that are not explicitly assigned to an application pool are assigned to the default application pool, which runs under the NetworkService process identity by default. Because LocalSystem has the same permissions and user rights as a member of the Administrators group, run Web sites and applications under the security context of the NetworkService account.

For each Web site or application that ran in Low or Medium isolation in IIS 5.0, do one of the following:

-   When the Web site or application is able to function under the identity of the NetworkService account in the default application pool, continue to host the Web sites or applications in the default application pool, named "DefaultAppPool."

-   When the Web site or application is unable to function under the identity of the NetworkService account in the default application pool, perform the following steps:

    1. Create a new application pool.

    2. Create a service account to be used as the identity for the application pool.

        For more information about how to create a service account to be used as an identity for an application pool, see "Create a Service Account" in "IIS Deployment Procedures" in this book.

    3. Configure the application pool identity to use the service account.

        For more information about how to configure the identity for an application pool, see "Configure Application Pool Identity" in "IIS Deployment Procedures" in this book.

    4. Place the Web site or application in the new application pool.

Configuring IIS 6.0 Properties

Up to this point in the migration process, you have migrated the Web site content and configuration settings from the source server — either manually or with the IIS 6.0 Migration Tool. However, you might need to further configure the IIS 6.0 properties on the target server so that the Web sites run as they did before they were migrated. In addition, you should configure your target server even further to utilize the enhanced security and availability capabilities of IIS 6.0.

Figure 6.7 illustrates the process for configuring the IIS 6.0 properties on the target server.

Figure 6.7   Configuring IIS 6.0 Properties

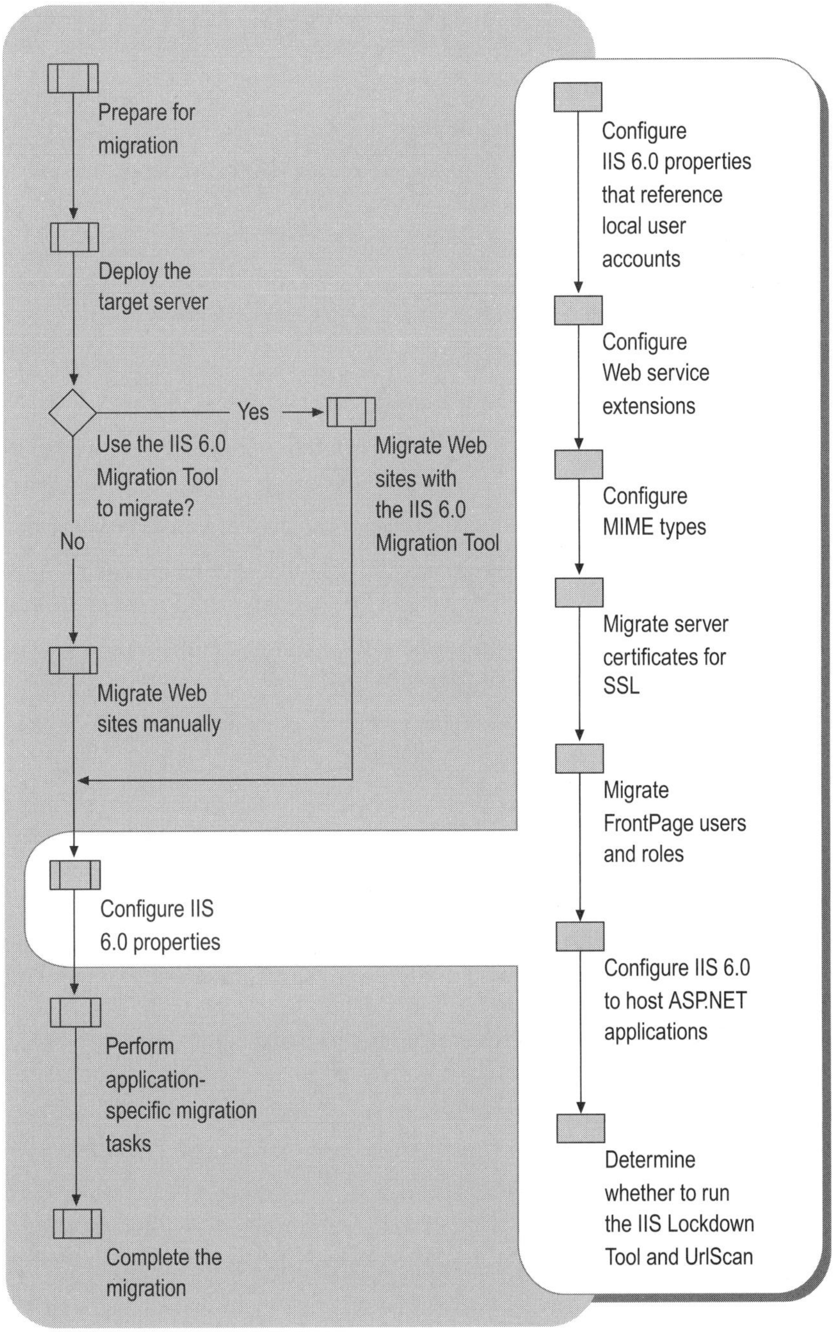

Prepare for migration

Deploy the target server

Use the IIS 6.0 Migration Tool to migrate?

Yes → Migrate Web sites with the IIS 6.0 Migration Tool

No

Migrate Web sites manually

Configure IIS 6.0 properties

Perform application-specific migration tasks

Complete the migration

Configure IIS 6.0 properties that reference local user accounts

Configure Web service extensions

Configure MIME types

Migrate server certificates for SSL

Migrate FrontPage users and roles

Configure IIS 6.0 to host ASP.NET applications

Determine whether to run the IIS Lockdown Tool and UrlScan

Configuring IIS 6.0 Properties That Reference Local User Accounts

The configuration of IIS and the Web sites on the source server can reference user accounts that are stored in the local account database on the source server. These accounts that are stored locally on the Web server are known as *local user accounts*. Local user accounts are valid only on the Web server where they are stored, not on any other Web servers.

As a result, when IIS, or any of the Web sites on the source server, reference local user accounts you must configure IIS 6.0 and the Web sites on the target server to reference:

- Domain-based user accounts that you create.

- Local user accounts that you create on the target server.

For each configuration that references a local account on the source server, you need to do the following on the target server:

1. Create, or designate, a domain-based or local user account that you can use to configure IIS.

    For more information about creating a service account that is domain-based or local to the target server, see "Create a Service Account" in "IIS Deployment Procedures" in this book.

2. Modify the IIS 6.0 properties, Web site properties, or content configuration settings, based on the type of property that you are configuring.

    The types of IIS 6.0 properties, Web site properties, or content configuration settings that can reference or use local user accounts include:

    - **NTFS permissions assigned to Web content.** Grant the same NTFS permissions to the account created in step 1on the target sever as were granted to the local user account on the source server. For more information about granting NTFS permission to content, see "Configure NTFS Permissions" in "IIS Deployment Procedures" in this book.

    - **Anonymous accounts for Web sites.** Configure the anonymous account identity for a Web site to use the account created in Step 1 on the target server. For more information about configuring the anonymous account identity, see "Configure Anonymous User Identity" in "IIS Deployment Procedures" in this book.

- **Application isolation settings.** Configure the application isolation identity based on the application isolation mode configured for the server.

  When the target server is configured to run in worker processor isolation mode, configure the identity properties of the application pools. For more information about configuring the application isolation settings when the target server is configured for worker process isolation mode, see "Configure Application Pool Identity" in "IIS Deployment Procedures" in this book.

  When the target server is configured to run in IIS 5.0 isolation mode, configure the identity properties of the COM+ applications that correspond to the Web site. For more information about configuring the application isolation settings when the target server is configured for IIS 5.0 isolation mode, see "Configure Application Isolation Settings in IIS 5.0 Isolation Mode" in "IIS Deployment Procedures" in this book.

Configuring Web Service Extensions

Many Web sites and applications that are hosted on IIS 6.0 have extended functionality beyond static Web pages, including the generation of dynamic content. Providing dynamic content and other enhanced capabilities requires executable code, such as ASP, ASP.NET, and ISAPI extensions. The handlers that extend IIS functionality beyond serving static pages are known as *Web service extensions*.

If you installed IIS 6.0 as described earlier in this chapter, all Web service extensions are disabled by default. If you used another method to install IIS 6.0, such as using Manage Your Server, the configuration of IIS might be different.

Enabling all of the Web service extensions ensures the highest possible compatibility with your Web sites. However, enabling all of the Web service extensions creates a security risk because it increases the attack surface of IIS by enabling functionality that might be unnecessary for your server.

Web service extensions allow you to enable and disable the serving of dynamic content. *MIME types* allow you to enable and disable the serving of static content. For more information about enabling and disabling the serving of static content, see "Configuring MIME Types" later in this chapter.

Tip

If the appropriate Web service extension is not enabled, the Web server returns a 404 error to the client when attempting to serve the dynamic content. When the 404 error is returned as a result of a Web service extension not being enabled, a 404.2 error entry is placed in the IIS log. For more information about troubleshooting IIS 6.0, see "Troubleshooting" in IIS 6.0 Help, which is accessible from IIS Manager.

Configure the Web service extensions by completing the following steps:

1. Enable the essential predefined Web service extensions based on the information in Table 6.3.

Table 6.3   Predefined Web Service Extensions

Web Service Extension	Description
Active Server Pages	Enable this extension when one or more of the Web sites or applications contains ASP content.
ASP.NET version 1.1.4322	Enable this extension when one or more of the Web sites or applications contains ASP.NET content.
FrontPage Server Extensions 2002	Enable this extension when one or more of the Web sites are FrontPage extended.
Internet Data Connector	Enable this extension when one or more of the Web sites or applications uses the Internet Data Connector (IDC) to display database information (content includes .idc and .idx files).
Server-Side Includes	Enable this extension when one or more of the Web sites uses server-side include (SSI) directives to instruct the Web server to insert various types of content into a Web page.
WebDAV	Enable this extension when you want to support Web Distributed Authoring and Versioning (WebDAV) on the Web server, but it is not recommended for dedicated Web servers.

2. For each Web service extension that is used by your applications and is not a one of the default Web service extensions, add a new entry to the Web service extensions list and configure the status of the new entry to **Allowed**.

   For example, one of your applications might use an ISAPI extension to provide access to a proprietary database. Set the ISAPI extension used by the application to **Allowed** to explicitly grant it permission to run. For information about how to add a Web service extension to the list, see "Configure Web Service Extensions" in "IIS Deployment Procedures" in this book.

3. Use a Web browser on a client computer to verify that the Web sites and applications run on the server.

Configuring MIME Types

IIS 6.0 serves only the static files with extensions that are registered in the Multipurpose Internet Mail Extensions (MIME) types list. IIS 6.0 is preconfigured to recognize a default set of global MIME types, which are recognized by all configured Web sites. You can define MIME types at the Web site and directory levels, independently of one another or the types defined globally. IIS also allows you to change, remove, or configure additional MIME types. For any static content file extensions used by the Web sites hosted by IIS that are not defined in the MIME types list, you must create a corresponding MIME type entry.

Configure the MIME types after migration by completing the following steps:

1. For each static file type used by your Web site, ensure that an entry exists in the MIME types list.

   When your application uses the standard MIME types that are included in IIS 6.0, no new MIME types entry is required. For information about how to add a MIME type to the MIME types list, see "Configure MIME Types" in "IIS Deployment Procedures" in this book.

2. Use a Web browser on a client computer to verify that the Web sites and applications run on the server.

Migrating Server Certificates for SSL

If you use Secure Sockets Layer to encrypt confidential information exchanged between the Web server and the client, you must migrate the server certificate from the source server to the target server, install the certificate on the target server, and then configure the Web site to use the certificate.

 Note

> Server certificates are installed on the Web server and typically require no additional configuration on client servers. Server certificates allow clients to verify the identity of the server. Alternatively, some Web sites and applications might require client certificates. Client certificates are installed on the client servers and allow the server to authenticate the clients. For more information about configuring client certificates, see "About Certificates" in IIS 6.0 Help, which is accessible from IIS Manager.

Migrate the server certificate for SSL by completing the following steps for each Web site and application that uses SSL:

1. Export the server certificate for the Web site from the source server.

   For more information about exporting a server certificate, see "Export a Server Certificate" in "Deployment Procedures" in this book.

2. Install the server certificate to be used by the Web site on the target server.

   For more information about installing the server certificate on the Web server by using the Certificate MMC snap-in, see "Install a Server Certificate" in "Deployment Procedures" in this book.

3. Assign the server certificate to the Web site.

   For more information about assigning the server certificate to the Web site, see "Assign a Server Certificate to a Web Site" in "IIS Deployment Procedures" in this book.

Migrating FrontPage Users and Roles

When the source server has Web sites that are FrontPage extended and FrontPage roles have been assigned to the Web site users, you need to migrate the FrontPage roles to the target server. The FrontPage roles control the types of access that users have on FrontPage extended Web sites. FrontPage 2002 Server Extensions are administered through the Microsoft SharePoint™ Team Services HTML administration tool, which is installed with FrontPage 2002 Server Extensions.

The predefined FrontPage roles include the following:

- **Administrator.** Users assigned this role can view, add, and change all server content; and manage server settings and accounts.

- **Advanced author.** Users assigned this role can view, add, and change pages, documents, themes, and borders; and recalculate hyperlinks.

- **Author.** Users assigned this role can view, add, and change pages and documents.

- **Contributor.** Users assigned this role can view pages and documents, and view and contribute to discussions.

- **Browser.** Users assigned this role can view pages and documents.

In addition to the predefined FrontPage roles, custom FrontPage roles might be defined on the source server.

Migrate FrontPage users and roles by completing the following steps:

1. Identify the FrontPage roles on the source server and compare them to the FrontPage roles on the target server.

2. Create any FrontPage roles on the target server that exist on the source server but do not exist on the target server.

3. For each FrontPage user on the source server that is local to the source server, create a corresponding user on the target server, and then assign that user the same FrontPage roles that are assigned to the corresponding user on the source server.

4. For each FrontPage user on the source server that is in Active Directory, assign the user the same FrontPage roles on the target server.

For more information about configuring the FrontPage 2002 Server Extensions users and roles, see "Configure FrontPage Server Roles" in "IIS Deployment Procedures" in this book. For more information about administering FrontPage 2002 Server Extensions, see the SharePoint Team Services Administrator's Guide link on the Web Resources page at http://www.microsoft.com/windows/reskits/webresources.

Configuring IIS 6.0 to Host ASP.NET Applications

If you migrated any ASP.NET applications to the target server, you need to configure IIS 6.0 to use the correct version of the .NET Framework, and you must configure the .NET Framework to support your applications.

Configure IIS 6.0 to host ASP.NET applications by completing the following steps:

1. Configure IIS 6.0 to use the correct version of the NET Framework.

2. Configure the .NET Framework.

3. Review how ASP.NET applications run in each application isolation mode.

4. Migrate Machine.config attributes to IIS 6.0 metabase property settings.

Configuring IIS to Use the Correct Version of the .NET Framework

If you have migrated ASP.NET applications that were developed with version 1.0 of the .NET Framework, you might have to install version 1.0 of the .NET Framework on the target server to ensure that your applications continue to function properly. After migration, version 1.1 of the .NET Framework is installed on the target server and the applications are configured to use version 1.1 of the .NET Framework. After installing version 1.0 of the .NET Framework, both version 1.0 and 1.1 of the .NET Framework are installed on the target server. This is referred to as *side-by-side support*.

Running versions 1.0 and 1.1 of the .NET Framework side-by-side is only supported when IIS is configured to run in IIS 5.0 isolation mode. If you have already configured IIS to run in worker process isolation mode, then you can only use version 1.1 of the .NET Framework on the target server. In most cases, ASP.NET applications function correctly with version 1.1 of the .NET Framework. For more information about possible application incompatibilities when migrating from version 1.0 to version 1.1 of the .NET Framework, see "Determining Application Compatibility with the .NET Framework" earlier in this chapter. When your ASP.NET application is incompatible with version 1.1 of the .NET Framework, configure the application to use version 1.0 of the .NET Framework and configure IIS to run in IIS 5.0 isolation mode.

You can configure each ASP.NET application to use a specific version of the .NET Framework by registering a *script map* in IIS for the application. A script map associates a file name extension and HTTP verb with the appropriate ISAPI for script handling. For example, when IIS receives a request for a .aspx file, the script map for the corresponding application directs IIS to forward the requested file to the appropriate version of the ASP.NET ISAPI for processing.

The script map for each ASP.NET application can be applied directly to an application, or inherited from a parent application. However, ASP.NET supports only one version of the .NET Framework for each application pool. For more information about how to configure the script map for an ASP.NET application, see "Configure an ASP.NET Application for ASP.NET" in "IIS Deployment Procedures" in this book.

Configuring the .NET Framework

The configuration method for the .NET Framework is determined by the application isolation mode that you use to configure IIS 6.0. Table 6.4 lists the methods for configuring the .NET Framework that are associated with each IIS 6.0 application isolation mode.

Table 6.4   Methods for Configuring the .NET Framework

Application Isolation Mode	Configuration Method for the .NET Framework
IIS 5.0 isolation mode	Configured by making changes to the Machine.config file in the *systemroot*\Microsoft.NET\Framework*VersionNumber*\Config folder.
Worker process isolation mode	Configured by making changes to the IIS 6.0 metabase.

When IIS 6.0 is configured to run in IIS 5.0 isolation mode, the .NET Framework uses the **<processModel>** section of the Machine.config file (in the *systemroot*\Microsoft.NET\Framework*versionNumber*\Config folder) for its configuration and no additional steps are required.

However, if you configured IIS 6.0 to run in worker process isolation mode, the .NET Framework ignores the **<processModel>** section of the Machine.config file, and instead gets its process configuration from the IIS 6.0 metabase. Because the migration process does not migrate the existing settings in the Machine.config file, you must manually convert any settings required by the ASP.NET applications.

For information about how to convert the Machine.config attribute settings to IIS 6.0 metabase property settings, see "Migrating Machine.config Attributes to IIS 6.0 Metabase Property Settings" later in this chapter. For more information about configuring IIS 6.0 for ASP.NET applications, see "Deploying ASP.NET Applications in IIS 6.0" in this book.

Reviewing How ASP.NET Applications Run in Each Application Isolation Mode

When running IIS 6.0 in worker process isolation mode, ASP.NET applications use the W3wp.exe worker process and application pool properties, which are stored in the IIS 6.0 metabase. When you configure IIS 6.0 to run in IIS 5.0 isolation mode, ASP.NET applications use the ASP.NET request processing model, Aspnet_wp.exe, and configuration settings. These configuration settings are stored in the Machine.config file.

Behavior of ASP.NET Applications That Are Running in IIS 5.0 Isolation Mode

By default, ASP.NET applications are configured to run in worker process isolation mode. If your application can only run in the ASP.NET process model, you must configure the server to run in IIS 5.0 isolation mode to be able to run the application on IIS 6.0. When IIS 6.0 is configured to run in IIS 5.0 isolation mode, ASP.NET applications behave as follows:

- The applications run within Aspnet_wp.exe.

  Aspnet_wp.exe is a request processing model that is similar to worker process isolation mode, and it contains worker process management capabilities similar to the WWW service in IIS 6.0. Aspnet_wp.exe includes most of the IIS application management features, such as recycling, health detection, and *processor affinity*. Processor affinity is the ability to force worker processes to run on specific microprocessors.

- The configuration settings are stored in the Machine.config file.

  When IIS 6.0 is running in IIS 5.0 isolation mode, the configuration settings for ASP.NET applications are managed by modifying the Machine.config file, not the IIS metabase file. Because there is no administrative console for the Machine.config settings, any configuration settings for ASP.NET must be made directly to the Machine.config file.

 Important

> In IIS 5.0 isolation mode, the .NET Framework ignores any configuration changes made in the IIS metabase. Administrative consoles, such as IIS Manager, make changes to the IIS 6.0 metabase, but those changes are not read by the .NET Framework.

When IIS 6.0 is configured to run in IIS 5.0 isolation mode, your ASP.NET applications should behave as they did in IIS 5.0. However, incompatibilities can result when running version 1.1 of the .NET Framework. For more information about configuring IIS to support ASP.NET applications that use version 1.0 of the .NET Framework, see "Running Different Versions of ASP.NET Side-by-Side" in "Deploying ASP.NET Applications in IIS 6.0" in this book.

Behavior of ASP.NET Applications That Are Running in Worker Process Isolation Mode

When IIS 6.0 is configured to run in worker process isolation mode, ASP.NET applications behave as follows:

- The process model within the ASP.NET ISAPI extension is disabled, and ASP.NET applications run using worker process isolation mode in IIS 6.0.

  In this configuration, the ASP.NET application runs in worker process isolation mode like any other application, such as an ASP application. In addition, IIS 6.0 provides all of the management features such as recycling, health detection, and processor affinity.

- The ASP.NET ISAPI extension is configured by a combination of configuration settings that are stored in the IIS metabase (MetaBase.xml) and configuration settings in the Machine.config file.

  When IIS 6.0 is running in worker process isolation mode, the majority of the application configuration settings are stored in the IIS metabase. You can adjust these settings directly in MetaBase.xml or from administrative consoles, such as IIS Manager, or scripts.

  However, if there are existing settings in the **<processModel>** section of the Machine.config file, those configuration settings must be converted to the appropriate application pool settings when the Web server is configured to run in worker process isolation mode Additionally, there are other configuration settings that are still modified in the Machine.config file, regardless of the application isolation mode. For more information about converting Machine.config attributes to worker process isolation mode settings, see "Migrating Machine.config Attributes to IIS 6.0 Metabase Property Settings" later in this chapter.

When IIS 6.0 is configured in worker process isolation mode, your ASP.NET applications should behave as they did on IIS 5.0. Before deploying your ASP.NET applications on your production Web servers, test compatibility with IIS 6.0 running in worker process isolation mode and version 1.1 of the .NET Framework. For more information about determining application compatibility with IIS 6.0 running in worker process isolation mode, see "Determining Application Compatibility with Worker Process Isolation Mode" earlier in this chapter. For more information about determining compatibility with version 1.1 of the .NET Framework see "Determining Application Compatibility with the .NET Framework" earlier in this chapter.

If you determine that your ASP.NET applications are incompatible with worker process isolation mode, reconfigure IIS to run in IIS 5.0 isolation mode. If your ASP.NET applications are incompatible with version 1.1 of the .NET Framework, configure IIS to use version 1.0 of the .NET Framework with your ASP.NET application.

For more information about configuring IIS 6.0 to run in IIS 5.0 isolation mode, see "Configure Application Isolation Modes" in "IIS Deployment Procedures" in this book. For more information about configuring IIS to use version 1.0 of the .NET Framework with your ASP.NET application, see "Running Different Versions of ASP.NET Side-by-Side" in "Deploying ASP.NET Applications in IIS 6.0" in this book.

Migrating Machine.config Attributes to IIS 6.0 Metabase Property Settings

When IIS 6.0 is configured to run in IIS 5.0 isolation mode, the .NET Framework uses the **<processModel>** section of the Machine.config file (in the *systemroot*\Microsoft.NET\Framework*versionNumber*\Config folder) for its runtime configuration. When the target server is running in IIS 5.0 isolation mode, you do not need to convert the attribute configuration settings on the source server to their equivalent IIS 6.0 metabase property settings on the target server so you can proceed to the next step in the migration process. To proceed to the next step in the migration process, see "Determining Whether to Run the IIS Lockdown Tool and UrlScan" later in this chapter.

However, if you configured IIS 6.0 to run in worker process isolation mode, the .NET Framework ignores the <**processModel**> section of the Machine.config file, and instead gets its process configuration from the IIS 6.0 metabase. Because the migration process does not migrate the existing settings in the Machine.config file, you must manually migrate any settings that are required by your ASP.NET applications.

For information about how to migrate the Machine.config settings to IIS 6.0 metabase settings, see "Migrating Machine.config Attributes to IIS 6.0 Metabase Property Settings" in "Upgrading an IIS Server to IIS 6.0" in this book.

Determining Whether to Run the IIS Lockdown Tool and UrlScan

The IIS Lockdown Tool and UrlScan are IIS security related programs designed for IIS 5.1 and earlier. Each tool provides different types of protection for earlier versions of IIS. The IIS migration process does not install the IIS Lockdown Tool and UrlScan on the target server.

IIS Lockdown Tool

The IIS Lockdown Tool is provided to assist administrators in configuring optimal security settings for existing IIS servers. You cannot install the IIS Lockdown Tool after migration because all of the default configuration settings in IIS 6.0 meet or exceed the security configuration settings made by the IIS Lockdown Tool.

UrlScan

UrlScan is a tool that is provided to reduce the attack surface of Web servers running earlier versions of IIS. By default, IIS 6.0 has features that significantly improve security by reducing the attack surface of the Web server. UrlScan provides flexible configuration for advanced administrators, while maintaining the improved security in IIS 6.0. When you need this flexibility in configuring your Web server, you can run UrlScan on IIS 6.0.

For more information about determining whether to run UrlScan after migrating your server to IIS 6.0, see the Using UrlScan link on the Web Resources page at http://www.microsoft.com/windows/reskits/webresources.

Performing Application-Specific Migration Tasks

When no setup or provisioning scripts exist for your applications, you might need to perform additional application-specific migration tasks, whether you have migrated content and metabase information manually or with the IIS 6.0 Migration Tool. Some of these tasks involve the modification of application code and might require the assistance of the application developers. Depending on your application, you might need to perform any combination of the steps in Figure 6.8.

Figure 6.8   Performing Application-Specific Migration Tasks

Prepare for migration

Deploy the target server

Use the IIS 6.0 Migration Tool to migrate?

Yes → Migrate Web sites with the IIS 6.0 Migration Tool

No

Migrate Web sites manually

Configure IIS 6.0 properties

Perform application-specific migration tasks

Complete the migration

Modify application code for compatibility with Windows Server 2003 and IIS 6.0

Install additional software required by applications

Migrate MTS packages, COM objects, and COM+ applications

Modify ODBC data connection strings and DSNs

Create IP addresses that are used by applications

Create users and groups that are used by applications

Create registry entries for applications

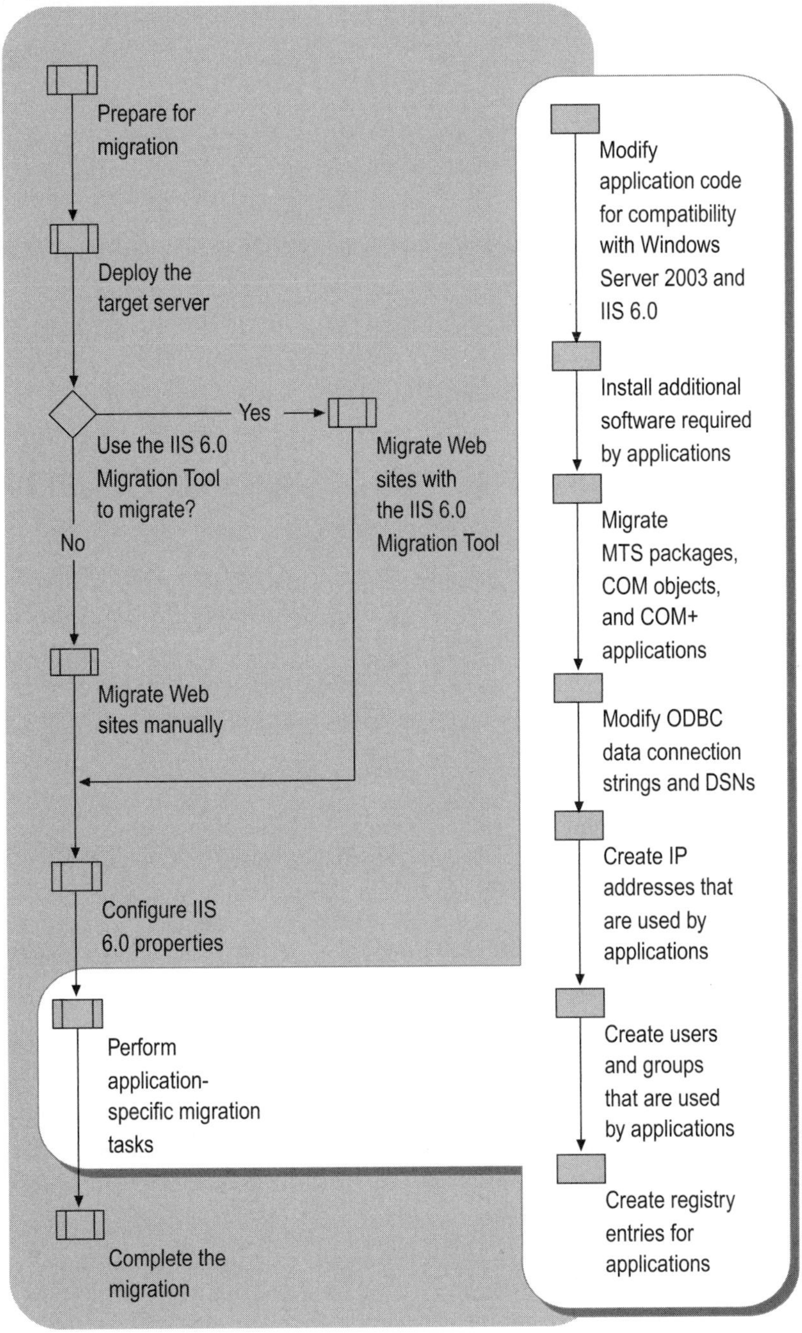

Modifying Application Code for Compatibility with Windows Server 2003 and IIS 6.0

If any application code needs to be changed or recompiled to run on Windows Server 2003, you must make those changes manually. The most common application code changes include the following:

- Code that references Windows platform components or APIs no longer supported in Windows Server 2003.

- Code that references IIS metabase properties that have changed or are no longer supported in IIS 6.0.

- Code that is incompatible with worker process isolation mode.

Modifying References to Windows Platform Components and APIs No Longer Supported in Windows Server 2003

Applications developed to run on earlier versions of Windows server operating systems and IIS can call APIs that are not supported in Windows Server 2003 and IIS 6.0. Usually these APIs are replaced with newer APIs that provide additional functionality.

If your Web sites and applications use an API that is not supported in Windows Server 2003 and IIS 6.0, you must modify your code to use an API that provides the same functionality and is supported in Windows Server 2003 and IIS 6.0.

For example, the APIs supported by the Collaboration Data Objects for Windows NT Server 4.0 (CDONTS) DLL are not supported in Windows Server 2003. The functionality provided by CDONTS is supported by Collaboration Data Objects for Windows 2000 (CDOSYS), which, in turn, is supported by Windows Server 2003. Therefore, if your applications use CDONTS, you can modify your code to use CDOSYS instead. For more information about modifying your application to use CDOSYS, see the Collaboration Data Objects Roadmap link on the Web Resources page at http://www.microsoft.com/windows/reskits/webresources.

Modifying References to IIS 6.0 Metabase Properties

Some metabase properties that were used to configure features in earlier versions of IIS are no longer supported in IIS 6.0. Because some features are eliminated, or implemented differently in IIS 6.0, the corresponding unused metabase properties are not referenced by any code in IIS 6.0. In cases where the feature is implemented differently in IIS 6.0, new metabase properties have been created to replace the obsolete, or unused, properties.

In addition, there is one IIS 5.0 metabase property — **CPUResetInterval** — whose behavior has changed because of architectural changes made to IIS 6.0.

To determine whether any of your Web sites, applications, or setup programs reference these changed or unsupported IIS metabase properties, see "Changes to Metabase Properties in IIS 6.0" in this book. You can then follow the recommendations associated with each changed metabase property listed in this appendix to accommodate functionality changes in IIS 6.0.

 Tip
The metabase properties that are no longer supported in IIS 6.0 are not available in IIS 6.0, even when IIS 6.0 is configured to run in IIS 5.0 isolation mode.

Modifying Applications To Be Compatible with Worker Process Isolation Mode

Most applications that were developed to run on earlier versions of IIS run in worker process isolation mode without modification. However, you might need to modify your applications to make them compatible with worker process isolation mode. For more information about the types of modifications that you might need to make to your applications, see "Application Changes Required for Worker Process Isolation Mode" earlier in this chapter.

Your applications can require other modifications that are not described in this chapter because of the myriad of approaches to developing applications. For the most current information about modifying your applications to be compatible with worker process isolation mode, see the MSDN Online link on the Web Resources page at http://www.microsoft.com/windows/reskits/webresources, and search for relevant articles.

Installing Additional Software Required by Applications

Some of your applications might require or be dependent upon additional software that is not in the same folder with the Web site content. This software can be developed by your organization, by Microsoft, or by other organizations. You must install this software on the target server by running the setup or installation program that accompanies the software.

Examples of this type of software include software that creates reports, integrates databases with dynamic content generation, or provides connectivity with applications running on other servers with non-Microsoft operating systems.

Migrating MTS Packages, COM Objects, and COM+ Applications

In addition to installing any software that you installed earlier in the migration process, there can be MTS packages, COM objects, and COM+ applications that need to be migrated. Table 6.5 lists the tasks that you need to complete to migrate MTS packages, COM objects, and COM+ application from earlier version of Windows.

Table 6.5   Migrating MTS Packages, COM Objects, and COM+ Applications

Source Server	Target Server	Migration Tasks
MTS packages on Windows NT 4.0 Server	COM + applications	Convert the MTS package to a COM+ application.
COM objects	COM objects	Copy COM object files (.dll or .exe) from the source server to the target sever and register the COM object by running the **regsrv32** command.
COM+ applications on Windows 2000 Server	COM + applications	Create the COM+ application on the target server and use the same configuration on the target server that existed on the source server.

For more information about migrating MTS packages, COM objects, and COM+ applications to Windows Server 2003, see the following articles: "COM: Delivering on the Promises of Component Technology", which you can find on the Microsoft Web site at http://www.microsoft.com; and "Microsoft .NET/COM Migration and Interoperability", which you can find by seeing the MSDN Online link on the Web Resources page at http://www.microsoft.com/windows/reskits/webresources.

An example of registering a COM object that is running on the source server is CDONTS. If you decide to not modify your code to us CDOSYS instead of CDONTS, you must copy the Cdonts.dll file from the source server to the target server and then register Cdonts.dll with Windows Server 2003. For more information about how to migrate CDONTS, see "Migrate CDONTS" in "IIS Deployment Procedures" in this book.

Modifying ODBC Data Connection Strings and DSNs

If your application establishes database connectivity through an ODBC data connection string or through an ODBC data source name (DSN), you must do any combination of the following:

- Manually modify ODBC DSNs when the ODBC data connection string references a database that is stored on the source server and the database has not been migrated to the target server.

- Manually create a system ODBC DSN on the target server for each system ODBC DSN on the source server.

Modifying ODBC DSNs

ODBC data connection strings might need to be modified if they reference the database or are migrated to a different location. For more information about modifying ODBC data connection strings, see the article "Connection String Format and Attributes." To find this article, see the MSDN Online link on the Web Resources page at http://www.microsoft.com/windows/reskits/webresources, and then search for "ODBC connection string".

Creating System ODBC DSNs

In addition, if you have system ODBC DSNs that are defined on the source server, you need to create corresponding ODBC DSNs on the target server. Table 6.6 lists methods for administering ODBC DSNs on different Windows server operating systems. You can administer ODBC DSNs on the source server and the target server by using the methods listed in this table.

Table 6.6 Administering ODBC DSNs on Source Servers and Target Servers

Operating System	Administered Through	Additional Information
Windows Server 2003	Data Sources (ODBC) in Administrative Tools	For more information about using Data Sources (ODBC) in Windows Server 2003, see Help and Support Center for Windows Server 2003.
Windows 2000 Server	Data Sources (ODBC) in Administrative Tools	For more information about using Data Sources (ODBC) in Windows 2000 Server, see Windows 2000 Server Help.
Windows NT 4.0 Server	ODBC Data Sources in Control Panel	For more information about using ODBC Data Sources in Windows NT 4.0 Server, see Help in the ODBC Data Source Administrator in the ODBC Data Sources, in Control Panel.

Creating IP Addresses That Are Used by Applications

You can uniquely identify a Web site or application by associating the Web site or application with a unique IP address, a unique combination of an IP address and a TCP port number, or host headers. For Web sites and applications on the source server that are uniquely identified by IP addresses, you must create corresponding IP addresses on the target server and then configure the Web sites and applications to use the newly created IP addresses.

To create IP addresses that are used by applications, complete the following steps:

1. Determine which Web sites and applications on the source server are uniquely identified by IP addresses.

    For more information about how to determine which Web sites and applications on the source server are uniquely identified by IP addresses see, "Determine Web Sites Uniquely Identified by IP Addresses" in "IIS Deployment Procedures" in this book.

2. For each Web site and application identified in Step 1, assign new a new IP address to the TCP/IP properties of the network adapter in the target server that the clients use to access the Web sites and applications.

    For more information about how to assign a new IP addresses to the network adapter in the target server that the clients use to access the Web sites and applications see, "Assign Additional IP Addresses to a Network Adapter" in "IIS Deployment Procedures" in this book.

3. Configure the migrated Web sites and applications on the target server to use the IP addresses assigned in Step 2.

    For more information about how to configure the IP addresses assigned to Web sites and applications see, "Configure IP Address Assigned to Web Sites" in "IIS Deployment Procedures" in this book.

Creating Users and Groups That Are Used by Applications

The Web sites and applications on the source server might be accessed by accounts that are local to the source server. The local user and group accounts need to be created on the target server so that the accounts can access the Web sites and applications on the target server.

In cases where the users and groups that are used by the applications exist in Active Directory, no steps are required and you can continue to the next migration step. To continue to the next step in the migration process, see "Creating Registry Entries for Applications" later in this chapter.

Create the users and groups that are used by applications and are local to the source server by completing the following steps:

1. Identify the users and groups that are local to the source server.

2. For each group on the source server, create a corresponding group on the target server.

3. For each user on the source server, create a corresponding user on the target server.

4. For each user created in Step 3, assign the user to the same groups as the corresponding user on the source server.

   For more information about viewing the users and groups on the source server, see "Creating user and group accounts" in Windows 2000 Server Help and Windows NT Server 4.0 Help. For more information about creating users and groups in Windows Server 2003, see "Create a Service Account" in "IIS Deployment Procedures" in this book.

5. For each user created in Step 3, assign the same user rights assigned to the corresponding user on the source server.

   For more information about assigning user rights to a user, see "Grant User Rights to a Service Account" in "IIS Deployment Procedures" in this book.

6. Assign the same NTFS permissions for the content on the target server as the NTFS permissions for the content on the source server.

   For more information about configuring NTFS permissions on the target server, see "Configure NTFS Permissions" in "IIS Deployment Procedures" in this book.

Creating Registry Entries for Applications

Some applications save configuration information in the Windows registry. If the setup program or provisioning script creates the registry entries, run the setup program or provisioning script on the target server. Otherwise, you must manually identify the registry entries and then re-create them on the target server.

 Caution

Do not edit the registry unless you have no alternative. The registry editor bypasses standard safeguards, allowing settings that can damage your system, or even require you to reinstall Windows. If you must edit the registry, back it up first and see the Registry Reference on the *Microsoft Windows Server 2003 Deployment Kit* companion CD or on the Web at http://www.microsoft.com/reskit.

Create application registry entries on the target server manually by completing the following steps:

1. Identify the registry entries required by the applications that are currently running on the source server.

   Earlier in the migration process, you identified the registry entries required by the applications on the source server. For more information about identifying registry entries, see "Identifying Which Web Site and Application Components to Migrate", earlier in the chapter.

2. Back up the registry entries on the source server that you identified in the previous step by using the registry editor Regedit.exe.

   For more information about backing up copies of registry entries, see "Back Up and Restore Registry Entries" in "IIS Deployment Procedures" in this book.

3. Copy the .reg backup file, created in Step 2, to the target server.

4. Modify the .reg backup file created in the previous step to accommodate for changes in disk volume letters, such a F:, or paths to folders by completing the following steps:

   a. In Notepad, open the .reg backup file created in Step 2.

   b. Search for specific references to disk volume letters or paths that you want to change, and update them to reflect the disk volume letters or paths on the target server.

   c. Save the .reg file.

5. Restore the registry backup on the target server.

   For more information about restoring registry entries, see "Back Up and Restore Registry Entries" in "IIS Deployment Procedures" in this book.

Completing the Migration

At this point in the process, you have migrated your Web sites and applications to the target server and configured the IIS 6.0 properties to settings on the source server. Now you need to verify that the migration completed successfully, capture the current configuration of the target server, and enable client access to the target server. After you complete these last steps, your migration is complete. Figure 6.9 illustrates the process for completing the migration to IIS 6.0.

Figure 6.9 Completing the Migration to IIS 6.0

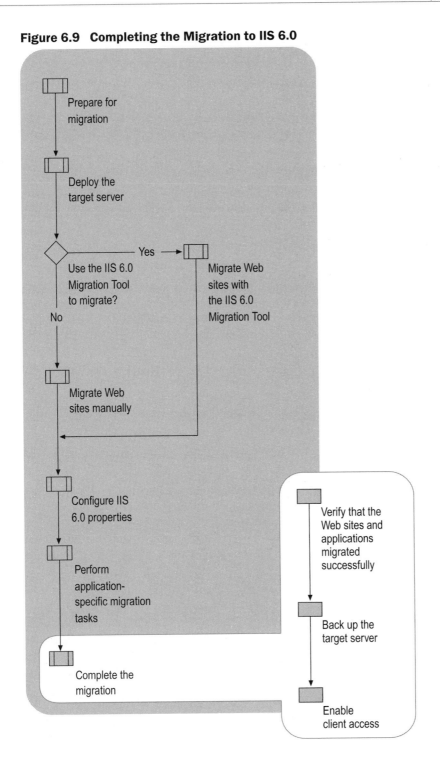

Verifying That the Web Sites and Applications Migrated Successfully

Before deploying the target server to a production environment, verify that the Web site content and configuration information migrated successfully by completing the following steps:

1. Review the system log in Windows Server 2003 on the target server to determine whether any of the Web sites did not start.

   IIS 6.0 creates entries in the system log when a Web site fails to start for any reason. Search the System log on the target server for to determine if any errors occurred. For more information about how to troubleshoot Web sites that fail to start, see "Troubleshooting" in IIS 6.0 Help, which is accessible from IIS Manager.

2. Verify that the Web site content migrated to the target server.

   Compare the files and folders for each Web site on the target server with the original files and folders on the source server to determine whether the Web site content has been migrated correctly. Ensure that the number and size of the files and folders on the target server approximates the number and size of the same files on the source server.

3. Verify that the Web site configuration migrated to the target server.

   View the Web site configuration information for a random sampling of the Web sites that were migrated. Compare the Web site configuration on the target server with the corresponding Web site configuration on the source server. Ensure that the configuration for the Web sites has been migrated correctly.

4. Perform functional testing of the migrated Web sites and applications to ensure that the Web sites and applications behave as expected.

   You can find possible causes of application failure by reviewing the Windows Server 2003 and IIS 6.0 Migration Tool logs and application configuration, but the only way to accurately assess whether your Web sites and applications migrated successfully is to perform functional testing. Functional testing is designed to ensure that Web sites and applications are functioning correctly in the most common usage scenarios (for example URLs and inputs).

   Procedures for performing functional testing of Web sites and applications are beyond the scope of this chapter. For more complete information about general testing, see the MSDN Online link on the Web Resources page at http://www.microsoft.com/windows/reskits/webresources, and search for "testing".

Backing Up the Target Server

Before you enable client access to the target server, perform a complete image backup of the target server. Performing this image backup provides you with a point-in-time snapshot of the Web server. If you need to restore the target server in the event of a failure, you can use this backup to restore the Web server to a known configuration.

 Important

Do not proceed further unless you have a successful backup of the entire target server. Otherwise, you can lose Web sites, applications, or data that you migrated to the target server.

For more information about how to back up the Web server, see "Back Up and Restore the Web Server to a File or Tape" in "IIS Deployment Procedures" in this book.

Enabling Client Access

After you have migrated your Web sites from the source server to the target server, you are ready to enable client access to the Web sites on the target server while maintaining the DNS entries to the source servers. After a period of time that meets your business needs, you can remove the DNS entries that point to the Web sites on the source server.

Enable client access to the Web sites that are on the target server by completing the following steps:

1. Create the appropriate DNS entries for the Web sites and applications running on the target server.

   For more information about how to create DNS entries for your Web sites and applications see "Managing resource records" in Help and Support Center for Windows Server 2003.

2. Monitor client traffic to determine whether clients are successfully accessing the target server.

   For more information about how to monitor client traffic to Web sites on the target server, see "Monitor Active Web and FTP Connections" in "IIS Deployment Procedures" in this book.

3. Establish a monitoring period, such as a few hours or a day, to confirm that clients accessing Web sites on the target server are experiencing response times and application responses that meet or exceed your requirements.

4. Remove the DNS entries that are pointing to the Web sites and applications on the source server.

   For more information about how to remove DNS entries for your Web sites and applications, see "Managing resource records" in Help and Support Center for Windows Server 2003.

5. Prevent new clients from accessing the Web sites on the source server by pausing the Web sites on the source server.

   For more information about how to pause Web sites on the source server, see "Pause Web or FTP Sites" in "IIS Deployment Procedures" in this book.

6. Monitor client traffic to the Web sites on the source server to determine when clients are no longer accessing the source server.

   For more information about how to monitor client traffic to Web sites on the source server, see "Monitor Active Web and FTP Connections" in "IIS Deployment Procedures" in this book.

7. When clients are no longer accessing the Web sites on the source server, decommission the hardware for the source server.

Additional Resources

These resources contain additional information and tools related to this chapter.

Related Information

- "Deploying ASP.NET Applications in IIS 6.0" in this book for information about configuring IIS 6.0 for ASP.NET applications.

- "IIS Deployment Procedures in this book for information about specific procedures for migrating IIS Web sites to IIS 6.0.

- "Migrating Apache Web Sites to IIS 6.0" in this book for information about migrating Apache Web sites.

- "Migrating Machine.config Attributes to IIS 6.0 Metabase Property Settings" in "Upgrading an IIS Server to IIS 6.0" in this book for information about how to migrate the Machine.config settings to IIS 6.0 metabase settings.

- "Securing Web Sites and Applications" in this book for information about improving the security of your IIS Web sites after migration.

- "Designing a Test Environment" in *Planning, Testing, and Piloting Deployment Projects* of the *Microsoft® Windows® Server 2003 Deployment Kit* for information about setting up a test lab.

- "COM: Delivering on the Promises of Component Technology", which you can find on the Microsoft Web site at http://www.microsoft.com, for information about migrating MTS packages, COM objects, and COM+ applications to Windows Server 2003.

- The Collaboration Data Objects Roadmap link on the Web Resources page at http://www.microsoft.com/windows/reskits/webresources for information about modifying your applications to use CDOSYS.

- The Compatibility Considerations and Version Changes link on the Web Resources page at http://www.microsoft.com/windows/reskits/webresources for a current list of possible compatibility issues when upgrading from version 1.0 to version 1.1 of the .NET Framework.

- The *Hardware Compatibility List* on the product CD-ROM or the Hardware Driver Quality link on the Web Resources page at http://www.microsoft.com/windows/reskits/webresources for information about the hardware devices supported by Windows Server 2003.

- "Microsoft .NET/COM Migration and Interoperability", which you can find by seeing the MSDN Online link on the Web Resources page at http://www.microsoft.com/windows/reskits/webresources, for information about migrating MTS packages, COM objects, and COM+ applications to Windows Server 2003.

- The SharePoint Team Services Administrator's Guide link on the Web Resources page at http://www.microsoft.com/windows/reskits/webresources for information about administering FrontPage 2002 Server Extensions.

- The Using UrlScan link on the Web Resources page at http://www.microsoft.com/windows/reskits/webresources for information about determining whether to run UrlScan after migrating your server to IIS 6.0.

- The Windows Server 2003 link on the Web Resources page at http://www.microsoft.com/windows/reskits/webresources for the latest information about compatibility with Windows Server 2003.

Related IIS 6.0 Help Topics

- "About Certificates" in IIS 6.0 Help, which is accessible from IIS Manager, for information about configuring client certificates.

- "Metabase Edit-While-Running Feature" in IIS 6.0 Help, which is accessible from IIS Manager, for information about the edit-while-running feature.

- "Troubleshooting" in IIS 6.0 Help, which is accessible from IIS Manager, for information about troubleshooting IIS 6.0.

Related Windows Server 2003 Help Topics

For best results in identifying Help topics by title, in Help and Support Center, under the **Search** box, click **Set search options**. Under **Help Topics**, select the **Search in title only** check box.

- "Features unavailable on 64-bit versions of the Windows Server 2003 family" in Help and Support Center for Windows Server 2003 for information about features, such as ASP.NET, that are not supported on 64-bit versions of Windows Server 2003.

- "Managing resource records" in Help and Support Center for Windows Server 2003 for information about how to create DNS entries for your Web sites and applications.

Related Tools

- The "IIS 6.0 Migration Tool User Guide" on the *Windows Server 2003 Deployment Kit* companion CD or the *Internet Information Services (IIS) 6.0 Resource Kit* companion CD for information about using the IIS 6.0 Migration Tool.

- The Windows Application Compatibility link on the Web Resources page at http://www.microsoft.com/windows/reskits/webresources to download the latest version of the Windows Application Compatibility Toolkit.

Migrating Apache Web Sites to IIS 6.0

Migration is the process of installing a Microsoft® Windows® Server 2003 operating system and Internet Information Services (IIS) 6.0 on a server and then moving or reinstalling existing Apache Web sites and applications to that server. Migrating Apache Web sites and applications to IIS 6.0 allows you to take advantage of the improved security, performance, and management provided by Windows Server 2003 and IIS 6.0. The migration process provides minimal outage of service to the users accessing the Web sites and applications, while ensuring that the existing configuration and content of the Web sites and applications are maintained.

In This Chapter

Related Information

- For information about upgrading IIS Web servers, see "Upgrading an IIS Server to IIS 6.0" in this book.

- For information about migrating Web sites on earlier versions of IIS to IIS 6.0, see "Migrating IIS Web Sites to IIS 6.0" in this book.

Overview of Migrating Apache Web Sites to IIS 6.0

The Apache Web site migration process is completed with the *Apache to IIS 6.0 Migration Tool*. This tool is a set of configurable modules to migrate Apache Web sites — including FrontPage® Server Extensions from Microsoft, .htaccess files, and user directories — to servers running IIS 6.0 on Microsoft Windows® Server 2003, Standard Edition; Windows® Server 2003, Enterprise Edition; Windows® Server 2003, Datacenter Edition; and Windows® Server 2003, Web Edition. The tool is a Perl-based command-line utility that migrates both Web content and configuration settings.

The Apache to IIS 6.0 Migration Tool supports Apache versions 1.3.0–1.3.22, as well as the following Linux distributions:

- Red Hat software (Linux versions 6.0, 6.2, 7.0, 7.1, and 7.2)

- Mandrake Linux (versions 8.0, 8.1, and 8.2)

- SuSE (versions 7.3 and 8.0)

You can use the Apache to IIS 6.0 Migration Tool to migrate site content and configuration settings from a *source server* (a server running a supported version of Linux and Apache) to a *target server* (a server running a Windows Server 2003 operating system and IIS 6.0). You can perform the migration from the source server, the target server, or on an *intermediate computer*. The intermediate computer must have File Transfer Protocol (FTP) access to the source and target servers.

The Apache to IIS 6.0 Migration Tool migrates only the Apache Web site content and configuration. If the Apache Web site is made up of only static content, such as Hypertext Markup Language (HTML) pages, the migration can most likely be completed with a few simple steps. However, Apache Web sites containing dynamic content, such as PHP: Hypertext Preprocessor (PHP) or Common Gateway Interface (CGI) scripts, might need modifications to the code in the dynamic content after migration. In addition, any existing provisioning scripts or setup programs for the existing Apache Web sites typically require modifications after the migration process is complete. Because each organization has different provisioning scripts and setup programs, you need to review and make modifications based on input from your developers, and then test the Web site after completing the modifications. For more information about possible necessary modifications to dynamic content, see "Determining Web Site Compatibility with IIS 6.0" later in this chapter.

For more information about the Apache to IIS 6.0 Migration Tool, including how to install it, see "Preparing for Migration" later in this chapter. For more information about the additional migration tasks that you must perform after running the Apache to IIS 6.0 Migration Tool, see "Migrating Apache-Specific Extensions" later in this chapter.

Process for Migrating Apache Web Sites to IIS 6.0

In addition to migrating the existing Web site content, the migration process automatically migrates the Web site configuration including FrontPage Server Extensions. Before performing the migration of the Web site, you need to evaluate the compatibility of the Apache Web sites with the software installed on your existing server, including dynamic content, database connections, and *external modules*. External modules are software components that are not shipped as a part of the Linux operating system.

If your Apache Web sites contain dynamic content or you want to further secure the Web sites, you can use the Apache to IIS 6.0 Migration Tool to customize the configuration of IIS 6.0 and migrate the dynamic content. Figure 7.1 illustrates the process for migrating existing Apache Web sites to IIS 6.0.

Figure 7.1 Migrating Apache Web Sites to IIS 6.0

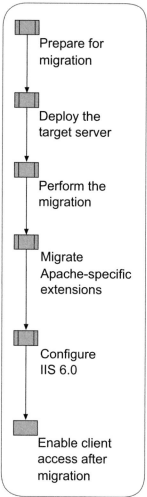

 Tip

To upgrade a Web farm, use the process described in this chapter to upgrade each server in the Web farm.

Depending on your familiarity with Linux, Windows Server 2003, Apache, IIS 6.0, and the migration process, you might require less guidance through the migration process. The following quick-start guide provides a detailed overview of the Apache to IIS migration process described in this chapter. You can use this guide to help identify the steps of the migration process where you need additional information and skip the information with which you are already familiar. In addition, all of the procedures required to complete the migration process are documented in "IIS Deployment Procedures" in this book.

Prepare for Migration

1. Determine Web site compatibility with IIS 6.0.
2. Determine application compatibility with worker process isolation mode by evaluating the differences between application isolation modes.
3. Identify the role of the Apache to IIS 6.0 Migration Tool in the migration process.
4. Select on of the following Apache to IIS 6.0 Migration Tool installation options:
   - The source server installation option
   - The target server installation option
   - The intermediate computer installation option

Deploy the Target Sever

1. Install Windows Server 2003.
2. Install IIS 6.0.
3. Configure the FTP service.

Perform the Migration

1. Install the Apache to IIS 6.0 Migration Tool:
   - Install the migration tool on computers running Linux.
   - Install the migration tool on computers running Windows.
   - Configure the target server for migration.
2. Verify that clients are not accessing the Web sites.
3. Migrate the Web site content.
4. Migrate the Web site configuration.
5. Recover from an interruption in the migration process:
   - Determine the cause of resolve any errors.
   - Restart the migration tool in recovery mode.

Migrate Apache-Specific Extensions

1. Migrate dynamic content.
2. Migrate database content and connectivity:
   - Migrate the database content.
   - Migrate the database connectivity.
3. Migrate external modules.

Configure IIS 6.0 After Migration

1. Configure Web service extensions.

2. Configure Multipurpose Internet Mail Extensions (MIME) types.

3. Configure Web site properties.

4. Configure server certificates for Secure Sockets Layer (SSL).

5. Back up the target server.

Enable Client Access After Migration

Preparing for Migration

Before initiating the migration, ensure that existing Apache Web sites are compatible with IIS 6.0 and Windows Server 2003. In addition, determine if the existing Web sites are compatible with worker process isolation mode in IIS 6.0. Then, you must identify which steps in the migration process are automated by the Apache to IIS 6.0 Migration Tool and which steps you need to complete after running the tool. Finally, you must decide which option to use to install the tool.

Figure 7.2 Preparing for Migration of Apache Web Sites to IIS 6.0

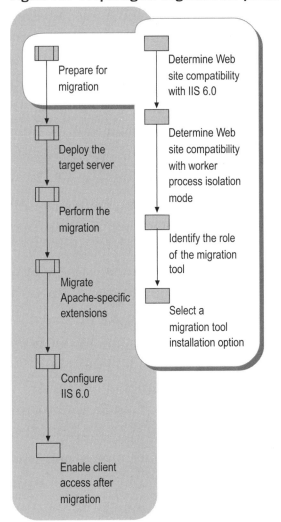

Determining Web Site Compatibility with IIS 6.0

Before you migrate to IIS, you must determine the compatibility of the Apache Web site with IIS 6.0. Because of architectural differences, Web sites hosted on Apache have different dependencies than Web sites hosted on IIS. For example, some PHP applications running on Apache use MySQL to connect to databases, whereas IIS Web sites use Microsoft ActiveX® Data Objects (ADO) or Open Database Connectivity (ODBC) to connect to databases. After you migrate an Apache Web site that uses MySQL for database connectivity, you must modify the Web site content to use ADO database connectivity.

Table 7.1 lists the Apache Web site components that you must consider before migrating the Apache Web site to IIS 6.0, along with brief descriptions of the compatibility issues, if any, that can result after migration.

Table 7.1   Apache Web Site Component Migration Compatibility Issues

Web Site Component	Description	Compatibility Issues
Static content	Static content contains no executable code. Examples of static content include HTML, .jpg, and .gif files.	Static content should migrate to IIS 6.0 without any modifications. However, IIS 6.0 MIME types might need to be configured to enable static content file types that are not well known. For more information about MIME types, see "Configuring MIME Types" later in this chapter.
Dynamic content	Dynamic content contains executable code. Examples of dynamic content include CGI and PHP files.	To run Apache dynamic content on IIS, you must do one of the following: ■ Run the executable code on an appropriate environment that is compatible with IIS 6.0. ■ Convert the executable code to an environment that is supported by IIS 6.0. For more information, see "Migrating Apache-Specific Extensions" later in this chapter.
Database connectivity	Database connectivity provides a standardized method of connecting to various database systems. MySQL is the most common database connectivity standard used in Apache Web sites.	To provide database connectivity on IIS 6.0, you must do one of the following: ■ Obtain a version of MySQL that is compatible with IIS 6.0. ■ Convert the executable code so that it uses ADO. ADO is the database connectivity standard supported by IIS 6.0. For more information, see "Migrating Apache-Specific Extensions" later in this chapter.
External modules	External modules provide extended features to Apache Web sites. These components include Cold Fusion and Wpoison.	To use the features provided by these external modules, you must do one of the following: ■ Obtain a version of the external module that is compatible with IIS 6.0. ■ Convert the external module to IIS 6.0. For example, Wpoison is written in CGI and can be converted to run on IIS 6.0. For more information, see "Migrating Apache-Specific Extensions" later in this chapter.

Determining Web Site Compatibility with Worker Process Isolation Mode

IIS 6.0 can run in one of two distinct modes of operation, which are called application isolation modes. *Application isolation* is the separation of applications by process boundaries that prevent the applications from affecting one another, and is configured differently for each of the two IIS isolation modes: IIS 5.0 isolation mode and worker process isolation mode.

Worker process isolation mode takes advantage of the redesigned architecture for IIS 6.0. This isolation mode runs all application code in an isolated environment; however, unlike earlier versions of IIS, IIS 6.0 provides isolation without a performance penalty because there are no added process hops. Worker process isolation mode is compatible with most existing Web sites and applications. Whenever possible, run IIS 6.0 in worker process isolation mode to take advantage of the enhanced performance and security in IIS 6.0. When IIS 6.0 is configured to use worker process isolation mode, the metabase property **Iis5IsolationModeEnabled** contains a value of **False**.

IIS 5.0 isolation mode provides compatibility for applications that depend upon the process behavior and memory model of IIS 5.0. Run IIS in this mode only when a Web site or application has compatibility issues when running in worker process isolation mode and you cannot resolve the problem. When IIS 6.0 is configured to use IIS 5.0 isolation mode, the metabase property **Iis5IsolationModeEnabled** contains a value of **True**.

 Important

IIS 6.0 cannot run both application isolation modes simultaneously on the same server. Therefore, on a single server running IIS 6.0, you cannot run some Web applications in worker process isolation mode and others in IIS 5.0 isolation mode. If you have applications that require separate modes, you must run them on separate servers.

After you install the target server, IIS is configured to use worker process isolation mode by default. *The only reason for configuring IIS to use IIS 5.0 isolation mode is if there are Apache extensions that run only in IIS 5.0 isolation mode.* For example, if the preprocessor for the dynamic content in an Apache Web site is incompatible with worker process isolation mode, you must configure IIS to use IIS 5.0 isolation mode. Determine Web site compatibility, in particular Apache-specific extensions to the Web sites, with IIS in your lab before migrating your existing Apache Web sites. In most cases, IIS hosts the Web sites in worker process isolation mode without any problems.

For more information about how to migrate Apache-specific extensions and how to determine compatibility of these extensions with worker process isolation mode, see "Migrating Apache Specific Extensions" later in this chapter.

 Note

Identifying a complete list of potential incompatibilities that Web sites can experience with worker process isolation mode is beyond the scope of this book. Even after following the guidelines in this chapter, you need to verify in your lab whether your Web sites are compatible with worker process isolation mode.

Identifying the Role of the Migration Tool

Before you migrate Apache Web sites to IIS 6.0, you must know which steps of the migration process are automated by the Apache to IIS 6.0 Migration Tool and which steps you must complete manually. This will allow you to have the appropriate tools and resources available when you are ready to start the migration. In addition, you need to determine the configuration and placement of your Web site after running the tool. The automation provided by the Apache to IIS 6.0 Migration Tool is the same for static and dynamic content. However, depending on the content in your Apache Web site, further configuration might be required after running the tool.

The following steps in the Apache Web site migration process are automated by the Apache to IIS 6.0 Migration Tool:

Copying of Web site content.   The migration tool creates a copy of the files and folders containing Web site content. The copied files are converted from standard UNIX text file format (end-of-line denoted by carriage return) on the server running Apache to standard Windows text file format (end-of-line denoted by carriage return and line feed characters) on the server running IIS. The Web site content is placed on the server running IIS in a location selected while running the tool.

Translation of Web site configuration.   The configuration of the Apache Web server and individual Web sites is translated to the corresponding IIS Web server and Web site configuration settings in the IIS metabase.

Migration of ~user directories.   ~user directories are private virtual Web directories that contain individual user Web sites. The tool migrates the contents of these directories, creates corresponding users, and converts permissions found in these virtual Web directories.

Translation of .htaccess permissions.   The htaccess file sets permissions for access for the virtual Web directories on an Apache Web server. The permissions in this file are translated by the tool into the corresponding directory permissions in the NTFS file system.

Migration of MIME types and port numbers.   MIME types define the types of *static* files that are served by the Web server. The tool automatically determines the MIME types defined on the Web server running Apache and then creates the associations of MIME types to extensions on the Web server running IIS.

Migration of FrontPage Server Extensions.   The tool detects the presence of FrontPage 2000 Server Extensions and FrontPage 2002 Server Extensions on the Apache Web server, enumerates the Web sites and subweb sites, enumerates the FrontPage Server Extensions settings, users, and roles, creates the Web sites and subweb sites, and recalculates the links for each Web site and subweb site.

Creation of status file.   The tool creates a file that contains the status of the migration steps completed by the tool. The status file can be used for confirming that the migration completed successfully or for troubleshooting any problems encountered while performing the migration with the tool.

The following steps in the Apache Web site migration process need to be completed after running the Apache to IIS 6.0 Migration Tool:

Convert code within dynamic content.   Dynamic content, such as PHP or CGI, on Apache needs to be modified to run on IIS 6.0.

Modify database connectivity within dynamic content.   For the Web sites and applications that have database connectivity, the content needs to be modified to use database connectivity provided by IIS 6.0 and Windows Server 2003.

Migrate external modules used by Web sites.   After migration, you need to migrate external modules that are used by the Web sites and applications.

Add Web service extensions used by the Web sites.   Any dynamic content types that are not automatically migrated by the tool must be added as Web service extensions. These new Web service extensions might be necessary for any modifications or conversions of dynamic code.

Configure advanced Web site properties.   After tool completes its migration tasks, the Web sites are configured comparably to how they were on Apache. You might want to configure the Web site to take advantages of the advanced security and availability features in IIS 6.0.

Obtain server certificates for SSL.   For each Web site on the Apache Web server that uses SSL, you must either renew the existing server certificates in a format that is compatible with IIS 6.0 or you must request new server certificates in a format that is compatible with IIS 6.0. This is because the server certificates on the Apache Web server are in a format that is incompatible with IIS. Once you have the server certificates, you must import the certificates into IIS and configure your Web sites to use the appropriate certificates.

Selecting a Migration Tool Installation Option

The Apache to IIS 6.0 Migration Tool supports four options you can choose from when determining how you want to migrate Apache Web sites to IIS. Your familiarity with the Linux or Windows operating systems and the access that you have to the Web servers involved in the migration will determine the process you should follow to install and then run the tool. In some cases, you might not have unrestricted access to the Web servers because another group manages the Apache servers or the Web servers are behind firewalls that prevent FTP traffic.

To install and run the Apache to IIS 6.0 Migration Tool for any of the installation options, you must be able to:

- Log on to the source server with an account that has root-level or super-user access.
- Log on to the target server with an account that is a member of the local Administrators group.

In addition, when you select the intermediate computer installation option, you must be able to:

- Log on to the intermediate computer running Linux with an account that has root-level or super-user access.
- Log on to the intermediate computer running Windows with an account that is a member of the local Administrators group.

Table 7.2 lists and describes the installation options for the Apache to IIS 6.0 Migration Tool. Read this table to select the installation option that best fits your needs.

Table 7.2   Apache to IIS 6.0 Migration Tool Installation Options

Installation Option	Installation Details
The source server (See Figure 7.3)	■ Install and run the Apache to IIS 6.0 Migration Tool on your Linux-based source server (you do not need to physically access the Windows-based target server). ■ Install Perl on both the Linux-based source server and the Windows-based target server. ■ Enable the FTP service on the Windows-based target server only.
The target server (See Figure 7.4)	■ Install and run the migration Apache to IIS 6.0 Migration Tool on the Windows-based target server (you do not need to physically access the Linux-based source server). ■ Install Perl on the Windows-based target server only. ■ Enable the FTP service on the Linux-based source server only.
An intermediate computer running Microsoft Windows 2000 or later (See Figure 7.5)	■ Install and run the Apache to IIS 6.0 Migration Tool on a Windows-based intermediate computer (you do not need to physically access either the Linux-based source server or the Windows-based target server). ■ Install Perl on both the Windows-based intermediate computer and the Windows-based target server. ■ Enable the FTP service on both the Windows-based target server and the Linux-based source server.
An intermediate computer running a supported version of Linux (See Figure 7.5)	■ Install and run the Apache to IIS 6.0 Migration Tool on a Linux-based intermediate computer (you do not need to physically access either the Linux-based source server or the Windows-based target server). ■ Install Perl on both the Linux-based intermediate computer and the Windows-based target server. ■ Enable the FTP service on both the Windows-based target server and the Linux-based source server.

The Apache to IIS 6.0 Migration Tool must be installed on the source server, target server, or intermediate computer. The high-level process for installing the tool includes the following:

1. Copying the compressed distribution files (.tar for Linux or .zip for Windows) to the appropriate computer based on the installation option selected.

2. Expanding the compressed distribution files.

3. Installing the Perl interpreter, if it is not already installed.

For more detailed information about the installation option that you have selected for the Apache to IIS 6.0 Migration Tool, see "Installing the Migration Tool" later in this chapter.

Source Server Installation Option

When you select the source server installation option, you install and run the Apache to IIS 6.0 Migration Tool on the source server, which runs Apache. In addition, you must install and configure the FTP service on the target server.

Figure 7.3 illustrates the migration process for the source server installation option.

Figure 7.3   Migrating from Apache to IIS 6.0 with the Source Server Installation Option

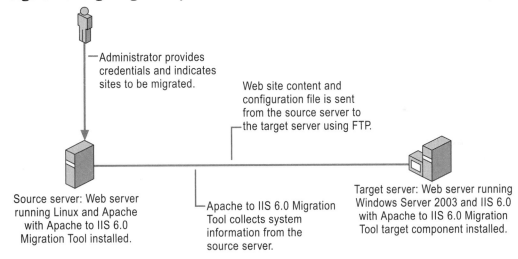

The process for migrating Apache Web sites when you select the source server installation option is as follows:

1. The Apache to IIS 6.0 Migration Tool prompts you for the appropriate user credentials for the source server and target servers.

2. The tool then transfers the Apache-based Web site content and the configuration information from the source server to the target server by way of FTP.

3. The tool applies the Web site configuration settings to the IIS Web sites on the target server.

Target Server Installation Option

When you select the target server installation option, you install and run the Apache to IIS 6.0 Migration Tool on the target server, which runs Windows Server 2003 and IIS 6.0. In addition, you must install and configure the FTP service on the source server.

Figure 7.4 illustrates the migration process for the target server installation option .

Figure 7.4   Migrating from Apache to IIS 6.0 with the Target Server Installation Option

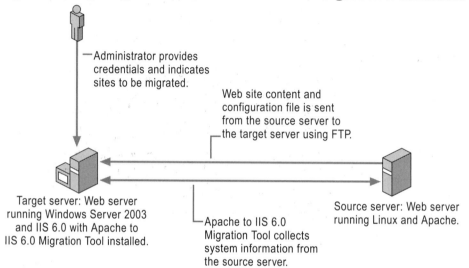

The process for migrating Apache Web sites when you select the target server installation option is as follows:

1.   The Apache to IIS 6.0 Migration Tool prompts you for the appropriate user credentials for the source and target servers.

2.   The tool then transfers the Apache-based Web site content and the configuration information from the source server to the target server by way of FTP.

3.   The tool applies the Web site configuration settings to the IIS 6.0 Web sites on the target server.

Intermediate Computer Installation Option

When you select the intermediate computer installation option, you install and run the Apache to IIS 6.0 Migration Tool on the intermediate computer, which runs either Windows or Linux. In addition, you must install and configure the FTP service on the source and target servers.

Figure 7.5 illustrates the migration process for the intermediate computer installation option.

Figure 7.5   Migrating from Apache to IIS 6.0 with the Intermediate Computer Installation Option

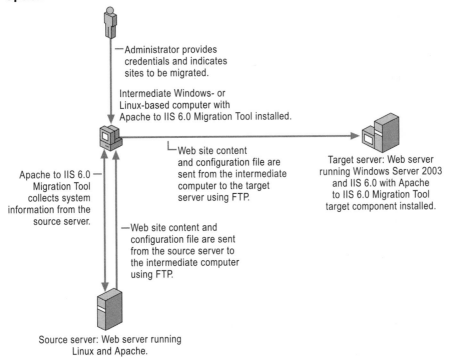

Administrator provides credentials and indicates sites to be migrated.

Intermediate Windows- or Linux-based computer with Apache to IIS 6.0 Migration Tool installed.

Web site content and configuration file are sent from the intermediate computer to the target server using FTP.

Target server: Web server running Windows Server 2003 and IIS 6.0 with Apache to IIS 6.0 Migration Tool target component installed.

Apache to IIS 6.0 Migration Tool collects system information from the source server.

Web site content and configuration file are sent from the source server to the intermediate computer using FTP.

Source server: Web server running Linux and Apache.

The process for migrating Apache Web sites when you select the intermediate computer installation option is as follows:

1. The Apache to IIS 6.0 Migration Tool prompts you for the appropriate user credentials for the source and target servers.

2. The tool transfers the Apache-based Web site content and the configuration information from the source server to the intermediate computer by way of FTP.

3. The tool applies the site configuration settings to the IIS Web sites on the target server.

Deploying the Target Server

The Web server running IIS 6.0 must be installed and configured before you can migrate the Apache Web sites. In addition to installing Windows Server 2003, you must install and configure IIS 6.0 and, based on the installation option you selected, install and configure the FTP service on the target server. The tool uses FTP to transfer Web site content between the source and target servers.

Figure 7.6   Deploying the Target Server

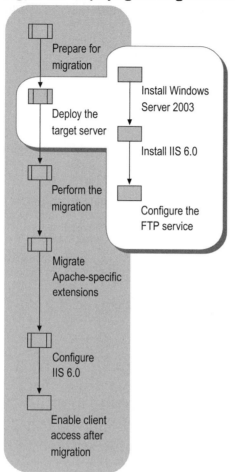

If the target server is already installed and configured, you can proceed to "Performing the Migration" later in this chapter.

Installing Windows Server 2003

The primary concern when installing Windows Server 2003 is to ensure that the security of the target server is maintained. When you install Windows Server 2003 as a dedicated Web server, the default components and services are configured to provide the lowest possible attack surface. You can further reduce the attack surface of the target server by enabling only the essential Windows Server 2003 components and services.

The migration process presented here assumes that you install Windows Server 2003 with the default options. If you use other methods for installing and configuring Windows Server 2003, such as unattended setup, the default configuration settings might be different.

 Note

When you complete the installation of Windows Server 2003, Manage Your Server automatically starts. The migration process assumes that you close Manage Your Server, and then further configure the Web server in **Add or Remove Programs** in Control Panel.

For more information about the essential components and services to enable in Windows Server 2003, see "Enabling Only Essential Windows Server 2003 Components and Services" in "Securing Web Sites and Applications" in this book.

Installing IIS 6.0

Because IIS 6.0 is not installed during the default installation of Windows Server 2003, the next step in deploying the target server is to install and configure IIS 6.0. The migration process presented here assumes that you install IIS 6.0 with the default options in **Add or Remove Programs** in Control Panel. If you use other methods for installing and configuring Windows Server 2003, such as Manage Your Server, the default configuration settings might be different.

Install and configure IIS 6.0 by completing the following steps:

1. Install IIS 6.0 with only the essential components and services.

    As with installing Windows Server 2003, the primary concern when installing and configuring IIS 6.0 is to ensure that the security of the target server is maintained. Enabling unnecessary components and services increases the attack surface of the target server. You can help ensure the target server is secure by enabling only the necessary components and services in IIS 6.0.

    For more information about how to install IIS 6.0, see "Install IIS 6.0" in "IIS Deployment Procedures" in this book. For more information about the necessary IIS 6.0 components and services, see "Enabling Only Essential IIS Components and Services" in "Securing Web Sites and Applications" in this book.

2. In addition to the necessary components and services recommendations in step 1, enable the File Transfer Protocol (FTP) Service.

    The FTP service migrates content to the target server when you install and run the Apache to IIS 6.0 Migration Tool on the source server or on an intermediate computer.

    For more information about how to enable the FTP service, see "Configure IIS Components and Services" in "IIS Deployment Procedures" in this book.

3. If the source server has Web sites that are FrontPage extended, enable FrontPage 2002 Server Extensions on the target server.

   For more information about how to enable FrontPage Server Extensions, see "Configure a Web Site to be FrontPage Extended" in "IIS Deployment Procedures" in this book.

Configuring the FTP Service

The Apache to IIS 6.0 Migration Tool requires the FTP service to migrate Apache Web sites to the target server. The installation option you previously selected will determine on which computers you need to enable the FTP service. Table 7.3 lists the FTP service requirements for each installation option.

Table 7.3   Methods for Installing and Configuring the FTP Service

If You Install and Run the Migration Tool On	Install and Configure FTP Service On
The source server	The target server
The target server.	The source server
An intermediate computer	Both the target and source server

Configure the FTP service on the target server   After you install the FTP service on the target server, no additional configuration is required. The Apache to IIS 6.0 Migration Tool works with the FTP service in the default configuration. Later in the deployment process, the tool creates a default FTP site to be used for Web site migration.

Configure the FTP service on the source server   Configuring the FTP service on the source server requires installing and configuring the FTP package from the Linux distribution disc. After the FTP service is installed, you must configure it to allow access to the Web sites.

For more information about how to install and configure the FTP service on the source computer, see the FTP documentation that accompanies the version of Linux that is installed on the source server.

Performing the Migration

In the next step of the migration process, the Apache to IIS 6.0 Migration Tool copies the Web site content from the source server to the target server. Then, the tool transfers the Apache Web site settings to the corresponding IIS 6.0 metabase properties.

Figure 7.7   Performing the Migration from Apache to IIS 6.0

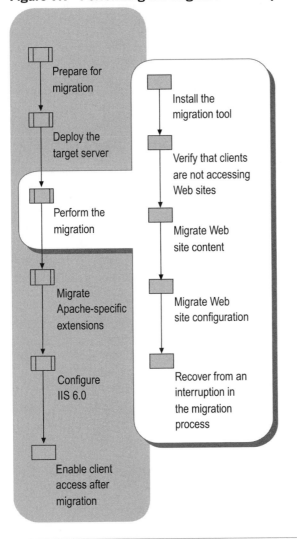

Installing the Migration Tool

Now you are ready to install the Apache to IIS 6.0 Migration Tool based on the method you selected earlier in the "Selecting a Migration Tool Installation Option" section of this chapter. You can install the tool on one of the following:

- Source server, which is running Linux

- Target server, which is running Windows Server 2003

- Intermediate computer, which can be running either Linux or Windows

The installation process is dependent on the operating system. So, for example, you can use the same procedure for installing the Apache to IIS 6.0 Migration Tool on the source server or for an intermediate computer running Linux.

Install the Apache to IIS 6.0 Migration Tool by completing the following steps:

1. Install the tool on a computer running Linux. Or, install the tool on a computer running Windows.

2. Configure the target server for migration.

Installing the Migration Tool on Computers Running Linux

The Apache to IIS 6.0 Migration Tool installation process on the source server and on an intermediate computer running Linux is identical. The versions of Linux supported by the tool are listed in "Overview of Migrating Apache Web Sites" earlier in this chapter.

Install the Apache to IIS 6.0 Migration Tool on the computer running Linux by completing the following steps:

1. Install the *Windows Server 2003 Deployment Kit* companion CD or the *Internet Information Services (IIS) 6.0 Resource Ki*t companion CD on a computer other than the target server.

2. Install Perl on the computer running Linux.

    Because the Apache to IIS 6.0 Migration Tool is written in Perl, you must install a Perl interpreter before you can run the tool. Install Perl on the computer running Linux and verify that the Perl interpreter is configured properly before installing the tool. To obtain a free copy of Perl, see the ActivePerl link on the Web Resources page at http://www.microsoft.com/windows/reskits/webresources.

3. Create a folder to contain the Apache to IIS 6.0 Migration Tool on the computer running Linux.

4. Change to the folder created in Step 3 so that the folder is the current working folder.

5. Copy **AIISMT_linux.tar.gz** from the *systemroot*\Program Files\AIISMT folder on the computer in Step 1 to the folder created in Step 3.

6. At a Linux command line type **tar -zxvf AIISMT_linux.tar.gz.**

    The compressed files are extracted to the folder created in step 3.

Installing the Migration Tool on Computers Running Windows

The Apache to IIS 6.0 Migration Tool installation process on the target server and on an intermediate computer running Windows is identical. The target server must be running Windows Server 2003. The intermediate computer can be running Microsoft Windows 2000 Professional, Microsoft Windows 2000 Server, Windows 2000 Advanced Server, or Microsoft Windows Server 2003.

Install the Apache to IIS 6.0 Migration Tool on the computer running Windows by completing the following steps:

1. Install the *Windows Server 2003 Deployment Kit* companion CD or the *Internet Information Services (IIS) 6.0 Resource Ki*t companion CD on a computer other than the target server.

2. Install Perl on the computer running Windows.

   Because the Apache to IIS 6.0 Migration Tool is written in Perl, you must install a Perl interpreter before you can run the tool. Install Perl on the computer running Windows and verify that the Perl interpreter is configured properly before installing the tool. To obtain a free copy of Perl, see the ActivePerl link on the Web Resources page at http://www.microsoft.com/windows/reskits/webresources.

3. Copy the **AIISMT_windows.exe** from the *systemroot*\Program Files\AIISMT folder on the computer in step 1 to the desktop of the target server.

4. Double-click **AIISMT_windows.exe**.

   The **WinZip Self-Extractor** dialog box appears.

5. In the **Unzip to folder** box, type the path of the folder where you want to extract the tool or click **Browse** to browse to the folder.

6. Click **Unzip**.

   The WinZip Self-Extractor extracts the Apache to IIS 6.0 Migration Tool into the folder selected in step 5.

Configuring the Target Server for Migration

You must configure the target server before you can perform the migration process. The configuration process creates virtual directories in the FTP root mapped to the physical drives of the server.

Configure the target server for migration by completing the following steps:

1. At the command line, type **cd *installation_path*, where *installation_path* is the fully qualified path where you installed the Apache to IIS 6.0 Migration Tool, and then press ENTER.

   This changes the default folder to the folder where you installed the tool. For more information about how the Apache to IIS 6.0 Migration Tool was installed, see "Installing the Migration Tool on Computers Running Windows" earlier in this chapter.

2. At the command line, type **aiismt_setup**, and then press ENTER.

3. When prompted to create a virtual directory, type **y** to create a virtual directory on the disk volume you want to use for migration.

    You must select at least one disk volume and create a virtual directory.

 Important
You cannot create a virtual directory on a drive formatted with the FAT file system because access rights to directories on that drive cannot be set.

The aiismt_setup program creates the virtual directories in the FTP site root and configures FTP to listen on TCP port 21.

Verifying that Clients Are Not Accessing Web Sites

The Apache to IIS 6.0 Migration Tool requires only read access to the Web site content and configuration settings on the source server; therefore, the source server can remain online in your production environment. However, you might need to remove the source server from your production network and move it to a private network segment that has direct network connectivity to the target server when:

-   The amount of files and configuration information being copied across the network can generate a high volume of traffic and slow the production network.

-   Firewalls that reside between the source and target servers prevent the migration tool from performing the migration. This is most commonly caused because the migration tool uses FTP for communicating with the source and target servers, and the FTP protocol is blocked by the firewalls.

-   Security-related configuration settings on the source server need to be changed to allow the migration tool to work. This can include enabling FTP on production Web servers that are directly connected to the Internet.

Migrating Web Site Content

The migration of your Apache Web site involves migrating both the Web site content and its configuration. Based on the installation option you selected, the Apache to IIS 6.0 Migration Tool prompts you for the information required to perform the migration of the Web site content.

To run the tool, do one of the following, depending on the operating system on the computer:

On Linux-based computers   From the Linux shell, change the current folder to the folder where you installed the tool, and then type **perl aiismt_main.pl**.

On Windows-based computers: At the command line, change the current folder to the folder where you installed the tool, and then type **aiismt**.

After the Apache to IIS 6.0 Migration Tool starts, it prompts you for information. Table 7.4 lists the information that the migration tool requires to migrate the Web site content.

Table 7.4 Information Required by Migration Tool During Web Site Content Migration

Information Required	Do the Following
Session name	Type a: ■ **Unique session name** to indicate that the tool should begin a new migration process. ■ **Previous session name** if you want to resume a previous migration. Supplying a previous session name causes the tool to run in recovery mode.
Source server IP address	If you run the tool on the: ■ **Target server or on an intermediate computer**, type the IP address of the source server. ■ **Source server**, press ENTER to see the default IP address displayed. If the tool cannot detect the source server's IP address, it will prompt you to confirm that the source server is running on a supported operating system.
Root user password	If you run the Apache to IIS 6.0 Migration Tool on the: ■ **Target server or on an intermediate computer**, type the root user password to gain access to the Linux-based source server's system files and FTP service. ■ **Source server**, you do not need to type the root user password.
Target server IP address	If you run the Apache to IIS 6.0 Migration Tool on the: ■ **Source server or on an intermediate computer**, type the IP address of the source server. ■ **Target server**, type the IP address of the target server or press ENTER to use the default (LocalHost) IP address.
User name and password for the target server	If you run the Apache to IIS 6.0 Migration Tool on the: ■ **Source server or on an intermediate computer**, type a user name that is a member of the local Administrator's group on the target server, and the associated password. ■ **Target server**, you do not need to type a user name and password.
Configuration file path	Type the complete path to the *httpd.conf* file, which is a file that contains configuration and settings for Apache on the source server. You can also press ENTER to see the default path (/Etc/Httpd/Conf/Httpd.conf).

(continued)

Table 7.4   Information Required by Migration Tool During Web Site Content Migration *(continued)*

Information Required	Do the Following
Web site directory on target server	Type the path of the directory on the target server where you want the Web site content to be migrated. You must supply a path for each Web site migrated.
	When a Web site has SSL certificates associated with it, the Apache to IIS 6.0 Migration Tool prompts you to indicate whether you want the certificates to be migrated as well.
Listening IP address and port number	When you want to change the listening IP address and port number, type the new values. The new IP address and port numbers are applied to all the sites you selected for migration.
Web site IP address	When you want to change the IP address at the site level, type the new IP address, or type "" to use all unassigned IP addresses.

 Note

If you run the Apache to IIS 6.0 Migration Tool on the source server, the target server credentials are authenticated. If you run the tool on the target server, the source server credentials are authenticated.

For more information about how to migrate Web sites using the Apache to IIS 6.0 Migration Tool, see the "Apache to IIS 6.0 Migration Tool User Guide" on the *Windows Server 2003 Deployment Kit* companion CD or the *Internet Information Services (IIS) 6.0 Resource Kit* companion CD.

If the migration tool is interrupted or fails at any point during the process, you can run it in recovery mode. For more information about the recovery process, see "Recovering from an Interruption in the Migration Process" later in this chapter.

Migrating Web Site Configuration

After migrating the Web site content, you must migrate the Web site configuration. Before you continue in the migration process, check the Apache to IIS 6.0 Migration Tool status file, Aiismt_Status.html in the session directory, to ensure the migration has completed successfully up to this point.

To start Web site configuration migration on the target server, at the command line, change the current folder to the folder where you installed the Apache to IIS 6.0 Migration Tool, and then type **aiismt**.

During the migration of the Web site configuration the tool, prompts you to supply the session name. The files with the configuration settings are located in a folder under the FTP root. The folder uses the name of the current migration session, which you specified when you migrated the Web site content in "Migrating Web Site Content" earlier in this chapter.

During the Web site configuration process on the target server, the Apache to IIS 6.0 Migration Tool does the following:

- Migrates Apache Web site directives and maps them to corresponding IIS configuration settings, including security settings.

- Migrates the FrontPage Server Extensions settings, users, and roles if any of the Apache Web sites are FrontPage extended.

- Sets the security settings on the sites by assigning user rights to the directories that contain site-related content.

- Verifies that settings have been correctly applied to the Web sites on the target server when the Web site configuration migration is complete.

Recovering from an Interruption in the Migration Process

If you received no error messages while migrating the Web site content and configuration, you can proceed to one of the following sections in this chapter:

- "Migrating Apache-Specific Extensions" if any of your Web sites contain dynamic content.

- "Configuring IIS 6.0 After Migration" if all of your Web sites contain static content.

If you received an error message while running the Apache to IIS 6.0 Migration Tool, do the following:

1. Determine the cause of the error and resolve the problem.

2. Restart the Apache to IIS 6.0 Migration Tool in recovery mode.

In addition to resolving migration errors, you can use the tool in recovery mode to:

- Perform another migration if the majority of the settings are the same.

  For example, you might run the tool to migrate a specific Web site on a Web server that hosts multiple Web sites. You can migrate subsequent Web sites by running the tool in recovery mode and change only the name of the Web site to be migrated. The remainder of the settings remains unchanged.

- Perform the actual migration of Web site content and configuration after a trial migration.

  You can perform a *trial migration* of the Web site and content by supplying all information except the Web sites to migrate. You can use this method to validate the majority of the migration settings. You can subsequently run the tool in recovery mode.

- Provide a scripted environment for automating the Apache to IIS 6.0 Migration Tool migration process.

  The tool creates an answer file that is used by the recovery process, which you can edit to automate the tool. The answer file has the naming convention of AIISMT_*session name*_Recovery.txt, where *session_name* is the session name for the migration.

Determining Cause of and Resolving Errors

The Apache to IIS 6.0 Migration Tool automatically creates a status file for each migration session in the session folder, located in the FTP root on the target server. The name of the session folder is identical to the migration tool session name. The status file, Aiismt_Status.html, contains information about every phase of the migration process.

If an interruption occurs while the tool is running:

1. Refer to the status file to determine the cause of the failure.

2. Resolve any errors before proceeding with the upgrade process.

Restarting the Migration Tool in Recovery Mode

If the Apache to IIS 6.0 Migration Tool is interrupted or fails at any point during the process, you can run it again in recovery mode. Recovery mode allows you to pick up the migration process from the point at which the tool was interrupted, rather than starting over from the beginning. Any of the following events can cause a failure or interruption in the migration tool:

- System failure.

- Network connection terminated.

- FTP access denied.

You can restart the migration tool in recovery mode when:

- An interruption occurs during data entry.

  If the tool terminates as you are entering information about the migration (such as IP addresses or file paths) you can restart it in recovery mode. The migration tool validates your user credentials, and the migration process proceeds from the point where the tool was interrupted. You do not need to retype the information you have already entered.

- An interruption occurs during file transfer.

  If the migration tool terminates during the process of transferring files from the source server to the target server, you can restart it in recovery mode. The tool resumes migration with the file that was being transferred during the interruption.

Migrating Apache-Specific Extensions

If the Apache Web site contains dynamic content, requires database connectivity, or includes external modules, you must separately migrate these Apache-specific extensions to complete the migration process.

Figure 7.8 illustrates the process for migrating Apache-specific extensions to IIS 6.0.

Figure 7.8   Migrating Apache-Specific Extensions to IIS 6.0

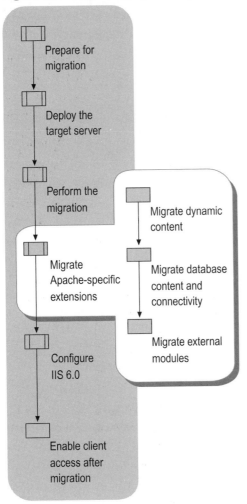

The Apache-specific extensions on Linux commonly include MySQL and PHP. The combination of Linux, Apache, MySQL, and PHP are often referred to as LAMP. LAMP is the application platform used for Linux systems. The migration of the Apache Web sites must include the migration of LAMP.

For more information about migrating Apache Web sites to IIS, see the Migration of Linux-Apache-MySQL-PHP Platform to Windows 2000 link on the Web Resources page at http://www.microsoft.com/windows/reskits/webresources. Although the white paper refers to IIS 5.0 and Windows 2000 Server, the processes and methods are applicable for IIS 6.0 and Windows Server 2003.

 Important

Test the migration of Apache-specific extensions in your lab environment before starting the Web site migration.

The Apache-specific extensions that you might need to migrate include:

- Dynamic content.

- Database content and connectivity.

- External modules.

Migrating Dynamic Content

The Apache to IIS 6.0 Migration Tool transfers the files that make up the dynamic content to the target server during the Web site content migration. However, the dynamic content typically cannot run on IIS and requires further steps. Table 7.5 describes the advantages and disadvantages of the methods for migrating dynamic content.

Table 7.5   Comparison of Methods for Migrating Dynamic Content

Migration Method	Advantages	Disadvantages
Run dynamic content on a preprocessor that ships with IIS and Windows Server 2003.	■ Requires minimal migration effort, depending on the extent of changes to the dynamic content. ■ Requires no purchase of additional preprocessor.	■ Might not run as efficiently as dynamic content written in ASP or ASP.NET.
Run dynamic content on a preprocessor external to IIS and Windows Sever 2003.	■ Requires minimal migration effort, depending on the extent of changes to the dynamic content.	■ Might not run as efficiently as dynamic content written in ASP or ASP.NET. ■ Requires purchase of an additional preprocessor.
Rewrite the dynamic content in ASP or ASP.NET.	■ Runs the dynamic content more efficiently than the other methods. ■ Requires no purchase of additional preprocessor.	■ Requires the most migration effort because the dynamic content must be completely rewritten.

Important

When you run dynamic content written in preprocessors, you need to enable the *Web service extensions* (request handlers, such as Perl and CGI, that extend IIS functionality beyond serving static pages) for the preprocessor. For more information, see "Configuring Web Service Extensions" later in this chapter.

Run Dynamic Content on a Preprocessor that Ships with IIS

When you select this method for migrating the dynamic content, you must have the source code to the dynamic content and you must use a preprocessor that ships with IIS 6.0 and Windows Server 2003, such as CGI or Perl. You might have to adjust the code to accommodate any differences between preprocessors on Apache and IIS and between Linux and Windows.

Ensure that the version of the preprocessor supported on IIS 6.0 and Windows Server 2003 is compatible with the version of the code in the dynamic content. You most likely need to make modifications to the code in the dynamic content to compensate for version and platform differences. For example, CGI scripts migrated from Apache Web sites typically require modification to run on IIS 6.0 and Windows Server 2003.

Run Dynamic Content on a Preprocessor External to IIS

This method for migrating the external module assumes that you have the source code to the dynamic content and you can purchase or obtain a version of the preprocessor that runs with IIS, such as PHP. You might have to adjust the code to accommodate any differences between preprocessors on Apache and IIS 6.0.

For example, if the dynamic content is written in PHP, you must obtain a version of a PHP preprocessor for IIS to install and configure the PHP preprocessor on IIS 6.0. You must then adjust the PHP code to accommodate any differences between the PHP preprocessors on Apache and IIS 6.0.

Rewrite the Dynamic Content in ASP or ASP.NET

When you select this method for migrating the dynamic content, you need to evaluate the function of the original dynamic content, draft a functional specification for the dynamic content, and then develop a version of the dynamic content in ASP or ASP.NET.

For more information about selecting either ASP or ASP.NET, see the Active Server Pages and ASP.NET links on the Web Resources page at http://www.microsoft.com/windows/reskits/webresources.

Migrating Database Content and Connectivity

Database connectivity provides a standardized method of connecting to various database systems. Although the Apache to IIS 6.0 Migration Tool migrated the Web site content and configuration, any database content and database connectivity must be migrated separately. Many Apache Web sites and applications use a database server, such as MySQL, the most common database connectivity standard used in Apache Web sites. Dynamic and static content can make requests to databases through MySQL.

For more information about how to migrate database content and connectivity to IIS, see the Migration of Linux-Apache-MySQL-PHP Platform to Windows 2000 link on the Web Resources page at http://www.microsoft.com/windows/reskits/webresources. Although the white paper refers to IIS 5.0 and Windows 2000 Server, the processes and methods are applicable for IIS 6.0 and Windows Server 2003.

Migrating the Database Content

The Apache to IIS 6.0 Migration Tool does not transfer the database content to the target computer. You must migrate the database content by other methods, whose advantages and disadvantages are described in Table 7.6.

Table 7.6   Comparison of Methods for Migrating Database Content

Migration Method	Advantages	Disadvantages
Obtain a copy of the database that is compatible with IIS 6.0 and Windows Server 2003.	▪ Requires minimal migration effort. ▪ Administrators are familiar with administering the database engine.	▪ Might not run as efficiently as Microsoft Data Engine (MSDE) or Microsoft SQL Server™ 2003. ▪ Requires purchase of an additional preprocessor.
Convert the database to MSDE or SQL Server 2000.	▪ Might run more efficiently than the original database engine on IIS 6.0 and Windows Server 2003. ▪ Requires no purchase of additional database when using MSDE.	▪ Requires more extensive conversion. ▪ Administrators might not be familiar with administering MSDE or SQL Server 2000.

Obtain a Copy of the Database Engine that is Compatible with IIS   Most database engines on Linux have compatible versions that are designed for Windows. The easiest method of converting the database is to run the same database engine because little or no modification to the dynamic content is required. For more information, see the Web site or product documentation for the database engine used by the source server to determine if there is a version for Windows.

Convert the Database to MSDE or SQL Server 2000   Microsoft SQL Server supports the importing of data stored in other databases into SQL Server 2000. For example, you can import MySQL data directly into SQL Server 2000. You can use ODBC connectivity between MySQL and MSDE or SQL Server 2000 to import data as well. Client applications, such as Microsoft Access XP, can be used to import data through ODBC to MSDE or SQL Server 2000.

For more information about importing data into SQL Server 2000, see the SQL Server link on the Web Resources page at http://www.microsoft.com/windows/reskits/webresources. You can use the same methods for migrating data into MSDE as SQL Server 2000 because MSDE is based on SQL Server 2000.

Migrating the Database Connectivity

You need to ensure the dynamic content migrated to the target computer by the Apache to IIS 6.0 Migration Tool can use a database connectivity supported on IIS 6.0 and Windows Server 2003. Table 7.7 describes the advantages and disadvantages of the methods for migrating database connectivity.

Table 7.7 Comparison of Methods for Migrating Database Connectivity

Migration Method	Advantages	Disadvantages
Obtain a version of the database that runs on IIS 6.0 and Windows Server 2003.	▪ Requires minimal migration effort.	▪ Requires purchase of the database that is compatible with IIS 6.0 and Windows Server 2003.
Convert the dynamic content to use ADO or ODBC.	▪ Requires no purchase of additional database.	▪ Requires more extensive conversion.

Obtain a Version of the Database Connectivity that Runs on IIS 6.0

The database connectivity for dynamic content is implemented on Apache as libraries that are called by the dynamic content. When you install a version of the database connectivity on IIS 6.0 and Windows Server 2003, the appropriate libraries are also installed. There should be minimal changes to the dynamic content.

 Note

This method assumes that you are installing a version of the database, such as MySQL, on the target server.

Convert the Dynamic Content to use Windows Database Connectivity

When you use this method, the assumption is that you are connecting to MSDE or SQL Server 2000 as the database engine through ODBC or ADO. If you are installing a version of the database engine on IIS 6.0 and Windows Server 2003, use the database connectivity libraries that accompany the database engine to reduce the effort required in the migration.

For example, there are ODBC drivers for MySQL; however, if you install MySQL on the target server, there is little or no conversion if you continue to use the MySQL libraries. In this case, converting your dynamic content to use ODBC has no long-term advantage unless you are planning to migrate to another database engine.

For more information about selecting ODBC, see the Open Database Connectivity (ODBC) link on the Web Resources page at http://www.microsoft.com/windows/reskits/webresources. For more information about selecting ADO, see the ActiveX Data Objects link on the Web Resources page at http://www.microsoft.com/windows/reskits/webresources.

Migrating External Modules

External modules, such as Cold Fusion and Wpoison, provide extended features to Apache Web sites. The Apache to IIS 6.0 Migration Tool transfers external modules to the target computer if they are in the same directory with the other Web site content. When the external modules are stored in other directories, you must manually transfer the external modules to the target server. After the external modules are transferred to the target server, you must complete additional steps so that the external modules run on IIS and Windows Server 2003. Table 7.8 describes the advantages and disadvantages of the methods for migrating external modules.

Table 7.8   Comparison of Methods for Migrating External Modules

Migration Method	Advantages	Disadvantages
Obtain a version of the external module that runs on IIS 6.0 and Windows Server 2003.	▪ Requires minimal migration effort. ▪ Source code for the external module is not required.	▪ Might not run as efficiently as external modules written in ASP or ASP. ▪ Requires purchase of another version of the external module. ▪ Might require minor modifications to the Web site content to accommodate version differences.
Convert the external modules to run on the same preprocessor as IIS 6.0 and Windows Sever 2003.	▪ Can require minimal migration effort, depending on the extent of changes to the code for the external module.	▪ Might not run as efficiently as external modules written in ASP or ASP.NET. ▪ Might require the purchase of an additional preprocessor. ▪ Requires the source code of the external module so that the module can be converted.
Rewrite the external module in ASP or ASP.NET.	▪ Runs the dynamic content produced by the original external module more efficiently. ▪ Requires no additional purchases.	▪ Requires the most migration effort because the external module must be completely rewritten.

Obtain Version of External Module that Runs on IIS 6.0 and Windows Server 2003

When you select this method for migrating the external module, you need to purchase a version of the external module for Windows. Install and configure the external module on the target server using the documentation that accompanies the external module.

For example, if an Apache Web site uses Cold Fusion, you would purchase a version of Cold Fusion for IIS 6.0 and Windows Server 2003. After installing and configuring Cold Fusion on the target server, you might have to adjust the code, such as PHP, CGI, or Perl, that calls the external module to accommodate any difference between Cold Fusion on Apache and IIS.

Convert External Modules to Run on Same Preprocessor as IIS 6.0 and Windows Sever 2003

This method for migrating the external module assumes you have the source code to the external modules. In addition, you must have a preprocessor on IIS that supports the code in which the external module is written, such as PHP, CGI, or Perl. You might have to adjust the code to accommodate any differences between preprocessors on Apache and IIS.

Important
When you run external modules written in preprocessors, you need to enable the Web service extensions for the preprocessor. For more information, see "Configuring Web Service Extensions" later in this chapter.

Rewrite the External Module in ASP or ASP.NET

Select this method if no version of the external module exists for IIS 6.0 and Windows Server 2003 and you do not have the source code to the external module, or if you want to rewrite the external module to take advantage of the enhanced performance offered by ASP or ASP.NET. You need to evaluate the functions of the external module, draft a functional specification for the external module, and then develop a version of the external module in ASP or ASP.NET.

For more information about selecting either ASP or ASP.NET, see the Active Server Pages and ASP.NET links on the Web Resources page at http://www.microsoft.com/windows/reskits/webresources.

Important
When you write ASP or ASP.NET applications, you must enable Web service extensions for ASP or ASP.NET. For more information, see "Configuring Web Service Extensions" later in this chapter.

Configuring IIS 6.0

After migrating the Web site content, configuration, and Apache-specific extensions, you must further configure IIS to allow proper operation of the Web sites. This post-migration configuration of IIS ensures that your Web sites run as they did on Apache before they were migrated to IIS 6.0.

Figure 7.9 illustrates the process for configuring IIS 6.0 after completing the migration of the Web sites from Apache.

Figure 7.9   Configuring IIS 6.0 After Migration

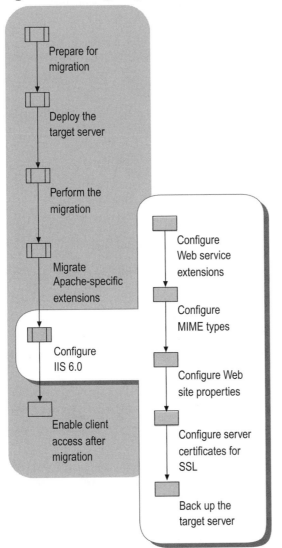

Configuring Web Service Extensions

Many Web sites and applications that you migrate have extended functionality beyond static pages, including the ability to generate dynamic content. Any request handlers, such as Perl and CGI, that extend IIS functionality beyond serving static pages are known as *Web service extensions*. Web service extensions allow you to enable and disable the serving of dynamic content and easily determine the content types on the Web server that can initiate code.

If you installed IIS 6.0 as described in "Installing and Configuring IIS 6.0" earlier in this chapter, all Web service extensions are disabled by default. If you used another method, such as using Manage Your Server, the configuration of IIS might be different.

Enabling all Web service extensions ensures the highest possible compatibility with your Web sites. However, enabling all Web service extensions creates a security risk because it increases the attack surface of IIS by enabling functionality that might be unnecessary for your server.

Web service extensions allow you to enable and disable the serving of dynamic content. *MIME types* allow you to enable and disable the serving of static content. For more information about enabling and disabling the serving of static content, see "Configuring MIME Types" later in this chapter.

 Tip

If the appropriate Web service extension is not enabled, the Web server returns a 404 error when attempting to serve the dynamic content.

Configure the Web service extensions by completing the following steps:

1. Enable the essential predefined Web service extensions based on the information in Table 7.9.

Table 7.9   Predefined Web Service Extensions

Web Service Extension	Enable When
Active Server Pages	Enable this extension when one or more of the Web sites or applications contains ASP content.
ASP.NET version 1.1.4322	Enable this extension when one or more of the Web sites or applications contains ASP.NET content.
FrontPage Server Extensions 2002	Enable this extension when one or more of the Web sites are FrontPage extended.
Internet Data Connector	Enable this extension when one or more of the Web sites or applications uses the Internet Data Connector (IDC) to display database information (content includes .idc and .idx files).
Server-Side Includes	Enable this extension when one or more of the Web sites uses server-side include (SSI) directives to instruct the Web server to insert various types of content into a Web page.
WebDav	Enable this extension when you want to support Web Distributed Authoring and Versioning (WebDAV) on the Web server, but it is not recommended for dedicated Web servers.

 Important

Enable only the Web service extensions that are required by the migrated Apache Web sites.

2. For each Web service extension used by your applications that is not a one of the default Web service extensions, add a new entry to the Web service extensions list and configure the status of the new entry to **Allowed**.

   For information about how to add a Web server extension to the list, see "Configure Web Service Extensions" in "IIS Deployment Procedures" in this book.

3. Use a Web browser on a client computer to verify that the Web sites and applications run on the server.

Configuring MIME Types

IIS serves only static files with extensions registered in the Multipurpose Internet Mail Extensions (MIME) types list. IIS is preconfigured to recognize a default set of global MIME types, which are recognized by all configured Web sites. You can define MIME types at the Web site and directory levels, independent of one another or the types defined globally. IIS also allows you to change, remove, or configure additional MIME types. For any static content file extensions used by the Web sites hosted by IIS that are not defined in the MIME types list, you must create a corresponding MIME type entry.

The Apache to IIS 6.0 Migration Tool migrates the MIME types for the Apache Web sites; however, you must add any MIME types for content that was added earlier in the Apache migration process by completing the following steps:

1. For each static file type used by your Web site, ensure that an entry exists in the MIME types list.

   When your application uses the standard MIME types included in IIS 6.0 or the MIME types migrated by the Apache to IIS 6.0 Migration Tool, no new MIME type entries are required. However, if you added new static content in earlier in the Apache migration process, then add the new MIME types. For information about how to add a MIME type to the MIME types list, see "Configure MIME Types" in "IIS Deployment Procedures" in this book.

2. Use a Web browser on a client computer to verify that the Web sites and applications run on the server.

Configuring Web Site Properties

After the Apache Web sites are migrated, they run in a configuration that approximates their configuration on the Apache Web server. All of the Web sites run in the default application pool with the default security identity, NetworkService. In this configuration, the Web sites do not take advantage of the enhanced security and availability of IIS 6.0.

You can further configure the Web sites to provide the following:

- **Improved security.** In many cases, you can improve the security of the Web sites by isolating and running each one with unique identities. For more information about improving the security of the Web sites, see "Securing Web Sites and Applications" in this book.

- **Enhanced availability.** In many cases, you can to improve the availability of your Web sites. For more information about improving the availability of your Web sites, see "Ensuring Application Availability" in this book.

Configuring Server Certificates for SSL

Some of the Web sites on the source server might use Secure Sockets Layer (SSL) to encrypt confidential information exchanged between the Web server and the client. For each SSL-encrypted Web site that you migrated from the source server, you need to ensure that you have a certificate for that Web site installed on the target server. You can either renew the existing certificates on the source server in a format that is compatible with IIS 6.0 or you can request new certificates. After you have installed the server certificates on the target server, you can import the certificates into the certificate store on the target server, and then configure your Web sites to use the appropriate certificates.

 Note

Server certificates are installed on the Web server and typically require no additional configuration on the client servers. Server certificates allow the clients to verify the identity of the server. Alternatively, some Web sites and applications might require client certificates. Client certificates are installed on the client servers and allow the server to authenticate the clients. For more information about configuring client certificates, see "Certificates" IIS 6.0 Help, which is accessible from IIS Manager.

For each Web site and application that uses SSL, configure the server certificate for SSL by completing the following steps:

1.   Obtain an SSL server certificate that is compatible with IIS 6.0 by doing one of the following:

- Renew an existing certificate in a format that is compatible with IIS 6.0.

   The format of the SSL server certificate on the source server is in a format that is incompatible with IIS. You can renew an existing certificate with your certification authority in a format that is compatible with IIS 6.0.

   For more information about renewing existing server certificates in a format that is compatible with IIS 6.0, contact your certification authority.

- Request a new certificate from a certification authority in a format that is compatible with IIS 6.0.

  You can use the Web Server Certificate Wizard either to generate a certificate request file (Certreq.txt, by default) that you send to a certification authority, or to generate a request for an online certification authority, such as Microsoft Certificate Services in Windows Server 2003. Depending on the level of identification assurance offered by your server certificate, you can expect to wait several days to several months for the certification authority to approve your request and send you a certificate file.

  For more information about requesting a server certificate by using the Web Server Certificate Wizard, see "Request a Server Certificate" in "IIS Deployment Procedures" in this book.

2. Install the SSL server certificate to be used by the Web site on the target server.

   After you obtain an SSL server certificate, you need to install the certificate on the target server. Install the SSL server certificate on the target server by using the Certificate MMC snap-in.

   For more information about installing the SSL server certificate on the Web server, see "Install a Server Certificate" in "IIS Deployment Procedures" in this book.

3. Assign the SSL server certificate to the Web site.

   For more information about assigning the SSL server certificate to the Web site, see "Assign a Server Certificate to a Web Site" in "IIS Deployment Procedures" in this book.

Backing Up the Target Server

Before you enable client access to the target server, perform a complete image backup of the target server. Performing this image backup provides you with a point-in-time snapshot of the Web server. If you need to restore the target server in the event of a failure, you can use this backup to restore the Web server to a known configuration.

 Important

Do not continue with the migration process unless you have a successful backup of the entire target server. Otherwise, you can lose Web sites, applications, or data that you migrated to the target server.

For more information about how to back up the Web server, see "Back Up and Restore the Web Server to a File or Tape" in "IIS Deployment Procedures" in this book.

Enabling Client Access After Migration

After you have migrated your Web sites from the source server to the target server, you are ready to enable client access to the Web sites on the target server, while maintaining the DNS entries to the source servers. After a period of time that meets your business needs, you can remove the DNS entries that point to the Web sites on the source server.

Figure 7.10 illustrates the final step of the process for migrating Web sites from Apache to IIS 6.0.

Figure 7.10   Enabling Client Access After Migration to IIS 6.0

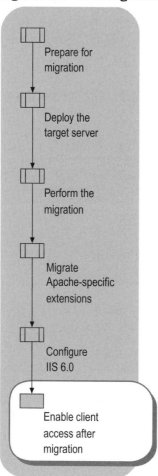

Prepare for migration

Deploy the target server

Perform the migration

Migrate Apache-specific extensions

Configure IIS 6.0

Enable client access after migration

Enable client access to the Web sites on the target server by completing the following steps:

1. Create the appropriate DNS entries for the Web sites and applications running on the target server.

   For more information about how to create DNS entries for your Web sites and applications, see "Managing resource records" in Help and Support Center for Windows Server 2003.

2. Monitor client traffic to determine whether clients are successfully accessing the target server.

   For more information about how to monitor client traffic to Web sites on the target server, see "Monitor Active Web and FTP Connections" in "IIS Deployment Procedures" in this book.

3. Establish a monitoring period, such as a few hours or a day, to confirm that clients accessing Web sites on the target server are experiencing response times and application responses that meet or exceed your requirements.

4. Remove the DNS entries pointing to the Web sites and applications on the source server.

   For more information about how to remove DNS entries for your applications, see "Managing resource records" in Help and Support Center for Windows Server 2003.

5. Monitor client traffic to the Web sites on the source server to determine when clients are no longer accessing the source server.

   For more information about how to monitor client traffic to Web sites on the source server, see "Monitor Active Web and FTP Connections" in "IIS Deployment Procedures" in this book.

6. When clients are no longer accessing the Web sites on the source server, decommission the hardware for the source server.

Additional Resources

These resources contain additional information and tools related to this chapter.

Related Information

- "Securing Web Sites and Applications in IIS 6.0" in this book for more information about securing your Web sites after migration.
- "Ensuring Application Availability" in this book for more information about improving the availability of your Web sites after migration.
- "Upgrading an IIS Server to IIS 6.0" in this book for information about upgrading IIS Web servers.
- "Migrating IIS Web Sites to IIS 6.0" in this book for information about migrating Web sites on earlier versions of IIS to IIS 6.0.

- "IIS Deployment Procedures in this book for more information about specific procedures for migrating Apache Web sites to IIS 6.0.

- The Active Server Pages and ASP.NET links on the Web Resources page at http://www.microsoft.com/windows/reskits/webresources for more information about selecting either ASP or ASP.NET to rewrite dynamic content.

- The Migration of Linux-Apache-MySQL-PHP Platform to Windows 2000 link on the Web Resources page at http://www.microsoft.com/windows/reskits/webresources for more information about migrating Apache Web sites to IIS.

- The SQL Server link on the Web Resources page at http://www.microsoft.com/windows/reskits/webresources for more information about importing data into SQL Server 2000.

Related IIS 6.0 Help topics

- "Certificates" in IIS 6.0 Help, which is accessible from IIS Manager, for more information about configuring client certificates.

Related Windows Server 2003 Help topics

For best results in identifying Help topics by title, in Help and Support Center, under the **Search** box, click **Set search options**. Under **Help Topics**, select the **Search in title only** check box.

- "Managing resource records" in Help and Support Center for Windows Server 2003 or more information about how to create DNS entries for your applications.

IIS Deployment Procedures

In This Appendix

Assign Additional IP Addresses to a Network Adapter

You can configure a network adapter to have additional IP addresses. When you assign a specific IP address to a network adapter, you can uniquely identify a Web site or application by associating the Web site or application with that unique IP address.

Requirements

- **Credentials**: Membership in the Administrators group on the local computer.

- **Tools**: Iis.msc.

Recommendation

As a security best practice, log on to your computer using an account that is not in the Administrators group, and then use the **Run as** command to run IIS Manager as an administrator. At the command prompt, type **runas /user:administrative_accountname "mmc %*systemroot*%\system32\inetsrv\iis.msc"**.

▶ **To assign additional IP addresses to a network adapter**

1. In Control Panel, click **Network Connections,** right-click the network adapter that connects to the client computers, and then click **Properties**.

2. On the **General** tab, click **Internet Protocol (TCP/IP)**, and then click **Properties**.

3. On the **General** tab, click **Advanced**.

4. On the **Advanced TCP/IP Settings** dialog box, click **Add**.

5. On the **TCP/IP Address** dialog box, enter the **IP address** and the **Subnet mask**, and then click **Add**.

6. Click **OK** twice, and then click **Close**.

Assign a Server Certificate to a Web Site

Server certificates contain information about the server that allows the client to positively identify the server before sharing sensitive information. After you obtain a server certificate from a trusted certification authority and install the server certificate on the Web server, you need to assign the server certificate to the Web site.

Requirements

- **Credentials**: Membership in the Administrators group on the local computer.

- **Tools**: Iis.msc.

Recommendation

As a security best practice, log on to your computer using an account that is not in the Administrators group, and then use the **Run as** command to run IIS Manager as an administrator. At the command prompt, type **runas /user:administrative_accountname "mmc %*systemroot*%\system32\inetsrv\iis.msc"**.

▶ **To assign a server certificate to a Web site**

1. In IIS Manager, expand the local computer, and then expand the **Web Sites** folder.

2. Right-click the Web site or file that you want, and then click **Properties**.

3. Depending on whether you are configuring a Web site or a file, select either the **Directory Security** or **File Security** tab, and under **Secure communications**, click **Server Certificate**.

4. In the Web Server Certificate Wizard, click **Assign an existing certificate**.

5. Follow the steps in the Web Server Certificate Wizard, which guides you through the process of installing a server certificate.

6. You can view the information about the certificate by clicking the **View Certificate** button on the **Directory Security** or **File Security** tab of the Web site's **Properties** page.

Back Up and Restore Registry Entries

Some COM objects, COM+ objects, Internet Server API (ISAPI) extensions, and other components save configuration information in the Windows registry. If no setup program or provisioning script exists to make the appropriate registry updates during migration, you must manually identify the registry entries and then recreate them on the target server. To accomplish this, once you have identified the registry entries required by the applications currently running on the source server, back up the registry entries on the source server by using the registry editor Regedit.exe. Modify the registry entries in the backup files created by the registry editor to reflect changes in disk volume drive letters or paths to directories, and then restore the updated registry backups to the target server. Restoring the registry entries is accomplished by merging the backup files into the registry on the target server.

Caution

The registry editor bypasses standard safeguards, allowing settings that can damage your system, or even require you to reinstall Windows. If you must edit the registry, back it up first and see the Registry Reference on the *Microsoft® Windows® Server 2003 Deployment Kit* companion CD or on the Web at http://www.microsoft.com/reskit.

▶ **To back up registry entries by using the registry editor**

1. In the **Run** dialog box, type **regedit**, and then click **OK**.

2. In the registry editor, right-click the registry key or subkey that contains the registry entries that you want to back up, and then click **Export**.

3. In the **Export Registry File** dialog box, select a location for the backup registry file. Click **Save** to save the registry file to that location.

4. Close the Registry Editor.

▶ **To restore registry entries**

1. Copy the backup registry file to any location on the target server.

2. In Windows Explorer, navigate to the backup registry file on the target server, and right-click the file name.

3. Click **Merge**. In the **Registry Editor** message box, click **Yes** to add the information in the file to the registry.

4. Click **OK** to finish.

Back Up and Restore the IIS Metabase

Metabase backup files are copies of the metabase configuration file (MetaBase.xml) and the matching metabase schema file (MBSchema.xml). The metabase can be restored from the backup files by using the metabase configuration backup and restore feature. You can create backup files by using IIS Manager or the command-line script **iisback.vbs**, which is stored in *systemroot*\System32.

The administrator can create a *portable backup* by providing a password that is used by IIS to encrypt the secure metabase properties in the backup files. Encrypting the secure properties in this way allows the backup files to be restored to another computer by using the password. Once a backup is created, the password within the backup file cannot be changed.

When creating a *non-portable backup*, the administrator does not provide a password. Instead, the machine key is used to encrypt secure metabase properties. Because a machine key is unique to the computer it belongs to, a backup created this way can only be restored to the original computer.

Requirements

- **Credentials**: Membership in the Administrators group on the local computer.

- **Tools**: Iis.msc, Iisback.vbs

Recommendation

As a security best practice, log on to your computer using an account that is not in the Administrators group, and then use the **Run as** command to run IIS Manager as an administrator. At the command prompt, type **runas /user:administrative_accountname "mmc %*systemroot*%\system32\inetsrv\iis.msc"**.

▶ **To create a portable backup (password required)**

1. In IIS Manager, right-click the local computer, click **All Tasks**, and then click **Backup/Restore Configuration**.

2. Click **Create Backup**.

3. In the **Configuration backup name** box, type a name for the backup file.

4. Select the **Encrypt backup using password** check box, type a password into the **Password** box, and then type the same password in the **Confirm password** box.

5. Click **OK**, and then click **Close**.

   The IIS metabase is created in the *systemroot***system32\inetsrv\MetaBack** folder.

▶ **To create a non-portable backup (password not required)**

1. In IIS Manager, right-click the local computer, click **All Tasks**, and click **Backup/Restore Configuration**.

2. Click **Create Backup**.

3. In the **Configuration backup name** box, type a name for the backup file.

4. Click **OK**, and then click **Close**.

   The IIS metabase is created in the *systemroot***system32\inetsrv\MetaBack** folder.

▶ **To restore the metabase backup**

1. In IIS Manager, right-click the local computer, click **All Tasks**, and click **Backup/Restore Configuration**.

2. In the **Backups** list box, click the version of the **Automatic Backup** file that you want to restore, and click **Restore**. If prompted for a password, type the password you chose to secure the backup.

   The IIS metabase is restored to the location from which it was backed up.

Back Up and Restore the Web Server to a File or Tape

You should back up a Web server before upgrading it or making configuration changes to it. A complete Web server backup includes all Web sites, applications, and data stored on the Web server. For example, before an upgrade, or before you enable client access to a target Web server, perform a complete image backup before you change any of the configuration settings on the existing Web server. The image backup provides a point-in-time snapshot of the Web server. If unforeseen problems occur during the upgrade or configuration process, you can use this backup to restore the Web server to a known configuration

A backup file can be saved to a hard disk, a floppy disk, or to any other nonremovable or removable media on which you can save a file. Backup files usually have the extension .bkf, but you can change it to any extension you prefer.

You should back up all boot and system volumes, including the System State, when you back up the Web server.

Requirements

- **Credentials**: Membership in the Administrators group on the local computer.
- **Tools**: ntbackup.exe

Recommendation

As a security best practice, log on to your computer using an account that is not in the Administrators group, and then use the **Run as** command to run IIS Manager as an administrator. At the command prompt, type **runas /user:administrative_accountname "mmc %systemroot%\system32\inetsrv\iis.msc"**.

▷ ### To back up to a file or tape

1. Open **Accessories**, click **System Tools**, and then click **Backup**.

2. Click the **Advanced Mode** link on the Backup or Restore Wizard.

3. Click the **Backup** tab, and then on the **Job** menu, click **New**.

4. In the **Click to select the check box for any drive, folder, or file that you want to back up** text box, click the box next to **System State** and any other items you would like to backup. You should back up all boot and system volumes along with the System State.

5. In **Backup destination**, do one of the following:

   - Choose **File** if you want to back up files and folders to a file. This is selected by default. You will not be able to choose any other option if you do not have a tape drive on your system.

     -or-

   - Click a tape device from the drop-down list if you want to back up files and folders to a tape. You cannot use this option if you do not have a tape device on your system.

6. In **Backup media or file name**, do one of the following:

   - If you are backing up files and folders to a file, type a path and file name for the backup (.bkf) file, or click the **Browse** button to find a file.

   - If you are backing up files and folders to a tape, select the tape you want to use from the drop-down list box.

7. Click **Tools**, and then click **Options** to select any backup options you want, such as the backup type and the log file type. When you have finished selecting backup options in the **Options** dialog box, click **OK**.

8. Click **Start Backup**, and then make any necessary changes to the **Backup Job Information** dialog box.

9. Click the **Advanced** tab if you want to set advanced backup options such as data verification or hardware compression. When you have finished setting advanced backup options, click **OK**.

10. Click **Start Backup** to start the backup operation.

▷ **To restore the Web server from a file or tape**

1. Open **Accessories**, point to **System Tools**, and then click **Backup**.

2. Click the **Advanced Mode** link on the Backup or Restore Wizard.

3. Click the **Restore and Manage Media** tab, and then in **Expand the desired media item, then check the box for the items to restore,** expand the media item that contains the backup file you wish to use, and select the check box next to **System State** for that file. This will restore the System State data along with any other data you have selected for the current restore operation.

4. In **Restore files to**, do one of the following:

   ▪ Click **Original location** if you want the backed up files and folders to be restored to the folder or folders they were in when they were backed up. Skip to step 6.

   -or-

   ▪ Click **Alternate location** if you want the backed up files and folders to be restored to a folder that you designate. This option will preserve the folder structure of the backed up data; all folders and subfolders will appear in the alternate folder you designate.

   -or-

   ▪ Click **Single folder** if you want the backed up files and folders to be restored to a folder that you designate. This option will not preserve the folder structure of the backed up data; the files will appear only in the folder that you designate.

5. If you selected **Alternate location** or **Single folder**, type a path for the folder under **Alternate location**, or click the **Browse** button to find the folder.

6. On the **Tools** menu, click **Options**, click the **Restore** tab, and then do one of the following:

   ▪ Click **Do not replace the file on my computer** if you do not want the restore operation to copy over files that are already on your hard disk.

   -or-

   ▪ Click **Replace the file on disk only if the file on disk is older** if you want the restore operation to replace older files on your disk with newer files from your backup.

   -or-

   ▪ Click **Always replace the file on my computer** if you want the restore operation to replace files on your disk regardless of whether the backup files are newer or older.

7. Click **OK** to accept the restore options you have set.

8. Click **Start Restore**.

9. Click the **Advanced** tab if you want to change any advanced restore options, such as restoring security settings and junction point data. When you are done setting advanced restore options, click **OK**.

10. Click **OK** to start the restore operation.

Configure an ASP.NET Application for ASP.NET

By default, when the Microsoft®.NET Framework is installed on a computer with an existing .NET Framework installation, most Microsoft ASP.NET applications are automatically updated to use the newly installed version. The exceptions are applications that are bound to an incompatible or later version of the .NET Framework. Although later versions of the .NET Framework are designed to be backward compatible, you might need to configure an ASP.NET application to use an earlier version, if it cannot run successfully on a later version of the .NET Framework.

When multiple versions of the .NET Framework are executing side-by-side on a single computer, the ASP.NET ISAPI version script that is mapped to an ASP.NET application determines which version of the common language .NET Framework is used for the application. The following sections describe the process for configuring an ASP.NET application to target a specific version of the .NET Framework.

Requirements

- **Credentials**: Membership in the Administrators group on the local computer.

- **Tools**: Iis.msc.

Recommendation

As a security best practice, log on to your computer using an account that is not in the Administrators group, and then use the **Run as** command to run IIS Manager as an administrator. At the command prompt, type **runas /user:administrative_accountname "mmc %*systemroot*%\system32\inetsrv\iis.msc"**.

Viewing the Script Map for an ASP.NET Application

When managing a computer with multiple versions of the .NET Framework installed, it is often useful to view the script map for an ASP.NET application to determine which version is used by the application.

▶ **To view the script map for an ASP.NET application**

1. Open IIS Manager, expand the local computer, and navigate to the Web site folder that contains the ASP.NET application.

2. Right-click the Web site folder, and then click **Properties**.

3. In the **Properties** dialog box, on the **Home Directory** tab, click the **Configuration** button.

4. In the **Application Configuration** dialog box, on the **Mappings** tab, select an ASP.NET application extension, such as .asmx or .aspx.

   The **Executable Path** column of the dialog box lists the path to the ASP.NET ISAPI version used by the selected application type. By default, the ASP.NET ISAPI is installed in the following location:

   systemroot**Microsoft.NET\Framework***versionNumber*

   The version number shown in the path indicates the version number of the ASP.NET ISAPI used by the application type. The first two digits of the ASP.NET ISAPI version number are the same as the first two digits of the version number of the .NET Framework used by the application.

Configure an ASP.NET Application for ASP.NET

When the .NET Framework is installed on a computer with an existing .NET Framework installation, by default all ASP.NET application script maps are automatically updated to use the newly installed version. To make it easier to reconfigure the script map for an ASP.NET application, each installation of the .NET Framework comes with an associated version of the ASP.NET IIS Registration tool (Aspnet_regiis.exe). Administrators can use Aspnet_regiis.exe to remap an ASP.NET application to the correct version of ASP.NET.

 Note

Because Aspnet_regiis.exe is linked to a specific version of the .NET Framework, administrators must use the appropriate version of Aspnet_regiis.exe to reconfigure the script map for an ASP.NET application.

Aspnet_regiis.exe can also be used to display the status of all installed versions of ASP.NET, register the associated version of ASP.NET, create client-script directories, and perform other configuration operations.

 To use Aspnet_regiis.exe to update a script map for an ASP.NET application

1. In the **Run** dialog box, type **cmd**, and then click **OK**.

2. At the command prompt, use the **cd** command to change to the directory of the Aspnet_regiis.exe version you want to use. Remember that each version of the .NET Framework comes with its own version of Aspnet_regiis.exe. By default, Aspnet_regiis.exe is located in the following directory:

   systemroot**Microsoft.NET\\Framework***versionNumber*

   You can check to see which version you are running by using the procedure "To view the script map for an ASP.NET application" earlier in this section.

3. Run **Aspnet_regiis.exe** using the **–s** or **–sn** option along with the path to the application to set up the script maps. The following command-line example updates the script maps for an application called SampleApp1.

   ```
   Aspnet_regiis.exe -s W3SVC/1/ROOT/SampleApp1
   ```

    Note

   The **-s** and **-sn** options allow you to install scriptmaps for ASP.NET at the specified path recursively (-s), which copies the scriptmaps to the subfolders, or nonrecursively (-sn), which does not copy the scriptmaps to the subfolders.

▷ **To get a list of the options available for Aspnet_regiis.exe**

- At the command prompt in the folder where Aspnet_regiis.exe is installed, type:

```
aspnet_regiis ?.
```

A list of options available for use with Aspnet_regiis.exe displays.

Configure Anonymous User Identity

When the Web sites and applications running on the Web server require anonymous access, IIS must be configured with a user account specifically for anonymous access. This user account can be stored in the local account database on the Web server or in a domain.

If, prior to upgrade, the anonymous user identity is configured to use an account stored in a domain you must configure the anonymous user identity to use the same domain-based account after the upgrade. This is necessary because the upgrade process automatically configures IIS to use the default anonymous user account IUSR_*computername*, where *computername* is the name of the computer on which IIS is running. You can configure the anonymous user identity to use the domain-based user account through IIS Manager. If the anonymous user identity does not use an account stored in a domain, it can be configured to use an account stored in the local account database on the Web server.

▷ **To configure the account used for Anonymous authentication**

1. In IIS Manager, expand the local computer, right-click the site, directory, or file that you want to configure, and then click **Properties**.

2. Click the **Directory Security** or **File Security** tab, depending on the level for which you are changing the security settings.

3. In the **Authentication and access control** section, click **Edit**.

4. Select the **Enable anonymous access** check box.

5. Type the valid Windows user account you want to use for Anonymous access, or click **Browse** to locate it.

6. Click **OK** twice.

Configure a Web Site to be FrontPage Extended

FrontPage 2002 Server Extensions from Microsoft provides Web-based and command-line administration for extending Web sites. *Extending* a Web site means enabling various FrontPage 2002 Server Extensions features to improve how you manage the content development and security of your site. Extending Web sites with FrontPage 2002 Server Extensions enables the Web site owner to author the site in the Microsoft® FrontPage® web site creation and management tool and delegate Web site ownership and administration credentials. After a Web site is extended, a FrontPage client can open the Web site and author it in FrontPage.

Before you can use FrontPage 2002 Server Extensions, you must create one or more Web sites to contain them. An extended Web site, formerly known as a virtual server, is an IIS Web site that receives additional functionality when it is extended by FrontPage Server Extensions. By default, IIS provides a working extended Web site called **Default Web Site**. This extended Web site points to the content directory *systemroot*\Inetpub\Wwroot.

Requirements

- **Credentials**: Membership in the Administrators group on the local computer.

- **Tools**: Iis.msc.

Recommendation

As a security best practice, log on to your computer using an account that is not in the Administrators group, and then use the **Run as** command to run IIS Manager as an administrator. At the command prompt, type **runas /user:administrative_accountname "mmc %systemroot%\system32\inetsrv\iis.msc"**.

Before extending a site, check to make sure that the FrontPage 2002 Server Extensions optional component is installed. In Control Panel, click **Add or Remove Programs**, and then click Windows Components Wizard. If the FrontPage 2002 Server Extensions component is not installed, add it by using the following procedure.

▶ **To add the FrontPage 2002 Server Extensions component**

1. In the **Windows Components Wizard** select **Application Server**, and then click **Details**.

2. In the **Application Server** subcomponents list, select **Internet Information Services,** and then click **Details**.

3. In the IIS subcomponents list, select the check box for **FrontPage 2002 Server Extensions**, and then click **OK** to complete the Windows Components Wizard and install FrontPage 2002 Server Extensions. You might need your Windows Server 2003 installation CD to complete the installation.

▷ **To extend a site by using the FrontPage Server Extensions 2002 Server Administration tool**

1. Open Administrative Tools, and then click **Microsoft SharePoint Administrator**.

    If the FrontPage 2002 Server Extensions optional component is not installed IIS returns error 404, "The page cannot be found." In this case, add the FrontPage 2002 Server Extensions component by using the procedure described earlier in this section.

2. On the **FrontPage Server Extensions 2002 Server Administration** site, verify that the extended Web site you created is listed in the **Virtual Servers** section.

3. To extend the Web site, click the **Extend** link next to the extended Web site name.

4. Click **Submit**. The **FrontPage Server Extensions 2002 Server Administration** tool adds FrontPage 2002 Server Extensions template directories to the content directory of your extended Web site, and adds other files that contain metadata.

Configure Application Identity for IIS 5.0 Isolation Mode

If you are running Internet Information Services (IIS) 6.0 in IIS 5.0 isolation mode, you also need to configure application identities for IIS 5.0 isolation mode. On your Microsoft® Windows® Server 2003–based server running in IIS 5.0 isolation mode, configure the application identity to the same settings as were set up on your server running IIS 5.0. You can do this by modifying the identity property of the COM+ object created for the Web site.

▷ **To configure Web site and application process identities in IIS 5.0**

1. In the **Run** dialog box, type **mmc**, and then click **OK** to start the Microsoft Management Console (MMC).

    If the Component Services Snap-in is not already loaded, on the **File** menu, click **Add/Remove Snap-in**, and then click **Add**. Under **Available Standalone Snap-ins**, click **Component Services**, and then click **Add**. Click **Close** and then click **OK**.

2. In MMC, in the console tree, expand **Component Services**, expand **Computers**, expand **My Computer**, and then expand **COM+ Applications**.

3. Right-click **IIS Out-of-Process Pooled Applications** and then click **Properties**.

4. Click the **Identity** tab.

5. In **User**, type the user name. In the **Password** and **Confirm password** text boxes, enter the password for the user account. To look up a valid user name, click **Browse**.

6. Click **OK**.

Configure Application Isolation Modes

You can run Internet Information Services (IIS) 6.0 in one of two modes: *worker process isolation mode* or *IIS 5.0 isolation mode*. Worker process isolation mode is the default mode the Web server runs in after a clean installation of the Microsoft® Windows® Server 2003 operating system. IIS 5.0 isolation mode is the default mode when you upgrade to IIS 6.0 from a previous version of IIS. Administrators should only run IIS in IIS 5.0 isolation mode when applications on the server are determined to be incompatible with worker process isolation mode.

Requirements

- **Credentials**: Membership in the Administrators group on the local computer.

- **Tools**: Iis.msc.

Recommendation

As a security best practice, log on to your computer using an account that is not in the Administrators group, and then use the **Run as** command to run IIS Manager as an administrator. At the command prompt, type **runas /user:administrative_accountname "mmc %systemroot%\system32\inetsrv\iis.msc"**.

Configuring IIS for Worker Process Isolation Mode

To complete the following procedure, you must restart IIS, which will temporarily interrupt the World Wide Web Publishing Service (WWW service).

▶ **To configure IIS for worker process isolation mode**

1. In IIS Manager, expand the local computer, right-click **Web Sites**, and then click **Properties**.

2. Click the **Service** tab, clear the **Run WWW service in IIS 5.0 isolation mode** check box, and then click **OK**.

3. To start the WWW service, click **Yes** when asked if you want to restart IIS now.

If the switch to worker process isolation mode is successful, a folder named Application Pools appears in the IIS Manager listing for your local computer. You can quickly determine which isolation mode IIS is running because the Application Pools folder is present in worker process isolation mode and absent in IIS 5.0 isolation mode.

Configuring IIS for IIS 5.0 Isolation Mode

After you complete the following procedure, you must restart the WWW service, which will temporarily interrupt the service.

▶ **To configure IIS for IIS 5.0 isolation mode**

1. In IIS Manager, expand the local computer, right-click **Web Sites**, and then click **Properties**.

2. Click the **Service** tab, select the **Run WWW service in IIS 5.0 isolation mode** check box, and then click **OK**.

3. To start the WWW Service, click **Yes** when asked if you want to restart IIS now.

Configure Application Isolation Settings for IIS 5.0 Isolation Mode

Isolating applications means configuring them to run in a process (memory space) that is separate from the Web server core (the core components required to run Internet Information Services (IIS), such as IISAdmin, the metabase, and so on) and other applications. You can configure applications into one of three levels of application protection:

- Low (IIS process)
- Medium (pooled)
- High (isolated)

Note that server-side includes (SSI), Internet Database Connector (IDC), and other InProcessISAPIApps applications (special applications that must be run in process) cannot be run in medium or high isolation.

Requirements

- **Mode:** This feature of IIS 6.0 is available only when IIS is running in IIS 5.0 isolation mode.
- **Credentials**: Membership in the Administrators group on the local computer.
- **Tools**: Iis.msc.

Recommendation

As a security best practice, log on to your computer using an account that is not in the Administrators group, and then use the **Run as** command to run IIS Manager as an administrator. At the command prompt, type **runas /user:administrative_accountname "mmc %systemroot%\system32\inetsrv\iis.msc"**.

▶ **To set or change the level of application protection**

1. In IIS Manager, expand the local computer, right-click the Web site or the starting-point directory for the application you want to configure, and then click **Properties**.

2. Click the **Home Directory**, **Virtual Directory**, or **Directory** tab, depending on whether you are configuring a Web site, a virtual directory, or an application.

3. In the **Application protection** box, click the appropriate level of protection, and then click **OK**.

The Web server finishes processing any current requests for the application before it creates a separate process. At the next request for the application, the application will run in the appropriate memory space.

Configure Application Pool Health

Monitoring the health of a worker process includes detecting whether the worker process is able to serve requests and then taking appropriate action. For example, if a worker process fails to respond to a ping request by the World Wide Web Publishing Service (WWW service), the worker process probably does not have threads available for processing incoming requests. You can monitor the health condition of an application pool by pinging the worker processes assigned to it at regular intervals. When a configurable unhealthy condition occurs, you can also set the following features to take corrective action:

- Rapid-fail protection

- Startup time limit

- Shutdown time limit

Requirements

- **Mode:** This feature of Internet Information Services (IIS) 6.0 is available only when IIS is running in worker process isolation mode.

- **Credentials**: Membership in the Administrators group on the local computer.

- **Tools**: Iis.msc.

Recommendation

As a security best practice, log on to your computer using an account that is not in the Administrators group, and then use the **Run as** command to run IIS Manager as an administrator. At the command prompt, type **runas /user:administrative_accountname "mmc %*systemroot*%\system32\inetsrv\iis.msc"**.

Consider the following when setting the configuration for recycling the worker processes assigned to an application pool:

- Worker process pinging is enabled by default. Adjust the ping interval to get timely information about application pool health without triggering false unhealthy conditions.

- When the WWW service detects that a worker process fails more than a set maximum number of times in a set time period, it places the worker process in a rapid-fail protection state. Placing application pools in rapid-fail protection state protects the availability of other applications on the server.

- When the WWW service detects that a worker process is unhealthy, it marks the worker process for termination. Within configured time limits, IIS terminates the worker process. It is important to tune the shutdown time period to fit the load characteristics of the applications that are being processed.

- After IIS terminates an unhealthy worker process, it starts a new worker process to replace the unhealthy one. It is important to tune the startup time period to fit the overlap desired between the unhealthy worker process and the new worker process.

▷ **To configure worker process pinging**

1. In IIS Manager, expand the local computer, right-click the application pool you want to configure, and then click **Properties**.

2. On the **Health** tab, select the **Enable pinging** check box.

3. In the text box to the right of **Ping worker process every (frequency in seconds)**, type the number of seconds to elapse before the worker process is pinged, and then click **OK**.

▷ **To configure rapid-fail protection**

1. In IIS Manager, expand the local computer, right-click the application pool you want to configure, and then click **Properties**.

2. On the **Health** tab, select the **Enable rapid-fail protection** check box.

3. In the text box to the right of **Failures**, type the maximum number of failures allowed.

4. In the box to the right of **Time period (in minutes)**, type the elapsed time, in minutes, during which the number of failures is counted, and then click **OK**.

▷ **To configure startup and shutdown time limits**

1. In IIS Manager, expand the local computer, right-click the application pool you want to configure, and then click **Properties**.

2. On the **Health** tab, under **Startup time limit**, in the text box to the right of **Worker process must startup within (time in seconds)**, type the time, in seconds, to elapse before starting up a new worker process.

3. On the **Health** tab, under **Shutdown time limit**, in the text box to the right of **Worker process must shutdown within (time in seconds)**, type the time, in seconds, to elapse before shutting down a failing worker process, and then click **OK**.

Configure Application Pool Identity

The identity of an application pool is the name of the service account under which the application pool's worker process runs. By default, application pools operate under the Network Service user account, which has low-level user access rights. You can configure application pools to run under the Local System user account, which is an account with more user rights than the Network Service or Local Service user accounts. However, be mindful that running an application pool under an account with increased user rights presents a high security risk.

Requirements

- **Credentials**: Membership in the Administrators group on the local computer.

- This feature of Internet Information Services (IIS) 6.0 is available only when IIS is running in worker process isolation mode.

- **Tools**: Iis.msc.

Recommendation

As a security best practice, log on to your computer using an account that is not in the Administrators group, and then use the **Run as** command to run IIS Manager as an administrator. At the command prompt, type **runas /user:administrative_accountname "mmc %systemroot%\system32\inetsrv\iis.msc"**.

By default, application pools operate under the Network Service user account, which has low-level user access rights. Consequently, this account provides better security against attackers or malicious users who might attempt to take over the computer on which the World Wide Web Publishing Service (WWW service) is running. The Local Service user account has low access rights as well, and is useful for situations that do not require access to resources on remote computers. You can, however, configure application pools to run under the Local System user account, which is an account with more user rights than the Network Service or Local Service user accounts.

▷ **To change the service account that an application pool runs under**

1. In IIS Manager, expand the local computer, and expand **Application Pools**.

2. Right-click the application pool you want to configure, and then click **Properties**.

3. Click the **Identity** tab, and click either **Predefined** or **Configurable**.

   Predefined refers to standard service accounts, such as Network Service (the default), which has low-level user access rights that can be used for access to resources on remote computers, Local Service, which has low-level access rights, and is used for situations that do not require access to resources on remote computers, or, Local System, which is an account with more user rights than the Network Service or Local Service account.

   Configurable refers to registered user names.

4. If you click **Predefined**, click a predefined account in the list box.

5. If you click **Configurable**, in the **User name** and **Password** boxes, type the user name and password of the account under which you want the worker process to operate.

6. Click **OK**.

Configure Application Pool Performance

In worker process isolation mode, Internet Information Services (IIS) 6.0 can be configured to optimize the performance of an application pool, allowing you optimize the performance of your Web applications. Some of the ways to accomplish this include configuring an application pool to limit the size of its request queue, enabling CPU monitoring to allow the server to take action when CPU usage exceeds maximum CPU use, configuring the server to shut down a worker process after being idle for a specified number of minutes, and creating a Web garden, which is an application pools with more than one worker process assigned. Setting these configurations helps you manage the resources on a Web server.

Requirements

- **Mode**: This feature of IIS 6.0 is available only when IIS is running in worker process isolation mode.

- **Credentials**: Membership in the Administrators group on the local computer.

- **Tools**: Iis.msc.

Recommendation

As a security best practice, log on to your computer using an account that is not in the Administrators group, and then use the **Run as** command to run IIS Manager as an administrator. At the command prompt, type **runas /user:administrative_accountname "mmc %*systemroot*%\system32\inetsrv\iis.msc"**.

When performance is degraded by too many requests or by problem applications, and you want to configure the application pool to improve the performance of the worker processes assigned to the pool, consider the following:

- When an application pool receives requests faster than it can handle them, the requests might consume all of the application pool's memory. This could happen when the requests queue size limit is large and legitimate requests are coming in at a rapid rate, or during a denial of service attack. To prevent requests from consuming all of an application pool's memory, limit the size of the request queue for the application pool.

- When problem applications consume excessive CPU resources, you need a way to manage them. In worker process isolation mode, you can enable CPU monitoring, configure CPU limits, and direct IIS to take action when a worker process exceeds the CPU limit set for it.

- Web gardens are application pools with more than one worker process assigned. Create a Web garden to achieve more robust performance when resources often get tied up with a single worker process, or when you need to smooth out the handling of a workload.

▷ **To configure idle timeout**

1. In IIS Manager, expand the local computer, right-click the application pool you want to configure, and then click **Properties**.

2. On the **Performance** tab, under **Idle Timeout**, select the **Shutdown worker process after being idle for (time in minutes)** check box.

3. In the text box to the right of **Shutdown worker process after being idle for (time in minutes)**, type the number of minutes to elapse before the worker process is recycled, and then click **OK**.

▷ **To configure a request queue limit**

1. In IIS Manager, expand the local computer, right-click the application pool you want to configure, and then click **Properties**.

2. On the **Performance** tab, select the **Limit the kernel request queue (number of requests)** check box.

3. In the text box to the right of **Limit the kernel request queue (number of requests)**, type the maximum number of requests to allow in the request queue, and then click **OK**.

▷ **To configure CPU monitoring**

1. In IIS Manager, expand the local computer, right-click the application pool you want to configure, and then click **Properties**.

2. On the **Performance** tab, select the **Enable CPU monitoring** check box.

3. In the box to the right of **Maximum CPU use (percentage)**, type the percent maximum CPU threshold.

4. In the text box to the right of **Refresh CPU usage numbers (in minutes)**, type the number of minutes before the CPU usage numbers are refreshed.

5. In the drop-down list box below **Action performed when CPU usage exceeds maximum CPU use**, select the action to take, and then click **OK**.

▷ **To configure a Web garden**

1. In IIS Manager, expand the local computer, right-click the application pool you want to configure, and then click **Properties**.

2. On the **Performance** tab, under **Web garden**, in the **Maximum number of worker processes** text box, type the number of worker processes to assign to the application pool., and then click **OK**

Configure Application Pool Recycling

Internet Information Services (IIS) can be configured to periodically restart worker processes assigned to an application pool, which recycles faulty Web applications. Recycling keeps problematic applications running smoothly, especially when it is not feasible to modify the application code. Recycling helps ensure that problematic applications do not cause other applications to fail, and that system resources can be recovered from unhealthy applications. Use the "Configure Application Pool Health" procedure earlier in this appendix to configure worker process shutdown and startup times to ensure that applications do not experience downtime.

Requirements

- **Mode**: This feature of IIS 6.0 is available only when IIS is running in worker process isolation mode.

- **Credentials**: Membership in the Administrators group on the local computer.

- **Tools**: Iis.msc.

Recommendation

As a security best practice, log on to your computer using an account that is not in the Administrators group, and then use the **Run as** command to run IIS Manager as an administrator. At the command prompt, type **runas /user:administrative_accountname "mmc %systemroot%\system32\inetsrv\iis.msc"**.

▷ **To recycle a worker process immediately on demand**

1. In IIS Manager, expand the local computer.

2. Expand **Application Pools**.

3. Right-click the appropriate application pool you want to recycle, and then click **Recycle**.

▷ **To configure a worker process to be recycled after a set elapsed time**

1. In IIS Manager, expand the local computer, and expand **Application Pools**.

2. Right-click the application pool you want to configure, and then click **Properties**.

3. On the Recycling tab, select the **Recycle worker processes (in minutes)** check box.

4. In the text box to the right of the **Recycle worker processes (in minutes)**, type the number of minutes that you want to elapse before the worker process is recycled, and then click **OK**.

▷ **To configure a worker process to be recycled after a set number of processing requests**

1. In IIS Manager, expand the local computer, and expand **Application Pools**

2. Right-click the application pool you want to configure, and then click **Properties**.

3. On the **Recycling** tab, select the **Recycle worker process (number of requests)** check box.

4. In the text box to the right of the **Recycle worker process (number of requests)**, type the number of requests to be processed before the worker process is recycled, and then click **OK**.

▷ **To configure a worker process to be recycled at scheduled times**

1. In IIS Manager, expand the local computer, expand **Application Pools**.

2. Right-click the application pool you want to configure, and then click Properties.

3. On the Recycling tab, select the Recycle worker processes at the following times check box.

4. Click **Add to add a time to the list, Remove to delete a time**, or **Edit to change an existing time when the worker process is recycled**, and then click **OK**.

 Note

When recycling is set to occur at scheduled times, it may occur off-schedule if the system time is manually altered. To avoid unintended changes in the time that recycling occurs, recycle the scheduled worker processes soon after the system time is changed.

▷   **To configure a worker process to be recycled after consuming a set amount of memory**

1.   In IIS Manager, expand the local computer, and expand **Application Pools**.

2.   Right-click the application pool you want to configure, and then click **Properties**.

3.   On the Recycling tab, under Memory recycling, select the Maximum virtual memory (in megabytes) check box.

4.   In the text box to the right of **Maximum virtual memory (in megabytes)**, type the maximum amount of virtual memory allowed before the worker process is recycled.

5.   Select the Maximum used memory (in megabytes) check box.

6.   In the text box to the right of **Maximum used memory (in megabytes)**, type the maximum amount of memory allowed before the worker process is recycled, and then click **OK**.

Configure FrontPage Server Roles

The configuration of Internet Information Services (IIS) and the Web sites on the source server might reference user accounts that are stored in the local account database on the source server. These accounts stored locally on the Web server are known as *local user accounts*. Local user accounts are only valid on the Web server where they exist, not on other Web servers. When you migrate your Web site to another server, these local user accounts must be recreated on the target server. Once the user accounts have been created, the roles that were assigned to the user accounts on the source server must be assigned to the user accounts on the target server.

You can manage roles from the **Site Administration** page for your Web site. On this page you can view a list of roles, change which rights are included in a role, add a new role, and delete a role.

▷   **To add a user account and assign FrontPage server roles to it**

1.   Open Administrative Tools, and click **Microsoft SharePoint Administrator**.

2.   On the **Server Administration** page, click the name of the extended Web site for which you want to assign user roles.

3.   On the **Site Administration** page for the Web site, click **Manage users**.

4.   On the **Manage Users** page, click **Add a user**.

5.   On the **Add a User** page, in the **User** section, click **Add user or group name (For example, DOMAIN\name)**, and enter a user name in the format *LocalComputerName\UserAccountName*.

6.   In the **User Role** section, select the check boxes for all roles that apply to this user account, and then click **Add User**.

▷   ### To assign FrontPage server roles to an existing user account

1. Open Administrative Tools, and click **Microsoft SharePoint Administrator**.

2. On the **Server Administration** page, click the name of the extended Web site for which you want to assign user roles.

3. On the **Site Administration** page for the Web site, click **Manage users**.

4. On the **Manage Users** page, click the name of the user for which you need to change the roles.

5. On the **Edit User Role Membership** page, next to **User Role**, select the check box for every role that applies to this user, and then click **Submit**.

Configure FTP Server Authentication

Internet Information Services (IIS) supports the following File Transfer Protocol (FTP) authentication methods:

- Anonymous FTP authentication

- Basic FTP authentication

Available authentication settings must be set at the site level for FTP sites. FTP service is not enabled by default in IIS 6.0.

  Important

> If you change the security settings for your FTP site or virtual directory, your Web server prompts you for permission to reset the security settings for the child nodes of that site or directory. If you choose to accept these settings, the child nodes inherit the security settings from the parent site or directory.

Requirements

- **Credentials**: Membership in the Administrators group on the local computer.

- **Tools**: Iis.msc.

Recommendation

As a security best practice, log on to your computer using an account that is not in the Administrators group, and then use the **Run as** command to run IIS Manager as an administrator. At the command prompt, type **runas /user:administrative_accountname "mmc %*systemroot*%\system32\inetsrv\iis.msc"**.

Enable Anonymous FTP Authentication

If you select Anonymous FTP authentication to secure FTP resources, all requests for that resource are accepted without prompting the user for a user name or password. For Anonymous authentication, IIS automatically creates a Windows user account called IUSR_*computername*, where *computername* is the name of the server on which IIS is running. If you have both Anonymous FTP authentication and Basic FTP authentication enabled, IIS tries to use the Anonymous FTP authentication user account first.

▷ **To enable the Anonymous FTP authentication method**

1. In IIS Manager, right-click the FTP site, directory, virtual directory, or file you want to configure, and click **Properties**.

2. Click the **Security Accounts** tab.

3. Select the **Allow anonymous connections** check box.

4. To allow your users to gain access by Anonymous authentication only, select the **Allow only anonymous connections** check box.

5. In the **User name** and **Password** boxes, enter the Anonymous logon user name and password you want to use, and then click OK

   The user name is the name of the anonymous user account, which is typically designated as **IUSR_computername**.

    Note

   > If the default **IUSR_computername** account will not be used for Anonymous FTP authentication, you must create a Windows user account appropriate for the authentication method. For more information about creating a new user account, see the procedure "Create a Service Account" in this chapter.

6. Set the appropriate NTFS permissions for the anonymous account.

   For more information about setting NTFS permissions, see the procedure "Configure NTFS Permissions" earlier in this appendix.

Enable Basic FTP Authentication

If you select the Basic FTP authentication method to secure your FTP resources, users must log on with a user name and password corresponding to a valid Windows user account. If the FTP server cannot verify a user's identity, the server returns an error message. Basic FTP authentication provides only low security because the user transmits the user name and password across the network in an unencrypted form.

▷ **To enable the Basic FTP authentication method**

1. Create a Windows user account appropriate for the authentication method. If appropriate, add the account to a Windows user group.

    For more information about creating a new user account, see the procedure "Create a Service Account" earlier in this appendix.

2. Configure NTFS permissions for the directory or file for which you want to control access.

    For more information about setting NTFS permissions, see the procedure "Configure NTFS Permissions" earlier in this appendix.

3. In IIS Manager, right-click the FTP site, directory, virtual directory, or file you want to configure, and click **Properties**.

4. Click the **Security Accounts** tab.

5. Clear the **Allow anonymous connections** check box, and then click **OK**.

Configure IIS Components and Services

Add or Remove Programs helps you manage programs and components on Microsoft® Windows® Server 2003 and Internet Information Services (IIS) 6.0. As you enable and disable the IIS protocols and services, you correspondingly increase and decrease the attack surface of the Web server.

 Tip

You can also add Windows components by using the Configure Your Server Wizard.

▷ **To configure IIS components and services**

1. In Control Panel, open **Add or Remove Programs**.

2. Click **Add/Remove Windows Components**.

3. On the Windows Components Wizard page, under **Components**, click **Application Server**, and then click **Details**.

4. Click **Internet Information Services (IIS)**, and then click **Details**.

5. Enable or disable the appropriate IIS components and services by selecting the check box to add the component or clearing the check box to remove the component.

6. Complete the Windows Components Wizard by following the instructions in the wizard.

Configure IP Address Assigned to Web Sites

You can configure your Web site to use a unique IP address that uniquely identifies the Web site.

Requirements

- **Credentials**: Membership in the Administrators group on the local computer.

- **Tools** Iis.msc.

Recommendation

As a security best practice, log on to your computer using an account that is not in the Administrators group, and then use the **Run as** command to run IIS Manager as an administrator. At the command prompt, type **runas /user:administrative_accountname "mmc %*systemroot*%\system32\inetsrv\iis.msc"**.

▶ **To configure the IP address assigned to a Web site**

1. In IIS Manager, expand the local computer, right-click the Web site you want to configure, and then click **Properties**.

2. Click the **Web Site** tab, and then click the drop-down arrow next to **IP Address**.

3. Click the IP address you want to use from the drop-down list of IP addresses, and then click **OK**.

Configure IP Address and Domain Name Restrictions

You can configure your Web site to grant or deny specific computers, groups of computers, or domains access to Web sites, directories, or files.

Requirements

- **Credentials**: Membership in the Administrators group on the local computer.

- **Tools** Iis.msc.

Recommendation

As a security best practice, log on to your computer using an account that is not in the Administrators group, and then use the **Run as** command to run IIS Manager as an administrator. At the command prompt, type **runas /user:administrative_accountname "mmc %*systemroot*%\system32\inetsrv\iis.msc"**.

Configure Restrictions Based on IP Address

You can use IIS Manager to grant or deny access to Web sites or applications for a computer or group of computers.

Grant or deny access to resources for a single computer

You can either deny or grant access for a single computer based upon its IP address.

▷ **To grant access to resources for a computer**

1. In IIS Manager, expand the local computer, right-click a Web site, directory, or file you want to configure, and click **Properties**.

2. Click the **Directory Security or File Security** tab. In the IP address and domain name restrictions section, click **Edit**.

3. Click **Granted access**.

4. When you select **Granted access**, you grant access to all computers and domains, except to those that you specifically deny access.

5. Click **Add**.

6. Click **Single computer**.

7. Click **DNS Lookup** to search for computers or domains by name, rather than by IP address.

8. Type the DNS name for the computer. IIS searches on the current domain for the computer, and if found, enters its IP address in the IP address box.

   The following information is important to remember when using the **DNS Lookup** feature:

   - Server performance decreases while DNS addresses are being looked up.

   - A user accessing your Web server through a proxy server will appear to have the IP address of the proxy server.

   - Some user server access problems can be corrected by using the "*.domainname.com" syntax rather than the "domainname.com" syntax.

9. Click **OK** three times.

▷   **To deny access to resources for a computer**

1. In IIS Manager, expand the local computer, right-click a Web site, directory, or file you want to configure, and click **Properties**.

2. Click the **Directory Security** or **File Security** tab. In the **IP address and domain name restrictions** section, click Edit.

3. Click **Denied access**.

   When you select **Denied access**, you deny access to all computers and domains, except to those that you specifically grant access.

4. Click **Add**.

5. Click **Single computer**.

6. Click **DNS Lookup** to search for computers or domains by name, rather than by IP address.

7. Type the DNS name for the computer.

   IIS searches on the current domain for the computer, and if found, enters its IP address in the **IP address** box.

   The following information is important to remember when using the **DNS Lookup** feature:

   - Server performance decreases while DNS addresses are being looked up.

   - A user accessing your Web server through a proxy server will appear to have the IP address of the proxy server.

   - Some user server access problems can be corrected by using the "*.domainname.com" syntax rather than the "domainname.com" syntax.

8. Click **OK** three times.

Grant or deny access to resources for a group of computers

A group of computers can be either denied or granted access based upon their network ID and a subnet mask. The network ID is the IP address of a host computer, usually a router for the *subnet*. The subnet mask determines which part of the IP address is a subnet ID, and which part is a host ID. All computers in a subnet have the same subnet ID, but have their own unique host ID. By specifying a network ID and a subnet mask, you can select a group of computers.

▷ **To grant access to resources for a group of computers**

1. In IIS Manager, expand the local computer, right-click a Web site, directory, or file you want to configure, and click **Properties**.

2. Click the **Directory Security** or **File Security** tab. In the **IP address and domain name restrictions** section, click **Edit**.

3. Click **Granted access**.

   When you select **Granted access**, you grant access to all computers and domains, except to those that you specifically deny access.

4. Click **Add**.

5. Click **Group of computers**.

6. In the **Network ID** box, type the IP address of the host computer.

7. In the **Subnet mask** box, type the subnet ID for the computer you want grant or deny access to.

8. Click **OK** three times.

▷ **To deny access to resources for a group of computers**

1. In IIS Manager, expand the local computer, right-click a Web site, directory, or file you want to configure, and click **Properties**.

2. Click the **Directory Security** or **File Security** tab. In the **IP address and domain name restrictions** section, click **Edit**.

3. Click **Denied access**.

   When you select **Denied access**, you deny access to all computers and domains, except to those that you specifically grant access.

4. Click **Add**.

5. Click **Group of computers**.

6. In the **Network ID** box, type the IP address of the host computer.

7. In the **Subnet mask** box, type the subnet ID for the computer you want grant or deny access to.

8. Click **OK** three times.

Configure Restrictions Based on Domain

Access to resources for a domain can be granted or denied by using IIS Manager.

▶ **To grant access to resources for a domain**

1. In IIS Manager, expand the local computer, right-click a Web site, directory, or file you want to configure, and click **Properties**.

2. Click the **Directory Security** or **File Security** tab. In the **IP address and domain name restrictions** section, click **Edit**.

3. Click **Granted access**.

   When you select **Granted access**, you grant access for all computers and domains, except for those that you specifically deny access.

4. Click **Add**.

5. Click **Domain name**. You will see a warning message saying that "Restricting access by domain name requires a DNS reverse lookup on each connection. This is a very expensive operation and will dramatically affect server performance." Click **OK** to close the message dialog box.

6. In the **Domain name** box, type the domain name.

7. Click **OK** three times.

▶ **To deny access to resources for a domain**

1. In IIS Manager, expand the local computer, right-click a Web site, directory, or file you want to configure, and click **Properties**.

2. Click the **Directory Security** or **File Security** tab. In the **IP address and domain name restrictions** section, click **Edit**.

3. Click **Denied access**.

   When you select **Denied access**, you deny access for all computers and domains, except for those that you specifically grant access.

4. Click **Add**.

5. Click **Domain name**.

6. In the **Domain name** box, type the domain name.

7. Click **OK** three times.

Configure MIME Types

Internet Information Services (IIS) serves only static files with extensions registered in the Multipurpose Internet Mail Exchange (MIME) types list. IIS is preconfigured to recognize a default set of global MIME types, and also allows you to configure additional MIME types and change or remove MIME types. These MIME types are recognized by all Web sites you create in IIS.

MIME types can also be defined at the Web site and directory levels, independent of one another or the types defined globally. When you view MIME types at the Web site or directory level, only the types unique to that level are displayed, not all types inherited from the next level up. If you apply a MIME type at the global level after modifying the same MIME type at a lower level, the global-level MIME type overrides the modified MIME type at the lower level.

When IIS delivers a mail message to a mail application, or a Web page to a client Web browser, it also sends the MIME type of the data it is sending. If there is an attached or embedded file in a specific format, IIS tells the client application the MIME type of the embedded or attached file. The client application then knows how to process or display the data being received from IIS. IIS returns error 404.3 if a client request refers to a file name extension that is not defined in the MIME types.

Requirements

- **Credentials**: Membership in the Administrators group on the local computer.
- **Tools**: Iis.msc.

Recommendation

As a security best practice, log on to your computer using an account that is not in the Administrators group, and then use the **Run as** command to run IIS Manager as an administrator. At the command prompt, type **runas /user:administrative_accountname "mmc %systemroot%\system32\inetsrv\iis.msc"**.

▶ To add a global MIME type

1. In IIS Manager, right-click the local computer, and click **Properties**.
2. Click the **MIME Types** button.
3. Click **New**.
4. In the **Extension** box, type the file name extension.
5. In the **MIME type** box, type a description that exactly matches the file type defined on the computer.

    Note

   You can also create a MIME type for files without an extension or for undefined MIME types. This is not recommended.

6. Click **OK**.

▷ **To add a MIME type to a Web site or directory**

1. In IIS Manager, right-click the Web site or Web site directory for which you want to add a MIME type, and click **Properties**.

2. Click the **HTTP Headers** tab.

3. Click **Mime Types**.

4. Click **New**.

5. In the **Extension** box, type the file name extension.

6. In the **MIME type** box, type a description that exactly matches the file type defined on the computer. If you define a MIME type that has already been defined at a higher level, you are prompted to select the level where the MIME type should reside.

7. Click **OK**.

▷ **To remove a MIME type from a Web site or directory**

1. In IIS Manager, right-click the Web site or Web site directory from which you want to remove a MIME type, and click **Properties**.

2. Click the **HTTP Headers** tab.

3. Click **Mime Types**.

4. From the **Registered MIME types** list, click the MIME type you want to remove, and then click **Remove**.

5. Click **OK** three times.

Configure NTFS Permissions

Use NTFS permissions to define the level of access to your directories and files that you want to grant to specific users and groups of users. Proper configuration of file and directory permissions is crucial for preventing unauthorized access to your resources.

Requirements

- **Credentials**: Membership in the Administrators group on the local computer.

- **Tools**: Iis.msc.

Recommendation

As a security best practice, log on to your computer using an account that is not in the Administrators group, and then use the **Run as** command to run IIS Manager as an administrator. At the command prompt, type **runas /user:administrative_accountname "mmc %*systemroot*%\system32\inetsrv\iis.msc"**.

▶ **To secure a Web site by using NTFS permissions**

1. In IIS Manager, expand the local computer, right-click the Web site or file you want to configure, and click **Permissions**.

2. To add a group or user that does not appear in the **Group or user names** list box, click **Add**, and in the **Enter the object names to select** text box, type the name of the user or group. Click **OK**.

    -OR-

3. To change or remove permissions from an existing group or user, click the name of the group or user in the **Group or user names** list box.

4. To allow or deny a permission such as **Read & Execute**, **List Folder Contents**, **Read**, or **Write**, in the **Permissions for** *group or user name* list box, select the **Allow** or **Deny** check box next to the appropriate permission, and then click **OK**.

 Important

Inherited Deny permissions do not prevent access to an object if the object has an explicit Allow permission entry. Explicit permissions take precedence over inherited permissions, including inherited Deny permissions.

With NTFS permissions, you also have the choice of assigning special permissions to groups or users. Special permissions are permissions on a more detailed level. For better management, you should assign broad-level permissions to users or groups, where it is applicable. For descriptions of permissions, see "Permissions for files and folders" in Help and Support Center for Windows Server 2003.

▷   ## To secure a Web site using NTFS special permissions

1. In IIS Manager, expand the local computer, right-click a Web site or file you want to configure, and click **Permissions**.

2. Click **Advanced**, and then do one of the following on the **Permissions** tab:

    - To set special permissions for an additional group or user, click **Add**, and in the **Enter the object name to select** text box, type the name of the user or group. Click **OK**.

    - To view or change special permissions for an existing group or user, click the name of the group or user, and then click **Edit**.

    - To remove an existing group or user and its special permissions, click the name of the group or user and then click **Remove**. If the **Remove** button is unavailable, clear the **Allow inheritable permissions from the parent to propagate to this object and all child objects. Include these with entries exclusively defined here**. check box, and then click **Remove**. Click **OK** and skip steps 3-6 below.

3. To allow or deny a permission such as **Read & Execute**, **List Folder Contents**, **Read**, or **Write**, in the **Permissions** list box, select the **Allow** or **Deny** check box next to the appropriate permission.

4. In the **Apply onto** list box, click the folders or subfolders you want these permissions to be applied to.

5. To prevent the subfolders and files from inheriting these permissions, clear the **Apply these permissions to objects and/or containers within this container only** check box, and then click **OK** three times.

   Important

It is recommended that you assign permissions to the highest-level folders as possible and then apply inheritance to propagate the settings to lower-level subfolders and files. For more information on inheritance, see "How inheritance affects file and folder permissions" in Help and Support Center for Windows Server 2003.

Configure the State Service on the ASP.NET State Server

The ASP.NET state service is used to manage session state on a computer. The ASP.NET state service is installed by default when Microsoft® Windows® Server 2003 is installed. The file aspnet_state.exe is installed on the remote server that will store session state information; the default location is *systemroot***Microsoft.NET\Framework***version***aspnet_state.exe**.

 To configure the ASP.NET state service

1. On the remote server that will store session state information, open Administrative Tools, and then click **Services**.

2. In the details pane, right-click **ASP.NET State Service**, and then click **Properties**.

3. On the **General** tab, in the **Startup type** list box, click **Automatic**.

4. Under **Service status**, click **Start**, and then click **OK**. The state service starts automatically when the Web server is restarted.

Configure the Registry

If a registry entry must be created or modified to correctly configure the server, you can edit the entry directly using the registry editor Regedit.exe.

Requirements

- **Credentials**: Membership in the Administrators group on the local computer.

- **Tools**: Regedit.exe.

Recommendation

As a security best practice, log on to your computer using an account that is not in the Administrators group, and then use the **Run as** command to run IIS Manager as an administrator. At the command prompt, type **runas /user:administrative_accountname "mmc %*systemroot*%\system32\inetsrv\iis.msc"**.

> **Caution**
>
> Do not edit the registry unless you have no alternative. The registry editor bypasses standard safeguards, allowing settings that can damage your system, or even require you to reinstall Windows. If you must edit the registry, back it up first and see the Registry Reference on the *Microsoft Windows Server 2003 Deployment Kit* companion CD or on the Web at http://www.microsoft.com/reskit.

▷   **To create a new registry entry by using the registry editor**

1.   In the **Run** dialog box, type **regedit**, and then click **OK**.

2.   In the registry editor, navigate to the key or subkey under which you wish to add an entry and select the name of the key or subkey by clicking on it.

3.   On the **Edit** Menu, point to **New** and then click the data type for the entry, such as **String Value**, **Binary Value**, or **DWORD Value**.

4.   In the details pane, type the name of the registry entry, and then press ENTER to create the entry.

5.   To assign a value to the registry entry, right-click the entry and then click **Modify**. If the entry has been defined as **Binary Value**, click **Modify Binary Data** instead.

6.   In the **Edit** *ValueType* **Value** dialog box, type an appropriate value in the **Value data** text box. Type or select the value of other options, such as the base (hexadecimal or decimal) for DWORD values, and then click **OK**.

▷   **To configure an existing registry entry by using the registry editor**

1.   In the **Run** dialog box, type **regedit**, and then click **OK**.

2.   In the registry editor, navigate to the registry entry that you want to modify.

3.   In the details pane, right-click the entry, and click **Modify**. If the entry has been defined as **Binary Value**, then click **Modify Binary Data** instead

4.   In the **Edit** *ValueType* **Value** dialog box, type an appropriate value in **Value data**. Type or select the value of other options, such as the base (hexadecimal or decimal) for DWORD values, and then click **OK**.

Configure the Web Site Identification Number

When a new site is created on Internet Information Services (IIS) 6.0, a Web site identification number is randomly generated based on the name of the Web site. In this way, Web sites of the same name usually generate the same Web site identification for IIS 6.0 servers in a Web farm. With IIS 5.0 and earlier versions, Web site identification numbers were incremental. For example, because the default Web site is created first, its site identification number is 1, and the next site to be created is identified as 2.

If you have administrative scripts that depend upon the IIS 5.0 method of generating Web site identification numbers, you can edit the registry entry **IncrementalSiteIDCreation** in the Windows registry to force IIS to use the incremental method of generating Web site identification numbers.

 Note

When you remotely administer a server running IIS, the value of the **IncrementalSiteIDCreation** registry entry on the local server is used to determine the generation of Web site identification numbers on the remote server.

Requirements

- **Credentials**: Membership in the Administrators group on the local and on the remote computer is required to make changes to the remote computer's registry. Network policy settings might prevent you from completing this procedure.

- **Tools**: Regedit.exe.

Recommendation

As a security best practice, log on to your computer using an account that is not in the Administrators group, and then use the **Run as** command to run IIS Manager as an administrator. At the command prompt, type **runas /user:administrative_accountname "mmc *%systemroot%*\system32\inetsrv\iis.msc"**.

 Caution

Do not edit the registry unless you have no alternative. The registry editor bypasses standard safeguards, allowing settings that can damage your system, or even require you to reinstall Windows. If you must edit the registry, back it up first and see the Registry Reference on the *Windows Server 2003 Deployment Kit* companion CD or on the Web at http://www.microsoft.com/reskit.

▷ **To configure the IncrementalSiteIDCreation registry entry**

1. To open the registry editor, in the **Run** dialog box, type **regedit**, and then click **OK**.

2. Expand **HKEY_LOCAL_MACHINE**, expand **SOFTWARE**, expand **Microsoft**, expand the **InetMGR** subkey, and then click **Parameters**.

3. Under **Parameters**, in the details pane, click **IncrementalSiteIDCreation**. If the entry does not exist, create it by doing the following:

   - Select **Parameters** by clicking on it.

   - On the **Edit** Menu, point to **New**, and then click **DWORD Value**.

   - Type **IncrementalSiteIDCreation** and press **ENTER** to create the entry.

4. With the entry **IncrementalSiteIDCreation** selected, on the **Edit** menu, click **Modify**.

5. In the **Value data** box, type **1** to force IIS to use the incremental method of generating Web site identification numbers, and then click **OK**.

Configure Web Server Authentication

You can set the authentication method for your Web resources with property sheets at the Web site, directory, or file level by using IIS Manager.

Requirements

- **Credentials**: Membership in the Administrators group on the local computer.

- **Tools**: Iis.msc.

Recommendation

As a security best practice, log on to your computer using an account that is not in the Administrators group, and then use the **Run as** command to run IIS Manager as an administrator. At the command prompt, type **runas /user:administrative_accountname "mmc %*systemroot*%\system32\inetsrv\iis.msc"**.

▷ **To configure Web server authentication**

1. In IIS Manager, right-click the **Web Sites** folder, Web site, directory, virtual directory, or file, and click **Properties**.

    Note

   Configuration settings made at the Web Sites folder level can be inherited by all Web sites

2. Click the **Directory Security** or **File Security** tab, depending upon the level at which you are configuring security settings.

3. In **Authentication and access control** , click **Edit**.

4. To configure Integrated Windows authentication, in **Authenticated access**, select the **Integrated Windows authentication** check box.

5. To configure Digest authentication, in **Authenticated access**, select the **Digest authentication for Windows domain servers** check box.

6. To configure **Advanced Digest authentication**, in the **Realm** text box, type the realm name, or click **Select** to browse for a domain.

    Note

   If Basic authentication is enabled for the site, virtual directory, or folder you are configuring, the **Default domain** text box will also be available. However, **Realm** is only meaningful for **Advanced Digest** authentication.

7. To configure Basic authentication, In the **Authenticated access** section, select the **Basic authentication (password is sent in clear text)** check box. Because **Basic authentication** sends passwords over the network unencrypted, a dialog box appears asking if you want to proceed. Click **Yes** to proceed. In the **Default domain** box, either type the domain name you want to use, or click **Select** to browse to a new default logon domain.

8. To configure .NET Passport authentication, select the **.NET Passport Authentication** check box. When .NET Passport authentication is selected, all other authentication methods are unavailable. .NET Passport cannot be used with other authentication methods because it validates user credentials in a fundamentally different way.

9. Click **OK** twice.

Configure Web Service Extensions

In order to take a more proactive stance against malicious users and attackers, Internet Information Services (IIS) is not installed on members of the Microsoft® Windows® Server 2003 family by default. Furthermore, when you initially install IIS, it is installed in a highly secure mode. By default, IIS serves only static content — features such as ASP, ASP.NET, server-side includes, WebDAV publishing, and FrontPage 2002 Server Extensions from Microsoft do not work unless they are specifically enabled. You can configure these features, also called Web service extensions, through the Web Service Extensions node in IIS Manager.

Requirements

- **Credentials**: Membership in the Administrators group on the local computer.

- **Tools**: Iis.msc.

Recommendation

As a security best practice, log on to your computer using an account that is not in the Administrators group, and then use the **Run as** command to run IIS Manager as an administrator. At the command prompt, type **runas /user:administrative_accountname "mmc %systemroot%\system32\inetsrv\iis.msc"**.

▶ **To enable and disable a Web service extension**

1. In IIS Manager, expand the local computer, and then click **Web Service Extensions**.

2. In the details pane, click the Web service extension that you want to enable or disable.

3. To enable a disabled Web service extension, click **Allow**.

4. To disable an enabled Web service extension, click **Prohibit**.

    A message box with a list of applications that will be prevented from running on the IIS Web server displays.

5. Click **OK** to disable the Web service extension.

To use, or to deny the use of, an HTTP request handler that is not in the list of Web service extensions, you must first register it by adding the HTTP request handler to the list of Web service extensions.

▷ **To add new Web service extensions**

1. In IIS Manager, expand the computer name, and then click **Web Service Extensions**.

2. In the details pane, click Add a new Web service extension.

3. In the **Extension name** text box, type the name of the new Web service extension, and then click **Add**.

4. In the **Path to file** text box, type the path or click **Browse** to navigate to any files that the new Web service extension requires, and then click **OK**.

5. Optionally, select the **Set extension status to Allowed** check box to automatically set the status of the new Web service extension to **Allowed**.

6. Click **OK** to add the new Web service extension.

▷ **To delete Web service extensions**

> ✎ | **Note**
> You cannot delete built-in extensions. You can delete only extensions that you have added to the Web extension list.

1. In IIS Manager, expand the computer name, and then click **Web Service Extensions**.

2. In the details pane, right click the Web Service Extension you want to delete, and then click **Delete**.

3. Click **Yes** to confirm the deletion.

You can also use IIS Manager to specify the applications that are allowed to call Web service extensions.

▷ **To allow an application to call Web service extensions**

1. In IIS Manager, expand the local computer, and then click **Web Service Extensions**.

2. In the details pain, click **Allow all Web service extensions for a specific application**.

3. From the **Application** list box, click the name of the application.

   The Web service extension that the application is allowed to call appears in the **Extensions to be allowed** box.

4. Click **OK** to allow the application to call Web service extensions.

You can disable all Web service extensions that are registered on the local computer with one setting in the Web Service Extension node of IIS Manager.

> **To disable all Web service extensions**

1. In IIS Manager, expand the local computer, and then click **Web Service Extensions**.

2. Click **Prohibit all Web service extensions**. The following message appears:

   If you prohibit all extensions, all Web service extensions in the list will be prohibited. This may prevent applications from running on your IIS Web server. Do you want to prohibit all extensions?

3. To disable all extensions, click **Yes**. To cancel the action, click **No**. For more information, click **Help**.

4. If you click **Yes**, the status of each Web service extension is **Prohibited**.

Configure Web Site Permissions

You can configure access permissions for specific Web sites, directories, and files. Unlike NTFS permissions, Web permissions affect everyone who tries to access your Web site. Web site permissions are not meant to be used in place of NTFS permissions, but are used in conjunction with them.

 Note

If Web site permissions conflict with NTFS permissions for a directory or file, the more restrictive settings are applied.

Requirements

- **Credentials**: Membership in the Administrators group on the local computer.

- **Tools**: Iis.msc.

Recommendation

As a security best practice, log on to your computer using an account that is not in the Administrators group, and then use the **Run as** command to run IIS Manager as an administrator. At the command prompt, type **runas /user:administrative_accountname "mmc %systemroot%\system32\inetsrv\iis.msc"**.

▷ **To set permissions for Web content**

1. In IIS Manager, right-click the **Web Sites** folder, Web site, directory, virtual directory, or file you want to configure, and click **Properties**.

2. On the **Home Directory**, **Virtual Directory**, or **File** property sheet, select or clear any of the following check boxes (if available), depending on the type of access you want to grant or deny:

   - **Script Source Access.** Users can access source files. If **Read** is selected, source can be read, if **Write** is selected, source can be written to. **Script Source Access** includes the source code for scripts. This option is not available if neither **Read** nor **Write** is selected.

   - **Read** (selected by default). Users can view directory or file content and properties.

   - **Write.** Users can change directory or file content and properties.

   - **Directory browsing.** Users can view file lists and collections.

   - **Log visits.** A log entry is created for each visit to the Web site.

   - **Index this resource.** Allows Indexing Service to index this resource. This allows searches to be performed on the resource.

3. In the **Execute Permissions** list box, select the appropriate level of script execution:

   - **None** Do not run scripts or executables on the server.

   - **Scripts only** Run only scripts on the server.

   - **Scripts and Executables** Run both scripts and executables on the server.

4. Click **OK**. If child nodes for a directory have different Web site permissions configured, the **Inheritance Overrides** box appears.

   If a child node belonging to the directory whose Web site permissions you have changed has also set the Web site permissions for a particular option, the permissions in the child node will override those you have set for the directory. If you want the Web site permissions at the directory level to apply to the child nodes, you must select those child nodes in the **Inheritance Overrides** box.

5. If the **Inheritance Overrides** box appears, select the child nodes in the **Child Nodes** list to which you want the directory's Web permissions to apply. You can also click **Select All** to set the property to apply the Web permissions to all child nodes.

6. You might see more than one **Inheritance Overrides** box if more than one property has been defined in the child nodes of the directory. Select the child nodes from the **Child Nodes** list or click **Select All**, and then click **OK** to apply the Web permissions for this property to the child nodes.

Configure Windows Server 2003 Services

You can use Add or Remove Programs in Control Panel to add or remove Microsoft® Windows® Server 2003 services, and you can use the Services console to enable or disable services. As you add and remove Windows Server 2003 services and enable and disable services, you increase and decrease the attack surface of the Web server correspondingly.

Tip

You can also add Windows Server 2003 services by using the Configure Your Server Wizard.

Requirements

- **Credentials**: Membership in the Administrators group on the local computer.

- **Tools**: Iis.msc.

Recommendation

As a security best practice, log on to your computer using an account that is not in the Administrators group, and then use the **Run as** command to run IIS Manager as an administrator. At the command prompt, type **runas /user:administrative_accountname "mmc %*systemroot*%\system32\inetsrv\iis.msc"**.

▶ **To add or remove Windows Server 2003 services**

1. From Control Panel, click **Add or Remove Programs**.

2. Click **Add/Remove Windows Components**.

3. On the Windows Components Wizard page, in the **Components** box, select or clear the check box next to the component to enable or disable the appropriate Windows Server 2003 services. You may need to select a higher level component and then click **Details** to locate the component you wish to add or remove.

4. Click **Next** to run the Windows Components Wizard.

5. Follow the instructions in the Windows Components Wizard to complete the addition or removal of the component.

Note

You may need to have your Windows Server 2003 CD-ROM available to complete the installation of the component.

▷ **To enable or disable Windows Server 2003 services**

1. Open Administrative Tools, and then click **Services**.

2. In the details pane, right-click the Windows Server 2003 service that you want to change, and then click **Properties**.

3. On the **General** tab, in the **Startup type** list box, click one of the following:

   ▪ **Automatic.** The service starts automatically when the Web server is restarted.

   ▪ **Manual.** The service can be started manually by an administrator or by another service.

   ▪ **Disabled.** The service cannot be started by an administrator or by another service unless the startup type is changed to **Automatic** or **Manual**.

4. Click **OK** to save the changes.

Convert Existing Disk Volumes to NTFS

The command-line tool **Convert.exe** converts FAT and FAT32 volumes to the NTFS file system, leaving existing files and folder intact. Volumes converted to the NTFS file system cannot be converted back to FAT or FAT32.

Requirements

▪ **Credentials**: Membership in the Administrators group on the local computer.

▪ **Tools**: Convert.exe

Recommendation

As a security best practice, log on to your computer using an account that is not in the Administrators group, and then use the **Run as** command to run IIS Manager as an administrator. At the command prompt, type **runas /user:administrative_accountname "mmc %systemroot%\system32\inetsrv\iis.msc"**.

▷ **To convert FAT and FAT32 volumes to NTFS**

▪ In the **Run** dialog box, type **convert** followed by the appropriate syntax, and then click **OK**.

Syntax

```
convert [Volume] /fs:ntfs
```

Parameters

```
Volume
```

Specify the drive letter (followed by a colon), mount point, or volume name to convert to NTFS. Required if the volume to be converted is not the current volume.

```
/fs:ntfs
```

Required. Converts the volume to NTFS.

Create a Service Account

A service account is a user account that is created explicitly to provide a security context for services running on Microsoft® Windows® Server 2003. Application pools use service accounts to assign permissions to Web sites and applications running on Internet Information Services (IIS). Administrators can manage service accounts individually to determine the level of access for each application pool in a distributed environment.

Use Active Directory Users and Computers to create service accounts in the Active Directory® directory service. Use Computer Management to create local service accounts on a local computer.

Requirements

- **Credentials**: Membership in the Administrators group on the local computer.
- **Tools**: Active Directory Users and Computers; Computer Management.

Recommendation

As a security best practice, log on to your computer using an account that is not in the Administrators group, and then use the **Run as** command to run IIS Manager as an administrator. At the command prompt, type **runas /user:administrative_accountname "mmc %*systemroot*%\system32\inetsrv\iis.msc"**.

▶ **To create a service account in Active Directory**

1. Open Administrative Tools, and then click **Active Directory Users and Computers**.
2. In the console tree, double-click the **Domain** node.
3. In the **Details** pane, right-click the organizational unit where you want to add the service account, point to **New**, and then click **User**.
4. In **First name**, type a first name for the service account.
5. In **Last name**, type a last name for the service account.
6. Modify **Full name** as desired.
7. In **User logon name**, type the name that the service account will log on with and, from the drop-down list, click the UPN suffix that must be appended to the service account logon name (following the @ symbol). Click **Next**.
8. In **Password** and **Confirm password**, type a password for the service account.
9. Select the appropriate password options, and then click **Next**.
10. Click **Finish** to complete creating a service account.

▶ **To create a service account on the local Web server**

1. Open Administrative Tools, and then click **Computer Management**.

2. In the console tree, expand **System Tools**, expand **Local Users and Groups**, and then click **Users**.

3. On the **Action** menu, click **New User**.

4. Type a **User name**, **Full name**, and a **Description** of the user account.

5. In **Password** and **Confirm password**, type a password for the user account.

6. Set the user account access by selecting the check box to set the option or clearing the check boxes to remove the option for:

   ■ **User must change password at next logon**

   ■ **User cannot change password**

   ■ **Password never expires**

   ■ **Account is disabled**

7. Click **Create**, and then click **Close**.

▶ **To create a service account for IIS_WPG Group**

1. Open Administrative Tools, and then click **Computer Management**.

2. In the console tree, expand **System Tools**, expand **Local Users and Groups**, and click **Groups**.

3. Click the IIS_WPG group and, on the **Action** menu, click **Add to Group**.

4. Under **Description**, type the name of the account and click **Add**.

5. In the **Select Users** dialog box, click the **Object Types** button, and select or clear the check box for the object types you want to find. Click **OK**.

6. Click the **Locations** button to select the location of the service account. Click **OK**.

7. Enter the name of the object under **Enter the object names to select**.

8. Click **OK**, and then click **OK** again.

Create A SQL Server Database for Storing ASP.NET Session State

ASP.NET SQL state server is used to manage session state on a computer running Microsoft® SQL Server™. All versions of Microsoft ASP.NET that are installed on the same computer share the same SQL state server. The SQL state server version of session state that is used is always the one that is installed with the latest version of ASP.NET. When this version of ASP.NET is uninstalled, the latest remaining version on the computer is then registered and used in its place.

Requirements

- **Credentials**: Membership in the Administrators group on the local computer.

- **Tools**: Iis.msc.

Recommendation

As a security best practice, log on to your computer using an account that is not in the Administrators group, and then use the **Run as** command to run IIS Manager as an administrator. At the command prompt, type **runas /user:administrative_accountname "mmc %*systemroot*%\system32\inetsrv\iis.msc"**.

▷ **Create an ASP.NET session state database with SQL Server Enterprise Manager**

1. On the **Start** menu, point to **Programs**, point to **Microsoft SQL Server**, and then click **Enterprise Manager**.

2. In **SQL Server Enterprise Manager**, connect to the server running SQL Server that will store the session state.

3. On the **Tools** menu, click **SQL Query Analyzer**.

4. In SQL Query Analyzer, on the **File** menu, click **Open**, and navigate to **InstallSqlState.sql** (the SQL script that builds the ASP.NET session state database).

   The InstallSqlState.sql file is located on the Web server in *systemroot***Microsoft.NET\Framework***version* (where *version* is the most recent version number of the .NET Framework installed on the Web server).

5. On the **Query** menu, click **Execute**.

   Ensure the query completed with no errors by reviewing the status in the lower window of the SQL Query Analyzer.

6. Close SQL Query Analyzer.

7. In **SQL Server Enterprise Manager**, in the console tree, expand the server node, and then click **Databases**.

8. In the details pane, verify that **ASPState** is listed.

9. Close SQL Server Enterprise Manager.

Create a Virtual Directory

In most cases, the content you publish to your Web site is located in a home directory on your computer, such as C:\Inetpub\Wwwroot\. However, there might be instances when the content is located in another directory, or even on a remote computer.

To be able to publish content from any directory not contained within your home directory, you must create a *virtual directory*. A virtual directory is a directory that is not contained in the home directory but appears to client browsers as though it were. You can create a virtual directory by using IIS Manager or by using Windows Explorer.

Requirements

- **Credentials**: Membership in the Administrators group on the local computer.

- **Tools**: Iis.msc.

Recommendation

As a security best practice, log on to your computer using an account that is not in the Administrators group, and then use the **Run as** command to run IIS Manager as an administrator. At the command prompt, type **runas /user:administrative_accountname "mmc %systemroot%\system32\inetsrv\iis.msc"**.

To create a virtual directory by using IIS Manager

1. In IIS Manager, expand the **Web Sites** folder, and expand the Web site to which you want to add a virtual directory.

2. Right-click the Web site or folder within which you wish to create the virtual directory, select **New**, and then click **Virtual Directory**. The Virtual Directory Creation Wizard appears.

3. Click **Next**.

4. In the **Alias** box, type a name for the virtual directory. This is the name the user types, and should be short and easy to type.

5. Click **Next**.

6. In the **Path** box, type the name of the physical directory or click **Browse** to navigate to the physical directory in which the content for the virtual directory resides.

7. Click **Next**.

8. Under **Allow the following permissions**, select the check boxes for the access permissions you want to assign to your users, and then click **Next**.

> **Note**
>
> For security purposes, when selecting access permissions, consider allowing only the default **Read** permission. By restricting permissions in this way, you can mitigate potential attacks against your Web site by malicious users.

9. Click **Finish**. The virtual directory is created below the currently selected folder level.

▷ **To create a virtual directory by using Windows Explorer**

1. Open Windows Explorer.

2. Right-click the folder you want to be a virtual directory, and select **Sharing and Security**.

3. On the **Web Sharing** tab, click Share this folder.

4. On the **Edit Alias** dialog box, in the **Alias** box, type the name for the virtual directory.

5. Under **Access permissions**, select the check boxes for the type of access you want to assign to the virtual directory.

6. Under **Application permissions**, select the check boxes for the type of application access you want to assign to the virtual directory.

7. Click **OK**, and then click **OK** again.

Create a Web Site

During installation of Internet Information Services (IIS), a default home directory and Web site configuration are created on your hard disk. Similarly, creating a Web site by using IIS Manager does not create content, but merely creates a directory structure and configuration files from which to publish the content To publish your Web content, you can place content in the default home directory, or you can create a different home directory or virtual directory and place content there.

Requirements

- **Credentials**: Membership in the Administrators group on the local computer.

- **Tools**: Iis.msc.

Recommendation

As a security best practice, log on to your computer using an account that is not in the Administrators group, and then use the **Run as** command to run IIS Manager as an administrator. At the command prompt, type **runas /user:administrative_accountname "mmc %*systemroot*%\system32\inetsrv\iis.msc"**.

▷ **To use the default Web site**

1. In IIS Manager, expand the local computer, and expand the **Web Sites** folder.

2. Right-click **Default Web Site**, and select **Properties**.

3. On the **Web Site** tab, under **Web site identification**, type the name of your Web site in the **Description** box.

4. Click **OK**. The new name of the site appears in IIS Manager.

▷ **To create a new Web site**

1. In IIS Manager, expand the local computer, and right-click the **Web Sites** folder.

2. Select **New**, and then click **Web Site**. The Web Site Creation Wizard appears.

3. Click **Next**.

4. In the **Description** box, type a name for your site, and then click **Next**.

5. Type or select the IP address (the default is **All Unassigned**), TCP port, and host header (for example, *www.mysite.com*) for your site.

6. Click **Next**.

7. In the **Path** box, type the name of the directory or click **Browse** to navigate to the directory that contains, or will contain, the site content.

8. Click **Next**.

9. Select the check boxes for the Web site access permissions you want to assign to your users, and then click **Next**.

10. Click **Finish**.

11. o change these and other settings later, right-click the Web site, and select **Properties**.

Debug Application Pool Failures

To enable *orphaning* of a worker process serving an application pool (which keeps failed applications running while your diagnostic tools monitor them), and to attach a debugger to the worker process, you must change the values of three metabase properties. The values of these metabase properties, which are set by running a script, must specified as follows:

- Set the **OrphanWorkerProcess** metabase property to TRUE to notify the WWW service to orphan the worker process when it fails.

- Set the **OrphanActionExe** metabase property to specify an executable to run when the worker process is orphaned.

- Set the **OrphanActionParams** metabase property to configure command-line parameters for attaching the debugger to the worker process.

Consider the following guidelines when you enable debugging of application pool failures:

- Debugging requires that you set all three metabase properties outlined above; enabling debugging is ineffective until you attach a debugger.

- When you no longer want to use the debugging feature, disable it. Putting an application in orphan state wastes resources if the diagnostics are not running or will not be used.

Requirements

- **Credentials**: Membership in the Administrators group on the local computer.

- **Tools**: Iis.msc.

Recommendation

As a security best practice, log on to your computer using an account that is not in the Administrators group, and then use the **Run as** command to run IIS Manager as an administrator. At the command prompt, type **runas /user:administrative_accountname "mmc %systemroot%\system32\inetsrv\iis.msc"**.

▷ **To enable and configure debugging on a worker process**

1. Copy the following ADSI script (written in VBScript) into a text editor or word processor.

```
set appPoolObj=GetObject("IIS://localhost/W3svc/AppPools/app pool name")
' Set the application pool properties:
appPoolObj.Put "OrphanWorkerProcess", TRUE
appPoolObj.Put "OrphanActionExe", "full path\ntsd.exe"
appPoolObj.Put "OrphanActionParams", "-g -p %1%"
' Save the property changes in the metabase:
appPoolObj.SetInfo
WScript.Echo "After: " & appPoolObj.OrphanWorkerProcess & ", " &
appPoolObj.OrphanActionExe & ", " & OrphanActionParams
```

2. Save the file with the extension .vbs.

3. In the **Run** dialog box, type **cmd**, and then click **OK**.

4. At the command prompt, run the script by typing the following command:

   `cscript //nologo` *filename*

   where *filename* is the fully qualified path of the script file.

   – or –

   You can call the script by using a batch file that contains the following command:

   `"cscript //nologo` *filename*`"`

   where *filename* is the fully qualified path of the script file.

Determine Web Sites Uniquely Identified by IP Addresses

You can determine whether you have any Web sites that are uniquely identified with an IP address by viewing the Properties sheet of the Web sites on your source server.

Requirements

- **Credentials**: Membership in the Administrators group on the local computer.

- **Tools**: Iis.msc.

Recommendation

As a security best practice, log on to your computer using an account that is not in the Administrators group, and then use the **Run as** command to run IIS Manager as an administrator. At the command prompt, type **runas /user:administrative_accountname "mmc %systemroot%\system32\inetsrv\iis.msc"**.

▷ **To determine Web sites that are uniquely identified by an IP address in IIS 5.0**

   1. Open Administrative Tools, and then click **Internet Service Manager**.

   2. In IIS Manager, expand the server, right-click the Web site, and then click **Properties**.

   3. On the **Web Site** tab, under **IP Address**, note whether there is a specific IP address assigned to this Web site. A specific IP address entry in this box denotes a uniquely identified Web site.

▷ **To determine Web sites that are uniquely identified by an IP address in IIS 4.0**

   1. Click **Start**, click **Programs**, click **Windows NT 4.0 Option Pack**, click **Microsoft Internet Information Server**, and then click **Internet Service Manager**.

   2. In Internet Service Manager, expand the server, right-click the Web site, and then click **Properties**.

   3. On the **Web Site** tab, under **IP Address**, note whether there is a specific IP address assigned to this Web site. A specific IP address entry in this box denotes a uniquely identified Web site.

Disable Network Adapters

To ensure that clients cannot connect to the Web server while it is being upgraded, disable the network adapter that connects the Web server to the clients before taking it offline for the upgrade.

Requirements

- **Credentials**: Membership in the Administrators group on the local computer.

- **Tools**: none

▷ **To disable the network adapter for IIS 5.0**

   1. Click **Start**, click **Settings**, and then click **Network Connections**.

   2. Locate the network adapter that connects the Web server to the clients.

   3. Right-click the network adapter, and then click **Disable**.

▷ **To disable the network adapter for IIS 4.0**

   1. In Control Panel, double-click **Network**.

   2. On the **Bindings** tab, click the network adapter, click **Disable**, and then click **OK**.

Enable ASP.NET

A server running a member of the Microsoft® Windows® Server 2003 family supports application server functionality, with Microsoft ASP.NET as an option that you can enable when configuring the application server role. To deploy ASP.NET Web applications to a production server, you must be sure to enable the ASP.NET and Internet Information Services (IIS) roles on the production server before you distribute the application.

> **Note**
>
> If you want to install ASP.NET on a domain controller, there are special steps you must take to make the installation work properly. For more information, see article 315158, "ASP.NET Does Not Work with the Default ASPNET Account on a Domain Controller," in the Microsoft Knowledge Base. To find this article, see the Microsoft Knowledge Base link on the Web Resources page at http://www.microsoft.com/windows/reskits/webresources.

ASP.NET, along with the .NET Framework version 1.1, is included with Windows Server 2003. You need to install it by using Add or Remove Programs, or enable it by using the Configure Your Server Wizard.

> **Note**
>
> When you use the Configure Your Server Wizard or the **Add or Remove Programs** dialog box to install ASP.NET on a server running Windows Server 2003, ASP.NET is automatically enabled in IIS Manager. However, if you install ASP.NET from a Web download or as part of an application such as Microsoft® Visual Studio®.NET, you must enable ASP.NET manually, as described later in this section.

▶ **To enable ASP.NET on a server running Windows Server 2003 by using the Configure Your Server wizard**

1. Click **Start**, and then click **Manage Your Server**.

2. In the **Manage Your Server** window, click **Add or remove a role**.

3. In the Configure Your Server wizard, click **Next**.

4. In the **Server Role** dialog box, click **Application Server (IIS, ASP.NET)** and then click **Next**.

5. In the **Application Server Options** dialog box, select the **Enable ASP.NET** check box.

6. Click **Next**, and then click **Next** again.

7. If you are prompted to do so, insert your Windows Server 2003 installation CD in the CD-ROM drive, and then click **Next**.

8. When the installation is complete, click **Finish**.

▷ **To enable ASP.NET on a server running Windows Server 2003 by using Add or Remove Programs**

1. In Control Panel, click **Add or Remove Programs**.

2. Click **Add/Remove Windows Components**.

3. In the **Components** box in the Windows Components Wizard, select the **Application Server** check box, and then click **Details**.

4. In the **Application Server** dialog box, select the **ASP.NET** check box, and then click **OK**.

5. In the Windows Components Wizard, click **Next** to begin installing ASP.NET.

6. When the Windows Components Wizard has finished configuring Windows Server 2003, click **Finish**.

Enable Logging

You can enable logging for individual Web and File Transfer Protocol (FTP) sites. After you enable logging for a Web or FTP site, all traffic to the site (including virtual directories) is written to the corresponding file for each site. You can also enable logging for specific virtual directories.

Requirements

- **Credentials**: Membership in the Administrators group on the local computer.

- **Tools**: Iis.msc.

Recommendation

As a security best practice, log on to your computer using an account that is not in the Administrators group, and then use the **Run as** command to run IIS Manager as an administrator. At the command prompt, type **runas /user:administrative_accountname "mmc %systemroot%\system32\inetsrv\iis.msc"**.

▷ **To enable logging on a Web or FTP site**

1. In IIS Manager, expand the local computer, expand the **Web or FTP Sites** directory, right-click the Web or FTP Site for which you want to enable logging, and then click **Properties**.

2. On the **Web Site** or **FTP Site** tab, click the **Enable logging** check box.

3. In the **Active log format** list box, click a format. By default, the format is **W3C Extended Log File Format**.

 Note

If you select Open Database Connectivity (ODBC) logging, click **Properties** and type the ODBC Data Source Name (DSN) and the name of the table within the database into the text boxes. If a user name and password are required to access the database, type the necessary credentials, and click OK.

4. Click **Apply**, and then click **OK**.

▷   **To enable logging for a specific virtual directory on a site**

1. In IIS Manager, expand the local computer, expand the **Web Sites** directory, right-click the virtual directory, and click **Properties**.

2. On the **Virtual Directory** or **Directory** tab, select the **Log visits** check box if it is not selected. By default, the check box is selected.

3. Click **Apply**, and then click **OK**.

Enable Network Adapters

After you have upgraded the Web server, you are ready to enable client access to the Web sites. During the upgrade process, you disabled the network adapter on the Web server to prevent users from accessing the Web server during the upgrade process. Now that you know the upgrade completed successfully, you can enable the network adapters.

Requirements

- **Credentials**: Membership in the Administrators group on the local computer.

- **Tools**: none.

▷   **To enable the network adapter for IIS 6.0**

1. In Control Panel, click **Network Connections**, and then click **Local Area Connection**.

2. The network adapter is automatically enabled.

Enable Security Auditing

Microsoft® Windows® Server 2003 uses security and system logs to store collected security events. Before enabling the system and security logs, you need to enable auditing for the system log and establish the number of events you want recorded in the security log. You customize system log events by configuring *auditing*. Auditing is the process that tracks the activities of users and processes by recording selected types of events in the security log of the Web server. You can enable auditing based on categories of security events such as:

- Any changes to user account and resource permissions.

- Any failed attempts for user logon.

- Any failed attempts for resource access.

- Any modification to the system files.

The most common security events recorded by the Web server are associated with user accounts and resource permissions.

Requirements

- **Credentials**: Membership in the Administrators group on the local computer.

- **Tools**: Microsoft Management Console (MMC); Local Security Policy

Recommendation

As a security best practice, log on to your computer using an account that is not in the Administrators group, and then use the **Run as** command to run IIS Manager as an administrator. At the command prompt, type **runas /user:administrative_accountname "mmc %*systemroot*%\system32\inetsrv\iis.msc"**.

▷ **To define or modify auditing policy settings for an event category on the local Web server**

1. Open Administrative Tools, and then click **Local Security Policy**.

2. In the console tree, click **Local Policies**, and then click **Audit Policy**.

3. In the details pane, double-click an event category for which you want to change the auditing policy settings.

4. On the **Properties** page for the event category, do one or both of the following:

   - To audit successful attempts, select the **Success** check box.

   - To audit unsuccessful attempts, select the **Failure** check box.

5. Click **OK**.

▷ **To define or modify auditing policy settings for an event category within a domain or organizational unit, when the Web server is joined to a domain**

This procedure is run on the domain controller.

1. Open Administrative Tools, and then click **Active Directory Users and Computers**

2. Right-click the appropriate domain, site, or organizational unit and then click **Properties**.

3. On the **Group Policy** tab, select an existing Group Policy object to edit the policy.

4. In **Group Policy Object Editor**, in the console tree, expand **Computer Configuration**, expand **Windows Settings**, expand **Security Settings**, expand **Local policy**, and then click **Audit Policy**.

5. In the details pane, double-click an event category for which you want to change the auditing policy settings.

6. If you are defining auditing policy settings for this event category for the first time, select the **Define these policy settings** check box.

7. Do one or both of the following:

   - To audit successful attempts, select the **Success** check box.

   - To audit unsuccessful attempts, select the **Failure** check box.

8. Click **OK**.

Enable the WWW Service After Upgrade

When you upgrade a Web server running Internet Information Services (IIS) 5.0 and the Microsoft® Windows® 2000 operating system, the World Wide Web Publishing Service (WWW service) is disabled unless, prior to upgrade, you elected to run the IIS Lockdown Tool or you added the entry **RetainW3SVCStatus** to the registry. However, if neither of those was done, then you need to enable the WWW service after the upgrade.

Requirements

- **Credentials**: Membership in the Administrators group on the local computer.
- **Tools**: Microsoft Management Console (MMC); Local Security Policy.

Recommendation

As a security best practice, log on to your computer using an account that is not in the Administrators group, and then use the **Run as** command to run IIS Manager as an administrator. At the command prompt, type **runas /user:administrative_accountname "mmc %systemroot%\system32\inetsrv\iis.msc"**.

▷ **To enable the WWW Service after upgrade**

1. Open Administrative Tools, and then click **Services**.

2. In the **Services** pane, double-click **World Wide Web Publishing Service**.

3. On the **Properties** page, on the **General** tab, select **Automatic** from the **Startup Type** drop-down box.

4. Under **Service Status**, click the **Start** button.

5. Click **OK**.

Enable Web Site Content Auditing

Once you have enabled security auditing, you must also enable auditing on the Web site content (files and folders) in order to track any modification or deletion of the content.

Before you set up auditing for files and folders, you must first enable object access auditing. This security setting determines whether to audit the event of a user accessing an object, such as a file, folder, or printer. Enabling object access auditing is accomplished by defining auditing policy settings for the object access event category of the Audit Policies in Local Security Settings. If you do not enable object access auditing, you receive an error message when you set up auditing for files and folders, and no files or folders are audited. After object access auditing is enabled, you can view the security log in Event Viewer to review the results of your changes. You can then set up Web site content auditing.

Tip

Because the security log is limited in size, carefully select the files and folders to be audited. In addition, consider the amount of disk space that you want to devote to the security log. The maximum size for the security log is defined in Event Viewer.

If file or folder auditing has been inherited from the parent folder, you will see the following.

- In the **Auditing Entry for** *File or Folder* dialog box, in the **Access** box, the check boxes are unavailable.

  -or-

- In the **Advanced Security Settings for** *File or Folder* dialog box, the **Remove** button is unavailable.

Requirements

- **Credentials**: You must be logged on as a member of the Administrators group or you must have been granted the **Manage auditing and security log** right in Group Policy to perform this procedure.

- **Tools**: Windows Explorer

- **File system:** To enable auditing of Web site content, the disk volumes on which the Web site is stored must use the NTFS file system.

Recommendation

As a security best practice, log on to your computer using an account that is not in the Administrators group, and then use the **Run as** command to run IIS Manager as an administrator. At the command prompt, type **runas /user:administrative_accountname "mmc %*systemroot*%\system32\inetsrv\iis.msc"**.

▷ To enable object access auditing

1. Open Administrative Tools, and then click **Local Security Policy**.

2. Expand **Local Policies**, and then click **Audit Policy**.

3. Right-click **Audit object access**, and then click **Properties**.

4. Enable auditing by clicking one of the following:

   - Click **Success** to generate an audit entry when a user successfully accesses an object.

   - Click **Failure** to generate an audit entry when a user unsuccessfully attempts to access an object.

   - If you clear both check boxes, object access auditing is turned off.

5. Click **OK**.

▷   **To apply or modify auditing policy settings for a local file or folder**

1. Open Accessories, and then click **Windows Explorer**.

2. Right-click the file or folder for which you want to set audit policy settings, click **Properties**, and then click the **Security** tab.

3. Click **Advanced**, and then click the **Auditing** tab.

4. Do one of the following:

   ▪ To set up auditing for a new user or group, click **Add**. In **Enter the object name to select**, type the name of the user or group that you want to audit, and then click **OK**.

   ▪ To remove auditing for an existing group or user, click the group or user name, click **Remove**, click **OK**, and then skip the rest of this procedure.

   ▪ To view or change auditing for an existing group or user, click the name of the group or user, and then click **Edit**.

5. In the **Apply onto** box, click the location where you want auditing to take place.

6. In the **Access** box, indicate what actions you want to audit by selecting the appropriate check boxes:

   ▪ To audit successful events, select the **Successful** check box.

   ▪ To stop auditing successful events, clear the **Successful** check box.

   ▪ To audit unsuccessful events, select the **Failed** check box.

   ▪ To stop auditing unsuccessful events, clear the **Failed** check box.

   ▪ To stop auditing all events, click **Clear All**.

7. If you want to prevent subsequent files and subfolders of the original object from inheriting these audit entries, select the **Apply these auditing entries to objects and/or containers within this container only** check box.

Export a Server Certificate

Web server certificates contain information about the server that allows the client to positively identify the server over a network before sharing sensitive information, in a process called *authentication*. Secure Sockets Layer (SSL) uses these certificates for authentication, and uses encryption for message integrity and confidentiality. SSL is a public key–based security protocol that is used by Internet services and clients to authenticate each other and to establish message integrity and confidentiality.

If you use SSL to protect confidential information exchanged between the Web server and the client, you must migrate or export the certificates and the associated private keys from the source server to the target server.

Requirements

- **Credentials**: Membership in the Administrators group on the local computer.
- **Tools**: Iis.msc.

Recommendation

As a security best practice, log on to your computer using an account that is not in the Administrators group, and then use the **Run as** command to run IIS Manager as an administrator. At the command prompt, type **runas /user:administrative_accountname "mmc %*systemroot*%\system32\inetsrv\iis.msc"**.

 To export a server certificate

1. In the **Run** dialog box, type **mmc**, and then click **OK**. The Microsoft Management Console (MMC) appears.

2. If you do not have **Certificate Manager** installed in MMC, you need to install it.

   For more information on how to add the Certificate snap-in to an MMC console, see the procedure "To add the Certificates Snap-in to MMC" in "Install a Server Certificate" in this appendix.

3. In the console tree, click the logical store where the certificate you want to export exists. Usually this is in the **Certificates** folder in the **Personal** directory under **Certificates (Local Computer)** on the Console Root.

4. Right-click the certificate you want to export, click **All Tasks**, and click **Export** to start the Certificate Export Wizard.

5. Click **Next**.

6. On Export Private Key, click Yes, export the private key.

   > ⬥ **Important**
   >
   > You must export the private key along with your certificate for it to be valid on your target server. Otherwise, you will have to request a new certificate for the target server.

7. In the **Export File Format** dialog box, click the format you want for the certificate. If the certificate has already been formatted, that format is selected as the default. Click **Next**.

   Do not select **Delete the private key if export is successful**, because this will disable the SSL site that corresponds to that private key.

8. Continue to follow steps in the wizard, and enter a password for the certificate backup file when prompted. Using a strong password is highly recommended because it ensures that the private key is well protected.

9. Type the name of the file you want to export, or click **Browse** to search for the file. Click **Next**.

10. Click **Finish** to complete the Certificate Export Wizard.

Gather and Display WWW Service Uptime Data

You can use Internet Information Services (IIS) 6.0 Performance Monitor to record and display data about the uptime of World Wide Web Publishing Service (WWW service) and Web sites by using the Service Uptime performance counter. These procedures support the task of determining the availability of the WWW service and Web sites running on IIS.

Use the following procedures to:

- Create a log file to record WWW service uptime data.
- Select a performance counter to generate uptime data for the WWW service and your Web sites.
- Start the Service Uptime performance counter.
- Connect System Monitor to the data in the log file you are using to gather WWW service and Web site uptime data.
- Read the display window in the details panel of System Monitor to display WWW service and Web site uptime data.

Requirements

- **Credentials**: Membership in the Administrators group on the local computer.
- **Tools**: Perfmon.msc; Iis.msc.

Recommendation

As a security best practice, log on to your computer using an account that is not in the Administrators group, and then use the **Run as** command to run IIS Manager as an administrator. At the command prompt, type **runas /user:administrative_accountname "mmc %systemroot%\system32\inetsrv\iis.msc"**.

Gathering WWW Service Uptime Data

You can use IIS 6.0 Performance Monitor to create a log file, and to select and start the Service Uptime performance counter.

▷ **To gather uptime data on the WWW service and Web sites**

1. Open Administrative Tools, and then click **Performance**.

2. In the console pane, click **Performance Logs and Alerts**, and then click **Counter Logs**.

3. Right-click in the details pane, and select **New Log Settings** from the menu.

4. Enter the name you want to use for the new log, for example, **WWWServiceUptime**, and then click **OK**.

   The property sheets for the new counter log open.

5. On the **General** tab, click **Add Counters**.

6. In the **Add Counters** window, if the performance counters you want to monitor are on the local computer, click **Use local computer counters**. If the performance counters you want to monitor are on a remote computer, click **Select counters from computer**, and then click. the remote computer in the drop-down list.

7. Under **Performance object**, click **Web Service** in the drop-down list.

8. Click **Select counters from list**, and then click the **Service Uptime** counter.

9. Click **All instances**.

10. Click **Add**, and then click **Close**.

    The **Service Uptime** counter for the computer you selected displays in the **Counters** window on the **General** tab.

11. Click **OK**.

12. To start logging data, select the log file on the **Performance** detail pane and, on the **Action** menu, click **Start**.

13. The counter log you created displays in green on the **Computer Logs** detail pane.

14. To manually stop logging data, select the log file and, on the **Action** menu, click **Stop** .

15. To start logging data again, select the log file and, on the **Action** menu, click **Start**.

Displaying WWW Service Uptime Data

Consider the following guidelines for displaying WWW service uptime data:

- This procedure reads a log file that gathers WWW service uptime data. Before you can read the log file, you must create the file and connect it to the performance counter, as described earlier in this section.

- The file logs data for all instances of the Service Uptime performance counter. One instance, named the Total instance, accumulates WWW service data. Each of the other instances accumulates data about a Web site. Each Web site is recorded by a separate instance.

▶ **To display data for WWW service uptime and Web site uptime**

1. Open Administrative Tools, and click **Performance**.

2. In the console pane, click **System Monitor**.

3. Right-click in the details pane, and then click **Properties**.

4. On the **Source** tab, under **Data Source**, click **Log files**, and then click **Add**.

5. In the **Select Log File** window, navigate to the log file that you created to gather WWW service and Web sites uptime data.

6. Select the log file name from the list, and then click **Open**.

7. Click the **Data** tab, and then click the **Add** button. Under **Performance object**, select **Web Service** from the drop-down list.

8. Click the **Select counter from list** button and click **Service Uptime**.

9. Click the **All instances** button.

10. Click **Add**, and then click **Close**.

11. On the **System Monitor Properties** window, click **OK**.

    The Service Uptime counter instances appear in the list in the **Performance** detail pane.

12. Select the instance desired to view the graph and statistics for WWW Service ("_Total"), or for each Web site.

Grant User Rights to a Service Account

Typically, the user rights assigned to the IIS_WPG group is sufficient for most Web sites or applications. However, when a Web site or application requires additional user rights to run properly, you must assign the required rights to the service account that is used as the identity for the Web sites and applications.

You grant user rights based on where the account is stored. If the service account is created locally on the Web server, you make changes in user rights through Local Computer Policy by using the Group Policy Object Editor MMC snap-in. When the service account is created in Active Directory, make the changes on the appropriate Group Policy object in Active Directory.

Requirements

- **Credentials**: Membership in the Administrators group on the local computer.

- **Tools**: Iis.msc.

Recommendation

As a security best practice, log on to your computer using an account that is not in the Administrators group, and then use the **Run as** command to run IIS Manager as an administrator. At the command prompt, type **runas /user:administrative_accountname "mmc %*systemroot*%\system32\inetsrv\iis.msc"**.

▶ **To add the Group Policy Object Editor to MMC**

1. In the **Run** dialog box, type **mmc**, and then click **OK**.

   The Microsoft Management Console appears.

2. On the **File** menu, click **Add/Remove Snap-in**.

3. On the **Standalone** tab, click **Add**.

4. In the **Available Standalone Snap-ins** list box, click **Group Policy Object Editor**, and then click **Add**.

5. In the **Select Group Policy Object** dialog box, in **Group Policy Object**, select **Local Compu**ter, and then click **Finish**.

6. Click **Close**, and then click **OK**.

▷   **To grant user rights to a service account when the service account is stored locally on the Web server**

1.   In MMC, open the **Group Policy Object Editor**.

2.   In the console tree, expand **Computer Configuration**, expand **Windows Settings**, expand **Security Settings**, expand **Local Policies**, and then click **User Rights Assignment**.

3.   In the details pane, double-click the user right that you want to grant to the service account.

4.   In the *user_right* **Properties** dialog box (where *user_right* is the user right you selected in Step 3), click **Add User or Group**.

5.   In the **Select Users, Computers, or Group** dialog box, type the name of the service account, and then click **OK**.

6.   In the *user_right* **Properties** dialog box (where *user_right* is the user right you selected in Step 3), click **OK**.

▷   **To grant user rights to a service account when the service account is stored in Active Directory**

1.   In MMC, open **Active Directory Users and Computers**.

2.   In the console tree, browse to the organizational unit that contains the Group Policy object that you want to modify, right click the organizational unit, and then click **Properties**.

3.   In the *organizational_unit* **Properties** dialog box (where *organizational_unit* is the organizational unit you selected in Step 2), click the **Group Policy** tab.

4.   Select the Group Policy object that you want to modify, and then click **Edit**.

     The Group Policy Object Editor appears.

5.   In the console tree, expand **Computer Configuration**, expand **Windows Settings**, expand **Security Settings**, expand **Local Policies**, and then click **User Rights Assignment**.

6.   In the details pane, double-click the user right that you want to grant to the service account.

7.   In the *user_right* **Properties** dialog box (where *user_right* is the user right you selected in Step 3), click **Add User or Group**.

8.   In the **Select Users, Computers, or Group** dialog box, type the name of the service account, and then click **OK**.

9.   In the *user_right* **Properties** dialog box (where *user_right* is the user right you selected in Step 3), click **OK**.

10.   Close the Group Policy Object Editor

11.   Click **OK**.

Install a Server Certificate

Web server certificates contain information about the server that allows the client to positively identify the server over a network before sharing sensitive information. This process is called *authentication*. If you use Secure Sockets Layer (SSL) to protect confidential information exchanged between the Web server and the client and you have exported the certificates from the source server to the target server, the server certificate needs to be installed on the Web server. before you can assign the server certificate to Web sites for use with SSL

Requirements

- **Credentials**: Membership in the Administrators group on the local computer.

- **Tools**: Certificates MMC snap-in.

Recommendation

As a security best practice, log on to your computer using an account that is not in the Administrators group, and then use the **Run as** command to run IIS Manager as an administrator. At the command prompt, type **runas /user:administrative_accountname "mmc %*systemroot*%\system32\inetsrv\iis.msc"**.

▶ **To add the Certificates Snap-in to MMC**

1. In the **Run** dialog box, type **mmc**, and then click **OK**.

   The Microsoft Management Console appears.

2. On the **File** menu, click **Add/Remove Snap-in**.

3. On the **Standalone** tab, click **Add**.

4. In the **Available Standalone Snap-ins** list box, click **Certificates**, and then click **Add**.

5. Click the **Computer account** option, and then click **Next**.

6. Click the **Local computer (the computer this console is running on)** option, and then click **Finish**.

7. Click **Close**, and then click **OK**.

To install a server certificate on a Web server

1. In MMC, open the **Certificates** snap-in.

2. In the console tree, click the logical store where you want to import the certificate.

    The default location of the logical store for certificates is on the Console Root in the **Certificates (Local Computer)/ Personal/Certificates** folder.

3. On the **Action** menu, point to **All Tasks**, and then click **Import** to start the Certificate Import Wizard.

    > **Important**
    >
    > You should only import certificates obtained from trusted sources. Importing an altered or unreliable certificate could compromise the security of any system component that uses the imported certificate.

4. Click **Next**.

5. Type the name of the file that contains the certificate to be imported, or click **Browse** and navigate to the file.

    Certificates can be stored in several different file formats. The most secure format is Public-Key Cryptography Standard (PKCS) #12, an encryption format that requires a password to encrypt the private key. It is recommended that you send certificates using this format for optimum security.

    If the certificate file is in a format other than PKCS #12, skip to step 8.

    If the certificate file is in the PKCS #12 format, do the following:

    -   In the **Password** box, type the password used to encrypt the private key. You must have access to the password that was originally used to secure the file.

    -   (Optional) If you want to be able to use strong private key protection, select the **Enable strong private key protection** check box, if available.

    -   (Optional) If you want to back up or transport your keys at a later time, select the **Mark key as exportable** check box.

6. Click **Next**.

7. In the **Certificate Store** dialog box, do one of the following:

    -   If the certificate should be automatically placed in a certificate store based on the type of certificate, select **Automatically select the certificate store based on the type of certificate**.

    -   If you want to specify where the certificate is stored, select **Place all certificates in the following store**, click **Browse**, and select the certificate store to use.

8. Click **Next**, and then click **Finish**.

The file from which you import certificates remains intact after you have completed importing the certificates. You can use Windows Explorer to delete the file if it is no longer needed.

Install IIS 6.0

You can install Internet Information Services (IIS) 6.0 by using **Add/Remove Windows Components** from Add or Remove Programs in Control Panel.

Requirements

- **Credentials**: Membership in the Administrators group on the local computer.

- **Tools**: Iis.msc.

Recommendation

As a security best practice, log on to your computer using an account that is not in the Administrators group, and then use the **Run as** command to run IIS Manager as an administrator. At the command prompt, type **runas /user:administrative_accountname "mmc *%systemroot%*\system32\inetsrv\iis.msc"**.

▶ **To install IIS 6.0 using Control Panel**

1. In Control Panel, double-click **Add or Remove Programs**.

2. Click **Add/Remove Windows Components**.

3. In the **Components** list box, click **Application Server,** and then click **Details**.

4. In the **Subcomponents of Application Server** box, click **Internet Information Services (IIS)**.

5. Click **OK** to start the installation of IIS 6.0.

Install Subauthentication

To use Digest authentication in Internet Information Services (IIS) 6.0 when the domain controller is running Microsoft® Windows® 2000, you must enable subauthentication, which is not installed by default on IIS 6.0. There are three requirements for enabling subauthentication:

- Install the subauthentication component, **iissuba.dll**.

- Set the **UseDigestSSP** metabase property to **False**.

- Set the identity of the application pool to **Local System**. For more information about setting application pool identity, see "Ensuring Application Availability" in this book.

Consider the following guidelines for enabling subauthentication:

- The requirement to use subauthentication applies to Digest authentication only. Using Advanced Digest authentication does not require subauthentication.

- When you no longer want to use subauthentication, unregister the sub-authentication component and set the identity of the application pool to Local System.

Requirements
- **Credentials**: Membership in the Administrators group on the local computer.

- **Tools**: Iis.msc.

Recommendation

As a security best practice, log on to your computer using an account that is not in the Administrators group, and then use the **Run as** command to run IIS Manager as an administrator. At the command prompt, type **runas /user:administrative_accountname "mmc %systemroot%\system32\inetsrv\iis.msc"**.

▶ **To install and register the subauthentication component**

1. In the **Run** dialog box, type **cmd**, and click **OK**.

2. At the command prompt, type:

   `rundll32 systemroot\system32\iissuba.dll,RegisterIISSUBA.`

3. Press ENTER.

4. For any application pools that use Digest authentication, set the application pool identity to **Local System**.

   For more information about Digest authentication, see "Configure Web Server Authentication" earlier in this appendix.

   For more information on configuring application pool identity, see "Configure Application Pool Identity" earlier in this appendix.

▶ **To unregister the subauthentication component**

1. In the **Run** dialog box, type **cmd**, and click **OK**.

2. At the command prompt, type:

   `rundll32 systemroot\system32\iissuba.dll,UnregisterIISSUBA`

3. Press ENTER.

Isolate Applications in Worker Process Isolation Mode

An *application pool* is a configuration that links one or more applications to a set of one or more worker processes. Because applications in an application pool are separated from other applications by worker process boundaries, an application in one application pool is not affected by problems caused by applications in other application pools.

By creating application pools and assigning Web sites and applications to them, you can improve the availability and reliability of your Web sites and applications.

Requirements

- **Credentials**: Membership in the Administrators group on the local computer.
- **Tools**: Iis.msc.

Recommendation

As a security best practice, log on to your computer using an account that is not in the Administrators group, and then use the **Run as** command to run IIS Manager as an administrator. At the command prompt, type **runas /user:administrative_accountname "mmc %*systemroot*%\system32\inetsrv\iis.msc"**.

▷ **To create a new application pool**

1. In IIS Manager, expand the local computer, right-click **Application Pools**, click **New**, and then click **Application Pool**.

2. If the ID that appears in the **Application pool ID** box is not the ID that you want, type a new ID.

3. Under **Application pool settings**, click one of the following options:

   - **Use default settings for the new application pool**

     -or-

   - **Use existing application pool as a template**.

4. If you click the **Use existing application pool as template** option, in the drop-down box, click the **Application pool name** of the application pool you want to use as a template.

5. Click **OK**.

▷ **To assign a Web site or application to an application pool**

1. In IIS Manager, right-click the application that you want to assign to an application pool, and then click **Properties**.

2. Click the **Virtual Directory**, **Directory**, or **Home Directory** tab, depending on the type of application you have selected.

3. If you are assigning a directory or virtual directory, verify that **Application name** is filled in. If the **Application name** box is not filled in, click **Create**, and then type a name.

4. In the **Application pool** list box, click the name of the application pool to which you want to assign the Web site.

5. Click **OK**.

Make a Service Account a Member of the Local Administrators Group

If an application requires specific user rights to run successfully, but the service account for the application cannot be assigned the appropriate permissions, make the service account a member of the local administrators group. This should give the service account sufficient user rights to allow the application to run successfully.

▶ **To add a service account to the local administrators group**

1. In Administrative Tools, click **Computer Management**.

2. In the console tree, expand **Local Users and Groups**, and then click **Groups**.

3. Right-click the **Administrators** group, and then click **Add to Group**.

4. Click **Add**.

5. Click **Look in** to display a list of domains from which users and groups can be added to the group.

6. In **Location**, click the domain containing the users and computers you want to add, and then click **OK**.

7. In **Enter the object names to select**, type the name of the user or group you want to add to the group, and then click **OK**.

8. If you want to validate the user or group names that you are adding, click **Check Names**.

Migrate CDONTS

Collaboration Data Objects (CDO) for Microsoft® Windows NT® Server (CDONTS) has been removed from Microsoft® Windows® Server 2003. If your Web applications use CDONTS, you can modify your code to use Collaboration Data Objects for Windows 2000 (CDOSYS), which is supported by Windows Server 2003. However, if you upgrade to Windows Server 2003, CDONTS remains on your server, because Cdonts.dll is not removed during an upgrade to Windows Server 2003. CDONTS is not installed when you perform a clean installation of Windows Server 2003, but if necessary, you can copy it to the computer running Windows Server 2003 and register it.

▷ **To copy CDONTS to a computer running Windows Server 2003**

1. On the source server, copy **Cdonts.dll** from the *%systemroot%*\system32 folder to a floppy disk.

2. On the target server, copy **Cdonts.dll** from the floppy disk to the folder *systemroot*\system32.

3. To register CDONTS, on the target server, in the **Run** dialog box, type **cmd**, and then click **OK**.

4. At the command prompt, change to the *systemroot*\system32 directory, and then type:

   ```
   regsvr32 %windir%\system32\cdonts.dll.
   ```

   If the process is successful, the following message displays:

   ```
   DllRegisterServer in cdonts.dll succeeded.
   ```

5. Click **OK**.

Modify the IIS Metabase Directly

If you need to modify the Internet Information Services (IIS) metabase, you can do so directly in the Metabase.xml file by using a text editor. Before you can modify the Metabase .xml file, you must enable the edit-while-running feature of the metabase by using IIS Manager. Once you have made your changes and saved the Metabase.xml file, disable the edit-while-running feature of the metabase. To implement changes to some metabase properties, you might need to restart the server.

Requirements

- **Credentials**: Membership in the Administrators group on the local computer.

- **Tools**: Iis.msc.

Recommendation

As a security best practice, log on to your computer using an account that is not in the Administrators group, and then use the **Run as** command to run IIS Manager as an administrator. At the command prompt, type **runas /user:administrative_accountname "mmc %systemroot%\system32\inetsrv\iis.msc"**.

▷ **To enable the edit-while running feature of the metabase by using IIS Manager**

1. In IIS Manager, right-click the local computer, and then click **Properties**.

2. Select the **Enable Direct Metabase Edit** check box, and then click **OK**.

▷ **To modify the IIS metabase**

1. Open the Metabase.xml file in a text editor. The default path to this file is
    %systemroot%\system32\inetserv\metabase.xml

2. Modify the metabase properties that you wish to change in the Metabase.xml file.

3. Save the changes to the file, and close the text editor.

Most changes to metabase properties are automatically recognized by IIS; in some cases, you must restart IIS for the metabase property changes to go into effect.

▷ **To disable the Edit-while running feature of the metabase by using IIS Manager**

1. In IIS Manager, right-click the local computer, and then click **Properties**.

2. Clear the **Enable Direct Metabase Edit** check box, and then click **OK**.

Monitor Active Web and FTP Connections

To ensure that service to clients is not interrupted, monitor the Web server for any active Web and File Transfer Protocol (FTP) connections before taking the Web server offline. Internet Information Services (IIS) 4.0, IIS 5.0, and IIS 6.0 include performance monitor counters that can be used to monitor the active Web and FTP connections. Monitor the active Web and FTP connections to ensure one of the following is true:

- The number of active Web and FTP connections is zero.

- All active Web or FTP sessions can be accounted for and can be terminated.

Requirements

- **Credentials**: Membership in the Administrators group on the local computer.

- **Tools**: Perfmon.msc, Perfmon.exe.

▷ **To monitor active Web and FTP connections in IIS 6.0**

1. Open Administrative Tools, and then click **Performance**.

2. Right-click the **System Monitor details** pane, and then click **Add Counters**.

3. Do one of the following:

   ▪ To monitor any computer on which the monitoring console is run, click **Use local computer counters**.

   -or-

   ▪ To monitor a specific computer, regardless of where the monitoring console is run, click **Select counters from computer,** and specify a computer name or IP address.

4. In **Performance object**, click:

   ▪ **Web Service** to monitor active Web connections.

   -or-

   ▪ **FTP Service** to monitor active FTP connections.

5. Click **Select counters from list**, and select **Current Connections**.

6. Click **All instances**.

7. Click **Add**, and then click **Close**.

▷ **To monitor active Web and FTP connections in IIS 5.0**

1. Open Administrative Tools, and then click **Performance**.

2. Right-click the **System Monitor details** pane and then click **Add Counters**.

3. Do one of the following:

   ▪ To monitor any computer on which the monitoring console is run, click **Use local computer counters**.

   -or-

   ▪ To monitor a specific computer, regardless of where the monitoring console is run, click **Select counters from computer,** and specify a computer name or IP address.

4. In **Performance object**, click:

   ▪ **Web Service** to monitor active Web connections.

   -or-

   ▪ **FTP Service** to monitor active FTP connections.

5. Click **Select counters from list**, and then click **Current Connections**.

6. Click **All instances**.

7. Click **Add**, and then click **Close**.

▶ **To monitor active Web and FTP connections in IIS 4.0**

1. Open Administrative Tools, and then click **Performance Monitor**.

2. Click **Edit**, and then click **Add to Chart**.

3. The local computer is listed in the Computers box. To monitor any other computer on which the monitoring console is run, click the button to the right of **Computers** and select a computer from the **Select Computer** list, and then click **OK**.

4. In **Performance object**, click:

   - **Web Service** to monitor active Web connections.

     -or-

   - **FTP Service** to monitor active FTP connections.

5. In **Counters**, click **Current Connections**.

    | **Note**

   The performance counters are not installed when IIS 4.0 is installed on Microsoft® Windows NT® version 4.0. In this case, if the performance counters have not been manually enabled, they do not appear in the Counters list. For more information about enabling the performance counters, see article 226512, "HOW TO: Reinstall IIS 4.0 Performance Monitor Counters," in the Microsoft Knowledge Base. To find this article, see the Microsoft Knowledge Base link on the Web Resources page at http://www.microsoft.com/windows/reskits/webresources.

6. In **Instances**, click **_Total**.

7. Click **Add**, and then click **Done**.

Pause Web or FTP Sites

To ensure that service to clients is not interrupted, pause all Web and File Transfer Protocol (FTP) sites on the Web server before taking the server offline. Pausing a site prevents the site from accepting new connections, but does not affect requests that are already being processed. Stopping a site does not interfere with other Internet services that are running.

You can pause a Web or FTP site by using either IIS Manager or a command-line script.

Requirements

- **Credentials**: Membership in the Administrators group on the local computer.

- **Tools**: Iis.msc.

Recommendation

As a security best practice, log on to your computer using an account that is not in the Administrators group, and then use the **Run as** command to run IIS Manager as an administrator. At the command prompt, type **runas /user:administrative_accountname "mmc %systemroot%\system32\inetsrv\iis.msc"**.

Pausing Web Sites

If you pause a Web site, you can temporarily reduce the load on the computer that hosts the site, and can make changes to the folder or document structure of the Web site.

▷ **To pause a Web site by using Internet Services Manager in IIS 4.0**

1. Click **Start**, click **Programs**, click **Windows NT 4.0 Option Pack**, click **Microsoft Internet Information Server**, and then click **Internet Services Manager**.

2. In Internet Services Manager, right-click the Web site you want to pause, and then click **Pause**.

▷ **To pause a Web site by using Internet Services Manager in IIS 5.0**

1. Open Administrative Tools, and then click **Internet Services Manager**.

2. In Internet Services Manager, right-click the Web site you want to pause, and then click **Pause**.

> **Note**
> If a site stops unexpectedly, Internet Services Manager might not correctly indicate the state of the site. In IIS, right-click the **Web Sites** folder and then click **Refresh** to see the current state of all Web sites.

Pausing FTP Sites

▷ **To pause an FTP site by using Internet Services Manager in IIS 4.0**

1. Click **Start**, click **Programs**, click **Windows NT 4.0 Option Pack**, click **Microsoft Internet Information Server**, and then click **Internet Services Manager**.

2. In Internet Services Manager, right-click the FTP site you want to pause; and then click **Pause**.

▷ **To pause an FTP site by using Internet Services Manager in IIS 5.0**

1. Open Administrative Tools, and then click **Internet Services Manager**.

2. In Internet Services Manager, right-click the FTP site you want to pause, and click **Pause**.

> **Note**
> If a site stops unexpectedly, Internet Services Manager might not correctly indicate the state of the site. In IIS, right-click the **FTP Sites** folder and click **Refresh** to see the current state of all FTP sites.

Publish Web Site Content with FrontPage

FrontPage Server Extensions from Microsoft provides a Web-based administration tool for extending Web sites. *Extending* a Web site means implementing features of FrontPage Server Extensions that enable the site owner to author the site in Microsoft® FrontPage® and delegate Web site ownership and Web site administration credentials. Making content available on an extended Web site is called *publishing* the Web site. A Web site that is not extended cannot be opened or authored in FrontPage.

Requirements

- **Credentials**: Membership in the Administrators group on the local computer.

- **Tools**: Iis.msc.

Recommendation

As a security best practice, log on to your computer using an account that is not in the Administrators group, and then use the **Run as** command to run IIS Manager as an administrator. At the command prompt, type **runas /user:administrative_accountname "mmc %systemroot%\system32\inetsrv\iis.msc"**.

Extending a Web site

You can use the FrontPage 2002 Server Administration tool to extend a Web site.

▶   **To extend a Web site by using the FrontPage 2002 Server Administration tool**

1. Open Administrative Tools, and then click **Microsoft SharePoint Administrator**.

    Note

   If IIS returns error 404, "The page cannot be found," check to make sure FrontPage 2002 Server Extensions is enabled by using **Add or Remove Programs** in Control Panel.

2. On the **FrontPage Server Extensions 2002 Server Administration** site, check to see that the Web site you created is listed in the **Virtual Servers** section.

3. To extend the Web site, click the **Extend** link next to the name of the Web site.

4. To specify an administrator account for the extended Web site, type the administrator name in **Administrator user name**.

5. Click **Submit**.

   The **FrontPage 2002 Server Administration** tool adds FrontPage Server Extensions template directories to the content directory of your extended Web site, and adds other files that contain metadata.

Publishing a Web site

If your Internet service provider (ISP) has FrontPage Server Extensions from Microsoft installed, you can publish to the Web server by using HTTP. Otherwise, you can use FrontPage to publish your Web site to a File Transfer Protocol (FTP) server.

 Note

If you publish to a location on your local computer, your Web site will not have the full FrontPage functionality unless your computer is a server that has FrontPage Server Extensions or SharePoint Team Services from Microsoft installed.

▶ **To publish to a Web server by using HTTP**

1. In Microsoft FrontPage, on the **File** menu, click **Publish Web**.

2. In the **Publish Destination** dialog box, do one of the following:

   ▪ Type the location of a Web server.

   -or-

   ▪ Click the drop-down arrow to select a location to which you have already published another Web site.

   -or-

   ▪ Click **Browse** to find the publishing location.

    Note

   If you have previously chosen a publishing destination for this Web site, the **Publish Destination** dialog box will not appear; proceed to step 4.

3. Click **OK**.

4. Specify the pages you want to publish by doing the following:

   a. In the **Publish Web** dialog box, click **Options** in the lower left corner.

   b. Click the **Publish** tab, and do one or more of the following:

   ▪ Under **Publish**, specify whether you want to publish only pages that have changed, or all pages.

   ▪ Under **Changes**, specify how you want FrontPage to determine which pages have been changed.

   ▪ If you want to create a log file for changes made during publishing, select that check box.

   c. Click **OK**.

5. To publish subwebs, select the **Include subwebs** check box.

6. Click **Publish**.

FrontPage publishes your Web site to the Web server you specified. If you want to verify that your Web site was successfully published, click the hyperlink that is displayed after the Web has been published — your Web browser will open to the Web site you just published.

 Note

If you cancel publishing in the middle of the operation, files that have already been published remain on the destination Web server.

 To publish to an FTP site

1. In FrontPage, on the **File** menu, click **Publish Web**.

2. In the **Publish Destination** dialog box, type the location of the FTP server, or click the drop-down arrow to select a location to which you have already published another web site.

    Note

   If you have previously chosen a publishing destination for this web site, the **Publish Destination** dialog box will not appear; proceed to step 4,

3. Click **OK**.

4. To specify the pages you want to publish, in the **Publish Web** dialog box, click **Options** in the lower left corner.

5. Click the **Publish** tab, and do one or more of the following:

   - Under **Publish**, specify whether you want to publish only pages that have changed, or all pages.

   - Under **Changes**, specify how you want FrontPage to determine which pages have been changed.

   - If you want to create a log file for changes made during publishing, select that check box.

6. Click **OK**.

7. To publish subwebs, select the **Include subwebs** check box.

8. Click **Publish**.

    Note

   If you cancel publishing in the middle of the operation, files that have already been published remain on the destination FTP server.

FrontPage publishes your Web site to the FTP server you specified.

Remove Virtual Directories

The Internet Information Services (IIS) Lockdown Tool works by turning off unnecessary IIS features and components to reduce the attack surface of the Web server. To assist in mitigating these potential risks, remove any unnecessary virtual directories.

▷ **To remove a virtual directory using IIS Manager**

1. In IIS Manager, expand the site containing the virtual directory you want to remove, right-click the virtual directory, and then click **Delete**.

2. Click **Yes**.

▷ **To remove a virtual directory using Windows Explorer**

1. In Windows Explorer, browse to the folder containing the virtual directory you want to remove, right-click the directory, and then click **Sharing and Security**.

2. Click the **Web Sharing** tab, click **Remove**, and then click **Yes**.

3. Click **OK**.

You can verify that the virtual directory was deleted by starting IIS Manager and expanding the Web site.

 Note

The following method does not work for root virtual directories

▷ **To delete a virtual directory using the Iisvdir.vbs administration script**

1. In the **Run** dialog box, type **cmd**, and then click **OK**.

2. At the command prompt, use the **cd** command to change to the directory where the **Iisvdir.vbs** script is installed. The default location for this file is *systemroot*/**system32/iisvdir.vbs**.

3. At the command prompt, type:

```
cscript iisvdir.vbs /delete "Sample Web Site" VirtualDirectoryName.
```

Substitute your Web site name and virtual directory name as appropriate. If there are spaces in the Web site name, use quotation marks around the Web site name, as shown in the preceding example.

4. Click **OK**.

Request a Server Certificate

To enable Secure Sockets Layer (SSL) on a Web site, you must first request a server certificate from a trusted certification authority. After you obtain the certificate, you need to install it on the Web server, and then assign it to one or more Web sites.

Requirements

- **Credentials**: Membership in the Administrators group on the local computer.
- **Tools**: Iis.msc.

Recommendation

As a security best practice, log on to your computer using an account that is not in the Administrators group, and then use the **Run as** command to run IIS Manager as an administrator. At the command prompt, type **runas /user:administrative_accountname "mmc %systemroot%\system32\inetsrv\iis.msc"**.

▷ **To request a server certificate**

1. In IIS Manager, expand the local computer, and then expand the **Web Sites** folder.
2. Right-click the Web site or file that you want, and then click **Properties**.
3. On the **Directory Security** or **File Security** tab, under **Secure communications**, click **Server Certificate**.
4. In the Web Server Certificate Wizard, click **Next**, and then click **Create a new certificate**.
5. Follow the steps in the Web Server Certificate Wizard, which guides you through the process of requesting a new server certificate.

Secure the Root Folder of Each Disk Volume

Immediately after a new installation of Microsoft® Windows® Server 2003, the special group Everyone has Read and Execute permissions on the root of the *system volume*, which is the disk volume where Windows Server 2003 is installed.

Any folders created beneath the root of the system volume automatically inherit the permissions assigned to the root of the system volume. This means that the Everyone group will have Read and Execute permissions on any new folders created immediately beneath the root of the system volume. To prevent an accidental breach in security, remove the permissions assigned to the special group "Everyone" on dedicated Web servers.

Requirements

- **Credentials**: Membership in the Administrators group on the local computer.
- **Tools**: Iis.msc.
- **File System:** The system volume must use the NTFS file system if you want to set file and folder permissions.

Recommendation

As a security best practice, log on to your computer using an account that is not in the Administrators group, and then use the **Run as** command to run IIS Manager as an administrator. At the command prompt, type **runas /user:administrative_accountname "mmc %systemroot%\system32\inetsrv\iis.msc"**.

▶ **To secure the root of the system volume by removing permissions**

1. Open Accessories, and then click **Windows Explorer**.

2. In Windows Explorer, locate the root of the system volume.

3. Right-click the root of the system volume, click **Properties**, and then click the **Security** tab.

4. In the **Group or user names** list box, click **Everyone**, and then click **Remove**.

5. Click **OK**.

Secure Windows Server 2003 Built-in Accounts

After the installation of Microsoft® Windows® Server 2003, the built-in accounts Administrator and Guest exist on the Web server. In some instances, potential attackers can exploit these well known accounts unless they are renamed or disabled.

The Administrator account can be renamed, but cannot be disabled. The Guest account can be renamed and disabled. To help prevent potential attackers from exploiting these accounts, do the following:

- Rename the Administrator account.

- Rename and disable the Guest account.

Requirements

- **Credentials**: Membership in the Administrators group on the local computer.

- **Tools**: Iis.msc.

Recommendation

As a security best practice, log on to your computer using an account that is not in the Administrators group, and then use the **Run as** command to run IIS Manager as an administrator. At the command prompt, type **runas /user:administrative_accountname "mmc %systemroot%\system32\inetsrv\iis.msc"**.

▶ **To rename the Administrator user account**

1. In Control Panel, click Administrative Tools, and then click **Computer Management**.

2. In the console tree, expand **Local Users and Groups**, and then click **Users**.

3. In the details pane, right-click **Administrator**, and then click **Rename**.

4. Type the new user name, and then press ENTER.

▷   **To disable and rename the Guest user account**

1. In Control Panel, click Administrative Tools, and then click **Computer Management**.

2. In the console tree, expand **Local Users and Groups**, and then click **Users**.

3. In the details pane, right-click **Guest**, and then click **Properties**.

4. In the **Guest Properties** dialog box, on the **General** tab, click the **Account is disabled** check box, and then click **OK**.

5. In the **Details** pane, right-click **Guest**, and then click **Rename**.

6. Type the new user name, and then press ENTER.

Set Processor Affinity

On a multi-CPU server, you can configure application pools to establish affinity between worker processes and CPUs in order to take advantage of more frequent CPU cache hits. You can use processor affinity to control processors when applications place demands on system resources.

Processor affinity is used when it is necessary to continue processing an application that is tied to a subset of the hardware, so that transitions from one processor to another are minimized. You can establish affinity on a server that is supporting multiple applications so that a processor is dedicated to each application.

Consider the following when setting processor affinity to enable debugging of application pool failures:

- By default, processor affinity is off, and the load is distributed across all available CPUs.

- Processor affinity is used in conjunction with the processor affinity mask setting that is used to specify the CPUs.

- The metabase property **SMPProcessorAffinityMask** is a hexadecimal number. The maximum value, FFFFFFFF, is equivalent to decimal 32, the largest number of processors currently allowed. The hexadecimal value, translated to binary, gives the processors that are connected to the worker process in the application pool. For example, the hexadecimal number FFFFFFFF translates to the binary number 1111 1111 1111 1111 1111 1111 11111111 . This means that all 32 processors are available to the worker processes in the application pool. If the hexadecimal value is 00000005, the binary value is 0000 0000 0000 0000 0000 0000 0000 0101, which means that processor 0 and processor 2 are connected to the worker processes in the application pool (processors are numbered from the right, beginning with 0).

Requirements

- **Credentials**: Membership in the Administrators group on the local computer.

- **Tools**: Iis.msc.

- **Mode:** The processor affinity feature of IIS 6.0 is available only when running in worker process isolation mode.

Recommendation

As a security best practice, log on to your computer using an account that is not in the Administrators group, and then use the **Run as** command to run IIS Manager as an administrator. At the command prompt, type **runas /user:administrative_accountname "mmc %systemroot%\system32\inetsrv\iis.msc"**.

▶ **To set processor affinity**

1. Copy the following ADSI script into a text editor or word processor. The script (written in VBScript) enables and configures processor affinity.

```
set appPoolObj=GetObject("IIS://localhost/W3svc/AppPools/app pool name")
' Set the properties. Enable processor affinity for processors 0,1,2,3:
appPoolObj.Put "SMPAffinitized", TRUE
appPoolObj.Put "SMPProcessorAffinityMask", &H0000000F
' Save the property changes in the metabase:
appPoolObj.SetInfo
WScript.Echo "After: " & appPoolObj.SMPAffinitized & ", " &
appPoolObj.SMPProcessorAffinityMask
```

2. In the text editor, change the value of the metabase property **SMPProcessorAffinityMask** to the hexadecimal value that corresponds to the CPU numbers of the CPUs that are used by the worker processes in the application pool.

3. Save the file with extension **.vbs**.

4. In the **Run** dialog box, type **cmd** and then click **OK**.

5. At the command prompt, run the script by typing:

   ```
   cscript //nologo filename.vbs
   ```

   where *filename* is the fully qualified path of the script file.

6. To ascertain that the metabase properties have changed, view the metabase properties in the **metabase.xml** file to see if the values have been correctly set. To do so, open the **metabase.xml** file in Notepad or another text editor. The default path to this file is *%systemroot%*\system32\inetserv\metabase.xml.

Stop the WWW Service

Once you have verified that no users are accessing your Web site, you can stop the World Wide Web Publishing Service (WWW service) on your source computer. You can then migrate your Web sites to the target server.

Requirements

- **Credentials**: Membership in the Administrators group on the local computer.
- **Tools**: Iis.msc.

Recommendation

As a security best practice, log on to your computer using an account that is not in the Administrators group, and then use the **Run as** command to run IIS Manager as an administrator. At the command prompt, type **runas /user:administrative_accountname "mmc %*systemroot*%\system32\inetsrv\iis.msc"**.

▶ **To stop the WWW Service in IIS 5.0**

1. Open Administrative Tools, and then click **Services**.

2. In the **Services** pane, double-click **World Wide Web Publishing Service**.

3. On the **Properties** page, on the **General** tab under **Service Status**, click the **Stop** button, and then click **OK**.

▶ **To stop the WWW Service in IIS 4.0**

1. Open Control Panel, and then double-click **Services**.

2. On the **Services** page, click **World Wide Web Publishing Service**, and then click the **Stop** button, and then click **Close**.

Upgrade FrontPage Extended Web Sites

You can upgrade Web sites to FrontPage 2002 Server Extensions from Microsoft from any previous version of FrontPage Server Extensions. During the upgrade process, changes are made to your Web site metadata and background structure, and some content is added to your Web site to enable it to work with FrontPage 2002 Server Extensions.

After you have installed FrontPage 2002 Server Extensions, you can upgrade your extended Web sites from the command-line, or by using Microsoft® SharePoint™ Administrator. To upgrade an extended Web site from the command-line, use the upgrade command.

▷ **To upgrade an extended Web site from the command line**

1. In the **Run** dialog box, type **cmd,** and then click **OK**.

2. At the command prompt, change to the FrontPage Extensions directory by typing:

    ```
    cd %CommonProgramFiles%\Microsoft Shared\Web Server Extensions\50\bin
    ```

3. Then, at the command prompt, type:

    ```
    owsadm -o upgrade -p Port -m WebSiteUrl
    ```

    where *Port* is the optional port number of the site to be upgraded (defaults to port 80), and *WebSiteUrl* is the URL for the Web site you are upgrading.

▷ **To upgrade an extended Web site by using SharePoint Administrator**

1. On the server, open Administrative Tools, and then click **Microsoft SharePoint Administrator**.

2. In the list of extended Web sites, next to the extended Web site you want to upgrade, click **Upgrade**.

3. In the **Administrator user name** box, type the user name for the administrator of the extended Web site.

4. Click **Submit**.

View Application Isolation Configuration

Before configuring Internet Information Services (IIS) 6.0 to run in worker process isolation mode, you need to document the configuration for existing Web sites and applications running on the source server so you can transfer the settings to the target server.

Requirements

- **Credentials**: Membership in the Administrators group on the local computer.

- **Tools**: Iis.msc.

▷ **To view application isolation settings in IIS 5.0**

1. Open Administrative Tools, and then click **Internet Services Manager**.

2. Expand the local computer, right-click the Web site for which you are documenting the settings, and then click **Properties**.

3. Click the **Home Directory** tab.

4. Under **Application Settings**, note the settings for **Application Protection**. Available settings are:

    - Low (IIS Process)

    - Medium (Pooled)

    - High (Isolated)

5. Click **OK**.

▷ **To view application isolation settings in IIS 4.0**

1. Click **Start**, click **Programs**, click **Windows NT 4.0 Option Pack**, click **Microsoft Internet Information Server**, and then click **Internet Services Manager**.

2. In Internet Services Manager, expand **Internet Information Server**, expand the local computer, right-click the Web site for which you are documenting the settings, and then click **Properties**.

3. On the **Home Directory** tab, under **Application Settings**, note whether the check box **Run in separate memory space (isolated process)** is selected.

4. Click **OK**.

View Web Site and Application Process Identities

Before configuring Internet Information Services (IIS) 6.0 to run in worker process isolation mode, you need to document the process identity used by the Web site and application. After configuring IIS 6.0 to run in worker process isolation mode, you will use the documented process identities to configure the application pools in worker process isolation mode.

Requirements

- **Credentials**: Membership in the Administrators group on the local computer.

- **Tools**: Internet Service Manager (ISM) for IIS 4.0 and IIS 5.0, and IIS Manager for IIS 6.0

▷ **To view Web site and application process identities in IIS 6.0 running in IIS 5.0 Isolation Mode**

1. In the **Run** dialog box, type **mmc**, and then click **OK**.

2. If you do not have the Component Services Snap-in installed, in MMC, on the **File** menu, click **Add/Remove Snap-ins**, and then click **Add**. Under **Available Standalone Snap-ins**, click **Component Services**, and then click **Add**.

3. In MMC, in the console tree, expand **Component Services**, expand **Computers**, expand **My Computer**, and then click **COM+ Applications**.

4. Right-click *WebSiteName* and then click **Properties** (where *WebSiteName* is the name of the Web site or application).

5. Click the **Identity** tab.

6. Document the identity for the Web site or application found in the **User** text box.

▷ **To view Web site and application process identities in IIS 5.0**

1. In the **Run** dialog box, type **mmc**, and then click **OK**

2. If you do not have the Component Services Snap-in installed, in the **File** menu click **Add/Remove Snap-ins**, and then click **Add**. Under **Add Standalone Snap-ins**, click **Component Services**, and then click **Add**. Click **Close** and then click **OK**.

3. In MMC, in the console tree, expand **Computers**, expand **My Computer** and expand **COM+ Applications**.

4. Right-click **IIS-{*WebSiteName//*Root}** and then click **Properties** (where *WebSiteName* is the name of the Web site or application).

5. Click the **Identity** tab.

6. Document the identity for the Web site or application found in the **User** text box.

▷ **To view Web site and application process identities in IIS 4.0**

1. Click **Start**, click **Programs**, click **Windows NT 4.0 Option Pack**, click **Microsoft Internet Information Server**, and then click **Internet Services Manager**.

2. In the console tree, expand **Microsoft Transaction Server**, expand **Computers**, expand **My Computer**, expand **Packages installed**, right-click *WebSiteName* and then click **Properties** (where *WebSiteName* is the name of the Web site or application).

3. Click the **Identity** tab.

4. Document the identity for the Web site or application found in the **User** text box.

Changes to Metabase Properties in IIS 6.0

B

There are IIS 5.0 metabase properties that are no longer supported in IIS 6.0. When upgrading or migrating from an earlier version of IIS, these properties are still in the metabase, but IIS 6.0 ignores the settings. On a new installation of IIS 6.0, these properties have been removed from the metabase, and they are not available even when IIS 6.0 is running in IIS 5.0 isolation mode.

In addition, there is one IIS 5.0 metabase property — **CPUResetInterval** — that still exists in the IIS 6.0 metabase, but it behaves differently in IIS 6.0.

Table B.1 lists metabase properties that have changed in IIS 6.0. If your Web sites, applications, or setup programs reference any of these IIS metabase properties, follow the recommendations described in the table to accommodate these changes and ensure compatibility with IIS 6.0.

Table B.1 IIS Metabase Properties That Have Changed Since IIS 5.0

IIS Metabase Properties	Recommendation
<ul><li>AspThreadGateEnabled</li><li>AspThreadGateLoadHigh</li><li>AspThreadGateLoadLow</li><li>AspThreadGateSleepMax</li><li>AspThreadGateTimeSlice</li></ul>	In IIS 5.0, these metabase properties are provided for the configuration of performance features. In IIS 6.0, these performance features are provided by other means. As a result, IIS 6.0 no longer uses these metabase properties. Remove any references to these metabase properties from Web sites, applications, or setup programs. For more information about improving performance in IIS 6.0, see "Designing Scalability into Server Environments" in IIS 6.0 Help, which is accessible from IIS Manager.
<ul><li>CPUAppEnabled</li><li>CPUCGIEnabled</li><li>CPUCGILimit</li><li>CPUEnableActiveProcs</li><li>CPUEnableAllProcLogging</li><li>CPUEnableAppLogging</li><li>CPUEnableCGILogging</li><li>CPUEnableEvent</li><li>CPUEnableKernelTime</li><li>CPUEnablePageFaults</li><li>CPUEnableProcType</li><li>CPUEnableTerminatedProcs</li><li>CPUEnableTotalProcs</li><li>CPUEnableUserTime</li><li>CPULimitLogEvent</li><li>CPULimitPause</li><li>CPULimitPriority</li><li>CPULimitProcStop</li><li>CPULimitsEnabled</li><li>CPULoggingInterval</li><li>CPULoggingMask</li><li>CPULoggingOptions</li></ul>	In IIS 5.0, these metabase properties are provided for the configuration of processor (CPU) management features. In IIS 6.0, processor management (CPU throttling) is provided by other means. As a result, IIS 6.0 no longer uses these metabase properties. Remove any references to these IIS metabase properties from Web sites, applications, or setup programs. The following metabase properties reference and implement CPU throttling in IIS 6.0: <ul><li>CPULimit</li><li>CPUResetInterval</li><li>CPUAction</li></ul>For more information about CPU throttling in IIS 6.0, see the **CPULimit**, **CPUResetInterval**, and **CPUAction** properties in the "Metabase Property Reference" in IIS 6.0 Help, which is accessible from IIS Manager.

(continued)

Table B.1   IIS Metabase Properties That Have Changed Since IIS 5.0 *(continued)*

IIS Metabase Properties	Recommendation
CPUResetInterval	In IIS 5.0, this property enables the monitoring of processor utilization at the Web site level. IIS 5.0 was unable to monitor individual processes for a Web site, such as multiple processes in an ASP.NET Web garden.
	In IIS 6.0, this property enables the monitoring of processor utilization at the worker process level. You cannot monitor the processor utilization for individual Web sites unless there is only one Web site in the application pool.
	For more information about how to configure this value for worker processes in an application pool, see the **CPUResetInterval** property in the "Metabase Property Reference" in IIS 6.0 Help, which is accessible from IIS Manager.
DisableSocketPooling	In IIS 4.0 and IIS 5.0, Windows Sockets (WinSock) listens for HTTP requests that use Transmission Control Protocol (TCP). WinSock uses the concept of *sockets* to provide TCP connectivity. As a result, IIS 4.0 and IIS 5.0 are bound to the scalability constraints of using sockets through WinSock. In IIS 5.0, socket pooling addresses these scalability problems, in cases where a large number of Web sites were configured with individual IP addresses.
	In IIS 5.0, socket pooling allows for socket resources to be shared between multiple Web sites and thus provides significant improvements — up to two to three times the scaling capacity of earlier versions of IIS.
	In IIS 6.0, HTTP.sys is responsible for listening for HTTP requests and provides similar functionality to the **DisableSocketPooling** metabase property.
	To configure HTTP.sys, use Httpcfg.exe.
	Note
	On new installations of Windows Server 2003 and IIS 6.0, the **DisableSocketPooling** metabase property still exists; however, IIS 6.0 ignores the property.
HcDoDynamicCompression	In IIS 6.0, the **DoDynamicCompresssion** metabase property replaces this property.
	For more information, see the **DoDynamicCompression** metabase property in the "Metabase Property Reference" in IIS 6.0 Help, which is accessible from IIS Manager.

(continued)

Table B.1   IIS Metabase Properties That Have Changed Since IIS 5.0 *(continued)*

IIS Metabase Properties	Recommendation
HcDoStaticCompression	In IIS 6.0, the **DoStaticCompression** metabase property replaces this property. For more information, see the **DoStaticCompression** property in the "Metabase Property Reference" in IIS 6.0 Help, which is accessible from IIS Manager.
HcMimeType	In IIS 5.0, this metabase property indicates which Multipurpose Internet Mail Extensions (MIME) types are supported by the compression scheme. IIS 6.0, HTTP compression is performed in a different way, and this metabase property is no longer used. Remove any references to this metabase property from Web sites, applications, or setup programs.
PutReadSize	In IIS 5.0, this metabase property is provided to support the Web Distributed Authoring and Versioning (WebDAV) component, but is untested and unsupported. In IIS 6.0, this functionality is integrated with the WebDAV component. As a result, IIS 6.0 no longer uses this metabase property. Remove any references to this metabase property from Web sites, applications, or setup programs. For more information about WebDAV in IIS 6.0, see "About WebDAV" in IIS 6.0 Help, which is accessible from IIS Manager.
UNCAuthenticationPassthrough	In IIS 5.0, this metabase property enables pass-through user authentication for Universal Naming Convention (UNC) virtual root access, which is for authentication schemes that support delegation. In IIS 6.0, pass-through authentication occurs automatically when the **UNCUserName** and **UNCPassword** metabase properties are not specified. As a result, IIS 6.0 no longer uses this metabase property. Remove any references to this metabase property from Web sites, applications, or setup programs. For more information, see the **UNCUserName** and **UNCPassword** properties in the "Metabase Property Reference" in IIS 6.0 Help, which is accessible from IIS Manager.

PART II at top right.

PART II

Internet Information Services (IIS) 6.0 Resource Guide

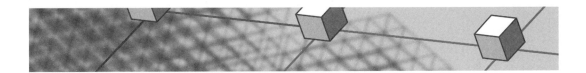

Part two of this book is a comprehensive technical resource that will help you effectively operate, maintain, and troubleshoot your servers running Internet Information Services (IIS) 6.0. This part delivers an in-depth description of the new IIS 6.0 architecture, as well as reference information about IIS 6.0 features and services. It also includes practical information and tools to help you accomplish everyday administrative tasks. Topics include running IIS 6.0 as a platform for Web applications, managing a secure IIS 6.0 solution, administering servers programmatically, and capitalizing on built-in scalability features to manage large-scale deployments. In addition, this part includes a thorough discussion of IIS 6.0 troubleshooting concepts, tools, and procedures.

In This Part

Introducing IIS 6.0

8

Internet Information Services (IIS) 6.0 is a significant new release. Completely redesigned — from its core components and architecture to its default locked-down installation — IIS 6.0 offers organizations significant advantages over previous versions for reliability, manageability, security, scalability, and performance. Whether you manage a single Web server or are a system administrator at a large Internet service provider, *Internet Information Services (IIS) 6.0 Resource Guide* provides the conceptual and practical information you need to work with IIS 6.0. You will find information about how IIS 6.0 is different from previous versions; how IIS 6.0 works and integrates with the Microsoft® Windows® Server 2003 operating system; and how to manage, maintain, and troubleshoot IIS effectively.

In This Chapter

Related Information

- For information about IIS 6.0 architecture, see "IIS 6.0 Architecture" in this book.
- For information about common tasks you can do in IIS 6.0, see "Common Administrative Tasks" in this book.

Internet Information Services 6.0

IIS 6.0 is tightly integrated with the Microsoft® Windows® Server 2003, Standard Edition; Windows® Server 2003, Enterprise Edition; Windows® Server 2003, Web Edition; and Windows® Server 2003, Datacenter Edition operating systems. Along with Windows Server 2003, IIS 6.0 provides Web server capabilities over an intranet, the Internet, or an extranet. A versatile tool for creating a reliable communications platform of dynamic network applications, IIS 6.0 can be deployed in many different environments. Small businesses and organizations might use one server running IIS 6.0 to host a single Web site and a small intranet. Large organizations, including Internet service providers (ISPs), corporations, and educational institutions, can manage many application servers, each hosting thousands of Web sites and applications.

Organizations also use IIS 6.0 to host File Transfer Protocol (FTP) sites and route news or e-mail by using the Network News Transfer Protocol (NNTP) and the Simple Mail Transfer Protocol (SMTP). Because IIS 6.0 supports the latest Web standards, such as ASP.NET, XML, and Simple Object Access Protocol (SOAP), it is a robust platform for the development, implementation, and management of new Web sites and applications.

Installing IIS as an Application Server

To help protect your systems from attackers who target unused or unmonitored services, IIS 6.0 is not installed on Windows Server 2003 by default. You must install IIS 6.0 manually when you are ready to deploy your Web solutions.

To install IIS 6.0, you can use the Configure Your Server wizard, which is included in Windows Server 2003. The wizard allows you to install or remove Windows Server 2003 services that are grouped into different *server roles*. These server roles include file server, print server, terminal server, DNS server, DHCP server, and application server. The application server role can include the following services:

- Internet Information Services (IIS) 6.0
- COM+ for remote transactions
- Distributed Transaction Coordinator (DTC) for remote access
- ASP.NET
- FrontPage Server Extensions

For more information about the application server role, see "Running IIS 6.0 as an Application Server" in this book. For information about installing IIS, see "Internet Information Services (IIS) 6.0 overview" in Help and Support Center for Windows Server 2003.

Enabling Web Service Extensions to Serve Dynamic Content

When you initially install IIS, Web service extensions are locked down, which means that IIS 6.0 only serves static content until you enable specific extensions. To protect your server, select and enable features like ASP, ASP.NET, Server-Side Includes, WebDAV publishing, and FrontPage® 2002 Server Extensions from Microsoft *only if you need them*. If you do not enable these features before you try to serve dynamic content, IIS returns an HTTP 404 level error message ("File or directory not found").

For information about enabling Web service extensions, see "Enabling Dynamic Content" in IIS 6.0 Help, which is accessible from IIS Manager.

What's Changed

IIS 6.0 core components and architecture are redesigned, which makes this version of IIS significantly different from previous versions. IIS 6.0 meets organizations' demands for the following improvements:

- **Reliability.** Greater reliability by providing a way to isolate one application from another.
- **Manageability.** Better manageability by providing a configurable XML-based metabase.
- **Security.** Tighter security by providing a locked-down security strategy.
- **Performance and scalability.** Improved performance by providing isolation in-process. Built-in scalability by offering an architecture that allows you to consolidate sites and applications on fewer servers.

Reliability Improvements

IIS 6.0 promotes greater reliability and reduces the chance of defective applications compromising overall server performance and application reliability. Applications that do not function properly can adversely affect any Web server, regardless of the reason for the application's faulty functionality. For example, one application can consume CPU resources, causing other applications to perform slowly. In addition, a Web application that fails can potentially bring down a Web server, including all its sites and applications. Web server administrators must sometimes restart the entire Web server, bringing down all its applications and sites, in an attempt to update or fix one faulty application. IIS 6.0 offers solutions for all these scenarios.

The IIS 6.0 redesigned architecture, which includes two new request processing models, worker process isolation mode and IIS 5.0 isolation mode, helps you avoid the problems caused by faulty applications. Worker process isolation mode, which is the default application isolation mode for IIS 6.0, separates key components of the World Wide Web Publishing Service (WWW service) from the effects of malfunctioning applications by using isolated worker processes. In IIS 5.0 isolation mode, requests are processed similarly to how they were processed in IIS 5.0. This process model is intended for existing applications that do not initially work when you test them during deployment testing in worker process isolation mode. For more information about IIS architecture changes, see "IIS 6.0 Architecture" in this book.

Worker process isolation mode is the default process model in IIS 6.0 because it enables the greatest number of benefits, many of which are achieved by using application pools. An *application pool* is a grouping of one or more URLs that are served by a worker process or set of worker processes. You can configure specific settings for each application pool and the worker processes that serve it.

If your server is running applications that contain imperfect code, using worker process isolation mode allows you to isolate a defective application in an application pool. You can then use health monitoring (a feature that makes an application pool self-healing), worker process recycling (periodic restarts of unstable applications or ones that leak memory), and rapid-fail protection (auto-restart of failed applications) to specifically address the application's faulty functionality, which results in fewer or no system restarts. For more information about how IIS improves reliability of applications, see "Running IIS 6.0 as an Application Server" in this book.

Manageability Improvements

Whether you are responsible for one Web server or for many clusters of Web servers, you can find new features and improvements in IIS 6.0 that will make your Web server easier to manage than with previous versions of IIS. For example, changes in the IIS metabase, additions to programmatic administration, logging enhancements, and debugging improvements can help you manage your Web servers more efficiently. From propagating configuration changes across multiple servers to pinpointing the problem in a slow-to-respond Web site, you can administer your Web servers more quickly and easily with IIS 6.0.

Metabase Improvements

The metabase configuration and schema for IIS 4.0 and IIS 5.0 were stored in a binary file, which was difficult to read or edit. IIS 6.0 replaces the single binary file (MetaBase.bin), with two XML files, which are named MetaBase.xml and MBSchema.xml. In IIS 6.0, administrators who want to manage IIS by editing the metabase directly can use a simple text editor, such as Microsoft Notepad, to edit MetaBase.xml (the metabase configuration file). Editing the metabase configuration file directly is a good solution for administrators who do not want to use scripts or code to administer IIS, and it is a faster administration solution than using IIS Manager when you are working remotely over a slow network connection. For more information about the IIS metabase, see "Working with the Metabase" in this book.

Programmatic Administration Additions

Many administrators prefer to manage IIS programmatically by using scripts and batch files, rather than by using IIS Manager, which provides a graphical user interface. Administrators working in an ISP environment with many servers — both local and remote — and thousands of Web sites, can save time by managing IIS programmatically.

IIS 6.0 includes a Windows Management Instrumentation (WMI) provider that allows administrators to control services and applications programmatically. In addition, you can still administer IIS programmatically by using Active Directory Services Interfaces (ADSI) and other custom scripts and batch files. For more information about ADSI and WMI, see "IIS 6.0 Administration Scripts, Tips, and Tricks" in this book.

 Note

In previous releases of IIS, IIS Manager was called the Internet Service Manager. For information about using IIS Manager to administer IIS, see "Common Administrative Tasks" in this book.

Logging Enhancements

You can manage and troubleshoot your Web server more effectively if you understand how to read and analyze log files. In IIS 6.0, logging differs from previous versions in several ways, so be sure to familiarize yourself with the changes before you configure logging on your server.

In IIS 5.0, Inetinfo.exe (a user-mode process) performed all logging. In the redesigned architecture of IIS 6.0, if a request is cached, the response is served from the HTTP.sys kernel-mode cache without passing through Inetinfo.exe or another user-mode component; therefore, HTTP.sys handles most logging in IIS 6.0 (Open Database Connectivity [ODBC] and custom logging are the exceptions) to ensure that responses are recorded.

IIS 6.0 provides the following additional enhancements to logging:

- Substatus error code logging allows you to record substatus error codes for requests that fail (substatus error codes are not returned to the client).

- Centralized binary logging provides a way to record detailed information about all your Web sites but to use a minimum of system resources. For example, you can use a single log file to record data for all your sites.

- HTTP.sys error logging ensures that all errors generated by HTTP.sys can be recorded, including error reasons.

- Remote logging allows you to write log data to a remote share over a network by using a Universal Naming Convention (UNC) path.

For more information about IIS logging, see "Analyzing Log Files" in this book.

Troubleshooting

Troubleshooting and debugging can be time-consuming tasks for an administrator. To help you troubleshoot effectively, be sure you are aware of the changes and new features in IIS 6.0 and Windows Server 2003 that can make troubleshooting easier. For example, Windows Server 2003 provides a new framework, Enterprise Tracing for Windows (ETW), which you can use for debugging and capacity planning. IIS 6.0 (through ETW) implements several different tracing providers to trace key transitions for an HTTP request, following its progress through the IIS service framework. These tracing providers include HTTP.sys, IIS Web Server, IIS ISAPI Filter, IIS ISAPI Extension, and IIS ASP traces. The information generated by these providers can help you determine where, in the lifetime of a request, a problem is occurring. For more information about troubleshooting, including how to use new and existing features, tools, and techniques with IIS 6.0, see "Troubleshooting IIS 6.0" in this book.

Security Improvements

Attackers and malicious users can take advantage of a system with services that are running but not being used. Such an attack is possible because if administrators do not use a service, they might forget to maintain it with current hotfixes, service packs, and patches. To reduce this security risk, IIS 6.0 is locked down by default — only request handling for static Web pages is enabled, and only the WWW service is installed. None of the applications that run on IIS — including ASP, ASP.NET, Common Gateway Interface (CGI) scripting, FrontPage 2002 Server Extensions, and WebDAV — are turned on by default.

IIS 6.0 improves security in other ways as well. Many aspects of IIS 6.0, including default functionality and settings, perform different than they did in previous versions. These changes can result in existing applications or sites performing in unexpected ways. To save troubleshooting time, familiarize yourself with the security features in IIS 6.0. For more information about IIS 6.0 security, see "Managing a Secure IIS 6.0 Solution" in this book.

Performance and Scalability Improvements

If you want to host many applications or Web sites on the same server or if you have applications that consume large amounts of system resources, such as bandwidth or CPU processing, you can host those applications on IIS 6.0 and still obtain good performance. IIS 6.0 architecture provides the foundation for a number of performance enhancements in the Web server. For example, Web gardens, processor affinity, idle timeout, bandwidth throttling, HTTP compression, and CPU monitoring are a few of the features that help you conserve system resources while optimizing performance.

When your Web server is running in worker process isolation mode, you can create *Web gardens*, which enable multiple worker processes to serve one application pool. Web gardens can improve performance because if one worker process in an application pool is busy processing a request, other worker processes can also accept and process requests for that application pool.

IIS 6.0 enables you to configure application pools to establish affinity between worker processes and specific processors in a multiprocessor computer. Processor affinity, when set, enables IIS to efficiently use the caches on multiprocessor servers. Also, you can configure an application pool to have its worker processes request a shutdown if the worker processes are idle for a configurable amount of time. Shutting down idle worker processes frees up unused resources, allowing CPU resources to be used where needed. For more information about idle timeout, see "Running IIS 6.0 as an Application Server" in this book.

If the network or Internet connection that your Web server uses is also used by other services, such as e-mail or news, you can monitor (and limit) the CPU usage of individual worker processes so that a portion of CPU resources are available for those other services. If your Web server hosts more than one Web site, you can individually throttle the bandwidth used by each site. If bandwidth is generally limited, you can enable HTTP compression, which allows faster transmission of pages between the Web server and compression-enabled clients. Also, IIS 6.0 supports HTTP Keep-Alives, an HTTP specification that increases server efficiency by reducing server activity and resource consumption.

If your server hosts applications that have workloads requiring large amounts of cached data, you can configure IIS 6.0 to cache up to 64 gigabytes (GB) on an x86-based (or compatible processor) system. For more information about these features and how to improve Web server performance, see "Optimizing IIS 6.0 Performance" in this book.

IIS supports Windows scalability solutions, such as clustering and network load balancing; however, IIS 6.0 also provides a number of specific changes that can improve Web server scalability. Scalability is particularly important for organizations that want to reduce overhead and maintenance costs by consolidating sites and applications on fewer servers.

Another way to extend a system is to store content in a remote location, such as on a UNC–based drive. IIS 6.0 provides caching, authentication, and administration changes that make it easier for you to create, secure, and manage centralized content storage.

For more information about these and other scalability features in IIS 6.0, see "Web Server Scalability" in this book.

IIS 6.0 Resource Guide Tools

The IIS 6.0 Resource Kit includes 14 tools to help you implement and administer IIS 6.0 more effectively. You can install the IIS 6.0 Resource Kit Tools, which includes Help documentation, by running IIS60rkt.exe from the companion CD. When you perform a default installation of the Resource Kit Tools, most of the files are installed in the *LocalDrive*: \Program Files\IIS Resources folder. A few tools are installed in other directories. Read the Help documentation that is included with the tools if you want to know the installation directory for a specific tool.

After installing the tools, you can access the tools and their documentation from the **Start** menu (point to **All Programs** and then **IIS Resources**).

The IIS 6.0 Resource Kit provides the following tools for migrating to IIS 6.0, troubleshooting IIS, testing and improving IIS performance, applying IIS security settings, and administering IIS.

 Important

These tools are provided as-is without a warranty of any kind. Use these tools at your own risk. Microsoft disclaims any implied warranty of merchantability and fitness for a particular purpose.

Migration Tools

The IIS 6.0 Resource Kit Tools includes two migration tools, the IIS 6.0 Migration Tool and the Apache to IIS 6.0 Migration Tool.

IIS 6.0 Migration Tool (IISmt.exe)   Use the IIS 6.0 Migration Tool to migrate Web site content and configuration settings from a server running IIS 4.0, IIS 5.0, or IIS 6.0 to a server running IIS 6.0. The IIS 6.0 Migration tool saves time and reduces the chance of errors by automating many of the repetitive processes involved with moving sites manually. This command-line tool is not documented in Resource Kit Tools Help, but a separate user guide is included in the IIS 6.0 Migration Tool folder and is also available from the Start menu.

Apache to IIS 6.0 Migration Tool (Wsmk_targ_virdir.exe and Wsmk_windows.exe)
Use this tool to migrate Web sites — for example, FrontPage Server Extensions, .htaccess files, and home directories — from Linux-based servers that run Apache Web applications to servers running IIS 6.0 on Windows Server 2003. Use this Perl-based command-line tool to migrate both Web content and configuration settings. This migration tool supports a variety of both Linux and Apache versions. The tool is not documented in Resource Kit Tools Help, but a separate user guide is included in the Apache to IIS 6.0 Migration Tool folder and is also available from the Start menu.

Performance and Troubleshooting Tools

The IIS 6.0 Resource Kit Tools provides several tools to help you improve performance and to troubleshoot an application server that is running IIS 6.0. These tools include the Web Capacity Analysis Tool (WCAT), Log Parser, IISState, Wfetch, and TinyGet.

WCAT (Wcclient.exe and Wcctl.exe)   Use the two WCAT tools, Wcclient.exe and Wcctl.exe, as a stress client to simulate clients and as a controller to initiate and monitor the testing. WCAT can test how your IIS 6.0-based server and your network configuration respond to a variety of client requests for content, data, or Web pages. Then use the test results to determine the optimal server and network configuration for your environment.

Log Parser (LogParser.exe or LogParser.dll)   Use Log Parser to perform many tasks related to log files, such as filtering entries, converting log files to other formats, and performing data mining. Log Parser supports many different input formats, including all the IIS log file formats and multiple output formats, such as text files and database tables. You can use Log Parser to obtain logging information for WCAT and TinyGet. Log Parser is available as a command-line tool (LogParser.exe) and as a set of COM objects that support scripting (LogParser.dll).

IISState (IISState.exe and IISState.log)   Use IISState to troubleshoot slow performance and application failures for applications running on IIS 6.0. IISState can also help you identify the causes of ASP0115 error messages and the causes of errors detected by Dr. Watson. For example, IISState can analyze an application like Inetinfo.exe as it executes, record all running threads, and display and log the analysis. IISState also identifies each thread, and displays the raw thread stack and the time that each thread spent executing in kernel and user modes. IISState is a command-line tool.

WFetch   Use WFetch to troubleshoot, test, and log HTTP connections between a server and client. For example, you can use Wfetch to test the performance of new Web sites or Web sites that contain new elements, such as ASP or wireless protocols. Because Wfetch provides only HTTP connection information, it provides a faster way to analyze and troubleshoot HTTP performance than by running a Network Monitor trace. Wfetch provides a graphical user interface (GUI).

TinyGet (TinyGet.exe)   Use TinyGet to troubleshoot, test, and log HTTP connections between a server and client. With TinyGet.exe, you can customize each test request by configuring many different factors, including the authentication method, HTTP version, and output format. You can also use scripts that specify looping and multithreading. TinyGet.exe is a command-line tool.

Security Tools

The IIS 6.0 Resource Kit Tools provides several tools to help secure your Web server and troubleshoot security issues, including CustomAuth, Permissions Verifier, SelfSSL, and IISCertDeploy.vbs.

CustomAuth (CustomAuth.dll and CustomAuth.ini)   Use CustomAuth as a Web client authentication alternative to Basic, NTLM, and other IIS authentication methods. With CustomAuth, you can create a custom logon form for collecting user credentials, or you can use or modify the logon form that is included with the tool. As an ISAPI filter that must also be installed as a wildcard application map, CustomAuth runs at the beginning of every request, regardless of the extension of the requested file. Because CustomAuth allows users to log off after they complete a session, it is a good solution for a public kiosk.

Permissions Verifier (Permissions Verifier.js)   Use Permissions Verifier and its accompanying XML sample to verify that IIS is configured with the minimum permissions required to run. The tool checks the access control lists (ACLs) set for users and groups to help you determine whether permissions issues are causing any Web server problems.

SelfSSL (SelfSSL.exe)   Use SelfSSL to generate and install a self-signed Secure Sockets Layer (SSL) certificate. Because SelfSSL.exe generates a self-signed certificate that does not originate from a commonly trusted source, use this tool only when you need to troubleshoot third-party certificate problems or when you need to create a secure private channel between your server and a limited, known group of users, such as exists in a software test environment. SelfSSL.exe is a command-line tool.

IISCertDeploy.vbs   Use IISCertDeploy.vbs to deploy and back up SSL certificates on servers running IIS 6.0.

Administration Tools

The IIS 6.0 Resource Kit Tools provides several tools to help you administer your Web server and manage your sites, including IIS Host Helper Service, RemapURL, and Metabase Explorer.

IIS Host Helper Service (IISHostsvc.exe)   Use IIS Host Helper Service to register IIS host header strings with name resolution services. You can use IIS Host Helper Service in corporate intranet settings when you want to allow users to access Web sites by using host header names, but you do not want to register each site's name statically with Windows Internet Name Service (WINS) or a DNS server. When you install the IIS 6.0 Resource Kit Tools, IISHostsvc.exe is placed in the *systemroot*\System32\Inetsrv directory, and an IIS Host Helper Service log file directory is created at *systemroot*\System32\LogFiles\Iishostsvc.

RemapURL (RemapUrl.ini and RemapUrl.dll)   Use RemapURL to redirect client HTTP requests for URLs. RemapURL is a sample ISAPI filter that redirects HTTP requests by using an ISAPI PREPROC_HEADERS notification. This method enables you to redirect client GET or POST requests in a way that is completely transparent to the user. You can also use RemapURL if you want to display custom error messages.

Metabase Explorer   Use Metabase Explorer for viewing and editing the IIS 6.0 metabase. You can also use this tool to edit security settings for keys, export and import keys and subkeys, copy and paste keys and subkeys, and compare records. Metabase Explorer provides a GUI.

Additional Resources

These resources contain additional information and tools related to this chapter.

Related Information

- "Analyzing Log Files" for information about improvements to IIS logging, including centralized binary logging.

- "Common Administrative Tasks" for information about how to perform frequently used administrative tasks.

- "Configuring Internet Sites and Services" for information about configuring Web, FTP, NNTP, and SMTP sites and services.

- "IIS 6.0 Administration Scripts, Tips, and Tricks" for information about configuring IIS programmatically. Includes steps for creating and configuring a site from a batch file.

- "IIS 6.0 Architecture" for information about IIS 6.0 architecture as it pertains to the application isolation modes. Includes diagrams of how request processing occurs in worker process isolation mode and in IIS 5.0 isolation mode.

- "Managing a Secure IIS 6.0 Solution" for information about improvements to IIS security.

- "Optimizing IIS 6.0 Performance" for information about specific performance counters and tools for monitoring and tuning performance. Includes information about managing system resources, such as setting connection timeouts, configuring HTTP compression, and enabling bandwidth throttling.

- "Running IIS 6.0 as an Application Server" for information about installing IIS 6.0, choosing and configuring an application isolation mode, using health monitoring features and application pools, and managing Web server resources.

- "Troubleshooting IIS 6.0" for information about troubleshooting IIS, including HTTP status codes.

- "Web Server Scalability" for information about improving scalability by optimizing IIS caches.

- "Working with the Metabase" for information about editing, backing up, and importing and exporting the IIS 6.0 metabase.

- *Internet Information Services (IIS) 6.0 Deployment Guide* of the *Microsoft® Windows® Server 2003 Resource Kit*, which is also a member of the *Internet Information Services (IIS) 6.0 Resource Kit*.

Related IIS 6.0 Help Topics

- "Common Administrative Tasks" in IIS 6.0 Help for detailed information about how to complete many of the tasks described in this chapter.

- "Enabling Dynamic Content" in IIS 6.0 Help, which is accessible from IIS Manager, for information about enabling features in the Web Service Extensions list.

- "Frequently Asked Questions" in IIS 6.0 Help for basic information about IIS 6.0.

- "Metabase Property Reference" in IIS 6.0 Help for reference information about metabase properties.

- "Server Administration Guide" in IIS 6.0 Help for information about administering IIS 6.0.

- "Site Setup" in IIS 6.0 Help for information about setting up IIS 6.0.

- "Web Application Guide" in IIS 6.0 Help for information about using ASP and ASP.NET with IIS 6.0.

Related Windows Server 2003 Help Topics

For best results in identifying Help topics by title, in Help and Support Center, under the **Search** box, click **Set search options**. Under **Help Topics**, select the **Search in title only** check box.

- "Internet Information Services (IIS) 6.0 overview" in Help and Support Center for Windows Server 2003 for information about installing IIS 6.0.

Related Tools

- Adsutil.vbs

  Obtain syntax, parameters, and examples for using Adsutil.vbs to configure and manage IIS from "IIS 6.0 Administration Scripts, Tips, and Tricks" in this book.

- IIS 6.0 Resource Kit tools (IIS60rkt.exe)

  Obtain the IIS 6.0 Resource Kit tools and their documentation (IISTools.chm,) from the *Windows Server 2003 Resource Kit* companion CD or the *Internet Information Services (IIS) 6.0 Resource Kit* companion CD. Install the Resource Kit Tools by running IIS60rkt.exe from the companion CD. When you perform a default installation of the Resource Kit Tools, the files are installed in the *LocalDrive*:\Program Files\IIS Resources folder.

- Windows Support Tools

  Obtain the Windows Support Tools by installing them from the \Support\Tools folder of the Windows Server 2003 operating system CD. See the Support Tools Help file for information about using these tools.

C H A P T E R 9

IIS 6.0 Architecture

Internet Information Services (IIS) version 6.0, which runs on all editions of the Microsoft® Windows® Server 2003 operating system, provides a new architecture that offers flexibility in the choice of two application isolation modes. The new architecture helps you run a faster Web service that is more reliable and secure. Read this chapter to obtain a detailed review of the new architecture so that you can understand how IIS works and can effectively deploy, manage, and troubleshoot IIS 6.0.

In This Chapter

Related Information

- For more information about running IIS as an application server, see "Running IIS 6.0 as an Application Server" in this book.
- For more information about what has changed since IIS 5.0, see "Introducing IIS 6.0" in this book.

Overview of IIS 6.0 Architecture

IIS 6.0 provides a redesigned World Wide Web Publishing Service (WWW service) architecture that can help you achieve better performance, reliability, scalability, and security for your Web sites, whether they run on a single server running IIS or on multiple servers.

IIS 6.0 runs a server in one of two distinct request processing models, called application isolation modes. *Application isolation* is the separation of applications by process boundaries that prevents one application or Web site from affecting another and reduces the time that you spend restarting services to correct problems related to applications.

In IIS 6.0, application isolation is configured differently for each of the two IIS application isolation modes. Both modes rely on the *HTTP protocol stack* (also referred to as *HTTP.sys*) to receive Hypertext Transfer Protocol (HTTP) requests from the Internet and return responses. HTTP.sys resides in *kernel mode*, where operating system code, such as device drivers, runs. HTTP.sys listens for, and queues, HTTP requests. For more information about HTTP.sys, see "HTTP Protocol Stack" later in this chapter.

The new request-processing architecture and application isolation environment enables individual Web applications, which always run in *user mode*, to function within a self-contained worker process. A *worker process* is user-mode code whose role is to process requests, such as returning a static page or invoking an Internet Server API (ISAPI) extension or filter. Worker processes use HTTP.sys to receive requests and send responses over HTTP. For more information about worker processes, see "Worker Processes" later in this chapter.

IIS 6.0 Request Processing Models

Worker process isolation mode is the new IIS request processing model. In this application isolation mode, you can group Web applications into *application pools*, through which you can apply configuration settings to the worker processes that service those applications. An application pool corresponds to one request routing queue within HTTP.sys and one or more worker processes.

Worker process isolation mode enables you to completely separate an application in its own process, with no dependence on a central process such as Inetinfo.exe to load and execute the application. All requests are handled by worker processes that are isolated from the Web server itself. Process boundaries separate each application pool so that when an application is routed to one application pool, applications in other application pools do not affect that application. By using application pools, you can run all application code in an isolated environment without incurring a performance penalty. For more information about application pools, see "How Application Pools Work" later in this chapter.

For a visual representation of worker process isolation mode architecture, see Figure 2.1.

Figure 2.1 Architecture of Worker Process Isolation Mode

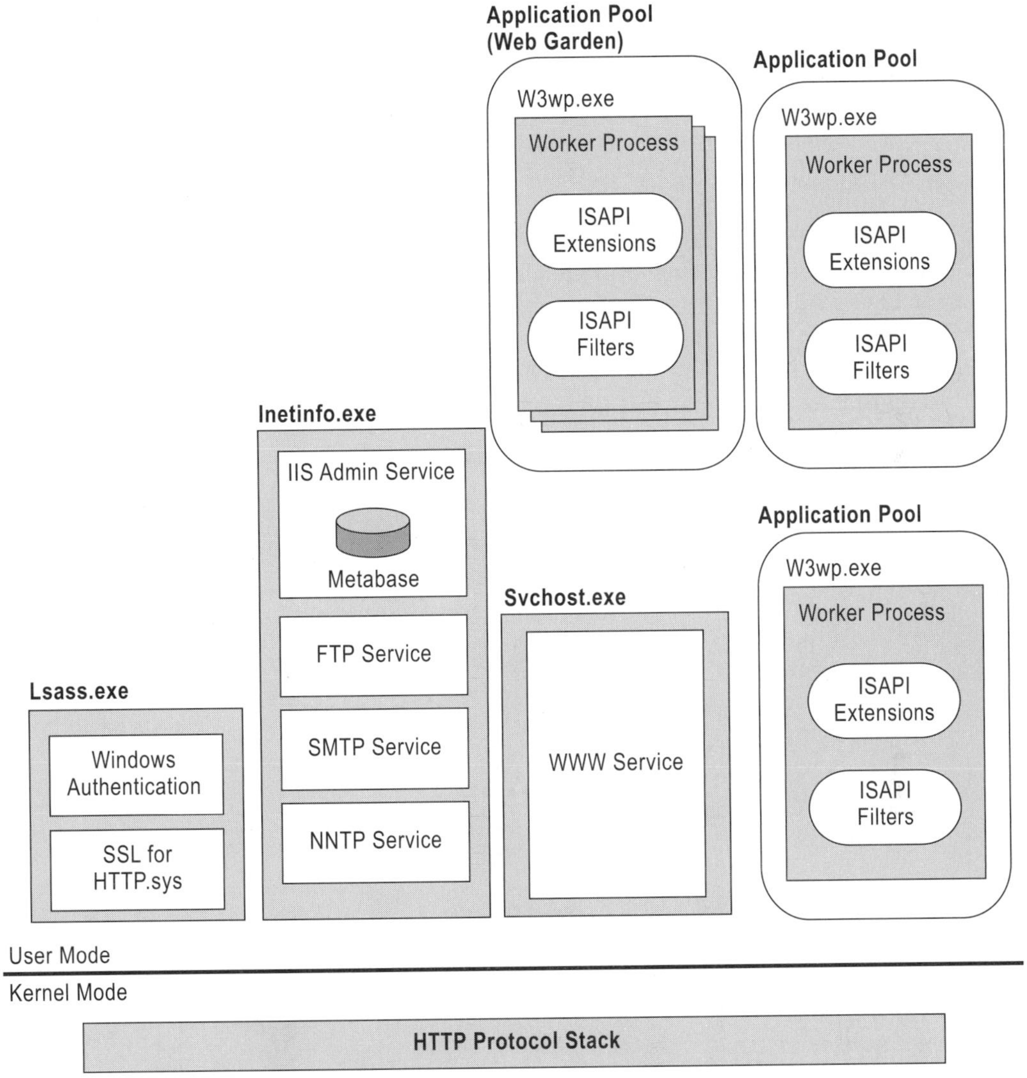

Worker process isolation mode delivers all the benefits of the new IIS 6.0 architecture, including multiple application pools, health monitoring and recycling, increased security and performance, improved scalability, and processor affinity. For example, the new health monitoring features can help you discover and prevent application failures, and can also help protect your Web server from imperfect applications.

IIS 5.0 isolation mode provides compatibility for applications that were designed to run in earlier versions of IIS. When IIS 6.0 is running in IIS 5.0 isolation mode, request processing is almost identical to the request processing in IIS 5.0. When a server is working in IIS 5.0 isolation mode, application pools, recycling, and health monitoring features are unavailable.

For a visual representation of IIS 5.0 isolation mode architecture, see Figure 2.2. The dashed line in Figure 2.2 indicates the dependency of the worker process on the WWW service, which manages the worker process. For more information about the role of the WWW service, see "WWW Service Administration and Monitoring" later in this chapter.

Figure 2.2   Architecture of IIS 5.0 Isolation Mode

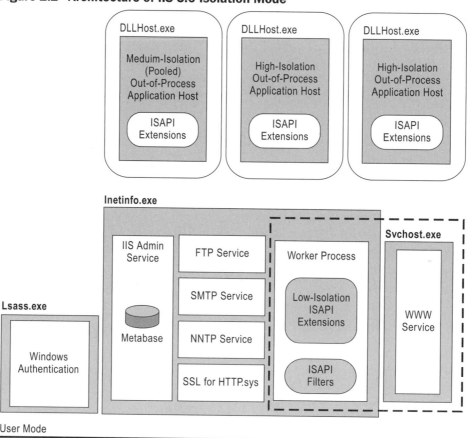

Use IIS 5.0 isolation mode only if components or applications do not function in worker process isolation mode. The latter mode is designed to provide an environment in which most existing applications or sites function correctly.

For more information about IIS 6.0 isolation modes, see "Application Isolation Modes" later in this chapter.

IIS 6.0 Services

IIS 6.0 provides four Internet services: the World Wide Web Publishing Service (WWW service) for hosting Internet and intranet content; the File Transfer Protocol (FTP) service for hosting sites where users can upload and download files; the Network News Transfer Protocol (NNTP) service for hosting discussion groups; and the Simple Mail Transfer Protocol (SMTP) service for sending and receiving e-mail messages.

After installing these services, you can create sites or virtual servers, configure properties and security settings, and set up components to further customize your system. For more information about IIS services, see "IIS 6.0 Services" later in this chapter and "Configuring Internet Sites and Services" in this book.

WWW Service Administration and Monitoring, which is a new set of features that were added to the WWW service in IIS 6.0, manages worker processes, supports the new request processing model, and is responsible for health management and maintenance, including application pool health monitoring, recycling worker processes, and rapid-fail protection.

IIS Admin service is a service of the Microsoft® Windows® Server 2003, Standard Edition; Microsoft® Windows® Server 2003, Enterprise Edition; Microsoft® Windows® Server 2003, Web Edition; and Microsoft® Windows® Server 2003, Datacenter Edition operating systems. The IIS Admin service manages the IIS metabase, which stores IIS configuration data. The IIS Admin service makes metabase data available to applications and the core components of IIS. For more information about the IIS metabase, see "The IIS Metabase" later in this chapter.

Comparing Basic Functionality Between IIS 6.0 and Earlier IIS Versions

For a quick preview of IIS architecture, comparing IIS 6.0 architecture with the architecture for earlier versions of IIS, see Table 2.1, which summarizes the basic functionality for different versions of IIS.

Table 2.1 Basic Functionality in Different Versions of IIS

Functionality	IIS 4.0	IIS 5.0	IIS 5.1	IIS 6.0
Platform	Microsoft® Windows NT® 4.0 operating system	Microsoft® Windows® 2000 Server operating system	Microsoft® Windows® XP Professional operating system	Windows Server 2003
Architecture	32-bit	32-bit	32-bit and 64-bit	32-bit and 64-bit
Network subsystem	TCP/IP kernel	TCP/IP kernel	TCP/IP kernel	HTTP.sys kernel

(continued)

Table 2.1   Basic Functionality in Different Versions of IIS *(continued)*

Functionality	IIS 4.0	IIS 5.0	IIS 5.1	IIS 6.0
Application request processing model	**MTX.exe:** Multiple DLL hosts in High application isolation. **Inetinfo.exe:** In-process as DLLs with Low isolation.	**DLLHost.exe:** Multiple DLL hosts in Medium or High application isolation. **Inetinfo.exe:** In-process as DLLs with Low isolation.	**DLLHost.exe:** Multiple DLL hosts in Medium or High application isolation. **Inetinfo.exe:** In-process as DLLs with Low isolation.	**W3wp.exe:** In worker process isolation mode (multiple worker processes). **Inetinfo.exe:** Only in IIS 5.0 isolation mode with *in-process* applications. **DLLHost.exe:** Only in IIS 5.0 isolation mode with *out-of-process* applications.
Metabase configuration	Binary	Binary	Binary	XML
Security	Windows authentication Secure Sockets Layer (SSL)	Windows authentication SSL Kerberos	Windows authentication SSL Kerberos	Windows authentication SSL Kerberos .NET Passport support
Remote administration	HTMLA[1]	HTMLA	No HTMLA Terminal Services	Remote Administration Tool (HTML) Terminal Services

1 Hypertext Markup Language Administration or HTML-based administration. HTMLA-based administration allows administrators to manage IIS Web servers by using a standard Web browser, such as Microsoft® Internet Explorer, as the client-side interface.

IIS 6.0 Services

IIS 6.0 offers four Internet services that you can use to create sites or virtual servers, configure properties and security settings, and set up components to customize your system.

When you install IIS 6.0 on a computer that does not contain an earlier version of IIS, IIS 6.0 automatically installs the following two services:

- The WWW service, which hosts Internet and intranet content.
- The IIS Admin service, which manages the IIS metabase.

You can also choose to install one or more of the following services:

- The FTP service for hosting sites from which users can upload and download files.
- The NNTP service for hosting discussion groups.
- The SMTP service for sending and receiving e-mail messages.

Table 2.2 lists the IIS services, their core components, and their service hosts.

Table 2.2   Basic Services Provided by IIS 6.0

Service Name	Description	Service Short Name	Core Component	Host
World Wide Web Publishing Service (WWW service)	Delivers Web publishing services.	W3SVC	Iisw3adm.dll	Svchost.exe
File Transfer Protocol (FTP)	Allows file uploads and downloads from remote systems.	MSFTPSVC	Ftpsvc2.dll	Inetinfo.exe
Simple Mail Transfer Protocol (SMTP)	Sends and receives electronic messages (e-mail).	SMTPSVC	Smtpsvc.dll	Inetinfo.exe
Network News Transfer Protocol (NNTP)	Distributes network news messages.	NNTPSVC	Nntpsvc.dll	Inetinfo.exe
IIS Admin Service	Manages the metabase.	IISADMIN	Iisadmin.dll	Inetinfo.exe

World Wide Web Publishing Service

The World Wide Web Publishing Service (WWW service) provides Web publishing for IIS, connecting client HTTP requests to Web sites running on an IIS-based Web server.

The WWW service manages and configures the IIS core components that process HTTP requests. These core components include the HTTP protocol stack (HTTP.sys) and the worker processes.

The WWW service includes these subcomponents: Active Server Pages (ASP), Internet Data Connector, Remote Administration (HTML), Remote Desktop Web Connection, server-side includes (SSI), Web Distributed Authoring and Versioning (WebDAV) publishing, and ASP.NET.

FTP Service

IIS provides an FTP service, which you can use to allow users on remote computer systems to copy files to and from your server on a network that uses TCP/IP. The IIS FTP service is an implementation of the File Transfer Protocol, RFC 959, "File Transfer Protocol (FTP)," and several extensions. The FTP protocol is implemented on top of TCP, which ensures that file transfers are complete and that data transfer is accurate.

You can deploy the FTP service across an arbitrary number of front-end and back-end servers, which increases reliability and availability. By adding virtual directories and servers, you can easily scale FTP without affecting end users.

In IIS 6.0, the FTP service allows you to isolate users at the site level, a feature known as *FTP user isolation*, to help administrators secure and commercialize their Internet sites. Because of the easy availability and wide adoption of FTP, Internet service providers (ISPs) and application service providers (ASPs) traditionally have used FTP to upload their Web content. IIS 6.0 allows the isolation of users into their own directory, thus preventing users from viewing or overwriting other users' Web content. The user's top-level directory appears as the root of the FTP site, thus restricting access by not allowing users to navigate farther up the directory tree or across to other users' home directories. Within the user's own site, the user can create, modify, or delete files and folders.

SMTP Service

The SMTP service in IIS processes messages by using the Simple Mail Transfer Protocol (SMTP), which is a TCP/IP protocol that is used to send and receive messages from one computer to another on a network. This protocol is used in intranets and on the Internet to route e-mail.

SMTP is the Internet standard for transporting and delivering electronic messages. Based on specifications in RFCs 2821 and 2822, Microsoft SMTP service is included in the Windows Server 2003 operating system. In Windows Server 2003, the SMTP service is actually a component of IIS and runs as part of Inetinfo.exe. Windows Server 2003 uses SMTP as its native transport protocol to route all messages internally and externally. SMTP is also the default transport for Microsoft® Exchange 2000 Server.

The SMTP component of IIS can send or receive SMTP e-mail messages. You can program the server to automatically send messages in response to events — for example, to confirm a successful form submission by a user. You can also use SMTP to receive messages — for example, to collect feedback from Web site customers.

SMTP does not provide a complete e-mail service. To obtain complete e-mail services for your users, use Microsoft® Exchange Server. For more information about Exchange Server, see the Microsoft Product Support Services link on the Web Resources page at http://www.microsoft.com/windows/reskits/webresources.

NNTP Service

IIS provides a Network News Transfer Protocol (NNTP) service, which you can use to distribute network news messages to NNTP servers and to NNTP clients (news readers) on the Internet. NNTP provides for the distribution, inquiry, retrieval, and posting of news articles by using a reliable stream-based transmission of news on the Internet. With NNTP, news articles are stored on a server in a central database from which users select specific items to read. Indexing, cross-referencing, and expiration of aged messages also are provided.

You can host NNTP local discussion groups on a single computer. Because this feature complies fully with the NNTP protocol, users can use any NNTP client to participate in the newsgroup discussions. The IIS NNTP service does not support news feeds or replication. To use news feeds or to replicate a newsgroup across multiple computers, use Microsoft Exchange Server.

 Note

For more information about these four IIS Internet services, see "Configuring Internet Sites and Services" in this book.

IIS Admin Service

IIS Admin service is a Windows Server 2003 service that manages the IIS metabase. The metabase stores IIS configuration data in a plaintext XML file that you can read and edit by using common text editors. IIS Admin service makes metabase data available to other applications, including the core components of IIS, applications built on IIS, and applications that are independent of IIS, such as management or monitoring tools. For more information about the IIS metabase, see "The IIS Metabase" later in this chapter and "Working with the Metabase" in this book.

IIS 6.0 Core Components

IIS 6.0 contains several core components that perform important functions in the new IIS architecture. The more that you know about these components, the better you can use IIS 6.0 to your advantage and effectively troubleshoot any issues that might arise.

Most of these core components were briefly described in "Overview of IIS 6.0 Architecture" earlier in this chapter. This section provides additional details, including how these core components interact with each other or how they function in each of the two application isolation modes. For example, you can read about the following topics in this section:

- **HTTP Protocol Stack (HTTP.sys).** How the HTTP protocol stack protects the operating system kernel from the effects of imperfect application code, and how it handles kernel-mode queuing.
- **Worker processes.** How the worker process is controlled by the WWW service in both application isolation modes, but in different ways.
- **WWW Service Administration and Monitoring.** How the WWW Service Administration and Monitoring component manages the lifetime of the worker process.
- **Inetinfo.exe.** How the role of Inetinfo.exe has changed since IIS 5.0.
- **IIS Metabase.** Benefits of the new XML metabase, especially in diagnosing possible metabase corruption or in reading and editing the metabase configuration.

HTTP Protocol Stack

The HTTP listener is implemented as a kernel-mode device driver called the HTTP protocol stack (HTTP.sys). IIS 6.0 uses HTTP.sys, which is part of the networking subsystem of the Windows operating system, as a core component.

Earlier versions of IIS use Windows Sockets API (Winsock), which is a user-mode component, to receive HTTP requests. By using HTTP.sys to process requests, IIS 6.0 delivers the following performance enhancements:

- **Kernel-mode caching.** Requests for cached responses are served without switching to user mode.
- **Kernel-mode request queuing.** Requests cause less overhead in context switching, because the kernel forwards requests directly to the correct worker process. If no worker process is available to accept a request, the kernel-mode request queue holds the request until a worker process picks it up.

Using HTTP.sys and the new WWW service architecture provides the following benefits:

- When a worker process fails, service is not interrupted; the failure is undetectable by the user because the kernel queues the requests while the WWW service starts a new worker process for that application pool.
- Requests are processed faster because they are routed directly from the kernel to the appropriate user-mode worker process instead of being routed between two user-mode processes.

How HTTP.sys Works

When you create a Web site, IIS registers the site with HTTP.sys, which then receives any HTTP requests for the site. HTTP.sys functions like a forwarder, sending the Web requests it receives to the request queue for the user-mode process that runs the Web site or Web application. HTTP.sys also sends responses back to the client.

Other than retrieving a stored response from its internal cache, HTTP.sys does not process the requests that it receives. Therefore, no application-specific code is ever loaded into kernel mode. As a result, bugs in application-specific code cannot affect the kernel or lead to system failures.

HTTP.sys provides the following services in IIS 6.0:

- Routing HTTP requests to the correct request queue.
- Caching of responses in kernel mode.
- Performing all text-based logging for the WWW service.
- Implementing Quality of Service (QoS) functionality, which includes connection limits, connection timeouts, queue-length limits, and bandwidth throttling.

How HTTP.sys Handles Kernel-Mode Queuing

When IIS 6.0 runs in worker process isolation mode, HTTP.sys listens for requests and queues those requests in the appropriate queue. Each request queue corresponds to one application pool. An *application pool* corresponds to one request queue within HTTP.sys and one or more worker processes.

When IIS 6.0 runs in IIS 5.0 isolation mode, HTTP.sys runs like it runs in worker process isolation mode, except that it routes requests to a single request queue.

If a defective application causes the user-mode worker process to terminate unexpectedly, HTTP.sys continues to accept and queue requests, provided that the WWW service is still running, queues are still available, and space remains in the queues.

When the WWW service identifies an unhealthy worker process, it starts a new worker process if outstanding requests are waiting to be serviced. Thus, although a temporary disruption occurs in user-mode request processing, an end user does not experience the failure because TCP/IP connections are maintained, and requests continue to be queued and processed.

Worker Processes

A *worker process* is user-mode code whose role is to process requests, such as processing requests to return a static page, invoking an ISAPI extension or filter, or running a Common Gateway Interface (CGI) handler.

In both application isolation modes, the worker process is controlled by the WWW service. However, in worker process isolation mode, a worker process runs as an executable file named W3wp.exe, and in IIS 5.0 isolation mode, a worker process is hosted by Inetinfo.exe. Figure 2.2, which depicts the architecture for IIS 5.0 isolation mode, uses a dashed line to suggest the relationship between the worker process and the WWW service.

Worker processes use HTTP.sys to receive requests and to send responses by using HTTP. Worker processes also run application code, such as ASP.NET applications and XML Web services. You can configure IIS to run multiple worker processes that serve different application pools concurrently. This design separates applications by process boundaries and helps achieve maximum Web server reliability.

By default, worker processes in worker process isolation mode run under the Network Service account, which has the strongest security (least access) compatible with the functionality that is required. For more information about Network Service accounts, including Windows Server 2003 built-in security accounts, see "Running IIS 6.0 as an Application Server" in this book and "IIS and Built-in Accounts" in IIS 6.0 Help.

WWW Service Administration and Monitoring

The WWW Service Administration and Monitoring component, which is hosted in Svchost.exe, is a set of new features contained in the WWW service. Like the worker process, this new component runs in user mode, and like HTTP.sys, this component contains critical IIS 6.0 functionality that never loads external code. IIS 6.0 completely isolates external application code from this component by running only the external code in worker processes.

 Note

Because the WWW Service Administration and Monitoring component implements and controls a set of new features contained in the WWW service, to simplify the text, the term *WWW service* is used when discussing these new features instead of the term *WWW Service Administration and Monitoring component*.

The WWW service is responsible for two roles in IIS: HTTP administration and worker process management.

HTTP administration

The WWW service interacts with the metabase to obtain the configuration data that is needed to set up HTTP.sys and that is used to manage the worker process.

When you start a server that is running IIS, and the WWW service is started, this service reads metabase information and initializes the HTTP.sys namespace routing table with one entry for each application. HTTP.sys then uses the routing table data to determine which application pool responds to requests from what parts of the namespace. When HTTP.sys receives a request, it signals the WWW service to start a worker process for the application pool.

When you add or delete an application pool, the WWW service processes the configuration changes, which includes adding or deleting the application pool queue from HTTP.sys. The WWW service also listens for and processes configuration changes that occur as a result of application pool recycling.

Managing the lifetime of the worker process

The WWW service is responsible for managing the worker processes, which includes starting the worker processes and maintaining information about the running worker processes. This service also determines when to start a worker process, when to recycle a worker process, and when to restart a worker process if it becomes blocked and is unable to process any more requests.

In worker process isolation mode, the WWW service is responsible for health management and maintenance, including application pool health monitoring, recycling worker processes, and rapid-fail protection. For more information about these new features, see "Features of Worker Process Isolation Mode" later in this chapter and "Running IIS 6.0 as an Application Server" in this book.

The WWW service runs under the Local System account. For more information about Local System accounts, including Windows Server 2003 built-in security accounts, see "Running IIS 6.0 as an Application Server" and "Managing a Secure IIS 6.0 Solution" in this book.

Inetinfo.exe

When IIS 6.0 runs in worker process isolation mode, Inetinfo.exe is a user-mode component that hosts the IIS metabase and that also hosts the non-Web services of IIS 6.0, including the FTP service, the SMTP service, and the NNTP service. Inetinfo.exe depends on IIS Admin service to host the metabase.

When IIS 6.0 runs in IIS 5.0 isolation mode, Inetinfo.exe functions much as it did in IIS 5.0. In IIS 5.0 isolation mode, however, Inetinfo.exe hosts the worker process, which runs ISAPI filters, Low-isolation ISAPI extensions, and other Web applications.

Important

In IIS 6.0, regardless of the application isolation mode used, the services that run in Inetinfo.exe run as dynamic-link libraries (DLLs) under the Local System account. Because a Local System account allows users access to every resource on the local computer, use caution when you run services in Inetinfo.exe, especially on computers that provide services on the Internet.

When you run services in Inetinfo.exe that can be accessed from the Internet, be sure to protect your system by using a firewall, such as Microsoft® Internet Security and Acceleration (ISA) Server, or by disabling services that you do not use.

The IIS Metabase

The IIS *metabase* is a plaintext, XML data store that contains most IIS configuration information. Although most of the IIS configuration settings are stored in the IIS metabase, a few settings are maintained in the Windows registry. If a configuration setting is one that you might need to configure or change, or if you can access the setting in the IIS 6.0 user interface, then the setting is typically stored in the IIS metabase.

The new XML metabase allows administrators to directly read and edit the configuration file without using scripts or code, by using a common text editor such as Notepad. The XML metabase makes it easier to diagnose potential metabase corruption, and to back up and restore your metabase files.

If you upgrade to IIS 6.0, the existing binary metabase is automatically converted to the new XML metabase. The metabase is 100 percent compatible with IIS 5.*x* metabase application programming interfaces (APIs) and Active Directory® directory service Service Interfaces (ADSI), ensuring that existing scripts and code continue to work.

For more information about the metabase, see "Working with the Metabase" in this book.

Metabase Elements

IIS 6.0 replaces the single binary file (MetaBase.bin) of earlier IIS versions with two XML files: MetaBase.xml and MBSchema.xml. IIS stores these files in the *systemroot*\System32\Inetsrv folder of your computer. To view and modify these files, you must be a member of the Administrators group.

The metabase consists of the following elements:

- **MetaBase.xml file.** This file stores IIS configuration information that is specific to an installation of IIS.
- **MBSchema.xml file.** This file contains the metabase schema. The MBSchema.xml file is a master configuration file that defines default attributes for all metabase properties and enforces rules for constructing and placing metabase entries within the metabase.
- **In-memory metabase.** The in-memory metabase contains the most current metabase and metabase schema configuration. The in-memory metabase accepts changes to the metabase configuration and schema, storing them in RAM, and periodically writing changes to the on-disk metabase and metabase schema files.

When IIS starts, the MetaBase.xml and MBSchema.xml files are read by the IIS storage layer and copied to the in-memory metabase. While IIS is running, any changes that you make to the in-memory metabase are periodically written to disk. IIS also saves the in-memory metabase to disk when you stop IIS.

The IIS Admin service makes the metabase available (by means of the Admin Base Object) to other applications, including the core components of IIS, applications built on IIS, and applications that are independent of IIS, such as management or monitoring tools.

For more information about what happens to the metabase when IIS starts or restarts, see "About the Metabase" in IIS 6.0 Help.

Automatic Versioning and History

IIS 6.0 also provides automatic versioning and history. This metabase history feature automatically tracks any changes to the metabase that are written to disk. When the metabase is written to disk, IIS marks the new MetaBase.xml file with a version number and saves a copy of the file in the history folder. Each history file is marked with a unique version number, which is then available, if needed, for metabase rollback or restore. The metabase history feature is enabled by default.

For more information about the metabase, see "Working with the Metabase" in this book.

Application Isolation Modes

IIS 6.0 runs a server in one of two distinct request processing models, called *application isolation modes*. In each isolation mode, IIS functions differently, although both application isolation modes rely on HTTP.sys as the HTTP listener.

Worker process isolation mode

Worker process isolation mode takes advantage of the redesigned architecture for IIS 6.0. In this application isolation mode, you can group Web applications into application pools, through which you can apply specific configuration settings to groups of applications and to the worker processes servicing those applications. By using application pools, you can run all application code in an isolated environment; however, unlike earlier versions of IIS, IIS 6.0 provides isolation without a performance penalty, because there are no added process hops.

Worker process isolation mode provides application (or site) compatibility for most existing applications. This application isolation mode is specified by a **false** value for the metabase property **IIs5IsolationModeEnabled**.

IIS 5.0 isolation mode

IIS 5.0 isolation mode is provided for applications that depend upon specific features and behaviors of IIS 5.0. Use this mode only if an application has a compatibility issue when it runs in worker process isolation mode and you cannot resolve the problem.

In this application isolation mode, you can isolate applications as you did in IIS 5.0: in Low isolation (in-process), Medium isolation (pooled out-of-process), or High isolation (out-of-process). This application isolation mode is specified by a **true** value for the **IIs5IsolationModeEnabled** metabase property.

Whenever possible, run your server in worker process isolation mode, which is more secure and reliable than IIS 5.0 isolation mode and is also the default application isolation mode for a clean installation of IIS 6.0. For more information about IIS 6.0 application isolation mode defaults, see "Application Isolation Mode Defaults" later in this chapter.

Choosing an Application Isolation Mode

The IIS application isolation mode that you choose affects performance, reliability, security, and feature availability. Worker process isolation mode is the recommended mode of operation for IIS 6.0 because it provides a more robust platform for applications and the ability to isolate applications in separate application pools without incurring a performance penalty. Also, in the default configuration, worker process isolation mode provides a higher level of security than does IIS 5.0 isolation mode because its default host process identity is Network Service.

Some applications might have compatibility problems when they run in worker process isolation mode. If compatibility problems occur, you might need to use IIS 5.0 isolation mode. For applications that run in IIS 5.0 isolation mode, Local System is the only available process identity when you run an application in-process in Inetinfo.exe. For more information about IIS security, see "Managing a Secure IIS 6.0 Solution" in this book. Also see "Configuring Worker Process Identities" and "IIS and Built-in Accounts" in IIS 6.0 Help.

 Important

> IIS 6.0 cannot run both application isolation modes simultaneously on the same computer. Therefore, on a single computer running IIS 6.0, you cannot run some Web applications in worker process isolation mode and others in IIS 5.0 isolation mode. If your applications require different modes, you must run them on separate computers.

When you are deciding which application isolation mode to use, follow these guidelines:

- Use worker process isolation mode unless you need to use IIS 5.0 isolation mode because of a specific compatibility problem. For example, an application that checks to see if an application is running in a process named Inetinfo.exe is incompatible with worker process isolation mode.
- For Web sites that contain static content and simple ASP applications, run the applications in worker process isolation mode because these Web sites usually require little or no modification.
- For applications that run correctly on IIS 5.0, try running them first in worker process isolation mode. If they do not work correctly, change them back to IIS 5.0 isolation mode until you can diagnose and fix the incompatibility.

Applications that cannot run in worker process isolation mode

Applications that run in worker process isolation mode can take advantage of all the worker process behaviors, which include multi-instancing, recycling, and configurable process identity. Certain application characteristics conflict with the architecture of worker process isolation mode and must be run in IIS 5.0 isolation mode until you can modify them.

The following applications or application characteristics conflict with worker process isolation mode:

- **Read raw data filters.** This type of filter can only be loaded in IIS 5.0 isolation mode.
- **Dependency on Inetinfo.exe.** Applications that must run in an Inetinfo.exe worker process can only run in IIS 5.0 isolation mode because applications cannot run in Inetinfo.exe in worker process isolation mode.
- **Requires Dllhost.exe.** Web applications that must run in a Dllhost.exe environment can run only in IIS 5.0 isolation mode because running Web applications in Dllhost.exe is not an option in worker process isolation mode.

Applications that require special handling to run in worker process isolation mode

Applications that you cannot load into multiple processes simultaneously have the following limitations:

- You cannot run them in application pools configured to perform overlapped recycling.
- You cannot run them in application pools configured as Web gardens.

Instead, run this type of application in an application pool that is not configured for overlapped recycling and that is not configured to run as a Web garden. For more information about overlapped recycling, see "Features of Worker Process Isolation Mode" later in this chapter. For information about configuring overlapped recycling, see "Recycling Worker Processes" in IIS 6.0 Help.

If the IIS 6.0 WWW service is running in worker process isolation mode (the IIS 6.0 default mode), and you must run applications that require a functionality that is available only in IIS 5.0 isolation mode, change to IIS 5.0 isolation mode until you can correct the incompatibility. When running your server in IIS 5.0 isolation mode, you cannot take advantage of worker process isolation and the other features of worker process isolation mode.

Application Isolation Mode Defaults

When you install IIS 6.0 on a computer that does not contain an earlier version of IIS, IIS 6.0 automatically sets the application isolation mode to worker process isolation mode. If you upgrade from a earlier version of IIS, IIS 6.0 sets the application isolation mode to IIS 5.0 isolation mode.

Table 2.3 lists the IIS 6.0 default settings for the two application isolation modes.

Table 2.3   Default IIS 6.0 Installation Settings for Each Application Isolation Mode

Type of Installation	Application Isolation Mode
New installation of IIS 6.0 (clean install)	Worker process isolation mode
Upgrade from an earlier version of IIS 6.0, such as a beta release	No change in isolation mode
Upgrade from IIS 5.0	IIS 5.0 isolation mode
Upgrade from IIS 4.0	IIS 5.0 isolation mode

Although IIS 5.0 isolation mode is the default application isolation mode when you upgrade from earlier versions of IIS, be sure to test your applications for compatibility issues so that, if possible, you can upgrade to worker process isolation mode.

Application Isolation Modes 435

Application Isolation Mode Functions

Use Table 2.4 to compare how certain IIS 6.0 functions run in worker process isolation mode with how they run in IIS 5.0 isolation mode. Knowing the host component for each iapplication solation mode can help you decide which application isolation mode to use. For example, if an application must run in DLLhost.exe, and you cannot change the application to remove this requirement, this table shows you the two available options, which are to run the application in Medium or High isolation in IIS 5.0 isolation mode.

Table 2.4   Comparison of IIS 6.0 Functions in the Two Application Isolation Modes

IIS 6.0 Function	Worker Process Isolation Mode Host/Component	IIS 5.0 Isolation Mode Host/Component
Worker process management	Svchost.exe/WWW service	Svchost.exe/WWW service
Worker process	W3wp.exe	Inetinfo.exe
Running Low-isolation ISAPI applications	W3wp.exe	Inetinfo.exe
Running Medium-isolation ISAPI applications	Not applicable (All ISAPI extensions are in-process.)	DLLHost.exe (1)
Running High-isolation ISAPI applications	Not applicable (All ISAPI extensions are in-process.)	DLLHost.exe
Running ISAPI filters	W3wp.exe	Inetinfo.exe
HTTP.sys configuration	Svchost.exe/WWW service	Svchost.exe/WWW service
HTTP protocol support	Windows kernel/HTTP.sys	Windows kernel/HTTP.sys
HTTP SSL (HTTPFilter)	Lsass.exe	Inetinfo.exe
IIS metabase	Inetinfo.exe	Inetinfo.exe
FTP	Inetinfo.exe	Inetinfo.exe
NNTP	Inetinfo.exe	Inetinfo.exe
SMTP	Inetinfo.exe	Inetinfo.exe

HTTP SSL (HTTPFilter)

When HTTP.sys receives requests that are encrypted by using Secure Sockets Layer (SSL), the kernel-mode HTTP service cannot decrypt the requests or encrypt the responses. Instead, HTTP SSL (HTTPFilter), which is a user-mode service, implements SSL for the HTTP service. HTTP SSL runs in the IIS 6.0 isolation modes as follows:

- In worker process isolation mode, Lsass.exe hosts HTTPFilter.
- In IIS 5.0 isolation mode, HTTP filter runs in Inetinfo.exe.

 Important

Lsass.exe cannot be stopped except during computer shutdowns — either planned or unexpected.

IIS 6.0 Identity *vs.* IIS 5.0 Identity

In IIS 6.0, worker processes use a different process identity than in IIS 5.0. *Process identity* is an operating system term used to denote the account that a process runs under. Every process that is running on a Windows NT operating system has a process identity that is used to control access to resources on the system.

The different process identity used by worker processes in IIS 6.0 can affect applications migrated from IIS 5.0 if the application expects the process identity to run as a specific account, such as IWAM_*ComputerName*. In addition, for Medium-isolation or High-isolation Web applications created in IIS 5.0 or run on IIS 6.0 in IIS 5.0 isolation mode, identity is configured by Component Services; however, when IIS 6.0 is running in worker process isolation mode, identity is configured in IIS Manager.

Worker Process Isolation Mode

IIS 6.0 worker process isolation mode takes the concept of application isolation, which was introduced in IIS 4.0, one step further. In IIS 6.0, you can isolate one application from another so that an error in one application does not affect another application running in a different process. This application isolation mode provides better isolation while not incurring a performance penalty for isolation.

Worker process isolation mode loads application code — for example, ASP and ASP.NET applications — into the worker process only. By isolating application code in the worker process, this application isolation mode ensures a reliable environment for an application server: the WWW service, IIS Admin service, and HTTP.sys can run continuously despite any service interruptions that occur in a worker process. Also, Web sites running in the worker processes are not affected by failures in other worker processes because they are isolated from each other through operating system process boundaries.

Worker process isolation mode uses all of the new IIS 6.0 core components and supports application pooling, recycling, and health monitoring features.

Benefits of Using Worker Process Isolation Mode

One benefit of isolating applications or sites into separate worker processes is to simplify management tasks, such as taking an application offline or putting an application back online (independent of all other sites or applications running on the system), changing a component that an application uses, debugging an application, and throttling (limiting) resources that an application uses.

IIS 6.0 worker process isolation mode improves on earlier versions of IIS in the following areas:

- **It is more robust.** Prevents Web applications and Web sites in an application pool from disrupting or harming applications or Web sites in another application pool.
- **It requires fewer or no reboots.** Does not force you to reboot the server or to shut down the WWW service. You can perform common tasks, such as upgrading site content or components, debugging Web applications, or dealing with faulty Web applications, without affecting service to other sites or applications on the server.
- **It is self-healing.** Supports autorestart of failed applications and periodic restart of unstable applications or applications that leak memory.

- **It is more scalable and reliable.** Supports scaling for ISPs, which sometimes run thousands of sites on a server, and offers better multiprocessor scalability.
- **It is application-oriented.** Makes the application the unit of administration and robustness by enabling application isolation and also by enabling resource throttling (limiting the amount of resources that an application can use) and scaling based on the application.

The result is a Web server that is more reliable and always available, even if applications cause their hosting worker processes to terminate.

Features of Worker Process Isolation Mode

Worker process isolation mode includes several features that you can use to improve IIS robustness, scalability, and reliability without reducing performance. These features include multiple application pools, application pool health monitoring, worker process recycling, and rapid-fail protection. When you run your Web server in worker process isolation mode, you can configure application pools to take advantage of these features, which can only be used when a Web server is running in worker process isolation mode.

Multiple Application Pools

In IIS 5.0, applications can be pooled together out-of-process, but only in one application pool (typically referred to as *a pooled out-of-process* in IIS 5.0, rather than an *application pool*). In IIS 6.0, worker process isolation mode allows customers to create multiple application pools, each with a different configuration, such as a unique recycling configuration or a unique process ID. In addition, all HTTP application run-time features, such as the services that support ISAPI extensions, are available in all application pools. This design prevents a malfunctioning Web application or Web site from disrupting other Web applications or Web sites on that server.

Application Pool Health Monitoring

You can configure an application pool to monitor not only the health of its worker process, but the health of the entire pool. The WWW service can detect an unhealthy application pool in these situations:

- If a worker process in the application pool terminates abnormally.
- If all of the available IIS threads in the worker process that is assigned to the application pool are blocked.
- If the application notifies IIS that a problem exists.

Monitoring the health of a worker process includes detecting that the worker process is not able to serve requests and taking corrective action. For example, if a worker process does not respond to a ping from the WWW service, the worker process probably does not have threads available for processing incoming requests. When this happens, the WWW service either terminates the worker process or releases the worker process and leaves it running. (You can configure IIS to attach a debugger to an unhealthy worker process when the WWW server releases it.) If requests are waiting in the request queue, the WWW service starts a new worker process to replace the one that was terminated or released.

For more information about configuring IIS for application pool health monitoring, see "Configuring Worker Process Health Monitoring" in IIS 6.0 Help and "Running IIS 6.0 as an Application Server" in this book.

Worker Process Recycling

Web applications sometimes leak memory, are poorly coded, or have other unidentified problems. In earlier versions of IIS, these faulty applications might force you to restart the Web server. In worker process isolation mode, you can use the recycling feature to periodically restart the worker processes in an application pool in order to manage faulty applications. You can schedule worker processes to restart based on several options, such as elapsed time or the number of requests served.

You can configure the WWW service so that it recycles a worker process in one of two ways:

- By default, the WWW service establishes an *overlapped recycle*, creating a new worker process to handle any new incoming requests *before* signaling the old worker process to finish processing its existing requests and shut down.
- Optionally, the WWW service first signals the old worker process to shut down and, after it shuts down, starts a new worker process.

In both types of recycling, the WWW service allows a configured amount of time for the old worker process to handle the requests that it has already taken from HTTP.sys before it shuts itself down.

In the default configuration, when a worker process requests a recycle, the WWW service initiates an overlapped recycle, creating a new worker process to replace the old process. While the new worker process is starting, the old process continues to serve requests. As soon as the new worker process starts and initializes successfully, the WWW service signals the old worker process to shut down. The old worker process then stops pulling new requests and begins to shut down. The WWW service gives the old worker process a configured time period in which to finish processing its requests and shut down, and it terminates the worker process if it does not shut down within the specified time.

For more information about worker process recycling, including when to use it and how to configure it, see "Recycling Worker Processes" in IIS 6.0 Help.

Rapid-Fail Protection

Rapid-fail protection stops an application pool when too many of the worker processes assigned to it are found to be unhealthy within a specified period of time. When an application pool is stopped, HTTP.sys either returns an out-of-service message ("503: Service Unavailable") or resets a connection based on the configuration of the **LoadBalancerCapabilities** property of the application pool. Also, when an application pool stops automatically, such as when rapid-fail protection engages, you can configure an action (a debugging action, for example) to notify the administrator that the application pool has stopped.

For more information about rapid-fail protection, including how to configure this feature, see "Running IIS 6.0 as an Application Server" in this book.

Orphaning Worker Processes

You can configure worker process isolation mode to "orphan" a worker process that the WWW service deems to be failing. The WWW service usually terminates a failing worker process and replaces it. If you enable orphaning, the WWW service allows a failing worker process to continue running, but separates it from the application pool (making it an orphan) and starts a new worker process in its place. You can configure the WWW service to run a command on the orphaned worker process — for example, launching a debugger.

For more information about orphaning worker processes, including how to configure this feature, see "Running IIS 6.0 as an Application Server" in this book and "OrphanWorkerProcess" in the Metabase Property Reference of IIS 6.0 Help.

Web Gardens

Web gardens are application pools that are configured to run multiple worker processes. By default, each application pool in IIS 6.0 has only one worker process. However, you can configure an application pool to have a set of equivalent worker processes that share the work, thus creating a *Web garden*. In a Web garden, HTTP.sys distributes the requests among the set of worker processes in the application pool.

 Note

Do not confuse a Web garden with a *Web farm*, which is a Web site or Web hosting service that runs off of more than one server and that uses clustering and load balancing.

The benefits of Web gardens are that they can handle more load, and that if one worker process stops responding, other worker processes are available to accept and process requests. Hence, Web gardens can enhance performance and reliability of the applications in the application pool.

The **MaxProcesses** metabase property determines the maximum number of worker processes that an application pool allows to service its requests. For more information about Web gardens, including how to create them, see "Running IIS 6.0 as an Application Server" in this book and "Configuring Web Gardens" in IIS 6.0 Help.

Processor Affinity

Processor affinity is an application pool property that forces worker processes to run on a specific set of microprocessors or CPUs. Processor affinity applies to all worker processes that serve a particular application pool and allows you to take advantage of more frequent CPU caching. If a Web garden is running on a multiprocessor computer, you can use processor affinity to dedicate certain application pools to specific clusters of CPUs.

To set up processor affinity, configure the **SMPAffinitized** and **SMPProcessorAffinityMask** metabase properties. For more information about assigning processor affinity, including how to configure these metabase properties, see "Running IIS 6.0 as an Application Server" in this book.

Idle Timeout

You can configure an application pool to have its worker processes request a shutdown if they are idle for a certain period of time. Configuring idle timeout can help you to free unused resources. New worker processes are started when demand exists for that application pool.

Use either IIS Manager or the **IdleTimeout** metabase property to configure this feature. For information about setting the **IdleTimeout** metabase property, see "IdleTimeout" in IIS 6.0 Help. For more information about configuring idle timeout for a worker process, see "Running IIS 6.0 as an Application Server" in this book.

Application Pool Identity

Application pool identity is the user account that the worker processes servicing the application pool use as their process identity. *Process identity* is the operating system term that is used to denote the account that a process runs under. Every running process on a Windows NT operating system has a process identity that is used to control access to resources on the system.

You can assign a predefined account for the application pool identity or create your own account for this purpose. For security reasons, choose an application pool identity with the minimum permissions that your application requires.

For more information about configuring process identities, see "Configuring Worker Process Identities" in IIS 6.0 Help.

How Application Pools Work

When you run IIS 6.0 in worker process isolation mode, you can separate different Web applications and Web sites into groups known as *application pools*. An a*pplication pool* is a group of one or more URLs that are served by a worker process or set of worker processes. Any Web directory or virtual directory can be assigned to an application pool.

Every application within an application pool shares the same worker process. Because each worker process operates as a separate instance of the worker process executable, W3wp.exe, the worker process that services one application pool is separated from the worker process that services another. Each separate worker process provides a process boundary so that when an application is assigned to one application pool, problems in other application pools do not affect the application. This ensures that if a worker process fails, it does not affect the applications running in other application pools.

Use multiple application pools when you want to help ensure that applications and Web sites are confidential and secure. For example, an enterprise organization might place its human resources Web site and its finance Web site on the same server, but in different application pools. Likewise, an ISP that hosts Web sites and applications for competing companies might run each company's Web services on the same server, but in different application pools. Using different application pools to isolate applications helps prevent one customer from accessing, changing, or using confidential information from another customer's site.

In HTTP.sys, an application pool is represented by a *request queue*, from which the user-mode worker processes that service an application pool collect the requests. Each pool can manage requests for one or more unique Web applications, which you assign to the application pool based on their URLs. Application pools, then, are essentially worker process configurations that service groups of namespaces.

Multiple application pools can operate at the same time. An application, as defined by its URL, can only be served by one application pool at any time. While one application pool is servicing a request, you cannot route the request to another application pool. However, you can assign applications to another application pool while the server is running.

Request Processing in Worker Process Isolation Mode

Figure 2.3 shows the standard request process for IIS 6.0 when it is running in worker process isolation mode.

Figure 2.3   Standard (HTTP) Request Processing in Worker Process Isolation Mode

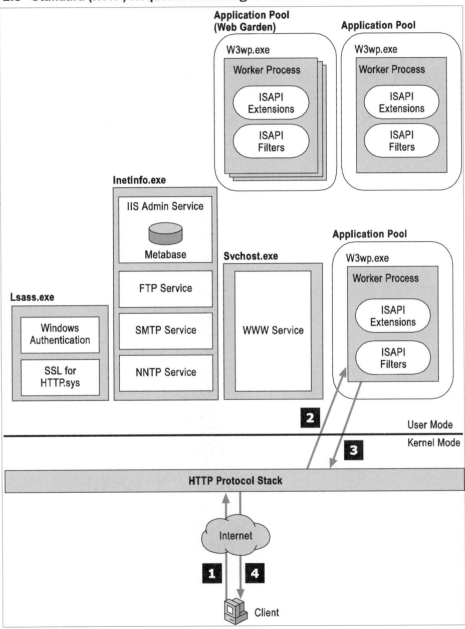

The HTTP protocol stack (HTTP.sys), which runs in kernel mode, receives client requests and routes them to the appropriate request queue. Worker processes, which run in user mode, pull the requests directly from their own kernel request queues, eliminating the process hops that occur in IIS 5.0 (and that also occur in IIS 5.0 isolation mode) when the Web server sends a request to a High-isolation, out-of-process application. Because these extra process hops are eliminated in worker process isolation mode, IIS can provide application isolation without sacrificing performance.

Note

Before routing a request to a queue, HTTP.sys checks to see if the response is located in its kernel-mode cache; if a response is cached, it is returned immediately.

To see a visual representation of the request process for the two application isolation modes, compare Figure 2.3 (worker process isolation mode) with Figure 2.6 (High isolation in IIS 5.0 isolation mode).

Note

In Figure 2.3, and also in Figure 2.4, 2.5, 2.6, and 2.7, the numbered arrows indicate the request process flow.

When HTTP.sys receives requests that are encrypted by using SSL, the kernel-mode HTTP service cannot decrypt the requests or encrypt the responses. Instead, HTTP SSL (HTTPFilter), which is a user-mode service, implements SSL for the HTTP service. In worker process isolation mode, the default host for HTTPFilter is Lsass.exe.

Figure 2.4 illustrates the process flow for an SSL request when IIS 6.0 is running in worker process isolation mode. The HTTP protocol stack receives the SSL request from the client and places it in the SSL queue. The HTTPFilter listens for requests to enter the queue, picks up any new request, uses SSL to decrypt the request, and then returns the decrypted request to HTTP.sys. HTTP.sys then places the decrypted request in the appropriate request queue. A worker process pulls the request directly from its own kernel request queue.

Figure 2.4 SSL Request Processing in Worker Process Isolation Mode

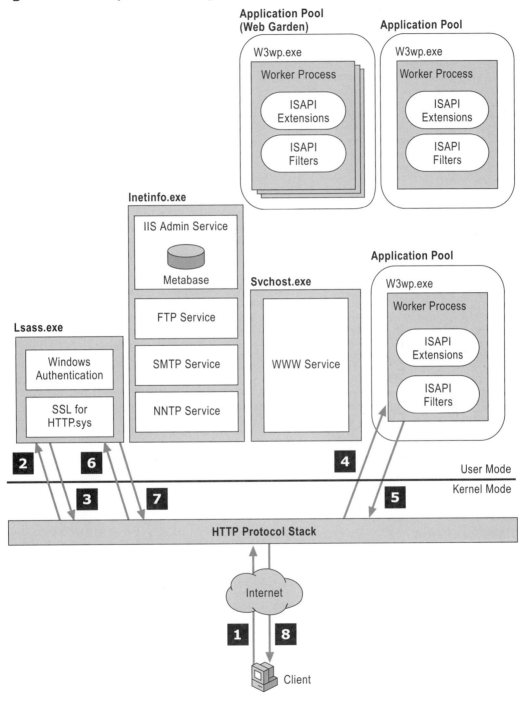

On the return trip, the worker process returns the response to HTTP.sys, which places it in the appropriate queue from which the HTTPFilter picks it up and performs SSL encryption. After encryption, the HTTPFilter again returns the response to HTTP.sys, which sends the encrypted response back to the client.

Keep in mind that SSL requires more resources than does standard HTTP. If you use SSL, ensure that the information being sent, such as credit card numbers or medical information, is sensitive enough to justify the added performance expense. For example, your home page or a search results page does not necessarily need to be run through SSL. However, you need to make sure that a checkout or purchase page is SSL-secured.

When you use SSL, the initial connection takes significantly longer than reconnecting. Reconnections use security information in the SSL session cache. The default timeout for the SSL session cache is changed to 5 minutes in Windows 2000 (10 hours in Windows 2000 with Service Pack 2) and 10 hours in Windows Server 2003. After cached data is deleted, the client and server must establish a completely new connection. You can change the default timeout by configuring the **ServerCacheTime** registry entry. For more information about configuring this registry setting, see "Optimizing IIS 6.0 Performance" in this book.

 Caution

Do not edit the registry unless you have no alternative. The registry editor bypasses standard safeguards, allowing settings that can damage your system, or even require you to reinstall Windows. If you must edit the registry, back it up first and see the Registry Reference on the *Microsoft Windows Server 2003 Deployment Kit* companion CD or on the Web at http://www.microsoft.com/reskit.

For more information about balancing performance and security, see "Performance and Security" in IIS 6.0 Help. For more information about encryption, see "About Encryption" in IIS 6.0 Help. For more information about the security features available in IIS 6.0, see "Managing a Secure IIS 6.0 Solution" in this book.

Table 2.5 provides additional details about how worker process isolation mode processes HTTP (standard) and HTTPS (SSL) requests.

Table 2.5 HTTP and HTTPS Request Processing

Step	Request Type	Description
I	HTTP & HTTPS	HTTP.sys receives the request from the client and determines the type of request (HTTP or HTTPS). (Corresponds to #1 in Figures 2.3 and 2.4.) If the request is an HTTPS request, HTTP.sys places it in the SSL queue.
	HTTPS (SSL) only	For an SSL request, the HTTPFilter performs these steps: ■ Listens for requests to be added to the SSL queue (see #2 in Figure 2.4). ■ Picks up any requests that are queued. ■ Uses SSL to decrypt the request. ■ Returns the decrypted request to HTTP.sys for processing (see #3 in Figure 2.4).
II	HTTP & HTTPS	HTTP.sys determines if the request is valid: ■ If the request is invalid, HTTP.sys sends a 400-class error message for an invalid request back to the client. [1] ■ If the request is valid, HTTP.sys checks to see if the response is located in its kernel-mode cache.
III	HTTP & HTTPS	HTTP.sys checks the kernel-mode cache for a response: ■ If the response is in the kernel-mode cache, HTTP.sys returns the response immediately, without transitioning to user mode. ■ If the response is not in the cache, HTTP.sys determines the correct request queue and places the request in that queue. ■ If the target request queue is out of service or if the queue is full, HTTP.sys returns a "503 Service Unavailable" message to the client.
IV	HTTP & HTTPS	If no worker process is available and listening in the request queue and if HTTP.sys is able to request that a new worker process be started, HTTP.sys signals the WWW service to start a worker process.
V	HTTP & HTTPS	The worker process pulls the request from the queue and processes the request. (Corresponds to #2 in Figure 2.3 and #4 in Figure 2.4.)
VI	HTTP & HTTPS	The worker process sends the response back to HTTP.sys and instructs HTTP.sys whether to cache the response. (Corresponds to #3 in Figure 2.3 and #5 in Figure 2.4.)
VII	HTTP & HTTPS	HTTP.sys determines the type of response (HTTP or HTTPS). If the request is an HTTPS response, HTTP.sys places it in the SSL queue.
	HTTPS (SSL) only	For an SSL response, the HTTPFilter performs the following steps: ■ Listens for responses to enter the SSL queue (see #6 in Figure 2.4). ■ Picks up any responses that enter the queue. ■ Uses SSL to encrypt the response. ■ Returns the encrypted response to HTTP.sys (see #7 in Figure 2.4).
VIII	HTTP & HTTPS	HTTP.sys sends the response back to the client and logs the request if logging is enabled. (Corresponds to #4 in Figure 2.3 and #8 in Figure 2.4.)

1 For information about 400-class error messages, including keys to the many substatus codes, see "Troubleshooting IIS 6.0" in this book.

IIS 5.0 Isolation Mode

IIS 5.0 isolation mode provides as much compatibility as possible for applications that were developed for IIS 5.0. For example, the request processing of IIS 6.0 when it is running in IIS 5.0 isolation mode is nearly identical to the request processing of IIS 5.0. Hence, in IIS 5.0 isolation mode, you can run read raw data filters and can run applications in Inetinfo.exe or in DLLHost.exe — all of which is not accommodated in worker process isolation mode.

Before you decide to run an application in IIS 5.0 isolation mode, carefully evaluate whether you can substitute other filters and applications for the ones that require IIS 5.0 architecture because when a server is running in IIS 5.0 isolation mode, application pools, recycling, and health monitoring features are unavailable.

For more information about choosing an application isolation mode, see "Choosing an Application Isolation Mode" earlier in this chapter.

Application Isolation in IIS 5.0 Isolation Mode

When IIS 6.0 is running in IIS 5.0 isolation mode, your options for isolation, which are similar to your options when you run an application on IIS 5.0, are as follows:

- **Low isolation (in-process).** Applications run in-process (on the Web server) as DLLs in Inetinfo.exe and are not protected from other applications running in-process. The process identity of the application (the account under which the application's process runs) is Local System.
- **Medium isolation (pooled out-of-process).** All pooled applications run as DLLs in one instance of DLLHost.exe and are protected from the effects of applications running in High isolation. However, because all pooled applications run in the same process, they are not protected from each other. The default application identity is IWAM_*ComputerName*.
- **High isolation (out-of-process).** Applications run as DLLs in DLLHost.exe and are protected from the effects of other applications running in Medium or High isolation. In addition, all other applications that run on the same computer are protected from the effects of applications that run in High isolation. The default application identity is IWAM_*ComputerName*.

Security Considerations

When IIS 6.0 runs in IIS 5.0, Web applications that are set to Low isolation run with the Local System account. The Local System account has access to all of the resources on the computer. This means that when an attack by a malicious user takes over a Web application that is set to Low isolation, all of the assets of the local computer are open to the attacker.

When you set Web applications to Medium or High isolation, they run with IWAM_*ComputerName* as the default account; however, you can configure these applications to run with other identities.

Performance Considerations

When you run IIS 6.0 in IIS 5.0 isolation mode, applications that run in Medium or High isolation incur a performance penalty. The penalty occurs because the Component Object Model (COM) uses a remote procedure call (RPC) during these parts of the cycle:

- When a request is sent to an application that is running in Medium or High isolation and the response is sent back.
- When a Web application that is running in Medium or High isolation communicates with the Web server during the processing of a request.

In contrast, when IIS 6.0 runs in worker process isolation mode, applications are loaded in-process to W3wp.exe. Therefore, no performance penalty occurs.

Request Processing in IIS 5.0 Isolation Mode

In IIS 5.0 isolation mode, HTTP.sys is used in almost the same way that it is in worker process isolation mode. The difference is that HTTP.sys routes requests to only a single request queue, which is maintained by the WWW Service Administration and Monitoring component of IIS. Depending on how you configure the IIS 5.0 isolation mode — as in-process or out-of-process — IIS processes the request in either Inetinfo.exe or in DLLHost.exe.

Figure 2.5 illustrates the processing of an SSL request for a Low-isolation application that is running in IIS 5.0 isolation mode. When HTTP.sys receives requests that are encrypted by using SSL, the kernel-mode HTTP service cannot decrypt the requests or encrypt the responses. Instead, HTTP SSL (HTTPFilter), which is a user-mode service, implements SSL for the HTTP service. In IIS 5.0 isolation mode, Inetinfo.exe, rather than Lsass.exe, hosts HTTPFilter.

Figure 2.5 Low-Isolation SSL Request Processing in IIS 5.0 Isolation Mode

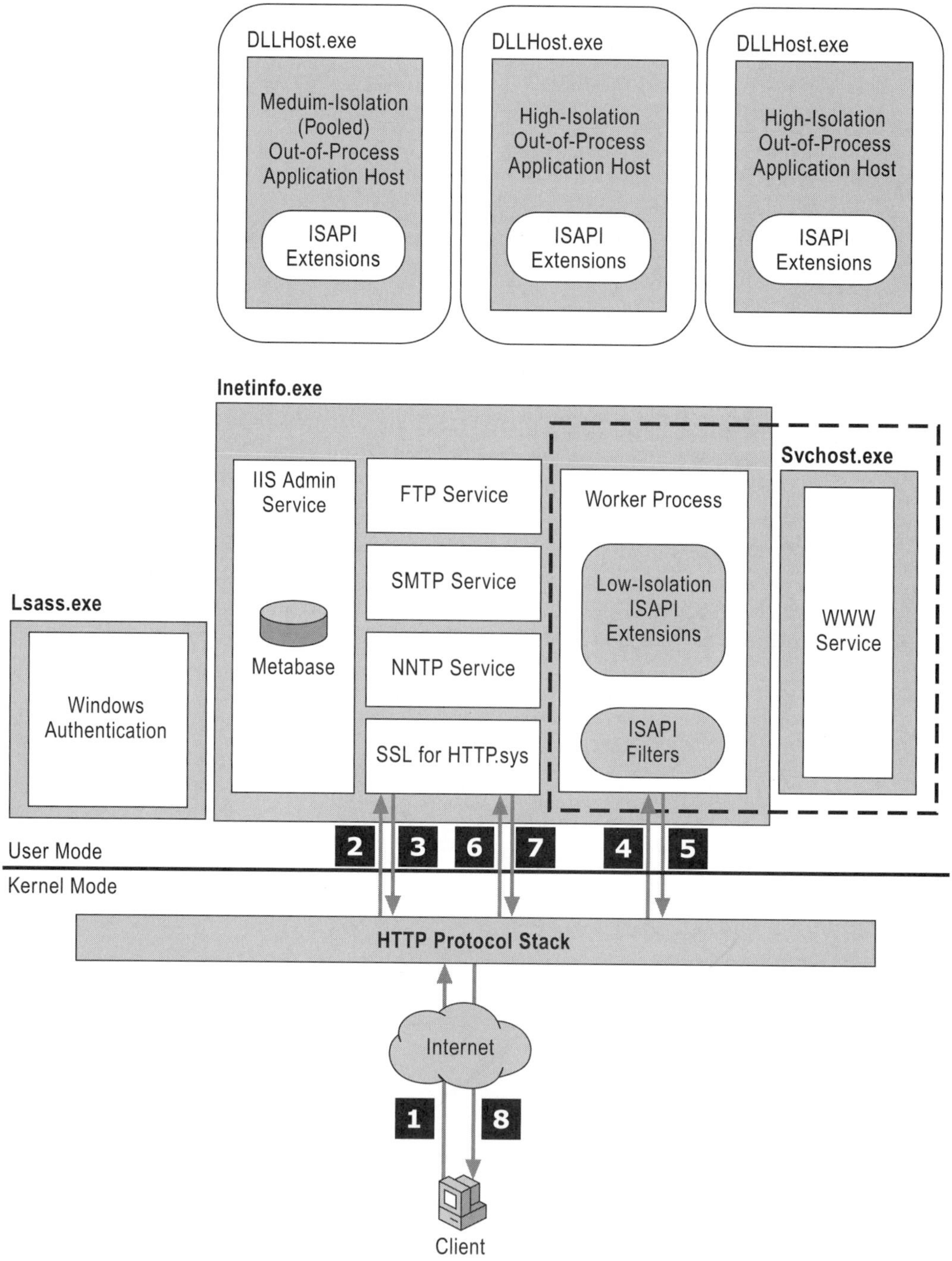

In Figure 2.5, if you eliminate the decrypting and encrypting steps that are required for SSL requests and follow only arrows 1, 4, 5, and 8, you see the standard (non-SSL) request process for a Low-isolation application that is running in IIS 5.0 isolation mode. For example, an HTTP request comes in to the HTTP protocol stack from the Internet, enters a single request-processing queue, and is picked up by a worker process that delivers the request to the Low-isolation application and returns it directly to the HTTP protocol stack.

Figure 2.6 illustrates request processing for an HTTP (non-SSL) request when IIS 6.0 is running in IIS 5.0 isolation mode. Note the extra process hops (represented by arrows 3 and 4) that occur when the request hops from the worker process, which is hosted by Inetinfo.exe and managed by the WWW service, to the High-isolation out-of-process application, which is hosted by DLLHost.exe.

Figure 2.6   High-Isolation Standard Request Processing in IIS 5.0 Isolation Mode

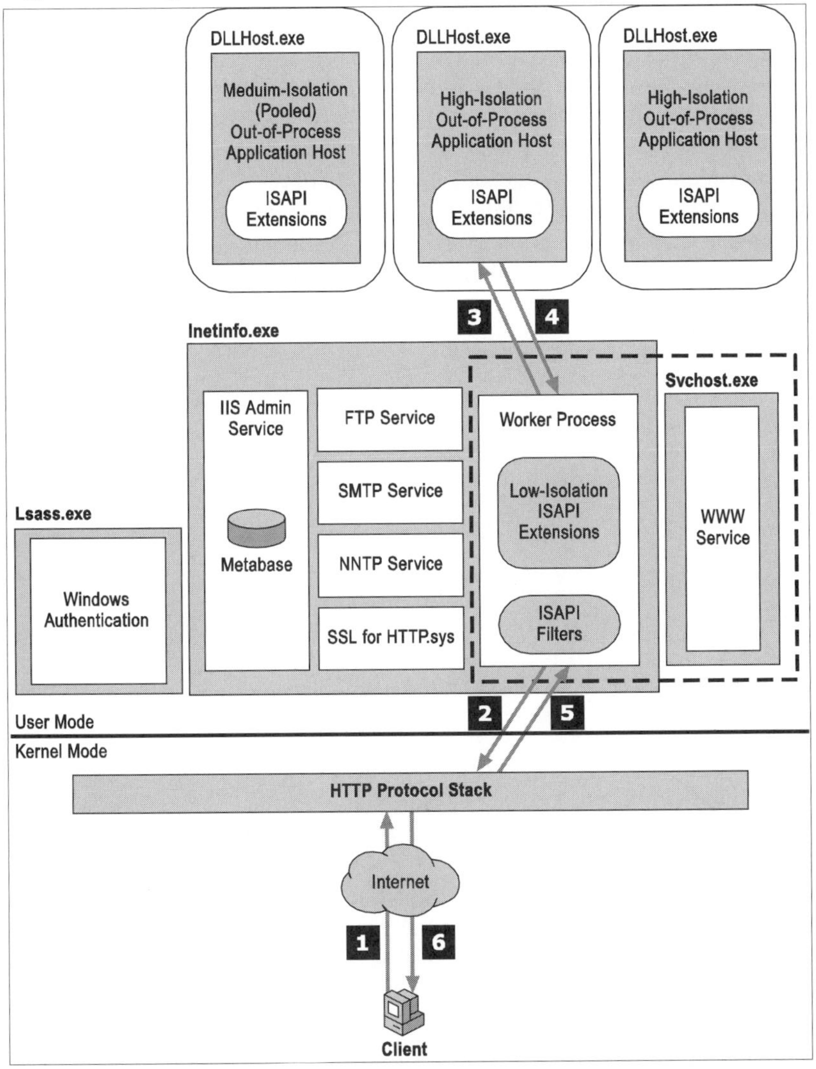

If you compare Figure 2.6 with Figure 2.3, you can see the advantage of using worker process isolation mode, in which application isolation occurs without a performance penalty (the additional process hops are not needed) and in which health monitoring and worker process recycling promote the stability of your application server and its applications.

 Note

In IIS 5.0 isolation mode, request processing is almost identical for High-isolation and Medium-isolation applications. The only differences between these two isolation methods are that multiple applications can run in the pool for Medium isolation and there can only be one Medium-isolation process; however, only a single application can run in the pool for High isolation and you can have multiple High-isolation applications on one computer.

Figure 2.7 illustrates the processing of an SSL request for a High-isolation application that is running in IIS 5.0 isolation mode. The HTTP protocol stack receives the SSL request from the client and places it in the SSL queue. The HTTPFilter listens for requests to be added to the SSL queue, picks up any requests that are queued, uses SSL to decrypt the request, and then returns the decrypted request to HTTP.sys. HTTP.sys then places the decrypted request in the worker process request queue (in this application isolation mode, there is only a single request queue), and a worker process pulls the request directly from the queue.

Figure 2.7 High-Isolation SSL Request Processing in IIS 5.0 Isolation Mode

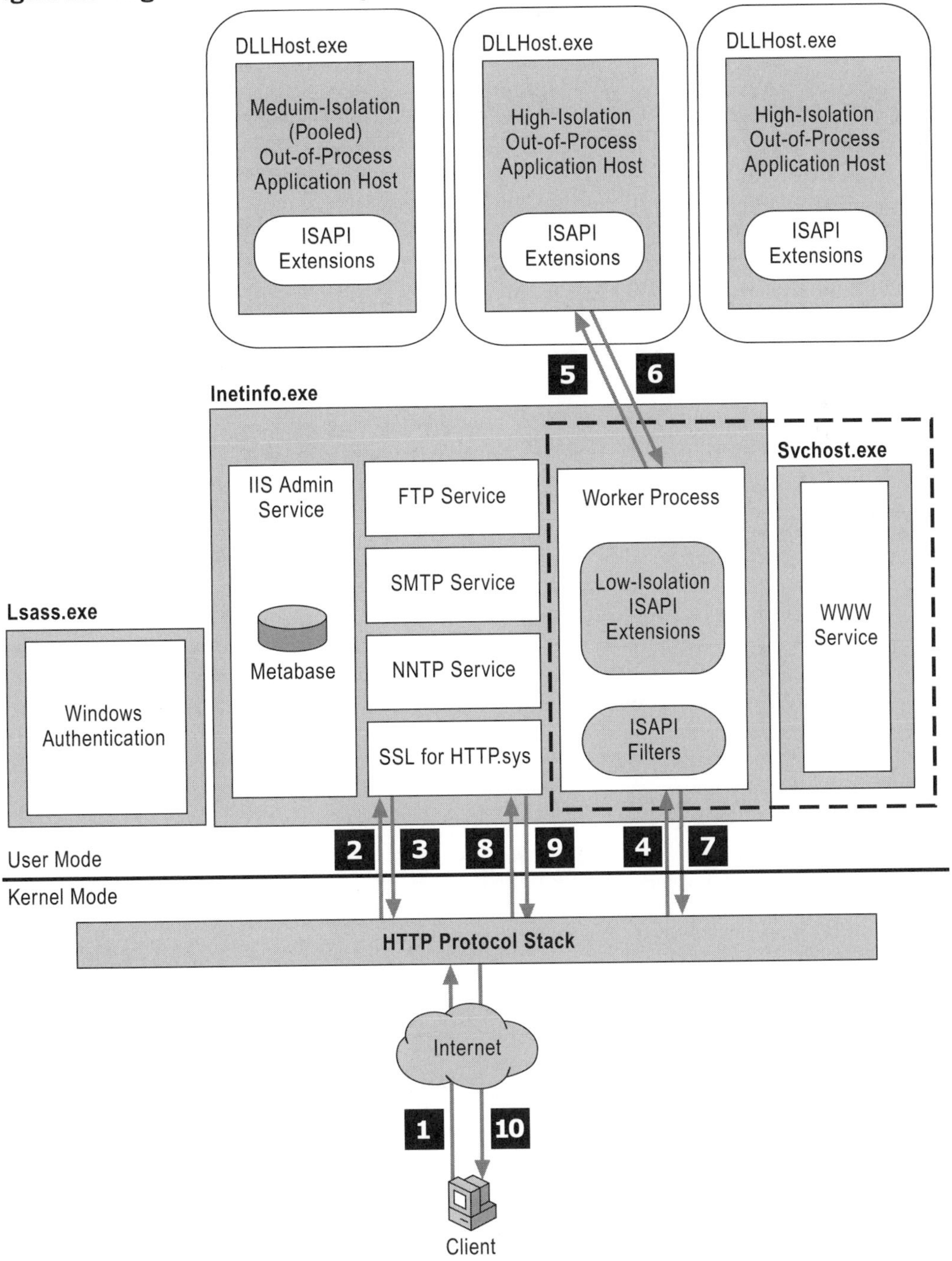

On the return trip, the worker process returns the response to HTTP.sys, which places it in the SSL queue, from which the HTTPFilter picks it up and performs SSL encryption. After encryption, the HTTPFilter returns the response to HTTP.sys, which sends the encrypted response back to the client.

If performance is a concern, and you are running applications in High isolation or Medium isolation on a computer that is running in IIS 5.0 isolation mode, keep in mind that using SSL requires more resources to process a request. In addition, the extra process hops required for High isolation and Medium isolation add to the resource requirements.

For more information about balancing performance and security, see "Performance and Security" in IIS 6.0 Help. For more information about configuring IIS 5.0 isolation mode, see "Running IIS 6.0 as an Application Server" in this book.

How ASP.NET Works with IIS 6.0

If you run your ASP.NET applications in IIS 6.0, you obtain a significant advantage over running your ASP.NET applications in IIS 5.0. For example, in IIS 5.0, you cannot isolate individual applications into their own worker processes; hence, if one ASP.NET application fails, it can affect all the other applications. IIS 6.0, however, provides a new architecture that allows you to isolate your ASP.NET applications without incurring a performance penalty.

Before you run ASP.NET applications on IIS 6.0, be sure that you understand how ASP.NET works with the two IIS 6.0 isolation modes. When running in IIS 5.0 isolation mode, ASP.NET uses its own request processing model and configuration settings in the Machine.config file — just as it does when ASP.NET runs on IIS 5.x. When running in worker process isolation mode, ASP.NET disables its own request processing model and uses the new worker process architecture of IIS 6.0.

 Important

The version of ASP.NET that is included with Windows Server 2003 is not available with the Microsoft® Windows® XP 64-Bit Edition and the 64-bit versions of Windows Server 2003. For more information, see "Features unavailable on 64-bit versions of the Windows Server 2003 family" in Help and Support Center for Windows Server 2003.

ASP.NET Request Processing Model

When ASP.NET is enabled on a server running Windows Server 2003, the ASP.NET request processing model depends on the application isolation mode in which IIS 6.0 is running. The preferred application isolation mode for IIS 6.0 is worker process isolation mode, which enables you to use application pools, worker process recycling, and application pool health monitoring. When IIS 6.0 is running in worker process isolation mode, ASP.NET uses the IIS 6.0 request processing model settings.

In almost all situations, if your ASP.NET applications are running on Windows Server 2003, configure them to run in worker process isolation mode. However, if your application has compatibility issues in this mode — for example, if your application depends upon read raw ISAPI data filters — you can change your configuration to run IIS 6.0 in IIS 5.0 isolation mode.

If you configure IIS 6.0 to run in IIS 5.0 isolation mode, ASP.NET runs in its own request processing model, Aspnet_wp.exe, and uses its own configuration settings for process configuration, which are stored in the Machine.config configuration file. When your server is running in IIS 5.0 isolation mode, the ASP.NET ISAPI extension implements a request processing model that is similar to worker process isolation mode and contains worker process management capabilities similar to those provided by the WWW service. ASP.NET also provides recycling, health monitoring, and processor affinity.

When ASP.NET is installed on servers running Windows XP or Windows 2000 Server, ASP.NET runs in IIS 5.1 or IIS 5.0, respectively, and runs in the Aspnet_wp.exe process by default. The ASP.NET request processing model provides process recycling, health detection, and support for affinities between worker processes and particular CPUs on a server with multiple CPUs. For more information about running ASP.NET in its own request processing model, see "Using the ASP.NET Process Model" in IIS 6.0 Help.

ASP.NET processModel Configuration Settings

If the processModel section of the Machine.config file includes specific configuration settings for your ASP.NET application, those settings are not used when the application is running in worker process isolation mode, with the exception of the following attributes:

- **maxIOThreads** configures the maximum number of I/O threads per processor that are used by the ASP.NET thread pool.
- **maxWorkerThreads** configures the maximum number of worker threads per processor that are used by the ASP.NET thread pool.
- **responseDeadlockInterval** specifies a time limit, after which ASP.NET reports a worker process as unhealthy when a deadlock condition is detected.

If developers create ASP.NET applications with processModel configurations that include other attributes, the developers must manually convert the applications to the appropriate application pool settings before they deploy the applications in IIS 6.0. Except for the attributes previously mentioned, the other health monitoring and recycling features available in processModel do not automatically transfer from an ASP.NET configuration to IIS 6.0.

When Different Versions of ASP.NET Share the Same Application Pool

When multiple versions of the .NET Framework are installed on a computer that uses IIS 6.0, you might encounter the following error message in the Application Event log:

```
It is not possible to run different versions of ASP.NET in the same IIS process.
Please use the IIS Administration Tool to reconfigure your server to run the
application in a separate process.
```

This error occurs when more than one version of ASP.NET is configured to run in the same process. Different versions of the .NET Framework and run time cannot coexist side by side within the same process. Therefore, an ASP.NET application that uses one version of the run time must not share a process with an application that uses a different version. This error commonly occurs when two or more applications are mapped to different versions of ASP.NET but share the same application pool.

For more information about using ASP.NET with IIS 6.0 application pools, see "Configuring an ASP.NET Application for an ASP.NET Version" in IIS 6.0 Help. For more information about deploying ASP.NET applications on IIS 6.0, see "Deploying ASP.NET Applications in IIS 6.0" in *Deploying Internet Information Services (IIS) 6.0* of the *Microsoft® Windows® Server 2003 Deployment Kit* (or see "Deploying ASP.NET Applications in IIS 6.0" on the Web at http://www.microsoft.com/reskit). For more information about ASP.NET, see "ASP.NET" in the Web Application Guide of IIS 6.0 Help.

Additional Resources

These resources contain additional information related to this chapter.

Related Information

- "Configuring Internet Sites and Services" in this book for information about the IIS FTP, NNTP, and SMTP services.
- "Managing a Secure IIS 6.0 Solution" in this book for information about the security features available in IIS 6.0.
- "Running IIS 6.0 as an Application Server" in this book for information about configuring application pool health monitoring, orphaning worker processes, creating Web gardens, configuring idle timeout, configuring worker process isolation mode and IIS 5.0 isolation mode, and using the built-in Network Service account.
- "Deploying ASP.NET Applications in IIS 6.0" in *Deploying Internet Information Services (IIS) 6.0* of the *Microsoft Windows Server 2003 Deployment Kit* (or see "Deploying ASP.NET Applications in IIS 6.0" on the Web at http://www.microsoft.com/reskit) for information about deploying ASP.NET applications on IIS 6.0.
- The Exchange Server link on the Web Resources page at http://www.microsoft.com/windows/reskits/webresources for information about the complete e-mail services that Exchange Server provides.
- The Microsoft Product Support Services link on the Web Resources page at http://www.microsoft.com/windows/reskits/webresources for information about Exchange Server and other Microsoft products.

Related IIS 6.0 Help Topics

- "About Encryption" in IIS 6.0 Help, which is accessible from IIS Manager, for information about how to use encryption to help reduce the attack surface of your Web server.
- "About the Metabase" in IIS 6.0 Help for information about the architecture of the IIS metabase.
- "ASP.NET" in the Web Application Guide of IIS 6.0 Help for information about ASP.NET.
- "Configuring an ASP.NET Application for an ASP.NET Version" in IIS 6.0 Help for information about using ASP.NET with IIS 6.0.
- "Configuring Web Gardens" in IIS 6.0 Help for information about creating Web gardens.
- "Configuring Worker Process Health Monitoring" in IIS 6.0 Help for information about configuring IIS 6.0 for application pool health monitoring.
- "Configuring Worker Process Identities" and "IIS and Built-in Accounts" in IIS 6.0 Help for information about IIS security, including the recommended use of the built-in Network Service account.
- "IdleTimeout" in the Metabase Property Reference of IIS 6.0 Help for information about using this property to specify how long a worker process runs idle if no new requests are received.
- "OrphanWorkerProcess" in the Metabase Property Reference of IIS 6.0 Help for information about using this property to separate (instead of terminate) a failing worker process from its application pool.
- "Performance and Security" in IIS 6.0 Help for information about successfully balancing performance and security.
- "Recycling Worker Processes" in IIS 6.0 Help for information about worker process recycling, including when to use it, how to configure it, and how to configure overlapped recycling.
- "Using the ASP.NET Process Model" in IIS 6.0 Help for information about running ASP.NET in its own request processing model.

Related Windows Server 2003 Help Topics

- For best results in identifying Help topics by title, in Help and Support Center, under the **Search** box, click **Set search options**. Under **Help Topics**, select the **Search in title only** check box.
- "Features unavailable on 64-bit versions of the Windows Server 2003 family" in Help and Support Center for Windows Server 2003.

Running IIS 6.0 as an Application Server

Internet Information Services (IIS) 6.0, running on Microsoft® Windows® Server 2003, helps provide a secure, reliable, and easily managed application server on which you can host sites over an intranet, the Internet, or an extranet. IIS helps you create a platform of dynamic network applications, allowing you to use the latest Web standards to develop, implement, and manage your Web applications.

To match the needs of your applications to your server, IIS offers an adjustable architecture that allows you to isolate applications within a self-contained worker process. The new process model helps prevent one application or Web site from stopping another and reduces the time that you spend restarting services to maintain the health of your server. If health issues arise, IIS helps you manage them, usually without restarting your Web server or affecting your users.

In This Chapter

Related Information

- For information about configuring sites, see "Configuring Internet Sites and Services" in this book.

- For information about IIS 6.0 architecture, see "IIS 6.0 Architecture" in this book.

Introduction to Running an Application Server

Establishing an application server begins with configuring the application server role, which includes deciding what Web-related technologies you want to use and then enabling those technologies on your server. Attackers often target unused or unmonitored services; so if you enable only what you need, your IIS 6.0 application server provides a reduced attack surface when it is connected to the Internet.

In IIS 6.0, deciding which request processing model to use is your next decision. Helping you make this decision is "IIS 6.0 Architecture," the chapter that introduces the two IIS 6.0 request processing models, known as *application isolation modes*. Where the earlier chapter provides architectural diagrams and descriptions of the two application isolation modes, this chapter offers guidelines for deciding where and when to use each mode and provides procedures for configuring the isolation modes and their features. For information about choosing and configuring an application isolation mode, see "Configuring an Application Isolation Mode" later in this chapter.

Your application server runs in one of two mutually exclusive application isolation modes: worker process isolation mode or IIS 5.0 isolation mode. Worker process isolation mode, which is the default request processing model, supports new features such as application pools, health monitoring, worker process recycling, and rapid-fail protection. These new features help provide more robust performance. For example, you can recycle faulty applications to prevent service disruption and can use application pools to isolate one application from another without incurring a performance penalty. For more information about using these new features, see "Creating Application Pools" and "Ensuring Application Health in Worker Process Isolation Mode" later in this chapter.

Worker process isolation mode also provides better default security for your Web applications — in particular, better balance between security and functionality. To help you evaluate the security differences between the two application isolation modes, see "Security Considerations When Choosing an Application Isolation Mode" later in this chapter.

Worker process isolation mode provides several features to help you manage system resources, including Web gardens, idle timeout, CPU monitoring, processor affinity, and startup and shutdown limits. For information about configuring these features, see "Managing Resources in Worker Process Isolation Mode" later in this chapter.

To help you migrate from earlier versions of IIS, IIS 6.0 provides IIS 5.0 isolation mode, which is a processing model that offers compatibility for applications that depend on certain request processing characteristics of IIS 5.0. For example, if an application must run within Inetinfo.exe, it can only run in IIS 5.0 isolation mode unless you modify the application, making it compatible with worker process isolation mode. For information about which applications might require a processing model like IIS 5.0 isolation mode, see "Evaluating Application Requirements" later in this chapter.

You can configure most IIS 6.0 features either by using a graphical user interface (GUI) or by using a programmatic interface. For the procedures included here, the method that uses the GUI (usually implemented through IIS Manager) appears first, and an optional method for configuring metabase properties programmatically (by using the administrative utility Adsutil.vbs) appears second.

Configuring an Application Server Role

You can use the Configure Your Server wizard to install or remove many services on a computer running the Microsoft® Windows® Server 2003, Standard Edition; Windows® Server 2003, Enterprise Edition; Windows® Server 2003, Datacenter Edition; or Windows® Server 2003, Web Edition operating system. The server roles that you can install by using this wizard include the following: file server, print server, application server (IIS, ASP.NET), terminal server, DNS server, and DHCP server.

The application server role can include IIS 6.0, COM+, ASP.NET, and FrontPage® Server Extensions from Microsoft. Before you install IIS 6.0 on your server, review the technologies offered in the application server role and decide which technologies you want to install and enable during initial installation, and which technologies you will install later as needed. Then prepare for the IIS 6.0 installation by reviewing security considerations.

Technologies Offered in the Application Server

When you install IIS 6.0 as an application server by using the Configure Your Server wizard, IIS, COM+, and Microsoft® .NET Framework are automatically installed. To help ensure the security of your system after a default installation, ASP.NET and FrontPage 2002 Server Extensions are installed but not enabled in a default installation; the wizard gives you the option of enabling these services.

Table 3.1 describes the technologies included in the IIS 6.0 application server role, noting which are installed and enabled by default when you use the Configure Your Server wizard to install an application server role on a computer running Windows Server 2003.

Table 3.1   Technologies That Make Up the Application Server Role

Technology	Enabled by Default
Internet Information Services (IIS). Gives you a full-featured Web server that provides the infrastructure for .NET and existing Web applications and Web services. IIS 6.0 is optimized to run Web applications and XML Web services in a hosting environment.	●
COM+ for remote transactions. Provides an extension to COM. COM+ builds on COM's integrated services and features, making it easier for developers to create and use software components in any language by using any tool.	●
Distributed Transaction Coordinator (DTC) for remote access. Coordinates COM+ transactions across multiple computers.	●
ASP.NET. Offers a unified Web development platform that provides the services necessary for developers to build enterprise-class Web applications.[1]	
FrontPage Server Extensions. Enables users on a client computer to publish and administer Web sites on a server remotely over a network.[1]	

1 To ensure a more secure server during default installations, ASP.NET and FrontPage Server Extensions are automatically installed but in a disabled state. You must enable each of these technologies before you can use them. You can optionally enable either ASP.NET or FrontPage Server Extensions (or both) when using the Configure Your Server wizard by selecting the appropriate check box.

Important

The version of ASP.NET that is included with Windows Server 2003 is not available in the Microsoft® Windows XP 64-Bit Edition and the 64-bit versions of Windows Server 2003. For more information, see "Features unavailable on 64-bit versions of the Windows Server 2003 family" in Help and Support Center for Windows Server 2003.

If you are unsure whether you need either of the optional technologies, you can install IIS by using the default installation, which installs them in a disabled state, and then enable the optional technologies when you need them by using **Add or Remove Programs** in Control Panel. For more information about installing IIS 6.0 by using Control Panel, see "Installing IIS" in IIS 6.0 Help, which is accessible from IIS Manager.

As with every functionality that you enable on your server, use caution and take appropriate steps to secure each new technology that you add. For more information about securing your application server, see "Managing a Secure IIS 6.0 Solution" in this book.

Benefits of Enabling ASP.NET

ASP.NET is an application environment that provides the services necessary to build and deploy enterprise-class Web applications. ASP.NET is installed but not enabled during a default installation; you must enable it before you can use your application server to host ASP.NET Web pages. ASP.NET is part of the .NET Framework, which simplifies application development in the highly distributed environment of the Internet.

ASP.NET offers several important benefits:

- **Manageability.** ASP.NET uses a text-based, hierarchical configuration system that makes it easier for you to apply settings to your server environment and Web applications. Because ASP.NET stores configuration information as plain text, you can apply new settings without using local administration tools.

- **Security.** ASP.NET provides default authorization and authentication schemes for Web applications. Developers can easily add to, remove, or replace these schemes.

- **Easy deployment.** You can deploy an ASP.NET application to a server by merely copying the necessary files to the server, without restarting the server.

- **Enhanced performance.** ASP.NET is compiled code that runs on the server. ASP.NET takes advantage of early binding, just-in-time (JIT) compilation, native optimization, and caching services out of the box.

- **Flexible output caching.** ASP.NET can cache page data, portions of a page, or entire pages. When ASP.NET is running on Windows Server 2003 with IIS 6.0, ASP.NET can cache entire pages in the high-performance IIS kernel cache.

- **Mobile device support.** ASP.NET supports any browser on any device.

- **Scalability and availability.** ASP.NET includes features specifically designed to improve performance in clustered and multiprocessor environments.

ASP.NET and ASP pages can run compatibly side by side on an IIS application server because they are serviced by different ISAPI extensions that do not interfere with each other. Installing ASP.NET does not corrupt any ASP applications; the ASP engine continues to process files with an .asp extension. You can isolate these two processing environments in separate application pools or run both types of application in the same application pool.

The security configurations for ASP.NET and IIS are complementary and in part interdependent. For example, when IIS is running in worker process isolation mode, the ASP.NET processes are secured by means of restrictions on worker process identities; when IIS is running in IIS 5.0 isolation mode, the ASP.NET processes are secured by means of the identity assigned within the Machine.config file. Additional IIS security features are configured in the IIS metabase, and additional ASP.NET security features are configured in XML-based Web.config files. To secure an ASP.NET Web application, you might need to configure security in both places.

For more information about ASP.NET, see "Introduction to ASP.NET" in IIS 6.0 Help.

Benefits of Installing FrontPage Server Extensions

FrontPage Server Extensions provides Web-based and command-line administration for extending virtual servers. Extending virtual servers with FrontPage Server Extensions enables the site owner to author the site in FrontPage and delegate site ownership and administrative credentials.

If you build and maintain Web sites for customers and coordinate these efforts with multiple authors, the features included in FrontPage Server Extensions can help you accomplish the following tasks:

- Manage Web sites either on the local server or remotely by using HTML Administration pages or a command-line interface.

- Secure Web sites, and grant authoring, browsing, site management, or other user rights to authorized users.

- Analyze site usage to find out which users are visiting the site and how often.

- Monitor the health of FrontPage Server Extensions and detect errors.

FrontPage Server Extensions is typically used on development, test, or staging servers but not on application servers in a production environment. Use appropriate caution if you install a publishing system like FrontPage Server Extensions on a production server.

If you are unsure whether you need FrontPage Server Extensions, you can install them after installing IIS 6.0 by using **Add or Remove Programs** in Control Panel. For more information about installing FrontPage 2002 Server Extensions, see "Using FrontPage 2002 Server Extensions with IIS 6.0" in this book.

Preparing to Install IIS 6.0

Before you install IIS and configure it as an application server, review the security considerations outlined in this section:

- Avoid installing IIS on a domain controller.

- Verify that all disk volumes on your application servers use the NTFS file system, not FAT or FAT32 file systems.

- Ensure that your computer has network connectivity and a static or dynamic IP address. For more information, see "Before Configuring IIS" and "Securing Sites with IP Address Restrictions" in IIS 6.0 Help.

Avoid installing IIS on a domain controller

Whenever possible, do not install IIS on a domain controller for the following reasons:

- The networking and processor load generated by authentication and other domain controller processes can degrade IIS performance.

- Adding users to a group that can log on locally to the domain controller can increase the attack surface that is exposed by a Web application. If security is compromised on the domain controller, security is compromised on the entire domain.

Verify that all disk volumes on your application servers use NTFS

To provide a more secure file system, use NTFS on your application servers. NTFS is a more powerful and secure file system than the FAT or FAT32 file system. When you use NTFS on your application servers, you can limit access to the files and directories on the server and configure the access level that you grant to a particular user or group. An added benefit of NTFS is that it allows larger volume sizes than FAT.

Table 3.2 compares the benefits of using the NTFS and FAT file systems.

Table 3.2   Comparison of Support Offered by NTFS and FAT File Systems

Type of Support	NTFS File System	FAT File System
Directory and file security	Enables more secure directories and files through the use of NTFS permissions, which you can set at both the file and directory levels.	Does not allow you to secure directories and files.
The Active Directory® directory service and domain-based security	Supports Active Directory and domain-based security.	No support.
File encryption	Supports file encryption, which enhances file security.	No support.

To determine the type of file system used by a disk volume, view the properties of the volume (open **My Computer**, right-click the disk volume, and then click **Properties**). Windows provides a conversion utility (Convert.exe) that you can use to convert an existing FAT or FAT32 volume to NTFS without losing data. For more information about converting FAT or FAT32 volumes to NTFS, see "Reformatting or converting a partition to use NTFS" in Help and Support Center for Windows Server 2003.

Installing IIS 6.0

To help protect the system from malicious users and attackers, IIS is not installed by default when you install Windows Server 2003. In addition, when you initially install IIS, the service is installed in a secure, "locked" mode.

In Windows Server 2003, you can install IIS by using either Control Panel or the Configure Your Server wizard. These options offer slightly different default installations:

- If you install IIS by using **Add or Remove Programs** in Control Panel, only IIS is installed and enabled, so the default installation serves only static content. Features such as ASP, ASP.NET, server-side includes (SSI), Web Distributed Authoring and Versioning (WebDAV) publishing, and FrontPage Server Extensions are either not installed or not enabled, and therefore do not work.

- If you install IIS by using the Configure Your Server wizard, ASP.NET and ASP are automatically installed with IIS. In addition, you have the option of enabling ASP.NET and installing FrontPage Server Extensions by using the wizard.

If you want to serve dynamic content, you can "unlock" applications such as ASP.NET, ASP, and FrontPage Server Extensions through the **Web Service Extensions** node in IIS Manager. For more information, see "Enabling Dynamic Content" later in this chapter.

 Note

When you upgrade from a previous version of IIS, most dynamic content features remain enabled. The installation program notes the exceptions.

Be sure to install IIS on an NTFS-formatted drive. NTFS is a more powerful and secure file system than FAT or FAT32. For more information about the advantages of using NTFS, see "Preparing to Install IIS 6.0" earlier in this chapter.

The following procedure tells how to install IIS 6.0 by using the Configure Your Server wizard. For information about installing IIS by using **Add or Remove Programs** in Control Panel, see "Installing IIS" in IIS 6.0 Help.

▷ To install IIS by using the Configure Your Server wizard

1. Open Control Panel, double-click **Administrative Tools**, and then double-click **Configure Your Server Wizard**.

2. Click **Next** to reach the Server Role page, click Application server (IIS, ASP.NET), and then click Next.

    By default, the wizard installs and enables IIS, COM+, and DTC.

3. If you want to serve either of the optional technologies (FrontPage Server Extensions or ASP.NET), on the **Application Server Options** page, select the appropriate check boxes, and then click **Next**.

4. Click **Finish**.

For more information about installing IIS by using Control Panel or the Configure Your Server wizard, see "Installing IIS" in IIS 6.0 Help.

Enabling Dynamic Content

The default installation of IIS 6.0 protects your system from malicious users and attackers by delivering IIS in a "locked" mode, in which IIS can only serve static HTTP content. After a default installation, the request handlers that process dynamic content are disabled, which means that features like ASP, ASP.NET, SSI, WebDAV publishing, and FrontPage Server Extensions do not work.

You can configure the request handlers (ISAPI extensions or Common Gateway Interface [CGI] programs), known as *Web service extensions*, by using either the **Web Service Extensions** node in IIS Manager or the command-line script Iisext.vbs, which is located in *systemroot*\System32.

Iisext.vbs can be used to perform the same operations that are available in IIS Manager. You can use either tool to administer dynamic content, performing the following tasks:

- Allow or prohibit Web service extensions on the local computer.

- Add new Web service extensions.

- Allow all the Web service extensions that an application requires.

- Prohibit the running of all Web service extensions on the local computer.

> ⬥ **Important**
>
> You must be a member of the Administrators group on the local computer to perform the following procedure or procedures, or you must have been delegated the appropriate authority. As a security best practice, log on to your computer by using an account that is not in the Administrators group, and then use the **runas** command to run IIS Manager as an administrator. At a command prompt, type **runas** /*User:Administrative_AccountName* "mmc %systemroot%\system32\inetsrv\iis.msc".

▷ **To enable or disable a Web service extension by using IIS Manager**

1. In IIS Manager, expand the local computer, and then click **Web Service Extensions**.

2. In the details pane, click the Web service extension that you want to enable or disable, and then do one of the following:

   - To enable a disabled Web service extension, click **Allow**.

   - To disable an enabled Web service extension, click **Prohibit**.

For more information about using IIS Manager to administer dynamic content, including instructions for adding new Web service extensions, allowing an application to call a Web service extension, or disabling all Web service extensions, see "Enabling and Disabling Dynamic Content" in IIS 6.0 Help.

To enable a Web service extension from the command line, use the Iisext.vbs command-line script. Before enabling a Web service extension or application type, obtain a list of all the defined Web service extensions on the computer. (To view a list in IIS Manager, expand the **Web Service Extensions** node.)

 Important

You must be a member of the Administrators group on the local computer to run scripts and executables, or you must have been delegated the appropriate authority. As a security best practice, log on to your computer by using an account that is not in the Administrators group, and then use the **runas** command to run your script or executable as an administrator. At a command prompt, type runas /profile /*User:MyMachine\Administrator* cmd to open a command window with administrator rights and then type cscript.exe *ScriptName* (including the full path with parameters, if any).

▷ **To view a list of a Web service extensions on the local computer by using Iisext.vbs**

1. In the **Run** dialog box, type **cmd**, and then click **OK**.

2. At the command prompt, type:

   ```
   cscript %SystemRoot%\system32\iisext.vbs /listapp
   ```

This command displays a list of all Web service extensions that are located on the local computer. For example, using the **/listapp** parameter might return the following:

```
Connecting to server ...Done.
Active Server Pages
Internet Data Connector
Server Side Includes
WebDAV
FrontPage Server Extensions
ASP.NET v1.1.4322
```

If you want to enable ASP pages, type the command-line syntax that is shown in the following procedure. If you want to enable another type of application, replace "Active Server Pages" with the name of that application. If the application name contains spaces, be sure to enclose the name with quotation marks.

▷ **To enable ASP pages (or other Web service extension)**

- At the command prompt, type:

```
cscript %SystemRoot%\system32\iisext.vbs /EnApp "Active Server Pages"
```

For more information about using the Iisext.vbs command-line script to administer dynamic content, such as enabling, disabling, or listing Web service extensions and their files, see "Managing Applications and Web Service Extensions" in IIS 6.0 Help.

Configuring an Application Isolation Mode

So that you can match the needs of your server configuration to the requirements of your applications, and to provide more flexibility if you are upgrading from an earlier version of IIS, IIS 6.0 offers an adjustable architecture for isolating your applications. IIS 6.0 can run an application server in one of two process models, called application isolation modes:

- Worker process isolation mode, which is the default application isolation mode for IIS 6.0, isolates key components of the World Wide Web Publishing Service (WWW service) from the effects of defective applications and protects applications from each other by using isolated worker processes.

- IIS 5.0 isolation mode, which processes requests in nearly the same way that IIS 5.0 does, is provided for applications that depend on specific features and behaviors of IIS 5.0 or earlier. Use this isolation mode only if an application has a compatibility problem, which you cannot resolve, when it runs in worker process isolation mode.

Both application isolation modes use the HTTP protocol stack, HTTP.sys, in almost identical ways. The primary difference is that in worker process isolation mode, HTTP.sys can route requests to multiple queues; in IIS 5.0 isolation mode, HTTP.sys routes requests to a single queue. For more information about IIS 6.0 request processing, see "IIS 6.0 Architecture" in this book.

Choosing an Application Isolation Mode

One of the most important decisions that you will make when you configure your application server is which application isolation mode to use. Although worker process isolation mode is recommended if your environment supports it, you must evaluate the relative capabilities of the two application isolation modes, considering their compatibility with the applications that the server will make available, the level of security that your organization requires, and performance requirements.

Evaluating the Capabilities of the Two Application Isolation Modes

Before you choose an application isolation mode for your application server, review the benefits of each mode and then review your ISAPI (Internet Server API) filters and applications to determine whether any conflicts exist with worker process isolation mode. Keep in mind that when an application server is running in IIS 5.0 isolation mode, many of the benefits of the new request-processing architecture — such as application pools, recycling, and health monitoring — are unavailable. If a filter or application cannot run in worker process isolation mode, evaluate whether you can substitute another filter or application that does not conflict with worker process isolation mode.

Benefits of Worker Process Isolation Mode

In worker process isolation mode, you can isolate an application within its own process, where it does not depend on a central process such as Inetinfo.exe. When you run IIS in this isolation mode, you can group Web applications into *application pools*, through which you can apply specific configuration settings to groups of applications and to the worker processes that service those application groups.

An application pool corresponds to one request routing queue within HTTP.sys and one or more worker processes. Process boundaries separate each application pool from the others so that when an application is routed to one application pool, applications in other application pools do not affect that application. Application pools allow you to run all application code in an isolated environment without incurring a performance penalty.

Worker processes operate independently; if one fails, it does not affect other worker processes. The pooling of applications protects applications from the effects of worker processes that support other application pools. In this way, applications are protected from each other.

In worker process isolation mode, a kernel-mode device driver called the HTTP protocol stack (HTTP.sys) routes HTTP requests directly to a kernel-mode request queue that is assigned to a specific application pool. Worker processes that serve the application pool pull incoming requests directly from the request queue, avoiding the overhead of user-mode process switching.

To protect the WWW service, IIS 6.0 isolates critical components, such as HTTP.sys and WWW Service Administration and Monitoring, from external application code that runs in worker processes. HTTP.sys receives and queues requests for Internet services.

When a worker process enters an unhealthy state and stops processing requests, HTTP.sys continues to queue requests. The WWW service detects that the worker process is unhealthy and shuts it down, starting a new worker process if requests are waiting in the queue or if new requests arrive. Because HTTP.sys continues to accept incoming requests even when worker processes fail, end users are shielded from the failure; the client can still connect to the WWW service while a replacement worker process is initialized.

IIS 6.0 worker process isolation mode delivers the following improvements over earlier versions of IIS:

- **Robust performance.** Isolation prevents Web applications and Web sites in an application pool from disrupting applications or Web sites in other application pools. Restarts of the operating system and WWW service are avoided.

- **Self-healing.** Automated management provides auto-restart of failed applications and periodic restart of unstable applications or applications that leak memory.

- **Scalability.** IIS 6.0 supports hundreds (even thousands) of sites on a server through features such as start on demand and idle timeout for a worker process. In addition, IIS 6.0 offers improved multiprocessor scalability.

- **Processor affinity.** You can bind worker processes to specific processors on multiprocessor servers.

- **Automated debugging.** You can configure debugging tools to start automatically when worker processes fail.

- **CPU monitoring.** You can limit the amount of CPU resources that an application pool can consume within a configured amount of time.

For more information about worker process isolation mode, including architectural diagrams, see "IIS 6.0 Architecture" in this book. For more information about automated debugging and CPU monitoring, see "Enabling Debugging" and "Enabling CPU Monitoring" later in this chapter.

Before you decide which application isolation mode to run on a server, read "Evaluating Application Requirements" later in this chapter.

Isolation Options in IIS 5.0 Isolation Mode

When IIS 6.0 is running in IIS 5.0 isolation mode, the following options for application isolation, which are similar to those in IIS 5.0, are available:

- **Low isolation (in-process).** Applications run in-process (on the Web server) as DLLs in Inetinfo.exe and are not protected from other applications that run in-process. The process identity (the security context of the process running the application) is LocalSystem.

- **Medium isolation (pooled out-of-process).** All pooled applications run as DLLs in the same single instance of DLLHost.exe and are protected from the effects of applications running in High isolation. However, because all pooled applications run in the same process, they are not protected from each other. The default application identity is IWAM_*ComputerName*.

- **High isolation (out-of-process).** Applications run as DLLs in their own DLLHost.exe and are protected from the effects of other applications running in Medium or High isolation. Also, all other applications that run on the same computer are protected from the effects of applications that run in High isolation. The default application identity is IWAM_*ComputerName*.

Note that only the parts of applications that are served by ISAPI extensions can be run out-of-process — that is, in a memory space that is separate from the Web server. Thus, if an ASP page that is set to High-isolation includes static files, those static files are served by Inetinfo.exe.

For more information about IIS 5.0 isolation mode, including architectural diagrams, see "IIS 6.0 Architecture" in this book.

Evaluating Application Requirements

IIS 6.0 cannot run both application isolation modes simultaneously on the same computer. Therefore, on a single computer running IIS 6.0, you cannot run some Web applications in worker process isolation mode and others in IIS 5.0 isolation mode. Applications that require different application isolation modes must be run on separate computers.

Guidelines for Optimizing Application Performance

When you are deciding which application isolation mode to use, follow these guidelines:

- Use worker process isolation mode unless you need to use IIS 5.0 isolation mode because of a specific compatibility issue. For example, read raw data filters only work in IIS 5.0 isolation mode.

- Run Web sites that contain static content or simple ASP applications in worker process isolation mode. These Web sites usually require little or no modification to run in worker process isolation mode.

- For applications that run correctly in IIS 5.0, try running them first in worker process isolation mode. If they do not work correctly, attempt to diagnose and resolve any compatibility issues. You can also turn off or scale down some of the features that worker process isolation mode provides. For example, you might turn off recycling or change the recycling settings so that the server does not perform an overlapped recycle.

If a server is running in IIS 5.0 isolation mode and you upgrade the server's applications so that they are compatible with worker process isolation mode, be sure to change the isolation mode on that server to worker process isolation mode. If, after changing the server from IIS 5.0 isolation mode to worker process isolation mode, you find that you cannot easily maintain a healthy server, change back to IIS 5.0 isolation mode while you diagnose and fix the compatibility issues. Then reconfigure the server to run in worker process isolation mode.

 Important

Before you change the application isolation mode, consider that each time you reconfigure a server to use a different mode, you must restart IIS, which temporarily interrupts the service and can cause loss of application state data.

Applications That Cannot Run in Worker Process Isolation Mode

Applications that run in worker process isolation mode can take advantage of all the worker process behaviors, which include multi-instancing, recycling, and configurable process identity. Certain application characteristics conflict with the architecture of worker process isolation mode. Applications with those characteristics must be run in IIS 5.0 isolation mode until you can modify them.

Applications with the following characteristics cannot run in worker process isolation mode:

- **Read raw data filters.** This type of ISAPI filter only works in IIS 5.0 isolation mode.

- **Dependency on Inetinfo.exe.** Applications that must run within an Inetinfo.exe worker process can only run in IIS 5.0 isolation mode.

- **Requires Dllhost.exe.** ISAPI applications that must run in a Dllhost.exe environment can only run in IIS 5.0 isolation mode because Dllhost.exe is not available for ISAPI applications in worker process isolation mode. (Dllhost.exe can still be used to host out-of-process COM+ applications, regardless of the mode in which IIS is running.)

If IIS 6.0 is running in worker process isolation mode (the default mode in IIS 6.0), and you must run applications that require a functionality that is only available in IIS 5.0 isolation mode, reconfigure the server to run in IIS 5.0 isolation mode until you can correct the incompatibility. Running your server in IIS 5.0 isolation mode means that you cannot take advantage of the reliability features in worker process isolation mode.

Security Considerations When Choosing an Application Isolation Mode

When you choose an application isolation mode, keep these security considerations in mind:

- **Worker process isolation mode.** Worker process isolation mode provides better default security for running Web applications than does IIS 5.0 isolation mode. In worker process isolation mode, worker processes run by default as Network Service, which is the account that provides a better balance between security and functionality.

- **IIS 5.0 isolation mode.** Web applications that are set to Low isolation, such as low-isolation ISAPI extensions, run in a process that runs as LocalSystem. The LocalSystem account can read, execute, and change all of the resources on the computer. Thus, if an attack by a malicious user takes over a Web application that runs in Low isolation, many assets of the local computer are open to the attacker. Also, if you set Web applications to Medium or High isolation, they run with IWAM_*ComputerName* as the default identity, which has fewer rights than LocalSystem.

Windows Server 2003 provides the following built-in system accounts, which you can use to provide the security context for worker processes:

- **Local Service.** Has limited rights on the local computer and limited access (Anonymous) to network resources. Use the Local Service account if the worker process does not require authenticated access to network resources.

- **Network Service.** Has limited rights on the local computer and authenticated access (as the computer account) to network resources.

- **LocalSystem.** Has full access to the system because it belongs to the Administrators group.

Table 3.3 provides additional details about the built-in system accounts that are available in IIS 6.0, and Table 3.4 shows the default security account for both application isolation modes.

Table 3.3   Built-in System Accounts in IIS 6.0

Built-in Account	Privilege Level	Group or Account Used	
		On the Local Machine	On the Network
Local Service	Least privileged	Users group	Anonymous access account
Network Service	More privileged	Users group	Computer account
LocalSystem	Most privileged	Administrator with full access account	Computer account

Table 3.4   Default Security Accounts for Each Application Isolation Mode

Mode or Options Within a Mode	Default Account
Worker process isolation mode	Network Service
IIS 5.0 isolation mode	
ISAPI extensions set to Low isolation that run in Inetinfo.exe	LocalSystem
ISAPI extensions set to Medium-isolation that run in pooled out-of-process application hosts	IWAM_*ComputerName*
ISAPI extensions set to High-isolation that run in out-of-process application hosts	IWAM_*ComputerName*
ASP.NET worker processes	ASPNET

For more information about built-in security accounts in IIS 6.0 and Windows Server 2003, including IWAM_*ComputerName*, see "Managing a Secure IIS 6.0 Solution" in this book and "IIS and Built-in Accounts" in IIS 6.0 Help.

Performance Considerations When Choosing an Application Isolation Mode

When you run IIS 6.0 in IIS 5.0 isolation mode, applications that run in Medium or High isolation incur a performance penalty when COM uses a remote procedure call (RPC) during these parts of the request processing cycle:

- When a request is sent to an application that is running in Medium or High isolation and the response is sent back.

- When a Web application that is running in Medium or High isolation communicates with the Web server during the processing of a request.

In contrast, when IIS 6.0 runs in worker process isolation mode, applications are loaded in-process to W3wp.exe and remain there. Therefore, no performance penalty is incurred.

 Note

You cannot run SSI and Internet Database Connector (IDC) applications out-of-process. You need to run these applications in-process.

For more information about performance issues, see "About Performance Tuning" in IIS 6.0 Help and "Optimizing IIS 6.0 Performance" in this book.

Configuring an Application Isolation Mode

After configuring the IIS application server role and enabling dynamic content, configure the application isolation mode for the server. IIS 6.0 can run in one of two application isolation modes: worker process isolation mode, which is the default mode for IIS 6.0, or IIS 5.0 isolation mode. To configure IIS 6.0 to run in a specific application isolation mode, use either IIS Manager or the Adsutil.vbs administrative utility.

If you are configuring IIS to run in IIS 5.0 isolation mode, after setting the application isolation mode, you must perform the additional task of setting the level of isolation for each application hosted on the server.

For information about choosing the appropriate application isolation mode for your environment, see "Choosing an Application Isolation Mode" earlier in this chapter.

 Important

You must be a member of the Administrators group on the local computer to perform the following procedure or procedures, or you must have been delegated the appropriate authority. As a security best practice, log on to your computer by using an account that is not in the Administrators group, and then use the **runas** command to run IIS Manager as an administrator. At a command prompt, type **runas** /*User:Administrative_AccountName* "mmc %systemroot%\system32\inetsrv\iis.msc".

After you configure the application isolation mode, you must restart IIS, which temporarily interrupts the WWW service.

▶ **To configure IIS for an application isolation mode by using IIS Manager**

1. In IIS Manager, expand the local computer, right-click **Web Sites**, and then click **Properties**.

2. On the **Service** tab, specify the appropriate application isolation mode by selecting or clearing the **Run WWW service in IIS 5.0 isolation mode** check box. Clearing this check box configures IIS to run in worker process isolation mode.

3. Click **OK**. To restart IIS, click **Yes**.

You can also configure IIS for an application isolation mode by setting the metabase property **IIs5IsolationModeEnabled** to **true** or **false**. Use the following procedure to configure this metabase property from a command line.

 Important

You must be a member of the Administrators group on the local computer to run scripts and executables, or you must have been delegated the appropriate authority. As a security best practice, log on to your computer by using an account that is not in the Administrators group, and then use the **runas** command to run your script or executable as an administrator. At a command prompt, type **runas /profile** /*User*.*MyMachine\Administrator* cmd to open a command window with administrator rights and then type **cscript.exe** *ScriptName* (including the full path with parameters, if any).

 To configure IIS for an application isolation mode by using Adsutil.vbs

1. In the **Run** dialog box, type **cmd**, and then click **OK**.

2. To set the application isolation mode, type one of the following commands at the command prompt:

   - To configure the server to run in worker process isolation mode, type:

     ```
     cscript %SystemDrive%\Inetpub\AdminScripts\adsutil.vbs set
     W3SVC/IIs5IsolationModeEnabled FALSE
     ```

   - To configure the server to run in IIS 5.0 isolation mode, type:

     ```
     cscript %SystemDrive%\Inetpub\AdminScripts\adsutil.vbs set
     W3SVC/IIs5IsolationModeEnabled TRUE
     ```

     ☑ **Note**

     If you configured the server to run in IIS 5.0 isolation mode, you will need to set the level of application protection, or isolation, for each application running on the server. For instructions, see the following procedure.

3. To restart IIS, at the command prompt, type:

   iisreset /noforce

   For more information about restarting IIS from the command line, see "Common Administrative Tasks" in this book.

To verify that you successfully changed to worker process isolation mode, check whether an Application Pools folder appears when you open IIS Manager on your local computer. You can always determine which isolation mode that IIS is running by the presence (in worker process isolation mode) or absence (in IIS 5.0 isolation mode) of the Application Pools folder.

Important

Do not confuse the DefaultAppPool application pool, which appears by default when you configure a computer to run in worker process isolation mode, with the MSSharePointAppPool application pool, which appears by default when you install FrontPage 2002 Server Extensions or SharePoint™ Team Services from Microsoft®.

Do not use, delete, or make changes to the MSSharePointAppPool application pool. It holds files that are used internally by FrontPage Server Extensions and SharePoint Team Services. For more information, see "Using FrontPage 2002 Server Extensions with IIS 6.0" in this book.

Setting Isolation for Applications Running in IIS 5.0 Isolation Mode

If you configured the server to run in IIS 5.0 isolation mode, you must now set the level of application protection, or isolation, for each application that runs on the server. Table 3.5 summarizes the security and performance considerations to take into account when you choose an application isolation mode. If you do not set an isolation level, by default, IIS 5.0 isolation mode runs an application in Medium isolation pooled out-of-process.

Table 3.5   Isolation Levels in IIS 5.0 Isolation Mode

Isolation Level/Host	Protection	Default Security Account	Performance Penalty?
Low/Inetinfo.exe	**In-process.** Not protected from other applications that run in-process.	LocalSystem	
Medium/ DLLHost.exe	**Pooled out-of-process.** Protected from the effects of applications that run in High isolation; however, the applications are not protected from each other.	IWAM_*Computer Name*	●
High/ DLLHost.exe	**Out-of-process.** Protected from the effects of other applications that run in Medium or High isolation; cannot affect other applications running on the same computer.	IWAM_*Computer Name*	●

For more information about the security and performance implications of running applications at each of these application levels, see "Security Considerations When Choosing an Application Isolation Mode" and "Performance Considerations When Choosing an Application Isolation Mode" earlier in this chapter.

▶ **To set or change the level of application protection for an application in IIS 5.0 isolation mode**

1. In IIS Manager, expand the local computer, right-click the Web site or the starting-point directory for the application, and then click **Properties**.

2. Click the **Home Directory**, **Virtual Directory**, or **Directory** tab. If you are in the directory that is listed as the **Starting Point** directory, the **Application name** box is filled in.

3. In the **Application protection** box, click the appropriate level of protection:

   - **Low (IIS Process)**

   - **Medium (Pooled)**

   - **High (Isolated)**

4. Click **OK**.

The WWW service finishes processing any active requests for the application before it creates a separate process. At the next request for the application, the application runs in the appropriate memory space.

You can also configure isolation by updating the **AppIsolated** metabase property setting for each application. For information about how to do this, see the **AppIsolated** property in the "Metabase Property Reference" in IIS 6.0 Help, and see "Code Examples to Configure Metabase Properties" in IIS 6.0 Help.

 Note

If you need to stop an application that has isolation set to Medium (pooled) or High, see "Stopping Isolated Applications" in IIS 6.0 Help.

Creating Application Pools

When you run IIS 6.0 in worker process isolation mode, you can isolate different Web applications or Web sites in pools, which are called *application pools*. An application pool is a group of URLs that are routed to one or more worker processes that share the same configuration. The URLs that you assign to an application pool can be for an application, a Web site, a Web directory, or a virtual directory.

In an application pool, process boundaries separate each worker process from other worker processes so that when an application is routed to one application pool, applications in other application pools do not affect that application.

By using an application pool, you can assign specific configuration settings to a worker process (or, in the case of a Web garden, to a set of worker processes) that services a group of applications. For example, you can configure worker process recycling, which offers several configuration options to match the needs of each application. If, for example, you suspect that an application has a memory leak, you might configure the application pool's worker process to recycle when its memory use reaches a certain threshold. If another application fails because of the volume of requests that it receives, you can set the application pool's worker process to recycle when the application exceeds a specified number of requests.

By creating new application pools and assigning Web sites and applications to them, you can make your server more efficient, reliable, and secure, and ensure that your applications remain available even when a worker process serving an application pool is recycled because of a faulty application.

For more information about the application pool architecture in IIS 6.0, including how application pools work, see "IIS 6.0 Architecture" in this book.

Guidelines for Creating Application Pools

Consider the following guidelines when you create application pools:

- To isolate Web applications on a Web site from Web applications on other sites running on the same computer, create an individual application pool for each Web site.

- To improve application security, you can specify a unique user account (process identity) for each application pool. If you specify a unique user account, be sure to add that account to the IIS_WPG group. When you use a built-in account, use Network Service if possible because it offers a better balance between security and functionality.

 Note

> If you specify a large number of unique user accounts, your Web server might reach a limit to the number of worker processes you can start under separate identities, in which case, all subsequent application pools fail with a message of "Service unavailable."

The use of unique user accounts also improves security auditing capabilities, because you can more easily trace security events to the corresponding applications that use the security context — that is, the process identity —of the account listed in the security events. For information about auditing security events, see "Auditing" in IIS 6.0 Help.

- If you want to configure an application to run with its own unique set of properties, create a unique application pool for that application.

- If you test an application on the same server on which the application is running, create separate application pools and be sure to use different virtual directories for the test and production versions of the application. Using a test application pool for the test virtual directory helps to isolate the test version of the application.

By running the test version in a separate application pool, you reduce the risk of the test version crashing or corrupting the production version because the applications are separated by process boundaries. However, separation by application pool does not protect any shared resources that both versions use, such as shared COM components or common data sources (for example, flat files, databases, or registry keys). You can improve the isolation of COM components by using side-by-side assemblies, but you must segregate data sources by some other means to completely isolate the applications. For information about using side-by-side assemblies, see "Configuring Applications to Use COM+ Services" in IIS 6.0 Help.

Configuring Application Pools

Use the following procedure to create an application pool for a Web site, a Web directory, or a virtual directory. Note that the application pool feature is only available when you run IIS in worker process isolation mode.

Important

You must be a member of the Administrators group on the local computer to perform the following procedure or procedures, or you must have been delegated the appropriate authority. As a security best practice, log on to your computer by using an account that is not in the Administrators group, and then use the runas command to run IIS Manager as an administrator. At a command prompt, type runas /*User:Administrative_AccountName* "mmc %systemroot%\system32\inetsrv\iis.msc".

▶ **To create a new application pool**

1. In IIS Manager, expand the local computer, right-click **Application Pools**, point to **New**, and then click **Application Pool**.

2. In the **Application pool ID** box, type a name for the new application pool.

3. Under **Application pool settings**, select one of the following settings:

    - To use the default application pool settings, click **Use default settings for new application pool.**

    - To use the settings from an existing application pool, click **Use existing application pool as template**, and in the **Application pool name** list, click the application pool to be used as a template.

4. Click **OK**.

For more information about creating application pools and configuring worker processes, see "Configuring Application Pools" and "Configuring Application Pool Identity" in IIS 6.0 Help.

Application pools allow you to apply configuration settings to groups of applications and the worker processes that service those applications. Any Web site, Web directory, or virtual directory can be assigned to an application pool.

▶   **To assign an application to an application pool**

1. In IIS Manager, right-click the application that you want to assign to an application pool, and then click **Properties**.

2. Click the **Virtual Directory**, **Directory**, or **Home Directory** tab.

3. If you are assigning a directory or virtual directory, verify that **Application name** is filled in. If the **Application name** box is not filled in, click **Create**, and then type a name.

4. In the **Application pool** list, click the name of the application pool to which you want to assign the application, and then click **OK**.

Alternatively, you can assign an application to an application pool by editing the metabase property **AppPoolId** directly. For more information about assigning applications in this way, see the **AppPoolId** property in the "Metabase Property Reference" in IIS 6.0 Help.

Ensuring Application Health in Worker Process Isolation Mode

Worker process isolation mode provides several features that can help you identify and correct faulty applications in your application pools before they affect your systems or your users. These features often do the work for you, ensuring that you have robust performance and healthy systems:

- **Application pool health monitoring.** Provides the basis for application pool health and health monitoring, including worker process health monitoring and debugging.

- **Recycling worker processes.** Periodically restarts worker processes in an application pool.

- **Rapid-fail protection.** Protects system resources when a worker process that is serving an application pool fails repeatedly within a short period of time.

IIS 5.0 isolation mode does not offer these features.

Monitoring Application Pool Health

The WWW service monitors the health of worker processes by periodically pinging them to determine their responsiveness. If a worker process fails to respond to a ping (for example, the worker process might not have available threads to process the incoming request), the WWW service either terminates the worker process and creates another worker process to replace it, or releases the worker process but lets it continue to run. You can configure IIS to perform a specified action when an unhealthy worker process is released — for example, you can specify that IIS attach a debugger to a released worker process.

Additionally, the WWW service maintains a communication channel to each worker process and can detect a drop in the communication channel, which indicates a worker process failure. When a worker process fails of its own accord, the WWW service starts another worker process in its place, provided the application pool does not go into rapid-fail protection.

In addition to monitoring the health of worker processes, the WWW service can detect ongoing problems with the entire application pool by using rapid-fail protection. For example, if worker processes are terminating abnormally every few seconds, the WWW service can determine that the application pool is unhealthy and disable it, preventing the unhealthy application pool from affecting applications in other pools.

The following conditions cause an application pool to start or stop:

- Initiation of rapid-fail protection causes an application pool to stop. For more information about rapid-fail protection, see "Configuring Rapid-Fail Protection" later in this chapter.

- CPU monitoring shuts down an application pool after it reaches the configured Maximum CPU use limit. When the limit is reached, the application pool shuts down and remains down until the **CPUResetInterval** time limit expires, at which time the application pool restarts. For more information about CPU monitoring, see "Enabling CPU Monitoring" later in this chapter.

- A configuration error occurs — such as when an incorrect user name or password, or a nonexistent or misconfigured account identity, is used — causing an application pool to stop. For more information about configuring worker process account identities, see "Managing a Secure IIS 6.0 Solution" in this book and "Configuring Worker Process Identities" in IIS 6.0 Help.

- A Windows administrator performs a demand stop or start on an application pool. For more information about performing demand stops and starts on an application pool, see the **IIsApplicationPool (WMI)** class and the **IIsApplicationPool (ADSI)** class in the "Programmatic Administration Reference" in IIS 6.0 Help.

You can enable health monitoring for an application pool by using IIS Manager or by using the Adsutil.vbs utility to update metabase properties from the command line. The following procedures give instructions for each approach.

 Important

You must be a member of the Administrators group on the local computer to perform the following procedure or procedures, or you must have been delegated the appropriate authority. As a security best practice, log on to your computer by using an account that is not in the Administrators group, and then use the **runas** command to run IIS Manager as an administrator. At a command prompt, type **runas** /*User:Administrative_AccountName* "mmc %systemroot%\system32\inetsrv\iis.msc".

▶ **To enable application pool health monitoring by using IIS Manager**

1. In IIS Manager, expand the local computer, expand **Application Pools**, right-click the application pool, and then click **Properties**.

2. On the **Health** tab, select the **Enable pinging** check box.

3. In the **seconds** box next to **Ping worker process every**, type the number of seconds that you want to elapse between pings. (The default value is 30 seconds.)

4. Click **OK**.

You can also configure the WWW service pinging feature and the frequency of the ping by setting the metabase properties **PingingEnabled** and **PingInterval**. Use the following procedures to configure these metabase properties from the command line.

 Important

You must be a member of the Administrators group on the local computer to run scripts and executables, or you must have been delegated the appropriate authority. As a security best practice, log on to your computer by using an account that is not in the Administrators group, and then use the runas command to run your script or executable as an administrator. At a command prompt, type runas /profile /User:MyMachine\Administrator cmd to open a command window with administrator rights and then type cscript.exe ScriptName (including the full path with parameters, if any).

▶ **To enable application pool health monitoring by using Adsutil.vbs**

1. In the **Run** dialog box, type **cmd**, and then click **OK**.

2. At the command prompt, type:

    ```
    cscript %SystemDrive%\Inetpub\AdminScripts\adsutil.vbs set
    W3SVC/AppPools/ApplicationPoolName/PingingEnabled TRUE
    ```

▶ **To change the ping interval by using Adsutil.vbs**

- At the command prompt, type:

    ```
    cscript %SystemDrive%\Inetpub\AdminScripts\adsutil.vbs set
    W3SVC/AppPools/ApplicationPoolName/PingInterval n
    ```

    In the preceding syntax, replace *n* with the number of seconds that you want to elapse between pings.

For more information about setting these metabase properties, see the **PingingEnabled** and **PingInterval** properties in the "Metabase Property Reference" in IIS 6.0 Help, and see "Code Examples to Configure Metabase Properties" in IIS 6.0 Help.

Using an ISAPI Extension That Declares Itself Unhealthy

You can use an ISAPI extension application that is built to programmatically signal the WWW service that it needs to be recycled. ISAPI developers can configure an ISAPI extension to signal the WWW service by using the **ServerSupportFunction** callback function together with the parameter HSE_REQ_REPORT_UNHEALTHY.

The ISAPI extension requires an internal mechanism for determining that it is unhealthy, such as monitoring the status of its internal thread pool. During the ping operation, the WWW service detects whether a worker process is hosting an ISAPI extension that is unhealthy and needs recycling; therefore, for this function to work, you must enable worker process pinging on the application pool that is running the ISAPI extension.

When you use this type of ISAPI extension and pinging is enabled, consider that it will cause a worker process recycle in which the ISAPI extension is running. This affects all applications that are running in that worker process.

The ASP and ASP.NET ISAPI extensions apply logic that takes advantage of this feature as it monitors the status of its internal thread pool. If too many of its threads enter a blocking state, it reports itself as unhealthy, which triggers a worker process recycle if pinging is enabled for the application pool.

For more information about the **ServerSupportFunction** callback function, see the MSDN Online link on the Web Resources page at http://www.microsoft.com/windows/reskits/webresources.

Enabling Debugging

By default, when a worker process is determined to be unhealthy, the WWW service terminates the unhealthy process and starts a new worker process to serve new or queued client requests. Optionally, you can allow an application pool to keep the worker process running, but release, or *orphan*, the worker process from the application pool for purposes of debugging while at the same time initializing a new worker process to handle incoming client requests. An orphaned worker process ceases to take new requests from HTTP.sys.

If you enable debugging on an application pool, the WWW service allows an unhealthy worker process to keep running when the WWW service releases the worker process from serving an application pool. When enabling debugging, you can also configure the WWW service to start an executable application or script for a released worker process. For example, the WWW service might start an application that sends you an e-mail notifying you of the failure.

Be sure to closely monitor any worker process that is released from its application pool but continues to run. The worker process can still terminate because the WWW service leaves it running but no longer monitors it, which effectively tells the worker process to shut down without forcing it to do so. If the worker process recovers from its unhealthy state, it detects that it has no relationship to the WWW service and self-terminates. When an orphaned worker process self-terminates, you might find an event log entry stating that a worker process was released but find no evidence of the worker process ever having run.

If you enable debugging on unhealthy worker processes, be sure to monitor these released worker processes, because IIS does not remove them from memory. If you do not correctly handle worker processes that you keep alive for debugging purposes, you can have large numbers of failed worker processes running on your computer. These worker processes can tie up resources needed by other processes. You might need to terminate them quickly to free those resources. In some cases, these worker processes can block metabase access and cause problems with other worker processes or with the WWW service itself.

For more information about setting a metabase property to configure the WWW service to release rather than terminate an unhealthy worker process, see the **OrphanWorkerProcess** property in the "Metabase Property Reference" in IIS 6.0 Help. For more information about configuring IIS to start an executable application or script when a worker process is orphaned, see "Troubleshooting IIS 6.0" in this book and the **OrphanActionParams** and **OrphanActionExe** properties in the "Metabase Property Reference" in IIS 6.0 Help.

Ensuring Application Pool Health

Health monitoring cannot detect application failures that do not cause the worker process to fail or do not block the available threads in the worker process. For example, an application can return an error response code, such as an HTTP 404 error (Not Found), but still respond normally to a ping from the WWW service. (The exception is an application like a custom ISAPI extension that implements specific code to indicate its unhealthy state.)

At a minimum, monitoring application pool health and taking corrective actions requires that you take the following steps:

- Allow the WWW service to detect unhealthy worker processes by enabling the WWW service to ping worker processes.

- Configure rapid-fail protection to disable application pools when the worker processes assigned to them fail a set number of times within a specified period.

For more information about rapid-fail protection, see "Configuring Rapid-Fail Protection" later in this chapter.)

Recycling Worker Processes

In worker process isolation mode, you can configure IIS to periodically restart worker processes so that you can recycle faulty Web applications. Recycling ensures that applications in those pools remain healthy and that system resources are recovered.

You can configure worker processes to restart based on one of several options, including elapsed time, the number of requests served, scheduled times, and memory usage.

IIS 5.0 isolation mode does not offer these features.

How Worker Process Recycling Works

The WWW service can recycle a worker process in one of two ways, both of which do not interrupt service:

- By default, the WWW service establishes an *overlapped recycle*, in which the worker process that is to be shut down is kept running until after a new worker process is started.

- If the applications in an application pool cannot tolerate multi-instancing, you can optionally configure the WWW service to shut down a worker process and then start a new worker process. Use this type of recycling only if the applications in the application pool cannot tolerate multi-instancing. To turn off overlapped recycling, set the **DisallowOverlappingRotation** metabase property to **true**.

When a worker process requests a recycle, the WWW service initiates an overlapped recycle, creating a new worker process to replace the old one. While the new worker process is starting, the old process continues to serve requests. After the new process starts and initializes successfully, the WWW service instructs the old worker process to shut down. At this point, the old worker process stops accepting new requests from HTTP.sys and begins to shut down. The WWW service allows the old worker process a configured time period in which to finish processing its requests before the worker process is shut down. The WWW service terminates the worker process if it fails to shut down within the configured time.

With overlapped recycling, the old worker process remains in communication with HTTP.sys to handle requests until the new worker process is running. HTTP.sys establishes and maintains TCP/IP connections. When the WWW service recycles a worker process, it does not disconnect the existing TCP/IP connection. However, because the shutdown timeout value of a shutdown or startup is configurable, the worker process can be terminated while it is still serving requests if it does not finish servicing existing requests within the time limit.

If the application pool is a Web garden, which uses a set of equivalent worker processes, and you configure worker process recycling based on elapsed time, all the worker processes are recycled during the elapsed time set, but they are not recycled all at once. Worker process recycling in a Web garden is spread over the time set to reduce interruptions of service to client requests and to reduce the impact of restarting all processes at the same time.

Similarly, when you configure a Web garden to recycle applications based on the number of requests processed, recycling takes place at intervals in order to spread out the overhead that is associated with the worker process recycling.

For more information about Web gardens and how to configure them, see "Configuring Web Gardens" later in this chapter. For more information about how you can recycle a Web garden based on length of time, including examples of Web garden recycling, see "Deploying ASP.NET Applications in IIS 6.0" in *Deploying Internet Information Services (IIS) 6.0* of the *Microsoft® Windows® Server 2003 Deployment Kit*.

When and How to Use Worker Process Recycling

Consider the following guidelines when you decide whether to enable worker process recycling. Worker process recycling is not intended as a replacement for fixing a faulty application; however, recoding is not always an option, especially in cases when other application code is running that cannot be modified.

Consider using recycling in these situations:

- Your Web server hosts faulty applications that you cannot fix.

- Your Web server is experiencing undetermined or intermittent problems.

- Performance monitoring suggests that an application is leaking memory.

- You have implemented a temporary reset solution, such as a scheduled execution of the IISReset utility or a scheduled restart.

You might not need to use recycling in these situations:

- You are hosting a Web site that contains static content only and no custom ISAPI applications.

- You are hosting an application that is thoroughly tested and does not have memory or resource allocation issues.

To effectively use recycling, see Table 3.6, which presents the criteria on which recycling can be based.

Table 3.6   When to Use Each Recycling Option

Recycle Trigger	Timing of Recycling	Conditions for Use
ISAPI unhealthy request	Recycles based on a request from an ISAPI extension in an application pool.	An ISAPI extension is built to declare itself unhealthy and pinging is enabled.
Elapsed time	Recycles after a specified number of minutes.	Applications cannot run for extended time periods.
Number of requests	Recycles when the number of HTTP requests exceeds a specified number of requests.	Applications fail because of the quantity of requests that they receive.
Scheduled times	Recycles at specified times within a 24-hour period.	Applications cannot run for an extended time period, or you want to periodically refresh applications during times of low use, such as on weekends or during late evening and early morning.
Virtual memory	Recycles when the worker process virtual memory (reserved plus used) reaches a specified maximum.	The memory heap becomes fragmented, which is caused by applications reserving memory multiple times. A steady increase in the use of virtual memory can indicate a fragmented memory heap.

(continued)

Table 3.6   When to Use Each Recycling Option (*continued*)

Recycle Trigger	Timing of Recycling	Conditions for Use
Used memory	Recycles when the memory that is used by the worker process reaches a specified maximum.	Some applications have memory leaks.
User demand	Recycles when you use IIS Manager to manually recycle all the worker processes in an application pool, or when you run a script that calls the Recycle() method for the application pool.	A single application is causing problems while other sites are running, and you need to act quickly. Consider recycling the application pool instead of resetting the entire WWW service.

▶   **To recycle a worker process immediately (on demand)**

- In IIS Manager, expand the local computer, expand **Application Pools**, right-click the application pool, and then click **Recycle**.

For information about configuring worker processes for recycling, see "Common Administrative Tasks" in this book, which provides detailed instructions for recycling worker processes based on the following criteria: elapsed time, number of processing requests, scheduled time, and maximum memory used. For additional information about configuring worker processes for recycling, see "Recycling Worker Processes" in IIS 6.0 Help.

Logging Worker Process Recycling Events

By setting the metabase property **LogEventOnRecycle**, you can direct the WWW service to log worker process recycling events in the Windows Server 2003 system log. You can use **LogEventOnRecycle** parameters to monitor and log recycle events based on the following criteria:

- Time consumed

- Requests processed

- Scheduled recycles

- On-demand recycles initiated by an administrator

- Memory consumed (both virtual and physical)

- Changes in application pool properties

- ISAPI unhealthy requests

For more information about logging worker process recycling events, see the **LogEventOnRecycle** property in the "Metabase Property Reference" in IIS 6.0 Help.

Configuring Rapid-Fail Protection

When a worker process fails, the WWW service detects the failure and takes action, such as logging the event and restarting the process. You can also configure IIS so that if a worker process fails multiple times within a specified time period, its application pool is disabled to protect other application pools that are running on the same computer. This feature, known as *rapid-fail protection*, stops application pools from a continuous cycle of failing and restarting, which uses up system resources.

Rapid-fail protection places the disabled application pool in out-of-service mode, and HTTP.sys returns a 503 error (Service Unavailable) message for requests to that portion of the namespace, including requests that have already been queued for the disabled application pool. In addition, you can configure IIS so that when an application pool is stopped automatically, a specified action occurs, such as running a debugger or notifying the administrator that the application pool has stopped.

 Note

Alternatively, HTTP.sys can do a connection reset based on the configuration of the **LoadBalancerCapabilities** property of the application pool. However, if a single computer hosts multiple applications, be sure to configure load balancers or switching hardware to reroute only the traffic intended for a failed application pool. Do not route requests away from healthy application pools, which can still receive and process requests.

The rapid-fail protection feature is unavailable when IIS 6.0 is running in IIS 5.0 isolation mode.

▶ **To configure rapid-fail protection for an application pool by using IIS Manager**

1. In IIS Manager, expand the local computer, expand **Application Pools**, right-click the application pool, and then click **Properties**.

2. On the **Health** tab, select the **Enable rapid-fail protection** check box.

3. In the **Failures** box, type the number of worker process failures to be detected before disabling the worker process. The default value is 5.

4. In the **Time period** box, type the number of minutes during which failure totals will be allowed to accumulate, and then click **OK**. The default interval is five minutes.

Configuring Rapid-Fail Protection from the Command Line

Use the following procedure to configure rapid-fail protection from the command line:

1. Set the **RapidFailProtection** metabase property to **true**, which enables rapid-fail protection.

   By default, when you set the **RapidFailProtection** property to **true**, the WWW service puts all applications in an application pool out of service if five failures occur within a five-minute interval.

2. Optionally, you can change the default settings for rapid-fail protection by setting either or both of the following:

   - Set the **RapidFailProtectionInterval** property, which specifies the number of minutes during which worker process failures are accumulated.

   - Set the **RapidFailProtectionMaxCrashes** property, which specifies the maximum number of failures allowed within the specified time limit.

If you set the **RapidFailProtection** metabase property to **true** but do not set either the **RapidFailProtectionInterval** property or the **RapidFailProtectionMaxCrashes** property, IIS applies the default settings for these properties.

▶ **To enable rapid-fail protection for an application pool by using Adsutil.vbs**

1. In the **Run** dialog box, type **cmd**, and then click **OK**.

2. At the command prompt, type:

   ```
   cscript %SystemDrive%\Inetpub\AdminScripts\adsutil.vbs set
   W3SVC/AppPools/ApplicationPoolName/RapidFailProtection TRUE
   ```

By default, rapid-fail protection is activated if five process failures occur within a five-minute interval. You can reset the accumulation interval by updating the **RapidFailProtection Interval** metabase property, or you can reset the maximum number of crashes to allow during the interval by updating the **RapidFailProtectionMaxCrashes** metabase property.

▶ **To specify the maximum number of minutes during which worker process failures are accumulated**

   - At the command prompt, type:

   ```
   cscript %SystemDrive%\Inetpub\AdminScripts\adsutil.vbs set
   W3SVC/AppPools/ApplicationPoolName/RapidFailProtectionInterval n
   ```

   In the preceding syntax, replace *n* with the number of minutes that you want to set for the accumulation interval.

The **RapidFailProtectionMaxCrashes** property specifies the maximum number of worker process failures that are allowed within the minutes specified by the **RapidFailProtectionInterval** property. The default value for the **RapidFailProtectionMaxCrashes** property is 5.

▶   **To specify the maximum number of worker process failures before rapid-fail protection occurs**

- At the command prompt, type:

```
cscript %SystemDrive%\Inetpub\AdminScripts\adsutil.vbs set
W3SVC/AppPools/ApplicationPoolName/RapidFailProtectionMaxCrashes n
```

In the preceding syntax, replace *n* with the number of process failures to allow within an accumulation interval before shutting down an application pool.

For more information about the **RapidFailProtection**, **RapidFailProtectionInterval**, and **RapidFailProtectionMaxCrashes** properties, see the "Metabase Property Reference" in IIS 6.0 Help.

Managing Resources in Worker Process Isolation Mode

IIS 6.0, when running in worker process isolation mode, offers several features that you can use to better manage your systems' resources and to help maintain healthy and robust systems:

- Configure Web gardens.
- Configure idle timeout for a worker process.
- Configure startup and shutdown time limits.
- Enable CPU monitoring.
- Assign processor affinity.

Configuring Web Gardens

In worker process isolation mode, you can configure an application pool to be supported by multiple worker processes. An application pool that uses more than one worker process is called a *Web garden*. (Web gardens are to be distinguished from *Web farms*, which use multiple servers for a Web site.)

 Important

Web gardens can reduce contention for system resources, such as threads, but they can also cause resource contention. For example, if application resources are designed for exclusive access by a single process, such as a flat file used for temporary storage, resource contention can occur between the worker processes within a Web garden. Also, there are documented application characteristics (singletons) for which Web gardens might cause increased contention.

Creating a Web garden for an application pool enhances performance and reliability in the following ways:

- **Robust processing of requests.** When a worker process in an application pool is tied up (for example, when a script engine stops responding), other worker processes can accept and process requests for the application pool.

- **Reduced contention for resources.** When a Web garden reaches a steady state, each new TCP/IP connection is assigned, according to a round-robin scheme, to a worker process in the Web garden. The round-robin scheme smoothes out workloads and reduces contention for resources that are bound to a worker process.

 Important

You must be a member of the Administrators group on the local computer to perform the following procedure or procedures, or you must have been delegated the appropriate authority. As a security best practice, log on to your computer by using an account that is not in the Administrators group, and then use the runas command to run IIS Manager as an administrator. At a command prompt, type runas / User:Administrative_AccountName "mmc %systemroot%\system32\inetsrv\iis.msc".

▶ To configure a Web garden by using IIS Manager

1. In IIS Manager, expand the local computer, expand **Application Pools**, right-click the application pool, and then click **Properties**.

2. On the **Performance** tab, under **Web garden**, in the **Maximum number of worker processes** box, type the number of worker processes that you want to assign to the application pool. (You must type a number greater than 1 for the application pool to become a Web garden.)

3. Click **OK**.

Optionally, you can configure a Web garden by setting the metabase property **MaxProcesses**. The **MaxProcesses** property determines the maximum number of worker processes that an application pool allows to service its requests. A value of zero indicates an unmanaged application pool that is not served by a worker process.

The default value for the **MaxProcesses** property is 1, which is the default number of worker processes that service an application pool. To configure an application pool so that it is a Web garden, set the **MaxProcesses** property to a value greater than 1.

 Important

You must be a member of the Administrators group on the local computer to run scripts and executables, or you must have been delegated the appropriate authority. As a security best practice, log on to your computer by using an account that is not in the Administrators group, and then use the runas command to run your script or executable as an administrator. At a command prompt, type runas /profile /User:MyMachine\Administrator cmd to open a command window with administrator rights and then type cscript.exe ScriptName (including the full path with parameters, if any).

▶ **To configure a Web garden by using Adsutil.vbs**

1. In the **Run** dialog box, type **cmd**, and then click **OK**.

2. At the command prompt, type:

```
cscript %SystemDrive%\Inetpub\AdminScripts\adsutil.vbs set
W3SVC/AppPools/ApplicationPoolName/MaxProcesses n
```

Replace *n* with the number of worker processes that you want to service the application pool.

For more information about configuring Web gardens, see the **MaxProcesses** property in the "Metabase Property Reference" in IIS 6.0 Help.

Configuring Idle Timeout for a Worker Process

You can conserve system resources by configuring worker processes to shut down after a specified period of inactivity. This feature, known as *idle timeout,* can be used to better manage system resources when the processing load is heavy, when identified worker processes are consistently idle, or when new processing space is not available. If an application pool is shut down due to inactivity and HTTP.sys receives a request for the idle application pool, the WWW service starts a new worker process to replace the one that timed out.

▷ **To configure application pool idle timeout**

1. In IIS Manager, expand the local computer, expand **Application Pools**, right-click the application pool, and then click **Properties**.

2. On the **Performance** tab, under **Idle timeout**, select the **Shutdown worker processes after being idle for** check box.

3. In the **minutes** box, type the number of idle minutes (with no processing requests) that you want to elapse before shutting down the idle worker process. The default value is 20 minutes.

4. Click **OK**.

Optionally, you can configure idle timeout by setting the **IdleTimeout** metabase property.

▷ **To configure application pool idle timeout by using Adsutil.vbs**

1. In the **Run** dialog box, type **cmd**, and then click **OK**.

2. At the command prompt, type:

```
cscript %SystemDrive%\Inetpub\AdminScripts\adsutil.vbs set
W3SVC/AppPools/ApplicationPoolName/IdleTimeout n
```

Replace *n* with the number of minutes of idle time to allow before shutting down the idle worker process; the default time-out interval is 20 minutes.

For more information about setting application pool idle timeout, see the **IdleTimeout** property in the "Metabase Property Reference" in IIS 6.0 Help.

Configuring Shutdown and Startup Time Limits

For a worker process that has a requested recycle, you can set the maximum time that the worker process continues to process requests before it shuts down. When you set the shutdown time limit (the default is 90 seconds), consider that a worker process shuts down gracefully when the configured shutdown time is long enough to allow it to finish processing its queued requests. Be sure you tune the shutdown time period to fit the load characteristics of the applications that are being processed. If the worker process cannot shut down within the configured time limit, a termination event appears in the event log even when the application shuts down gracefully.

You can also configure a startup time limit (the default is 90 seconds), which specifies how long the WWW service waits for a worker process to start before identifying the worker process as unhealthy and in need of being shut down.

▷ **To configure a worker process to shut down or start up within a specified time period**

1. In IIS Manager, expand the local computer, expand **Application Pools**, right-click the application pool, and then click **Properties**.

2. On the **Health** tab, do one of the following:

   ▪ To set a shutdown time limit, under **Shutdown time limit**, in the **seconds** box next to **Worker process must shutdown within**, type the number of seconds you want.

   ▪ To set a startup time limit, under **Startup time limit**, in the **seconds** box next to **Worker process must startup within**, type the number of seconds you want.

3. Click **OK**.

Optionally, you can configure shutdown and startup time limits by setting the **StartupTimeLimit** or **ShutdownTimeLimit** metabase properties.

▷ **To set a worker process to shut down or start up within a specified time by using Adsutil.vbs**

1. In the **Run** dialog box, type **cmd**, and then click **OK**.

2. To set a shutdown time limit, at the command prompt, type:

   ```
   cscript %SystemDrive%\Inetpub\AdminScripts\adsutil.vbs set
   W3SVC/AppPools/ApplicationPoolName/ShutdownTimeLimit n
   ```

3. To set a startup time limit, at the command prompt, type:

   ```
   cscript %SystemDrive%\Inetpub\AdminScripts\adsutil.vbs set
   W3SVC/AppPools/ApplicationPoolName/StartupTimeLimit n
   ```

   Replace *n* with the number of seconds that you want to elapse before shutting down or starting the worker process.

For more information about setting startup and shutdown times for worker processes, see the **StartupTimeLimit** and **ShutdownTimeLimit** properties in the "Metabase Property Reference" in IIS 6.0 Help.

Enabling CPU Monitoring

By using CPU monitoring, you can monitor worker processes for CPU usage and optionally shut down the worker processes that consume large amounts of CPU time. CPU monitoring is only available in worker process isolation mode.

To configure CPU monitoring for individual application pools, choose between two monitoring options: error event logging or the shutdown of all worker processes in the application pool that is consuming more CPU time than the specified limit.

Event logging

When the CPU usage for a specific application pool reaches a set limit, the WWW service writes an error to the Windows Server 2003 system log, which can be viewed in Event Viewer. The entry includes the worker process identifier and the name of the application pool that exceeded the CPU limit.

To view the event log, open Control Panel and access **Event Viewer** through Administrative Tools. Then double-click the system event log.

Shut down the unhealthy application pool (also includes event logging)

When you choose this option, IIS logs an error in the system log and shuts down all worker processes in the application pool. After the application pool shuts down, HTTP.sys returns an out-of-service message (503: Service Unavailable) for any request that is received during the interval when the application pool is stopped. The application pool remains shut down until the CPU reset interval (set by the **CPUResetInterval** metabase property) elapses. IIS then restarts the application pool, and CPU monitoring starts over again.

Obtaining more detailed CPU monitoring

If your Web server is running Windows Server 2003, Enterprise Edition or Windows Server 2003, Datacenter Edition, you can use Windows System Resource Manager to obtain more detailed CPU monitoring. Using Windows System Resource Manager, you can control how CPU resources are allocated to applications, services, and processes. For more information, see the Windows System Resource Manager — Fast Facts link on the Web Resources page at http://www.microsoft.com/windows/reskits/webresources.

Enabling CPU Monitoring by Using IIS Manager

When you enable CPU monitoring by using IIS Manager, IIS allows, by default, a maximum CPU use of 50 percent. To change the default value, follow this procedure.

 To enable CPU monitoring for an application pool by using IIS Manager

1. In IIS Manager, expand the local computer, expand **Application Pools**, right-click the application pool for which you want to enable CPU accounting, and then click **Properties**.

2. On the **Performance** tab, select the **Enable CPU monitoring** check box.

3. In the **Maximum CPU use** box, type the maximum percentage of CPU use to allow for the application pool.

4. In the **Refresh CPU usage numbers (in minutes)** box, type a refresh rate. The default value is five minutes.

5. In the **Action performed when CPU usage exceeds maximum CPU use** box, click the appropriate action for the designated application pool:

   - To have IIS write an event to the system log when the application pool reaches the maximum CPU usage, without shutting the application pool down, click **No Action**.

   - To shut down the application pool in addition to logging an event in the system log, click **Shutdown**.

   By default, **No Action** is selected.

   > **Important**
   >
   > Shutting down the application pool shuts down all worker processes that serve that application pool.

6. Click **Apply**, and then click **OK**.

Enabling CPU Monitoring from the Command Line

Enabling CPU monitoring from the command line can take as many as three steps:

1. Set the **CPULimit** metabase property, which limits the worker processes in a specified application pool to a percentage of CPU time.

2. Set the **CPUResetInterval** metabase property, which specifies the time interval for CPU monitoring.

3. Set the **CPUAction** metabase property, which specifies the type of action you want IIS to take, such as write to the event log or shut down worker processes that exceed the CPU limit.

Set the CPU Limit

The **CPULimit** property configures the maximum percentage of CPU time that the worker processes in an application pool are allowed to consume over the period of time set by the **CPUResetInterval** property. If the limit set by the **CPULimit** property is exceeded, an event is written to the event log and an optional set of events can be triggered as determined by the **CPUAction** property. Setting the value of the **CPULimit** property to zero disables CPU monitoring.

To start CPU monitoring for an application pool, set the **CPULimit** property to a value greater than zero. To calculate the value to set, determine the maximum percentage of CPU time that you want the worker processes in an application pool to use — for example, 50 percent (which is the default value). Next multiply that percentage by 1,000 (50 × 1,000 = 50,000). Hence, to limit CPU use to 50 percent, set a value of 50000 for the CPU limit.

▶ **To set the CPU limit for CPU monitoring by using Adsutil.vbs**

1. In the **Run** dialog box, type **cmd**, and then click **OK**.

2. At the command prompt, type:

   ```
   cscript %Systemroot%\Inetpub\AdminScripts\adsutil.vbs set
   W3SVC/AppPools/ApplicationPoolName/CPULimit n
   ```

   Replace *n* with the maximum percentage of CPU use to allow for the application pool in 1/1,000ths of a percentage.

Set the CPU Reset Interval

After turning on CPU monitoring for the application, use Adsutil.vbs to set a value for the **CPUResetInterval** property, which specifies the reset period (in minutes) for CPU monitoring and throttling limits on the application pool. When the number of minutes elapsed since the last CPU monitoring reset equals the number specified by this property, IIS resets the CPU timers for both the logging and limit intervals. The default value is five minutes. Setting the value of this property to zero disables CPU monitoring.

Important

The value of the CpuResetInterval property must be greater than the time between logging operations; otherwise, IIS resets counters before logging has occurred, and CPU monitoring does not occur.

▷   **To set the CPU monitoring reset interval by using Adsutil.vbs**

- At the command prompt, type:

```
cscript %SystemDrive%\Inetpub\AdminScripts\adsutil.vbs set
W3SVC/AppPools/ApplicationPoolName/CPUResetInterval n
```

Replace *n* with the number of minutes for the reset interval. To disable CPU monitoring, type **0**.

Set the CPU Action

Finally, set the **CPUAction** property, which configures the actions that IIS takes when Microsoft® Windows NT® job objects run. Only one Windows NT job object exists per application pool; therefore, you must configure the **CPUAction** property separately for each application pool. Table 3.7 lists the possible values for **CPUAction**. Use only one value from the table for each application pool. If you do not set the **CPUAction** metabase property, IIS assigns the default value, which is zero (event logging only).

Table 3.7   Values for the CPUAction metabase property

Value	Description
0	Writes a warning to the system log in Event Viewer when the worker processes for the application pool exceed the CPU limit, but takes no other action.
1	Writes a warning to the system log, and shuts down worker processes in the application pool, when the worker processes exceed the CPU limit.

▷   **To set the CPUAction value by using Adsutil.vbs**

- At a command prompt, type:

```
cscript %SystemDrive%\Inetpub\AdminScripts\adsutil.vbs set
W3SVC/AppPools/ApplicationPoolName/CPUAction ActionValue
```

Replace *ActionValue* with the appropriate value: **0** logs an error without shutting down the process; **1** logs an error and shuts down the process.

For more information about setting the CPU action, see the **CPULimit**, **CPUResetInterval**, and **CPUAction** properties in the "Metabase Property Reference" in IIS 6.0 Help.

Assigning Processor Affinity

To efficiently use CPU caches on multiprocessor servers, you can configure application pools to establish affinity between worker processes and the processors, a feature known as *processor affinity*. Processor affinity forces worker processes to run on specific CPUs, and applies to all worker processes serving a particular application pool. You can also use processor affinity with Web gardens that run on multiprocessor computers where specific application pools are dedicated to specific clusters of CPUs.

Processor affinity typically yields the greatest performance benefits when you configure affinity on a computer that has eight or more processors.

You can set processor affinity from the command line by using the **set** command with Adsutil.vbs. To set processor affinity, configure the **SMPAffinitized** and **SMPProcessorAffinityMask** metabase properties. Assigning processor affinity involves these steps:

1. Enable processor affinity. Set the **SMPAffinitized** metabase property to **true,** which indicates that a particular worker process assigned to an application pool can also be assigned to a specified CPU.

2. Assign processor affinity. Set the **SMPProcessorAffinityMask** metabase property, which configures a hexadecimal processor mask that indicates which CPU the worker processes in an application pool are bound to.

▶ **To enable processor affinity for an application pool**

1. In the **Run** dialog box, type **cmd**, and then click **OK**.

2. At the command prompt, type:

```
cscript %SystemDrive%\Inetpub\AdminScripts\adsutil.vbs set
W3SVC/AppPools/ApplicationPoolName/SMPAffinitized TRUE
```

▶ **To assign processor affinity by binding an application pool to a specified processor**

▪ At a command prompt, type:

```
cscript %SystemDrive%\Inetpub\AdminScripts\adsutil.vbs set
W3SVC/AppPools/ApplicationPoolName/SMPProcessorAffinityMask MaskValue
```

Replace *MaskValue* with the hexadecimal value that binds the application pool to the appropriate processor or processors. See Table 3.8 for sample hexadecimal mask values.

For example, if you want to bind the worker processes that serve your FinanceAppPool to processors 0, 1, 2, and 3 of an eight-processor computer, type the following command:

```
cscript %SystemDrive%\Inetpub\AdminScripts\adsutil.vbs set
W3SVC/AppPools/FinanceAppPool/SMPProcessorAffinityMask 0xF
```

Table 3.8 shows which processors, on a computer with eight processors, are made available to worker processes that serve an application pool when various processor affinity masks are assigned.

Table 3.8 Sample Processor Affinity Mask Values for Binding an Application Pool to Specific Processors on an Eight-Processor Computer

Hexadecimal Mask (Binary Representation)	Processor[1]							
	7	6	5	4	3	2	1	0
0x2 (0010)							•	
0x5 (0101)						•		•
0xD (1101)					•	•		•
0xF (1111)					•	•	•	•
0x11 (00010001)				•				•
0x1E				•	•	•	•	
0xF0 (11110000)	•	•	•	•				
0xFE	•	•	•	•	•	•	•	
0xFF	•	•	•	•	•	•	•	•

1 Processor numbering begins with 0.

If you extend the table, a hexadecimal value of 0xFFFFFFFF (maximum value) allows all processors up to 32 to be available to worker processes that serve an application pool.

For more information about processor affinity mask settings, see the **SMPProcessorAffinityMask** and **SMPAffinitized** properties in the "Metabase Property Reference" in IIS 6.0 Help. For more information about using the **set** command with Adsutil.vbs, see "IIS 6.0 Administration Scripts, Tips, and Tricks" in this book.

Running Web Applications

With IIS 6.0 as your application server, you can use the latest Web application platforms and standards, such as ASP.NET, XML, and Simple Object Access Protocol (SOAP), to develop, implement, and manage your Web applications. While continuing to build on the ISAPI programming model, IIS 6.0 provides several new features, including custom errors, server-side redirection, streamlined file and buffer response, and improved Unicode support.

Enhancements to ISAPI Support

IIS 6.0 supports both ISAPI extensions and ISAPI filters:

- **ISAPI extensions** are DLLs that handle specific requests.

- **ISAPI filters** are DLLs that you can register with IIS to modify the behavior of the server.

ISAPI extensions and filters load the first time a client requests resources that are processed by the ISAPIs and are kept in memory to handle future requests. ISAPI extensions handle specific requests from the client.

Like ISAPI extensions, ISAPI filters are programs that respond when the application server receives an HTTP request. Unlike ISAPI extensions, ISAPI filters are driven by Web server events instead of client requests. For example, you can write an ISAPI filter to control which files are mapped to a URL, modify the response sent by the server, and perform other actions to modify the behavior of the server.

IIS 6.0 supports these programmatic enhancements to ISAPI extensions:

- HSE_REQ_EXEC_URL

- HSE_REQ_VECTOR_SEND

- HSE_REQ_REPORT_UNHEALTHY

- HSE_REQ_SEND_CUSTOM_ERROR

These enhancements are new **ServerSupportFunction** callback functions, known as *support functions*. The **ServerSupportFunction** function, which returns data for several auxiliary functions that are not covered by other callback functions, is supplied in the EXTENSION_CONTROL_BLOCK structure that is associated with HTTP requests. IIS and the ISAPI extensions use the EXTENSION_CONTROL_BLOCK structure to exchange information.

For more information about ISAPI filters and extensions, including the **ServerSupportFunction** callback functions, see the MSDN Online link on the Web Resources page at http://www.microsoft.com/windows/reskits/webresources.

Using HSE_REQ_EXEC_URL to Call Other URLS on the Server

The HSE_REQ_EXEC_URL support function (also known as ExecuteURL) allows ISAPI extensions to rewrite any part of the request, including the entity body, and have IIS reprocess this modified request. As long as the rewritten URL is in the same application pool and uses the same authentication, IIS can successfully reprocess the modified request.

This new support function gives ISAPI developers greater flexibility in transparently rewriting URLs on the server without the client's knowledge, allows an arbitrary number of URLs to be executed in a chain, and supports custom authentication. When used with wildcard application mapping, this support function can replace most read raw data filters by offering easy examination and modification of request entity body prior to request reprocessing. For information about wildcard application mapping, see "Setting Application Mappings" later in this chapter.

Using HSE_REQ_VECTOR_SEND to Consolidate Multiple Buffers

The HSE_REQ_VECTOR_SEND support function (also known as VectorSend) allows developers to group and send, in order, a list of buffers and file handles. This list is handed to IIS 6.0 and passed on to HTTP.sys, which compiles all the buffers and file handles within the kernel and then directly sends the group in one kernel-mode transition. This new functionality frees ISAPI from building large memory buffers or making multiple WriteClient calls.

In earlier versions of IIS, ISAPI developers have only two possibilities if they have multiple buffers that make up a response: they can either call WriteClient multiple times or assemble the response in one big memory buffer. The first approach causes a performance bottleneck because there is one kernel-mode transition for each WriteClient function call. The second approach also affects performance and uses additional memory. VectorSend is a more all-purpose transmit function for IIS 6.0 customers.

Using HSE_REQ_REPORT_UNHEALTHY to Recycle a Worker Process

The HSE_REQ_REPORT_UNHEALTHY support function (also known as ReportUnhealthy) allows an ISAPI extension to request that its worker process be recycled. Developers can use this new function to request a recycle if their ISAPI application becomes unstable or enters an unknown state. Note that in order to cause a recycle after an ISAPI calls ReportUnhealthy, health monitoring must be enabled for the ISAPI extension's application pool. When calling ReportUnhealthy, the developer can also pass in a string representing the reason why the ISAPI extension is calling ReportUnhealthy. This string is then added to the event that the worker process writes to the application log, which you can view in Windows Server 2003 Event Viewer.

Using HSE_REQ_SEND_CUSTOM_ERROR to Send Custom Error Messages

The HSE_REQ_SEND_CUSTOM_ERROR support function (also known as SendCustomErrors) allows ISAPI developers to send the client a specific IIS-configured custom error message, including all sub-error codes. This support function allows an ISAPI extension to better integrate its error messages with a Web site's custom error configuration.

Using the New Unicode ServerSupportFunctions

In addition to the preceding enhancements, IIS 6.0 allows ISAPI extensions to retrieve server variable values that are encoded as Unicode characters. In particular, ISAPI extensions can retrieve the request URL in Unicode, which can benefit international companies that have multilanguage Web sites for which the URL is not in the same code page as the server.

The following are new **ServerSupportFunction** callback functions that support values encoded as Unicode characters:

HSE_REQ_EXEC_UNICODE_URL   The HSE_REQ_EXEC_UNICODE_URL support function is functionally identical to HSE_REQ_EXEC_URL except that it expects the URL to be in Unicode instead of ANSI. This support function, when used with the new Unicode GetServerVariable, easily substitutes for HSE_REQ_EXEC_URL.

HSE_REQ_MAP_UNICODE_URL_TO_PATH   Allows your ISAPI extension to map a logical URL path to a physical path.

HSE_REQ_MAP_UNICODE_URL_TO_PATH_EX   Allows your ISAPI extension to map a logical URL path to a physical path, as well as gather several types of attributes that are associated with that physical path, such as access-control or cache-control flags.

Using ASP in IIS 6.0

ASP is a server-side scripting environment that you can use to create dynamic and interactive Web pages, and powerful Web applications. When the server receives a request for an ASP file, it processes the server-side script code contained in the ASP file to build a Hypertext Transfer Protocol (HTML) Web page, which is sent to the browser.

In addition to server-side script code, ASP files can contain HTML (including related client-side scripts) and calls to COM components that perform a variety of tasks, such as connecting to a database or processing business logic.

Because ASP scripts run on the server rather than on the client, your Web server does all the work involved in generating the HTML pages sent to browsers. Because only the result of the script is returned to the browser, the client cannot access the server-side scripts; therefore, users cannot view the script commands that created the page they are viewing.

For more information about ASP pages, see the IIS Software Development Kit (SDK). For information about writing server-side scripts with ASP and creating ASP applications, see the MSDN Online link on the Web Resources page at http://www.microsoft.com/windows/reskits/webresources.

Improvements to the ASP Programming Environment

In IIS 6.0, you can make use of the following enhancements to the ASP programming environment:

- **Improved international and UTF-8 support.** UTF-8 support has been expanded to include all ASP built-in object properties and methods. The previous version of ASP supported UTF-8 only for Response.Write.

- **Improved POST support.** ASP can now read chunked-encoded POST data from a client.

- **UNC enhancements.** If your ASP scripts reside on a Universal Naming Convention (UNC) share, ASP has improved performance in executing those scripts. For information about configuring IIS 6.0 with remotely stored content on UNC servers, see the UNC Servers Accessed by Using IIS 6.0 link on the Web Resources page at http://www.microsoft.com/windows/reskits/webresources.

- **Optional script source access in ASP pages.** *Script source access,* which allows access to the source code of scripts in ASP pages and other scripts, is new and is disabled by default. To enable script source access, you must select either Read or Write permission.

- **COM+ services in ASP.** You can now configure your ASP applications to use the following COM+ services without having to create a COM component:

    - Apartment model selection

    - Side-by-side assemblies

    - COM+ partitions

    - COM+ tracker

COM+ Services in ASP

In previous versions of IIS, if you wanted to use COM+ services from an ASP application, you had to create a COM component to call the methods of those services. In IIS 6.0, COM+ services are separate from the components. This separation allows ASP applications to use a set of COM+ services without instantiation by any COM components. Because of this separation, you can configure your ASP application to use the following COM+ services without having to create a COM component.

Apartment model selection

ASP is now capable of running all of its threads in a multithreaded apartment (MTA). If your COM components are primarily free-threaded or both-threaded, running the ASP threads as MTA can improve performance significantly.

To enable an ASP application to run in an MTA, set the **AspExecuteInMTA** metabase property at the application level. This enables you to have one application running on ASP MTA threads and a second application running on ASP single-threaded apartment (STA) threads. By default, ASP runs applications in the STA.

 Important

When you switch an ASP application from running in STA to MTA (or from MTA to STA), the impersonation token becomes obsolete, which can cause the application to run with no impersonation. Without impersonation, the application runs with the identity of the process, which might allow access to other resources. If you must switch threading models, disable and unload the application before you make the change.

Side-by-side assemblies

Side-by-side (SxS, in metabase property names) assemblies allow ASP applications to specify which version of a system DLL or shared COM component to use. For example, if your ASP application relies on MSXML version 2.0, you can ensure that your application still uses MSXML 2.0 even if a later version is installed on the computer for use by other applications.

Configuring SxS assemblies requires that you know the path to the DLL, and that the COM+ manifest file exists in every virtual directory that requires the use of the DLL. The COM+ manifest is an XML file that contains information about where a DLL is installed. IIS does not verify that the manifest exists.

You can enable side-by-side assemblies either programmatically or by using IIS Manager. To programmatically enable side-by-side assemblies, set the **AspEnableSxs** flag of the **AspAppServiceFlags** metabase property to **true**. Also, set the **AspSxsName** metabase property to the name of the COM+ manifest. Set both metabase properties at the application level.

Important

Even though this feature is configurable at the application level, you must not use more than one version of a system DLL in any IIS 6.0 application pool. If you load more than one version of a system DLL in an application pool, the application that is loaded first has its version loaded and the other applications are forced to use that DLL until the applications are unloaded.

COM+ partitions

You can use COM+ partitions to isolate Web applications in their own COM+ partitions. Isolation is useful to prevent one Web application from accessing the private COM+ applications, configuration information, and data of another Web application.

COM+ partitions can hold different versions of your own custom COM components. For example, if you host Web sites for two competing companies that both use COM+ in their Web applications, you can use COM+ partitions to ensure that one company's Web application cannot access the COM+ components in the other company's Web applications. If one of those companies asks you to change certain features in a COM+ application that both companies use, you can isolate the new version of that COM+ application in the partition that is linked to that company's Web application.

To enable COM+ partitions in IIS, set the **AspUsePartition** flag of the **AspAppServiceFlags** metabase property at the application level. The partition is identified by a globally unique identifier (GUID) (created by using the Component Services Manager snap-in), which is set by the **AspPartitionID** metabase property. If no partition is specified, the default system partition is used.

 Important

Even though you can configure this feature at the application level, use only one version of a COM+ component in any application pool. For example, if application App1 uses version 1.0 of a custom COM+ application called Shop.dll, and application App2 uses version 2.0 of Shop.dll, App1 and App2 cannot be in the same application pool. If you put them in the same application pool, the application that you load first has its version of Shop.dll loaded, and the other application is forced to use that version until the applications are unloaded.

COM+ tracker

COM+ tracker allows you to debug ASP applications. For example, if you need to diagnose and fix a faulty Web application, you can enable COM+ tracker to determine when ASP pages are being loaded, when COM components are loaded, and when threads leave a page. After debugging your application, you can disable COM+ tracker to return your application to normal performance speed.

To enable COM+ tracker on the IIS side, set the **AspEnableTracker** flag of the **AspAppServiceFlags** metabase property at the application level.

For more information about these enhancements to COM+ services in ASP, including application examples of each, see "What's New in ASP" in IIS 6.0 Help.

New Metabase Properties for ASP

Table 3.9 describes the metabase properties for ASP that are new in IIS 6.0.

Table 3.9   New ASP Metabase Properties in IIS 6.0

Property	Purpose
AspAppServiceFlags	Contains the flags that must be set to enable COM+ services on your IIS applications.
AspDiskTemplateCacheDirectory	Specifies the location of the ASP disk cache.
AspExecuteInMTA	Enables ASP threads to execute in an MTA.
AspKeepSessionIDSecure	Sends the ASP session cookie to a browser securely.
AspMaxDiskTemplateCacheFiles	Specifies the maximum number of compiled ASP templates that can be stored.
AspPartitionID	Sets the COM+ partition to use for the application.
AspRunOnEndAnonymously	Enables ASP to run the Global.asa Application_OnEnd and Session_OnEnd events anonymously.
AspBufferingLimit	Specifies the buffer size limit.
AspMaxRequestEntityAllowed	Specifies the maximum number of bytes allowed in the entity body of an ASP request.
AspSxsName	Allows ASP applications to specify which version of a system DLL or COM component to use.

For more information about how to use these new metabase properties, see the "Metabase Property Reference" in IIS 6.0 Help.

Security and Performance Enhancements in ASP

In IIS 6.0, ASP has undergone several important changes to improve security and performance:

- **Default disabling of ASP pages during clean installations of IIS 6.0.** In a default installation, the IIS service is installed in a secure mode, and only serves static content. You must enable features such as ASP, ASP.NET, CGI, ISAPI, and WebDAV if you need them. For more information about these features, including how to enable them, see "Enabling Dynamic Content" earlier in this chapter.

- **Secure ASP built-in functions.** All ASP built-in functions always run as the low-privileged account, IUSR_*ComputerName*, or under an authenticated user account if one is selected and has valid credentials.

- **Default disabling of parent paths.** As a security precaution, the metabase property **AspEnableParentPaths** is now set to zero by default. This new default setting affects Web pages that contain or use the ".." notation to refer to a parent directory in the #include SSI directive. Unless you explicitly set this property to **true**, such Web pages do not respond to a client request (they instead generate a "Disallowed Parent Path" message).

- **ASP hang detection.** When an IIS Web site is busy, there might be instances when the maximum number of ASP threads are spawned and some of the ASP threads hang, resulting in degraded performance. (Threads are considered to be hung if they do not respond to a timeout.) If sufficient ASP requests hang so that ASP cannot service requests quickly, ASP detects this unhealthy state and requests that the worker process recycle itself.

- **Monitoring of disk-based caching.** The Active Server Pages performance object now provides the Templates Cached counter to monitor disk-based caching in addition to in-memory caching. This counter counts the number of cached ASP files, both on disk and in memory. A new ASP counter, In Memory Templates Cached, reports the number of ASP pages in the memory cache. The default location of the ASP disk cache is *systemroot*\System32\Inetsrv\ASP Compiled Templates. You can change the cache location by setting the **AspDiskTemplateCacheDirectory** metabase property.

- **Anonymous user access for Global.asa events.** Earlier versions of ASP executed events in the security context (or user identity) of the host process because during these events there was not necessarily a user context. This sometimes caused access denied errors when writing to a file in the Application_OnEnd or Session_OnEnd event. By default, ASP now runs the Global.asa events, Application_OnEnd and Session_OnEnd, anonymously. Setting the **AspRunOnEndAnonymously** metabase property to **true** allows these global ASP functions to run as anonymous user.

- **Performance enhancements.** To limit the amount of memory allocated to ASP pages, IIS 6.0 sets the default value of the **AspScriptFileCacheSize** metabase property to 500 ASP pages and the default value of the **AspScriptEngineCacheMax** metabase property to 250 script engines. For sites that include a large set of frequently requested ASP pages, you can increase the number of ASP pages allowed by the **AspScriptFileCacheSize** property, which improves performance because ASP page compilation is substantially slower than retrieving pages from cache. On a site with only a small number of frequently requested ASP pages, you can save memory by setting a smaller value.

ASP Metabase Properties No Longer in Use in IIS 6.0

The following metabase properties are no longer used by ASP, even though they are still in the metabase for compatibility with existing administration scripts:

- **AspAllowOutOfProcComponents**
- **AspTrackThreadingModel**
- **AspExceptionCatchEnable**

In IIS 6.0, all properties that relate to ASP thread gating, such as the **ASPThreadGatingModel** property, were removed from ASP and the metabase. If you are using scripts to upgrade from IIS 5.0, you might need to make manual adjustments for the properties that were removed.

Setting Application Mappings

Because you can choose from many programming and scripting languages when you develop Web applications, IIS uses the file name extension of a requested resource on your Web site to determine which ISAPI or CGI program to run to process a request. For example, a request for a file with a .aspx extension causes the Web server to call the ASP.NET ISAPI (Aspnet_isapi.dll) to process the request. The association of a file name extension with an ISAPI or CGI program is called *application mapping* (or sometimes *script mapping* or *application extension mapping*).

IIS 6.0 is preconfigured to support common application mappings. You can add or remove mappings for all of the applications on a Web site or for an individual application. Use IIS Manager to map a file name extension to an application or remove an application mapping. For more information about setting application mappings, including step-by-step instructions, see "Setting Application Mappings" in IIS 6.0 Help.

Benefits of Using Wildcard Application Mappings Instead of ISAPI Filters

You can configure a Web site or virtual directory to run any number of ISAPI applications at the beginning of every request to that Web site or virtual directory, regardless of the file name extension of the requested file. This type of configuration, which can only be an ISAPI application, is called *wildcard application mapping*.

When an IIS Web server receives a request from a client, the Web server looks at the file name extension for the requested file to determine whether an ISAPI or CGI application handles that file type. For example, if a request comes in for a Web page called Default.asp, IIS knows from its default application mappings that ASP files are handled by the Asp.dll ISAPI extension.

Prior to wildcard application mapping, if you wanted certain tasks to be executed for every client request before the requested page was sent to its mapped application, you had to write an ISAPI filter that intercepted requests as they arrived. Wildcard application mapping offers an alternative to ISAPI filters. Although ISAPI filters are excellent for the functions that they perform, they have a more narrow use than do ISAPI applications.

For example, when you use wildcard application mapping, your ISAPI application:

- Can easily access the entity body of a request.

- Can be configured for virtual directories.

- Can contain long-running operations.

- Offers greater flexibility because the ISAPI extension API, which is used to write ISAPI applications, has more functionality than does the ISAPI filter API.

For more information about ISAPI filters, see "Installing ISAPI Filters" in IIS 6.0 Help.

Request Handling with Wildcard Application Mappings

Highly secure Web applications, such as banking applications, require that every user who makes a request be authenticated against a database of user names, passwords, and account numbers. After the user is authenticated, certain rules are applied that specify what information the user can access. If the wildcard application map determines that the user has no rights, it can prevent the request from going any farther, or it can redirect the request to a new Web page.

You can implement a custom authentication and authorization scheme like this in an ISAPI application that you install as a wildcard application mapping, and all users must go through authentication regardless of the file type of their requests. For example, when you install wildcard application mappings, IIS processes a client request in this way:

1. An incoming request is handled by any existing ISAPI filters that are installed at the global and Web site levels. IIS executes the ISAPI filters in priority order from global to Web site.

2. The request is sent to any existing wildcard application mappings, which IIS also executes in order.

   - If the incoming request for a Web file triggers wildcard application mappings at multiple levels — such as Web site, virtual directory, or nested virtual directories — IIS only executes the wildcard application mappings installed in the virtual directory closest to the Web file. That is, if wildcard application mappings exist at the Web site and virtual directory level, a request for a Web file in the virtual directory only triggers the wildcard application mappings for the virtual directory.

   - If no custom application mappings are installed in a virtual directory, that virtual directory inherits the effective application mappings, including wildcard application mappings, from its parent.

3. The IIS server looks at the application mappings table to determine which ISAPI application or CGI script specifically processes the requested resource.

Inserting Wildcard Application Mappings

By inserting wildcard application mapping, you can instruct IIS to allow ISAPI applications known as *interceptors* to intercept and examine every request before the requested page is sent to its mapped application. The effect is an application mapping that handles every file name extension.

 Important

You must be a member of the Administrators group on the local computer to perform the following procedure or procedures, or you must have been delegated the appropriate authority. As a security best practice, log on to your computer by using an account that is not in the Administrators group, and then use the **runas** command to run IIS Manager as an administrator. At a command prompt, type **runas** /*User:Administrative_AccountName* "mmc %systemroot%\system32\inetsrv\iis.msc".

 To insert a wildcard application map to a Web server or Web site

1. In IIS Manager, expand the local computer, and then expand the **Web sites** folder.

2. Right-click the Web site or virtual directory that you want to map, and then click **Properties**.

3. Click the appropriate tab: Home Directory, Virtual Directory, or Directory.

4. In the **Application settings** area, click **Configuration**, and then click the **Mappings** tab.

5. To install a wildcard application map:

   a. On the **Mappings** tab, click **Insert**.

   b. In the **Executable** text box, type the path to the DLL.

   c. Click **OK**.

    Important

   Do not list the same application more than once in your list of wildcard application maps unless it is designed to be listed so.

Table 3.10 presents the steps for performing three additional tasks for managing wildcard application maps. The steps are performed on the **Mappings** tab in the application property sheet. Begin each task by completing steps 1 through 4 of the preceding procedure.

Table 3.10   Steps for Performing Additional Tasks for Wildcard Application Maps

Task	Steps To Follow
To edit a wildcard application map	1. In the **Application extensions** list, click the script map that you want to change. 2. Click **Edit** to display a copy of the script map for editing.
To change the order in which the wildcard application maps execute	▪ Rearrange the wildcard application maps in the **Wildcard application maps (order of implementation)** box by selecting wildcard application maps and clicking the **Move up** or **Move down** button until the maps match the execution order that you want.
To remove a wildcard application map	1. In the **Application extensions** list, click the script map that you want to remove. 2. Click **Remove**.

For information about developing wildcard application maps, see the IIS Software Development Kit (SDK) link on the Web Resources page at http://www.microsoft.com/windows/reskits/webresources. Then search for these topics: "Developing ISAPI Extensions and Filters" and the "ISAPI Reference."

For more information about application mapping in general, see "Setting Application Mappings" in IIS 6.0 Help.

Additional Resources

These resources contain additional information and tools related to this chapter.

Related Information

- "Configuring Internet Sites and Services" in this book for information about configuring the File Transfer Protocol (FTP), Network News Transfer Protocol (NNTP), and Simple Mail Transfer Protocol (SMTP) services.

- "IIS 6.0 Architecture" in this book for information about the IIS 6.0 application isolation modes.

- "Using FrontPage 2002 Server Extensions with IIS 6.0" in this book for information about installing and using FrontPage 2002 Server Extensions.

- "Deploying ASP.NET Applications in IIS 6.0" in *Deploying Internet Information Services (IIS) 6.0* of the *Microsoft® Windows® Server 2003 Deployment Kit* for information about how you can recycle a Web garden based on length of time, including examples of Web garden recycling.

- The MSDN Online link on the Web Resources page at http://www.microsoft.com/windows/reskits/webresources for information about the **ServerSupportFunction** callback function.

Related IIS 6.0 Help Topics

- "Configuring Application Pools" and "Recycling Worker Processes" in IIS 6.0 Help, which is accessible from IIS Manager, for information about worker process isolation mode features.

- "IIS and Built-in Accounts" and "Configuring Application Pool Identity" in IIS 6.0 Help for security-related information that pertains to running your application server.

- "Installing IIS" and "Enabling and Disabling Dynamic Content" in IIS 6.0 Help for information about installing IIS 6.0 and enabling the features and services necessary for your applications to run properly.

- "Installing ISAPI Filters" in IIS 6.0 Help for information about ISAPI filters.

- The "Metabase Property Reference" and "Code Examples to Configure Metabase Properties" in IIS 6.0 Help for information about configuring metabase properties.

- The "Programmatic Administration Reference" in IIS 6.0 Help for information about performing demand stops and starts on an application pool.

- "Setting Application Mappings" in IIS 6.0 Help for information about setting application mappings, including step-by-step instructions.

- "What's New in ASP" and "Introduction to ASP.NET" in IIS 6.0 Help for information about using ASP and ASP.NET with IIS 6.0.

Related Windows Server 2003 Help Topics

For best results in identifying Help topics by title, in Help and Support Center, under the **Search** box, click **Set search options**. Under **Help Topics**, select the **Search in title only** check box.

- "Features unavailable on 64-bit versions of the Windows Server 2003 family" in Help and Support Center for Windows Server 2003 for information about features, such as ASP.NET, that are not supported on 64-bit versions of Windows Server 2003.

- "Reformatting or converting a partition to use NTFS" in Help and Support Center for Windows Server 2003 for information about converting FAT or FAT32 volumes to NTFS.

Related Tools

- Adsutil.vbs

  You can use the Adsutil.vbs command-line tool, which is an unsupported IIS administrative utility that is provided as a learning tool, to configure your application server. For more information about this tool, including a description of its syntax, commands, and parameters, see "IIS 6.0 Administration Scripts, Tips, and Tricks" in this book.

Working with the Metabase

The metabase is a hierarchical store of configuration information and schema that are used to configure Internet Information Services (IIS) 6.0. Read this chapter for an overview of the metabase structure and terminology, as well as detailed information about effectively managing the IIS 6.0 metabase by using the graphical user interface (GUI)–based and command-line utilities that are available with IIS 6.0.

In This Chapter

Related Information

- For step-by-step instructions and information to help you complete many of the tasks described in this chapter, see "Common Administrative Tasks" in this book.

- For information about how the metabase fits into the overall architecture of IIS 6.0, see "IIS 6.0 Architecture" in this book.

- For information about the IIS 6.0 metabase properties, see the "Metabase Property Reference" in IIS 6.0 Help, which is accessible from IIS Manager.

Overview of the IIS 6.0 Metabase

The Internet Information Services (IIS) 6.0 metabase comprises two plaintext XML files that store IIS configuration values and schema. The metabase can be edited manually, by using IIS Manager, or it can be edited programmatically. In addition, the IIS 6.0 metabase is extensible in a highly efficient manner — as your IIS deployment grows, so does the metabase. By using an inheritance model, explicit declarations of duplicate values are avoided, which reduces overhead when IIS reads configuration values from the metabase.

The metabase is a hierarchical store of configuration information and schema that are used to configure IIS. The metabase configuration and schema for IIS 4.0 and IIS 5.0 were stored in a single binary file named MetaBase.bin, which was not easy to read or edit. IIS 6.0 replaces MetaBase.bin with two XML files named MetaBase.xml and MBSchema.xml. These files are stored on your computer in the *systemroot*\System32\Inetsrv folder. Only users who are members of the Administrators group can view and modify these files.

The metabase configuration file, MetaBase.xml, stores most of the IIS configuration. Some IIS configuration values are also stored in the Windows registry. If a configuration value is one that you might need to configure or change, or if you can access the setting in the IIS 6.0 user interface, then the setting is typically stored in the IIS metabase.

The MetaBase.xml file is organized in a hierarchical structure, which can vary depending on the choices that are made when IIS is installed and, if needed, reconfigured. When IIS is started or restarted, the configuration settings are read from MetaBase.xml and copied into the IIS cache in-memory, which is referred to as the *in-memory metabase*. When IIS Manager or programmatic interfaces are used to change IIS configuration, the changes are made to the in-memory metabase and persisted to MetaBase.xml after a previously configured number of changes, or according to regular time intervals.

In physical terms, the metabase is a combination of the MetaBase.xml and MBSchema.xml files and the in-memory metabase. The IIS configuration information is stored in the MetaBase.xml file, while the metabase schema is stored in the MBSchema.xml file. When IIS is started, these files are read by the storage layer and then written to the in-memory metabase through Admin Base Objects (ABOs), as shown in Figure 4.1.

Figure 4.1   Metabase Communication Layers

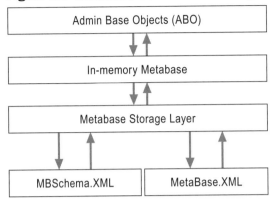

The metabase configuration and schema are stored in separate nodes in the in-memory metabase. The in-memory metabase itself resides in the IIS file cache in your computer's RAM. While IIS is running, changes that are made to the in-memory metabase are periodically saved to disk. The in-memory metabase is also saved to disk when IIS is stopped.

IIS 6.0 Metabase Features

The IIS 6.0 metabase includes the following features:

The metabase schema can be modified by an administrator

Active Directory® Service Interfaces (ADSI) and Windows Management Instrumentation (WMI) use the metabase schema to enforce which properties can be written at a particular key in the metabase. The schema also enforces the data types that can be used for a particular property attribute. You can modify the metabase schema by using ADSI or WMI to customize this enforcement, or to allow out-of -schema properties to be written in the metabase. For information about extending the metabase schema, see "Extending the Metabase Schema" in IIS 6.0 Help, which is accessible from IIS Manager.

The metabase is 100 percent compatible with IIS 5.0 metabase APIs

Because the XML metabase in IIS 6.0 is fully compatible with IIS 5.0 metabase application programming interfaces (APIs), existing scripts and code will continue to work.

Metabase performance and scalability are improved

The IIS 6.0 metabase improves performance and scalability over earlier versions of IIS in the following ways:

- Comparable or better disk footprint size compared to the IIS 5.0 metabase

- Faster read times on Web server startup than the IIS 5.0 binary metabase

- Equivalent write performance to the IIS 5.0 binary metabase

The metabase incorporates rich functionality

The metabase incorporates rich functionality with the following features:

- Property inheritance

- Data typing of property values

- Change notification when metabase properties change

- Security

- Simplified backup and restore of your IIS configuration

- Easier import and export of individual nodes to other computers

Benefits of Plaintext XML Files

Plaintext XML metabase files offer the following benefits:

Metabase files can be edited directly by using common text editors

The metabase configuration file, MetaBase.xml, can be easily read and edited by using common text editors, such as Notepad, which is provided as part of the Microsoft® Windows® operating system. Editing the metabase configuration file directly will be of interest primarily for administrators who do not want to use scripts or code to administer IIS. In addition, editing the metabase configuration file directly is faster than using IIS Manager when administering IIS over a slow network connection. It is recommended that you become familiar with the structure of MetaBase.xml before you attempt to configure IIS by editing the MetaBase.xml file.

 Important

Editing the MBSchema.xml file directly is not supported. Changes made to the metabase schema must be made programmatically by using the IIS ADSI provider.

Improved metabase corruption recovery and troubleshooting

The metabase makes it easier to diagnose potential metabase corruption because the metabase is stored in a plaintext file, and it can be analyzed by using tools such as the WinDiff utility. The WinDiff utility is located in the Deploy.cab file in the \Support\Tools folder of your Microsoft® Windows® Server 2003, Standard Edition; Windows® Server 2003, Enterprise Edition; Windows® Server 2003, Datacenter Edition; or Windows® Server 2003, Web Edition operating system CD. As the metabase is edited and saved to disk, IIS makes copies of each version of the MetaBase.xml and MBSchema.xml files in the History folder. In other words, the metabase history feature is like an automatic backup mechanism. You can use history files to compare changes that have been made to the MetaBase.xml and MBSchema.xml files.

Improved metabase backup and restore capabilities

By using Backup/Restore Configuration, administrators can back up the metabase and encrypt it with any password. If a critical failure occurs, the metabase can be restored on a different computer or on a different installation of the operating system. Additionally, the metabase can be restored by using an earlier version of the MetaBase.xml and MBSchema.xml files from the History folder.

Metabase Terminology

MetaBase.xml is structured by using keys. *Keys* are analogous to file folders in a file system or registry keys in the registry. Each key contains a **Location** attribute, which specifies its hierarchical location in the metabase. Properties, which define the values for configuring IIS, are contained in keys. Because MetaBase.xml is structured hierarchically, a particular property can be configured differently at different keys. Properties contain attributes, such as the **Value** attribute.

Table 4.1 summarizes the metabase terminology that is used to describe the structure of the IIS metabase. These terms are discussed in more detail later in this chapter.

Table 4.1   Metabase Terminology

Term	Description
Key	A hierarchical container in MetaBase.xml that is used to contain properties. Each key contains the **Location** attribute within the start tag of the key, specifying the hierarchical position of the key in MetaBase.xml. A metabase key is analogous to a file folder or registry key.
Location	Each key contains a **Location** attribute — a sequence of location names separated by one or more forward slashes (/) — that uniquely identifies the hierarchical position of the key in MetaBase.xml. For example /LM is the location of the **IisComputer** key, and /LM/W3SVC is the location of the **IisWebService** key. The latter is a child key of the LM location. A child key is a key that is contained by another key.
Property or Custom Property	A property or custom property defines values that are used to configure IIS. Properties contain attributes; some properties, such as **AccessFlags**, also contain flags. Properties are contained by keys and can be written, in MetaBase.xml, as schema-defined or custom.
Attributes	Metabase properties contain several attributes that describe some characteristics of the property. Keys also contain attributes, such as the **Location** attribute or the **DefaultDoc** attribute found within the **IisWebService** key. Do not confuse the term *attributes* as used here to describe IIS metabase properties with XML attributes, which describe general XML structure.
Flag	A flag is a bit within the DWORD value of a property that contains flags. Each flag within a property is used to configure particular functionality of the property, such as read or write access. The sum of the flag values for a property becomes the sum of the value attribute for that property.

Keys and Locations

Metabase keys are analogous to registry keys or a directory in a file system. Each metabase key is identified by its name and location, which are defined within the start tag of the key. The following example shows two keys, **IIsConfigObject** and **IIsLogModules**, each having a unique location as defined by the value of its respective **Location** attribute:

Most key names are the same as the value of the **KeyType** property, also known as the ABO class name, which relates to the type of key. The **IIsLogModules** key, seen in the example above, is named this way. If you change the **KeyType** value of a metabase key programmatically, the name of the key changes in MetaBase.xml when the in-memory metabase is saved. This **KeyType** value is important because the schema-defined collection that is named by using the same **KeyType** enforces which properties the key can contain.

Keys named **IIsConfigObject** are special because they are not named by using a **KeyType** value. Because all properties are schema-defined in the **IIsConfigObject** collection, keys in MetaBase.xml that are named **IIsConfigObject** can contain any property. You can specify a **KeyType** value for a key named **IIsConfigObject** by writing the **KeyType** property in the key as a custom property. This is not a recommended method, however, because it does not work with ADSI. Preferably, use a real object, not **IIsConfigObject**.

Some key names describe the type of data at a unique location in the metabase, and thus might appear at multiple locations. For example, because you can have more than one virtual directory, **IIsWebVirtualDir** is a key that can appear at multiple locations. The **Location** attribute defines the hierarchical position of a key in MetaBase.xml. The value of the **Location** attribute, with only two exceptions, is a sequence of location names separated by one or more forward slashes (/) that uniquely identifies the hierarchical position of the key in MetaBase.xml.

The exceptions are the **IIS_Global** key, which has the highest hierarchical position in MetaBase.xml (**Location** = "."), and the **IIS_ROOT** key, which has the next-highest hierarchical position in MetaBase.xml (**Location** = "/"). The next-highest hierarchical position is the **IIsComputer** key (Location = "/LM"). All remaining keys in MetaBase.xml are contained by the **IIsComputer** key; therefore, their location always begins with /LM/*LocationName*, where *LocationName* is the name of the location.

The hierarchical position of any metabase key can be determined by looking at its **Location** attribute. For example /LM" is the location of the **IIsComputer** key, and /LM/W3SVC is the location of the **IIsWebService** key. Because the /LM/W3SVC location begins with /LM followed by a forward slash character (/) and another location name (W3SVC), the **IIsWebService** key at location /LM/W3SVC is a child of the **IIsComputer** key. A *child key* is a key that is contained by another key. A key that contains another key is also called a *parent key*.

XML Terminology Related to IIS

Because MetaBase.xml is an XML file constructed with XML elements, it helps to be familiar with XML terminology and metabase terminology to understand how MetaBase.xml is structured. Table 4.2 identifies and defines the XML terms and relates them to their use in MetaBase.xml.

Table 4.2   XML Terminology and How It Relates to the IIS Metabase

Term	XML Description	Relation to MetaBase.xml
XML declaration	A processing instruction at the start of an XML document, such as `<?xml version = "1.0"?>`, that declares the file to be XML code.	The first line in MetaBase.xml is an XML declaration.
Element	A logical unit of information. Elements are surrounded by <*ElementName*> and </*ElementName*> tags, where *ElementName* is the name of the element. Elements can contain attributes.	Keys and custom properties are written by using XML elements.
Root element	A single element that contains all the other elements and character data that make up an XML document; also known as a *document element*.	MetaBase.xml contains a root element named <configuration>.
Start tag	A tag that marks the start of an element, such as <*ElementName*>, where *ElementName* is the name of the element.	In MetaBase.xml, start tags are used to identify the start of a key or custom property.
End tag	A tag that marks the end of an element, such as </*ElementName*>, where *ElementName* is the name of the element.	In MetaBase.xml, end tags are used to identify the end of a key or custom property.
Element type	Indicated by the name that occurs in its start tag and end tag.	In MetaBase.xml, the element type for metabase keys is actually the value of the **KeyType** property. For example, **IIsWebService** is the **KeyType** that is used to identify the World Wide Web Publishing Service (WWW service) key. Custom properties use the name **Custom** as the element type.
Attribute	A name and value pair that is associated with an XML element and that provides more information about the content of that element. Do not confuse the term *attribute* as used here to describe XML structure with an IIS metabase property attribute that describes an IIS property.	A metabase property contains several attributes that describe the characteristics of the property, such as the data type or value. Keys also contain attributes, such as the **Location** attribute or the **DefaultDoc** attribute found within the **IIsWebService** key.
Comment	Text that is not to be treated as part of the document. Comments are delimited by <!-- and --> tags.	In MetaBase.xml, comments are delimited by <!-- and --> tags, and must be written above the key to which they pertain. If you put a comment inside an XML node, it is removed by IIS. In addition, no comments are allowed above the IIS_Global node.

Metabase Structure

The XML declaration `<?xml version = "1.0"?>` occupies the first line in MetaBase.xml and indicates that the file is formatted as XML. The root element, named <configuration>, contains all other elements.

The **IIS_Global** key is the highest-level key in the metabase that contains properties. Consider the **IIS_Global** key to be read-only; do not configure its properties.

The **IIS_ROOT** key (Location = "/") is the highest-level key in which you can configure properties. Properties that are configured at the **IIS_ROOT** key affect the general operation of IIS.

The **IIsComputer** key (Location = "/LM") contains all remaining metabase locations. Table 4.3 lists, in hierarchical order, child locations that can exist within the namespace of the /LM location. The File Transfer Protocol (FTP), Network News Transfer Protocol (NNTP), and Simple Mail Transfer Protocol (SMTP) components are not installed with IIS by default. Therefore, the /LM/MSFTPSVC, /LM/NNTPSVC, and /LM/SmtpSvc locations do not exist in MetaBase.xml unless their respective components have been installed.

The Local Machine Namespace

The local machine ("LM") namespace is the parent location in the hierarchical structure of keys where all services and sites are organized. These keys, each of which contains their own unique location, are organized in the following format:

/LM/*Service*/*Site*/*ROOT*/*VirtualDirectory*/*Directory*/*File*

Where the replaceable parameters are:

- *Service* = MSFTPSVC, NNTPSVC, SmtpSvc, or W3SVC
- *Site* = unique number identifier for the FTP, NNTP, SMTP, or Web, site
- *ROOT* = root virtual directory of the site
- *VirtualDirectory* = virtual directory
- *Directory* = physical directory
- *File* = file name

Each site is a server instance, and is referred to by the number used in its namespace. For example, /LM/W3SVC/1 specifies the location of the key that contains the first Web site, and /LM/MSFTPSVC/3 specifies the location of the key that contains the third FTP site.

Table 4.3 lists the locations of the parent keys that are contained in the "LM" namespace. Because their child keys are too numerous, they are not listed here.

Table 4.3 Local Machine Locations

Location	Keys at this location
/LM/EventManager	Keys at the /LM/EventManager location and its child locations configure Microsoft Exchange Server. You should not configure keys at the /LM/EventManager location or its child keys by editing the MetaBase.xml file.
/LM/IISADMIN	Keys at the /LM/IISADMIN location and its child locations record DCOM extensions to IIS. Because the /LM/IISADMIN location is internally configured by IIS, you should not configure keys at /LM/IISADMIN or its child locations.
/LM/Logging	Keys at the /LM/Logging location and its child locations configure IIS logging.
/LM/MimeMap	Keys at the /LM/MimeMap location configure the **MimeMap** property.
/LM/MSFTPSVC	Keys at the /LM/MSFTPSVC location and its child locations configure the FTP service and sites.
/LM/NNTPSVC	Keys at the /LM/NNTPSVC location and its child locations configure the NNTP service and sites.
/LM/SmtpSvc	Keys at the /LM/SmtpSvc location and its child locations configure the SMTP service and sites.
/LM/W3SVC	Keys at the /LM/W3SVC location configure properties that are global to the WWW service.
/LM/W3SVC/1	Keys at the /LM/W3SVC/1 location and its child locations configure properties that are specific to the first Web site.
/LM/W3SVC/AppPools	Keys at the /LM/W3SVC/AppPools location configure properties that are global to all application pools. Keys at child locations, such as /LM/W3SVC/AppPools/DefaultAppPool, configure properties that are specific to a particular application pool.
/LM/W3SVC/Filters	Keys at the /LM/W3SVC/Filters location and its child locations configure Internet Server API (ISAPI) filters and compression schemes.
/LM/W3SVC/Info	Keys at the /LM/W3SVC/Info location configure properties that are global to all Web sites.
/LM/W3SVC/Info/Templates	The /LM/W3SVC/Info/Templates location and its child locations were used by the IIS Permissions Wizard in earlier versions of IIS. It remains solely for legacy compatibility. You should not configure keys at the /LM/W3SVC/Info/Templates location by editing the MetaBase.xml file.

Property Inheritance

Property inheritance configures IIS by using as few property settings as possible. The benefits of using a minimal number of property settings to configure IIS are as follows:

- Faster IIS cache performance
- Reduced memory consumption
- Reduced time required for IIS administration

Metabase properties are used to provide detailed control of IIS functionality. All metabase properties contain attributes, such as the **DefaultValue** attribute, which specify the configuration of the properties. Most metabase properties are inheritable, and they are specified as inheritable in MBSchema.xml by using the string value "**INHERIT**" as part of the value of the **Attributes** attribute. The following example shows the default attributes for the **HttpErrors** property in MBSchema.xml:

```
<Property
    InternalName = "HttpErrors"
    ID = "6008"
    Type = "MULTISZ"
    UserType = "IIS_MD_UT_FILE"
    Attributes = "INHERIT"
    MetaFlagsEx = "CACHE_PROPERTY_MODIFIED"
    DefaultValue = ""/
>
```

Hierarchical Relationship of Keys

The metabase is designed so that properties can be set differently at different keys. To understand how property inheritance works, it is necessary to first understand the hierarchical relationship of keys in the MetaBase.xml file. In relation to other keys, a key can be located in MetaBase.xml at a higher level, lower level, or the same level. The **Location** attribute of each key determines the level in which a key exists in the hierarchical structure.

The following example illustrates the relationship between the **IIsWebService**, **IIsWebServer**, and **IIsWebVirtualDir** keys. The example uses indentation to illustrate the hierarchical relationship of the keys.

```
<IIsWebService Location = "/LM/W3SVC"
    <IIsWebServer Location = "/LM/W3SVC/1">
        <IIsWebVirtualDir Location = "/LM/W3SVC/1/ROOT">
    <IIsWebServer Location = "/LM/W3SVC/2">
        <IIsWebVirtualDir Location = "/LM/W3SVC/2/ROOT">
```

In this example, the **IIsWebService** key is the highest-level key. The **IIsWebServer** keys are at a lower level than **IIsWebService**, and the **IIsWebVirtualDir** keys are at a lower level than the **IIsWebServer** keys. Keys that are at the same level cannot inherit properties from each other. Therefore, because the **IIsWebServer** keys are at the same hierarchical level in the metabase, they cannot inherit properties from each other. The **IIsWebVirtualDir** keys are also at the same level in relation to each other, and therefore they cannot inherit properties from each other.

Note

The hierarchical structure of the metabase is determined by the **Location** attribute of the keys themselves, not the class name of the keys.

Inheritance

Inheritable properties that are not explicitly set at a lower-level key are automatically inherited from the key at the next-higher level in which the property is configured. The **IIS_ROOT** key is the highest key in MetaBase.xml from which a property can be inherited.

The following example illustrates properties that are configured differently in different keys in MetaBase.xml, as well as properties that are inherited. The names of properties that are set at a specific metabase key appear in **bold** text. Otherwise, the names of properties that are inherited from the next-highest key that has the inheritable property set appear in plain text. XML comments precede the property or properties to which they correspond.

```
<IIsWebService Location = "/LM/W3SVC"
<!-- The DefaultDoc and ContentIndexed properties are specifically set at this
key. -->
DefaultDoc = "Default.htm,Default.asp,index.htm,Default.aspx"
ContentIndexed = "TRUE"
   <IIsWebServer Location = "/LM/W3SVC/1">
   <!-- The DefaultDoc property is specifically set at this key. -->
   DefaultDoc = "Default.htm,Default.asp,index.htm,iisstart.htm,Default.aspx"
   <!-- The ContentIndexed property is inherited from the IIsWebService key and
   does not appear here -->
   </IIsWebServer>

<IIsWebVirtualDir Location = "/LM/W3SVC/1/ROOT"
<!-- The DefaultDoc and ContentIndexed properties are inherited from the
/LM/W3SVC/1 location and do not appear here. -->
</IIsWebVirtualDir>
>
   <IIsWebServer Location = "/LM/W3SVC/2"
   <!-- The DefaultDoc and ContentIndexed properties are inherited from the
   IIsWebService key. -->
   </IIsWebServer>
   >
   <IIsWebVirtualDir Location = "/LM/W3SVC/2/ROOT"
   <!-- The DefaultDoc property is inherited from the /LM/W3SVC/2 location. -->
   <!-- The ContentIndexed property is specifically set at this key. -->
   ContentIndexed = "TRUE"
   >
</IIsWebVirtualDir>
</IIsWebService>
```

The Metabase Schema

The metabase schema defines what properties can exist in the metabase configuration file. The metabase schema also enforces which properties can be set at which keys. The metabase schema provides this enforcement only for *schema-defined* properties, which are properties written to the metabase configuration file that adhere to the rules of metabase schema. Properties that are not schema-defined can be written in the metabase configuration file as *custom properties*. Custom properties can be used in the metabase configuration file to override schema enforcement or to configure a property with values other than the default values that are defined by the schema.

Collections

The metabase schema is organized into containers called *collections*. Collections are defined in MBSchema.xml by using <Collection> start and end tags, and they are written in the following format:

```
<Collection InternalName = "CollectionName" MetaFlagName = "MetaFlagValue" …>
    <Property PropertyName = "PropertyValue" …>
        <Flag FlagName = "FlagValue" …>

    .
    .
    .
</Collection>
```

In the example above, *CollectionName* is the name of the entire collection. *MetaFlagName* and its associated *MetaFlagValue* apply to the entire collection. *PropertyName* and its associated *PropertyValue* are individual settings within the collection. *FlagName* and its associated *FlagValue* are individual settings within a property.

All collections exist at the same hierarchical level in MBSchema.xml. Therefore, no collection is a parent of another. Reading the MBSchema.xml file from top to bottom, the first collection, named **MetabaseBaseClass**, defines global settings in the schema.

The following code example is taken from the metabase schema file to illustrate how collections are defined.

```
<Collection InternalName = "IIsConfigObject" MetaFlagsEx =
"NOTABLESCHEMAHEAPENTRY" MetaFlags = "HASUNKNOWNSIZES | HIDDEN">
    <Property InternalName = "AccessFlags" ID = "6016" Type = "DWORD"
    UserType = "IIS_MD_UT_FILE" Attributes = "INHERIT"
    MetaFlagsEx = "CACHE_PROPERTY_MODIFIED" DefaultValue = "AccessRead"
    EndingNumber = "0">
        <Flag InternalName = "AccessExecute" Value = "4" ID = "6209"/>
</Collection>
```

The collection directly below **MetabaseBaseClass** is named **IIsConfigObject**. The **IIsConfigObject** collection is unique, because it is where all properties are defined. Only properties that are defined in the **IIsConfigObject** collection can be written to the metabase configuration as schema-defined properties.

Properties

Properties are configuration objects that are associated with IIS Admin Objects and their corresponding ABOs. All properties that are defined in the **IIsConfigObject** collection contain attributes. The default values of these attributes for each property are also defined.

 Note

The default values that are assigned to property attributes in the IIsConfigObject collection are not necessarily the values that are written to the metabase configuration when IIS is installed. The default values of attributes, which are defined by the IIsConfigObject collection, are used when you write a schema-defined property to the metabase configuration file after IIS is installed.

Each property that is defined in the **IIsConfigObject** collection contains the following attributes: **ID**, **Type**, **UserType**, **Attributes**, **InternalName**, and **DefaultValue**. Some properties also contain the following attributes: **MetaFlags**, **MetaFlagsEx**, **StartingNumber**, and **EndingNumber**. Property attributes are contained in the <Property> start tag. The following example from the **IIsConfigObject** collection illustrates how a property is defined.

```
<Property
    InternalName = "ServerComment"
    ID = "1015"
    Type = "STRING"
    UserType = "IIS_MD_UT_SERVER"
    Attributes = "INHERIT"
    MetaFlagsEx = "CACHE_PROPERTY_MODIFIED | WAS_NOTIFICATION"
    DefaultValue = ""/>
```

Flags

In addition to attributes, some properties also contain *flags*. Each flag configures a unique functionality of the property, such as read or write access. Each flag is identified by the ABO that uses unique *bitmask identifier* of the flag.

Flags contain attributes named **Value** and **ID**. Flags are defined in the property's start and end tags, and they are identified by using <Flag> tags. The sum value of all flags that are set for a property determines the value of the property's **DefaultValue** attribute, which is also called the default value of the property. The following example illustrates a property that contains flags.

```
<Property InternalName = "PasswordChangeFlags"
   ID = "2068"
   Type = "DWORD"
   UserType = "IIS_MD_UT_SERVER"
   Attributes = "INHERIT"
   MetaFlagsEx = "CACHE_PROPERTY_MODIFIED"
   DefaultValue = "0"
   EndingNumber = "0">
      <Flag InternalName = "AuthChangeUnsecure" Value = "1" ID = "6292"/>
      <Flag InternalName = "AuthChangeDisable" Value = "2" ID = "6293"/>
      <Flag InternalName = "AuthAdvNotifyDisable" Value = "4" ID = "6294"/>
</Property>
```

> **Note**
>
> Flags and their attributes are written in the start and end tags of a property. A property that does not contain a flag is encapsulated in the start tag of the property, and it does not use end tags.

Remaining Collections

All remaining collections, which are below the **IIsConfigObject** collection, are organized by key type. These collections enforce at which keys in the metabase configuration a schema-defined property can be written. For example, if a collection named **IIsWebServer** contains the **ServerComment** property, IIS allows the **ServerComment** property to be written to any key in the metabase configuration that uses the **IIsWebServer** key type. Therefore, only properties that are contained in these remaining collections can be written (as schema-defined properties) in a metabase key of the same key type in MetaBase.xml.

The exception to this rule is the **IIsConfigObject** key type, described earlier. Because all properties are contained in the **IIsConfigObject** collection, all properties can be written to any key in the metabase configuration of the **IIsConfigObject** key type.

Properties are written in these remaining collections in the following format:

```
<Property InheritsPropertiesFrom = "IIsConfigObject:PropertyName"/>
```

where *PropertyName* is the name of the property.

All of the properties that are contained by these remaining collections inherit their default values from the **IIsConfigObject** collection, because the **IIsConfigObject** collection is where all properties are defined.

You cannot use ADSI or WMI, which are not defined in metabase schema, to update properties in the metabase configuration. Changes written directly to the MetaBase.xml file that do not comply with metabase schema rules might not be written to the in-memory metabase. If this occurs, an error or warning is sent to the event log.

Metabase Security

A default installation of IIS 6.0 ensures metabase security by setting strict access control entries (ACEs) on the metabase files and by encrypting sensitive data within the files. If you maintain this level of security, perform regular backups, use a strong administrator password, and limit the number of users who have administrative credentials, you are taking the proper precautions to protect your metabase files.

File-Level Security

As described in Table 4.4, IIS installs the metabase files with strict ACEs set to prevent anyone but administrators from viewing your configuration data. An access control list (ACL) is a container for ACEs.

Table 4.4   Metabase files, purpose, and permissions

File	Purpose	ACL
systemroot\System32\Inetsrv\MetaBase.xml	Stores configuration data for the IIS services.	NT AUTHORITY\SYSTEM : Full control BUILTIN\Administrators : Full control
systemroot\System32\Inetsrv\MBSchema.xml	Stores the schema for the configuration file. The schema defines what IIS properties can be set at certain metabase keys.	NT AUTHORITY\SYSTEM : Full control BUILTIN\Administrators : Full control
systemroot\System32\Inetsrv\History*HistoryFile*	Stores the metabase history files that are created automatically by IIS.	NT AUTHORITY\SYSTEM : Full control BUILTIN\Administrators : Full control
systemroot\System32\Inetsrv\MetaBack*BackupFile*	Stores the metabase backup files that are created on demand by using Backup/Restore Configuration.	NT AUTHORITY\SYSTEM : Full control BUILTIN\Administrators : Full control

Encrypted Properties

IIS encrypts sensitive data in the metabase configuration file, MetaBase.xml, so that it cannot be viewed even if an unauthorized user gains access to the file.

> **Important**
>
> Do not manually change encrypted properties in MetaBase.xml. There is no way to encrypt your data before inserting it by using Notepad or another text editor. Only WMI, ADSI, or ABOs can be used to change the data in encrypted properties.

Metabase properties are marked for encryption by an attribute that is set on the property in the metabase schema file. The following example from the metabase schema file shows how the **AnonymousUserPass** property is marked for encryption with a **SECURE** attribute:

```
<Property InternalName = "AnonymousUserPass" ID = "6021" Type = "STRING"
UserType = "IIS_MD_UT_FILE"
   Attributes = "INHERIT|SECURE" MetaFlagsEx = "CACHE_PROPERTY_MODIFIED"
   DefaultValue = ""/>
```

> **Caution**
>
> You cannot use WMI, ADSI, or ABOs to add an attribute to an existing property in the metabase schema. For example, you cannot add the **SECURE** attribute to an existing property. If you attempt to use WMI, ADSI, or ABOs to remove a property in the metabase schema and then create it again with the **SECURE** attribute, the metabase configuration data for that property is lost. You can, however, use ADSI to create new properties in the metabase schema with the **SECURE** attribute. Manual changes made to the metabase schema are not supported and might cause an error.

The following metabase properties are encrypted:

- **ADConnectionsPassword**
- **AdminACL**
- **AdminACLBin**
- **AnonymousUserPass**
- **ImapDsPassword**
- **LogOdbcPassword**
- **Pop3DsPassword**
- **RoutePassword**
- **SmtpDsPassword**

- **UNCPassword**
- **FeedPassword**
- **WAMUserPass**

Checklist: Metabase Security

Table 4.5 is a list of recommended steps to ensure the security of the metabase.

Table 4.5   Steps to ensure metabase security

Step	Reference
☐ Make sure that the passwords for all accounts on your computer are strong and not written anywhere near the computer or within view.	See "Passwords" in Help and Support Center for Windows Server 2003.
☐ Maintain strict access control permissions on the metabase files that are listed in Table 4.4. Only the LocalSystem account and the Administrators group should be listed in the ACLs as having full control of the metabase files, including the history files and backups. IIS sets this access control by default.	See "Access control" in Help and Support Center for Windows Server 2003.
☐ Employ the concept of *least permission* on your computer. Allow only one person to know the Administrator password, and limit the number of people whose accounts are in the Administrators group. Set ACLs on all folders and files so that the fewest users have the lowest-level permission needed to run required tasks. Set IIS security on all IIS applications and virtual directories so that the least permission necessary exists to allow proper clients to view your content.	See "Access control" and "Security" in Help and Support Center for Windows Server 2003.
☐ Do not run the **cipher** command or use Encrypting File System (EFS) on the metabase files. Sensitive data, such as passwords that are stored in MetaBase.xml, are already encrypted. Encrypting the entire MetaBase.xml file slows down your IIS server and might cause errors.	See the "Cipher" and "Encrypting File System" topics in Help and Support Center for Windows Server 2003.
☐ When you edit the MetaBase.xml file manually, copy the MetaBase.xml file first, and then work on the copy. When you have checked your changes, replace MetaBase.xml with your copy.	See "Editing the MetaBase.xml File While IIS Is Running" later in this chapter.
☐ Create backups of your metabase files using Backup/Restore Configuration whenever you make a significant change in the metabase. If you allow other people to configure the metabase, make it a policy that they create a backup with their name in the title whenever they make a change. IIS periodically makes its own backup files, called history files, but history files might not be created for every change to the metabase.	See "Backing Up the Metabase" later in this chapter.

(continued)

Table 4.5   Steps to ensure metabase security *(continued)*

	Step	Reference
☐	Do not use the metabase import and export feature to create regular backup files. This feature is meant to transport sections of the metabase to other computers However, it is recommended that you create an export file for your entire metabase periodically in the event that your computer hardware fails and you must move your Web sites to another computer.	See "Metabase Import and Export" later in this chapter.
☐	Remember that backing up or exporting the metabase does not back up your content (.htm files, .asp files, components, and so on). The metabase only holds configuration data, such as where your content is stored. To back up your content, use Windows Backup.	See "Backing up and restoring data" in Help and Support Center for Windows Server 2003.
☐	Monitor your event log for IIS event messages. For example, if you attempt to make changes to the metabase when there is a write-lock on the in-memory database, a metabase history file is created and an error is written to the event log. If you successfully create an FTP virtual directory, but IIS cannot enumerate the physical directory, an error is written to the event log.	See "Event Viewer" in Help and Support Center for Windows Server 2003.
☐	Set up file auditing on the various files that affect the metabase. This way, if the metabase becomes corrupted, you can identify the account of the last user who made a change. Select your auditing choices carefully for the files listed below, and monitor the audit logs for a period of time to determine if the settings are meeting your needs. *systemroot*\System32\Inetsrv\MetaBase.xml If you choose to audit the MetaBase.xml file, only users who edit the metabase manually are identified in the audit logs by their own account name. Users who edit the metabase by using IIS Manager or other tools are logged as accessing the metabase under the LocalSystem account. Because IIS itself is constantly accessing the metabase, audit logs can grow very quickly unless you limit auditing to specific users, such as the local Administrators group, and specific access attempts, such as writing to a file. Auditing MetaBase.xml is still valuable for determining when changes were made, but you might have to audit the other files listed here to find the exact identity of the user. **Custom tools and script files that use WMI, ADSI, or ABO s to edit the metabase** Auditing should be set on these tools to identify who executes them. If you audit MetaBase.xml and want to find out who made a change at 3:01 P.M. on a certain day, you can look in the audit logs for your scripts and tools to see if someone ran one of them at 3:01 P.M. *systemroot*\System32\Inetsrv\Inetmgr.exe Audit this file for the same reason you audit custom tools and script files, above.	See "Auditing overview" in Help and Support Center for Windows Server 2003.

Backing Up and Restoring the Metabase

Creating backups of the metabase is a vital part of maintaining metabase reliability. The ability to create backup files and to restore the metabase by using backup files has been enhanced in IIS 6.0. You can now restore the backup on other computers if portable backup has been chosen. History file copies of the metabase are created automatically by IIS, and an IIS administrator using IIS Manager can create them on demand. All backups, regardless of how they were created, are stored together and displayed together in IIS Manager.

Restoring a backup from an earlier version of IIS is not supported. After you install or upgrade to IIS 6.0, it is recommended that you perform a metabase backup as soon as possible to preserve your configuration data.

Backing up the metabase should be supplemented with proper metabase security practices. For more information about metabase security, see "Metabase Security" earlier in this chapter.

Backing Up the Metabase

Using Backup/Restore Configuration, you can create complete backup copies of the IIS metabase. The backup files are either portable or non-portable copies of the metabase configuration file (MetaBase.xml) and the matching metabase schema file (MBSchema.xml). Metabase backup files provide a way to restore your metabase configuration and schema data in the event that the metabase becomes corrupted. Portable backup files can be restored either to the computer on which the backup was made or to other installations of Windows Server 2003, while non-portable backup files can only be restored to the same system from which it was made.

Backup files contain only configuration data; they do not include your content. To back up your content as well, use Windows Backup. For more information about using Windows Backup, see "Backing up and restoring data" in Help and Support Center for Microsoft® Windows® Server 2003.

 Note
The metabase is locked while the backup is in progress.

Portable Backup

When creating a portable backup, the administrator provides a password that is used by IIS to encrypt the backup files. The password is encrypted and stored in the header of the backup file. Only the administrator password and secure properties within the backup files are encrypted; all other information within the backup files is plain text. After the backup file is encrypted, the password within the backup file cannot be changed.

Non-portable Backup

When creating a non-portable backup, the administrator does not supply a password. Therefore, non-portable backup files are encrypted with a blank password, which allows any member of the Administrators group to restore the metabase. Only the blank password and secure properties are encrypted; all other information within the backup file is plain text.

Important

You must be a member of the Administrators group on the local computer to perform the following procedure or procedures, or you must have been delegated the appropriate authority. As a security best practice, log on to your computer by using an account that is not in the Administrators group, and then use the runas command to run IIS Manager as an administrator. At a command prompt, type runas /*User:Administrative_AccountName* "mmc %systemroot%\system32\inetsrv\iis.msc".

▶ To back up the IIS metabase

1. In IIS Manager, right-click the local computer, point to **All Tasks**, and click **Backup/Restore Configuration**.

2. Click **Create Backup**, and then type a name for the backup file in the **Configuration backup name** box. Note that the backup name is not case-sensitive.

3. To restore the backup to a different computer, select the **Encrypt backup using password** check box, type a password in the **Password** box, and then type the same password in the **Confirm password** box.

4. Click **OK**.

When a backup is created, a set of two files is created and named in the following way:

```
Name.mdx and Name.scx
```

In the syntax above, *Name* is the name that the administrator uses to name the backup set, and x is the version number of the backup set, starting with 0 (zero). The version number is increased by one for each backup set that uses the same name, up to 999. For example, if you use the name *MyBackup* as the name of your backup set twice, MyBackup.md0 and MyBackup.sc0 are created on the first backup; on the second backup, the files are named MyBackup.md1 and MyBackup.sc1. By default, backup files are stored in the *systemroot*\System32\Inetsrv\MetaBack folder.

The Metabase History Feature

IIS automatically maintains a record of metabase changes in history files that are saved to disk. You can also configure the number of metabase history files to save. By using the metabase history feature, you can revert the metabase through any number of changes to restore a particular configuration, or to see what has changed between revisions.

By marking each new metabase file with a unique version number and saving a copy of the file in the History folder, the metabase history feature automatically keeps track of metabase changes that are saved to disk. Each history file is then available for restoring the MetaBase.xml and MBSchema.xml files from the History folder, editing the MetaBase.xml file while IIS is running, and troubleshooting event log errors. The metabase history feature is enabled by default.

History Folder

The History folder stores versioned copies of the MetaBase.xml and MBSchema.xml files. These copies can only be viewed by members of the Administrators group. The location of the History folder is *systemroot*\System32\Inetsrv\History.

A *history file pair* consists of a MetaBase.xml and MBSchema.xml file of the same major and minor version numbers. The default setting allows for a maximum of 10 versioned history file pairs to be stored in the History folder, but you can configure this number. However, before increasing the number of versioned sets of files stored in the History folder, you should ensure that you have adequate hard disk space on the drive volume where the History folder is located. (You can estimate the amount of hard disk space that is required by multiplying the average combined file size of MetaBase.xml and MBSchema.xml files by the number of versions that you want to store in the History folder.) You should not decrease the value of the **MaxHistoryFiles** property to below 10.

When the in-memory metabase is written to disk, IIS checks to determine whether the number of history file pairs that are contained in the History folder exceeds the value of the **MaxHistoryFiles** property. If the number of history file pairs exceeds the value of the **MaxHistoryFiles** property, the oldest history file pair is deleted.

For information about backing up your entire operating system, including special steps that must be performed to include IIS in that backup, see "Backing up and restoring data" in Help and Support Center for Windows Server 2003. For information about the event log, see "Event log" in Help and Support Center for Windows Server 2003.

Configuring the Metabase History Feature

By default, the metabase history feature is enabled and the number of history file pairs that are saved within the History folder is defined by the default value of the **MaxHistoryFiles** property. A history file pair is the combination of a copy of a MetaBase.xml file and an MBSchema.xml file of the same version in the History folder. If the **EnableHistory** property is not written in the MetaBase.xml file, IIS interprets the absence of the property to mean that the history feature is enabled, and the **MaxHistoryFiles** property is set to the default value.

▷ **To change the metabase history default settings**

- Add the **EnableHistory** and **MaxHistoryFiles** metabase properties to the /LM level of the metabase.

▷ **To disable metabase history**

- Set the value of the **EnableHistory** property to **0** (zero).

▷ **To enable metabase history**

- Set the value of the **EnableHistory** property to **1**.

▷ **To change the number of history files that are stored in the History folder**

- Change the value of the **MaxHistoryFiles** property.

> **Caution**
>
> Disabling history files can have serious consequences in the event that the metabase becomes corrupted by improper editing. Without backup files, the IIS server might have to be reconfigured from an empty state. However, keeping backup files can also be a security risk if you do not ensure that the files are protected by ACLs. By default, only members of the Administrators group can view the history files, but if you copy history files to a new location, you must duplicate those settings. For information about configuring ACLs, see "Access control" in Help and Support Center for Windows Server 2003.

Naming the Metabase History Files

To keep track of metabase history, IIS uses the following versioning scheme to enumerate the copies of MetaBase.xml that are stored in the History folder.

Metabase Version Numbers

The value of the **HistoryMajorVersionNumber** metabase property, also referred to as the major version number, increases when the in-memory metabase is written to disk.

The minor version number increases when the edit-while-running feature is enabled and an administrator changes and saves the MetaBase.xml file directly with an application such as Notepad.

HistoryMajorVersionNumber Property

The **HistoryMajorVersionNumber** property is located under the IIS_Global node in the metabase, as shown in the following example:

```xml
<?xml version = "1.0"?>
<configuration xmlns = "urn:microsoft-catalog:XML_Metabase_V54_0">
<MBProperty>
<IIS_Global Location = "."
   BINSchemaTimeStamp = "9676376defb8c201"
   ChangeNumber = "1023"
   HistoryMajorVersionNumber = "154"
   SessionKey = "4585thge754u4509853743hg0948054ug6t095"
   XMLSchemaTimeStamp = "444e436defb8c201"
   >
</IIS_Global>
```

 Important

IIS uses the HistoryMajorVersionNumber property to track the versions of the metabase. Thus, manually changing the value of the HistoryMajorVersionNumber property is not recommended.

Minor Version Number

The minor version number is not a property that is stored in the metabase. IIS calculates the minor version number when the MetaBase.xml file is edited and saved directly, and if edit-while-running is enabled, as follows:

IIS looks in the History folder to determine the last minor version number that was used for a history file with the same **HistoryMajorVersionNumber** number as MetaBase.xml. IIS then uses the next sequential minor version number when naming the new history file.

When a history file is created because the in-memory metabase is written to disk, either through the regular timed history algorithm, or by the user explicitly saving the current configuration to disk, the major version number is incremented by 1, and the minor version number is reset to zero.

Naming the History Files

When a copy of MetaBase.xml is written to the History folder, the value of the **HistoryMajorVersionNumber** property is incremented and added to the names of the file pair. If edit-while-running is enabled, and the user makes a manual change to the metabase, the minor version number is incremented and added to the names of the file pair.

The file names of versioned MetaBase.xml files and MBSchema.xml files are created in the following format, respectively, where both the value of the **HistoryMajorVersionNumber** property and the minor version number are 10-digit numbers:

```
MetaBase_HistoryMajorVersionNumber_MinorVersionNumber.xml

MBSchema_HistoryMajorVersionNumber_MinorVersionNumber.xml
```

When either the **HistoryMajorVersionNumber** or the minor version number value is less than 10 digits, the number is padded with zeros in the file name to create a 10-digit number. This keeps the file names aligned and in numerical order when you sort by file name, making the contents of the History folder easier to read.

The following is an example of file names in the History folder:

```
MetaBase_0000000001_0000000000.xml
MetaBase_0000000001_0000000001.xml
MetaBase_0000000002_0000000000.xml
MetaBase_0000000002_0000000001.xml
MetaBase_0000000002_0000000002.xml
MetaBaseError_0000000000.xml
MetaBaseError_0000000001.xml
MBSchema_0000000001_0000000000.xml
MBSchema_0000000001_0000000001.xml
MBSchema_0000000002_0000000000.xml
MBSchema_0000000002_0000000001.xml
MBSchema_0000000002_0000000002.xml
```

For each instance of a MetaBase_*MajorVersion_MinorVersion*.xml file within the History folder, there is an MBSchema_*MajorVersion_MinorVersion*.xml file of the same version that is used with the metabase configuration.

Metabase Error Files

File names that contain the word *error* are created in the History folder under the following circumstances:

- Edit-while-running is enabled.

- You edit MetaBase.xml directly by using an application, such as Notepad.

- An error, such as (but not limited to) the following occurs:

    - An XML tag is omitted in MetaBase.xml.

    - A property name is misspelled in MetaBase.xml.

    - The corresponding history file with the same **HistoryMajorVersionNumber** value as MetaBase.xml is not found.

Error files are named in the following format, where *TenDigitNumber* is the version number of the error file, starting with version number 0000000000:

```
MetaBaseError_TenDigitNumber.xml
```

The version number increases by one for each additional error file that is created.

Restoring the Metabase

Restoring the metabase from history files is similar to restoring it from backup files. For a comparison of the two methods of restoring the metabase, see Table 4.6.

Table 4.6   Comparison of Metabase Restore Methods

Using Backup Files	Using History Files
If a password is provided by the user to encrypt secure properties, the metabase can be restored to a different installation of Windows, even on a different computer.	The metabase can be restored only on the same installation of Windows from which the history files were created. This is because data is encrypted with the machine key in the backups.
Backup files can be created on demand, scheduled, or created by using a programmatic administration script.	History files can be created automatically (when the IIS history feature is enabled) or by using a programmatic administration script.
Backup files can be restored from IIS Manager, by using APIs or by using programmatic administration scripts.	History files can be restored manually or by using IIS Manager.

Restoring the Metabase from History Files

The following procedures describe how to use automatically generated history files to restore your IIS configuration.

 To restore the metabase using IIS Manager

1. In IIS Manager, right-click the local computer, point to **All Tasks**, and click **Backup/Restore Configuration**.

2. In the **Backups** list, click the Automatic Backup you want to restore, and then click **Restore**.

3. Read the message that appears, and click **Yes** if you want to continue.

4. Click **OK**.

You might find it necessary to restore the metabase without using IIS Manager. For example, if a configuration change is made improperly or if it is made with incorrect XML syntax, and IIS Manager is unable to enumerate the metabase, use the following procedure to restore the metabase. Note that this method should be used only as a last resort. If at all possible, use metabase history or backup files to restore the metabase.

> **Important**
>
> You must be a member of the Administrators group on the local computer to run scripts and executables, or you must have been delegated the appropriate authority. As a security best practice, log on to your computer by using an account that is not in the Administrators group, and then use the runas command to run your script or executable as an administrator. At a command prompt, type runas /profile /User:MyMachine\Administrator cmd to open a command window with administrator rights and then type cscript.exe ScriptName (including the full path with parameters, if any).

▷ **To manually restore the metabase**

1. From the **Start** menu, click **Run**.

2. In the **Open** box, type **cmd**, and then click **OK**.

3. At the command prompt, type **iisreset /stop /noforce**, and then press ENTER.

4. If the IIS services do not stop, and it is possible to restart the computer, type **iisreset /stop /rebootonerror**, and then press ENTER.

5. At the command prompt, type **cd %systemroot%\System32\Inetsrv**, and then press ENTER to navigate to the folder where the files are. Next, type **copy MBSchema.xml Mbschema.old**, and then press ENTER to copy the schema file. Finally, type **copy MetaBase.xml Metabase.old**, and then press ENTER to copy the metabase configuration file.

6. At the command prompt, type **cd %systemroot%\System32\Inetsrv\History**, and then press ENTER.

7. At the command prompt, type **dir**, and then press ENTER. All of the files appear in the following format:

   ```
   <Date> <Time> <FileSize> MBSchema_<MajorVersion>_MinorVersion.xml
   ```

8. Select the version of history files that you want. When you restore the IIS metabase to an earlier version, you need matching metabase schema and configuration files. Select matching files by their major version number.

9. At the command prompt, type **copy /y mbschema_<majorversion>_minorversion.xml %systemroot%\System32\Inetsrv\MBSchema.xml**, and then press ENTER. With this command, you copy the file and rename it at the same time.

10. At the command prompt, type **copy /y Metabase_<majorversion>_minorversion.xml %systemroot%\System32\Inetsrv\MetaBase.xml**, and then press ENTER. Again, this command copies the file and renames it at the same time.

    Important
   If you mix up the names or copy a schema and configuration file that do not match, the metabase restoration might fail when you start the IIS services.

11. At the command prompt, type **iisreset /start**, and then press ENTER.

   If the IIS services do not restart, repeat these steps beginning at step 4, and copy a different set of history files over the current metabase files.

Restoring the Metabase from Backup Files

You can restore a metabase backup to the same computer on which the backup was made or, if the backup was created with a password, onto a different computer. Because a metabase backup does not include content files, if you restore a metabase backup to a different server you must copy your content files as well. The content files must exist in the same location and on the same drive used on the original server. Restoring a backup from an earlier version of IIS is not supported.

 Important

Before restoring a metabase from one computer to a different computer, you must first delete or alter the machine-specific information from the metabase file. For important information about this issue, see "Machine-Specific and System-Specific Information" later in this chapter.

▶ **To restore an IIS metabase backup**

1.   In IIS Manager, right-click the local computer, point to **All Tasks**, and click **Backup/Restore Configuration**.

2.   In the **Backups** list, click the backup you want to restore, and then click **Restore**.

3.   Read the message that appears, and click **Yes**.

4.   If you are restoring a portable backup, you are prompted for the password you typed when the backup was created. Type the password, and then click **OK**. Note that passwords are case-sensitive.

5.   Click **OK**.

The IIS services, except the IIS Admin service, are restarted.

SSL Certificates

If you use a Secure Sockets Layer (SSL) certificate on your Web server and you restore the metabase backup to a different installation of the operating system, an error occurs if the certificate is not available or installed. If a site's SSL certificate is missing, connections are dropped, and the browser displays a "page unavailable" message. The solution is to reinstall the certificate into the same certificate store as on the original computer, and restart IIS.

Restoring a Section of the Metabase

You can make fixes to specific sections of the metabase in two ways:

- You can use the import feature without the merge option to import metabase elements over damaged data.

- If the damaged section prevents IIS from loading the metabase, you can manually edit the MetaBase.xml file in any text editor by copying sections from an export or backup file and pasting them into the MetaBase.xml file.

  For information about importing and exporting metabase elements, see "Metabase Import and Export" later in this chapter.

You can be prepared to make fixes to the metabase by creating a template of your entire metabase, as well as by creating export files of new sections of your metabase file at various stages of its life, so that you have something to work from if a section becomes corrupted.

To create a template of your entire metabase, first create a backup file. Remove any machine-specific and system-specific information from your backup file, and then remove extraneous information and configuration information that is specific to applications, sites, and virtual directories.

What you are left with is a template of top-level configuration information that might not be recoverable using metabase import/export. Together with the export files of specific sections that you created, you are prepared for any loss of data or corruption. One way to identify where XML syntax corruption exists, open the MetaBase.xml file with Internet Explorer. Internet Explorer will identify the line at which it encountered invalid xml syntax.

Editing the Metabase

Editing the MetaBase.xml file directly by using common text-editing tools is an efficient way to configure the metabase over low-bandwidth connections. Editing MetaBase.xml with Notepad is more efficient than using IIS Manager, because IIS Manager is relatively slow over low-bandwidth lines, such as a 56 KB modem. Additionally, editing the metabase file directly is faster than through user interfaces (UIs), such as IIS Manager, when hundreds or thousands of sites are running on the same computer. Editing the MetaBase.xml file directly is particularly useful for administrators who do not want to use programmatic methods to administer IIS but want an alternative to the UI methods. Editing the Metabase directly over a remote connection is not recommended because a dropped connection can leave the Metabase in an indeterminate state.

You can make changes to the MetaBase.xml file while IIS is running only if the edit-while-running feature is enabled. If edit-while-running is not enabled, you must stop IIS before you edit the MetaBase.xml file. This is inefficient and not a recommended practice.

Best Practices for Maintaining Metabase Integrity

The following practices can greatly reduce the chance that the metabase will become corrupted.

- Enable edit-while-running. This ensures that changes made to the metabase configuration while IIS is running are written to the on-disk metabase.

- Always back up the metabase before making configuration changes. Make the right kind of backup. A password-protected backup is cleanly transportable to other systems, while a backup made without a password is tied to the system on which the backup was made.

- When editing the metabase with a text editor, use a text editor that write-locks the open file. This prevents the possibility of more than one person editing the metabase at a time.

- After editing the metabase, open the file in Internet Explorer 6 or above. Any errors in the XML syntax will be displayed when Internet Explorer opens the file.

- Never allow changes to the metabase by more than one entity at a time. For example, do not edit the metabase by hand at the same time an administrative script that changes metabase settings is running.

- If you make changes to the metabase and it does not load properly, use a file comparison tool to compare the backup you made before editing the metabase with the edited metabase. This can help pinpoint any unintended changes.

Note the following about editing the metabase:

- Recoverable metabase schema errors occur when text editing yields well-formed XML but one or more properties are invalid, according the metabase schema.

- Editing the metabase schema is not supported.

- If the metabase contains incorrectly formatted XML, IIS cannot read the metabase and will not run. You can restore the last good history file to correct this problem.

- If an invalid configuration is created in MetaBase.xml, the error "cannot read property" is logged to Event Viewer, but the rest of IIS keeps running.

Configuring the Metabase

The IIS metabase is a plaintext XML file containing most IIS configuration values. The metabase can be configured manually, by using IIS Manager or a text editor, or programmatically, using the IIS WMI and ADSI providers. Deciding the method you use to configure the metabase depends on the task you want to accomplish. For a one-time, one-step configuration task, editing the metabase file directly in a text editor might be easiest; for repetitive tasks that require a number of steps, a programmatic approach is most efficient. Another important aspect of configuring the metabase is knowing how to back up and restore the metabase if changes result in an error.

IIS includes several methods for changing values in the metabase. As shown in Figure, you can set or view metabase values programmatically by using any of the following resources:

- **IIS Manager.** The user interface (UI) that you can use to update the in-memory metabase. This is the safest way to update the metabase. However, it does not expose all available metabase properties.

- **IIS ADSI provider.** A set of scripting interfaces that you can run from a script.

- **IIS WMI provider.** A set of scripting interfaces that you can run from a script.

- **Admin Base Objects (ABOs).** A set of binary COM interfaces.

- **IIS MetaEdit 2.2 Utility.** MetaEdit is a metabase editing tool available for download from Microsoft. For information about obtaining MetaEdit, see article 232068, "Download, Install, and Remove the IIS MetaEdit 2.2 Utility," in the Microsoft Knowledge Base. To find this article, see the Microsoft Knowledge Base link on the Web Resources page at http://www.microsoft.com/windows/reskits/webresources.

All configuration settings are written to the metabase through ABOs, as illustrated in Figure 4.2.

Figure 4.2   Interfaces to the In-Memory Metabase

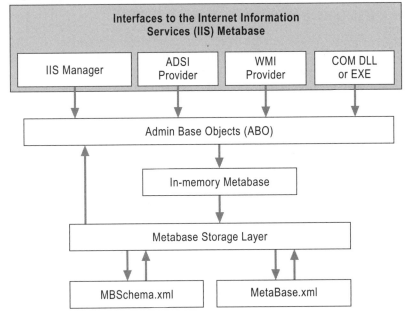

About the IIS ABOs

As shown in Figure 4.2, the ABOs are central to updating the in-memory metabase. An ABO is a set of binary COM objects that are used to write IIS configuration values that are stored in the IIS metabase. Each object has properties, and each property is stored in the metabase. You can manipulate IIS configuration by using ABOs to add new virtual directories, new Web sites, and so forth.

IIS Manager and the other resources in the illustration that are used to update the in-memory metabase write directly to the ABOs. The ABOs then write the changes to the in-memory metabase. You can also access ABOs directly by using C or Microsoft® Visual C++® development system, Microsoft® Visual Basic® development system, Delphi, or any COM-compliant language to programmatically update the in-memory metabase. You cannot use scripting language code to programmatically update the in-memory metabase.

Metabase Storage Layer

The in-memory metabase is periodically written to disk through the metabase storage layer. The metabase storage layer is the part of IIS that reads the metabase files into the in-memory metabase and also writes the in-memory metabase to the metabase files. The storage layer writes the in-memory metabase directly to the metabase files when a write-to-disk event occurs or when IIS is shut down.

 Important

You cannot edit the MBSchema.xml file directly by using edit-while-running. Changes to MBSchema.xml must be made programmatically by using ADSI.

Adding Comments to the Metabase

A metabase comment must be stored in the in-memory metabase in the correct XML format and associated with a particular node within the metabase, so the context of the comment is preserved during subsequent writes of the metabase to disk. Put node-specific comments right above the node. If you delete the node, the comments about the node are deleted as well.

When loading the metabase, the configuration system loads comments as a generic property into the metabase, along with other metabase data. If comments are found at the bottom of the file (below all nodes), that set of comments will always be preserved at the bottom of the file.

Comments are added in the following format:

```
<!-- your comment goes here -->
```

The following is a list of rules concerning metabase comments:

- Comments that are added above the **MBProperty** node are not picked up by edit-while-running.

- Comments that are added between the **MBProperty** node and the **IIS_Global** node cause an error file to be created.

- Comments that are added between **IIS_Global** and **IIS_ROOT** are picked up by edit-while-running.

- Adding comments between start and end XML tags results in an error file and the in-memory metabase being flushed to disk.

Editing Metabase Properties

You can write metabase properties in MetaBase.xml as either schema-defined or custom properties. Writing schema-defined properties results in an efficient use of the IIS cache, which is where the in-memory metabase and schema are stored, because the attributes are inherited from the schema rather than rewritten for each instance of a property. Using custom properties is not recommended, because they might not show up in the UI and ADSI cannot access them after they have been created.

A schema-defined property is contained in the start tag of a key, and only the property name and value are defined. Attributes for a schema-defined property come from the metabase schema. In the following example, the **EnableEditWhileRunning** property is a schema-defined property with a value of zero, and it is written in the **IIs_Computer** key:

```
<IIs_Computer Location = "/LM"
    EnableEditWhileRunning = "0">
```

A custom property defines some or all of the attributes of a property. Unlike a schema-defined property, a custom property is written between the XML start tag and the end tag of a metabase key. Custom properties are easy to identify because the name of the element that contains the custom property is **Custom**. The name and attributes of a custom property are contained in an XML element named **Custom**.

At a minimum, the **Name** and **ID** attributes must be defined in a custom property. Other than the name of the property and the **ID** attribute, all remaining attributes for a custom property come from the schema, if they are undefined. You need to define the other attributes only when you want them to contain a different value than the schema-defined attribute values. In the following example, the **Win32Error** property is defined as a custom property with a value of zero, and it is written within the **IIsFtpVirtualDir** key.

```
<IIsFtpVirtualDir Location = "/LM/MSFTPSVC/1/ROOT">
    <Custom
        Name = "Win32Error"
        ID = "1099"
        Value = "0"
        Attributes = "INHERIT"/>
</IIsFtpVirtualDir>
```

 Important

Each property that is defined in the schema (MBSchema.xml) has a unique ID attribute. When you define a known property as a custom property, you must specify the unique ID number for that property.

General Notes for Editing the Metabase

Keep the following points in mind when editing the metabase.

- Properties with the **SECURE** attribute set are stored encrypted.

- All text in MetaBase.xml is case sensitive.

- The **KeyType** property contained in a node is used to determine the element or node type that is applied to the metabase path.

- Nodes that do not contain a **KeyType** property are stored as the generic object **IISConfigObject**, which can contain any property, and any node can be contained within any other node.

- Custom properties are allowed for any node type.

- The **IIS_Global** node must not be edited.

- A schema-defined property that violates the schema — for example, a misspelled property name — is logged and the property is ignored.

- Custom properties require a metabase **ID** attribute.

- The **Multi-SZ** attribute is replaced with the multistring value.

- Flags contain bitmask identifiers.

- The internal metabase implementation is Unicode. To support international and non-ASCII characters, the MetaBase.xml file is encoded in UTF-8 text format.

Changing Schema-Defined or Out-of-Schema Properties

You can use custom properties for the following purposes:

- To use properties that are not schema-defined.

- To use properties with different attribute values than what is available in the schema-defined properties.

When you write a property by using different attribute values than what is schema-defined, you must write the property as a custom property. Only the attributes that are different from the schema should be defined in MetaBase.xml.

The following example shows a schema-defined property:

```
AccessFlags = AccessWrite
```

The following example shows a custom property:

```
<Custom Name = "AccessFlags"
    ID = "6016"
    Type = "DWORD"
    Value = "1"
    UserType = "IIS_MD_UT_FILE"
    Attributes = "INHERIT"/>
```

Starting or Stopping IIS

When IIS is started or restarted, the metabase configuration that is stored in MetaBase.xml and the schema information that is stored in MBSchema.xml is read by the storage layer and then written to the in-memory metabase through ABOs, as shown in Figure 4.2.

If the MetaBase.xml file cannot be parsed when IIS is started or restarted, an error is sent to the event log and IIS does not start. The reasons that MetaBase.xml might not be parsed correctly include — but are not limited to — missing XML tags, misspelled property names, or corruption of the MetaBase.xml file. To determine the cause of failure, you can use the last history file to determine what has changed in the MetaBase.xml file. If the metabase cannot be parsed, you can also restore it to an earlier version by using the last manual backup or an automatically generated history file.

When IIS is stopped, it checks to determine whether the configuration node or the schema node have changed in the in-memory metabase since the last time the in-memory metabase was written to disk. The configuration node contains the metabase configuration, which is stored in the MetaBase.xml file. The schema node contains the metabase schema, which is stored in the MBSchema.xml file.

To minimize the amount of time that is required to stop IIS, the MetaBase.xml file is not written to disk if the configuration node in the in-memory metabase has not changed. If the configuration node in the in-memory metabase has changed since the last time the in-memory metabase was saved to disk, the MetaBase.xml file is overwritten with the contents of the configuration node, and a new history file is created. For more information about history files, see "Naming the Metabase History Files" earlier in this chapter.

Editing the MetaBase.xml File While IIS Is Running

This section contains information about the metabase edit-while-running feature, which is also known as Direct Metabase Edit. The ability to edit the metabase while IIS is running makes administration simpler and avoids site down time, because you do not have to stop IIS when you need to change the metabase configuration.

The Edit-While-Running Process

IIS uses Windows file change notification to determine when the MetaBase.xml file has been saved. When IIS detects that the metabase configuration file has been saved, a series of checks are made, as illustrated in Figure 4.3. Several possible scenarios are presented, based on the results of the steps shown in the illustration, to demonstrate the behavior of edit-while-running.

 Important

The MBSchema.xml file cannot be edited directly by using edit-while-running. Changes made to metabase schema must be made programmatically.

Figure 4.3   The Edit-While-Running Process

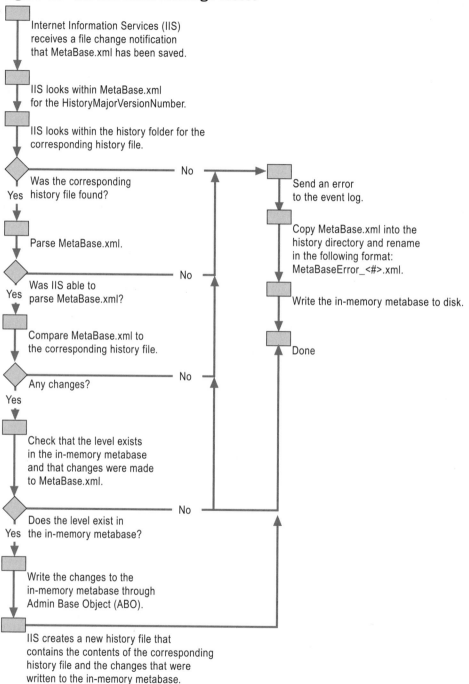

Step 1: IIS receives a file change notification that MetaBase.xml has been saved.

IIS receives a file change notification from Windows when the metabase configuration file is saved. If MetaBase.xml is write-locked and you attempt to save MetaBase.xml directly with an application such as Notepad, an error is generated and a file change notification does not occur.

Step 2: IIS looks in MetaBase.xml for the HistoryMajorVersionNumber value.

IIS reads the value of the **HistoryMajorVersionNumber** property in MetaBase.xml to determine the major version number.

Step 3: IIS looks in the History folder for the corresponding history file.

The corresponding history file is named with the highest minor version number with the same **HistoryMajorVersionNumber** value found in MetaBase.xml in step 2. If the corresponding history file is found, IIS proceeds to step 4.

Step 4: Parse MetaBase.xml.

IIS parses MetaBase.xml to determine whether there are fatal XML errors, such as missing XML end tags. If MetaBase.xml can be parsed successfully, IIS proceeds to step 5.

Step 5: Compare MetaBase.xml to the corresponding history file.

IIS compares MetaBase.xml to the corresponding history file of the same major version within the History folder. IIS determines the differences between the two files and does one of the following:

- If no changes were made to MetaBase.xml, a history file is not created and no further action is taken.

- If changes were made to MetaBase.xml, IIS proceeds to step 6.

Step 6: Check that the level exists in the in-memory metabase that changes were made to in MetaBase.xml.

IIS determines whether the level/node exists within the in-memory metabase that changes were made to in the MetaBase.xml file. If the level/key exists within the in-memory metabase, IIS proceeds to step 7.

Step 7: Write the changes to the in-memory metabase through ABO.

The changes are written to the in-memory metabase through ABOs.

A change that was made to MetaBase.xml might not be sent to the in-memory metabase for any of the following reasons:

- The change violates metabase schema; for example, a property name is misspelled.

- The in-memory metabase is write-locked by someone making a simultaneous change by using ADSI, ABO, or WMI to modify the same metabase node or property.

- The key in the in-memory metabase that changes were made to in MetaBase.xml does not exist. This could occur if an administrator deletes the key in the in-memory metabase, by using a programmatic interface or IIS Manager, before MetaBase.xml is changed and saved to disk.

If a change is not written to the in-memory metabase for any of the reasons listed above, an error or warning is sent to the event log.

Step 8: IIS creates a new history file that contains the contents of the corresponding history file and the changes that were written to the in-memory metabase.

A history file is created in the History folder. This new file includes the combination of contents of the corresponding history file plus the changes that were written to the in-memory metabase in step 7. The new history file is named with the major version number that was found within MetaBase.xml (the value of the **HistoryMajorVersionNumber** property that was determined in step 2) and the next highest minor version number. IIS looks within the History folder to find the highest minor version number that was used for the same major version number, and it uses the next sequential minor version number to name the new history file. This naming convention permits succeeding edits to the same major version of the file to work correctly.

Simultaneous Updates

IIS supports simultaneous updates between programmatic interfaces such as ADSI and WMI. However, under some circumstances, errors can occur as described in step 7 above. The rule is that the last write always wins.

IIS does not support simultaneous updates between the programmatic interfaces and an administrator who directly edits MetaBase.xml. Simultaneous writes to the same metabase node or property can result in an error because of the resulting race condition. You can protect against this type of error by allowing only one administrator to edit the metabase at a time.

Enabling Edit-While-Running

Edit-while-running can be enabled by using either IIS Manager or a command prompt. Before you can enable edit-while-running, the metabase history feature must be enabled and set to a value of at least 10 (the default metabase history setting).

It is important to note that all text within MetaBase.xml is case sensitive.

 Important

You must be a member of the Administrators group on the local computer to perform the following procedure or procedures, or you must have been delegated the appropriate authority. As a security best practice, log on to your computer by using an account that is not in the Administrators group, and then use the **runas** command to run IIS Manager as an administrator. At a command prompt, type **runas** / *User.Administrative_AccountName* "mmc %systemroot%\system32\inetsrv\iis.msc".

To enable edit-while-running by using IIS Manager

1. In IIS Manager, right-click the local computer, and then click **Properties**.

2. Select the **Enable Direct Metabase Edit** check box.

> ◆ **Important**
>
> You must be a member of the Administrators group on the local computer to run scripts and executables, or you must have been delegated the appropriate authority. As a security best practice, log on to your computer by using an account that is not in the Administrators group, and then use the **runas** command to run your script or executable as an administrator. At a command prompt, type **runas /profile /***User:MyMachine\Administrator* cmd to open a command window with administrator rights and then type **cscript.exe** *ScriptName* (including the full path with parameters, if any).

▷ **To enable edit-while-running from the command line**

The following procedure requires IIS to be restarted. Restarting IIS stops all sites for a short time. To enable direct metabase edit without interruption of service, use IIS Manager, as described in the previous procedure.

1. From the **Start** menu, click **Run**.

2. In the **Open** box, type **cmd**, and then click **OK**.

3. At the command prompt, type **iisreset /stop**, and press ENTER. Leave the command window open.

4. Open MetaBase.xml with a plain text editor. By default, MetaBase.xml is located in the *systemroot*\System32\Inetsrv folder.

5. In the **IIsComputer** node, change the value of the **EnableEditWhileRunning** property from **0** (FALSE) to **1** (TRUE). The change should look as follows:

```
<IIsComputer   Location = "/LM"
   EnableEditWhileRunning = "1"
   EnableHistory = "1"
   MaxBandwidth = "4294967295"
   MaxHistoryFiles = "10">
</IIsComputer>
```

6. Save changes to MetaBase.xml.

7. At the command prompt, type **iisreset /start**, and then press ENTER.

Writing the In-Memory Metabase and Schema to Disk

The metabase is written to disk either when MetaBase.xml is edited directly and manually saved to disk, or when the in-memory metabase is saved to disk.

 Important

MetaBase.xml can be edited by hand and saved to disk only when edit-while-running is enabled or when the IIS Admin service is stopped before the MetaBase.xml file is edited and saved.

The in-memory metabase is written to disk only under the following circumstances:

- When the IIS Admin service is stopped, and there are changes pending in the in-memory metabase.

- The in-memory metabase is written to disk 60 seconds after a change is made to the metabase; however, if more than 30 changes occur during those 60 seconds, the write-to-disk event is postponed for another 60 seconds. The in-memory metabase write-to-disk event is postponed a maximum of five times, after which it is written to disk.

- When saved programmatically, as when using a resource such as ADSI, WMI, or ABO.

Figure 4.4 and the following discussion describe how the in-memory metabase is written to disk. The verification checks can influence how IIS saves the in-memory metabase to disk, as illustrated by the possible scenarios.

Writing the In-Memory Metabase to Disk

Figure 4.4 shows the process IIS uses to determine when to write the in-memory metabase to disk.

Figure 4.4   How the In-Memory Metabase Is Written to Disk

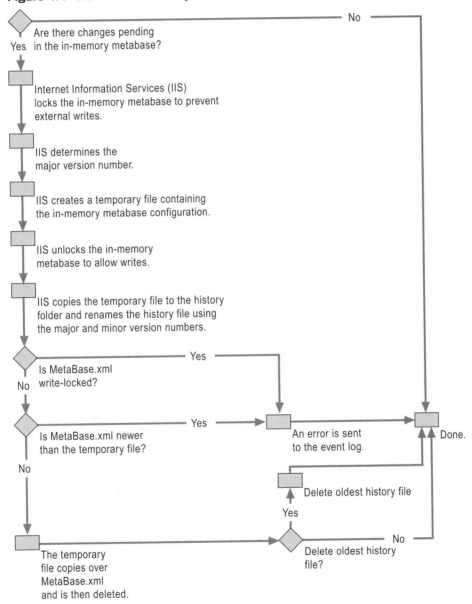

Step 0: A change is made to the metabase, which schedules a write-to-disk event 60 seconds in the future.

Step 1: Are there changes pending in the in-memory metabase?

When a write-to-disk event occurs, IIS first checks for pending changes that occurred after the first change in the in-memory metabase. Changes that are written to the MetaBase.xml file when edit-while-running is enabled are counted as pending changes in the in-memory metabase. If there are no pending changes in the in-memory metabase, no further action is taken and the in-memory metabase is written to disk; otherwise, IIS proceeds to step 2.

Step 2: IIS locks the in-memory metabase to prevent external writes.

The in-memory metabase is write-locked, meaning that no writes can occur but the metabase can still be read; this prevents writes while the in-memory metabase is written to disk and ensures that a valid copy of the in-memory metabase is saved.

Step 3: IIS determines the major version number.

IIS increases the value of the **HistoryMajorVersionNumber** property in the in-memory metabase by one. IIS then verifies whether a file in the History folder is named with the same major version number. If a file that uses the same major version number exists in the History folder, IIS increases the value of the **HistoryMajorVersionNumber** property in the in-memory metabase again by one, and checks the History folder to determine whether the major version number is available. This process is repeated until an available major version number is found.

This method of determining the major version number prevents the possibility of overwriting a file in the History folder. Although unlikely under normal circumstances, the possibility exists that a file in the History folder has a nonsequential version number for one of the following reasons:

- An administrator changes the value of the **HistoryMajorVersionNumber** property, which causes the value of the **HistoryMajorVersionNumber** property to roll over to 1 or to the lowest available major version number.

- An administrator copies an old history file into the History folder.

Step 4: IIS creates a temporary file that contains the in-memory metabase configuration.

When the major version number is determined, a temporary file named Xml.tmp is created in the same folder as MetaBase.xml. The major version number that was determined in step 3 is written in the temporary file.

Step 5: IIS unlocks the in-memory metabase to allow writes.

After the temporary file is created, the in-memory metabase is unlocked to allow writes through ABOs.

Step 6: IIS copies the temporary file to the History folder and renames the history file by using the major and minor version numbers.

The temporary file is copied to the History folder and renamed in the following format, where *HistoryMajorVersionNumber* is the major version number that was determined in step 3 and the minor version number is reset to 0.

MetaBase_*HistoryMajorVersionNumber_MinorVersionNumber*.xml

Step 7: Is MetaBase.xml write-locked?

The MetaBase.xml file can become write-locked if edit-while-running is not enabled and an administrator uses an application to open MetaBase.xml for editing, and the editing application enforces a write-lock. An application that enforces a write-lock releases the lock when the file is closed. However, in most circumstances, MetaBase.xml is not write-locked.

If MetaBase.xml is write-locked by an application, IIS cannot write changes to the file. Instead, a history file is created and an error is sent to the event log.

Step 8: Is MetaBase.xml newer than the temporary file?

IIS checks to determine whether the MetaBase.xml file is newer than the temporary file. The MetaBase.xml file can be newer than the temporary file when the in-memory metabase is written to disk at about the same time that an administrator saves changes to the MetaBase.xml file when edit-while-running is enabled.

If the MetaBase.xml file is newer than the temporary file, the MetaBase.xml file is not overwritten with the temporary file. Instead, an error is sent to the event log.

Step 9: The temporary file copies over MetaBase.xml, and is then deleted.

If all verification tests are passed, the MetaBase.xml file is overwritten with the temporary file and the temporary file is deleted.

Step 10: Delete oldest history file?

IIS checks to determine whether the number of history file pairs in the History folder exceeds the value of the **MaxHistoryFiles** property. (A history file pair is a MetaBase.xml file and an MBSchema.xml history file that are named by using the same major and minor version numbers.) If the number of history file pairs exceeds the value of the **MaxHistoryFiles** property, the oldest history file pair is deleted.

Writing the In-Memory Schema to Disk

IIS can distinguish changes that are made to the in-memory metabase schema separately from changes that are made to the in-memory metabase configuration. The process of writing the in-memory metabase schema to disk is similar to writing the in-memory metabase configuration to disk, as follows:

- If there are no pending changes within the in-memory metabase schema when a write-to-disk event occurs, the in-memory metabase schema node is not written to disk. Instead, the MBSchema.xml file is copied to the History folder and renamed with the same major and minor version numbers that are used to name the metabase configuration history file in step 6 above.

- If changes are made to the in-memory metabase schema, the following occurs:

    - The MBSchema.xml file is renamed to a temporary schema file.

    - The in-memory schema is written to MBSchema.xml.

    - The temporary schema file is copied to the History folder and renamed with the same major and minor version numbers that are used in step 6 above.

Metabase Import and Export

The metabase import and export feature enables administrators to create an export file, named MetaBase.xml by default, which contains specifically selected elements of a metabase configuration file. This export file can later be imported into the metabase configuration file of the same computer, or to another computer running Windows Server 2003.

Additionally, you can use the metabase export feature to create a metabase template, which can be used to configure multiple computers with the same IIS configuration settings, excluding machine-specific and system-specific information. For more information about metabase templates, see "Restoring a Section of the Metabase" in this chapter.

Metabase export does not replace the functionality of metabase backup. You use metabase backup to create a backup file of the entire metabase configuration and schema, which can be restored only in its entirety (including encrypted properties). Metabase export does not export the metabase schema.

 Note

Neither metabase backup nor export can be used to save or copy content files, scripts, or binaries. To back up your entire server — including content files, scripts, and binaries — use Windows Backup. To simply copy these files to a new location, use Windows Explorer or the Windows xcopy command. Remember to reregister any components that you copy to a new computer.

Specifying Metabase Elements for Import or Export

You can import and export the following metabase elements:

- All Web site configurations or a single site configuration
- All FTP site configurations or a single FTP site configuration
- All SMTP site configurations or a single SMTP site configuration
- All NNTP site configurations or a single NNTP site configuration
- An IIS application configuration
- A directory, virtual directory, or file configuration properties
- All application pool configurations or a single application pool configuration

Importing and Exporting a Metabase Element

To import or export a metabase element, you can use any of the following:

- IIS Manager

- The Iiscnfg.vbs tool that is included with IIS

- A custom script that uses the **Export** method of the WMI provider for IIS or the **Export** method of the ADSI provider for IIS

- A custom application that uses ABO

Regardless of whether you use a programmatic interface, a script, or IIS Manager to import and export metabase elements, there are specific choices you must make. The following list outlines both the required and optional steps needed to import and export a metabase element. The inheritance and merge options are discussed after the list. When a metabase element is exported, IIS creates an XML file that contains the exported element.

Before exporting a metabase element

1. Select a metabase element to export.

2. Specify the name and location of the XML file to contain the exported element.

3. Optionally choose to export inherited properties.

4. Optionally choose to export lower-level child keys recursively (recommended).

5. Optionally encrypt the export file with a password that you provide (recommended).

Before importing a metabase element

1. Specify a metabase export file to import.

2. Specify an element within the export file to import.

3. Optionally choose to import inherited properties.

   The export file must contain inherited properties for this option to be available.

4. Optionally choose to import lower-level child keys recursively.

   The export file must contain lower-level child keys for this option to be available.

5. Specify the password, if any, that was used to encrypt the export file.

6. Optionally choose to merge the settings from the export file into the metabase configuration.

7. If you intend to import a metabase element to another computer, you must first change the machine-specific and system-specific information in the export file.

Setting Inherit and Merge Flags

If you set the inherit flag during a metabase export, inheritable properties that are applicable to the metabase element are saved as part of the export file. If the inherit flag is set during an import operation, these inheritable properties are imported into the metabase.

The behavior of importing inheritable properties differs, depending on whether the merge flag is used along with the inherit flag.

For example:

- If you import a metabase element by using the inherit flag without the merge flag, inheritable properties are imported into the metabase, unless the property already exists at the same location in MetaBase.xml. (If the value of an imported property differs between the export file and the MetaBase.xml file, the value of the property in the MetaBase.xml file remains unchanged.)

- If you import a metabase element by using the inherit flag with the merge flag, inherited properties are imported into the metabase and the value of the properties that already exist at the same location in MetaBase.xml are overwritten. (If the value of an imported property differs between the export file and the MetaBase.xml file, the value of the property in the MetaBase.xml file is overwritten with the value from the export file.)

 Important

Inherited properties in the destination metabase affect the configuration of all sites. Use caution when you import a metabase element without using the inherit flag. To avoid unintended changes to other sites, import to a unique location that has no child nodes.

Exporting Lower-Level Child keys

When specifying a metabase element to export, you can optionally export lower-level child keys. If an element is exported by using this option, you can optionally import the element and all recursive child keys.

Importing and Exporting Metabase Elements with IIS Manager

You can use the metabase import/export feature to create an export file that contains specifically selected elements of a metabase configuration file. This exported file can later be imported into the metabase configuration file on the same computer or another computer running Windows Server 2003.

The simplest way to use the metabase import/export feature is through IIS Manager. However, if you need to use this feature on numerous machines quickly, you can use one of the following:

- The Iiscnfg.vbs tool that is included with IIS 6.0

- A custom script that uses the **Export** method of the WMI provider for IIS or the **Export** method of the ADSI provider for IIS

- A custom application that uses ABO

Important

You must be a member of the Administrators group on the local computer to perform the following procedure or procedures, or you must have been delegated the appropriate authority. As a security best practice, log on to your computer by using an account that is not in the Administrators group, and then use the **runas** command to run IIS Manager as an administrator. At a command prompt, type **runas** / *User:Administrative_AccountName* "mmc %systemroot%\system32\inetsrv\iis.msc".

 **To export metabase elements**

1. In IIS Manager, expand the **Local Computer**; right-click the application pool, Web site, FTP site, or virtual directory that you want to export; point to **All Tasks**; and then click **Save Configuration to a File**.

2. In the **File name** box, type the name you want to give to your export file.

3. In the **Path** box, type or browse to the path where you want the export file saved. For security purposes, select a folder on which you have already restricted access by setting strict access control permissions. Any files created in such a folder inherit the ACL.

4. If you want to encrypt your export file for increased security, select the **Encrypt configuration using password** check box, and type a strong password in the **Password** and **Confirm password** boxes. For more information about strong passwords, see "Passwords" in Help and Support Center for Windows Server 2003.

5. Click **OK**, and then verify that your export file has been created.

▷ **To import metabase elements**

Before importing metabase elements from a file, make sure you have removed or changed all machine-specific and system-specific information.

1. In IIS Manager, expand the **Local Computer**; right-click the Web site, FTP site, virtual directory, or application pool node to which you want to import configuration data; point to **New**; and click **Web Site (from file)**, **FTP Site (from file)**, **Virtual Directory (from file)**, or **Application Pool (from file)** — depending on the type of node to which you want to import configuration data.

2. In the **File** box, type the path to your import file or click **Browse** to locate it.

3. Click **Read File**. The importable nodes are displayed under **Select a configuration to import**.

4. Click the object whose configuration you want to import, and then click **OK**.

5. If the element already exists in the metabase, a message that states **This *<element>* already exists** appears. Click **Create a new *<element>*** or **Replace the existing *<element>***, and then click **OK**. Note that if you choose to replace the existing element, you lose all previous configuration settings.

Moving Sites and Applications to Another Computer

You can use the metabase export feature to configure multiple computers with the same basic IIS configuration settings. The procedure below illustrates how to create a metabase template for the WWW service — though any service, site, virtual directory, or application can be moved.

The following procedure creates a complete, system-independent copy of the metabase configuration and saves it to a file. The file can then be moved to other IIS 6.0 servers.

 Important

You must be a member of the Administrators group on the local computer to run scripts and executables, or you must have been delegated the appropriate authority. As a security best practice, log on to your computer by using an account that is not in the Administrators group, and then use the runas command to run your script or executable as an administrator. At a command prompt, type runas /profile /*User*:*MyMachine**Administrator* cmd to open a command window with administrator rights and then type cscript.exe *ScriptName* (including the full path with parameters, if any).

▷ **To port an entire system-independent metabase configuration to another computer**

1. Open a command prompt, and then switch to the \Windows\System32 folder.

2. Type **cscript iiscnfg.vbs /f** *filename***.xml /d** *password* **/inherited /children**

3. Copy the XML file you created to a temporary directory on the target system.

4. On the target system, open a command prompt, and then switch to the \Windows\System32 folder.

5. Type **cscript iiscnfg.vbs /import /f** *path\filename***.xml /dp** *password* **/children /inherited /merge**

The Iiscnfg.vbs tool contains many options for exporting and importing metabase configurations. For more information about metabase import and import options, see "Iiscnfg.vbs" in Help and Support Center for Windows Server 2003.

▷ **To port specific metabase elements to another computer**

1. Configure an IIS server to the state that you want to port to other computers.

2. Export a metabase element to a file by using IIS Manager, the iiscnfg.vbs tool that is included with IIS, a custom script that uses the **IIsComputer.Export** method of the WMI provider for IIS or the **Export** method of the ADSI provider for IIS, or a custom application that uses ABO. IIS Manager includes inherited settings by default. If you are not using IIS Manager, you can specify the inherit flag if you want to include all inherited settings.

3. Clean up the export file by removing or changing all the machine-specific and system-specific information and removing all other settings that you do not want applied to other computers. This cleaned-up export file becomes your import file.

4. On the new computers, create any physical folders that are needed for site and virtual directory paths, copy any content files (such as ASP files and ISAPIs) that need to be ported, and register any components that were copied over.

5. Import your file on each computer to which you want to apply the settings. Make sure to use the merge flag if you do not want settings in the import file to overwrite any existing settings on the computer. Choose the inherit flag if you used it to create the export file.

Always test your computers after you import metabase elements to be sure your import file works as intended.

Metabase Import/Export Behavior

When using the metabase import/export feature, you need to be aware of the following behaviors with which the feature operates:

- If you attempt to import a property to a computer whose metabase schema file does not include the property, the import process continues, but errors are logged in Event Viewer. If you are using a script or application to perform the import, the script or application issues a warning.

- If the key type of any imported metabase element does not match the destination element, an error occurs.

- If you use a script or application that uses the inherited option, inherited settings are imported and applied to the top element. If you do not use the inherited option, only the elements that are explicitly set are imported.

- If you import configuration data by using a script or application and you use the merge flag, existing elements are not overwritten, and new ones are added. If you do not use the merge flag, existing elements are deleted or overwritten.

Machine-Specific and System-Specific Information

When importing a metabase element to another computer, you must change or remove machine-specific and system-specific information in the import file before you use it, otherwise IIS cannot use these values.

 Important

Never include password properties in import files. If you use an import file with a blank password property, the new computer subsequently stores encrypted properties as plain text.

Metabase properties that contain paths to resources in the file system might not match the paths on other computers. For example, the following properties might be written in the import file in the following way:

```
LogFileDirectory = "c:\windows\system32\logfiles"
Path = "c:\inetpub\ftproot"
HttpErrors = "400,*,FILE,c:\windows\help\iishelp\common\400.htm
    more HTTP errors
InProcessIsapiApps = "c:\windows\system32\inetsrv\httpext.dll
    more ISAPI applications
ScriptMaps = ".asp,c:\windows\system32\inetsrv\asp.dll,1,GET,HEAD,POST,TRACE
    more script maps
```

Change the paths in bold above to the path used by the computer to which you want to import the metabase element. Search for other paths in your import file before using it.

Metabase properties that specify the IWAM and IUSR accounts might not match the user accounts used by other computers. If your import file contains these properties, delete or alter them so that their values do not overwrite the existing valid properties. These properties might be written in the import file in the following way:

```
<IIsWebService
    Location = "/LM/MSFTPSVC"
    WAMUserName = "AccountName"
    AnonymousUserName = "AccountName">
```

The **ServerBindings** property, which is used to configure the port number for a site, might not be set the same way on another computer. However, you might want to import these settings to the new computer so that the computers will be configured the same way. The **ServerBindings** property is set at the site level, and can be written in the import file in the following way:

```
<IIsFtpServer
    Location = "/LM/MSFTPSVC/1"
    ServerBindings = ":21:" >
<IIsWebServer
    Location = "/LM/W3SVC/1"
    ServerBindings = ":80:">
```

Metabase properties that contain ACLs cannot be moved to another computer. If your import file contains these properties, delete them so that their values do not overwrite the existing valid properties. These properties might be written in the import file in the following way:

```
AdminACL = "LongNumber"
```

Metabase properties that contain passwords cannot be moved to another computer. If your import file contains properties with passwords, delete them so that their values do not overwrite the existing valid properties. These properties might be written in the import file in the following way:

```
<IIsWebService
    Location = "/LM/W3SVC"
    WAMUserPass = "LongNumber"
    AnonymousUserPass = "LongNumber"
    LogOdbcPassword = "LongNumber">
```

Additional Resources

These resources contain additional information and tools related to this chapter.

Related Information

- "Common Administrative Tasks" in this book for step-by-step instructions to help you complete many of the tasks described in this chapter.

- "IIS 6.0 Architecture" in this book for information about how the metabase fits into the overall architecture of IIS 6.0.

Related IIS 6.0 Help Topics

- "About the Metabase" in IIS 6.0 Help, which is accessible from IIS Manager, for general information about the IIS 6.0 metabase

- "Extending the Metabase Schema" in IIS 6.0 Help for information about extending the metabase schema.

- "Metabase Property Reference" in IIS 6.0 Help for information about the IIS 6.0 metabase properties.

- "Metabase Schema" in IIS 6.0 Help for information about the IIS 6.0 metabase schema.

Related Windows Server 2003 Help Topics

For best results in identifying Help topics by title, in Help and Support Center, under the **Search** box, click **Set search options**. Under **Help Topics**, select the **Search in title only** check box.

- "Access control" in Help and Support Center for Windows Server 2003 for information about configuring ACLs.

- "Backing up and restoring data" in Help and Support Center for Windows Server 2003 for information about backing up your entire operating system, including special steps that must be performed to include IIS in that backup.

- "Passwords" in Help and Support Center for Windows Server 2003 for information about strong passwords.

Related Tools

- The IIS MetaEdit 2.2 Utility

  MetaEdit is a metabase editing tool available for download from Microsoft. For information about obtaining MetaEdit, see article 232068, "Download, Install, and Remove the IIS MetaEdit 2.2 Utility," in the Microsoft Knowledge Base. To find this article, see the Microsoft Knowledge Base link on the Web Resources page at http://www.microsoft.com/windows/reskits/webresources.

Managing a Secure IIS 6.0 Solution

Proper security safeguards on your Web server can reduce or eliminate various security threats from malicious users and from well-intentioned users who can accidentally gain access to restricted information or inadvertently alter important files. Internet Information Services (IIS) 6.0 provides the elements for a secure IIS solution, including a new approach to server configuration that emphasizes installing only the services that you know you will run on your server.

In This Chapter

Related Information

- For information about interpreting substatus error codes, see "Analyzing Log Files" in this book.

- For information about configuring security for host header–based sites, see "Configuring Internet Sites and Services" in this book.

- For information about IIS 6.0 metabase security, see "Working with the Metabase" in this book.

What's Changed

To improve the security of your Web server, many aspects of IIS 6.0, including default behavior and settings, function differently than in earlier versions of IIS. Some of the most notable changes were made to take a more proactive stance against malicious users and attackers. A significant change is that IIS is not installed by default on Microsoft® Windows® Server 2003, Standard Edition; Windows® Server 2003, Enterprise Edition; and Windows® Server 2003, Datacenter Edition operating systems, and many services and features of IIS are not installed or enabled by default when you install IIS. Other security changes in IIS 6.0 affect components of Active Server Pages (ASP), authentication, and access control methods. As a result of these changes, some existing applications and sites might require you to enable services, change settings, or make other adjustments before they run as expected. However, if you change default settings, you should do so carefully in order to manage the most secure solution possible.

The most significant security-related changes are as follows:

- IIS installs in a locked-down mode.

- Restrictive Multipurpose Internet Mail Extensions (MIME) types reduce the attack surface of IIS.

- Multiple worker processes affect Internet Server API (ISAPI) filter status display.

- ASP and ASP.NET functionality are disabled by default.

- Parent paths are disabled by default.

- Global.asa events are run as anonymous user.

- Anonymous password synchronization is disabled by default.

- Advanced Digest authentication requires Windows Server 2003.

- Microsoft® .NET Passport authentication requires LocalSystem user account rights.

- Kerberos authentication requires service principal names (SPNs) for multiple worker processes.

- Access is restricted for executables.

- Access is restricted for non-default identities for Common Gateway Interface (CGI) processes.

The following sections describe the security-related changes and provide information about how to customize your IIS work environment.

IIS Installs in a Locked-Down Mode

When you install IIS 6.0, it is locked down — only request handling for static Web pages is enabled, and only the World Wide Web Publishing Service (WWW service) is installed. None of the features that sit on top of IIS are turned on by default, including ASP, ASP.NET, CGI scripting, FrontPage® 2002 Server Extensions from Microsoft, and Web Distributed Authoring and Versioning (WebDAV). This locked-down state minimizes the attack surface that is available to intruders who sometimes target computers by attacking services that are running, but that are unused. Such an attack is possible because if an administrator does not use a service, then he or she might forget to maintain it with current hotfixes, service packs, and patches, and the service might become vulnerable to attackers.

You can install and enable services when you need them. All of the Internet services, with the exception of the WWW service, are not installed by default; you must install them before you can enable them. Other services, such as CGI scripting, are installed by default and can be enabled using the Web Service Extensions node in IIS Manager.

 Important

It is possible to use the Web Service Extensions node to allow all unknown ISAPI and CGI extensions, but this presents a security risk and is not recommended. This option is available for use in a development environment, but it should never be enabled on a production server.

IIS Lockdown Tool Capabilities Are Built-in

You cannot install the IIS Lockdown Tool in IIS 6.0. However, to prevent the WWW service from being disabled after an upgrade, you can run the IIS Lockdown Tool prior to upgrading from an earlier version of IIS. When you upgrade from a server running Microsoft Windows® 2000 Server and IIS 5.0, IIS 6.0 runs in IIS 5.0 isolation mode by default, and IIS implements the following security measures:

- UrlScan functionality is left unchanged. UrlScan is a tool that is provided to reduce the attack surface of Web servers running earlier versions of IIS. By default, IIS 6.0 has features that significantly improve security by reducing the attack surface of the Web server. UrlScan provides flexible configuration for advanced administrators, while maintaining the improved security in IIS 6.0. When you need this flexibility in configuring your Web server, you can run UrlScan on IIS 6.0.

- Web service extensions that are mapped to 404.dll are mapped to their original location and added to the Web service extensions list with a prohibited status.

- Access control lists (ACLs) for WebDAV are reset correctly, and WebDAV is added to the Web service extensions list with a prohibited status.

- Indexing Service is left disabled, and existing ACLs are unchanged.

Restrictive MIME Types Reduce the Attack Surface of IIS

To prevent attackers from sending files that could compromise the security of your Web server, the IIS static file handler serves only the files that are explicitly listed in the list of Multipurpose Internet Mail Extensions (MIME) types. IIS is preconfigured to recognize a default set of global MIME types that are recognized by all of the Web sites that you create with IIS.

 Important

You must be a member of the Administrators group on the local computer to perform the following procedure or procedures, or you must have been delegated the appropriate authority. As a security best practice, log on to your computer by using an account that is not in the Administrators group, and then use the runas command to run IIS Manager as an administrator. At a command prompt, type runas / User.Administrative_AccountName "mmc %systemroot%\system32\inetsrv\iis.msc".

▷ **To see a list of all available MIME types**

1. In IIS Manager, right-click the local computer, and then click **Properties**.

2. In **MIME types**, click **MIME Types**.

    The registered MIME types are displayed in **Registered MIME types (file extensions)**. You can add, change, or remove MIME types from the list.

Alternatively, you can query the metabase using the Adsutil.vbs command-line script to see a list of all available MIME types.

To query the metabase using Adsutil.vbs, type **Adsutil.vbs enum/MimeMap** at the command prompt. For more information about MIME types, see "MIME Types" later in this chapter.

Adding MIME Types

If the default list of registered MIME types is too restrictive and you want to allow IIS to serve other file types, then you can add allowable MIME types on a global basis or for a specific Web site or directory.

▷ **To add a MIME type on a global basis**

1. In IIS Manager, right-click the local computer, and then click **Properties**.

2. In **MIME types**, click **MIME Types**, and then click **New**.

3. In the **Extension** box, type the file name extension.

4. In the **MIME type** box, type a description that exactly matches the file type defined on the client, and then click **OK**.

▷ **To add a MIME type for a specific Web site or directory**

1. In IIS Manager, right-click the site or directory to which you want to add a MIME type, and then click **Properties**.

2. Click the **HTTP Headers** tab, and then, in **MIME types**, click **MIME Types**, and then click **New**.

3. Follow steps 3 and 4 in the preceding procedure.

Allowing All Extensions

In IIS 5.0, if a request fell through the static file handler, then IIS served the file, regardless of its extension. IIS 6.0 does not automatically serve file requests that fall through the static file handler. Although it is not generally recommended as a best security practice, you may want to allow all file extensions in some scenarios — for example, if you want to serve files that have ascending extensions such as .001, .002, and so on. If you want to serve all files, then you can add a wildcard character (*) to the MIME types list. Files that do not have extensions can be served only if the wildcard character is added to the list.

You can add a wildcard character using IIS Manager or programmatically, using the Adsutil.vbs command-line script.

▷ **To add a wildcard character through IIS Manager**

1. In IIS Manager, double-click the local computer, right-click the computer on which you want to add a MIME type, and then click **Properties**.

2. Click **MIME Types**, and then click **New**.

3. In the **Extension** box, type an asterisk.

4. In the **MIME type** box, type the following: **application/octet-stream**

5. Click **OK**.

To add a wildcard programmatically by using Adsutil.vbs, use the customizable text file provided in Listing 5.1.

 Important

You must be a member of the Administrators group on the local computer to run scripts and executables, or you must have been delegated the appropriate authority. As a security best practice, log on to your computer by using an account that is not in the Administrators group, and then use the **runas** command to run your script or executable as an administrator. At a command prompt, type **runas /profile** /*User.MyMachine\Administrator* **cmd** to open a command window with administrator rights and then type **cscript.exe** *ScriptName* (including the full path with parameters, if any).

Listing 5.1   Sample Script for Adding Wildcards

```
c:\inetpub\adminscripts\adsutil.vbs set /w3svc/MimeMap ".*,common/type"
Sample
' VBScript source code
Const ADS_PROPERTY_UPDATE = 2
Set MimeMapObj = GetObject("IIS://LocalHost/MimeMap")
aMimeMap = MimeMapObj.GetEx("MimeMap")
' Add a new mapping.
i = UBound(aMimeMap) + 1
Redim Preserve aMimeMap(i)
Set aMimeMap(i) = CreateObject("MimeMap")
aMimeMap(i).Extension = ".*"
aMimeMap(i).MimeType = "common/type"
MimeMapObj.PutEx ADS_PROPERTY_UPDATE, "MimeMap", aMimeMap
MimeMapObj.SetInfo
```

Multiple Worker Processes Affect ISAPI Filter Status Display

As a routine security practice, you should monitor the status of your ISAPI filters to ensure that they are functioning correctly. In IIS 6.0, you can use IIS Manager to check the ISAPI filter status. Because multiple worker processes are supported in IIS 6.0, be careful when you interpret the status as it is displayed. For example, if a red arrow appears, that indicates that the last ISAPI filter failed to load; it does not indicate that all of the ISAPI filters for all of the worker processes failed.

▷ **To check the ISAPI filter status**

1. In IIS Manager, right-click the Web site or virtual server on which the ISAPI filter is installed, and then click **Properties**.

2. Click the **ISAPI Filters** tab, and then, in the **Status** column, check the ISAPI filter status.

    A green arrow indicates that the last ISAPI filter installed correctly. A red arrow indicates that a filter failed the last time the worker process started.

ASP-Related Security Changes

There are several important changes to the way IIS interacts with ASP that improve security and reduce the attack surface of IIS.

ASP and ASP.NET Are Disabled by Default

In IIS 6.0, ASP and ASP.NET are disabled by default. If you want to serve ASP or ASP.NET content from IIS 6.0, then you must first enable ASP or ASP.NET in the Web Service Extensions node.

▷ **To enable ASP or ASP.NET**

1. In IIS Manager, double-click the local computer, and then click **Web Service Extensions**.

2. In the details pane, click **Active Server Pages** or **ASP.NET**, and then click **Allow**.

 Note

If your content requires ISAPI, CGI, WebDAV, or other extensions, then you will need to enable those extensions as well.

Parent Paths Are Disabled by Default

When parent paths are enabled, ASP pages allow you to include files with paths that are relative to the current directory (using the ..\ notation). This constitutes a potential security risk because a server-side include (SSI) path can provide access to critical or confidential files that are outside the root directory of the application. When parent paths are enabled, a Web server is more susceptible to *traversal attacks*, which allow a malicious user to execute commands or view data that is outside the intended target path.

In IIS 6.0, because parent paths are disabled by default, an existing application that has a Web page that contains the #include SSI directive and uses ..\ notation to refer to a parent directory will not work unless you enable parent paths. The parent paths correspond to the **AspEnableParentPaths** metabase property. For more information about SSI directives, see "Using Server-Side Include Directives" in IIS 6.0 Help, which is accessible from IIS Manager.

▷ **To enable parent paths**

1. In IIS Manager, double-click the local computer, right-click the starting-point directory of the application that you want to configure, and then click **Properties**.

2. Click the **Home Directory** tab, and then click **Configuration**.

3. Click the **Options** tab, and, in **Application configuration**, select the **Enable parent paths** check box, and then click **OK**.

Global.asa Events Are Run As Anonymous User

In earlier versions of IIS, ASP executes events in the security context (or user identity) of the host process because during ASP-executed events there is no user context. Global.asa executes events in earlier versions of IIS as follows:

Application_OnStart Impersonated user

Application_OnEnd Host identity

Session_OnStart Impersonated user

Session_OnEnd Host identity

In IIS 6.0, ASP executes the Global.asa events **Application_OnEnd** and **Session_OnEnd** anonymously by default. This change prevents user code from running as the base identity of the worker process. For example, if **Application_OnEnd** and **Session_OnEnd** run under the host identity context, and an Internet service provider (ISP) allows users to upload Global.asa files, a malicious user might be able to use the FileSystemObject to access files that are otherwise inaccessible in the anonymous context.

If you want to change this default setting, then you can do so by using the **AspRunOnEndAnonymously** metabase property. For more information about this setting, see the **AspRunOnEndAnonymously** property in the "Metabase Property Reference" of IIS 6.0 Help, which is accessible from IIS Manager.

Security-Related Changes in Authentication

IIS 6.0 introduces a number of changes to the way that user authentication functions. These changes include new default settings and requirements for different authentication methods.

Anonymous Password Synchronization is Disabled by Default

For security reasons, IIS 6.0 does not allow anonymous password synchronization by default. Anonymous password synchronization is accomplished with the IIS subauthentication component, Iissuba.dll, which is installed by default in earlier versions of IIS. The subauthentication component allows IIS to authenticate an anonymous user even if the password in the IIS metabase does not match the password in the Windows local account database. Because this involves a security risk, the subauthentication component is not installed by default in IIS 6.0. However, some administrators need to use anonymous password synchronization, in, for example, large ISP settings where thousands of anonymous IIS accounts are used to isolate Web sites. To enable anonymous password synchronization, make sure that your system meets the following requirements:

- The application pool of the Web site runs as the LocalSystem user account. However, running as the LocalSystem user account might be a security risk because it allows the worker process full access to the entire system.

- The subauthentication component, Iissuba.dll, must be registered.

- The **AnonymousPasswordSynch** metabase property must be enabled (set to TRUE).

To enable anonymous password synchronization

1. Install the subauthentication component by doing the following:

   a. From the **Start** menu, click **Run**.

   b. In the **Open** box, type **cmd**, and click **OK**.

   c. At the command prompt, type the following:

   rundll 32 %systemroot%\system32\iissuba.dll,RegisterIISSUBA

   d. Press ENTER.

2. Set the identity of the application pool to the LocalSystem user account. For step-by-step information about setting the application pool identity, see "Configuring Application Pool Identity" later in this chapter.

> **Important**
>
> Running as the LocalSystem user account might pose a security risk because it allows the worker process full access to the entire system.

3. Set the **AnonymousPasswordSynch** metabase property to TRUE.

When you no longer want to use subauthentication, revoke the subauthentication component's registration.

To revoke the subauthentication component's registration

1. From the **Start** menu, click **Run**.

2. In the **Open** box, type **cmd**, and click **OK**.

3. At the command prompt, type the following:

   rundll32 %systemroot%\system32\iissuba.dll,UnregisterIISSUBA

4. Press ENTER.

Advanced Digest Authentication Requires Windows Server 2003

To use Advanced Digest authentication, the domain infrastructure and the server running IIS must both be running Windows Server 2003. If you upgraded to IIS 6.0, the default digest authentication is Digest authentication. If you performed a clean installation of IIS 6.0, the default digest authentication is Advanced Digest authentication. For more information about Advanced Digest authentication, see "Advanced Digest Authentication" later in this chapter.

.NET Passport Authentication Requires LocalSystem User Account Rights

Microsoft .NET Passport authentication works only when the account that is used for the IIS worker process has *trusted computing base* (TCB) rights, which means that the account acts as part of the operating system. Only the LocalSystem user account has TCB rights by default. You can add TCB rights to an account by using the Local Security Settings snap-in. However, because a worker process running with TCB rights acts as part of the operating system, this account has a very high level of access, which presents a security risk.

Kerberos Authentication Requires SPNs for Multiple Worker Processes

You can isolate Web sites that are in different worker processes and running under different identities; however, unexpected IIS behavior might occur if you use Integrated Windows authentication. Integrated Windows authentication attempts to use Kerberos authentication, which might not work, depending upon the identity of the worker process. To use Kerberos authentication, a service must register its SPN in the account in the Microsoft Active Directory® directory service under which the service is running. By default, Active Directory registers the NetBIOS name or computer name and allows the Network Service or LocalSystem user accounts to use Kerberos. However, for Kerberos to work with the following configurations, you must first register an SPN:

- If your site is referenced by a Windows Internet Name Service (WINS) or Domain Name System (DNS) name that is different from the computer name of the server running IIS (a Web farm, for example), then authentication defaults to NTLM (which is also known as Microsoft Windows NT® Challenge/Response authentication).

- If you configure the worker process for the Web site to run as a domain account, and you did not use a WINS or DNS name, then authentication will fail. This is because the SPN can be found, but it is registered for the Network Service and LocalSystem user accounts, not for the domain account under which the worker process is running.

You can use the Setspn.exe command-line tool to register an SPN on the account under which the worker process is running. You must be a domain administrator to set an SPN. The Setspn.exe tool is included in Resource Kit Tools for Windows Server 2003, available on the *Windows Server 2003 Deployment Kit* companion CD, or on the Web at http://www.microsoft.com/reskit.

Using Setspn.exe

The following is the basic syntax for using Setspn.exe, where *AccountName* can be either the account name or *Domain\AccountName*.

```
setspn [-R ComputerName] [-A ComputerName] [-D ComputerName] [-L ComputerName]
[AccountName]
```

Table 5.1 lists the parameters that you can use with Setspn.exe.

Table 5.1   Setspn.exe Parameters

Parameter	Function
-R	Resets the HOST SPN.
-A	Adds an arbitrary SPN.
-D	Deletes an arbitrary SPN.
-L	Lists registered SPNs.

The following example uses Setspn.exe to register (add) an application pool running as Domain\UserAccount, where Host/<*your computer name*> refers to the name of the computer to which you want to add the SPN:

```
setspn -A Host/<your computer name> Domain\UserAccount
```

The following example resets SPNs HOST/Server1 and HOST/{DNS of Server1}:

```
setspn -R server1
```

The following example lists registered SPNs for computer Server1:

```
setspn -L server1
```

The following example deletes SPN http/Server from computer Server1:

```
setspn -D http/server server1
```

Forcing NTLM

When you isolate Web sites on a virtual directory level by configuring worker process identities as different domain accounts, Kerberos fails. If you are using Integrated Windows authentication, are not using a WINS or DNS name for the server running IIS, and you want to use a local user account or the Local Service user account as a worker process identity, Kerberos authentication fails because Active Directory does not trust the accounts.

To work around these issues, you can force IIS to use NTLM authentication by setting the **NTAuthenticationProviders** metabase property to NTLM.

Security-Related Changes in Access Control

IIS 6.0 improves security by changing access control requirements for executables and CGI processes. These changes can affect existing applications that might require less restrictive permissions.

Access Is Restricted for Executables

Windows Server 2003 requires a user to be a member of the Administrators group to run most command-line executables in the System folder, so remote access is limited to administrators. This might affect you if your application uses command-line tools from a Web page. To work around this issue, change the ACL for the executable by using an ACL editing tool, such as the **cacls** command. For more information about ACLs and ACL editing tools, see "Access Control" later in this chapter.

Access Is Restricted for Nondefault Identities for CGI Processes

IIS 6.0 worker processes use the CreateProcessAsUser API to start CGI processes. The CreateProcessAsUser API must have the SE_ASSIGNPRIMARYTOKEN_NAME and SE_INCREASE_QUOTA_NAME user rights to succeed. The Network Service, Local Service, and LocalSystem user accounts have these user rights. If you change the identity of a worker process and want to run CGI processes, then make sure that the new identity has these two user rights. You can assign user rights using the Local Security Settings snap-in in Windows Server 2003.

▷ **To assign user rights to an account on the local computer**

1. From the **Start** menu, point to **Administrative Tools**, and then click **Local Security Policy**.

2. In the **Local Security Settings** dialog box, double-click **Local Policies**, and then double-click **User Rights Assignment**.

3. In the details pane, double-click **Adjust memory quotas for a process**. This is the SE_INCREASE_QUOTA_NAME user right.

4. Click **Add User or Group**, and, in the **Enter the object names to select** box, type the user or group name to which you want to assign the user right, and then click **OK**.

5. Click **OK** again, and then, in the details pane, double-click **Replace a process level token**. This is the SE_ASSIGNPRIMARYTOKEN_NAME user right.

6. Click **Add User or Group**, and, in the **Enter the object names to select** box, type the user or group name to which you want to assign the user right, and then click **OK**.

Automatic Installation of Security Patches

As a security best practice, keep IIS up-to-date with the current security patches that Microsoft releases. With Windows Server 2003 Automatic Updates, you can install patches automatically so that your computer is updated with the most critical code, based on a schedule that you specify. You do not need to be logged on to the computer for the installation to occur. By minimizing the time that you spend logged on to your computer as a member of the Administrators group, your computer is less vulnerable to attack.

The only IIS patches that are available for scheduled automatic installation are critical security-related hotfixes. Because these hotfixes might require restarting the operating system , you can delay or change the time of the scheduled installation. You must be logged on as an administrator to change the scheduled installation time.

When an update is available for automatic installation, two events occur:

- At the scheduled installation time, the Priority 0 Critical security hotfix is installed.

- After the scheduled installation takes place, an event is logged notifying you that the hotfix has been installed successfully.

▷ **To schedule automatic updates**

1. From the **Start** menu, click **Control Panel**, and then click **System**.

2. Click the **Automatic Updates** tab, and, in **Settings**, click **Automatically download the updates, and install them on the schedule that I specify**, and then use the drop-down lists to set your schedule.

For more information about Windows Server 2003 Automatic Updates, see "Windows Automatic Updates" in Help and Support Center for Windows Server 2003.

 Note

The new request and memory processing model in IIS 6.0 includes process recycling, which makes it easier to install all patches, hotfixes, and updates. With process recycling, the administrator can install most patches and new worker process dynamic-link libraries (DLLs) without any interruption of service.

Authentication

IIS 6.0 supports multiple methods of authentication so that you can confirm the identity of everyone who requests access to your Web sites. For example, IIS 6.0 supports the following authentication methods:

- **Anonymous authentication.** This authentication method allows everyone access to your Web sites, without asking for a user name or password.

- **Basic authentication.** This authentication method prompts the user for a user name and a password, which are sent unencrypted over the network.

- **Digest authentication.** This authentication method operates much like Basic authentication, except that passwords are sent as a hash value. Digest authentication is available only on domains with domain controllers running Windows server operating systems.

- **Advanced Digest authentication.** This authentication method is identical to Digest authentication, except Advanced Digest authentication stores the client credentials as an MD5 hash in Active Directory on your domain controller running Windows Server 2003.

- **Integrated Windows authentication.** This authentication method uses hashing technology to identify your users. Credentials are not sent over the network.

- **UNC authentication.** This authentication method passes users' credentials through to the computer with the Universal Naming Convention (UNC) share.

- **.NET Passport Authentication.** This authentication method is a user-authentication service that lets Web site users create a single sign-in name and password for access to all .NET Passport–enabled Web sites and services. .NET Passport–enabled sites rely on the .NET Passport central server to authenticate users; .NET Passport–enabled sites do not host and maintain their own proprietary authentication systems.

You can use these authentication methods to grant access to public areas of your site while preventing unauthorized access to your private files and directories. Each authentication method is covered in detail in the following sections.

Anonymous Authentication

Anonymous authentication gives users access to the public areas of your Web or File Transfer Protocol (FTP) site without prompting the users for a user name or password. When a user attempts to connect to your public Web or FTP site, your Web server assigns the connection to the Windows user account that is specified for anonymous connections. By default, this account is named IUSR_*ComputerName*, where *ComputerName* is the name of the computer on which IIS is running, and it is included in the Windows user group, Guests. This group has security restrictions, imposed by NTFS file system permissions, which designate the level of access and the type of content that is available to public users.

 Important

Do not confuse the anonymous user context that Windows Server 2003 provides with the anonymous user account that IIS provides. The IIS anonymous user account is configurable; the default is IUSR_*ComputerName.* The operating system also provides a notion of anonymous access across the network.

When you use Anonymous authentication, the IUSR_*ComputerName* account is added to the Guests group on the computer running IIS during setup. When IIS receives a request, it impersonates the IUSR_*ComputerName* account before executing any code. IIS can impersonate the IUSR_*ComputerName* account because it recognizes the user name and password for this account. Before returning a page to the client, IIS checks NTFS and directory permissions to see whether the IUSR_*ComputerName* account is allowed access to the file. If access is allowed, the access process, which is also called authorization, completes, and the resources are made available to the user. If access is not allowed, IIS returns a 401.3 error message to the browser.

You can change the account that is used for Anonymous authentication in IIS Manager, either at the Web server service level or for individual virtual directories and files. However, when you change the IUSR_*ComputerName* account, the changes affect every anonymous HTTP request that a Web server services, so use caution if you modify this account.

In IIS 6.0, NETWORK_CLEARTEXT is the default logon type for Anonymous authentication. As a result, Anonymous authentication no longer requires the Allow log on locally user right. More information about the NETWORK_CLEARTEXT logon type is provided in the next section.

Basic Authentication

The Basic authentication method is a widely used industry-standard method for collecting user name and password information. When you use Basic authentication, the browser displays a dialog box into which users are required to enter a previously assigned Windows account user name and password, which are also known as *credentials*. The browser then attempts to establish a connection to a server using the user's credentials. The plaintext password is Base64-encoded before it is sent over the network.

Note that Base64 encoding is not encryption. If a Base64-encoded password is intercepted over the network by a network sniffer, unauthorized users can easily decode and reuse the password. Therefore, Basic authentication is not recommended unless you are confident that the connection between the user and your Web server has been secured, such as with a dedicated line or an SSL connection. For more information about SSL, see "SSL and Certificates" later in this chapter.

If a user's credentials do not correspond to a valid Windows user account, then Internet Explorer displays a dialog box into which the user re-enters his or her credentials. Internet Explorer — not IIS — allows the user three connection attempts before it terminates the connection and reports an error to the user. If a user's credentials correspond to a valid Windows user account, then a connection is established.

Basic authentication does not automatically configure your Web server to authenticate users; to require authentication, you must also disable anonymous access. As a best security practice, you should create Windows user accounts with NTFS permissions properly set. For step-by-step instructions for configuring Basic authentication, see "Basic Authentication" in IIS 6.0 Help, which is accessible from IIS Manager.

Logon Types

In IIS 6.0, the default logon type for Basic authentication (and Anonymous authentication) is NETWORK_CLEARTEXT. This is a change from earlier versions of IIS, in which the default logon type is INTERACTIVE. As a result of this change, when you use the default logon type for Basic authentication, users no longer need interactive logon rights. Basic authentication works with domain controllers, and the NETWORK and NETWORK_CLEARTEXT settings no longer require logon rights. Table 5.2 lists the logon types that are available for Basic authentication and Anonymous authentication.

Table 5.2 Logon Types for Basic Authentication and Anonymous Authentication

Logon Type	LogonMethod Setting	Logon Right Required	Security Identifier (SID) Added to Access Token	Outbound Credentials
NETWORK_ CLEARTEXT (default)	3 - MD_LOGON_NETWORK_ CLEARTEXT	Network	NT AUTHORITY\NETWORK_ CLEARTEXT	Yes
NETWORK	2 - MD_LOGON_NETWORK	Network	NT AUTHORITY\NETWORK	No
BATCH	1 - MD_LOGON_BATCH	Batch	NT AUTHORITY\BATCH	Yes
Interactive	0 - MD_LOGON_INTERACTIVE	Interactive	NT AUTHORITY\INTERACTIVE	Yes

For more information, see the **LogonMethod** property in the "Metabase Property Reference" of IIS 6.0 Help, which is accessible from IIS Manager.

Token Cache Security Considerations

When you use Basic authentication, user tokens are cached in the token cache. By default, tokens remain in the cache for 15 minutes. If you want to change the amount of time that tokens remain in the cache, then complete either of the following steps:

- Disable user token caching by setting the global registry entry, **UserTokenTTL,** to zero (0).

 Caution

Do not edit the registry unless you have no alternative. The registry editor bypasses standard safeguards, allowing settings that can damage your system, or even require you to reinstall Windows. If you must edit the registry, back it up first and see the Registry Reference on the *Microsoft Windows Server 2003 Deployment Kit* companion CD or on the Web at http://www.microsoft.com/reskit.

- Change the **UserTokenTTL** metabase property to less than the default of 15 minutes. Note that time is expressed in seconds for this metabase property. For more information about the **UserTokenTTL** property, see "Global Registry Entries" in IIS 6.0 Help, which is accessible from IIS Manager.

 Important

If you use Basic authentication and disable the token cache, IIS must log on for every request made — potentially thousands for a requested Web page. This will have a negative effect on performance.

Digest Authentication

Digest authentication offers the same functionality as Basic authentication; however, Digest authentication provides a security improvement because a user's credentials are not sent across the network in plaintext. Digest authentication sends credentials across the network as a Message Digest 5 (MD5) hash, which is also known as the MD5 message digest, in which the credentials cannot be deciphered from the hash.

If you have an earlier version of IIS with Digest authentication enabled and you upgrade to IIS 6.0, Digest authentication remains the default authentication method. In all other instances, you must enable Digest authentication.

Requirements for Digest Authentication

You not need to install additional client software to use Digest authentication, but Digest authentication relies on the HTTP 1.1 protocol, as defined in the RFC 2617 specification at the World Wide Web Consortium Web site, and not all browsers support that protocol. If a non–HTTP 1.1–compliant browser requests a file from a server that uses Digest authentication, the server requests that the client provide Digest authentication credentials. The non–HTTP 1.1–compliant browser rejects the request because the client cannot support Digest authentication.

You do need to meet the following minimum requirements before you enable Digest authentication on your IIS server:

- All of the clients that need access to a resource that is secured with Digest authentication are using Internet Explorer 5.*x* or Internet Explorer 6.

- The user and the server running IIS are members of, or are trusted by, the same domain.

- Users have a valid Windows user account that is stored in Active Directory on the domain controller, with reversible encryption enabled.

- The domain has a domain controller running the Microsoft® Windows® 2000 Server operating system or Windows Server 2003.

 Important

If the authenticating domain controller is on a computer running Windows 2000 Server, IIS 6.0 requires subauthentication for Digest authentication to work. For more information about subauthentication, see "What's Changed" earlier in this chapter.

- The server running IIS is running Windows 2000 Server or Windows Server 2003.

- If the server operates in worker process isolation mode, the LocalSystem user account is used as the identity.

- The Iissuba.dll file is registered on the server running IIS.

 Note

Only domain administrators can verify that the domain controller requirements are met. Check with your domain administrator if you are unsure about whether your domain controller meets the preceding requirements.

For step-by-step instructions for configuring Digest authentication, see "Digest Authentication" in IIS 6.0 Help, which is accessible from IIS Manager.

Advanced Digest Authentication

When Advanced Digest authentication is enabled, user credentials are stored on the domain controller as an MD5 hash. Advanced Digest authentication does not require that credentials are stored using reversible encryption. Instead, Advanced Digest authentication stores a few precalculated hashes in Active Directory, so user passwords cannot feasibly be discovered by anyone with access to the domain controller, including the domain administrator.

When you perform a clean installation of IIS 6.0, Advanced Digest authentication is enabled as the default authentication method, and it is recommended over Digest authentication because passwords are not stored in plaintext on the domain controller.

Requirements for Advanced Digest Authentication

As with Digest authentication, you do not need to install additional client software to use Advanced Digest authentication. Because Advanced Digest authentication relies on the HTTP 1.1 protocol as defined in the RFC 2617 specification at the World Wide Web Consortium Web site, your browsers should be HTTP 1.1 compliant.

Advanced Digest authentication, like Digest authentication, will not work unless the following minimum requirements are met:

- All of the clients that need access to a resource that is secured with Advanced Digest authentication are using Internet Explorer 5 or Internet Explorer 6.

- The user and the server running IIS are members of the same domain, or the user is a member of a trusted domain.

- Users have a valid Windows user account that is stored in Active Directory on the domain controller.

- The domain controller and the server running IIS are both running Windows Server 2003. If either your domain controller or the server running IIS is running Windows 2000 Server or earlier, IIS defaults to Digest authentication and does not notify you of this action.

Note

Only domain administrators can verify that the domain controller requirements are met. Check with your domain administrator if you are unsure about whether your domain controller meets these requirements.

Advanced Digest authentication uses the **UseDigestSSP** property to switch between Digest and Advanced Digest security support provider interface (SSPI) code. If this property is set to false, Digest authentication is used. In all other cases (true, empty, or not set), IIS uses Advanced Digest authentication.

Important

If you use Digest authentication and select worker process isolation mode, you must use the LocalSystem user account as the application pool identity.

Integrated Windows Authentication

With Integrated Windows authentication (formerly called NTLM, and also known as Windows NT Challenge/Response authentication), the user name and password (credentials) are hashed before they are sent across the network. When you enable Integrated Windows authentication, the client browser proves its knowledge of the password through a cryptographic exchange with your Web server, involving hashing.

In Windows Server 2003, Integrated Windows authentication is the default authentication method.

Integrated Windows authentication uses Kerberos v5 authentication and NTLM authentication. Kerberos is an industry-standard authentication protocol that is used to verify user or host identity. If Active Directory is installed on a domain controller running Windows 2000 Server or Windows Server 2003, and the client browser supports the Kerberos v5 authentication protocol, Kerberos v5 authentication is used; otherwise, NTLM authentication is used.

Integrated Windows authentication includes the Negotiate wrapper, which supports Kerberos v5 and NTLM. Negotiate allows the client application to select the best security support provider for the situation. Kerberos v5 and NTLM have the following restrictions:

- NTLM can get past a firewall, but it is generally stopped by proxies because NTLM is connection-based, and proxies do not necessarily keep connections established.

- Kerberos v5 requires that the client has a direct connection to Active Directory, which is generally not the case in Internet scenarios.

- Kerberos v5 requires that both the client and the server have a trusted connection to a Key Distribution Center (KDC) and be Active Directory–compatible.

- Kerberos v5 requires SPNs for multiple worker processes. If your Web site uses multiple worker processes, you can use Kerberos authentication, but you must manually register service names. More information about Kerberos and service registration is provided later in this section.

Integrated Windows authentication has the following limitations:

- Integrated Windows authentication is supported by only Internet Explorer 2 and later.

- Integrated Windows authentication does not work over HTTP proxy connections.

Therefore, Integrated Windows authentication is best suited for an intranet environment, where both user and Web server computers are in the same domain and where administrators can ensure that every user has Internet Explorer 2 or later.

Client Authentication Process

Unlike Basic authentication, Integrated Windows authentication does not initially prompt for a user name and password. The current Windows user information on the client is used for Integrated Windows authentication. If the authentication exchange initially fails to authorize the user, then Internet Explorer prompts the user for a Windows account user name and password, which it processes using Integrated Windows authentication. Internet Explorer prompts the user for the correct user name and password up to three times.

Kerberos and Service Registration

Kerberos employs the concept of services. If a service wants to leverage Kerberos, the service needs to register its SPN in Active Directory. The NetBIOS name of the server is registered in Active Directory. If the SPN uses a different name, then the registration has to be performed manually. You can accomplish this using Setspn.exe. A service is also registered under a particular account if the account changes. For example, if you run the application pool under a different identity, you must also use Setspn.exe. You must be a domain administrator to use Setspn.exe.

Before the Kerberos authentication service can authenticate a service, the service must be registered on only one account object. If the logon account of a service instance changes, the service must be reregistered under the new account. Therefore, only one application pool that has the service registered can authenticate with Kerberos. As a result, you cannot isolate sites from one another on the virtual directory level in an application pool. For more information about this limitation and using Setspn.exe, see "Security-Related Changes in Authentication" earlier in this chapter.

UNC Authentication

The UNC authentication method, which is also known as UNC Passthrough authentication, determines the credentials to use for gaining access to a UNC share on a remote computer. If you use IIS Manager to create a Web site or virtual directory and you specify a UNC path for the content, then IIS Manager prompts you to type a user name and a password for the network resource. If you specify a user name and password, the **UNCUserName** and **UNCPassword** metabase properties are set. In IIS 6.0, UNC authentication works by looking at the requesting user and the credentials that are stored in the **UNCUserName** and **UNCPassword** properties of the metabase to determine the credentials to pass through to the computer with the UNC share.

If **UNCUserName** is specified (not empty) and **UNCPassword** is valid, then the metabase user credentials are sent as the user identity for access to the remote share. If **UNCUserName** is specified (not empty) and **UNCPassword** is not valid, then a 500 "Internal Server Error: Invalid Username or Password" message is sent to the client. If **UNCUserName** is empty, then the credentials of the request user, which can be either an authenticated set of credentials for authenticated requests or IUSR_*ComputerName* credentials for anonymous requests, are sent as the user identity for access to the remote share.

> **Note**
>
> The UNCAuthenticationPassthrough metabase property is no longer used for UNC authentication.

Constrained Delegation

Delegation is the act of allowing a service to impersonate a user account or computer account in order to access resources throughout the network. When a service is trusted for delegation, that service can impersonate a user to use other network services. *Constrained delegation* is a new option for Windows Server 2003 that allows you to specify the SPNs to which an account can delegate. A service can be trusted for delegation, but the domain administrator can limit that trust to a select group of explicitly specified services. By allowing delegation only to specific services, you can control the specific network resources the service or computer can use.

Figure 5.1 shows how constrained delegation works in a simple configuration.

Figure 5.1 Constrained Delegation

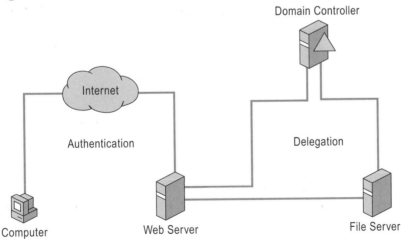

Deciding Whether to Use Constrained Delegation

Constrained delegation is best implemented in a Windows Server 2003 domain. Although you can use constrained delegation in a Windows 2000 Server mixed domain, there are significant limitations. In a Windows 2000 Server mixed domain, constrained delegation works only for users that are authenticated using Basic or Kerberos authentication. In addition, you cannot restrict delegation to a specific set of services on a computer running Windows 2000 Server, which makes it difficult to implement this feature and reduce the attack surface of your server.

Constrained delegation is particularly useful in scenarios in which a site that requires authentication — a site that does not allow anonymous access — contains content that is housed on a remote UNC file server. With constrained delegation, you can enable Integrated Windows authentication, which can use NTLM authentication or send credentials across the network as a Kerberos token. For more information about Integrated Windows authentication, see "Integrated Windows Authentication" earlier in this chapter.

If you do not use constrained delegation but you enable Integrated Windows authentication, the token that the Web server obtains from the security infrastructure of Windows does not have sufficient permissions to access another computer, such as your file server. However, with constrained delegation and Integrated Windows authentication, the token received by the Web server from the security infrastructure of Windows is a Kerberos-based token with permission to access other computers, including the file server. Essentially, constrained delegation allows an NTLM-based token to be upgraded to a Kerberos-based token.

If you use Basic authentication, you probably do not need constrained delegation because the tokens achieved by Basic authentication have sufficient permissions to access other computers in the domain, including the file server. However, in some situations you do not need to allow clients to authenticate with Integrated Windows authentication, but you might need constrained delegation. For example, you might have applications that need to access a file server using computer accounts, such as an enterprise intranet application that impersonates the client to gain access to information on various servers in the enterprise and then presents the consolidated data to the client over HTTP.

If you are running IIS 6.0 in IIS 5.0 isolation mode and you have an out-of-process application, this process normally runs as the local IWAM account, which prevents constrained delegation from working properly. One example of an application that might fail to perform as expected in this scenario is an ASP application that accesses a remote computer running Microsoft® SQL Server™ on which you intend for the authenticated user's credentials to be used. To fix this, switch IIS to run in worker process isolation mode.

Configuring Constrained Delegation for IIS

You can configure your server to allow clients to authenticate using any authentication protocol, and IIS will access content on the file server on behalf of the authenticated clients.

 Important

You must be a domain administrator to perform the following procedure.

▷ **To configure constrained delegation for IIS**

1. From the **Start** menu, point to **Administrative Tools**, and then click **Active Directory Users and Computers**.

2. In the **Active Directory Users and Computers** dialog box, ensure that your domain is in the **Windows Server 2003** mode by doing the following:

   a. In the left pane, click your domain name.

   b. From the **Action** menu, select **Raise Domain Functional Level**.

   c. In the **Raise Domain Functional Level** dialog box, if your domain is in Windows 2000 native or Windows 2000 mixed mode, click **Windows Server 2003** from the **Select an available domain functional level** list box, and then click **Raise**.

    Important

   After you change your domain level, you cannot reverse the action. The change can take up to 15 minutes to propagate. For more information about domain functional levels, see "Domain and forest functionality" in Help and Support Center for Windows Server 2003.

3. In each of the two **Raise Domain Functional Level** dialog boxes that appear, click **OK**.

4. Double-click the domain, and then click the **Computers** folder. A list of computers in the domain appears in the right pane.

5. Right-click the Web server computer name, and then select **Properties**.

6. Click the **Delegation** tab, and then select the **Trust this computer for delegation to specified services only** check box.

7. Click the authentication type that you want to use, and then click **Add**.

8. **In the Add Services** dialog box, click **Users or Computers**.

9. In the **Select Users or Computers** dialog box, in the **Enter the object names to select** text box, search for or type the name of the file server that you want to use, and then click **OK**.

10. In the **Properties** dialog box, click **Add** to add the HOST and CIFS services for the target file server. Add only the services that you are sure need to present delegated credentials, and then click **OK**.

.NET Passport Authentication

Microsoft .NET Passport is a user-authentication service and a component of the Microsoft .NET Framework. The .NET Passport single sign-in service and express purchase service enable organizations to deliver a fast and convenient way for consumers to sign in and make transactions on a Web site. With the .NET Passport single sign-in service, you can map sign-in names to information in your databases, which enables you to offer .NET Passport members a personal Web experience through targeted content, advertisements, and promotions. The .NET Passport single sign-in service is similar to the forms-based authentication model that is commonly used on the Web today. The .NET Passport network extends this model to work across a distributed set of participating sites while helping to preserve the privacy and security of its members. In addition, organizations can customize and brand the sign-in experience.

Microsoft .NET Passport uses standard Web technologies, such as SSL, HTTP redirects, cookies, Microsoft® JScript® development software, and strong symmetric key encryption to deliver the single sign-in service. In addition, .NET Passport is compatible with Internet Explorer 4 and later, Netscape Navigator version 4.0 and later, and some versions of UNIX.

.NET Passport–enabled sites rely on the .NET Passport central server to authenticate users. However, the .NET Passport central server does not authorize or deny the access of a user to individual .NET Passport–enabled sites. It is the responsibility of the Web site to control user access rights.

After .NET Passport authentication is verified, a Windows Server 2003 Passport user can be mapped to a user of Active Directory through the user's Windows Server 2003 Passport identification, if such a mapping exists. A token is created by the Local Security Authority (LSA) for the user, and is set by IIS for the HTTP request. Application developers and Web site administrators can use this security model for authorization based on users of Active Directory. You can also delegate these credentials through the constrained delegation feature supported by Windows Server 2003. For more information about constrained delegation, see "Constrained Delegation" earlier in this chapter.

Users can register at a .NET Passport–enabled site, and their user information is then stored in encrypted profiles on .NET Passport servers. When .NET Passport users register at a participating site, their personal information can be shared with the site to speed up the registration process. When the .NET Passport users sign in to that site again, their .NET Passport profiles can enable access to personalized accounts or services on that site.

For more information about .NET Passport authorization, see the Microsoft .NET Passport link on the Web Resources page at http://www.microsoft.com/windows/reskits/webresources.

Access Control

You can control which users and computers can access your Web server and its resources. There are two main types of access control: NTFS permissions, which are controlled by the operating system, and Web site permissions, which are controlled by IIS. To help secure your Web server, you should use a defense-in-depth strategy, combining proper authentication methods with tools such as firewalls and the appropriate NTFS permissions and Web site permissions. IIS built-in accounts and features, such as URL authorization, help you control access to resources on multiple levels, from entire Web and FTP sites to individual files or specific URLs.

How Access Control Works

Access control involves both user rights and permissions. *User rights* are rights that allow a user to perform specific actions on a computer or network. *Permissions* are rules that are associated with an object, such as a file or folder, to regulate which accounts can gain access to that object. After you configure your Windows file system and Web server security features, when a user attempts to access your Web server, the server carries out several access-control processes to identify the user and determine the allowed level of access.

Figure 5.2 shows how the access-control process works.

Figure 5.2   Access-Control Process

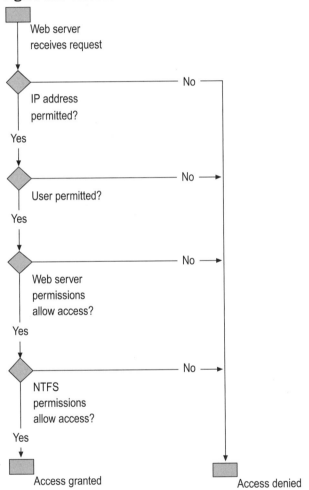

The following steps outline the access-control process:

1. The client requests a resource on the server.

2. The IP address of the client is checked against any IP address restrictions in IIS. If the IP address is denied access, the request fails, and a "403 Access Forbidden" message is returned to the user.

3. The server, if configured to require it, requests authentication information from the client. The browser either prompts the user for a user name and password or offers this information automatically.

4. IIS checks whether the user has a valid Windows user account. If the user does not, the request fails, and a "401 Access is denied" message is returned to the user.

5. IIS checks whether the user has Web permissions for the requested resource. If the user does not, then the request fails, and a "403 Access Forbidden" message is returned to the user.

6. Any security modules, such as ASP.NET impersonation, are added.

7. IIS checks the NTFS permissions on static files, ASP, and Common CGI files for the resource. If the user does not have NTFS permissions for the resource, then the request fails, and a "401 Access is denied" message is returned to the user.

8. If the user has NTFS permissions, the request is fulfilled.

NTFS Permissions

With NTFS access permissions as the foundation of your Web server's security, you can define the level of file and directory access that is granted to Windows users and groups. For example, if a business decides to publish its catalog on your Web server, you need to create a Windows user account for that business and then assign permissions for the specific Web site, directory, or file. The permissions should permit only the server administrator and the owner of the business to update the contents of the Web site. Public users should be allowed to view the Web site, but not to alter its contents. To control access to directories and files in this manner, you must be using drives formatted in NTFS, not FAT32. Using FAT32 is strongly discouraged because it allows users access to every file on your hard drive, which is a serious security risk. For more details about setting NTFS permissions, see "Setting NTFS Permissions for Directories or Files" in IIS 6.0 Help, which is accessible from IIS Manager.

Access Control Lists

NTFS permissions are set and managed using ACLs. An *ACL* is a list that indicates which users or groups are able to access or modify a particular file. An ACL is made up of access control entries (ACEs).

ACL Tools

Many tools, such as the **cacls** command and the Xcacls.exe command-line tool, are available to help you set and manage ACLs.

Cacls

Cacls is a Windows Server 2003 command that allows you to display or modify discretionary access control lists (DACLs). For more information about the **cacls** command, see "Cacls" in Help and Support Center for Windows Server 2003.

Xcacls.exe

Xcacls.exe is a Windows Server 2003 command-line tool that you can use to set all file-system security options that are accessible in Windows Explorer from the command line. Xcacls.exe does this by displaying and modifying the ACLs of files. For more information about Xcacls.exe, including where to download it, see the Xcacls.exe link on the Web Resources page at http://www.microsoft.com/windows/reskits/webresources.

IIS Default ACLs

When you install IIS, some ACLs are set automatically. Table 5.3 lists the ACLs that are set by default for the IIS_WPG group.

Table 5.3   IIS Default ACLs

IIS Component	NTFS Permission
\INETPUB\WWWROOT	Read & Execute (Applies to any Web content, not just WWWROOT [default Web site content])
\WINDOWS\HELP\IISHELP\COMMON	Read & Execute (Applies to error messages)
\WINDOWS\IIS TEMPORARY COMPRESSED FILES	Full Control (Applies to the default location of compressed files)
\WINDOWS\MICROSOFT.NET\FRAMWORK\V1.0.3705	Read & Execute (Applies to the current .NET Framework)
\WINDOWS\MICROSOFT.NET\FRAMWORK\V1.0.3705\TEMPORARY ASP.NET FILES	Full Control (Applies to the current .NET Framework)
\WINDOWS\SYSTEM32\INETSRV\ASP COMPILED TEMPLATES	Full Control (Applies to the default location of cached ASP pages)
\WINDOWS\SYSTEM32\MICROSOFTPASSPORT	Special Permissions — no Change, no Take Ownership (Applies to the location of the .NET Passport account)

(continued)

Table 5.3   IIS Default ACLs *(continued)*

IIS Component	NTFS Permission
\WINDOWS\TEMP	Full Control (Applies to the default TEMP directory)
Metabase Settings	**Permissions**
IIS://localhost/W3SVC	Read
Unsecured properties	Read, Enumerate
Registry Keys	**Permissions**
HKEY_LOCAL_MACHINE\SOFTWARE\Microsoft\Passport	Read (QENR)
HKEY_LOCAL_MACHINE\SYSTEM\CurrentControlSet\Services\ASP	Read (QENR)
HKEY_LOCAL_MACHINE\SYSTEM\CurrentControlSet\Services\ASP.NET_ 1.1.4322\Names	QSCEN R
HKEY_LOCAL_MACHINE\SYSTEM\CurrentControlSet\Services\HTTP	Read (QENR)
HKEY_LOCAL_MACHINE\SYSTEM\CurrentControlSet\Services\InetInfo	Read (QENR)
HKEY_LOCAL_MACHINE\SYSTEM\CurrentControlSet\Services\W3SVC	Read (QENR)

In addition, IIS sets restrictive ACLs on log files. For more information about log file permissions, see "Analyzing Log Files" in this book.

Metabase ACLs

IIS installs the metabase files with strict ACLs set to prevent anyone but administrators from viewing your configuration data. You can use the MetaACL.vbs command-line tool to change the ACLs and grant granular permissions on a site-by-site or application-by-application basis. For more information about MetaACL.vbs, see the MetaACL.exe Sample link on the Web Resources page at http://www.microsoft.com/windows/reskits/webresources. For more information about metabase security, see "Working with the Metabase" in this book.

 Important

Before you edit the metabase, verify that you have a backup copy that you can restore if a problem occurs. For information about how to do this, see "Working with the Metabase" in this book.

Web Site Permissions

When configuring access control for your servers, it is important to understand the distinction between Web site permissions and NTFS permissions. Unlike NTFS permissions, Web site permissions apply to all of the users that access your Web sites. NTFS permissions apply only to a specific user or group of users with a valid Windows account. NTFS permissions control access to physical directories on your server, whereas Web site permissions control access to virtual directories on your Web site. For example, you can use Web site permissions to control whether users visiting your Web site are allowed to view a particular page, upload information, or run scripts on the site.

 Note

If Web site permissions conflict with NTFS permissions for a directory or file, the more restrictive settings are applied.

The following Web site permissions are supported by IIS 6.0:

- **Read.** Users can view file content and properties. This permission is set by default.

- **Write.** Users can change content and properties of directories or files

 Important

Allowing users to have Read and Write access to source code can compromise the security of your server.

- **Script source access.** Users can access the source code for files, such as the scripts in an ASP application. This option is available only if Read or Write permissions are assigned. If the Read permission is assigned, then users can view the source code. If the Write permission is assigned, then users can view and modify the source code.

- **Directory browsing.** Users can view file lists and collections.

- **Log visits.** A log entry is created for each visit to the Web site.

- **Index this resource.** Allows Indexing Service to index this resource.

Whereas Web site permissions control whether users can access sites, code, or pages, another set of permissions, which are known as *Execute permissions*, control whether scripts and other executables can be run.

The following Execute permissions are supported by IIS 6.0:

- **None.** Prevents all scripts and executables from running.

- **Scripts only.** Enables applications that are mapped to a script engine to run in this directory, even if the applications are not assigned permissions for executables.

- **Scripts and Executables.** Enables any application to run in this directory, including applications that are mapped to script engines and Windows binaries (.dll and .exe files).

The Scripts only permission is more secure than the Scripts and Executables permission because the Scripts only permission allows you to limit the applications that can be run in the directory. For information about how to configure Web site permissions, see "Securing Sites with Web Site Permissions" in IIS 6.0 Help, which is accessible from IIS Manager.

IIS and Built-in Accounts

IIS uses a number of built-in Windows accounts, as well as accounts that are specific to IIS. For security reasons, you should be aware of the different accounts and their default user rights. It can be a security risk to change the identity of a worker process so that it runs as an account with a high level of access, such as the LocalSystem user account.

LocalSystem

The built-in LocalSystem user account has a high level of access rights; it is part of the Administrators group. If a worker process identity runs as the LocalSystem user account, then that worker process has full access to the entire system. LocalSystem has one default user right, Full access.

Network Service

The built-in Network Service user account has fewer access rights on the system than the LocalSystem user account, but the Network Service user account is still able to interact throughout the network with the credentials of the computer account. For IIS 6.0, it is recommended that the worker process identity that is defined for application pools runs as the Network Service user account, which is the default setting. Network Service has the following default user rights:

- Replace a process-level token (SeAssignPrimaryTokenPrivilege)

- Adjust memory quotas for a process (SeIncreaseQuotaPrivilege)

- Generate security audits (SeAuditPrivilege)

- Bypass traverse checking (SeChangeNotifyPrivilege)

- Access this computer from a network (SeNetworkLogonRight)

- Log on as a batch job (SeBatchLogonRight)

- Log on as a service (SeInteractiveLogonRight)

- Allow log on locally (SeInteractiveLogonRight)

Local Service

The built-in Local Service user account has the same access rights on the computer as the Network Service user account, but the user rights are limited to the local computer. Use the Local Service user account if the worker process does not require access outside the server on which it is running. Local Service has the following default user rights:

- Replace a process-level token (SeAssignPrimaryTokenPrivilege)
- Adjust memory quotas for a process (SeIncreaseQuotaPrivilege)
- Generate security audits (SeAuditPrivilege)
- Bypass traverse checking (SeChangeNotifyPrivilege)
- Access this computer from a network (SeNetworkLogonRight)
- Log on as a batch job (SeBatchLogonRight)

IIS_WPG

The IIS IIS_WPG group account has the minimum permissions and user rights that are necessary to start up and run a worker process on a Web server. IIS_WPG has the following default user rights:

- Bypass traverse checking (SeChangeNotifyPrivilege)
- Log on as a batch job (SeBatchLogonRight)
- Access this computer from a network (SeNetworkLogonRight)

IUSR_*ComputerName*

The IIS IUSR_*ComputerName* user account is for anonymous access to IIS. By default, when a user accesses a Web site that uses Anonymous authentication, that user is mapped to the IUSR_*ComputerName* account. IUSR_*ComputerName* has the following default user rights:

- Access this computer from a network (SeNetworkLogonRight)
- Bypass traverse checking (SeChangeNotifyPrivilege)
- Log on as a batch job (SeBatchLogonRight)
- Allow log on locally (SeInteractiveLogonRight)

IWAM_*ComputerName*

The IIS IWAM_*ComputerName* user account is for starting out-of-process applications in IIS 5.0 isolation mode. IWAM_*ComputerName* has the following default user rights:

- Replace a process-level token (SeAssignPrimaryTokenPrivilege)
- Adjust memory quotas for a process (SeIncreaseQuotaPrivilege)
- Bypass traverse checking (SeChangeNotifyPrivilege)
- Access this computer from a network (SeNetworkLogonRight)
- Log on as a batch job (SeBatchLogonRight)

ASPNET

The built-in ASPNET user account is for running the ASP.NET worker process in IIS 5.0 isolation mode. ASPNET has the following default user rights:

- Access this computer from a network (SeNetworkLogonRight)

- Log on as a batch job (SeBatchLogonRight)

- Log on as a service(SeInteractiveLogonRight)

- Deny logon locally (SeDenyInteractiveLogonRight)

- Deny logon through Terminal Services (SeDenyRemoteInteractiveLogonRight)

Configuring Application Pool Identity

The identity of an application pool is the name of the account under which the worker process of the application pool runs. By default, application pools run under the Network Service user account, which has low-level user access rights, so it provides better security against attackers or malicious users who might attempt to take over the computer on which the WWW service is running.

 Important

This feature of IIS 6.0 is available only when IIS is running in worker process isolation mode.

The Local Service user account also has low-level access rights, and you might want to configure application pools to run as the Local Service user account in situations that do not require access to resources on remote computers. You can configure application pools to run as the LocalSystem user account, which has more user rights than the Network Service or Local Service user account. However, running an application pool under an account with increased user rights presents a high security risk.

For example, suppose an ISP wants to allow customers to upload CGI applications and then add them to an application pool. You can run CGI-enabled applications in a separate application pool under the Network Service user account, which has lower user rights, to reduce the risk that these applications will be used to attack the server.

 Important

You must be a member of the Administrators group on the local computer to perform the following procedure or procedures, or you must have been delegated the appropriate authority. As a security best practice, log on to your computer by using an account that is not in the Administrators group, and then use the **runas** command to run IIS Manager as an administrator. At a command prompt, type runas */User:Administrative_AccountName* "mmc %systemroot%\system32\inetsrv\iis.msc".

▷ **To change the account under which an application pool runs**

1. In IIS Manager, double-click the local computer, double-click **Application Pools**, right-click the application pool, and then click **Properties**.

2. Click the **Identity** tab, and then do one of the following:

   - To change the account to a standard user account name, such as the Network Service (the default), LocalSystem, or Local Service user accounts, click **Predefined**, click a predefined account in the list box, and then click **OK**.

   - To change the account to a registered user name, click **Configurable**, and then, in the **User name** and **Password** boxes, type the user name and password of the account under which you want the worker process to operate, and then click **OK**. Then you must add the user to the IIS_WPG group. For more information about adding users to groups, see "Add a member to a local group" in Help and Support Center for Windows Server 2003.

You can change the worker process identity programmatically by using the Microsoft® Visual Basic® Scripting Edition (VBScript) development system sample script provided in Listing 5.2. Listing 5.2 provides a customizable VBScript-based file that creates an application that runs in an application pool under the supplied identity. Then the script starts Task Manager to show the worker process, and it attempts to access the newly created application using Internet Explorer. When the script is complete, you should see, in Task Manager, a new worker process that serves the request and that runs under the supplied identity.

 Important

You must be a member of the Administrators group on the local computer to run scripts and executables, or you must have been delegated the appropriate authority. As a security best practice, log on to your computer by using an account that is not in the Administrators group, and then use the **runas** command to run your script or executable as an administrator. At a command prompt, type **runas /profile** /*User*.*MyMachine\Administrator* **cmd** to open a command window with administrator rights and then type **cscript.exe** *ScriptName* (including the full path with parameters, if any).

Listing 5.2   Sample Script for Configuring Worker Process Identity

```
' VBScript source code
option explicit

if WScript.Arguments.Count < 4 OR WScript.Arguments.Count > 5 then
   WScript.Echo "Usage:"
   WScript.Echo WScript.ScriptFullName & " username password AppPoolName
vdirname <physical path for vdir>"
   WScript.Quit
end if
dim basepath          :    basepath = "IIS://localhost/w3svc/1/root"
dim username          :    username = WScript.Arguments(0)
dim password          :    password = WScript.Arguments(1)
dim AppPoolName       :    AppPoolName = WScript.Arguments(2)
dim vdirname          :    vdirname = WScript.Arguments(3)
dim VDirPhysicalPath

if WScript.Arguments.Count < 5 then
   VDirPhysicalPath = "c:\inetpub\wwwroot"
else
   VDirPhysicalPath = WScript.Arguments(4)
end if

if CreateNewUser(username, password) = false then
   WScript.Echo "Error creating user " & username & ". "
   WScript.Quit
end if

if AddUserToIIS_WPG(username) = false then
   WScript.Echo "Error adding user " & username & " IIS_WPG. "
   WScript.Quit
end if

if CreateNewAppPool(username, password, AppPoolName) = false then
   WScript.Echo "Error creating AppPool " & AppPoolName & " running as user " &
username & ". "
   WScript.Quit
end if

if CreateNewVDir(vdirname, vdirphysicalpath) = false then
   WScript.Echo "Error creating new virtual directory " & vdirname & ". "
   WScript.Quit
end if
```

(continued)

Listing 5.2 Sample Script for Configuring Worker Process Identity *(continued)*

```
if AssignAppPool(vdirname, AppPoolName) = false then
   WScript.Echo "Error assigning Application Pool " & AppPoolName & " to vdir "
& vdirname & ". "
   WScript.Quit
end if
'we don't have to reset the server in RC1 anymore
dim wsh : set wsh = CreateObject("WScript.Shell")
WScript.Echo "Waiting for iisreset to return"
wsh.Run "iisreset /restart",,true
wsh.Run "http://localhost/" & vdirname
wsh.Run "taskmgr"

function AssignAppPool(vdirname, AppPoolName)
   dim vdirobj

   set vdirobj = GetObject(basepath & "/" & vdirname)
   vdirobj.AppPoolId = AppPoolName
'   vdirobj.SetInfo
   if err = 0 then
      AssignAppPool = true
   else
      AssignAppPool = false
   end if
end function

function CreateNewVDir (vdirname, vdirphysicalpath)
   dim VdirObj, VRoot
   set VRoot = GetObject(basepath)
   set VdirObj = VRoot.Create("IIsWebVirtualDir", vdirname)
   VdirObj.AccessRead = True
   VdirObj.AccessScript = True
   VdirObj.Put "Path", vdirphysicalpath
   VdirObj.SetInfo
   'why why why????
   vdirobj.AppCreate true
   vdirobj.SetInfo
   if err = 0 then
      CreateNewVDir = True
   else
      CreateNewVdir = false
   end if
end function
```

(continued)

Listing 5.2   Sample Script for Configuring Worker Process Identity *(continued)*

```
function CreateNewAppPool(username, password, AppPoolName)
   dim AppPools, newAppPool
   set AppPools = GetObject("IIS://localhost/w3svc/AppPools")
   set newAppPool = AppPools.Create("IIsApplicationPool", AppPoolName)
   newAppPool.WamUserName = username
   newAppPool.WamUserPass = password
   'LogonMethod will not be required in RC1
   newAppPool.LogonMethod =1
   newAppPool.AppPoolIdentityType=3
   newAppPool.SetInfo
   if err = 0 then
      CreateNewAppPool = True
   else
      CreateNewAppPool = false
   end if
end function

function AddUserToIIS_WPG (username)
   dim nw : set nw = CreateObject("WScript.Network")
   dim computername : computername = nw.Computername
   dim MyUser
   dim IIS_WPG

   set IIS_WPG = GetObject("WinNT://" & computername & "/IIS_WPG,group")
   set MyUser = GetObject("WinNT://" & computername & "/" & username & ",user")
   if not IIS_WPG.IsMember(MyUser.AdsPath) then
      IIS_WPG.Add(MyUser.AdsPath)
   end if
   if err = 0 then
      AddUserToIIS_WPG = True
   else
      AddUserToIIS_WPG = false
   end if

end function
```

(continued)

Listing 5.2 Sample Script for Configuring Worker Process Identity *(continued)*

```
function CreateNewUser(username, password)
   dim nw              :    set nw = CreateObject("WScript.Network")
   dim computername    :    computername = nw.Computername
   dim container       :    set container = GetObject("WinNT://" & computername)
   dim newuser         :    set newuser = container.Create( "user", username)
   newuser.SetPassword(password)
   newuser.SetInfo
   if err = 0 then
      CreateNewUser = True
   else
      WScript.Echo "Error: " & err.Description & " - " & err.number
      CreateNewUser = false
   end if

end function
```

URL Authorization

A new authorization framework is available with Windows Server 2003. Implemented through the Windows Server 2003 Authorization Manager, role-based access control is designed to make it easier to manage access control for Web-based or line-of-business applications in enterprise environments.

For example, for an expense-reporting or Web-based shopping application, the authorization decisions often do not involve determining access to persistent objects. Instead, the applications might need to verify a workflow, or they might involve multiple distinct operations, such as querying a database and sending mail. Access decisions often are made based not only on token group membership but also on business logic, such as the amount that is submitted in an expense application or verification of workflow completion. For applications such as these, which do not have well-defined persistent objects, object-oriented ACLs are not effective.

IIS extends the use of role-based authentication by providing gatekeeper authorization to specific URLs. IIS URL authorization allows you to authorize user access to the URLs that make up a Web application. When a user requests access to a URL, URL authorization validates the user's access based on the roles of that user, which can be defined in Lightweight Directory Access Protocol (LDAP) queries, custom user roles, and the Authorization Manager rules (scripts that are written in VBScript or JScript, which you can include in role definitions and task definitions). This allows you to control all user access to URLs instead of controlling access per ACL, on each resource.

Additionally, Web applications can use URL authorization together with Authorization Manager to control — from within the same policy store — access to the URLs that make up a Web application and the application-specific tasks and operations. Maintaining the policy in the same policy store allows you to manage access to the URLs and application features from a single point of administration while leveraging the store-level application groups and user-programmable business rules.

URL authorization is task-based, allowing you to create flexible authorization schemes that selectively allow or deny access to parts of the URL namespace for certain sets, users, or roles. The **URLAuthorizationModule** class maps users and roles to pieces of the URL namespace. This module implements both positive and negative authorization assertions and is available for use anytime. You need only to list users or roles in the <allow> or <deny> elements of the <authorization> section of a configuration file.

URL authorization is implemented as an ISAPI interceptor. When an application, virtual directory, or URL is configured to use URL authorization, each request to a URL is routed to the URL authorization ISAPI interceptor. The URL authorization wildcard script map uses Authorization Manager to authorize access to the requested URL. The URL must be associated with an Authorization Manager policy store that contains the authorization policy for the URL. After the client has been authorized to access the URL, the Execute URL feature of the URL authorization ISAPI passes the request to the appropriate handler for the URL, such as ASP.dll, another ISAPI, or the static file handler. Figure 5.3 shows this process. In this figure, the wildcard script map is named URL Authz ISAPI, Authorization Manager is named .NET Authz Framework, and the Execute URL feature is named ExecURL.

Figure 5.3   URL Authorization

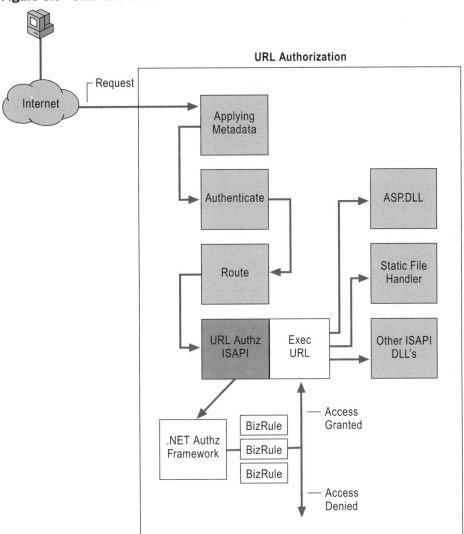

By using URL authorization, you can control access based on information that is available only at run time. For example, if you have a Web page that should be available only to employees in a given cost center or to employees of a certain age, you can assign roles to the correct users based on LDAP queries that check the cost center or age attributes on a user object. If employees can access only certain pages on certain days of the week or during a certain time of day, you can create a BizRule that grants access to the URL based on these values or any value that can be asserted at run time, including IIS server variables.

For more information about Authorization Manager, see "Authorization Manager" in Help and Support Center for Windows Server 2003.

Using URL Authorization

IIS 6.0 does not provide graphical user interface (GUI) support for URL authorization. To use URL authorization in IIS 6.0, you must enable the wildcard script map, Urlauth.dll. In addition, you must set the following metabase properties on the application, virtual directory, or URL (Web site):

- **AzEnable.** This property enables URL authorization for the virtual directory, application, or URL that corresponds to the entry in the metabase.

- **AzStoreName.** This property associates an Authorization Manager store with the virtual directory, application, or URL.

- **AzScopeName.** This property associates the virtual directory, application, or URL with a scope. This scope will be the name of a scope in the IIS 6.0 URL authorization application in the Authorization Manager policy store referred to in the **AzStoreName** property. If no scope or an empty string is specified, the default scope of the URL authorization is used.

- **AzImpersonationLevel.** This property determines the impersonation behavior for the application, allowing you to configure the Web application to impersonate the client user, the IIS worker process, or the IUSER_*ComputerName* account for the worker process. Each setting significantly changes the environment and implied design of the Web application.

For more information about these metabase properties, see "URL Authorization" in IIS 6.0 Help, which is accessible from IIS Manager.

Listing 5.3 provides a customizable text file, written in VBScript, that you can use to mark the root of the first site as a URL in MyAZScope, which is defined in the MyAZStore.xml file. Users with URLAccess rights in this scope will be able to access the site.

Listing 5.3 Sample Script for URL Authorization

```
var objVDir = GetObject("IIS://localhost/w3svc/1/root");
objVDir.AzEnable = true;
objVDir.AZStoreName = "MSXML://d:\MyAZStore.xml";
objVDir.AzScopeName = "MyAZScope";
objVDir.AZImpersonationLevel = 0;
objVDir.SetInfo();
```

Although URL authorization controls access to other forms of authorization, such as settings for IIS directory security or ACL permissions, the application context still requires the correct IIS directory security and ACL permissions. URL authorization allows the IIS directory security and ACL permissions to be more easily maintained.

When URL authorization is configured, the **AzStoreName** property in the IIS metabase entry for the application, virtual directory, or URL identifies an Authorization Manager policy store. To manage the authorization policy, you must run Authorization Manager in Developer mode and use the **Open Policy Store** command from the **Action** menu. URL authorization is an application in this store. The **AzScopeName** property in the metabase entry is an Authorization Manager scope in URL authorization. Use this scope to manage access to the corresponding URL. When you configure an application, virtual directory, or URL for URL authorization, you must create a scope in the *authorization policy store*, a database that stores the authorization manager policies and that has the same name as the name that is specified in the **AzScopeName** property of the corresponding metabase entry.

Enabling the Wildcard Script Map

To use the URL authorization wildcard script map (Urlauth.dll), you must first enable it for each Web site that requires URL authorization.

▶ **To enable the URL authorization wildcard script map**

1. In IIS Manager, double-click the local computer, double-click **Web Sites**, right-click the Web site that you want, and then click **Properties**.

2. Click the **Home Directory** tab, and then, in **Application settings**, click **Configuration**.

3. On the **Mappings** tab, click **Insert**.

4. In the **Add/Edit Application Extension Mapping** dialog box, click **Browse**, and browse to the Windows\System32\Inetsrv directory.

5. Click **urlauth.dll**, click **Open**, and then click **OK**.

Encryption

You can use encryption to help protect the private information that clients exchange with your server, such as credit card numbers or phone numbers. Encryption scrambles the information before it is sent, and decryption unscrambles the information after it is received. The foundation for this encryption in IIS is the *SSL protocol*, which establishes an encrypted communication link with users. SSL confirms the authenticity of your Web site and, optionally, the identity of users that access restricted Web sites.

Certificates are digital identification documents that allow both servers and clients to authenticate each other. If you want the server and client browser to set up an SSL connection over which encrypted information can be sent, then certificates are required. Certificates include keys that are used to establish an SSL-encrypted connection. A *key* is a unique value that is used to authenticate the server and the client in establishing an SSL connection. A public key and a private key form an *SSL key pair*. Your Web server uses this key pair to negotiate an encrypted connection with the client browser.

For this type of connection, both your Web server and the client browser must be equipped with compatible encryption and decryption capabilities. During the key exchange, an encryption key, which is also known as a session key, is created. Both your server and the browser use the session key to encrypt and decrypt transmitted information. The degree of encryption, which is also known as strength, of the session key is measured in bits. The greater the number of bits, the greater the level of encryption and security. Although greater encryption key strengths offer greater security, they also require more server resources to implement. The session key for your Web server is typically 128 bits long. For more information, see "Encryption" in IIS 6.0 Help, which is accessible from IIS Manager.

SSL and Certificates

The certificate-based SSL features in IIS consist of a server certificate, a client certificate, and various digital keys. You can use Certificate Services to create certificates, or you can obtain certificates from a mutually trusted third-party organization called a certification authority (CA). For more information about setting up certificates and keys, see "Configuring SSL on Servers" in IIS 6.0 Help, which is accessible from IIS Manager.

Server certificates provide a way for users to confirm the identity of your Web site. A server certificate contains detailed identification information, such as the name of the organization that is affiliated with the server content, the name of the organization that issued the certificate, and a public key that is used to establish an encrypted connection. This information helps to assure users of the authenticity of Web server content and the integrity of the SSL-secured connection. For more information, see "About Certificates" in IIS 6.0 Help, which is accessible from IIS Manager.

With SSL, your Web server also has the option of authenticating users by checking the contents of their client certificates. A typical client certificate contains detailed identification information about a user and the organization that issued the certificate and a public key. You can use client certificate authentication, along with SSL encryption, to implement a highly secure method for verifying the identity of your users. For more information, see "Certificate Authentication" in IIS 6.0 Help, which is accessible from IIS Manager.

Managing Certificates Programmatically

IIS 6.0 includes the new certificate object, **IISCertObj**, which allows you to use scripts to process SSL certificates on your local computer or on a remote computer. You can use scripts in conjunction with **IISCertObj**, a COM object, to perform the following tasks:

- Import copies of a certificate from a .pfx file (a file containing a PFX-encrypted certificate and a private key) from one server onto multiple servers.

- Save backup copies of certificates on a central site.

- Copy a certificate from one server onto multiple servers.

For more information about **IISCertObj**, including supported properties and methods, see "Managing Server Certificates Programmatically" in IIS 6.0 Help, which is accessible from IIS Manager.

Listing 5.4 provides a customizable text file that you can use to import a certificate from a .pfx file and assign it to the desired site.

 Important

You must be a member of the Administrators group on the local computer to run scripts and executables, or you must have been delegated the appropriate authority. As a security best practice, log on to your computer by using an account that is not in the Administrators group, and then use the **runas** command to run your script or executable as an administrator. At a command prompt, type **runas /profile** /*User.MyMachine\Administrator* cmd to open a command window with administrator rights and then type **cscript.exe** *ScriptName* (including the full path with parameters, if any).

Listing 5.4 Sample Script for Importing Certificates

```
' certimp.vbs
'
' author: uladm   05/03/2002
'
' certimp.vbs for usage info
'


REM
REM LOCALIZATION
REM

L_SWITCH_PFX        = "-c"
L_SWITCH_PFX_PASSWORD   = "-p"
L_SWITCH_INSTANCE_ID   = "-i"
L_SWITCH_SERVER      = "-s"
L_SWITCH_USER       = "-u"
L_SWITCH_PASSWORD    = "-pwd"

L_DESC_PROGRAM   = "certimp - imports a certificate from a pfx file and assigns
it to the desired site"

L_DESC_PFX      = "Specify pfx file name"
L_DESC_PFX_PASSWORD   = "pfx password"
L_DESC_INSTANCE_ID   = "<site> Specify server instance (site) name"
L_DESC_SERVER      = "<server> Specify computer to configure"
L_DESC_USER     = "User name"
L_DESC_PASSWORD      = "User password"

L_DESC_EXAMPLES        = "Examples:"
L_DESC_EXAMPLE1        = "certimp.vbs -c cert.pfx -p pfxpassword -i w3svc/1 -s
iisserver1 -u Administrator -pwd aal34290"
```

(continued)

Listing 5.4   Sample Script for Importing Certificates *(continued)*

```
L_ERR_IMPORT_ERROR    = "Error importing certificate: "
L_ERR_IMPORT_SUCCESS  = "Import succeeded."

REM
REM END LOCALIZATION
REM

REM
REM --- Globals ---
REM

dim g_dictParms
set g_dictParms = CreateObject ( "Scripting.Dictionary" )

REM
REM --- Set argument defaults ---
REM

g_dictParms(L_SWITCH_PFX)          = ""
g_dictParms(L_SWITCH_PFX_PASSWORD)     = ""
g_dictParms(L_SWITCH_INSTANCE_ID)    = "w3svc/1"
g_dictParms(L_SWITCH_SERVER)       = ""
g_dictParms(L_SWITCH_USER)       = ""
g_dictParms(L_SWITCH_PASSWORD)        = ""

REM
REM --- Begin Main Program ---
REM

if NOT ParseCommandLine ( g_dictParms, WScript.Arguments ) then
   usage
   WScript.Quit ( 0 )
end if

pfxfile = g_dictParms(L_SWITCH_PFX)
pfxfilepassword = g_dictParms(L_SWITCH_PFX_PASSWORD)
instance = g_dictParms(L_SWITCH_INSTANCE_ID)
server = g_dictParms(L_SWITCH_SERVER)
user = g_dictParms(L_SWITCH_USER)
userpassword = g_dictParms(L_SWITCH_PASSWORD)

REM
REM    Check arguments
REM
if ( pfxfile = "" ) then
   usage
   WScript.Quit 0
end if
```

(continued)

Listing 5.4 Sample Script for Importing Certificates *(continued)*

```
REM
REM    Import certificate
REM
dim iiscertobj
set iiscertobj = WScript.CreateObject( "IIS.CertObj" )
if (user <> "") then
   iiscertobj.UserName = user
   if (userpassword <> "") then
      iiscertobj.UserPassword = userpassword
   end if
end if
if (server <> "") Then
   iiscertobj.ServerName = server
end if
iiscertobj.InstanceName = instance
iiscertobj.Import pfxfile, pfxfilepassword, true, true

REM
REM    Show Result
REM
if (err.number <> 0) then
   WScript.echo L_ERR_IMPORT_ERROR
   WScript.echo Err.Description & " (Error 0x" & Hex(Err.Number) & ")"
else
   WScript.echo L_ERR_IMPORT_SUCCESS
end if
WScript.Quit 0

REM
REM
REM --- End Main Program ---
REM
REM

REM
REM ParseCommandLine ( dictParameters, cmdline )
REM      Parses the command line parameters into the given dictionary
REM
REM Arguments:
REM      dictParameters  - A dictionary containing the global parameters
REM      cmdline - Collection of command line arguments
REM
REM Returns - Success code
REM
```

(continued)

Listing 5.4 Sample Script for Importing Certificates *(continued)*

```
Function ParseCommandLine ( dictParameters, cmdline )
    dim     fRet
    dim     cArgs
    dim     i
    dim     strSwitch
    dim     strArgument

    fRet    = TRUE
    cArgs   = cmdline.Count
    i       = 0

    do while (i < cArgs)

        REM
        REM Parse the switch and its argument
        REM

        if i + 1 >= cArgs then
            REM
            REM Not enough command line arguments - Fail
            REM

            fRet = FALSE
            exit do
        end if

        strSwitch = cmdline(i)
        i = i + 1

        strArgument = cmdline(i)
        i = i + 1

        REM
        REM Add the switch,argument pair to the dictionary
        REM

        if NOT dictParameters.Exists ( strSwitch ) then
            REM
            REM Bad switch - Fail
            REM

            fRet = FALSE
            exit do
        end if
```

(continued)

Listing 5.4   Sample Script for Importing Certificates *(continued)*

```
        dictParameters(strSwitch) = strArgument


    loop

    ParseCommandLine = fRet
end function


REM
REM Usage ()
REM      prints out the description of the command line arguments
REM

Sub Usage
    WScript.Echo L_DESC_PROGRAM

    WScript.Echo vbTab & L_SWITCH_PFX & " " & L_DESC_PFX
    WScript.Echo vbTab & L_SWITCH_PFX_PASSWORD & " " & L_DESC_PFX_PASSWORD
    WScript.Echo vbTab & L_SWITCH_INSTANCE_ID & " " & L_DESC_INSTANCE_ID
    WScript.Echo vbTab & L_SWITCH_SERVER & " " & L_DESC_SERVER
    WScript.Echo vbTab & L_SWITCH_USER & " " & L_DESC_USER
    WScript.Echo vbTab & L_SWITCH_PASSWORD & " " & L_DESC_PASSWORD

    WScript.Echo L_DESC_EXAMPLES
    WScript.Echo L_DESC_EXAMPLE1
end sub
```

Server-Gated Cryptography

Server-Gated Cryptography (SGC) offers financial institutions a solution for worldwide, secure financial transactions using 128-bit encryption. SGC is an extension of SSL that allows financial institutions with export versions of IIS to use strong encryption.

SGC does not require an application to run on the client browser and will allow export clients to connect with 128-bit strength. Although SGC capabilities are built into IIS 4.0, 5.0, and 6.0, an SGC certificate is required to use SGC. Contact your CA for availability information.

If you want to support clients that run software without strong encryption support, you need only SGC certificates. On January 14, 2000, the United States government eliminated the remaining export controls for most computer hardware and software products that incorporate *strong encryption*, which was defined as products that implemented symmetric key encryption with key lengths of over 64 bits. Windows 2000 Server was the first platform to be shipped internationally under the new regulations with 128-bit+ encryption. For information about United States export regulations, visit the United States Commerce Department Bureau of Industry and Security link on the Web Resources page at http://www.microsoft.com/windows/reskits/webresources. For more information about exporting Microsoft products, see the Exporting Microsoft Products link on the Web Resources page at http://www.microsoft.com/windows/reskits/webresources.

 Note

> If you are running Windows 2000 and you open your SGC certificate, then you might receive the following notice on the **General** tab: "The certificate has failed to verify for all of its intended purposes." This notice is issued because of the way SGC certificates interact with Windows 2000 Server and does not necessarily indicate that the certificate does not work properly.

Cryptographic Service Provider

Cryptographic service provider (CSP) allows you to select a Microsoft or third-party cryptographic provider to handle cryptography and certificate management. Each cryptographic provider can create a public and private key to encrypt the data that is sent to and from the Web server. The private key is stored at the server on hardware, on a Peripheral Component Interconnect (PCI) card, on a smart card, or in the registry, as it is for the two default providers that Microsoft installs: Microsoft DH SChannel Cryptographic Provider and Microsoft RSA SChannel Cryptographic Provider. The Microsoft Cryptographic API (CryptoAPI) for every cryptographic provider contains identical methods and properties. This allows you to switch between cryptographic providers without having to rewrite code. For more information about CSP and managing installed third-party cryptographic providers, see "About Security" in IIS 6.0 Help, which is accessible from IIS Manager.

Client Certificate Mapping

You can authenticate users who log on with a client certificate by creating *mappings*, which relate the information that is contained in the certificate to a Windows user account. There are three ways to map client certificates: Directory Service (DS) mapping, one-to-one mapping, and many-to-one mapping.

Directory Service Mapping

Directory Service (DS) certificate mapping uses native Windows Active Directory features to authenticate users with client certificates. There are advantages and disadvantages to using DS mapping. For example, an advantage is that the client certificate information is shared across many servers. A disadvantage, however, is that wildcard matching is not as advanced as it is in the IIS mapper.

You can enable DS mapping only at the **Master** properties level, and only if you are a member of a Windows domain. Activating DS mapping will exclude the use of one-to-one and many-to-one mapping for the entire World Wide Web Publishing Service (WWW service).

One-to-One Mapping

One-to-one mapping maps individual client certificates to accounts. The server compares the copy of the client certificate it holds with the client certificate that is sent by the browser. The two must be absolutely identical for the mapping to proceed. If a client gets another certificate containing all of the same user information, it must be mapped again.

Many-to-One Mapping

Many-to-one mapping uses wildcard matching rules that verify whether a client certificate contains specific information, such as issuer or subject. This mapping does not compare the actual client certificate, but rather accepts all client certificates fulfilling the specific criteria. If a client gets another certificate containing all of the same user information, the existing mapping will work.

TCP/IP Port Filtering

TCP/IP port filtering is the practice of selectively enabling or disabling Transmission Control Protocol (TCP) ports and User Datagram Protocol (UDP) ports on computers or network devices. When used in conjunction with other security practices, such as deploying firewall software at your Internet access point, applying port filters to intranet and Internet servers insulates those servers from many TCP/IP-based security attacks, including internal attacks by malicious users.

An Internet or intranet host, such as a computer or network device on a TCP/IP-based network, uses a combination of an IP address and port number to communicate with an application or service running on another Internet or intranet host. Together, an IP address and port number make up a *socket*. Because TCP/IP hosts are assigned a unique IP address, and standard TCP/IP-based applications and services typically use a specific TCP or UDP port number, sockets can direct communications between specific applications or services running on specific hosts.

A port number is identified in a TCP or UDP packet header and represents the transport protocol address of a specific application and service that uses TCP or UDP. For example, HTTP services use TCP port 80 by default, Telnet uses TCP port 23 by default, and Simple Network Management Protocol (SNMP) uses UDP port 161 by default.

The Internet Assigned Numbers Authority (IANA) categorizes TCP and UDP ports into three categories. Table 5.4 lists these categories.

Table 5.4   IANA Categories of TCP and UDP Ports

Port Category	Port Number	Range Description
Well-known ports	0–1023	Typically used by standard system processes or programs that are executed by users with administrator credentials. Assigned by IANA.
Registered ports	1024–49151	Used by ordinary user processes or programs that are executed by ordinary users. IANA does not assign these ports, but registers use of them as a convenience for the TCP/IP community.
Dynamic or private ports	49152–65535	Unassigned and unregistered ports used for private applications, client-side processes, or other processes that dynamically allocate port numbers.

Typically, the server side of a TCP or UDP process listens to the associated well-known port number. The client side of the process uses either the well-known port number or, more commonly, a dynamically allocated port number that is assigned only for the duration of the process.

To enable communications with the applications and services that your servers use, you must ensure that the associated ports are enabled. However, because malicious users on your internal network can attempt to exploit enabled ports to attack your servers, you should disable the TCP and UDP ports on your servers that are not used. This reduces the avenues of attack to your servers and improves the security of hosts that connect to your servers.

Important

Server-based port filtering is not the only method you should use to secure your servers and network from TCP/IP-based security attacks. To provide a more complete network security solution, you should also deploy network firewall software at your Internet access point. For more information about network firewalls, see the ISA Server link on the Web Resources page at http://www.microsoft.com/windows/reskits/webresources.

Table 5.5 lists some of the default TCP port numbers for processes that are commonly used with Internet services.

Table 5.5 TCP Ports and Associated Services

Default TCP Port Number	Internet Service
20	FTP Data Channel
21	FTP Control Channel
23	Telnet (enabled on some intranet or Internet servers)
25	Simple Mail Transfer Protocol (SMTP)
80	HTTP for World Wide Web
119	Network News Transfer Protocol (NNTP)
443	Hypertext Transfer Protocol over TLS/SSL (HTTPS) for secure World Wide Web
563	Network News Transfer Protocol over TLS/SSL (NNTPS)

Note

Windows Media Services can provide streaming media services over unicast or multicast IP through a variety of static or dynamic UDP and TCP ports, or through a single port, depending on the configuration. You can also configure Windows Media Services to provide HTTP streaming media services through the default HTTP port, which is TCP port 80. For more information about Windows Media Services, see Help and Support Center for Windows Server 2003, and search for "Using Windows Media Services".

Table 5.6 lists the well-known UDP port numbers for the processes that are commonly used with Internet services.

Table 5.6 UDP Ports and Associated Services

UPD Port Number	Service
53	DNS name queries (supports some Internet services)
161	SNMP

For a list of TCP and UDP port numbers that are used by Windows Server 2003, see the services.txt file in the *systemroot*\System32\Drivers\Etc folder.

Creating an IPSec Policy to Restrict Ports

Internet Protocol security (IPSec) is designed to encrypt data as it travels between two computers, protecting it from modification and interpretation. To use IPSec, you must define how computers that attempt to connect will trust each other and how the computers will secure their traffic. To implement these specifications, create and apply an IPSec policy. IPSec policies support policy-based stateful packet filtering rules that can be used with IPSec authentication and encryption to provide robust end-to-end security.

Example: Creating an IPSec Policy

This section provides step-by-step instructions for creating an example IPSec policy that allows inbound requests to connect only to ports 80 and 443. Port 80 is the default port for HTTP requests, and port 443 is the default port for HTTPS requests. The policy blocks requests for all other ports on the server.

In contrast with typical firewall or packet filtering rules, there is no way to order the list of rules in an IPSec policy. The rule engine matches traffic with rules according to specificity. If a packet matches more than one rule, the engine will apply the most specific rule to the packet. In the following example, packets that match the filter list that allows connections to port 80 also match the filter list that blocks all incoming traffic. Because the former list is more specific, the rule engine uses that list to make its decision. Therefore, traffic that connects to port 80 or port 443 is passed to the server, while everything else is blocked. You need to create multiple filter lists to make the policy effective.

There are several steps to creating an IPSec policy:

1. Create IPSec filter lists. Filter lists include ports, protocols, and directions and trigger a decision when traffic matches an item in the list. This example requires you to create three filter lists. The first two filter lists apply to inbound traffic that attempts to connect to port 80 or 443, and the third filter list applies to all ports.

2. Set filter actions. Filter actions are the required response when traffic matches a filter list. You will only use "permit" and "block" actions for your IIS IPSec policy.

3. Create the IPSec policy. The IPSec policy is a collection of rules, which are the correlation of a filter list with a filter action. You can have only one active, or assigned, policy at any particular time.

The following steps are for creating IPSec policies using the Local Security Settings snap-in in Windows Server 2003. You can also create IPSec policies using the **Netsh commands for IPSec.** For more information about Netsh commands for IPSec, see "Managing IPSec from the command line" in Help and Support Center for Windows Server 2003.

To create IPSec filter lists, begin by changing the security settings on the local computer.

▷ **To create the IPSec filter lists**

1. From the **Start** menu, point to **All Programs**, point to **Administrative Tools**, and then select **Local Security Policy**.

2. In the **Local Security Settings** dialog box, click **IP Security Policies on Local Computer**. The right pane displays the default Windows Server 2003 policies.

3. Right-click the right pane, and then click **Manage IP filter lists and filter actions**.

4. In the **Manage IP filter lists and filter actions** dialog box, on the **Manage IP Filter Lists** tab, click **Add**.

5. In the **IP Filter List** dialog box, in the **Name** box, type a name for your filter list, such as "Inbound HTTP," and type a description if you want one. This is the filter list that applies to all inbound HTTP connections.

6. Click **Add**. The IP Filter Wizard appears. Create a filter list with the following specifications:

   - Description: Optional.

   - Source address: **Any IP Address**.

   - Destination address: **My IP Address**. Or click **A specific IP address**, and then type the IP address of the interface that's connected to the Internet.

   - Protocol type: **TCP**.

   - Protocol Port: **From any port**.

   - To this port: **80**.

7. In the **Completing the IP Filter Wizard** screen, clear the **Edit properties** check box, and then click **Finish**.

8. In the **IP Filter List** dialog box, click **OK**.

9. Repeat steps 1 through 8, except create a filter list that applies to destination port 443 for HTTPS connections. Name the filter list "Inbound HTTPS," or something similar.

10. Repeat steps 1 through 8, except create a filter list that applies to all destination ports. This filter list will apply to the policy that blocks all inbound traffic. Name the filter list "All Inbound," or something similar.

After you create the IPSec filter list, you must create a filter action that will occur when incoming traffic matches the criteria in your filter lists. For this example, two actions are necessary. The first is a permit action for allowing requests to connect to ports 80 and 443. The action to permit traffic is an existing default, so you do not need to create it. You must create the second action, which is to block traffic to all other ports.

▷ **To set the filter actions**

1. After you create the filter lists, in the **Local Security Settings** dialog box, right-click the right pane, and then click **Manage IP filter lists and filter actions**.

2. In the **Manage IP filter lists and filter actions** dialog box, click the **Manage Filter Actions** tab, and then click **Add**. The Filter Action Wizard appears.

3. Create a filter action with the following specifications:

   ▪ Name: **Block**

   ▪ Description: Optional

   ▪ Filter Action General Options: **Block**

4. In the **Completing the IP Security Filter Action Wizard** screen, clear the **Edit properties** check box, and then click **Finish**.

5. In the **Manage IP filter lists and filter actions** dialog box, click **Close**.

After you create the IPSec filter lists and filter actions, you must create the IPSec policies and define the rules that link the lists to the actions.

▷ **To create the IPSec policies**

1. After you set the filter actions, in the **Local Security Settings** dialog box, right-click the right pane, and then select **Create IP Security Policy**. The IP Security Policy Wizard appears.

2. Create a policy with the following specifications:

   ▪ Name: **Packet Filter**

   ▪ Description: Optional

3. In the **Requests for Secure Communication** screen, clear the **Activate the default response rule** check box, and then click **Next**.

4. In the **Completing the IP Security Policy Wizard** screen, make sure that the **Edit properties** check box is selected, and then click **Finish**. The **New IP Security Policy Properties** dialog box appears. Do not close this dialog box.

After you create the IPSec filter lists, filter actions, and IPSec policies, you must add rules to the policy and associate the IPSec filter lists that you created with the rules.

▷ **To add rules to the policy**

1. After you create the IPSec policies, in the **New IP Security Policy Properties** dialog box, click **Add**. The Security Rule Wizard appears.

2. Create a rule with the following specifications:

   ▪ Tunnel endpoint: **This rule does not specify a tunnel**.

   ▪ Network type: **All network connections**.

   ▪ IP filter lists: **All Inbound** (or the name of your filter list that applies to inbound traffic on any port).

   ▪ Filter Action: **Block**.

3. In the **Completing the Security Rule Wizard** screen, clear the **Edit properties** check box, and then click **Finish**.

4. In the **New IP Security Policy Properties** dialog box, click **Close**.

5. Repeat steps 1 through 4 to create rules that apply to the Inbound HTTP and Inbound HTTPS filter lists. For these rules, choose the Permit filter action.

After you create the IPSec filter lists, filter actions, and policies and add rules to the policy and associate the IPSec filter lists with rules, you must assign the IPSec policy to the server. Only one policy can be assigned at any time.

▷ **To assign the IPSec policy**

   ▪ In the **Local Security Settings** dialog box, right-click the policy you created, and click **Assign**.

   The policy is applied immediately, and IPSec starts processing packets according to the rules in the policy. You do not need to reboot the server. To stop the policy, right-click the policy in the **Local Security Settings** dialog box, and click **Un-assign**.

Secure Code

No matter how secure your server is, if the applications that it hosts are not programmed according to best security practices, your network might be vulnerable to attacks. As part of a defense-in-depth strategy, IIS administrators should work with developers to ensure that the code that the server running IIS hosts is as secure as possible. For example, developers can reduce the risk of certain types of attacks, such as cross-site scripting and SQL injection, by validating user input.

Cross-site scripting occurs when an attacker sends a link in e-mail to a user or otherwise points the user to a Web site, and the link actually contains malicious script code, which can be VBScript or JScript. As a result of cross-site scripting, an attacker potentially can perform such actions as reading cookies, instantiating browser plug-ins or native code and scripting it with untrusted data, and intercepting user input. Potential targets are any browsers that support scripting and any Web servers that support HTML forms.

In a *SQL-injection attack*, an attacker finds a way to modify a SQL command that is used in a dynamic Web page. The attacker typically crafts user input in a way that modifies the logic of the SQL command, so that the attacker is able to obtain information that would otherwise be unavailable.

Developers who write the applications that are hosted on your Web site must know how to include safeguards against these types of attacks. It is paramount that all user input be validated thoroughly. The book *Writing Secure Code* covers these and other Web application security issues in depth. For more information about *Writing Secure Code*, see "Additional Resources" later in this chapter.

MIME Types

To reduce the available attack surface, IIS serves only a small number of default, static file types unless you approve an extension and that extension appears in the MIME types list. MIME types instruct a browser or mail application about how to handle the files received from a server. For example, when a browser requests an item on a server, the browser also requests the MIME type of the object. When IIS delivers a Web page to a client browser, IIS also sends the MIME type of the data it is sending. If there is an attached or embedded file in a specific format, then IIS also tells the client application the MIME type of the embedded or attached file. The client application then knows how to process or display the data being received from IIS.

Known extensions are handled somewhat differently for static pages and for dynamic content, but you can add, change, or remove allowable extensions for both static and dynamic content. Also, if a user requests a file with an extension that is not permitted, the user receives a 404 error (File not found), rather than a 403 error (Access is denied). This reduces the amount of information that is supplied to a would-be attacker. For more information about interpreting substatus error codes, see "Analyzing Log Files" in this book.

Inheritance and Merge Behavior

IIS merges the MIME mappings that it finds on different levels to one in-memory representation. For example, when IIS receives a request, it looks up the **MimeMap** property for the level, such as lm/w3svc/1/root/MimeMap, and the closest inherited level. If the MIME type for an extension is not in the resulting array, then IIS looks for the MIME type in the registry (HKEY_CLASSES_ROOT\<extension). If a matching MIME type is not found, then IIS can use a wildcard mapping if one is configured. Otherwise, the user receives a 404 error. The default wildcard for IIS is .*,application/octet-stream.

Merge considerations

When you configure MIME types, be aware of the restrictive MIME merge behavior of IIS 6.0. Values that are set on nodes are inherited by default by child nodes, but values that are set on child nodes do not propagate back up to parent nodes. For example, if you allow the .ini MIME type on *LocalComputer*/Directory, but you do not allow this MIME type on the root directory, then users might not receive the files that you expect. In this situation, if a user requests http://server/directory/default.ini, the user receives the file. However, if the user requests http://server/default.ini, the user does not receive the file because IIS uses the **MimeMap** property for *LocalComputer*/Directory and does not merge it with entries in *LocalComputer*/Root. Instead, the user receives a 404 error.

Additional Resources

These resources contain additional information and tools related to this chapter.

Related Information

- "Analyzing Log Files" in this book for information about interpreting substatus error codes.

- "Configuring Internet Sites and Services" in this book for information about configuring host header–based sites.

- "Working with the Metabase" in this book for information about metabase security.

- The ISA Server link on the Web Resources page at http://www.microsoft.com/windows/reskits/webresources for information about network firewalls.

- The Microsoft .NET Passport link on the Web Resources page at http://www.microsoft.com/windows/reskits/webresources for information about .NET Passport authorization.

- The MetaACL.exe Sample link on the Web Resources page at http://www.microsoft.com/windows/reskits/webresources for information about MetaACL.vbs.

- *Writing Secure Code* by Michael Howard and David LeBlanc, 2002, Redmond: Microsoft Press.

Related IIS 6.0 Help Topics

- "About Certificates" in IIS 6.0 Help, which is accessible from IIS Manager, for information about certificate-based authentication.

- "About Security" in IIS 6.0 Help, which is accessible from IIS Manager, for information about securing your IIS 6.0 servers.

- The **ASPRunOnEndAnonymously** property in the "Metabase Property Reference" of IIS 6.0 Help, which is accessible from IIS Manager, for information about ASP OnEnd routines.

- "Basic Authentication" in IIS 6.0 Help, which is accessible from IIS Manager, for information about the Basic authentication method.

- "Digest Authentication" in IIS 6.0 Help, which is accessible from IIS Manager, for information about the Digest authentication method.

- "Encryption" in IIS 6.0 Help, which is accessible from IIS Manager, for information about SSL encryption features.

- "Global Registry Entries" in IIS 6.0 Help, which is accessible from IIS Manager, for information about the **UserTokenTTL** property.

- "Securing Sites with Web Site Permissions" in IIS 6.0 Help, which is accessible from IIS Manager, for information about Web site permissions.

Related Windows Server 2003 Help Topics

For best results in identifying Help topics by title, in Help and Support Center, under the **Search** box, click **Set search options**. Under **Help Topics**, select the **Search in title only** check box.

- "Add a member to a local group" for information about adding users to groups.

- "Authorization Manager" for information about Authorization Manager.

- "Cacls" for information about the **cacls** command.

- "Domain and forest functionality" for information about domain functional levels.

- "Managing IPSec from the command line" for information about Netsh commands for IPSec.

- "Using Windows Automatic Updates" for information about scheduled installation of security patches.

Related Tools

- The Xcacls.exe command-line tool

  See the Xcacls.exe link on the Web Resources page at http://www.microsoft.com/windows/reskits/webresources for information about Xcacls.exe, including instructions for downloading this command-line tool.

C H A P T E R   1 3

Optimizing IIS 6.0 Performance

13

When you monitor your application servers to maintain a baseline of performance data, you can spot performance trends as they develop, take steps to prevent unsatisfactory performance, decide how to best tune or upgrade your servers, and determine whether your changes are beneficial. By tuning your Internet Information Services (IIS) version 6.0 application servers, you improve the client experience, help avoid bottlenecks, and can extend the interval between hardware upgrades.

In This Chapter

Related Information

- For information about using IIS logs to monitor and tune performance, see "Analyzing Log Files" in this book.

- For information about troubleshooting performance, see "Troubleshooting IIS 6.0" in this book.

- For information about IIS 6.0 capacity planning and scalability, see "Web Server Scalability" in this book.

Overview of Performance Monitoring and Tuning

Performance monitoring is the process of capturing and analyzing performance data from different areas of your server environment, which include applications, memory, processors, hardware, and your network. You obtain performance data to help you recognize trends as they develop, prevent unsatisfactory performance, and optimize the use of your system resources. Monitoring also helps you decide when to upgrade your hardware and whether upgrades are actually improving your server's performance.

Although some performance problems and their solutions are immediate and obvious, others develop over time and require careful monitoring and tuning. First, monitor to establish a performance baseline against which to judge and compare the performance of your server; without a baseline, your tuning efforts might not give you optimal performance.

By monitoring performance and analyzing performance data, you can identify performance patterns to help you locate bottlenecks and to identify underused or overused resources. After locating a bottleneck, you can make changes to the component to improve performance. Bottlenecks can occur anywhere in your server environment at any time, so you must regularly monitor performance to capture baseline information about your system.

To get started with performance monitoring, familiarize yourself with the tools used, which include System Monitor, Performance Logs and Alerts, and Network Monitor; with the counters that are available for monitoring performance objects; and with the basics of setting up monitoring in order to collect useful data.

Using Performance Tools to Obtain a Baseline

Using the appropriate tools, you can monitor your application server to collect data on performance, make specific changes in order to tune your server and its Web applications, evaluate the results of changes, and plan additional changes to help your application server run optimally. Which tools you should use, and when you should use them, depends on the data you need and your purpose in collecting it.

The Microsoft® Windows® Server 2003, Standard Edition; Windows® Server 2003, Enterprise Edition; Windows® Server 2003, Datacenter Edition; or Windows® Server 2003, Web Edition operating system provides the Performance console, which includes System Monitor, Performance Logs and Alerts, and Task Manager. System Monitor and Performance Logs and Alerts are Microsoft Management Console (MMC) snap-ins. In addition, you can access these tools through the **Run** dialog box by using the **perfmon** command.

From the Performance console, you can examine the output of *performance counters*, which monitor the activity of *performance objects*. Each performance counter is named based on the object from which it collects data (for example, a processor, process, or thread) and the type of data that it collects (for example, the Processor\% Processor Time performance counter reports the average percentage of processor time in use for the Processor performance object).

Windows Server 2003 provides several command-line tools that you can use to monitor performance. This section cites two command-line tools for performing event tracing. For more information about using command-line tools to monitor performance, see "Monitoring performance from the command line" in Help and Support Center for Windows Server 2003.

System Monitor

System Monitor enables you to collect and display real-time performance data for a local computer or remote computers according to criteria that you define. System Monitor can also display data that is collected in counter logs.

You can use System Monitor to monitor your server's activity and summarize its performance at selected intervals. You can display performance data in real-time charts or reports, collect data in files, and generate alerts when critical events occur. Use the data to determine the cause of system bottlenecks and to fine-tune system and application performance.

By default, the System Monitor graph is plotted on a scale of 0 through 100. For counters that register small values, you might need to change the scale. When interpreting the counters, remember that most of them show the most recently observed value, not a long-term average. Use Performance Logs and Alerts to log data over time and determine average values.

For more information about using System Monitor, see "Setting Up Monitoring" later in this chapter and "System Monitor overview" in Help and Support Center for Windows Server 2003.

Performance Logs and Alerts

Use Performance Logs and Alerts to automatically collect performance data in logs and to send alerts based on criteria that you set:

- Create custom log files that automatically log the values for specified counters based on the start and stop times that you provide.

- Set an alert on a counter that defines what action you want the system to take (for example, send an alert, run a program, make an entry in a log file, or initiate logging) when the alert condition is met.

- View counter data during or after collection. After collecting data in logs, use System Monitor to view the data, or export the data to a spreadsheet or database application.

A binary log file format is provided for circular logging or for logging instances, such as threads or processes, that begin after the system starts logging data. (*Circular logging* is the process of continuously logging data to a single file, overwriting previous data with new data.)

For more information about Performance Logs and Alerts, see "Performance Logs and Alerts overview" in Help and Support Center for Windows Server 2003.

 Note

You can also monitor your server by examining IIS logs. For information about IIS logs, see "Analyzing Log Files" in this book.

Task Manager

Use Task Manager to monitor key indicators of your computer's performance.

The **Performance** tab displays a dynamic overview of your computer's performance, including usage history for CPU and memory; the total number of handles, threads, and processes currently running on the computer; and physical memory, kernel memory, and commit memory usage.

The **Processes** tab shows information about the processes running on your computer. You can select columns to display. For example, display information about CPU and memory usage, page faults, handle count, and a number of other parameters.

For more information about Task Manager, see "Task Manager" in Help and Support Center for Windows Server 2003.

Event Tracing with Log Manager and Trace Report

A Web request goes through many layers of the operating system, most of which can be tuned. By tracing IIS and kernel events, you can pinpoint Web bottlenecks on the server, and can often determine where to tune your server for improved performance. You can use the trace data with performance monitors, capacity planning tools, and applications that analyze information relating to system resource usage.

Use the Log Manager and Trace Report command-line tools in Windows Server 2003 to collect and report trace data relating to IIS and kernel events:

- Use the Log Manager tool (Logman.exe) to collect trace data for specified IIS and kernel events.

- Then use the Trace Report tool (Tracerpt.exe) to process the event trace log and to generate trace analysis reports and comma-delimited files for the events.

For information about Logman.exe and Tracerpt.exe, in Help and Support Center for Windows Server 2003, click **Tools**, and then click **Command-line reference A-Z**. For information about using Log Manager and Trace Report with IIS 6.0, including syntax examples and analysis of output reports, see "Capacity Planning Tracing" in IIS 6.0 Help, which is accessible from IIS Manager.

Network Monitor

Network Monitor is a useful tool for conducting a network analysis of your Web applications. Use this tool to document the number of roundtrips that are required for a client to download a specific Web page from your server. Make adjustments to your applications, such as the changes recommended in "Optimizing Application Design and Administration" later in this chapter, and then rerun Network Monitor to verify that the adjustments improved performance.

Network Monitor collects data about the network traffic that flows to and from the network adapter of the computer on which it is installed. By capturing and analyzing that data, you not only can improve performance, you can prevent, diagnose, and solve many types of network problems.

You can configure Network Monitor to provide only the information that is most relevant to you. For example, you can configure *capture triggers*, which cause Network Monitor to start or stop capturing data when a circumstance or set of circumstances occurs, and you can configure *capture filters* to control the types of data that Network Monitor captures or displays.

Network Monitor monitors the frames in which data is sent over the network, which, in addition to the data, contain the addresses of the source and destination computers and the protocols in use.

Because using Network Monitor can affect server performance, you might want to run this tool when usage is low or for short periods during peak usage. Use capture filters so that you collect only the data that you need, then repeat each network capture one or more times to verify that the data you obtained accurately reflects network activity.

For more information about using Network Monitor, including how to design capture filters and set capture triggers, see the checklist "Monitoring network traffic on your local computer" in Help and Support Center for Windows Server 2003.

Monitoring with Performance Counters

Both System Monitor and Performance Logs and Alerts allow you to examine the output of *performance counters*, which monitor the activity of specific *performance objects*. Each performance counter is named for the object for which it collects data and the type of data that it collects. For example, the Processor\% ProcessorTime counter is the primary indicator of processor activity, displaying the average percentage of busy time observed during the sample interval.

A performance object often offers a choice of more than one *instance*. Using the Processor object as an example, if you are monitoring a dual-processor computer, the first processor instance is 0 and the second processor instance is 1. A commonly used instance is the _Total instance, which monitors the sum of the values of a specific counter's instances.

Components of a counter path

The counter path contains the computer name, and the performance object, instance, and counter. It is typically represented in the following way:

```
\\ComputerName\Object(Instance)\Counter
```

The computer name is optional. If you do not designate a computer name, the counter monitors the local computer.

Again, using the Processor object as an example, if you want to monitor the percentage of processor time that your #0 processor uses, your selection is represented in the following way:

```
Processor(#0)\% ProcessorTime
```

Sampling methods for counters

Performance counters collect and display their data in one of two ways:

- **Instantaneous counters.** These counters display the most recent measurement of an aspect of resource use. For example, the Process\Thread Count counter shows the number of threads for a particular process as of the last time it was measured. An instantaneous counter might have a name containing the word "Current." Unless the server has a steady workload, these counters might not provide meaningful data.

- **Averaging counters.** Based on the previous two measurements, averaging counters derive an average value for the interval between the measurements. These counters typically calculate a percentage or the number of occurrences per second. For example, the Memory\Pages/sec counter shows the number of memory pages read over the sample interval, divided by the number of seconds in the interval. When you start one of these counters, no value is displayed until the second measurement is taken.

Counters Provided by Windows and by IIS

Windows Server 2003 provides hundreds of counters. Frequently used performance objects include cache, memory, process, and server. For more information about Windows performance objects and counters, see "Performance objects and counters" in Help and Support Center for Windows Server 2003.

When you install IIS, you automatically install the IIS performance counters, which include the following:

- Web Service counters to monitor the World Wide Web Publishing Service (WWW service).

- Web Service Cache counters to monitor the WWW service cache.

- FTP Service counters to monitor the File Transfer Protocol (FTP) service.

- Active Server Pages counters to monitor applications that run as Active Server Pages (ASP pages).

If you use Simple Network Management Protocol (SNMP) services to monitor your Web services, IIS makes available a set of counters by means of SNMP. They include SNMP FTP service counters and SNMP HTTP service counters, which you can use to monitor an SNMP WWW service. However, you cannot view the SNMP counters in System Monitor or Performance Logs and Alerts; you must use Windows Management Instrumentation (WMI) or a management information base (MIB) browser tool instead. For more information about specific IIS counters, including how to locate and view the SNMP counters, see "IIS 6.0 Performance Counters" in this book.

Suggested Performance Counters to Watch

Table 6.1 and Table 6.2 list some of the counters that are typically used for monitoring application servers. The tables include the preferred value of each counter and suggest values that might indicate performance problems.

Most of the values provided in this section are relative: Optimal values vary with the Web application, system, and network architecture. For example, data collected by the PhysicalDisk\Avg Disk Bytes/Transfer counter is different for different kinds of controllers and drives. Some counters may not be relevant to your applications. For example, data collected by the Active Server Pages\Transactions/sec counter is not relevant to a Web site with only static content.

In Table 6.1 and Table 6.2 (as in most of the tables in this chapter), *ComputerName* is omitted to conserve space. For example, the first counter in Table 6.1 is actually *ComputerName*\Memory\Pages/sec.

Table 6.1   Preferred Values for Frequently Used Performance Counters

Object\Counter	Preferred or Ideal Value
Memory\Pages/sec	0–20. (Unhealthy if greater than 80; probably indicates not enough RAM.)
Memory\Available Bytes	10% of physical memory.
Memory\Committed Bytes	No more than 75 percent of physical memory.
Memory\Pool Nonpaged Bytes	A steady value. (A slow rise might indicate a memory leak.)
Processor\% Processor Time	Less than 75 percent.
Processor\Interrupts/sec	Depends on the processor, and on network hardware and drivers. Up to 3,500 for a 90-megahertz (MHz) Pentium; more than 19,000 for a 500-MHz Pentium or more than 58,000 for a 1.5-gigahertz (GHz) Pentium. Lower is better. If the value is too high, try moving some hardware devices to a different server.
Processor\System Processor Queue Length	4 or less.
LogicalDisk\% Disk Time PhysicalDisk\% Disk Time	As low as possible.
LogicalDisk\Avg. Disk Queue Length PhysicalDisk\Avg. Disk Queue Length	Less than 4.
LogicalDisk\Avg. Disk Bytes/Transfer PhysicalDisk\Avg. Disk Bytes/Transfer	As high as possible.
System\Context Switches/sec	Compare this value with the value of Web Service\Total Method Requests/sec. Context switches per request (Context Switches/sec divided by Total Method Requests/sec) should be low.
System\System Calls/sec	As low as possible.
Web Service\Bytes Total/sec	As high as possible.
Web Service\Total Method Requests/sec	As high as possible.
Web Service\Current Connections	As high as possible.

(continued)

Table 6.1 Preferred Values for Frequently Used Performance Counters *(continued)*

Object\Counter	Preferred or Ideal Value
Web Service Cache\File Cache Hits %	As high as possible for static content. **Note:** This value might be low if the Kernel URI cache hits percentage is high.
Web Service Cache\Kernel:URI Cache Flushes	As low as possible, relative to the number of requests. **Note:** This number increases every time a file is flushed from the HTTP.sys response cache (HTTP.sys is the kernel-mode device driver in IIS 6.0), which means that the content has not been accessed in the past 2–4 minutes. The only way to decrease this number is to flush the cache less often, although frequent flushing can cause HTTP.sys to use more memory for content that is not being accessed.
Web Service Cache\Kernel:URI Cache Misses	As low as possible. (Each request for dynamic content increases the value of the counter by one.)
Web Service Cache\Kernel:URI Cache Hits %	As high as possible. (Applies to static unauthenticated content and dynamic content that is marked as cacheable.)
Active Server Pages\Request Wait Time	As low as possible.
Active Server Pages\Requests Queued	As low as possible.
Active Server Pages\Transactions/sec	As high as possible. **Note:** ASP transactions degrade overall server performance because each transaction requires interaction with a database. If you are concerned about server performance, use ASP transactions sparingly.

The counters listed in Table 6.2 are useful for monitoring your FTP servers.

Table 6.2 Preferred Values for Useful FTP Performance Counters

Object\Counter	Preferred or Ideal Value
FTP Service\Bytes Sent/sec	As high as possible.
FTP Service\Bytes Received/sec	As high as possible.
FTP Service\Bytes Total/sec	As high as possible.

In addition to the counters in Table 6.1 and Table 6.2, the following system counters are useful for monitoring your server's use of system resources:

- System\Threads
- System\Processes
- System\Context Switches/sec

For a discussion of system-related counters and how their data relates to the performance of your Web server, see "Identifying Processor Bottlenecks" later in this chapter.

For more information about choosing which counters to monitor, including suggested counters for monitoring the main components of your server's operating system, see "Setting up a monitoring configuration" in Help and Support Center for Windows Server 2003.

Setting Up Monitoring

Use the counters listed in Table 6.1 and Table 6.2 to generate a baseline log that typifies your server's performance under ordinary conditions. Be sure to obtain multiple logs so that your baseline data contains enough information to give you a good sense of your server's behavior. For example, you might log the recommended counters for one week of typical operation. Shorter logs, which you need to periodically create, can help you monitor how changes in network activity are affecting your system performance.

Viewing Counter Data in the Performance Console

If you are new to Windows Server 2003 performance monitoring, open the Performance console and take a look at the data provided by a few counters.

▷ **To select performance objects and counters to view in System Monitor**

1. In Control Panel, double-click **Administrative Tools**, and then double-click **Performance**.

2. On the System Monitor toolbar, click the **Add** button (+) to open the **Add Counters** dialog box.

3. Click the **Performance object** list box to view a list of available performance objects, and then select an object to monitor.

   When you select an object, the list box on the left shows the available counters for that object and the list box on the right displays the instances for that object.

4. To select specific counters for the performance object, click **Select counters from list** (the default option), and then select the counters that you want to view.

   After you select a counter, you can click **Explain** to view a description.

5. If you want to monitor one or more specific instances of the counter (when available), select from the list of instances in the box on the right. Windows provides a default selection if you do not select a specific instance.

6. Click **Add** to begin monitoring.

In its default view, System Monitor provides a list of active counters, including their object and instance, directly below the graphical display of counter data. Remember that many counters display the last observed value or a cumulative count, not an average value or rate.

Using the Predefined System Overview Log

To get started quickly, use the predefined System Overview log that Windows Server 2003 provides under Counter Logs. The System Overview log is configured to create a binary log in the *systemroot*\Perflogs folder that, after manual startup, is updated every 15 seconds until the log reaches a maximum size. To minimize the system resources used during logging, the System Overview log provides *circular logging*, which overwrites older data with new data.

By default, the log includes three counters: Memory\Pages/sec, PhysicalDisk(_Total)\Avg. Disk Queue Length, and Processor(_Total)\% Processor Time.

Interpreting the data from a binary log requires the use of a parser, such as the Log Parser tool (LogParser.exe), to extract the data and convert it to formatted text. You can obtain the Log Parser tool from the *Internet Information Services (IIS) 6.0 Resource Kit* companion CD.

For information about creating counter logs, including baseline IIS logs, see article 313064, "Monitor Web Server Performance by Using Counter Logs in System Monitor in IIS," in the Microsoft Knowledge Base. To find this article, see the Microsoft Knowledge Base link on the Web Resources page at http://www.microsoft.com/windows/reskits/webresources.

For information about using Performance Logs and Alerts to create custom logs, see "Performance Logs and Alerts overview" in Help and Support Center for Windows Server 2003. For information about analyzing log data and a list of acceptable values for counters, see "Analyzing performance data" in Help and Support Center for Windows Server 2003.

Collecting Useful Data

When you set up performance monitoring, keep the following guidelines in mind:

- Be selective when choosing which counters to run, because several counters running at the same time can cause a small decrease in performance and can consume disk space.

- For routine monitoring, start by sampling data every 15 minutes.

- If you are monitoring for a specific problem, try varying the length of the interval until you find the optimal setting for obtaining the data that you need.

  For example, if you are monitoring the activity of a specific process at a specific time, set a frequent update interval; however, if you are monitoring a problem that reveals itself slowly, such as a memory leak, use a longer interval.

- When deciding the logging interval, consider the overall length of time over which you want to monitor.

  For example, you might sample data every 15 seconds for monitoring that is 4 hours or less. If you plan to monitor for 8 hours or more, set an interval longer than 300 seconds.

When you decide to change your system in any way, such as by tuning settings, adding hardware, or upgrading your system, follow these guidelines:

- **Always make changes one at a time.** Unsatisfactory performance that appears to relate to a single component might be the result of bottlenecks involving multiple components. However, if you make multiple changes simultaneously, it is often impossible to assess the impact of each change. For this reason, even when you are troubleshooting performance problems that involve multiple components, you might need to address each problem individually, making changes one at a time.

- **Repeat monitoring after every change.** Because tuning one resource can affect other resources, it is recommended that you monitor after every change that you make, being sure to monitor not only the area you changed but also more globally. Unless you monitor after you make a change, you cannot determine whether your change improved performance.

- **Review event logs.** Sometimes poor or unsatisfactory performance generates output in event logs. Use Event Viewer to monitor events that appear in event logs, such as application, system, and security logs. In addition, IIS logs can provide you with information about your changes. For more information about Event Viewer, see "Event Viewer" in Help and Support Center for Windows Server 2003. For more information about IIS logs, see "Analyzing Log Files" in this book.

- **Test your changes in a lab.** When your changes are significant, test them in a performance lab before making the changes in a production environment.

- **Periodically, obtain a new performance baseline.** After making several changes, monitor again to update your performance baseline. Compare the new baseline to previous logs to observe the actual effects your changes are having on performance and capacity.

Managing Network Activity

Creating and maintaining a Web site involves using hardware, software, and network bandwidth to manage network traffic. Servers send out pages in response to requests. In order to issue a request, a browser first establishes a Transmission Control Protocol (TCP) connection with the server and then sends the request through the connection. Network traffic, as the term applies to Web servers, is the mixture of incoming requests and outgoing responses.

Network traffic typically occurs in bursts and clumps that are only partly predictable. For example, many intranet sites have activity peaks at the beginning and end of the day, and around lunchtime. However, the exact size of these peaks varies from day to day, and the actual traffic load changes from moment to moment. There is a direct relationship between the amount of traffic and the network bandwidth needed. *Network bandwidth* is the capacity of the transmission medium stated in bits per second (bps). On computer networks, greater bandwidth means faster data-transfer capability. The more visitors your site has and the larger the pages the site provides, the more network bandwidth your server requires.

Estimating Bandwidth Requirements and Connection Speed

Data traveling on a network is split into packets. In addition to the data that it carries, each packet includes about 20 bytes of header information and other network protocol information (this extra information is known as *overhead*). The amount of data in a packet is not fixed, and thus the ratio of overhead to data can vary. Most incoming HTTP requests are small. A typical request (for example, `GET http://www.microsoft.com/default.asp`), including the TCP/IP overhead, consists of no more than a few hundred bytes as it travels across the network.

Overhead can become an important consideration when you are estimating your site's bandwidth requirements and deciding how fast a connection you need. If current usage is close to the limits of your connection's capacity, an extra 20 percent for overhead might mean that you need the next faster type of connection.

Think of a server that displays static Hypertext Markup Language (HTML) text-only pages that average 5 kilobytes (KB), which is nearly equivalent to a full page of printed text. The server is connected to the Internet through a DS1/T1 line, which can transmit data at 1.536 megabits per second. Inherent overhead makes it impossible to use the full-rated T1 bandwidth of 1.544 megabits per second. For this 5-KB file, protocol overhead is significant, amounting to about 30 percent of the file's size. For larger files, the overhead accounts for a smaller percentage of network traffic.

Table 6.3 shows the traffic generated by a typical request for a 5-KB page. Note that all the figures for overhead are estimates. The precise number of bytes sent varies with each request.

Table 6.3   Network Traffic Generated by a Request for a 5-KB Page

Traffic Type	Bytes Sent
TCP connection	180 (approx.)
GET request	256 (approx.)
5-KB file	5,120
Protocol overhead	1,364 (approx.)
Total	6,920

To calculate the number of bits for this 5-KB page, multiply the total number of bytes sent by 8 bits per byte:

$6,920 \times 8 = 55,360$

As stated previously, a T1 line can transmit 1.536 megabits per second. Dividing bits per second by bits per page (1,536,000/55,360) indicates a maximum transmission rate of just under 28 pages per second. (Because modems add a start bit and a stop bit to each byte, the transmission rate through a modem is slower than the raw numbers appear to indicate.) For this small text-only page, Table 6.4 shows the relative speed for connections to several types of network interfaces and an estimated page delivery rate for each connection type.

Table 6.4   Relative Network Interface Speeds to Request a 5-KB Page

Connection Type	Connection Speed	5-KB Pages Sent per Second
Dedicated PPP/SLIP via modem	28.8 kilobits per second (Kbps)	About half of 1 page
Frame Relay or fast modem	56 Kbps	Almost 1 page
Integrated Services Digital Network (ISDN)	128 Kbps	Just over 2 pages
Typical DSL	640 Kbps	Almost 11 pages
DS1/T1	1.536 megabits per second (Mbps)	26 pages
10-megabit Ethernet	8 Mbps (best case)	(Up to) 136 pages
DS3/T3	44.736 Mbps	760 pages
OC1	51.844 Mbps	880 pages
100-megabit Ethernet	80 Mbps (best case)	(Up to) 1,360 pages
OC3	155.532 Mbps	2,650 pages
OC12	622.128 Mbps	10,580 pages
1-gigabit/sec Ethernet	800 Mbps (best case)	(Up to) 13,600 pages

If you add a small graphic to the 5-KB page, the results are considerably different. An image, in the form of a .jpg file that appears on-screen as a 1-inch by 2-inch rectangle (the actual physical size depends on monitor settings), takes up about as much disk space as the original text file. Adding one such image file to each page nearly doubles the average page size and also the number of requests that are needed. This increased size reduces the number of pages that the server can send to the Internet on a DS1/T1 line to a maximum of about 15 pages per second, regardless of how fast the computer itself runs.

If a page contains several images, if the images are relatively large, or if the page contains multimedia content, the page can take much longer to download. You can often find simple solutions for improving download time, such as consolidating, removing, sizing down, or compressing images or converting images to a more compact graphics format. You might also connect to the network by using a faster interface (this change can improve performance for the server, but not necessarily for the client, as is discussed later in this section).

A site that serves primarily static HTML pages, especially pages with a simple structure, is likely to run out of network bandwidth before it runs out of processing power. In contrast, a site that performs a lot of dynamic page generation, or that acts as a transaction or database server, uses more processor cycles and can create bottlenecks in its processor, memory, disk, or network.

For more information about how to create more efficient Web pages, see "Creating a More Efficient Web Site" later in this chapter.

Browser Download Time

Up to this point, the bandwidth discussion has focused on the number of pages that a *server* can send in a specified amount of time. The second part of this discussion focuses on how long it takes a *browser* to download a page.

Consider how much time a browser needs to download a page that, including overhead, amounts to 90 KB, which equals about 720 kilobits. If you ignore *network latency*, which is the amount of time required for a packet or signal to travel from one point on a network to another (latency typically adds a few seconds before any of the data arrives), and if everything is working perfectly, a 720-kilobit page downloads over a 28.8-Kbps connection in about 25 seconds. The download takes longer if any blocking or bottlenecks occur at the server, if the network is overloaded and slow, or if the user's connection is slower than 28.8 Kbps (due to poor line quality, for example).

If the client computer has a higher bandwidth connection on an intranet, the download time is usually much shorter. If your Web site is on the Internet, however, you cannot count on a majority of users having faster connections.

Server-Side Request Processing

It takes about 52 connections at 28.8 Kbps to saturate a DS1/T1 line. Not accounting for delays (which are fairly typical), if no more than 52 clients simultaneously request the page used in the preceding example, and if the server can keep up with the requests, the clients all receive the 90-KB page in the 25 seconds calculated in the example.

If 100 clients simultaneously request that same page, however, the total number of bits to be transferred is $100 \times 737,280$ (720 kilobits). It takes between 47 and 48 seconds for that many bits to travel over a DS1/T1 line. When that many bits are involved, the network connection for the server, not the client, becomes the limiting factor.

A DS3/T3 line carries nearly 45 Mbps, about 30 times the capacity of a DS1/T1 line, and it takes more than 1,500 clients at 28.8 Kbps to saturate its bandwidth. Moreover, the increase in download time for each new client is much smaller on a DS3/T3 line. When there are 2,000 simultaneous 28.8-Kbps connections, for example, it still takes less than 33 seconds for a client to download the page.

This example assumes that the server is capable of performing the relevant processing and handling of 2,000 simultaneous connections, which is not the same as handling 2,000 simultaneous users: users occasionally stop to read or think, and typically spend only a small percentage of their time downloading, except while receiving streaming multimedia content. Because of this difference between users and connections, IIS 6.0 can support more users than the figures appear to indicate. A Web server on a DS1/T1 line can typically handle several hundred users connecting at 28.8 Kbps, and with a DS3/T3 line the number typically climbs to 5,000 or more. Although these numbers are derived from actual servers, you can expect performance to vary with differing content types and user needs, and with the number and type of services that a particular computer is performing.

These network performance differences scale linearly, and the scaling continues at higher data-transfer rates. Two DS3/T3 lines, for example, can serve approximately twice as many clients as one line can, provided that processor power is sufficient to keep up with user demand and no bottlenecks prevent your servers from operating at maximum processing power. Connecting to the network by using a faster interface often resolves any performance problems for the server, but not necessarily for the client, as is shown later in this section.

Perceived Delay, Acceptable Delay, and Site Performance

The amount of time in which a user perceives that a Web page appears, known as *perceived delay*, is not identical to the actual time that is required to fully display the page. If the first thing that the user sees when opening a page is a set of buttons that allow further navigation, the user might never know or care that the rest of the page takes longer than a minute to download. If, on the other hand, the page takes longer than a minute to download, and the navigation buttons do not appear until after the rest of the page, users might not wait for the download.

The length of an *acceptable delay* depends partly on the kind of information that the page provides, but no more than 30 seconds is usually considered acceptable. If the information is important, users are more likely, but still reluctant, to wait.

As a best practice, set minimum performance goals that specify the acceptable performance for each of your sites. For example, the managers of certain Microsoft e-commerce Internet sites test their site performance against the following minimum performance goals:

- All pages must load within 10 seconds.
- Average CPU usage for each server must be less than 70 percent.
- Available memory must remain stable throughout the test period.
- The site must maintain 10 customer checkouts per second.

Monitoring Network Activity

The primary functions of IIS 6.0 are to establish connections for clients, to receive and interpret requests, and to deliver files — all as quickly as possible. The pace at which these vital functions are performed depends, in large part, on two factors: the effective bandwidth of the link between the server and the network, and the capacity of this link and the server to support network resources.

The speed of the network interfaces also affects the pace. Some servers have two or more network interfaces, which are frequently called front-end and back-end servers. *Front-end servers* are client-accessible Web servers that run application server software, such as IIS, to handle traffic coming from the Internet. Front-end servers can add a layer of protection for your *back-end servers*, which include database servers, file servers, domain controllers, and WINS servers. Different interfaces do not necessarily run at the same speed. This is the case, for example, if a Web server is connected to a database server by means of a private network.

If more bandwidth is needed, the network must be upgraded or — in the case of shared-resource networks such as Ethernet — the network must be broken into subnets.

Bandwidth and Capacity

The main purpose of most Web servers is to manage input/output (I/O): Requests come in, and pages go out. Handling I/O requires a certain amount of bandwidth and other server resources as well. In addition to IIS 6.0, network I/O involves TCP/IP, which is implemented by Windows Server 2003 TCP/IP.

Network capacity is measured, in part, by the number of connections that the server establishes and maintains. Bandwidth is measured in several ways:

- By the rate at which bytes are transferred to and from the server.

- By the rate at which the server sends data packages, which include frames, packets, segments, and datagrams.

- By the rate at which the server sends and receives files.

Effective bandwidth varies widely and depends upon the transmission capacity of the link, the server configuration, and the server workload. The values for a single server also change as it operates in response to demand and to competition for shared network resources.

To ensure that your network has sufficient bandwidth and capacity for the network activity it must support, monitor the following performance indicators:

- Data transmission rates at the different Open Systems Interconnection (OSI) layers, because the components that transmit data reside in different layers.

- File transfer rates, because a Web page often requires multiple file transfers.

- TCP connections, because a plateau in connections established, or increases in connection failures and connection resets, can indicate insufficient bandwidth.

Monitoring Data Transmission Rates at Different OSI Layers

The simplest measure of the effective bandwidth of a server is the rate at which the server sends and receives data. System Monitor displays counts of data transmissions that are collected by many components of the server computer.

The components that collect data reside in different layers of the OSI reference model:

- Counters on the Web, FTP, and Simple Mail Transfer Protocol (SMTP) services performance objects measure data transmitted at the OSI application layer.

- Counters on the TCP object measure data transmitted at the transport layer.

- Counters on the IP object measure data at the network layer.

- Counters on the Network Interface object measure data at the data-link layer.

As a result of their different positions in the OSI stack, the counters collect different data. For example, the counters at the application layer measure data in the form in which the application sends it, counting the bytes sent before the data is divided into packets and prefixed with protocol headers and control packets. Counters at the application layer do not include retransmitted data.

In addition, the counters display the data in units native to the component being measured. For example, the Web Service object displays data in bytes, and the TCP object displays data in segments.

For more information about TCP/IP and about the OSI reference model, see "Additional Resources" at the end of this chapter.

Tables 6.5 through 6.8 list and describe some of the counters that can be used to measure transmission rates. These counters display the transmission rates observed during the last sample interval; they do not display a rolling or cumulative average of the rate.

Counters for Monitoring Data Transmission Rates at the Application Layer

Table 6.5 lists counters at the application layer. As with all the Web Service counters, these collect data that shows the rate at which the WWW service (a user-mode service) is sending and receiving bits. These counters do not measure the transmittal rates for HTTP.sys.

Table 6.5   Counters for Measuring Data Transmission Rates at the Application Layer

Object\Counter	Value
Web Service\Bytes Sent/sec	The rate at which the WWW service is sending data, in bytes per second.
Web Service\Bytes Received/sec	The rate at which the WWW service is receiving data, in bytes per second.
Web Service\Bytes Total/sec	The rate at which the WWW service is sending and receiving data, in bytes per second (the sum of Web Service\Bytes Sent/sec and Web Service\Bytes Received/sec).
FTP Service\Bytes Sent/sec	The rate at which the FTP service is sending data, in bytes per second.
FTP Service\Bytes Received/sec	The rate at which the FTP service is receiving data, in bytes per second.
FTP Service\Bytes Total/sec	The rate at which the FTP service is sending and receiving data, in bytes per second (the sum of FTP Service\Bytes Sent/sec and FTP Service\Bytes Received/sec).
SMTP Server\Bytes Sent/sec	The rate at which the SMTP server is sending data, in bytes per second.
SMTP Server\Bytes Received/sec	The rate at which the SMTP server is receiving data, in bytes per second.
SMTP Server\Bytes Total/sec	The rate at which the SMTP server is sending and receiving data, in bytes per second (the sum of SMTP Service\Bytes Sent/sec and SMTP Service\Bytes Received/sec).

Analyzing the data

The IIS 6.0 service counters listed in Table 6.5 display the number of bytes transmitted on behalf of each service that runs on the server. To calculate the total number of bytes sent or received by all IIS 6.0 services, calculate the sum of the values for each service. To determine the proportion of bytes transmitted by each service, compute the ratio of bytes for one service to the sum of bytes for all services or for the network.

Data collected by the IIS 6.0 service counters underestimates the total number of bytes that the IIS 6.0 services actually transmit to the network. Because these values are collected at the application layer, they measure data only. They do not measure protocol headers, control packets, or retransmitted bytes. In general, the bytes counted by the services represent 60 to 70 percent of the total number of bytes transmitted by the services on the network. If the sum of bytes for all services accounts for two-thirds or more of total network bandwidth, you can assume that your network is running at or near the total capacity of its communications link.

If you are using bandwidth throttling to limit the amount of bandwidth that the WWW service or an individual Web site uses, or you want to evaluate whether bandwidth throttling might be useful, monitor the Web Service\Bytes Total/sec and the Web Service\Bytes Sent/sec counters. These counters can indicate whether your Web server has sufficient bandwidth to handle its load. If it does not, consider using bandwidth throttling to redistribute network availability.

For information about using bandwidth throttling, see "Throttling Bandwidth to Manage Service Availability" later in this chapter.

Counters for Monitoring Data Transmission Rates at the Transport and Network Layers

Table 6.6 lists the counters on the TCP object. These counters monitor *TCP segments* — the unit of data that TCP sends down the protocol stack to IP. Windows Server 2003 provides two TCP objects, TCPv4 and TCPv6. Choose the counter that monitors the version of TCP that your server uses.

Table 6.6   Counters for Measuring Data Transmission Rates at the Transport Layer

Object\Counter	Value
TCPv4\Segments Sent/sec TCPv6\Segments Sent/sec	The rate at which TCP segments are sent by using the TCP protocol.
TCPv4\Segments Received/sec TCPv6\Segments Received/sec	The rate at which TCP segments are received by using the TCP protocol.
TCPv4\Segments/sec TCPv6\Segments/sec	The rate at which TCP segments are sent and received by using the TCP protocol (the sum of Segments Sent/sec and Segments Received/sec).
TCPv4\Segments Retransmitted/sec TCPv6\Segments Retransmitted/sec	The rate at which segments are transmitted that contain one or more bytes that TCP recognizes as having been transmitted before. Segments Retransmitted/sec is a subset of Segments Sent/sec and Segments/sec. To determine the proportion of transmissions caused by failed transmission attempts, divide Segments Retransmitted/sec by Segments Sent/sec.

Table 6.7 describes lists some of the datagram counters for the IP object. These counters monitor *IP datagrams,* which are the units of data that IP sends down the protocol stack to the network interface, such as a network adapter. The sum of IP\Datagrams/sec and IP\Datagrams Forwarded/sec represents the rate at which the server handles all IP datagrams.

Table 6.7 Counters for Measuring Data Transmission Rates at the Network Layer

Object\Counter	Value
IPv4\Datagrams Sent/sec IPv6\Datagrams Sent/sec	The rate at which IP datagrams are sent to the network interfaces. This counter does not include datagrams forwarded to another server.
IPv4\Datagrams Received/sec IPv6\Datagrams Received/sec	The rate at which IP datagrams are received from the network interfaces. This counter does not include datagrams forwarded to another server.
IPv4\Datagrams/sec IPv6\Datagrams/sec	The overall transmission rate for IP datagrams being sent and received over the network interfaces (the sum of IP\Datagrams Sent/sec and IP\Datagrams Received/sec).
IPv4\Datagrams Forwarded/sec IPv6\Datagrams Forwarded/sec	The rate, in incidents per second, at which the server attempts to find routes over which to forward IP datagrams to their final destination.

Analyzing the data

Counters on the TCP and IP performance objects display the rate at which data is sent and received over a TCP/IP connection at the transport and network layers, but the rate is not expressed in bytes. Counters on the IP performance object display data in datagrams, and counters on the TCP performance object display data in segments. It is difficult to convert segments to bytes because bytes per segment can vary from 8 KB to 64 KB (the size can increase to 1 gigabyte [GB] if a window scaling option is in effect), depending upon the size of the TCP/IP receive window and the maximum segment size negotiated when each connection is established.

Counters for Monitoring Data Transmission Rates at the Data-Link Layer

Table 6.8 lists several counters on the Network Interface performance object that might be useful for obtaining data about the network adapters on the server. The first instance of the Network Interface object that you see in System Monitor represents the *loopback* — a local path through the protocol driver and the network adapter; all other instances represent installed network adapters.

Table 6.8 Counters for Measuring Data Transmission Rates at the Data-Link Layer

Object\Counter	Value
Network Interface (*Adapter ID*)\Bytes Sent/sec	The rate, in seconds, at which bytes are sent over this network adapter. The counted bytes include framing characters. This counter is a subset of Network Interface\Bytes Total/sec.
Network Interface (*Adapter ID*)\Bytes Received/sec	The rate, in seconds, at which bytes are received over this network adapter. The counted bytes include framing characters. This counter is a subset of Network Interface\Bytes Total/sec.
Network Interface (*Adapter ID*)\Bytes Total/sec	The rate, in bytes per second, at which bytes are sent and received over this network adapter (the sum of Network Interface\Bytes Sent/sec and Network Interface\Bytes Received/sec).
Network Interface\Packets Sent/sec	The rate, in seconds, at which packets are sent over the network adapter.
Network Interface\Packets Received/sec	The rate, in seconds, at which packets are received over the network adapter.

Analyzing the data

Counters for the Network Interface performance object display the rate at which bytes are transmitted over a TCP/IP connection by monitoring the counters on the network adapter at the data-link layer. The values of these Network Interface counters include all prepended frame header bytes and bytes that have been retransmitted. They provide a relatively accurate estimate of the number of bytes transmitted over the network, but do not measure the bytes transmitted by a specific IIS 6.0 service.

It is useful to compare the data produced by these counters with other performance measures, such as the total number of connections served at a given bandwidth or processor use at different throughput rates.

Monitoring File and Message Transfers

Most static Web pages include multiple files, such as a file of text and one or more graphics files. File counters are available for each IIS 6.0 service. The counters for the WWW and FTP services count the total number of files that the services send and receive. The counters for the SMTP service tally total messages sent and total messages received, but not total messages sent and received.

Table 6.9 lists the counters for monitoring file and message transfers.

Table 6.9   Counters for Monitoring IIS 6.0 File and Message Transfers

Object\Counter	Value
Web Service\Total Files Sent FTP Service\Total Files Sent SMTP Server\Messages Sent Total	For the WWW and FTP services, the total number of files sent by the service since service startup. For the SMTP service, the total number of outbound messages sent since service startup.
Web Service\Files Received FTP Service\Total Files Received SMTP Server\Messages Received Total	For the WWW and FTP services, the total number of files received by the service since service startup. For the SMTP service, the total number of inbound messages received since service startup.
Web Service\Total Files Transferred FTP Service\Total Files Transferred	For the WWW and FTP services, the sum of Total Files Sent and Total Files Received by the service since service startup. The SMTP service does not provide a sum total counter.

Analyzing the Data

The file counters for a particular service are an indicator of the network activity generated by that service. This data can also be associated with other performance measures to determine the effects of high and low file activity on server components.

The file counters in Table 6.9 display a cumulative total for all traffic since the service was started, regardless of when System Monitor was started. These counters do not display the current value or the rate at which files are transmitted. In IIS 6.0, the Web Service object (but not the FTP Service object) provides counters to measure the rate, in seconds, at which files are sent and received. The SMTP service provides similar counters that measure the rate at which messages are received and sent.

To calculate file transmission rates for the FTP service, you can use Performance Logs and Alerts to log the values for the file counters and the times at which measurements are taken. To derive the transmission rates, you can export the log files to a spreadsheet that associates the time of the measurement with the file count.

Monitoring TCP Connections

If the bandwidth of your server is insufficient to handle its workload, clients usually become aware of this before the server does. Client requests to the server might be rejected or time out, or the response might be delayed. On the server side, the indicators are less clear because the server continues to establish connections, receive requests, and transmit data.

Bandwidth shortages are not uncommon. You can detect one on your server (perhaps even before clients do) by monitoring the success and failure of connections established and rejected by TCP. With ample bandwidth, the server can establish and serve connections before they time out. If bandwidth is insufficient, the connections fail.

Table 6.10 lists the counters that monitor the success and failure of connections to TCP. Windows Server 2003 provides two TCP objects, TCPv4 and TCPv6; choose the counter that monitors the version of TCP that your server is using.

Table 6.10   Counters for Monitoring the Success or Failure of TCP Connections

Object\Counter	Value
TCPv4\Connections Established TCPv6\Connections Established	The number of simultaneous connections supported by TCP. This counter displays the number of connections last observed to be in the ESTABLISHED or CLOSE-WAIT state. This counter displays the last observed value (indicating the current state); its value is not an average.
TCPv4\Connection Failures TCPv6\Connection Failures	The number of connections that have failed since the service was started (regardless of when you started System Monitor). TCP counts a connection as having failed when it goes directly from sending (SYN-SENT) or receiving (SYN-RCVD) to CLOSED, or from receiving (SYN-RCVD) to listening (LISTEN).
TCPv4\Connections Reset TCPv6\Connections Reset	The number of connections reset since the service was started (regardless of when you started System Monitor). TCP counts a connection as having been reset when it goes directly from ESTABLISHED or CLOSE-WAIT to CLOSED.

The counters on the TCPv4 and TCPv6 objects are the best indicators of the success of connection requests. The counters on the Web Service and FTP Service performance objects monitor connections maintained by each IIS 6.0 service, but display only successful connection requests, not failed attempts. Like all counters at the application layer, they do not have information about connections until the connections are established.

For a discussion of performance counters that display the number of simultaneous connections maintained by IIS 6.0, see "Preventing Processor Bottlenecks" later in this chapter.

Analyzing the Data

If your server does not support current or increasing demand, look for the following patterns when you analyze the data from the TCP\Connections counters:

- **Look for a plateau in the Connections Established counter value.** If the counter value of TCP\Connections Established often reaches, but rarely exceeds, a maximum value (that is, the line in the graph rises and then reaches a plateau), the peak value is likely to indicate the maximum number of connections that can be established with the current bandwidth and application workload. If you observe such a pattern, the server probably cannot support any greater demand.

- **Look for consistent increases of the Connection Failures and Connections Reset counter values.** An increasing number of failures and resets, or a consistently increasing rate of failures and resets, can indicate a bandwidth shortage. The counters that monitor failures and resets show cumulative values, but you can use Performance Logs and Alerts to set alerts on the values or to log values over time. You can then use a spreadsheet to calculate the rates at which connections are rejected and reset.

Note

Be cautious when interpreting the number of reset connections shown by the TCP\Connections Reset counter. Resets do not always indicate dropped or failed connections. To minimize connection overhead, many browsers routinely close connections by sending a TCP reset (RST) packet rather than by using a normal close operation. The TCP\Connections Reset counter does not distinguish between connections that are reset because they are dropped and those that are reset in order to be closed abruptly.

Administering Network Resources

IIS 6.0 provides a set of Quality of Service (QoS) features to help you maintain acceptable service levels of data transmission on your network. The goal of QoS is to ensure that particular sites or applications do not monopolize server resources, such as memory or CPU cycles, which can adversely affect performance. QoS helps administrators control how IIS components — such as sites, application pools, or the WWW service as a whole — use resources.

If the bandwidth on your server is not sufficient to support demand, you can increase overall server bandwidth. You can also increase the effective bandwidth of existing communication links. Some suggestions on how to do so follow; many involve setting parameters that can only be modified by editing the Windows registry or the IIS 6.0 metabase.

It is frequently possible to reduce your use of bandwidth by optimizing Web application scripts or content. This option is worth looking into as an interim solution, partly because it can also improve response time and the user experience; however, if your client base is growing, you might eventually have to increase the bandwidth of your network connection anyway.

You can sometimes effectively increase existing bandwidth by limiting connections, by increasing the length of the connection queues, or by enabling HTTP Keep-Alives.

QoS in IIS provides the following methods for managing and maintaining network performance:

- **Limit connections in order to manage resources.** Set limits on the number of connections allowed to a Web or FTP server or to specific sites. Use this feature to ensure that all your services remain active during periods of peak use and to protect against malicious attack.

- **Enable HTTP Keep-Alives in order to keep browser connections open.** To maintain an open connection when browsers send multiple requests to download a Web page, be sure that HTTP Keep-Alives are enabled.

- **Set connection timeouts to save resources.** To reduce the loss of processing resources consumed by idle connections, set connection timeouts on your Web server.

- **Use HTTP compression for faster downloads.** To provide faster transmission time between IIS and compression-enabled browsers, use HTTP compression.

- **Throttle bandwidth to manage service availability.** Limit the bandwidth used by your Web server so that the server remains available for other services, such as e-mail or news, even during periods of peak use.

- **Use other IIS features to enhance performance.** In addition to the QoS features, use other IIS features, including Web gardens, idle timeout, CPU monitoring, and processor affinity, to help you manage system resources and enhance performance:

For more information about IIS QoS features, see "Quality of Service" in IIS 6.0 Help.

Limiting Connections to Manage Resources

Connection limits restrict the number of simultaneous connections to your Web sites and your Web server. If the number of connections reaches the maximum allotted, all subsequent connection attempts return an error and then are disconnected.

By limiting connections, you can conserve bandwidth for other uses, such as e-mail servers, news servers, or another Web site running on the same installation. Limiting connections also conserves memory and protects against malicious attacks designed to overload your Web server with thousands of client requests.

To determine whether you need to limit connections, use System Monitor to log the Current Connections, Maximum Connections, and Total Connection Attempts counters on the Web Service and FTP Service objects. Continue logging until you have a good sense of the normal range; typically, logging can take several days to a week or more and must be repeated at regular intervals. For more information about performance logging, see "Enabling Logging" in IIS 6.0 Help and "Analyzing Log Files" in this book.

You can establish global WWW service or FTP service connection limits for all Web and FTP sites, or you can establish connection limits on individual Web or FTP sites. IIS checks for a global connection limit before checking for connection limits on individual sites. If the global connection limit is exceeded, IIS returns error message 403.9 (Forbidden - Too Many Users) regardless of the connection limit set for individual sites. (You can customize the connection limit error message in IIS 5.0; however, IIS 6.0 does not offer that option.)

The following procedure tells how to set an overall connection limit for the WWW service. To set connection limits on the FTP service, follow the same procedure, but enter the connection limits on the **FTP** tab rather than the **Performance** tab.

 Important

You must be a member of the Administrators group on the local computer to perform the following procedure or procedures, or you must have been delegated the appropriate authority. As a security best practice, log on to your computer by using an account that is not in the Administrators group, and then use the **runas** command to run IIS Manager as an administrator. At a command prompt, type **runas** /*User.Administrative_AccountName* "mmc %systemroot%\system32\inetsrv\iis.msc".

To set a global connection limit for the WWW service

1. In IIS Manager, expand the local computer, right-click the **Web Sites** folder, and then click **Properties.**

2. On the **Performance** tab, select the **Connections limited to** check box, and in the box next to it, type the maximum number of simultaneous connections to allow for the WWW service.

3. Click **Apply**, and then click **OK.**

 Caution

If you set the Unlimited connections option on the Performance tab, IIS permits as many simultaneous connections as your memory, network bandwidth, and processor memory can support. Allowing an unlimited number of simultaneous connections to your Web server exposes all the sites on the server to the threat of a malicious attack, such as when thousands of clients are instructed to connect to the server, which delays subsequent service by consuming memory and bandwidth resources.

For more information about setting global and individual site connection limits, see "Limiting Connections" in IIS 6.0 Help.

Another way to limit connections to your Web server is through bandwidth throttling. For information about using this feature, see "Throttling Bandwidth to Manage Service Availability" later in this chapter. For a list of counters related to performance, see "IIS 6.0 Performance Counters" in this book. For information about connection timeouts, see "Setting Connection Timeouts to Save Resources" later in this chapter.

Enabling HTTP Keep-Alives to Keep Connections Open

A browser typically makes multiple requests in order to download an entire Web page. To enhance server performance, most Web browsers request that the server keep the connection open across these multiple requests, which is a feature known as *HTTP Keep-Alives*.

Without HTTP Keep-Alives, a browser that makes numerous requests for a page containing multiple elements, such as graphics, might require a separate connection for each element. These additional requests and connections require extra server activity and resources, decreasing server efficiency. The additional connections also make a browser much slower and less responsive, especially across a slow connection.

HTTP Keep-Alives are enabled by default in IIS 6.0, which complies with the HTTP/1.1 specification for HTTP Keep-Alives. IIS holds open an inactive connection for as long as the **ConnectionTimeout** metabase property specifies (the default value is 120 seconds).

If you disable HTTP Keep-Alives, the server ignores a client's request to keep the connection open. Therefore, disable HTTP Keep-Alives only for a specific reason and if you clearly understand how this change affects your server.

HTTP Keep-Alives are required for integrated security or connection-based authentication services, such as Integrated Windows authentication. If you disable HTTP Keep-Alives for Web sites that use Integrated Windows authentication, requests to the Web site fail.

To verify that your server is running with HTTP Keep-Alives enabled, or to enable HTTP Keep-Alives if this feature is disabled, use the following procedure.

▷   **To enable HTTP Keep-Alives**

1. In IIS Manager, expand the local computer, expand the **Web Sites** folder, right-click the Web site for which you want to enable HTTP Keep-Alives, and then click **Properties**.

2. On the **Web Site** tab, under **Connections**, select the **Enable HTTP Keep-Alives** check box.

3. Click **Apply**, and then click **OK**.

Alternatively, you can enable HTTP Keep-Alives by setting the **AllowKeepAlive** metabase property to **true** (the default value).

Setting Connection Timeouts to Save Resources

Connection timeouts help reduce the amount of memory resources that are consumed by idle connections. Time-out settings also allow you to specify how long server resources are allocated to specific tasks or clients. When you enable connection timeouts, IIS 6.0 enforces the following types of connection timeouts at the connection level:

- A *connection timeout*, in which the client has sent data to the server, but the client is now idle. Use the **ConnectionTimeout** metabase property to set a connection timeout limit for the WWW, FTP, Network News Transfer Protocol (NNTP), and SMTP services.

- A *request timeout*, which prevents clients from issuing unreasonably slow requests to the server (for example, 1 bit per second). Use the **HeaderWaitTimeout** metabase property to set a request timeout for the WWW service.

- A *response timeout*, which prevents malicious or malfunctioning clients from consuming resources by holding a connection open with minimal data. Use the **MinFileBytesPerSec** metabase property to set a response timeout for the WWW service.

Monitoring with Counters to Evaluate Connection Limits

In IIS 6.0, the default connection timeout settings are more restrictive than in earlier versions of IIS, which helps prevent denial of service attacks on the server. To determine whether you can improve performance by changing a default connection timeout setting or by adding an optional setting, begin by obtaining a baseline of how your server performs with the current connection limits. For example, use System Monitor to log the Current Connections, Maximum Connections, and Total Connection Attempts counters on the Web Service and FTP Service objects. Continue logging until you have a good sense of the normal range; typically, logging can take several days to a week or more and must be repeated at regular intervals.

After obtaining baseline performance data for the default configuration, make incremental changes to the connection timeout settings, and then collect additional performance data by using these same counters. Compare the results to determine if changing the connection limits improves performance, keeping in mind that more aggressive limits can increase protection against malicious attacks.

Setting Connection Timeouts by Using IIS Manager

Use the following procedure to set a global connection timeout for the WWW or FTP service.

▶ **To set a global connection timeout for the WWW or FTP service**

1. In IIS Manager, expand the local computer, right-click the **Web Sites** or **FTP Sites** folder, and then click **Properties**.

2. On the **Web Site** or **FTP Site** tab, in the **Connection timeout** box, type the maximum number of seconds that IIS will maintain an idle connection before resetting the connection. (The default value for both Web and FTP sites is 120 seconds.)

   For the WWW service, verify that the **Enable HTTP Keep-Alives** check box is selected.

3. Click **Apply**, and then click **OK**.

You can also set global connection timeouts on SMTP and NNTP servers. In addition, you can set connection timeouts for an individual Web or FTP site. For more information about setting these connection timeouts, see "Setting Connection Timeouts" in IIS 6.0 Help.

Setting Connection Timeouts by Editing the Metabase

IIS 6.0 provides three metabase properties, **ConnectionTimeout**, **HeaderWaitTimeout**, and **MinFileBytesPerSec**, which you can use to set different types of connection timeouts. In IIS 6.0, these properties replace the **ServerListenTimeout** metabase property, which is no longer used for the WWW service but can be used for the FTP, SMTP, and NNTP services.

Setting connection timeouts

The **ConnectionTimeout** metabase property specifies the amount of time (in seconds) that the server waits before disconnecting an inactive connection. IIS applies this timeout limit after the client sends the first request to the server and the client is idle. The default value is 120 seconds for the WWW and FTP services (global settings); 120 seconds for individual Web and FTP sites; and 10 minutes for the SMTP and NNTP services. (In IIS Manager, when you change the value of the **ConnectionTimeout property**, you change this setting.)

For security reasons, the **ConnectionTimeout** property cannot be disabled. Thus, if you try to set the **ConnectionTimeout** property to 0, the property retains its previous setting.

Setting request timeouts

The **HeaderWaitTimeout** metabase property specifies the amount of time (in seconds) that the server waits for the client computer to send all HTTP headers for a request (indicated by a double carriage return) before HTTP.sys resets the connection. The purpose of this property is to help impede a type of denial of service attack that attempts to exhaust connection limits and keep those connections connected. You can apply this connection timeout only at the WWW service level.

For security reasons, the **HeaderWaitTimeout** property cannot be disabled. Thus, if you try to set the **HeaderWaitTimeout** property to 0, the property retains its previous setting.

Setting response timeouts

The **MinFileBytesPerSec** metabase property determines the length of time that the client has to receive the server's entire response to its request. If the client computer does not receive the entire HTTP response within the interval set by the time-out value (by default, 240 bytes per second), HTTP.sys terminates the connection. You can apply this connection timeout only at the WWW service level.

Configuring the **MinFileBytesPerSec** metabase property prevents a client computer from sending a request for a large response (such as a file download) and then receiving the response at a maliciously slow rate that is meant to consume resources on the server and potentially interrupt service for other client computers.

The time-out period is calculated by dividing the size of the entire response (including headers) by the value of the **MinFileBytesPerSec** property to obtain a maximum allowable response time, in seconds. For example, a 2-KB response (2,048 bytes) is allowed 8.5 seconds to complete if **MinFileBytesPerSec** has the default value of 240 bytes per second.

To accommodate very slow applications, you can disable the **MinFileBytesPerSec** property by setting the value to 0.

Reference to Default Time-out Settings

Additional IIS 6.0 metabase properties set time-out values for ASP, Common Gateway Interface (CGI) scripts, and Internet database connection pooling. Table 6.11 gives a summary of the metabase properties for setting timeouts and the default time-out limit for each property. For information about configuration options, see "Code Examples to Configure Metabase Properties" in IIS 6.0 Help. The final column of the table indicates which properties can alternatively be updated in IIS Manager.

Table 6.11   Default Time-out Values for IIS 6.0

Metabase Property	Default Time-Out Value	Configured in IIS Manager
AspQueueTimeout	Unlimited	
AspScriptTimeout	90 seconds	●
AspSessionTimeout	20 minutes	●
CGITimeout	300 seconds	●
ConnectionTimeout	120 seconds (Web and FTP); 10 minutes (SMTP and NNTP)	●
HeaderWaitTimeout	None (Turned off by default.)	
MinFileBytesPerSec[1]	240 bytes per second	
PoolIdcTimeout	None (Turned off by default.)	

1 This metabase property cannot be modified in IIS Manager, but it can be modified by adding the **MinFileBytesPerSec** entry to the Windows registry.

For more information about ASP–related properties and counters, see "Monitoring ASP Performance" later in this chapter. For information about the registry path for the **MinFileBytesPerSec** entry, see "Global Registry Entries" in IIS 6.0 Help.

Another way to limit connections to your Web server is to use bandwidth throttling. For information, see "Throttling Bandwidth to Manage Service Availability" later in this chapter. A related way to manage resources is to limit the number of simultaneous connections to your sites and server. For information about limiting connections, see "Limiting Connections to Manage Resources" earlier in this chapter.

Using HTTP Compression for Faster Downloads

If your Web sites use large amounts of bandwidth, or if you want to use bandwidth more effectively, consider enabling HTTP compression, which provides faster transmission times between IIS and compression-enabled browsers. If your network bandwidth is restricted, HTTP compression can be beneficial unless your processor usage is already very high.

IIS provides the following compression options:

- Static files only.

- Dynamic application responses only.

- Both static files and dynamic application responses.

Dynamic processing can affect CPU resources because IIS does not cache compressed versions of dynamic output. If compression is enabled for dynamic responses and IIS receives a request for a file that contains dynamic content, the response that IIS sends is compressed every time it is requested. Because dynamic compression consumes considerable CPU time and memory resources, use it only on servers that have slow network connections but CPU time to spare.

Compressed static responses can be cached and therefore do not affect CPU resources like dynamic responses do.

How HTTP Compression Works

When IIS receives a request, it checks whether the browser that sent the request is compression-enabled. (Recent versions of Microsoft® Internet Explorer and most other browsers typically send the following header if they are compression-enabled: Accept-Encoding: gzip, deflate.) IIS then determines whether the request is for a static file or for dynamic content.

If the content of the file is static, IIS checks whether the file has previously been requested and is already stored in a compressed format in the temporary compression directory. If a compressed version of the requested file is not found, IIS sends an uncompressed version of the requested file to the client browser while a background thread compresses the requested file. The newly compressed file is then stored in the compression directory, and subsequent requests for that file are serviced directly from the compression directory. In other words, an uncompressed version of the file is returned to the client unless a compressed version of the file already exists in the compression directory.

If the file contains dynamic content, IIS compresses the response as it is generated and sends the compressed response to the browser. No copy of the file is cached by the Web server.

The performance cost of compressing a static file is modest and is typically incurred only once, because the file is then stored in the temporary compression directory. The cost of compressing dynamically generated files is somewhat higher because the files are not cached and must be regenerated with each request. The cost of expanding the file at the browser is minimal. Compressed files download faster, which makes them particularly beneficial to the performance of any browser that uses a network connection with restricted bandwidth (a modem connection, for example).

When you enable HTTP compression, compressed files are given a default expiration date of Jan. 1, 1997. This expiration date prevents proxy servers from serving cached copies of compressed files to browsers that are not compression-enabled. This expiration date also forces browsers to return to the server for a fresh copy of the file when the user makes a new request instead of displaying a cached copy of the file. When you enable HTTP compression, the default settings for the **HcExpiresHeader**, **HcCacheControlHeader**, and **HcSendCacheHeaders** metabase properties ensure that older clients and proxy servers do not attempt to cache compressed files. Before you change these settings, see "Metabase Property Reference" in IIS 6.0 Help for information about these and related metabase properties.

Determining Whether HTTP Compression Will Improve Performance

If your server generates a large volume of dynamic content, consider whether the additional processing cost of HTTP compression is one that you can reasonably afford. If the % Processor Time counter is already 80 percent or higher, enabling HTTP compression is not recommended.

To evaluate how much of your processor is typically being used, follow these steps:

1. Establish a baseline for your processor usage by using System Monitor to log the following counters over several days. If you use Performance Logs and Alerts, you can log the data to a database and then query the data, examining the results in detail.

    - **Processor\% Processor Time.** This counter has a total instance and a separate instance for each processor in the system. If your server has more than one processor, you need to watch the individual processors as well as the total to discover any imbalance in the workload.

    - **Network Interface\Bytes Sent/sec.** Counters for the Network Interface performance object display the rate at which bytes are transmitted over a TCP/IP connection by monitoring the counters on the network adapter. For information about additional counters to monitor for this object, see Table 6.8.

2. Enable compression, and continue to log the values for these counters for an extended period — preferably for several days — so you have a good basis for comparison.

    Collect a broad sample to determine how compression affects various aspects of performance. Conduct the following tests:

    - Enable static compression only, dynamic compressions only, and both.

    - Change the list of files that you use for compression testing for both static and dynamic content.

    - Vary the compression level. Try this on all content types.

3. Compare the data from monitoring with and without compression, and with different types of compression, different compression levels, and different files.

 Important

If you see signs of blocking or bottlenecking during the preceding testing, promptly stop the test. A significant drop in the value of either counter indicates that performance with compression enabled has decreased relative to performance without compression enabled.

Choosing Compression Options

When you configure HTTP compression by using IIS Manager, IIS 6.0 automatically applies the default settings shown in Table 6.12. You can configure custom settings for each compression option by editing the metabase or alternatively — in the case of the compression directory — by using IIS Manager.

Table 6.12   Default Settings When HTTP Compression Is Enabled

Compression Options	File Type	Default Configuration	Configuration Method
File types compressed	Static	.txt, .htm, and .html	Metabase
	Dynamic	.exe, .dll, and .asp	Metabase
Compression schemes	Static	Both gzip and deflate	Metabase
	Dynamic	Both gzip and deflate	Metabase
Compression level	Static	10	Metabase
	Dynamic	0	Metabase
Compression directory	Static	Size: 95 MB Location[1]: %Windir%\IIS Temporary Compressed Files	Metabase or IIS Manager
	Dynamic	No directory[2]	N.A.

1 The compression directory must reside on an NTFS file system volume.

2 When dynamic files are compressed, they are not cached.

If the default HTTP compression configuration does not meet the needs of your organization, you can make the following changes to the configuration:

- **Specify additional file types to compress.** Edit the **HcFileExtensions** metabase property (for static files) and the **HcScriptFileExtensions** metabase property (for dynamic files) to apply compression to additional file types.

- **Enable or disable the gzip or deflate compression scheme.** When you use IIS Manager to enable compression, IIS enables both compression schemes (gzip and deflate), so that IIS can apply whichever compression scheme the client requests. You can edit the metabase to specify a particular compression scheme. If you disable a compression scheme, the server replies with an uncompressed file, which is an acceptable response to any client requests for that compression scheme.

- **Change the level of compression for static or dynamic files.** Compression levels range from 0 through 10. Higher compression levels produce smaller compressed files but use more CPU and memory. Lower compression levels produce slightly larger compressed files, but with less impact on CPU and memory usage. To configure a compression level other than 10 for static files and other than zero for dynamic files, edit the **HcOnDemandCompLevel** and **HcDynamicCompressionLevel** metabase properties.

  For dynamic compression, increasing the compression level can significantly increase CPU usage. The default compression level of zero uses the least amount of CPU resources and can increase performance if network bandwidth is adequate. Raise the dynamic compression level above zero only if you need more network bandwidth and have sufficient CPU capacity to handle the extra load.

- **Change the location or size of the compression directory.** To change the location and size of the compression directory for static files, edit the **HcCompressionDirectory**, **HcDoDiskSpaceLimiting**, and **HcMaxDiskSpaceUsage** metabase properties.

The procedures in the following sections tell how to enable HTTP compression and make the following configuration changes:

- Use IIS Manager to enable HTTP compression, using the default HTTP compression configuration, for static and dynamic files.

- Configure compression at specific levels of the metabase (for example, compression at the Web site level).

- Specify which file types to compress and the compression scheme to apply.

- Specify the location and size of the compression directory.

- Disable HTTP compression for requests that come through certain proxy servers.

Enabling Global HTTP Compression

When you enable HTTP compression by using IIS Manager, IIS applies compression according to the default settings shown in Table 6.12. With the exception of the location and size of the compression directory, you cannot change the default settings by using IIS Manager; you must edit the metabase to change the defaults.

 Important

After enabling HTTP compression (either by using IIS Manager or by editing the metabase), you must restart IIS for the change to take effect.

▷ **To enable HTTP compression of static files by using IIS Manager**

1. In IIS Manager, expand the local computer, right-click the **Web Sites** folder, and then click **Properties**.

2. On the **Service** tab, under **HTTP compression**, select the **Compress static files** check box.

3. In the **Temporary directory** box, either accept the default location (which is %Windir%\IIS Temporary Compressed Files), type the path to a local folder, or click **Browse** to locate a temporary folder in which to store the compressed files.

   The folder must be on a local drive of an NTFS–formatted partition. The folder cannot be a compressed directory and must not be shared. The access control lists (ACLs) for the folder must include Full Control access to the identity of the application pool or to the IIS_WPG group.

4. Under **Maximum temporary directory size**, click a folder size option. If you specify a maximum size under **Limited to (in megabytes)** (the default setting is 95 MB), when the limit is reached, IIS automatically cleans up the temporary directory by using the "least recently used" rule.

5. Click **Apply**, and then click **OK**.

Alternatively, you can enable HTTP compression of static files by setting the **HcDoStaticCompression** metabase property to **true**.

▷ **To enable HTTP compression of dynamic files by using IIS Manager**

1. In IIS Manager, expand the local computer, right-click the **Web Sites** folder, and then click **Properties**.

2. On the **Service** tab, under **HTTP compression**, select the **Compress application files** check box.

3. Click **Apply**, and then click **OK**.

Alternatively, you can enable HTTP compression of dynamic files by setting the **HcDoDynamicCompression** metabase property to **true**.

Configuring HTTP Compression at Specific Metabase Levels

All the compression configurations discussed so far are located under W3SVC/Filters/Compression in the metabase and are used to apply *global* HTTP compression, which is applied by using IIS Manager or by using one of the metabase properties that are used for global compression (beginning with **Hc…**). IIS 6.0 offers two new metabase properties, **DoStaticCompression** and **DoDynamicCompression** (beginning with **Do…**), which can reside at the service, site, virtual directory, directory, and file levels. Use these two new properties to apply compression to *individual* namespaces. Hence, you can enable global compression by using IIS Manager or the **Hc…** global properties and then disable one of the **Do…** properties (or vice versa) to obtain compression at a specific location in the IIS metabase.

 Important

You must be a member of the Administrators group on the local computer to run scripts and executables, or you must have been delegated the appropriate authority. As a security best practice, log on to your computer by using an account that is not in the Administrators group, and then use the runas command to run your script or executable as an administrator. At a command prompt, type runas /profile/ *User.MyMachine\Administrator* cmd to open a command window with administrator rights and then type cscript.exe *ScriptName* (including the full path with parameters, if any).

To enable static compression for a single directory, you need to first disable global static compression and then enable static compression at that directory. For example, to enable static compression for a directory at http://www.contoso.com/Home/StyleSheets, you need to perform the following steps:

1. Disable global static compression by executing the following command at a command prompt:

   ```
   adsutil set w3svc/filters/compression/parameters/HcDoStaticCompression false
   ```

2. Create, if it does not already exist, the metabase node for the "www.contoso.com/Home/StyleSheets" directory by executing the following commands at a command prompt:

   ```
   adsutil create w3svc/1/root/Home IIsWebDirectory

   adsutil create w3svc/1/root/Home/StyleSheets IIsWebDirectory
   ```

3. Enable static compression at this directory by executing the following command at a command prompt:

   ```
   adsutil set w3svc/1/root/Home/StyleSheets/DoStaticCompression true
   ```

Specifying File Types and Compression Schemes by Editing the Metabase

After enabling HTTP compression, you can use the Adsutil.vbs command-line utility (located in the *systemroot*\Inetpub\Adminscripts folder) to edit the metabase, specifying which static or dynamic file types to compress and which compression scheme to apply.

Using Adsutil.vbs, you can customize HTTP compression in the following ways:

- Apply the gzip or deflate compression scheme, or both. To apply both schemes, you must execute a separate **set** command for each compression scheme.

- Customize the file types to which both static and dynamic compression are applied. You must execute a separate **set** command for each compression type. If you use IIS Manager to enable compression and you then use Adsutil.vbs to specify specific static or dynamic file types, you replace any default values that were applied by IIS Manager.

Note

For compression to be performed, the **HcDoStaticCompression** metabase property must be set to **true** (for static compression) and the **HcDoDynamicCompression** metabase property must be set to **true** (for dynamic compression). You can set these by using IIS Manager or Adsutil.vbs. For instructions, see the procedures in the preceding section.

The following syntax enables compression at the W3SVC level (which means it is applied to all Web sites and virtual directories on the Web server):

```
cscript.exe adsutil.vbs set W3svc/Filters/Compression/{GZIP|DEFLATE}/
{HcFileExtensions "StaticFileType" ...}|{HcScriptFileExtensions "DynamicFileType"
...}
```

You must restart the WWW service before any changes take effect. For information about restarting a service, see "Common Administrative Tasks" in this book. Table 6.13 describes the parameters for customizing file types and compression schemes.

Table 6.13   Parameters for Setting Compression Schemes and File Types for HTTP Compression

Parameter	Description
`GZIP|DEFLATE`	Specifies which compression scheme (either gzip or deflate) to apply to the specified file types. To enable both compression schemes, you must run this command once for each compression scheme.
`HcFileExtensions` *"StaticFileType"* `...`	Specifies which static file types to apply the compression scheme to — for example, .txt, .js, .css, .doc, or .xls files. To specify a file type, enclose the file name extension (without the leading period) in quotation marks. Separate multiple file types with a space. This parameter cannot be executed together with the **HcScriptFileExtensions** " *DynamicFileType*" parameter.
`HcScriptFileExtensions` *"DynamicFileType"* `...`	Specifies which dynamic file types to apply the compression scheme to — for example, .exe, .dll, or .asp files. To specify a file type, enclose the file name extension (without the leading period) in quotation marks. Separate multiple file types with a space. This parameter cannot be executed together with the **HcFileExtensions** " *StaticFileType*" parameter. **Important:** Setting the **HcScriptFileExtensions** parameter to an empty string can adversely affect your server's performance. If this parameter is empty, all dynamic responses are sent compressed. In addition, any static file type not specified in **HcFileExtensions** is dynamically compressed and therefore not cached.

For example, the following command uses a deflate compression scheme to apply static compression at the W3SVC level to text files (.txt) and cascading style sheets (.css):

```
cscript.exe adsutil.vbs set w3svc/Filters/Compression/DEFLATE/HcFileExtensions
"txt" "css"
```

Specifying the Location and Size of the Compression Directory for Static Compression

Three metabase properties enable you to change the location of the default directory for static compression and to limit its size.

Changing the location of the compression directory

The **HcCompressionDirectory** metabase property specifies the folder where compressed versions of static files are temporarily cached. By default, the compression directory is at %Windir%\IIS Temporary Compressed Files.

Due to a number of differences between NTFS and FAT volumes — such as differences in time stamping and access control mechanisms, and the efficiency with which NTFS handles directories that contain large numbers of files — the compression directory must reside on an NTFS volume. In addition, the access control lists (ACLs) for the folder must include Full Control access to the identity of the application pool or to the IIS_WPG group. If a requested file resides on an NTFS volume and the compression directory is on a FAT volume, IIS does not perform HTTP compression on that file.

Setting a size limit for the compression directory

In addition, you can configure the **HcDoDiskSpaceLimiting** and **HcMaxDiskSpaceUsage** metabase properties to limit the amount of disk space that all files in the compression directory can occupy. **HcDoDiskSpaceLimiting** enables disk space limiting. If it is set to **true**, IIS limits compressed files to no more than the number of bytes specified by **HcMaxDiskSpaceUsage**. After the limit is reached, compressed files are removed from the compression directory on a "least recently used" basis. If **HcDoDiskSpaceLimiting** is set to **false**, no disk space limit is enforced for the compression directory.

HcDoDiskSpaceLimiting is relevant only if you have set the property **HcDoOnDemandCompression** to **true**. For more information about these metabase properties, see "Metabase Property Reference" in IIS 6.0 Help.

 Important

Limiting the use of disk space has a significant impact on performance because additional overhead is required to check for the limit. Use this feature only when you lack adequate disk space to cache all content files on your Web server.

Disabling HTTP Compression for Requests That Come Through Certain Proxy Servers

Certain HTTP proxy servers, including some advertised as HTTP 1.1–compliant, do not handle the caching of compressed objects correctly. The **HcNoCompressionForProxies** metabase property allows you to disable the HTTP 1.1 response for compression requests that come through proxy servers.

In addition, you can use the **HcNoCompressionForHttp10** metabase property to disable compression for requests that contain an HTTP 1.0 version number. HTTP 1.0, as described in RFC 1945, "Hypertext Transfer Protocol — HTTP/1.0," provides a minimal level of support for certain types of compression. However, some confusion exists concerning HTTP 1.0 compression, especially with regard to proxy servers. To minimize the chance of inappropriately returning a compressed file to a client that cannot decompress it, you can use the **HcNoCompressionForHttp10** metabase property to disable compression in questionable scenarios.

For more information about the many metabase properties that you can set when configuring HTTP 1.1 compression, including a complete list of all the properties you can set, see "IIsCompressionSchemes (ADSI)" in IIS 6.0 Help.

Throttling Bandwidth to Manage Service Availability

If the network or Internet connection used by your Web server is also used by other services, such as e-mail or news, you can limit the bandwidth used by your Web server so that the server is available for those other services. If your Web server hosts more than one Web site, you can individually throttle the bandwidth used by each site. However, keep in mind that the IPv6 network traffic handled by your Web sites is not throttled.

Bandwidth throttling uses Packet Scheduler to manage when data packets are sent. When you configure a site to use bandwidth throttling by using IIS Manager, Packet Scheduler is automatically installed, and IIS automatically sets bandwidth throttling to a minimum of 1,024 bytes per second. However, if you use another method, such as Active Directory® Service Interfaces (ADSI) or WMI, you must install Packet Scheduler in order for bandwidth throttling to work correctly.

When using ADSI or WMI to configure bandwidth throttling, you must set bandwidth throttling to 1,024 or more bytes per second, because Packet Scheduler cannot enforce bandwidth throttling settings below that level. Also, you need to uninstall Packet Scheduler if it is not in use by individual sites or the WWW service as a whole.

Determining When and Where to Use Bandwidth Throttling

Before enabling bandwidth throttling, determine your Web server's typical load by using System Monitor to log the following counters over several days:

- Bytes Total/sec or Current Bandwidth counter on the Network Interface object. To compare incoming and outgoing traffic, examine both Bytes Sent/sec and Bytes Received/sec.

- Compare the values from the Network Interface object counters with the total bandwidth of your network connection.

If you use Performance Logs and Alerts, you can log the data to a database and then query the data, examining the results in detail.

For a typical load, your server should use no more than 50 percent of its total available bandwidth. If your server is subject to large peaks in use, keep your typical load lower than 50 percent. The remaining bandwidth can be used during peak periods.

If testing of your servers' typical loads shows that a server or a particular site is consistently using more than 50 percent of the available bandwidth, use the procedures that follow to throttle bandwidth.

In addition, before you set global bandwidth throttling, be sure that you understand the following:

- Individual sites throttle bandwidth according to their established maximum; the global setting limits the total network bandwidth that is available for all unthrottled Web sites on a server. Setting a global WWW service maximum bandwidth does not override established bandwidth maximums for individual Web sites on the server.

- Global bandwidth throttling settings for the WWW service do not affect FTP sites or the FTP service as a whole.

Enabling Bandwidth Throttling

The following procedures tell how to globally enable bandwidth throttling for the WWW service or to enable bandwidth throttling for a specific Web site, and how to disable bandwidth throttling on an individual site in order to override global bandwidth throttling.

▷ **To globally throttle WWW service bandwidth**

1. In IIS Manager, expand the local computer, right-click the **Web Sites** folder, and then click **Properties**.

2. On the **Performance** tab, under **Bandwidth throttling**, select the **Limit the total network bandwidth available for all Web sites on this server** check box.

3. In the **Maximum bandwidth (in kilobytes per second)** box, type the maximum number of kilobytes per second that you want to allow for each site contained in the folder.

4. Click **Apply**, and then click **OK**.

▷   **To throttle the bandwidth used by an individual Web site**

1. In IIS Manager, expand the local computer, expand the **Web Sites** folder, right-click the Web site, and then click **Properties**.

2. On the **Performance** tab, under **Bandwidth throttling**, select the **Limit the network bandwidth available to this Web site** check box.

3. In the **Maximum bandwidth (in kilobytes per second)** box, type the maximum number of kilobytes per second that you want the site to use.

4. Click **Apply**, and then click **OK**.

5. The following procedure tells how to disable bandwidth throttling for an individual site. The procedure is slightly different if you are overriding global bandwidth throttling. Either task can also be performed by using ADSI or WMI to update the **MaxBandwidth** metabase property for the site.

▷   **To disable bandwidth throttling on an individual site**

-   If global bandwidth throttling is not in effect, on the **Performance** tab, under **Bandwidth throttling**, clear the **Limit the network bandwidth available to this Web site** check box. Alternatively, you can set the **MaxBandwidth** metabase property to –1 by using ADSI or WMI.

-   If global bandwidth throttling is in effect, but you want an individual site to have virtually unlimited bandwidth, on the **Performance** tab, under **Bandwidth throttling**, do not clear the **Limit the network bandwidth available to this Web site** check box (the global setting automatically applies to the individual site when the check box is cleared). Instead, enter a very high number in the **Maximum bandwidth (in kilobytes per second)** box. Alternatively, you can set the **MaxBandwidth** metabase property to –2 by using ADSI or WMI.

> **Note**
>
> Bandwidth throttling is not supported for requests that come to a site by means of an IPv6 address. The MaxBandwidth metabase property does not affect IPv6 network traffic.

For more information about administering IIS with ADSI or with WMI, see "Using the IIS ADSI Provider" or "Using the IIS WMI Provider" in IIS 6.0 Help. For more information about configuring the **MaxBandwidth** metabase property, see "Metabase Property Reference" in IIS 6.0 Help.

Using Other Features to Enhance Performance

IIS 6.0, when running in worker process isolation mode, offers several features that you can use in addition to the QoS feature to better manage your systems' resources:

- Use Web gardens to enhance performance.

- Conserve processor resources by using idle timeout.

- Enable CPU monitoring to conserve processing time.

- Assign processor affinity to better use CPU caching.

Using Web Gardens to Enhance Performance

If the server is running in worker process isolation mode, you can configure an application pool to be supported by multiple worker processes. An application pool that uses more than one worker process is called a *Web garden*. Creating a Web garden for an application pool enhances performance and reliability by providing the following enhancements:

- **Robust processing of requests**. When a worker process in an application pool is tied up (for example, when a script engine stops responding), other worker processes can accept and process requests for the application pool.

- **Reduced contention for resources**. When a Web garden reaches a steady state, each new TCP/IP connection is assigned, according to a round-robin scheme, to a worker process in the Web garden. The round-robin scheme smooths out workloads and reduces contention for resources that are bound to a worker process.

For more information about Web gardens, including how to configure them, see "Running IIS 6.0 as an Application Server" in this book.

Conserving Processor Resources by Using Idle Timeout

If the server is running in worker process isolation mode, you can conserve system resources by terminating idle worker processes; that is, you can configure an application pool's worker process to shut down after a specified period of inactivity. Use this feature to better manage your resources when the processing load is heavy, when identified worker processes are consistently idle, or when new processing space is not available. If an application pool times out because the inactivity of its worker process exceeds a configured limit for idle timeout, and if HTTP.sys then receives a request for the idle application pool, the WWW service starts a new worker process to replace the one that timed out.

For more information about configuring idle timeout for a worker process, see "Running IIS 6.0 as an Application Server" in this book.

Enabling CPU Monitoring to Conserve Processing Time

Through CPU monitoring of application pools, you can monitor the CPU usage of worker processes and, if you configure it to do so, automatically shut down worker processes that consume large amounts of CPU processing time. CPU monitoring logs and throttles only the applications that are isolated in a process that is separate from IIS; hence, this feature is only available when your server is running in worker process isolation mode.

When you configure CPU monitoring for an application pool, you can choose from two monitoring options:

- **Perform only event logging.** When the CPU usage for an application pool exceeds the Maximum CPU use limit, the WWW service writes an error to the Windows event log. The log entry identifies the specific worker process and the application pool that exceeded the CPU limit.

- **Log events, and also shut down the unhealthy application pool.** After an application pool reaches the configured Maximum CPU use limit, CPU monitoring writes an error to the event log and shuts down the application pool. The application pool remains down until the **CPUResetInterval** time limit expires, at which time the application pool restarts. If any requests are received while the application pool is stopped, HTTP.sys returns a 503 error (Server Too Busy).

For more information about CPU monitoring, including how to configure it, see "Running IIS 6.0 as an Application Server" in this book.

Obtaining more detailed CPU monitoring

If your Web server is running the Windows Server 2003, Enterprise Edition, or Windows Server 2003, Datacenter Edition, operating system, you can use the Windows System Resource Manager to monitor different types of CPU activity more closely. With this feature, you can control how CPU and memory resources are allocated to applications, services, and processes. However, Windows System Resource Manager cannot manage system resources correctly if the computer is already being managed by another resource manager, such as IIS CPU monitoring. For best results, if you use Windows System Resource Manager, do not use any other resource manager on that computer.

For more information about Windows System Resource Manager, see the Windows System Resource Manager — Fast Facts link on the Web Resources page at http://www.microsoft.com/windows/reskits/webresources.

Controlling Memory Usage

With memory, more is almost always better. However, just adding more RAM to your server does not optimize performance. You must first determine whether you are making good use of the memory that the server has.

The biggest performance gains with IIS occur when you resolve issues related to insufficient memory. Before changing your hardware configuration, rule out memory problems. Monitor memory first to verify that your server has enough memory, and then move on to other parts of your server environment. Problems caused by memory shortages can often appear to be problems in other parts of the system.

Minimum Memory Requirements for IIS 6.0

To run IIS 6.0 with the Windows Server 2003 operating system, a dedicated Web server must have a minimum of 128 MB of RAM. However, your server might require more RAM to handle the resource needs of custom applications. If your custom applications require large amounts of memory, provide 256 MB or more of RAM. Additional memory is particularly beneficial for e-commerce sites, sites with a lot of content, and sites with a high volume of traffic.

Memory Management and Memory Allocation in Windows Server 2003

In order to use memory most efficiently, the Windows Server 2003 memory system is largely self-tuning. Similarly, IIS 6.0 regulates the size of the IIS object cache. Therefore, the primary purpose of monitoring memory on a Windows Server 2003–based server running IIS 6.0 is not to adjust the size of each memory component, but rather to make sure that the system as a whole has enough memory and is using it efficiently.

The largest "chunk" of activity in Windows Server 2003 is a *process*. The physical RAM available to a process is known as its *working set*. If the needs of a process exceed its working set — that is, if the process is not able to store all its code and frequently used data in RAM — some of the information is stored elsewhere, usually on disk as virtual memory.

Storing information on disk instead of in memory increases disk activity, which slows down the server. Some memory contains information that is frequently used, and sending that data to disk instead of retaining it in memory can degrade performance.

In addition, a section of system memory, known as *pool memory*, is reserved for use by the operating system. Pool memory is either *paged* or *nonpaged*. *Nonpaged pool* is the section of pool memory that is not pageable. Data in a nonpaged pool is always stored in physical memory and never saved to the disk. This section is usually reserved for device drivers or other critical system components that cannot wait for memory to be paged. *Paged pool* is the section of pool memory that can be managed in the same way as other virtual memory — that is, it is *pageable* in that inactive memory can reside on the disk, and the current or active memory can reside in physical memory.

Within each process, Windows Server 2003 uses threads to accomplish particular tasks. The memory occupied by threads is part of the working set of the process, except for some special threads that run in nonpageable memory. Threads that service connections in IIS 6.0, for example, cannot be paged.

This section tells how to monitor various aspects of overall server memory — available memory, paging, use of the file system cache, the size of paging files, the IIS working set, and disk I/O — and, based on your observations, how to optimize memory usage.

Monitoring Overall Server Memory

Use System Monitor to check the values of the counters described in the following sections. This will help you determine if the current amount of memory on your server is sufficient for your needs.

To evaluate memory usage on your Web server, look at available memory, paging, the size of the file system cache, the size of the paging files, the size of the components of the IIS 6.0 working set, and disk I/O.

Monitoring Available Memory

Monitor the counter in Table 6.14 to determine whether the server has performance bottlenecks associated with memory.

Table 6.14 Counter for Monitoring Available Memory

Object\Counter	Value
Memory\Available Bytes	The amount of physical memory, in bytes, available to processes running on the computer. This counter displays the last observed value only; it is not an average.

Compare the total physical memory that is available to Windows Server 2003 with the available memory remaining when all server services are running. To gather reliable data, log this value over time, being sure to include periods of peak activity. Try to reserve at least 10 percent of available memory for peak use.

Monitoring Paging

If a process requests a page in memory and the system cannot find the page at the requested location, a page fault occurs. If the page is elsewhere in memory, the fault is a *soft page fault*. If the page must be retrieved from disk, the fault is a *hard page fault*. Most processors can handle large numbers of soft page faults without consequence. However, hard page faults can cause significant delays. Continuous high rates of disk paging indicate a memory shortage.

Table 6.15 lists the counters that are available for monitoring hard and soft page faults.

Table 6.15 Counters for Monitoring Page Faults, Pages Input, and Page Reads

Object\Counter	Value
Memory\Page Faults/sec	The overall rate at which the processor handles both hard and soft page faults.
Memory\Pages Input/sec	The total number of pages read from disk to resolve hard page faults.
Memory\Page Reads/sec	The number of times that the disk was read to resolve hard page faults.
Memory\Transition Faults/sec	The rate at which page faults are resolved by recovering pages without incurring additional disk activity. *Transition faults*, which measure soft page faults, are counted in numbers of faults because only one page is faulted in each operation; the number of transition faults is equal to the number of pages faulted.

Hard page faults increment the Page Faults/sec counter (which reports the rate of hard and soft page faults combined) in addition to the Pages Input/sec and Page Reads/sec counters (which report the rate of hard page faults only). The Transition Faults/sec counter is only incremented by soft page faults.

The value of the Memory\Pages Input/sec counter (the number of pages read from disk as a result of hard page faults) will be greater than or equal to the value of Page Reads/sec (the number of times the disk was read as a result of hard page faults), and can give you a good idea of your hard page fault rate. If these numbers are low, your server is responding to requests quickly. If these numbers are high, investigate whether you have dedicated too much memory to the caches, leaving too little memory for the rest of the system. If reducing cache sizes does not improve system performance, you might need to increase the amount of RAM on your server.

Monitoring the File System Cache

Monitor the counters in Table 6.16 to determine whether a server has a performance bottleneck associated with the size of the file system cache. These counters display the last observed value only; they do not display an average value.

Table 6.16 Counters for Monitoring the File System Cache

Object\Counter	Value
Memory\Cache Bytes	The current size, in bytes, of the file system cache. By default, the cache uses up to 50 percent of available physical memory. The counter value is the sum of Memory\System Cache Resident Bytes, Memory\System Driver Resident Bytes, Memory\System Code Resident Bytes, and Memory\Pool Paged Resident Bytes.
Memory\System Cache Resident Bytes	The current size, in bytes, of the pageable operating system code in the file system cache. This value includes only current physical pages and excludes any virtual memory pages not currently resident.
Memory\System Driver Resident Bytes	The current size, in bytes, of the pageable physical memory in use by device drivers. This represents the *working set* (physical memory area) of the drivers. This value is a component of Memory\System Driver Total Bytes.
Memory\System Code Resident Bytes	The current size, in bytes, of the operating system code currently in physical memory that can be written to disk when it is not in use. This value is a component of Memory\System Code Total Bytes.
Memory\Pool Paged Resident Bytes	The current size, in bytes, of the paged pool. The paged pool is an area of *system memory* (physical memory used by the operating system) reserved for objects that can be written to disk when they are not in use. The space that is used by the paged and nonpaged pools is taken from physical memory; thus, a pool that is too large denies memory space to processes.

The value of the Memory\System Cache Resident Bytes counter equals the System Cache value shown on the **Performance** tab in Task Manager. As a result, this value can be smaller than the actual amount of virtual memory in use by the file system cache.

Windows Server 2003 automatically trims the cache when memory is scarce and enlarges the cache when memory is ample. Use the Memory\Cache Bytes counter to monitor the size of the file system cache. A log of cache size readings reveals how the size of the file system cache changes over time. Compare the log data to a measure of general memory availability, such as data from the Memory\Available Bytes counter. By monitoring these counters and watching the trends, you can expose memory shortages in a server.

When examining the logs, note when the cache is smallest. Track how small the cache gets and how often its size is reduced. Also, note how much system memory is available when the cache size is reduced. By watching these trends, you can begin to associate the size of the cache with the server's performance. For example, if performance degrades when the cache is large, consider adding RAM. If performance degrades when the cache is small, consider increasing the time interval during which objects remain in the cache before being flushed. For more information about monitoring and tuning IIS file cache, see "Web Server Scalability" in this book.

Monitoring the Size of the Paging Files

The counters in Table 6.17 are useful in examining paging file usage. *Paging files* store pages of memory used by a process that are not contained in other files. Paging files are shared by all processes, and the lack of space in paging files can prevent processes from allocating memory.

Table 6.17   Counters for Monitoring Page Files

Object\Counter	Value
Process\Page File Bytes	The current amount of virtual memory, in bytes, that this process has reserved for use in the paging files.
Process\Page File Bytes Peak	The maximum amount of virtual memory, in bytes, that this process has reserved for use in the paging files.
Paging File\% Usage	The percentage of the Page File instance that is in use.
Paging File\% Usage Peak	The peak usage of the Page File instance, expressed as a percentage of total file size.

Windows Server 2003 creates a paging file (with the file name Page File) on the system drive. You can create a paging file on each logical disk. By striping a paging file across separate physical drives, you can improve paging file performance by using drives that do not contain your site's content or log files.

You can change the sizes of existing paging files. The larger the paging file, the more memory the system commits to it. Be sure that the paging file on the system drive is at least twice the size of the physical memory, so that the system can write the entire contents of RAM to disk if the system unexpectedly locks up or shuts down.

Monitoring the IIS 6.0 Working Set

If free memory on the computer is above a threshold, pages are left in the working set of a process even if they are not in use. When free memory falls below that threshold, pages are trimmed from working sets. If the trimmed pages are later needed, they are soft-faulted back into the working set before leaving main memory.

When available memory falls below about 4 MB, the system attempts to make more memory available by taking memory away from the working sets of processes. This strategy increases the rate of page faults, because each process must now retrieve data that was once in its working set either from disk or from elsewhere in memory. When the rate of page faults for a particular process rises, however, the system attempts to expand the working set of that process to lower the page fault rate. As the system tries to maintain this balance, the size of the working set of each process fluctuates accordingly.

The Process\Working Set counters measure the number of memory pages that each process uses. If the system has sufficient memory, it can maintain enough space in the working set so that IIS 6.0 rarely must perform disk operations. One indicator of memory sufficiency is how much the size of the process working set fluctuates in response to general memory availability on the server. Significant fluctuation can indicate a lack of available memory.

The system's memory pools hold objects created and used by applications and the operating system. The contents of the memory pools are accessible only in privileged mode — that is, only the kernel of the operating system can directly use the memory pools; user processes cannot.

Table 6.18 describes the counters that are available for monitoring the IIS 6.0 working set.

Table 6.18   Counters for Monitoring the IIS 6.0 Working Set

Object\Counter	Value
Memory\Pool Paged Bytes Memory\Pool Non-paged Bytes	Pool Paged Bytes and Pool Non-paged Bytes monitor the pool space for all processes on the server.
Process(W3wp[1])\Virtual Bytes Process(Inetinfo)\Virtual Bytes	The amount of virtual address space, in bytes, reserved directly by IIS, either by the Inetinfo.exe process (where IIS runs when set to IIS 5.0 isolation mode) or by the W3wp.exe process (where isolated or pooled applications run when IIS is set to worker process isolation mode) instantiated on your server.
Process(W3wp[1])\Working Set Process(Inetinfo)\Working Set	Size, in bytes, of the working set of the W3wp.exe or Inetinfo.exe process. These counters display the last observed value, not an average over time.

1 Monitor the W3wp instance if you are running your Web server in worker process isolation mode. If you are running your server in IIS 5.0 isolation mode, monitor either the Inetinfo instance (for in-process applications) or the Dllhost instance (for out-of-process applications).

 Important

You can run IIS 6.0 in one of two request processing models: *worker process isolation mode* and *IIS 5.0 isolation mode*. IIS typically performs better while running in worker process isolation mode, although results depend on a variety of factors, including the design of your applications. Also note that each mode uses different instances of a counter to monitor performance. For more information about the two request processing models, see "Running IIS 6.0 as an Application Server" in this book.

Be sure that you monitor Process\Working Set counters for all instances of W3wp.exe (the component that hosts the worker process when IIS runs in worker process isolation mode) on your server; otherwise, you might obtain an inaccurate reading of the virtual memory used by IIS.

You can use the Memory\Available Bytes counter (in Table 6.14) as an indicator of memory availability and the Process\Working Set counters (in Table 6.18) as an indicator of the size of the IIS 6.0 working set. These counters display the last value observed, rather than an average, so be sure to examine data collected over time.

Monitoring Disk I/O

IIS 6.0 writes its logs to disk, so there is almost always some activity, even when requests are processed out of the cache 100 percent of the time. Under ordinary circumstances, disk activity other than that generated by logging might indicate a problem in other areas. For example, if your server has insufficient RAM, you see lots of disk activity because many hard page faults are occurring.

Under certain conditions, disk activity is normal. Examples include a large site that serves more content than your server can cache and any site that serves large amounts of static content that is not cacheable. You are also likely to notice lots of disk activity if your server hosts a database or if your users request many different Web pages.

Typically, you use the Physical Disk counters in Table 6.1 to watch for spikes in the number of disk reads when the server is busy. If the server has enough RAM, most connections result in cache requests, unless the server also hosts a database and clients are making dissimilar queries, which precludes caching.

If the server does not host any application or service that is obviously disk-intensive, but you see lots of disk activity anyway, you need to check RAM use immediately to make sure that the server has enough memory.

Optimizing Memory Usage

Servers running IIS 6.0 benefit from ample physical memory. Generally, the more memory that you add, the more the servers use and the better they perform. IIS 6.0 requires a minimum of 128 MB of memory; at least 256 MB is recommended. If you are running memory-intensive applications, your server might require much more memory to run optimally — more than the recommended 256 MB of memory.

Adding RAM to your system is not the only option, however. The following methods can be used to optimize memory performance without adding memory.

Improve Data Organization

To improve the performance of the file system cache, keep related Web files on the same logical partitions of a disk.

Use Disk Defragmenter to consolidate fragmented files and folders on the server's hard disk so that each occupies a single, contiguous space on the volume. As a result, the system can gain access to files and folders and save new ones more efficiently.

Increase the Efficiency of High-Traffic Web Sites

Evaluate your high-traffic Web sites to find ways to increase their efficiency. For more information about creating efficient Web sites, see "Creating a More Efficient Web Site" later in this chapter.

Try Disk Mirroring or Striping

The optimum configuration is to have enough physical memory to hold all static Web pages. However, if pages must be retrieved from disk, use mirroring or striping to make reading from disk sets faster. In some cases, a caching disk controller is helpful. For more information about mirrored or striped volumes, see "Using mirrored volumes" or "Using striped volumes" in Help and Support Center for Windows Server 2003.

Add or Enlarge Paging Files

Add paging files, or increase the size of existing ones. Windows Server 2003 creates one paging file on the system disk, but you can also create a new paging file on each logical partition of each disk. By striping a paging file across separate physical drives, you can improve paging file performance by using drives that do not contain your site's content or log files.

You can change the sizes of existing paging files. The larger the paging file, the more memory the system commits to it. Be sure that the paging file on the system drive is at least twice the size of the physical memory, so that the system can write the entire contents of RAM to disk if the system unexpectedly locks up or shuts down.

For information about resizing paging files, see "Change the size of the virtual memory paging file" in Help and Support Center for Windows Server 2003.

Retime the IIS Object Cache

Consider shortening the period of time that an unused object remains in the cache, or lengthening the time that a used object remains in the cache, by adding the **ObjectCacheTTL** entry to the registry.

 Caution

Do not edit the registry unless you have no alternative. The registry editor bypasses standard safeguards, allowing settings that can damage your system, or even require you to reinstall Windows. If you must edit the registry, back it up first and see the Registry Reference on the *Windows Server 2003 Resource Kit* companion CD or on the Web at http://www.microsoft.com/reskit.

The value of **ObjectCacheTTL** controls the static file cache by specifying the Time To Live (TTL), which sets the length of time that objects are held in cached memory. If an object in the memory cache has not been referenced for the defined period, that object is phased out of the cache.

The default value is 30 seconds. If system memory is limited or if the contents of the server are dynamic, you can use a lower TTL to prevent system memory from being used to cache a large number of volatile objects. Setting the **ObjectCacheTTL** entry to unlimited disables the object-cache scavenger and allows cached objects to remain in the cache until the cached object changes. Disabling the cache scavenger is useful if your server has ample system memory and your data is relatively static.

Use the following procedure to reset the time that an unused object remains in the object cache by adding the **ObjectCacheTLL** entry to the registry.

 Important

You must be a member of the Administrators group on the local computer to run scripts and executables, or you must have been delegated the appropriate authority. As a security best practice, log on to your computer by using an account that is not in the Administrators group, and then use the **runas** command to run your script or executable as an administrator. At a command prompt, type **runas /profile** */User:MyMachine\Administrator* **cmd** to open a command window with administrator rights and then type **cscript.exe** *ScriptName* (including the full path with parameters, if any).

▶ **To reset the period that unused objects remain in the cache**

1. From the **Start** menu, click **Run**, type **regedit.exe**, and then click **OK**.

2. In the registry editor, navigate to the following subkey:

   HKEY_LOCAL_MACHINE\SYSTEM\CurrentControlSet\Services\InetInfo\Parameters

3. Right-click the Parameters subkey, point to **New**, and then click **DWORD Value**.

4. In the **New Value** box, type **ObjectCacheTTL**

5. Right-click **ObjectCacheTTL**, and then click **Modify**.

6. Under **Base**, click **Decimal**.

7. In the **Value Data** box, type the number of seconds that you want an unused object to remain in the cache, and then click **OK**.

   The default value is 30 (seconds). You can enter any value from zero, to disable caching, through 4,294,967,295 (unlimited), to disable the object-cache scavenger and allow cached objects to remain in the cache until the cached object changes.

Change the Balance of the File System Cache to the IIS 6.0 Working Set

By default, servers running Windows Server 2003 are configured to give preference to the file system cache over the working sets of processes when allocating memory (through the server property **Maximize data throughput for file sharing**). Although IIS 6.0–based servers benefit from a large file system cache, giving the file system cache preference often causes the IIS 6.0 pageable code to be written to disk, which results in lengthy processing delays. To avoid these processing delays, set server properties to maximize data throughput for network applications.

▷   **To maximize data throughput on the server for network applications**

1. In Control Panel, double-click **Network Connections**, right-click **Local Area Connection**, and then click **Properties**.

2. Select **File and Printer Sharing for Microsoft Networks**, and then click **Properties**.

3. Under **Optimization**, select **Maximize data throughput for network applications**.

Limit Connections

If your server does not have enough memory, limiting the number of connections on the server might help alleviate the shortage because some physical memory (about 10 KB per connection) is consumed by the data structures that the system uses to keep track of connections. For more information about limiting connections to save memory, see "Limiting Connections to Manage Resources" earlier in this chapter.

Limit the Queue Length for Application Pools

If you are running your server in worker process isolation mode, you can limit application pool queue lengths to prevent large numbers of requests from queuing up and overloading your server. When the queue length limits feature is enabled (it is enabled by default), IIS monitors the number of requests in a designated application pool queue before queuing a new request. Use IIS Manager to change the default limit of 1,000 requests for application pool request queues.

If adding a new request to the queue exceeds the maximum queue length, the server rejects the request and sends a 503 error (Server Too Busy) to the client. However, requests that are already queued remain queued even if the limit is changed to a value that is less than the current queue length.

Use the following procedure to set a limit on the queue length for an application pool.

 Important

You must be a member of the Administrators group on the local computer to perform the following procedure or procedures, or you must have been delegated the appropriate authority. As a security best practice, log on to your computer by using an account that is not in the Administrators group, and then use the **runas** command to run IIS Manager as an administrator. At a command prompt, type **runas** /*User:Administrative_AccountName* "mmc %systemroot%\system32\inetsrv\iis.msc".

To change an application pool's queue length limit

1. In IIS Manager, expand the local computer, expand the **Application Pools** folder, right-click the application, and then click **Properties**.

2. On the **Performance** tab, under **Request queue limit**, select the **Limit the kernel request queue to** check box.

3. In the **requests** box, type or select the maximum number of queued requests to allow. The default limit is 1,000 requests.

> ◆ **Important**
>
> If you clear the Limit the kernel request queue to check box, IIS does not apply a request limit. Without a limit, IIS might queue requests until your server runs out of memory.

4. Click **Apply**, and then click **OK**.

For information about configuring application pool queue length limits by using metabase properties, see the **AppPoolQueueLength** property in the "Metabase Property Reference" in IIS 6.0 Help.

Adjust Resource Allocation in Windows

System processing is managed by Windows Server 2003, which can allocate processor and memory resources among tasks. If your server needs a temporary performance boost, you can temporarily adjust resource allocation in Windows to allocate the resources where you need them:

- To obtain a faster response time, you can set Windows to allocate more processor time to the program that you are currently running.

- If you want to run background programs, such as printing or disk backup, while you work, you can have Windows share processor resources equally between background and foreground programs.

For more information about changing the way that Windows allocates processor resources, see "Change the performance of foreground and background programs" in Help and Support Center for Windows Server 2003.

Limit Performance Logging

Always keep in mind that performance logging uses system resources. When you are not actively checking performance, disable performance-related logging to squeeze a bit more performance from your server.

Preventing Processor Bottlenecks

Servers running IIS 6.0 rely on the speed and efficiency of their processors. IIS 6.0 code is multithreaded for efficient scaling on uniprocessor and multiprocessor computers, and is largely self-tuning. Even so, processor bottlenecks can occur on very active servers.

A *processor bottleneck* occurs when one or more processes consume the majority of the processor time. This forces threads that are ready to be executed to wait in a queue for processor time. Processor bottlenecks can occur on multiprocessor computers even when only a single processor is fully loaded, if the work in the queue cannot be — or is not — distributed to the other processors. Because a processor bottleneck is not centered in other components, such as memory, disks, or network connections, upgrading or adding to those components does not fix this performance problem, and can sometimes make it worse.

The processors on a server running IIS 6.0 must support the operating system and processes unrelated to Internet services, in addition to IIS 6.0 processes. The processors must also support applications related to Internet services, such as those that assemble data from Microsoft® SQL Server™ databases or generate dynamic Web pages.

To identify processor bottlenecks on the server, you need to monitor process activity, connections, and threads. After evaluating the data, determine the appropriate measures for improving processor performance through hardware upgrades, software configuration changes (limiting connections or allowing a higher thread count), or the redesigning of Web sites to reduce the processor workload.

Identifying Processor Bottlenecks

The relationships among threads, connections, and requests are complex, especially in IIS 6.0, which uses the worker thread model rather than the simpler, and less efficient, thread-per-client model. Because of the complexity of the model, it is important to obtain a baseline from which to evaluate your system if a bottleneck occurs.

To identify performance bottlenecks, perform the following types of monitoring activity:

- Monitor processor activity by using performance counters and other tools.

- Monitor connections to determine how your server responds to managing different numbers of connections.

- Monitor threads, including context switches, interrupts, and deferred procedure calls.

Monitoring Processor Activity

Several tools are available for monitoring processor performance:

- Use the Web Capacity Analysis Tool (WCAT) to perform stress tests. For information about using WCAT, see "Using WCAT as a Stress Client" later in this chapter.

- To monitor process performance on servers running Windows Server 2003, you can use Task Manager, System Monitor, and Performance Logs and Alerts.

Remember that all monitoring tools use system resources. Monitor the processor use of the process in which the tool runs; then, before you analyze your data, subtract the processor time of the tool process from the data.

To collect data about processor activity, monitor the counters that are listed in Table 6.19. The % Processor Time counter is the primary indicator of processor activity, displaying the average percentage of busy time observed during the sample interval.

Table 6.19   Counters for Monitoring Processor Activity

Object\Counter	Value
System\Processor Queue Length	The number of threads in the processor queue. Shows ready threads only, not threads that are running. Even multiprocessor computers have a single queue for processor time; thus, for multiprocessors, you need to divide this value by the number of processors servicing the workload. A sustained processor queue of less than two threads per processor is normally acceptable, depending upon the workload.
System\Context Switches/sec	The combined rate at which all processors on the computer are switched from one thread to another.
Processor (_Total)\% Processor Time	The average percentage of time that all processors are active. This counter is the primary indicator of average processor activity. This value is derived by calculating the percentage of time during the sample interval that all processors spent in executing their idle thread (which consumes cycles on a processor when no other threads are ready to run), and then subtracting the result from 100 percent.
Processor\% Processor Time	The average percentage of processor use for each processor (#0, #1, and so on).
Processor\% Privileged Time	The average percentage of processor time that is spent in privileged mode. In Windows Server 2003, only privileged mode code has direct access to hardware and memory. Application threads can be switched to privileged mode to run operating system services.

(continued)

Table 6.19 Counters for Monitoring Processor Activity *(continued)*

Object\Counter	Value
Processor\% User Time	The average percentage of processor time that is spent in user mode. *User mode* is a restricted processing mode designed for applications, environment subsystems, and integral subsystems. The alternative, *privileged mode*, is designed for operating system components, allowing direct access to hardware and memory. The operating system switches application threads to privileged mode to access operating system services.
Process\% Processor Time	The average percentage of processor use attributable to each processor, either for a particular process or for the total for all processes (shown in the list of instances).

Tip

A memory bottleneck can sometimes look like a processor or disk bottleneck. If the system does not have enough physical memory to store the code and data that are needed, the processor spends substantial time paging. Before adding or upgrading processors or disks, you need to monitor the memory on your server. For more information about monitoring memory, see "Monitoring Overall Server Memory" earlier in this chapter.

Analyzing Processor Activity Data

Of the counters listed in Table 6.19, the System\Processor Queue Length counter is probably the most important for analyzing processor activity data. This counter displays the number of threads waiting to be processed in the single queue shared by all processors. Sustained high rates of processor activity, which leave little excess capacity to handle peak loads, are often associated with processor bottlenecks. Processor activity itself only indicates that the resource is being used, not that maximum use of the resource is a problem. However, a long, sustained queue indicates that threads are being kept waiting because a processor cannot handle the load assigned to it.

A sustained processor queue length of two or more threads (as indicated by the System\Processor Queue Length counter) typically indicates a processor bottleneck. You can set an alert in Performance Logs and Alerts to notify administrators when the processor queue length is unacceptably high.

The Processor\% Processor Time counter is most often used as a general measure of processor activity on both uniprocessor and multiprocessor computers. On a multiprocessor server, use this counter to reveal unequal distribution of processor load. You might have a processor bottleneck if % Processor Time numbers are high while usage of the network adapter and disk I/O remain well below capacity.

On multiprocessor computers, use the total instance of the Processor\% Processor Time counter — for example, Processor(_Total)\% Processor Time — to monitor systemwide processor use. For multiprocessor use, this counter represents the active time of all processors divided by the number of processors. If the server workload is shared equally among all processors, the total instance time is an excellent measure of processor activity.

Windows Server 2003 is designed for efficient scaling and includes several strategies for balancing processor load. An application, however, can create an imbalance by setting a processor affinity, which binds a process to a single processor. To identify processor bottlenecks related to processor affinity, chart Processor\% Processor Time for each processor on the computer.

 Note

Though processor affinity can overload a single processor, it can improve performance by reducing the number of processor cache flushes as threads move from one processor to another. You will need to assess, through monitoring, whether the trade-off is acceptable. For information about assigning processor affinity to an application pool or Web garden, see "Improving Processor Performance" later in this chapter.

Optimizing Processor Activity

If data shows a large processor queue with all processors busy, view a histogram of Process\% Processor Time for each process. To do this, click the **View Histogram** button on the toolbar in System Monitor. The histogram shows the processor time consumed by each process.

Based on the histogram readings, consider making the following adjustments to optimize performance:

- If a single bar in the histogram rises above all of the others, the process represented by the bar might be consuming a disproportionate share of processor time and causing a bottleneck. Consider replacing the application running in that process, or moving the process to another server.

- If the processors are being shared equally by several processes, consider upgrading or adding processors. (Multithreaded processes benefit most from additional processors.)

For more information about processor use by applications related to IIS, see "Improving Application Performance" later in this chapter.

Monitoring Connections

It is important to determine how your server responds when it is managing different numbers of connections. After collecting data on connection trends, you can associate data about general server performance with the number of connections being served.

Each connection that an IIS 6.0 service establishes consumes processor time. The network adapter interrupts the processor to signal that a client has requested a connection. Further processing is required to establish and maintain the connection, to fulfill client requests sent over the connection, and — when the connection is closed — to delete the structures that serviced the connection. Each time a connection is established, the load on the server increases.

IIS 6.0 includes several features to optimize its handling of connections. For example, the HTTP Keep-Alives feature, which is enabled by default, maintains an open connection between the server and browser across multiple requests until an entire Web page is downloaded. This feature significantly improves bandwidth performance on most servers and improves response times for clients. For more information about HTTP Keep-Alives, see "Enabling HTTP Keep-Alives to Keep Connections Open" earlier in this chapter.

You can use IIS 6.0 logging to monitor the number of connections that your server makes and to track patterns of client demand for your server. Table 6.20 lists the counters that you can use with Performance Logs and Alerts to monitor connections to IIS 6.0.

Table 6.20   Performance Counters for IIS 6.0 Service Connections

Object\Counter	Value
Web Service\Current Connections FTP Service\Current Connections	The number of connections maintained by the service during the most recent sample interval.
Web Service\Maximum Connections FTP Service\Maximum Connections	The maximum level of simultaneous connections since the server started up.

Because these counters display the last observed value, and not an average, you must log their values over time to get a reliable sample. These counters can exaggerate the number of simultaneous connections because, at any given moment, some entries may not have been deleted even though the connections on which they are based have been closed.

For more information about configuring and interpreting IIS 6.0 logs, see "Analyzing Log Files" in this book.

Analyzing Connection Data

Identify patterns of client demand for your server by monitoring the number of connections. Log connection data at regular time intervals, and look at the number of connections served during each interval. Observe the size of the processor queue and the usage on each processor during periods of small, moderate, and large numbers of connections. This data shows how your configuration responds to each load level.

You can identify a processor bottleneck during a given time interval by observing one of the following:

- A long, sustained processor queue (with more than two threads).

- High usage rates on one or more processors.

- A curve in the graph of the Current Connections counter on any IIS 6.0 service performance object that reaches a high value and then plateaus. This pattern often indicates that additional connections are being blocked or rejected.

The Active Server Pages, Web Service, FTP Service, and SMTP Server counters collect data at the OSI application layer. If any connections are blocked, rejected, or reset between the transport and application layers, counts of TCP/IP connections might not equal the sum of HTTP, FTP, and SMTP connections. For information about monitoring connections at lower layers, see "Monitoring Network Activity" earlier in this chapter.

Optimizing Connections

To prevent processor bottlenecks, make certain that a lengthy processor queue is not forming when you serve large numbers of connections. You can usually avoid a bottleneck during peak usage by setting the connection limit to twice the average value of the Current Connections counter.

If the processor regularly develops a bottleneck when servicing large numbers of connections, consider upgrading or adding processors, or limit the maximum number of connections on the server. Limiting connections can cause the server to block or reject connections, but it helps to ensure that accepted connections are processed promptly.

For information about limiting connections, including how to configure this setting, see "Limiting Connections to Manage Resources" earlier in this chapter.

Monitoring Threads

IIS 6.0 runs in a set of multithreaded processes designed for efficient scaling on uniprocessor and multiprocessor systems. *Threads* are the sequences of execution in each process that run the process code on the processor. In the IIS 6.0 process, there is no simple association between threads and connections or between threads and requests, nor is there an easily quantifiable relationship between the optimum number of threads in the process and the number of files served, the number of requests filled, or the number of connections maintained.

Because IIS 6.0 uses the worker thread model (rather than the simpler, thread-per-client model), which dedicates a thread to each connection or request), a pool of threads, known as the *worker threads*, is dedicated to accepting and monitoring all connections. This frees other threads to do the remaining work of the application, such as authenticating users; parsing client requests; locating, opening, and transmitting files; and managing internal data structures.

Even though you cannot associate individual threads with connections or requests, you can:

- Count the number of threads in the IIS 6.0 process.

- Measure the amount of processor time that each thread gets.

- Associate the number of threads (and processor activity) with the number of current connections, number of files served, and other measures of server activity and performance.

Several tools — including Performance Logs and Alerts, Task Manager, and System Monitor — monitor or enumerate the threads in a process. Individual threads are difficult to monitor, especially if they frequently start and stop. Monitoring threads is also costly. Be sure to monitor the overhead of the process in which your tool runs (by monitoring the Process\% Processor Time counter), and subtract this from the overall processor time for the data that you collect.

Monitoring Threads and Context Switches

Table 6.21 lists the counters that monitor threads and context switches. You can add to this list any counters that you use to associate numbers of threads with performance, such as Web Service\Current Connections, Web Service\Bytes/sec, or Server\Logon/sec.

Table 6.21   Counters for Monitoring IIS 6.0 Threads

Object\Counter	Value
Process (W3wp[1])\Thread Count	The number of threads created by the process. This counter does not indicate which threads are busy and which are idle. It displays the last observed value, not an average.
Thread (W3wp[1:] *Thread* #)\% Processor Time	The percentage of processor time that each thread of the worker process is using.
Thread (W3wp[1]/ *Thread* #)\Context Switches/sec	The rate of switches from one thread to another. Thread switches can occur either inside of a single process or across processes.
System\Context Switches/sec	The combined rate at which all processors on the computer are switched from one thread to another.

1 Monitor the W3wp instance if you are running your Web server in worker process isolation mode. If you are running your server in IIS 5.0 isolation mode, monitor either the Inetinfo instance (for in-process applications) or the Dllhost instance (for out-of-process applications).

Balancing threads against overall performance as measured by connections and requests can be difficult. Any time that you tune threads, follow up with overall performance monitoring to see whether performance increases or decreases.

You can chart the Process\Thread Count: W3wp value over time to see how many threads the worker process creates and how the number of threads varies. Then, observe the processor time for each thread in the process (Thread\% Processor Time: W3wp/*Thread #*) during periods of high, medium, and low server activity (as indicated by the other performance measures).

To determine if you need to adjust the thread count, compare the number of threads and the processor time for each thread in the process to the total processor time. If the threads are constantly busy, but are not fully using the processor time, you might improve performance by allowing more threads. However, if all the threads are busy and the processors are operating at close to their maximum capacity, it is best to distribute the load across more servers instead of increasing the number of threads.

Context switch counters are provided for the System and Thread objects. If you decide to increase the maximum size of any of the thread pools, it is important to monitor the counters for context switches. *Context switches* occur when a running thread voluntarily relinquishes the processor, is preempted by a higher priority ready thread, or switches between user mode and kernel mode to use an Executive or subsystem service. Switching to the subsystem process causes one context switch in the application thread; switching back causes another context switch in the subsystem thread.

Increasing the number of threads can increase the number of context switches to the point that performance decreases rather than increases. Ten thousand or more context switches per second is high. If you see numbers in that range, consider reducing the maximum thread pool size.

You should also observe the patterns of context switches over time, which indicate that the kernel has switched the processor from one thread to another. A large number of threads is likely to increase the number of context switches. Although they allow multiple threads to share the processor, context switches also interrupt the processor and might interfere with its performance, especially on multiprocessor computers.

Controlling processor affinity can improve performance by reducing the number of processor cache flushes as threads move from one processor to another. For example, you might be able to reduce cache flushes for dedicated servers by assigning processor affinity. However be aware that dedicating a program to a particular processor might prevent other program threads from migrating to the least-busy processor.

Monitoring Interrupts and Deferred Procedure Calls

You also need to monitor the counters for interrupts and deferred procedure calls (DPCs). Table 6.22 lists the counters to use.

Table 6.22 Counters to Monitor Interrupts and Deferred Procedure Calls

Object\Counter	Value
Processor\Interrupts/sec	The rate, in average number of interrupts in incidents per second, at which the processor received and serviced hardware interrupts. It does not include deferred procedure calls, which are counted separately.
Processor\% DPC Time	The percentage of time that the processor spent receiving and servicing deferred procedure calls during the sample interval. Deferred procedure calls are interrupts that run at a lower priority than standard interrupts.

The value of the Processor\Interrupts/sec counter is an indirect indicator of the activity of devices that generate interrupts, such as the system clock, the mouse, disk drivers, data communication lines, network adapters, and other peripheral devices. These devices normally interrupt the processor when they have completed a task or require attention, suspending normal thread execution. The system clock typically interrupts the processor every 10 milliseconds, creating a background of interrupt activity.

Use the Processor\Interrupts/sec and Processor\% DPC Time counters to determine how much time the processor is spending on interrupts and deferred procedure calls. These two factors can be another source of load on the processor. Client requests can be a major cause of interrupts and deferred procedure calls. Some new network adapters include interrupt moderation, which accumulates interrupts in a buffer when the level of interrupts becomes too high.

Optimizing Thread Values

By default, the IIS 6.0 process creates as many as four threads per processor. IIS 6.0 continually adjusts the number of threads in its process in response to server activity. For most systems, this tuning is sufficient to maintain the optimum number of threads, but you can change the maximum number of threads per processor if your system requires this. If the threads in the IIS 6.0 process appear to be overworked or underutilized, consider these tuning strategies:

- If nearly all of the threads of the IIS 6.0 process are busy nearly all of the time, and the processors are at or near their maximum capacity, consider distributing the workload among more servers. You can also add processors.

- If nearly all threads appear busy, but the processors are not always active, consider increasing the maximum number of threads per processor. Do not increase the maximum number of threads unless you have processors with excess capacity. More threads on the same number of processors cause more interrupts and context switches, and result in less processor time per thread.

To adjust the maximum number of threads in the IIS 6.0 service process, use a registry editor to add the **MaxPoolThreads** entry to the following registry path:

HKEY_LOCAL_MACHINE\SYSTEM\CurrentControlSet\Services\Inetinfo\Parameters

Caution

Do not edit the registry unless you have no alternative. The registry editor bypasses standard safeguards, allowing settings that can damage your system, or even require you to reinstall Windows. If you must edit the registry, back it up first and see the Registry Reference on the *Windows Server 2003 Resource Kit* companion CD or on the Web at http://www.microsoft.com/reskit.

The **MaxPoolThreads** entry is calculated in units of threads per processor. Do not set this value below 2 or above 20. You can try setting the **MaxPoolThreads** entry to a higher value if back-end latency is higher; set the entry to a lower value for applications that are CPU-intensive. Continue monitoring the system carefully to make sure that changing the number of threads allowed achieves the effect that you want.

Improving Processor Performance

If your data on processor performance indicates that processor queues are developing regularly or while a server is handling large numbers of connections, start by monitoring the server's memory. Rule out a memory bottleneck or add more memory before (or in addition to) adding or upgrading processors.

In addition to the methods for optimizing thread values (discussed earlier in "Monitoring Threads"), consider making the following adjustments.

Upgrade the L2 cache

When adding or upgrading processors, choose processors with a large secondary (L2) cache. Server applications, such as IIS, benefit from a large processor cache because their instruction paths involve many different components. A large processor cache (2 MB or more if external, up to the maximum available if on the CPU chip) is recommended to improve performance on active servers running IIS 6.0.

Add network adapters

If you are administering a multiprocessor system that does *not* distribute interrupts symmetrically, you can improve the distribution of the processor workload by adding network adapters so that there is one adapter for every processor. Generally, you only add adapters when you need to improve the throughput of your system. Network adapters, like any additional hardware, have some intrinsic overhead. However, if one of the processors is nearly always active (that is, if Processor\% Processor Time = 100) and more than half of its time is spent servicing deferred procedure calls (if Processor\% DPC Time > 50), then adding an adapter is likely to improve system performance, as long as the available network bandwidth is not already saturated.

Upgrade network adapters

If you are adding or upgrading network adapters, choose those with drivers that support interrupt moderation cards, which can perform transfers in the background without processor help. Interrupt moderation prevents the processor from being overwhelmed by bursts of interrupts. Consult the driver manufacturer for details. Also, if at all possible, use adapters that support TCP checksum offloading.

Upgrade to a multiprocessor computer

A server-application environment, such as e-commerce sites running COM+ applications, is much more processor-intensive than a typical file or print server environment because much more processing is taking place at the server. For that reason, high-end multiprocessor computers can increase performance in server-application environments. IIS 6.0 introduces a new kernel-mode driver for HTTP parsing and caching that is tuned to increase Web server throughput and scalability of multiprocessor computers.

Assign processor affinity to better use CPU caching

To efficiently use CPU caches on multiprocessor servers, you can configure application pools to establish affinity between worker processes and the processors. *Processor affinity* forces worker processes to run on a specific microprocessor or CPU, and applies to all worker processes serving a particular application pool. You can also use processor affinity with Web gardens that run on multiprocessor computers where clusters of CPUs are dedicated to specific application pools.

Controlling processor affinity can improve performance by reducing the number of processor cache flushes as threads move from one processor to another. For example, you might be able to reduce cache flushes for dedicated servers by assigning processor affinity. However, the performance trade-off is that dedicating a program to a particular processor might prevent other program threads from migrating to the least-busy processor.

If you want to assign a particular process or program to a single processor to improve its performance — possibly at the expense of other processes — configure the **SMPAffinitized** and **SMPProcessorAffinityMask** metabase properties. For more information about assigning processor affinity, including how to configure these metabase properties, see "Running IIS 6.0 as an Application Server" in this book.

Limit connections

If you cannot upgrade or add processors, consider reducing the maximum number of connections that each IIS 6.0 service accepts. Limiting connections can result in connections being blocked or rejected, but it helps ensure that accepted connections are processed promptly.

Adjust the maximum number of threads

IIS 6.0 tunes the number of threads in its process dynamically. The dynamic values are usually optimal; in extreme cases of very active or underused processors, however, it might help to adjust the maximum number of threads. If you change the maximum number of threads, continue careful testing to make sure that the change has improved performance. The difference is usually quite subtle.

Redesign the Web site

You can improve performance and reduce the processor workload by optimizing database use, calling compiled components from scripts in ASP pages, using Internet Server API (ISAPI) instead of ASP (and ASP or ISAPI instead of CGI applications), and eliminating large bitmapped images or optimizing them to reduce file size. For more information about optimizing Web site performance, see "Improving Application Performance" later in this chapter.

Improving Application Performance

Web applications continue to increase in popularity, constituting an ever larger proportion of the average Web server file base. The challenge for administrators is to preserve speed and efficiency while serving complex applications. By monitoring and tuning different types of applications, in addition to static HTML pages, you can estimate application overhead during periods of varying activity to ensure that your server is prepared for the workload.

Use the tools and counters that are included with IIS 6.0, such as those discussed here, to help you optimize application performance:

- **Test applications with stress tools.** Use a stress client like the Web Capacity Analysis Tool (WCAT) to test your applications under a variety of workloads.

- **Monitor and tune applications.** When you enable ASP.NET and ASP pages on a Web server, IIS provides application-specific counters for monitoring and tuning their performance.

Testing Applications with Stress Tools

If Web applications are an important part of your site, the performance of those applications is critical in determining the capacity of the site. In turn, testing is the only way to find out the capacity and performance of a Web application.

If you are unfamiliar with stress testing or need a refresher, look at the following sections:

- **Measuring performance by using a stress client.** Provides an introduction to performing stress testing.

- **Using WCAT as a stress client.** Details how to obtain the WCAT tool and its documentation. WCAT is a stress client provided in the IIS 6.0 Resource Kit Tools.

- **Estimating baseline performance for applications.** Compares the relative performance capabilities of specific application types to help you proactively develop applications that provide optimal performance.

Measuring Performance by Using a Stress Client

Use a stress client to test different server and network configurations under a variety of workloads. For example, use a stress client to test how your server responds to different workloads or to test the same workload with varying configurations of the server. Some stress clients include prepared test workloads; optionally, you can create your own workloads.

A stress client simulates clients and servers communicating over a network, and usually requires at least four primary subsystems:

- At least one computer that simulates a client, which runs one or more virtual clients.

- One computer that acts as a server.

- One computer, called a *controller*, that initiates and monitors the test.

- A network.

Both the client and controller components can run on one computer. (You can also run the server component on the same computer, but doing so might provide inaccurate results.)

To produce a more realistic test of your server, link it to client computers that are powerful enough to drive the server. The processors in the client computers must be fast enough to prevent a client bottleneck when accessing the server computer. If the client processors are slower than the server, you might need to link more client computers to each server.

Stress clients usually work best if the network that connects the computers has little or no traffic that is unrelated to the test. If possible, use a link dedicated only to the test, and run the tests on a 100 megabits per second — or faster — network.

Test different performance features to observe the effect they have on your server. To test a feature, first run a stress client test with the feature, then run the same test without it. Be sure to run the "with feature" and "without feature" versions of the test on varying workloads and multiple clients. For example, use a stress client to test the following features:

- Set different connection limits, such as HTTP Keep-Alives and connection timeouts.

- Test several compression combinations. For example, compress only static files, only dynamic files, or both; allow different compression schemes (gzip, deflate, or both); and compress at different compression levels for both file types.

- Test bandwidth throttling at different times and on different services.

- Test different hardware combinations, including multiprocessor machines with and without processor affinity.

- Compare the benefits of running different health-monitoring features, such as rapid-fail protection and worker process recycling.

- Test security-related features, such as SSL.

Repeat each test several times, and average the results to eliminate the effects of unintended variations in the test conditions. Then compare the results of the "with feature" and "without feature" tests. Consistent differences in the results of the tests are likely to indicate the overhead associated with the feature. You can use these results for planning configuration changes.

Using WCAT as a Stress Client

The *Internet Information Services (IIS) 6.0 Resource Kit* companion CD includes a stress client called the Web Capacity Analysis Tool (WCAT), which is a script-driven command-line tool. WCAT includes a stress client tool (Wcclient.exe) to simulate the clients and a controller tool (Wcctl.exe) to initiate and monitor the testing.

You can install the Resource Kit Tools by running IIS60rkt.exe from the companion CD. When you perform a default installation of the Resource Kit Tools, the WCAT client and controller files are installed in the *LocalDrive:*\Program Files\IIS Resources folder.

A WCAT test begins with the controller locating and interpreting input files. A controller input file includes three required sections (Configuration, Script, and Distribution) and one optional section (Performance, for specifying which performance counters to monitor). The controller uses the input files to send instructions to the clients, including which tests to run. WCAT includes a prepared input file (Sample.ubr, in the *LocalDrive:*\Program Files\IIS Resources\WCAT Controller\Scenarios folder) that contains a test for stressing the default IIS Web page.

When a WCAT test is complete, the controller collects the test results and writes them to output files. Output files include a log file, which you can optionally configure as an XML-formatted file, and an optional performance results file, which contains data collected from performance counters on the server.

If you specify performance counters in the Performance section of the .ubr file, WCAT logs the counter data in its usual report but also produces a performance log file in a tab-separated format, so that you can import the logged counter data into a spreadsheet or data-processing application. The log of performance data that WCAT generates is stored, by default, in the WCAT Controller\Scenarios folder. You can open this log, which is a text file, by using any word processor.

For more information about obtaining and using WCAT, see Internet Information Services (IIS) 6.0 Resource Kit Tools Help (IISTools.chm), which is located in the folder where you install the tools.

Estimating Baseline Performance for Applications

Before you develop a new application, it is useful to understand the performance capabilities of different types of Web applications. Table 6.23 provides a guide to the relative performance of different types of applications, where n represents the fastest application, and all other application types are rated relative to its performance.

Table 6.23   Relative Performance of Different Application Types

Application Type	Relative Cost	Comments
Static page (kernel mode)	n	Fastest and simplest Web page.
Static page (user mode)	$2n$	
ISAPI	$2n$	Relative speed for a simple ISAPI application.
ASP.NET	$5n$	Relative speed for a simple ASP.NET application.
ASP	$10n$	Relative speed for a simple ASP application.
CGI	$100n$	Slowest.

Microsoft® Visual Studio® .NET provides Application Center Test (ACT) to help you test and monitor the performance of your Web application. ACT simulates a large group of users by opening multiple connections to a Web server and rapidly sending HTTP requests. ACT is designed to stress-test Web servers and to analyze performance and scalability problems with Web applications. For more information about ACT, see the MSDN Library link on the Web Resources page at http://www.microsoft.com/windows/reskits/webresources. On the MSDN Library Web page, search for "ACT."

For more information about Web application development, including ASP.NET and ASP applications, see the "Web Application Guide" in IIS 6.0 Help.

Monitoring and Tuning Applications

To ensure that all of your Web applications run reliably and efficiently during peak hours as well as normal usage periods, you should monitor and tune your applications, obtaining baseline data to compare the performance of different types of applications. If you uncover applications or groups of applications that appear to run inefficiently, review the suggestions for improving application performance in "Optimizing Application Design and Administration" later in this chapter.

You can also improve application performance by using the connection timeout and HTTP compression features that IIS provides. Certain applications, such as ASP pages, provide metabase properties for customizing these features. For more information about using these features to improve application performance, see "Administering Network Resources" earlier in this chapter.

When you make changes to your applications or to the hardware on which your applications run, be sure to test the changes in a nonproduction environment before implementing them on production servers.

IIS provides application-specific counters that you can monitor to obtain performance data about different types of applications that run on your servers.

- Monitor applications that use the WWW service by observing counters that monitor ISAPI extensions, CGI requests, and so forth.

- Monitor ASP pages, and tune metabase properties for ASP.

- Monitor ASP.NET applications.

Monitoring Applications That Use the WWW Service

Monitor the counters in Table 6.24 to determine how the WWW service is processing ISAPI, CGI, POST, and GET requests.

Table 6.24   Counters That Provide Data About WWW Service Applications

Object\Counter	Value
Web Service\ISAPI Extension Requests/sec Web Service\CGI Requests/sec	The rates at which the server is processing ISAPI and CGI application requests. If these values decrease due to increasing loads, you might need to redesign the applications. Note: ASP is an ISAPI extension; therefore ASP requests are included in the first counter.
Web Service\Get Requests/sec Web Service\Post Requests/sec	The rate at which these two common HTTP request types are made to the server. POST requests are generally used for forms and are sent to ISAPIs (including ASP) or CGIs. GET requests make up almost all other requests from browsers and include requests for static files, ASPs and other ISAPIs, and CGI requests.

Monitoring ASP Performance

If you are running ASP pages on your server, the counters listed in Table 6.25 can help you determine how well the applications are performing. These counters provide the sum of the ASP performance counters for all processes hosting ASP; the data cannot be broken down by process. For information about monitoring the performance of your ASP.NET applications, see "Monitoring ASP.NET Performance" later in this chapter.

Table 6.25   Counters Used to Monitor ASP Performance

Object\Counter	Value
Active Server Pages\Requests/sec	The number of ASP responses during the past second. This counter excludes requests for static files or other dynamic content, and can fluctuate considerably based on the complexity of the ASP pages and the capacity of your Web server.
Active Server Pages\Requests Executing	The number of ASP requests currently executing (for example, the number of active worker threads).
Active Server Pages\Request Wait Time	The number of milliseconds that the most recent ASP request was waiting in the queue.
Active Server Pages\Request Execution Time	The number of milliseconds that the most recent ASP request took to execute. This value can be somewhat misleading because it is not an average.
Active Server Pages\Requests Queued	The number of queued ASP requests that are waiting to be processed. The maximum number for this counter is determined by the metabase property **AspRequestQueueMax**.

Analyzing the Data

The Active Server Pages\Requests/sec counter excludes requests for static files or other dynamic content, and can fluctuate considerably based on the complexity of the ASP pages and the capacity of your Web server. If this counter is low during spikes in traffic on your server, your applications might be causing a bottleneck.

It is difficult to give an ideal value for the Active Server Pages\Requests Executing counter. Some factors to consider include:

- If pages execute quickly and do not wait for I/O (for example, loading a file or making a database query), the number of ASP requests that are currently executing is likely to be low — little more than the number of processors when the computer is busy.

- If pages must wait for I/O, the number of pages executing is likely to be higher —up to the maximum thread count allowed for an ASP processor (set by the **AspProcessorThreadMax** metabase property) multiplied by the number of processors, multiplied by the number of processes hosting ASP. (The default **AspProcessorThreadMax** value is 25.)

- If the Requests Executing counter value equals the value of the **AspProcessorThreadMax** property, if Requests Queued is large, and if CPU usage is low, you might need to increase the value of the **AspProcessorThreadMax** metabase property.

 Important

The value of the AspProcessorThreadMax metabase property can significantly influence the scalability of your Web applications and the performance of your server. Before changing the setting, be sure to read about this property and its use in IIS 6.0 Help.

The Request Execution Time counter can be misleading because it is not an average. For example, if you regularly receive 30 requests for a page that executes in 10 milliseconds (ms) to every one request for a page that executes in 500 ms, the counter is likely to indicate 10 ms even though the average execution time is over 25 ms.

Ideally, the Requests Queued and Request Wait Time counters remain close to zero; however, they can vary under varying loads (depending on the application) while the server still provides good performance. If these numbers vary too much from their expected range, you might need to rewrite your ASP applications. If the queue size and wait time increase, or if the queue limit is reached, browsers display the message "HTTP 500/Server Too Busy."

For more information about ASP performance counters, including additional ASP counters, see "IIS 6.0 Performance Counters" in this book.

Tuning ASP Metabase Settings

If your Web server is running ASP applications, you can help optimize server performance by tuning the metabase properties described in this section. You can retrieve and change these properties by using WMI or ADSI, or by directly editing the metabase with a text editor. Changes to most of these properties do not take effect until you restart the WWW service.

For more information about the default values of these metabase properties, see "Metabase Property Reference" in IIS 6.0 Help.

AppAllowDebugging

The **AppAllowDebugging** metabase property specifies whether ASP debugging is enabled on the server. When this property is enabled, IIS application threads are serialized; only one thread can execute for each application at one time. Serialized threads adversely affect Web server performance. You should retain the default setting for this property, which is **false,** on all production servers. Set this property to **true** only on a test server when you are debugging an application during its deployment phase.

AspBufferingOn

The **AspBufferingOn** metabase property turns on buffering in ASP, so that all output from an application is collected in the ASP output buffer before the buffer is flushed to the client browser (default behavior). If this property is set to **false**, output from ASP scripts is written to the client browser as the client browser becomes available. Set this property to **true** on all production Web servers.

AspProcessorThreadMax

The **AspProcessorThreadMax** metabase property specifies the maximum number of worker threads per processor that IIS can create. To find out the maximum number of worker threads that IIS allows per ASP process, multiply this value by the number of processors on your server. If you decrease this value, monitor performance to make sure that the lower thread limit does not degrade performance. If it does, increase the value again.

AspQueueConnectionTestTime

The **AspQueueConnectionTestTime** metabase property specifies the maximum time, in seconds, that a request remains queued before ASP checks to determine whether a client is still connected. If a request is in the queue longer than the queue connection test time, the server checks whether the client is still connected before beginning execution.

This feature can help you handle impatient users who fill up the request queue with numerous attempts at the same page. Often, users do not wait more than a few seconds for ASP pages to process. Although the maximum waiting time varies from user to user, the generally accepted maximum is about 10 seconds; so set a small value — for example, 3 seconds.

This property is useful for making ASP processing efficient only up to the point at which ASP begins to process the script. After the script is running, your application should continue to check for client connection at appropriate times, by using the **IsClientConnected** method of the ASP built-in **Response** object. For long-running pages, make cautious use of **Response.Flush** to ensure that users perceive that the page is still alive and doing productive work. For more information about using this property, see the **AspQueueConnectionTestTime** property in the "Metabase Property Reference" in IIS 6.0 Help.

AspRequestQueueMax

The **AspRequestQueueMax** metabase property specifies the maximum number of ASP requests that are permitted in a queue. The default value is 3,000, but the optimal setting depends on the behavior of the application. If the execution time of the request is very short and the time in the queue is short, it is reasonable to decrease this value.

AspScriptEngineCacheMax

The **AspScriptEngineCacheMax** metabase property specifies the maximum number of scripting engines that ASP pages keep cached in memory (excludes currently running script engines). The default value is 250. Adjust the value according to the type of content in the application. If you are serving thousands of unique pages, server performance might improve if you increase the cache size so that the most frequently requested pages are accessed easily. A hit in the script engine cache means that you can avoid recompiling the template into byte code.

AspScriptFileCacheSize

The **AspScriptFileCacheSize** metabase property specifies the number of precompiled script files that can be stored in the ASP template cache. If you set the property to 4,294,967,295 (unlimited), all requested script files are cached. The default value is 500. Increase the value if you have many ASP pages. Do not set the value of this property to zero, which turns off all ASP caching and can severely impair your server's performance.

AspDiskTemplateCacheDirectory

The **AspDiskTemplateCacheDirectory** metabase property specifies the name of the directory where ASP stores compiled ASP templates to disk when the in-memory cache overflows. If you change the default directory, you must ensure that the identity of the processes running Asp.dll is assigned Full Control permission to the new directory. Typically, the identity of the worker processes running Asp.dll is the LocalSystem or Network Service account. You must specify a local path; ASP template caching fails if this property is set to a Universal Naming Convention (UNC) or mapped network path.

AspSessionTimeout and AspSessionMax

The metabase property **AspSessionTimeout** specifies, in minutes, the default amount of time that a session object is maintained after the last request associated with the object is received. **AspSessionMax** specifies the maximum number of concurrent sessions that IIS permits. For applications that take advantage of sessions, you might want to decrease the session timeout in order to reduce server overhead. If decreasing the session timeout causes the number of concurrent sessions to increase too much, you might need to set a lower session maximum.

AspTrackThreadingModel

The **AspTrackThreadingModel** metabase property specifies whether IIS checks the threading model of any components that your application creates. ASP no longer uses this metabase property, although it is still in the metabase to provide compatibility with existing administrative scripts. It is recommended that you retain this property's default value, which is **false,** to avoid the overhead incurred by the ASP track threading model and to help improve performance of your ASP application.

CacheISAPI

The **CacheISAPI** metabase property indicates whether ISAPI extensions are cached in memory after first use. If the value of this property is **true** (the default setting), ISAPI extensions, after they are loaded, remain in the cache until the server is stopped. If the value is **false**, extensions are unloaded from memory after the ISAPI extension is no longer in use.

ISAPI extensions are cached or not cached based on the value of this property when they are loaded into memory. Thus, if this property is changed after an extension is loaded and cached, the change has no effect on that extension until the Web server is restarted.

Although you might temporarily set this property to **false** to help with debugging, you need to keep this value set to **true** on all production Web servers. Because the ASP.dll is an ISAPI extension, disabling this property — which requires that every request be reloaded — degrades performance.

Monitoring ASP.NET Performance

ASP.NET includes a number of performance counters that you can use to track the execution of your Web applications. When you do steady-state running analysis, you might want to ignore the first request and also any one-time initialization costs for objects. For example, when an ASP.NET page is requested for the first time, there is always the cost of compiling an instance of the **Page** class. After the initial cost is incurred, performance improves for subsequent requests.

 Note
You can also use the built-in ASP.NET tracing feature to track code execution for a page or an application.

Two performance objects are defined for ASP.NET, supporting two types of performance counters:

- The ASP.NET performance object contains system counters that monitor events on the state server. These global counters are not bound to a particular application instance.

- The ASP.NET Applications performance object contains application counters.

For example, there is a significant difference between the State Server Sessions counters for the ASP.NET performance object, which apply only to the computer on which the state server is running, and the Sessions counters for the ASP.NET Applications performance object, which apply only to user sessions that occur in process.

Unlike the ASP performance counters discussed earlier, which are exposed globally for the entire server computer, most of the ASP.NET performance counters are exposed per application.

Use System Monitor to view the counters for ASP.NET. If your Web server serves multiple applications, you need to specify a particular application instance when selecting a counter to monitor. In addition, System Monitor provides a __**Total**__ application instance, which aggregates the counter values for all applications on a server.

Useful Counters for Monitoring ASP.NET Applications

When monitoring the performance of your ASP.NET Web applications, try tracking the performance counters described in Table 6.26.

Table 6.26 ASP.NET Performance Counters

Object\Counter	Value
ASP.NET\Application Restarts	The aggregate number of restarts for all ASP.NET applications during the Web server's lifetime.
ASP.NET\Requests Queued	The number of ASP.NET requests waiting to be processed.
ASP.NET\Worker Process Restarts	The number of times that a worker process has restarted on the computer.
ASP.NET Applications\Errors Total	The total number of errors that have occurred in ASP.NET applications.
ASP.NET Applications\Requests/Sec	The number of requests executed per second for ASP.NET applications.

Application restarts, as reported by the ASP.NET\Application Restarts counter, are incremented with each **Application_OnEnd** event. An application restart can occur because changes were made to the Web.config file or to assemblies stored in the application's \Bin directory, or because too many changes occurred in Web Forms pages. A sudden increase in this counter can mean that your Web application is shutting down. If an unexpected increase occurs, be sure to investigate it promptly. This value is reset every time that IIS is restarted.

 Note

The value of each ASP.NET performance counter is updated every 400 milliseconds.

Useful Counters for Troubleshooting ASP.NET Performance Problems

Table 6.27 describes some additional performance counters that you can use to troubleshoot performance problems with your Web applications.

Table 6.27   Performance Counters for Troubleshooting ASP.NET Applications

Object\Counter	Indicates
ASP.NET Applications\Pipeline Instance Count	The number of active pipeline instances.
.NET CLR Exceptions\# of Exceps Thrown	The total number of exceptions thrown since the start of the application. Collects data both on .NET exceptions and on unmanaged exceptions that are converted to .NET exceptions. For example, a null pointer reference exception in unmanaged code is rethrown in managed code as a .NET SystemNullReferenceException. Exceptions that are rethrown are recounted. This counter collects data from both handled and unhandled exceptions.
System\Context Switches/sec	The rate at which thread contexts are switched by all CPUs in the Web server. A high number usually indicates either high contention for locks or many switches between user and kernel mode by the thread. Be sure to investigate these problems by using sampling profiles and other tools.

Although exceptions occur infrequently, you might want to monitor the # of Exceps Thrown counter, because exceptions can have performance implications. Some code paths, however, rely on exceptions for their proper functioning. For example, the **HttpResponse.Redirect** method always throws an exception, **ThreadAbortException**. Therefore, it can be more useful to track the number of exceptions thrown by using the Errors Total counter to see if the exception generated an error for the application.

For more information about the ASP.NET performance counters discussed in this section, as well as other ASP.NET performance counters, see "IIS 6.0 Performance Counters" in this book.

Balancing Performance and Security

Balancing performance with concerns about the security of your Web applications can be an important issue, particularly if you run an e-commerce Web site. Secure Web communications require more resources than do Web communications that are not secure, so you need to know when to use security techniques such as SSL certificates or any of the Windows authentication methods. Because SSL uses complex encryption, and encryption requires considerable processor resources, it takes much longer to retrieve and send data from SSL-enabled directories. Therefore, you should place only those files that contain or receive sensitive information in your SSL-enabled directory, keeping pages free of resource-consuming elements such as images.

If you use SSL, be aware that establishing the initial connection takes five times longer than reconnecting by using security information in the SSL session cache. The default time-out interval for the SSL session cache is 10 hours in Windows Server 2003. After secure data is deleted from the cache, the client and server must establish a new connection.

Configuring ServerCacheTime for SSL Sessions

If you plan to support long SSL sessions, consider lengthening the SSL cache time-out interval by adding the **ServerCacheTime** entry to the registry. If you expect thousands of users to connect to your site by using SSL, estimate how long you expect SSL sessions to last, and then set the value of the **ServerCacheTime** entry to a number slightly higher than your estimate. Do not set the value much higher than your estimate, because the resulting time-out interval might cause your server to retain stale data in the cache.

 Caution

> The registry editor bypasses standard safeguards, allowing settings that can damage your system, or even require you to reinstall Windows. If you must edit the registry, back it up first and see the Registry Reference on the *Windows Server 2003 Resource Kit* companion CD or on the Web at http://www.microsoft.com/reskit.

One reason for changing the default value for the SSL session cache is to force the client to authenticate more often. More frequent caching is sometimes useful, for example, if you know that the client is using a smart card and you want the Web page to be accessible only when the user inserts the smart card in the reader.

Before changing the SSL cache time-out interval, make sure that HTTP Keep-Alives are enabled (HTTP Keep-Alives are enabled by default). SSL sessions do not expire when you use them with HTTP Keep-Alives except when the browser closes the connection.

 Important

You must be a member of the Administrators group on the local computer to run scripts and executables, or you must have been delegated the appropriate authority. As a security best practice, log on to your computer by using an account that is not in the Administrators group, and then use the **runas** command to run your script or executable as an administrator. At a command prompt, type **runas /profile** */User:MyMachine\Administrator* **cmd** to open a command window with administrator rights and then type **cscript.exe** *ScriptName* (including the full path with parameters, if any).

▶ To configure the ServerCacheTime registry entry

1. From the **Start** menu, click **Run**, type **regedit.exe**, and then click **OK**.

2. In the registry editor, navigate to the following subkey:

   HKEY_LOCAL_MACHINE\SYSTEM\CurrentControlSet\Control\SecurityProviders \SCHANNEL.

3. Right-click the SCHANNEL subkey, point to **New**, and then click **DWORD Value**.

4. In the **New Value** box, type the following: **ServerCacheTime**

5. Right-click the **ServerCacheTime** entry and then click **Modify**.

6. Under **Base**, click **Decimal**.

7. In the **Value Data** box, type the value (in milliseconds) that you want to assign for the cache time (1 minute = 60,000 milliseconds), and then click **OK**. See Table 6.28 for commonly used cache times converted to milliseconds.

Table 6.28 Calculating ServerCacheTime Values for Secure Session Caching

Desired Cache Time (1 minute = 60,000 milliseconds)	ServerCacheTime Value (in Milliseconds)
No secure session caching	0 (turns off session caching)
2 minutes (default setting for the Microsoft® Windows NT® version 4.0 operating system)	120000
5 minutes (default setting for the Microsoft® Windows® 2000 operating system)	300000
10 hours (default setting for Windows Server 2003, Windows 2000 with Service Pack 2 [SP2] or later, and Windows XP)	36000000

For more information about configuring SSL session caching, including how to set the **ClientCacheTime** registry setting, see article 247658, "Configure Secure Sockets Layer Server and Client Cache Elements," in the Microsoft Knowledge Base. To find this article, see the Microsoft Knowledge Base link on the Web Resources page at http://www.microsoft.com/windows/reskits/webresources.

Testing How Security Features Affect Performance

The security services in Windows Server 2003 and IIS 6.0 are integrated into a number of operating system services. This means that you cannot monitor security features separately from other aspects of those services. Instead, the most common way to measure security overhead is to run tests that compare server performance with and without a security feature. Run the tests with fixed workloads and a fixed server configuration so that the security feature is the only variable.

In your tests of the effects of security services on performance, measure the following:

- **Processor activity and the processor queue**. Security features like authentication, certificates, encryption, and the SSL protocol require significant processing; so it is important to balance the performance costs associated with these security features with your performance objectives.

   When using security features, you are likely to see increased processor activity, in both privileged mode and user mode, and an increase in the rate of context switches and interrupts. If the processors on the server are not sufficient to handle the increased load, queues are likely to form.

   If the SSL protocol is being used, Lsass.exe might consume an unexpected amount of CPU resources because SSL processing occurs in the Lsass.exe process. Custom hardware, such as cryptographic accelerators that perform encryption, can help. When you create certificates by using the certificate wizards provided in IIS, you can select a cryptographic service provider that uses cryptographic accelerators.

- **Physical memory used.** Security features require that the system store and retrieve more user information.

- **Network traffic.** You are likely to see an increase in traffic between the IIS-based server and the domain controller that is used for authenticating logon passwords and verifying IP addresses.

- **Latency and delays.** The most obvious performance degradation resulting from complex security features like SSL is the time and effort involved in encryption and decryption, both of which use many processor cycles. Downloading files from servers by using the SSL protocol can be 10 to 100 times slower than downloading from servers that are not using SSL.

 Important

It is recommended that you do not use a domain controller as a Web server. If a domain controller is running IIS, the proportion of processor use, memory, and network and disk activity consumed by domain services is likely to increase significantly. The increased activity can be enough to prevent IIS services from running efficiently.

For more information about IIS certificate wizards, see "Using Certificate Wizards" in IIS 6.0 Help.

Measuring Security Overhead by Using a Stress Client

To test a security feature like SSL, first run a stress client test with the security feature; then run the same test without it. Be sure to run the "with feature" and "without feature" versions of the test on varying workloads and multiple clients.

To eliminate the effects of unintended variations of the test conditions, repeat each test several times and average the results. Then, compare the results of the "with feature" and "without feature" tests. Consistent differences in the results of the tests are likely to indicate the overhead associated with the security feature. You can use these results for planning configuration changes in order to handle the security overhead.

For more information about testing with a stress client, see "Testing Applications with Stress Tools" earlier in this chapter.

WCAT is a particularly useful tool for determining security overhead. Run IIS 6.0 logging together with WCAT to count the number of logons and file accesses. In addition, you might use System Monitor, which includes a set of counters for monitoring user authentication.

For more information about obtaining and using WCAT, see "Using WCAT as a Stress Client" earlier in this chapter.

Tracking Anonymous and Nonanonymous Requests

The Web Service and FTP Service performance objects include counters that report the number of anonymous and nonanonymous requests that are sent to each of these IIS 6.0 services. (The term *nonanonymous* is used instead of *authenticated* to account for custom authentication schemes that require data from the client other than, or in addition to, the user name and password, as is also the case with authentication.)

By themselves, these counters help you determine the number and proportion of each type of request. You can also use the counter values to estimate the effect of changing how you handle anonymous and nonanonymous users. For example, if most connections are anonymous, prohibiting anonymous requests has a more significant impact than if most requests are nonanonymous.

Analysis of data from these counters, together with general measures of server performance — such as the use and allocation of processor time, the size of processor queues, memory use, the number of disk reads and writes, and throughput — is even more useful. By analyzing the combined data, you can associate the effects of varying numbers and proportions of anonymous and nonanonymous users with changes in the performance of system components.

The counters that report the number of anonymous and nonanonymous requests are called Current Anonymous Users and Current NonAnonymous Users. In IIS 5.0, these counters actually displayed connections. In IIS 6.0, these counters count each request as a unique user.

Table 6.29 describes the counters for monitoring anonymous and nonanonymous requests. These counters are associated with the Web Service and FTP Service performance objects. The Anonymous Users and Nonanonymous Users counters display the number of anonymous and nonanonymous requests to the IIS 6.0 service when the values were last observed. They do not report averages or rates. These counters can exaggerate the number of requests because closed requests might not yet have been deleted when the counter is displayed.

Table 6.29   Counters for Anonymous and Nonanonymous Users

Object\Counter	Indicates
Web Service\Anonymous Users/sec Web Service\NonAnonymous Users/sec	The number of requests per second that anonymous or nonanonymous users sent to the IIS 6.0 service. (These counters provide an instantaneous value rather than an average.) Note that IIS 6.0 counts each request as a new user.
Web Service\Current Anonymous Users Web Service\Current NonAnonymous Users FTP Service\Current Anonymous Users FTP Service\Current NonAnonymous Users	The number of requests from anonymous or nonanonymous users that the server is currently processing. Note that IIS 6.0 counts each request as a new user.
Web Service\Maximum Anonymous Users Web Service\Maximum NonAnonymous Users FTP Service\Maximum Anonymous Users FTP Service\Maximum NonAnonymous Users	The maximum number of anonymous or nonanonymous users that made concurrent requests to the service since the service was started. Note that IIS 6.0 counts each request as a new user.
Web Service\Total Anonymous Users Web Service\Total NonAnonymous Users FTP Service\Total Anonymous Users FTP Service\Total NonAnonymous Users	The total number of requests that anonymous or nonanonymous users sent to the service since the service was started. Note that IIS 6.0 counts each request as a new user.
Web Service\Total Logon Attempts FTP Service\Total Logon Attempts	The total number of requests that both anonymous *and* nonanonymous users sent to the service since the service was started.

If you prefer to use SNMP services to monitor the WWW and FTP services, IIS provides a set of SNMP counters that monitor anonymous and nonanonymous users. For more information about the SNMP Web counters, see "IIS 6.0 Performance Counters" in this book.

Watching 404 Not-Found Errors

The Web Service performance object includes a counter that displays not-found errors. *Not-found errors* result from client requests that were not satisfied because they included a reference to a Web page or a file that does not exist. These errors are identified by their HTTP status code number, which is 404. Many not-found errors occur because Web pages and files have been deleted or moved to another location.

You can use the Web Service\Not Found Errors/sec counter, described in Table 6.30, to track the rate at which not-found errors are occurring on your server. Alternatively, set an alert in Performance Logs and Alerts to notify the administrator when the rate of not-found errors exceeds a threshold.

Table 6.30   Counters for Not-Found Errors

Object\Counter	Indicates
Web Service\Not Found Errors/sec	The number of client read requests that were not satisfied because the URL did not point to a valid file.

An increase in not-found errors might indicate that a file has been moved without its link being updated. However, it can also indicate failed attempts to access protected documents, such as user lists and file directories.

An increase in not-found errors might also be related to IIS 6.0 security measures. When you perform a clean installation of IIS 6.0, the default settings ensure that IIS is installed in a secure, locked mode. This default installation serves only static HTTP content, such as .htm files; the request handlers for dynamic content, such as ISAPI and CGI, are disabled.

IIS 6.0 provides new substatus error codes that can help you determine why an HTTP 404 error (file or directory not found) occurred. For example, if a request is denied because an ISAPI extension or CGI is locked, a 404.2 error is returned, and a 404.3 substatus code indicates a MIME map restriction policy.

For more information about analyzing substatus codes, see "Troubleshooting IIS 6.0" in this book. For more information about unlocking dynamic content, see "Common Administrative Tasks" in this book.

Analyzing Security Data and Planning Upgrades

After you collect data to assess the effects of adding security features to your server configuration, use the results of your analysis to plan configuration changes that can help you handle the additional workload that is required to support security features. Consider the following options.

Upgrade or add processors

Security features in general and the SSL protocol in particular are usually processor-intensive. Because Windows Server 2003 security features are multithreaded, they can run simultaneously on multiple processors. Thus, adding processors can improve performance significantly and prevent the processors from becoming a bottleneck.

For best results, choose processors with large secondary (L2) cache space (up to 2 MB). When a security feature like SSL encrypts and decrypts data, much of the processor's time goes to reading and writing small units of data to and from main memory. If your server can store this data in the processor cache, the data is retrieved much faster.

Add memory

If security features cause increased paging or shortages in virtual memory, adding more memory can help. The physical memory used to support the security service consumes space that can be used to cache files. To accommodate peak use, allow for twice as much memory as required during times of average use while still maintaining 10 MB of available memory.

 Important

Avoid adding disk space for security-related activity. Do not add disk space solely to support security features. Any increased disk activity associated with security features is likely to result from a shortage of physical memory, not from an actual need for more disk space. Security features such as the SSL protocol rely primarily on processors and physical memory, as opposed to disk space.

Use custom hardware

Custom hardware, such as cryptoaccelerator cards, can make a significant difference in the way that your server handles security overhead. Be sure to thoroughly test any nonstandard hardware to make sure that it is compatible with the other hardware and software that you use.

For more information about IIS security features, see "Security" in IIS 6.0 Help. For more information about setting up certificates and keys, see "Configuring SSL on Servers" in IIS 6.0 Help. For more information about enabling HTTP Keep-Alives, see "Enabling HTTP Keep-Alives to Keep Connections Open" later in this chapter.

Optimizing Performance Through Design

In addition to monitoring and tuning your server, you can optimize performance by improving the design and administration of your Web applications, by optimizing Web page design to create efficient Web pages, and by partnering with other groups in your organization who share the same network.

Optimizing Application Design and Administration

You can often improve the performance of your Web server by paying attention to the design and administration of your Web applications and by upgrading hardware components to support fast application response times.

Upgrading Hardware to Improve Application Performance

Several types of hardware upgrade can significantly improve application response times on your Web servers:

- Upgrade or add processors. Web applications benefit from faster processors.

- Add memory. Adding memory can improve application response times if applications are running within their own processes.

Optimizing Application Design

Check this list for general application design guidelines that can optimize performance.

- Use static files wherever possible. Typically, static files require much less processor time than do files with dynamic content.

  If you are generating pages dynamically to satisfy user preferences, consider substituting as many as 10 or 20 static variations for a single dynamic page. If you are generating dynamic pages to provide frequently updated data, redesign your application so that it generates a single static page on a fixed schedule and stores that page for retrieval until the next update.

- Use managed code (C# or Microsoft® Visual Basic® .NET), Microsoft ASP.NET, or ISAPI applications. C# and Visual Basic .NET applications usually run faster than ASP applications because the run-time environment executes compiled code. All of these types of applications typically run faster than equivalent CGI applications.

- Enable ISAPI and ASP.NET output caching where possible, which allows HTTP.sys to cache the response and serve requests for the applications from the kernel instead of transitioning to user mode. For more information about tuning ISAPI output caching, see "Tuning ASP Metabase Settings" earlier in this chapter.

- Avoid transitions from managed code to unmanaged code in your applications, if possible.

- Enhance database-driven performance by using Microsoft SQL Server. Create and maintain good indexes to minimize I/O during database queries. Also, use stored procedures, which take much less time to execute and are easier to write than ASP scripts designed to do the same task.

- Design your site so that applications push the processing load onto the client.

  Client-side checks reduce roundtrips and help to avoid network latencies, conserve server-side resources, and allow changes to appear instantaneously to the user. For example, add client-side code to validate that forms are filled out with good data, such as checking that credit-card numbers have a correct checksum. However, the server must still validate the data, because malicious clients can send malformed data.

Optimizing the Design of ASP Applications

Check this list for ASP application design guidelines that can optimize performance.

- Turn off ASP debugging, and verify that both the **AppAllowDebugging** and **AppAllowClientDebug** metabase properties are set to **false**.

- Avoid storing apartment-threaded components in ASP application or session state. Remove Visual Basic objects from ASP Session state if they are apartment threaded.

- Cache output from ASP if possible; if not, cache inputs to ASP if possible.

- Convert scripts in ASP pages into COM objects. Scripts in ASP pages are interpreted; if a script involves one or more loops, converting it to a COM object can improve its performance considerably.

- ASP is now able to run all of its threads in a multithreaded apartment (MTA) If your COM components are primarily free-threaded or both-threaded, running the ASP threads as MTA can improve performance significantly. To enable all ASP applications to run in an MTA, you can use the metabase property **AspExecuteInMTA** at the application level. For more information about designing ASP to run its threads in MTA, see "Configuring Applications to Use COM+ Services" in IIS 6.0 Help.

- If an ASP script is more than 100 lines (counting lines of code in included files), consider creating a COM+ component to provide the same function. If COM+ components are written efficiently and debugged properly, they can offer 20 to 30 times the processing speed of a script for the same dynamic page.

 Tip

The easiest way to measure the size of an ASP script with #include directives is to change the file name extension of the page from .asp to .stm, and then open the .stm file by using your browser. Use your browser's View Source command to display the .asp file and lines of code from the included files.

Optimizing Network Administration and Design

Check this list for network administration and design guidelines that can optimize performance.

- Set HTTP expire headers for all images and for HTML so that proxy servers and browsers make fewer calls to the Web server. For information about setting an expiration date for Web site content, see "Using Content Expiration" in IIS 6.0 Help.

- Use SSL certificates only when needed and only for content that requires security. Because SSL uses complex encryption that consumes considerable processor resources, it takes much longer to retrieve and send data from SSL-enabled directories. Therefore, only secure the files that contain or receive sensitive information, such as credit-card numbers or medical information. Also, keep these pages free of other elements that consume resources, such as images. For more information about implementing an acceptable level of security while preserving performance, see "Balancing Performance and Security" earlier in this chapter.

- Minimize initialization processing wherever possible. For example, enable caching, when appropriate; on multiprocessor computers, assign processor affinity to better use CPU caching; and use HTTP compression for faster downloads. For information about caching, see "Monitoring Overall Server Memory" earlier in this chapter. For information about using compression on different file types, see "Using HTTP Compression for Faster Downloads" earlier in this chapter.

- Run IIS in worker process isolation mode, which allows you to periodically restart worker processes assigned to an application pool (either manually or automatically by using preconfigured settings). Recycling worker processes can help minimize problems attributed to faulty Web applications.

- Establish Web gardens, which are application pools that can run multiple worker processes.

- Stress-test applications in your lab before you place them on a production server.

- If you have a large installation with many FTP sites, each attached to a different IP port, your server might create too many backlog monitor threads (the system creates a thread for every 64 sites). The workaround for this is to disable the backlog monitor. To disable the backlog monitor, set the value of the **DisableBacklogMonitor** registry entry to 1 and then restart the FTP services. The **DisableBacklogMonitor** entry is located in the following registry subkey:

  HKEY_LOCAL_MACHINE\SYSTEM\CurrentControlSet\Services\Inetinfo\Parameters

Caution

The registry editor bypasses standard safeguards, allowing settings that can damage your system, or even require you to reinstall Windows. If you must edit the registry, back it up first and see the Registry Reference on the *Windows Server 2003 Resource Kit* companion CD or on the Web at http://www.microsoft.com/reskit.

- If you expect a large spike in traffic on a particular page or set of pages, you can change that page or set it to static HTML for a few days. Switching from a dynamic page to static HTML can involve some redesign, but the effort is often worthwhile. For example, when many thousands of people, during a short period, traverse three or four scripted pages to get to a particular download page, your server uses a lot more resources than it needs to. To save time for your users, you can instead provide a temporary static front page that has simple navigation.

Creating a More Efficient Web Site

Creating a page-load performance profile provides a systematic way of looking at a Web page and recording its performance characteristics across a wide area network (WAN). A page-load performance profile incorporates the distance, congestion, and limited bandwidth that 99 percent of your users experience when accessing your site.

Page-load performance profiles can help you determine the following:

- The impact of not setting expiration dates.

- Which files are taking the longest to load.

- Whether you have unneeded file content.

- Where to reduce and consolidate files.

- How long your pages take to load (on first access and second access).

To perform a page-load test, install the appropriate tools to collect data so that you can develop performance profiles by analyzing HTTP traffic. Network Monitor is a protocol analyzer that looks into packet-level detail. For more information about obtaining and using this tool, see "Network Monitor overview" in Help and Support Center for Windows Server 2003.

After obtaining page-load performance profiles for your Web pages, you can use the performance data to identify changes that you can make in order to optimize the performance of the Web pages.

Obtaining a Page-Load Performance Profile

Measure your page-load times by using the procedures that follow. After obtaining a page-load performance profile, analyze the data and remove obstacles to the page's efficient performance by using the information in "Optimizing a Page-Load Performance Profile" later in this chapter.

To obtain an accurate picture of a Web page's performance during normal use, you must obtain page-load performance data for the second access to a Web page as well as the first access. The first-access load time is usually much longer in duration than second-access load times. When a first-time user visits a Web page, the user's computer does not hold cached files from previous visits; hence, the user's browser must load all the files that are a part of the Web page. The procedure for measuring a Web page's first-access load time differs slightly from the procedure for measuring second-access load times.

Use this procedure to measure a Web page's first-access load time.

To measure a Web page's first-access load time

1. Set up your WAN simulator to represent your 50th percentile domestic user. For example, your settings might be 60 milliseconds roundtrip delay, 50 kilobits per second, and no packet loss.

2. Set the site that you want to test as the default home page for your browser.

3. Browse to a site other than the one you are testing.

   If you are still on the test site when you clear your cache, the site refreshes after you clear the cache, reloading the files that you want to clear.

4. Clear the cache of all files by doing the following:

   a.   On the **Tools** menu of Internet Explorer, click **Internet Options**.

   b.   On the **General** tab, under **History**, click **Clear History**.

5. Close your browser.

   You must close TCP connections between tests, or your tests will be affected by TCP's slow-start algorithm, which retains the window size from the previous page load, producing inaccurate results.

6. Start your Network Monitor capture.

7. Open your browser to the test site (your new home page).

8. Stop the capture when the page is fully loaded and run Network Monitor. Determine how much total time elapsed while the page was loading.

9. Copy your data into a Microsoft® Excel worksheet for further analysis.

> **Important**
>
> Do not use CTRL+F5 (refresh the Web page — regardless of time stamp) as a substitute for this procedure. Although using CTRL+F5 is similar to this process in that it forces a full reload, it does not disconnect the TCP connections before the new page load.

When you test a Web page for its second-access load time, you can use files that are saved in the client's cache.

To measure a Web page's second-access load time

1. Use the same WAN parameters and browser default settings that you used to determine first-access load time.

2. Close your browser without clearing the cache.

3. Restart your Network Monitor capture.

4. Open your browser to the test page.

5. Stop the capture when the page is fully loaded, and measure the time from the first TCP SYN from the client to the server, until the last byte is received.

6. Copy the results to a second Excel worksheet for further analysis.

> ◆ **Important**
>
> Do not use F5 (refresh the Web page) as a substitute for this procedure because it does not provide the same results as a second page-load. Using F5 forces Internet Explorer to check the date on all cached files regardless of whether the dates will expire in the future.

After you complete your own page-load performance profiles, perform a page-load test against your competitors' sites, compare the results with your own performance data, and ask:

- Which site is faster?

- Does speed contribute to ratings?

- Which sites will users choose to come back to?

Optimizing a Page-Load Performance Profile

By optimizing page-load performance profiles, you can provide more efficient Web sites for your users. Begin by making sure that HTTP Keep-Alives are enabled, enabling HTTP compression if appropriate for your Web sites, and setting expiration dates on the files associated with your Web pages. Then identify your slow-loading files, reviewing them for unneeded file content. Next measure your file quantity and size. Finally, determine port usage and minimize unneeded screen refreshes. After reviewing all these factors and optimizing your Web sites, obtain a new page-load profile to determine whether the changes significantly improve the efficiency of your Web site.

For additional tips for optimizing your Web sites, see "Best Practices for Creating Efficient Sites" later in this chapter. For instructions telling how to obtain a page-load profile, see "Obtaining a Page-Load Performance Profile" earlier in this chapter.

Verify That HTTP Keep-Alives Are Enabled

Another item to verify is the "connection = keep-alive" state for each TCP connection. If keep-alive connections are turned off, every file requires a new TCP connection. For small files, enabling HTTP Keep-Alives in IIS effectively doubles the number of roundtrips. For more information about HTTP Keep-Alives, see "Enabling HTTP Keep-Alives to Keep Connections Open" earlier in this chapter.

Set HTTP Compression

If you have Web sites that use large amounts of bandwidth, consider enabling HTTP compression to obtain faster transmission times between your server and compression-enabled browsers. The performance cost of compressing a static file is small and is typically incurred only once because the compressed file is stored in a compression cache.

The cost of expanding the file at the browser is minimal. Compressed files download faster, which makes them especially beneficial to the performance of any browser that uses a network connection with restricted bandwidth, such as a modem connection.

For more information about enabling HTTP compression, see "Using HTTP Compression for Faster Downloads" earlier in this chapter.

Set Expiration Dates on Files

A common performance mistake is omitting to set the expiration dates on the files associated with Web pages. When a user returns to a Web page, Internet Explorer already has most of the files for the page in its cache, but it does not use these files if the expiration dates are in the past. Instead, Internet Explorer sends a GET request to the server for the file, indicating the date of the file in the cache. If the file has not changed, the server sends a Not Modified message. This GET/Not-Modified sequence costs the client a roundtrip. For small files of 3 KB or less, this roundtrip is as expensive as getting the original file.

 Important

You must be a member of the Administrators group on the local computer to perform the following procedure or procedures, or you must have been delegated the appropriate authority. As a security best practice, log on to your computer by using an account that is not in the Administrators group, and then use the **runas** command to run IIS Manager as an administrator. At a command prompt, type **runas** /*User.Administrative_AccountName* "**mmc** %systemroot%\system32\inetsrv\iis.msc".

▷ **To set the expiration date in IIS 6.0**

1. In IIS Manager, right-click the file, and then click **Properties**.

2. On the **HTTP Headers** tab, select the **Enable Content Expiration** check box, and then choose the option you want for setting a date.

   You can set a specific date or you can choose to have IIS expire the file within a specified time, such as 30 days after the user loads it. For very small files, you can set the header to expire immediately.

To verify that expiration dates are working correctly, look for Not Modified messages in the HTTP response packet of your Network Monitor capture summary.

Identify Slow-Loading Files

Identifying which files are taking the longest to load often provides the best clues about what you need to improve. Causes of very long load times can include server capacity issues, network congestion, and large file content. Use the data that you collect from Network Monitor captures to identify how long each file takes to load. Visit a Web page several times and observe which files are regularly loaded most slowly. Multiple visits to a page help improve statistical veracity.

Remove Unneeded File Content

Files often contain clutter, such as tabs, spaces, new lines, and comments, that consumes up to 15 percent or more of a page. For production Web sites that are visited by millions of users, remove every bit of file content that is not absolutely necessary for the rendering of the page.

View the packet contents of your files with Network Monitor. Look for repetitive text such as <Option Value = data> statements that are used to insert text into drop-down lists. It takes much less space to add a few lines of code that sends an array (that reads the drop-down lists) to the client.

Measure File Quantity and Size

The number and size of files that you load on your Web site have a large impact on page-load times. Fewer large files load faster than many small files, as follows:

- **Number of files.** For each file, HTTP must perform a GET-File. Each GET-File is at least a single roundtrip. If the files are on a new server that the user has not previously connected to, HTTP must also make another roundtrip to create a new connection. Roundtrips across a modem cost 250 milliseconds or more.

  The optimal minimum number of files for a Web site is about four. Consider consolidating like files; for example, have only one .js or .css file instead of two or three.

- **Size of files.** The TCP slow-start algorithm favors larger files. When a new connection is first opened, TCP sends a small number of packets in response to a GET-File. Thereafter, for each acknowledgement received by the server, TCP increases the number of response packets sent to the client.

  Small files of 3 KB or less are complete in one roundtrip. Files larger than 20 KB receive only about 16 KB of data per roundtrip. The size of a file can make the difference between a very small bit rate of 1 to 10 kilobits per second (Kbps) and a high bit rate of 40 to hundreds of Kbps.

Determine Your Port Usage

Using HTTP 1.1, Internet Explorer can open a maximum of two ports to any one server and a maximum of four ports total. The best performance occurs when four ports are opened and are kept open to be reused by all the files. Reusing a port is a good thing; when TCP slow-start increases the window size for a file, the next file that uses the same port can also use the increased window size.

View your Network Monitor capture summary to determine how many ports were used during your page-load tests, and by which files. Keep in mind that measuring Web pages through a proxy server hides the true number of ports being used. The best tests from your office are conducted by using a direct connection to the Internet without a proxy.

Control Screen Refreshes

In a refresh request, Internet Explorer (the client) tells the server the date stamp of the version of a file that it has in its cache by using the "If-Modified-Since" header. IIS 6.0 then determines whether the file has been modified since that time. If the file is unmodified, IIS 6.0 replies with a brief "Not Modified" response.

In routine file updates for your Web site, do not copy files that have not been modified. A static HTML page is not retrieved during a screen refresh if it has not been updated. Some publication processes copy files that have not been modified, which gives the files new time stamps and thus "updates" them as far as the system is concerned. These files are downloaded even though they are actually unchanged. When you set up your publication process, make every effort to avoid this waste of resources.

Best Practices for Creating Efficient Sites

For important, often-used Web pages, do the following.

Optimize settings

- Set file expiration dates. By setting future expiration dates on each file at the IIS server, you can reduce second-access load times by 50 to 70 percent.

- Enable HTTP Keep-Alives in IIS.

- Author hyperlinks consistently because the Internet Explorer cache is case sensitive.

- Use cache-control extensions. Internet Explorer version 5 introduced support for two extensions to the cache-control HTTP response header: pre-check and post-check.

Use design elements judiciously

- Standardize images. For example, if your site uses two images that are slightly different from each other, either in size, color, or design, standardize to a single image.

- Reduce Graphics Interchange Format (GIF) image color depth or consider using Portable Network Graphics (PNG) format.

- Eliminate unnecessary images that appear below the scroll bar. Users view these images less frequently; so weigh their value against their performance cost. For example, use text rather than images for arrows, lines, and bullets. Incorporate several small images into one large graphic (or remove some of the images). Substitute smaller images for large ones.

- Use the most compact graphics format that supports the quality of image that you need. Images saved as a file type that is inherently large, such as a Tagged Image File Format (.tif), can increase download times; consider substituting a more compact format such as a Graphics Interchange Format (.gif) or a Joint Photographic Experts Group (.jpg) file. You might also consider compressing existing images.

Ensure that developers design scripts and code that load quickly

- Reduce clutter. Space characters, tabs, and remarks often consume more than 20 percent of an .htm or an .asp file. Delete this clutter before you load the files on production servers.

- Remove redundant tags. Consider using arrays to fill drop-down lists instead of repeating [<Option Value = data> data</Option>] again and again.

- Use JavaScript (.js) files to consolidate commonly used scripts.

- Reduce the number of small files. Build whole images instead of multiple component images. For tabs, use a single image map.

- Consolidate multiple images and adjacent images into a single file.

- Do not use nested <table> tags.

Test load times for your pages

You can use the following tools to test the load times for your Web pages:

- WAN simulators

- Network Monitor

- Load simulators for the Internet environment

- Reporting tools

Partnering with Other Groups to Improve Performance

In enterprise organizations, where corporate intranets might be accessed by employees in far-reaching parts of the country or the world, IT administrators in areas that share the intranet must work together to ensure optimal performance for all users. Take time to find out how the performance of other areas is affecting the performance of your applications and systems; then work with IT administrators in other areas to coordinate efforts to improve performance.

If the systems and applications that you manage depend on the performance of other systems and applications, use this guide to help you collaborate with your IT partners:

1. Identify your partners:

    - Start early in the IT cycle to contact partners and find performance allies in other groups and on your own team. Obtain agreement to work together to maintain and improve performance, including upgrading, adding to, or changing your network components.

    - Determine how the performance of other systems and applications affects your systems and applications, and vice versa; then document the dependencies and share the data with your partners.

2. Before you begin your design, obtain information about your users. You must know your users in order to set realistic goals for response times and system preferences. If possible, conduct usability tests to discover the actual needs, behaviors, and preferences of real users.

3. Set performance goals for your group, and establish a timeline:

    - Set performance goals and test plans for your group.

    - Discuss key milestones in your timeline.

    - Identify competing priorities, especially conflicting priorities of partners outside your immediate group.

4. Coordinate your plans and goals with your partners' plans and goals:

    - Share your goals, timeline, and milestones with your partners; then synchronize goals and timelines with them. Define terminology to ensure that everyone understands each goal and service level. Include a plan for communicating with your partners.

    - Write contracts, if needed, to set service level agreements for performance and to balance competing priorities so that other groups' priorities do not adversely affect yours (and vice versa).

    - Establish baseline requirements for operating systems and hardware.

    - Establish guidelines for how to monitor any mutual performance dependencies. Establish minimum testing standards. Establish a system for logging bugs against performance problems.

5. Design the systems and applications for your group to minimize their impact on other components:

- Design your client systems so they do not put unnecessary load on servers. For example, ensure that clients' browsers are compression-enabled, and enable HTTP compression of static files on your Web server to provide faster transmission times.

- Test to identify and minimize unnecessary client requests, such as requests from impatient users who make numerous attempts to access the same page. It is recommended that you set the **AspQueueConnectionTestTime** metabase property so that your server does not process abandoned requests, enable HTTP Keep-Alives, and set up caching to minimize requests from clients' Web browsers.

Additional Resources

These resources contain additional information and tools related to this chapter.

Related Information

- "Analyzing Log Files" in this book for information about using IIS logs to monitor and tune performance.

- "Common Administrative Tasks" in this book for step-by-step instructions to help you complete many of the tasks described in this chapter.

- "Troubleshooting IIS 6.0" in this book for information about troubleshooting performance.

- "Web Server Scalability" in this book for information about IIS 6.0 capacity planning and scalability.

- Article 247658, "Configure Secure Sockets Layer Server and Client Cache Elements," in the Microsoft Knowledge Base for information about configuring SSL session caching, including how to set the **ClientCacheTime** registry setting. To find this article, see the Microsoft Knowledge Base link on the Web Resources page at http://www.microsoft.com/windows/reskits/webresources.

- Article 313064, "Monitor Web Server Performance by Using Counter Logs in System Monitor in IIS," in the Microsoft Knowledge Base for information about creating counter logs, including baseline IIS logs. To find this article, see the Microsoft Knowledge Base link on the Web Resources page at http://www.microsoft.com/windows/reskits/webresources.

- The Windows System Resource Manager — Fast Facts link on the Web Resources page at http://www.microsoft.com/windows/reskits/webresources for information about using Windows System Resource Manager.

- Microsoft Application Consulting and Engineering (ACE) Team, *Performance Testing Microsoft .NET Web Applications*. Redmond, WA: Microsoft Press, 2003. Read this source for information about how to perform stress testing by using Microsoft Application Center Test (ACT), how to use System Monitor and Network Monitor, and how to conduct an application network analysis.

Related IIS 6.0 Help Topics

- "Enabling Logging" in IIS 6.0 Help, which is accessible from IIS Manager, for information about performance logging.

- "Limiting Connections" in IIS 6.0 Help for information about setting global and individual site connection limits.

- "Quality of Service" in IIS 6.0 Help for information about the QoS features in IIS 6.0.

- "Security" in IIS 6.0 Help for information about IIS 6.0 security features.

- "Web Application Guide" in IIS 6.0 Help for information about Web application development, including ASP.NET and ASP applications.

Related Windows Server 2003 Help Topics

For best results in identifying Help topics by title, in Help and Support Center, under the **Search** box, click **Set search options**. Under **Help Topics**, select the **Search in title only** check box.

- "Analyzing performance data" in Help and Support Center for Windows Server 2003 for information about analyzing log data and a list of acceptable values for counters.

- "Performance console overview" in Help and Support Center for Windows Server 2003 for information about Windows performance monitoring tools.

- "Monitoring performance from the command line" in Help and Support Center for Windows Server 2003 for information about command-line tools that you can use to monitor performance.

- "The TCP/IP model" in Help and Support Center for Windows Server 2003 for information about how the OSI model relates to the TCP/IP reference model.

Related Tools

- The **logman** command

  Use the **logman** command to schedule performance counter and event trace log collections on local and remote systems. For more information about the **logman** command, see "Logman" in Help and Support Center for Windows Server 2003.

- Log Parser tool (LogParser.exe)

  Use the Log Parser tool to extract data from the raw file. The Log Parser tool and its accompanying user documentation are included in the IIS 6.0 Resource Kit Tools. You can install the IIS 6.0 Resource Kit Tools, which include Help documentation, by running IIS60rkt.exe from the *Internet Information Services (IIS) 6.0 Resource Kit* companion CD.

- The **start netmon** command

  Use the **start netmon** command to start the Network Monitor user interface from the command line. You can also specify parameters for capturing and filtering frames. For more information about using this command-line option, see "Managing Network Monitor from the command line" in Help and Support Center for Windows Server 2003.

- Web Capacity Analysis Tool (WCAT), which contains a stress client tool (Wcclient.exe) and a controller tool (Wcctl.exe).

  Use WCAT to perform stress testing. You can obtain WCAT and its documentation from the *Internet Information Services (IIS) 6.0 Resource Kit* companion CD. You can install the Resource Kit Tools by running IIS60rkt.exe from the companion CD.

CHAPTER 14

Web Server Scalability

Internet Information Services (IIS) 6.0, running on the Microsoft® Windows® Server 2003 operating system, includes a new architecture and new features to help your application server scale. *Scaling* is the ability of a system to handle increasing demands at an acceptable performance level. If an application server and the underlying infrastructure scale, the application can handle steady traffic growth, in addition to occasional peaks in traffic volumes, while maintaining good performance. If an application server and the underlying infrastructure do not scale, clients connecting to that application can experience poor response times, errors, or other problems that might ultimately frustrate end users.

In This Chapter

Related Information

- For information about performance monitoring and tuning, see "Optimizing IIS 6.0 Performance" in this book.

Scaling IIS 6.0

Changes in the Internet Information Services (IIS) 6.0 architecture have led to dramatic improvements in how IIS scales. During preliminary testing, IIS 6.0 scaled better than earlier versions of IIS. Those preliminary results showed that on a default installation, while running in worker process isolation mode, IIS 6.0 was capable of the following:

- Hosting as many as 20,000 static-content sites.

- Hosting as many as 2,000 application pools.

- Processing 25,000 requests per second for a 15-KB cached static file with Hypertext Transfer Protocol (HTTP) Keep-Alives enabled.

- Running hundreds — or potentially thousands — of simultaneous worker processes.

 Note

Performance and scalability results vary depending on hardware and software configurations. Microsoft does not make any warranties or guarantees about these preliminary results.

Additionally, processing throughput has greatly improved for installations with up to eight processors. Default thread pool, queue, and cache settings have all been tuned to increase throughput. Startup and shutdown times are faster than earlier versions. Simply put, your IIS Web server installation should scale better on a default installation of IIS 6.0 than on any earlier version of IIS. However, there are many variables in a Web server installation that can affect how IIS 6.0 scales. Scalability is dependent on the least scalable part in your server installation. Factors such as network latency, slow back-end processing, a shortage of RAM on your servers, or poorly designed and untested applications can all undermine how IIS 6.0 scales. If one part does not scale, the whole installation suffers.

This section provides a brief overview of the many changes and features that help IIS scale, and also describes some of the changes and features in the Microsoft® Windows® Server 2003, Standard Edition; Windows® Server 2003, Enterprise Edition; Windows® Server 2003, Web Edition; and Windows® Server 2003, Datacenter Edition operating systems that can increase the scalability of your server installation. Be aware that scaling an application server is a process much like tuning the performance of your server. Performance and scalability are intricately linked, and both goals require long-term planning, testing, and monitoring. For more information about performance monitoring and tuning, see "Optimizing IIS 6.0 Performance" in this book.

Scalability Features in IIS 6.0

This section describes features in IIS 6.0 that can improve the scalability of your application server.

 Important

Do not enable the features described in this chapter on a production server before you establish a performance baseline in a test environment. If enabling any of these features degrades performance, continue testing or disable the feature and return your server to the pre-change configuration.

Worker process isolation mode

IIS 6.0 introduces worker process isolation mode, which runs all Web applications in an isolated environment. When you run IIS in worker process isolation mode, you can configure applications to run in separate application pools. An *application pool* is a grouping of URLs routed to one or more worker processes. An application pool allows specific configuration settings to apply to these worker processes.

Worker processes operate independently: if one fails, it does not affect other worker processes. The pooling of applications protects applications from the effects of worker processes that support other application pools. In this way, applications are protected from each other.

When a worker process enters an unhealthy state and stops processing requests, the HTTP protocol stack (HTTP.sys) continues to queue requests. The World Wide Web Publishing Service (WWW service) detects that the worker process is unhealthy and shuts it down, starting a new worker process if requests are waiting in the queue or if new requests arrive. Hence, even when a worker process fails, the WWW service, by means of HTTP.sys, continues to accept requests and shields the user from loss of service because the client can still connect to the WWW service.

For more information about IIS 6.0 application isolation modes, including how to enable and configure worker process isolation mode, see "Running IIS 6.0 as an Application Server" in this book. For more information about how IIS 6.0 processes requests, see "IIS 6.0 Architecture" in this book.

On-demand process start

IIS 6.0 does not allocate resources at initialization time; instead, it allocates resources as needed, which increases site scalability. In particular, IIS 6.0 application pools only start processes when the first request for a URL is served by the application pool.

HTTP Keep-Alives

IIS 6.0 supports HTTP Keep-Alives, an HTTP specification that can significantly improve server performance. Most Web browsers request that the server keep the connection open across multiple requests; this is called a *Keep-Alive*. Without this feature, a browser must make numerous connection requests for a page that contains multiple elements, such as graphics. A separate connection might need to be made for each element. HTTP Keep-Alives increase server efficiency by reducing server activity and resource consumption. HTTP Keep-Alives can also increase browser responsiveness across a slow connection. For more information about HTTP Keep-Alives, see "Optimizing IIS 6.0 Performance" in this book.

Web gardens

When running in worker process isolation mode, IIS can be configured to have multiple worker processes servicing requests for an application pool. This configuration is known as a "Web garden." When a worker process in an application pool is busy processing a request, other worker processes can accept and process requests for the application pool. For more information about Web gardens, including how to enable or configure this feature, see "Running IIS 6.0 as an Application Server" in this book.

Processor affinity

To efficiently use resources on large multiprocessor servers, IIS 6.0 enables you to configure application pools to establish affinity between worker processes and individual processors. When set, processor affinity forces worker processes to run on specific microprocessors or CPUs. This affinity applies to all worker processes that serve the Web sites and applications of an application pool. For more information about processor affinity, including how to enable or configure this feature, see "Optimizing IIS 6.0 Performance" in this book.

Idle timeout for worker processes

An IIS 6.0 application pool can be configured so that its worker processes request a shutdown if they are idle for a configurable amount of time. Shutting down worker processes frees up unused resources and reduces CPU load. For more information about idle timeout, including how to enable or configure this feature, see "Running IIS 6.0 as an Application Server" in this book.

Bandwidth throttling

If the network or Internet connection used by your Web server is also used by other services, such as e-mail or news, you can limit the bandwidth used by your Web server so it is available for those other services. If your Web server hosts more than one Web site, you can individually throttle the bandwidth used by each site. For more information about bandwidth throttling, including how to enable or configure this feature, see "Optimizing IIS 6.0 Performance" in this book.

HTTP compression

HTTP compression allows faster transmission of pages between the Web server and compression-enabled clients. This is useful in situations where bandwidth is limited. For more information about HTTP compression, including how to enable or configure this feature, see "Optimizing IIS 6.0 Performance" in this book.

64 GB cache capacity

For workloads that require large amounts of cached data, the IIS 6.0 kernel-mode driver, HTTP.sys, can be configured to cache up to 64 gigabytes (GB) on an x86-based or compatible processor–based system. For more information about IIS caches, see "Improving Scalability by Optimizing IIS 6.0 Caches" later in this chapter.

Centralized binary logging

IIS 6.0 supports centralized binary logging, where multiple Web sites send binary, unformatted log data to a single log file. When many Web sites are hosted on the same server, the process of creating hundreds or thousands of formatted log files and writing the log data to disk can quickly consume valuable CPU and memory resources, thereby creating performance and scalability problems. Centralized binary logging in IIS 6.0 minimizes the server resources that are used for logging, while providing detailed log data for organizations that require it. For more information about centralized binary logging, including how to enable or configure this feature, see "Analyzing Log Files" in this book.

Scalability Features in Windows Server 2003

This section describes features in Windows Server 2003 that can improve the scalability of your application server.

 Important

Do not enable features described here on a production server before you establish a performance baseline in a test environment. If enabling any of these features degrades performance, continue testing or disable the feature and return your server to the pre-change configuration.

Kernel-mode driver

Windows Server 2003 introduces a new kernel-mode driver, HTTP.sys, for HTTP parsing and caching. IIS 6.0 is built on top of HTTP.sys. HTTP.sys is specifically tuned to increase Web server throughput by directly processing requests in the kernel (in specific circumstances) or by efficiently routing requests to user-mode worker processes. The combination of kernel request processing and efficient user-mode routing have dramatically improved how IIS 6.0 scales and performs. For more information about HTTP.sys, see "IIS 6.0 Architecture" in this book.

64-bit support

The complete Windows Server 2003 code base is compiled for both 32-bit and 64-bit platforms. Organizations that need highly scalable applications can take advantage of an operating system that runs — and is supported — on these two platforms.

WSRM

Windows System Resource Manager (WSRM) is a feature of Windows Server 2003, Enterprise Edition and Windows Server 2003, Datacenter Edition.

With WSRM, you can control how CPU and memory resources are allocated to applications, services, and processes. Managing resources in this way improves system performance and reduces the chance that applications, services, or processes will interfere with the rest of the system; it also creates a more consistent and predictable experience for users of applications and services running on the computer.

WSRM can be installed from the Windows Server 2003, Enterprise Edition or Windows Server 2003, Datacenter Edition operating system CD. For more information about WSRM, see the Help files that are included in the WSRM snap-in.

DFS

Distributed File System (DFS) unifies files on different computers into a single namespace, making it easy to build a single, hierarchical view of multiple file servers and file server shares on a network. To use DFS as the file system for IIS, select the root for the Web site as a DFS root. You can then move resources within a DFS tree without affecting any HTML links. For more information about DFS, see Help and Support Center for Windows Server 2003.

FRS

The File Replication service (FRS) provides multimaster file replication for designated directory trees between designated servers running Windows Server 2003. The designated directory trees must be on disk partitions formatted with the version of the NTFS file system used with Windows Server 2003. FRS must be used with DFS. DFS uses FRS to automatically synchronize content between assigned replicas. The combination of DFS and FRS can also work with the Active Directory® directory service to automatically synchronize the content of system volume information across domain controllers. For more information about FRS, see Help and Support Center for Windows Server 2003.

Improving IIS 6.0 Scalability and Availability with Network Load Balancing

The best way to guarantee the scalability and availability of your Internet services is to host your site with more than one computer. Microsoft Windows Server 2003 includes the Network Load Balancing service. Network Load Balancing enhances the availability and scalability of Internet server applications such as those used on Web, File Transfer Protocol (FTP), firewall, proxy, and virtual private network (VPN) servers, in addition to other mission-critical servers. A single computer running Windows can provide a limited level of server reliability and scalable performance. However, by combining the resources of two or more computers running Windows Server 2003 into a single cluster, Network Load Balancing can deliver the reliability and performance that Web servers and other mission-critical servers need. Figure 7.1 shows two connected Network Load Balancing clusters. The first cluster consists of two hosts and the second cluster consists of four hosts.

Figure 7.1 Load Balanced Clusters

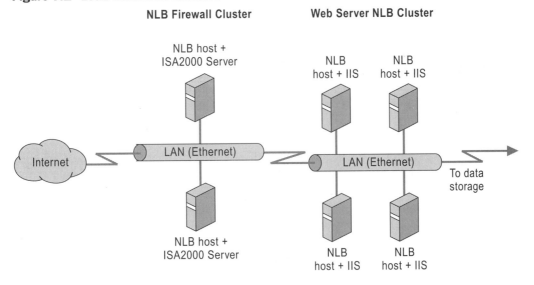

Each host runs separate copies of the server applications, such as those for a Web, FTP, or Telnet server. Network Load Balancing distributes incoming client requests across the hosts in the cluster. The load weight to be handled by each host can be configured as necessary. You can also dynamically add hosts to the cluster to handle the increased load. In addition, Network Load Balancing can direct all traffic to a designated single host, called the default host.

Network Load Balancing allows all of the computers in the cluster to be addressed by the same cluster IP address (but also maintains their existing unique, dedicated IP addresses). For more information about Network Load Balancing, see Help and Support Center for Windows Server 2003.

 Note

FrontPage® Server Extensions from Microsoft do not work in a Network Load Balancing environment. Also, FrontPage Server Extensions do not work side-by-side with SharePoint™ Team Services from Microsoft on the same virtual server or Web site. For more information about upgrading your FrontPage-extended Web sites, see the SharePoint Team Services Administrator's Guide link on the Web Resources page at http://www.microsoft.com/windows/reskits/webresources.

IIS Responses to Load-Balanced Application Pool Behaviors

IIS 6.0 is designed to work with a variety of hardware and software network load balancers. However, the introduction of application pools and health-monitoring features such as rapid-fail protection in IIS 6.0 has the potential to confuse load balancers when an application pool fails to respond to a request, or when IIS health-monitoring features act on a faulty application pool. This section describes how HTTP.sys and IIS respond to load balancers for various application pool failures or problems.

For Layer 3 and Layer 4 load balancers (that is, basic load balancers such as Network Load Balancing), when an application pool fails, IIS causes the load balancer to run a TCP reset command. For Layer 7 load balancers (more advanced load balancers that balance the load based on higher-level application data, such as URLs, session data, and cookies) HTTP.sys sends a 503 error and attempts to connect to the application pool again after a specified period of time. IIS can also be configured to shut down the faulty application pool altogether. These responses can remedy application failures at the application pool level instead of forcing the load balancer to fail over the entire server. These responses also allow healthy application pools to continue processing requests without forcing the load balancer to fail over the entire server.

Table 7.1 summarizes how HTTP.sys and IIS respond to load balancers for various application pool failures.

Table 7.1 IIS Responses to Load-Balanced Application Pool Behaviors

Condition	Auto-Shutdown of Application Pool?	Layer 7 Load Balancer Behavior	Layer 3 and Layer 4 Load Balancer Behavior
The application pool entered rapid-fail protection.	Yes	HTTP 503 error	IIS resets the TCP connection.
The application pool CPU threshold was exceeded.	Yes	HTTP 503 error	IIS resets the TCP connection.
An administrator disabled the application pool or shut down the WWW service.	No	HTTP 503 error	IIS resets the TCP connection.
The kernel-mode request queue is full.	No	HTTP 503 error	IIS resets the TCP connection.

By default, the IIS metabase property **LoadBalancerCapabilities** is configured for Layer 7 responses (**LoadBalancerCapabilities** = 2). If your organization uses Layer 3 or Layer 4 load balancers, you will need to change this property in the IIS metabase to a value of 1.

 Important

> It is recommended that you back up the IIS metabase before you change the metabase. For additional information, see "Working with the Metabase" in this book.

For more information about configuring load balancing, see the **LoadBalancerCapabilities** property in the "Metabase Property Reference" in IIS 6.0 Help, which is accessible from IIS Manager. For more information about the IIS 6.0 metabase, including how to change a metabase property, see "Working with the Metabase" in this book.

IIS Response When a Load-Balanced Application Pool Enters Rapid-Fail Protection

When an application pool enters the rapid-fail protection state, HTTP.sys responds to requests with a 503 error. If IIS is configured to shut down the application pool when the application pool enters the rapid-fail protection state, IIS executes the auto-shutdown application pool command. For more information about rapid-fail protection, see "Running IIS 6.0 as an Application Server" in this book. For load-balanced applications, HTTP.sys responds to requests in one of the following ways:

- **Layer 7 response.** When HTTP.sys receives requests for an application pool that is in the rapid-fail protection state, HTTP.sys sends a 503 error. If IIS is configured to shut down the application pool when it enters the rapid-fail protection state, IIS executes the auto-shutdown application pool command. When the error has been resolved, the administrator must restart the application pool.

- **Layer 3 and Layer 4 response.** When HTTP.sys receives requests for an application pool that is in the rapid-fail protection state, HTTP.sys resets the TCP connection that carried the request. If IIS is configured to shut down the application pool when it enters the rapid-fail protection state, IIS executes the auto-shutdown application pool command. When the error has been resolved, the administrator must restart the application pool.

For information about rapid-fail protection, see "Running IIS 6.0 as an Application Server" in this book.

IIS Response When a Load-Balanced Application Pool Exceeds a Configured CPU Threshold

The IIS CPU monitoring feature allows you to configure a CPU threshold for a specific application pool. The IIS CPU monitoring feature includes the option to shut down an application pool if the CPU exceeds a configured maximum. For load-balanced applications, HTTP.sys responds to requests in one of the following ways:

- **Layer 7 response.** When HTTP.sys receives subsequent requests for an application pool that has exceeded the configured CPU maximum, HTTP.sys sends a 503 error. If IIS is configured to shut down the application pool when it exceeds its CPU threshold, IIS executes the auto-shutdown application pool command. When the error has been resolved, the administrator must restart the application pool.

- **Layer 3 and Layer 4 response.** When HTTP.sys receives requests for an application pool that has exceeded the configured CPU maximum, HTTP.sys resets the TCP connection that carried the request. If IIS is configured to shut down the application pool when it exceeds its CPU threshold, IIS executes the auto-shutdown application pool command. When the error has been resolved, the administrator must restart the application pool.

For information about CPU monitoring, see "Running IIS 6.0 as an Application Server" in this book.

IIS Response When a Load-Balanced Application Pool Is Disabled by an Administrator or an Administrator Shuts Down the WWW Service

When an application pool is shut down, the requests that have already been queued in kernel mode are lost. A shutdown of this nature indicates serious application failure and presents a potential threat to the rest of the system if the application continues processing. Such an application failure can affect the integrity of data in custom applications. For this reason, all requests to that application pool should be stopped.

- **Layer 7 response.** When HTTP.sys receives requests for a disabled application pool, or if the administrator shuts down the WWW service, HTTP.sys sends a 503 error. When the error has been resolved, the administrator must restart the application pool.

- **Layer 3 and Layer 4 response.** When HTTP.sys receives requests for a disabled application pool, or if the administrator shuts down the WWW service, HTTP.sys resets the TCP connection that carried the request.

IIS Response When the Kernel-Mode Request Queue Is Full

A full kernel-mode request queue is a temporary state. After application queues finish processing other requests, the kernel-mode request queue will begin accepting new requests.

- **Layer 7 response.** When HTTP.sys receives requests for an application pool but the request queue is full, HTTP.sys sends a 503 error.

- **Layer 3 and Layer 4 response.** When HTTP.sys receives requests for an application pool but the request queue is full, HTTP.sys resets the TCP connection that carried the request.

Preserving Session State in Network Load Balancing Web Server Clusters

IIS enables a Web application to maintain user session data (also called *session state*) across multiple requests. For example, an online ordering application might maintain the user's shopping cart as part of the user's session. IIS uses *session cookies*, which are text files supplied by the user's browser and stored on the user's computer for each request to keep track of which session belongs to which user.

 Note
Worker processes lose session state if the worker process is recycled. The ideal configuration for storing session state with IIS 6.0 is to store user session data in a back-end database.

Ideally, Network Load Balancing always routes connections from a user who has an active session to the server where that session is stored. However, Network Load Balancing and other Layer 4 network load balancers do not use sessions or cookies to decide which Web server should handle an incoming request. For this reason, sessions can be lost between requests in a Network Load Balancing server cluster.

There are several ways to avoid losing sessions:

- Design the Web site application to store session state on the client. For more information, see "Preserving Session State with ASP Web Applications in Network Load Balancing" and "Preserving Session State with ASP.NET Web Applications in Network Load Balancing" later in this chapter.

- Store session state on a central server-side store, such as a database.

- Use the client affinity feature. When client affinity is enabled, Network Load Balancing directs all TCP connections to the same cluster host. This allows session state to be maintained in host memory. You can enable client affinity in the **Add/Edit Port Rules** dialog box in Network Load Balancing Manager. Choose either **Single** or **Class C** affinity to ensure that only one cluster host will handle all connections that are part of the same client session. This is important if the server application running on the cluster host maintains session state (such as server cookies) between connections. For more information about Network Load Balancing affinity, see Help in the Network Load Balancing snap-in.

Preserving Session State with ASP Web Applications in Network Load Balancing

You can enable session state persistence for Active Server Pages (ASP) applications. If you enable session state, the server creates a new Session object for each connection, session state is accessible, session storage is allowed, **Session_OnStart** and **Session_OnEnd** occurs, and the **ASPSessionID** cookie is sent to the client. If you do not enable session state, state access and storage are not allowed, events are not processed, and no cookie is sent. By default, session state is enabled with the session timeout set to 20 minutes. The corresponding metabase property is **AspAllowSessionState**.

Important

You must be a member of the Administrators group on the local computer to perform the following procedure or procedures, or you must have been delegated the appropriate authority. As a security best practice, log on to your computer by using an account that is not in the Administrators group, and then use the runas command to run IIS Manager as an administrator. At a command prompt, type runas /*User.Administrative_AccountName* "mmc %systemroot%\system32\inetsrv\iis.msc".

▷ **To enable session state for an ASP application**

1. In IIS Manager, expand the local computer, right-click the starting-point directory of the application you want to configure, and then click **Properties**.

2. Click the appropriate tab: **Home Directory**, **Virtual Directory**, or **Directory**.

3. In the **Application settings** area, click **Configuration**, and then click the **Options** tab.

4. On the **Options** tab, under **Application configuration**, select the **Enable session state** check box.

5. In the **Session timeout** box, set the number of minutes until the session expires.

6. Click **OK**.

Preserving Session State with ASP.NET Web Applications in Network Load Balancing

If you use **SqlServer** or **StateServer** session state mode, session state might be lost when you run an ASP.NET Web application in a Network Load Balancing server cluster. To maintain session state across different Web servers in the cluster, the application path of the Web site (for example, \LM\W3SVC\2) in the IIS metabase must be the same for all of the Web servers in the cluster.

On one Web server, the instance ID of the Web site where the ASP.NET application is hosted might be 1 (where the application path is \LM\W3SVC\1). On another Web server, the instance ID of the Web site might be 5 (where the application path is \LM\W3SVC\5).

 Note

Web sites created on a clean installation of IIS 6.0 will maintain their individual site numbers, as determined by the **ServerComment** metabase property, across the load-balanced installation. For more information about the **ServerComment** metabase property, see the "Metabase Property Reference" in IIS 6.0 Help.

For **SqlServer** or **StateServer** session state mode to properly store session state, you must synchronize the application path for the Web site in the IIS metabase for all Web servers in the Web farm. You can change the Web site instance ID by manually editing the metabase on each Web server or by using the script Moveinstance.vbs as described in this section. For more information about manually editing the IIS metabase, see "Working with the Metabase" in this book.

Important

You must be a member of the Administrators group on the local computer to run scripts and executables, or you must have been delegated the appropriate authority. As a security best practice, log on to your computer by using an account that is not in the Administrators group, and then use the **runas** command to run your script or executable as an administrator. At a command prompt, type **runas /profile** */User.MyMachine\Administrator* cmd to open a command window with administrator rights and then type **cscript.exe** *ScriptName* (including the full path with parameters, if any).

▶ **To synchronize the application path of a Web site**

1. Create a text file, and then name the file Moveinstance.vbs.

2. Add to Moveinstance.vbs the following script code, which modifies the instance IDs of the Web sites so that they are the same:

```
Dim WebService
Dim oldstr
Dim newstr
Dim args
Set args = WScript.Arguments
If args.Count < 1 Then
    Wscript.Echo "Must have original instance id and new instance id" &
chr(10) & chr(13) & _
    "usage:  moveinstance.vbs 1 5"  & chr(10) & chr(13) & _
"Moves instance 1 to instance 5"
    WScript.Quit()
End If
Set WebService = GetObject("IIS://LocalHost/W3SVC")
oldstr = args(0) 'old instance
newstr = args(1) 'new instance
WebService.MoveHere oldstr,newstr
WebService.SetInfo
Set WebService = nothing
Set args=nothing
WScript.echo "DONE"
```

3. Save Moveinstance.vbs.

4. From the same directory in which you saved Moveinstance.vbs, run the script from a command prompt. For example, at the command prompt, type the following:

cscript moveinstance.vbs 1 5

and then press ENTER. This changes the instance ID of a Web site from 1 to 5 in the metabase.

Note

When you use **StateServer** mode, make sure that the [machineKey] section in the Machine.config file has the same keys on every server in the Web farm.

Improving Scalability by Optimizing IIS 6.0 Queues

A request queue holds a collection of one or more requests waiting to be executed. Request queues can develop when your site experiences high traffic volumes, or if your site blocks to wait for database processing. Large queues, or queues that are not cleared quickly, impact scalability by limiting the number of requests the server can process and by reducing throughput. More importantly, if users are forced to wait for a response from your server, they might perceive that the site is not available and click the **Stop** button on their Web browser. In this situation, the queuing problem grows because clicking the **Stop** button can fill a queue with requests that are no longer connected to a client's browser. If your site routinely develops queues, you might dramatically improve scalability and availability by adjusting the number of requests that can wait in a queue. You can set limits for the following request queues:

- TCP/IP queue

- Kernel request queue

- ASP request queue

- ASP.NET request queues

TCP/IP Queue

At the TCP/IP layer, high-priority threads respond to client requests by validating that the server is or is not accepting and processing requests. If the server is accepting requests, the thread maintains the customer connection and attempts to hand off the request to HTTP.sys. The only reason you might need to adjust the TCP/IP queue is if users cannot connect to your site on the Web. Monitor the TCPv4\Connection Failures and TCPv4\Connections Reset counters (for TCPv6, use the same counters for the TCPv6 object). If the Connection Failures and Connections Reset counters increase steadily, examine your TCP/IP settings. For more information about TCP/IP, see Help and Support Center for Windows Server 2003.

Kernel Request Queue

After HTTP.sys detects the TCP/IP thread, it either begins serving the request with content stored in the HTTP.sys cache, if available (this is called a *cache hit*), or puts the request in a kernel request queue for the designated application pool. Because the request is still in the kernel, but is waiting in a queue for a specific application pool, this queue is sometimes called the *application pool queue*. In IIS Manager, this queue is called the *kernel request queue*.

When IIS 6.0 runs in worker process isolation mode, by default HTTP.sys checks the number of requests for a designated application pool queue before it adds a new request to the queue. If adding the new request to the queue exceeds the queue limit, the server rejects the request, logs a QueueFull error in the HTTP error log, and sends a 503 error (Service Unavailable) to the client. This 503 error response cannot be customized. During times of high traffic, if you experience this 503 error, try adjusting the number of requests that wait in the queue. Increase the number to a large value such as 16,000 and test to see if the 503 errors persist.

Requests in the application pool queue remain in the queue if you lower the queue maximum to a number less than 1,000 by using the following procedure.

 Important

You must be a member of the Administrators group on the local computer to perform the following procedure or procedures, or you must have been delegated the appropriate authority. As a security best practice, log on to your computer by using an account that is not in the Administrators group, and then use the **runas** command to run IIS Manager as an administrator. At a command prompt, type **runas** / *User.Administrative_AccountName* "mmc %systemroot%\system32\inetsrv\iis.msc".

▷ **To adjust the number of requests that can wait in the kernel request queue**

1. In IIS Manager, right-click the **Application Pools** folder, and then click **Properties**.

2. Click the **Performance** tab.

3. Under **Request queue limit**, select the **Limit the kernel request queue to** check box, and then set the maximum number of queued requests.

> **Note**
>
> If you clear the Limit the kernel request queue to check box, or if you set the AppPoolQueueLength metabase property to zero, IIS does not enforce a kernel request limit. Without a kernel request limit, IIS could queue an unlimited number of requests and your server could potentially run out of memory. For this reason, you should set kernel request-queue limits on all production servers.

4. Click **Apply**, and then click **OK**.

ASP Request Queue

For requests to ASP pages, after the worker process picks up the request in the application pool queue, the request is sent to the Internet Server API (ISAPI) handler, which passes the request along to Asp.dll. If a thread is available, the ASP request is processed. If a thread is not available, the request waits in the ASP request queue. Requests are processed in the order in which they are received. If the ASP request queue fills to 3,000 requests (the default metabase value of **AspRequestQueueMax**) the server rejects the request, logs the error in the IIS log, and sends a 500 error (Server Too Busy) to the client.

If the number of queued requests is under 3,000, users with the last requests are forced to wait (called *queue latency*) as other requests are pulled from the queue and executed. This is an acceptable condition if the queue is cleared within a few seconds. After a few seconds, most users believe the server is not responding and click the **Stop** button on their Web browser. High queue latency results in poor performance for all ASP requests for the entire time the queue is saturated, because all ASP requests in a worker process share the same queue. Additionally, CPU utilization tends to spike when the queue is saturated, which results in slower response times.

You can improve ASP queuing by adjusting the default values for the **AspProcessorThreadMax** and **AspRequestQueueMax** metabase properties. **AspProcessorThreadMax** represents the maximum number of threads per processor, and **AspRequestQueueMax** represents the maximum size of the request queue. For more information about these metabase properties, see "AspProcessorThreadMax" and "AspRequestQueueMax" in IIS 6.0 Help.

Table 7.2 describes performance counters and their ideal values for ASP queuing. Monitor these counters in System Monitor by using a chart with one-second intervals before you change any metabase properties on your server. For more information about IIS 6.0 counters, see "Performance Counters Reference" in IIS 6.0 Help.

Table 7.2   Preferred Values for Active Server Pages Queuing Performance Counters

Object\Counter	Preferred or Ideal Value
Active Server Pages\Request Wait Time	As low as possible. This counter determines how long clients connecting to your site must wait before the page starts executing. If this number is high, users connected to your site might be frustrated by slow response times.
Active Server Pages\Requests Queued	As low as possible. If large queues develop, or if this number fluctuates, you might need to adjust the metabase properties that affect ASP queuing, as described later in this chapter. This counter is not as important as the Request Wait Time counter. Queues can clear quickly, but long wait times can frustrate users connected to your site.
Active Server Pages\Requests Rejected	As low as possible. If this number is high and Requests Queued is high, you might be reaching the ASP request queue default maximum of 3,000. You might need to adjust the metabase properties that affect ASP queuing, as described later in this chapter.
Active Server Pages\Requests/second	Application-specific. You want this number to be as high as possible. If Requests Queued is high, this number will typically be lower. Adjusting the metabase properties that affect ASP queuing can increase it.
Processor\% Processor Time (for each processor)	Application-specific. If Requests Queued never increases and % Processor Time is low, it is likely that ASP queuing is not affecting the performance of your site.

Tuning AspProcessorThreadMax

If the number of requests in the ASP queue is fluctuating and your CPUs are running below 50 percent, your requests might be blocking. *Blocking* occurs when a request that is being processed is forced to wait for an available thread to perform component processing or back-end processing. For example, an ASP page using ActiveX® Data Objects (ADO) to access a computer running Microsoft® SQL Server™ located on a separate computer will typically be blocked. If the SQL request executes a query that takes five seconds, and if dozens of requests arrive every second to execute this same query, soon all available threads will be allocated and each thread will wait five seconds for the query to be completed. Typically, you can reduce blocking by increasing the number of threads. Increasing the number of threads increases concurrency, which means that the server has more threads available to process requests (especially nonblocking requests), which might reduce queuing and improve response times. On a site with minor blocking (that is, the queue only occasionally reaches the value of **ASPRequestQueueMax**), increasing the threads can have a dramatic effect; in fact, it might eliminate all ASP queuing, because there are always enough threads to handle the blocking and nonblocking requests.

 Important

It is recommended that you back up the IIS metabase before you change the metabase. For additional information, see "Working with the Metabase" in this book.

▶ **To increase the number of ASP threads**

1. In the IIS metabase, change **ASPProcessorThreadMax** from 25 (the default) to 50 threads.

2. Restart the WWW service.

You should expect to see a slight increase in CPU utilization, and the queue should fluctuate more quickly. If, after increasing the number of threads, Requests Queued increases and stays high and % Processor Time decreases, a significant percentage of your requests are being blocked. You might want to reexamine your application code and determine whether the source of the blocking can be mitigated or worked around. Or you might want to simply add more servers to your Web farm to reduce contention.

If your queue decreases and CPU utilization increases, continue increasing **AspProcessorThreadMax** until you hit your target CPU utilization (do not exceed 70 percent, and keep **AspProcessorThreadMax** below 100). Ultimately, you might discover that the network input/output (I/O) or another factor is placing a limit on your server's performance. You might not be able to improve this limit.

Tuning AspRequestQueueMax

The goal of tuning **AspRequestQueueMax** is to ensure good response time while minimizing how often the server sends the HTTP 503 error (Server Too Busy) to clients when the ASP request queue is full. If the value of **AspRequestQueueMax** is too low, the server will send the HTTP 503 error too often. If the value of **AspRequestQueueMax** is too large, users might perceive that the server is not responding when in fact their request is waiting in the queue. By watching the queue during periods of high traffic, you should see a pattern of ups and downs. Make note of the peak value, and set the value of **AspRequestQueueMax** just above the peak value. Use the queue to handle short-term spikes, ensure response time, and throttle the system to avoid overload when sustained, unexpected spikes occur. If you do not have data for adjusting **AspRequestQueueMax**, a good initial setting seems to be a one-to-one ratio of queue to total threads. For example, if **AspProcessorThreadMax** is set to 25 and you have four processors ($4 \times 25 = 100$ threads), set **AspRequestQueueMax** to 100 and tune from there.

▶ **To adjust the number of requests that can wait in the ASP request queue**

1. In the IIS metabase, change the value of **AspRequestQueueMax**.

2. Restart the WWW service.

Additional Metabase Properties

The following metabase properties also affect queuing.

AspQueueTimeout

The **AspQueueTimeout** property specifies the amount of time (in seconds) that an ASP script request is allowed to wait in the queue. When requests are pulled from the queue, they are checked to see if they have expired (that is, they have waited longer than the value of this property). Expired requests are rejected with a 503 error (Service Unavailable). By default, ASP does not reject requests from valid connections, no matter how long they have been in the queue.

AppPoolQueueLength

The **AppPoolQueueLength** property indicates to HTTP.sys how many requests to queue up for an application pool before it rejects future requests. When the limit for this property is exceeded, IIS rejects the additional requests with a 503 error. Setting the **AppPoolQueueLength** value to 0 means there is no maximum request queue length. This is not recommended.

For more information about these properties, see the "Metabase Property Reference" in IIS 6.0 Help.

ASP.NET Request Queues

ASP.NET uses two request queues:

- The *global queue*, which is managed by the process that runs ASP.NET (Aspnet_wp). The global queue is configured in the Machine.config file by the **<processModel requestQueueLimit>** property.

- The *application queue*, or *virtual directory queue*, which is managed by the HttpRuntime class. The HttpRuntime class provides run-time services for ASP.NET applications. There is one queue for each virtual directory. The application queue is configured in Machine.config by the **<httpRuntime appRequestQueueLimit>** property.

When either queue exceeds its default limit, the request is rejected with a 503 error (Service Unavailable).

Worker processes that handle ASP.NET requests might run more threads than needed for ASP requests. Also, ASP.NET might queue requests more readily than ASP queues requests, but this should not be regarded as a scalability or performance issue. ASP.NET requests are executed more quickly than ASP requests. This means that with ASP.NET it is actually better to have fewer concurrent requests and more serial requests. Because ASP.NET maximizes the overall work on the CPU, this leads to fewer context switches.

Overall, ASP.NET is very self-tuning. For the global queue (Aspnet_wp process), the default ASP.NET thread numbers on four-processor and eight-processor servers should not require additional tuning. For servers with more than eight processors, you might want to decrease the default thread numbers by modifying the values of the **<processModel maxworkerthreads>** and **<processModel maxiothreads>** properties in Machine.config.

ASP.NET Counters

Use the following counters to monitor queuing for all ASP.NET applications on your server.

Request Execution Time

The value of this counter is the number of milliseconds taken to execute the latest request. In the Microsoft .NET Framework version 1.0, request execution time begins when the worker process receives the request and stops when the ASP.NET ISAPI sends HSE_REQ_DONE_WITH_SESSION to IIS. This counter includes the time taken to write the response to the client for IIS 5.0, but not for IIS 6.0. Consequently, for IIS 5.0, a client with a slow network connection increases the value of this counter considerably.

In .NET Framework version 1.1, request execution time begins when the HttpContext for the request is created and stops before the response is sent to IIS. Assuming that user code does not call HttpResponse.Flush, this means that request execution time stops before any bytes are sent to IIS or to the client.

There is no threshold for this counter. The value of this counter should be stable. Experience will help you set a threshold for a particular site.

Requests Queued

The value of this counter is the number of requests currently in the queue. It includes requests in all ASP.NET queues. The Aspnet_wp process queue is a named pipe through which the request is sent from one process to the other. The number of requests in this queue increases if there is a shortage of available I/O threads in the Aspnet_wp process. When the limit specified by **<processModel requestQueueLimit=/>** is exceeded, requests will be rejected with a 503 error (Service Unavailable). Note that if a request is rejected for this reason, it will never reach managed code, and error handlers will not be notified. Normally this only occurs when the server is under a very heavy load.

Virtual directory queues maintain the availability of worker and I/O threads. The number of requests in these queues increases if the number of available worker threads or available I/O threads falls below the limit specified by **<httpRuntime minFreeThreads=/>**. When the limit specified by **<httpRuntime appRequestQueueLimit=/>** is exceeded, the request is rejected with a 503 error and the client is sent an HttpException with the message "Service Unavailable."

Requests Rejected

The value of this counter is the number of rejected requests. Requests are rejected when one of the queue limits is exceeded. Back-end latency, such as that caused by a slow computer running SQL Server, is often preceded by a sudden increase in the number of pipeline instances and a decrease in % Processor Time and Requests/second. A server might be overwhelmed during times of heavy load due to processor or memory constraints that ultimately result in the rejection of requests.

The value of this counter should be 0. Values greater than this should be investigated.

Request Wait Time

The number of milliseconds that the most recent request spent waiting in the global queue. This does not include any time the request spent waiting in the application queues.

The threshold for this counter is 1,000. The average request should spend 0 milliseconds waiting in the queue.

ASP.NET Application Counters

Use the following counters to monitor queuing for individual ASP.NET applications.

Requests Executing

The number of requests currently being executed. This counter is incremented when the ASP.NET request pipeline begins to process the request and is decremented after the ASP.NET request pipeline finishes the request.

Requests In Application Queue

The number of requests in the application request queue. In addition to Requests Executing, Requests In Application Queue provides a warning when requests will be rejected. If there are only a few virtual directories, increasing the default value of the **appRequestQueueLimit** property in the Machine.config file to 200 or 300 might be suitable, especially for slow applications under heavy load.

Pipeline Instance Count

The number of active pipeline instances. Only one thread of execution can run within a pipeline instance, so this number gives the maximum number of concurrent requests that are being processed for a given application. The number of pipeline instances should not fluctuate. Sudden increases are indicative of back-end latency.

Registry Entries for Thread Pool Queuing

The following entries in the Windows registry determine the number of threads in the IIS thread pool. Tuning thread pools can produce dramatic improvement in IIS performance and scalability. For more information about these registry entries, including their locations, see "Optimizing IIS 6.0 Performance" in this book.

MaxPoolThreads

Specifies the maximum number of pool threads per processor. This is not an absolute limit; that is, IIS can increase the number of threads if the current load would benefit from having more threads available. Pool threads monitor the network for requests and process incoming requests. The value of **MaxPoolThreads** does not include threads that are consumed by ISAPI applications.

PoolThreadLimit

Specifies the maximum number of pool threads that can be created in the system. Pool threads monitor the network for requests and process incoming requests. **PoolThreadLimit** is an absolute limit that includes all core Web service threads. It is always greater than or equal to the value of **MaxPoolThreads**.

Improving Scalability by Optimizing IIS 6.0 Caches

A cache is a special subsystem that stores frequently requested data. Without caches or caching, IIS can potentially impose three time-consuming processes on each request, which can cause poor response times. These processes include:

- Reading metadata for each request, which results in a time-consuming remote procedure call (RPC) to the IIS Admin service.

- Retrieving the authentication token for the IUSR_*computername* account with a time-consuming RPC to Lsass.exe.

- Opening and reading the file.

To mitigate these time-consuming processes, HTTP.sys and IIS use caches. These caches are all enabled by default and should not require much tuning by administrators. If, while monitoring Web Service Cache counters in System Monitor, you begin to see rising numbers of cache misses or very low cache hit rates, you can adjust settings for the following:

- URI cache (user-mode URI cache)

- Token cache

- File cache

- HTTP.sys response cache (kernel URI cache)

- ASP caches, including the ASP template cache and the ASP script engine cache

- Global cache registry entries

For information about Universal Naming Convention (UNC) caching see, "Caching UNC-Based Files" in this chapter. For information about IIS cache counters, see the "Performance Counters Reference" in IIS 6.0 Help.

URI Cache

The user-mode URI cache is known as the URI cache. The URI cache stores metadata about a URL. Metadata can include a variety of configuration data, including data about headers and authentication. This configuration data is stored in the IIS Admin service. The URI cache stores the metadata as an object. For each request that reaches IIS user mode, the worker process checks the URI cache to see if the object for the requested URL has been cached. If the object has not been cached, the worker process must call the IIS Admin service for the appropriate metadata. This call is expensive from a performance and scalability standpoint. If the URI cache has a stored object for the URL, the request pulls in the object and continues processing.

The IIS Admin service is responsible for URI cache change notification. If, for example, Default.htm changes, the IIS Admin service tells the worker process to flush the URI cache for that specific URL. Subsequent requests for that URL are cached in the URI cache. Table 7.3 describes the preferred or ideal values for URI cache counters. For more information about IIS 6.0 counters, see the "Performance Counters Reference" in IIS 6.0 Help.

Table 7.3 Preferred Values for URI Cache Counters

Object\Counter	Preferred or Ideal Value
Web Service Cache\URI Cache Hits	Depends on content. If content cannot be cached in the HTTP.sys response cache, the value of this counter should be as high as possible. If your content can be stored in the HTTP.sys response cache, the value of this counter should be low.
Web Service Cache\URI Cache Hits%	Depends on content. If content cannot be cached in the HTTP.sys response cache, the value of this counter should be as high as possible. If your content can be stored in the HTTP.sys response cache, the value of this counter should be low.
Web Service Cache\URI Cache Misses	Low is better. The value of this counter increases when IIS cannot locate requested content in either the HTTP.sys response cache or the IIS file cache, and must locate the requested content on the hard disk. If the value of this counter is low, responses are being sent from either the IIS file cache or the HTTP.sys response cache.

Token Cache

When a request is made to the server, the security credentials for the request (or the configured anonymous user) are used to create a user token on the server. The server impersonates this user token when accessing files or other system resources. The token is cached in what is commonly called the *token cache*, so that the Windows logon only takes place the first time the user accesses the system or after the user's token has been flushed from the cache. If a token does not exist in the cache for an incoming request, IIS must call the Lsass.exe process to get the token. This call is expensive from a performance and scalability standpoint.

 Note

Integrated Windows authentication tokens are not cached.

The IIS worker process is responsible for flushing the token cache. The worker process monitors the **UserTokenTTL** registry entry for change notification (*TTL* stands for "time to live"). If the token has expired (the default time to live is 15 minutes) or if the token has changed in any way, IIS flushes the token cache. Currently, there are no performance counters that monitor the token cache.

File Cache

The IIS file cache stores file contents in memory. If the file is larger than the 256 KB default maximum file size, IIS creates a file handle, passes the handle to HTTP.sys, and then closes the handle. The maximum file size is controlled by the **MaxCacheFileThreshhold** metabase property.

The IIS 6.0 file cache uses an algorithm that attempts to cache only frequently requested files. The algorithm requires that a file be requested at least twice in a 10-second activity period, or the file will not be cached. In the case of a request for a Default.htm file, the activity-period algorithm works in this way:

1. The worker process receives the request for Default.htm.

2. The worker process checks to see if the file is in the IIS file cache table. At this point, the file has not been cached yet (that is, no cache entry is found).

3. The IIS file cache checks the activity table to see if Default.htm has been requested within the last 10 seconds. Because the file has not been requested, the file cache enters Default.htm in the activity table and serves out the file handle.

4. Three seconds later, the worker process receives another request for Default.htm.

5. The file cache does not find the cache entry in the cache table, but the activity table contains an entry that is within the 10-second activity period.

6. The file cache again serves out the file handle, but this time the file cache gets the cache entry from the worker process and stores the cache entry in the cache table (the cache table flushes all unused entries every 30 seconds).

7. A third request for Default.htm is served directly from the file cache.

You can configure the activity period (which is 10 seconds by default) by modifying the **ActivityPeriod** registry entry. If you set the value of **ActivityPeriod** to 0, IIS always caches files. The **ActivityPeriod** registry entry is located in the following subkey:

HKEY_LOCAL_MACHINE\System\CurrentControlSet\Services\Inetinfo\Parameters

 Caution

Do not edit the registry unless you have no alternative. The registry editor bypasses standard safeguards, allowing settings that can damage your system, or even require you to reinstall Windows. If you must edit the registry, back it up first and see the Registry Reference on the *Microsoft Windows Server 2003 Deployment Kit* companion CD or on the Web at http://www.microsoft.com/reskit.

Windows provides file cache change notification at the directory level. This means Windows monitors the parent file directory and informs IIS when a file in the directory or any subdirectory has changed. When IIS gets the change notification, the worker process flushes the file from the IIS file cache.

Table 7.4 describes the preferred or ideal values for file cache counters. For more information about IIS 6.0 counters, see the "Performance Counters Reference" in IIS 6.0 Help.

Table 7.4 Preferred Values for File Cache Counters

Object\Counter	Preferred or Ideal Value
Web Service Cache\Current Files Cached	Depends on content. A low value can indicate that HTTP.sys is caching a majority of static files, which is ideal. If the content files cannot be cached by HTTP.sys, a high value is good.
Web Service Cache\File Cache Flushes	Note that this counter value represents the number of times the cache was flushed, and not the number of files flushed. This value will continue to increase over time. If you edit files or change files often, this value will increase more rapidly.
Web Service Cache\File Cache Hits	Depends on content. If the content files cannot be cached by HTTP.sys, a high value is good.
Web Service Cache\File Cache Hits%	If the Kernel: Cache Hits % counter is low, this value should be high. If Kernel: Cache Hits % is low and this value is low, examine your file set and determine why your files are not being cached. Note that this counter does not include dynamic content, only static files. If your static files are not being cached, you might want to lengthen the activity period for this cache.
Web Service Cache\File Cache Misses	A *file cache miss* means the request for the file must go to the hard disk. File cache misses negatively impact performance and scalability. This value should be as low as possible. Also note that kernel cache hits will cause this value to be low.
Web Service Cache\Total Flushed Files	As low as possible. This value will increase if you edit or change content files, which results in a cache flush.
Web Service Cache\Maximum File Cache Memory Usage	The value of this counter and the value of Web Service Cache\Current File Cache Memory Usage should be the same. If the numbers are different, the cache was flushed. If this counter is significantly higher than Web Service Cache\Current File Cache Memory Usage, you might consider recycling the worker process because the application might have a memory leak.
Web Service Cache\Total Files Cached	Ideally, this value will be the same as Web Service Cache\Current Files Cached. If you edit or change your content files and subsequently flush the file cache, this value will decrease.

HTTP.sys Response Cache

Kernel caching with the HTTP.sys response cache can be one of the most effective means of scaling and improving Web server performance. Cached responses are served from the kernel, which greatly improves response times and increases the number of requests per second that IIS can serve because requests for cached content never enter IIS user mode.

 Note

The HTTP response cache is known as the kernel URI cache in System Monitor.

For each request, the IIS worker process tells HTTP.sys whether or not to cache a response based on the activity-period cache algorithm. If a file is requested twice within 10 seconds (the default value for the **ActivityPeriod** registry entry) the IIS worker process tells HTTP.sys to cache the full response by URI. All subsequent requests for the cached response will be served from the cache. For more information about the activity-period cache algorithm, see "File Cache" earlier in this chapter.

Every 120 seconds, the HTTP.sys response cache runs a flush algorithm, which flushes cached files that have not been requested within the 120-second interval. The flush algorithm is also called when IIS receives change notification for a file — that is, when the file has been edited or changed in some way.

HTTP.sys Cache Counters

Table 7.5 describes the preferred or ideal values for HTTP.sys response cache counters. For more information about IIS 6.0 counters, see the "Performance Counters Reference" in IIS 6.0 Help.

Table 7.5   Preferred Values for HTTP.sys Response Cache Counters

Object\Counter	Preferred or Ideal Value
Web Service Cache\Kernel: Current URIs Cached	The value of this counter should nearly equal the total number of cacheable responses on the server (presuming that all cacheable responses have been cached). If this value is considerably lower than the total number of cacheable responses on the server, make sure the corresponding files are not larger than the default size, 256 KB. For information about the criteria that determine which files cannot be cached in the HTTP.sys response cache, see "Events and Conditions That Disable HTTP.sys Response Caching" later in this chapter.
Web Service Cache\Kernel: Total Flushed URIs	As low as possible. The value of this counter represents the number of times a response was flushed. Note that responses are flushed from the cache if the associated file is edited or changed in any way, or if the file is not requested within 120 seconds.

(continued)

Table 7.5   Preferred Values for HTTP.sys Response Cache Counters *(continued)*

Object\Counter	Preferred or Ideal Value
Web Service Cache\Kernel: Total URIs Cached	Depends on content, but the value of this counter should nearly equal the total number of cacheable responses on the server (presuming all cacheable responses have been cached). If this value is significantly larger than the total number of cacheable responses on the server, the HTTP.sys response cache is caching responses, flushing responses, and then caching responses again, which can impact performance and scalability. Investigate why responses are being flushed from the cache. If the value of this counter is significantly lower than the total number of cacheable responses on your sites, determine why some of the corresponding content files are not being cached.
Web Service Cache\Kernel: URI Cache Flushes	As low as possible. This counter denotes the number of times the flush algorithm has been called. Note that a response will be flushed from the cache if the corresponding file is edited or changed in any way, or if the file was not requested within 120 seconds.
Web Service Cache\Kernel: Cache Hits	As high as possible. This counter is incremented continually. If the value of this counter is very low, investigate why requests are not finding the cached response.
Web Service Cache\Kernel: Cache Hits %	Depends on content. The value of this counter should reflect the ratio of requests for cacheable content to requests for content that is not cacheable. If, for example, roughly half the requests to your sites are for cacheable content, the value of this counter should be close to 50 percent.
Web Service Cache\Kernel: URI Cache Hits/sec	As high as possible.
Web Service Cache\Kernel: URI Cache Misses	Depends on content. All requests for content that cannot be cached result in a cache miss. If the value of this counter is high and the value of Cache Hits is low, investigate why your responses are not being cached.

Events and Conditions That Disable HTTP.sys Response Caching

The HTTP.sys response cache will cache any response that has the appropriate flag in the request header; however, HTTP.sys will not cache the response if one the following applies:

 Note

This cache is disabled on a per-request basis.

- The request is not an anonymous request.
- The request required authentication (that is, there was an "Authorization:" header present in the request).

- The site is configured to use a footer.

- Dynamic compression is enabled and is used for the response. (Static compression can be used for HTTP.sys caching.)

- The static file is a UNC file and the **DoDirMonitoringForUnc** registry entry is not enabled (the entry is not enabled by default). Note: this default might change in future releases of IIS.

- There is a query string in the request.

- The request verb was not GET.

- The cache is disabled (the **MD_VR_NO_CACHE** metabase property equals 1).

- The request has an entity body.

- Certificate mapping is enabled for the URL in question.

- Custom logging is enabled for the site in question.

- The request HTTP version was neither 1.1 nor 1.0.

- There was a "Translate: f" header in the request (that is, it was a Web Distributed Authoring and Versioning [WebDAV] request).

- There was an "Expect:" header that did not contain exactly "100 continue."

- There was either an "If-Range" or "Range" header in the request. HTTP.sys processes only whole responses; it does not attempt to send ranged responses.

- The response spanned multiple SendResponse/SendResponseEntityBody calls. A cacheable response must come down in a single, vectored SendResponse call.

- The total response size was greater than the per-response maximum size, which is set by using the **UriMaxUriBytes** registry key. The default value is 256 KB.

- The size of the response header was greater than the per-response maximum header size. The default maximum value is 1024 bytes.

- The cache is already full. The default size of the cache is proportional to the physical memory in the computer.

- The response is zero length.

- There is an ISAPI filter installed that is not cache-aware. By default, ISAPI filters are not cache-aware, but you can set the **FilterEnableCache** metabase property for the filter to make it cache-aware. All filters that are included with IIS 6.0, including FrontPage and ASP.NET filters, are cache-aware.

- The static file is accessed as a default document. For example, Default.htm exists in the root directory. Accessing the specific file by name (Default.htm) causes HTTP.sys to cache the file. Accessing the site by requesting the root folder (/) and no specific file results in an uncached response. Note: this might change in future releases of IIS.

ASP Caching

The process of creating compiled ASP script files (called *templates*) and script engines each time an ASP page is requested can consume memory and CPU resources, which in turn can impact performance and scalability. The following section describes how you can improve ASP performance and scalability by caching ASP templates and ASP script engines.

ASP Template Caching

ASP processes the templates or template files that contain ASP scripts. ASP stores these templates in a template cache and then serves the cached templates for subsequent client requests. Caching ASP templates enhances performance and scalability, because cached templates are not compiled each time they are called.

The ASP template cache uses a least-recently-used algorithm for determining which templates are cached. This means that if the cache is full, the template that has been in the cache and has not been requested for the longest amount of time is replaced by the next template to enter the cache. Every time a new template is added to the cache, the template goes to the "beginning" of the cache. The ASP template cache stores up to 500 templates by default (as determined by the **AspScriptFileCacheSize** metabase property). Templates are moved to the beginning of the cache when they are requested. In the case where the 501st template is bumped from the cache, the template is written to disk. By default, the ASP disk cache can hold 2,000 templates (as determined by the **AspMaxDiskTemplateCacheFiles** metabase property). If a template in the disk cache is referenced, the template is moved back to the ASP template cache.

In worker process isolation mode, **AspScriptFileCacheSize** and **AspMaxDiskTemplateCacheFiles** are global settings, which means they apply to all ASP pages on the Web server. (They are process-level settings in IIS 5.0 isolation mode.) ASP pages can contain **#include** files and these **#include** files can make the ASP files very large. The default 500-file limit established by the ASP template cache applies only to ASP pages and not **#include** files. However, ASP files that contain **#include** files can grow large enough to cause memory shortages and errors. ASP will flush the ASP template cache if IIS runs out of memory. If the ASP template cache is flushed, each subsequent request to an ASP page will need to be recompiled before it is cached again. In these situations, you might see ASP queuing. If you display the Active Server Pages\In Memory Templates Cached counter in System Monitor and see spikes followed by a severe reduction in the number of cached templates, your ASP pages might be too big. This could cause your system to run out of memory, flush the cache, recompile, and then run out of memory again. To remedy this situation, reduce the size of the ASP template cache to a number less than 500. Table 7.6 lists the preferred or ideal values for ASP template cache counters. For more information about IIS 6.0 counters, see the "Performance Counters Reference" in IIS 6.0 Help.

Table 7.6   Preferred Values for ASP Template Cache Counters

Object\Counter	Preferred or Ideal Value
Active Server Pages\In Memory Templates Cached	The value of this counter should reflect the number of frequently requested ASP files on your site (also known as your *hot set*).
Active Server Pages\In Memory Template Cache Hit Rate	As high as possible.
Active Server Pages\Templates Cached	The value of this counter should be close to the value of the **AspMaxDiskTemplateCacheFiles** metabase property; however, this value represents the total number of templates cached in memory and cached to disk, so this value could be higher than **AspMaxDiskTemplateCacheFiles**.
Active Server Pages\Template Cache Hits	As high as possible.
Active Server Pages\Template Cache Hit Rate	If this value is low and the Active Server Pages\In Memory Template Cache Hit Rate is high, a majority of user requests are being served from the memory cache. Performance and scalability should show a positive impact by not having to read the template from disk. If the value of Active Server Pages\Templates Cached equals the value of the **AspMaxDiskTemplateCacheFiles** metabase property, the cache has reached its maximum value. When the cache has reached its maximum value, this value should be high, otherwise the cache is being flushed.

 Important

You must be a member of the Administrators group on the local computer to perform the following procedure or procedures, or you must have been delegated the appropriate authority. As a security best practice, log on to your computer by using an account that is not in the Administrators group, and then use the **runas** command to run IIS Manager as an administrator. At a command prompt, type **runas** */User:Administrative_AccountName* "mmc %systemroot%\system32\inetsrv\iis.msc".

To change the settings for caching ASP templates

1. In IIS Manager, right-click the **Web Sites** folder, and then click **Properties**.

2. Click the **Home Directory** tab.

3. In the **Application Settings** area, click **Configuration**, and then click the **Cache Options** tab.

> **Note**
>
> If the **Configuration** button is not active, the directory or starting point does not contain an isolated application. You can create a new application by clicking **Create**.

4. In the **ASP File Cache** section, configure the ASP cache setting by doing one of the following:

   - To cache all requested ASP files, select the **Cache all ASP files in memory** check box. The maximum number of files that can be cached is 2,000,000,000.

   - To set the maximum number of files cached in memory, select the **Cache limited ASP files in memory** check box, and then set the maximum number of files. Files in excess of this number are persisted to the disk cache if you select the **Cache remaining ASP files on disk** check box. Or you can limit the total number of ASP files cached by selecting the **Cache limited ASP files on disk** check box, and then setting the maximum number of files.

   - To turn off the cache, select the **Do not cache ASP files** check box.

5. Click **OK**.

The ASP disk cache begins caching files into a directory when the ASP memory cache is full. Furthermore, a file has to be requested at least twice before it becomes a candidate for the ASP disk cache. The corresponding metabase property, **AspMaxDiskTemplateCacheFiles**, specifies the maximum number of compiled ASP templates that can be stored. **AspDiskTemplateCacheDirectory** contains the name of the directory that ASP uses to store compiled ASP templates to disk after overflow of the in-memory cache.

> ◆ **Important**
>
> In order for disk caching to work, ASP needs a properly configured disk cache directory in which to store the compiled ASP files. This means that the Administrators and IIS_WPG groups have Read/Write and Delete permission on the disk cache directory, and the disk cache directory is a local directory on the Web server.

The default location of the disk cache is *systemroot*\System32\inetsrv\ASP Compiled Templates. In worker process isolation mode, subdirectories under the disk cache directory are created for each application pool. In IIS 5.0 isolation mode, the default disk cache directory is *windir*\system32\inetsrv\ASP Compiled Templates.

▷ **To create an ASP disk cache directory**

1. In IIS Manager, expand the local computer, expand the **Web Sites** folder, right-click the Web site that you want, and then click **Properties**.

2. Click the appropriate tab: **Home Directory**, **Virtual Directory**, or **Directory**.

3. In the **Application Settings** area, click **Configuration**.

4. Click the **Cache Options** tab, and in the **Disk cache directory** box, browse to the directory used for disk caching.

5. Click **OK**.

 Note

ASP requests might fail unless the IIS_WPG group has Read/Write and Delete permission for the ASP template cache directory.

Script Engine Caching

ASP code is compiled and executed by Microsoft® Visual Basic® Scripting Edition (VBScript) by default. To improve performance and scalability of ASP code, ASP creates script engines. ASP script engines contain the object and marshalling data that VBScript.dll needs to execute the request. Each entry in the ASP script file cache can point to one or more entries in the ASP script engine cache.

Table 7.7 describes the preferred or ideal values for the ASP Script Engine Cache counter. For more information about IIS 6.0 counters, see "Performance Counters Reference" in IIS 6.0 Help.

Table 7.7   Preferred Value for ASP Script Engine Cache Counter

Object\Counter	Preferred or Ideal Value
Active Server Pages\Script Engines Cached	The value of this counter should be greater than or equal to the value of Active Server Pages\Requests Executing. If this number is low, the server might not have enough memory to store the script engines in the cache. Performance and scalability will suffer because the server must create script engines often.

To change the settings for caching ASP script engines

1. In IIS Manager, right-click the **Web Sites** folder, and then click **Properties**.

2. Click the **Home Directory** tab.

3. In the **Application Settings** area, click **Configuration**, and then click the **Cache Options** tab.

> ✎ | **Note**
>
> If the Configuration button is not active, the directory or starting point does not contain an isolated application. You can create a new application by clicking **Create**.

4. Set the value for **Number of script engines cached**.

To programmatically change the maximum number of script engines ASP pages will keep cached in memory, use the **AspScriptEngineCacheMax** metabase property.

Setting the ASP Cache Metabase Property and Registry Entry

The following metabase property and Windows registry entry impact ASP caching on your server. In most cases, these settings should not require tuning or adjusting. If you find it necessary to adjust these settings, monitor performance and scalability after making changes.

AspScriptFileCacheSize

The **AspScriptFileCacheSize** metabase property specifies the number of precompiled script files to cache. If set to 0, no script files are cached. If set to 4,294,967,295, all script files requested are cached. This property is used to tune performance, depending on the amount of available memory and the number of script file cache hits.

The metabase represents "unlimited" as the DWORD value of 4,294,967,295 (0xFFFFFFFF); however, VBScript represents unlimited in hexadecimal format as &HFFFFFFFF. Earlier versions of IIS represented unlimited as -1.

> | **Caution**
>
> Do not edit the registry unless you have no alternative. The registry editor bypasses standard safeguards, allowing settings that can damage your system, or even require you to reinstall Windows. If you must edit the registry, back it up first and see the Registry Reference on the *Microsoft Windows Server 2003 Deployment Kit* companion CD or on the Web at http://www.microsoft.com/reskit.

DisableLazyContentPropagation

Windows registry path: HKLM\SYSTEM\CurrentControlSet\Services\ASP\Parameters

Data type: REG_DWORD

Default value: 0 (lazy propagation enabled)

Range: 0 - 1

Lazy propagation refers to the action that IIS takes when a large amount of content is updated at one time. IIS has an internal limit on the amount of content that can be updated in the in-memory template cache. If the size of the updated content exceeds that limit, IIS marks each of the files in the in-memory template cache as invalid. When it receives the first request to an invalid file, IIS begins to compile a new template, but it serves the expired template until the new template is compiled.

If you set the value of the registry entry **DisableLazyContentPropagation** to 1, IIS behaves as it does for IIS 5.0 and IIS 5.1 when a large amount of content is updated at one time. IIS flushes the in-memory template cache, and performance can slow to a standstill as each new request to the server forces IIS to compile new templates.

If you are developing Web pages and making changes to a few files at a time, you do not have to refresh your pages twice to see new changes because lazy propagation only applies when a large amount of content is updated at one time.

Global IIS Caching Registry Entries

The following registry entries impact caching on your server. In most cases, these settings should not require tuning or adjusting. If you find it necessary to adjust these settings, use caution and monitor performance and scalability after making changes.

 Caution

Do not edit the registry unless you have no alternative. The registry editor bypasses standard safeguards, allowing settings that can damage your system, or even require you to reinstall Windows. If you must edit the registry, back it up first and see the Registry Reference on the *Microsoft Windows Server 2003 Deployment Kit* companion CD or on the Web at http://www.microsoft.com/reskit.

DisableMemoryCache

Windows registry path: HKLM\SYSTEM\CurrentControlSet\Services\InetInfo\Parameters

Data type: REG_DWORD

Default value: 0 (disabled)

Range: 0 - 1

Disables server static file caching, which negatively impacts performance and scalability. It is not recommended that you disable caching unless you are troubleshooting an issue or debugging application code.

MemCacheSize

Windows registry path: HKLM\SYSTEM\CurrentControlSet\Services\InetInfo\Parameters

Data type: REG_DWORD

Default value: approximately one-half of available physical memory, in megabytes (MB)

Range: 0 - 2500 MB

Controls the size of the static file cache. The default value is dynamically adjusted every 60 seconds.

ObjectCacheTTL

Windows registry path: HKLM\CurrentControlSet\Services\InetInfo\Parameters

Data type: REG_DWORD

Default value: 30 (seconds)

Range: 0 - 4,294,967,295 (unlimited)

Controls the TTL setting, which defines the length of time that objects are held in the cache. If an object in the memory cache has not been referenced for the specified period, that object will be phased out of the cache. If system memory is limited, or the contents of the server are dynamic, you can use a lower TTL to prevent system memory from being used to cache a large number of volatile objects. Setting **ObjectCacheTTL** to 0xFFFFFFFF disables the *object-cache scavenger* (the process that routinely reads the items in the cache to determine which items should stay in the cache and which items should be flushed) and allows cached objects to remain in the cache until they are overwritten. Disabling the cache scavenger is useful if your server has ample system memory and your data is relatively static.

ISP Scaling — Strategies for Hosting Thousands of Sites

The ability for IIS to scale up to thousands of sites on one server depends on the type of content the site hosts and the number of application pools on the server. Your business model and service agreements with customers will also determine how many sites you can put on one server. There are three common Internet service provider (ISP) installation strategies you can use when IIS is running in worker process isolation mode:

- Shared static hosting
- Shared static and dynamic hosting
- Dedicated hosting

Shared Static Hosting

The *shared static hosting* strategy involves collecting large numbers of static sites together on one server. These static sites are typically personal home pages or business pages that experience very low traffic volumes on a daily basis, so performance and scalability issues are rarely an issue. Before provisioning your server, consider the following guidelines.

Administer IIS by using command-line administration scripts or batch files

Using IIS Manager to perform tasks such as provisioning thousands of new sites or configuring sites is extremely inefficient. If your server hosts a few thousand sites, IIS Manager can take several minutes to refresh as it reads configuration data from the metabase. In this case, it is more efficient to administer IIS by using command-line tools. For information about command-line administration tools in IIS 6.0, see "IIS 6.0 Administration Scripts, Tips, and Tricks" in this book, or see "Using Command-Line Administration Scripts" in IIS 6.0 Help. For general information about Web site and virtual directory configuration, see "Configuring Internet Sites and Services" in this book.

Create a logical folder structure

A logical folder structure, for example Domain/Username, will alleviate some of the administration overhead in locating sites when they require configuration changes.

Use host header names to create multiple sites on one server

Static IP addresses are in limited supply, and obtaining thousands of static IP addresses can be problematic. Static IP addresses are only necessary when a site requires Secure Sockets Layer (SSL). Also, static IP addresses have performance overhead costs. The WWW service must manage an endpoint for every site identified by a unique IP address, and this consumes memory from the nonpaged pool.

Put all static sites in one application pool

Static sites, if they are truly static, pose little or no crash risk for an application pool because static sites do not execute code. By putting the sites in one application pool, you limit the resource overhead that multiple application pools impose. You also limit the administrative overhead that comes with multiple application pools.

Run all static sites with the same anonymous user account

For static, public Web sites, the anonymous user account provides ample security. Before returning a page to the client, IIS checks NTFS file and directory permissions to see whether the IUSR_*computername* account is allowed access to the file. If access is not allowed, IIS attempts to use another authentication method. If none is selected, IIS returns an HTTP 403 error (Access Denied) to the browser.

Recycle the application pool worker process (optional)

You will need to monitor site traffic to determine a regular recycle schedule, if a regular recycle is needed. Ideally, you should recycle the worker process during low-traffic times, for example 3:00 A.M. local time. For more information about worker process recycling, see "Running IIS 6.0 as an Application Server" in this book.

Monitor startup times

Although you should not need to restart your server very often, monitor startup times when you do restart the server. When an IIS server hosts thousands of Web sites, the size of the metabase grows significantly and the task of reading configuration data from the metabase while IIS is starting can strain your CPU resources. Your startup times might be a determining factor for when you need to add a new server to your installation.

Monitor performance

As you provision sites, regularly monitor site traffic and resource consumption. In this way, you will be able to see how the system scales and proactively determine when it is time to add a new server to your installation.

Enable centralized binary logging

Centralized binary logging writes all log file data in binary format to one centralized file, and preserves memory and CPU resources by not creating and writing to thousands of individual log files. For more information about centralized binary log files, see "Analyzing Log Files" in this book.

Partition log files on multiple disks

If you choose not to use centralized binary logging, partition log files on multiple disks to minimize I/O. With multiple disk controllers writing log data to different disks, you will minimize I/O and preserve memory resources for other needs.

Shared Static and Dynamic Hosting

The *shared static and dynamic hosting* strategy mixes static and dynamic sites on the same server. If your customer base requires you to host a mix of static and dynamic sites on the same server, the following guidelines can help you maximize the number of sites and application pools you can host on one server. Most of the guidelines in "Shared Static Hosting" earlier in this chapter apply to this strategy as well.

Separate static and dynamic content sites in different application pools

If you need to host static and dynamic sites on the same server, put the static sites in one or more application pools and the dynamic sites in one or more different application pools. By isolating the static sites from the dynamic sites, you mitigate the possibility of a poorly developed application crashing the static content application pool.

Set content quotas for sites

Your business model and customer service agreement should define content quotas, for example 200 MB for each site. Set disk quotas in the properties of each physical hard disk by using the Quota service available in Windows Server 2003.

Consider enabling Quality of Service (QoS) features for sites that are resource-intensive

Features such as CPU monitoring, bandwidth throttling, and idle timeout will ensure that one site does not consume a majority of the resources and cause errors for other sites on the same server. For more information about these features, including how to enable them, see "Optimizing IIS 6.0 Performance" in this book.

Configure one unique anonymous user per site

Configuring one unique anonymous user per site adds a security layer by ensuring that users cannot access content on sites to which they are not permitted access.

Develop processes for handling service packs, security patches, and hotfixes

If your customers will be using IIS 6.0 to administer their own dynamic sites, set up a process for handling service packs, security patches, and hotfixes to minimize downtime for your customers and to ensure the security of your installation. Windows Server 2003 has improved patch management with Auto Update version 1.0, which provides you with three options:

- Notify you of patch availability the moment a patch is available.

- Download the patch and notify you of its availability.

- Scheduled installation (this option enables the patch to be downloaded and automatically installed at a time you choose).

For ASP content, allow ASP pages to run on MTA instead of STA

Because of the overhead memory and CPU cost of running dynamic applications, your server will reach a limit in the number of application pools it can host. With ASP content, you can mitigate this limitation on application pools by enabling ASP pages to run on multithreaded apartment (MTA) threads instead of single-threaded apartment (STA) threads. ASP is capable of running all of its threads in an MTA. If your COM components are primarily free-threaded or both-threaded, running the ASP threads as MTA can improve performance significantly. By default, the **AspExecuteInMTA** metabase property is set to 0, which means that ASP does not execute in MTA. Set this property to 1 at the application level to enable ASP to run in MTA.

 Note

MTA has some limitations with respect to components that can be instantiated. Objects that are strictly Apartment might show a performance regression because marshalling will occur and the potential for STA thread contention will increase.

If you need to set up more than 60 application pools where each pool is running as a unique identity on a server, change the UseSharedWPDesktop registry key

If you are setting up your application pools with unique identities, depending on the applications and memory resources on your server, you will reach a limit of about 60 application pools. There are finite limits to some system resources that get allocated with each new logon session. This means that 60 processes can run concurrently as distinct accounts. IIS 6.0 supports running these processes in a single shared workstation and desktop, at a cost of sharing a single encapsulation of a user session among all parties.

Caution

Do not edit the registry unless you have no alternative. The registry editor bypasses standard safeguards, allowing settings that can damage your system, or even require you to reinstall Windows. If you must edit the registry, back it up first and see the Registry Reference on the *Microsoft Windows Server 2003 Deployment Kit* companion CD or on the Web at http://www.microsoft.com/reskit.

To scale beyond 60 application pools and to share a single desktop, change the value of the registry entry **UseSharedWPDesktop**, of data type DWORD, to 1. The registry entry is located in the subkey HKLM\System\CurrentControlSet\Services\W3SVC\Parameters\UseSharedWPDesktop. After changing this registry entry, you should be able to scale to hundreds of application pools and hundreds of concurrently running worker processes.

If IIS is spinning up too many worker processes and your server is running out of resources, set a maximum number of concurrent worker processes

With the IIS 6.0/HTTP.sys architecture and with a request load distributed across many application pools, IIS might attempt to start more worker processes than the server can sustain without running out of memory or CPU resources. The **DemandStartThreshold** metabase property (also called *concurrent process gating*), when set to a value less than the default, applies a hard limit to the number of IIS worker processes that can run concurrently. If the hard limit is exceeded, HTTP.sys returns an HTTP 503 error (Service Unavailable).

Locate misbehaving applications and isolate them in their own application pool

You can use Event Viewer and IIS logs to locate misbehaving applications, or you can use Log Manager and Trace Report, which are general-purpose tools supplied with Windows Server 2003. Log Manager creates trace data, which is then processed by the Windows Trace Report utility. The Trace Report utility creates a formatted, detailed report that is useful in assessing IIS and IIS-related activity in the operating system. Once you have located a misbehaving application, isolate the application in its own application pool so it doesn't affect other applications. Recycle the application pool regularly. For more information about Log Manager and Trace Report, see "Capacity Planning Tracing" in IIS 6.0 Help. For more information about viewing and interpreting log files, see "Analyzing Log Files" in this book.

Dedicated Hosting

Dedicated hosting is typically reserved for those customers who have the greatest availability, security, and performance requirements for their dynamic Web sites. In some cases, you might put only one or two sites on an IIS server to ensure there are enough memory and CPU resources to meet customer requirements. In other cases, dedicated hosting means the customer pays to have their own server or servers. Dedicated hosting can be configured in the following ways.

Configure one unique application pool per Web site

Process boundaries separate each worker process so that problems in one application pool do not affect other application pools on the server. By configuring each Web site in a different application pool, you ensure greater reliability, availability, and security. For information about how to configure application pools, see "Running IIS 6.0 as an Application Server" in this book.

Configure one unique anonymous user per site

Configuring one unique anonymous user per site adds a security layer by ensuring that users cannot access content on sites to which they are not permitted access.

Configure one unique user to run as the process identity of the application pool

Configuring one unique user to run as the process identity of the application pool adds an additional layer of security by ensuring that one site cannot access content on another site. If you specify a unique user account, be sure to add that account to the IIS_WPG group. When you use a built-in account, try to use Network Service because it offers the best balance between security and functionality.

If you experience scalability issues on a dedicated hosting computer, see "Shared Static and Dynamic Hosting" earlier in this chapter.

Improving Scalability Through UNC–Based Centralized Content Storage

IIS 6.0 delivers several technical changes that make it easier for ISPs or other organizations to create UNC-based centralized storage solutions. Centralized content storage can make it much easier to scale your installation to thousands of Web sites. Centralized storage can also help minimize time commitments for server management and administration. This section describes the following:

- **Caching Changes.** For UNC content, IIS 6.0 provides the new last-modified caching algorithm for both static and ASP files. In addition, IIS 6.0 improves the performance of change-notification-based caching for ASP files.

- **UNC Authentication.** IIS 6.0 now performs UNC authentication, formerly called Passthrough authentication, by default.

- **Constrained Delegation.** With constrained delegation, you can allow delegation only to certain services, so you can control the specific network resources that a service or computer can use.

Caching UNC–based Files

When you can create UNC-based virtual directories, the IIS caches must treat each UNC path as a separate directory structure, and therefore ASP and static file caches must monitor each directory individually. In a centralized-content architecture with many different UNC shares, this has the potential to exhaust system resources.

The Web server and the file server are connected with a Server Message Block (SMB) connection. Only one SMB connection is created between a Web server and a file server; however, within that SMB connection, there are a finite number of work items. Work items can be consumed in a variety of ways and for varying amounts of time. For example, performing an operation — such as a **CreateFile** or **GetFileAttributes** command — on a file consumes an I/O work item for a short amount of time, but asking for a change notification on a directory structure consumes a work item for as long as the connection is intact. Each change-notification instance uses a work item until the connection is lost, and each request from a Web server to the file server uses a work item only temporarily. However, the scalability impact of the SMB connection is reduced by using last-modified caching.

Last-Modified Caching

To allow for greater scalability of UNC-based storage systems, IIS 6.0 implements a new last-modified cache algorithm for static and ASP files. The new caching algorithm does not request change notification for each directory structure; instead, it requests only the last-modified date of the cached file. If the file is new, the cache entry is updated with the new content and served. If the file has not changed, IIS serves the cached version of the file. By default, IIS checks the last-modified date for both ASP and static files if more than five seconds have elapsed since the file was last checked. Otherwise, IIS assumes the file has not changed, and it serves the existing content.

 Note

The server side includes (SSI) file handler (Ssinc.dll) makes use of the static file cache, so this behavior occurs for .stm, .shtml, and any other files that are mapped to this DLL.

IIS 6.0 uses the last-modified caching algorithm by default. To specify change-notification caching or to change the TTL value of the cached files, you must edit the registry.

 Caution

The registry editor bypasses standard safeguards, allowing settings that can damage your system, or even require you to reinstall Windows. If you must edit the registry, back it up first and see the Registry Reference on the *Microsoft Windows Server 2003 Deployment Kit* companion CD or on the Web at http://www.microsoft.com/reskit.

▷ **To set change-notification tracking or TTL for static files**

1. From the **Start** menu, click **Run**.

2. In the **Open** box, type **Regedit.exe**, and then click **OK**.

3. Navigate to the following subkey:
    HKLM\System\CurrentControlSet\Services\Inetinfo\Parameters

4. Do one or both of the following:

    -   To enable change-notification caching, modify the value of the registry entry **DoDirMonitoringForUnc** by setting it to **1**.

    -   To change the TTL setting from the default of five seconds, change the value of the registry entry **FileAttributeCheckThreshold** to the number of seconds you want to use.

5. Close the registry editor.

ASP Change-Notification Caching

IIS 6.0 provides a scalable change-notification mechanism for ASP pages. Because change notification occurs for unique directory structures, instead of for every directory, the number of work items required for change notification is reduced.

To specify change-notification caching or to change the TTL value of the cached files, you must edit the registry.

▶ **To set change-notification tracking or TTL for ASP files**

1. From the **Start** menu, click **Run**.

2. In the **Open** box, type **Regedit.exe**, and then click **OK**.

3. Navigate to the following subkey:
   HKLM\System\CurrentControlSet\Services\ASP\Parameters

4. Do one or both of the following:

   ▪ To enable change-notification caching, change the value of the registry entry **EnableChangeNotificationForUNC** by setting it to **1**.

   ▪ To change the TTL setting from the default of five seconds, change the value of the registry entry **FileMonitoringTimeoutSeconds** to the number of seconds you want to use.

5. Close the registry editor.

UNC–based Caching Considerations

You should decide which caching method to use based on your network architecture and your scalability and performance requirements. In general, last-modified caching is the most reliable method. It is recommended that you use this caching method when you require scalability for a system with a Web server that points to different file structures. You can also experience performance gains by using change-notification caching if your system uses a file server that reliably reports change notifications and you have only a few sites or virtual directories. For example, if you have a single Web site with one or two applications, and all of your content is stored on a Windows Server 2003–based file server, use change-notification caching.

To configure caching for optimum scalability and performance, you must edit the registry entries **MaxMpxCt**, **MaxWorkItems**, and **MaxCmds**. On the server running IIS, these entries are stored in the subkey HKLM\System\CurrentControlSet\Services\LanmanWorkstation\Parameters. On the remote file server running Windows Server 2003, these entries are stored in the subkey HKLM\System\CurrentControlSet\Services\LanmanServer\Parameters.

MaxMpxCt

The **MaxMpxCt** registry entry permits a server to provide a specified maximum number of simultaneous client requests to itself, and then enforces that limit. Because each client connection generates multiple instances (for example, Windows shell and Explorer.exe), with multiple clients connecting to the server, the number of client requests can be greater than the default **MaxMpxCt** value of 50. As soon as this limit is reached for that server, additional requests are refused until the number of requests drops below the limit again.

MaxWorkItems

The value of the registry entry **MaxWorkItems** should be at least four times as large as that for **MaxMpxCt**. For example, if **MaxMpxCt** has a value of 1,024, **MaxWorkItems** should have a value of at least 4,096.

Some resources, including Microsoft Knowledge Base articles, recommend setting the value of **MaxWorkItems** to 16,000. However, this could consume up to 250 MB of nonpaged pool memory, which could starve the system. To increase your system's reliability, it is recommended that you set the value of **MaxWorkItem** lower than 16,000.

To determine the number to set for the value of **MaxWorkItems**, monitor the Server object performance counters. The Work Item Shortages counter will indicate if you need to make these values larger or increase the load capability of your file server by adding memory or clustering the file server. You must allow enough work items for two activities: change notifications and normal I/O requests.

MaxCmds

The **MaxCmds** registry entry sets the limit for the number of concurrent outstanding network requests between the SMB client and server that the client can support. The general formula for calculating the value of MaxCmds is as follows:

(number of distinct physical directories that IIS needs to monitor for change notifications) × (1(if static files exist) + 1 (if ASP content exists) + 1 (if ASP.NET content exists) + 50 (for concurrent default/regular file I/O)

This formula is merely a starting point for tuning your servers. You might need to increase your settings depending on concurrent traffic. For better scaling, you typically need to modify the values of the **MaxCmds**, **MaxMpxCt**, and **MaxWorkItems** registry entries on both the server running IIS and the remote file server. Before you modify the entries, however, watch the Server object performance counters while you stress-test your system. Carefully monitor the Work Item Shortages counter to see if you need to increase the values of the entries or increase the load capability of your file server by adding memory or clustering the file server. If you are using the non-default change-notification option for caching, you must allow enough work items for two activities: change notifications and normal I/O requests for the file.

UNC-based Caching Scenarios

The following three scenarios illustrate the different UNC–based caching options in more detail and provide recommendations for setting maximum values:

- **Wide content, low traffic.** This scenario is an example of a typical low-end shared hosting server.

- **Wide content, high traffic.** This scenario represents an enterprise Web site that hosts hundreds of small applications and receives a high volume of traffic consisting mainly of anonymous users.

- **Narrow content, high traffic.** This scenario represents a dedicated hosted Web site with fewer than 10 applications, but with a very high volume of traffic consisting only of anonymous users.

When evaluating the settings in the tables in the following sections, consider the number of simultaneous work items that are opened from the server running IIS to the remote file server, but reflected (inversely) by the value of the **MaxCmds** entry. You should calculate all other remote file server settings based on that result.

 Important

The settings in the following scenarios are intended as guidelines only. Changing the registry settings listed here will produce different results, depending on your specific system configuration. You should test your application with the default settings, and then increase the maximum settings accordingly.

Scenario 1: Wide Content, Low Traffic

In this scenario, each site has its own directory structure, and there are no virtual directories below each site. Each server running IIS might have up to 20,000 sites, but only approximately 1,000 sites are active at any given time. Each site runs in its own process. Users are authenticated if they are publishing on the Web; otherwise, they are anonymous. The content is primarily ASP and static files, with a few ASP.NET applications.

If you enable file caching with the change-notification algorithm, you might use the following equation to calculate **MaxCmds**:

20,000 physical directories × (1(static) + 1(ASP) +1(ASP.NET) + 50 = approximately 60,000 for MaxCmds

However, this setting would jeopardize server performance and scalability because it would consume hundreds of megabytes of nonpaged pool memory.

If you use caching with the default last-modified algorithm, no work items are used for change notification. Depending on active traffic for file I/O and your analysis of the performance counters, you might still need to increase the values of **MaxCmds**, **MaxWorkItems**, and **MaxMpxCt** from their default values. Table 7.8 lists the recommended settings for the wide-content, low-traffic scenario that uses the default last-modified caching algorithm.

Table 7.8   Recommended Registry Settings for Wide Content, Low Traffic

Registry Entry	Server Running IIS	Remote File Server
MaxCmds	3,072 (0xC00). This is the maximum number of work items allowed by this computer.	Default setting.
MaxMpxCt	Default setting.	3,072 (0xC00). This is the maximum number of work items allowed per client computer. The client computer in this case is the server running IIS.
MaxWorkItems	Default setting.	12,288(0x3000). This value must be four times MaxMpxCt.

Scenario 2: Wide Content, High Traffic

In this scenario, a large Web site has 300 applications. The site contains static files, ASP content and ASP.NET content. Most users access the site anonymously.

If you enable file caching with the change-notification algorithm, this site will consume approximately three work items per cache, per application, for a total of 900 work items.

If you enable file caching with the last-modified algorithm, the site will not consume any work items that would be consumed for long periods, but there will be temporary work items and heavy traffic between the Web server and the file server. The caches are all frequently used.

Because there are a manageable number of applications in this scenario that use less than 1,000 work items per client, you might attempt to use the change-notification caching algorithm. This would reduce the back-end network traffic.

Table 7.9 lists the recommended settings for the wide-content, high-traffic scenario that uses the change-notification algorithm.

Table 7.9   Recommended Registry Settings for Wide Content, High Traffic

Registry Entry	Server Running IIS	Remote File Server
MaxCmds	2,048 (0x800). This is the maximum number of work items allowed by this computer.	Default setting.
MaxMpxCt	Default setting.	2,048 (0x800). This is the maximum number of work items allowed per client computer. The client computer in this case is the server running IIS.
MaxWorkItems	Default setting.	8,192 (0x2000). This value must be four times MaxMpxCt.

Note

The value listed in Table 7.9 for MaxCmds is higher than the value that results when you use the general formula for calculating MaxCmds because the value in the table was rounded.

If you have too many applications to use the change-notification algorithm, you can use the last-modified algorithm. You should extend the cache TTL value to approximately 30 seconds to reduce the traffic between the Web server and the file server. This scenario is the most difficult to tune properly.

Scenario 3: Narrow Content, High Traffic

In this scenario, a small site contains 10 applications and static, ASP, and ASP.NET files that receive a very high number of hits.

If you enable file caching with the change-notification algorithm, this site will consume approximately three work items per cache, per application, for a total of 30 work items.

If you enable file caching with the last-modified algorithm, the site will not consume any work items, but there will be heavy traffic between the Web server and the file server. The caches are all frequently used.

Because this scenario requires only a few work items to cache the content reliably, change notification is the recommended caching algorithm. You do not need to increase the default maximum settings by very much. Table 7.10 lists the recommended settings for the narrow-content, high-traffic scenario that uses the change-notification algorithm.

Table 7.10 Recommended Registry Settings for Narrow Content, High Traffic

Registry Entry	Server Running IIS	Remote File Server
MaxCmds	512 (0x200). This is the maximum number of work items allowed by this computer.	Default setting.
MaxMpxCt	Default setting.	512 (0x200). This is the maximum number of work items allowed per client computer. The client computer in this case is the server running IIS.
MaxWorkItems	Default setting.	2,048 (0x800). This value must be four times MaxMpxCt.

Note

The value listed in Table 7.10 for MaxCmds is higher than the value that results when you use the general formula for calculating MaxCmds because the value in the table was rounded.

UNC Authentication

The UNC authentication method, also called UNC Passthrough authentication, determines the credentials to be used for gaining access to a UNC share on a remote computer. In IIS 6.0, UNC authentication works by looking at the request user and the credentials stored in the **UNCUserName** and **UNCPassword** metabase properties to determine the credentials to pass through to the computer with the UNC share.

If you use IIS Manager to create a Web site or virtual directory and specify a UNC path for the content, IIS Manager prompts you to type a user name and password for the network resource. If you specify a user name and password, the **UNCUserName** and **UNCPassword** metabase properties are set.

If **UNCUserName** is specified (not empty) and **UNCPassword** is valid, the metabase user credentials are sent as the user identity for access to the remote share. If **UNCUserName** is specified (not empty) and **UNCPassword** is not valid, a 500.13 error (Internal Server Error: Invalid Username or Password) is sent to the client.

If **UNCUserName** is empty, the credentials of the request user — which can be either an authenticated set of credentials for authenticated requests or IUSR_*computername* credentials for anonymous requests — are sent as the user identity for access to the remote share. In other words, by default in IIS 6.0, you do not need to specify user name and password credentials.

Note

The UNCAuthenticationPassthrough metabase key is no longer used for UNC authentication.

For more information about enabling UNC authentication, see "Securing Virtual Directories" in IIS 6.0 Help.

Constrained Delegation for UNC File Content

Delegation is the act of allowing a service to impersonate a user account or computer account in order to access resources throughout the network. When a service is trusted for delegation, that service can impersonate a user to use other network services. *Constrained delegation* is a new option for Windows Server 2003, and it is recommended that you use it with a Windows Server 2003 domain. With this option, you can specify the Service Principal Names (SPNs) to which an account can delegate. With this option, a service can be trusted for delegation, but the domain administrator can limit that trust to a select group of explicitly specified services. By only allowing delegation to specific services, you can control the specific network resources the service or computer can use.

Constrained delegation is particularly useful in scenarios where a site that requires authentication — that is, a site that does not allow anonymous access — contains content that is housed on a remote UNC file server. With constrained delegation, you can enable Windows Integrated authentication, which can use NTLM authentication or send credentials across the network as a Kerberos-based token.

If you do not use constrained delegation, but you enable Windows Integrated authentication and NTLM, the token that the Web server obtains from the Windows security infrastructure does not have sufficient permissions to access another computer, such as your file server. However, with constrained delegation and Windows Integrated authentication, the token received by the Web server from the Windows security infrastructure is a Kerberos-based token with permission to access other computers, including the file server. Essentially, constrained delegation allows an NTLM-based token to be upgraded to a Kerberos-based token. Be aware, however, that Kerberos-based authentication can degrade performance because each access check occurs on the file server.

For more information about constrained delegation, see "Managing a Secure IIS 6.0 Solution" in this book.

When you set up a UNC-based virtual directory and specify a user name and password for that directory, you might receive an error message when you attempt to access the directory by using IIS Manager. This error occurs because IIS Manager sends the current Windows user credentials when it accesses the virtual directory. The credentials of the current Windows user might not be the same as those you specified for the UNC-based virtual directory. However, if you access your Web server over the Internet by using IIS Manager on a remote computer, the contents of the virtual directory will be displayed without error. Because using IIS Manager is not a reliable method of verifying whether your customers can access the content stored on the remote computer, you should test your virtual directories by making requests with a Web browser.

Case Study: Scaling an ASP.NET Web Application on IIS 6.0

The following case study illustrates how to monitor and tune IIS 6.0 for improved performance and scalability. In this study, network administrators in a fictional company, Contoso, were getting ready to roll out a new Web application for the purpose of selling books online. The application code had been extensively tested, but performance and scalability statistics were still unknown. To gather performance and scalability metrics, the administrators stress-tested the site by using the Microsoft Web Capacity Analysis Tool (WCAT).

Stress testing helps administrators locate performance and scalability bottlenecks in their Web application installation. By using a tool such as WCAT or the Microsoft Application Center Test (ACT) in a test environment to simulate the server load they can expect in a production environment, administrators can isolate and fix potential bottlenecks that might undermine the customer experience. Administrators can also plan the installation capacity.

The administrators in this study were preparing to roll out the Duwamish 7.0 ASP.NET application, a fictitious online bookseller application. Their rollout consisted of the following phases:

- Capacity planning
- Tuning production servers
- Scaling up
- Scaling out

 Note

This case study does not provide information about how to create a WCAT script or how to perform stress testing by using WCAT. WCAT ships on the *Internet Information Services (IIS) 6.0 Resource Kit* companion CD. The WCAT guide (Wcatguide.doc) contains information about how to create a WCAT script and how to use WCAT for stress testing.

Capacity Planning

The administrators initially wanted to see how their application scaled on a server with four 500-MHz processors running IIS 6.0 in worker process isolation mode. Their goal was to stress the site to see how many requests per second the installation processed at (or close to) 100 percent CPU saturation. By understanding how the application performed when the CPU was saturated, they could begin to understand how the site would scale under a heavy load, and they could begin to plan the capacity of the installation based on traffic estimates. Table 7.11 describes the software and hardware used for this case study.

Table 7.11   Case Study Software and Hardware

Software	Hardware
Web Servers Windows Server 2003 (RC1) Default installation of IIS 6.0 (running in worker process isolation mode) ASP.NET Duwamish.NET 7.0 Web application	**Web Servers** Four 550-MHz Intel Pentium 3 processors Compaq Proliant 6400R 512 MB RAM Single 3COM Gigabyte Ethernet Server network adapter Eight 900-MHz Pentium 3 processors Compaq Proliant 6400R 8 GB RAM Intel Pro Gigabit Optic Fiber Server network adapter
Database SQL Server 2000	**Database** Two 1000-MHz Pentium 3 processors Compaq DL360 264 MB RAM

Preparing to Test

The administrators set up their WCAT configuration file to run 40 virtual clients (four client computers running 10 threads each). They set up their WCAT distribution file to imitate real-world customer use of their site. Table 7.12 shows the breakdown of the WCAT distribution file.

Table 7.12   Description of WCAT Distribution File Classes for Contoso Stress Tests

Class Number	Percentage of Requests	Class Description
<class> 1	60	User browses for books. The administrators assigned the highest percentage of requests to this action to reflect what they expect to be the highest percentage of real-world traffic to their site.
<class> 2	10	User creates an account and buys a book.
<class> 3	20	User logs on to an existing account, puts five books in the shopping cart, takes two books out of the shopping cart, and then completes the purchase.
<class> 4	10	Invalid searches and other user mistakes.

The administrators ran the stress test for 10 minutes. If they had wanted to locate bugs or bottlenecks in their Web application, they would have run the test for much longer; however, because they were not concerned about bugs in the application, the 10-minute test run was sufficient.

While the test ran, the administrators monitored the network to make sure the connection (with a capacity of 1 GB) was not saturated. In Windows Task Manager, on the **Networking** tab, the administrators noted that network traffic was steady at about 4 percent, which meant that the network was not a bottleneck.

The administrators then opened System Monitor and monitored the Processor(_Total)\% Processor Time counter. The counter showed that the CPU was saturated at 100 percent. The administrators ran the test several more times with fewer virtual clients and the CPU did not reach 100 percent saturation, so they concluded that the data from the test that ran 40 virtual clients would suit their needs for capacity planning, provided the WCAT log did not reveal test errors.

The log revealed no errors, so the administrators concluded the bottleneck is the CPU. The server installation could not scale beyond the 40 virtual clients because the server did not have sufficient processing power. If the administrators had failed to saturate the CPU, they would have looked elsewhere in the installation for the bottleneck — for example, disk I/O (reading and writing from disk) or database activity. Also, a badly written application can be the source of a bottleneck in cases where the CPU is not saturated during stress testing.

Interpreting Test Data

In a situation where the CPU constrains maximum performance, the WCAT results can be used to perform a cycles-per-request calculation for capacity planning. The WCAT log showed 893 requests per second on a server with four 550-MHz processors. Test results can be summarized as follows:

- 4×550 megacycles/second = 2,200 megacycles/second.

- 2,200,000,000 cycles/second divided by 893 requests/second = 2,463,606 cycles/request (on average). Rounded up, the server used 2.5 million cycles/request while the CPU was at 100 percent saturation.

- At this point, the administrators spoke with the business managers and marketing managers to learn about expected traffic loads per day. The managers explained that after extensive research, they expected 200,000 customers per day. Each customer will send roughly 60 requests per session, so the total requests/day is $60 \times 200,000$, or 12,000,000 total requests/day (estimated).

- 12,000,000 divided by 24×60 minutes $\times 60$ seconds = 139 anticipated requests per second.

- Rounding to 150 requests/second $\times 2.5$ megacycles per request = 375 MHz needed to process the expected traffic at any given time (on average).

The administrators did not want their Web server to run at 100 percent CPU utilization. Furthermore, the administrators knew from experience that all Web sites have a pattern to their traffic. In order to accurately assess their capacity needs, they would need to know how much CPU power would be needed to handle traffic spikes. After researching other online booksellers, the administrators determined that their site would be busiest in the evening hours from 6 P.M. to midnight (local time) and that their peaks would be around 300 requests per second. The administrators also knew that according to their company's policy, maximum CPU utilization during peak loads should rarely exceed 30 percent. This maximum helps to assure quality of service during times of heavy traffic.

With a goal of 300 requests per second and a maximum CPU utilization of 30 percent, the administrators adjusted their WCAT distribution and configuration files and then ran the stress test again. The tests showed that at 275 requests per second, CPU utilization approached 30 percent. In this way, the administrators determined that their current capacity on the server with four 550-MHz processors is sufficient for expected regular traffic and peak loads. In other words, the installation scales well for their current needs, and the installation should have sufficient resources available to handle peak loads.

Tuning Production Servers

Contoso best practices mandate that each server be configured for optimum performance and scalability before the server is put into production. These best practices specifically target disk setup, services running on the server by default, network setup, and caches.

Use RAID

To begin with, the administrators set up the site content on a redundant array of independent disks (RAID). RAID is a data storage method in which data — along with information used for error correction, such as parity bits — is distributed among two or more hard disk drives to improve performance and reliability. For information about setting up RAID, see Help and Support Center for Windows Server 2003.

If using RAID is not an option, consider moving the site content to a disk other than the system disk (that is, the disk on which the operating system is installed). By storing your site content on a disk other than the system disk, you reduce contention for disk access between the operating system and the Web sites. This further increases performance.

Delete unused default documents

The administrators knew that if a user tried to access the Web site by using a trailing slash — for example, http://www.contoso.com/website/ — the server would read each item listed in the default document list (such as Default.htm, Default.asp, and Index.htm) and perform a search to see if each document existed. As a best practice, the administrators deleted all the documents in the default document list that do not exist. They left only the default document that does exist — for Contoso, this is Default.aspx. You can delete unnecessary default documents by using IIS Manager to modify the **Documents** tab on the **Web Sites** property pages.

Shut down unused services

To conserve memory and CPU resources for the Web service, the administrators shut down unnecessary services. The server will host only the Contoso Web application, so the administrators stopped other IIS services such as the FTP, Simple Mail Transfer Protocol (SMTP), and Network News Transfer Protocol (NNTP) services. Using the Services snap-in, the administrators stopped the Automatic Updates, Task Scheduler, Wireless Configuration, and Print Spooler services (because they would not be printing from that server).

 Important

Refer to Help and Support Center for Windows Server 2003 to ensure that you understand the role of each service before you stop it. Monitor performance after stopping each service to ensure that the change does not negatively impact performance.

Change file and printer sharing defaults

The administrators changed the default File and Printer Sharing for Network properties from **Maximize data throughput for file sharing** to **Maximize data throughput for network applications**. This small change resulted in a 10 percent increase in throughput. For information about how to change these properties, see Help and Support Center for Windows Server 2003.

For more information about performance tuning, see "Optimizing IIS 6.0 Performance" in this book.

Scaling Up

Scaling up means adding hardware, such as RAM or CPUs, to a Web server to increase the number of sites a server can host. Scaling up can be an inexpensive way to boost performance, especially if you host static-content Web sites.

Shortly after moving the server with four 550-MHz processors into production, the Contoso Marketing department finalized plans for a major television advertisement campaign. The marketing director informed the administrators that site traffic would likely double in the next few weeks. The administrators needed to determine whether the server with four 550-MHz processors could handle sustained traffic loads of 600 requests per second while staying within the 30 percent CPU restriction. The cycles-per-request analysis is as follows:

- 4×550 megacycles/second = 2,200 megacycles/second.

- 2,200,000,000 cycles/second divided by 893 requests/second = 2,463,606 cycles/request (on average). Rounded up, the server performed 2.5 million cycles/request while the CPU was at 100 percent saturation.

- 600 requests/second $\times$ 2.5 million cycles/request = 1500 MHz.

- 1500 MHz divided by 30 percent CPU saturation maximum (1500/.3) = 5000 megacycles/second.

As a result of this analysis, the administrators realized they needed a server that could perform 5,000 megacycles/second in order to use 1,500 megacycles/second at 30 percent CPU. The server with four 550-MHz processors could only achieve 2,200 megacycles/second. Consequently, they would need to scale up, scale out, or both.

To determine the results of scaling up, the administrators tested a server with eight 900-MHz processors. This new server was capable of 7,200 megacycles/second, which covered their current needs.

The administrators migrated the application and performed their WCAT stress test again. In an effort to saturate the CPU at 100 percent, the administrators ran the test with 48, then 72, and finally 120 virtual clients. CPU utilization never exceeded 70 percent. The administrators checked Task Manager and found that the network hovered around 11 percent. The administrators determined at this point that they had a bottleneck somewhere in the system, but for the purpose of their tests, the result of 1,904 requests/second with an average response time of 630 milliseconds was sufficient test data.

The server with four 550-MHz processors performed 893 requests/second. The server with eight 900-MHz processors performed 1,900 requests/second. The installation scaled at a ratio of 1 to 1.6 [(7200/1900)/(2200/893)] when moving from four to eight processors. The administrators understood this to be an acceptable scaling ratio. Realistically, the overhead in system resources and issues such as lock contention do not allow a system to scale linearly; and so they did not expect to see a scale ratio of 1 to 2 when moving from four to eight processors. According to their calculations, the administrators determined that the server with eight 900-MHz processors, barring any unforeseen problems, should scale and perform satisfactorily for their application.

Scaling Out

Scaling out is the process of adding servers to an existing server environment to improve performance and to increase the number of Web sites that the system can host or publish. Scaling out reduces bottlenecks and lock contention because requests coming into the system do not share resources. The request load is balanced among servers.

The Contoso administrators understood that although scaling up to an eight-processor server would meet their performance and scalability needs, they would potentially gain more throughput and increased reliability by hosting their Web application on multiple servers. They decided to use two four-processor servers (one with four 550-MHz processors and one with four 900-MHz processors) with Network Load Balancing for load balancing and failover. After installing and configuring Network Load Balancing on both servers, the administrators ran their WCAT stress test using 500 virtual clients (five client computers running 100 threads each).

As one Network Load Balancing node, the two servers processed (on average) 1,900 requests per second when the Processor(_Total)\% Processor Time counter approached 100 percent. The administrators were initially concerned that the requests per second had not increased beyond the results of the eight-processor server by itself. After looking at the actual megacycles per request, as shown in Table 7.13, the administrators realized they actually had an 18 percent increase in throughput, because the number of megacycles per request had decreased in the Network Load Balancing test.

Table 7.13   Megacycles/Request Calculations

Server	Megacycles/Second (of Processors/MHz)	Requests/Second	Megacycles/Request
4 × 550 MHz	2,200	900	2.45
8 × 900 MHz	7,200	1,900	3.8
4 × 550 MHz + 4 × 900 MHz	5,800	1,900	3.1

With the 18 percent increase in throughput and the added reliability of hosting the Web application on two servers, the administrators asked themselves, Are we done? Is this good enough? Have we scaled this installation as much as we can scale it? They realized that the only truly accurate benchmark they could use for their application was the application itself. In other words, they had scaled the installation out to the point where they could readily process the expected traffic loads while staying within the 30 percent CPU utilization guideline. They had increased reliability by hosting the site on two servers, and they had executed their stress testing with no errors. Unless they began to experience errors from clients, or they noticed — during regular performance monitoring — that traffic loads were increasing and CPU usage was surpassing the 30 percent restriction, they had achieved their objective.

Additional Resources

These resources contain additional information and tools related to this chapter.

Related Information

- "IIS 6.0 Administration Scripts, Tips, and Tricks" in this book for information about command-line administration tools in IIS 6.0.

- "IIS 6.0 Architecture" in this book for information about IIS 6.0 request processing modes.

- "Optimizing IIS 6.0 Performance" in this book for information about performance tuning.

- "Running IIS 6.0 as an Application Server" in this book for information about IIS 6.0 application isolation modes, including how to enable and configure worker process isolation mode.

- "Working with the Metabase" in this book for information about the IIS 6.0 metabase, including how to change a metabase property.

- The Capacity Planning link on the Web Resources page at http://www.microsoft.com/windows/reskits/webresources for information about capacity planning.

- The Duwamish 7.0 link on the Web Resources page at http://www.microsoft.com/windows/reskits/webresources for information about Duwamish 7.0.

- The Scalability link on the Web Resources page at http://www.microsoft.com/windows/reskits/webresources for information about scalability.

- The SharePoint Team Services Administrator's Guide link on the Web Resources page at http://www.microsoft.com/windows/reskits/webresources for information about upgrading your FrontPage-extended Web sites.

- *Performance Testing Microsoft .NET Web Applications* by Microsoft Application Consulting and Engineering (ACE) Team, 2003, Redmond: Microsoft Press.

Related IIS 6.0 Help Topics

- "Performance Counters Reference" in IIS 6.0 Help for information about IIS cache counters.

- "Metabase Property Reference" in IIS 6.0 Help for information about specific IIS 6.0 properties.

- "Using Command-Line Administration Scripts" in IIS 6.0 Help for information about administering IIS 6.0 programmatically.

- "Performance Counters Reference" in IIS 6.0 Help for information about IIS 6.0 counters.

Related Tools

- WCAT

  The Microsoft Web Capacity Analysis Tool (WCAT) runs simulated workloads on client/server configurations. Using WCAT, you can test how IIS and network configurations respond to a variety of different client requests for content or data. The results of these tests can be used to determine the optimal server and network configuration for your server. WCAT and its documentation (Wcatguide.doc) are included on the *Internet Information Services (IIS) 6.0 Resource Kit* companion CD.

Configuring Internet Sites and Services

15

Internet Information Services (IIS) provides four Internet services: the World Wide Web Publishing Service (WWW service) for hosting Internet and intranet content, the File Transfer Protocol (FTP) service for hosting sites from which users can upload and download files, the Network News Transfer Protocol (NNTP) service for hosting discussion groups, and the Simple Mail Transfer Protocol (SMTP) service for sending and receiving e-mail messages. The WWW service is installed by default. Otherwise, install only the services that you need. After you install IIS–based Internet services, you can create sites or virtual servers, configure properties and security settings, and set up components to further customize your server.

In This Chapter

Related Information

- For information about the WWW service and IIS core components, see "IIS 6.0 Architecture" in this book.

- For information about creating a Web site, see "Common Administrative Tasks" in this book.

- For information about IIS security, see "Managing a Secure IIS 6.0 Solution" in this book.

- For information about creating Web sites programmatically, see "IIS 6.0 Administration Scripts, Tips, and Tricks " in this book.

DNS Overview

The Internet employs Transmission Control Protocol/Internet Protocol (TCP/IP) to locate and connect to network hosts, which are computers or other network devices. Each network host is identified by a unique IP address. For users to reach your IIS-based Internet site or service, you must have a unique IP address.

IP addresses are expressed in dotted-decimal notation and segmented into four 8-bit octets, for example, 192.168.1.42. It is difficult to remember and use numeric IP addresses, and many people prefer to use alphanumeric names. To address this issue, Domain Name System (DNS) provides a standard naming convention for locating IP-based computers. When you use DNS, clients can connect to an Internet site or service by typing a DNS domain name (such as www.microsoft.com) in their browsers, rather than an IP address (such as 192.168.1.42). A DNS domain name such as www.microsoft.com is easier to remember and type correctly.

The process of mapping a DNS domain name to an IP address is called *name resolution*. DNS name resolution is performed by a DNS service, such as the DNS service provided with the Microsoft® Windows® Server 2003, Standard Edition; Windows® Server 2003, Enterprise Edition; and Windows® Server 2003, Datacenter Edition, operating systems. For more information about Windows Server 2003 DNS, see "DNS" in Help and Support Center for Windows Server 2003.

Before you can set up an IIS-based Internet site or service, you must obtain an IP address, and if you want users to be able to use a DNS domain name to connect to your Internet site or service, you must also register a unique DNS domain name. Before you request a DNS domain name to register, decide on a plan for your DNS namespace.

Namespace Planning for DNS

DNS uses a namespace that is hierarchically structured and based on the concept of a tree of named domains. The tree has multiple levels:

- **The root domain**. The root domain is the top-level organizational domain. Root domain names include com, org, and gov.

- **Second-level domains**. Second-level domains provide an identifying name. For example, if your company is named Contoso Pharmaceuticals, then the second-level domain can be *contoso* in contoso.com.

- **Subdomains**. Subdomains are arranged according to departments, geography, or other logical divisions to help users find information as quickly as possible. For example, you can create a subdomain of research.contoso.com.

The DNS namespace includes globally unique identifiers — Internet domain names, IP address numbers, protocol parameter and port numbers, and others — that are assigned to the organizations that request them. These identifiers must be unique for the Internet to function.

To effectively plan your DNS namespace, consider the long-term organization of your network architecture, as well as how users might look for information. For more information about namespace planning, see "Namespace planning for DNS" in Help and Support Center for Windows Server 2003.

Registering a DNS Domain Name

Your Internet service provider (ISP) should assign you an IP address for your server that you will use when you configure IIS to host your Internet site or sites. To register a DNS domain name, you can work directly with a naming authority. Many ISPs can register a DNS domain name for you. The InterNIC Web site maintains a list of registrars that are currently taking registrations for all available top-level domains. The InterNIC Web site organizes and lists these registrars alphabetically, by name, by location, and by supported languages. After you register your DNS domain name, your ISP or registrar can host the domain, or you can host the domain yourself (if you are a more advanced user). For more information about domain name registration services, see the InterNIC link on the Web Resources page at http://www.microsoft.com/windows/reskits/webresources.

Configuring Web Sites

The IIS WWW service allows you to publish content on the Internet or an intranet. You can publish a static Web site or a dynamic application. The primary function of the WWW service is to connect client Hypertext Transfer Protocol (HTTP) requests to your Web site or sites. The WWW service is installed at *SystemDrive*:\Windows\System32 by default when you start IIS.

For more information about the WWW service and IIS core components, see "IIS 6.0 Architecture" in this book.

Note

If you want to install the WWW service somewhere other than at the default location, you must use an unattended installation answer file and specify the alternative path using the **PathWWWRoot** parameter. For more information, see "Unattended Setup" in this book.

Creating and Setting Up Web Sites

When you use the Manage Your Server Wizard to install the application server role, the default Web site is created automatically. You can use this Web site as it is, change it, or create and use new Web sites. For step-by-step instructions for creating your first Web site, see "Common Administrative Tasks" in this book or see "How to Create Web or FTP Sites" in IIS 6.0 Help, which is accessible from IIS Manager.

Whether you plan to publish your site on an intranet or the Internet, the principles of providing content are the same. You place your Web files in directories on your server and configure IIS to serve those directories. Then users establish an HTTP connection and view the files with a browser. The first step in creating a Web site, therefore, is to design your server, directory, and file structure.

The two main types of directories in IIS are physical directories and virtual directories. Each Web site must have one home directory, which is the central location for the published pages of the site. In addition, you can create Web Distributed Authoring and Versioning (WebDAV) publishing directories, where users can publish, lock, and manage resources.

Home Directories

The *home directory* is the central location for your published pages. It contains the pages or applications that you will publish. When you install the application server role, IIS creates a default home directory for the default Web site. The home directory for the default Web site is *SystemDrive*:\Inetpub\Wwwroot. You can change the home directory to another local directory or a shared directory on another computer, or you can redirect requests to a URL if your content is located on a different server on the Internet. For step-by-step instructions for setting the home directory, see "Setting Home Directories" in IIS 6.0 Help.

If you set your home directory as a shared directory on another computer, then users might need to enter a user name and password to access the resource. If you set the home directory as a shared directory on another computer, it is important to use an account that has only the minimum credentials that are required to run the application. If you use an account with administrative credentials when you create this directory, then clients can gain access to server operations, which seriously jeopardizes the security of your network. For more information about security credentials, see "Managing a Secure IIS 6.0 Solution" in this book.

If you have a simple Web site, you can set up subdirectories under the home directory. You can create subdirectories for the different elements used on your Web site, such as images, scripts, and server-side includes. Alternatively, in a simple Web site setting, you can set up virtual directories instead.

Virtual Directories

To publish from any directory not contained within your home directory, you must create a *virtual directory*. A *virtual directory* is an *alias*, either for a physical directory on your server hard disk that does not reside in the home directory or for the home directory on another computer. An *alias* is a name that Web browsers use to access the virtual directory. Because an alias is usually shorter than the path name of the directory, it is more convenient for users to type. A client simply adds the alias to the URL of the Web site to browse the Web content in that virtual directory.

Using virtual directories offers several benefits. Not only is an alias usually easier for users to type and remember, but also it is a good security practice to use virtual directories because an alias hides the physical location of your files from unauthorized users. In addition, virtual directories make it easier for you to change and manage the directories on your site. If you change the name or location of a directory, you can simply change the mapping between the alias and the physical directory, rather than change the URL of the Web site.

In addition, virtual directories allow administrators to store content in different locations. Users can access the directories using simple URLs. For example, if a default Web site is located at C:\Inetpub\WWWRoot, an administrator can create a virtual directory as a subdirectory of the default Web site, but the virtual directory can have a physical directory in a different location, such as D:\Data. If the virtual directory has an alias of *Data*, and the server name is *MyWeb*, users can access the default Web site and the virtual directory by typing **http://MyWeb** and **http://MyWeb/Data**, respectively.

If you have a simple Web site housed on one directory, using virtual directories is an optional, although recommended, practice. However, if you have a complex site that spans multiple directories, drives, or computers, or if you want to specify different URLs for different parts of the site, you must use virtual directories. To set up a virtual directory that maps to a directory on another computer, you must specify the Universal Naming Convention (UNC) name of the directory and provide a user name and password.

For step-by-step instructions for creating and deleting virtual directories, see "Using Virtual Directories" in IIS 6.0 Help.

WebDAV Publishing Directories

WebDAV is an industry-standard set of extensions to HTTP 1.1. WebDAV is a good alternative to FTP if you need a secure solution for publishing resources because it enables the same strong authentication, encryption, proxy support, and caching capabilities as any other HTTP-based Web site. In addition, with WebDAV, you can send multiple file transfers through a single TCP connection, whereas FTP requires a new connection for each file transferred. For more information about the WebDAV standard, see the WebDAV Resources link on the Web Resources page at http://www.microsoft.com/windows/reskits/webresources.

WebDAV is integrated into IIS, but it is disabled by default. For step-by-step instructions for enabling WebDAV in IIS, see "Web Authoring with WebDAV" in IIS 6.0 Help. For information about securing WebDAV, see "Securing WebDAV Publishing Directories" later in this chapter.

With WebDAV, you can create Web publishing directories where users can publish, lock, and manage resources. To set up a WebDAV publishing directory, enable WebDAV, and then set up a virtual directory using IIS Manager in the same way that you set up a virtual directory for a standard Web site. For security purposes and to configure DAV custom properties, which are special properties that users can search on, a WebDAV publishing directory must reside on an NTFS file system partition. For step-by-step instructions for setting up a WebDAV publishing directory, see "Creating Publishing Directories" in IIS 6.0 Help.

Making the WebDAV Publishing Directory Available to Users

After you enable WebDAV and set up a publishing directory, users can use the directory on your server as a collaborative work environment. Users with the correct permissions can copy and move files, and they can search for and modify the content and the properties of files. Multiple users can read a file concurrently, but the WebDAV lock and unlock capabilities allow only one person to modify the file at a time.

Users can access a WebDAV publishing directory through clients running Microsoft® Windows® 2000 or Microsoft® Windows® XP Professional operating systems, Microsoft® Internet Explorer 5 and 6, Microsoft® Office 2000 or Office XP products, and through any other client that supports the industry-standard WebDAV protocol.

For more information about WebDAV clients, including how they can access your WebDAV publishing directory, see "About WebDAV" in IIS 6.0 Help.

Enabling WebDAV Redirector

WebDAV Redirector is a remote file system that allows clients running Windows XP Professional or Windows Server 2003 to connect to your WebDAV publishing directory through the command line. Once the client is connected, a user can create, modify, and save files on the WebDAV publishing directory using any existing applications that are written for a Windows 32-bit operating system. WebDAV Redirector enables users to access files on the Web as though they are on a mapped network drive. When enabling the WebDAV Redirector, you must ensure that the WebClient service is started.

For the WebDAV Redirector to work, the site that contains the virtual directory that is mapped to your WebDAV publishing directory must be set up exclusively as a WebDAV site. Therefore, you must delete all custom headers on that site, including custom headers for the Microsoft® FrontPage® 2002 Server Extensions. If your WebDAV Web site is set up as both a WebDAV site and a site running FrontPage 2002 Server Extensions, IIS will send the FrontPage custom header and the WebDAV Redirector will assume that the server is not a proper WebDAV site.

Configuring Web Site Properties

Every Web site is configured with default properties. You can change the default properties at the WWW service level (which affects all the Web sites on a server), the site level, the directory level, or the file level. IIS employs property inheritance to reduce Web site administration tasks. Lower-level properties are automatically inherited from higher-level properties. For example, the default **Connection Timeout** property is 900, which means that every file on every Web site on the server will time out after 900 seconds. If you want to reduce the time-out period for a certain Web site, you can change the setting at the site level and the change will be replicated to all the files and directories on that site. You can edit settings at lower levels individually to override inherited settings from the next level up. If you change a setting at a lower level, and then you later change a setting at a higher level that conflicts with the lower-level setting, you will be prompted to choose whether you want to change the lower-level setting to match the new higher-level setting. For step-by-step instructions for changing default settings using IIS Manager, see "Changing Default Web Site Settings" in IIS 6.0 Help.

Modifying the Default Web Site

When you install IIS, it creates the default Web site automatically. This Web site is configured with default settings that are not optimal for every environment. You can do one of three things with the default Web site:

- **Use it as is, without changing any of the settings**. This practice is not recommended for a production Internet or intranet site. It is recommended that you use the default Web site only in test or demonstration situations.

- **Delete the default Web site, and create new sites**. Many ISPs will delete the default Web site and then use custom scripts to create new Web sites as needed. For more information about creating Web sites programmatically, see "IIS 6.0 Administration Scripts, Tips, and Tricks" in this book.

- **Modify the default Web site to work in your environment**. If you choose to modify the default Web site, then, as a best practice, change the properties immediately, before you create any directories or virtual directories. Directories and virtual directories inherit the properties of the default Web site.

You can modify properties of the default Web site as appropriate for your environment.

Modifying Default Web Site Identity Settings

You can use the Web Site tab of the **Web Site Properties** dialog box to configure several key Web site identity settings.

Description   Change the description of the Web site, using a name that is appropriate for your environment. This name will appear only in IIS Manager.

IP address   Enter an IP address if you are creating a Web site bound to a specific IP address on the computer and you do not want to use the All Unassigned default setting, or if you recently changed the IP address of the server.

TCP and SSL port   Change the value for TCP, User Datagram Protocol (UDP), or both TCP and UDP ports only if you have special requirements. It is recommended that you leave the default TCP and SSL (Secure Sockets Layer) port settings (80 and 443, respectively) for production servers.

Host header   Enter a host header value if you plan to host multiple Web sites on the same server, or if you plan to publish the site so that users can access it by using a DNS name rather than the computer name. To create a host-header value, click **Advanced**, and then in the **Advanced Web Site Configuration** dialog box, click **Add to type in a host header value**. Any subsequent Web sites that you create cannot use the host header value that you enter for the default Web site. For more information about using host headers to host multiple Web sites, see "Hosting Multiple Web Sites on the Same Server" later in this chapter.

Modifying the Default Authentication Method

You can use the **Directory Security** tab of the **Web Site Properties** dialog box to change the authentication method. The authentication method determines whether users are identified, and how users must be identified to access your site. The authentication method you select varies, depending on the kind of site you are creating and the purpose of the site. For a complete discussion of authentication, see "Managing a Secure IIS 6.0 Solution" in this book.

Modifying the Default Physical File Location

You can use the **Home Directory** tab of the **Web Site Properties** dialog box to specify the path to the home directory for your Web site and whether the home directory resides on the local computer or on a network computer. The default Web site home directory is *SystemDrive*:\Inetpub\Wwwroot.

Enabling and Configuring Log File Formats

You can use the **Web Site** tab of the **Web Site Properties** dialog box to enable logging and to specify the log format that you want to use. For more information about IIS logs, see "Analyzing Log Files" in this book.

Specifying the Application Pool

You can use the **Home Directory** tab of the **Web Site Properties** dialog box to specify the application pool. For more information about application pools, see "IIS 6.0 Architecture" and "Running IIS 6.0 as an Application Server" in this book.

Extending Web Sites with FrontPage 2002 Server Extensions

You can install and enable FrontPage 2002 Server Extensions for Web sites. FrontPage 2002 Server Extensions provide Web-based and command-line administration that allow you to *extend* your virtual servers, which means that the site owner can author the site in FrontPage and delegate site ownership and administrative credentials for Web sites. FrontPage 2002 Server Extensions are not installed by default. For more information about FrontPage 2002 Server Extensions, including information about installing and enabling, see "Using FrontPage 2002 Server Extensions with IIS 6.0" in this book.

Redirecting Requests

Redirecting refers to the process of configuring the Web server to issue an HTTP 302 redirect message to the client, which instructs the client to resubmit the request for a new location. This process helps ensure that users always receive the Web page that they want, even if you changed the location of the page and did not update all of the links.

It is useful to redirect requests when the content is not hosted on the Web server or when you are updating your Web site and want to make a portion of the site temporarily unavailable. In addition, you can use a redirect when you have changed the name of a virtual directory and you want users to be able to access files using the old URL.

You can use redirect wildcards to perform basic rewriting operations for the redirected URL. For example, to redirect all requests for /Scripts/Filename.stm to a single file named Default.stm, and to redirect all requests for /Scripts/Filename.htm to a single file named Default.htm, you would type the following in the **Redirect to** box for the /Scripts virtual directory:
*;Filename.stm;/Default.stm;Filename.htm;/Default.htm

 Important

You must be a member of the Administrators group on the local computer to perform the following procedure or procedures, or you must have been delegated the appropriate authority. As a security best practice, log on to your computer by using an account that is not in the Administrators group, and then use the **Run as** command to run IIS Manager as an administrator. At a command prompt, type runas / *User.Administrative_AccountName* "mmc %systemroot%\system32\inetsrv\iis.msc".

▷ **To use redirect wildcards**

1. In IIS Manager, click the local computer, right-click the Web site or directory that you want to redirect, and then click **Properties**.

2. In the **Web Site Properties** dialog box, click the **Home Directory** tab, the **Virtual Directory** tab, or the **Directory** tab.

3. In **The content for this resource should come from**, click **A redirection to a URL**.

4. In the **Redirect to** box, type the wildcard character (*), a semicolon (;), and then the URL. Separate pairs of wildcard characters and destination URLs with a semicolon.

5. In **The client will be sent to**, select the **The exact URL entered above** check box.

For more information about redirecting requests, see "Redirecting Requests to Files, Directories, or Programs" in IIS 6.0 Help.

Redirecting to Dynamic Content

You can also redirect requests to dynamic content, which is useful for sending users to Common Gateway Interface (CGI) scripts, Active Server Pages (ASP), and .aspx pages. If you want to redirect to dynamic content, make sure that dynamic content is enabled on your server running IIS. To redirect to dynamic content, use redirect variables to pass parameters to the page. For example, to redirect all requests for scripts in the Scripts folder to a logging program named Logger.exe that records the requested URL and any parameters that are passed with the URL, type: **/Scripts/Logger.exe?URL=$V+PARAMS=$P**. In this example, $V and $P are redirect variables. For more complete information about redirect variables, see "Redirect Reference" in IIS 6.0 Help.

Securing Web Sites

To secure your Web sites, implement a defense-in-depth strategy that combines many different security measures. Use appropriate settings for authentication methods, Web site access control, IP address and domain name restrictions, and secure communications, including certificates and encryption. In addition, implement tools such as firewalls, and lock the rooms that contain hardware. You can use the **Directory Security** tab in the **Web Site Properties** dialog box to configure authentication, Web site access control, and IP address and domain name restrictions, and to enable secure communications. For a thorough discussion of IIS security, including how to configure security settings, see "Managing a Secure IIS 6.0 Solution" in this book.

There are a number of considerations for configuring authentication and access-control settings for WebDAV-based remote publishing. These considerations are outlined in this section.

Securing WebDAV Publishing Directories

Just as with a standard Web site, you can use the **Directory Security** tab in the **Web Site Properties** dialog box to configure WebDAV authentication, Web site access control, and IP address and domain name restrictions, and to enable secure communications. Furthermore, for security reasons and to enable WebDAV custom search properties, your WebDAV publishing directory must reside on an NTFS file system partition. For more information about NTFS partitions, see "Choosing a file system: NTFS, FAT, or FAT32" in Help and Support Center for Windows Server 2003.

Setting the Client Authentication Method

Because WebDAV is an HTTP-based protocol, the same authentication methods are available for your WebDAV publishing directory as for your Web sites. When you create a WebDAV virtual directory, the authentication settings will be set by default to Anonymous authentication and Integrated Windows authentication.

 Important

Change the default authentication settings for your WebDAV site.
Anonymous authentication and Integrated Windows authentication are
appropriate for Web sites, but not for resources on a WebDAV publishing
directory.

Use the following best practices as guidelines when configuring client authentication for WebDAV. For more information about authentication, see "Web Site Authentication" in IIS 6.0 Help.

Anonymous authentication   Turn off Anonymous authentication to your WebDAV publishing directory. Without controlling access, your directory might be vandalized by unknown clients.

Basic authentication Turn on Basic authentication only if you encrypt passwords through SSL. Basic authentication sends passwords over the connection in plaintext, so passwords can be intercepted and read. For more information about SSL, see "Configuring SSL on Servers" in IIS 6.0 Help.

Digest authentication Turn on Digest authentication if users access your WebDAV publishing directory over the Internet and through firewalls because Digest authentication sends the passwords over the network as an MD5 hash. However, passwords are stored as plaintext in the Active Directory® directory service.

Advanced Digest authentication Turn on Advanced Digest authentication if users access your WebDAV publishing directory over the Internet and through firewalls. Advanced Digest authentication is the best choice because, in addition to sending passwords over the network as an MD5 hash, the passwords are also stored in Active Directory as an MD5 hash rather than as plaintext.

Integrated Windows authentication Turn off Integrated Windows authentication unless users access your WebDAV publishing directory only from an intranet.

.NET Passport authentication Turn off .NET Passport authentication. Microsoft® .NET Passport authentication uses cookies to validate user credentials against a central .NET Passport server. However, the central .NET Passport server does not authorize or deny the access of a specific user to individual .NET Passport–enabled sites.

Configuring Access Control

You can control access to your WebDAV publishing directory by coordinating permissions in IIS and Windows Server 2003. The following information can help you set the correct permissions depending on what kind of content your WebDAV publishing directory contains and what you want to allow users to do with that content. For step-by-step instructions for setting permissions, see "Securing Sites with Web Site Permissions" in IIS 6.0 Help.

Read, Write, Directory browsing enabled Set these permissions if you want clients to see a list of resources, modify them (except for resources that do not have Write permission), publish their own resources, or manipulate files.

Write enabled; Read and Directory browsing disabled Set these permissions if you want clients to publish private information on the directory, but you do not want others to see what has been published. This configuration works well if clients are submitting ballots or performance reviews.

Read and Write enabled; Directory browsing disabled Set these permissions only if you want to obscure file names as a security method. However, be aware that security by obscurity is a low-level security precaution because an attacker or a malicious user can guess file names by trial and error.

Index this resource enabled   Enable Indexing Service if you plan to let clients search directory resources.

You can also control access to your WebDAV publishing directory through discretionary access control lists (DACLs). When you set up a WebDAV publishing directory on an NTFS file system disk, the server running Windows Server 2003 is configured with a secure set of defaults that can be too restrictive for Web publishing. If you change the defaults, assign Write permission only to the specific users or groups that absolutely need Write permission. (Whenever possible, assign permissions to groups rather than users.) By default, the Users group is assigned only Read permission for most portions of the file system.

If you have script files in your WebDAV publishing directory that you do not want users to access, you can deny access to these files by verifying that the Script Source Access permission is not assigned. The extensions of your script files are listed in the Applications Mapping list. All other executable files, including files with .exe extensions, are treated as static HTML files unless the Scripts and Executables permission is assigned to the directory.

You can prevent users from downloading and viewing .exe files as HTML files but still allow clients to run them by assigning the Scripts and Executables permission. To do so, on the **Virtual Directory** tab of the publishing directory, on the **Execute permissions** list, click **Scripts and Executables**. When you assign the Scripts and Executables permission to the directory, all of the executable files are subject to the Script Source Access permission setting. You can assign the Script Source Access permission on the **Home Directory** tab of the **Web Site Properties** dialog box of the Web site that you are configuring. When the Script Source Access permission is assigned, clients with Read permission can see all the executables, and clients with Write permission can edit and run all the executables.

If you want clients to be able to write to an executable file that does not appear in the Application Mapping list, assign the Write permission and the Scripts Only Execute permission to the directory.

If you want clients to be able to write to any executable file, regardless of whether it appears in the Application Mapping list, assign the Script Source Access permission and the Scripts and Executables Execute permission to the directory.

Hosting Multiple Web Sites on the Same Server

You can host and manage multiple Web sites on one server running Windows Server 2003 and IIS 6.0. To host multiple Web sites on a single Web server, you must configure a unique identity for each Web site by using one of three methods:

- Port-based routing
- IP-based routing
- Host-header routing

By using one of these three methods, you can create unique identities for multiple Web sites without installing a dedicated Web server for each site. You can also create a unique home directory for each site and store the content on the local server or on remote network shares. By doing so, you configure each Web site as a separate entity or virtual server.

For each server hosting multiple Web sites, choose one of the three routing methods listed earlier. When you use one method per server, performance improves because cache and routing lookups are optimized. Conversely, when you use a combination of nonstandard port numbers, unique IP addresses, and host headers to identify multiple Web sites on the same server, performance is degraded for all of the Web sites on the server. For more information about Web site performance, see "Optimizing IIS 6.0 Performance" in this book.

You can add Web sites to a server by using IIS Manager or by using the Iisweb.vbs command-line script. For step-by-step instructions for adding Web sites, see "Adding Web Sites to Your Server" in IIS 6.0 Help.

Port-Based Routing

You can use a nonstandard TCP port number for each Web site. Some administrators use ports other than port 80 for development and testing purposes or for running other server applications that require exclusive access to port 80.

When using port-based routing to host multiple Web sites on the same server, consider the following:

- A server can listen on a maximum of 64 ports at one time. The actual number of ports a server can listen on varies depending on the available RAM on the computer. Therefore, you cannot use port-based routing to route a large number of sites.

- Port-based routing consumes a vast amount of kernel resources and can degrade server performance.

- If you use a nonstandard TCP port number to identify a Web site, users cannot reach the site by using a standard name or URL. Instead, users must know the nonstandard TCP port number assigned to the Web site and add it to the name or IP address of the Web site in their browser. For example, to reach a private Web site named Contoso with an IP address of 10.0.0.02 and HTTP assigned to the nonstandard TCP port 8080, users would have to type **http://contoso:8080** or **http://10.0.0.02:8080** in their browser to reach the site.

If you choose to use a nonstandard port for a nonproduction server, use a port number higher than 1023 so that it does not conflict with the well-known port numbers that the Internet Assigned Numbers Authority (IANA) assigns.

IP-Based Routing

With IIS 6.0, you can configure Web sites to listen on all available IP addresses or on an individual IP address. If you use multiple IP addresses to distinguish between different Web sites on the same server, you must configure IIS to assign each site a unique, static IP address.

Although it is simple to configure IP–based routing, this strategy typically is viable only for large corporations and ISPs. Unique IP addresses are in short supply, so it can be difficult and expensive to obtain a block of static IP addresses.

One advantage of IP–based routing is that it enables you to host multiple Web sites that require SSL on the same server. However, hosting a large number of sites that require SSL on the same server can degrade performance because so many requests have to be encrypted and decrypted.

Host-Header Routing

You can use one IP address (or the **All Unassigned** setting) for multiple Web sites and distinguish the Web sites with unique host-header names. This option is easy to configure by using IIS Manager. To use host-header names, your computer or network must be using a name resolution system such as DNS.

When a client sends a request for an HTTP connection to the server running IIS, the client request includes a field in the HTTP header called HOST. This field contains the host name of the requested Web server. For example, when you type **http://www.microsoft.com** into your browser, your browser sends a packet with an HTTP header that includes the following field: HOST: www.microsoft.com. Because the name of the field is **HOST** and it is in the HTTP header of the client, it is referred to as the *host header*. For more information on the HTTP 1.1 standard, see the RFC link on the Web Resources page at http://www.microsoft.com/windows/reskits/webresources, and search for RFC 2616.

With host-header routing, when a client request reaches the server, IIS uses the host name, rather than only the IP address as it does with IP–based routing, to determine which Web site the client is requesting. To set up multiple Web sites on the same server to take advantage of host-header routing, the host-header names must be DNS domain names that are publicly available and registered with an authorized Internet naming authority. For more information about obtaining a DNS name, see "DNS Overview" earlier in this chapter.

 Note
To set up an intranet site for host-header routing, the host-header name can be an intranet site name.

Host-Header Routing and SSL

When a client requests a Web site by using Secure Hypertext Transfer Protocol (HTTPS) over Transport Layer Security (TLS) or over SSL, the HTTP header with the **HOST** field is contained in the encrypted part of the packet. Therefore, the Web server cannot decrypt the host-header name to determine which Web site the client requested. For this reason, when you use SSL connections, you cannot use host headers as the primary means of identifying a Web site.

Configuring FTP Sites

IIS includes the FTP service for publishing and managing files. FTP uses TCP at the transport layer, so all the data that is exchanged between the server and the client is guaranteed not only to be delivered but also to be delivered intact, as originally sent.

The IIS Admin service, which is physically part of the Inetinfo.exe process, manages the protocols in IIS that are not related to the Web, including FTP. By default, the FTP service is not installed on a server running Windows Server 2003. Once it is installed, the FTP sites start automatically the next time you restart the IIS services.

Installing the FTP Service

Before you can set up an FTP site, you must install the FTP service from Add or Remove Programs in Control Panel. For information about how to install the FTP service, see "FTP Site Setup" in IIS 6.0 Help.

When you install the FTP service, a default FTP site directory is created with the home directory *SystemDrive:*\Inetpub\Ftproot.

There are two kinds of directories for FTP site content: user home directories and shared virtual directories. Each FTP site, except for those in Active Directory Isolation mode, must have a home directory that serves as the initial directory for users connecting to the site. In most configurations, each user has an individual directory under this site home directory. Create a virtual directory to hold additional content that is accessible to every user that logs on to the site, or if you want to use different URLs for different parts of the site. This virtual directory is different than the anonymous user home directory that is accessible to all anonymous users. Home and virtual directories for FTP sites function similarly to Web site directories. For more information about directories, see "Creating and Setting Up Web Sites" earlier in this chapter.

 Note
Virtual directory names do not show up when listing the home directory of a user. Instead, virtual directories are used as if they were subdirectories of the user's home directory. A site administrator can publish these virtual directories in the site welcome message.

Configuring FTP Site Properties

The FTP service uses inherited default property settings, much like the WWW service does. Settings on lower levels automatically inherit higher-level settings, and you can edit lower-level settings individually to override inherited settings from the next level up. If you use IIS Manager to change a setting at a lower level and then later change a setting at a higher level that conflicts with the lower-level setting, you are prompted to choose whether you want to change the lower-level setting to match the new higher-level setting. For step-by-step instructions for changing settings, see "Changing Default FTP Site Settings" in IIS 6.0 Help.

Configuring Site Messages

When you set up an FTP site, you can configure IIS to send messages when a user accesses the FTP site. You can create the following messages:

- **Banner**. This message is sent to users as they connect but before they log on to an FTP site. A banner message usually informs users about what kind of information is available on the FTP site.

- **Welcome**. This message welcomes users to an FTP site after they have logged on.

- **Exit**. This message appears when users log off from an FTP site.

- **Maximum connections**. This message is sent to users when the maximum number of connections for the FTP site has been reached.

Setting the Directory Output Style

You can set the directory output style of your FTP site. The directory output style can be either Microsoft® MS-DOS® operating system-based or UNIX-based, and the output style defines the format that is used when an FTP client sends a **list** command.

By default, the MS-DOS directory output style displays the year in a two-digit format, for example, 03. You can change this setting to display the year in a four-digit format, for example, 2003, by enabling the **FtpDirBrowseShowLongDate** metabase property. For more information, see "FtpDirBrowseShowLongDate" in IIS 6.0 Help.

The UNIX directory output style displays the year in a four-digit format when the date of the file is different from the year of the FTP server. The year is not returned in cases where the file date is the same as the year of the FTP server.

Setting the Authentication Method

Two types of users can connect to an FTP site: anonymous users and authenticated users. Set the authentication method to allow only anonymous users, authenticated users, or both anonymous users and authenticated users. If you want to allow only anonymous users, in the **FTP Sites Properties** dialog box, on the **Security Accounts** tab, select the **Allow anonymous connections** check box and the **Allow only anonymous connections** check box. If you want to allow only authenticated users, clear the **Allow anonymous connections** check box. If you want to allow anonymous users and authenticated users, select only the **Allow anonymous connections** check box. Anonymous access to FTP resources works similarly to anonymous access to Web sites. If anonymous access is allowed, all client connections with the user name *anonymous* or *ftp* are accepted and authenticated as the anonymous user. By default, the user account that is configured as the anonymous user is IUSR_*ComputerName*. As an Internet convention for anonymous FTP user identification, the anonymous user is prompted for a password, which is used as a user name.

If a site uses FTP User Isolation and a user connects with a user name and password, then the user is authenticated with his or her Windows account and mapped to individual home directories. This practice is not secure because credentials are transmitted over the network in plaintext and can therefore be intercepted and read. For step-by-step instructions for setting the FTP authentication method, see "FTP Site Authentication" in IIS 6.0 Help.

Note

You cannot set the authentication method and the anonymous user properties using IIS Manager for FTP sites that are configured for the Isolate users using Active Directory mode. The Isolate users using Active Directory mode is explained in more detail later in this chapter.

Setting the Passive Connection Port Range

FTP clients connect to FTP servers through a well-known service port — TCP port 21 — and establish a control channel for sending requests and receiving replies. For actual file data transfers, a second connection is established: a *data channel*. By default, the server connects back to the client to establish the data connection, which is an active-mode connection. However, to support clients that are behind firewalls and cannot accept incoming connections, the FTP protocol allows the client to connect to the server to establish the data channel, which is a passive-mode connection. Passive-mode connections are established through the following process: the client requests a passive mode (PASV), the server replies with a unique port number, and the client connects to that port.

By default, the FTP server allocates ports for passive-mode connections from the WinSock dynamic range, 1024 to 5000. If the server itself is behind a firewall, the 1024 to 5000 port range must be open for incoming connections at the firewall. This requirement can expose the server to potential attack because many applications share the WinSock dynamic port range. To reduce the attack surface, you can configure the FTP service to allocate ports for passive-mode connections from a port range above 5000, which allows you to assign a port range to be used exclusively by FTP passive-mode connections and to create firewall and router policies that open that range for incoming TCP connections.

To set the port range for passive-mode connections, edit the **PassivePortRange** property in the metabase. When you set the port range, consider the number of anticipated concurrent file transfers because each client might need a distinct port. For performance reasons, the port range should be at least two times the number of anticipated concurrent file transfers.

For more information about setting the port range used for FTP passive-mode connections, see "PassivePortRange" in IIS 6.0 Help.

Securing FTP Sites

FTP is not a secure means of transferring data. Although you can configure the FTP service to require a valid user name and password combination, neither the credentials that are specified at log on nor the data itself is encrypted or encoded in any way. The credentials are sent across the network in plaintext and can be intercepted and analyzed by any station on any network between the FTP client and the FTP server. If your plaintext credentials are intercepted and analyzed by a malicious user, then someone other than the intended user can log on to your FTP site and download the files that you placed there or gain access to other network resources, even network resources that require Windows account authentication. For more information about setting the authentication method for your FTP site, see "Configuring FTP Site Properties" earlier in this chapter.

If you intend to place sensitive data on your FTP site or if secure communication between clients and your FTP server is important, consider using FTP over an encrypted channel, such as a virtual private network (VPN) secured with Point-to-Point Tunneling Protocol (PPTP) or Internet Protocol security (IPSec). To learn how to set up a private network over the Internet using PPTP or how to set up secure IP communications with a VPN and IPSec, see the PPTP, VPN, and IPSec topics in Help and Support Center for Windows Server 2003. For more information about IPSec and IIS, see "Managing a Secure IIS 6.0 Solution" in this book.

If you need to authorize users or host sensitive content, then WebDAV is a good alternative to FTP because WebDAV can take advantage of SSL for secure communications. For more information about WebDAV, see "Securing WebDAV Publishing Directories" earlier in this chapter.

Creating Additional FTP Sites

When you install the FTP service, the default FTP site is created with a default directory that is located at *SystemDrive*:\Inetpub\Ftproot. If you want to add additional FTP sites, then you can use the FTP Site Creation Wizard or the Iisftp.vbs command-line script, which is stored in the *SystemDrive*:\Windows\System32 directory. Iisftp.vbs sets up the home directory and configuration in the metabase for the new FTP site. For step-by-step instructions for creating new FTP sites with the wizard or the command-line script, see "Adding FTP Sites to Your Server" in IIS 6.0 Help.

Each FTP site must have a unique IP and port number combination, so each site must have a unique IP address or a unique TCP port number (other than 21, which is the default port number for FTP connections). It is recommended that you create multiple sites with unique IP addresses instead of multiple sites with unique port numbers because when you use a port other than the default port 21, users must type the port number, in addition to the computer name, to locate the site.

If you use a name resolution system, such as Windows Server 2003 DNS, and you use port 21 for FTP, then visitors can type **ftp://** followed by your computer name in their browsers to reach your site. If you use a port other than port 21, then users have to type **ftp://** followed by the port number and the name of your computer. If you have multiple sites with multiple IP addresses, then each address needs to have a corresponding registered domain name, which users type instead of your computer name. For more information about registering a domain name, see "DNS Overview" earlier in this chapter.

Hosting Multiple FTP Sites with FTP User Isolation

You can host multiple FTP sites on the same server running IIS. If you are an ISP or an application service provider in a multisite Internet hosting scenario and you want to ensure that your customers cannot access the FTP directories of one another, then you can enable FTP User Isolation. When you enable FTP User Isolation, the user's top-level directory appears as the root of the FTP site, so other users cannot view or overwrite content. Within the user's specific site, the user can create, modify, or delete files and folders.

FTP User Isolation supports three isolation modes: **Do not isolate users**, **Isolate users**, and **Isolate users using Active Directory**. You can select the isolation mode during FTP site setup using the FTP Site Creation Wizard. You can use Iisftp.vbs to configure FTP User Isolation, using the **/isolation** parameter. When you use the **/isolation** parameter, specify either **AD**, for Active Directory isolation, or **Local**, for local isolation. If you do not include the **/isolation** parameter, the site will not isolate users.

You can select a different isolation mode for each FTP site. For step-by-step instructions for configuring FTP User Isolation, see "Isolating FTP Users" in the IIS 6.0 Help.

 Important

After you set the FTP User Isolation mode and finish the FTP Site Creation Wizard or create the site using Iisftp.vbs, do not change the isolation setting manually.

Do Not Isolate Users Mode

The **Do not isolate users** mode does not enforce FTP User Isolation and is designed to work like earlier versions of the FTP service in IIS. Because isolation is not enforced among the different users that log on to your FTP server, this mode is ideal for a site that offers only download capabilities for shared content or for sites that do not require protection of data between users.

In this mode, all user directories are in one level as a subdirectory of the FTP site directory. The site directory can reside either on the local computer or on a network share. When a user accesses the FTP site, the home directory is determined as follows:

- By default, the initial user directory is set to the physical path configured as the FTP site directory. If this directory does not exist, the user connection is denied.

- If a user name is supplied, the home directory is derived from the user name. For anonymous users, the derived name is *anonymous*. For local computer users, the derived name is the user name. For domain users, the derived name is the user name without the domain name.

- If a directory with the derived name exists in the site directory, then that directory becomes the initial log-on directory for the user.

 Important

The user is not restricted to this subdirectory and can navigate up to the site directory and into other subdirectories unless you have set ACLs to prevent users from accessing them.

Isolate Users Mode

The **Isolate users** mode determines a unique home directory for each user derived from the user name. The home directory of the user is treated as a root directory for the user, and the user cannot navigate or access the physical file system outside of the root directory. If users need access to dedicated shared folders, then you can establish a virtual directory.

User home directories are located in a two-level directory structure under the FTP site directory. The site directory can reside either on the local computer or on a network share. When a user accesses the FTP site, the home directory is determined in one of three ways:

- For anonymous users, the home directory is **LocalUser\Public** under the FTP root directory.

- For local users, the home directory is **LocalUser***UserName* under the FTP root directory.

- For users that log on with *Domain\UserName*, the home directory is *Domain\UserName* under the FTP root directory.

The user home directory must be created before the user logs on. If the directory does not exist when the user attempts to connect, the connection is denied.

Important

You must be a member of the Administrators group on the local computer to perform the following procedure or procedures, or you must have been delegated the appropriate authority. As a security best practice, log on to your computer by using an account that is not in the Administrators group, and then use the **Run as** command to run IIS Manager as an administrator. At a command prompt, type **runas** /*User:Administrative_AccountName* "mmc %systemroot%\system32\inetsrv\iis.msc".

▷ **To create a new FTP site with Isolate users mode**

1. In IIS Manager, click the local computer, right-click the **FTP Sites** folder, point to **New**, and then click **FTP Site**.

2. In **Welcome to the FTP Site Creation Wizard**, click **Next**.

3. In **FTP Site Description**, type a description for the FTP site, and then click **Next**.

4. In **IP Address and Port Settings**, type an IP address and port number, and then click **Next**.

5. In FTP User Isolation, click Isolate users, and then click Next.

6. Follow the directions in the FTP Site Creation Wizard.

7. To complete the process of creating a new FTP site with **Isolate users** mode, do any of the following:

   - If anonymous access is allowed, create the subdirectories **LocalUser** and **LocalUser\Public** under the FTP site home directory.

   - If users of the local computer log on with their individual account user names (rather than as anonymous users), create the subdirectory **LocalUser** and a separate directory **LocalUser***UserName* under the FTP site home directory for each user allowed to connect to the FTP site.

- If users of different domains log on with their explicit *Domain\UserName* credentials, create a subdirectory for each domain (by using the name of the domain) under the FTP site root directory. Under each domain directory, create a directory for each user. For example, to support access by user Contoso\user1, create the Contoso and Contoso\user1 directories.

You can convert an existing FTP site to **Isolate users** mode after you upgrade to Windows Server 2003.

 To convert an existing FTP site to Isolate users mode

1. In IIS Manager, click the local computer, double-click the **FTP Sites** folder, right-click the FTP site that you want to convert, and then click **Stop**.

   > **⬥ Important**
   >
   > You must stop the FTP service because you need to move user directories to new locations.

2. If users log on to the FTP site with local machine accounts or if you allow anonymous access to the FTP site, complete the following steps:

   a. Under the FTP home directory, create a subdirectory named **LocalUser**.

   b. If you allow anonymous access to the site, create a subdirectory under **LocalUser** named **Public**. This will be the home directory for anonymous users.

   c. Move the content for the anonymous user from the existing location to the new **Public** subdirectory.

   d. For each FTP user with a local computer account, create a subdirectory under **LocalUser** with the user account name. Move content from existing user directories to these new directories.

3. If domain users access the site, complete all of the following steps:

   a. Create a subdirectory under the FTP home directory for each domain for which users are accessing the site. The subdirectories must be named by the domain names.

   b. For each user, create a subdirectory under the corresponding domain-named subdirectory, and move existing content into the new subdirectories.

4. To finish the conversion, do one of the following:

- Use the FTP Site Creation Wizard to create a new FTP site, and point the site path to the FTP home directory (recommended).

- Edit the metabase, set the **UserIsolationMode** property to **1** for the site and the path in the corresponding **/Root** virtual root section to the new site home directory.

Important

Before you edit the metabase, verify that you have a backup copy that you can restore if a problem occurs. For information about how to do this, see "Working with the Metabase" in this book.

5. In IIS Manager, click the local computer, double-click the **FTP Sites** folder, right-click the converted FTP site, and then click **Start**.

Isolate Users Using Active Directory Mode

In the **Isolate users using Active Directory** mode, the FTP service is integrated with Active Directory to retrieve home directory information for users. To accomplish this integration, the Active Directory user object is extended with two properties: **msIIS-FTPRoot** and **msIIS-FTPDir**. The **msIIS-FTPRoot** property stores the file server share, and the **msIIS-FTPDir** property stores the relative physical path to the home directory for each user. You can use Iisftp.vbs to get and set these properties.

Information that is frequently retrieved from Active Directory is cached by the FTP service. The default caching interval is 10 minutes. You can adjust the caching interval by editing the registry entry **DsCacheRefreshSecs**.

Caution

Do not edit the registry unless you have no alternative. The registry editor bypasses standard safeguards, allowing settings that can damage your system or even require you to reinstall Windows. If you must edit the registry, back it up first and see the Registry Reference on the *Microsoft® Windows® Server 2003 Resource Kit* companion CD or at http://www.microsoft.com/reskit.

If the FTP service successfully accesses the path, it becomes the home directory for the user. The user cannot access the file system outside this directory. The user is denied access if either the **msIIS-FTPRoot** or **msIIS-FTPDir** property does not exist, or if the resulting home directory cannot be accessed.

This configuration option provides maximum flexibility and control over user home directories in an ISP environment. For example, John Doe connects to his FTP site at ftp.example.com. The example.com network load-balancing server (NLBS) resolves this request to the server FTPS3. John Doe enters the user name JohnDoe. FTPS3 is configured with the default domain name Domain4, so the user Domain4\JohnDoe is authenticated and the home directory information for John Doe is retrieved from Active Directory as \\FS1\Share2\Users\u2\johndoe_dir. From now on, FTPS3 will access the data under this home directory for all the FTP requests from John Doe. This example is illustrated in Figure 8.1.

Figure 8.1   FTP User Isolation Example: Isolate Users by Using Active Directory Mode

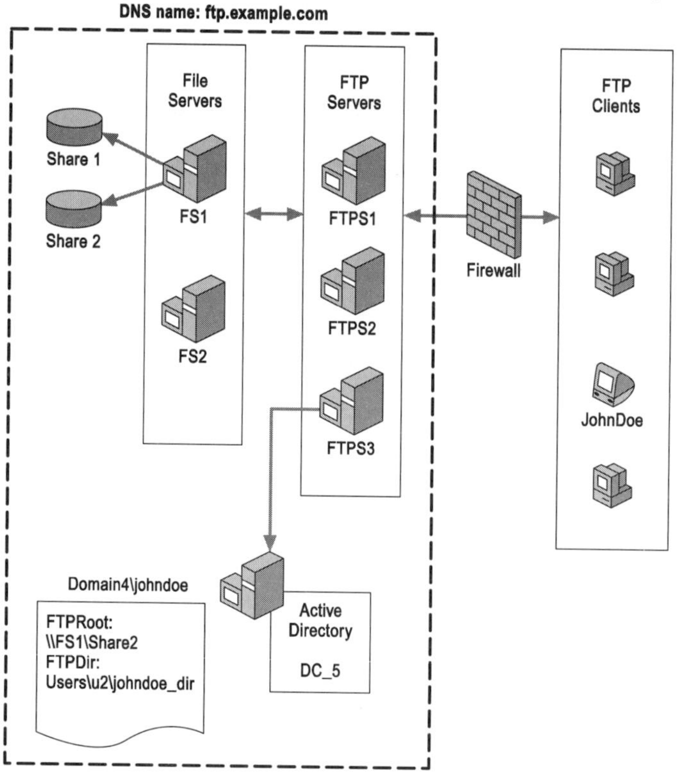

User Home Directories

In the **Isolate users using Active Directory** mode, each user's home directory resides on an arbitrary network path, which provides you with the flexibility to distribute user home directories across multiple servers, volumes, and directories. In addition, you can move users' home directories transparently from one location to another, which affects the service for the users only during the duration of the move. You can also set the **msIIS-FTPRoot** and **msIIS-FTPDir** properties so that the user's home directory maps to a local folder on the FTP server; for example, **msIIS-FTPRoot** is set to **E:\FTPUsers**.

Configuring Isolate Users Using Active Directory Mode

There are three main steps to configuring the **Isolate users using Active Directory** mode:

- Configure the file servers.

- Configure Active Directory.

- Create and configure the FTP sites to be isolated.

When you configure the file servers, you must create the shares and user directories for all the users that are permitted to connect to the FTP service, including the user configured to impersonate anonymous users. Before you complete this step, consider factors such as expected disk space usage, storage management, and network traffic.

To configure Active Directory, you need a server running Windows Server 2003, Standard Edition, and Active Directory. Configure the user object in Active Directory for each user, including the user configured to impersonate the anonymous user, by setting the **msIIS-FTPRoot** and **msIIS-FTPDir** properties to point to the home directories that you previously created. You can do this by using the Iisftp.vbs command-line utility with the **/SetADProp** command. To learn more about setting up Active Directory, see "Active Directory" in Help and Support Center for Windows Server 2003.

▶ **To create FTP sites with Isolate users using Active Directory mode**

1. In IIS Manager, click the local computer, right-click the **FTP Sites** folder, point to **New**, and click **FTP Site**.

2. In the **Welcome to the FTP Site Creation Wizard**, click **Next**.

3. In **FTP Site Description**, type a description for the FTP site, and then click **Next**.

4. In **IP Address and Port Settings**, type an IP address and port, and then click **Next**.

5. In **FTP User Isolation**, click **Isolate users using Active Directory**, and then click **Next**.

6. In the **User name** text box, type the user name, using the *Domain\User* format. Choose a user with minimal domain privileges. This user name is used to access Active Directory and read the home directory properties.

7. In the **Password** text box, type the password of the user.

8. In the **Enter the default Active Directory domain** text box, type the default domain name.

   This domain name is used for the users who do not specify their user domain when they log on. In other words, a user connecting with the user name Domain1\User1 is authenticated against Domain1, while a user connecting as User2 is authenticated against the default logon domain. If a default domain is not named and a user does not specify a domain name, access is denied for all but anonymous users. Type the base domain name only, not the fully qualified name. For example, type **MyDomain**, not **MyDomain.dept.microsoft.com**.

9. Click **Next**. You are prompted to re-enter the password for the user entered in the previous steps.

10. Follow the directions to complete the wizard.

By default, anonymous access is disabled to sites created in this isolation mode.

▷ **To enable anonymous access for the FTP site configured with Isolate users using Active Directory mode**

1. Configure the metabase properties as shown in the following example. You can do so by using the adsutil.vbs SET command-line tool.

   - adsutil set /msftpsvc/6634/AllowAnonymous "TRUE"

   - adsutil set /msftpsvc/6634/AnonymousOnly "FALSE"

   - adsutil set /msftpsvc/6634/AnonymousUserName "MyDomain\LowPrivUser"

   - adsutil set /msftpsvc/6634/AnonymousUserPass "PaSsWoRd"

> ☑ | **Note**
>
> When a site is created with Isolate Users Using Active Directory mode, the **Path** property of the root FTP virtual directory (which, for the other isolation modes identifies the home directory) is set to " ", or empty. Also, the **AccessFlags** property of the root FTP virtual directory contains the **AccessNoPhysicalDir** flag. Do not alter these two values. If you change or remove them, further access to the site is not allowed.

You can convert an existing FTP site to **Isolate users using Active Directory** mode after you upgrade to Windows Server 2003. Before you convert an existing FTP site to the **Isolate users using Active Directory** mode, complete the following procedure.

▷ **To prepare to convert an existing FTP site to Isolate users using Active Directory mode**

1. Plan user distribution over your network file server resources.

2. Create server shares and user directories for all users that have access to FTP.

3. Make sure to create a directory for anonymous access (if you want to enable anonymous user connections).

4. For each user, set the **msIIS-FTPRoot** and **msIIS-FTPDir** properties in Active Directory to point to the new home directory using Iisftp.vbs, by typing the following at the command line:

   Iisftp.vbs /SetADProp *UserName* **FTPRoot** *Server\Share*

   Iisftp.vbs /SetADProp *UserName* **FTPDir** *Directory*

   For complete Iisftp.vbs syntax, see "Setting Active Directory User Isolation" in IIS 6.0 Help, or type **Iisftp.vbs /SetADProp /?** at the command prompt.

▷ **To convert an existing FTP site to Isolate users using Active Directory mode**

1. In IIS Manager, click the local computer, double-click the **FTP Sites** folder, right-click the FTP site that you want to convert, and then click **Stop**.

2. Move existing user content into the new directories.

3. Complete the conversion by doing one of the following:

   - Use the FTP Site Creation Wizard to create a new FTP site (recommended).

- Edit the metabase directory or use adsutil.vbs to configure the following metabase properties:

  o **UserIsolationMode**: Set to **2**.

  o **ADConnectionUserName**: Set to a user that has permission to read Active Directory properties. Use *Domain\UserName* format.

  o **ADConnectionPassword**: Set to the password for the user in **ADConnectionUserName**.

  o **DefaultLogonDomain**: Set to the default domain name.

  o For the site root virtual directory: Set the **Path** property to an empty string, and add the value **AccessNoPhysicalDir** to the **AccessFlags** property, using the | operator; for example: **AccessFlags = AccessRead | AccessNoPhysicalDir**.

  o **AllowAnonymous**, **AnonymousUserName**, and **AnonymousPassword**: See "To enable anonymous access for the Isolate Users Using Active Directory FTP site" earlier in this chapter for information on how to set these properties.

Important

Before you edit the metabase, verify that you have a backup copy that you can restore if a problem occurs. For information about how to do this, see "Working with the Metabase" in this book.

4. In IIS Manager, click the local computer, double-click the **FTP Sites** folder, right-click the converted FTP site, and then click **Start**.

Configuring the NNTP Service

The IIS NNTP service enables you to create a news server to host discussion groups. NNTP is the protocol for distributing, posting, and retrieving news items between a news server and client.

You can use the NNTP service to host local discussion groups, called *newsgroups*, on a single computer. For example, you can create departmental newsgroups where company department members can discuss projects and issues. Or you can create a newsgroup and allow customers to access it over the Internet for technical or customer support. Because the NNTP service is in complete compliance with the NNTP protocol, users can use any newsreader client, such as the Microsoft® Outlook® Express messaging and collaboration client, to participate in newsgroup discussions.

You can also configure the NNTP service for *newsfeeds*. Newsfeeds enable users of different newsgroups to read and post articles to other newsgroups, as if the users were using a single group. An article that is posted to one newsgroup gets sent to other newsgroups, where it can be read.

The NNTP service is hosted by Inetinfo.exe. Clients connect to the NNTP service through TCP port 119 by default. If you enable encrypted SSL connections, the default port is 563.

Installing the NNTP Service and Setting Up NNTP Virtual Servers

The NNTP service is not installed by default. You must install the NNTP service using Control Panel, which creates a default NNTP configuration that you can customize using IIS Manager. For step-by-step instructions for installing the NNTP service, see "NNTP Server Setup" in IIS 6.0 Help.

The NNTP service stores newsgroup articles on virtual servers with one or more directory hierarchies. Each virtual server has its own virtual directory or directories, which contain newsgroup articles, or messages, stored as files. In addition, the NNTP service involves other file types, which include internal files as well as the public newsgroup message files. When you install the NNTP service, a default NNTP virtual server configuration is created with a message store in *SystemDrive*:\Inetpub\Nntpfile\Root.

Virtual Servers

You can have multiple NNTP virtual servers running on IIS. Each virtual server has its own properties, expiration policies, and virtual directories. Create as many NNTP virtual servers as you need. Consider creating multiple virtual servers to host different types of newsgroups on the same server. For example, you might want to host internal departmental newsgroups on the same server with Internet-based customer service newsgroups. Because those newsgroups will have different settings, it is easiest to set them up on different virtual servers. However, if you have many different departmental newsgroups that have the same property settings, consider hosting all of them on the same virtual server.

Each virtual server should have a unique IP address/TCP port combination. Although it is possible to host multiple NNTP virtual servers on a single IP address by using a different TCP port for each one, this configuration is not recommended because users will have to configure their client software specifically to use the nonstandard TCP port.

File and Message Types

The NNTP service involves several file and message types, including:

- **Message files**. Message files are messages that are posted to newsgroups, receive an .nws extension, and are stored in the directory that the NNTP service creates for them.

- **Internal files**. Users never see or use internal files, which are files that the NNTP service creates that list the subjects of the stored articles. These internal files have an .xix extension, and the NNTP service creates one subject file for every 128 articles in a newsgroup. The NNTP service also uses .tag files to mark folders as newsgroups or virtual roots. In addition, the NNTP service maintains a number of internal data structure files with .hsh, .hdr, .lst, and .txt extensions. These files are essential for the NNTP service; do not delete them. If you accidentally delete the internal files or if they become corrupted, you can restore them by rebuilding the NNTP service. For more information about rebuilding the NNTP service, see "Rebuilding the NNTP Service" later in this chapter.

- **Control messages**. Control messages are specially formatted messages that direct the NNTP service to delete a specific article from a newsgroup or to add or delete an entire newsgroup. Control messages are stored in directories that the NNTP service creates. For more information about control messages, see "Using Control Messages" later in this chapter.

When you create an NNTP virtual server, you are prompted to enter two directory paths: a path for internal files and a path for newsgroup message files. If possible, put these two paths on different disk partitions because the internal files can be corrupted if the disk partition runs out of disk space. Also, if you expect a high volume of traffic on your NNTP virtual server, you can place the files on a drive in a redundant array of independent disks (RAID) to improve performance.

Virtual Directories

A virtual directory is a directory on a local or remote disk drive that acts as the root of a part of the newsgroup hierarchy. Virtual directories enable you to store newsgroup files on multiple disk drives. Using more than one disk drive can improve the performance of a heavily used disk drive and can provide more storage. Virtual directories also enable you to change the physical location of the directory without changing the name of the newsgroup.

Virtual directories can be located on a local disk drive or on a network drive. However, if you store content in a remote location, then you must configure the remote computer with at least Read and Write permissions for the user name that you provide. Make sure that the remote location is secure and maintained by a trusted administrator. There is no advantage to creating a virtual directory on the same physical drive as the home directory. For step-by-step instructions for creating virtual directories, see "Creating Virtual Directories" in IIS 6.0 Help.

Configuring NNTP Virtual Server Properties

The **NNTP virtual server properties** dialog box in IIS Manager allows you to configure many different settings for your virtual server, including access control, logging, newsgroup limits, and security. Use the **General** tab to set the IP address and, optionally, the port number for the NNTP virtual server. You can also set connection limits and time-outs, specify a path header, and enable logging. Auditing server activity with log files is a good way to detect if unauthorized external users are attempting to access your virtual server or if internal users are trying to access resources that they do not have authority to access. Use the **Settings** tab for management tasks, such as enabling moderated newsgroups and control messages. For more information, see "Creating and Managing Newsgroups" later in this chapter. Use the **Access**, **Settings**, and **Security** tabs to configure security-related settings. For more information about setting properties that affect security, see "Securing NNTP Virtual Servers" later in this chapter.

For a detailed description of each property on every **Properties** tab and for more information about logging, see "Configuring NNTP Virtual Servers" in IIS 6.0 Help.

Securing NNTP Virtual Servers

By configuring the properties of your NNTP virtual server correctly, you can increase the security of your NNTP server and your network. The **Access**, **Settings**, and **Security** tabs each have security-related properties that you can use to configure access-related settings, set post and connection limits, and assign administrative credentials. You can also increase security through the use of access control lists (ACLs).

Configuring Access-Related Settings

The **Access** tab has three important security-related settings: Authentication, Certificate, and Connection.

Authentication

The Authentication option allows you to select from the following authentication methods for newsgroup users:

Anonymous access. Anonymous access is enabled by default. If you do not disable Anonymous access, everyone is able to access all of the newsgroups on this virtual server.

- **Basic authentication**. If you enable Basic authentication and you disable anonymous access, users must enter a valid Windows user name and an authorized password to access the newsgroup. However, those credentials are not encrypted when they are sent across the network (credentials are sent in plaintext). Basic authentication leaves your server vulnerable to a dictionary attack. Use this option only if your newsgroups are internal.

- **Integrated Windows authentication**. If you enable Integrated Windows authentication and you disable anonymous access, users must enter a valid Windows user name and an authorized password to access the newsgroup, and those credentials are encrypted when they are sent over the network. Integrated Windows authentication can also leave your Web server vulnerable to a dictionary attack. Outlook Express supports this protocol.

- **SSL client authentication**. SSL provides a secure, encrypted connection between the NNTP service and the client. SSL support requires that an SSL certificate is installed on the computer running Windows Server 2003 and that the client software supports SSL. (Outlook Express supports SSL.) If a server certificate is installed, then the NNTP service uses SSL whenever a client requests it. You have the option to require SSL for all newsgroups or for newsgroups located in a virtual directory.

Certificate

The Certificate option starts the Web Server Certificate Wizard, which you can use to create and administer server certificates used in secure Web communications, such as those that require SSL.

Connection

The Connection option allows you to restrict access to the virtual server based on the IP address of the client. By default, all IP addresses have access to the NNTP service. You can either allow or deny access to a specific list of IP addresses, and you can specify the IP addresses individually or as a group using a subnet mask. You can also specify IP addresses using a domain name, but doing so adds the overhead of a DNS lookup for each connection. For more information about domain names and DNS, see "DNS Overview" earlier in this chapter.

Setting Post and Connection Limits

There are several options on the **Settings** tab that affect the security of your NNTP virtual server. You can set the post size, in kilobytes, of the largest single article a user can post. You can also set the connection size, in megabytes, of the maximum amount of data that a user can post to a newsgroup during a connection. When you set limits on the size of posts and connections, you help prevent a malicious individual from trying to overload your server resources by posting extremely large articles.

Assigning Administrative Credentials

You can use the **Security** tab to grant administrative credentials to Windows user accounts. By default, the Windows Administrator account is granted administrative credentials. For more information about security and access control, see "Managing a Secure IIS 6.0 Solution" in this book.

Creating ACLs

After you set the authentication requirements for your virtual server, you can further restrict access to newsgroups with ACLs. For example, in the case of departmental newsgroups, ACLs can prevent non-executives from reading the executive newsgroup. You can control access to individual newsgroups or sets of newsgroups by assigning permissions on your computer running Windows Server 2003 for the directories that contain those newsgroups. You can set permissions for an individual directory or for a set of directories. For more information about ACLs, see "Access control" in Help and Support Center for Windows Server 2003.

Creating and Managing Newsgroups

A *newsgroup* is the organizational structure for a group of related news articles. For example, if you are creating departmental newsgroups, then you can create the accounting, human resources, and executive newsgroups. If you expect a lot of newsgroup activity, then you can break down the newsgroups into narrower categories. However, because articles within each newsgroup are organized by subject, you do not need to create a separate newsgroup for each subject.

Creating Newsgroups

There are three ways to create a newsgroup:

- Use the New Newsgroup Wizard in IIS Manager. For step-by-step instructions for creating a newsgroup with the wizard, see "Creating Newsgroups" in IIS 6.0 Help.

- Use the Rgroup.vbs command-line script.

- Use a control message. For more information about using control messages, see "Using Control Messages" later in this chapter.

When you create a newsgroup, the NNTP service creates the directory for the newsgroup automatically.

Creating Newsgroups Using Rgroup.vbs

You can use Rgroup.vbs to create newsgroups. You can also use Rgroup.vbs to delete and modify newsgroups. Table 8.1 lists and describes the parameters that you can use with Rgroup.vbs.

 Important

You must be a member of the Administrators group on the local computer to run scripts and executables, or you must have been delegated the appropriate authority. As a security best practice, log on to your computer by using an account that is not in the Administrators group, and then use the **Run as** command to run your script or executable as an administrator. At a command prompt, type **runas /profile** /*User:MyMachine\Administrator* **cmd** to open a command window with administrator rights and then type **cscript.exe** *ScriptName* (including the full path with parameters, if any).

Table 8.1   Rgroup.vbs Parameters

Parameter	Description
-t *Operation*, where *Operation* is one of the following arguments: ■ f ■ a ■ d ■ g ■ l	Finds a group. Adds a group. Deletes a group. Gets the properties of a newsgroup. Loads newsgroups from an active file.
-s *Server*	Specifies the name of the server that is affected by this change.
-v *VirtualServerID*	Specifies the ID of the virtual server.
-c *CreationDate*	Specifies the date on which the newsgroup is created.
-g *Group*	Specifies the group to be modified or deleted. The wildcard character (*) can be used during searches (**Rgroup.vbs –t f**).
-n *NumberOfResults*	Specifies the maximum number of newsgroups to return for a search (required with **Rgroup.vbs –t f**).
-m *Moderator*	Specifies the full e-mail address of the moderator.
-d *Description*	Provides a description of the newsgroup.
-p *Description*	Specifies the response to the **List PrettyNames** command.
-r true | false	Indicates whether the newsgroup is read-only.
-u true | false	Indicates whether the group is moderated by the default moderator.
-a *FileName*	Specifies the names of the active file.

Table 8.2 lists examples of how to use Rgroup.vbs.

Table 8.2   Rgroup.vbs Script Examples

Command-line Script	Function
Rgroup.vbs -t f -g alt.*	Finds all newsgroups beginning with *alt.*
Rgroup.vbs -t d -g my.old.group	Deletes the newsgroup my.old.group.
Rgroup.vbs -t a -g my.new.group	Adds the newsgroup my.new.group.

Moderating Newsgroups

If you want to control which articles are posted to a newsgroup or if you want to designate someone to control the articles, then create a moderated newsgroup. Articles submitted to a moderated newsgroup are not posted until they are approved by the moderator that you choose for that newsgroup. The moderator can filter inappropriate material and can detect if someone is trying to compromise information on the server or the server itself. To use moderated newsgroups, you must specify either an SMTP mail server to send articles directly to the moderator or a directory where the articles are stored for the moderator.

When a user submits an article to a moderated newsgroup, the NNTP service sends the article to the newsgroup moderator. The moderator can either approve the article and send it back to the NNTP service to be posted or discard the article. For discarded articles, the moderator can send a message to the author of the article to explain why the article was rejected. Any NNTP client can be used to post messages to a moderated newsgroup. However, the moderator needs to use an NNTP client that supports moderating functions.

Alternatively, you can specify a default moderator domain. If you choose to use the default moderator for a newsgroup, articles are sent to *Newsgroup_Name@DefaultDomain*, where *Newsgroup_Name* is the name of the newsgroup. (The periods are replaced by underscores.) For example, articles posted to the newsgroup rec.sports.tennis, with a default domain of contoso.com, are sent to rec_sports_tennis@contoso.com.

Use the **Settings** tab in the **NNTP virtual server properties** dialog box to enable moderated newsgroups. For step-by-step instructions for enabling and setting up moderated newsgroups, see "Moderating Newsgroups" in IIS 6.0 Help.

Managing Newsgroup Messages

You can set expiration policies to delete newsgroup messages automatically after a certain period of time. You can also delete messages that are no longer needed.

Setting Expiration Policies

You can specify how long articles are kept in an NNTP service newsgroup by defining expiration policies. An expiration policy can apply to a single newsgroup or to any number of newsgroups. You can define as many policies as you need. In each case, the oldest articles are deleted first.

If you are hosting a newsgroup that is intended for internal project tracking or to record organizational information, then do not set an expiration policy. Manually delete and save articles. If you are hosting a busy newsgroup that receives many articles, set a short expiration policy to avoid overloading your server resources.

If you do not specify an expiration policy for a newsgroup, then delete articles manually when they are no longer needed. You can set and modify expiration policies using IIS Manager, or you can use Rexpire.vbs. To set expiration policies in IIS Manager, right-click **Expiration Policies**, point to **New**, and click **Expiration Policy**.

Setting Expiration Policies Using Rexpire.vbs

You can use Rexpire.vbs to set expiration policies. You can also use this command to delete and modify expiration policies. Table 8.3 lists and describes the parameters you can use with Rexpire.vbs.

Table 8.3 Rexpire.vbs Parameters

Parameter	Description
-t *Operation*, where *Operation* is one of the following arguments:	
▪ a	Adds the expiration policy.
▪ d	Deletes the expiration policy.
▪ g	Gets the expiration policy.
▪ s	Sets the expiration policy.
▪ e	Enumerates the expiration policies.
-s *Server*	Specifies the name of the server to be configured.
-v *VirtualServerID*	Specifies the ID of the virtual server.
-i *ExpireID*	Specifies the ID of the expiration policy.
-h *ExpireTime*	Specifies the number of hours until articles are discarded.
-d *MegabytesExpireSize*	Specifies the limit, in megabytes, of the size of the data in the virtual directory at which articles begin to be deleted. The default is 500 MB.
-n *Newsgroups*	Specifies the newsgroups to which the command is applied. NOTE: You can use strings that contain the wildcard character (*).
-p *PolicyName*	Specifies the name of the expiration policy.
o- **true	false**	Indicates whether this is a one-time expiration policy.

Table 8.4 lists examples of how you can use Rexpire.vbs.

Table 8.4   Rexpire.vbs Script Examples

Command Script	Function
Rexpire.vbs -t e -v 1	Enumerates the expiration policies for NNTP site 1.
Rexpire.vbs -t a -n alt.binaries.* -h 24	Creates an expiration policy that expires articles on alt.binaries that are older than 24 hours.
Rexpire.vbs -t s -i 1 -h 24	Sets policy 1, which expires any articles older than 24 hours.
Rexpire.vbs -t d -i 1	Deletes expiration policy 1.

Deleting Messages Using Rcancel.vbs

You cannot delete messages in IIS Manager, but you can delete messages using Rcancel.vbs or control messages. For more information about control messages, see "Using Control Messages" later in this chapter.

Table 8.5 lists and describes the parameters you can use with Rcancel.vbs. You must supply the message ID to cancel the message.

Table 8.5   Rcancel.vbs Parameters

Parameter	Description
-m *MessageID*	Specifies the ID of message to cancel.
-s *Server*	Specifies the computer to configure.
-l *VirtualServerID*	Specifies the ID of the virtual server.

The following example shows how you would use Rcancel.vbs:

```
rcancel.vbs -m "<uqjWStxCBHA.1240@example.microsoft.com>"
```

Limiting Newsgroup Enumeration

If you host many newsgroups on one server, then you might want to limit or filter the newsgroups that are displayed in IIS Manager. You can specify how many newsgroups to display, or you can filter the display to show only newsgroups of a certain type. For example, if you have many different departmental newsgroups that are broken down into subgroups, then you might want to filter the display to show only the top-level departmental newsgroups. To limit or filter newsgroup enumeration, in IIS Manager, right-click **Newsgroups**, and then click **Limit groups enumeration**. For more information, see "Limiting Newsgroup Enumeration" in IIS 6.0 Help.

Managing Sessions

There might be times when you need to manage or monitor sessions as an administrator. You can terminate a session or all current sessions, or you can enumerate users. For example, if a specific user is posting inappropriate messages to an unmoderated newsgroup, you can terminate the session for that user.

You can manage sessions in IIS Manager or by using the Rsess.vbs command-line script. To manage sessions in IIS Manager, right-click the session, and then click the appropriate action.

Managing Sessions Using Rsess.vbs

Table 8.6 lists and describes the parameters that you can use with Rsess.vbs.

Table 8.6   Rsess.vbs Parameters

Parameter	Description
-t *Operation*, where *Operation* is one of the following arguments: ■ e ■ d ■ a	Enumerates current sessions. Deletes the session. (You must also specify -u *UserName* or -I *IPAddress*.) Deletes all sessions and terminates the client connection.
-u *UserName*	Specifies the user name to delete.
-i *IPAddress*	Specifies the IP or host name to delete.
-s *Server*	Specifies the name of the server to configure.
-v *VirtualServerID*	Specifies the ID of the virtual server (an integer).

Table 8.7 lists examples of how you can use Rsess.vbs.

Table 8.7   Rsess.vbs Script Examples

Command Script	Function
`Rsess.vbs -t e -v 1`	Lists the current sessions for NNTP site 1.
`Rsess.vbs -t d -u john_doe`	Terminates the session for the user john_doe.
`Rsess.vbs -t a`	Terminates all sessions.

 Note

Rsess.vbs -t e returns a list of the local feed (that is, the inbound push feed) as an anonymous connection.

Using Control Messages

Control messages are specially formatted newsgroup messages that can create newsgroups, delete newsgroups, and delete posts. You can enable or disable control messages for newsgroups and for newsfeeds. If you enable control messages, then they are enabled for every user. If you want to restrict access to control messages to administrators only, then set appropriate ACLs for the control groups and enable either Basic authentication or Integrated Windows authentication.

In IIS Manager, use the **Settings** tab in the **NNTP virtual server properties** dialog box to enable or disable control messages for newsgroups. Use the Rfeed.vbs command-line script to enable or disable control messages for newsfeeds. Control messages are disabled by default in IIS 6.0. However, if you have upgraded from the Microsoft® Windows® 2000 operating system and you enabled control messages in that operating system, control messages are enabled in IIS 6.0.

Generating Control Messages

Control messages are generated automatically by NNTP client software, NNTP servers, and special utility programs. You can also generate control messages manually by connecting to the NNTP server using Telnet and entering the control messages directly.

The NNTP service accepts the following basic control messages:

Cancel   Deletes a specified article.

Newgroup   Creates a newsgroup.

Rmgroup   Deletes an existing newsgroup.

The Cancel control message is generated by client programs. The Newgroup and Rmgroup messages are typically generated by NNTP servers.

Control messages look like other newsgroup messages, but control messages have the following headers:

From   The name of the user or service from which this message originated.

Subject   A description of the subject.

Newsgroups   The name of the newsgroup affected by the control message, such as control.cancel|newgroup|rmgroup or any other valid newsgroup.

Approved   The user or administrator who created the message. If the newsgroup is moderated, the name of the moderator must appear. If the group is not moderated, any name can be used.

Control   The control header. Control messages must contain one of the following control headers:

- **newgroup** *<name of new group>*. Creates a new group, for example, `newgroup Test.One`.

- **rmgroup** *<name of group to delete>*. Deletes an existing newsgroup, for example, `rmgroup Test.One`.

- **cancel** *<MessageID>*. Deletes the message that is referenced by the message ID, for example, `cancel <BMO2mVOECHA.2772@server.domain.microsoft.com>`.

A blank line separates the headers from the message body. The message body can contain any text, or it can be blank. The following appears at the end of the control message:

`{CRLF}.{CRLF}`

Restricting Access to Control Messages

When the NNTP service receives Cancel, Newgroup, and Rmgroup control messages, it posts them into the following newsgroups, respectively: control.cancel, control.newgroup, and control.rmgroup. These newsgroups are created automatically. Control messages are sent to the control newsgroups regardless of where they were originally posted. The NNTP service also automatically creates a control virtual directory.

Restrict access to control messages to prevent unauthorized users from changing your newsgroups or deleting messages. You can restrict access by configuring the control newsgroups as moderated newsgroups or by restricting access to a limited group of users. For more information about moderating and restricting access, see "Moderating Newsgroups" and "Configuring NNTP Virtual Server Properties " earlier in this chapter.

In addition, any ACLs that you have in place for your existing newsgroups apply to control messages. For example, if you have a newsgroup named Microsoft.Software and you have secured the \Inetpub\Nntpfile\Root\Microsoft\Software directory with ACLs that restrict anonymous users from creating subfolders, then when an anonymous user posts a newsgroup control message in Microsoft.Software, the control message is not processed.

Rebuilding the NNTP Service

You can fix several common problems with the NNTP service by rebuilding it. Rebuild the NNTP service when:

- The virtual server does not start.
- You delete internal newsgroup files accidentally.
- You recover the system after a disk failure occurs.
- Users cannot gain access to articles that they are authorized to read.
- An error message that is written to the Event Viewer system log tells you to rebuild the server.

You can rebuild the IIS NNTP service by using IIS Manager.

You can choose one of two rebuild types:

- **Standard**. Rebuilds only group.lst files, based on the contents of the virtual directories. This is the faster of the two options.
- **Thorough**. Rebuilds all internal files, such as .hsh and .lst files.

First run the standard rebuild. If the problem is not fixed when you run the standard rebuild, run a thorough rebuild.

 Note

You must stop the NNTP service news server before you can rebuild it.

▶ **To rebuild the NNTP service by using IIS Manager**

1. In IIS Manager, click the local computer, right-click the NNTP virtual server, and then click **Stop**.

2. Right-click the NNTP virtual server again, point to **All Tasks**, and then click **Rebuild Server**. If **Rebuild Server** is not available, then the server might still be running. Check to make sure that it is stopped.

3. In the **Rebuild NNTP Virtual Server** dialog box, do one of the following:
   - To run a standard rebuild, in **Rebuild type**, move the slider to **Standard**, and then click **Start**.
   - To run a thorough rebuild, in **Rebuild type**, move the slider to **Thorough**, and then click **Start**.

Backing Up and Restoring an NNTP Virtual Server

You can back up your locally hosted NNTP virtual servers so that you can restore them in case of a serious system failure.

To back up an NNTP virtual server, use the **ntbackup** command or the Backup or Restore wizard to back up everything under *LocalDrive*:\Inetpub\Nntpfile. For more information about backing up and restoring Windows Server 2003–based files and directories, see "Backing up and restoring data" in Help and Support Center for Windows Server 2003.

Enabling and Managing Newsfeeds

Newsfeeds send articles between the IIS NNTP service and other NNTP servers. With newsfeeds, the articles that are posted to one server can be read by users of the other servers. There are several different kinds of newsfeeds:

Usenet   Usenet is a network of NNTP servers that share thousands of newsgroups throughout the world. The articles that are posted to a newsgroup on an NNTP-based server that participates in Usenet are shared with all the other NNTP-based servers that subscribe to that newsgroup.

You can create an external newsfeed to Usenet to enable users of your news site to access the articles that are posted to any Usenet news site. A Usenet provider uses one or more NNTP servers to push new articles to the NNTP service. The NNTP service pushes the articles that are posted by your users to your Usenet provider.

Peer newsfeed   If your organization has more than one news site, you can share articles between the sites. A peer newsfeed is ideal for private newsgroups that are not appropriate for public distribution on Usenet.

Master/slave newsfeed   If the volume of traffic on your news site exceeds the capacity of a single computer, you can use multiple computers and share articles among them. A single master news site pushes articles to and from multiple subordinate sites. All clients connect to the subordinate sites.

The master site controls the article numbers and keeps all the subordinate sites synchronized. Because all the subordinate sites have the same data, a master/slave newsfeed also provides a backup in case one of the computers fails.

Enabling Newsfeeds

Newsfeeds are not enabled by default.

▷ **To enable newsfeeds**

1. In IIS Manager, click the local computer, right-click the NNTP virtual server, and then click **Properties**.

2. Click the **Settings** tab, select the **Allow feed posting** check box, and then do any of the following:

   - To limit the size of articles posted to this news site, select the **Limit post size (KB)** check box, and type or select the size (1 to 32,000 kilobytes) of the largest article that is accepted.

   - To limit the size of a newsfeed, select the **Limit connection size (MB)** check box, and type or select the size (1 to 4000 megabytes) of the largest newsfeed to accept.

   - To allow servers to pull articles from this news site, select the **Allow servers to pull news articles from this server** check box.

Adding, Deleting, and Modifying Newsfeeds

Use Rfeed.vbs to add, delete, and modify newsfeeds. Table 8.8 lists and describes the parameters that you can use with Rfeed.vbs.

Table 8.8   Rfeed.vbs Parameters

Parameter	Description
-t *Operation*, where *Operation* is one of the following: ▪ a ▪ d ▪ g ▪ s ▪ e	 Adds a feed. Deletes a feed. Gets information about a feed. Sets feed information. Enumerates feeds.
-s *Server*	Specifies the computer name of the server to configure.
-v *VirtualServerID*	Specifies the ID of the virtual server.
-f peer | master | slave	Indicates the feed type.
-r *FeedServer*	Specifies the server that you push newsfeeds to or pull newsfeeds from.

(continued)

Table 8.8   Rfeed.vbs Parameters *(continued)*

Parameter	Description
-u *UucpName*	Specifies the name that you put in the path header. (The default is the host name of the server.)
-a *AuthInfoAccount*	Specifies the user name to use when you connect.
-b *AuthInfoPassword*	Specifies the password to use when you connect.
-i *FeedID*	Specifies the ID of the specified feed.
Parameters for inbound feed settings: ▪ -ia pull | accept | none ▪ -in NewsgroupPatterns ▪ -ix *#Minutes* ▪ -iz true | false ▪ -im *#Connections* ▪ -io *Date* ▪ -ic true | false ▪ -ip *PortNumber* ▪ -it *Directory*	Indicates whether to enable or disable pull feeds. Specifies newsgroup patterns. Specifies the amount of time (in minutes) between feed runs. Indicates whether to process control messages. Specifies the maximum number of connection attempts that are allowed. Gets articles after this date (pull feed only). Indicates whether to create newsgroups automatically during pull feeds. Specifies the outbound IP port for pull feeds. Specifies the temporary files directory.
Parameters for outbound feed settings: ▪ -oa push | none ▪ -on Patterns ▪ -ox *#Minutes* ▪ -oz true | false ▪ -om *#Connections* ▪ -op *PortNumber* ▪ -ot *Directory*	Indicates whether to enable a push feed. Specifies newsgroup patterns. Specifies the amount of time (in minutes) between feed runs. Indicates whether to process control messages. Specifies the maximum number of connection attempts allowed. Specifies the outbound IP port for push feeds. Specifies the temporary files directory.

Table 8.9 lists examples of how you can use Rfeed.vbs.

Table 8.9   Rfeed.vbs Script Examples

Command Script	Function
Rfeed.vbs -t e	Enumerates feeds.
Rfeed.vbs -t a -r FeedServer.microsoft.com -f peer -ia pull -in *	Adds a pull feed from peer server FeedServer.microsoft.com, from which the articles from all the newsgroups are to be pulled.
Rfeed.vbs -t d -i 1	Deletes feed 1.
Rfeed.vbs -t -s -i 1 -ix 120	Sets the wait time between feed runs to 120 minutes.

Configuring the SMTP Service

The IIS SMTP service is a simple component for delivering and receiving e-mail messages. A message is transferred to a designated SMTP server to initiate the delivery. The originating SMTP server initiates communications with a DNS server, based on the domain name of the recipient e-mail address. The DNS server looks up and then returns the host name of the destination SMTP server for that domain.

Next, the originating SMTP server communicates with the destination SMTP server directly through TCP/IP port 25. If the user name of the recipient e-mail address matches one of the authorized user accounts on the destination SMTP server, the message is transferred to the destination SMTP sever, where it waits for the recipient to pick up the message through a client program.

The SMTP service also can transfer messages through one or more intermediate relay SMTP servers. A *relay SMTP server* receives the original message and then delivers it to the destination SMTP server or redirects it to another relay server. This process is repeated until the message is delivered or a designated time-out period passes.

The IIS SMTP service is commonly used to create a *smart host*, which is an SMTP server through which all outgoing messages are routed. For example, you can set up a smart host as a stand-alone SMTP server that sits between the Microsoft® Exchange server at your organization and the Internet. In this scenario, the smart host routes all e-mail from the Exchange server to the Internet and provides an added layer of protection between the Internet and the internal network. A smart host can also operate within a network.

Another common use for the SMTP service is to enable e-mail messages to be delivered from a Web site. For example, a company can provide an e-mail link for sending feedback messages or for requesting information. The SMTP service receives and routes those messages to the appropriate mailbox or to another SMTP server. Collaboration Data Objects (CDO) provides a simple object model that applications can leverage to submit mail to the SMTP server. For more information about CDO, see the Collaboration Data Objects link on the Web Resources page at http://www.microsoft.com/windows/reskits/webresources.

Installing the SMTP Service and Creating an SMTP Virtual Server

The IIS SMTP service is not installed by default. Use Control Panel to install the SMTP service, and use IIS Manager to change the default SMTP configuration. For step-by-step instructions for installing the SMTP service, see "SMTP Server Setup" in IIS 6.0 Help.

When you install the SMTP service, IIS creates the default SMTP virtual server automatically. In most cases, you need only one SMTP virtual server so that you can modify the default SMTP virtual server to work in your environment. However, if you are hosting multiple domains and want to have more than one default domain, for example, then you can create multiple SMTP virtual servers. To an end user, each SMTP virtual server appears as a separate server with a unique IP address/TCP port combination. To create a new virtual server, right-click **Default SMTP Virtual Server**, point to **New**, and click **Virtual Server**.

Default Settings

The default SMTP virtual server has the following default settings.

Name   The name of the virtual server that appears in IIS Manager. You can change the name of the virtual server to anything that you want by right-clicking the virtual server in IIS Manager and then clicking **Rename**.

IP address/TCP port   All unassigned/25. You can use the **General** tab in the **SMTP virtual server properties** dialog box to change this setting. If you change this setting, you must specify an IP address/TCP port combination that is not being used by another SMTP virtual server. TCP port 25 is both the default TCP port and the recommended TCP port. More than one virtual server can use the same TCP port, provided that they are configured with different IP addresses. If you do not set a unique IP address/TCP port combination, the SMTP virtual server will not start.

Default domain   The domain name that is listed on the **Computer Name** tab in **System Properties**. The default domain is used to stamp messages from addresses that do not have a domain. An SMTP virtual server can have only one default domain, and it cannot be deleted. To change the name of the default domain, double-click the virtual server, and double-click **Domains**. Right-click the local (default) domain, and click **Rename**. For more information about domains, see "Organizing Messages Using SMTP Domains" later in this chapter.

Home directory   *LocalDrive*:\Inetpub\Mailroot. The home directory is the root of your SMTP content directories, and it must be local to the computer on which the SMTP service runs.

If you create a new virtual server, you can configure default settings using the New Virtual Server Wizard.

Configuring an SMTP Virtual Server as a Smart Host

This section provides information about configuring an SMTP virtual server as a smart host. Only the properties for which there are special considerations for the smart host scenario are covered. For more complete information about configuring every virtual server property, see "SMTP Administration" in IIS 6.0 Help.

Setting Delivery Properties

Delivery properties govern how the SMTP service handles outbound e-mail messages and are especially important when you configure a smart host.

To designate a smart host for delivering messages, in the **SMTP virtual server properties** dialog box, click the **Delivery** tab, and then click **Advanced**. In the **Advanced Delivery** dialog box, type the name of the virtual server that will act as the smart host. If the server you are currently configuring will be the smart host, then type its name.

You can also designate a masquerade domain in the **Advanced Delivery** dialog box. In a *masquerade domain*, e-mail that is sent from one domain looks as though it were sent from another. For example, if you have one SMTP virtual server named mail.contoso.com and you want all e-mail to look as though it were sent from contoso.com, then configure a masquerade domain.

If you configure a smart host that sits outside your firewall, click **Outbound Connections** to set the authentication type and provide the necessary credentials for the SMTP server to which your smart host will connect. For more information about authentication methods, see "Securing SMTP Virtual Servers" later in this chapter.

Securing SMTP Virtual Servers

There are many steps you can take to make your SMTP virtual server more secure, including configuring access-related settings such as the authentication method, limiting administrative access, and setting connection limits.

Configuring Access-Related Settings

You can restrict access to your SMTP server by requiring authentication, limiting access according to IP address, or both. Restrict access by using the **Access** tab of the **SMTP virtual server properties** dialog box. The **Access** tab has five important security-related settings: Authentication, Certificate, Communication, Connection, and Relay.

Authentication

The Authentication option allows you to select from the following methods for authenticating users who attempt to connect to your SMTP server:

- **Anonymous access**. Anonymous access does not require users to enter a user name and password. This option is intended for servers that accept mail from outside the network.

   For example, if you are creating a stand-alone smart host that sits outside of your firewall and in front of your Exchange server, then you might select Anonymous access. Or, if you are creating a server to receive e-mail from a public Web site, then you might select Anonymous access.

- **Basic authentication**. Basic authentication requires users to enter a valid user name and password; however, the credentials are sent across the network unencrypted. If you select Basic authentication, then select **Requires TLS encryption**, which encrypts the user credentials. To require TLS encryption, you must have a valid SSL certificate installed on the server.

- **Integrated Windows authentication**. Integrated Windows authentication requires users to enter a valid Windows user name and password to connect to your SMTP server. Credentials are sent across the network encrypted. You can select Integrated Windows authentication if you are setting up a smart host to relay messages within your network or if you are setting up a server to receive e-mail from internal sites, such as a company intranet.

Certificate and Communication

The Certificate and Communication options allow you to secure communication by installing security certificates and requiring encryption. To install a certificate, click **Certificate** to start the New Certificate Wizard. Then, if you want to require the SMTP service to use SSL to encrypt every message, click **Communication**.

Connection

The Connection option allows you to restrict access to your server based on IP address. For example, if you are setting up a smart host that works inside your network, then you can use the **Only the list below** option to restrict access to the range of IP addresses for your network. If you are setting up a smart host that relays external e-mail or if you are setting up a server to accept e-mail from a public Web site, then connection control can be an effective way to restrict unsolicited commercial e-mail. After you identify the IP address or addresses of computers that send bulk e-mail, you can use the **All except the list below** option to prevent computers with specific IP addresses from connecting to your server. Although you can restrict access based solely on the domain name, this practice is not recommended because of the resources required to perform a reverse DNS lookup to identify the IP address of the computer attempting to connect.

Relay

The Relay option allows you to send e-mail to an SMTP server, which then sends it to the destination server or to another SMTP relay server. By default, the SMTP service blocks all computers from relaying unwanted mail through the virtual server, except those that meet the authentication requirements you designated in the **Authentication** dialog box. If you are setting up a smart host, enable only authenticated users to relay messages. If you are setting up a server to receive e-mail from the Internet, do not allow relaying, which can make you vulnerable to outside users who attempt to send unsolicited commercial e-mail through your SMTP server.

Limiting Administrative Access

You can restrict access to your server to only trusted administrators and make sure that administrators are granted only the access that they need to accomplish their work. Limit administrator access by using the **Security** tab of the **SMTP virtual server properties** dialog box.

Setting Messages Limits

You can set message limits to prevent large, incoming messages from affecting the performance of your server. Set message limits by using the **Messages** tab of the **SMTP virtual server properties** dialog box.

There are two message limit settings. The first limits the message size. If a mail client sends a message that exceeds the limit, then the mail client receives an error. The second limits the session size, the maximum amount of data that is accepted during the total connection. This setting applies to the sum of all the messages that are sent during the connection and to only the message body.

To help protect against users who send unsolicited, commercial e-mail to your SMTP server, you can limit the maximum number of recipients for a single message sent in one connection. For more information about setting message and recipient limits, see "Managing Messages" in IIS 6.0 Help.

Organizing Messages Using SMTP Domains

SMTP domains are used for organizing messages for delivery. There are two main types of domains: local and remote.

Organizing Messages Using Local Domains

A *local domain* is a DNS domain that is serviced by the local SMTP server. Any message with a local domain name that arrives at an SMTP server must be delivered to a local mailbox or drop directory, forwarded to another local address, or returned to the sender with a nondelivery report.

You can specify local domains to be either default or alias. The SMTP service uses the default domain to stamp message headers that lack a domain specification. An alias domain is an alias for the default domain. For example, if Contoso Pharmaceuticals merges with Contoso Corporate, then customers might not know which domain to use. If ContosoPharmaceuticals.com is the default domain, then you can set ContosoCorporate.com as an alias domain, which allows users to send mail to either the ContosoPharmaceuticals.com domain or the ContosoCorporate.com domain so that the mail is still delivered to the correct recipient.

Organizing Messages Using Remote Domains

A **remote domain** is a domain that is not served by the local SMTP server. When mail is routed to a remote domain and the address is found, the SMTP service sends the mail to another server. Therefore, if you are setting up a smart host as a stand-alone server in front of your Exchange server, then you need to create a remote domain using the domain of your Exchange server.

▶ **To create a new domain**

1. Double-click the smart host virtual server, and right-click **Domains**.

2. Point to **New**, and click **Domain**. The New SMTP Domain Wizard starts.

3. In **Welcome to the New SMTP Domain Wizard**, ensure that the **Remote** option is selected, and click **Next**.

4. In **Domain Name**, in the **Name** text box, type a name for the new domain, and then click **Finish**.

   You can use a wildcard character. For example, type ***contoso.com** if you want mail to be delivered to any of the contoso.com SMTP servers.

5. Right-click the domain you just created, and then click **Properties**.

6. Select the **Allow incoming mail to be relayed to this domain** check box.

7. Click **Outbound Security**, and then configure the authentication and provide the credentials required by the SMTP server to which the smart host will connect.

Additional Resources

These resources contain additional information and tools related to this chapter.

Related Information

- "Analyzing Log Files" in this book for information about IIS logs.

- "Common Administrative Tasks" in this book for information about creating a Web site.

- "IIS 6.0 Administration Scripts, Tips, and Tricks " in this book for information about creating Web sites programmatically.

- "IIS 6.0 Architecture" in this book for information about the WWW service and IIS core components.

- "Managing a Secure IIS 6.0 Solution" in this book for information about IIS security.

- "Running IIS 6.0 as an Application Server" in this book for information about application pools.

- "Unattended Setup" in this book for information about unattended installation.

- "Working with the Metabase" in this book for information about the IIS metabase.

Related Windows Server 2003 Help Topics

For best results in identifying Help topics by title, in Help and Support Center, under the **Search** box, click **Set search options**. Under **Help Topics**, select the **Search in title only** checkbox.

- "Access control" in Help and Support Center for Windows Server 2003.

- "Active Directory" in Help and Support Center for Windows Server 2003 for information about using Active Directory.

- "Backing up and restoring data" in Help and Support Center for Windows Server 2003 for information about how to back up servers running Windows Server 2003.

- "Choosing a file system: NTFS, FAT, or FAT32" in Help and Support Center for Windows Server 2003 for information to help you decide which file system is the best solution for your server.

- "DNS" in Help and Support Center for Windows Server 2003 for information about the Windows Server 2003 DNS feature.

- "Namespace planning for DNS" in Help and Support Center for Windows Server 2003 for information about planning namespaces for DNS.

IIS 6.0 Administration Scripts, Tips, and Tricks

Day-to-day administration of Internet Information Services (IIS) 6.0 includes tasks such as creating and configuring Web and File Transfer Protocol (FTP) sites, managing server certificates, and backing up IIS–based content and configuration. To work more efficiently, you can perform most of these administration tasks programmatically and remotely, whether you are administering IIS in a single-site or multi-site environment.

In This Chapter

Related Information

- For information about specific commands, including command syntax, see "Command-line reference A-Z" in Help and Support Center for Microsoft® Windows® Server 2003.

- For information about configuring Web sites as well as the File Transfer Protocol (FTP), Network News Transfer Protocol (NNTP), and Simple Mail Transfer Protocol (SMTP) services, see "Configuring Internet Sites and Services" in this book.

- For information about installing and using FrontPage® 2002 Server Extensions from Microsoft, see "Using FrontPage 2002 Server Extensions with IIS 6.0" in this book.

Creating and Configuring a Site Programmatically

One of the most common tasks for Internet service providers (ISPs) and administrators who manage complex intranet sites hosted on servers running Internet Information Services (IIS) 6.0 is creating and configuring new Web sites and File Transfer Protocol (FTP) sites. Although you can create these sites by using IIS Manager, if you create sites often or create many sites at once, it can be faster and easier to create sites programmatically. For more information about creating Web sites and FTP sites by using IIS Manager, see "Configuring Internet Sites and Services" in this book.

You can use a combination of scripts and tools to create a batch file that will automate all of the creating and configuring tasks. The steps for creating the batch file are as follows:

- Set up and configure DNS.
- Create directories.
- Add temporary content.
- Create Web sites.
- Set up FrontPage® 2002 Server Extensions from Microsoft.
- Create FTP sites.
- Set access control lists (ACLs).
- Include verification and error checking.

The following sections provide details, including sample scripts, for each step of the process for creating a batch file. In the final section, a complete batch file that you can customize for your environment is provided.

Variables

Some of the sample scripts in the following sections contain one or more of the following variables:

%1 = User

%2 = Domain

%3 = .com (extension)

%4 = y or n (indicates whether FrontPage 2002 Server Extensions should be installed)

If you type **newsite.bat user domain.com y** at a command prompt, after you save the complete batch file in a text editor, each entry becomes a variable in the script. The variable %1 represents User; the variable %2%3 represents Domain.com; and the variable %2 represents Domain.

Setting Up and Configuring DNS

Domain Name System (DNS) is an important part of creating new sites, especially if you host many sites on a single server with one Internet Protocol (IP) address. For more information about DNS and IP addresses, see "Configuring Internet Sites and Services" in this book.

One tool that can be helpful in managing DNS is the Dnscmd.exe command-line tool that is provided with the Support Tools for Microsoft® Windows® Server 2003, Standard Edition; Microsoft® Windows® Server 2003, Enterprise Edition; and Microsoft® Windows® Server 2003, Datacenter Edition operating systems. You can use Dnscmd.exe to view, manage, and update existing DNS server configurations or to set up and configure new DNS servers on your network. Before you use Dnscmd.exe, decide how best to configure DNS zones for your network, or, if you have a designated DNS administrator for the network, ask him or her which parameters to use. For more information about using Dnscmd.exe, see "Server administration using Dnscmd" in Help and Support Center for Microsoft® Windows® Server 2003.

Listing 9.1 shows how you can use Dnscmd.exe to set up a DNS zone for contoso.com, create entries for contoso.com and www.contoso.com that point to IP address 10.1.1.1, and then set up a canonical name (CNAME) for www.contoso.com that instructs the DNS server to use the same IP address that is configured for contoso.com.

 Important

You must be a member of the Administrators group on the local computer to run scripts and executables, or you must have been delegated the appropriate authority. As a security best practice, log on to your computer by using an account that is not in the Administrators group, and then use the runas command to run your script or executable as an administrator. At a command prompt, type runas /profile /User:MyMachine\Administrator cmd to open a command window with administrator rights and then type cscript.exe ScriptName (including the full path with parameters, if any).

Listing 9.1   Sample Script for Setting Up and Configuring DNS

```
dnscmd PRIMARY /zoneadd contoso.COM /primary /file contoso.COM.dns
//sets up the overall zone contoso.COM on the primary name server

dnscmd SECONDARY /zoneadd contoso.COM /secondary /file contoso.COM.dns
//sets up the zone on the secondary

dnscmd PRIMARY /recordadd contoso.COM @ A 1.1.1.1
//sets up the record on the primary server for contoso.COM pointing to the IP
10.1.1.1

dnscmd PRIMARY /recordadd contoso.COM www CNAME contoso.COM
//sets up a CNAME record for WWW.contoso.com to point to the same IP as
// contoso.COM
```

Creating Directories

After you set up and configure DNS, you should create the physical directory for your sites. You can use the **mkdir** command to create a directory programmatically. For more information about **mkdir**, including command syntax, see "Mkdir" in the command-line reference section of Help and Support Center for Windows Server 2003.

Although it is simple to create a directory, the task requires advanced planning to create logical structures. Listing 9.2 uses C:\Web\UserName\Domain, where a user's content is in a directory that has the same name as the user name. Each user's domain is a subdirectory of the user name directory. This structure allows users to use FTP to download files to their folders and access other directories as necessary.

Listing 9.2   Sample Script for Setting Up Directories

```
mkdir  C:\WEB\USERNAME\
mkdir  C:\WEB\USERNAME\DOMAIN\
```

To prevent mistakes, such as unintentionally overwriting an existing directory, include error handling in your script. You can use the **if [not] exist** command in batch programs to check for and respond to certain conditions, as seen in Listing 9.3. For more information about the **if** commands, including command syntax, see "If" in the command-line reference section of Help and Support Center for Windows Server 2003.

Listing 9.3   Sample Script for Error Handling

```
If NOT exist C:\WEB\USERNAME\ goto errornofolder1
If NOT exist C:\WEB\USERNAME\DOMAIN\ goto errornofolder2
'errornofolder1 and errornofolder2 refer to locations in the script where those
'errors are handled.
```

Creating Directories Remotely

 Important

As a best security practice, use the **net use** command to authenticate with the remote computer before you use **mkdir** remotely. For more information about the **net use** command, including command syntax, see "Net services commands" in the command-line reference section of Help and Support Center for Windows Server 2003.

To create directories on a remote computer, use the following command-line syntax:

mkdir \\Server\c$\Web\UserName\

Adding Temporary Content

When you create sites, you can add temporary content files that users can replace with their own content when they are ready. An example of a temporary content file is a home page that says "Coming Soon" or "Under Construction." Use the Adsutil.vbs command-line script to add temporary content files.

Adsutil.vbs is a flexible tool that uses the Microsoft® Visual Basic® development system, Scripting Edition (VBScript), with Microsoft® Active Directory® Service Interfaces (ADSI) to manipulate the IIS configuration. Note that Adsutil.vbs is not a Microsoft-supported product. The documentation for, and the format of, Adsutil.vbs can change at any time. For more information about Adsutil.vbs, including syntax and parameters, see "Adsutil.vbs IIS Administration Utility" later in this chapter.

You must use the CScript.exe command-line tool, which is installed with Windows Script Host, to run Adsutil.vbs. You can set CScript.exe as the default run-time program by typing **CScript //h:cscript //nologo //s** at the command prompt. The optional **//nologo** parameter disables the display of the CScript copyright banner. Alternatively, you can type **Cscript.exe** at the beginning of the Adsutil.vbs script. For more information about using Adsutil.vbs, including commands and parameters, see "Adsutil.vbs Commands" in IIS 6.0 Help, which is accessible from IIS Manager.

Listing 9.4 uses Adsutil.vbs to add a file named temp.htm to the list of default documents. Although you do not have to use the name temp.htm, do not name the file default.htm because default.htm would take precedence if the user added only index.htm as the home page. The sample script adds the temp.htm file as the last file on the **Documents** tab in the Web site properties so that temp.htm can never override a user's home page, even if the user never deletes temp.htm. You must type the complete Adsutil.vbs script on one line.

Listing 9.4   Sample Script for Setting Up Temporary Files

```
Adsutil.vbs set w3svc/defaultdoc
"default.htm,default.html,default.asp,default.aspx,index.htm,index.html,index.
asp,index.aspx,temp.htm"
```

After you add a temporary file, use the **copy** command to copy the file to the user's directory. For example, to copy temp.htm to the user's directory, at the command prompt, type **copy temp.htm C:\WEB\USERNAME\DOMAIN\temp.htm**.

Adding Temporary Content Remotely

You can run any of the Adsutil.vbs commands remotely. To add temporary content to a remote computer, add **-s:**_Server_ to the end of the command, where _Server_ is the name of the target server.

Creating Web Sites

After you configure DNS, create the directories, and populate the directories with temporary content, you need to create the Web sites. You can use IIS Manager to create Web sites, or you can use the Iisweb.vbs command-line script, which is stored in the *systemroot*\System32 folder.

When you use Iisweb.vbs to create a Web site, you specify only the basic properties that are needed to create the site and identify its contents. Iisweb.vbs uses the same default properties that IIS Manager uses when creating new Web sites, and it adheres to the same rules for inheriting properties. For more information about default Web site properties, see "Configuring Internet Sites and Services" in this book. For more information about Iisweb.vbs, including command syntax, see "Creating Web Sites" in IIS 6.0 Help. For example, to create a Web site on the local computer using the directory specified in the preceding sample scripts, at a command prompt, type **iisweb /create C:\WEB\USER\DOMAIN "contoso.COM" /d www.contoso.COM**.

Creating Web Sites Remotely

To create a Web site on a remote computer, type **/s** *Server* after the **/create** parameter, where *Server* is the name of the target computer. To specify the IP address of the target computer, type **/i** *IPAddress* after the **/s** parameter, where *IPAddress* is the IP address.

Providing Additional Host Headers

Many users request additional host headers, such as contoso.com, without the www prefix. You can use Adsutil.vbs to set host headers, but you need to specify the site identification (ID). Although you can find out the site ID by parsing it from Adsutil.vbs output, an easier way is to integrate the Translate.js command-line script, which uses the IIS Windows Management Instrumentation (WMI) provider, into your Adsutil.vbs command. For more information about the IIS WMI provider, see "Managing IIS 6.0 Programmatically by Using WMI" later in this chapter.

The Translate.js script appears below. Copy it exactly as it is shown, and then save it in the same location as your other scripts. If you do not specify a location, it will be saved to C:\Windows\System32 by default. You need to use CScript.exe to run Translate.js. For information about using CScript.exe, see "Adding Temporary Content" earlier in this chapter.

```
TRANSLATE.JS
var serverComment = WScript.Arguments(0);
var query = "SELECT Name, ServerComment FROM IIsWebServerSetting WHERE
ServerComment='" + serverComment + "'";
var providerObj = GetObject("winmgmts:/root/MicrosoftIISv2");
var sites = providerObj.ExecQuery(query);

if (sites.Count != 0)
{
   for(e = new Enumerator(sites); ! e.atEnd(); e.moveNext())
   {
      var item = e.item();
      // Print the site ID only by leaving the "W3SVC/" prefix out.
      WScript.Echo(item.Name.substr(6));
   }
}
else
{
   WScript.Echo("No sites found.");
}
```

After you save Translate.js, you can integrate it with Adsutil.vbs to provide additional host headers. Listing 9.5 uses 80:contoso.com to designate the site IP binding as All Unassigned. If you want to designate a specific IP address, type the IP address followed by a colon (:) in front of this string, as in **IPAddress:80:contoso.com**.

Listing 9.5 Sample Script for Setting Up Host Headers

```
cscript //nologo translate.js "CONTOSO.COM" > siteid.txt

for /f %%I in (siteid.txt) do SET SITEID=%%I

Adsutil set w3svc/%SITEID%/serverbindings ":80:WWW.CONTOSO.COM"
":80:CONTOSO.COM"

Del siteid.txt
```

Providing Additional Host Headers Remotely

 Important

To provide additional host headers remotely while logged in with a domain account, you must have administrative credentials on both computers. When logged in with a local user account, you must have an account with the same user name and password on the remote computer, as well as administrative credentials on both computers.

To modify Translate.js to access a remote server, add the server name when you get the object by changing **GetObject("winmgmts:/root/MicrosoftIISv2");** to **GetObject("winmgmts://***Server***/root/MicrosoftIISv2");**, where *Server* is the name of the remote server.

Installing and Setting Up FrontPage 2002 Server Extensions

FrontPage 2002 Server Extensions provide Web-based and command-line administration for extending virtual servers. *Extending* a virtual server means enabling various FrontPage 2002 Server Extensions features to improve the way that you manage the content development and security of your site. Extending virtual servers with FrontPage 2002 Server Extensions enables the site owner to author the site in FrontPage and delegate site ownership and administration credentials.

FrontPage 2002 Server Extensions include new security features, such as roles and rights, and new features for monitoring server health and Web site use. For more information about improvements in FrontPage 2002 Server Extensions, see "Using FrontPage 2002 Server Extensions with IIS 6.0" in this book.

Listing 9.6 enables both FrontPage 2002 Server Extensions and FTP on the same site. The sample script sets up FTP by default and checks the *%4* variable. If the *%4* variable is **y**, the script goes to the FrontPage 2002 Server Extensions setup section. Otherwise, FrontPage 2002 Server Extensions setup is skipped.

Listing 9.6   Sample Script for Setting Up FTP and FrontPage 2002 Server Extensions

```
:iffp
if "%4"=="y" goto fpse
goto skipfp
```

There are two options for setting up FrontPage 2002 Server Extensions. You can add the full FrontPage 2002 Server Extensions path to System Properties, or you can include the path in the batch file each time you run it. The locations are as follows:

- For FrontPage 2002 Server Extensions: *Drive*:\Program Files\Common Files\Microsoft Shared\Web Server Extensions\50\Bin

- For FrontPage 2000 Server Extensions: *Drive*:\Program Files\Common Files\Microsoft Shared\Web Server Extensions\40\Bin

▶ **To add the FrontPage 2002 Server Extensions path to System Properties**

1. From the **Start** menu, right-click **My Computer**, and then click **Properties**.

2. In the **System Properties** dialog box, click the **Advanced** tab, and then click **Environment Variables**.

3. In the **Environment Variables** dialog box, in **System variables**, click the path, and then click **Edit**.

4. In the **Edit System Variable** dialog box, in the **Variable value** box, type a semicolon (**;**) at the end of the path, and then do one of the following:

   - For FrontPage 2002 Server Extensions, type:

     *Drive***:\Program Files\Common Files\Microsoft Shared\Web Server Extensions\50\bin**

   - For FrontPage 2000 Server Extensions, type:

     *Drive***:\Program Files\Common Files\Microsoft Shared\Web Server Extensions\40\bin**

To include the FrontPage 2002 Server Extensions path in the batch file each time you run it, run a script like Listing 9.7. This sample script does not add the path to System Properties.

Listing 9.7 Sample Script for Installing FrontPage 2002 Server Extensions Batch Files

```
@set path=%path%;%SYSTEMDRIVE%\inetpub\adminscripts;%SystemDrive%\Program
Files\Common Files\Microsoft Shared\Web Server Extensions\50\bin
```

After you set up FrontPage 2002 Server Extensions, you can use SharePoint™ Team Services from Microsoft command-line tools to install and administer FrontPage 2002 Server Extensions from the local server or from a remote computer. The Owsadm.exe command-line tool runs on only the server, and the Owsrmadm.exe command-line tool can be run from a remote computer. These tools are available at *systemroot*\Program Files\Common Files\Microsoft Shared\Web Server Extensions\50\Bin.

Installing FrontPage 2002 Server Extensions Locally

To view the command-line options for Owsadm.exe, at the command prompt, change the directory to the *systemroot*\Program Files\Common Files\Microsoft Shared\Web Server Extensions\50\Bin folder, and then type **owsadm.exe -h**.

 Note

In the following sample scripts, "CONTOSO.COM" is case sensitive.

Listing 9.8 uses Owsadm.exe to install FrontPage 2002 Server Extensions on the local server.

Listing 9.8   Sample Script for Installing FrontPage 2002 Extensions System Properties

```
:fpse
owsadm -o install -p 80 -m www.CONTOSO.COM -t msiis -u USER
```

To install FrontPage 2000 Server Extensions, use Listing 9.9.

Listing 9.9   Sample Script for Installing FrontPage 2000 Extensions System Properties

```
:fpse
fpsrvadm -o install -p 80 -m www.CONTOSO.COM -t msiis -u USER
```

Security Considerations for Installing FrontPage 2002 Server Extensions Remotely

Be aware of security considerations when using Owsrmadm.exe. When you administer a server remotely, a wider community of users is given greater access to the Web server from the Internet, which can create a security risk. During remote administration of Windows SharePoint Team Services and FrontPage 2002 Server Extensions, an unauthorized person can gain access to Web sites, based on the Windows SharePoint Team Services or FrontPage 2002 Server Extensions on your server, and modify Web site settings, and even delete Web sites. To increase security when administering FrontPage 2002 Server Extensions remotely, you should use a Secure Sockets Layer (SSL) connection, and you should use a nonstandard administration port to access Fpadmdll.dll.

To require SSL security for authoring and site administration tasks, use the **Require SSL for authoring and administration** option on the **Set Installation Defaults** tab in **Server Administration**, or set the **RequireSSL** property by using the **setproperty** command.

When you install FrontPage 2002 Server Extensions, a nonstandard administration port is created. Use this administration port to access Fpadmdll.dll, which, on the Web server, acts as the form handler for any of the FrontPage 2002 Server Extensions HTML–based administration pages.

For more information about using Owsrmadm.exe, see the Using the Administration Tools Remotely link on the Web Resources page at http://www.microsoft.com/windows/reskits/webresources.

Creating FTP Sites

The directory structures for the sample scripts in this chapter include an overall user folder that contains a folder for each of the user's domains. For example, if the user has two domains, the structure would be *C:\Web\User\Domain1* and *C:\Web\User\Domain2*. For the purposes of uploading content through FTP, you need to set up an FTP virtual directory — instructions for which are provided later in this section — that points to *C:\Web\User* so that the user can upload to either domain easily.

You can have only one FTP site per IP address on TCP port 21, so you need to use virtual directories and ACLs to ensure that users are sent to the correct directory. You can create and host multiple FTP sites with the same IP address, as long as they have different ports. This configuration can be difficult to manage. It requires making sure that the port number is explicitly defined in the URL, and you might also need to open the port at the firewall.

If you want to configure multiple users to a single FTP site but also ensure that users cannot access and download from the directories of other users, you can create FTP sites by using FTP isolation. Some of the benefits of FTP isolation include added security and easier migration of users to different servers.

FTP user isolation supports two isolation modes: Isolate users and Isolate users using Active Directory. You can also create FTP sites with no isolation. You can configure FTP user isolation with the Iisftp.vbs command-line script by using the **/isolation** parameter. To use the parameter, type either **AD**, for Active Directory isolation, or **Local**, for local isolation, after **/isolation**. If you do not include the **/isolation** parameter, the site will not isolate users. For more detailed information about creating multiple FTP sites and setting up FTP user isolation, see "Configuring Internet Sites and Services" in this book.

Setting Up FTP Virtual Directories

You can set up an FTP virtual directory by using Iisftpdr.vbs. The directory structure in these sample scripts has a domain beneath each user folder. If you set up your directory this way, when your users upload content they can change directories into any domain they own. For more information about Iisftpdr.vbs, including command syntax, see "Creating FTP Virtual Directories" in IIS 6.0 Help.

For example, to use one FTP site that points to the same IP address as the Web sites and creates a virtual directory for a user named USER, at the command prompt, type **iisftpdr /create "FTPSITENAME" USER C:\WEB\USER**. In Listing 9.10, Translateftp.js gets the site ID and uses an Adsutil.vbs command to assign write permissions for the user on the new virtual directory. The sample script creates Translateftp.js by copying Translate.js, renaming it Translateftp.js, and changing two elements.

The first element that is changed is the IISWebServerSetting class. Translate.js queries the IISWebServerSetting class by using WMI. For FTP, you must switch to the IISFtpServerSetting class. This class corresponds to the IIsFtpServer IIS Admin object, and it contains the read/write properties for the object. For more information about the IISWebServerSetting element, see "IIsWebServerSetting (WMI)" in IIS 6.0 Help.

The second element that is changed is the JavaScript *item.Name*.substr() call. The substr() method returns a specified part of a string. By changing the setting from six (6) to nine (9) for Translateftp.js, the script will return the FTP site ID as a return string.

Listing 9.10   Sample Script for Setting UP FTP Virtual Directories

```
TRANSLATEFTP.JS
var serverComment = WScript.Arguments(0);
var query = "SELECT Name, ServerComment FROM IIsFTPServerSetting WHERE
ServerComment='" + serverComment + "'";
var providerObj = GetObject("winmgmts:/root/MicrosoftIISv2");
var sites = providerObj.ExecQuery(query);

if (sites.Count != 0)
{
   for(e = new Enumerator(sites); ! e.atEnd(); e.moveNext())
   {
      var item = e.item();
      //Print the site ID only by leaving the "MSFTPSVC/" prefix out.
      WScript.Echo(item.Name.substr(9));
   }
}
else
{
   WScript.Echo("No sites found.");
}

The ADSUTIL command and integration with translateftp.js.

cscript //nologo translate.js "FTPSITEID" > ftpsiteid.txt

for /f %%I in (ftpsiteid.txt) do SET FTPSITEID=%%I

adsutil.vbs set msftpsvc/%FTPSITEID%/root/USER/accesswrite "true"

del ftpsiteid.txt
```

Setting Up FTP Remotely

 Important

To set up FTP remotely while logged in with a domain account, you must have administrative credentials on both computers. When logged in with a local user account, you must have an account with the same user name and password on the remote computer, as well as administrative credentials on both computers.

To modify Translateftp.js to access a remote server, add the server name when you get the object by changing **GetObject("winmgmts:/root/MicrosoftIISv2");** to **GetObject("winmgmts://*Server*/root/MicrosoftIISv2");**, where *Server* is the name of the remote server.

Setting ACLs

Depending on the requirements of your Web sites and services, you might want to explicitly set ACLs for groups and accounts in IIS. For example, you might need to ensure that ASP.NET can run on a Web site. For a list of the default IIS ACLs, see "Managing a Secure IIS 6.0 Solution" in this book.

You can use one of several tools to programmatically display and modify ACLs for your physical folders. For a list of popular ACL tools, see "Managing a Secure IIS 6.0 Solution" in this book.

 Important

If you use FrontPage 2002 Server Extensions and FTP on the same site (which is not recommended), you should set ACLs after you install FrontPage 2002 Server Extensions to prevent FrontPage 2002 Server Extensions from changing the permissions.

For example, to edit the ACLs instead of replacing them, so that the defaults will be inherited from C:\WEB and the FrontPage 2002 Server Extensions permissions will be left intact, at the command prompt, type **cacls C:\WEB\USER /t /e /g USER:c networkservice:r <y.txt**.

You will need to use a text file to simulate pressing ENTER+Y+ENTER, which confirms the operation. To do so, create a .txt file named Y, and type the following:

<enter>

Y

<enter>

Because this sample script uses **cacls**, the account name is specified as "networkservice" instead of "Network Service," but both names refer to the same account.

Recommended and Inherited ACLs

Table 9.1 lists several accounts or groups with ACLs that you might need to change, as well as an explanation for the recommendation.

Table 9.1 Recommended ACLs

Account or Group Name	Recommended ACL	Explanation
IUSR_*ComputerName*	Read	Anonymous browsing account (used by default).
Network Service	Read	ASP.NET requires read access on the Network Service account. Note: IIS 6.0 runs under this account by default when IIS is running in worker process isolation mode. In IIS 5 compatibility mode, the default account is ASPNET.
USER	Change	Account for the site administrator.

Table 9.2 lists the ACLs that are inherited from the folder structure, but that can be added in the script.

Table 9.2   Inherited ACLs

Account or Group Name	Inherited ACL	Explanation
Administrators	Full	Account for users in the Administrators group.
System	Full	Account for users who need system access.

Setting ACLs Remotely

To run **cacls** remotely, use the following command-line syntax, where *Server* is the name of the target server:

```
cacls \\Server\c$\web
```

Including Verification and Error Checking

As a best practice, you should place error-checking and verification code at the start of and throughout your batch file. If you plan to be present while you run the batch file, you do not need extensive verification.

One way to have your batch file check for errors is to include a **net user** command that verifies that the user name is in the domain and then parses the command output for any text that says the user does not exist. For example, use the following command-line syntax to verify that the user name is in the domain:

```
net user User/Domain > user.txt
```

Then, parse the command output for the text string "The user name could not be found," which would indicate that the user is not in the domain. You can use the **findstr** command to parse a file for a text string.

Another way to have your batch file check for errors is to include the **if not exist** command and other commands that ensure that the previous portion of the script succeeded. Ideally, you should run this script after each series of commands to check, for example, that the DNS entries were created, and then to check that the directories were created, and so on. You should also include error-handling code after the error-checking code, such as a loop that waits a few minutes to attempt to complete a series of commands again, or a more complex series of commands, while the batch file parses a specific error.

Listing 9.11 provides simple error checking for the existence of all variables. In addition, this sample script allows another administrator, who might not be familiar with your script, to run **/?** if he or she does not know how to use the script.

Listing 9.11 Sample Script for Error Checking

```
if "%1" == "?" goto usage
if "%1" == "/?" goto usage
if "%1" == "-?" goto usage


if "%1" == "" goto errormissingvariable
if "%2" == "" goto errormissingvariable
if "%3" == "" goto errormissingvariable
if "%4" == "" goto errormissingvariable
```

The Complete Batch File

Listing 9.12 provides the complete batch file named newsite.bat. The complete batch file includes the series of commands that are documented in the preceding sections, variables for elements such as the server IP address and DNS servers, and the @ symbol in front of certain lines to hide them from the console window.

After you save newsite.bat, type the following at the command prompt to run it:

newsite.bat USER DOMAIN .COM N

%1 = USER

%2 = DOMAIN

%3 = .COM (extension)

%4 = y|n (to indicate whether to install FrontPage 2002 Server Extensions)

Listing 9.12 NEWSITE.BAT: Sample Batch File

```
@SET PRIMARYNS=dns.contoso.com
@SET SECONDARYNS=dns1.contoso.com
@SET IP=1.1.1.1
@SET LOC=C:\WEB
@SET FTPSITE=ftp_computername
@SET ANONACCT=IUSR_computername
@SET IIS_ASPNET_ACCT=networkservice

@if "%1" == "?" goto usage
@if "%1" == "/?" goto usage
```

(continued)

Listing 9.12 NEWSITE.BAT: Sample Batch File *(continued)*

```
@if "%1" == "" goto errormissingvariable
@if "%2" == "" goto errormissingvariable
@if "%3" == "" goto errormissingvariable
@if "%4" == "" goto errormissingvariable

@set path=%path%;%SYSTEMDRIVE%\inetpub\adminscripts;%SystemDrive%\Program
Files\Common Files\Microsoft Shared\Web Server Extensions\50\bin

:dns
dnscmd %PRIMARYNS% /zoneadd %2%3 /primary /file %2%3.dns
dnscmd %SECONDARYNS% /zoneadd %2%3 /secondary /file %2%3.dns
dnscmd %PRIMARYNS% /recordadd %2%3 @ NS %SECONDARYNS%
dnscmd %PRIMARYNS% /recordadd %2%3 @ A %IP%
dnscmd %PRIMARYNS% /recordadd %2%3 www CNAME %2%3

:dir
mkdir %LOC%\%1
mkdir %LOC%\%1\%2
copy temp.htm %LOC%\%1\%2\temp.htm

:web
iisweb /create %LOC%\%1\%2 "%2%3" /d www.%2%3

cscript //nologo translate.js "%2%3" > siteid.txt
for /f %%I in (siteid.txt) do SET SITEID=%%I
Adsutil set w3svc/%SITEID%/serverbindings ":80:WWW.%2%3" ":80:%2%3"
Del siteid.txt

:iffp
if "%4"=="y" goto fpse
goto skipfp

:fpse
owsadm -o install -p 80 -m www.%2%3 -t msiis -u %1

:skipfp

:ftp
Iisftpdr /create "%FTPSITE%" %1 %LOC%\%1

or /f %%I in (ftpsiteid.txt) do SET FTPSITEID=%%I
adsutil.vbs set msftpsvc/%FTPSITEID%/root/%1/accesswrite "true"
del ftpsiteid.txt
```

(continued)

Listing 9.12 NEWSITE.BAT: Sample Batch File *(continued)*

```
:acls
cacls %LOC%\%1 /t /e /g %1:c %IIS_ASPNET_ACCT %:r <y.txt
@goto end

:errormissingvariable
@echo You are missing a variable.
@goto usage

:usage
@echo Creates a domain on the LOCAL server.
@echo var1=username, var2=domain (without extension!), var3=extension, var4=y
(for FrontPage 2002 Server Extensions, n  for none.)
@echo EXAMPLE myusername mydomain .com y
@goto end

:end
```

Creating a Web Site from a Template

If you have a standard Web site configuration that you use or plan to use frequently, you can use IIS Manager to create a Web site template. To do this, export the configuration of the site to a file, and then use that file to create new sites. The exported configuration is stored as a metabase XML configuration file; it does not contain content. After you export the configuration file, you can import that file into a different directory on the same Web server or to a different Web server.

You can also export and import sites and application pools as configuration files to quickly migrate sites and application pools between servers. This feature allows you to import Web applications if the developer stored the application in a configuration file.

 Important

You must be a member of the Administrators group on the local computer to perform the following procedure or procedures, or you must have been delegated the appropriate authority. As a security best practice, log on to your computer by using an account that is not in the Administrators group, and then use the **runas** command to run IIS Manager as an administrator. At a command prompt, type **runas** /*User.Administrative_AccountName* "mmc %systemroot%\system32\inetsrv\iis.msc".

▶ **To create a Web site template file**

1. In IIS Manager, double-click the local computer, right-click the site or application that you want to back up, point to **All Tasks**, and then click **Save Configuration to a File**.

2. In the **Save Configuration to a File** dialog box, in the **File name** box, type a file name.

3. In the **Path** box, type the full path to the configuration file, or click **Browse** to browse to the location where you want to save the file, and then click **OK**.

▶ **To create a new site from a template file**

1. In IIS Manager, double-click the local computer, right-click the **Web Sites** folder, point to **New**, and then click **Web Site (from file)**.

2. In the **Import Configuration** dialog box, in the **File** box, type the full path to the configuration file, or click **Browse** to browse for the file.

3. Click **Read File**.

   The **Select a configuration to import** box is populated.

4. In **Select a configuration to import**, click the configuration that you want to import, and then click **OK**.

Managing IIS 6.0 Programmatically by Using ADSI

In Windows Server 2003 and Microsoft® Windows® 2000 Server, ADSI is a directory service model and a set of COM interfaces. ADSI enables Windows applications and clients of the Microsoft® Active Directory® directory service to access several network directory services, including Active Directory. ADSI is supplied as a software development kit (SDK). For more information about the SDK, see the Microsoft Platform SDK link on the Web Resources page at http://www.microsoft.com/windows/reskits/webresources.

Most enterprises already have many different directories in place. For example, network operating systems and e-mail systems have their own directories. When a single enterprise deploys multiple directories, issues, such as usability, data consistency, development cost, and support cost, can arise. ADSI provides a solution for these issues by offering a single, consistent, open set of interfaces for managing and using multiple directories.

IIS 6.0 includes the IIS ADSI provider, which delivers ADSI objects for IIS programmatic administration. IIS ADSI objects are based on Windows ADSI, are Automation-compatible, and can be accessed and manipulated by any language that supports Automation, such as VBScript, Microsoft® JScript® development software, Perl, Active Server Pages (ASP), Visual Basic, Java, or the Microsoft® Visual C++® development system.

Any script or code that uses ADSI needs to use some basic Windows ADSI interfaces. The Windows ADSI interfaces include methods and properties that are frequently used. For example, the ADSI object Get and Put methods allow you to change properties in a data store such as the IIS metabase, and the ADSI object **SetInfo** commits the changes to the directory.

ADSI is fully scriptable for ease of use by administrators. When you are writing scripts and code that use ADSI, it can save time to keep open a reference to the Windows ADSI interfaces. For reference information about each of the IIS ADSI objects, see "IIS ADSI Provider Reference" in IIS 6.0 Help.

IIS ADSI Objects

IIS ADSI objects are COM Automation objects that you can use in command-line scripts, ASP pages, or custom applications to change the IIS configuration values that are stored in the IIS metabase. For example, instead of using IIS Manager to set permissions for the **AppRoot**, **LogType**, and **ConnectionTimeout** properties in the metabase, you can write a script to set these permissions.

Each IIS ADSI object corresponds to a key in the metabase schema. For example, the **IIsWebServer** ADSI object corresponds to the **IIsWebServer** collection key in the metabase schema file. IIS uses the metabase schema as a guide to build your metabase configuration file, add Web sites and virtual directories, and make other configuration changes as your Web server grows.

If you find that no existing ADSI object class meets your management needs, you can extend the IIS ADSI schema. The IIS ADSI schema is implemented as a group of objects that are stored in the metabase. Because extending the IIS ADSI schema is a complex operation, you can usually obtain the best results by using existing classes. For more information about extending the IIS ADSI schema, see "Extending the Metabase Schema" in IIS 6.0 Help.

IIS ADSI objects are organized in a hierarchical structure that mirrors the structures that are defined in the IIS metabase configuration file. Most objects inherit characteristics or properties from the parent object, but the child objects can contain unique characteristics that are implemented by extending the schema. For more information about this hierarchical structure, including a diagram of the structure, see "IIS ADSI Object Hierarchy" in IIS 6.0 Help.

Because of the hierarchical structure of the metabase and its property inheritance feature, you can easily configure properties for a single file, a single server, all Web servers, all FTP servers, or the common properties of many other groups of objects.

IIS ADSI Security

By default, only server administrators can use ADSI to change metabase values. If you are using ADSI in command-line scripts, the scripts work only when an administrator runs them. If you are using ADSI in a compiled program, set the account of the application to an administrative account. For increased security, set ACLs on your scripts and compiled administrative programs to restrict access to the Administrators group only.

If you are using ADSI in an ASP page to configure the metabase, you must disable anonymous access to the Web application that contains the ASP page. Then create a server or directory for your administrative ASP files, and set the authentication method to use Integrated Windows authentication for the server or directory.

For security purposes, out-of-process Web applications cannot access the metabase unless the user specified in the **WAMUserName** property is recognized as an administrator; however, this is not a recommended configuration. The **WAMUserName** property specifies the account user name that IIS uses by default as the COM+ application identity for newly created IIS out-of-process Web applications. The values of this property and its companion property, **WAMUserPass**, are set when IIS is installed, and they match the user name and password values in the Windows user account, which is established at the same time. Changing the value of this property is not recommended. If you do alter the value, change it to a valid Windows user account, and change **WAMUserPass** to the corresponding password for the new account.

As an alternative, change the identity of the specific out-of-process package to some other account identity, and give only that account administrative access to the metabase. This method introduces less potential risk, but it must be implemented for each out-of-process package.

Important

If a computer is running in IIS 5.0 isolation mode, do not make the IWAM_*ComputerName* account an Administrator account unless special circumstances require you to do so. When the IWAM_*ComputerName* account is an Administrator account, anyone who uses an out-of-process Web application to access your server is granted administrative credentials on your computer.

Adsutil.vbs IIS Administration Utility

Adsutil.vbs is an IIS administration utility that uses VBScript with ADSI to manipulate IIS configuration by modifying the metabase. You must use CScript, which is installed with Windows Script Host, to run this script. Be aware that Adsutil.vbs is not a Microsoft-supported product. The documentation for, and the format of, Adsutil.vbs can change at any time.

Important

You must be a member of the Administrators group on the local computer to run scripts and executables, or you must have been delegated the appropriate authority. As a security best practice, log on to your computer by using an account that is not in the Administrators group, and then use the **runas** command to run your script or executable as an administrator. At a command prompt, type **runas** */profile* /*User:MyMachine\Administrator* **cmd** to open a command window with administrator rights and then type **cscript.exe** *ScriptName* (including the full path with parameters, if any).

To run Adsutil.vbs, use the following command-line syntax:

```
cscript.exe adsutil.vbs COMMAND [Path|PropertyPath] [-s:ServerNamer]
```

Parameters for Adsutil.vbs

Table 9.3 lists and describes the Adsutil.vbs parameters: *Path*, *PropertyPath*, and **-s:***ServerName*. The **-s:***ServerName* parameter is optional. Either the *Path* parameter or the *PropertyPath* parameter is valid for certain designated commands, as Table 9.3 and Table 9.4 show. If you specify more than one parameter for a command, place the *Path* or *PropertyPath* parameter directly following the command (so that it precedes all other parameters).

For more information about metabase terminology, including definitions of metabase keys, values, and KeyTypes, see "Working with the Metabase" in this book and also see "Metabase Configuration File" in IIS 6.0 Help.

Table 9.3   Adsutil.vbs Parameters

Parameter	Description
Path	Specifies the metabase path that is contained within a metabase key. A metabase path is a sequence of location names, each name separated by a forward slash (for example, W3SVC/1/ROOT). Location attributes specify the hierarchical position of the key in Metabase.xml. A key is analogous to a file folder or registry key.
	The *Path* parameter is required for, and can be used with, the **ENUM, ENUM_ALL, DELETE, CREATE, APPCREATEINPROC, APPCREATEOUTPROC, APPCREATEPOOLPROC, APPDELETE, APPUNLOAD, APPDISABLE, APPENABLE, APPGETSTATUS, CREATE_VDIR, CREATE_VSERV, START_SERVER, STOP_SERVER, PAUSE_SERVER**, and **CONTINUE_SERVER** commands.
PropertyPath	Specifies the metabase property path. A metabase property path is a sequence of location names that are separated by a forward slash, each sequence ending with the name of a metabase property (for example, /W3SVC/ServerBindings).
	If you do not precede the property name with a specific location (for example, if you type: **/ServerBindings**), the utility searches the entire metabase.
	The *PropertyPath* parameter is required for, and can be used with, the **GET, SET**, and **FIND** commands.
-s:*ServerName*	Optional. Executes the command on a remote computer. If you use this parameter without specifying a server name, the utility executes the command on the local computer.
	For example, if you want to delete Web site 3 on a remote computer that is named ComputerA, type the following at the command prompt:
	`cscript.exe adsutil.vbs DELETE W3SVC/3 -s:ComputerA`

Commands for Adsutil.vbs

Table 9.4 describes the Adsutil.vbs commands and their valid parameters. In the preceding syntax, substitute one of the following commands for *COMMAND* and include any applicable parameters.

Table 9.4   Adsutil.vbs Commands with Valid Parameters

Command with Valid Parameters	Description

GET *PropertyPath*	Displays the property value for the specified property path.
	
	For example, type the following at the command prompt to determine the network endpoints that Web site 1 uses:
	
	`cscript.exe adsutil.vbs GET W3SVC/1/ServerBindings`
	
	The string format for ServerBindings is *IP:Port:HostName*. If you run the preceding query on a computer that has a Web site running on port 80, the utility might return the following:
	
	`serverbindings       : <LIST> <1 Items>`
	`":80:"`

SET *PropertyPath Value*	Assigns a new value for the specified property path. If *Value* contains spaces, you must enclose *Value* in quotation marks.
	
	For example, if you want to set the **ServerComment** metabase property to Web server number 1, type the following at the command prompt:
	
	`cscript.exe adsutil.vbs SET w3svc/1/ServerComment`
	`"Web Server Number 1"`
	
	The next time you open IIS Manager, it shows the name of the Web server as Web Server Number 1.

ENUM *Path* [/P]	Lists all metabase paths (subkeys) and all properties for the specified path. If you use the optional **/P** parameter with this command, the utility lists the paths (subkeys) only and does not list properties. For example, if you want to enumerate only the subkeys under W3SVC, type the following at the command prompt: `cscript.exe adsutil.vbs ENUM W3SVC /P`
ENUM_ALL *Path* [/P]	Recursively lists all subkeys and properties for the specified path. If you use the optional **/P** parameter with this command, the utility enumerates the paths (subkeys) only and does not list properties. **Important**: If you do not include the *Path* parameter with this command, the utility lists all the subkeys and properties for the entire metabase.

(continued)

Table 9.4   Adsutil.vbs Commands with Valid Parameters *(continued)*

Command with Valid Parameters	Description
DELETE *Path*	Deletes the specified path from the metabase, and also deletes all the subkeys and properties that belong to the path.
CREATE *Path* [*KeyType*]	Creates the specified path and assigns it the specified **KeyType** property. The **KeyType** property specifies the class of the object that is associated with the key, such as IIsWebServer or IIsWebVirtualDir. If the value that you substitute for *KeyType* contains spaces, you must enclose the entire value in quotation marks.
	For example, if you want to create a subkey called /MyVDir under W3SVC for a **KeyType** of IIsWebVirtualDir, type the following at the command prompt:
	`cscript.exe adsutil.vbs CREATE W3SVC/1/ROOT/MyVdir "IIsWebVirtualDir"`
	For more information about the **KeyType** property, see "KeyType" in IIS 6.0 Help.
APPCREATEINPROC *Path*	Creates an in-process application on the specified path.
	Important: Use this command only on a computer that is running in IIS 5.0 isolation mode.
APPCREATEOUTPROC *Path*	Creates an out-of-process application on the specified path.
	Important: Use this command only on a computer that is running in IIS 5.0 isolation mode.
APPCREATEPOOLPROC *Path*	Creates a pooled out-of-process application on the specified path.
	Important: Use this command only on a computer that is running in IIS 5.0 isolation mode.
APPDELETE *Path*	Deletes the application, if one is present, on the specified path.
APPUNLOAD *Path*	Unloads an out-of-process (medium-isolation or high-isolation) application for the specified path.
	Important: Use this command only on a computer that is running in IIS 5.0 isolation mode.
APPGETSTATUS *Path*	Gets the status of the application. Returns the value Stopped, Running, or Not defined. The value Not defined is received if no application is defined for the specified path.

(continued)

Table 9.4   Adsutil.vbs Commands with Valid Parameters *(continued)*

Command with Valid Parameters	Description
FIND *PropertyPath*	Lists the paths where the specified property (as defined in *PropertyPath*) is set. If a specific location does not precede the property name, the utility searches the entire metabase.
	For example, if you type the following at the command prompt, the utility looks for and returns all occurrences of the **ServerComment** property within the entire metabase:
	`cscript.exe adsutil.vbs FIND /ServerComment`
	However, if you type the following code sample at the command prompt, the utility looks for and returns only the occurrences of **ServerComment** underneath the /W3SVC path:
	`cscript.exe adsutil.vbs FIND W3SVC/ServerComment`
START_SERVER*Path*	Starts the Web site defined by the specified path.
	For example, if you want to start the Web site defined by the W3SVC/1 metabase path, type the following code sample at the command prompt:
	`cscript.exe adsutil.vbs START_SERVER W3SVC/1`
STOP_SERVER*Path*	Stops the Web site defined by the specified path.
PAUSE_SERVER*Path*	Pauses the Web site defined by the specified path.
CONTINUE_SERVER *Path*	Restarts the Web site defined by the specified path.
HELP	Displays and describes all available commands for the Adsutil.vbs utility.

Managing IIS 6.0 Programmatically by Using WMI

WMI is a management infrastructure that lets you monitor and control system resources through a common set of interfaces. WMI is the Microsoft implementation of Web-Based Enterprise Management (WBEM), an industry initiative to establish standards for accessing and sharing management information over an enterprise network. WMI is WBEM-compliant and provides integrated support for the Common Information Model (CIM) — the data model that describes the objects that exist in a management environment.

WMI includes an *object repository*, which is the database of object definitions, and an *object manager* that handles the collection and manipulation of objects in the repository and gathers information from WMI providers. *WMI providers* act as intermediaries between WMI and components of the operating system, applications, and other systems. A WMI provider extends the WMI schema of classes to allow WMI to work with new types of objects.

IIS 6.0 includes the IIS WMI provider, which delivers a set of interfaces that let you use scripts and programs to administer Web sites. The IIS WMI provider defines classes for querying and configuring IIS. You can use it to manipulate managed objects, such as IIS metabase keys, or to retrieve information about managed objects.

IIS WMI Provider

In previous versions of IIS, you can programmatically administer IIS with Admin Base Objects from compiled C++ applications or with ADSI from C++ applications or script files. The IIS WMI provider in IIS 6.0 offers functionality similar to that of the IIS ADSI provider for editing the metabase and is likely to replace the IIS ASDI provider as the preferred interface for IIS administration.

The IIS WMI provider reads the metabase as a database of records, where each record is represented as an instance of a class. You can query each instance to determine content, state, associations, and properties. The IIS WMI provider establishes relationships among objects, allowing you to use the various objects and all the objects contained within them together to perform more complex actions. You can perform management tasks by using a single instance of the class or by using many instances of the class.

Advantages of Using the IIS WMI Provider

The IIS WMI provider offers the following advantages over other available management technologies, such as the IIS ADSI provider:

- **Query support**. You can select the objects or properties that you want to see, and WMI will return only the requested data. This level of detail saves time because you no longer need to sort through unwanted data.

- **Association**. In WMI, an association describes a relationship between classes and is, in itself, defined by a class. This allows you to view and traverse data about an entire system of associated components, such as troubleshooting. Because objects and properties can be associated outside the boundaries of a containment model, WMI allows selections and modifications by association across containment boundaries.

- **Global object model**. A single COM API exposes managed objects in IIS and other systems and applications depending only on the availability of appropriate WMI providers.

Comparing the IIS WMI Provider with the IIS ADSI Provider

The schema of the IIS WMI provider is compatible with the IIS ADSI provider, although the two technologies differ in architecture and features. Table 9.5 compares the architecture and features of the IIS WMI provider and the IIS ADSI provider.

Table 9.5   Comparing the IIS WMI Provider with the IIS ADSI Provider

Issue	IIS WMI Provider	IIS ADSI Provider
Query support	IIS WMI allows you to query on metadata key types to obtain only the data that you need.	IIS ADSI does not provide support for queries.
Object model and access routes	IIS WMI uses COM, which allows you to develop scripts, programs, and user interface (UI) tools. The WMI Object Browser, which you can obtain in the WMI SDK, is a tool that helps you perform all operations through any WMI provider.	IIS ADSI uses COM, which allows you to develop scripts and programs.
Extensible schema	IIS WMI returns existing schema extensions; however, you cannot use IIS WMI to extend the metabase schema.	IIS ADSI supports metabase schema extensions.
How properties are related to metabase keys	IIS WMI allows you to relate properties to metabase keys by containment or by association.	IIS ADSI allows you to relate properties to metabase keys by containment only.
Association or containment of related data	When you use the IIS WMI provider with other providers, IIS WMI supports associations with managed objects that are not in the metabase. Containment does not limit your ability to navigate associations to other classes.	IIS ADSI allows you to use the IIS ADSI container object methods to manipulate keys in the IIS metabase. You can create, delete, and move keys by creating, deleting, and moving IIS Admin Base Objects within container objects. You can also enumerate contained objects, such as virtual directories or servers, by using container object methods. IIS ADSI supports property inheritance.

For more information about the WMI provider, including the WMI Object Browser, see the Microsoft Windows Management Instrumentation (WMI) SDK link on the Web Resources page at http://www.microsoft.com/windows/reskits/webresources.

Object Hierarchy in IIS WMI Provider

Each WMI provider maintains its own namespace for classes that are specific to that provider. Each WMI provider namespace is a collection of class definitions that describe objects hierarchically in a domain. The namespace for IIS WMI provider classes is *MicrosoftIISv2*. Script writers and programmers use the MicrosoftIISv2 namespace to read and configure the IIS metabase.

WMI Class Types

The classes defined in the MicrosoftIISv2 namespace correspond to the IIS metabase schema, which means that at least one WMI class is defined for every unique metabase key. More than one WMI class is defined for most metabase keys: a WMI element class, containing read-only properties; a WMI setting class, containing writable properties; and a WMI association class, containing relationships between element classes and setting classes and between element classes and other element classes.

Table 9.6 lists some commonly used metabase keys and their corresponding WMI element classes (which have the same names as ADSI classes) and setting classes.

Table 9.6   Commonly Used Metabase Keys as They Relate to WMI Element and Setting Classes

Metabase Key	WMI Element Class	WMI Setting Class
Computer	IIsComputer	IIsComputerSetting
WWW service	IIsWebService	IIsWebServiceSetting
Web server	IIsWebServer	IIsWebServerSetting

The following sections describe the three types of WMI classes and how they are used.

WMI Element Classes

Use WMI element classes to navigate or enumerate objects, create new metabase nodes, call methods, and query read-only properties. WMI element classes expose the following types of properties, which you cannot change:

- Read-only properties, which belong to the element class.

- Inherited properties, which belong to the parent class.

- System properties, which belong to the system.

WMI element classes also expose methods for working with real instances of the objects they represent. For example, you can use WMI to start or stop an application pool.

WMI Setting Classes

Use WMI setting classes to change metabase properties, create new metabase nodes, and to set writable metabase properties. WMI setting classes expose read and write properties, which you can change by using a script or program. For example, the **IIsWebVirtualDirSettings** setting class, a counterpart to the **IIsWebVirtualDir** element class, exposes several writable metabase properties, including **AccessFlags**, **AccessSSL**, and **CacheISAPI**. WMI setting classes do not contain methods.

WMI Association Classes

Use WMI association classes to find WMI element classes or WMI setting classes that are associated with any WMI element class. For example, by using the association of **IIsWebDirectory**, you can find the IP security settings (**IPSecuritySetting**) for each of the files contained in a Web directory. Similarly, you can find all of the child classes of an element class. For example, to find the **IISWebVirtualDir** child classes of a Web virtual directory, use the association class **IIsWebVirtualDir_IIsWebVirtualDir**. Association class names are distinguished by an underscore separating two names, such as **IIsComputer_IIsComputerSetting** or **IIsComputer_IIsMimeMap**.

Sample WMI Scripts

This section includes sample scripts to perform the common tasks of enumerating virtual directories and recycling application pools. You can use these scripts as starting points to create custom scripts to perform tasks in your own environment.

Enumerating Virtual Directories

Listing 9.13 is a WMI sample script that uses Ccode to enumerate all executable virtual directories. You need a development environment such as the Microsoft® Visual Studio® .NET development system to compile Ccode.

 Important

You must be a member of the Administrators group on the local computer to run scripts and executables, or you must have been delegated the appropriate authority. As a security best practice, log on to your computer by using an account that is not in the Administrators group, and then use the runas command to run your script or executable as an administrator. At a command prompt, type runas /profile / *User:MyMachine\Administrator* cmd to open a command window with administrator rights and then type cscript.exe *ScriptName* (including the full path with parameters, if any).

Listing 9.13   Sample Script for Enumerating Virtual Directories

```
using System;
using System.Management;

namespace wmi1
{
     class Sample_SelectQuery
     {
          public static int Main(string[] args)
          {
               ManagementObjectSearcher s = new ManagementObjectSearcher(
                    "root\\MicrosoftIISv2",
                    "SELECT name FROM IISWebVirtualDirSetting where
AccessExecute=true",
                    new EnumerationOptions());

               foreach (ManagementObject vdir in s.Get())
               {
                    Console.WriteLine(vdir.ToString());
               }
               return 0;
          }
     }
}
```

Recycling Application Pools

Listing 9.14 is a VBScript sample script that recycles all application pools. For more information about application pools and performance issues, see "Running IIS 6.0 as an Application Server" or "Optimizing IIS 6.0 Performance" in this book.

Listing 9.14   Sample Script for Recycling Application Pools

```
strServer = WScript.arguments(0)

set Locator = CreateObject("WbemScripting.SWbemLocator")
set Service = locator.connectserver(strServer,"root/MicrosoftIISv2")
set APCollection = Service.InstancesOf("IISApplicationPool")
For each APInstance in APCollection
 APInstance.Recycle
Next
```

For more information about the IIS WMI provider, including a tutorial on the IIS WMI provider and sample scripts, see "IIS WMI Provider Tutorial" in IIS 6.0 Help.

For more information about WMI, and to download the WMI SDK, which contains WMI reference material and WMI object browsing tools, see the WMI SDK link on the Web Resources page at http://www.microsoft.com/windows/reskits/webresources.

Managing Server Certificates Programmatically

There are many ways to manage server certificates programmatically. This section provides a description of two different methods, including sample scripts for performing management tasks related to server certificates. One method uses the **IISCertObj** COM object, and the other method uses a CAPICOM-based script. *CAPICOM* is a CryptoAPI interface.

Managing Server Certificates by Using IISCertObj

You can use **IISCertObj** to perform the following tasks:

- Import copies of a server certificate from a .pfx file (a file containing a PFX-encrypted server certificate and a private key) from a server to multiple servers.

- Save backup copies of server certificates on a central site.

- Copy a server certificate from one server to multiple servers.

When using **IISCertObj**, you must set properties for the methods that you call. The following sections outline the necessary properties and the methods that you need to manage server certificates.

Setting IISCertObj Properties

Because a method will return an error message if the required properties for that method are not available when the method is called, you should set properties before you call methods. Table 9.7 lists the **IISCertObj** properties that you need to generate server certificate requests.

Table 9.7   Required IISCertObj Properties

Property Attribute	Name Attribute	Value	Description
ServerName	Data Type	String, write only	Contains the name of the computer on which server certificate operations are executed.
UserName	Data Type	String, write only	Specifies the user name that is used to log on to the remote computer. If UserName is empty, the credentials of the user that is currently logged on are used.
UserPassword	Data Type	String, write only	Specifies the password that is used for logging onto the remote computer.
InstanceName	Data Type	String, write only	Identifies the targeted metabase instance. W3svc/1 is an example.

Applying IISCertObj Methods

You can apply the following methods to the **IISCertObj** object: Copy, Export, GetCertInfo, Import, ImportToCertStore, IsExportable, IsInstalled, Move, and RemoveCert.

Copy

The Copy method allows you to copy a server certificate from one instance of IIS to another and from one computer to another. Use the following syntax with the Copy method:

```
Copy bAllowExport, bOverwriteExisting, DestinationServerName,
DestinationServerInstance, DestinationServerUserName, DestinationServerPassword
```

Table 9.8 lists the parameters that the Copy method uses.

Table 9.8   Copy Method Parameters

Parameter	Data Type	Description
bAllowExport	Boolean	Indicates whether the imported server certificate will be exportable (**true**) or not exportable (**false**).
bOverwriteExisting	Boolean	Indicates whether, if an identical server certificate already exists, it is overwritten (**true**) or not overwritten (**false**).
DestinationServerName	String	Specifies the computer name of the server to which the server certificate will be moved.
DestinationServerInstance	String	Specifies the IIS metabase instance at which the server certificate will be pointed. For example, w3svc/1.
DestinationServerUserName	String	Specifies the user name for the destination server. If empty, the user name of the user who is currently logged on will be used.
DestinationServerPassword	String	Specifies the password for the destination server when the *DestinationServerUserName* parameter is used.

Export

The Export method exports a copy of a server certificate to a file. The target file can be on a local or remote computer. Use the following syntax with the Export method:

```
ExportFileName, Password, bPrivateKey, bCertChain, bRemoveCert
```

Table 9.9 lists the parameters that the Export method uses.

Table 9.9   Export Method Parameters

Parameter	Data Type	Description
FileName	String	Specifies the name of the targeted file. For example, C:\Mydir\Mycert.pfx.
Password	String	Specifies the password that is used to secure the file specified as *FileName*.
bPrivateKey	Boolean	Indicates whether the private key is exported (**true**) or not exported (**false**).
bCertChain	Boolean	Indicates whether the certificate trust chain is exported (**true**) or not exported (**false**).
bRemoveCert	Boolean	Indicates whether the binding of a server certificate is removed (**true**) or not removed (**false**).

GetCertInfo

The GetCertInfo method allows you to acquire information on a server certificate that is installed on the computer specified by the **IISCertObj** properties, **ServerName** and **InstanceName**.

The GetCertInfo method uses no parameters.

Import

The Import method imports a copy of a server certificate from a file to a local or remote computer. Use the following syntax with the Import method:

```
Import FileName, Password, bAllowExport, bOverWriteExisting
```

Table 9.10 lists the parameters that the Import method uses.

Table 9.10   Import Method Parameters

Parameter	Data Type	Description
FileName	String	Specifies the name of the server certificate file to import.
Password	String	Specifies the password that is used to secure the file specified as *FileName*.
bAllowExport	Boolean	Indicates whether the imported server certificate is exportable (**true**) or not exportable (**false**).
bOverwriteExisting	Boolean	Indicates whether, if an identical server certificate already exists, it is overwritten (**true**) or not overwritten (**false**).

ImportToCertStore

The ImportToCertStore method imports a copy of a server certificate from a file to the certificate store on a local or remote computer. Use the following syntax with the ImportToCertStore method:

```
ImportToCertStoreFileName, Password, bAllowExport, bOverwriteExisting,
```

Table 9.11 lists the parameters that the ImportToCertStore method uses.

Table 9.11 ImportToCertStore Method Parameters

Parameter	Data Type	Description
FileName	String	Specifies the name of the server certificate file to import.
Password	String	Specifies the password that is used to secure the file specified as *FileName*.
bAllowExport	Boolean	Indicates whether the imported server certificate is exportable (**true**) or not exportable (**false**).
bOverwriteExisting	Boolean	Indicates whether, if an identical server certificate already exists, it is overwritten (**true**) or not overwritten (**false**).

IsExportable

The IsExportable method allows you to determine whether a server certificate is exportable from a computer that is specified by the IIS **ServerName** and **InstanceName** properties.

The IsExportable method uses no parameters.

IsInstalled

The IsInstalled method allows you to determine whether a server certificate is installed on a computer that is specified by the **IISCertObj** properties, **ServerName** and **InstanceName**.

The IsInstalled method uses no parameters.

Move

The Move method allows you to move a server certificate from one instance of IIS to another, and from one computer to another. Use the following syntax with the Move method:

```
Move bAllowExport, bOverwriteExisting, DestinationServerName,
DestinationServerInstance, DestinationServerUserName, DestinationServerPassword
```

Table 9.12 lists the parameters that the Move method uses.

Table 9.12   Move Method Parameters

Parameter	Data Type	Description
bAllowExport	Boolean	Indicates whether the imported server certificate is exportable (**true**) or not exportable (**false**).
bOverWriteExisting	Boolean	Indicates whether, if an identical server certificate already exists, it is overwritten (**true**) or not overwritten (**false**).
DestinationServerName	String	Specifies the computer name of the server to which the server certificate will be moved.
DestinationServerInstance	String	Specifies the IIS metabase instance at which the server certificate will be pointed. For example, w3svc/1.
DestinationServerUserName	String	Specifies the user name for the destination server. If no user name is entered, the user name of the user that is currently logged on will be used.
DestinationServerPassword	String	Specifies the password for the destination server when the *DestinationServerUserName* parameter is used.

RemoveCert

The RemoveCert method allows you to delete a server certificate from a certificate store. Use the following syntax with the RemoveCert method:

```
Copy bRemoveFromCertStore, bPrivateKey
```

Table 9.13 lists the parameters that the RemoveCert method uses.

Table 9.13   RemoveCert Method Parameters

Parameter	Data Type	Description
bRemoveFromCertStore	Boolean	Indicates whether the server certificate is removed (**true**) or not removed (**false**).
bPrivateKey	Boolean	Indicates whether the private key of the server certificate is removed (**true**) or not removed (**false**).

Sample Server Certificate Management Scripts

In IIS, if you use Windows Script Host or ASP, you can execute scripts that communicate with **IISCertObj** programmatically to import, archive, or export server certificates.

Importing server certificates to multiple servers

Large sites often need to use one server certificate for secure user logon to multiple servers. It would be time-consuming to use the Microsoft Management Console (MMC) to add copies of the server certificate to each server. By using the **IISCertObj** Import method, you can install copies of the same server certificate on all of the targeted servers.

To import a server certificate from a certificate store on one server to other servers, first save the following script in your text editor as CertImport.vbs.

 Important

You must be a member of the Administrators group on the local computer to run scripts and executables, or you must have been delegated the appropriate authority. As a security best practice, log on to your computer by using an account that is not in the Administrators group, and then use the **runas** command to run your script or executable as an administrator. At a command prompt, type **runas /profile** /*User.MyMachine\Administrator* cmd to open a command window with administrator rights and then type **cscript.exe** *ScriptName* (including the full path with parameters, if any).

```
Option Explicit
Dim iiscertobj, pfxfile, pfxfilepassword, InstanceName, WebFarmServers,
IISServer
Set iiscertobj = WScript.CreateObject("IIS.CertObj")
pfxfile = WScript.Arguments(0)
pfxfilepassword = WScript.Arguments(1)
InstanceName = WScript.Arguments(2)
WebFarmServers = split(WScript.Arguments(3), ",")
iiscertobj.UserName = WScript.Arguments(4)
iiscertobj.UserPassword = WScript.Arguments(5)
For Each IISServer in WebFarmServers
  iiscertobj.ServerName = IISServer
  iiscertobj.InstanceName = InstanceName
  iiscertobj.Import pfxfile, pfxfilepassword, true, true
Next
```

After you save the script as CertImport.vbs, run this command:

```
Certimport.vbs cert.pfx pfxPassword w3svc/1 iisserver1,iisserver2,iisserver3
Administrator aa134290
```

Saving backup copies of server certificates in a central archive

Using the **IISCertObj** Export method, you can archive a backup of each server certificate on your server farm to a central site.

To export copies of server certificates to the central site, first save the following script in your text editor as Save_all_certs.vbs.

```
Option Explicit
Dim iiscertobj, targetServer, targetServers, pfxbasename, pfxpassword,
InstanceName
Set iiscertobj = WScript.CreateObject("IIS.CertObj")
pfxbasename = WScript.Arguments(0)
pfxpassword = WScript.Arguments(1)
InstanceName = WScript.Arguments(2)
targetServers = split(WScript.Arguments(3), ",")
iiscertobj.UserName = WScript.Arguments(4)
iiscertobj.UserPassword = WScript.Arguments(5)
iiscertobj.InstanceName = InstanceName
For Each targetServer in targetServers
  iiscertobj.ServerName = targetServer
  iiscertobj.Export pfxbasename + targetServer + ".pfx", pfxpassword, true,
false, false
Next
```

After you save the script as Save_all_certs.vbs, run this command:

```
Save_all_certs.vbs C:\certbackup\ pfxpassword w3svc/1
iisserver2,iisserver3,iisserver4 Administrator aal34290
```

Copying a server certificate from an existing server to a new server

Using the **IISCertObj** Copy method, you can copy a server certificate to a new server after you add the server to a server farm.

To copy a server certificate from an existing server to a new server, first save the following script in your text editor as Certcopy.vbs.

```
Option Explicit
Dim iiscertobj, targetServer, targetServers, targetInstance
Set iiscertobj = WScript.CreateObject("IIS.CertObj")
iiscertobj.ServerName = WScript.Arguments(0)
iiscertobj.Instancename = WScript.Arguments(1)
targetServers = split(WScript.Arguments(2), ",")
targetInstance = WScript.Arguments(3)
iiscertobj.UserName = WScript.Arguments(4)
iiscertobj.UserPassword = WScript.Arguments(5)
For Each targetServer in targetServers
  iiscertobj.Copy true, true, targetServer, targetInstance
Next
```

After you save this script as Certcopy.vbs, run this command:

```
Certcopy.vbs iisServer1 w3svc/1 iisServer2 w3svc/1 Administrator asdf-0324
```

Extracting Server Certificate Information with a CAPICOM-Based Script

CAPICOM is an easy-to-use interface into CryptoAPI. CAPICOM allows you to incorporate Public Key Infrastructure (PKI) functionality into your applications by providing a simple interface for searching the certificate store and using server certificates to sign or encrypt data. Applications using CAPICOM objects call interfaces into CAPICOM.dll. CAPICOM.dll must be present and registered at run time to use CAPICOM objects. If you use CAPICOM objects in a Visual Basic project, you should add CAPICOM.dll to the project references. CAPICOM.dll is available with the Platform SDK. For more information about CAPICOM, see the CAPICOM link on the Web Resources page at http://www.microsoft.com/windows/reskits/webresources.

Registering CAPICOM.dll

To register CAPICOM.dll, at the command prompt, change directories to the directory where CAPICOM.dll is stored, and then type **regsvr32 CAPICOM.dll**.

You can use CAPICOM to create any number of server certificate–related management scripts. Listing 9.15 uses CAPICOM to extract SSL script information from IIS.

Listing 9.15 Sample Script for Extracting CAPICOM SSL Script Information

```
REM
Option Explicit
on error resume next
Const CAPICOM_MY_STORE = "My"
Const CAPICOM_LOCAL_MACHINE_STORE   = 1
Const CAPICOM_CURRENT_USER_STORE   = 2
Const CAPICOM_STORE_OPEN_READ_ONLY = 0
Const CAPICOM_EKU_CLIENT_AUTH = 2
Const CAPICOM_EKU_CODE_SIGNING = 3
Const CAPICOM_EKU_EMAIL_PROTECTION = 4
Const CAPICOM_EKU_SERVER_AUTH = 1
Const CAPICOM_EKU_OTHER = 0
Const CR_DISP_ISSUED   = &H3
Const CR_OUT_CHAIN = &H100
Const CR_OUT_BASE64 = &H1
Const CERT_SYSTEM_STORE_LOCAL_MACHINE = &H20000
Const CR_IN_BASE64   = &H1
Const CR_IN_PKCS10   = &H100
Dim oCert, oStore
Set oStore = CreateObject ("CAPICOM.Store")
if Err.Number <> 0 Then
    wscript.echo "CAPICOM NOT detected"
    Wscript.Quit(1)
End if
```

(continued)

Listing 9.15 Sample Script for Extracting CAPICOM SSL Script Information (continued)

```
oStore.Open CAPICOM_LOCAL_MACHINE_STORE, CAPICOM_MY_STORE,
CAPICOM_STORE_OPEN_READ_ONLY
For Each oCert in oStore.Certificates
    WScript.Echo "  Subject Name: " & oCert.SubjectName
        WScript.Echo "  Issuer Name: " & oCert.IssuerName
        WScript.Echo "  SHA-1 Thumbprint: " & oCert.Thumbprint
        WScript.Echo "  Serial Number: " & oCert.SerialNumber
        WScript.Echo "  Version: " & oCert.Version
        WScript.Echo "  Valid From: " & oCert.ValidFromDate
        WScript.Echo "  Valid To: " & oCert.ValidToDate
Next
```

Managing IIS 6.0 Remotely

You can remotely administer your server running IIS on an intranet or the Internet by using WMI or ADSI scripts, or you can use one of the following tools to manage IIS remotely:

- **IIS Manager**. You can use IIS Manager on your server to remotely connect to and administer an intranet server running IIS 5.0, IIS 5.1, and IIS 6.0. (IIS 3.0 and IIS 4.0 are not supported.)

- **Terminal Services**. Terminal Services does not require you to install IIS Manager on the remote client computer because once you are connected to the server running IIS, you use IIS Manager on the Web server as if you are logged on locally.

- **Remote Administration (HTML) tool**. You can use the Remote Administration (HTML) tool to administer your Web server from any Web browser on your intranet. This version of the Remote Administration (HTML) tool runs only on servers running IIS 6.0.

 Important

You must be a member of the Administrators group on the local computer to perform the following procedure or procedures, or you must have been delegated the appropriate authority. As a security best practice, log on to your computer by using an account that is not in the Administrators group, and then use the **Runas** command to run IIS Manager as an administrator. At a command prompt, type **runas** /*user:administrative_accountname* "mmc %*systemroot*%\system32\inetsrv\iis.msc".

▶ **To administer your intranet server remotely by using IIS Manager**

1. In IIS Manager, right-click the local computer, and click Connect.

2. In the **Connect to Computer** dialog box, in the **Computer name** box, type the name of the computer to which you want to connect, or click **Browse** to browse to the computer, and then click **OK**.

 Note

If you do not have TCP/IP and a name resolution server such as DNS installed, you might not be able to connect to an IIS computer by using the computer name. You can also use the IP address of the IIS computer, or you can add the host name and IP address to the local hosts file on the computer, which is located at *systemroot*\Windows\system32\drivers\etc\hosts. For more information, see "TCP/IP" in Help and Support Center for Windows Server 2003.

▶ **To administer your server remotely by using Terminal Services**

1. Install the Terminal Services client on the computer that you are using to connect to the server running IIS.

2. While the server is running, start Terminal Services and identify the name of the remote computer.

3. In Terminal Services, administer IIS as you would locally. You can start IIS Manager on any computer that is on your network and running Windows, or open a Web-based server-management appliance. You can also run scripts from the Terminal Services window.

▶ **To enable the Remote Administration (HTTP) tool through Control Panel**

1. In **Control Panel**, click **Add or Remove Programs**.

2. In the **Add or Remove Programs** dialog box, click **Add/Remove Windows Components**.

3. In the **Windows Components Wizard** dialog box, in **Components**, click **Application Server**, and then click **Details**.

4. In the **Application Server** dialog box, in **Subcomponents of Application Server**, click **Internet Information Services (IIS)**, and then click **Details**.

5. In the **Internet Information Services (IIS)** dialog box, in **Subcomponents of Internet Information Services (IIS)**, click **World Wide Web Service**, and then click **Details**.

6. In the **World Wide Web Service** dialog box, in **Subcomponents of World Wide Web Service**, select the **Remote Administration (HTML)** check box, and then click **OK**.

7. Click **OK** two more times, and then, in the **Windows Components Wizard** dialog box, click **Next.**

8. After setup is complete, click **Finish** to close the wizard.

▷ **To view the Remote Administration (HTML) tool from IIS Manager**

- In IIS Manager, double-click the local computer, double-click **Web Sites**, right-click **Administration**, and then click **Browse**.

▷ **To administer a Web server remotely by using the Remote Administration (HTML) tool**

- Open your intranet site from a Web browser, and type the following in the address bar: **http://***HostName***:8099**, where *HostName* is the name of the computer that you want to connect to and administer.

For more information about how to manage servers remotely by using the Remote Administration (HTML) tool, see the Remote Administration (HTML) Tool link on the Web Resources page at http://www.microsoft.com/windows/reskits/webresources.

Scheduling IIS 6.0 Backups

Using available tools, you can create a simple script to back up your IIS content and configuration as often as is required in your environment. After you create this script, you can type one additional command to schedule the backup to occur regularly.

Backing Up IIS Content

You can include the **xcopy** command in a simple script for copying IIS and backing up content. **Xcopy** offers useful parameters for copying permissions, auditing settings, and copying hidden files.

 Important

You must be a member of the Administrators group on the local computer to run scripts and executables, or you must have been delegated the appropriate authority. As a security best practice, log on to your computer by using an account that is not in the Administrators group, and then use the runas command to run your script or executable as an administrator. At a command prompt, type runas /profile /*User:MyMachine\Administrator* cmd to open a command window with administrator rights and then type cscript.exe *ScriptName* (including the full path with parameters, if any).

To back up content with **xcopy**, use the following command-line syntax:

```
xcopy Source [Destination] [/o] [/x] [/e] [/h] [/y] [c]
```

Table 9.14 lists relevant **xcopy** parameters.

Table 9.14 Xcopy Parameters

Parameter	Description
Source	Specifies the name of the source server.
Destination	Specifies the name of the destination server.
o	Copies ACLs.
x	Copies auditing settings (used with /o).
e	Copies the empty directories.
h	Copies the hidden directories.
y	Overwrites without prompting.
c	Continues to copy even if errors occur.

Backing Up IIS Configuration

To back up the metabase, you can run the Iisback.vbs command-line script with the **/backup** parameter, which places a backup file in *systemroot*\System32\Inetsrv\Metaback. After you run Iisback.vbs, you should copy the backup file to your main backup location. These examples use the backup location \\Mybackupserver\Share$.

If you want to create a batch file, you can set the name with dynamic variables, such as **%date%**, and static, user-defined variables, such as **%server%**.

Next, copy the backup files that are created in the *systemroot*\System32\Inetsrv\Metaback folder. The files that are created are named *Name*.MD and *Name*.SC#, where *Name* is the name you specify and is the version number of the backup set, starting with zero (0). If you use the same name for subsequent backups, the version number will be incremented by 1 for each backup set that uses the same name. For more information about backing up the metabase, see "Working with the Metabase" in this book.

Listing 9.16 is an example of a backup batch file that copies both content and configuration.

Listing 9.16 BACKUP.BAT: Sample Backup Batch File

```
BACKUP.BAT

SET SERVER=MyServer
SET NAME=%DATE%-%SERVER%
iisback /backup /b %NAME% /e %PASSWORD%
Xcopy %windir%\system32\inetsrv\metaback\%NAME%.*
\\mybackupserver\share$\%SERVER%
Xcopy /o /x /e /h /y /c c:\WEB \\mybackupserver\share$\%SERVER%
```

This batch file copies the backup files and all of the Web content — one or more Web sites that are subfolders of C:\WEB\ — to the backup location that is a subfolder of the folder that has the same name as the server. The defined variables **%server%** and **%name%** allow you to change the server name quickly without having to go through the batch file.

To schedule this backup process as a nightly task, type **at 9:00p /every:m,t,w,th,f,s,su "c:\backup.bat"** at the command prompt.

For more information about backing up a computer running Windows Server 2003, see "Backup" in Help and Support Center for Windows Server 2003.

Restarting and Alternatives to Restarting IIS 6.0

In earlier versions of IIS, if an application became unavailable, restarting IIS by using the IISReset.exe command-line tool was a common recovery practice. However, restarting or stopping IIS, or rebooting your Web server is a severe action. When you restart IIS, all of the sessions that are connected to your Web server, including the World Wide Web Publishing service (WWW service), FTP, Simple Mail Transfer Protocol (SMTP), and Network News Transfer Protocol (NNTP), are dropped. Any data held in Web applications is lost, and all of the Internet sites are unavailable until the Internet services are restarted. To avoid this, IIS 6.0 requires fewer restarts than earlier versions of IIS.

For more information about restarting IIS and alternatives to restarting IIS, see "Restarting IIS" in IIS 6.0 Help.

 Important

Although using IISReset.exe is not recommended, if you do use IISReset.exe, always use the **/noforce** parameter. The **/noforce** parameter is recommended as a safeguard against data loss in case the IIS services cannot all be stopped within the one-minute time-out period.

Automatic Restart

In IIS 6.0, the WWW service is hosted by the service host, Svchost.exe. The FTP, NNTP, and SMTP services and the IIS metabase, known as the IIS Admin service (IISAdmin.dll), live in Inetinfo.exe. If the IIS Admin service terminates abnormally, IIS restarts automatically. This feature is known as Automatic Restart.

In IIS 5.0, if the IIS Admin service terminated abnormally, both the WWW service and the IIS Admin service had to be restarted because they shared the same application space. In IIS 6.0, if the IIS Admin service terminates abnormally, the WWW service does not go down because the IIS Admin service and the WWW service run in separate process spaces. In this case, the WWW service acknowledges that the metabase has terminated abnormally and checks to see whether IISReset.exe is configured on the IIS Admin service. If IISReset.exe is configured on the IIS Admin service, IIS waits for the IIS Admin service to start again and then reconnects the WWW service.

Worker Process Isolation Mode

Worker process isolation mode is the default service mode in IIS; it is designed to ensure that your applications do not interfere with other services and cause the need to restart IIS. If you are running IIS in worker process isolation mode, you can configure it to periodically restart worker processes in the application pool. You can also recycle application pools manually. In addition, you can configure worker process isolation mode so that if a particular application pool experiences consecutive multiple failures, the application can be automatically disabled, allowing for rapid-fail protection. Finally, in worker process isolation mode you can use CPU monitoring, which is a tool for monitoring and automatically shutting down worker processes that consume large amounts of CPU time.

Additional Resources

These resources contain additional information and tools related to this chapter.

Related Information

- "Configuring Internet Sites and Services" in this book for information about configuring the File Transfer Protocol (FTP), Network News Transfer Protocol (NNTP), and Simple Mail Transfer Protocol (SMTP) services.

- "IIS 6.0 Architecture" in this book for information about the IIS 6.0 application isolation modes.

- "Managing a Secure IIS 6.0 Solution" in this book for information about setting ACLs.

- "Using FrontPage 2002 Server Extensions with IIS 6.0" in this book for information about installing and using FrontPage 2002 Server Extensions.

- "Working with the Metabase" in this book for information about metabase terminology, including definitions of metabase keys, values, and KeyTypes.

- The CAPICOM link on the Web Resources page at http://www.microsoft.com/windows/reskits/webresources for information about using CAPICOM.

- The Microsoft Windows Management Instrumentation (WMI) SDK link on the Web Resources page at http://www.microsoft.com/windows/reskits/webresources for information about the WMI provider, including the WMI Object Browser.

- The Remote Administration (HTML) Tool link on the Web Resources page at http://www.microsoft.com/windows/reskits/webresources for information about how to manage servers remotely by using the Remote Administration (HTML) tool.

- The Using the Administration Tools Remotely link on the Web Resources page at http://www.microsoft.com/windows/reskits/webresources for information about using Owsrmadm.exe.

Related IIS 6.0 Help Topics

- "Creating Web Sites" in IIS 6.0 Help, which is accessible from IIS Manager, for information about creating Web sites by using the Iisweb.vbs command-line script.

- "Creating FTP Virtual Directories" in IIS 6.0 Help for information about setting up FTP virtual directories.

- "Restarting IIS" in IIS 6.0 Help for information about restarting IIS 6.0 and alternatives to restarting IIS 6.0.

- "Using the IIS ADSI Provider" in IIS 6.0 Help for information about how to use the IIS ADSI provider to programmatically administer IIS 6.0.

- "Using the IIS WMI Provider" in IIS 6.0 Help for information about how to use the IIS WMI provider to programmatically administer IIS 6.0.

Related Windows Server 2003 Help Topics

For best results in identifying Help topics by title, in Help and Support Center, under the **Search** box, click **Set search options**. Under **Help Topics**, select the **Search in title only** check box.

- "Backup" in Help and Support Center for Windows Server 2003 for information about backing up a computer running Windows Server 2003.

- "Command-line reference A-Z" in Help and Support Center for Windows Server 2003 for information about specific commands, including command syntax.

- "Server administration using Dnscmd" in Help and Support Center for Windows Server 2003 for information about using Dnscmd.exe.

C H A P T E R   1 7

Analyzing Log Files

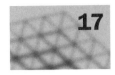

17

Internet Information Services (IIS) 6.0 offers a number of ways to record the activity of your Web sites, File Transfer Protocol (FTP) sites, Network News Transfer Protocol (NNTP) service, and Simple Mail Transfer Protocol (SMTP) service and allows you to choose the log file format that works best for your environment. IIS logging is designed to be more detailed than the event logging or performance monitoring features of the Microsoft® Windows® Server 2003, Standard Edition, Windows® Server 2003, Enterprise Edition, and Windows® Server 2003, Datacenter Edition, operating systems. IIS log files can include information such as who has visited your site, what was viewed, and when the information was last viewed. You can monitor attempts to access your sites, virtual folders, or files and determine whether attempts were made to read or write to your files. IIS log file formats allow you to record events independently for any site, virtual folder, or file.

In This Chapter

Related Information

- For information about centralized binary log file format, see "Centralized Binary Log File Format" in this book.

- For information about the IIS architecture and core components, see "IIS 6.0 Architecture" in this book.

New in Logging

Logging in IIS 6.0 differs from logging in previous versions of IIS in several ways. The redesigned IIS architecture, which allows for multiple worker processes, affects how the IIS core components handle logging. In addition, IIS 6.0 provides new logging features and log file formats.

Events Are Logged by HTTP.sys

In IIS 5.0, all logging is done by the Inetinfo.exe component and is accomplished using Component Object Model (COM) modules that are written for logging. This system is effective in IIS 5.0 because there is only one server process model, Inetinfo.exe. However, in IIS 6.0, logging is done by the HTTP protocol stack (HTTP.sys). IIS 6.0 passes user-mode events to HTTP.sys through application programming interfaces (APIs), and then the user-mode events are logged by HTTP.sys.

HTTP.sys handles logging for two main reasons. When IIS 6.0 is running in worker process isolation mode, each worker process can perform its own logging and a site's applications can spread across multiple application pools. If Inetinfo.exe performed logging in this environment, multi-instance or synchronization problems could occur. Such problems can be avoided because HTTP.sys performs logging. In addition, in IIS 6.0, requests can be served completely from the HTTP.sys kernel-mode cache without ever passing through Inetinfo.exe, so logging from HTTP.sys ensures that cached responses are recorded.

The log file format for which HTTP.sys does not perform logging is only Open Database Connectivity (ODBC) logging. For more information about how ODBC logging is handled, see "ODBC Logging" later in this chapter. For more information about the IIS 6.0 architecture and core components, see "IIS 6.0 Architecture" in this book.

Substatus Error Code Logging

To reduce the possibility that a malicious user might use the information provided by substatus error codes to attack the Web server, substatus error codes are not returned to the client in IIS 6.0. Instead, administrators using the World Wide Web Consortium (W3C) Extended log file format can record substatus error codes when requests fail. Substatus error code logging is turned on by default for the W3C Extended log file format. For more information about substatus error code logging, see "Substatus Error Codes" later in this chapter.

Centralized Binary Logging

Centralized binary logging is a process in which IIS creates a single log file that contains binary, unformatted log data for all of the Web sites that are hosted on a server. In contrast, the other available IIS logging methods create one formatted, human-readable log file per Web site. Centralized binary logging provides organizations with a way to record detailed information about all of their Web sites, using a minimum of system resources. For more information about centralized binary logging, see "Centralized Binary Logging" later in this chapter.

HTTP.sys Error Logging

HTTP.sys sometimes generates its own errors that, because of the IIS 6.0 architecture, are not recorded with the worker-process-driven events. To account for these errors, IIS 6.0 supports HTTP.sys error log files. One example of an event that would trigger a log file entry in the HTTP.sys error log file is a connection time-out. For more information about HTTP.sys error log files, see "HTTP.sys Error Log Files" later in this chapter.

Remote Logging

You can write log data to a remote share over a network using a full, Universal Naming Convention (UNC) path. For example, you can specify *Servername**LogFiles* as the storage directory for your log files, where *Servername* represents the name of the remote server, and *LogFiles* represents the name of the directory where the log files are stored.

For more information about remote logging, see "Remote Logging" in IIS 6.0 Help, which is accessible from IIS Manager.

Log File Formats in IIS

IIS provides six different log file formats that you can use to track and analyze information about your IIS-based sites and services. In addition to the six available formats, you can create your own custom log file format. For more information about custom logging, see "Custom Logging Modules" later in this chapter.

The following six log file formats are available in IIS:

- **W3C Extended log file format.** Text-based, customizable format for a single site. This is the default format.

- **National Center for Supercomputing Applications (NCSA) Common log file format.** Text-based, fixed format for a single site.

- **IIS log file format.** Text-based, fixed format for a single site.

- **ODBC logging.** Fixed format for a single site. Data is recorded in an ODBC-compliant database.

- **Centralized binary logging.** Binary-based, unformatted data that is not customizable. Data is recorded from multiple Web sites and sent to a single log file. To interpret the data, you need a special parser.

- **HTTP.sys error logging.** Fixed format for HTTP.sys-generated errors.

You can read text-based log files using a text editor such as Notepad, which is included with Windows, but administrators often import the files into a report-generating software tool for further analysis.

For step-by-step instructions on how to enable logging, see "Enabling Logging" in IIS 6.0 Help. For more information about the log file formats, see "W3C Extended Log File Format," "NCSA Common Log File Format," "IIS Log File Format," "ODBC Logging," "HTTP.sys Error Log Files," and "Centralized Binary Logging" later in this chapter.

UTF-8 Format for Non-English Languages and Security

UTF-8 is a method of character encoding that allows for both single and multibyte characters in one string. If you want to read text-based (W3C Extended, IIS, and NCSA Common) log files in a language other than English, you can enable the UTF-8 format. You also need the UTF-8 format if you serve URLs in a language other than the native server code page, for example, if you serve Chinese URLs on a Japanese system. In addition, because IIS 6.0 tries to serve URLs in code pages other than the server default code page by default, you might want to enable the UTF-8 format for security reasons. It is a good security practice to enable the UTF-8 format in case of an attack based on URLs in UTF-8 that might not translate correctly to the default code page.

Note

IIS does not support the UTF-8 format for FTP site log files.

▶   **To enable UTF-8 format**

Important

You must be a member of the Administrators group on the local computer to perform the following procedure or procedures, or you must have been delegated the appropriate authority. As a security best practice, log on to your computer by using an account that is not in the Administrators group, and then use the **runas** command to run IIS Manager as an administrator. At a command prompt, type **runas** /*User.Administrative_AccountName* "mmc %systemroot%\system32\inetsrv\iis.msc".

1. In IIS Manager, right-click the local computer, and then click **Properties**.

2. In **UTF-8 Logging**, select the **Encode Web logs in UTF-8** check box, and then click **OK**.

Log File Locations and ACLs

If you create a log file directory of C:\LogFiles for HTTP.sys-generated logging (W3C Extended log file format, NCSA Common log file format, IIS log file format, centralized binary logging, or HTTP.sys error logging), then HTTP.sys generates the following subdirectories, and the log files are created under these subdirectories:

- For the W3C Extended, NCSA Common, and IIS log file formats, HTTP.sys generates the subdirectory C:\LogFiles\W3SVC#, where # is the site ID.

- For centralized binary logging, HTTP.sys generates the subdirectory C:\LogFiles\W3SVC.

- For HTTP.sys error logging, HTTP.sys generates the subdirectory C:\WINDOWS\System32\LogFiles\HTTPErr.

By default, the log file directory has the following access control lists (ACLs):

- NT Authority\System: Full access

- Built-in\Administrators: Full access

- Everyone: No access (Although the No access permission is the effective permission, this setting is not explicitly set by HTTP.sys.)

Individual log files in the log file directory have the following controls:

- NT Authority\System: Full access

- Built-in\Administrators: Read and delete access

- Everyone: No access (Although the No access permission is the effective permission, this setting is not explicitly set by HTTP.sys.)

Important

The default log file directory ACLs (DACLs) are set for optimum security. If you choose to create log file directories with less restrictive ACLs, your system might be more vulnerable to attack.

If you are using the W3C Extended, NCSA Common, or IIS log file formats and it is necessary to do so, you can create a subdirectory called W3SVC# of the C:\LogFiles directory and set ACLs for that directory that are different from the defaults. For example, if you need to allow a site administrator to read the log files, create a W3SVC# subdirectory of the C:\LogFiles directory and set Read ACLs for the site's administrator.

Important

The owner of the W3SVC# subdirectory must be a member of the Local Administrators group. If not, HTTP.sys writes an error to the NT Event log and disables logging.

For more information about file and directory security and access control, see "Managing a Secure IIS 6.0 Solution" in this book.

W3C Extended Log File Format

The W3C Extended log file format is the default log file format for IIS. It is a customizable ASCII text-based format. You can use IIS Manager to select which fields to include in the log file, which allows you to keep log files as small as possible. Because HTTP.sys handles the W3C Extended log file format, this format records HTTP.sys kernel-mode cache hits.

Table 10.1 lists and describes the available fields. Default fields are noted.

Table 10.1   W3C Extended Log File Fields

Field	Appears As	Description	Default Y/N
Date	date	The date on which the activity occurred.	Y
Time	time	The time, in coordinated universal time (UTC), at which the activity occurred.	Y
Client IP Address	c-ip	The IP address of the client that made the request.	Y
User Name	cs-username	The name of the authenticated user who accessed your server. Anonymous users are indicated by a hyphen.	Y
Service Name and Instance Number	s-sitename	The Internet service name and instance number that was running on the client.	N
Server Name	s-computername	The name of the server on which the log file entry was generated.	N
Server IP Address	s-ip	The IP address of the server on which the log file entry was generated.	Y
Server Port	s-port	The server port number that is configured for the service.	Y
Method	cs-method	The requested action, for example, a GET method.	Y
URI Stem	cs-uri-stem	The target of the action, for example, Default.htm.	Y
URI Query	cs-uri-query	The query, if any, that the client was trying to perform. A Universal Resource Identifier (URI) query is necessary only for dynamic pages.	Y
HTTP Status	sc-status	The HTTP status code.	Y
Win32 Status	sc-win32-status	The Windows status code.	N

(continued)

Table 10.1 W3C Extended Log File Fields *(continued)*

Field	Appears As	Description	Default Y/N
Bytes Sent	sc-bytes	The number of bytes that the server sent.	N
Bytes Received	cs-bytes	The number of bytes that the server received.	N
Time Taken	time-taken	The length of time that the action took, in milliseconds.	N
Protocol Version	cs-version	The protocol version —HTTP or FTP —that the client used.	N
Host	cs-host	The host header name, if any.	N
User Agent	cs(User-Agent)	The browser type that the client used.	Y
Cookie	cs(Cookie)	The content of the cookie sent or received, if any.	N
Referrer	cs(Referrer)	The site that the user last visited. This site provided a link to the current site.	N
Protocol Substatus	sc-substatus	The substatus error code.	Y

For information about status codes, see the IIS Status Codes link on the Web Resources page at http://www.microsoft.com/windows/reskits/webresources.

 Note

FTP log files do not record the following fields:

- cs-uri-query
- cs-host
- cs(User-Agent)
- cs(Cookie)
- cs(Referrer)
- sc-substatus

You can select as many of the W3C Extended log file fields as you want. However, not all fields will contain information. For fields that are selected but for which there is no information, a hyphen (-) appears as a placeholder. If a field contains a nonprintable character, HTTP.sys replaces it with a plus sign (+) to preserve the log file format. This typically occurs with virus attacks, when, for example, a malicious user sends carriage returns and line feeds that, if not replaced with the plus sign (+), would break the log file format.

Fields are separated by spaces. Field prefixes have the following meanings:

- **s-** Server actions
- **c-** Client actions
- **cs-** Client-to-server actions
- **sc-** Server-to-client actions

 Note

For the **time-taken** field, the client-request timestamp is initialized when HTTP.sys receives the first byte, but before HTTP.sys begins parsing the request. The client-request timestamp is stopped when the last IIS send completion occurs. Time taken does not reflect time across the network. The first request to the site shows a slightly longer time taken than other similar requests because HTTP.sys opens the log file with the first request.

For more information about the W3C Extended log file format, see the W3C Extended Log File Format link on the Web Resources page at http://www.microsoft.com/windows/reskits/webresources.

W3C Extended Log File Examples

Example of an Intranet Site

The following example shows a W3C Extended log file entry from an intranet site, as viewed in a text editor. The log file includes only the default fields.

```
#Software: Microsoft Internet Information Services 6.0
#Version: 1.0
#Date: 2002-05-02 17:42:15
#Fields: date time c-ip cs-username s-ip s-port cs-method cs-uri-stem cs-uri-
query sc-status cs(User-Agent)
2002-05-02 17:42:15 172.22.255.255 - 172.30.255.255 80 GET /images/picture.jpg -
200 Mozilla/4.0+(compatible;MSIE+5.5;+Windows+2000+Server)
```

You can interpret the preceding log file entry as follows:

#Software: Microsoft Internet Information Services 6.0   This indicates the version of IIS that is running.

#Version: 1.0   This indicates the log file format.

#Date: 2002-05-02 17:42:15   This indicates when the first log file entry was recorded, which is when the entire log file was created.

#Fields: date time c-ip cs-username s-ip s-port cs-method cs-uri-stem ...   This indicates the fields that are recorded in the log file entry and the order in which they are recorded

Table 10.2 lists and describes the fields that are recorded in this example.

 Note

Use the order shown in the Fields log file entry to parse all entries until the next log file entry begins. The field order is subject to change and is different in IIS 6.0 than it was in IIS 5.0.

Table 10.2 Example of a W3C Extended Log File Entry from an Intranet Site

Field	Appears As	Description
date	2002-05-02	This log file entry was recorded on May 2, 2002.
time	17:42:15	This log file entry was recorded at 5:42 P.M. UTC. Entries are recorded to the log file when the send completion for the last IIS send occurs.
c-ip	172.22.255.255	The IP address of the client.
cs-username	-	The user was anonymous.
s-ip	172.30.255.255	The IP address of the server.
s-port	80	The server port.
cs-method	GET	The user issued a **GET**, or download, command.
cs-uri-stem	/images/picture.jpg	The user wanted to download the picture.jpg file from the Images folder.
cs-uri-query	-	The URI query did not occur. (URI queries are necessary only for dynamic pages, such as ASP pages, so this field usually contains a hyphen for static pages.)
sc-status	200	The request was fulfilled with no errors.
cs(User-Agent)	Mozilla/4.0+ (compatible;MSIE+5.5;+ Windows+2000+Server)	The type of browser that the client used, as represented by the browser.

Example of an Internet Site

The following example shows a W3C Extended log file entry from an Internet site, as viewed in a text editor. The log file contains several fields in addition to the default fields and is typical of the kind of log file you would run to monitor an Internet site.

```
#Software: Microsoft Internet Information Services 6.0
#Version: 1.0
#Date: 2002-05-24 20:18:01
#Fields: date time c-ip cs-username s-ip s-port cs-method cs-uri-stem cs-uri-
query sc-status sc-bytes cs-bytes time-taken cs(User-Agent) cs(Referrer)
2002-05-24 20:18:01 172.224.24.114 - 206.73.118.24 80 GET /Default.htm - 200 7930
248 31 Mozilla/4.0+(compatible;+MSIE+5.01;+Windows+2000+Server)
http://64.224.24.114/
```

You can interpret the preceding log file entry as follows:

#Software: Microsoft Internet Information Services 6.0   This indicates the version of IIS that is running.

#Version: 1.0   This indicates the log file format.

#Date: 2002-05-24 20:18:01   This indicates when the first log file entry was recorded, which is when the entire log file was created.

#Fields: date time c-ip cs-username s-ip s-port cs-method cs-uri-stem ...   This indicates the fields that are recorded in the log file entry and the order in which they are recorded. Table 10.3 lists and describes the fields recorded in this example.

Table 10.3   Example of a W3C Extended Log File Entry from an Internet Site

Field	Appears As	Description
date	2002-05-24	This log file entry was recorded on May 24, 2002.
time	20:18:01	This log file entry was recorded at 8:18 P.M. UTC.
c-ip	172.224.24.114	The IP address of the client.
cs-username	-	The user was anonymous.
s-ip	206.73.118.24	The IP address of the server.
s-port	80	The server port.
cs-method	GET	The user issued a **GET**, or download, command.
cs-uri-stem	/Default.htm	The user wanted to download the contents of Default.htm.
cs-uri-query	-	The URI query did not occur.
sc-status	200	The request was fulfilled without error.
sc-bytes	7930	The number of bytes that the server sent to the client.
cs-bytes	248	The number of bytes that the client sent to the server.
time-taken	31	The action was completed in 31 milliseconds.
cs(User-Agent)	Mozilla/4.0+(compatible;+MSIE+5.01;+Windows+2000+Server)	The type of browser that the client used, as represented by the browser.
cs(Referrer)	http://62.224.24.114/	The Web page that provided the link to the Web site.

Example of an FTP Site

The following example shows a W3C Extended log file entry from an Internet FTP site, as viewed in a text editor. The example does not include all of the default fields and is typical of the kind of log file that you would run to monitor an FTP site.

```
#Software: Microsoft Internet Information Services 6.0
#Version: 1.0
#Date: 2002-06-04 16:40:23
#Fields: time c-ip cs-method cs-uri-stem sc-status
16:40:23 10.152.10.200 [6994]USER anonymous 331
16:40:25 10.152.10.200 [6994]PASS anonymous@example.net 530
```

You can interpret the preceding log file example as follows:

#Software: Microsoft Internet Information Services 6.0   This indicates the version of IIS that is running.

#Version: 1.0   This indicates the log file format.

#Date: 2002-06-04 16:40:23   This indicates when the first log file entry was recorded, which is when the log was created.

#Fields: time c-ip cs-method cs-uri-stem sc-status   This indicates the fields that are recorded in the log file entry and the order in which they are recorded. Table 10.4 lists and describes the fields recorded in this example.

Table 10.4   Example of a W3C Extended Log File Entry from an FTP Site

Field	Appears As	Description
time	16:40:23	This log file entry was recorded at 4:40 P.M. UTC.
c-ip	10.152.10.200	The IP address of the client.
cs-method	[6994]USER	The **USER FTP** command was used, which requests a user name and is always followed by a **PASS FTP** command. 6994 is the connection number corresponding to an anonymous user.
cs-uri-stem	anonymous	The user (the target of the **USER** command) was anonymous.
sc-status	331	The user name was accepted.
time	16:40:25	The next recorded action occurred at 4:40 P.M. UTC.
c-ip	10.152.10.200	The IP address of the client.
cs-method	[6994]PASS	The **PASS FTP** command was used, which supplies a password for the user name and is always preceded by a **USER** command.
cs-uri-stem	anonymous@example.net	The password (the target of the **PASS** command) supplied.
sc-status	530	The user was not logged on.

Substatus Error Codes

In an effort to reduce the attack surface of IIS, in IIS 6.0, error messages do not return specific error message content, including the substatus error code, to clients. However, to allow administrators to track errors and debug failed requests, IIS provides the ability to record substatus error codes in the W3C Extended log file format. Substatus error code logging is enabled by default. For more information about enabling and disabling substatus error code logging, see "Substatus Error Codes in Log Files" in IIS 6.0 Help.

If an error message contains too much information about the server and an explanation of why a particular request failed to execute, malicious users can use the information from the error message to attack the server. For example, an error code such as 404.2 indicates that a file or directory is not returned because the server lockdown policy restricts it. In IIS 6.0, a 404.2 error is returned to the client as a 404 error message. The simple 404 error message does not provide a malicious user with any details about the configuration of the server.

When substatus error code logging is enabled by default, only members of the Administrators group and users with LocalSystem user accounts can access log files that contain substatus error codes. To analyze an error, the administrator locates the error and substatus error code in the log file and checks the code against the Custom Error Messages table. For example, if a client request to an Active Server Pages (ASP) page returned a 403 error, the administrator can determine that the actual error was 403.9 by viewing the log file. The administrator checks the Custom Error Messages table and learns that, in this situation, the file or directory was not found because too many clients were trying to connect to the server at once. The administrator can remedy the situation quickly and easily by changing the maximum number of connections setting to unlimited. To see the Custom Error Messages table, see "About Custom Error Messages" in IIS 6.0 Help.

NCSA Common Log File Format

The NCSA Common log file format is a fixed ASCII text-based format, so you cannot customize it. The NCSA Common log file format is available for Web sites and for SMTP and NNTP services, but it is not available for FTP sites. Because HTTP.sys handles the NCSA Common log file format, this format records HTTP.sys kernel-mode cache hits.

The NCSA Common log file format records the following data:

- Remote host address
- Remote log name (This value is always a hyphen.)
- User name
- Date, time, and Greenwich mean time (GMT) offset
- Request and protocol version

- Service status code (A value of 200 indicates that the request was fulfilled successfully.)

- Bytes sent

- Not all fields will contain information. For fields for which there is no information, a hyphen (-) appears as a placeholder. If a field contains a nonprintable character, HTTP.sys replaces it with a plus sign (+) to preserve the log file format. This typically occurs with virus attacks, when, for example, a malicious user sends carriage returns and line feeds that, if not replaced with the plus sign (+), would break the log file format.

Fields are separated by spaces, and time is recorded as local time with the GMT offset.

NCSA Common Log File Example

The following example shows an NCSA Common log file entry, as viewed in a text editor.

```
172.21.13.45 - Microsoft\JohnDoe [08/Apr/2001:17:39:04 -0800] "GET
/scripts/iisadmin/ism.dll?http/serv HTTP/1.0" 200 3401
```

Table 10.5 lists and describes the fields recorded in this example.

Table 10.5   Example of an NCSA Common Log File Entry

Field	Appears As	Description
Remote host address	172.21.13.45	The IP address of the client.
Remote log name	-	The name is unavailable.
User name	Microsoft\JohnDoe	The name of the user is JohnDoe.
Date, time, and GMT offset	[08/Apr/2001:17:39:04 -0800]	The log file entry was created on April 8, 2001 at 5:39 P.M. The difference between the local time and the GMT is eight hours.
Request and protocol version	"GET /scripts/iisadmin/ism.dll?http/serv HTTP/1.0"	The client issued a **GET** command for the Ism.dll file using HTTP version 1.0.
Service status code	200	The request was fulfilled successfully.
Bytes sent	3401	The number of bytes sent.

IIS Log File Format

The IIS log file format is a fixed ASCII text-based format, so you cannot customize it. Because HTTP.sys handles the IIS log file format, this format records HTTP.sys kernel-mode cache hits.

The IIS log file format records the following data:

- Client IP address
- User name
- Date
- Time
- Service and instance
- Server name
- Server IP address
- Time taken
- Client bytes sent
- Server bytes sent
- Service status code (A value of 200 indicates that the request was fulfilled successfully.)
- Windows status code (A value of 0 indicates that the request was fulfilled successfully.)
- Request type
- Target of operation
- Parameters (the parameters that are passed to a script)

Not all fields will contain information. For fields for which there is no information, a hyphen (-) appears as a placeholder. If a field contains a nonprintable character, HTTP.sys replaces it with a plus sign (+) to preserve the log file format. This typically occurs with virus attacks, when, for example, a malicious user sends carriage returns and line feeds that, if not replaced with the plus sign (+), would break the log file format.

Fields are separated by commas, making the format easier to read than the other ASCII formats, which use spaces for separators. The time is recorded as local time. A Web site instance is displayed as W3SVC#, and an FTP site instance is displayed as MSFTPSVC#, where # is the instance of the site. Time taken is recorded in milliseconds. For more information about the **time taken** field, see "W3C Extended Log File Format" earlier in this chapter.

IIS Log File Example

The following example shows an IIS log file entry, as viewed in a text editor:

```
192.168.114.201, -, 03/20/01, 7:55:20, W3SVC2, SERVER, 172.21.13.45, 4502, 163,
3223, 200, 0, GET, /DeptLogo.gif, -,
```

Table 10.6 lists and describes the fields recorded in this example.

Table 10.6   Example of an IIS Log File Entry

Field	Appears As	Description
Client IP address	192.168.114.201	The IP address of the client.
User name	-	The user is anonymous.
Date	03/20/01	This log file entry was made on March 20, 2001.
Time	7:55:20	This log file entry was recorded at 7:55 A.M.
Service and instance	W3SVC2	This is a Web site, and the site instance is 2.
Server name	SERVER	The name of the server.
Server IP	172.21.13.45	The IP address of the server.
Time taken	4502	This action took 4,502 milliseconds.
Client bytes sent	163	The number of bytes sent from the client to the server.
Server bytes sent	3223	The number of bytes sent from the server to the client.
Service status code	200	The request was fulfilled successfully.
Windows status code	0	The request was fulfilled successfully.
Request type	GET	The user issued a **GET**, or download, command.
Target of operation	/DeptLogo.gif	The user wanted to download the DeptLogo.gif file.
Parameters	-	There were no parameters passed.

ODBC Logging

ODBC logging records a fixed set of data fields in an ODBC-compliant database, such as Microsoft® Access or Microsoft® SQL Server™. With ODBC logging, you must set up a database to receive the data, and then specify this database as the database to which log files should be recorded.

When ODBC logging is enabled, IIS disables the HTTP.sys kernel-mode cache. For this reason, implementing ODBC logging will degrade overall server performance. ODBC logging is not recommended unless your database limits you to this option.

IIS includes a Structured Query Language (SQL) template file that you can run in a SQL database to create a table that accepts log file entries from IIS. The file is named Logtemp.sql and is available in the \Inetsrv directory. If you accepted the defaults when you installed IIS, the \Inetsrv directory is a subdirectory of *systemroot*\System32.

 Important

For security reasons, do not use the well-known SQL Server administrator account name SA for ODBC logging. If a malicious user accessed the worker process, that user could use the SA account to access the SQL Server. Remove the SA account, and create a new account with the least necessary rights. For more information, see the SQL Server link on the Web Resources page at http://www.microsoft.com/windows/reskits/webresources.

Table 10.7 lists the fields, data types, and descriptions of the fields recorded in the ODBC logging format.

Table 10.7   ODBC Logging Fields

Field	Data Type	Description
ClientHost	varchar(255)	The IP address of the client.
UserName	varchar(255)	The domain name of the client.
LogTime	datetime	The connection date and time.
Service	varchar(255)	The IIS service.
Machine	varchar(255)	The name of the computer.
ServerIP	varchar(50)	The IP address of the server.
ProcessingTime	integer	The processing time, in milliseconds.
BytesRecvd	integer	The number of bytes that the server received.

(continued)

Table 10.7   ODBC Logging Fields (*continued*)

Field	Data Type	Description
BytesSent	integer	The number of bytes that the server sent.
ServiceStatus	integer	The service status or reply code. A value of 200 indicates that the request was fulfilled successfully.
Win32Status	integer	The Windows status or error code. A value of 0 indicates that the request was fulfilled successfully.
Operation	varchar(255)	The command that the user requested.
Target	varchar(255)	The recipient.
Parameters	varchar(255)	The request parameters that the client sent.

For more complete information about enabling ODBC logging, see "About Logging Site Activity" in IIS 6.0 Help.

Centralized Binary Logging

Centralized binary logging is a process where multiple Web sites send binary, unformatted log data to a single log file. In contrast, the other IIS logging methods create one log file per Web site.

 Important

FTP, NNTP, and SMTP do not support centralized binary logging.

When a server running IIS hosts many Web sites, the process of creating hundreds or thousands of formatted log files and writing the log data to a disk can quickly consume valuable CPU and memory resources, thereby creating performance and scalability problems. Centralized binary logging minimizes the amount of system resources that are used for logging, while at the same time providing detailed log data for organizations that require it.

Centralized binary logging is a server property, not a site property, so when you enable centralized binary logging on a server, all of the Web sites on that server are configured to write log data to the central log file. When you enable centralized binary logging, you cannot record data from individual Web sites in a different format. The centralized binary logging log file has an Internet binary log (.ibl) file name extension. This file name extension ensures that text utilities do not try to open and read the central binary logging log file.

When to Use Centralized Binary Logging

Centralized binary logging is particularly useful when many Web sites are hosted on the same server or where server resources are at a premium. With centralized binary logging, an administrator can maximize the number of Web sites that a server can host and record activity for because centralized binary logging reduces the amount of system resources that are consumed during logging and decreases code paths in IIS, thus increasing performance and scalability.

Centralized binary logging can also reduce administration burdens for Internet service providers (ISPs) for whom collecting and storing logged data is imperative. For example, if an ISP has six servers with 10,000 Web sites per server, the ISP would have to manage 10,000 log files per day per server running IIS. With centralized binary logging, the ISP would have to manage and store only one file per server, per day.

Log files can be vital to troubleshooting applications. However, an organization might not want to take up system resources for log files that are used only in debugging situations. For example, a Web application team at an enterprise organization uses ASP and Microsoft® Visual Basic® development system to develop COM components that access a SQL database. The application team needs to maximize the response time of individual requests and maximize the amount of concurrent work that a group of servers can handle. Central binary logging can help the team achieve these goals.

 To enable centralized binary logging for all Web sites hosted on a server running IIS 6.0

> ⚠ **Important**
>
> You must be a member of the Administrators group on the local computer to run scripts and executables, or you must have been delegated the appropriate authority. As a security best practice, log on to your computer by using an account that is not in the Administrators group, and then use the **runas** command to run your script or executable as an administrator. At the command prompt, type **runas /profile /user:***MyMachine\Administrator* **cmd** to open a command window with administrator rights, and then type **cscript.exe** *ScriptName* (including the full path with parameters, if there are any).

1. To enable centralized binary logging, do the following:

   a. From the **Start** menu, click **Run**.

   b. In the **Open** box, type the following: **cscript.exe adsutil.vbs SET W3SVC/CentralBinaryLoggingEnabled true**

   c. Click **OK**.

2. To stop the World Wide Web Publishing Service (WWW service) so that the change can take effect, do the following:

   a. From the **Start** menu, click **Run**.

   b. In the **Open** box, type **cmd**, and then click **OK**.

   c. At the command prompt, type the following: **net stop W3SVC**

   d. Press ENTER.

3. To restart the WWW service with centralized binary logging enabled, do the following:

    a. At the command prompt, type the following: **net start W3SVC**

    b. Press ENTER.

    The binary log file is created in the W3SVC folder located at *systemroot*\WINDOWS\System32\LogFiles\.

When you are ready to extract data from a raw log file, you can do one of the following:

- Create a tool that locates and extracts the data that you want from the raw file and converts the data into formatted text. You can view a header file and log file format descriptions in the IIS 6.0 Software Development Kit, which is located on MSDN® Online. For more information, see the Software Development Kit (SDK) Information in the MSDN Library link on the Web Resources page at http://www.microsoft.com/windows/reskits/webresources.

- Use the Log Parser tool to extract data from the raw file. The Log Parser tool and its accompanying user documentation are included in the IIS 6.0 Resource Kit Tools. You can install the IIS 6.0 Resource Kit Tools, which include Help documentation, by running IIS60rkt.exe from the *Internet Information Services (IIS) 6.0 Resource Kit* companion CD.

Centralized Binary Logging File Format

The raw centralized binary logging log file is made up of fixed-length records or index records that contain string identifiers. The index records appear because, in an effort to record as much information as possible, variable-length string fields are replaced by numeric identifiers — indexes — that map the variable-length string to the logged identifier.

The raw log file is not human-readable, and it cannot be read using most available log analyzers. To extract data from a raw log file, you can create a tool that locates and extracts the data and then converts it into formatted text. For more information about the header file and log file format descriptions that you need to create such a tool, see "Centralized Binary Log File Format" in this book.

Centralized binary logging records the following information, which is similar, but not identical, to the W3C Extended log file format:

- Date
- Time
- Client IP address
- User name
- Site ID
- Server name
- Server IP address
- Server port
- Method
- URI stem

- URI query

- Protocol status

- Windows status

- Bytes sent

- Bytes received

- Time taken

- Protocol version

- Protocol substatus

For information about the **Time Taken** field, see "W3C Extended Log File Format" earlier in this chapter.

 Note

The following fields are reported in W3C Extended log files, but they are not recorded in centralized binary logging log files:

- **Host.** The host header.

- **User agent.** The browser type of the client; this string is too large to be practical for the binary format.

- **Cookie.** The content of the cookie that was sent.

- **Referrer.** The site that the user last visited.

HTTP.sys Error Log Files

For the W3C Extended, IIS, and NCSA Common log file formats and for centralized binary logging, the log data is generated from the worker processes, passed to HTTP.sys through APIs, and then recorded in log files. However, because of the separation of the HTTP protocol stack in kernel mode and the worker processes in user mode, HTTP.sys-initiated error responses are not recognized by the user mode and are, therefore, not passed back to HTTP.sys for logging. To record these error responses, HTTP.sys needs its own error logging scheme that comes directly from the kernel mode. This is accomplished with HTTP.sys error logging. By default, HTTP.sys error logging is turned on.

Common HTTP.sys Error Log File Entries

There are a number of cases where HTTP.sys will generate its own errors. For example, when HTTP.sys sends an error response back to a client and a site is not yet associated with the request, an error is recorded in the HTTP.sys error log files. This error usually happens when there is a parse error in the request that was last received on the connection and HTTP.sys disconnects the connection after sending the response.

Another example of an HTTP.sys-generated error is a connection time-out. If a time-out occurs during a request, the request is recorded in the HTTP.sys error log file to provide more information about the connection.

Also, if a worker process in user mode unexpectedly terminates or closes its application pool handle while there are still outstanding requests that were queued and routed to this worker process, the outstanding requests are recorded in the HTTP.sys error log files. In this case, you can use the **site ID** field entry to identify the problematic site.

HTTP.sys error log files will sometimes contain connection errors that occur when IIS does not immediately destroy connections that the client terminates before a response for the last request on these connections is complete. HTTP.sys cannot resolve these connections (sometimes known as zombie connections) until IIS completes its send or passes the last send call containing the logging information. Typically, unresolved connections are recorded in normal IIS log files. However, if IIS never sends the logging information back to HTTP.sys, unresolved connections are dropped after 30 seconds to one minute. HTTP.sys records these dropped connections in the HTTP.sys error log file to alert the administrator to their presence.

Configuring HTTP.sys Error Logging

To change the configuration of HTTP.sys error logging, you must edit the registry. HTTP.sys reads the configuration only once during startup. If you change the configuration, HTTP.sys can pick up the change only at the next startup. The HTTP.sys error logging configuration is global.

You must have administrative credentials to edit the HTTP.sys configuration in the registry.

 Caution
Do not edit the registry unless you have no alternative. The registry editor bypasses standard safeguards, allowing settings that can damage your system, or even require you to reinstall Windows. If you must edit the registry, back it up first and see the Registry Reference on the *Microsoft Windows Server 2003 Deployment Kit* companion CD or on the Web at http://www.microsoft.com/reskit.

Registry Parameters

Three parameters control HTTP.sys error logging. They are located under the following registry key: **HKEY_LOCAL_MACHINE\System\CurrentControlSet\Services\HTTP\Parameters**.

There are three entries that can be set:

- **EnableErrorLogging (DWORD)**. The default value is **TRUE**.

- **ErrorLogFileTruncateSize (DWORD)**. The default value is **1 * 1024 * 1024 bytes**. The value cannot be smaller than this, and it must be specified in bytes.

- **ErrorLoggingDir (String)**. The default value is *\systemroot*\System32\LogFiles. When specified, this value must be a fully qualified directory string, but you can use *\systemroot*. For example:

    C:\LogFiles

    — or —

    \systemroot\LogFiles

Although you can specify the directory, HTTP.sys will create a subdirectory named HTTPERR under the given log directory and put the error log files in this subdirectory. By default, members of the Administrators group and users with a LocalSystem user account have full access to the log files and directories. No other users have access rights.

The log file naming convention for HTTP.sys error logging is *httperr* followed by the sequence number. HTTP.sys error log files have a .log extension. For example, Httperr1.log. The error log files are recycled, based on their sizes. The default recycle size for error log files is 1 megabyte (MB). You can configure the value in the registry, but it cannot be smaller than 1 MB.

When the following events occur, HTTP.sys records them in the Windows Event log:

- HTTP.sys cannot create an error log file.

- The administrator sets an unacceptable configuration in the registry.

- There is not enough disk space.

- There is any other write failure.

Log File Format for HTTP.sys Error Logging

HTTP.sys error log files contain a fixed set of fields. Table 10.8 lists the fields that are recorded in HTTP.sys error logging log files and describes them.

Table 10.8   HTTP.sys Error Logging Fields

Field	Description
Date	The date, in UTC time. This entry is always 10 characters long, for example, `2000-01-31`.
Time	The time, in UTC time. This entry is always eight characters long, for example, `00:12:23`.
Client IP	The IP address of the client. The version of the IP address can be either IPv4 or IPv6. If it is IPv6, the Scope ID field also appears.
Client Port	The port number of the client.
Server IP	The IP address of the server. The server IP address can be either IPv4 or IPv6. If it is IPv6, the Scope ID field also appears.
Server Port	The port number of the server.
Protocol version	The protocol version, if the last request on the connection has been parsed enough to identify the protocol version. If either the major or the minor version is greater than or equal to 10, the driver records the version as "HTTP/?.?".
Verb	The verb, if the last request that was parsed passed the verb state. Unknown verbs are also recorded. HTTP.sys enforces a length limit of 255 bytes for the verb; anything longer is truncated.
CookedURL and query	The URL and its query, if both exist. A question mark (?) separates the URL from the query. If the URL of the request is completely processed (also known as *cooked*), then the processed URL is recorded with a local code page conversion and is treated as a Unicode field.
	If only the unprocessed (raw) URL was present at the time of logging, then it is recorded as is, without a local code page conversion. HTTP.sys enforces a length limit of 4096 bytes for the URL; anything longer is truncated.
Protocol status	The protocol status of the response for the request, if it is available. The value cannot be greater than 999.
Site ID	The site ID, as a numeric value. For example, instead of recording W3SVC1, the field contains "1." There is no maximum value for the site ID. (This value can be as large as a MAX_ULONG.)
Reason phrase	Detailed information about why the error occurred, depending on the error type. This field can never be empty. For more information about reason phrases, see "HTTP.sys Reason Phrases" later in this chapter.

For fields for which information is unavailable, a hyphen (-) appears as a placeholder. Fields are separated by spaces. If a field contains a nonprintable character, HTTP.sys replaces it with a plus sign (+) to preserve the log file format.

HTTP.sys Reason Phrases

The following reason phrases can appear in an HTTP.sys error log file to describe the error that caused the log file entry:

Connection_Abandoned_By_AppPool

This reason phrase indicates that the error was caused by a worker process stopping unexpectedly and orphaning requests.

Connection_Dropped

This reason phrase indicates that a zombie connection was dropped by IIS and not resolved correctly.

Various connection time-out errors

These reason phrases include the following various connection time-out errors:

- **Timer_ConnectionIdle**. There has been no new data sent over the connection since the last send from the client to server, and the connection timed out.

- **Timer_HeaderWait**. A connection was initiated with the server, but the headers for the request were not received in a timely manner.

- **Timer_MinBytesPerSecond**. The minimum throughput rate was not maintained.

- **Timer_EntityBody**. The connection expired while waiting for the entity body to arrive.

- **Timer_AppPool**. The connection expired because the request waited too long in an application pool queue.

Various errors

These reason phrases include the following errors, most of which are parse errors:

- BadRequest
- Verb
- URL
- Header
- Hostname
- Invalid_CR/LF

- Number
- FieldLength
- RequestLength
- Forbidden
- LengthRequired
- Precondition
- EntityTooLarge
- URL_Length
- Internal
- N/I

Internal

This reason phrase indicates that an HTTP Error 500, internal server error, occurred.

N/I

This reason phrase indicates that an HTTP Error 501, not implemented, occurred.

All 503 errors

The 503 errors are service unavailable errors. These reason phrases include the following 503 errors:

- **N/A**. The service is unavailable.
- **ConnLimit**. The site connection limit has been reached.
- **AppOffline**. Because of rapid fail protection, the application was taken offline by IIS.
- **QueueFull**. The application request queue is full.
- **Disabled**. The administrator has taken the application offline.
- **AppShutdown**. The application was automatically shut down because of an administrator policy.
- **AppPoolTimer**. The application pool process is too busy to handle the request.

Version_N/S

This reason phrase indicates that an HTTP error 505, HTTP version not supported, occurred.

HTTP.sys Error Log File Examples

The following example shows an HTTP.sys error log file entry, as viewed in a text editor:

```
2002-07-05 18:45:09 172.31.77.6 2094 172.31.77.6 80 HTTP/1.1 GET /qos/1kbfile.txt
503 - ConnLimit
```

Table 10.9 lists and describes the fields that are recorded in this example.

Table 10.9   Example of an HTTP.sys Error Log File Entry

Field	Appears As	Description
Date	2002-07-05	This log file entry was recorded on July 5, 2002.
Time	18:45:09	This log file entry was recorded at 6:45 P.M.
Client IP	172.31.77.6	The IP address of the client.
Client port	2094	The client port number.
Server IP	172.31.77.6	The IP address of the server.
Server port	80	The server port number.
Protocol version	HTTP/1.1	The protocol version.
Verb	GET	The user requested a **GET**, which requests a file.
Cooked URL and query	/qos/1kbfile.txt	The query was unavailable, and the URL of the request was completely processed (also known as *cooked*), so /qos/1kbfile.txt is the local code page conversion.
Protocol status	503	The service was unavailable.
Site ID	–	The site ID was unavailable.
Reason Phrase	ConnLimit	The connection limit was reached.

Custom Logging Modules

IIS supports custom logging modules that are COM objects that must expose a base set of methods for IIS to use. These methods are defined in the ILogPlugin, ILogPluginEx, and ILogUIPlugin interfaces. You can implement custom logging modules when you create your own log file formats or when you manipulate log data. For more information about the methods for the ILogPlugin, ILogPluginEx, and ILogUIPlugin interfaces, see the Custom Logging Module Interface Reference link on the Web Resources page at http://www.microsoft.com/windows/reskits/webresources. For information about creating custom logging modules, see the Creating a Custom Logging Module link on the Web Resources page at http://www.microsoft.com/windows/reskits/webresources.

Custom Logging Considerations

Before you create and use custom logging modules, it is important to consider the following:

- If you want to implement custom logging for a site, consider synchronization issues. For example, different instances of a logging module can record information for different applications within the same site — but from different worker processes. To avoid synchronization problems, you can write a per-application pool log instead of a per-site log or you can use Microsoft® Win32® application programming interface synchronization primitives. Alternatively, for existing custom logging modules that you cannot change, all of the site's applications must be assigned to the same application pool to avoid the possibility of multiple worker processes writing entries to the same log file. In addition, the application pool must have the following configuration:

    - **MaxProcesses** = 1
    - **DisallowOverlappingRotation** = True

- Because the worker process, not HTTP.sys, handles custom logging modules, the HTTP.sys kernel-mode cache is disabled for the site for which a custom logging module is specified.

- In IIS 6.0, HTTP.sys uses the LocalSystem user account when writing log data to the currently selected LogFiles directory. Custom logging modules, however, use the accounts of the application pool in which they are running. The default account for application pools is the Network Service user account. For this reason, custom logging modules can cause write problems or errors when writing to the default LogFiles folder. You can correct this problem by configuring your custom logging modules to write to a different folder.

- If you choose to have custom logging modules write to a different folder, be sure to set a proper ACL on the new folder. Consider giving write permissions to the IIS_WPG group, which is a built-in user group that has the minimum set of permissions that IIS requires. If the identity account is not in the IIS_WPG group and has not been assigned appropriate rights, then the worker process fails to start. For more information about ACLs, see "Managing a Secure IIS 6.0 Solution" in this book.

 Important

When a custom logging module is loaded, IIS disables the HTTP.sys kernel-mode cache. For this reason, implementing a custom logging module can degrade overall server performance.

Once you have created a custom logging module, you can add your format to the Active Log Format list in IIS Manager. To add the custom format to the Active Log Format list, you must edit the metabase with the Adsutil.vbs command-line script. For more information about custom logging, including the step-by-step process for adding your custom logging module to the Active Log Format list, see "Custom Logging Modules" in IIS 6.0 Help.

Additional Resources

These resources contain additional information and tools related to this chapter.

Related Information

- "Centralized Binary Log File Format" in this book for information about centralized binary logging.

- "IIS 6.0 Architecture" in this book for information about the IIS 6.0 architecture and core components.

- "Managing a Secure IIS 6.0 Solution" in this book for information about file and directory security and access control.

- The W3C Extended Log File Format link on the Web Resources page at http://www.microsoft.com/windows/reskits/webresources for information about the W3C Extended log file format.

- The Creating a Custom Logging Module link on the Web Resources page at http://www.microsoft.com/windows/reskits/webresources for information about creating custom logging modules.

Related Help Topics

- "Enabling Logging" in IIS 6.0 Help, which is accessible from IIS Manager, for information about how to enable logging.

- "Substatus Error Codes in Log Files" in IIS 6.0 Help for information about enabling and disabling substatus error code logging.

- "About Custom Error Messages" in IIS 6.0 Help for information about the Custom Error Messages table.

- "About Logging Site Activity" in IIS 6.0 Help for information about enabling ODBC logging.

- "Custom Logging Modules" in IIS 6.0 Help for information about custom logging and how to add your custom logging module to the Active Log Format list.

Related Tools

- Log Parser tool (LogParser.exe)

  Use the Log Parser tool to extract data from the raw file. The Log Parser tool and its accompanying user documentation are included in the IIS 6.0 Resource Kit Tools. You can install the IIS 6.0 Resource Kit Tools, which include Help documentation, by running IIS60rkt.exe from the *Internet Information Services (IIS) 6.0 Resource Kit* companion CD.

Troubleshooting IIS 6.0

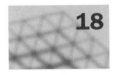

When administering Web applications, you will have problems to solve — whether fixing a service interruption, analyzing a configuration problem, or working around system resource contention problems. Whether the application is an internal corporate Web-presence or a widely available, scaled-out, data-intensive Web application, any problems that you encounter can seem nearly impossible to resolve, and attempting to do so consumes valuable time and resources.

This chapter describes how to troubleshoot Web applications on production computers running the Microsoft® Windows® Server 2003 operating system and Internet Information Services (IIS) 6.0. It explains how to use troubleshooting tools to administer IIS and discusses in detail service and program areas that might require troubleshooting, such as security, service startup, the IIS metabase, HTTP, and ASP.

In This Chapter

Related Information

- For more information about troubleshooting, see "Troubleshooting" in IIS 6.0 Help, which is accessible from IIS Manager.

Overview of Troubleshooting IIS 6.0

Problems that occur when administering Internet Information Services (IIS) 6.0 might be difficult to solve for any of the following reasons:

- Problem reports from end users might be vague or incomplete, lacking such information as the content of error messages, how frequently a problem occurs, or the specific conditions under which the problem occurred.

- Logs do not record information that reveals the cause of the problem.

- The problem occurs in a complex, widely distributed application, which is difficult to track comprehensively.

The goal of troubleshooting is to isolate and determine the causes of problems that interfere with normal operation. This section describes a troubleshooting methodology and some of the tools that you can use to troubleshoot a server running IIS 6.0 and the Web applications that it hosts.

Troubleshooting Methodology

To efficiently troubleshoot Web applications, you need to apply and consistently use a troubleshooting framework, or methodology. Doing so helps you to streamline your troubleshooting activities and approach problems with confidence.

The fundamental troubleshooting methodology has five phases:

- **Phase 1: Discovery.** Gather information about the problem.

- **Phase 2: Planning.** Create a plan of action.

- **Phase 3: Problem Reproduction.** Reproduce the problem, or determine that you cannot reproduce it. If you cannot reproduce the problem, then you might not have enough information to confirm that there is a problem.

- **Phase 4: Problem Isolation.** Isolate the variables that relate directly to the problem.

- **Phase 5: Analysis.** Analyze your findings to determine the cause of the problem.

Phase 1: Discovery

Most problems are discovered by the end user. Problems might also be revealed by the operating system or by application logging and event tracking utilities. When a problem is reported, begin the troubleshooting process by gathering information to confirm that a problem exists.

Interview the user who reported the problem

If an end user reported the problem, ask that user for detailed information about what occurred. If possible, get the exact text of any error messages. If the problem recurs, ask the user to provide screen shots for error-message information or other symptoms that appeared on a screen. If the problem is behavioral and does not generate an error message, ask very specific, closed-ended questions. For example, you might ask the following questions:

- What time did the problem occur? (You can use this information to locate proximate events a large log file or to correlate the problem with external causes.)

- Which button(s) or link(s) did you click just before the problem occurred?

- Did you refresh or re-request the Web page to recover from the problem?

Examine the records

The Microsoft® Windows® Server 2003, Standard Edition; Windows® Server 2003, Enterprise Edition; Windows® Server 2003, Web Edition; and Windows® Server 2003, Datacenter Edition operating systems provide logging and event tracking. Check the logs for entries around the time that the problem occurred. Additionally, the application itself might log events. For example, the IIS logs and the HTTP error log record this information. For more information, see "Analyzing Log Files" in this book.

Phase 2: Planning

Creating a plan of action is quite possibly the most important phase in the troubleshooting process. In this phase, you list the steps that you will follow as you proceed through the other troubleshooting phases. Stick to this plan and refer to it often. When you are bogged down in the tasks of the problem isolation phase, referring to your plan will help you remember where you are in the troubleshooting process and avoid getting sidetracked. Revise the plan as you progress — in most cases one step will dictate later steps.

When troubleshooting IIS–related problems, your plan might consist of configuring IIS logging to log extra details and then setting up a Performance Monitor log to run during a specific period of time. Based on the results of these actions, the next step might involve making a configuration change.

Phase 3: Problem Reproduction

Determine whether the problem is readily reproducible. The ability to reproduce the problem on demand is fundamental to properly and efficiently troubleshooting the problem. Use the information that you gathered in Phase 1 to reproduce the problem, most often by repeating the actions taken by the end user before the problem occurred. If you can readily reproduce the problem, the isolation phase is more manageable. When you have determined a set of steps or events that trigger the problem, move to the isolation phase.

If you cannot readily reproduce the problem, the problem isolation phase can be tedious or isolating the problem can be impossible. If you cannot reproduce the problem, prepare to gather the right kind of information the next time it happens. Consider doing any or all of the following:

- Enable more detailed event tracking.

- Ask users to watch for the problem and pay close attention to what they are doing if it occurs.

- Write additional code in the application that looks for and highlights the problem if it happens again.

For example, when dealing with a Web application problem, you might add extra tracing code to your ASP pages or you might configure Windows security auditing for specific failures. The goal is to gather enough information so that the next time the problem occurs, the information that you obtain will be sufficient to correctly diagnose the problem.

Phase 4: Problem Isolation

In the problem isolation phase, you reproduce the problem as efficiently as possible by using repetitive steps. In this phase, you eliminate variables — such as settings, file actions, component starts/stops, or any change in the execution — that do not cause the problem, narrowing the variables down to those that are responsible for the problem.

You have succeeded in isolating the problem when you achieve the following conditions:

- The problem can be reproduced consistently when you take a fixed series of actions.

- The problem cannot be reproduced when you omit any of those actions.

For example, when troubleshooting IIS–related problems, you might do the following:

- Configure a Web application to be hosted in its own worker process or configure a component to execute in an isolated host process like a COM+ Dllhost.exe in order to determine which part of an application is consuming CPU time or leaking memory.

- Configure security settings on a URL in varying degrees through repetitive tests to isolate authentication problems.

- Capture performance data to determine whether a problem lies in the core Web server or in a Web service extension–based application, such as ASP or ASP.NET.

Phase 5: Analysis

Depending on the nature of the problem, the analysis phase can be the most difficult phase of the troubleshooting process. In the analysis phase, you use everything that you learned in the previous phases to do the following:

- Determine the cause of the problem.

- Explore how the problem affects the application.

- Determine the best way to solve the problem.

  This step might be a simple formality if, after Phase 3 is complete, you know what the problem is and how to fix it. If not, you must perform additional analysis of the data you have gathered. You might find that you must spend more time in the isolation phase.

  You might find that there are several ways to fix the problem. Take what you have learned about the problem and decide which actions to take. Ask yourself these kinds of questions:

  - What is the impact of the problem?

  - Do the benefits of fixing the problem outweigh the costs of fixing it?

  - Is there an acceptable workaround?

- Record your progress and the data that you have gathered.

  As you obtain information about a problem, you will make decisions about the steps that you need to take that will often alter your plan of action. It is important to record the information that you collect so that you have a way to account for your decisions as you move through the process of troubleshooting. If you find yourself taking the wrong path, having this information will allow you to backtrack to the point where you made the wrong decision. In addition, your ability to explain the changes or improvements in the problem is often important to other stakeholders.

Tools for Troubleshooting IIS 6.0

Good tools are an indispensable part of any troubleshooting effort. This section identifies tools that you can use to help troubleshoot problems that you encounter on applications running on IIS 6.0. It also provides tips for getting the most benefit from each tool. Specific tool usage scenarios are discussed later in this chapter.

The following tools are useful for troubleshooting problems that occur with IIS 6.0:

- **WFetch (WFetch.exe).** This tool allows you to generate customized HTTP requests and view request and response data.

- **File Monitor (FileMon.exe).** This tool allows you to view and capture real-time file system activity.

- **Registry Monitor (RegMon.exe).** This tool allows you to view and capture real-time system registry activity.

- **IIS Enterprise Tracing for Windows.** This tool allows you to enable tracing for various providers. IIS includes a set of providers that can be used to troubleshoot various internal processes in addition to application performance. IIS Enterprise Tracing for Windows is new in Windows Server 2003. Logman.exe and Tracerpt.exe are the tools used to enable IIS ETW tracing.

- **Network Monitor.** This network tracing utility allows you to view activity in the network stack. Network Monitor is included with Windows Server 2003.

- **System Monitor.** This tool allows you to view and collect system performance data. System Monitor is included with Windows Server 2003.

- **HRPlus.** This tool provides error lookup functionality.

- **Microsoft Debugging Tools for Windows.** This tool allows you to debug and diagnose application problems.

WFetch

A simple HTTP request that is issued by typing a URL in the address bar of a browser might produce multiple network requests to the target server running IIS. However, the user does not see all of the resulting response data because the browser does not display it. WFetch allows you to fully customize an HTTP request and send it to a Web server so that you can see the raw HTTP request and response data. WFetch is included in the *Internet Information Services (IIS) 6.0 Resource Kit*.

For more information about using WFetch in a testing environment, see article 284285, "How To: Use Wfetch.exe to Troubleshoot HTTP Connections" in the Microsoft Knowledge Base. To find this article, see the Microsoft Knowledge Base link on the Web Resources page at http://www.microsoft.com/windows/reskits/webresources.

File Monitor and Registry Monitor

When troubleshooting IIS 6.0, you can use File Monitor and Registry Monitor to obtain two specific types of information:

- Verification that a specific file (File Monitor) or registry key (Registry Monitor) is being accessed by a given process.

- Information about whether that access results in an Access Denied error.

Both File Monitor and Registry Monitor can be downloaded from the System Internals Web site.

To install File Monitor and Registry Monitor, unzip and copy each .exe file to a desired location. To use one of these tools, double-click the appropriate executable file (FileMon.exe or RegMon.exe). Both utilities start in capture mode, which means that they display all file system (File Monitor) or registry (Registry Monitor) activity from all processes as it happens. Before you begin troubleshooting a problem, stop the capture and clear the entries that have been written.

▶ **To stop or start a capture in FileMon.exe or RegMon.exe**

- On the **Options** menu, click **Capture Events**.

▶ **To clear the current capture in FileMon.exe or RegMon.exe**

- On the **Edit** menu, click **Clear Display**.

Tips for Using File Monitor and Registry Monitor for Troubleshooting

Use the following tips to streamline the troubleshooting process when using File Monitor and Registry Monitor:

- **Isolate your task as much as possible.** The output from a capture comes very quickly and at a high volume. The larger the capture, the harder it is to find the information that you want. When you are ready, perform only the tasks that will produce the file or registry access that you are trying to verify.

- **Avoid unnecessary clicking or activity.** Performing extraneous operations while File Monitor or Registry Monitor is running will produce unrelated and unnecessary data in the output.

- **Start a capture as closely as possible to when you perform the task.** Separate your utility window from the workspace that contains the process that you are using to troubleshoot so that you can easily switch between programs. If possible, press ALT+TAB to quickly switch programs.

- **Create a capture filter for the process name that you are working with.** Registry Monitor and File Monitor both have capture filter functionality, which you can use to remove extraneous activity from the capture. You can filter on any string in an entry. For example, a common filter is the IIS 6.0 worker process name, W3wp.exe.

▷   **To set a capture filter for W3wp.exe**

1.   On the **Edit** menu of the appropriate tool, click **Filter/Highlight**.

2.   In the **Include** box, type **W3wp.exe** and then click **Apply**.

When you have finished the task, stop the capture and scan the results for specific output. Usually, your objective will be to verify whether the problem is being caused by or is related to an access denial. In either tool, you can see whether this is the case by looking for the text "ACCESS DENIED" in the Result column.

If you need to compare the time that an event occurred with some other activity on your network, change the time format of the capture from the elapsed time, which is the default, to the literal time of day.

IIS 6.0 Enterprise Tracing for Windows

Windows Server 2003 includes Enterprise Tracing for Windows (ETW), a new framework for implementing tracing providers that can be used for debugging and capacity planning. IIS 6.0 implements a number of providers to trace key transitions and the progress that an HTTP request makes as it moves through the IIS service framework. These providers include the following:

- **HTTP Service Trace.** This provider traces new connections, new HTTP requests from a given connection, HTTP kernel cache hits, application pool routing, and HTTP request completion.

- **IIS: WWW Server.** This provider traces the transition of a request from HTTP.sys to the worker process, start and stop events surrounding Common Gateway Interface (CGI) requests, and the transition of a request back to HTTP.sys from the worker process. This information reveals the type of request that is being processed.

- **IIS: SSL Filter.** This provider traces calls into and out of the SSL Filter, which is used for SSL traffic.

- **IIS ISAPI Extension.** This provider traces the transition of a request into and out of ISAPI extension processing.

- **IIS ASP.** Traces the start and completion of the execution of an ASP request.

These tracing providers allow you to follow a request through all of its phases. This information is very useful in the problem isolation phase of troubleshooting. For example, ISAPI filters can often cause delays or hangs in HTTP request processing. The tracing functionality can help to determine which ISAPI filter is causing the delay for a given request.

Use the LogMan utility, which is included with Windows Server 2003, to configure and control ETW. All of the tracing providers are enabled through their Globally Unique ID (GUID), which you can find by using LogMan. A GUID is a 128-bit number that is generally represented by a 32 character string of hexadecimal numbers.

The following procedure demonstrates one way that ETW tracing can be used.

▷ **To capture an ETW tracing session**

1. List the GUIDs of the providers by using the LogMan utility. At a command prompt, type the following: **logman.exe query providers**

   The output will look similar to the following:

```
D:\>logman.exe query providers


Provider                        GUID
----------------------------------------------------------------------------
---

ACPI Driver Trace Provider           {dab01d4d-2d48-477d-b1c3-daad0ce6f06b}
Active Directory: Kerberos           {bba3add2-c229-4cdb-ae2b-57eb6966b0c4}
IIS: SSL Filter                  {1fbecc45-c060-4e7c-8a0e-0dbd6116181b}
IIS: WWW Server                  {3a2a4e84-4c21-4981-ae10-3fda0d9b0f83}
IIS: Active Server Pages (ASP)       {06b94d9a-b15e-456e-a4ef-37c984a2cb4b}
Local Security Authority (LSA)       {cc85922f-db41-11d2-9244-006008269001}
Windows Kernel Trace             {9e814aad-3204-11d2-9a82-006008a86939}
ASP.NET Events                  {AFF081FE-0247-4275-9C4E-021F3DC1DA35}
NTLM Security Protocol            {C92CF544-91B3-4dc0-8E11-C580339A0BF8}
IIS: WWW ISAPI Extension           {a1c2040e-8840-4c31-ba11-9871031a19ea}
HTTP Service Trace               {dd5ef90a-6398-47a4-ad34-4dcecdef795f}
Active Directory: NetLogon          {f33959b4-dbec-11d2-895b-00c04f79ab69}
Spooler Trace Control            {94a984ef-f525-4bf1-be3c-ef374056a592}

The command completed successfully.

D:\>
```

2. Copy the GUIDs of the providers that you want to use into a text file, specify flags and levels, and then save the file using an appropriate name, such as iis_providers.guid. For information about setting flags and levels, see "Create and Configure Trace Logs" in Help and Support Center for Windows Server 2003.

   The file should look similar to the following, where the # character delimits comments:

```
#GUID           #flags #level    #provider
{1fbecc45-c060-4e7c-8a0e-0dbd6116181b}   0 5    #IIS: SSL Filter
{3a2a4e84-4c21-4981-ae10-3fda0d9b0f83}   0 5    #IIS: WWW Server
{06b94d9a-b15e-456e-a4ef-37c984a2cb4b}   0 5    #IIS: Active Server Pages
(ASP)
{AFF081FE-0247-4275-9C4E-021F3DC1DA35}   0 5    #ASP.NET Events
{a1c2040e-8840-4c31-ba11-9871031a19ea}   0 5    #IIS: WWW ISAPI Extension
{dd5ef90a-6398-47a4-ad34-4dcecdef795f}   0 5    #HTTP Service Trace
```

3. Start the tracing session. At the command prompt, type the following:

logman.exe start iis_trace -pf iis_providers.guid -ct perf -o iis_output.etl -bs 64 -nb 200 400 -ets

The output should look similar to the following:

```
D:\>logman start iis_trace -pf iis_providers.guid -ct perf -o iis_output.etl
-bs
 64 -nb 200 400 -ets


Name:            iis_trace
Age Limit:        15
Buffer Size:      64
Buffers Written:   1
Clock Type:       Perf
Events Lost:      0
Flush Timer:      0
Buffers Free:     159
Buffers Lost:     0
File Mode:        Sequential
File Name:        D:\iis_output.etl
Logger Id:        3
Logger Thread Id:   3732
Maximum Buffers:    160
Maximum File Size:   0
Minimum Buffers:    160
Number of buffers:   160
Real Time Buffers Lost:  0


Provider                 Flags          Level
-------------------------------------------------------------------------------
---
* "HTTP Service Trace"        0x00000000       0x05
  {DD5EF90A-6398-47A4-AD34-4DCECDEF795F} 0x00000000        0x05


* "IIS: SSL Filter"          0x00000000       0x05
  {1FBECC45-C060-4E7C-8A0E-0DBD6116181B} 0x00000000        0x05


* "IIS: WWW Server"          0x00000000       0x05
  {3A2A4E84-4C21-4981-AE10-3FDA0D9B0F83} 0x00000000        0x05


* "IIS: WWW ISAPI Extension"      0x00000000       0x05
  {A1C2040E-8840-4C31-BA11-9871031A19EA} 0x00000000        0x05


* "IIS: Active Server Pages (ASP)"   0x00000000       0x05
  {06B94D9A-B15E-456E-A4EF-37C984A2CB4B} 0x00000000        0x05


The command completed successfully.
D:\>
```

4. Attempt to reproduce the problem that you are troubleshooting.

5. After you have reproduced the problem, stop the tracing session. At a command prompt, type the following:

logman.exe stop iis_trace –ets

 Note

> When tracing is enabled, it is enabled for *all* requests. If you need trace data for only the request that is having problems, you should disconnect the server from the network before running the test.

Tracing generates a binary file. To obtain readable information, use a report generation tool like TraceRpt.exe.

► To generate an ETW tracing report

- Using the preceding output file as an example, at a command prompt, type the following:

tracerpt.exe iis_output.etl -o iis_logdump.csv -summary iis_trace_summary.txt -report iis_trace_report.txt

This command generates the specified reports, as follows:

```
D:\>tracerpt iis_output.etl -o iis_logdump.csv -summary
iis_trace_summary.txt -r
export iis_trace_report.txt

Input
----------------
File(s):
    iis_output.etl


100.00%

Output
----------------
Text (CSV):     iis_logdump.csv
Summary:        iis_trace_summary.txt
Report:         iis_trace_report.txt

The command completed successfully.
```

You can examine the .txt files for high-level information that was captured in the trace. The .csv file can be opened in Microsoft Excel or imported to a database, such as Microsoft SQL Server™.

Network Monitor

When troubleshooting IIS–related problems, you can use Network Monitor to start a capture, reproduce a problem, and view the capture. Network Monitor is included with Windows Server 2003.

▶ **To install Network Monitor**

1. From the **Start** menu, click **Control Panel**.

2. Double-click **Add or Remove Programs**.

3. In the left pane, click **Add/Remove Windows Components**.

4. Click **Management and Monitoring Tools** and then click **Details**.

5. Select the **Network Monitor Tools** check box and then click **OK**.

6. Click **Next**.

7. When installation is complete, click **Finish**.

    Network Monitor is now available on the Administrative Tools menu.

> ☑ | **Note**
>
> Network Monitor, unlike WFetch, is a good tool for analyzing TCP connection management or three-way handshake information. For more information about using Network Monitor in this way, see article 172983, "Explanation of the Three-Way Handshake Via TCP/IP" in the Microsoft Knowledge Base. To find this article, see the Microsoft Knowledge Base link on the Web Resources page at http://www.microsoft.com/windows/reskits/webresources.

Tips for Using Network Monitor for Troubleshooting

Consider the following tips when using Network Monitor for troubleshooting:

- As with any utility that captures large volumes of data, it is important to plan your Network Monitor capture and to time the beginning and end of captures so that they minimize extraneous network traffic.

- Network Monitor, like File Monitor and Registry Monitor, can display the timestamp instead of the elapsed time in the capture. Displaying the timestamp along with synchronizing system clocks on participating computers can help you accurately isolate problems.

- Increase the capture buffer size from its default of 1 MB to 20 MB.

▷ **To adjust Network Monitor capture settings**

1. On the **Capture** menu, click **Buffer Settings**.

2. In the **Buffer Size (MB)** box, type **20**.

3. Click **OK**.

Applying filters to captures allows you to record only relevant data. You can also apply a filter after the capture has completed to filter the data that is displayed. Filtering by protocol and by network addresses are the two most common ways to quickly filter Network Monitor capture data.

▷ **To filter capture data by HTTP protocol**

1. While viewing a saved capture file, on the **Display** menu, click **Filter**.

2. In the **Display Filter** dialog box, click **Protocol == Any**, and then click **Edit Expression**.

3. In the **Expression** dialog box, click **Disable All**.

4. In the **Disabled Protocols** list box, click **HTTP**, and then click **Enable**.

5. Click **OK** twice.

   Network Monitor filters and then displays only HTTP traffic.

▷ **To filter capture data by network addresses**

1. While viewing a saved capture file, on the **Display** menu, click **Filter**.

2. In the **Display Filter** dialog box, click **ANY<-->ANY**, and then click **Edit Expression**.

3. In the **Expression** dialog box, choose the source and destination network. If you don't see the one you want, type the address that you want in the **Edit Addresses** box.

By default, Network Monitor only parses traffic on port 80 as HTTP traffic. You can customize Network Monitor to parse traffic on other ports, for example, on port 8080, as HTTP traffic.

▷ **To configure Network Monitor to parse traffic on non-standard HTTP ports**

1. Open Notepad.

2. Open the Tcpip.ini file, which is located in the **Parsers** folder under the Network Monitor installation point (by default, *systemroot*\System32\Netmon).

3. Locate the [TCP_HandoffSet] section.

4. Below the **80=HTTP** line, type the following new line: **8080=HTTP**

5. Save and then close the Tcpip.ini file.

6. Open the Http.ini file, which is located in the same folder as Tcpip.ini.

7. Locate the [Ports] section.

8. Immediately after the text **SrcPorts=80**, type the new port, preceded by a comma. The line now reads **SrcPorts=80,8080**.

9. Save and then close the Http.ini file.

To start any new parsing activity, close and reopen your captures.

For more information about HTTP traffic and Network Monitor, see article 252876, "How to View HTTP Data Frames Using Network Monitor" in the Microsoft Knowledge Base. For more information about capturing network traffic, see article 148942, "How to Capture Network Traffic with Network Monitor" in the Microsoft Knowledge Base. To find these articles, see the Microsoft Knowledge Base link on the Web Resources pageat http://www.microsoft.com/windows/reskits/webresources.

System Monitor

System Monitor is part of the Performance snap-in, which is accessible through Administrative Tools. When generating a performance log for troubleshooting, add, at a minimum, the following counter objects:

- .NET CLR (Common Language Runtime)
- Active Server Pages (ASP)
- ASP.NET
- Memory
- Process
- Processor
- Thread
- Web Service

Alternatively, you can observe real-time data on the display, if doing so meets your troubleshooting needs.

▷ **To start System Monitor**

- From the **Start** menu, point to **Administrative Tools**, and click **Performance**.

 Note
If System Monitor does not open by default, on the console tree, click System Monitor.

HRPlus

HRESULTS are a type of 32-bit error code returned from various parts of the Windows Server 2003 operating system and its components. HRPlus is a free tool that is used primarily for decoding HRESULT values returned by COM applications, but it also can be used to generate custom HRESULT values for use in your own applications. Additionally, you can use HRPlus to decode Win32 error codes.

To obtain a copy of HRPlus, see the CNET Shareware.com link on the Web Resources page at http://www.microsoft.com/windows/reskits/webresources, and then search for "hrplus".

Microsoft Debugging Tools for Windows

The Microsoft Debugging Tools for Windows toolkit provides a robust suite of utilities for troubleshooting and debugging software. To download Microsoft Debugging Tools for Windows, see the Debugging Tools link on the Web Resources page at http://www.microsoft.com/windows/reskits/webresources.

For more information about Microsoft Debugging Tools for Windows, see "Advanced Troubleshooting" later in this chapter.

IIS Fundamentals

IIS is an HTTP protocol server, which means that it accepts and replies to HTTP requests. IIS processes three types of HTTP requests:

- Static content (like HTM document) requests
- CGI requests
- ISAPI requests

By understanding the fundamentals of IIS architecture and the related functionality, you can discover and isolate problems much more quickly. You will also be better equipped to differentiate between real problems and expected behavior. This section explores the following functionality, which any IIS troubleshooter must understand:

- **HTTP protocol basics.** Explains the way Internet browsers and servers running IIS communicate with each other.
- **IIS service startup.** Sometimes problems arise even before IIS starts servicing requests. This section describes the startup process and typical startup behavior, which can help you determine the causes of problems.
- **HTTP request walkthrough.** Explains the various phases that a typical request passes through as it moves through the service.

HTTP Protocol Basics

Troubleshooting IIS often requires that you examine the communications between a Web client and the server running IIS. By understanding the fundamentals of this communication, you can easily interpret network monitor traces and similar records.

Hypertext Transfer Protocol (HTTP) is the communication protocol used to exchange information between a client system and a Web server across a TCP/IP connection. The interchange is generally referred to as an HTTP transaction. In an HTTP transaction, the client system opens a TCP connection with the Web server and submits an HTTP request. The Web server, in turn, issues an HTTP response, completing one HTTP transaction. HTTP is "stateless," in that there is no provision in the protocol's design for information about any single request persisting beyond one transaction.

The following code segment is an example of an HTTP GET request.

```
GET /default.htm HTTP/1.1\r\n
Host: rhynoruv\r\n
Accept: */*\r\n
\r\n
```

The request line contains an HTTP method, a Uniform Resource Identifier (URI), and the HTTP version number, followed by carriage return and line feed characters. Typically, the request line is followed by a series of HTTP headers. Depending on the type of request, an HTTP request can have a variety of headers. With HTTP 1.1, the simplest GET request consists of the request line and only one HTTP header — the Host header. Two carriage returns/line feeds designate the end of the HTTP request header. In a simple GET request, these indicate the end of the request. Some requests include data, which is called the *entity body,* in addition to the HTTP headers. In the HTTP request, the division between the headers and the entity body is designated by two carriage returns/line feeds.

The following code sample shows an HTTP response, which is similar to a request:

```
HTTP/1.1 200 OK\r\n
Content-Length: 50\r\n
Content-Type: text/html\r\n
Last-Modified: Sun, 20 Oct 2002 22:52:16 GMT\r\n
Accept-Ranges: bytes\r\n
ETag: "255591568b78c21:5cd"\r\n
Server: Microsoft-IIS/6.0\r\n
MicrosoftOfficeWebServer: 5.0_Pub\r\n
X-Powered-By: ASP.NET\r\n
Date: Sun, 20 Oct 2002 22:52:35 GMT\r\n
\r\n

<HTML>\r\n
<BODY>\r\n
\r\n
Hello World.\r\n
\r\n
</BODY>\r\n
</HTML>
```

The first line is the status line, which consisting of the HTTP version, a numeric HTTP status code, and then a reason phrase that briefly explains the status code. The status code is often the first indicator of a problem. For information about status codes, see "HTTP Status Codes" later in this chapter.

There are two other important aspects of the HTTP protocol that you must understand before you attempt troubleshooting: the provisions for managing TCP connections and how credential management (authentication) occurs.

HTTP Connection Management

Because the TCP/IP protocol is so robust, establishing a new TCP connection for every HTTP request is relatively expensive in terms of network "roundtrips." The two versions of HTTP (1.0 and 1.1) avoid incurring this overhead differently.

HTTP 1.0 transactions typically involved a client opening a TCP connection with the Web server and issuing an HTTP request. The server would then send its response and close the TCP connection. The client could optionally ask that the TCP connection remain open beyond the first transaction with the HTTP header **Connection: keep-alive**.

Starting with HTTP 1.1, persistent connections are implicit; in other words, the Web client and Web server keep the underlying TCP connection open until either sends an indication that the connection can be closed with the **Connection: close** header. Because the connection remains open, a way to designate the end of the entity-body is required. The **Content-Length** header performs this function by specifying the size of the entity-body, in bytes.

HTTP Authentication

HTTP contains provisions for negotiating access to a secured resource, a process called *authentication*. Typically, an initial request from a client will not contain any authentication information; such a request is considered an *"anonymous"* request. If the requested resource is secured, the Web server can respond with a 401-Access Denied error and, optionally, can include one or more **WWW-Authenticate** HTTP headers. Each **WWW-Authenticate** header indicates a type of authentication scheme the server uses. The client can then choose to engage in one of these authentication schemes; doing so sometimes requires several more HTTP roundtrips.

For more information about authentication schemes, see "401.1 and 401.2-Authentication Problems" later in this chapter. For more information about IIS authentication types, see "Managing a Secure IIS 6.0 Solution" in this book.

Internet RFC 2616, *Hypertext Transfer Protocol — HTTP/1.1* is the governing specification for the current version of HTTP (1.1). For more detailed information about HTTP, see the Request for Comments (RFC) link on the Web Resources page at http://www.microsoft.com/windows/reskits/webresources.

IIS Service Startup

On rare occasions, you might encounter problems related to starting the IIS services infrastructure. The IIS services are generally robust enough to handle problems and recover from them gracefully. If a problem does occur and if it is appropriate, an event is logged to the application/system event log explaining the failure. Typically, the startup process never needs troubleshooting beyond examining messages written to the event log and taking the required corrective action. However, because it is helpful to understand the inner workings of an application in order to recognize problematic behavior, this section describes the major stages of the IIS services infrastructure startup process.

For information about the components of the services infrastructure, see "IIS 6.0 Architecture" in this book.

The Windows Service Control Manager (SCM) performs Windows operating system service management operations. Among other things, SCM is responsible for signaling services to begin the startup process and for managing service dependencies. Some services are configured to *auto-start*, which means that SCM asks those services to start when the system is restarted. Other services are configured to manually start (or *demand-start*), which means that SCM starts those services only when prompted by an external request or when a service dependency demands it.

IIS services startup begins when the computer restarts. The IIS Admin service, which is hosted by Inetinfo.exe, is configured as an auto-start service. This is the first service in the IIS service infrastructure that is asked by SCM to start. The IIS Admin service depends upon the Remote Procedure Call (RPCSS) service and the Security Accounts Manager (SAMSS) service, which means that SCM guarantees that these are started before the IIS Admin service.

The next auto-start service in the IIS services infrastructure that starts is the World Wide Web Publishing Service (WWW service). It is hosted by Svchost.exe. In addition to the IIS Admin and RPCSS services, the WWW service has dependencies on the HTTP SSL (HTTPFilter) service. The IIS Admin service and RPCSS were started earlier, but before SCM starts the WWW service, it needs to "demand-start" the HTTPFilter service.

The HTTPFilter service has dependencies on the IIS Admin service and the HTTP service. It is this dependency on HTTP that causes SCM to start the HTTP.sys kernel-mode driver. Consequently, SCM starts the HTTPFilter service, which runs in Lsass.exe (or Inetinfo.exe if you are running in IIS 5.0 isolation mode), and then starts the WWW service.

The following sections describe what happens when these services start.

HTTP.sys

In IIS 6.0, unlike in earlier versions of IIS, the HTTP.sys kernel-mode device driver is not part of the core IIS services. In Windows Server 2003, the HTTP.sys driver actually exposes an API set that any application or service, not just IIS, can leverage. However, since IIS 6.0 is the major client, so to speak, of HTTP.sys, it is beneficial to understand how HTTP.sys relates to IIS 6.0.

The primary responsibility of HTTP.sys is to listen for and respond to HTTP requests on the network endpoints on which it is requested to do so. When HTTP.sys starts, by default it listens for HTTP requests on all IP addresses configured on the system. In some cases, though, it is beneficial for HTTP.sys to listen only on specific addresses — for example, if Windows Media Services needs to listen on port 80 of a specific IP address, outside of the HTTP.sys driver. To accommodate this need, HTTP.sys has an IP inclusion list. This list, when it contains entries, tells HTTP.sys which IP addresses to listen on, and, thereby, which IP addresses *not* to listen on. At startup, HTTP.sys examines this list and configures itself accordingly. As a result, changes to this list take effect only when the service is restarted.

Tip

You can use the HttpCfg.exe utility to configure the IP inclusion list. For information about HttpCfg.exe, in Help and Support Center for Windows Server 2003, click **Tools**, and then click **Windows Support Tools**.

IIS Admin Service

The IIS Admin service primarily is responsible for managing the IIS metabase. During startup, it reads the MetaBase.xml file and creates its in-memory representation. Because the IIS Admin service creates this in-memory snapshot, if the metabase file is corrupt or if the XML code in the file is not syntactically well-formed, the IIS Admin service will fail to start. The IIS Admin service is responsible for synchronizing access to the metabase through the various control interfaces, even when manual updates are made directly to the MetaBase.xml file. During startup, the IIS Admin service sets up the control interfaces, like IMSAdmin, and registers for necessary file change notifications from the Windows Server 2003 operating system in order to monitor changes to the XML file.

WWW Service

The WWW service recognizes the following entities:

- **URLs.** The combined application and site binding information.

- **Applications.** Unique URLs that, when merged with a site's bindings and endpoints, provide full mapping information that enables HTTP.sys to determine which application pool requests that application should be directed to, and the metadata that should be used to support them.

- **Sites.** The specific bindings and endpoints that HTTP.sys should listen to. Sites contain one or more applications.

- **Application pools.** Sets of applications that are routed to the same set of worker processes. Application pools are also a common configuration for the worker processes that serve the applications in the pool.

- **Application root.** Also known as the Web application starting point, an application root is designated when you create and configure an application on a node in a Web site directory structure. You can have more than one application per Web site. The root of a newly created Web site, including the default Web site that is created when you install IIS, is an application starting point. Every file and directory beneath the starting-point directory in your Web site is considered part of the application until another starting-point directory is found. Thus, directory boundaries define the scope of an application.

When the WWW service starts, it performs the following operations:

1. Reads WWW Service configuration information from the IIS Admin service. This information includes global data, application pool data, Web site data, and application data.

2. Validates this data and logs any errors to the event log, choosing to ignore a record or to alter properties in the record to the defaults.

3. Configures HTTP.sys for all sites, applications, and application pools that are registered, and starts the ones that are set to start automatically.

4. Enables HTTP.sys configuration all at once, allowing IIS to accept requests.

5. If IIS 5.0 isolation mode is enabled, starts a worker process in Inetinfo.exe and waits for the worker process to start.

At this point, IIS can accept incoming HTTP requests. The first HTTP request to an application pool launches the worker process (W3wp.exe). In other words, an application pool can be started even though a worker process is not running.

Worker Process Startup

The fundamental aspects of a worker process startup routine are fairly straightforward. The worker process typically does the following:

1. Starts the metabase listener and listens for change notifications.

2. Initializes the IIS thread pool.

3. Obtains the application pool, which was specified in the command-line parameters, and then sets up the communication mechanism that it will use to receive requests from HTTP.sys.

4. Sets up communication with the WWW service to enable pinging and recycling.

5. Initializes other internal caches and structures that are used to process HTTP requests.

6. Initializes the Web service extension restriction list.

7. Begins accepting requests from HTTP.sys.

HTTP Request Walkthrough

An HTTP request takes only one of three basic paths through the WWW service depending on whether the request is for a static file, an ISAPI extension, or for CGI processing. This section describes these paths. Understanding the request flow is invaluable during the problem isolation phase of the troubleshooting process.

Common Request Operations

All HTTP requests arrive from the network and are passed up to the HTTP.sys listener from the TCP protocol stack. HTTP.sys parses the HTTP headers and makes sure that the request is well formed and valid. In most cases, HTTP.sys then determines into which application request queue to place the request.

Worker processes are signaled by the presence of requests in the HTTP request queue to start processing the requests. Using the HTTP headers, the worker process determines first which kind of authentication needs to be performed. It is here that the HTTP request goes through the process of getting a user context. All HTTP requests are authenticated (except in the case of anonymous requests served from the HTTP.sys kernel-mode cache) and have a Windows security context, which becomes the *user context* of the request. Even a request for content that has anonymous access enabled acquires the security context of the configured anonymous account; it is not anonymous in that there is no Windows user whatsoever. Through the authentication process, the worker process obtains a security token for the user by means of a Windows logon API. The user context and the associated Windows security token are fundamental and have a wide-reaching effect on how the rest of the request proceeds. Failures in this area and in areas related to security typically manifest themselves as HTTP 401 errors. For information about troubleshooting this type of error, see "HTTP Status Codes" later in this chapter.

After a user context has been obtained, the worker process determines from the HTTP headers the kind of content the request is requesting, and then chooses the appropriate handler. At this point, the three request types become relevant.

Requests for Static Content

A request for static content is the most basic kind of request that IIS handles. For this request type, IIS validates that the user has access to the file and then returns the file.

This request type also involves validation against the Multipurpose Internet Mail Exchange (MIME) type restriction feature. If the request is for a restricted file type, IIS returns a 404.3-MIME Map Policy Prevents This Request error. For more information, see "Requests for Static Files Return 404 Error" in IIS 6.0 Help.

IIS can also cause a response to be cached in the HTTP.sys kernel-mode cache. For more information, see the "HTTP.sys Response Cache" section in "Web Server Scalability" in this book.

Requests Handled by ISAPI Extensions

Active Server Pages (ASP) and ASP.NET requests are handled by ISAPI extensions. A request is designated an ISAPI request when it requests a file whose extension is mapped to an ISAPI extension DLL in the **ScriptMaps** metabase property. A request is also designated an ISAPI request when it requests an ISAPI DLL directly in the URL or when a wildcard **ScriptMaps** entry exists, whereby *all* requests go through the mapped ISAPI DLL. IIS calls a well-known entry point in the ISAPI DLL and passes a structure containing all of the information required about a request. When IIS is configured for IIS 5.0 isolation mode, ISAPI requests also can be passed out-of-process to a Dllhost.exe worker process. Before an ISAPI request is executed, IIS checks the **WebSvcExtRestrictionList** metabase property to ensure that the ISAPI is allowed. If the ISAPI is not allowed, IIS returns a 404.2 error.

In this kind of request, the ISAPI extension DLL is responsible for processing the HTTP request and then sending the response. When an ISAPI extension DLL processes a request, any number of things can happen. In the case of ASP and ASP.NET, the user context obtained during authentication is typically impersonated before the ScriptMap file is opened. These kinds of requests, where distributed and dynamic operations are performed, often involve custom-built components and backend data stores.

CGI Requests

CGI requests directly request a CGI executable. They are similar to ISAPI requests in that the CGI performs all of the execution work and also has to be enabled in the **WebSvcExtRestrictionList** metabase property. Unlike ISAPI requests, CGI requests involve launching a new process for each request. However, this design does not perform or scale very well — especially not on heavily trafficked Web sites. Consequently, CGI requests are typically used less often than other kinds of requests.

Common Troubleshooting Tasks

Several basic IIS troubleshooting tasks are helpful in many different troubleshooting situations. These tasks include: disabling HTTP friendly error messages in Internet Explorer, generating a custom HTTP request, checking basic request functionality, browsing with different host name styles, using substatus and Win32 errors in W3C extended logging, configuring the WWW service to log worker process recycling events, checking Windows NT system and application event logs, checking the HTTP error and IIS logs, restarting the IIS service, and identifying the process ID of the worker process. Perform these tasks during the initial steps of the discovery phase, or when initially diagnosing a problem.

Disabling HTTP Friendly Error Messages in Internet Explorer

Internet Explorer displays friendly error messages when it encounters a problem during communication with an HTTP server. Although friendly error messages are appropriate for the end user, they prevent you, the administrator, from seeing the literal HTTP error codes and explanations, which makes troubleshooting difficult, if not impossible. During the discovery phase of troubleshooting, you can gather and record the HTTP errors that have occurred if you have disabled friendly messages.

▷ **To disable friendly HTTP error messages in Internet Explorer**

1. On the **Tools** menu in Internet Explorer, click **Internet Options**.

2. Click the **Advanced** tab.

3. In the list of options under **Browsing**, clear the **Show friendly HTTP error messages** check box.

4. Click **Apply**, and then click **OK**.

Generating an HTTP Request

To observe the raw HTTP traffic between a browser and IIS, use WFetch. Commonly, you might use WFetch when a user receives an HTTP 403-Forbidden error. In such a situation, you might begin troubleshooting by checking the access control list (ACL) configuration on the requested content. If that does not reveal the cause, you most likely would start troubleshooting the problem as an authentication problem. However, the 403 message indicates that these are the wrong actions to take. Disabling friendly HTTP error messages in Internet Explorer and re-trying the request with WFetch would have yielded a much more meaningful error: "Directory Listing Denied. This virtual directory does not allow contents to be listed." You would then immediately realize that Directory Browsing is disallowed for that virtual directory and that either Default Documents is disabled or it is enabled, but none of the configured documents are present in that directory.

▶ **To generate a simple HTTP request using WFetch**

1. Start WFetch.

2. From the **Verb** list box, click **GET**.

3. In the **Host** box, type a host name — for example, *www.contoso.com*.

4. In the **Path** box, type the following: **/**

5. In the **Auth** list box, click **Anonymous**.

    The **Port**, **Ver** (HTTP Version), and **Connect** settings can be left at their defaults.

6. Click **Go**.

WFetch sends an HTTP request to the local instance of IIS and then receives the response. In the Log Output window, you can view the HTTP request and response data. Notice the individual headers in both the request and response, and the entity body in the response. Figure 11.1 shows WFetch in the default startup state.

Figure 11.1   WFetch Startup Screen

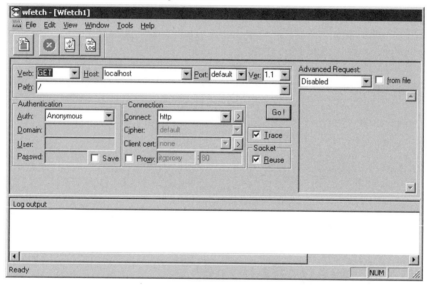

Checking Basic Functionality with Test Request Files

Occasionally, you might need to assess the core functional health of the various request types in IIS. Determining which kinds of requests work and which do not is a fundamental step in the isolation phase. The easiest way to accomplish this is to create several test files that can be placed in various application roots in your various Web sites.

Making these test requests from different locations is as important as making requests of different types. Consider that a directory location determines which application, URL, and application pool a request will be routed through. These locations can indicate at which point a particular kind of request is failing. The following examples are test request files for static content, ASP ISAPI, and ASP.NET ISAPI requests, respectively.

Static Content Test Request File

To create a static content test request file, create an HTML file with the following HTML code:

```
<HTML>
<BODY>
<H3>Hello World</H3>
</BODY>
</HTML>
```

Save this code in a file called Simple_Request.htm and use it to troubleshoot static content problems.

ASP Test Request File

For an ASP test file, you need include only dynamic ASP code inside of <% %> delimiters. However, output that returns the current time, user, and application pool is useful, too. To create an ASP request file that returns this information, create an HTML file with the following code:

```
<%@ Language=VBScript %>
<html>
<body>
<%
Response.Write ("The time is now: " & Now() & "<p>")
Response.Write ("The authenticated user is (blank if anonymous) : " & _
        Request.ServerVariables("LOGON_USER") & _
        "<p>")
Response.Write ("The application pool that served this request is: " & _
        Request.ServerVariables("APP_POOL_ID") & _
        "<p>")
%>
</body>
</html>
```

Save this code in a file called Simple_Request.asp.

ASP.NET Test Request File

The code for an ASP.NET test request is similar to that of an ASP test request:

```
<%@ Page Language="VB" Debug="True" Trace="True" %>
<%@ Import Namespace=System.Web%>

<HTML>
   <script language="VB" runat="server">

     Sub Page_Load(Src As Object, E As EventArgs)

     dim ctx as HttpContext = HttpContext.Current

     lblTime.Text = Now()
       lblUserIdentity.Text = ctx.Request.ServerVariables("LOGON_USER")
       lblAppPool.Text = ctx.Request.ServerVariables("APP_POOL_ID")

     End Sub

   </script>
   <body style="FONT: 8pt verdana">
    <form runat="server">
     The time is now:
    <asp:Label id="lblTime" runat="server" /><p>
     The authenticated user is (blank if anonymous):
    <asp:Label id="lblUserIdentity" runat="server" /><p>
      The application pool that served this request is:
     <asp:Label id="lblAppPool" runat="server" /><p>
    </form>
   </body>
</HTML>
```

Save this code in a file called Simple_Request.aspx.

Testing Simple Object Creation

A simple COM or .NET object that returns a basic "hello world" string is a useful troubleshooting tool. Placing that object locally on the server running IIS or remotely on your application tier, and then testing from ASP or from a simple script file or compiled client can help you determine where problems exist in your distributed application's architecture.

Testing Application Code Outside of IIS

Another way to test basic functionality is to test your applications completely outside of IIS. For example, if you are testing COM object creation failures, you can create a simple Microsoft Visual Basic® Scripting Edition (VBScript) file that contains your object creation code and then run the script when you log on to the IIS Web server. Variations might involve creating other custom applications by using other development tools.

Browsing with Different Host Name Styles

Connectivity and authentication problems can be related to Domain Name System (DNS) issues, the configuration of host headers, and general network anomalies. To understand the nature of a problem, it is sometimes helpful to vary the way that you type the host name in the requested Uniform Resource Locator (URL). Use any of the following variations:

- **Fully Qualified Domain Name (FQDN).** A fully qualified DNS name that uniquely identifies the computer. This name is a combination of the DNS host name and the DNS domain name, in the format *HostName.DomainName*. For example, if the DNS host name is "host1" and the DNS domain name is "example.contoso.com," the fully qualified DNS name is "host1.example.contoso.com."

- **Network BIOS (NetBIOS) name.** The computer name recognized by Windows Internet Name Service (WINS) in the format *HostName,* which maps the name to an IP address. For example, the NetBIOS name for "host1.example.contoso.com" is "host1."

- **IP address.** The address used to identify a unique node on an IP network. This address is typically represented with the decimal value of each octet, separated by a period (for example, 192.168.7.27).

 Note

IIS 6.0 also supports IPv6 addressing. For more information, see "IPv6 and IIS 6.0" in this book.

Browsing with different host name styles is useful for the following reasons:

- Certificate authentication requires matching the host name from the URL to the Common Name (CN) imprinted in the server certificate.

- In Kerberos authentication, the requested Kerberos service ticket is keyed off of the host name entered in the URL. If the wrong host name is used, a service ticket might not be obtainable.

- The host header configuration in the **ServerBindings** metabase property dictates how an HTTP request is routed into the service. This relies upon matching the requested host name with an appropriate host header configuration.

- The simple name resolution process can differ when you use a NetBIOS name instead of an FQDN. Using a NetBIOS name in the URL is similar to pinging to test name resolution of the NetBIOS name to the IP address.

- Internet Explorer can unexpectedly prompt for credentials during NTLM authentication (also referred to as Windows NT Challenge/Response authentication) when the host name portion of the requested URL contains a period. Using the NetBIOS name rather than an FQDN or IP address might indicate the cause. For more information, see article 258063, "Internet Explorer May Prompt You for a Password" in the Microsoft Knowledge Base. To find this article, see the Microsoft Knowledge Base link on the Web Resources page at http://www.microsoft.com/windows/reskits/webresources.

- Browsing by IP address is a foolproof way to rule out name resolution problems. However, the host header (set with the **ServerBindings** property) must be appropriately configured.

Using Substatus and Win32 Errors in W3C Extended Logging

To reduce the attack surface of IIS 6.0, custom error messages do not return specific error message information, including the substatus code, to remote client computers. If a custom error message contains too much information about the core Web server and an explanation of why a particular request failed to execute, malicious users can use the information to attack the Web server. As an example, an error code such as 404.2-Web Service Extension Lockdown Policy Prevents This Request is returned to a Web client as 404-File or Directory Not Found, and, thereby, gives the Web client no indication of why the request failed.

Although this change to error message reporting reduces the possibility of an attack by a malicious user, it makes it difficult to debug a failed request. For this reason, you can enable substatus error codes logging to IIS log files when appropriate. Note that on clean installs, substatus code logging for W3C Extended format files is enabled by default. Doing so is particularly useful when the logging of Win32 error codes is enabled. Then, to obtain the information that you need, you simply locate the specific request in the log file and check the Win32 error code and substatus code. This feature is called W3C extended logging. Figure 11.2 shows substatus codes as they appear on the extended logging properties sheet.

Figure 11.2   Extended Logging Properties Sheet

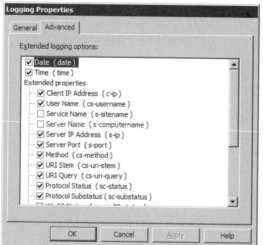

> **Important**
>
> You must be a member of the Administrators group on the local computer to perform the following procedure or procedures, or you must have been delegated the appropriate authority. As a security best practice, log on to your computer by using an account that is not in the Administrators group, and then use the **runas** command to run IIS Manager as an administrator. At a command prompt, type **runas** / *User.Administrative_AccountName* "mmc %systemroot%\system32\inetsrv\iis.msc".

▶ **T o log substatus error codes**

1. In IIS Manager, double-click the local computer, double-click the **Web Sites** folder, right-click the Web site, and click **Properties**.

2. On the **Web Site** tab, ensure that the **Enable logging** check box is selected.

3. In the Active log format list box, **click W3C Extended Log File Format**.

4. Click **Properties**.

5. Click the **Advanced** tab, and under **Extended properties**, select the **Protocol Substatus** check box.

6. Click **OK** twice.

Configuring the WWW Service to Log Worker Process Recycling Events

Proper configuration of IIS is always essential to successful troubleshooting. By setting the **LogEventOnRecycle** metabase property, you can direct the WWW service to log worker process recycling events in the event log. To accomplish this, you can set the **LogEventOnRecycle** property directly as a bitmask or you can set individual **AppPoolRecycle** property settings to **true**. The **LogEventOnRecycle** property is set to **AppPoolRecycleMemory** by default.

This is important as there could be occasions when the problem reported happened at or near the same time as a worker process recycle for the application. Having this information makes it easier to troubleshoot exactly what happened at the time of the problem to the entire server.

Table 11.1 summarizes the event IDs that are logged, and the related metabase properties and their bitmasks.

Table 11.1   LogEventOnRecycle Configuration

Recycle Condition	Event ID	Metabase Property	Bitmask
Elapsed time	1074	AppPoolRecycleTime	1 (0x1)
Number of requests processed	1075	AppPoolRecycleRequests	2 (0x2)
Scheduled recycle	1076	AppPoolRecycleSchedule	4 (0x4)
Virtual memory consumed	1077	AppPoolRecycleMemory	8 (0x8)
ISAPI reported itself unhealthy	1078	AppPoolRecycleIsapiUnhealthy	16 (0x10)
Recycled on demand	1079	AppPoolRecycleOnDemand	32 (0x20)
Recycled due to configuration change	1080	AppPoolRecycleConfigChange	64 (0x40)
Private memory consumed	1117	AppPoolRecyclePrivateMemory	128 (0x80)

Checking NT System and Application Event Logs

When looking for information about a problem, always consult the event logs for the application.

▶   **To access the event logs**

1.   From the **Start** menu, point to **Administrative Tools**, and click **Event Viewer**.

2.   In the console tree, click one of the three log types: **Application**, **Security**, or **System**.

Checking the HTTP Error Log

In IIS 6.0, HTTP.sys logs errors in the HTTP error log. The HTTP error log is the first place you should look when IIS returns an HTTP 503–Service Unavailable error, for example. The HTTP error log is located in *systemroot*\System32\LogFiles\HTTPERR.

For information about HTTP errors, see "HTTP Status Codes" later in this chapter.

Checking the IIS Logs

The IIS logs provide a great deal of information about the activity of a Web application. You can find the IIS logs in *systemroot*\System32\LogFiles\W3SVC*number,* where *number* is the site ID for the Web site.

Restarting IIS Services

During troubleshooting, you might need to restart the IIS services. You can use IIS Manager to start or to stop any Web site on your server running IIS, to stop or recycle an application pool, or to restart the WWW service, which restarts the complete IIS service base.

Restarting a Web Site

Stopping a Web site causes the WWW service to remove the URLs for that site from the HTTP.sys configuration. The WWW service then marks the Web site as stopped in the metabase and directs the Web site not to start again automatically when the WWW service is restarted. Stopping a Web site does not cause loaded segments of the applications to unload, nor does it affect the worker processes that might be running when you stop the site. Additionally, requests that are waiting in the application pool queue in HTTP.sys will still be processed. However, new requests will either generate HTTP 404-Not Found errors, or, if no other Web site is listening on the port, will send the client a socket connection error.

Web sites can be stopped and started by using either IIS Manager or the IisWeb.vbs command-line script.

▶ **To stop and restart a Web site by using IIS Manager**

1. In IIS Manager, double-click the local computer, double-click **Web Sites**, right-click the Web site that you want to restart, and click **Stop**.

    (**Stopped**) appears next to the site name in IIS Manager.

2. To restart the Web site, right-click the Web site, and click **Start**.

▶ **To stop and restart a Web site by using IisWeb.vbs**

1. To stop a Web site, at a command prompt, type the following:

    iisweb.vbs /stop *WebSiteName*

2. To restart the Web site, at a command prompt, type the following:

    iisweb.vbs /start *WebSiteName*

Recycling an Application Pool

Application pools are made up of a listening and routing structure in HTTP.sys and one or more ready-to-start worker processes that are waiting to process incoming requests. In worker process isolation mode, you can configure IIS to periodically restart worker processes under certain conditions. This automatic restarting of worker processes is called *recycling*.

Recycling an application pool causes the WWW service to shut down all running worker processes that are serving the application pool, and then start new worker processes. Whether the WWW service starts the new worker processes before it stops the existing one depends on the **DisallowOverlappingRotation** property in the metabase. Recycling an application pool does not alter any state in HTTP.sys or change any configuration in the metabase.

> **Note**
>
> When an application pool is serviced by more than one worker process, the recycle operation is staggered in some scenarios. Only when a worker process is recycled on demand or when all of the worker processes hit their memory limits at the same time would they be restarted simultaneously.

▷ **To recycle an application pool on demand**

- In IIS Manager, double-click the local computer, double-click **Application Pools**, right-click the application pool that you want to restart, and click **Recycle**.

For more information about when to manually recycle an application pool or worker process, see "Recycling Worker Processes" in IIS 6.0 Help.

Stopping an Application Pool

Stopping an application pool causes the WWW service to shut down all running worker processes serving that application pool. HTTP.sys is then directed to return HTTP 503-Service Unavailable errors for any requests currently queued for this pool, and to return HTTP 503 errors for all future requests. The application pool is marked as stopped in the metabase and is configured not to start automatically when the WWW service is restarted. You must manually start the application pool to cause it to serve requests again.

Restarting the WWW Service

Sometimes, as a last resort, you need to restart the WWW service.

▷ **To restart the WWW service**

1. In IIS Manager, right-click the local computer, point to **All Tasks**, and click **Restart IIS**.

2. Click **Restart Internet Services on *servername***, where *servername* is the name of your server.

3. Click **OK**.

Identifying Worker Process Process ID

The nature of some problems, especially those in which an application is hanging, leaking memory, or generally misbehaving, make it necessary to know which application pool goes with which worker process (or processes, if Web gardens are enabled). With the advent of the new worker process isolation mode in IIS 6.0, a Web server potentially can have thousands of individual instances of W3wp.exe running at any given time. Looking for the process ID in Task Manager is pointless in such a case because it is impossible to differentiate between the different worker processes servicing the application pools.

In earlier versions of IIS and when IIS 6.0 is running in IIS 5.0 isolation mode, identifying the process ID is relatively easy. If a component installed in a COM+ library application has been activated from a worker process, the procedure for identifying the process ID is the same.

▶ **To find the process ID in versions prior to IIS 6.0 and in IIS 5.0 isolation mode**

1. From the **Start** menu, point to **Administrative Tools,** and click **Component Services**.

2. In the console tree of the **Component Services** window, double-click **Component Services**, double-click **Computers**, double-click **My Computer**, and double-click **Running Processes**.

   Under this node, you see the various COM+ applications and their associated process IDs.

In worker process isolation mode, you can find the process ID by using the command-line script Iisapp.vbs, which is stored in *systemroot*\System32, and is designed specifically for this purpose.

 Important

You must be a member of the Administrators group on the local computer to run scripts and executables, or you must have been delegated the appropriate authority. As a security best practice, log on to your computer by using an account that is not in the Administrators group, and then use the runas command to run your script or executable as an administrator. At a command prompt, type **runas /profile** */User:MyMachine\Administrator* cmd to open a command window with administrator rights and then type **cscript.exe** *ScriptName* (including the full path with parameters, if any).

▶ **To find a worker process ID by using Iisapp.vbs**

- Run Iisapp.vbs with no parameters.

  This displays a listing of running worker processes, their process IDs, and the application pool names.

For more information about using Iisapp.vbs, see "Listing Running Web Applications" in IIS 6.0 Help.

HTTP Status Codes

HTTP status codes provide the best information about what is happening with IIS. On an active Web server, HTTP status codes provide a continuous feed of up-to-the-moment information about the activity and health of the server.

Most HTTP status codes have three digits, for example, 401. Some status codes have three digits followed by a decimal point, and one or two more digits (for example, 300.12). In such a case, the number that follows the decimal point is called the substatus code.

Codes within each hundred-number range provide specific types of information, as summarized in Table 11.2.

Table 11.2   HTTP Status Codes

Status Code Range	Type of Code
100	Informational
200	Successful
300	Redirection
400	Client Error
500	Server Error

As an administrator, at some point you will inevitably need to determine which HTTP status codes are being returned by IIS. There are a number of ways to do this. Your choice of method depends on the amount of information that you need and the type of problem that you are troubleshooting. If you have a problem that is limited to one or a few clients, viewing the status codes from the client's Web browser or issuing a reproduced HTTP request with WFetch might best serve your needs. However, if you need to look for an individual request or for a collection of multiple requests over a period of time, you should examine the IIS logs. Viewing IIS logs allows you to see not only the main HTTP status code, but the Win32 error code and the HTTP substatus code (if logging is configured to do so). The Win32 error codes and the HTTP substatus codes often contain information that is critical to your troubleshooting effort.

The following sections describe the HTTP status codes and provide troubleshooting suggestions.

HTTP 1*xx*-2*xx* — Informational and Success Codes

HTTP status codes in the 1*xx* are typically informational. Status codes in the 2*xx* range indicate that the transaction was successful. Because the codes in both ranges are self-explanatory, they do not require further discussion.

HTTP 3*xx*— Redirection Codes

HTTP status codes in the 3*xx* range pertain to *redirection* (telling the browser to issue a new request at a different location). These codes do not indicate that a problem has occurred.

Table 11.3 lists the HTTP redirection codes that IIS returns.

Table 11.3   HTTP 300-Class Error Codes Returned by IIS

Status Code	Condition
301	Permanent Redirect.
302	Object Moved
304	Not Modified.
307	Temporary redirect.

301-Permanent Redirect

This redirection status code tells the Web client that the location for the requested resource has permanently changed. The new location is specified in the **Location** HTTP header. This is primarily useful for Web clients that keep record of HTTP URL links. Upon receiving this status code, the Web client can update the stored URL with the new location.

302-Object Moved

This standard redirection status code tells the Web client to issue a new request to the location specified in the **Location** HTTP header.

304-Not Modified

RFC 2616, *Hypertext Transfer Protocol — HTTP/1.1* provides functionality for "conditional GET requests." For example, an HTTP client can specify an **If-Modified-Since** HTTP header that consists of a time and date stamp, which tells the server that it has a cached copy of the content being requested. If the request meets the condition specified in the **If-Modified-Since** header, the server will not return a body, but will return the 304-Not Modified result.

307-Temporary Redirect

The temporary redirect option, which is new in IIS 6.0, is used to prevent a Web browser from losing data when the browser issues an HTTP POST request. Normally, when a Web browser issues a POST request and then receives a 302-Object Moved redirect message from the Web server, the browser issues a GET request for the new location and loses the data in the POST request. With a 307 redirect, the browser reissues the POST request with the original data to the new location.

For more information about temporary HTTP redirects, see "HttpRedirect" in IIS 6.0 Help.

Courtesy Redirects

When a browser makes an HTTP request, the request sometimes takes the form http://example.contoso.com/vdir1. Notice that there is no trailing "/" at the end of the URL. In this case, vdir1 is a directory, instead of a file. As a courtesy to the Web browser, IIS responds to this request with a 302-Object Moved redirect message with the HTTP header: **Location:** */vdir1/.* This is known as a courtesy redirect.

Courtesy redirection can produce unexpected behavior when the Web server is behind a Network Address Translation (NAT) device —a proxy server, for example. Suppose, for example, that the Web site is configured to listen on port 8080 and the NAT device is configured to forward HTTP requests on port 80 to the Web server on port 8080. In this configuration, the NAT device accepts the Web browser's request, but when the courtesy redirect occurs, IIS appends the port number to the host name. The NAT device needs to be aware of this and alter the response appropriately before returning it to the client.

For more information, see article 298408, "IIS Generates Courtesy Redirect When Folder Without Trailing Slash Is Requested" and article 313074, "How To: Redirect Browser Requests in Internet Information Services 5.0" in the Microsoft Knowledge Base. To find these articles, see the Microsoft Knowledge Base link on the Web Resources page at http://www.microsoft.com/windows/reskits/webresources.

HTTP 40*x*— Client Error Codes

HTTP status codes in the 4*xx* range indicate that a problem occurred with the request. Request problems can range from the request not meeting authentication requirements to the request being malformed. RFC 2616, *Hypertext Transfer Protocol — HTTP/1.1* refers to request problems as client errors because the requests originate from the client.

Table 11.4 lists the client error codes that IIS returns. The descriptions for most codes are self-explanatory. When additional information about a code is required, it is provided in one of the following sections.

Table 11.4 HTTP 400-Class Client Error Codes Returned by IIS

Status Code	Condition
400	Cannot resolve the request.
401.x	Unauthorized.
403.x	Forbidden.
404.x	File or directory not found.
405	HTTP verb used to access this page is not allowed.
406	Client browser does not accept the MIME type of the requested page.
407	Initial proxy authentication required by the Web server.
412	Precondition set by the client failed when evaluated on the Web server.
413	Request entity too large.
414	Request URL is too large and therefore unacceptable on the Web server.
415	Unsupported media type.
416	Requested range not satisfiable.
417	Expectation failed.
423	Locked error.

HTTP 400-Cannot Resolve the Request

IIS returns a 400 error code when the request is malformed. Though there are a variety causes for this error, the most common reason is that the request does not comply with RFC 2616. For example, if the request is made in HTTP 1.1, RFC 2616 requires that the request include a **Host** header. The simplest HTTP 1.1 request would look similar to the following:

```
GET / HTTP/1.1
Host: example.contoso.com
```

You can use WFetch to issue such a custom-built request. Most HTTP clients adhere to HTTP RFC 2616 and issue well-formed requests. However, if you are developing a custom HTTP client and are experiencing HTTP 400 problems, use WFetch to make test requests.

▷ **To issue a simple HTTP 1.1 request using WFetch**

1. Start **WFetch**.

2. From the **Advanced Request** list box, click **Raw Request**.

3. In the box, type the following text, where *ComputerName* is the name of your server running IIS:

```
GET / HTTP/1.1\r\n
Host: ComputerName\r\n
\r\n
```

4. Ensure that the **Host** box contains the same *ComputerName* as noted above.

5. Click **Go**.

This sends the most basic HTTP 1.1 GET request to the server.

HTTP.sys records some errors in its own log file. Table 11.5 lists the HTTP.sys reason codes and explanations for each of the 400 errors. These errors are not recorded in the IIS logs.

Table 11.5   HTTP.sys Logged Reason Codes for HTTP 400 Errors

Reason Code	Condition
BadRequest	The request could not be understood by the server because the syntax was incorrect.
Verb	Invalid verb.
URL	Invalid URL.
Header	Invalid header name.
Hostname	Invalid hostname.
Invalid_CR/LF	Invalid carriage return or line feed.
Number	Invalid number.
FieldLength	A header field in the request was too long.
RequestLength	The request length was too long.

HTTP 401.*x*-Unauthorized

Authentication is one of the first operations performed when an HTTP request is issued. *Authentication* is the process whereby IIS creates a user context for an HTTP request, typically by obtaining credentials from the HTTP client using a preconfigured authentication method, and then calling a Windows logon API using those credentials. The API then returns a security token for the request, which represents the user context.

After the authentication process concludes, IIS determines where the HTTP request goes next based on the resource that is being requested. Regardless of this choice, IIS issues an authorization check against the requested resource. IIS checks to ensure that the user context associated with this request is allowed to make the request. Usually, IIS performs a file ACL check to authenticate the request.

When IIS cannot authenticate a request, it returns a 401.*x*-Unauthorized code. The substatus codes provide detailed information about why the request failed, as shown in Table 11.6. The descriptions for most substatus codes are self-explanatory. When additional information about a substatus code is required, it is provided in one of the following sections.

Table 11.6   HTTP 401-Substatus Codes

401 Substatus Code	Condition
1	Access is denied due to invalid credentials.
2	Access is denied due to server configuration favoring an alternate authentication method.
3	Access is denied due to an ACL set on the requested resource.
4	Authorization failed by a filter installed on the Web server.
5	Authorization failed by an ISAPI/CGI application.
7	Access denied by URL authorization policy on the Web server.

401.1 and 401.2 — Authentication Problems

Typically, HTTP 401.1 and 401.2 errors are encountered when the authentication process fails in some way — either because the mechanism that IIS used to obtain the credentials has failed or because the credentials themselves are invalid. This is an important distinction that is a critical to the problem isolation process. These errors tell you that, before performing any other function, IIS has failed to authenticate the user.

For a brief overview of the authentication options available in IIS, see "Managing a Secure IIS 6.0 Solution" in this book.

Initial Isolation

When you know that authentication has failed, gather the following information:

- The URL that is being requested.

- The authentication method that is configured for that node in the metabase.

  When you know the requested URL, you can use IIS Manager to verify the authentication methods that are enabled. Alternatively, you can use the Adsutil.vbs command-line script to check the **AuthFlags** metabase property. For information about the settings for this property, see "AuthFlags" in IIS 6.0 Help.

Multiple Authentication Methods

Typically, initial HTTP requests to a server are anonymous. In most cases, a Web browser does not know to send authentication information, and, therefore, it issues a request without this information. If Anonymous authentication is enabled for the requested resource, IIS does not attempt to use other authentication protocols, but instead attempts to obtain a security token for the IUSR_*ComputerName* account by calling one of the Windows logon APIs. If this fails, then IIS looks to see if other authentication methods are enabled for the URL and sends back a 401.2 response to the browser that includes a list of **WWW-Authenticate** HTTP headers that specify the authentication schemes IIS is configured to accept for that URL.

At this stage, typically it is up to the HTTP client to choose to continue the HTTP transaction, to pick a protocol from the list, and to proceed to authenticate with that protocol. If this process is successful, IIS then calls a logon API and obtains a security token that it can use to associate a user context with the HTTP request.

LogonMethod Default Has Changed

The **LogonMethod** metabase property designates the kind of logon token that IIS asks for when calling the Windows logon APIs for Anonymous or Basic authentication. In earlier versions of IIS, the default was set to **0**, which caused IIS to request an INTERACTIVE token. This sometimes caused problems when the IUSR_*ComputerName,* or, in the case of Basic authentication, the user credentials did not have the Log on locally user right. In such a case, IIS returns a 401.1 error.

In IIS 6.0, the default value of **LogonMethod** has changed to **3**, which evaluates to a NETWORK_CLEARTEXT token. This token is very similar to an INTERACTIVE token; however, it does not allow the user to physically log on to the system console and does not require the Log on locally user right.

For more information, see "Securing Sites with Web Site Permissions" in IIS 6.0 Help.

No Authentication Methods Selected (AuthFlags=0)

IIS returns a 401.2 error when no authentication methods are enabled. If you receive this error, ensure that an authentication method is enabled.

Anonymous Accounts (IUSR_*ComputerName*) Attempting Sub-authentication Logon Receive the 401.1 Error: Logon Failed

By default, the sub-authentication component, Iissuba.dll, is not enabled in IIS 6.0. In earlier versions, Iissuba.dll allowed IIS to manage passwords on anonymous accounts, which created a potential security risk. In IIS 6.0, you can use sub-authentication to manage passwords for anonymous accounts. To do so, your configuration must meet the following requirements:

- For applications for which you grant anonymous access, the worker process must run as LocalSystem.

- The sub-authentication component, Iissuba.dll, must be registered.

- The **AnonymousPasswordSync** metabase property must be enabled (set to **true**).

The actions taken to meet these requirements are different for clean installations of IIS 6.0 and upgrades to IIS 6.0 than they are for installations of IIS with sub-authentication configured. For more information about configuring sub-authentication, see "Anonymous Authentication" in IIS 6.0 Help.

Additionally, when you encounter a 401.1 error, ensure that the account configured for anonymous authentication has not expired or is not locked out.

Non-Anonymous authentication

Initially, a Web browser issues an anonymous request. If Anonymous authentication is not enabled or if Anonymous authentication fails, IIS sends a list of supported authentication protocols as a group of **WWW-Authenticate** HTTP headers. At this point, the browser chooses the protocol to use, and then continues processing the request.

Basic authentication

Basic authentication is the simplest authentication protocol. Because of its simplicity, it is a good authentication method to enable temporarily when you are troubleshooting authentication problems. Use this authentication protocol if you want to quickly verify that a password is correct or that communication with a domain controller is working.

If the user name is a domain account, IIS contacts a domain controller to verify the credentials. If this fails, IIS returns a 401.2 error. If communication with the domain controller is successful, but the user name or password is invalid, IIS returns a 401.1 error.

Internet Explorer — not IIS — allows the user three connection attempts before rejecting the connection request and reporting an error to the user. When the Web server verifies that the user name and password correspond to a valid Windows Server 2003 user account, a connection is established.

Integrated Windows authentication

Integrated Windows authentication actually encompasses two different authentication protocols:- Kerberos and Windows NT Challenge/Response, also known as NTLM. When this authentication protocol is enabled, IIS sends the following HTTP headers to the browser:

- WWW-Authenticate: Negotiate
- WWW-Authenticate: NTLM

The **Negotiate** header indicates that IIS can negotiate which of the two Windows authentication protocols to use. Internet Explorer 5, or later, recognizes this authentication header and determines which of the two authentication protocols to use. The **NTLM** authentication header is used as a fallback for browsers that do not support the **Negotiate** authentication header.

Kerberos protocol authentication   Authentication with the Kerberos protocol occurs as follows:

1. IIS requests authentication.

2. If the Windows user has not logged on to a domain, a dialog box requesting credentials appears in Internet Explorer, and then IIS contacts the Ticket Granting Server or Key Distribution Center (KDC) to request and receive a Ticket Granting Ticket. It then sends the Ticket Granting Ticket along with information about the server running IIS to the KDC.

3. If the Windows user has already successfully logged on to the domain and received a Ticket Granting Ticket, IIS sends this ticket along with information about the IIS server to the KDC.

4. The KDC issues the client a Resource Ticket.

5. The client passes this ticket to the server running IIS.

When troubleshooting Kerberos, ensure that the browser can make a trusted connection to the KDC by meeting the requirements listed in article 326985, "How To: Troubleshoot Kerberos-related Issues in IIS" in the Microsoft Knowledge Base. To find these articles, see the Microsoft Knowledge Base link on the Web Resources page at http://www.microsoft.com/windows/reskits/webresources.

Additionally, consider potential problems with the following:

▪   **Service Principal Names.** Kerberos uses a service for authentication. When the client passes the Ticket Granting Ticket and the information about IIS to the KDC, part of this information includes the server name from the URL that the browser is attempting to reach. By default, upon installation a system's NetBIOS name is registered in Active Directory® directory service. This is the name that a KDC uses to recognize IIS. It is called the Service Principal Name (SPN). If the browser is accessing the Web server by using some other host name — either the FQDN or another host header name — that name must be registered with Active Directory. You can do this by using the Setspn.exe command-line utility. For more information about Setspn.exe, in Help and Support Center for Windows Server 2003, click **Tools**, and then click **Windows Support Tools**.

- **Kerberos authentication.** If you suspect that you are having a problem with the SPN, test Kerberos authentication by using the NetBIOS computer name. If the test is successful, you probably need to use the Setspn.exe command-line utility.

  To run Setspn.exe, at a command prompt, type the following:

  Setspn -A HOST/*ServicePrincipalName ServiceAccount*

  In the above syntax, *ServicePrincipalName* is the new host name that you want to register and *ServiceAccount* is the identity under which the process that is hosting the service will be running. For computer accounts, like NetworkService or LocalSystem, use the NetBIOS name of the computer.

  Note

  The LocalService account, along with any other local accounts on an IIS server, cannot be authenticated by a KDC. Therefore, you cannot use the Kerberos protocol for authentication if the worker process identity is set to LocalService or to another account on the local computer.

- **Trust for delegation configuration.** When troubleshooting Kerberos authentication, also ensure that the IIS computer is configured to be trusted for delegation in Active Directory. If the server running IIS is a member of the domain and is not a domain controller, then it must be trusted for delegation in order for Kerberos to work properly.

▷ **To configure a computer to be trusted for delegation**

1. On the Domain controller, click **Start**, point to **Administrative Tools**, and click **Active Directory Users and Computers**.

2. Under the domain, double-click the **Computers** folder, right-click the server that is running IIS, and then click **Properties**.

3. Click the **General** tab.

4. Select the **Trusted for delegation** check box.

5. Click **OK**.

The computer account is now trusted for delegation.

- **Security auditing.** By enabling security auditing on the server running IIS, you can use the events that are logged to discover whether problems are occurring.

  For information about using the security log to troubleshoot Kerberos, see article 326985, "How To: Troubleshoot Kerberos-related Issues in IIS" in the Microsoft Knowledge Base. To find these articles, see the Microsoft Knowledge Base link on the Web Resources page at http://www.microsoft.com/windows/reskits/webresources.

Windows NT Challenge/Response protocol Windows NT Challenge/Response (NTCR) protocol differs from Kerberos in that the server presents the HTTP client with a "challenge" and the client responds with its response. This way, the client's password is never sent over the network. Authentication with the NTCR protocol occurs as follows:

1. Typically, the client issues an initial anonymous request. When the anonymous request is rejected, IIS returns a 401.2 error and the **WWW-Authenticate** headers.

2. If the client fails or does not support Kerberos, the **Negotiate** and **NTLM** header values initiate an NTCR authentication exchange. The client closes the TCP connection, opens a new one, and sends a request that includes an **Authorization: NTLM** header. This header also includes encoded text that represents the user's *UserName*, *ComputerName*, and *Domain*. This text is used by the Windows Security Support Provider Interface (SSPI) to generate the challenge. If the user account is not a local Windows account on the IIS server, the data is passed on to an appropriate domain controller, which then generates the challenge.

3. The challenge is sent to the client and IIS returns another 401.2 error.

4. The client uses its password and the challenge to create a mathematical hash. The client sends the hash back to the server in another **Authorization: NTLM** header.

5. The server accepts the response, and the local security provider or the appropriate domain controller recreates the same hash and compares the two. If they match, the user is successfully authenticated.

When troubleshooting NTCR authentication, note the following:

- **Point-to-point connections.** NTCR authentication requires point-to-point connection between the client and the server that is running IIS. Consequently, the NTRC protocol will not work with some Conseil Europeen pour la Recherche Nucleaire (CERN) proxies and other Internet devices. As a result, NTCR is not suitable for use over the Internet. If a connection is broken during authentication, IIS returns a 401.2 error.

- **HTTP keep-alives.** A connection must be maintained through the entire authentication sequence. Therefore, HTTP keep-alives must be enabled on the server running IIS. If they are not enabled, IIS continues to return 401.2 errors until the browser fails the authentication sequence.

- **Security privileges.** The user account accessing the server must have the **Access this computer from the network** privilege. If this is not the case, IIS returns a 401.1 error.

- **Domain controller communication.** As with Basic authentication, if the credentials presented by the client are for a domain user account, the server running IIS needs to contact a domain controller.

Note

In earlier versions of IIS, to enhance performance, administrators could use the **AuthPersistence** metabase property to force IIS to negotiate one-time-per-client connections, and then use the same credentials for subsequent requests over the same connection. For security reasons, this feature has been removed from IIS 6.0. Now the only valid setting for the **AuthPersistence** property is *AuthPersistSingleRequest*.

401.3-Unauthorized: Access Is Denied Due to an ACL Set on the Requested Resource

A 401.3 error is a catchall "access denied" error. To troubleshoot this error, first check the authentication method that is enabled on the requested URL. This will help you determine the security context under which the request is expected to execute: as an anonymous user or as an authenticated user. How you proceed depends on whether the user is authenticated or not.

Verify file and directory ACLs. When the requested URL is a directory, not a file, check the default document(s) that are configured for that URL. Sometimes, if the first document in the default document list is missing, the second document in the list might generate a 401.3 error.

After verifying the ACLs, you have a few options. You can enable security auditing for object access failures. This can be difficult, though, because you have to enable auditing on the individual objects (files, directories, and so on) that you want to monitor. Alternatively, you can use File Monitor and Registry Monitor to look for access denied problems in the registry or file system.

Simplified UNC authentication model

The Universal Naming Convention (UNC) authentication method, also called UNC Pass-through authentication, determines the credentials used for gaining access to a UNC share on a remote computer. Beginning with IIS 6.0, the UNC authentication method looks at the request user and the credentials stored in the **UNCUserName** and **UNCPassword** properties of the metabase to determine the credentials to pass through to the computer with the UNC share. This occurs in the following way:

1. If the **UNCUserName** is specified (not empty) and **UNCPassword** is valid, the request user credentials are sent as the user identity for access to the remote share. If the **UNCUserName** is specified and the **UNCPassword** is not valid, a 500-Internal Server Error message is sent to the client. For information about troubleshooting this error, see "HTTP 500.x-Internal Server Error" later in this chapter.

2. If the **UNCUserName** is not specified, then the credentials of the request user (either an authenticated set of credentials for authenticated requests or *IUSR_ComputerName* credentials for anonymous requests) are sent as the user identity for access to the remote share.

Note

The UNCAuthenticationPassthrough metabase property is no longer used for UNC authentication.

For more Information about authentication and authorization, see the following articles in the Microsoft Knowledge Base:

- Article 264921, "Info: How IIS Authenticates Browser Clients"

- Article 326985, "How To: Troubleshoot Kerberos-Related Issues in IIS"

- Article 294382, "Authentication May Fail with "401.3" Error If "Host Header" Differs from Server's NetBIOS Name"

- Article 811889, "How To: Troubleshoot the "Cannot Generate SSPI Context" Error Message

- Article 325358, "How To: Configure User and Group Access on an Intranet in Windows 2000 or Windows NT 4.0"

To find these articles, see the Microsoft Knowledge Base link on the Web Resources page at http://www.microsoft.com/windows/reskits/webresources.

HTTP 403.*x*-Forbidden

Typically, 403 errors occur when an operation or request is disallowed because a requirement other than proper authentication credentials is not met. Commonly, this error occurs when a script request is made to a Web directory for which script access is not enabled. In such a case, first verify for which resource the request is being made. If the request is, indeed, for script code, such as ASP or ASP.NET, check the **execute permissions** for that directory in IIS Manager and ensure that at least **Script** is selected.

Table 11.7 lists the HTTP 403 error substatus codes.

Table 11.7 HTTP 403 Substatus Codes

403 Substatus Code	Description
None	Access is denied.
1	Execute access is denied.
2	Read access is denied.
3	Write access is denied.
4	SSL is required to view this resource.
5	SSL 128 is required to view this resource.

(continued)

Table 11.7 HTTP 403 Substatus Codes *(continued)*

403 Substatus Code	Description
6	IP address of the client has been rejected.
7	SSL client certificate is required.
8	DNS name of the client is rejected.
9	Too many clients are trying to connect to the Web server.
10	Web server is configured to deny Execute access.
11	Password has been changed.
12	Client certificate is denied access by the server certificate mapper.
13	Client certificate has been revoked on the Web server.
14	Directory listing is denied on the Web server.
15	Client access licenses have exceeded limits on the Web server.
16	Client certificate is ill-formed or is not trusted by the Web server.
17	Client certificate has expired or is not yet valid.
18	Cannot execute requested URL in the current application pool.
19	Cannot execute CGIs for the client in this application pool.
20	Passport logon failed.

HTTP 404.x-File or Directory Not Found

A HTTP 404 error indicates that the requested resource was not found. Table 11.8 lists the substatus codes for the 404 error. The descriptions for most substatus codes are self-explanatory. When additional information about a substatus code is required, it is provided in one of the following sections.

Table 11.8   HTTP 404 Substatus Codes

404 Substatus Code	Condition
None	File or directory not found.
1	Web site not accessible on the requested port.
2	Web service extension lockdown policy prevents this request.
3	MIME map policy prevents this request.

Whether the requested resource is a file or a directory, begin by checking the following potential causes:

- **Verify the file or directory.** Examine the requested URL and check the physical path to which it maps.

- **Check for unexpected host header routing.** Problems with host headers occur when you have created more than one virtual Web server and rely on host header routing to serve content from the appropriate server. A 404 error results when you request a URL that exists on only one virtual server and, because of the configuration of the host header, the request is routed to the other virtual server.

- **Verify that the request has been made on the correct port.** The 404.1 error is returned when a request is made to a port on which the WWW service is not listening.

- **Ensure that the requested file is not hidden.** IIS sends a 404 error if the **Hidden** file attribute for a requested file is set.

- **Validate (*ScriptMaps) Web service extension requests.** 404 errors are sometimes returned when you have a *ScriptMap Web service extension and the Verify that file exists option is set to **true**. Because no file is actually associated with a *ScriptMap request, IIS cannot check for the file, so it returns a 404 error.

Both the Web service extension lockdown policy and **MimeMap** restriction features can cause a 404 error to be returned to the client making the request. If one of these features is the cause of an HTTP 404 error, do the following:

- **Check the sc-substatus field for the request in the IIS W3C extended log.** For information about enabling substatus logging, see "Using Substatus and Win32 Errors in W3C Extended Logging" earlier in this chapter.

- **Check the Win32 error in the IIS W3C extended log.** By default, IIS logs all Win32 errors associated with the request that are returned by the underlying operating system.

- **Enable a modified custom error for the HTTP 404 error that you suspect.** You can configure IIS to return a response to the client that contains the substatus code by editing the custom error page for the 404 error, and placing some custom text into the file. The custom error pages are located in *systemroot*\Help\IisHelp\Common.

 Important

Enabling a custom error that provides substatus information undermines the security strategy used by IIS and should be done temporarily and only for troubleshooting purposes.

404.1-Web Site Not Accessible on the Requested Port

The 404.1 error can occur only on computers with multiple IP addresses. If a specific IP address/port combination receives a client request, and the IP address is not configured to listen on that particular port, IIS returns a 404.1 HTTP error.

For example, if a computer has two IP addresses and only one of those IP addresses is configured to listen on port 80, any requests received on the other IP address with port 80 causes IIS to return a 404.1 error. This error should be set only at the service level because it is returned to clients only when multiple IP addresses are used on the server.

404.2-Lockdown Policy Prevents This Request

If a request is denied because the associated ISAPI or CGI has not been unlocked, a 404.2 error is returned. When substatus logging is enabled, if you look at this request in the IIS logs, you will see an entry similar to the following:

```
2002-11-25 05:46:15 127.0.0.1 GET /default.asp - 80 - 127.0.0.1 - 404 2 1260
```

If IIS logging is not configured to log the substatus code, you can check the Win32 error to verify this condition. When a 404.2 error occurs, IIS logs the Win32 error 1260, which is an ERROR_ACCESS_DISABLED_BY_POLICY error.

For information about how to enable an application that has been locked down, see "IIS 6.0 Administrative Scripts, Tips, and Tricks" in this book.

404.3-MIME Map Policy Prevents This Request

If a request is denied because a MIME map restriction is in effect, a 404.3 error is returned. When substatus logging is enabled, if you look at this request in the IIS logs, you will see an entry similar to the following:

```
2002-11-25 05:46:27 127.0.0.1 GET /somefile.unkext - 80 - 127.0.0.1 - 404 3 50
```

As with a 404.2 error, a 404.3 error causes a Win32 error to be logged. In this case, the error is 50, which is an ERROR_NOT_SUPPORTED error.

Another quick way to verify that a MIME map restriction is in effect is to add a wildcard MIME type to the virtual directory in question. This enables all MIME types to be served without restriction. Then, repeat the failed HTTP request and verify that it is served successfully.

 Note

Adding a wildcard MIME type to the virtual directory is a troubleshooting step not a final solution to the problem. Leaving the wildcard in place and allowing all MIME types to be served compromises the security of the server.

For more information about adding a wildcard MIME type, see "Working with MIME Types" in IIS 6.0 Help.

405-HTTP Verb Used to Access This Page Is Not Allowed

This HTTP code is returned when the client makes an HTTP request that contains a verb that is not allowed. This condition can occur when:

- A request for static content contains verbs other than GET or HEAD, and the request is made to a URL that did not end with a "/". Instead performing a courtesy redirect, IIS sends the 405 error.

- An HTTP request for an ISAPI application contains a verb not listed in the **ScriptMaps** configuration for that ISAPI.

407-Initial Proxy Authentication Required by the Web Server

This error indicates that an intermediary proxy server between the HTTP client and the Web server requires some form of authentication. How you troubleshoot this kind of error depends upon the proxy server itself. Generally speaking, running a network trace with Network Monitor is helpful. If the Web client is a custom client, ask its developer to ensure that it is handling security appropriately.

413-Request Entity Is Too Large

For security reasons, you can limit the size of the *entity-body* of an HTTP request by modifying the **MaxRequestEntityAllowed** metabase property. When an entity-body of a client request exceeds the size that is specified in the **MaxRequestEntityAllowed** property, IIS returns a 413 error. If this error is logged for an individual request, an application on the Web server might have encountered an unexpected event and generated a request that is too large. If this error is logged for many requests, a malicious user might be attempting to compromise your Web server.

414-Request URL Is Too Large and Therefore Unacceptable on the Web Server

Just as the entity body of a request can be too large for IIS to process, a URL can be too long for IIS to process. IIS returns a 414 error if this occurs.

HTTP 5xx Server Error Codes

Error codes in the 5xx range indicate server problems. Table 11.9 lists the HTTP 5xx-class codes that IIS returns. The descriptions for most codes are self-explanatory. When additional information about a code is required, it is provided in one of the following sections.

Table 11.9   HTTP 500-Class Client Error Codes Returned by IIS

Status Code	Condition
500.x	Internal server error.
501	Header values specify a configuration that is not implemented.
502	Bad gateway.
503	Service unavailable.
504	Gateway timeout.
505	HTTP version not supported.

HTTP 500.x— Internal Server Error Codes

Table 11.10 lists the most common 500 substatus codes returned by IIS. The descriptions for most substatus codes are self-explanatory. When additional information about a substatus code is required, it is provided in one of the following sections.

Table 11.10   HTTP 500 Substatus Codes

500 Substatus Code	Condition
11	Application is shutting down on the Web server.
12	Application is busy restarting on the Web server.
13	Web server is too busy.
14	Invalid application configuration on the server.
15	Direct requests for Global.asa are not allowed.
16	UNC authorization credentials are incorrect.
17	URL authorization store cannot be found.
18	URL authorization store cannot be opened.
100	Internal ASP error.

500.11 and 500.12-Application State Issues

Users rarely encounter 500.11 and 500.12 errors in their browser. These errors indicate that the ASP application to which the requested ASP page belongs is in the process of shutting down, restarting, or both. Restarts and shutdowns can be triggered directly from code when the built-in APIs available to ASP developers are used. Occasionally, these errors occur when the Global.asa file for the application (if one exists) is updated or altered in such a way that a file change notification is issued. Because IIS monitors for file change notifications on ASP content, IIS receives this notification, and because the file is the Global.asa file, IIS restarts the application.

If users often encounter these errors in their browser and you are certain that the code in the Global.asa file is not being updated, virus scanning and backup software, which sometimes sweep the ASP content and trigger a notification, might be causing these errors. For more information, see article 248013, "Err Msg: HTTP Error 500-12 Application Restarting" in the Microsoft Knowledge Base. To find this article, see the Microsoft Knowledge Base link on the Web Resources page at http://www.microsoft.com/windows/reskits/webresources.

500.13-Web Server Too Busy

ASP requests are executed by threads from a pool of threads whose size is limited to 25 threads per processor, by default. If more ASP requests arrive than there are threads available to execute them, ASP places the extra requests in a queue, where they wait until a thread becomes available. By default, this queue is limited to 3000 requests. If the queue becomes full, the next ASP request, instead of being queued, causes a 500.13-Web server too busy error. The number of requests that can wait in the queue is controlled by the **AspRequestQueueMax** metabase property. Change the **AspRequestQueueMax** property to produce the desired user experience — a smaller queue allows users to more quickly see the 500.13 error when ASP requests are backed up.

If users encounter this error, select the **Active Server Pages/Requests Queued** performance counter check box. If the queue fills up, but ultimately empties again, or if the queue remains partially filled but requests move through very quickly, there probably is not a problem, just a spike in traffic. However, if the queue remains partially or completely full for a sustained period and requests don't appear to be moving through quickly enough, there might be a problem.

Diagnosing a problem of this type can be a complex process. For information about diagnosing such problems, see "Advanced Troubleshooting" later in this chapter.

500.16-UNC Authorization Credentials Are Incorrect

Problems with content stored on remote file servers can be more complex than problems with locally stored content. The 500.16 error indicates that there is a specific configuration problem with remotely stored content. When IIS is configured to use specific credentials to access the UNC path in the metabase, it uses those credentials to open the content on the remote file server. To do this, IIS uses a Windows logon API to obtain a security token that it can use to impersonate a security identity when accessing the remotely stored content. If the call to the Windows logon API fails, indicating that there is a problem with the user name or password, IIS returns an HTTP 500.16 error.

500.17 and 500.18-IIS URL Authorization Issues

IIS URL Authorization is a security feature that is new in IIS 6.0. Among other administrative tasks, IIS URL Authorization configures the Authorization Manager store by setting the **AzStoreName** metabase property. This store can be an XML file or an LDAP location. It is configured by setting the **AzStoreName** property to an appropriate string that represents the path to a store. For example: *msxml://c:\MyStore.xml* or *msldap://CN=MyAzStore, CN=Program Data, DC=MyDomain, DC=com.*

The 500.17 and 500.18 errors pertain to problems accessing the Authorization Manager store. A 500.17 error indicates that the store could not be found. To begin troubleshooting one of these errors, try to verify the path specified in the string by either opening the XML file or testing the LDAP path with a simple client, such as LDP.exe. For more information about LDP.exe, in Help and Support Center for Windows Server 2003, click **Tools**, and then click **Windows Support Tools**.

A 500.18 error typically indicates that the store was found, but could not be opened. The error description might contain information such as an HRESULT and description. However, this error generally occurs because there is an ACL–related problem. The security context that is used to open the store is that of the worker process identity. To troubleshoot, verify that the configured worker process identity is a member of the built-in IIS_WPG group and that this group has access to the store. File Monitor is a good utility to use in such a case.

For more information about IIS URL Authorization, see "URL Authorization" in IIS 6.0 Help.

503-Service Unavailable

HTTP 503 errors are returned more often in IIS 6.0 than in earlier versions of IIS. Typically, the HTTP 503-Service Unavailable error is returned directly from HTTP.sys when there is a problem with getting the request up to the worker process. However, this error can occur for a variety of reasons, as listed in Table **11.11**.

Table 11.11 HTTP 503 Errors from HTTP.sys

Reason String	Text in HTTP.sys Error Log	Cause(s) of Error
Service unavailable.	N/A	▪ IIS cannot start any new worker processes because of limited system resources or because starting a new worker process would exceed the **DemandStartThreshold** property. ▪ Bandwidth throttling is enabled, but the filter addition fails. ▪ The control channel or internal configuration group for the URL is inactive. ▪ The send for a request that was serviced from the cache failed (typically under low memory conditions).
Too many users.	ConnLimit	The connection limit for the site or server as a whole has been reached.
Application taken offline.	AppOffline	The application pool has been put into Rapid Fail Protection and has been disabled automatically.
Application request queue full.	QueueFull	The application pool's request queue has been exceeded and the request cannot be queued.
Administrator has taken application offline.	Disabled	The administrator has stopped the application pool.
Application automatically shut down due to administrator policy.	AppShutdown	The application pool has been shut down because it exceeded its CPU usage limit.
Request timed out in app pool queue.	AppPoolTimer	The application pool is too busy to handle the request. The request has, therefore, timed out in the queue and has been returned with a 503 error.

For security purposes, the description that is sent back to the client (Service Unavailable) does not fully describe the error. HTTP.sys keeps its own error log. Requests that generate 503 errors never pass into user mode; therefore, the HTTP error log is the only place these problems are documented. To troubleshoot the cause of the 503 error, use the following procedure.

▶   **To check for possible causes of HTTP 503 errors**

1. Check the HTTP.sys error log for information about the error being returned. See Table **11.11** for error descriptions.

2. Check the event logs. Typically, the event logs contain more detailed information about the cause of a 503 error.

3. Verify that health/recycling issues are not causing the error.

4. Check for server binding conflicts.

5. Check the IP inclusion list for errors.

Other HTTP.sys Error Log Errors

In some cases, HTTP.sys generates entries in its error log that are not associated with a specific HTTP request and that do not have HTTP error codes. Table 11.12 lists these errors.

Table 11.12   Other HTTP.sys Errors

Logged Reason Code	Condition
Timer_ConnectionIdle	The connection was reset as its idle time exceeded the **ConnectionTimeout** property.
Timer_HeaderWait	The headers for the request were not received within the time limit specified by the **HeaderWaitTimeout** property.
Timer_MinBytesPerSecond	The throughput rate of this connection has dropped below the limit specified in the **MinFileBytesPerSec** property.
Timer_EntityBody	The entity body was not received within the specified timeout.
Timer_Response	The connection was reset because the response was not processed within the specified time limit.
Timer_AppPool	The connection was reset because the request stayed in the request queue of the application pool longer than the specified time limit.

For complete information about the errors logged in the HTTP error log, see the topic, "Error Logging in the HTTP API" on MSDN. To find this information, see the MSDN Library link on the Web Resources page at http://www.microsoft.com/windows/reskits/webresources.

For further information about available configuration options in HTTP.sys, see article 820129, "Inf: Http.sys Registry Settings for IIS" in the Microsoft Knowledge Base. To find this article, see the Microsoft Knowledge Base link on the Web Resources page at http://www.microsoft.com/windows/reskits/webresources.

Troubleshooting Configuration Problems

Configuration problems present their own unique troubleshooting challenges. This section provides information about troubleshooting common configuration problems that occur with the integrity of XML in the IIS metabase and with UNC content.

Preserving the Integrity of XML in the IIS Metabase

With the introduction of the XML-based IIS configuration store, administrators now have the ability to directly edit XML in a text editor. This feature is called edit-while-running. Because XML has very strict rules about syntax, the XML store needs to be well-formed at all times. Manually editing the XML store with a text editor can introduce syntax errors in the MetaBase.xml file. Therefore, when manually editing the MetaBase.xml file with a text editor, observe the following guidelines:

- If a syntax error in the XML file creates a problem, use the metabase backup/restore feature to restore the metabase from the backup files.

- Open the MetaBase.xml file in Internet Explorer, which has a built-in XML parser. If a syntax error occurs, Internet Explorer displays it and notes its location.

For information about XML syntax, see "Writing Changes to MetaBase.xml" in IIS 6.0 Help. For information about the metabase edit-while-running feature of IIS, see "Enabling Edit-While-Running" in IIS 6.0 Help. For information about the metabase backup/restore feature, see "Restoring the Metabase from Backup Files" in IIS 6.0 Help.

Troubleshooting Problems with UNC Content

Traditionally, situations that involve Universal Naming Convention (UNC) content have experienced configuration and performance problems related to security, user delegation, and file caching. Improvements in IIS 6.0 affect how these problems are resolved. Figure 11.3 illustrates the logic IIS 6.0 uses to manage and serve content from a UNC file share.

Figure 11.3 IIS 6.0 UNC Authentication

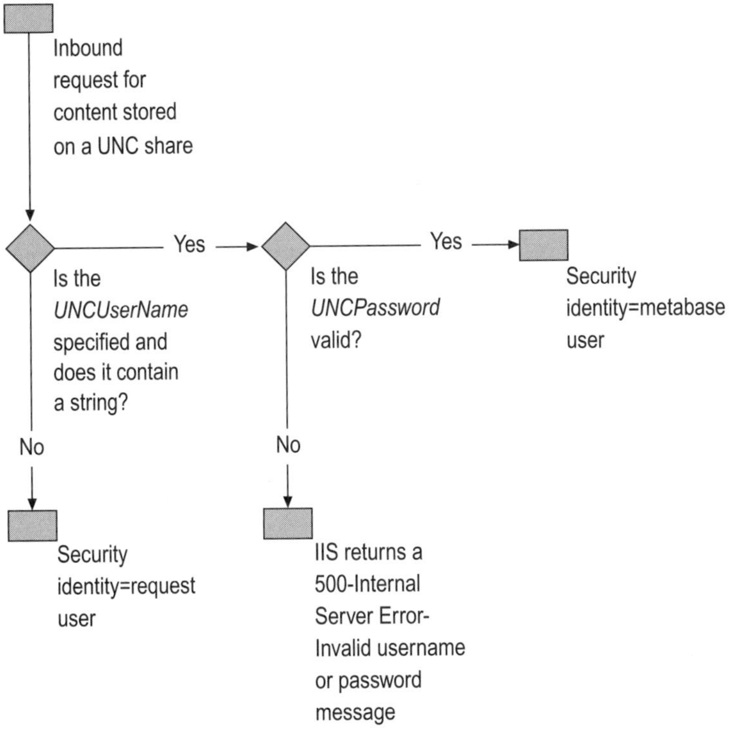

Accessing and Executing Remote Content

When IIS accesses content stored on a remote file server, user delegation becomes a factor because IIS uses the client's credentials to access content on the file server. In effect, the Web client passes the user's credentials to IIS, which then delegates them to the file server for the authorization check. In IIS 6.0, user delegation is easier because, by default, IIS uses the credentials of the request user (the anonymous user identity for anonymous requests and the authenticated user's identity for authenticated requests) to access the content on the remote file server. So, by default, IIS does *pass-through authentication*, which means that IIS passes the user credentials through to the remote file server. If you want IIS to use a specific user when accessing remote content, set the **UNCUsername** and **UNCPassword** properties in the IIS metabase. For information about setting these properties, see "**UNCUsername**" and "**UNCPassword**" properties in the Metabase Property Reference of IIS 6.0 Help.

Logging On

In Figure 11.3, the "request user" is the identity of the request coming into the Web server, such as a GET request for http://www.contoso.com/staticfile.txt. If anonymous access is enabled, this request uses the identity of the AnonymousUser as specified in the metabase (typically, IUSR_*MachineName*). If anonymous access is disabled and a valid authenticated request comes in, IIS uses that user's account to log on. However, in the case of UNC content, at this stage, IIS checks if **UNCUserName** is specified in the metabase. If so, IIS logs on as that user. If **UNCUserName** is not specified in the metabase or if it is set to an empty string, then IIS logs on as the user who originally made the request (that is, as an anonymous user or as an authenticated user).

 Note

The UNCPassthroughAuthentication metabase property has been removed from IIS 6.0. In IIS 6.0, pass-through authentication is enabled by default. To disable pass-through authentication, use the UNCUserName and UNCPassword properties.

Accessing the Remote Server

After IIS has a user identity, it must access the remote file server. The type of authentication (Anonymous, Basic, NTLM, Kerberos) enabled on the server can significantly affect how successful this step is. In almost all cases, Basic authentication enables IIS to access a remote file server (although you must always use SSL with Basic authentication since user names and passwords are sent in plain text). Using Basic authentication can help you verify that everything else is working properly.

Executing the Remote Content

So far, we have discussed how remote content is *accessed*. Remote content must also be *executed* in the context of this user account. In other words, if **UNCUserName** and **UNCUserPassword** are set, then all remote content will be accessed and executed in the context of **UNCUserName**. This might not be desirable for most applications, because with this approach you lose the identity of the originating Internet/Intranet user. If pass-through authentication is being used, then the request is processed under the identity of the "request user."

The process illustrated in Figure 11.3 applies to all content that is executed or retrieved by the server. Consequently, static content, such as Graphics Interchange Format (GIF) and Hypertext Markup Language(HTML) pages, Script-Mapped files, CGI executables, and ISAPI Extension DLLs (like ASP, ASP.Net, and so on) runs under this user context. (ISAPI filters run under the context of the worker process identity. By default, the worker process runs as NetworkService, which is a local account.)

Working in a Domain Environment

In most cases, you will want to run your Web servers and file server in a domain environment because it is much simpler to use a domain environment in which you can control one set of users and groups from the domain controller. Furthermore, if you want to use Windows Integrated Authentication in this scenario, then you need to use a domain environment to take advantage of the new "constrained delegation" feature of Windows Server 2003. Instructions on setting up constrained delegation follow. For more information about constrained delegation, see "Delegating authentication" in Help and Support Center for Windows Server 2003.

Working in a Workgroup Environment

Web servers and a file server used in a workgroup environment are difficult to manage and maintain. In a workgroup environment, because one user account has access to another computer only if that computer has a user with the same user name and password, you have added administrative overhead. To add a new user to your environment, you have to add the user to both servers and you need to ensure that both accounts have the same password.

For a complete look at using remote content on a UNC share, see the whitepaper "Deploying and Configuring Internet Information Services (IIS) 6.0 with Remotely Stored Content on UNC Servers and NAS Devices". You can find this article by seeing the UNC Servers Accessed by Using IIS 6.0 link on the Web Resources page at http://www.microsoft.com/windows/reskits/webresources.

Troubleshooting File Caching Problems

There are two causes for problems with file caching of UNC content:

- **Vendors' implementation and support for file change notifications**. Usually non-Windows-powered Network Attached Storage (NAS) vendors provide fixes for known problems; however, as a workaround, caching is typically disabled to prevent those problems.

- **The number of simultaneous distinct file structures that the ASP and static file caches can monitor for changes**. Because each "monitor" takes up a work item indefinitely from the Server Message Block (SMB) connection with the file server, IIS can exhaust a system's SMB resources by trying to cache a wide and disparate set of directories.

To address these problems, several changes have been made to the way IIS caches content. These changes improve performance and reliability in most cases; however, these changes can have unexpected effects on UNC stored content.

ASP and Static File Caching Changes

IIS 6.0 has a new caching algorithm for the ASP script and static file cache when the content is being stored on a UNC share. In earlier versions, IIS registered for a file change notification from the operating system for each directory structure so that it would be notified when a file changed. In IIS 6.0, the Web server simply checks the Last-Modified date on the cached file instead of requesting these notifications. If the Last-Modified date has not changed, the cached version of the file is sent out. If the file is new, the cache is updated with the new version of the file and is sent to the client.

To further improve performance, the algorithm has a "staleness" aspect that causes IIS to check the Last-Modified date only if more than five seconds have passed since the last check. Otherwise, IIS assumes that the file has not changed, and serves the cached version. For more information about this algorithm, see "Troubleshooting Performance Problems with UNC Content" later in this chapter.

 Note

> The server-side includes file handler (Ssinc.dll) makes use of the static file cache, so you see this file caching behavior for files with .stm and .shtml file name extensions, and for any other files that you have mapped to Ssinc.dll

Troubleshooting Problems with Stale Content

When stale content is being served by the Web Server even though the content has been updated on the remote file server, disable the Web Server cache as the first step in isolating the problem.

 Note

> First ensure that your results aren't being affected by the 5-second staleness factor.

▶ **To disable the ASP file cache**

1. In IIS Manager, double-click the local computer, right-click **Web Sites**, and click **Properties**.

2. Click the **Home Directory** tab.

3. Click **Configuration**.

4. On the **Cache Options** tab, click the **Do not cache ASP files** option.

5. Click **OK** twice.

To disable the static file cache

1. Navigate to the following subkey:

   HKLM\System\CurrentControlSet\Services\Inetinfo\Parameters

2. Add **DisableMemoryCache**, a DWORD value, and set it to **1**.

> **Caution**
>
> Do not edit the registry unless you have no alternative. The registry editor bypasses standard safeguards, allowing settings that can damage your system, or even require you to reinstall Windows. If you must edit the registry, back it up first and see the Registry Reference on the *Microsoft Windows Server 2003 Deployment Kit* companion CD or on the Web at http://www.microsoft.com/reskit.

Troubleshooting Performance Problems with UNC Content

Using the Last-Modified time to check for changes (instead of monitoring each virtual directory for change notifications) permits greater scalability when many virtual directories are mapped to UNC shares. Checking the Last-Modified time on the remote file server every time IIS wants to send a file is relatively expensive in terms of processing overhead. IIS checks the Last-Modified time on a file every five seconds by default; otherwise, it assumes that nothing has changed and serves the content from the cache, even though it might be stale.

For some sites, a five-second window will be too large a window, and for others, too small. The sampling interval is configurable with the following registry keys, which are not present by default:

- **Static pages** Set the registry property, **FileAttributeCheckThreshold**, a DWORD value, located at **HKEY_LOCAL_MACHINE\System\CurrentControlSet\Services\Inetinfo\Parameters**.

- **ASP Scripts** Set the registry property, **FileMonitoringTimeoutSeconds**, a DWORD value, located at **HKEY_LOCAL_MACHINE\System\CurrentControlSet\Services\ASP\Parameters**.

Using the last-modified cache update mechanism will result in more reliable and secure delivery of content. Additionally, it will scale well on a wide application structure (where your Web server has lots of applications pointing at thousands of different directories). There is, however, a performance penalty that might be noticeable in regards to static content.

Even with these new file-caching algorithms, overall performance of UNC-based content can still be slightly slower than that of local content. However, depending on the content size, the difference is usually negligible.

If you think that the performance of your server has diminished due to these changes, you can enable change notification–based caching by adding the following registry keys, which are not present by default:

- **Static Pages** Set the registry property, **DoDirMonitoringForUNC**, a DWORD value, located at **HKEY_LOCAL_MACHINE\System\CurrentControlSet\Services\Inetinfo\Parameters**.

- **ASP Scripts** Set the registry property, **EnableChangeNotificationForUNC**, a DWORD value, located at **HKEY_LOCAL_MACHINE\System\CurrentControlSet\Services\ASP\Parameters**.

These entries do not exist in the registry by default. To add it to the registry, use the registry editor, Regedit.exe.

However, note that this option is not always recommended because it can cause the operating system to suffer from the scalability problems that were present in earlier version of IIS. Additionally, share-level permissions will no longer be honored by the Web server (NTFS ACLs are always honored). Consider modifying this registry entry only if you have a small directory structure, are not concerned about share-level permissions, and consider performance the most important metric.

When deciding which caching mechanism to use, consider the following tradeoffs. The most reliable and secure method is using the default: Last-Modified-based caching. It is reliable because it does not rely on the change-notification functionality of the file server and it scales well on a wide application structure (where your Web server has lots of applications pointing at thousands of different directories). It is more secure because share-level permission changes are honored (the cache accesses the file often, which automatically triggers the authorization check against the current file system ACL and the current share ACL).

However, if you are using a file server that reliably reports change notifications *and* if you have few sites or virtual directories, using change-notification is significantly faster. For example, if you have a single Web site with a couple of applications and all of your content is stored on a Windows Server 2003 file server, it is recommended that you use the change-notification method of caching.

For a complete look at using remote content on a UNC share, see the whitepaper "Deploying and Configuring Internet Information Services (IIS) 6.0 with Remotely Stored Content on UNC Servers and NAS Devices". You can find this article by seeing the UNC Servers Accessed by Using IIS 6.0 link on the Web Resources page at http://www.microsoft.com/windows/reskits/webresources.

Troubleshooting IIS Manager and UNC Content Problems

Because of the way that IIS Manager displays the virtual directory, managing Web content that is stored on remote UNC shares can be confusing. IIS Manager uses the credentials of the logged-in user (the user actually running IIS Manager), who might not necessarily have the right credentials to access the remote file share. In this case, IIS Manager displays a stop-sign icon for the virtual directory. If this occurs, test UNC access by making requests with a Web browser.

You might want to create virtual directories that reference UNC-mapped drives. IIS does not support mapped drives because they are user-specific. For more information, see article 257174, "Using Mapped Drives with IIS" in the Microsoft Knowledge Base. To find this article, see the Microsoft Knowledge Base link on the Web Resources page at http://www.microsoft.com/windows/reskits/webresources.

Troubleshooting Errors That Occur When UNC Content Is Under High Load

If the Web server and the remote file server are not configured properly for high stress conditions, errors might occur. The following configuration errors might be reported in the browser, in the event log on the IIS server or remote file server, or the IIS logs.

```
"Windows cannot find the network path. Verify that the network path is correct
and the destination computer is not busy or turned off. If Windows still cannot
find the network path, contact your network administrator. Error code
0x80070033:"
```

```
"The network location cannot be reached. For information about network
troubleshooting, see Windows Help.Error code: 0x800704CF"
```

```
"Not enough server storage is available to process this command. Error code:
0x8007046"
```

Modifying the MaxUserPort Registry Entry

The first two errors are returned when the server running IIS has a shortage of outbound TCP ports when it attempts to make the UNC connection. In this case, the Web server returns HTTP 500 errors for all requests until TCP ports are available again. To fix this problem, you can modify the **MaxUserPort** registry entry on the server running IIS to specify an increase in the number of available ports. This entry does not exist in the registry by default. To add it to the registry, use the registry editor, Regedit.exe.

 Caution

Do not edit the registry unless you have no alternative. The registry editor bypasses standard safeguards, allowing settings that can damage your system, or even require you to reinstall Windows. If you must edit the registry, back it up first and see the Registry Reference on the *Microsoft Windows Server 2003 Deployment Kit* companion CD or on the Web at http://www.microsoft.com/reskit.

For example, if you have many concurrent authenticated users, a different SMB connection is opened from the computer running IIS to the remote file server for each individual user. These SMB connections use ports. By default, you are limited to ports from 1024 to 5000 for outbound TCP connections (slightly fewer than 4,000 ports are available), so you might need to increase this value to a higher number, such as 10000 or 20000, to provide additional ports for SMB connections. Be aware that this might cause problems with applications that create sockets on these higher ports. For more information, see Microsoft Windows 2000 TCP/IP Implementation Details.

Checking the File Server Setting

If you receive the "Not enough server storage is available to process this command. Error code: 0x8007046A" message, check your file server settings. This IIS error usually accompanies event log messages like the following:

```
"The server was unable to allocate from the system nonpaged pool because the pool
was empty."
```

```
"The server was unable to allocate a work item <n> times in the last 60 seconds."
```

Normally, these messages indicate that your file server is set to use too much nonpaged system memory. This can be quickly verified by opening Task Manager, clicking the **Performance** tab and checking the **Nonpaged** value in the **Kernel Memory** frame. Limit the amount of kernel memory that the Server service can use by configuring the SMB settings as discussed later in this section.

When troubleshooting this kind of error, check the following performance counters on the computer running the Web server:

- Server\Files Open
- Server\Server Sessions
- Server\Work Item Shortages

Modifying the Work Item Configuration

When two computers communicate, one SMB connection is used for each user. However, within an SMB connection, there are a finite number of work items. Work items can be consumed in a variety of ways and for varying amounts of time. For example, performing an operation against a file (by using **CreateFile**, **GetFileAttributes**, or other similar Windows APIs) takes up an I/O work item for a short period of time, but asking for a change notification on a directory structure takes up a work item for as long as the connection is maintained.

The "The network location cannot be reached. For information about network troubleshooting, see Windows Help.Error code: 0x800704CF" and "Not enough server storage is available to process this command. Error code: 0x8007046" errors usually can be fixed by changing the following registry entries, which are related to SMB configuration: **MaxCmds**, **MaxMpxCt**, and **MaxWorkItems**.

On the remote file server, you can update these registry entries in the following location: HKLM\System\CurrentControlSet\Services\LanmanServer\Parameters.

On the server running IIS, you can update these registry entries in the following location: HKLM\System\CurrentControlSet\Services\LanmanWorkstation\Parameters.

The **MaxCmds**, **MaxMpxCt**, **MaxWorkItems** registry entries do not exist in the registry by default. To add them to the registry, use the registry editor, Regedit.exe.

Note

For these registry values to take effect, you must stop and start the Server service on the remote file server and the Workstation service on the server running IIS. You do not need to restart the computers.

Before changing the **MaxCmds**, **MaxMpxCt**, and **MaxWorkItems** registry entries to troubleshoot work item shortages and system memory consumption, you need to understand how work items are consumed. Work item consumption occurs as follows:

- Only one SMB connection is created per Web server/file server connection per user.

- Each change notification instance uses a work item until the connection is ended.

- Each request from the Web server to the file server uses a work item temporarily.

- Typically, each work item takes up about 20K of non-paged pool memory. Although certain Microsoft Knowledge Base articles specify setting the value of the **MaxWorkItems** registry entry to 16000, doing so consumes approximately 320 MB of non-paged pool memory, which could overwhelm system resources. To increase the reliability of your system, always set this number lower than this recommended value.

- To calculate the value of the **MaxCmds** registry entry, use the following formula:

  (the number of distinct physical directories that IIS needs to monitor for change notifications) * (1 (if static files exist) + 1 (if ASP content exists) + 1 (if ASP.Net content exists)) + 50 (for concurrent default/regular file IO)

Note

This formula approximates a recommended value. Depending on the amount of concurrent traffic, you might need to increase your values.

Table 11.13 lists the default and maximum values for the relevant SMB settings on Windows Server 2003. These SMB settings also apply to the Microsoft Windows® 2000 Server operating system.

Table 11.13   Values for SMB Settings

Registry Entry	Default Value	Maximum Value
MaxCmds	50	65535
MaxMpxCt	50	65535
MaxWorkItems	Scaled on memory size, usually between 1KB and 4KB.	65535

Troubleshooting Logging Problems

Historically, IIS administrators have rarely had to troubleshoot logging problems. In earlier versions of IIS, log configuration was simple and straightforward, and in most cases, the default settings were adequate.

In IIS 6.0, new logging functionality, such as centralized binary logging and UTF-8 logging, and the fact that logging is now performed by HTTP.sys instead of the WWW Service (W3SVC) present new configuration options and architectural elements as well as new troubleshooting challenges. This section explores some of the problems that can occur with HTTP.sys logging.

Table 11.14 lists and describes HTTP.sys logging-related Event Log errors, and provides troubleshooting recommendations for each.

Table 11.14   HTTP.sys Logging-Related Event Log Errors

Event ID	Description	Recommendation
15000	Unable to create log file *%2*.	Ensure that the logging directory is correct and this computer account has write access to that directory.
15001	Unable to create the log file for site W3SVC *%2*.	Ensure that the logging directory for the site is correct and this computer has write access to that directory.
15002	Unable to write to the log file *%2* for site W3SVC *%3*. The disk might be full.	If this is a network path, ensure that network connectivity is not broken. Otherwise, the disk is full.
15003	Unable to create the centralized binary log file.	Ensure that the logging directory is correct and this computer has write access to that directory.
15004	Unable to write to the centralized binary log file *%2*. The disk might be full. .	If this is a network path, make sure that network connectivity is not broken. Otherwise, the disk is full.
15006	Owner of the log file or directory *%2* is invalid. Another user might have already created the log file or the directory.	Check for the existence of the logging directory and ensure that the owner is the local Administrators group.

Logging Security Configuration

One of the fundamental aspects of IIS logging design involves the expected security configuration of the log file directory or UNC share when logging to UNC.

Configuration process

Upon first receiving an HTTP request, HTTP.sys begins logging. On this initial request, if the appropriate logging subdirectory and file does not exist, HTTP.sys creates them, giving System and local Administrators full control. For each, the owner is the Local Administrators account. If the directory and file already exist, HTTP.sys performs an access check for security purposes and verifies that the owner of the file and directory is the local Administrators group. If not, HTTP.sys logs event ID 15006 to the event log and disables logging for that site. If the ownership check passes, HTTP.sys then ensures that System and local Administrators have full control.

When configuring logging to a UNC share, HTTP.sys does not perform an ownership check. Instead, the administrator is responsible for ensuring that security on the log file share and directory is configured appropriately. HTTP.sys sets the ACLs on the remote share to allow the Web server's system account the appropriate access.

Event ID 15000, 15001, and 15003

These errors occur when the log file and directory do not have proper security settings. When the IIS logging configuration settings are changed, if the file and directory security settings are not correct (if the System and Administrators do not have full control), HTTP.sys writes event ID 15001 or event ID 15003 (if binary logging is enabled) to the Event Log. HTTP.sys writes an event ID 15000 to the event log if security settings change during operation, for example, if the file ACLs are altered manually.

Event ID 15002 and Event ID 15004

Event ID 15002 and Event ID 15004 errors are similar. Both occur when HTTP.sys is unable to write to the log file because the disk is full. When binary logging is enabled, HTTP.sys writes an event ID 15004 error to the Event Log. An event ID 15004 also is written to the Event Log if a network problem prevents HTTP.sys from writing to the log file.

Logging Headers

In the past, the logging headers that were written to a log file typically indicated the restarting of the Web service. In IIS 6.0 this is not the case. After waiting for 15 minutes for a given site, HTTP.sys stops logging. When the next request for that site arrives, HTTP.sys restarts logging and writes a new set of headers to the log file.

"..." Present in Log Files

In rare cases, you might see "..." in an IIS log file entry. When a query string or a header value is longer than 4 KB, HTTP.sys writes the string as "..." instead of writing the entire string.

UTF-8 Logging Problems

When using the UTF-8 logging feature, note the following:

- A log file logged in UTF-8 does not contain a Byte Order Mark (BOM). File editors use this mark to identify text as UTF-8 text. Therefore, if you attempt to open a log file that is logged in UTF-8 in Notepad by double-clicking the file or by using the **Open With** option, the file might not display correctly. To open the file in a way that displays it correctly, use the **Open** command on the **File** menu and then select **UTF-8** in the **Encoding** box.

- Because IIS 6.0 now supports UTF-8 URLs, you can now log those URL requests to an ASCII log file. UTF-8 is a double-byte character set standard. Because ASCII is a single-byte character set standard, logging UTF-8 information to an ASCII file presents a problem. In such a case, "?" is logged for the characters that cannot be converted to the codepage of the server.

Troubleshooting HTTP.sys Problems

HTTP.sys can provide information through three mechanisms: HTTP status codes, Windows Event Logs, and the HTTP error log. Preceding sections discussed the HTTP status codes and several event log errors that are related to logging. This section addresses the initial startup process of IP addresses binding and the mechanism other services use to ask HTTP to listen to specific URL endpoints through the HTTP API.

Configuring the IP Inclusion List

The HTTP.sys IP inclusion list allows administrators to limit the IP addresses to which HTTP.sys automatically binds when it starts. This provides functionality similar to the functionality provided by the **DisableSocketPooling** property that was available in IIS 5.0. At startup, HTTP.sys checks to determine if there are any entries in the IP inclusion list. If there are, HTTP.sys attempts to listen only on these IP addresses and only at initial startup. If the list has no entries, HTTP.sys listens on all available IP addresses.

To configure the IP inclusion list, use the HttpCnfg.exe utility. For information about HttpCfg.exe, in Help and Support Center for Windows Server 2003, click **Tools**, and then click **Windows Support Tools**.

Table 11.15 lists and describes the HTTP.sys IP binding event log errors. Only the errors that require additional explanation are addressed below.

Table 11.15   HTTP.sys IP Binding Event Log Errors

Event ID	Description
15005	Unable to bind to the underlying transport for *%2*. The IP Listen-Only list might contain a reference to an interface that might not exist on this computer. The data field contains the error number.
15007	Reservation for the namespace identified by URL prefix *%2* was successfully added.
15008	Reservation for namespace identified by URL prefix *%2* was successfully deleted.
15009	An error occurred while initializing namespace reservations. The error status code is contained within the returned data.
15010	An error occurred while initializing a namespace reservation identified by URL prefix *%2*. The error status code is contained within the returned data.
15014	Unable to convert IP Listen-Only list entry *%2*. The data field contains the error number.
15015	Unable to convert all entries on IP Listen-Only list. The driver will listen on all available interfaces.

Event ID 15014

If the IP inclusion list contains entries, HTTP.sys iterates through the list and, for each entry, it first checks to ensure that the IP address is valid and is assigned to one of the system's network interfaces. If this check fails, HTTP.sys logs Event ID 15014 to the event log.

Event ID 15015

This error is logged to the event log when HTTP.sys parses the IP inclusion list and finds that all of the entries in the list are invalid. If this happens, as the description in Table 11.15 notes, HTTP.sys listens to all IP addresses.

Services that use the HTTP listening functionality — namely IIS — have to configure HTTP and, through available APIs, tell HTTP.sys which endpoints to listen to. If a service requests an endpoint where HTTP.sys is not listening, HTTP.sys logs an event to the event log that states this. In the case of IIS, the WWW service also makes note of these kinds of errors.

 Note

Once the IP inclusion list is set, HTTP.sys never reverts to listening on all IP addresses.

Troubleshooting HTTP.sys Communication Problems

In rare cases, the WWW service might encounter problems when communicating with the HTTP service. If this occurs, the WWW service logs errors to the event log. These errors are summarized in Table 11.16

Table 11.16 WWW Service to HTTP Communication Errors

Event ID	Description
1020	The World Wide Web Publishing Service encountered difficulty configuring the HTTP.sys control channel property ' *%1*'. The data field contains the error number.
1109	The World Wide Web Publishing Service failed to set the control channel's filter configuration. The data field contains the error number.
1062	The World Wide Web Publishing Service encountered a failure configuring the logging properties on the HTTP Control Channel. Logging Enabled is ' *%1*'. Log File Directory is ' *%2*'. Log Period is ' *%3*'. Log Truncate Size is ' *%4*'. The data field contains the error number.
1037	A failure occurred while opening the HTTP control channel for the World Wide Web Publishing Service. The data field contains the error number.

Troubleshooting Miscellaneous Problems

Additional problems that might require troubleshooting include unexpected metabase site IDs, CGI process difficulties, server connection problems, and client request timeout and error-out problems.

Metabase Site IDs Are Unexpected Numbers

When you create a new Web site in IIS Manager, the newly generated site ID in the metabase is a random number. In earlier versions of IIS, the site ID was incremented with each new site. If you have an application that in some way relies on the old behavior, you can change the current behavior by adding the registry entry **IncrementalSiteIDCreation**, a DWORD value, to the registry with a value of 1. Add **IncrementalSiteIDCreation** to the following subkey:

HKEY_LOCAL_MACHINE\SOFTWARE\Microsoft\InetMgr\Parameters

> **Caution**
>
> Do not edit the registry unless you have no alternative. The registry editor bypasses standard safeguards, allowing settings that can damage your system, or even require you to reinstall Windows. If you must edit the registry, back it up first and see the Registry Reference on the *Microsoft Windows Server 2003 Deployment Kit* companion CD or on the Web at http://www.microsoft.com/reskit.

When generating a new site ID, IIS uses a hash of the Web site name. This new design ensures that all IIS 6.0 servers in a Web farm have a good chance of generating the same site identification numbers for sites with the same name. For more information, see article 332122, "IIS 6.0: Web Site Identification Numbers Are Not Incremental" in the Microsoft Knowledge Base. To find this article, see the Microsoft Knowledge Base link on the Web Resources page at http://www.microsoft.com/windows/reskits/webresources.

Anonymous Users Performance Counters in IIS 6.0

The Current Anonymous Users performance counter is often used for capacity planning and performance troubleshooting. The counter is incremented differently in IIS 6.0 than it was in IIS 5.0.

In IIS 5.0. Current Anonymous Users is the number of current anonymous HTTP connections. This number decreases when the connection is closed (for various reasons, such as when the connection explicitly closes or times out).

In IIS 6.0. Current Anonymous Users is the number of current anonymous requests being processed. This number decreases when the request is completed. (HTTP.sys and IIS user mode both provide numbers for this counter.)

In short, IIS 6.0 counts each request as a user, whereas IIS 5.0 counts each connection as a user.

CGI Processes Will Not Start

In order for CGI processes to run, the account that starts the CGI processes (the worker process identity) must be assigned certain user rights. You can add the account as a member of the IIS_WPG group and assign the account these two necessary user rights:

- Adjust memory quotas for a process
- Replace a process-level token

▶ **To assign user rights to an account on the local computer**

1. From the **Start** menu, point to **Administrative Tools**, and click **Local Security Policy**.

2. In the console tree, double-click **Security Settings**, double-click **Local Policies**, and then double-click **User Rights Assignment**.

3. In the details pane, double-click the policy that you want to change.

4. Click **Add User or Group**.

5. In the **Enter the object names to select** box, type the user or group name.

6. Click **OK**.

 Note

CGI processes might also fail to start when they are not configured correctly in the Web Service Extension Restriction List. CGI processes require their image name and any parameters to be set in the list. For example, to allow a typical CGI request for Perl.exe, use **perl.exe "%s" %s**.

Clients Cannot Connect to the Server

Windows Server 2003 provides a software-based firewall to help prevent unauthorized connections to your server from remote computers. By default, the Internet Connection Firewall (ICF) is disabled. However, if you have enabled the firewall in its default configuration after installing Windows Server 2003 and before installing IIS 6.0, clients will not be able to connect to your server. Use the following procedure to configure the ICF to allow clients to initiate Web and other IIS–related connections to your server.

▶ **To configure ICF for IIS**

1. From the **Start** menu, click **Control Panel**.

2. In the **Control Panel** dialog box, double-click **Network Connections**.

3. In the Network Connections dialog box, right-click **Local Area Connection**, and click **Properties**.

4. In the **Local Area Connection Properties** dialog box, click the **Advanced** tab and then do one of the following:

   - If you do *not* want to use the ICF, ensure that the **Protect my computer and network by limiting or preventing access to this computer from the Internet** check box is not available, and click **OK**. The procedure is complete.

   - If you do want to use the ICF, ensure that the **Protect my computer and network by limiting or preventing access to this computer from the Internet** check box is available and selected, click **Settings**, and proceed to step 5.

5. On the **Services** tab, enable a service to which you want to allow access to clients.

6. In the **Service Settings** dialog box that appears after enabling a service, do one of the following:

   ▪ If you are enabling a service on the same computer on which you are working, the correct computer name is already filled in. Click **OK**.

   ▪ If you are enabling a service on a different computer on your network, type the name or IP address of the computer hosting the service that you are enabling, and click **OK**.

7. Repeat steps 5 and 6 until all of the services that you want to be accessible to clients are enabled.

Client Requests Error Out or Time Out

In IIS 6.0, settings are set to aggressive and secure defaults to minimize attacks due to timeouts and limits that were previously too generous. IIS enforces the following timeouts at the connection level:

▪ Limits on response buffering. The metabase property **ASPBufferingLimit** is 4 MB, by default. If ASP scripts buffer more than this, they generate an error. Prior to IIS 6.0, there was no limit to buffering.

▪ Limits on posts. The metabase property **AspMaxRequestEntityAllowed** enforces a maximum ASP POST size of 204800 bytes, with each individual field limited to 100 KB. Prior to IIS 6.0, there was no limit to posts.

▪ The **ServerListenTimeout** property is no longer available. The metabase property **ServerListenTimeout** has been replaced by the following metabase properties:

   ▪ **ConnectionTimeout.** This property specifies the amount of time, in seconds, that the server waits before disconnecting an inactive connection.

   ▪ **MinFileBytesPerSec.** When IIS responds to a client request, the **MinFileBytesPerSec** property determines the length of time that the client has to receive the entire response. If the client computer takes too long to receive the entire response, the kernel-mode driver, HTTP.sys, terminates the connection according to the timeout value.

   ▪ **HeaderWaitTimeout.** When a client connects to the Web server, the client computer is given a time limit to send in all headers for the request (demarked by a final double \r\n). If the complete header set for the request is not received within the time period indicated by **HeaderWaitTimeout**, HTTP.sys resets the connection. You can configure the value of **HeaderWaitTimeout**.

▪ **Header size limitation.** By default, HTTP.sys accepts only requests where the size of the request header is less than 16 KB. This means that if HTTP.sys does not receive the terminating carriage return/line feed (CRLF) pair sequence within 16 KB, HTTP.sys considers the request malicious and terminates the connection. You can change the header size limitation by adjusting the value of the registry entry **MaxRequestBytes**. Note that this entry does not exist in the registry by default. To add it to the registry, use the registry editor, Regedit.exe.

Advanced Troubleshooting

Up to this point, this chapter has explored problems and issues that are specific to IIS, its interaction with various Windows operating system mechanisms (like the file system and security), and its implementation of the HTTP protocol. These types of problems are identified by definitive error messages and demonstrate specific faulty behaviors. In addition, these types of problems usually reveal themselves early — during either application development or initial configuration of the IIS application environment. For example, problems with permissions usually appear during security configuration, which usually occurs during application deployment. Problems like these display symptoms immediately, making it is easy to identify the problem.

Today's Web-based applications often have many components and systems that interact. This complexity provides greater opportunity for components to fail or to behave in unexpected ways. Further complicating matters, large and complex applications often exhibit subtle or non-specific symptoms. The effects of such problems are abstract and might seem random. For example, a problem with data access synchronization might cause an application to stop responding in one instance, but a crash in another. Such "quirks" can occur deep within an application's processing, often masking or distorting symptoms and ultimately hiding the root cause of the problem.

IIS is the primary runtime environment for the execution of application logic implemented in custom ISAPI applications, ASP, ASP.NET, or a Web service. These components often communicate with middle-tier business logic servers and database servers. Consequently, IIS is often the main execution environment for the core workings of an application and, therefore, IIS is the environment where problems begin or symptoms are propagated.

Given that such problems are application specific, it is not possible to provide troubleshooting guidelines for all problems. However, most problems can be attributed to a few general causes: low CPU hangs, high CPU hangs, crashes, and memory problems. In addition to discussing these problems and suggesting how to troubleshoot them, this section explains how to use a debugger to troubleshoot.

Troubleshooting with a Debugger

Advanced troubleshooting activities will sometimes require a debugging tool. A debugging tool allows you to peer inside an executing Win32 process to observe what is happening. You can use the debugging tool to capture a record of the memory space of the process that is hosting the faulty application. In IIS 6.0, the process is usually W3WP.EXE. This memory "dump" is written to a DMP file.

The Microsoft Debugging Tools for Windows include a script file, named Adplus.vbs, which is a scripted front-end to the Microsoft Console Debugger (CDB). Adplus.vbs makes capturing dump files easy.

The key to using any debugger is understanding the kind of problem that you are troubleshooting. Once you identify the kind problem you are troubleshooting, you can decide what to do with the debugger and what kind of dump file to obtain. After you have obtained a dump file, it is recommended that you then have it debugged by a developer or a Microsoft support professional.

The IIS resource kit contains a tool called IISState. This tool is like a debugger and can also be used to look at a running process. IISState contains some heuristic functionality that attempts to figure out what is happening in the process for you. For more information, see the readme.txt that comes with IISState.

For detailed information about troubleshooting with Adplus.vbs, see article 286350, "How To: Use ADPlus to Troubleshoot 'Hangs' and 'Crashes'" in the Microsoft Knowledge Base. To find this article, see the Microsoft Knowledge Base link on the Web Resources pageat http://www.microsoft.com/windows/reskits/webresources.

Troubleshooting Low CPU Hangs

An application that becomes unresponsive to any kind of request while the process hosting the application is consuming little or no system processor(s) CPU time is in a low CPU hang state. This type of problem can be caused by unrecoverable lock situations in program code (deadlocks) or by threads that are waiting on an external resource, such as a database.

To capture a memory dump of the offending process, at a command prompt, type the following:
C:\debuggers\> cscript.exe adplus.vbs -hang -p <pid>

If you know that the hung process is an IIS process but do not know which process is causing the problem, instead of specifying a specific PID or process name, specify the **-iis** parameter. Specifying this parameter will cause Adplus.vbs to capture all IIS–related processes.

Troubleshooting High CPU Hangs

An application that becomes unresponsive to any kind of request while the process hosting the application is consuming a great deal of system processor(s) CPU time, usually near 100%, is in a high CPU hang state. This problem can be caused by an endless loop in script code or by some other intensive kind of processing.

In such a case, it is useful to identify the thread that is consuming the CPU before you attempt to capture a memory dump. To identify the offending thread, you can use a tool like QSlice.exe. For information about QSlice.exe, in Help and Support Center for Windows Server 2003, click **Tools**, and then click **Windows Support Tools**. Alternatively, you can check the .log file that is generated by the Adplus.vbs script. This log file contains output generated by the "!runaway" debugger command. The !runaway command lists the CPU consumption times of the various running threads. For information about debugging and the debugger commands, see Debugging Tools for Windows Help.

To capture a memory dump, at a command prompt, type the following: **C:\debuggers\> cscript.exe adplus.vbs -hang -p <PID>**

Troubleshooting Crashes

A crash can occur when code executing in the process hosting the application encounters an unexpected event that causes an exception and results in a process shutdown. Examples of such events include a stack overflow, encountering an invalid memory address (an access violation), or executing an invalid instruction. Because these situations are unexpected and, thus, unobservable, you need to run Adplus.vbs in monitoring, or *crash,* mode before the problem occurs again.

To run Adplus.vbs in crash mode, at the command prompt, type:

C:\debuggers\> cscript.exe adplus.vbs -crash -p <PID>

If you do not know which process is crashing, use the **-iis** parameter, which causes Adplus.vbs to monitor all of the IIS–related processes for crashes. When a crash occurs, the dump files are written to disk.

Troubleshooting Memory Problems

In a typical memory problem, application code consumes too much physical system memory or too much of the virtual address space for the process in which the application is running. These problems are called "memory leaks." Memory leaks can also cause the other crash and hang problems, as described earlier in this section. High CPU hangs can occur when the memory allocations of the application are intensive and consume a disproportionately great amount of CPU time. Crashes can occur when memory has been mismanaged and corruption has occurred.

IIS 6.0 Debugging Features

ISAPI application developers that take advantage of the **ServerSupportFunction** callback function with the HSE_REQ_REPORT_UNHEALTHY parameter can make debugging their ISAPI applications easier. When worker process pinging is enabled, you can also enable orphaning to aide in obtaining memory dumps. This is explained in the next section.

The ASP and ASP.NET ISAPI extensions apply logic that takes advantage of this feature as well. For example, ASP monitors the status of its internal thread pool. If too many of its threads enter a blocking state, it reports itself as unhealthy, which triggers a worker process recycle if pinging is enabled for the application pool. ASP.NET also has several algorithms to detect an unhealthy state.

For more information about the **ServerSupportFunction**, callback function see the MSDN Online link on the Web Resources page at http://www.microsoft.com/windows/reskits/webresources and then search for "**ServerSupportFunction**".

Enabling Debugging

By default, when a worker process is determined to be unhealthy, the WWW service terminates it and starts a new worker process to serve new or queued client requests. Optionally, you can allow an application pool to keep the worker process running, but release, or *orphan*, the worker process from the application pool for purposes of debugging while at the same time initializing a new worker process to handle incoming client requests. An orphaned worker process ceases to take new requests from HTTP.sys.

If you enable debugging on an application pool, the WWW service allows an unhealthy worker process to keep running when the WWW service releases the worker process from serving an application pool. When enabling debugging, you can also configure the WWW service to start an executable application or script for a released worker process. For example, the WWW service might start an application that sends you an e-mail notifying you of the failure.

To enable debugging, set the **OrphanWorkerProcess** property to **true**. Use the **OrphanActionExe** and **OrphanActionParams** properties to configure the application that will run when the worker process is orphaned. For example, to use Adplus.vbs to obtain a memory dump, you could set the properties as follows:

OrphanActionExe: %SystemRoot%\System32\CScript.exe

OrphanActionParams: C:\debuggers\adplus.vbs -quiet -hang -p %1%

Be sure to closely monitor any worker process that is released from its application pool but continues to run. The worker process can terminate because the WWW service leaves it running but no longer monitors it, which effectively tells the worker process to shut down without forcing it to do so. If the worker process recovers from its unhealthy state, it detects that it has no relationship to the WWW service and self-terminates. When an orphaned worker process self-terminates, you might find an event log entry stating that a worker process was released, but find no evidence of the worker process ever having run.

If you enable debugging on unhealthy worker processes, be sure to monitor these released worker processes, because IIS does not remove them from memory. If you do not correctly handle worker processes that you keep alive for debugging purposes, you can have many failed worker processes running on your computer. These worker processes can tie up resources needed by other processes. In such a case, you might need to terminate those worker processes quickly to free those resources. In some cases, these worker processes can block metabase access and cause problems with other worker processes or with the WWW service itself.

The **OrphanActionExe** and **OrphanActionParams** property settings shown above will leave an orphaned worker process running after obtaining a dump file. As an alternative, you can use CDB directly from a .cmd script file. For example, paste the following text into a new text file and save the file as *LocalDrive*\debuggers\action.cmd:

```
@if "%_echo%"=="" echo off
setlocal

set WORKINGDIR=c:\debuggers
set TIMESTAMP=%DATE:~-9%_%TIME%
set TIMESTAMP=%TIMESTAMP:/=_%
set TIMESTAMP=%TIMESTAMP::=_%
set TIMESTAMP=%TIMESTAMP:.=_%
set TIMESTAMP=%TIMESTAMP: =_%
set FILENAME=%WORKINGDIR%\crash_%TIMESTAMP%.dmp
set LOG=%WORKINGDIR%\log.txt
set COMMAND=c:\debuggers\cdb.exe -c ".dump /o /mhf %FILENAME%;q" -p %1

echo %COMMAND% > %LOG%
%COMMAND%

endlocal
```

Then you can set the orphaning properties as follows:

OrphanActionExe: C:\Debuggers\action.cmd

OrphanActionParams: %%1%%

Using the *.dump* command combined with the *q* command with the CDB debugger will capture the dump file and terminate the worker process.

Limitations of Health Detection

Health detection cannot be used to determine application failures that do not cause the worker process to crash or to block the available threads in the worker process. As an example, an application that returns invalid response codes, such as HTTP 500 errors, but otherwise functions normally, will still respond to being pinged from the WWW service, unless the application is a custom ISAPI extension that implements specific code to indicate its unhealthy state.

Additional Resources

These resources contain additional information and tools related to this chapter.

Related Information

- "IIS 6.0 Administrative Scripts, Tips, and Tricks" in this book for information about how to enable an application that has been locked down.

- "IIS 6.0 Architecture" in this book for information about the components of the IIS services infrastructure.

- "Managing a Secure IIS 6.0 Solution" in this book for a brief overview of the authentication options that are available in IIS 6.0.

The following links on the Web Resources page at http://www.microsoft.com/windows/reskits/webresources for up-to-date information about a variety of topics:

- The CNET Shareware.com link to download a copy of the HRPlus utility.

- The Debugging Tools link to download Microsoft Debugging Tools for Windows.

- The Requests for Comments (RFC) link for detailed information about RFC 2616, *Hypertext Transfer Protocol — HTTP/1.1*.

- The UNC Servers Accessed by Using IIS 6.0 link for a complete look at using remote content on a UNC share.

- The Microsoft Knowledge Base link provides access to the following articles:

  - Article 148942, "How to Capture Network Traffic with Network Monitor" for information about capturing network traffic.

  - Article 172983, "Explanation of the Three-Way Handshake Via TCP/IP" for information about using Network Monitor in this way.

  - Article 248013, "Err Msg: HTTP Error 500-12 Application Restarting" for information about errors that occur when the ASP application to which the requested ASP page belongs is in the process of shutting down, restarting, or both.

- Article 252876, "How to View HTTP Data Frames Using Network Monitor" for information about HTTP traffic and Network Monitor.

- Article 257174, "Using Mapped Drives with IIS."

- Article 258063, "Internet Explorer May Prompt You for a Password" for information about using the NetBIOS name instead of an FQDN or IP address during NTLM authentication.

- Article 264921, "Info: How IIS Authenticates Browser Clients" for information about authentication and authorization.

- Article 284285, "How To: Use Wfetch.exe to Troubleshoot HTTP Connections" for information about using WFetch in a testing environment.

- Article 294382, "Authentication May Fail with '401.3' Error If 'Host Header' Differs from Server's NetBIOS Name" for information about authentication and authorization.

- Article 298408, "IIS Generates Courtesy Redirect When Folder Without Trailing Slash Is Requested" for information about courtesy redirects.

- Article 313074, "How To: Redirect Browser Requests in Internet Information Services 5.0" for information about courtesy redirects.

- Article 325358, "How To: Configure User and Group Access on an Intranet in Windows 2000 or Windows NT 4.0" for information about authentication and authorization.

- Article 326985, "How To: Troubleshoot Kerberos-related Issues in IIS" for information about using the security log to troubleshoot Kerberos authentication.

- Article 811889, "How To: Troubleshoot the "Cannot Generate SSPI Content" Error Message" for information about authentication and authorization.

Related IIS 6.0 Help Topics

- "AuthFlags" in IIS 6.0 Help for information about the settings for the AuthFlags property.

- "Enabling Edit-While-Running" in IIS 6.0 Help for information about the metabase edit-while-running feature in IIS 6.0.

- "HttpRedirect" in IIS 6.0 Help for information about temporary HTTP redirects.

- "Listing Running Web Applications" in IIS 6.0 Help for information about using Iisapp.vbs.

- "Recycling Worker Processes" in IIS 6.0 Help for information about when to manually recycle an application pool or worker process.

- "Requests for Static Files Return 404 Error" in IIS 6.0 Help for information about troubleshooting static content problems.

- "Restoring the Metabase from Backup Files" in IIS 6.0 Help for information about the metabase backup/restore feature.

- "Securing Sites with Web Site Permissions" in IIS 6.0 Help for information about securing the Web sites hosted on your IIS 6.0 server.

- "Troubleshooting" in IIS 6.0 Help, which you can access from IIS Manager, for additional information about troubleshooting strategies for IIS 6.0.

- "Working with MIME Types" in IIS 6.0 Help for information about adding a wildcard MIME type.

Related Windows Server 2003 Help Topics

For best results in identifying Help topics by title, in Help and Support Center, under the **Search** box, click **Set search options**. Under **Help Topics**, select the **Search in title only** check box.

- "Create and Configure Trace Logs" for information about setting flags and levels in IIS Enterprise Tracing for Windows.

- "Delegating authentication" for information about constrained delegation.

Related Tools

- IIS 6.0 Resource Kit tools (IIS60rkt.exe)

  Obtain the IIS 6.0 Resource Kit tools, including WFetch, and their documentation (IISTools.chm,) from the *Internet Information Services (IIS) 6.0 Resource Kit* companion CD. Install the Resource Kit Tools by running IIS60rkt.exe from the companion CD. When you perform a default installation of the Resource Kit Tools, the files are installed in the *LocalDrive:*\Program Files\IIS Resources folder.

- Windows Support Tools

  Obtain the Windows Support Tools by installing them from the \Support\Tools folder of the Windows Server 2003 operating system CD. See the Support Tools Help file for information about using these tools.

Common Administrative Tasks

If you are already familiar with running Internet Information Services (IIS) 6.0 and need only a quick refresher to perform an administrative task, or if you are learning how to use IIS and want to know the most common tasks that follow an IIS installation, use this appendix as a quick reference. IIS 6.0 provides a wealth of tools and features, many of which are outlined in this appendix, to help you create a strong and secure communications platform of dynamic network applications.

In This Appendix

Related Resources

- For information about configuring Web sites as well as the FTP, NNTP, and SMTP services, see "Configuring Internet Sites and Services" in this book.

- For information about configuring IIS 6.0 programmatically, see "IIS 6.0 Administration Scripts, Tips, and Tricks".

Overview of Common Administrative Tasks

Although this appendix is a reference for the common tasks you frequently perform when administering IIS as your Web server, most tasks in this appendix do not include guidelines for their use or detailed explanations. A few tasks include brief conceptual information, although they are the exception. However, all topics include cross-references to IIS Help topics, and to chapters and other appendices in this book so that you can quickly find additional information on a task.

Table A.1 outlines the tasks that are included in this appendix.

Table A.1   Overview of the Tasks in This Appendix

Task Group	Task	Describes How To
Important First Tasks In IIS 6.0	Starting IIS Manager	Open IIS Manager (provides three options).
	Starting and stopping services and sites	Start and stop IIS services and sites.
	Enabling dynamic content services	Enable dynamic content services, such as Active Server Pages and ASP.NET (includes information about default installations).
	Creating a Web or FTP site	Create Web site configurations, and install and use File Transfer Protocol (FTP) services.
	Creating virtual directories	Create virtual directories within Web and FTP sites.
Tasks New to IIS 6.0 (tasks that are new or significantly different than they were in IIS 5.0)	Creating and isolating applications	Create and manage applications.
	Creating application pools	Group Web applications into application pools.
	Configuring recycling	Periodically restart worker processes assigned to an application pool.
	Backing up and restoring metabase configurations	Save metabase and application configurations, including portable backups.
	Saving and copying site configurations	Back up your site configurations.

(continued)

Table A.1 Overview of the Tasks in This Appendix *(continued)*

Task Group	Task	Describes How To
Security-related Tasks	Setting authentication settings	Set up and use user authentication methods.
	Obtaining and backing up server certificates	Set up and use Secure Sockets Layer (SSL) certification on your sites.
	Controlling access to applications	Help reduce the attack surface of your applications with permissions and restrictions.
Tasks for Managing Servers and Applications	Hosting multiple Web sites	Create and host multiple Web sites.
	Redirecting Web sites	Automatically direct users to the correct page on your site.
	Assigning resources to applications	Control the amount of resources an application uses.
Tasks for Administering Servers	Administering servers from the command line	Use powerful scripting and programming tools to access and configure settings.
	Administering servers remotely	Use tools to remotely administer your sites.

When performing these tasks — especially security-related tasks — be sure that you are familiar with best practice guidelines and that you apply those guidelines to these tasks.

To perform most of the tasks described in this appendix, you must be a member of the Administrators group on the local computer, or you must be delegated the appropriate authority. If you log on to your computer as a member of the Administrators group, you might make your system vulnerable to malicious programs that could cause security risks. Instead, use the **Run as** feature to perform administrative tasks so that you do not need to log on to your computer as a member of the Administrators group. Using this feature, you can open and execute a program that uses a different account and security context than the one you logged on with.

You can use **Run as** through the user interface (UI) or as a command-line tool. The **Run as** feature that is built into the UI is a shortcut that you access by right-clicking some programs (files with the .exe file name extension), some Control Panel items (files with the .cpl file name extension), and Microsoft Management Console (MMC) (files with the .msc file name extension) snap-ins.

▶ **To use the Run as feature to run IIS Manager as an administrator**

- From the **Start** menu, point to **Administrative Tools**, right-click **Internet Information Services (IIS) Manager**, and then click **Run as**.

The **runas** command provides the same capabilities as the built-in **Run as** feature.

▶ **To use the runas command to run IIS Manager as an administrator**

1. From the **Start** menu, click **Run.**

2. In the **Open** box, type **cmd,** and then click **OK.**

3. At the command prompt, type the following:

   runas /*User*:*Administrative_AccountName* **"mmc %systemroot%\system32\inetsrv\iis.msc"**

▶ **To use the runas command to run a command-line script as an administrator**

1. From the **Start** menu, click **Run.**

2. In the **Open** box, type **cmd,** and then click **OK.**

3. At the command prompt, type the following:

   runas /**profile** /*User*:*MyMachine**Administrator* **cmd**

   A new command window, which has administrative rights, opens.

4. In the new command window, type the following at the command prompt:

   cscript.exe *ScriptName* (including the full path with parameters, if any)

For more information about using the **Run as** feature or the **runas** command to perform procedures, see "Using Run as," "Runas," and "Create a shortcut using the runas command" in Help and Support Center for Microsoft® Windows® Server 2003.

Important First Tasks in IIS 6.0

After you install IIS, if you want to quickly build a few Web sites and virtual directories, this section introduces the first steps for these basic tasks:

- **Starting IIS Manager.** Learn three ways to open IIS Manager.

- **Starting and stopping services.** Start and stop IIS services.

- **Enabling dynamic content.** Enable Web service extensions, such as Active Server Pages (ASP) and Microsoft® ASP.NET, so you can serve dynamic content. Includes information about default installations.

- **Creating Web or FTP sites.** Create Web site configurations, and install and use FTP services.

- **Creating virtual directories.** Create virtual directories within Web and FTP sites.

Starting IIS Manager

IIS Manager is a graphical user interface (GUI) for configuring your application pools or your Web, FTP, Simple Mail Transfer Protocol (SMTP), or Network News Transfer Protocol (NNTP) sites. You can use IIS Manager to configure IIS security, performance, and reliability features. For example, you can add or delete sites; start, stop, and pause sites; back up and restore server configurations; and create virtual directories for better content management.

In earlier versions of IIS, this tool was called the Internet Service Manager.

 Important

You must be a member of the Administrators group on the local computer to perform the following procedure or procedures, or you must have been delegated the appropriate authority. As a security best practice, log on to your computer by using an account that is not in the Administrators group, and then use the **runas** command to run IIS Manager as an administrator. At a command prompt, type **runas** / *User.Administrative_AccountName* "mmc %systemroot%\system32\inetsrv\iis.msc".

▷ **To start IIS Manager**

- From the **Start** menu, point to **All Programs**, point to **Administrative Tools**, and then click **Internet Information Services (IIS) Manager**.

▷ **To start IIS Manager from the Run dialog box**

1. From the **Start** menu, click **Run**.

2. In the **Open** box, type **inetmgr**, and click **OK**.

▷ **To start IIS Manager from the Computer Management window**

1. From the **Start menu**, right-click **My Computer**, and then click **Manage**.

2. In the console tree, expand the **Services and Applications** node.

3. In the console tree, click **Internet Information Services (IIS) Manager**. The names and statuses of your sites, application pools, and Web service extensions appear in the details pane.

4. In the console tree, expand the **Internet Information Services (IIS) Manager** node and any site nodes within it to see a list of directories and virtual directories for each site.

For more information about using IIS Manager to administer IIS, see the "Server Administration Guide" in IIS 6.0 Help, which you can access from IIS Manager. For more information about administering IIS remotely, see "How to Administer the Server Remotely" in IIS 6.0 Help, which is accessible from IIS Manager.

Starting and Stopping Services and Sites

Infrequently, you might make configuration changes in IIS 6.0 that require you to restart IIS before the changes can take effect. For example, if you change the application isolation mode in which your server is running, such as when you change from worker process isolation mode to IIS 5.0 isolation mode or vice versa, you need to restart IIS. If you make this configuration change by using IIS Manager, you are prompted to restart IIS after you click **OK** to confirm the change. If you make this configuration change by using a command-line utility, such as Adsutil.vbs, you can use the **IISReset** command-line utility to complete the change. Both methods — using the Restart IIS command in IIS Manager or using a command-line utility — allow you to stop, start, and restart IIS Internet services, as well as restart your computer.

When you restart the Internet service, all sessions connected to your Web server (including Internet, FTP, SMTP, and NNTP) are dropped. Any data held in Web applications is lost. All Internet sites are unavailable until Internet services are restarted. For this reason, avoid restarting, stopping, or rebooting your server.

For a list of features designed to improve IIS reliability and remedy the need to restart IIS, see the "Alternatives to Restarting IIS" section in the "Restarting IIS" topic in IIS 6.0 Help, which is accessible from IIS Manager.

Saving Your Configuration to Disk

As a safeguard, if you must stop or restart IIS, save your configuration to disk before you perform the restart. Your configuration is automatically saved if you enable the edit-while-running feature (this feature is not enabled by default). For more information about the edit-while-running feature, see "Writing the Metabase to Disk" in IIS 6.0 Help, which is accessible from IIS Manager.

Alternatively, you can manually save your configuration to disk by performing the following procedure.

▶ **To manually save your configuration to disk**

- In IIS Manager, right-click the local computer, point to **All Tasks**, and then click **Save Configuration to Disk**.

If You Receive an Error Stating That IISReset Is Disabled

If the **IISReset** command-line utility is disabled, then the command-line or IIS Manager calls that require IISReset.exe fail and return an error stating that **IISReset** is disabled. Actions that fail include the **Restart IIS** command in IIS Manager and Service Control Manager (SCM) recovery configuration actions that use the **IISReset** command-line utility (for example, the default IIS Admin SCM recovery path). However, SCM recovery actions that do not use the **IISReset** command-line utility continue to function (for example, the default World Wide Web Publishing Service [WWW service] SCM recovery path that restarts the WWW service).

Starting or Stopping IIS Services and Sites

▷ **To restart, stop, or start IIS services**

1. In IIS Manager, right-click the local computer, point to **All Tasks,** and then click **Restart IIS.**

2. In the **What do you want IIS to do list,** click the action that you want to perform, such as **Restart Internet Services on** *ComputerName.*

    You can also choose to restart the computer, stop the Internet service, or start the Internet service. IIS attempts to stop all services before restarting.

▷ **To start, stop, or pause individual sites**

- In IIS Manager, right-click the site you want to start, stop, or pause; and then click **Start, Stop,** or **Pause.**

> **Important**
>
> You must be a member of the Administrators group on the local computer to run scripts and executables, or you must have been delegated the appropriate authority. As a security best practice, log on to your computer by using an account that is not in the Administrators group, and then use the runas command to run your script or executable as an administrator. At a command prompt, type runas **/profile** */User.MyMachine\Administrator* cmd to open a command window with administrator rights and then type cscript.exe *ScriptName* (including the full path with parameters, if any).

▷ **To restart IIS by using the IISReset command-line utility**

1. From the **Start** menu, click **Run.**

2. In the **Open** box, type **cmd,** and then click **OK.**

3. At the command prompt, type the following:

    Iisreset /noforce *ComputerName*

    If you are logged on locally, the *ComputerName* parameter is not required. If you are remotely administering a server running IIS, the *ComputerName* parameter is the NetBIOS name of the computer on which you want to restart IIS.

> ◆ **Important**
>
> Use the /noforce parameter to help prevent data loss in case the IIS services cannot be stopped within the one minute time-out period. If you are certain that it is safe to force IIS to restart, you can omit the /noforce parameter. However, be aware that you could lose data if you do not include this parameter.

4. IIS attempts to stop all services before restarting. The **IISReset** command-line utility waits up to one minute for all services to stop if you do not include the /noforce parameter. If the services cannot be stopped within one minute, all IIS services are terminated, and IIS restarts.

The **iisreset** command provides several additional parameters. For example, you can adjust the time-out value by using the **iisreset/timeout** command. For more information about the parameters that are available with the **IISReset** command-line utility, open a command-prompt window, and type **iisreset /?** at the command prompt.

For more information about starting and stopping services or using the **IISReset** command-line utility to restart IIS, see "Restarting IIS" in IIS 6.0 Help, which is accessible from IIS Manager, and also see "IIS 6.0 Administration Scripts, Tips, and Tricks" in this book.

Enabling and Disabling Dynamic Content

To help reduce the attack surface of systems, IIS 6.0 is not installed by default on the Microsoft® Windows® Server 2003, Standard Edition; Microsoft® Windows® Server 2003, Enterprise Edition; and Microsoft® Windows® Server 2003, Datacenter Edition. After installing these products, administrators must manually install IIS 6.0.

When you perform a clean installation of IIS 6.0, the default settings help protect your system from malicious users and attackers. When you install IIS 6.0, it is locked down — only request handling for static Web pages (HTTP content, such as .htm and .html files) is enabled, and only the World Wide Web Publishing Service (WWW service) is installed. The request handlers that process dynamic content are disabled, which means that features like ASP, ASP.NET, server-side includes (SSI), FrontPage® 2002 Server Extensions from Microsoft, and Web Distributed Authoring and Versioning (WebDAV) do not work by default.

You can configure the request handlers (for example, Internet Server API [ISAPI] extensions or Common Gateway Interface [CGI] programs), which are called Web service extensions, by using the Web Service Extensions node in IIS Manager or by using the command-line script Iisext.vbs, which is stored in the *systemroot*\System32 folder. You can individually enable or disable a Web service extension if it is registered in the Web Service Extensions node in IIS Manager.

▶ **To enable or disable dynamic content**

1. In IIS Manager, expand the local computer, and then click **Web Service Extensions**.

2. In the details pane, click the Web service extension that you want to enable or disable.

3. Do one of the following:

   - To enable a disabled Web service extension, click **Allow**.

   - To disable an enabled Web service extension, click **Prohibit**.

   - To view the properties of a Web service extension, click **Properties**.

For more information about using IIS Manager to administer dynamic content, including step-by-step documentation for adding new Web service extensions, allowing an application to call a Web service extension, or disabling all Web service extensions, see "Enabling and Disabling Dynamic Content" in IIS 6.0 Help, which is accessible from IIS Manager.

For more information about using the Iisext.vbs command-line script to administer dynamic content, such as enabling, disabling, or listing Web service extensions and their files, see "Managing Applications and Web Service Extensions" in IIS 6.0 Help.

Enabling ASP Pages

Active Server Pages (ASP) is a server-side scripting environment that you can use to create dynamic and interactive Web pages, and build powerful Web applications. When the server receives a request for an ASP file, it processes server-side script code contained in the file to build the Hypertext Markup Language (HTML) Web page that is sent to the browser. In addition to server-side script code, ASP files can contain HTML (including related client-side scripts), as well as calls to Component Object Model (COM) components that perform a variety of tasks, such as connecting to a database or processing business logic.

▷ **To enable ASP pages**

1.   In IIS Manager, expand the local computer, and then click **Web Service Extensions**.

2.   In the details pane, click **Active Server Pages**, and then click **Allow**.

If your Web applications require ISAPI, ASP, CGI, ASP.NET, WebDAV, or other extensions to operate, you must enable those extensions also.

For more information about ASP, including an introduction to ASP concepts, see the "ASP" section in IIS 6.0 Help, which is accessible from IIS Manager. For information about creating ASP pages and developing Web applications, see the "Web Application Guide" in IIS 6.0 Help.

Installing and Enabling ASP.NET

Microsoft ASP.NET is a unified Web development platform that provides the services necessary for developers to build enterprise-class Web applications. Although ASP.NET is largely syntax compatible with ASP, it also provides a new programming model and infrastructure for more secure, scalable, and stable applications. You can augment your existing ASP applications by incrementally adding ASP.NET functionality to them.

ASP.NET is a compiled, .NET-based environment; you can author applications in any .NET compatible language, including Microsoft® Visual Basic® .NET, Microsoft® Visual C#®, and Microsoft® JScript® .NET.

▷ **To enable ASP.NET by using IIS Manager**

1.   In IIS Manager, expand the local computer, and then click **Web Service Extensions**.

2.   In the details pane, click **ASP.NET**, and then click **Allow**.

▶ **To install and enable ASP.NET on a server running Windows Server 2003**

1. From the **Start** menu, click **Manage Your Server**.

2. In the Manage Your Server window, click Add or remove a role.

3. In the **Configure Your Server Wizard**, click Next.

4. In the Server Role dialog box, click Application server (IIS, **ASP.NET**), and then click Next.

5. In the **Application Server Options** dialog box, select the **Enable ASP.NET** check box, click **Next**, and then click **Next** again.

6. If necessary, insert your Windows Server 2003 operating system CD in the CD-ROM drive and then click **Next**.

7. When the installation is complete, click **Finish**.

If your applications require ISAPI, CGI, ASP, WebDAV, or other extensions to operate, you must enable those extensions also. For more information about ASP.NET, see "ASP.NET" in IIS 6.0 Help, which is accessible from IIS Manager.

Creating a Web Site or an FTP Site

IIS creates a default Web site on your computer during installation. You can use the *LocalDrive:*\Inetpub\Wwwroot directory to publish your Web content, or you can create any directory or virtual directory you choose. Because the FTP service is not installed by default, , you must first install and start the File Transfer Protocol (FTP) service to create an FTP site.

Creating a Web or FTP site by using IIS Manager does not create content but merely creates a directory structure and configuration files from which to publish the content.

▶ **To use the default Web site**

1. In IIS Manager, expand the local computer, expand the **Web Sites** folder, right-click **Default Web Site**, and then click **Properties**.

2. On the **Web Site** tab, under **Web site description**, type the name of your Web site in the **Description** box.

3. Click **OK**. The name of the new site appears in IIS Manager.

▶ To create a new Web site

1. In IIS Manager, expand the local computer, right-click the **Web Sites** folder, point to **New**, and then click **Web Site**. The **Web Site Creation Wizard** appears.

2. Click **Next**.

3. In the **Description** box, type the name of your site, and then click **Next**.

4. Type or click the IP address (the default is **All Unassigned**), TCP port, and host header (for example, *www.mysite.com*) for your site, and then click **Next**.

 Important

To help ensure that user requests reach the correct Web site, configure a unique identity for each site on the server by distinguishing each Web site with at least one of three unique identifiers: a host header name, an IP address, or a TCP port number.

Using unique host header names is the preferred way to identify multiple Web sites on a single server. For more information about choosing unique identifiers, see "Hosting Multiple Web Sites on a Single Server" and "Adding Web Sites to Your Server" in IIS 6.0 Help, which is accessible from IIS Manager.

---

5. In the **Path** box, type or browse to the directory that contains, or will contain, the site content, and then click **Next**.

6. Select the check boxes for the Web site access permissions you want to assign to your users, and then click **Next**.

7. Click **Finish**.

To change these and other settings later, right-click the Web site, and click **Properties**.

▷ **To install FTP services**

1. From the **Start** menu, click **Control Panel,** and then double-click **Add or Remove Programs**.

2. Click **Add/Remove Windows Components**.

3. In the **Components** box, click **Application Server**, and then click **Details**.

4. In the **Subcomponents of Application Server** box, click **Internet Information Services (IIS),** and then click **Details**.

5. In the **Subcomponents of Internet Information Services (IIS)** box, select the **File Transfer Protocol (FTP) Service** check box.

6. Click **OK** twice.

7. If necessary, insert your Windows Server 2003 operating system CD in the CD-ROM drive and then click **Next**. You might also be prompted for the network install path.

8. Click **Finish**.

When you install the FTP service, IIS creates a default FTP site at *LocalDrive*:\Inetpub\Ftproot. You can use that site to publish your content, or you can create a new FTP site.

▷ **To create a new FTP site**

1. In IIS Manager, expand the local computer, right-click the **FTP Sites** folder, point to **New,** and click **FTP Site**. The **FTP Site Creation Wizard** appears.

2. Click **Next**.

3. In the **Description** box, type the name of your site, and then click **Next**.

4. Type or click the IP address (the default is **All Unassigned**) and TCP port for your site, and then click **Next**.

5. Click the user isolation option you want, and then click **Next**.

6. In the **Path** box, type or browse to the directory that contains or will contain shared content, and click **Next**.

7. Select the check boxes for the FTP site access permissions you want to assign to your users, and then click **Next**.

8. Click **Finish**.

You can use IIS Manager to change the site settings by right-clicking the FTP site and then clicking **Properties**.

For more information about configuring Web and FTP sites, see "Configuring Internet Sites and Services" in this book, and also see "Web Site Setup" and "FTP Site Setup" in IIS 6.0 Help, which is accessible from IIS Manager.

Creating Virtual Directories

In most cases, the content you publish to your Web or FTP site is located in a root or home directory on your computer, such as *LocalDrive*:\Inetpub\Wwwroot\. However, you might need to publish content that is located elsewhere, such as on a remote computer.

To publish from a directory that is not contained within your home or root directory, you can create a virtual directory. A virtual directory is a directory that is not contained in the home directory but appears to client browsers as though it were.

To create a virtual directory by using IIS Manager

1. In IIS Manager, expand the local computer, expand the Web site or FTP site to which you want to add a virtual directory, right-click the site or folder within which you want to create the virtual directory, point to **New**, and then click **Virtual Directory**. The **Virtual Directory Creation Wizard** appears.

2. Click **Next**.

3. In the **Alias** box, type a name for the virtual directory. (Choose a short name that is easy to type because the user types this name.)

4. Click **Next**.

5. In the **Path** box, type or browse to the physical directory in which the virtual directory resides, and then click **Next**.

6. Under **Allow the following permissions**, select the check boxes for the access permissions you want to assign to your users, and then click **Next.**

7. Click **Finish**.

> **Important**
>
> For security reasons, when selecting access permissions, consider allowing only the default Read permission. By restricting permissions in this way, you can help avoid attacks against your Web site by malicious users. For more information about setting access permissions, see "Securing Virtual Directories" and "Access Control" in Help and Support Center for Windows Server 2003.

To locate the virtual directory that you just created, look in the console tree below the currently selected level.

If you are using the NTFS file system, you can also create a virtual directory by using Windows Explorer.

▷ **To create a virtual directory by using Windows Explorer**

1. In Windows Explorer, right-click the folder you want to be a virtual directory, and then click **Sharing and Security**.

2. Click the **Web Sharing** tab, and then click **Share this folder**.

3. In the **Alias** box, type the name for the virtual directory.

4. Click **OK** twice.

▷ **To create a Web virtual directory by using the Iisvdir.vbs script**

1. From the **Start** menu, click **Run.**

2. In the **Open** box, type **cmd,** and then click **OK**.

3. At the command prompt, type the following:

   cscript %SystemRoot%\system32\iisvdir.vbs /create *SampleWebSite*[*/Path*] *VirtualDirectory drive:\path*

   where *SampleWebSite, VirtualDirectory,* and *path* is the physical directory, as appropriate.

For more information about creating Web virtual directories by using the Iisvdir.vbs command and its parameters, type the following at the command prompt: **iisvdir /create /?**

▷ **To create an FTP virtual directory by using the Iisftpdr.vbs script**

1. From the **Start** menu, click **Run.**

2. In the **Open** box, type **cmd,** and then click **OK**.

3. At the command prompt, type the following:

   cscript %SystemRoot%\system32\iisftpdr.vbs /create *FTPSite*[*/Path*] *VirtualDirectory drive:\path*

   where *FTPSite, VirtualDirectory*, and *path* is the physical directory, as appropriate.

For more information about creating FTP virtual directories by using the Iisftpdr.vbs command and its parameters, type the following at the command prompt: **iisftpdr /create /?**

For more information about creating a virtual directory, including alternate ways to create a Web or FTP virtual directory, see "Using Virtual Directories" in IIS 6.0 Help, which is accessible from IIS Manager. For more information about using command-line scripts to create Web or FTP virtual directories, see "Creating Web Virtual Directories" or "Creating FTP Virtual Directories" in IIS 6.0 Help.

Tasks New to IIS 6.0

If you upgrade from an earlier version of IIS, you need to learn the tasks that are new to IIS 6.0. This section introduces the basic tasks that are new, or significantly different, in IIS 6.0:

- **Creating and isolating applications.** Create and manage applications.

- **Creating application pools.** Group Web applications into application pools.

- **Configuring recycling.** Periodically restart worker processes assigned to an application pool.

- **Backing up and restoring metabase configurations.** Save metabase and application configurations.

- **Saving and copying site configurations.** Copy site configurations for use on new sites.

Creating and Isolating Applications

To create an application, you designate a directory as the starting point (application root) for the application. You can then set properties for the application. Each application can have a friendly name; this name appears in IIS Manager and gives you a way to distinguish between applications.

Web sites are root-level applications by default. When you create a Web site, a default application is created at the same time. You can use this root-level application, remove it, or replace it with a new application by removing it and creating a new application.

 Important

You must be a member of the Administrators group on the local computer to perform the following procedure or procedures, or you must have been delegated the appropriate authority. As a security best practice, log on to your computer by using an account that is not in the Administrators group, and then use the **runas** command to run IIS Manager as an administrator. At a command prompt, type **runas** /*User:Administrative_AccountName* "mmc %systemroot%\system32\inetsrv\iis.msc".

▷ **To create an application**

1. In IIS Manager, expand the local computer, right-click the directory that is the application starting point, and then click **Properties**.

2. Click the Home Directory, Virtual Directory, or Directory tab.

3. In the Application settings section, click Create.

   Note that if you see the **Remove** button instead of the **Create** button, an application has already been created.

4. In the **Application name** box, type a name for your application.

5. In the **Execute Permissions** list box, set permissions by doing one of the following:

   - Click **None** to prevent any programs or scripts from running.

   - Click **Scripts only** to enable applications mapped to a script engine to run in this directory without having permissions set for executables. Setting permissions to **Scripts only** is more restrictive than setting them to **Scripts and Executables** because you can limit the applications that can be run in the directory.

   - Click **Scripts and Executables** to allow any application to run in this directory, including applications mapped to script engines and Microsoft® Windows® binaries (.dll and .exe file name extensions).

6. Click **OK**.

To isolate an application means that you configure it to run in a process (memory space) separate from the Web server and other applications. You can run IIS 6.0 in one of two application isolation modes: *worker process isolation mode* or *IIS 5.0 isolation mode*. IIS cannot run both application isolation modes simultaneously on the same computer. If you have applications that require different modes, you must run them on separate computers.

Worker process isolation mode is the default application isolation mode that the server runs in on a clean installation. In this mode, you can isolate an application by adding it to an application pool that includes isolation settings. For more information about creating and configuring application pools, see "Configuring Application Pools" in IIS 6.0 Help, and also see "Running IIS 6.0 as an Application Server" in this book.

 Tip

Before you isolate an application, verify in which application isolation mode the computer is running. You can determine the application isolation mode in which IIS is running by the presence (worker process isolation mode) or absence (IIS 5.0 isolation mode) of the Application Pools folder.

▶ **To isolate an application in worker process isolation mode**

1. In IIS Manager, expand the local computer, expand the **Web Sites** folder, right-click the application you want to isolate, and then click **Properties**.

2. Click the **Home Directory**, **Virtual Directory**, or **Directory** tab (depending on the application).

3. In the **Application settings** section, in the **Application pool** list box, click an application pool.

4. Click **Apply**, and then click **OK**.

IIS 5.0 isolation mode is provided for applications that depend on specific features and behaviors of IIS 5.0. Use this mode only if an application has a compatibility issue when it runs in worker process isolation mode and you cannot resolve the problem.

▶ **To isolate an application in IIS 5.0 isolation mode**

1. In IIS Manager, expand the local computer, expand the **Web Sites** folder, right-click the application you want to isolate, and click **Properties**.

2. Click the **Home Directory**, **Virtual Directory**, or **Directory** tab (depending on the application). If you are in the directory listed as the **Starting Point** directory, the **Application name** box is already filled in.

3. In the **Application protection** list box, click the appropriate process option.

4. Click **OK**.

    The Web server finishes processing any current requests for the application before creating a separate process. At the next request for the application, the application runs in the appropriate memory space.

For more information about creating and isolating applications, including guidelines for when to use each isolation mode, see "Running IIS 6.0 as an Application Server" in this book. Also see "Creating Applications" and "Web Application Isolation" in IIS 6.0 Help, which is accessible from IIS Manager.

Creating Application Pools

When you run IIS 6.0 in worker process isolation mode, you can group Web applications into application pools. An *application pool* is a grouping of URLs routed to one or more worker processes that share the same configuration. Application pools allow you to apply specific configuration settings to groups of applications and the worker processes servicing those applications. Any Web site, Web directory or virtual directory can be assigned to an application pool.

By creating new application pools and assigning Web sites and applications to them, you can make your server more efficient and reliable. In addition, your other applications are always available, even when the applications in the new application pool terminate.

▷   **To create a new application pool**

1. In IIS Manager, expand the local computer, right-click **Application Pools**, point to **New**, and then click **Application Pool**.

2. In the **Application pool ID** box, type the name of the new application pool.

3. Under **Application pool settings**, click either **Use default settings for new application pool** or **Use existing application pool as template**.

4. If you selected **Use existing application pool as template** from the **Application pool name** list box, click the application pool to be used as a template.

5. Click **OK**.

For more information about creating application pools and configuring worker processes, see "Running IIS 6.0 as an Application Server" in this book. Also see "Configuring Application Pools" and "Configuring Application Pool Identity" in IIS 6.0 Help, which is accessible from IIS Manager.

Configuring Recycling

In worker process isolation mode, you can configure IIS to periodically restart the worker processes that are assigned to an application pool in order to manage faulty Web applications. Recycling keeps problematic applications running smoothly, especially when it is not practical to modify the application code. Recycling ensures that application pools remain healthy and that system resources are recovered.

You can configure worker processes to restart based on one of several options, including elapsed time, number of requests served, scheduled times, and memory usage; or you can configure worker processes to start on demand. In IIS 6.0, worker process recycling is available only when IIS is running in worker process isolation mode.

▷   **To set a worker process to recycle after a specified elapsed time**

1. In IIS Manager, expand the local computer, expand **Application Pools,** right-click the application pool, and click **Properties**.

2. On the **Recycling** tab, select the **Recycle worker processes (in minutes)** check box.

3. Click the up or down arrow to set the number of minutes you want to elapse before the worker process is recycled.

4. Click **OK**.

▷   **To configure a worker process to recycle after a set number of processing requests**

1. In IIS Manager, expand the local computer, expand **Application Pools,** right-click the application pool, and then click **Properties**.

2. On the **Recycling** tab, select the **Recycle worker process (number of requests)** check box.

3. Click the up or down arrow to set the number of requests to be processed before the worker process recycles.

4. Click **OK**.

▷ **To configure a worker process to recycle at scheduled times**

1. In IIS Manager, expand the local computer, expand **Application Pools,** right-click the application pool, and click **Properties**.

2. On the **Recycling** tab, select the **Recycle worker processes at the following times** check box.

3. Do one of the following:

   ■ Click **Add** to add a recycle time to the list.

   ■ Click **Remove** to delete a recycle time from the list.

   ■ Click **Edit** to change an existing time at which the worker process is recycled.

4. Click **OK**.

When recycling is set to occur at scheduled times, it can occur off-schedule if you alter the system time. To avoid unintended changes in scheduled recycling times, recycle the scheduled worker processes right after you change the system time.

▷ **To configure a worker process to recycle after it consumes a specified amount of memory**

1. In IIS Manager, expand the local computer, expand **Application Pools,** right-click the application pool, and click **Properties**.

2. On the Recycling tab, under Memory recycling, select the Maximum virtual memory (in megabytes) or Maximum used memory (in megabytes) check box.

3. Click the up or down arrow to set memory limits.

4. Click **OK**.

For more information about recycling worker processes, see "Running IIS 6.0 as an Application Server" in this book and also see "Recycling Worker Processes" in IIS 6.0 Help, which is accessible from IIS Manager.

Backing Up and Restoring the Metabase

Metabase backup files provide a way to restore your metabase configuration and schema data if your metabase becomes corrupted. You can create backup files by using IIS Manager or an administration script. The backup files are copies of the metabase configuration file (MetaBase.xml) and the matching metabase schema file (MBSchema.xml). Use the metabase configuration backup and restore feature to restore the metabase from backup files.

You can create two types of metabase backups:

- **Portable backups.** When you create a portable backup, you provide a password that is used by IIS to encrypt the backup files. IIS encrypts the password and stores it in the header of the backup file. Only the administrator password and secure properties within the backup files are encrypted; all other information within the backup files are plaintext. After the backup file is encrypted, you cannot change the password of the backup file.

- **Non-portable backups.** When you create a non-portable backup, you do not supply a password. Therefore, IIS encrypts non-portable backup files with a blank password, which allows any member of the Administrators group to restore the metabase by using non-portable backup files. Only the blank password and secure properties are encrypted; all other information within the backup file is plaintext.

You can restore a metabase backup to the computer on which the backup was made or to a different computer that is running Microsoft® Windows® Server 2003, Standard Edition; Windows® Server 2003, Enterprise Edition; Windows® Server 2003, Datacenter Edition; and Windows® Server 2003, Web Edition. However, before you restore a metabase backup from one computer to another, you must first delete the machine-specific information from the metabase file. For more information about restoring a metabase backup to a different computer, see "Machine-Specific and System-Specific Information" in IIS 6.0 Help, which is accessible from IIS Manager.

Before you create a backup of the metabase, consider the following:

- A non-portable backup can only be restored to the computer on which the backup was made.

- The metabase is locked while the backup is in progress.

- Backup files contain only configuration data; they do not include your content.

To back up your content, use the Windows Backup feature. For more information about Windows Backup, see "Backing up and Restoring Data" in Help and Support Center for Windows Server 2003.

► To create a portable backup (password required)

1. In IIS Manager, right-click the local computer, point to **All Tasks**, and click **Backup/Restore Configuration**.

2. Click **Create Backup**.

3. In the **Configuration backup name** box, type a name for the backup file.

4. Select the **Encrypt backup using password** check box, type a password into the **Password** box, and then type the same password in the **Confirm password** box.

5. Click **OK**, and then click **Close**.

► To create a non-portable backup (password not required)

1. In IIS Manager, right-click the local computer, point to **All Tasks**, and click **Backup/Restore Configuration**.

2. Click **Create Backup**.

3. In the **Configuration backup name** box, type a name for the backup file.

4. Click **OK**, and click **Close**.

▷ **To restore the metabase backup**

1. In IIS Manager, right-click the local computer, point to **All Tasks**, and click **Backup/Restore Configuration**.

2. In the **Backups** list box, click a backup version that you previously created, or select an **Automatic Backup** file (IIS periodically creates these), and then click **Restore**. If prompted for a password, type the password you that you used to make the backup portable.

3. When a confirmation message appears, click **Yes**.

4. Click **OK**, and then click **Close**.

For more information about backing up and restoring the metabase, see "Working with the Metabase" in this book, and "Backing Up and Restoring the Metabase" in IIS 6.0 Help, which is accessible from IIS Manager.

Saving and Copying Site Configurations

After your site and applications are running the way you want, you can save all or part of the configurations for a backup copy, or for import and export to other sites or computers. You can use the following procedure to save site configurations for Web or FTP sites, as well as Web or FTP virtual directories.

IIS automatically makes a backup copy of the metabase configuration and schema files each time you make changes to the metabase. Backup files contain only configuration data; they do not include your content (.asp files, .htm files, .dll files, and so on). You can also create backup files on demand, or create backup copies of individual site or application configurations and then export and import them to and from other sites or computers.

For more information about backing up the metabase, including step-by-step procedures, see "Backing Up and Restoring the Metabase" earlier in this appendix.

▷ **To save a site or application configuration**

1. In IIS Manager, right-click the site or application you want to back up, point to **All Tasks**, and click **Save Configuration to a File**.

2. In the **File name** box, type a file name.

3. In the **Path** box, type or browse to the location where you want to save the file.

4. To make the configuration that you are saving portable, select the **Encrypt backup using password** check box, type a password in the **Password** box, and then type the same password in the **Confirm password** box.

5. Click **OK**.

For more information about importing and exporting site and application configurations, see "Managing IIS Configurations" in IIS 6.0 Help.

Security-Related Tasks

IIS 6.0 and Windows Server 2003 provide several ways to help secure your application servers and their content. This section provides information about the following security-related topics:

- **Setting Web site authentication.** Set up Web site authentication for your Web sites.

- **Setting FTP site authentication.** Set up FTP site authentication to validate users who request access to your FTP sites.

- **Obtaining and backing up server certificates.** Set up Secure Sockets Layer (SSL) certification on your sites. SSL certificates enable Web servers and users to authenticate each other before establishing a connection.

- **Controlling access to applications.** Reduce the attack surface of your applications with permissions and restrictions; control which users and computers are allowed to access your Web server and its resources.

Before you do any of these security-related tasks, be sure that you are familiar with best practice guidelines and that you apply those guidelines to these tasks. If you are new to using IIS or if you are unfamiliar with any of the following security-related tasks, be sure to read the cross-references to additional information that are provided in this section.

Setting Web Site Authentication

You can require users to provide a valid Windows user account name and password before they access any information on your server. This identification process is called *authentication*. Authentication, like many of the features in IIS, can be set at the Web site, directory, or file level.

This section contains step-by-step procedures for configuring Web site authentication. For information about configuring FTP sites, see "Setting FTP Site Authentication" later in this appendix.

To set Web authentication, choose from the following authentication methods:

- **Anonymous authentication.** This authentication method gives users access to the public areas of your Web site without prompting them for a user name or password.

- **Basic authentication.** This authentication method requires a previously assigned Windows account user name and password, also known as *credentials*.

- **Digest authentication.** This authentication method offers the same functionality as Basic authentication, while providing an additional level of security because the user's credentials are not sent over the network in plaintext.

- **Advanced Digest authentication.** This authentication method offers similar functionality to Digest authentication; however, collects user credentials and stores them on the domain controller as an MD5 hash, or message digest. Advantages of this authentication are that the worker process does not need to run as local system and the user password is not stored as plaintext on the domain controller. This authentication method requires a Windows Server 2003 domain controller infrastructure.

- **Integrated Windows authentication.** This authentication method collects information through a method where the user name and password are hashed before being sent across the network.

- **Certificate authentication.** This authentication method adds SSL security through client or server certificates. For information about this type of authentication, see "Obtaining and Backing Up Server Certificates" later in this appendix.

- **.NET Passport authentication.** This authentication method provides a single sign-in service that is HTTP cookie-based.

Configuring Anonymous Authentication

Anonymous authentication gives users access to the public areas of your Web or FTP site without prompting users for a user name or password. When a user attempts to connect to your public Web or FTP site, your Web server assigns the connection to the Windows user account IUSR_*computername*, where *computername* is the name of the computer on which IIS is running. By default, the IUSR_*computername* account is included in the Users and Guests user groups.

 Important

You must be a member of the Administrators group on the local computer to perform the following procedure or procedures, or you must have been delegated the appropriate authority. As a security best practice, log on to your computer by using an account that is not in the Administrators group, and then use the **runas** command to run IIS Manager as an administrator. At a command prompt, type **runas** / *User.Administrative_AccountName* "mmc %systemroot%\system32\inetsrv\iis.msc".

▶ **To enable Anonymous authentication**

1. In IIS Manager, expand the local computer, right-click a site, directory, or file, and then click **Properties**.

2. Depending on the security setting level that you are changing, click either the **Directory Security** or the **File Security** tab.

3. In the **Authentication and access control** section, click **Edit**.

4. Select the **Enable anonymous access** check box.

5. Click **OK** twice.

▶ **To change the account used for Anonymous authentication**

1. In IIS Manager, expand the local computer, double-click a site, directory, or file, and then click **Properties**.

2. Depending on the security setting level that you are changing, click the **Directory Security** or the **File Security** tab.

3. In the **Authentication and access control** section, click **Edit**.

4. Select the **Enable anonymous access** check box.

5. Click **Browse** and type or browse to the valid Windows user account that you want to use for anonymous access.

   Before you can change the account, you must create the user account; IIS does not create the account for you.

6. Click **OK** three times.

For more information about configuring Anonymous authentication, see "Anonymous Authentication" in IIS 6.0 Help, which is accessible from IIS Manager.

Configuring Basic Authentication

The Basic authentication method transmits user names and passwords across the network in an unencrypted form. You need to use SSL, in combination with Basic authentication, to encrypt user account information that is transmitted across the network.

Configuration settings made at the Web Sites folder level can be inherited by all Web sites unless you specify otherwise at the individual Web site level. Enabling Basic authentication does not automatically configure your Web server to authenticate users. You must also create Windows user accounts and set NTFS permissions.

▷ **To enable Basic authentication**

1. In IIS Manager, right-click the **Web Sites** folder, Web site, directory, virtual directory, or file, and click **Properties**.

2. Depending on the security setting level that you are configuring, click either the **Directory Security** or **File Security** tab.

3. In the **Authentication and access control** section, click **Edit**.

4. In the **Authenticated access** section, select the **Basic authentication** check box.

5. Because Basic authentication sends passwords over the network unencrypted, a dialog box appears asking if you want to proceed. Click **Yes** to proceed.

6. In the **Default domain** box, do either of the following:

   ▪ Type the domain name you want to use.

   ▪ Click **Select** to browse to a new default logon domain.

   If the **Default domain** box is filled in, the name is used as the default domain. If the **Default domain** box is left empty, IIS uses the domain of the computer that is running IIS as the default domain. IIS configures the value of the **DefaultLogonDomain** property, which determines the default domain that is used to authenticate clients who access your IIS server by using Basic authentication. However, the domain specified by the **DefaultLogonDomain** property is used only when a client does not specify a domain in the logon dialog box that appears on the client computer.

    Note

   Optionally, you can enter a value in the Realm box, which configures the value of the Realm property. If the Realm property is set, its value appears on the client's logon dialog box when Basic authentication is used. The value of the Realm property is sent to the client for informational purposes only and is not used to authenticate clients that use Basic authentication.

7. Click **OK** twice.

For more information about configuring Basic authentication, see "Basic Authentication" in IIS 6.0 Help, which is accessible from IIS Manager.

Configuring Digest Authentication

Digest authentication offers the same functionality as Basic authentication; however, Digest authentication provides a means to help ensure that user credentials are not sent across the network in plaintext. Digest authentication transmits credentials across the network as an MD5 hash, or message digest, where the original user name and password cannot be deciphered from the hash. Digest authentication is available to WebDAV directories.

Digest authentication is enabled by default for upgrades from an earlier version of IIS. If you need to enable Digest authentication on a server running IIS 6.0, do the following:

1. Enable Digest authentication for Windows domain servers.

2. Configure the realm name.

 To enable Digest authentication for Windows domain servers

1. In IIS Manager, right-click the **Web Sites** folder, Web site, directory, virtual directory, or file, and then click **Properties**.

   > **Note**
   >
   > Configuration settings made at the Web Sites folder level are inherited by all Web sites unless you specify otherwise at the individual Web site level.

2. Depending on the security settings level that you are configuring, click the **Directory Security** or **File Security** tab.

3. In the **Anonymous access and authentication control** section, click **Edit**.

4. In the **Authenticated access** section, select the **Digest authentication for Windows domain servers** check box.

5. In the **Realm** box, type the realm name, or click **Select** to browse for a domain.

6. Click **OK** twice.

If Basic authentication is enabled for the site, virtual directory, or folder that you are configuring, the **Default domain** box is also available. However, only **Realm** is meaningful to Digest authentication.

Configuring the Realm Name

In addition to using IIS Manager to enable Digest authentication on a Windows domain server, you can use scripting to configure the realm name at any level of the metabase, as shown in the Table A.2.

If a child key in the metabase is not configured with a realm name, that child key inherits the realm name from the next parent key that has the realm name configured. If the realm name is not configured, IIS sends its own computer name as the realm name. If IIS sends its own name as the realm name and IIS is not running on a Windows Server 2003 domain controller with Active Directory® directory service, Digest authentication fails. As a best practice, avoid running IIS on a domain controller; whenever possible, physically separate a server that is running IIS from a domain controller.

Table A.2   Configuring the Realm Name at Any Level of the Metabase

Metabase Level	Description
W3SVC	The W3SVC level, also known as the **IISWebService** level, is the highest level in the metabase where Digest authentication can be configured. Lower levels that do not have specific configuration settings inherit configurations set at this level.
W3SVC/*n*	The W3SVC/*n* level, also known as the **IISWebService** level, is a specific Web site, where *n* is the number of the site. Sites are numbered starting at 1. The default Web site is 1.
W3SVC/*n*/root	The W3SVC/*n*/Root level, known as the **IISWebVirtualDir** level, is the starting point for a Web Site, where *n* is the number of the site.
W3SVC/*n*/root/vdir	The W3SVC/*n*/Root/WebVirtualDir level, known as the **IISWebVirtualDir** level, is a virtual directory within a Web Site, where *n* is the number of the site.
W3SVC/*n*/root/vdir/webdir	The W3SVC/*n*/Root/WebVirtualDir/WebDir level, also known as the **IISWebDirectory** level, is a physical directory within a virtual directory within a Web site, where *n* is the number of the site.
W3SVC/*n*/root/vdir/file	The W3SVC/*n*/Root/Vdir/file level is an individual file within the W3SVC/*n*/Root/WebVirtualDir level, where *n* is the number of the site.
W3SVC/*n*/root/vdir/webdir/file	The W3SVC/*n*/Root/Vdir/file level is an individual file within the W3SVC/*n*/Root/WebVirtualDir/WebDir level, where *n* is the number of the site.

You can configure either single or multiple realm names on a server running IIS. You might want to configure multiple realm names if the domains do not have a trusted relationship. If you configure multiple realm names, you must configure them at different levels of the metabase.

For more information about Digest authentication, see "Digest Authentication" in IIS 6.0 Help, which is accessible from IIS Manager.

Configuring Advanced Digest Authentication

Under Advanced Digest authentication, user credentials are stored on the domain controller as an MD5 hash. Because credentials are stored in Active Directory as an MD5 hash, user passwords cannot be discovered by anyone with access to the domain controller, not even by the domain administrator. Advanced Digest authentication is available to WebDAV directories.

In IIS 6.0, Advanced Digest authentication is preferred over Digest authentication; however, you can use Digest authentication where your systems do not meet the requirements for Advanced Digest authentication.

Advanced Digest authentication is enabled by default on a clean installation of IIS 6.0. If you need to enable Advanced Digest authentication on a server running IIS 6.0, do the following:

1. Enable Digest authentication for Windows domain servers.

2. Configure the realm name.

3. Set the **UseDigestSSP** metabase property to TRUE.

 Important

If you perform the two procedures that precede this note but do not configure the UseDigestSSP metabase key, you are using Digest authentication, not Advanced Digest authentication.

Enabling Digest authentication and Configuring the Realm Name

For step-by-step instructions to enable Digest authentication for Windows domain servers and configure the realm name, see "Configuring Digest Authentication" earlier in this appendix.

Setting the UseDigestSSP Metabase Property

Advanced Digest authentication uses a metabase key called **UseDigestSSP**. This metabase key is a switch between Digest and Advanced Digest Security Support Provider Interface (SSPI) code.

After you set the key, the only valid property values are 1 (TRUE), 0 (FALSE), or empty. If you set the property to TRUE, IIS uses the new SSPI code for Advanced Digest authentication. In all other cases (FALSE, empty, or not set), IIS uses the Digest authentication code.

You can configure the **UseDigestSSP** metabase property at the W3SVC level of the metabase. A child key inherits its configuration from the level above it.

For more information about Advanced Digest authentication, see "Advanced Digest Authentication" in IIS 6.0 Help, which is accessible from IIS Manager.

Configuring Integrated Windows Authentication

Integrated Windows authentication (formerly called NTLM, and also referred to as Windows NT Challenge/Response authentication) is a form of authentication that hashes the user name and password before they are sent across the network. When you enable Integrated Windows authentication, the client submits the password through a cryptographic exchange with your Web server that involves hashing. Integrated Windows authentication is the default authentication method used in Windows Server 2003.

Integrated Windows authentication has the following limitations:

- Only Microsoft® Internet Explorer version 2.0 and later support this authentication method.

- This authentication method might not work over HTTP proxy connections.

Therefore, Integrated Windows authentication is best suited for an intranet environment, where both user and Web server computers are in the same domain and where administrators can ensure that every user has Internet Explorer version 2.0 or later.

▷ **To enable Integrated Windows authentication**

1. In IIS Manager, right-click the **Web Sites** folder, Web site, directory, virtual directory, or file, and then click **Properties**.

☑ | **Note**
Configuration settings made at the **Web Sites** folder level are inherited by all Web sites unless you specify otherwise at the individual Web site level.

2. Depending on the security settings level that you are configuring, click the **Directory Security** or the **File Security** tab.

3. In the **Authentication and access control** section, click **Edit**.

4. In the **Authenticated access** section, select the **Integrated Windows Authentication** check box.

5. Click **OK** twice.

For more information about configuring Integrated Windows authentication, see "Integrated Windows Authentication" in IIS 6.0 Help, which is accessible from IIS Manager.

Enabling .NET Passport Authentication

You can enable Microsoft® .NET Passport authentication on a Web site by using IIS Manager. When .NET Passport is enabled, requests coming into IIS must contain .NET Passport credentials on either the query string or within a cookie. The credentials also have to be valid, meaning the ticket has not expired. If IIS does not detect .NET Passport credentials, requests are redirected to the .NET Passport sign-in page.

.NET Passport uses cookies, which contain information that can be compromised. However, you can use .NET Passport authentication over a SSL connection, which reduces the potential of replay attacks.

▷ **To enable .NET Passport authentication on a Web site**

1. In IIS Manager, expand the local computer, expand the **Web Sites** folder, right-click the Web site on which you want to enable .NET Passport authentication, and then click **Properties**.

2. Click the **Directory Security** tab.

3. In the **Authentication and access control** section, click **Edit**.

4. In the **Authenticated access** section, select the **.NET Passport Authentication** check box.

   You cannot use .NET Passport authentication with other authentication methods because .NET Passport validates user credentials in a fundamentally different way. Hence, when you select .NET Passport authentication, all other authentication methods are unavailable.

5. Click **OK**.

For information about configuring .NET Passport authentication, see ".NET Passport Authentication" in IIS 6.0 Help.

Setting FTP Site Authentication

Based on your security requirements, you can select an IIS authentication method to validate users who request access to your FTP sites. To set FTP site authentication, choose from the following authentication methods:

- **Anonymous FTP authentication.** This authentication method gives users access to the public areas of your FTP site without prompting them for a user name or password.

- **Basic FTP authentication.** This authentication method requires users to log on with a user name and password corresponding to a valid Windows user account.

You cannot use Digest or Integrated Windows authentication with FTP sites, and you must set available authentication settings at the site level for FTP sites.

Enabling Anonymous FTP Authentication

You can configure your FTP server to allow anonymous access to FTP resources. If you select Anonymous FTP authentication for a resource, all requests for that resource are accepted without prompting the user for a user name or password. This is possible because IIS automatically creates a Windows user account called IUSR_*computername*, where *computername* is the name of the server on which IIS is running. This is very similar to Web-based Anonymous authentication. If Anonymous FTP authentication is enabled, IIS always try to use it first, even if you enable Basic FTP authentication.

▷ **To enable the Anonymous FTP authentication**

1. If the IUSR_*computername* account is not used for Anonymous FTP authentication, you must create a Windows user account appropriate for the authentication method and add the account to a Windows user group.

2. Configure NTFS permissions for the directory or files for which you want to control access by using the user account you selected in step 1.

3. In IIS Manager, right-click the FTP site, directory, virtual directory, or file, and then click **Properties**.

4. Click the **Security Accounts** tab.

5. Select the **Allow anonymous connections** check box.

6. To allow your users to gain access by Anonymous authentication only, select the **Allow only anonymous connections** check box.

7. In the **User name** and **Password** boxes, enter the anonymous logon user name and password you want to use. The user name is the name of the anonymous user account, which is typically designated as IUSR_*computername*.

8. Click **OK**.

9. Set the appropriate NTFS permissions for the anonymous account.

Important

If you change the security settings for your FTP site or virtual directory, your FTP server prompts you for permission to reset the security settings for the child keys of that site or directory. If you choose to accept these settings, the child keys inherit the security settings from the parent site or directory.

For more information about creating Windows user accounts, see "Securing Files with NTFS" in IIS 6.0 Help, which is accessible from IIS Manager. For more information about setting NTFS permissions, see "Setting NTFS Permissions for Directories or Files" in IIS 6.0 Help.

Enabling Basic FTP Authentication

To establish an FTP connection with your Web server by using Basic FTP authentication, users must log on with a user name and password corresponding to a valid Windows user account. If the FTP server cannot verify a user's identity, the server returns an error message. Basic FTP authentication transmits the user name and password across the network in an unencrypted form.

 To enable Basic FTP authentication

1. Create a Windows user account appropriate for the authentication method. If appropriate, add the account to a Windows user group.

2. Configure NTFS permissions for the directory or file for which you want to control access.

3. In IIS Manager, right-click the FTP site, directory, virtual directory, or file, and then click **Properties**.

4. Click the **Security Accounts** tab.

5. Clear the **Allow anonymous connections** check box.

6. Click **OK**.

7. Set the appropriate NTFS permissions for the account.

 Important

If you change the security settings for your FTP site or virtual directory, your FTP server prompts you for permission to reset the security settings for the child keys of that site or directory. If you choose to accept these settings, the child keys inherit the security settings from the parent site or directory.

For more information about setting Basic FTP site authentication, see "FTP Site Authentication" in IIS 6.0 Help, which is accessible from IIS Manager.

Obtaining and Backing Up Server Certificates

Server certificates contain information used in establishing identities over a network, which is a process called *authentication*. Similar to conventional forms of identification, certificates enable Web servers and users to authenticate each other before establishing a SSL connection.

Server certificates contain information about the server that allows the client to positively identify the server before sharing sensitive information. *Client certificates* contain personal information about the clients requesting access to your site that allow you to positively identify them before allowing them access to the site.

Certificates include *keys* used in establishing an SSL secure connection. A *key* is a unique value used to authenticate the server and the client in establishing an SSL connection. A *public key* and a *private key* form an SSL *key pair*. Your Web server uses this key pair to negotiate a secure connection with the user's Web browser to determine the level of encryption required for securing communications.

For more information about obtaining client certificates, see "Obtaining Client Certificates" in IIS 6.0 Help, which is accessible from IIS Manager.

You can obtain a server certificate in one of two ways: issue your own server certificate or obtain a server certificate from a certification authority.

Issue your own server certificate

To request and install your own server certificate, use the Web Server Certificate Wizard to create a customizable service for issuing and managing certificates. You can create server certificates for the Internet or for corporate intranets, giving your organization complete control over certificate management policies.

Obtain a server certificate from a certification authority

To obtain a server certificate from a certification authority, follow these steps:

1. Do either of the following:

    -   Find a certification authority that provides services that meet your business needs and request a server certificate.

    -   –Or–

    -   Use the Web Server Certificate Wizard to create a certificate request that you can send to the certification authority.

2. After the certificate is processed and returned to you, use the Web Server Certificate Wizard to install the certificate.

> ◆ **Important**
>
> To help safeguard the certificate and your private and public keys, always back them up and keep the backup copy in a safe place.

▷ **To obtain a new server certificate by using the Web Server Certificate Wizard**

1. In IIS Manager, expand the local computer, expand the **Web Sites** folder, right-click the Web site or file for which you want to obtain a certificate, and then click **Properties**.

2. Depending on the resource for which you are requesting a certificate, click the **Directory Security** or **File Security** tab.

3. Under **Secure communications**, click **Server Certificate**.

   The Web Server Certificate Wizard appears.

4. Click **Next**.

5. Accept the default option, which is **Create a new certificate**, and then click **Next**.

6. Follow the instructions in the Web Server Certificate Wizard, which guides you through the process of requesting a new server certificate.

▷ **To install a server certificate by using the Web Server Certificate Wizard**

1. In IIS Manager, expand the local computer, expand the **Web Sites** folder, right-click the Web site or file for which you want to install a certificate, and then click **Properties**.

2. Depending on the resource for which you are installing a certificate, click the **Directory Security** or **File Security** tab.

3. Under **Secure communications**, click **Server Certificate**.

   The Web Server Certificate Wizard appears.

4. Click **Next**.

5. Accept the default option, which is **Assign an existing certificate**, and then click **Next**.

   The Web Server Certificate Wizard describes this step as *assigning* a certificate to a resource (such as a file, directory, or site), not as *installing*.

6. Follow the instructions in the Web Server Certificate Wizard, which guides you through the process of installing a server certificate.

▷ **To create a backup copy of your server certificate and private key**

1. Locate the correct certificate store. This is typically the Local Computer store in Certificate Manager.

   If you do not have Certificate Manager installed in MMC, install it by following the steps outlined in the next procedure.

2. Right-click the certificate in the Personal store, point to **All Tasks**, and then click **Export**.

3. Select the **Yes, export the private key** check box.

   When you install a certificate, you can import it by marking the certificate as non-exportable. In such cases, the option to export the private key does not appear when you try to create a backup copy of the certificate, which prevents you from creating the backup.

4. Follow the wizard default settings, and enter a password for the certificate backup file when prompted.

   Do not select **Delete the private key if export is successful** check box because doing so disables your current server certificate.

5. Complete the wizard to export a backup copy of your server certificate.

If you already have Certificate Manager installed in MMC, it points to the correct Local Computer certificate store.

▷ **To add Certificate Manager to MMC**

1. From the **Start** menu, click **Run**.

2. In the **Open** box, type **mmc**, and then click **OK**. The **Microsoft Management Console** appears.

3. In the **File** menu, click **Add/Remove Snap-in**.

4. On the **Standalone** tab, click **Add**.

5. From the **Available Standalone Snap-ins** list box, click **Certificates**, and then click **Add**.

6. Click the **Computer account** option, and then click **Next**.

7. Click the **Local computer: (the computer this console is running on)** option, and then click **Finish**.

8. Click **Close**, and then click **OK**.

For more information about SSL certificates, including how to obtain, install, and back up server certificates, see "Certificates" in IIS 6.0 Help, which is accessible from IIS Manager. For more information about Microsoft Certificate Services, see "Certificate Services" in Help and Support Center for Windows Server 2003.

Controlling Access to Applications

You can control which users and computers are allowed to access your Web server and its resources. You can use both the NTFS file system and Web server security features to assign users specific permissions to directories and files. You can also use IP address restrictions to limit access by specific computers or groups of computers.

- **Securing your files with NTFS permissions.** With the NTFS file system, you can limit access to your Web server's files and directories. You can configure the file and directory permissions that set the access level assigned to a particular user account or user group. For example, you can configure your Web server to enable a specific user to view and execute a file, while excluding all other users from accessing that file.

- **Securing your Web site with Web permissions.** Web permissions, unlike NTFS permissions, apply to all users accessing your Web sites. NTFS permissions apply only to a specific user or group of users with a valid Windows account. NTFS controls access to physical directories on your server, whereas Web permissions control access to virtual directories on your Web site.

- **Restricting access to your Web site by using IP addresses.** With IP address restrictions, you can configure your Web server to assign or deny specific computers, groups of computers, or domains access to Web sites, directories, or files. For example, if your intranet server is connected to the Internet, you can prevent Internet users from accessing your Web server by assigning access only to members of your intranet, and explicitly denying access to outside users.

Securing Your Files with NTFS Permissions

You can control access to your Web site's directories and files by setting NTFS access permissions. You can use NTFS permissions to define the level of access that you want to assign to specific users, and groups of users. Correct configuration of file and directory permissions is crucial for preventing unauthorized access to your resources.

▷ **To secure a Web site by using NTFS permissions**

1. In IIS Manager, expand the local computer, right-click a Web site or file, and then click **Permissions**.

2. Do one of the following, as shown in Table A.3:

Table A.3 Options for Securing a Web Site by Using NTFS Permissions

Task	Procedure
Add a group or user that does not appear in the **Group or user names** list box.	1. Click **Add**. 2. In the **Enter the object name to select** box, type the name of the user or group, and then click **OK**.
Change or remove permissions from an existing group or user.	In the **Group or user names** list box, click the name of the group or user.

3. To allow or deny a permission, in the **Permissions for *User or Group*** list box, select the **Allow** or **Deny** check box.

Inherited Deny permissions do not prevent access to an object if the object has an explicit Allow permission entry. Explicit permissions take precedence over inherited permissions, including inherited Deny permissions.

With NTFS permissions, you also have the choice of assigning special permissions to groups or users. Special permissions are permissions on a more detailed level. For better management, assign broad-level permissions to users or groups, where it is applicable. For descriptions of permissions, see "Permissions for Files or Folders" in Help and Support Center for Windows Server 2003.

Securing Your Web Site with Web Permissions

You can also use Web permissions to help secure your Web site. When you configure your Web site's access permissions for specific sites, directories, and files, keep in mind the following:

- Web permissions are not meant to be used in place of NTFS permissions; instead, use Web permissions *with* NTFS permissions.

  Although you can use Web permissions with both the NTFS and FAT file systems, use NTFS whenever possible.

- Unlike NTFS permissions, Web permissions affect everyone who tries to access your Web site.

- Disabling permissions restricts all users. For example, disabling the Read permission restricts all users from viewing a file, regardless of the NTFS permissions applied to those users' accounts. However, enabling the Read permission can allow all users to view that file, unless NTFS permissions that restrict access have also been applied.

- If Web permissions conflict with NTFS permissions for a directory or file, the more restrictive settings are applied. For example, if you set both IIS and NTFS permissions, the permissions that explicitly deny access take precedence over permissions that grant access.

- If you want to set permissions for a WebDAV directory, keep in mind the following:

  - You must enable WebDAV before you can publish in a WebDAV directory.

  - You must turn off Anonymous access to your WebDAV directory. Protect your WebDAV directory by using one of the following authentication methods in IIS 6.0, such as Integrated Windows authentication and the discretionary access control lists (DACL) in NTFS. For more information about WebDAV security, see "Managing WebDAV Security" in IIS 6.0 Help, which is accessible from IIS Manager.

▷ **To set permissions for Web content (including WebDAV)**

1. In IIS Manager, right-click a Web site, virtual directory, or file, and then click **Properties**.

2. Depending on the permissions that you are assigning, click the **Home Directory**, **Virtual Directory**, or **File** tab.

3. Select or clear any of the following check boxes (if available):

   - **Read.** Users can view directory or file content and properties (default selection).

   - **Write.** Users can change directory or file content and properties.

   - **Script source access.** Users can access source files. If **Read** is selected, then source can be read, if **Write** is selected, then source can be written to. **Script source access** includes the source code for scripts. This option is not available if neither **Read** nor **Write** is selected.

      Important
     When you select Script source access, users might be able to view sensitive information, such as a user name and password. They might also be able to change source code that runs on your server, and significantly affect your server configuration and performance.

   - **Directory browsing.** Users can view file lists and collections.

   - **Log visits.** A log entry is created for each visit to the Web site.

   - **Index this resource.** Allows Indexing Service to index this resource. This allows searches to be performed on the resource.

4. In the **Execute Permissions** list box, select the appropriate level of script execution:

   - **None.** Do not run scripts or executables on the server.

   - **Scripts only.** Run only scripts on the server.

   - **Scripts and Executables.** Run both scripts and executables on the server.

5. Click **OK**.

Restricting Access to Your Web Site by Using IP Addresses

You can configure your Web site to grant or deny specific computers, groups of computers, or domains access to Web sites, directories, or files. For example, if your intranet server is connected to the Internet, you can prevent Internet users from accessing your Web server by assigning access only to members of your intranet, and explicitly denying access to outside users.

IP address restrictions apply only to Internet Protocol version 4 (IPv4) addresses.

▶ **To grant or deny access to a computer**

1. In IIS Manager, expand the local computer, right-click a Web site, directory, or file, and then click **Properties**.

2. Depending on the resource for which you are granting or denying access, click the **Directory Security** or **File Security** tab.

3. Under IP address and domain name restrictions, click Edit.

4. Click either **Granted access** or **Denied access**.

    If you select **Denied access**, you deny access to all computers and domains, except those to which you specifically *grant* access. If you select **Granted access**, you grant access to all computers and domains, except those to which you specifically *deny* access.

5. Click **Add**, and then click **Single computer.**

6. Click **DNS Lookup** to search for computers or domains by name, rather than by IP address.

7. Type the Domain Name System (DNS) name for the computer. IIS searches on the current domain for the computer, and if found, enters its IP address in the **IP address** box.

    The following information is important to remember when using the **DNS Lookup** feature:

    - It causes a performance decrease on your server while it is looking up DNS addresses.

    - A user accessing your Web server through a proxy server appears to have the IP address of the proxy server.

    - Some user server access problems can be corrected by entering the "*.domainname.com" syntax, rather than the "domainname.com" syntax.

8. Click **OK** three times.

► **To grant or deny access to a domain**

1. In IIS Manager, expand the local computer, right-click a Web site, directory, or file, and click **Properties**.

2. Depending on the resource for which you are granting or denying access, click the **Directory Security** or **File Security** tab.

3. Under **IP address and domain name restrictions**, click **Edit**.

4. Do one of the following:

   ▪ Click **Granted access**. When you select **Granted access**, you grant access to all computers and domains, except to those that you specifically deny access.

   ▪ –or–

   ▪ Click **Denied access.** When you select **Denied access**, you deny access to all computers and domains, except to those that you specifically grant access.

5. Click **Add**.

6. Click **Domain name**.

7. In the **Domain name** box, type the domain name.

8. Click **OK** three times.

For more information about granting or denying access to computers or to groups of computers, see "Securing Sites with IP Address Restrictions" in IIS 6.0 Help, which is accessible from IIS Manager.

Tasks for Managing Servers and Applications

Use the following tasks to manage your servers and applications:

▪ **Using host header names to host multiple Web sites.** Create and host multiple Web sites.

▪ **Redirecting Web sites.** Automatically direct users to the correct page on your site.

▪ **Assigning resources to applications.** Control the amount of resources an application uses.

Using Host Header Names to Host Multiple Web Sites

IIS supports multiple Web sites on a single server. To create and host multiple Web sites, you must configure a unique identity for each site on the server. To assign a unique identity, distinguish each Web site with at least one of three unique identifiers: a host header name, an IP address, or a TCP port number.

One method for providing each site with a unique identifier is to use IIS Manager to assign multiple host header names. Browsers must comply with HTTP 1.1 to support the use of host header names. Microsoft® Internet Explorer 3.0, Netscape Navigator 2.0, and later versions of both browsers support host header names.

 Important

Avoid assigning a host header name to the Default Web Site; instead, use an IP address of All Unassigned, a TCP port of 80, and no host header name.

Table A.4 briefly describes and compares the three ways that you can uniquely identify your Web sites.

Table A.4   Ways You Can Uniquely Identify Multiple Web Sites

Web Site Identifier	Description
Host header name	Recommended for most situations. Requires that your computer or network use a name resolution system. Organizations typically use DNS name resolution.
Unique IP Address	Used primarily for Internet services that host SSL on the local server. Typically, only large corporations and Internet service providers (ISPs) obtain and maintain multiple IP addresses.
Nonstandard TCP port number	Generally not recommended. Can be used for private Web site development and testing purposes but rarely used on production Web servers because users must add the port to the URL and the port must be opened on the firewall.

Choose one method of uniquely identifying Web sites for each server. Using one method for each server improves performance by optimizing cache and routing lookups. Conversely, using any combination of host headers, unique IP addresses, or non-standard port numbers to identify multiple Web sites degrades the performance of all Web sites on the server.

If you use host header names to identify a new Web site, select a unique name as follows:

- **On the Internet.** The host header must be a publicly available DNS name, such as support.microsoft.com. Register a public DNS name with an authorized Internet name authority. For more information about using DNS names to identify your site, see "Domain Name Resolution" in IIS 6.0 Help, which is accessible from IIS Manager.

- **On a private network.** The host header can be an intranet site name. To resolve host names to an IP address, register the host header name with your intranet's DNS administrator. Alternatively, you can resolve host names to an IP address by using a locally stored database file called the Hosts file, which is located in the *systemroot*\System32\Drivers\Etc folder. The following is an example of the contents of a Hosts file:

```
#
Table of IP addresses and host names
#
IP Address     TCP Port   Host Header Name
#
192.168.0.100    80        www.example1.com
192.168.0.100    80        example1.com
```

Use Windows Explorer to create a home directory for your Web site content. Create subdirectories to store HTML pages, image files, and other content as needed. To organize home directories for multiple Web sites on the same server, you can create a top-level directory for storing all home directories, and then create subdirectories for each site.

 Important

You must be a member of the Administrators group on the local computer to perform the following procedure or procedures, or you must have been delegated the appropriate authority. As a security best practice, log on to your computer by using an account that is not in the Administrators group, and then use the **runas** command to run IIS Manager as an administrator. At a command prompt, type runas / *User.Administrative_AccountName* "mmc %systemroot%\system32\inetsrv\iis.msc".

▷ **To assign multiple host header names to a single Web site**

1. In IIS Manager, expand the local computer, click the **Web Sites** folder, right-click the Web site for which you want to assign a host header name, and then click **Properties.**

2. Click the **Web Site** tab.

3. In the **IP Address** list, select the IP address that you want assigned to this Web site.

4. Click **Advanced**.

5. Under **Multiple identities for this Web Site**, select the IP address, and then click **Edit.**

6. In the **Host Header Value** box, type the host header name (for example, www.example1.com).

7. Click **OK** twice.

For more information about using host header names to host multiple Web sites, see "Hosting Multiple Web Sites on a Single Server" in IIS 6.0 Help, which is accessible from IIS Manager. Also see article 324287, "Use Host Header Names to Configure Multiple Web Sites in Internet Information Services 6.0" in the Microsoft Knowledge Base. To find this article, see the Microsoft Knowledge Base link on the Web Resources page at http://www.microsoft.com/windows/reskits/webresources.

Redirecting Web Sites

When a browser requests a page or program on your Web site, the Web server locates the page identified by the URL and returns it to the browser. When you move a page on your Web site, you cannot always correct all the links that refer to the old URL. To make sure that browsers can find the page at the new URL, you can instruct the Web server to *redirect* the browser to the new URL.

You can redirect requests for files in one directory to a different directory, to a different Web site, or to another file in a different directory. When the browser requests the file at the original URL, the Web server instructs the browser to go to the new URL.

▶ **To redirect requests to another Web site or directory**

1. In IIS Manager, expand the local computer, right-click the Web site or directory you want to redirect, and click **Properties**.

2. Depending on the resource you want to redirect, click the **Home Directory**, **Virtual Directory**, or **Directory** tab.

3. Under **The content for this source should come from**, click **A redirection to a URL.**

4. In the **Redirect to** box, type the URL of the destination directory or Web site.

    For example, to redirect all requests for files in the Catalog directory to the NewCatalog directory, type **/NewCatalog**.

▶ **To redirect all requests to a single file**

1. In IIS Manager, expand the local computer, right-click the Web site or directory you want to redirect, and then click **Properties**.

2. Click the **Home Directory**, **Virtual Directory**, or **Directory** tab.

3. Under **The content for this source should come from**, click **A redirection to a URL**.

4. In the **Redirect to** box, type the URL of the destination file.

5. Select **The exact URL entered above** check box to prevent the Web server from appending the original file name to the destination URL.

You can use wildcards and redirect variables in the destination URL to precisely control how the original URL is translated into the destination URL.

You can also use the redirect method to redirect all requests for files in a particular directory to a program. Generally, you need to pass any parameters from the original URL to the program, which you can do by using redirect variables.

▷   **To redirect requests to a program**

1.   In IIS Manager, expand the local computer, right-click the Web site or directory that you want to redirect, and then click **Properties**.

2.   Depending on the resource you want to redirect, click the **Home Directory**, **Virtual Directory**, or **Directory** tab.

3.   Under **The content for this source should come from**, click **A redirection to a URL**.

4.   In the **Redirect to** box, type the URL of the program, including any redirect variables needed to pass parameters to the program.

   For example, to redirect all requests for scripts in a Scripts directory to a logging program that records the requested URL and any parameters passed with the URL, type:

   ```
   /Scripts/Logger.exe?URL=$V+PARAMS=$P
   ```

   where **$V** and **$P** are redirect variables.

5.   Select **The exact URL entered above** check box to prevent the Web server from appending the original file name to the destination URL.

For more information about redirect variables, see "Redirect Reference" and "Redirecting Requests to Files, Directories, or Programs" in IIS 6.0 Help, which is accessible from IIS Manager.

Assigning Resources to Applications

There are several ways to assign, or limit, the amount of resources an application can use. You can use application property sheets to control performance, cache, and process options of individual applications, or you can use *bandwidth throttling* to limit resources for an entire site or application pool. A third alternative is to control access to your application through the NTFS file system and Web server security features.

▷   **To assign resources by using property sheets**

1.   In IIS Manager, expand the local computer, right-click the Web site or root directory of an application, and then click **Properties**.

2.   Depending on the location of the application, click the **Home Directory**, **Virtual Directory**, or **Directory** tab.

3.   In the **Application settings** section, click **Configuration**.

4.   On the **Mappings** and **Options** tabs, select the appropriate check boxes to enable or disable caching, session states, buffering, and side-by-side assemblies.

▶ **To globally assign resources by using bandwidth throttling**

1. In IIS Manager, expand the local computer, right-click the **Web Sites** folder, and then click **Properties**.

2. Click the **Performance** tab.

3. Under **Bandwidth throttling**, select the **Limit the total network bandwidth available for all Web sites on this server** check box.

4. In the **Maximum bandwidth** box, type or click the up and down arrows to set the maximum number of kilobytes per second that you want each site contained in the directory to use.

5. Under **Web site connections**, click either **Unlimited** or **Connections limited to**. If you select **Connections limited to**, type or click the up and down arrows to set the maximum number of kilobytes per second that you want each site contained in the directory to use.

▶ **To assign resources to an individual Web site by using bandwidth throttling**

1. In IIS Manager, expand the local computer, expand the **Web Sites** folder, right-click the Web site to which you want to assign resources, and then click **Properties**.

2. Click the **Performance** tab.

3. Under **Bandwidth throttling**, select the **Limit the network bandwidth available to this Web site** check box.

4. In the **Maximum bandwidth** box, type or click the up and down arrows to set the maximum number of kilobytes per second you want each site contained in the directory to use.

5. Under **Web site connections**, select either **Unlimited** or **Connections limited to**. If you select **Connections limited to**, type or click the up and down arrows to set the maximum number of Web site connections.

Bandwidth throttling is not supported on Internet Protocol Version 6 (IPv6) Web sites. For more information about bandwidth throttling, see "Throttling Bandwidth" in IIS 6.0 Help, which is accessible from IIS Manager.

Tasks for Administering Servers

IIS 6.0 and Windows Server 2003 provide several tools to help you administer your servers. This section provides task-based information about the following:

- **Administering servers from the command line.** Use the following powerful scripting and programming tools to access and configure settings:

  - **Supported command-line scripts.** Supplied scripts for the IIS Windows Management Instrumentation (WMI) provider to manage and set IIS metabase configurations.

  - **Adsutil.vbs IIS administration utility.** Uses VBScript and Active Directory Service Interfaces (ADSI) as a learning tool to manipulate the IIS configuration.

- **Administering servers remotely.** Use the following tools to remotely administer your sites:

  - **IIS Manager.** Remotely connect to and administer an intranet server.

  - **Terminal Services.** After you use Terminal Services to connect to the server that is running IIS, you can use IIS Manager on the Web server as if you were logged on locally.

  - **Remote Administration (HTML) tool.** Administer your IIS Web server from Web browsers on your intranet.

  - **Supported command-line scripts.** Use with the IIS WMI provider to remotely manage an IIS machine. Each command-line script supports the **/s** parameter, which you can use to specify the remote server against which you want to perform the command.

Administering Servers from the Command Line

IIS provides powerful scripting and programming tools that you can use to access and configure settings from within a command-line script or compiled application. You can use these tools to create, delete, start, stop, pause, and list various sites and applications, as well as to copy, import, and export configurations.

 Important

You must be a member of the Administrators group on the local computer to run scripts and executables, or you must have been delegated the appropriate authority. As a security best practice, log on to your computer by using an account that is not in the Administrators group, and then use the **runas** command to run your script or executable as an administrator. At a command prompt, type **runas /profile** */User:MyMachine\Administrator* **cmd** to open a command window with administrator rights and then type **cscript.exe** *ScriptName* (including the full path with parameters, if any).

IIS provides the following command-line tools:

- **Supported command-line scripts.** Use the supplied scripts for the IIS WMI provider to manage and set IIS metabase configurations.

- **Adsutil.vbs IIS administration utility.** Uses Microsoft® Visual Basic® Scripting Edition (VBScript) with ADSI to manipulate the IIS configuration.

Supported Command-Line Scripts

IIS 6.0 includes supported scripts that you can find in the *systemroot*\System32 directory. These VBScript scripts use the IIS WMI provider to manage configuration settings in the IIS metabase.

When you use these scripts to create a new site or virtual directory, you can specify the basic properties that are needed to create the site or directory and identify its contents. The scripts apply the same default properties that IIS Manager uses to create new sites or virtual directories, and they adhere to the same rules for inheriting properties.

To configure more advanced properties for a site or virtual directory, use IIS Manager. Alternatively, you can build an XML template that contains the properties you want to apply to a new Web site or virtual directory and then use the Iiscnfg.vbs script to apply this template to any Web site or virtual directory in the IIS metabase.

The computer that runs the command must be running Microsoft® Windows® XP Professional or Windows Server 2003. The computer that the command affects must be running Windows Server 2003 with IIS 6.0. You cannot use these scripts to manage IIS 6.0 on clients running Windows XP Professional because Windows XP runs with IIS 5.1.

Table A.5 lists the supported command-line scripts for IIS 6.0.

Table A.5 Supported Command-Line Scripts for IIS 6.0

Script	For These Areas	Tasks	IIS Help Topics
Iisweb.vbs	Web sites	Create, delete, start, stop, pause, and query or list Web sites.	"Managing Web Sites"
Iisftp.vbs	FTP sites	Create, delete, start, stop, pause, and query or list FTP sites. Query and set Active Directory properties for a user's FTP home directory (use in FTP user isolation).	"Managing FTP Sites" "Setting Active Directory User Isolation"
Iisvdir.vbs	Web virtual directories	Create, delete, or list the Web virtual directories of a given root.	"Managing Web Virtual Directories"
Iisftpdr.vbs	FTP virtual directories	Create, delete, or list the FTP virtual directories of a given root.	"Managing FTP Virtual Directories"
Iisback.vbs	Back up and restore IIS configuration	Create, delete, restore, and list backup copies of IIS configuration.	"Managing IIS Configurations"
Iiscnfg.vbs	Export or import IIS configuration	Export or import an IIS configuration to or from an XML file; copy the metabase and schema to another computer; and save configuration changes to disk.	"Managing IIS Configurations"
Iisext.vbs	Applications and dynamic content services	Configure and manage applications, Web service extensions (like ASP and ASP.NET), and individual files.	"Managing Applications and Web Service Extensions"
Iisapp.vbs	Application pools and their worker processes	List the worker processes (W3wp.exe) currently running and the application pool each one serves.	"Listing Running Web Applications"

Adsutil.vbs IIS Administration Utility

Adsutil.vbs is an IIS administration utility that uses VBScript with ADSI to manipulate the IIS configuration and modify the metabase. You must run this script by using CScript, which is installed with Windows Script Host.

Adsutil.vbs is a flexible and generic command-line tool. Because Adsutil.vbs is not supported (its documentation and format can change at any time), use Adsutil.vbs primarily as a learning tool.

For more information about how to use Adsutil.vbs, including Adsutil.vbs syntax, parameters, commands and examples, see "IIS 6.0 Administration Scripts, Tips, and Tricks" in this book.

Administering Servers Remotely

When you run IIS on an intranet or the Internet, you can administer your server remotely by using the following tools:

- **IIS Manager.** Use on your server to remotely connect to and administer an intranet server running IIS 5.*x* or IIS 6.0.

- **Terminal Services.** Does not require you to install IIS Manager on the remote client computer because, after you are connected to the server that is running IIS, you can use IIS Manager on the Web server as if you are logged on locally.

- **Remote Administration (HTML) tool.** Use to administer your IIS Web server from any Web browser on your intranet. This version of the tool runs only on servers running IIS 6.0.

- **Supported command-line scripts.** Use the IIS-supported command-line scripts with the IIS WMI provider to remotely manage a server running IIS. Each command-line script supports the **/s** parameter, which you can use to specify the remote server against which you want to perform the command.

 Important

You must be a member of the Administrators group on the local computer to perform the following procedure or procedures, or you must have been delegated the appropriate authority. As a security best practice, log on to your computer by using an account that is not in the Administrators group, and then use the **runas** command to run IIS Manager as an administrator. At a command prompt, type **runas** /*User:Administrative_AccountName* "mmc %systemroot%\system32\inetsrv\iis.msc".

▶ **To administer your intranet server remotely by using IIS Manager**

1. In IIS Manager, right-click the local computer, and then click **Connect**.

2. In the **Computer name** box, type or browse to the computer you want to connect to.

3. Click **OK**.

If you do not have TCP/IP and a name resolution server, such as Windows Internet Name Service (WINS) installed, you might not be able to connect to a server running IIS by using the computer name. As an alternative, you can use the IP address of the server running IIS. For more information about IP addresses and name resolution, see "Name resolution for TCP/IP" .in Help and Support Center for Windows Server 2003.

▶ **To administer your intranet server remotely by using Terminal Services**

1. Install the Terminal Services client on the local computer.

2. While the remote computer is running, start Terminal Services and identify the name of the remote computer.

3. From the **Terminal Services** window, administer IIS as you do locally.

   You can start IIS Manager on any network computer that is running Windows. You can also run scripts from the Terminal Services window.

▶ **To enable the Remote Administration (HTML) tool through Control Panel**

1. From the **Start** menu, click **Control Panel**.

2. Double-click **Add or Remove Programs**.

3. In the left pane, click **Add/Remove Windows Components**.

4. Click **Application Server**, and then click **Details**.

5. Click **Internet Information Services (IIS)**, and then click **Details**.

6. Click **World Wide Web Publishing Service**, and then click **Details**.

7. Select the **Remote Administration (HTML)** check box, and click **OK**.

8. Click **OK** two more times, click **Next**, and then click **Finish** to complete the Windows Components Wizard.

▶ **To view the Remote Administration (HTML) tool from IIS Manager**

- Expand the local computer, expand the **Web Sites** folder, right-click the **Administration** Web site, and then click **Browse**.

▶ **To administer an IIS Web server by using the Remote Administration (HTML) tool**

- Open your intranet site from a Web browser and type the following in the address bar: **http://*HostName*: 8098**

  In this procedure, *HostName* is the name of the computer that you want to connect to and administer.

For more information about remotely managing servers by using this tool, from the **Help** menu in the Remote Administration (HTML) tool, click **Help Topics**.

Unattended Setup

Internet Information Services (IIS) 6.0 is not installed by default when you install the Microsoft® Windows® Server 2003 operating system. To simplify the setup process on multiple computers, you can set up IIS 6.0 while the server is unattended. To do so, you can either create and use an answer file to install IIS 6.0 at the same time that you install Windows Server 2003, or you can perform an unattended installation of IIS 6.0 after you install Windows Server 2003.

In This Appendix

Related Resources

- For information about common tasks you can do in IIS 6.0, see "Common Administrative Tasks" in this book.

- For information about configuring Web, File Transfer Protocol (FTP), Network News Transfer Protocol (NNTP), and Simple Mail Transfer Protocol (SMTP) sites and services, see "Configuring Internet Sites and Services" in this book.

Creating an Answer File

To set up unattended installation for IIS 6.0, you must create an answer file containing parameters with appropriate settings, depending on how you want to customize your installation of IIS. You have two options for unattended installation of IIS 6.0:

- Install and set up IIS 6.0 at the same time that you install the Windows Server 2003 operating system.

- Install IIS 6.0 after the Windows Server 2003 operating system has been installed.

If you install IIS 6.0 simultaneously with the operating system, you need to create a complete answer file and include a [Components] section, as well as an optional [InternetServer] section that contains IIS–related parameters. Use the Winnt32.exe command-line utility to run your answer file. For more information about using Winnt32.exe, see "Installing IIS 6.0 with the Operating System" later in this appendix. For more information about creating and using a Windows unattended setup answer file, see "Planning for Unattended Setup" in Help and Support Center for Microsoft Windows Server 2003.

If you install IIS 6.0 after the Windows Server 2003 operating system has been installed, you can create an answer file containing only the [Components] and optional [InternetServer] sections. Use the Sysocmgr.exe command-line utility to run this answer file. For more information about using Sysocmgr.exe, see "Installing IIS 6.0 After the Operating System" later in this appendix.

Table B.1 lists the unattended installation parameters for IIS that you include in the [Components] section of the answer file. The default setting for all of the following parameters is **off** unless a component is required by some other component that you are installing. For example, if you are installing the World Wide Web Publishing Service (WWW service), then Common Files, IIS Manager, and network COM+ access are turned on by default.

Table B.1   IIS Unattended Installation Parameters

Parameter	Description
aspnet = on/off	Enable ASP.NET .
complusnetwork = on/off	Enable network COM+ access.
dtcnetwork = on/off	Enable network Distributed Transaction Coordinator (DTC) network access.
bitsserverextensionsisapi = on/off	Enable the BITS Server Extensions ISAPI.
bitsserverextensionsmanager = on/off	Enable the BITS Server Extensions snap-in.
iis_common = on/off	Enable Common Files.
iis_ftp = on/off	Enable the File Transfer Protocol (FTP) service.
fp_extensions = on/off	Enable FrontPage® 2002 Server Extensions from Microsoft.
iis_inetmer = on/off	Enable IIS Manager.
iis_nntp = on/off	Enable the Network News Transfer Protocol (NNTP) service.
iis_smtp = on/off	Enable the Simple Mail Transfer Protocol (SMTP) service.
iis_asp = on/off	Enable Active Server Pages (ASP).
iis_internetdataconnector = on/off	Enable Internet Data Connector (IDC).
sakit_web = on/off	Enable Remote Administration (HTML). You cannot perform an unattended installation of this feature simultaneously with performing an unattended installation of the operating system. You can perform an unattended installation of this feature if you install IIS after you have installed the operating system by using the Sysocmgr.exe command-line utility. This feature is not available on Itanium-based computers running Windows XP 64-Bit Edition; the 64-bit version of Windows Server 2003, Enterprise Edition; or the 64-bit version of Windows Server 2003, Datacenter Edition.
tswebclient = on/off	Enable remote desktop Web connection.
iis_serversideincludes = on/off	Enable server-side includes (SSI).
iis_webdav = on/off	Enable WebDAV publishing.
iis_www = on/off	Enable the WWW service.
appsrv_console = on/off	Enable Application Server Console. This feature is not available on Itanium-based computers running Windows XP 64-Bit Edition.

Table B.2 lists the optional IIS unattended installation parameters. You include these parameters in the [InternetServer] section.

Table B.2 Optional IIS Unattended Installation Parameters

Parameter	Description
SvcManualStart = www and/or ftp	If WWW or FTP is present, those services will be set to manual start. If you specify both **www** and **ftp**, separate them with a comma (,). When installed, the default service state is to automatically start.
PathFTPRoot = path to FTProot	Alternative path to which the FTP service is installed. The default is *systemroot*\Inetpub\Ftproot.
PathWWWRoot = path to WWWroot	Alternative path to which the WWW service is installed. The default is *systemroot*\Inetpub\Wwwroot.
ApplicationDependency = *ApplicationName, GroupID, GroupID*	Adds application and dependencies. For example: ApplicationDependency = CommerceServer, ASP, IndexingService ApplicationDependency = ExchangeServer, ASP60 ApplicationDependency = MyApp, ASP.NET v1.1.4322 This example makes Commerce Server dependent on ASP and the Indexing Service, Exchange Server dependent on ASP, and MyApp dependent on ASP.NET v1.1.4322.
ExtensionFile = <*Enabled Flag*>,<*File Path*>[,<*UI Deletable Flag*> [,<*Group ID*> [,<*Description*>]]]	Specifies an extension file. The *UI Deletable Flag, Group ID*, and *Description* settings are all optional. However, if you specify any of the optional settings, you must include all of the previous settings. The parameters represent the following: *Enabled Flag* is set to **0** (zero) for disabled and **1** for enabled. *File Path* is the path to the file, and it can contain environment variables. *UI Deletable Flag* specifies whether the item can be deleted using IIS Manager. Set to **0** for not deletable and **1** for deletable. *Group ID* allows you to group different dynamic-link libraries (DLLs) and Common Gateway Interfaces (CGIs) and have dependencies for the applications. *Description* is the description of the extension file. For example: ExtensionFile = 1, windir\MyISAPIS\Myisapi.dll, 1, MyGroup, My Custom ISAPI –Or– ExtensionFile = 1, windir\MyCGIs\Mycgi.cgi, 1, MyGroup, My Custom CGI

(continued)

Table B.2   Optional IIS Unattended Installation Parameters *(continued)*

Parameter	Description
DisableWebServiceOnUpgrade = True/False	The default for this parameter is **True** for upgrades from the Microsoft® Windows® 2000 Server operating system, unless you have run the IIS Lockdown Tool or added the registry entry **RetainW3SVCStatus** to the registry. Please see Caution below.
	For more information about when the WWW service is disabled after an upgrade has been performed, see "Upgrading an IIS Server to IIS 6.0" in *Deploying Internet Information Services (IIS) 6.0* of the *Microsoft® Windows® Server 2003 Deployment Kit* (or see "Upgrading an IIS Server to IIS 6.0" on the Web at http://www.microsoft.com/reskit).

Caution

Do not edit the registry unless you have no alternative. The registry editor bypasses standard safeguards, allowing settings that can damage your system, or even require you to reinstall Windows. If you must edit the registry, back it up first and see the Registry Reference on the *Microsoft Windows Server 2003 Deployment Kit* companion CD or on the Web at http://www.microsoft.com/reskit.

Installing IIS 6.0 with the Operating System

Use the Winnt32.exe command-line utility to install IIS 6.0 by using an unattended answer file that includes a [Components] section with the unattended setup parameters listed in Table B.1 and — optionally — an [InternetServer] section with the parameters listed in Table B.2.

Important

You must be a member of the Administrators group on the local computer to run scripts and executables, or you must have been delegated the appropriate authority. As a security best practice, log on to your computer by using an account that is not in the Administrators group, and then use the **runas** command to run your script or executable as an administrator. At a command prompt, type **runas /profile** */User:MyMachine\Administrator* **cmd** to open a command window with administrator rights and then type **cscript.exe** *ScriptName* (including the full path with parameters, if any).

▷ **To use the Winnt32.exe command-line utility**

- At a command prompt, type:

  winnt32 /unattend:<*AnsweFile*> **/s:**<*InstallSource*>

  where <*AnswerFile*> is a file that contains answers to questions that should be automated during installation, and <*InstallSource*> is the location of the Windows 2000 installation files.

▷ **To use an x86-based computer to view the command options available for Winnt32.exe**

1. On a computer running Microsoft® Windows® 95, Windows® 98, Windows® Millennium Edition, Microsoft® Windows NT®, Windows 2000, Windows XP, or Windows Server 2003 operating systems, insert the Setup CD for Windows Server 2003 in the CD-ROM drive.

2. On the **Start** menu, click **Run**.

3. In the **Open** box, type

   cmd

   and then click **OK**.

4. At the command prompt, change to the CD-ROM drive, change to the I386 directory, type

   winnt32 /?

   and then press ENTER.

▷ **To use an Itanium-based computer to view the command options available for Winnt32.exe**

1. On an Itanium-based computer running Windows XP 64-Bit Edition; the 64-bit version of Windows Server 2003, Enterprise Edition; or the 64-bit version of Windows Server 2003, Datacenter Edition, insert the Setup CD for the 64-bit version of the product into the CD-ROM drive.

2. On the **Start** menu, click **Run**.

3. In the **Open** box, type

   cmd

   and then click **OK**.

4. At the command prompt, change to the CD-ROM drive, change to the IA64 directory, type

   winnt32 /?

   and then press ENTER.

Installing IIS 6.0 After the Operating System

To install IIS by using scripts after you have installed and set up Windows Server 2003, use the Sysocmgr.exe command-line utility with an unattended answer file that includes a [Components] section with the unattended setup parameters listed in Table B.1 and, optionally, an [InternetServer] section with the parameters listed in Table B.2.

> **Important**
>
> You must be a member of the Administrators group on the local computer to run scripts and executables, or you must have been delegated the appropriate authority. As a security best practice, log on to your computer by using an account that is not in the Administrators group, and then use the **runas** command to run your script or executable as an administrator. At a command prompt, type **runas /profile** /*User:MyMachine\Administrator* cmd to open a command window with administrator rights and then type **cscript.exe** *ScriptName* (including the full path with parameters, if any).

▶ **To install IIS 6.0 by using scripts after the operating system has been installed**

1. On the **Start** menu, click **Run**.

2. In the **Open** box, type

   cmd

   and then click **OK**.

3. At the command prompt, type

   Sysocmgr.exe /i:sysoc.inf /u:%*PathToUnattendFile***%**

   and then press ENTER.

4. At the command prompt, type

   Sysocmgr.exe/?

   and then press ENTER to view Sysocmgr.exe Help.

Using FrontPage 2002 Server Extensions with IIS 6.0

FrontPage® 2002 Server Extensions from Microsoft® is a technology that works with Internet Information Services (IIS) to support administering, authoring, and browsing Web sites. FrontPage Server Extensions provides you with tools for managing site security, organizing your content into subwebs, and checking site usage. Users who are running the FrontPage client can create and manage professional-looking Web pages for corporate Internet or intranet sites.

In This Appendix

Related Information

- For information about configuring sites on IIS 6.0, see "Configuring Internet Sites and Services" in this book.

Overview of FrontPage 2002 Server Extensions

FrontPage 2002 Server Extensions is a set of server-side applications that extend the functionality of a Web server and support authoring in Microsoft FrontPage. FrontPage 2002 Server Extensions enables you and your customers to use advanced features without writing complex *server-side* programs, which are applications and programs that run on the Web server rather than on the client computer. Using this technology allows you to deploy content over HTTP without requiring a virtual private network (VPN) or an unsecured method, such as File Transfer Protocol (FTP).

FrontPage 2002 Server Extensions includes new features, such as roles and user rights, and server health monitoring.

A FrontPage client (a computer that is running FrontPage) communicates with a Web server by using WinSock and TCP/IP and with the server extensions by using HTTP. FrontPage implements a remote procedure call mechanism on top of the HTTP POST request, so that the FrontPage client can request documents, add new authors, and so on.

A Web server with FrontPage 2002 Server Extensions recognizes POST requests addressed to the server extension's Internet Server API (ISAPI) or Common Gateway Interface (CGI) applications and directs those requests accordingly. FrontPage can communicate between clients and servers even through proxy servers (firewalls).

Why Use FrontPage 2002 Server Extensions?

When you use FrontPage 2002 Server Extensions on your Web server, you can divide Web content on a single server into multiple content areas, called *subwebs*, each with its own set of authors and users. In addition, if you build and maintain Web sites for customers and you coordinate with multiple authors, the features included with FrontPage 2002 Server Extensions can help you do the following:

- Host Web sites that are created by using FrontPage-based Web authoring.

- Manage Web sites either on the local server or remotely by using HTML administration pages or a command-line interface.

- Grant authoring, browsing, site management, or other user rights to authenticated users.

- Create, delete, and rename FrontPage-extended subwebs.

- Analyze site usage to find out who is viewing the site and how often.

When you install FrontPage 2002 Server Extensions on your Web server, your users can do the following:

- Create Web pages and subwebs directly on your Web server.

- Enhance their sites with FrontPage components, such as hit counters, link bars, form handlers, full-text searches, and top 10 lists.

- Publish content directly to your Web servers by means of the Internet.

- Collaborate with other users on the same Web site and check files in and out of a FrontPage-extended subweb.

- Save directly to a Web server when using Microsoft Office programs.

- Use search functionality that provides a full-text index.

  For more information about the search capabilities of FrontPage 2002 Server Extensions, see article 820896, "Using Index Server in Scaleable Mode on Windows Server 2003" in the Microsoft Knowledge Base. To find this article, see the Microsoft Knowledge Base link on the Web Resources pageat www.microsoft.com/windows/reskits/webresources.

For more information about how you can use FrontPage 2002 Server Extensions in your organization, see the FrontPage 2002 Server Ext Support Center link on theWeb Resources page at http://www.microsoft.com/windows/reskits/webresources.

FrontPage Server Extensions Terminology

FrontPage 2002 Server Extensions uses the term *virtual server* to describe what IIS documentation typically calls an extended Web site. In this appendix, the term *extended Web site,* rather than the term *virtual server,* is used to describe a Web site that is extended with FrontPage Server Extensions. However, where using IIS terminology might be confusing, such as when documenting procedures that use the FrontPage 2002 Server Extensions user interface, this appendix refers to an extended Web site as a virtual server. Just remember that an IIS extended Web site is the same as a FrontPage 2002 Server Extensions virtual server.

A FrontPage-extended Web site is also known as the *rootweb* because it is the top-level content directory of one or more subwebs. Hence, if you are using FrontPage terminology, every virtual server contains a rootweb, which can have many levels of subdirectories and subwebs that contain its content.

When you extend a Web site with FrontPage 2002 Server Extensions, each extended Web site can have multiple subwebs. A *subweb* is a subdirectory of the rootweb or of another subweb. Subwebs are the FrontPage mechanism for breaking up a Web site so that different areas can be owned and maintained by different people or groups. Each subweb can have many levels of subdirectories.

Several extended Web sites, or rootwebs, can reside on one server. Each extended Web site has its own name and can be accessed through its domain name, IP address, or host header. For more information about using host headers, see "Common Administrative Tasks" in this book.

Preparing to Extend Web Sites

FrontPage 2002 Server Extensions provides Web-based and command-line administration for extending Web sites, which enables site owners to author Web sites in FrontPage and delegate site ownership and administration credentials. *Extending* a Web site means enabling FrontPage 2002 Server Extensions features to augment how you manage the content development and security of your sites. Extending a Web site can add an additional level of security management to a Web site and enable a FrontPage client to open the site and author it in FrontPage.

Before you can extend a Web site by using server extensions, you need to install and enable FrontPage 2002 Server Extensions.

Installing and Enabling FrontPage Server Extensions

By default, IIS 6.0 is installed in a *locked* mode that serves only static HTTP content, thus protecting your systems from malicious users and attackers. When your server receives a default installation, the request handlers that process dynamic content are disabled, which means that features like FrontPage Server Extensions and ASP.NET do not work.

If you use the Configure Your Server Wizard to install IIS 6.0, you can elect to install and enable FrontPage Server Extensions at the time you configure your server role. If you do not install FrontPage Server Extensions at that time, you can add them to your application server at a later time.

IIS 6.0 Application Isolation Modes

An IIS 6.0 Web server always runs in one of two mutually exclusive *application isolation modes*. When you install FrontPage 2002 Server Extensions on an IIS 6.0 Web server, the server extensions run in the application isolation mode that you have chosen to run on the server. The application isolation mode you choose depends on what mode best fits your needs, and you can change the isolation mode after installation. At the time you install IIS 6.0, a default application isolation mode is assigned as follows:

- For clean installations, *worker process isolation* mode is the default mode.

- For upgrade installations, *IIS 5.0 isolation mode* is the default mode.

For more information about choosing an IIS 6.0 isolation mode, see "Running IIS 6.0 as an Application Server" in this book.

Installing FrontPage 2002 Server Extensions

Before you install FrontPage 2002 Server Extensions, consider the following guidelines:

- You must run FrontPage 2002 Server Extensions on a computer that uses only the NTFS file system.

  Before you install FrontPage 2002 Server Extensions on an application server, verify that all disk volumes on the computer are formatted with the NTFS file system. Windows provides a conversion utility (Convert.exe) that you can use to convert an existing file allocation table (FAT) or FAT32 volume to NTFS without losing data. If you try to install FrontPage 2002 Server Extensions to a disk drive that is formatted with FAT, your default Web site is not extended.

  For more information about converting FAT or FAT32 volumes to NTFS, see "Reformatting or converting a partition to use NTFS" in Help and Support Center for Windows Server 2003.

- If you upgrade from an earlier version of FrontPage Server Extensions, you must manually upgrade each FrontPage-extended Web site.

  If you are running multiple extended Web sites and you upgrade from FrontPage 2000 Server Extensions running on the Microsoft® Windows® 2000 Server operating system to FrontPage 2002 Server Extensions running on Microsoft® Windows® Server 2003, Standard Edition; Microsoft® Windows® Server 2003, Enterprise Edition; Microsoft Windows Server 2003, Web Edition; or Microsoft® Windows® Server 2003, Datacenter Edition operating system, you must manually upgrade each FrontPage-extended Web site. If you have a single FrontPage-extended Web site and you upgrade to FrontPage 2002 Server Extensions running on Windows Server 2003, the extended Web site automatically upgrades to FrontPage 2002 Server Extensions.

If you have a Web server that runs on Windows Server 2003 and that has multiple extended Web sites, you must upgrade all your extended Web sites to FrontPage 2002 Server Extensions.

 Note

In FrontPage 2002 Server Extensions, the lightweight server extensions option is no longer supported. When you upgrade an extended Web site to FrontPage 2002 Server Extensions, it receives a full (not a lightweight) implementation.

For more information about upgrading your FrontPage-extended Web sites, see "Installation" in the SharePoint Team Services Administrator's Guide link on the Web Resources page at http://www.microsoft.com/windows/reskits/webresources.

▶   **To install and enable FrontPage 2002 Server Extensions**

1. From the **Start** menu, click **Control Panel**.

2. Double-click **Add or Remove Programs.**

3. Click **Add/Remove Windows Components**.

4. In the Windows Components Wizard, double-click **Application Server**, double-click **Internet Information Services**, and then select the **FrontPage 2002 Server Extensions** check box.

5. Click **OK** twice, click **Next**, and then click **Finish**.

For more information about installing and setting up FrontPage 2002 Server Extensions, including sample scripts to automate installation, see "IIS 6.0 Administration Scripts, Tips, and Tricks" in this book.

Enabling Web Service Extensions

If you have FrontPage 2002 Server Extensions installed on your Web server but they do not work, check that you have them enabled.

To enable Web service extensions

1. In IIS Manager, click the **Web Service Extensions** folder.

2. In the details pane, select the Web service extension that you want to enable, and then click **Allow**.

3. To see the properties of a Web service extension, select an extension, and then click **Properties**.

For more information about enabling dynamic content, such as FrontPage Server Extensions, see "Enabling and Disabling Dynamic Content" in IIS 6.0 Help.

Creating Web Sites to Extend as Virtual Servers

Before you can use FrontPage 2002 Server Extensions with your Web sites, you must create one or more IIS Web sites to contain them. By default, IIS provides a working Web site called *Default Web Site*, which points to the content directory *systemroot*\Inetpub\Wwwroot. To create a new Web site, you must create a content directory.

Be sure that you do not nest Web sites that you want to extend as FrontPage virtual servers because FrontPage Server Extensions does not recognize Web sites nested within each other. For example, if you need to create two extended Web sites, you can locate the first content directory in *systemroot*\Inetpub*Test* and the second content directory in *systemroot*\Inetpub*Test2*. If you place the *Test2* directory within the *Test* directory, the permissions in the *Test* directory overwrite all the permissions in the *Test2* directory.

When you create new Web sites, assign them to the default IIS application pool (DefaultAppPool) or to another IIS application pool of your choice.

 Important

Do not use, or make changes to, the MSSharePointAppPool, which is created by default in IIS Manager when you enable FrontPage 2002 Server Extensions. MSSharePointAppPool holds special files that are used internally by FrontPage Server Extensions.

FrontPage 2002 Server Extensions does not support Unicode content directory names or Web Distributed Authoring and Versioning (WebDAV).

Securing FrontPage 2002 Server Extensions

FrontPage 2002 Server Extensions relies on the security features of the Windows Server 2003 family to provide security for Web site content. FrontPage Server Extensions uses the following two elements of Windows security:

- **User authentication.** Validates the user account that is attempting to gain access to a Web site or network resource.

- **File system security**. Controls which users can access specific files and folders in the file system.

In addition to these elements of Windows security, FrontPage 2002 Server Extensions includes a new security feature: *user roles*. With user roles, you do not have to control the file and folder permissions separately or be concerned about keeping your local groups synchronized with your list of Web users. You use roles to give users permissions on your Web site, and use FrontPage 2002 Server Extensions administration tools to add new users directly. For more information about managing users and user roles, see "Using Roles to Manage User Rights" later in this appendix.

User Authentication

When you use FrontPage 2002 Server Extensions with IIS 6.0 on a computer running Windows Server 2003, user authentication is based on one or more of the following Windows authentication methods: Anonymous authentication, Basic authentication, Integrated Windows authentication, Digest authentication, Advanced Digest authentication, or Certificate authentication.

When you set up your Web server, choose the authentication method you want to use for FrontPage 2002 Server Extensions. With the exception of Anonymous authentication, you cannot change the authentication method by using the FrontPage 2002 Server Extensions administration tools; you must instead use IIS Manager to change the authentication method.

FrontPage 2002 Server Extensions supports connectivity through firewalls. Make sure your firewall is open for the standard HTTP ports 80 and 443 (which port you use depends on your configuration). If you use a firewall and want to use NTLM Integrated Windows authentication (formerly called NTLM and also referred to as Windows NT Challenge/Response authentication), make sure your firewall supports NTLM. Otherwise, configure your Web sites with Basic authentication, preferably with SSL.

For more information about these authentication methods, including brief descriptions of each, see "Common Administrative Tasks Tasks" in this book. For additional information about security options for IIS 6.0, see "Managing a Secure IIS Solution" in this book.

File System Security

FrontPage 2002 Server Extensions relies in part on the Windows operating system to help secure the file system for your Web sites. The Windows Server 2003 family uses access control lists (ACLs) to help secure files and folders. Because ACLs require the NTFS file system, your Web servers must use NTFS when you run FrontPage 2002 Server Extensions on IIS 6.0. For more information about access control, see "Understanding access control" in Help and Support Center for Windows Server 2003. For more information about setting ACLs for FrontPage 2002 Server Extensions, see "Windows Security Model" in the SharePoint Team Services Administrator's Guide link on the Web Resources page at http://www.microsoft.com/windows/reskits/webresources.

 Caution

When you build FrontPage-extended Web sites and subwebs, all the ACLs for those sites are maintained by FrontPage Server Extensions. Do not try to change the ACLs in Windows Server 2003. Instead, in order to maintain security, always make permissions changes and other security-related changes by using the FrontPage 2002 Server Administration tools.

Extending and Configuring Web Sites

After you install FrontPage 2002 Server Extensions, you can extend a Web site and then customize the Web site by configuring several options. To configure FrontPage Server Extensions, use one of the HTML administration pages, such as the Server Administration page, which you can access through Microsoft SharePoint Administrator. You can also use the FrontPage Server Extensions command-line tools. For more information about using the command-line tools, see "Using Command-Line Tools" later in this appendix.

The HTML administration pages, which are automatically created when you install FrontPage 2002 Server Extensions, replace the Microsoft Management Console (MMC) interface for administering the FrontPage 2000 Server Extensions. You must be a member of the Administrators group on the local computer to view and use these HTML administration pages. For more information about accessing the HTML administration pages, see "Extending Web Sites" later in this appendix.

icrosoft SharePoint Administrator provides the following HTML administration pages to help you administer your FrontPage-extended Web sites:

- **Server Administration pages.** Allow you to extend a Web site (make it a FrontPage virtual server) and administer settings for your Web server. You can also view a list of virtual servers on your Web server and obtain information about each one.

  For example, you can specify default settings for extended Web sites. You can also reset user passwords and specify which rights are available to assign to roles and users.

- **Virtual Server Administration pages.** Allow you to globally control settings for any extended Web site (FrontPage virtual server) on your computer.

  A newly created extended Web site inherits settings from defaults set on the Server Administration pages. You can use the Virtual Server Administration pages to change these default settings and to specify what settings to use for subwebs of the extended Web site. For example, you can individually upgrade an extended Web site to FrontPage 2002 Server Extensions. You can also change configuration settings and set user account limits.

- **Site Administration pages.** Control settings for each individual Web site that is part of a FrontPage rootweb or subweb.

  For example, you can manage users and roles; perform usage analysis tasks; create, merge, or delete subwebs; and perform server health checks on virtual servers.

Extending Web sites

After creating a Web site in IIS, you can use the Server Administration pages provided by FrontPage 2002 Server Extensions to extend the Web site and administer settings for your Web server.

To extend a Web site by using the Server Administration pages

1. From the **Start** menu, point to **Administrative Tools**, and then click **Microsoft SharePoint Administrator**.

   If the message "The page cannot be found" appears, check that the FrontPage 2002 Server Extensions optional component is enabled. For more information about enabling FrontPage 2002 Server Extensions, see "Installing and Enabling FrontPage Server Extensions" earlier in this appendix.

2. On the **Server Administration** site, check to see that the Web site you created earlier is listed in the **Virtual Servers** section.

    Note

   Optionally, you can access the Server Administration pages by using IIS Manager:

   - In IIS Manager, expand the local computer, expand the **Web Sites** folder, right-click **Microsoft SharePoint Administration**, point to **All Tasks**, and then click **Configure Server Extensions 2002**.
   - At the top left, click **Administration** to open the **Server Administration** site.

3. To extend the Web site (make it a FrontPage virtual server), click the **Extend** link beside the Web site name.

4. Specify a valid account to add to the Administrators role for the extended Web site.

5. Click **Submit**.

This administration tool adds FrontPage 2002 Server Extensions template directories to the content directory of your extended Web site and adds other files that contain metadata.

Configuring Extended Web Sites

Any changes that you make to an extended Web site at the rootweb level affect all sites and subwebs for that rootweb. You can set the following options at the rootweb level by using the Virtual Server Administration pages.

- **Authoring options.** Turn authoring on or off for an extended Web site. When authoring is turned on, users can add new pages, edit pages, and remove pages for a Web site. When authoring is turned off, FrontPage client users cannot perform any of these tasks.

- **Mail settings.** Specify the Simple Mail Transfer Protocol (SMTP) mail server, the mail encoding option, and the **From** and **Reply-to** address to use for e-mail messages related to FrontPage Server Extensions.

- **Performance tuning options.** Use default settings to manage the performance of your FrontPage-extended Web sites, or specify settings for several performance tuning options, including caching limits for documents, images, and files.

- **Client scripting options.** Control the types of scripts that authors can run on your site, including ISAPI, CGI, ASP, and others.

- **Security settings.** Change security options, track authoring data by creating logs, and specify whether users can store executable files on your server.

If you do not change these configuration settings, the extended Web site inherits the settings from the Set Installation Defaults administration page (in the Server Administration pages). Use the Change Configuration Settings page in the Virtual Server Administration pages to configure your extended Web site.

▶ **To configure FrontPage-extended Web sites by using the Virtual Server Administration pages**

1. From the **Start** menu, point to **Administrative Tools**, and then click **Microsoft SharePoint Administrator**.

2. On the **Server Administration** page, next to the FrontPage-extended Web site name, click **Administration**.

3. Click **Change configuration settings**.

4. On the **Change Configuration Settings** page, click the options you want, and then click **Submit**.

Configuring Web Sites

In addition to configuring the settings for an extended Web site (FrontPage virtual server), you can configure the settings for individual Web sites that are part of a rootweb (these Web sites become extended because they are contained in, or in a subdirectory of, the rootweb). Use the Site Administration page or the command-line tools to configure the following features:

- **User and role settings**. Add or delete users and roles, and change which roles a user is assigned to. For more information about how FrontPage 2002 Server Extensions manages user rights, see "Using Roles to Manage User Rights" later in this appendix.

- **Usage analysis settings**. Configure usage analysis to track how many users visit your site; track the type and number of hits that your site receives, and track other site-usage information. The usage reports rely on a log file that is generated by your IIS application server.

- **Server health check settings**. Detect and repair certain functionalities relating to extended Web sites, such as checking role configurations, managing security, or checking anonymous access.

▶ **To configure Web sites by using the Site Administration page**

- **If you are a server administrator**

    1. From the **Start** menu, point to **Administrative Tools**, and then click **Microsoft SharePoint Administrator**.

    2. On the **Server Administration** page, click the name of the extended Web site (FrontPage virtual server) that you want to manage, which takes you to the Site Administration page for the rootweb of that extended Web site.

- **If you are a site administrator**

    1. Open your Web site in the FrontPage client.

    2. On the **Tools** menu, point to **Server**, and then click **Administration Home**.

Using Command-Line Tools

FrontPage 2002 Server Extensions provides two new tools for command-line administration:

- **Owsadm.exe**. Administers FrontPage 2002 Server Extensions from the local server. You must have administrative credentials on the local server to use this tool.

- **Owsrmadm.exe**. Administers FrontPage 2002 Server Extensions from a remote computer. The Web server must be running before you can use this tool. You must have administrative credentials on the server to use this tool. In addition, you must have a copy of the tool on your local computer, which must be running Windows.

When you run Owsadm.exe, you supply an operation and a set of command-line parameters in the following form:

```
-operation CommandName -parameter value
```

Each parameter for the command line also has a short form that you can use instead of the full parameter name. For example, you can use the following command to add a specified user to the Web site on port 80:

owsadm.exe –o users -c add –u *username* **-p 80**

To configure settings for an extended Web site (FrontPage virtual server) from the command line, use the **SetProperty** parameter with Owsadm.exe or Owsrmadm.exe. You can set authoring, performance tuning, client scripting, mail settings, and security settings properties by using the command line. For example, to turn on authoring for an extended Web site at port 1088, configure the **Authoring** property by using the following command:

owsadm.exe –o setproperty -p 1088 –pn Authoring –pv enabled

For more information about using these command-line tools to extend and administer sites, including links to command-line parameters, operations, and properties, see "Command-line Administration," in the SharePoint Team Services Administrator's Guide link on the Web Resources page at http://www.microsoft.com/windows/reskits/webresources. For more information about using FrontPage 2002 Server Extensions with IIS 6.0 and for additional links to FrontPage-related Web sites, see "Using FrontPage Server Extensions to Extend Web Sites" in IIS 6.0 Help, which is accessible from IIS Manager.

Configuring Advanced Security and Customization

In addition to choosing a Windows authentication method for your extended Web sites, you need to manage user access by configuring user rights. FrontPage 2002 Server Extensions are designed to be scalable so that you can configure Web site permissions to be as simple or as complex as you need.

FrontPage 2002 Server Extensions also provides advanced customization, which Internet service providers (ISPs) and Web Presence Providers (WPPs) might find especially useful. For example, you can authenticate users separately for each extended Web site (FrontPage virtual server), which allows you to better manage anonymous user access to Web sites on separate virtual servers. In addition, you can create extended Web sites that have access to shared folders on your network by using the Universal Naming Convention (UNC) standards. Customizing FrontPage 2002 Server Extensions by using UNC network shares can be helpful if your Web server is hosting many large Web sites and subwebs.

All these advanced customizations are intended for experienced IT administrators who are familiar with Windows authentication methods and with configuring FrontPage 2002 Server Extensions.

 Note

Registered WPPs for Microsoft® FrontPage® version 2002 are companies that provide hosting services for FrontPage–based sites. Many WPPs also provide technical support, training and consulting, 24-hour monitoring, maintenance and traffic reporting, security management, or other Web-based services.

Using Roles to Manage User Rights

FrontPage 2002 Server Extensions uses roles to manage user rights. Each user is assigned at least one role with corresponding rights. You can edit or customize the rights assigned to a role, create a new role, or delete an unused role.

You can add users to a Web site without assigning them to a role. For example, if you are creating new user accounts for a Web site, you can create the user accounts and then assign or remove roles at any time.

Not only does FrontPage 2002 Server Extensions offer greater flexibility in assigning roles, it also provides user-friendly management tools. In earlier versions, you managed user roles from within the Microsoft FrontPage client by using the **Security** command on the **Tools** menu. With FrontPage 2002 Server Extensions, you can manage roles by using the HTML administration pages or the command-line tool.

You must be both a Web site administrator and an administrator on the local computer to perform administrative tasks that affect settings for all extended Web sites and subwebs in a rootweb. FrontPage 2002 Server Extensions includes the following roles by default:

- **Browser.** Has rights to view pages, view Web document discussions, and read lists.

- **Author.** Has Browser rights, plus rights to edit pages, directories, and lists.

- **Advanced Author.** Has Author rights, plus rights to define and apply themes and borders, link style sheets, and recalculate a Web site (check the links). This role appears as "advauthor" on the command line.

- **Administrator.** Has all Browser, Author, and Advanced Author rights, plus rights to configure roles, create local computer user accounts, manage source control, create subwebs, manage server health, and manage usage analysis. This role appears as "admin" on the command line and is a Web site administrator role, not a server administrator role.

For more information about user roles, including a complete list of user rights, their default settings, and how to configure them, see "Managing Roles," "Managing Users," and "User Rights" in the SharePoint Team Services Administrator's Guide link on the Web Resources page at http://www.microsoft.com/windows/reskits/webresources.

Authenticating Users Separately for Each Extended Web Site

When you use FrontPage 2002 Server Extensions on Windows Server 2003, you can take advantage of a new feature that allows you to better manage anonymous user access for Web sites on separate extended Web sites (FrontPage virtual servers). You can use group accounts to separate anonymous access for each extended Web site, so that only anonymous users and registered users on the same extended Web site have access to the source files. When you use this new feature, the users on one extended Web site can no longer read source files on another extended Web site.

This is an advanced feature and is intended for use by Internet service providers (ISPs) and Web Presence Providers (WPPs) who allow users direct access to the file system of their Web sites through methods such as FTP, ASP, and Perl.

To take advantage of this new feature, you must create a group account to track all user accounts that have access to a virtual server. To turn on this feature and to specify the name for the group account, you must edit the Windows registry. For more information about using this new feature, including step-by-step instructions for enabling group accounts, see "Authenticating Users Separately for Each Virtual Server" in the SharePoint Team Services Administrator's Guide link on the Web Resources page at http://www.microsoft.com/windows/reskits/webresources.

Connecting Web Sites to UNC Network Shares

When you run FrontPage 2002 Server Extensions on Windows Server 2003, you can create FrontPage-extended Web sites that have access to shared folders on your network by using the Universal Naming Convention (UNC) standard. A configuration that uses UNC shares is often advantageous when you set up a server that hosts many large Web sites and subwebs. You can create Web sites on your Web server and have the files for the Web sites distributed across multiple file servers on your network. Connecting Web sites to UNC network shares requires that you configure the file server and the Web server.

You must be a local administrator of both servers to perform the steps needed for this advanced configuration. Both servers must be running Microsoft® Windows® Server 2003, Standard Edition; Windows® Server 2003, Advanced Edition; or Windows® Server 2003 Enterprise Edition.

For more information about connecting a FrontPage extended Web site to a UNC network share, see "Connecting Web Sites to UNC Network Shares," in the SharePoint Team Services Administrator's Guide link on the Web Resources page at http://www.microsoft.com/windows/reskits/webresources.

For more information about configuring Web sites that have content stored on a file server, see the UNC Servers Accessed by Using IIS 6.0 link on the Web Resources page at http://www.microsoft.com/windows/reskits/webresources.

A P P E N D I X   F

IIS 6.0 Performance Counters

The Microsoft® Windows® Server 2003 operating system obtains performance data from components in your computer as those components are utilized. This data is described as a performance object and is typically named for the component that is generating the data. For example, the Web Service performance object is a collection of performance data about Internet Information Services (IIS) 6.0. Each performance object provides performance counters that represent data on specific aspects of a system or service. When you install IIS 6.0, all of the IIS performance counters, with the exception of the SNMP counters, appear in System Monitor and in Performance Logs and Alerts. You can also use Windows Instrumentation Management (WMI) to view and use these counters and the SNMP counters.

In This Appendix

Related Information

- For information about performance monitoring and tuning, see "Optimizing IIS 6.0 Performance" in this book.

Web Service Counters for the WWW Service

The Web Service counters help you determine how well the World Wide Web Publishing Service (WWW service) processes requests. The WWW service is a user-mode service. These counters also reflect the processing that occurs in the kernel-mode driver, HTTP.sys.

Configure these counters to monitor performance for individual Web sites or for all sites on a server (by using the _Total instance). Note that some counters that were included with IIS 5.x are now obsolete and, therefore, return a zero value. Obsolete counters are listed in Table D.8 and Table D.9.

Table D.1 describes the Bytes counters for the Web Service performance object.

Table D.1   Bytes (Sent, Received, and Transferred) Counters

Counter	Description
Total Bytes Sent	The number of data bytes that have been sent by the WWW service since the service started. This counter is new in IIS 6.0.
Bytes Sent/sec	The rate, in seconds, at which data bytes have been sent by the WWW service.
Total Bytes Received	The total bytes of data that have been received by the WWW service since the service started. This counter is new in IIS 6.0.
Bytes Received/sec	The rate, in seconds, at which data bytes have been received by the WWW service.
Total Bytes Transferred	The total number of bytes of data that have been sent and received by the WWW service since the service started. This counter is new in IIS 6.0.
Bytes Total/sec	The sum of Bytes Sent/sec and Bytes Received/sec.

Table D.2 describes the Files counters for the Web Service performance object.

Table D.2   Files (Sent, Received, and Transferred) Counters

Counter	Description
Total Files Sent	The number of user-mode files that have been sent by the WWW service since the service started. This counter does not include cache hits. Note that this counter does not increment when files are being served from the kernel-mode cache. For more information, see Kernel: URI Cache Hits in Table D.13.
Files Sent/sec	The rate, in seconds, at which files have been sent.
Total Files Received	The number of files that have been received by the WWW service since the service started.

(continued)

Table D.2   Files (Sent, Received, and Transferred) Counters *(continued)*

Counter	Description
Files Received/sec	The rate, in seconds, at which files have been received by the WWW service.
Total Files Transferred	The sum of Total Files Sent and Total Files Received by the WWW service since the service started. Note that this counter does not increment when files are being served from the kernel-mode cache. For more information, see Kernel: URI Cache Hits in Table D.13.
Files/sec	The rate, in seconds, at which files have been sent and received by the WWW service.

Table D.3 describes the Anonymous Users and NonAnonymous Users counters for the Web Service performance object. In this context, nonanonymous users are authenticated users.

 Note

With Anonymous and NonAnonymous Users counters, IIS 6.0 counts each request as a new user. This behavior differs from IIS 5.x, which counted each connection as a new user.

Table D.3   Anonymous Users and NonAnonymous Users Counters

Counter	Description
Current Anonymous Users	The number of users who currently have an anonymous request pending with the WWW service. In IIS 6.0, Current Users (Anonymous or NonAnonymous) is the number of requests currently being worked on by the server.
Current NonAnonymous Users	The number of users who currently have a nonanonymous request pending with the WWW service. In IIS 6.0, Current Users (Anonymous or NonAnonymous) is the number of requests currently being worked on by the server.
Total Anonymous Users	The number of users who have established an anonymous request since the WWW service started. This counter does not increment when files are being served from the kernel cache. For more information, see Kernel: URI Cache Hits in Table D.13.
Anonymous Users/sec	The rate, in seconds, at which users have made anonymous requests to the WWW service.
Total NonAnonymous Users	The number of users who have made nonanonymous requests to the WWW service since the service started. For more information, see Kernel: URI Cache Hits in Table D.13.
NonAnonymous Users/sec	The rate, in seconds, at which users have made nonanonymous requests to the WWW service.
Maximum NonAnonymous Users	The maximum number of users who have made concurrent nonanonymous requests to the WWW service since the service started.

Table D.4 describes the Connections and Attempts counters for the Web Service performance object.

Table D.4   Connections and Attempts Counters

Counter	Description
Current Connections	The number of active connections to the WWW service.
Maximum Connections	The maximum number of simultaneous connections made to the WWW service since the service started.
Total Connection Attempts	The number of connections to the WWW service that have been attempted since the service started.
Connection Attempts/sec	The rate, in seconds, at which connections to the WWW service have been attempted since the service started.
Total Logon Attempts	The number of attempts to log on to the WWW service that have occurred since the service started.
Logon Attempts/sec	The rate, in seconds, at which attempts to log on to the WWW service have occurred.

Table D.5 describes the Requests counters for the Web Service performance object.

Table D.5   Requests Counters

Counter	Description
Total Options Requests	The number of HTTP requests that have used the **OPTIONS** method since the WWW service started.
Options Requests/sec	The rate, in seconds, at which HTTP requests that use the **OPTIONS** method have been made.
Total Get Requests	The number of HTTP requests that have used the **GET** method since the WWW service started.
Get Requests/sec	The rate, in seconds, at which HTTP requests that use the **GET** method have been made to the WWW service.
Total Post Requests	The number of HTTP requests that have used the **POST** method since the WWW service started.
Post Requests/sec	The rate, in seconds, at which requests that use the **POST** method have been made to the WWW service.
Total Head Requests	The number of HTTP requests that have used the **HEAD** method since the WWW service started.
Head Requests/sec	The rate, in seconds, at which HTTP requests that use the **HEAD** method have been made to the WWW service.

(continued)

Table D.5   Requests Counters *(continued)*

Counter	Description
Total Put Requests	The number of HTTP requests that have used the **PUT** method since the WWW service started.
Put Requests/sec	The rate, in seconds, at which HTTP requests that use the **PUT** method have been made to the WWW service.
Total Delete Requests	The number of HTTP requests that have used the **DELETE** method since the WWW service started.
Delete Requests/sec	The rate, in seconds, at which HTTP requests that use the **DELETE** method have been made to the WWW service.
Total Trace Requests	The number of HTTP requests that have used the **TRACE** method since the WWW service started.
Trace Requests/sec	The rate, in seconds, at which HTTP requests that use the **TRACE** method have been made to the WWW service.
Total Move Requests	The number of HTTP requests that have used the **MOVE** method since the WWW service started.
Move Requests/sec	The rate, in seconds, at which HTTP requests that use the **MOVE** method have been made to the WWW service.
Total Copy Requests	The number of HTTP requests that have used the **COPY** method since the WWW service started.
Copy Requests/sec	The rate, in seconds, at which HTTP requests that use the **COPY** method have been made to the WWW service.
Total Mkcol Requests	The number of HTTP requests that have used the **MKCOL** method since the WWW service started.
Mkcol Requests/sec	The rate, in seconds, at which HTTP requests that use the **MKCOL** method have been made to the WWW service.
Total Propfind Requests	The number of HTTP requests that have used the **PROPFIND** method since the WWW service started.
Propfind Requests/sec	The rate, in seconds, at which HTTP requests that use the **PROPFIND** method have been made to the WWW service.
Total Proppatch Requests	The number of HTTP requests that have used the **PROPPATCH** method since the WWW service started.
Proppatch Requests/sec	The rate, in seconds, at which HTTP requests that use the **PROPPATCH** method have been made to the WWW service.
Total Search Requests	The number of HTTP requests that have used the **SEARCH** method since the WWW service started.

(continued)

Table D.5   Requests Counters (continued)

Counter	Description
Search Requests/sec	The rate, in seconds, at which HTTP requests that use the **SEARCH** method have been made to the WWW service.
Total Lock Requests	The number of HTTP requests that have used the **LOCK** method since the WWW service started.
Lock Requests/sec	The rate, in seconds, at which HTTP requests that use the **LOCK** method have been made to the WWW service.
Total Unlock Requests	The number of HTTP requests that have used the **UNLOCK** method since the WWW service started.
Unlock Requests/sec	The rate, in seconds, at which HTTP requests that use the **UNLOCK** method have been made to the WWW service.
Total Other Request Methods	The number of HTTP requests that did not use the **OPTIONS, GET, HEAD, POST, PUT, DELETE, TRACE, MOVE, COPY, MKCOL, PROPFIND, PROPPATCH, SEARCH, LOCK,** or **UNLOCK** methods since the WWW service started. Can include **LINK** or other methods supported by gateway applications.
Other Request Methods/sec	The rate, in seconds, at which HTTP requests that do not use the methods listed for the Total Other Requests Methods counter have been made to the WWW service.
Total Method Requests	The number of HTTP requests that have been made since the WWW service started.
Total Method Requests/sec	The rate, in seconds, at which all HTTP requests have been received.

Table D.6 describes the Errors counters for the Web Service performance object.

Table D.6   Errors (Not Found and Locked) Counters

Counter	Description
Total Not Found Errors	The number of requests that have been made since the service started that were not satisfied by the server because the requested document was not found. Usually reported as HTTP error 404.
Not Found Errors/sec	The rate, in seconds, at which requests were not satisfied by the server because the requested document was not found.
Total Locked Errors	The number of requests that have been made since the service started that could not be satisfied by the server because the requested document was locked. Usually reported as HTTP error 423.
Locked Errors/sec	The rate, in seconds, at which requests were not satisfied because the requested document was locked.

Table D.7 describes the Common Gateway Interface (CGI) Requests and ISAPI Extension Requests counters for the Web Service performance object.

Table D.7   CGI Requests and ISAPI Extension Requests Counters

Counter	Description
Current CGI Requests	The number of CGI requests that are being processed simultaneously by the WWW service.
Total CGI Requests	The number of all CGI requests that have been made since the WWW service started.
CGI Requests/sec	The rate, in seconds, at which CGI requests are being processed simultaneously by the WWW service.
Maximum CGI Requests	The maximum number of CGI requests that have been processed simultaneously by the WWW service since the service started.
Current ISAPI Extension Requests	The number of ISAPI extension requests that are being processed simultaneously by the WWW service.
Total ISAPI Extension Requests	The number of ISAPI extension requests that have been made since the WWW service started.
ISAPI Extension Requests/sec	The rate, in seconds, at which ISAPI extension requests are being processed by the WWW service.
Maximum ISAPI Extension Requests	The maximum number of ISAPI extension requests that were processed simultaneously by the WWW service.

Table D.8 lists the CAL (client access license) Count counters for the Web Service performance object, which are not valid in IIS 6.0. The value of these counters is always zero.

Table D.8   CAL Count Counters

Counter
Current CAL count for authenticated users
Maximum CAL count for authenticated users
Total count of failed CAL requests for authenticated users
Current CAL count for SSL connections
Maximum CAL count for SSL connections
Total count of failed CAL requests for SSL connections

Table D.9 describes other miscellaneous counters, some of which are no longer valid, for the Web Service performance object.

Table D.9 Async I/O Requests, Bandwidth Bytes, and Miscellaneous Counters

Counter	Description
Total Allowed Async I/O Requests	This counter is no longer valid; its value is always zero.
Total Blocked Async I/O Requests	This counter is no longer valid; its value is always zero.
Total Rejected Async I/O Requests	This counter is no longer valid; its value is always zero.
Current Blocked Async I/O Requests	This counter is no longer valid; its value is always zero.
Measured Async I/O Bandwidth Usage	This counter is no longer valid; its value is always zero.
Total Blocked Bandwidth Bytes	This counter is no longer valid; its value is always zero.
Current Blocked Bandwidth Bytes	This counter is no longer valid; its value is always zero.
Service Uptime	The uptime for the WWW service or a Web site.
MaxCalSsl	This counter is no longer valid; its value is always zero.

Web Service Cache Counters for the WWW Service

The WWW service and FTP service do not share a common cache. Instead, the caches are split into two separate performance objects: one for FTP service and one for the WWW service. WWW service cache counters are designed to monitor server performance only; therefore, you cannot configure them to monitor individual sites.

For information about FTP service counters, see "Internet Information Services Global Counters" later in this appendix.

Table D.10 describes the File counters for the Web Service Cache performance object. These counters are new in IIS 6.0.

Table D.10 File Counters for the Web Service Cache Object

Counter	Description
Active Flushed Entries	The number of user-mode cache entries that have been flushed, though memory is still allocated for these entries. The allocated memory will be released after all current transfers complete.
Current File Cache Memory Usage	The number of bytes currently used for the user-mode file cache.
Current Files Cached	The number of files whose content is currently in the user-mode cache.

(continued)

Table D.10   File Counters for the Web Service Cache Object *(continued)*

Counter	Description
Total Files Cached	The number of files whose content has been added to the user-mode cache since the WWW service started.
File Cache Hits	The number of successful lookups in the user-mode file cache that have occurred since the WWW service started.
File Cache Hits %	The ratio of user-mode file cache hits to total cache requests that have been made since the WWW service started up.
File Cache Misses	The number of unsuccessful lookups in the user-mode file cache that have been made since the WWW service started.
File Cache Flushes	The number of files that have been removed from the user-mode cache since the WWW service started.
Maximum File Cache Memory Usage	The maximum number of bytes that have been used for the user-mode file cache since the WWW service started.
Total Flushed Files	The number of file handles that have been removed from the user-mode cache since the WWW service started.

Table D.11 describes the URI counters for the Web Service Cache performance object. These counters are new in IIS 6.0.

Table D.11   URI Counters for the Web Service Cache Object

Counter	Description
Current URIs Cached	The number of URI information blocks that are currently stored in the user-mode cache.
Total URIs Cached	The number of URI information blocks that have been added to the user-mode cache since the WWW service started.
URI Cache Hits	The number of successful lookups that have been made in the user-mode URI cache since the WWW service started.
URI Cache Misses	The number of unsuccessful lookups that have been made in the user-mode URI cache since the WWW service started.
URI Cache Hits %	The ratio of URI Cache Hits to total cache requests that have occurred since the WWW service started.
URI Cache Flushes	The total number of URI cache flushes that have occurred since the WWW service started.
Total Flushed URIs	The number of URI information blocks that have been removed from the user-mode cache since the WWW service started.

Table D.12 describes the Metadata counters for the Web Service Cache performance object. These counters are new in IIS 6.0.

Table D.12   Metadata Counters for the Web Service Cache Object

Counter	Description
Current Metadata Cached	The current number of metadata information blocks in the user-mode cache.
Total Metadata Cached	The number of metadata information blocks that have been added to the user-mode cache since the WWW service started.
Metadata Cache Hits	The number of successful lookups in the user-mode metadata cache that have occurred since the WWW service started.
Metadata Cache Misses	The number of unsuccessful lookups in the user-mode metadata cache that have occurred since the WWW service started.
Metadata Cache Hits %	The ratio of successful lookups to total metadata cache requests.
Metadata Cache Flushes	The number of user-mode metadata cache flushes that have occurred since the WWW service started.
Total Flushed Metadata	The number of metadata information blocks that have been removed from the user-mode cache since the WWW service started.

Table D.13 describes the Kernel counters for the Web Service Cache performance object. These counters are new in IIS 6.0.

 Note

Kernel counters reflect all HTTP.sys activity, not just IIS activity.

Table D.13   Kernel Counters for the Web Service Cache Object

Counter	Description
Kernel: Current URIs Cached	The number of URI information blocks currently cached by the kernel.
Kernel: Total URIs Cached	The number of URI information blocks that have been added to the kernel URI cache since the WWW service started.
Kernel: URI Cache Hits	The number of successful lookups in the kernel URI cache that have occurred since the WWW service started.
Kernel: URI Cache Hits%	The ratio of Kernel: URI Cache Hits to total cache requests since the WWW service started.
Kernel: URI Cache Hits/sec	The average number of kernel URI cache hits that are being made per second.

(continued)

Table D.13   Kernel Counters for the Web Service Cache Object *(continued)*

Counter	Description
Kernel URI Cache Misses	The number of unsuccessful lookups in the kernel URI cache that have occurred since the WWW service started.
Kernel: URI Cache Flushes	The number of kernel URI cache flushes that have occurred since the WWW service started.
Kernel: Total Flushed URIs	The number of URI information blocks that have been removed from the kernel cache since the WWW service started.

FTP Service Counters

Use the counters in the following tables to monitor FTP service performance. You can configure the counters to monitor a server or an individual FTP site.

Table D.14 describes Bytes and Total Files counters for the FTP Service performance object.

Table D.14   Bytes and Total Files Counters

Counter	Description
Bytes Sent/sec	The rate at which data bytes are being sent by the FTP service.
Bytes Received/sec	The rate at which data bytes are being received by the FTP service.
Bytes Total/sec	The sum of Bytes Sent/sec and Bytes Received/sec.
Total Files Sent	The total number of files that have been sent by the FTP service since the service started.
Total Files Received	The total number of files that have been received by the FTP service since the service started.
Total Files Transferred	The sum of Total Files Sent and Total Files Received. This is the total number of files transferred by the FTP service since the service started.

Table D.15 describes Anonymous and NonAnonymous Users counters for the FTP Service performance object.

Table D.15 Anonymous and NonAnonymous Users Counters

Counter	Description
Current Anonymous Users	The number of users who currently have an anonymous connection that was made by using the FTP service.
Current NonAnonymous Users	The number of users who currently have a nonanonymous connection that was made by using the FTP service.
Total Anonymous Users	The number of users who have established an anonymous connection with the FTP service since the service started.
Total NonAnonymous Users	The number of users who have established nonanonymous connections with the FTP service since the service started.
Maximum Anonymous Users	The maximum number of users who have established concurrent anonymous connections using the FTP service since the service started.
Maximum NonAnonymous Users	The maximum number of users who have established concurrent nonanonymous connections using the FTP service since the service started.

Table D.16 describes Connections, Attempts, and Uptime counters for the FTP Service performance object.

Table D.16 Connections, Attempts, and Uptime Counters

Counter	Description
Current Connections	The current number of connections that have been established with the FTP service.
Maximum Connections	The maximum number of simultaneous connections that have been established with the FTP service.
Total Connection Attempts (all instances)	The number of connections that have been attempted by using the FTP service since the service started. This counter applies to all instances listed.
Total Logon Attempts	The number of logons that have been attempted by using the FTP service since the service started.
FTP Service Uptime	The amount of time, in seconds, that the FTP service has been running.

Internet Information Services Global Counters

Use the Internet Information Services Global counters described in Table D.17 through Table D.20 to monitor FTP, SMTP, and NNTP services as a whole. You cannot configure these counters to monitor individual sites. This differs from IIS 5.x, in which global counters monitored the WWW and FTP services.

If the service that you want to monitor (FTP, SMTP, or NNTP) is not installed or is not running, the counters return a zero value.

Table D.17 lists the Async I/O counters that are no longer valid for the Internet Information Services Global performance object. The value of these counters is always zero.

Table D.17   Async I/O Counters

Counter
Measured Async I/O Bandwidth Usage
Total Blocked Async I/O Requests
Total Rejected Async I/O Requests
Current Blocked Async I/O Requests
Measured Async I/O Bandwidth Usage

Table D.18 describes File Cache counters for the Internet Information Services Global performance object.

Table D.18   File Cache Counters

Counter	Description
Current Files Cached	The number of files whose content is currently in the cache.
Total Files Cached	The number of files whose content has been added to the cache since the service started.
File Cache Hits	The number of successful lookups in the file cache.
File Cache Misses	The number of unsuccessful lookups in the file cache.
File Cache Hits %	The ratio of File Cache Hits to the total number of cache requests.
File Cache Flushes	The number of file cache flushes that have occurred since the service started.
Current File Cache Memory Usage	The current number of bytes used for the file cache.
Maximum File Cache Memory Usage	The maximum number of bytes used for the file cache.

Table D.19 describes Flushed and URI Cached counters for the Internet Information Services Global performance object.

Table D.19   Flushed and URI Cached Counters

Counter	Description
Active Flushed Entries	The number of cached file handles that will close when all current transfers are complete.
Total Flushed Files	The number of file handles that have been removed from the cache since the service started.
Current URIs Cached	The number of URI information blocks that are currently in the cache.
Total URIs Cached	The number of URI information blocks that have been added to the cache.
URI Cache Hits	The number of successful lookups in the URI cache.
Uri Cache Misses	The number of unsuccessful lookups in the URI cache.
URI Cache Hits %	The ratio of URI Cache Hits to the total number of cache requests.
URI Cache Flushes	The number of URI cache flushes that have occurred since the server started.
Total Flushed URIs	The number of URI information blocks that have been removed from the cache since the service started.

Table D.20 describes the BLOBs counters for the Internet Information Services Global performance object. A *BLOB* is a binary large object.

Table D.20   BLOBs Counters

Counter	Description
Current BLOBs Cached	The BLOB information blocks currently in the cache.
Total BLOBs Cached	The number of BLOB information blocks that have been added to the cache.
BLOB Cache Hits	The number of successful lookups in the BLOB cache.
BLOB Cache Misses	The number of unsuccessful lookups in the BLOB cache.
BLOB Cache Hit %	The ratio of BLOB Cache Hits to the total number of cache requests.
BLOB Cache Flushes	The number of BLOB cache flushes that have occurred since the service started.
Total Flushed BLOBs	The number of BLOB information blocks that have been removed from the cache since the service started.

SNMP Counters

IIS exposes the following counters for Simple Network Management Protocol (SNMP) services. These counters are defined in more detail in three .mib files — Inetsrv.mib, Http.mib and Ftp.mib — which you can find in the *Windir*\System32 folder. Inetsrv.mib is a container object for the other two files and, therefore, does not contain counters. To view the contents of the .mib files, open the files by using Notepad.

You cannot view the SNMP counters in System Monitor or Performance Logs and Alerts. Use WMI or a management information base (MIB) Browser tool instead.

For information about installing and using the SNMP service, see "Checklist: Implementing the SNMP service" in Help and Support Center for Microsoft® Windows® Server 2003.

SNMP FTP Service Counters

Use the SNMP counters in Table D.21 through Table D.23 to monitor FTP service performance.

Table D.21 describes the totalBytes and totalFiles counters that you can use to monitor an SMTP FTP service.

Table D.21   totalBytes and totalFiles Counters

Counter	Description
totalBytesSentHighWord	The high 32-bits of the total number of bytes sent by the FTP server.
totalBytesSentLowWord	The low 32-bits of the total number of bytes sent by the FTP server.
totalBytesReceivedHighWord	The high 32-bits of the total number of bytes received by the FTP server.
totalBytesReceivedLowWord	The low 32-bits of the total number of bytes received by the FTP server.
totalFilesSent	The total number of files sent by this FTP server.
totalFilesReceived	The total number of files received by this FTP server.

Table D.22 describes the AnonymousUsers and NonAnonymousUsers counters that you can use to monitor an SNMP FTP service.

Table D.22 AnonymousUsers and NonAnonymousUsers Counters

Counter	Description
currentAnonymousUsers	The number of anonymous users currently connected to the FTP server.
currentNonAnonymousUsers	The number of nonanonymous users currently connected to the FTP server.
totalAnonymousUsers	The total number of anonymous users that have been connected to the FTP server.
totalNonAnonymousUsers	The total number of nonanonymous users that have been connected to the FTP server.
maxAnonymousUsers	The maximum number of anonymous users that have been simultaneously connected to the FTP server.
maxNonAnonymousUsers	The maximum number of nonanonymous users that have been simultaneously connected to the FTP server.

Table D.23 describes the Connections and Attempts counters that you can use to monitor an SNMP FTP service.

Table D.23 Connections and Attempts Counters

Counter	Description
currentConnections	The current number of connections to the FTP server.
maxConnections	The maximum number of simultaneous connections that have been made to the FTP server.
connectionAttempts	The number of attempts that were made to connect to the FTP server.
logonAttempts	The number of attempts that were made to log on to the FTP server.

SNMP HTTP Service Counters

Use the SNMP HTTP counters in Table D.24 through Table D.31 to monitor WWW service performance.

Table D.24 describes the totalBytes and totalFiles counters that you can use to monitor an SNMP WWW service.

Table D.24   totalBytes and totalFiles Counters

Counter	Description
totalBytesSentHighWord	The high 32-bits of the total number of bytes that have been sent by the WWW service since the service started.
totalBytesSentLowWord	The low 32-bits of the total number of bytes that have been sent by the WWW service since the service started.
totalBytesReceivedHighWord	The high 32-bits of the total number of bytes that have been received by the WWW service since the service started.
totalBytesReceivedLowWord	The low 32-bits of the total number of bytes that have been received by the WWW service since the service started.
totalFilesSent	The total number of files that have been sent by the WWW service since the service started.
totalFilesReceived	The total number of files that have been received by the WWW service since the service started.

Table D.25 describes the AnonymousUsers and NonAnonymousUsers counters that you can use to monitor an SNMP WWW service.

Table D.25   AnonymousUsers and NonAnonymousUsers Counters

Counter	Description
currentAnonymousUsers	The number of users who currently have an anonymous connection by using the WWW service.
currentNonAnonymousUsers	The number of users who currently have a nonanonymous connection by using the WWW service.
totalAnonymousUsers	The total number of users who have made an anonymous connection by using the WWW service since the service started.
totalNonAnonymousUsers	The total number of users who have made a nonanonymous connection by using the WWW service since the service started.
maxAnonymousUsers	The maximum number of users who have made concurrent anonymous connections by using the WWW service since the service started.
maxNonAnonymousUsers	The maximum number of users who have made concurrent nonanonymous connections to the WWW service since the service started up.

Table D.26 describes the Connections and Attempts counters that you can use to monitor an SNMP WWW service.

Table D.26   Connections and Attempts Counters

Counter	Description
currentConnections	The current number of connections made with the WWW service.
maxConnections	The maximum number of concurrent connections that have been made with the WWW service since the service started.
connectionAttempts	The number of connections that have been attempted by using the WWW service since the service started.
logonAttempts	The number of attempts to log on to the WWW service that have been made since the service started.

Table D.27 describes the total counters (totalOptions, totalGets, and others) that you can use to monitor an SNMP WWW service.

Table D.27   total Counters

Counter	Description
totalOptions	The number of HTTP requests that have been made using the **OPTIONS** method since the service started.
totalGets	The number of HTTP requests that have been made using the **GET** method since the service started.
totalPosts	The number of HTTP requests that have been made using the **POST** method since the service started.
totalHeads	The number of HTTP requests that have been made using the **HEAD** method since the service started. Head requests generally indicate that a client is querying the state of a document it already has to see if it needs to be refreshed.
totalPuts	The number of HTTP requests that have been made using the **PUT** method since the service started.
totalDeletes	The number of HTTP requests that have been made using the **DELETE** method since the service started. Delete requests are typically used for file removal.
totalTraces	The number of HTTP requests that have been made using the **TRACE** method since the service started. Trace requests allow the client to see what is being received at the end of the request chain and to use this information for diagnostic purposes.
totalMove	The number of HTTP requests that have been made using the **MOVE** method since the service started. Move requests move files and directories.
totalCopy	The number of HTTP requests that have been made using the **COPY** method since the service started. Copy requests copy files and directories.

(continued)

Table D.27   total Counters (continued)

Counter	Description
totalMkcol	The number of HTTP requests that have been made using the **MKCOL** method since the service started. Mkcol requests create directories on the server.
totalPropfind	The number of HTTP requests that have been made using the **PROPFIND** method since the service started. Propfind requests retrieve property values for files and directories.
totalProppatch	The number of HTTP requests that have been made using the **PROPPATCH** method since the service started. Proppatch requests set property values for files and directories.
totalSearch	The number of HTTP requests that have been made using the **SEARCH** method since the service started. Search requests query the server to find resources that match a set of conditions provided by the client.
totalLock	The number of HTTP requests that have been made using the **LOCK** method since the service started. Lock requests lock a file so that only the user who locked it can modify the file.
totalUnlock	The number of HTTP requests that have been made using the **UNLOCK** method since the service started. Unlock requests remove locks from files.
totalOthers	The number of HTTP requests that have been made by methods other than **OPTIONS, GET, HEAD, POST, PUT, DELETE, TRACE, MOVE, COPY, MKCOL, PROPFIND, PROPPATCH, SEARCH, LOCK,** or **UNLOCK** methods since the service started.

Table D.28 describes the CGIRequests and BGIRequests counters that you can use to monitor an SNMP WWW service.

Table D.28   CGIRequests and BGIRequests Counters

Counter	Description
currentCGIRequests	The current number of CGI requests being processed simultaneously by the WWW service.
currentBGIRequests	The current number of ISAPI requests being processed simultaneously by the WWW service.
totalCGIRequests	The total number of CGI requests that have been made since the service started.
totalBGIRequests	The total number of ISAPI requests that have been received since the service started.
maxCGIRequests	The maximum number of CGI requests that have been processed simultaneously by the WWW service since the service started.
maxBGIRequests	The maximum number of ISAPI requests that have been processed simultaneously by the WWW service since the service started.

Table D.29 lists the Requests counters (Blocked, Allowed, and Rejected), which are no longer valid in IIS 6.0. The value for these counters is always zero.

Table D.29   Requests Counters (Blocked, Allowed, and Rejected)

Counter
currentBlockedRequests
totalBlockedRequests
totalAllowedRequests
totalRejectedRequests

Table D.30 describes the Errors and Bandwidth counters that you can use to monitor an SNMP WWW service.

Table D.30   Errors and Bandwidth Counters

Counter	Description
totalNotFoundErrors	The number of requests made since the service started that the server did not satisfy because the requested document was not found. This type of request is usually reported to the client as an HTTP 404 error message.
totalLockedErrors	The number of requests made since the service started that the server did not satisfy because the requested document was locked. This type of request is usually reported to the client as an HTTP 423 error message.
measuredBandwidth	The I/O bandwidth that the WWW service used, averaged over a minute.

Table D.31 lists the CAL-related counters that are no longer valid for the SNMP WWW service. The value of these counters is always zero.

Table D.31   CAL-related Counters

Counter
currentCALsforAuthenticatedUsers
maxCALsforAuthenticatedUsers
totalCALFailedAuthenticatedUser
currentCALsforSecureConnections
maxCALsforSecureConnections
totalCALFailedSecureConnection

Active Server Pages Performance Counters

If you are running Active Server Pages (ASP) on your server, the ASP counters can help you determine how well the server or site is responding to ASP requests. The ASP counters are designed to monitor server performance; you cannot monitor individual ASP applications because ASP counters collect global data across the entire WWW service.

Table D.32 describes the ASP Debugging and Errors counters for the Active Server Pages performance object.

Table D.32   ASP Debugging and Errors Counters

Counter	Description
ASP Debugging Requests	The number of requests for debugging documents that have been made since the WWW service started.
Errors During Script Runtime	The number of requests that failed because run-time errors occurred.
Errors From ASP Preprocessor	The number of requests that failed because preprocessor errors occurred.
Errors From Script Compilers	The number of requests that failed because script compilation errors occurred.
Errors/sec	The average number of errors that occurred per second.

Table D.33 describes the Requests counters for the Active Server Pages performance object.

Table D.33   Requests Counters for ASP Pages

Counter	Description
Request Bytes In Total	The total size, in bytes, of all requests.
Request Bytes Out Total	The total size, in bytes, of responses sent to clients. This total does not include standard HTTP response headers.
Request Execution Time	The number of milliseconds that it took to execute the most recent request.
Request Wait Time	The number of milliseconds that the most recent request waited in the queue.
Requests Disconnected	The number of requests that were disconnected because communication failed.
Requests Executing	The number of requests that are currently executing.

(continued)

Table D.33   Requests Counters for ASP Pages *(continued)*

Counter	Description
Requests Failed Total	The number of requests that failed due to errors, authorization failure, and rejections.
Requests Not Authorized	The number of requests that failed because access rights were insufficient.
Requests Not Found	The number of requests that were made for files that were not found.
Requests Queued	The number of requests that are waiting in the queue for service.
Requests Rejected	The number of requests that were not executed because there were insufficient resources to process them.
Requests Succeeded	The number of requests that executed successfully.
Requests Timed Out	The number of requests that timed out.
Requests Total	The number of requests that have been made since the service was started.
Requests/sec	The average number of requests that were executed per second.

Table D.34 describes miscellaneous counters for the Active Server Pages performance object.

Table D.34   Script Engines, Sessions, Templates, and Transactions Counters

Counter	Description
Script Engines Cached	The number of script engines in the cache.
Script Engine Cache Hit Rate	The percentage of requests that were found in the script engine cache.
Engine Flush Notifications	The number of engines invalidated in the cache because change notification occurred.
Session Duration	The length of time that the most recent session lasted, in milliseconds.
Sessions Current	The number of sessions currently being serviced.
Sessions Timed Out	The number of sessions that have timed out.
Sessions Total	The number of sessions that have run since the service was started.
Templates Cached	The number of templates that are currently cached.
Template Cache Hit Rate	The percentage of requests that have been found in the template cache.
Template Notifications	The number of templates that have been invalidated in the cache because change notification occurred.
In Memory Templates Cached	The number of compiled templates that are cached in memory.
In Memory Template Cache Hit Rate	The percentage of requests that have been found in the memory cache.

(continued)

Table D.34   Script Engines, Sessions, Templates, and Transactions Counters *(continued)*

Counter	Description
Transactions Aborted	The number of transactions that have been aborted.
Transactions Committed	The number of transactions that have been committed. This counter increments after page execution if the transaction does not abort.
Transactions Pending	The number of transactions that are in progress.
Transactions Total	The number of transactions that have occurred since the service was started.
Transactions/sec	The average number of transactions that have been started, per second.

Note

The Templates Cached counter, Template Cache Hit Rate counter, and Template Notifications counter provide information about the total number of templates cached on disk and in memory. To determine the number of requests cached on disk only, subtract the value of the In Memory Templates Cached counter from the value of the Templates Cached counter.

ASP.NET Performance Counters

ASP.NET supports the following ASP.NET system performance counters, which aggregate information for all ASP.NET applications on a Web server computer, or, alternatively, apply generally to a system of ASP.NET servers running the same applications.

ASP.NET Counters

Use the ASP.NET counters in Table D.35 through Table D.38 to monitor ASP.NET system performance.

Table D.35 describes the Application Restarts and Applications Running counters for the ASP.NET performance object.

Table D.35   Application Restarts and Applications Running Counters

Counter	Description
Application Restarts	The number of times that an application has been restarted since the Web service started. Application restarts are incremented with each **Application_OnEnd** event. An application restart can occur because changes were made to the Web.config file or to assemblies stored in the application's \Bin directory, or because too many changes occurred in Web Forms pages. Sudden increases in this counter can mean that your Web application is shutting down. If an unexpected increase occurs, be sure to investigate it promptly. This value resets every time IIS is restarted.
Applications Running	The number of applications that are running on the server computer.

Table D.36 describes the Requests counters for the ASP.NET performance object.

Table D.36   Requests Counters

Counter	Description
Requests Disconnected	The number of requests that were disconnected because a communication failure occurred.
Requests Queued	The number of requests in the queue waiting to be serviced. If this number increases as the number of client requests increases, the Web server has reached the limit of concurrent requests that it can process. The default maximum for this counter is 5,000 requests. You can change this setting in the computer's Machine.config file.
Requests Rejected	The total number of requests that were not executed because insufficient server resources existed to process them. This counter represents the number of requests that return a 503 HTTP status code, which indicates that the server is too busy.
Request Wait Time	The number of milliseconds that the most recent request waited in the queue for processing.

Table D.37 describes the State Server Sessions counters for the ASP.NET performance object. These counter are available only on a computer on which the state server service (aspnet_state) is running.

Table D.37   State Server Sessions Counters

Counter	Description
State Server Sessions Abandoned	The number of user sessions that were explicitly abandoned. These are sessions that have been ended by specific user actions, such as closing the browser or navigating to another site.
State Server Sessions Active	The number of active user sessions.
State Server Sessions Timed Out	The number of user sessions that are now inactive. In this case, the user is inactive, not the server.
State Server Sessions Total	The number of sessions created during the lifetime of the process. This counter represents the cumulative value of State Server Sessions Active, State Server Sessions Abandoned, and State Server Sessions Timed Out counters.

Table D.38 describes the worker process counters for the ASP.NET performance object.

Table D.38 Worker Process Counters

Counter	Description
Worker Process Restarts	The number of times that a worker process restarted on the server computer. A worker process can be restarted if it fails unexpectedly or when it is intentionally recycled. If worker process restarts increase unexpectedly, investigate immediately.
Worker Processes Running	The number of worker processes that are running on the server computer.

ASP.NET Applications Performance Counters

ASP.NET supports the following application performance counters, which you can use to monitor the performance of a single instance of an ASP.NET application. A unique instance of these counters, named __Total__, aggregates counters for all applications on a Web server. The __Total__ instance is always available. When no applications are running on the server, the counters display zero.

Table D.39 describes the Anonymous Requests counters for the ASP.NET Applications performance object.

Table D.39 Anonymous Requests Counters

Counter	Description
Anonymous Requests	The number of requests that use anonymous authentication.
Anonymous Requests/sec	The average number of requests that have been made per second that use anonymous authentication.

Table D.40 describes the Cache Total counters for the ASP.NET Applications performance object.

Table D.40 Cache Total Counters

Counter	Description
Cache Total Entries	The total number of entries in the cache. This counter includes both internal use of the cache by the ASP.NET framework and external use of the cache through exposed APIs.
Cache Total Hits	The total number of responses served from the cache. This counter includes both internal use of the cache by the ASP.NET framework and external use of the cache through exposed APIs.
Cache Total Misses	The number of failed cache requests. This counter includes both internal use of the cache by ASP.NET and external use of the cache through exposed APIs.
Cache Total Hit Ratio	The ratio of cache hits to cache misses. This counter includes both internal use of the cache by ASP.NET and external use of the cache through exposed APIs.
Cache Total Turnover Rate	The number of additions to and removals from the cache per second. Use this counter to help determine how efficiently the cache is being used. If the turnover rate is high, the cache is not being used efficiently.

Table D.41 describes the Cache API counters for the ASP.NET Applications performance object.

Table D.41   Cache API Counters

Counter	Description
Cache API Entries	The total number of entries in the application cache.
Cache API Hits	The total number of requests served from the cache when it was accessed only through the external cache APIs. This counter does not track use of the cache internally by ASP.NET.
Cache API Misses	The total number of requests to the cache that failed when the cache was accessed through the external cache APIs. This counter does not track use of the cache internally by ASP.NET.
Cache API Hit Ratio	The cache hit-to-miss ratio when the cache was accessed through external cache APIs. This counter does not track use of the cache internally by ASP.NET.
Cache API Turnover Rate	The number of additions to and removals from the cache per second, when it is used through the external APIs (excluding internal use by the ASP.NET framework). This counter is useful for determining how effectively the cache is being used. If the turnover is great, then the cache is not being used effectively.

Table D.42 describes the Errors counters for the ASP.NET Applications performance object.

Table D.42   Errors Counters

Counter	Description
Errors During Preprocessing	The number of errors that occurred during parsing. Excludes compilation and run-time errors.
Errors During Compilation	The number of errors that occurred during dynamic compilation. Excludes parser and run-time errors.
Errors During Execution	The total number of errors that occurred during the execution of an HTTP request. Excludes parser and compilation errors.
Errors Unhandled During Execution	The total number of unhandled errors that occurred during the execution of HTTP requests. An *unhandled error* is any uncaught run-time exception that escapes user code on the page and enters the ASP.NET internal error-handling logic. Exceptions occur in the following circumstances: • When custom errors are enabled, an error page is defined, or both. • When the **Page_Error** event is defined in user code and either the error is cleared (by using the **HttpServerUtility.ClearError** method) or a redirect is performed.

(continued)

Table D.42   Errors Counters *(continued)*

Counter	Description
Errors Unhandled During Execution/sec	The number of unhandled exceptions that occurred per second during the execution of HTTP requests.
Errors Total	The total number of errors that occurred during the execution of HTTP requests. Includes parser, compilation, or run-time errors. This counter represents the sum of the Errors During Compilation, Errors During Preprocessing, and Errors During Execution counters. A well-functioning Web server should not generate errors.
Errors Total/sec	The average number of errors that occurred per second during the execution of HTTP requests. Includes any parser, compilation, or run-time errors.

Table D.43 describes the Output Cache counters for the ASP.NET Applications performance object.

Table D.43   Output Cache Counters

Counter	Description
Output Cache Entries	The total number of entries in the output cache.
Output Cache Hits	The total number of requests serviced from the output cache.
Output Cache Misses	The number of output-cache requests that failed per application.
Output Cache Hit Ratio	The percentage of total requests that were serviced from the output cache.
Output Cache Turnover Rate	The average number of additions to and removals from the output cache per second. If the turnover is great, the cache is not being used effectively.

Table D.44 describes the Request Bytes counters for the ASP.NET Applications performance object.

Table D.44   Request Bytes Counters

Counter	Description
Request Bytes In Total	The total size, in bytes, of all requests.
Request Bytes Out Total	The total size, in bytes, of responses sent to a client. This does not include standard HTTP response headers.

Table D.45 describes the Requests counters for the ASP.NET Applications performance object.

Table D.45   Requests Counters

Counter	Description
Requests Executing	The number of requests that are currently executing.
Requests Failed	The total number of failed requests. All status codes greater than or equal to 400 increment this counter. Note: Requests that cause a 401 status code increment this counter and the Requests Not Authorized counter. Requests that cause a 404 or 414 status code increment this counter and the Requests Not Found counter. Requests that cause a 500 status code increment this counter and the Requests Timed Out counter.
Requests In Application Queue	The number of requests in the application request queue.
Requests Not Found	The number of requests that failed because resources were not found (status code 404, 414).
Requests Not Authorized	The number of requests that failed because of lack of authorization (status code 401).
Requests Succeeded	The number of requests that executed successfully (status code 200).
Requests Timed Out	The number of requests that timed out (status code 500).
Requests Total	The total number of requests that have been made since the service started.
Requests/sec	The average number of requests that have been executed per second. This counter represents the current throughput of the application.

Table D.46 describes the Session State and SQL Server Connections counters for the ASP.NET Applications performance object.

Table D.46   Session State and SQL Server Connections Counters

Counter	Description
Session State Server Connections Total	The total number of session-state connections that were made to a computer on which out-of-process session-state data is stored.
Session SQL Server Connections Total	The total number of session-state connections that were made to the Microsoft® SQL Server™ database in which session-state data is stored.

Table D.47 describes the Sessions counters for the ASP.NET Applications performance object. These counters are supported only with in-memory session state.

Table D.47 Sessions Counters

Counter	Description
Sessions Active	The number of sessions that are active.
Sessions Abandoned	The number of sessions that have been explicitly abandoned.
Sessions Timed Out	The number of sessions that timed out.
Sessions Total	The total number of sessions.

Table D.48 describes the Transactions counters for the ASP.NET Applications performance object.

Table D.48 Transactions Counters

Counter	Description
Transactions Aborted	The number of transactions that were aborted.
Transactions Committed	The number of transactions that were committed. This counter increments after page execution if the transaction does not abort.
Transactions Pending	The number of transactions that are in progress.
Transactions Total	The total number of transactions that have occurred since the service was started.
Transactions/sec	The average number of transactions that were started per second.

Table D.49 describes a few miscellaneous counters for ASP.NET Applications.

Table D.49 Miscellaneous Counters for ASP.NET Applications

Counter	Description
Compilations Total	The total number of times that the Web server process dynamically compiled requests for files with .aspx, .asmx, .ascx, or .ashx extensions (or a code-behind source file).
	Note: This number initially climbs to a peak value as requests are made to all parts of an application. After compilation occurs, however, the resulting binary compilation is saved on disk, where it is reused until its source file changes. This means that, even when a process restarts, the counter can remain at zero (be inactive) until the application is modified or redeployed.
Debugging Requests	The number of requests that occurred while debugging was enabled.
Pipeline Instance Count	The number of active request pipeline instances for the specified ASP.NET application. Because only one execution thread can run within a pipeline instance, this number represents the maximum number of concurrent requests that are being processed for a specific application. In most circumstances, it is better for this number be low when the server is busy, because this means that the CPU is well used.

IIS 6.0 Event Messages

Internet Information Services (IIS) 6.0 generates events in Event Viewer so that you can verify the performance of IIS. Event Viewer tracks the following: error events, warning events, and informational events. The logs in Event Viewer provide an audited record of all services and processes in the Microsoft® Windows® Server 2003 operating system, such as logon and connection times.

In This Appendix

Related Information

- For information about viewing and interpreting log files, see "Analyzing Log Files" in this book.

- For information about performance monitoring and tuning, see "Optimizing IIS 6.0 Performance" in this book.

Event Logging Overview

By default, a computer running the Microsoft® Windows® Server 2003, Standard Edition; Windows® Server 2003, Enterprise Edition; Windows® Server 2003, Web Edition; or Windows® Server 2003, Datacenter Edition operating system records events in three kinds of logs:

- **Application.** Contains events logged by applications or programs.
- **Security.** Records events such as valid and invalid logon attempts, as well as events related to resource use.
- **System.** Contains events logged by Windows system components.

Logging begins automatically when Windows is started. For each type of log, you can filter the events to be viewed, designate the number of entries to view, specify how long to save entries, and specify whether to automatically overwrite existing events when the log becomes full.

You view Windows event logs through Event Viewer. You can open Event Viewer by using any one of the following methods:

- From the **Start** menu, click **Run**. In the **Open** box, type **eventvwr**, and then click **OK**.
- At the command prompt, type **start eventvwr**, and then press ENTER.
- From the **Start** menu, point to **Administrative Tools**, and then click **Event Viewer**.
- From the **Start** menu, point to **Administrative Tools**, and then click **Computer Management**. Event Viewer is listed under the **System Tools** node. The benefit of this display is that IIS Manager is in the same window under the **Services and Applications** node.

For more information about event logs and Event Viewer, see "Event Log Overview" in Help and Support Center for Windows Server 2003.

Operating system events related to IIS are logged in the event logs. These logs are not the same as the IIS logs that record specific information about Web site usage and activity. For more information about IIS logs, see "Analyzing Log Files" in this book.

 Note

When messages appear in the event log or Web browser, the symbols that appear in the tables in this chapter (such as |, %s, %X, %1, %2, %2!.20s!, and so on) are replaced with details about the error at the time that the error actually occurs.

WWW Service Events

Table E.1 lists the events that are generated by the part of the World Wide Web Publishing Service (WWW service) that handles internal administration of the W3SVC. The WWW service events are listed in the System log, with the source name W3SVC.

Table E.1   WWW Service Events

Event ID	Description
1001	The WWW service's InetInfo process monitor encountered an error and has shut down. This condition prevents the WWW service from detecting an unexpected termination of the InetInfo process and, therefore, it might not detect changes to the metabase as expected. Restart the WWW service.
1002	Application pool %1 is being automatically disabled because of a series of failures in the processes serving that application pool.
1003	Cannot register the URL prefix %1 for site %2. The URL might be invalid. The site has been deactivated. The data field contains the error number.
1004	Cannot register the URL prefix %1 for site %2. The site has been deactivated. The data field contains the error number.
1005	The WWW service is exiting because an error occurred. The data field contains the error number.
1007	Cannot register the URL prefix %1 for site %2. The necessary network binding might already be in use. The site has been deactivated. The data field contains the error number.
1009	A process serving application pool %1 was terminated unexpectedly. The process ID was %2. The process exit code was '0x%3.
1010	A process serving application pool %1 failed to respond to a ping. The process ID was %2.
1011	A process serving application pool %1 suffered a fatal communication error with the WWW service. The process ID was %2. The data field contains the error number.
1012	A process serving application pool %1 exceeded time limits during start up. The process ID was %2.
1013	A process serving application pool %1 exceeded time limits during shut down. The process ID was %2.
1014	The WWW service encountered an internal error in its process management of worker process %2 serving application pool %1. The data field contains the error number.
1015	A process serving application pool %1 was orphaned, but the specified orphan action %2 could not be executed. The data field contains the error number.

(continued)

Table E.1   WWW Service Events *(continued)*

Event ID	Description
1016	Unable to configure logging for site %1. The data field contains the error number.
1017	The WWW service has terminated because of a worker process failure.
1018	The WWW service was not able to initialize performance counters. The service will run without the performance counters. Restart the WWW service to reinitialize the performance counters. The data field contains the error number.
1019	The WWW service encountered difficulty initializing performance counters. Performance counters will function; however, some counter data might be inaccurate. The data field contains the error number.
1020	The WWW service encountered difficulty configuring the HTTP.sys control channel property %1. The data field contains the error number.
1021	The identity of application pool %1 is invalid. If it remains invalid when the first request for the application pool is processed, the application pool will be disabled. The data field contains the error number.
1022	The WWW service failed to create a worker process for the application pool %1. The data field contains the error number.
1024	Virtual site %1 is configured to truncate its log every %2 bytes. Because this value must be at least 1,048,576 bytes (1 megabyte), 1,048,576 bytes will be used.
1025	Application pool %1 exceeded its job limit settings.
1026	An error occurred securing the handle of application pool %1'; therefore, the application pool was not secured as expected. Change the identification information to cause the WWW service to secure the handle of the application pool again. The data field contains the error number.
1027	The WWW service's request of HTTP.sys to enable the application pool %1 failed. The data field contains the error number.
1028	The WWW service failed to add the worker process %1 to the job object representing application pool %2. The data field contains the error number.
1029	A failure occurred while configuring an application's bindings for site %1. The site has been deactivated. The data field contains the error number.
1030	InetInfo was terminated unexpectedly, and the system was not configured to restart the IIS Admin service. The WWW service has shut down.
1032	A failure occurred while configuring the logging properties for the site %1. Probable cause: A mapped network path is being used for the site's log file directory path, which is not supported by IIS. Use a UNC path instead.
1033	A failure occurred while configuring the logging properties for the site %1. Probable cause: The site's log file directory contains an invalid machine or share name.

(continued)

Table E.1 WWW Service Events *(continued)*

Event ID	Description
1034	A failure occurred while configuring the logging properties for the site %1. The server does not have access permissions to the site's log file directory.
1035	A failure occurred while configuring the logging properties for the site %1. The site's log file directory is not fully qualified. Probable cause: It is missing the drive letter or other crucial information.
1036	A failure occurred while initializing the configuration manager for the WWW service. The data field contains the error number.
1037	A failure occurred while opening the HTTP control channel for the WWW service. The data field contains the error number.
1039	A process serving application pool %1 reported a failure. The process ID was %2. The data field contains the error number.
1041	The %1 %2 failed range validation for property %3. The configured value %4 is outside of the range %5 to %6. The value will default to %7.
1042	The **AppPoolCommand** property set on the application pool %1 is not a valid value. It is %2. It must be either MD_APPPOOL_COMMAND_START = 1 or MD_APPPOOL_COMMAND_STOP = 2.
1043	The virtual site %1 has been invalidated and will be ignored because valid site bindings could not be constructed, or no site bindings exist.
1044	The virtual site %1 has been invalidated and will be ignored because the site's **AppPoolID** is null.
1046	The server command property for virtual site %1 is not a valid value. It is set to %2. It must be one of the following: MD_SERVER_COMMAND_START = 1, MD_SERVER_COMMAND_STOP = 2, MD_SERVER_COMMAND_PAUSE = 3, or MD_SERVER_COMMAND_CONTINUE = 4.
1047	The application %2 belonging to site %1 has an **AppPoolId** set, but the property is empty; therefore, the application will be ignored.
1048	The application %2 belonging to site %1 has an invalid **AppPoolId** %3 set; therefore, the application will be ignored.
1049	The application pool %1 has an **IdleTimeout** %2 greater than the **PeriodicRestartTime** %3. The defaults (**IdleTimeout** = %4 & PeriodicRestartTime %5) will be used.
1050	The application pool ID %1 exceeds length limits. It is %2 characters and cannot be more than %3 characters. The application pool will, therefore, be ignored.
1051	An application pool ID was defined as a zero-length string. An application pool ID must not be a zero-length string. The application pool will, therefore, be ignored.
1052	The application %2 belongs to an invalid site %1'; therefore, the application will be ignored.

(continued)

Table E.1 WWW Service Events *(continued)*

Event ID	Description
1053	The WWW service received a change notification, but was unable to process it correctly. The data field contains the error number.
1054	The WWW service failed to run the auto-stop action %2 for application pool %1. The data field contains the error number.
1055	The site %1 was disabled because the application pool defined for the site %2 is not a valid application pool.
1056	The site %1 was disabled because the application pool %2 defined for the site's root application is not a valid application pool.
1057	The identity of application pool %1 is invalid, so the WWW service cannot create a worker process to serve the application pool; therefore, the application pool has been disabled.
1058	The WWW service encountered a failure while setting the affinity mask of application pool %1. Probable cause: The mask does not contain any processors available on this machine. The data field contains the error number.
1059	A failure was encountered while launching the process serving application pool %1. The application pool has been disabled.
1060	The job object associated with application pool %1 encountered an error during configuration. CPU monitoring might not function as expected. The data field contains the error number.
1061	The job object attached to application pool %1 failed to start its timer. The application pool's CPU usage is being monitored and will eventually reach the limit and report a failure. The data field contains the error number.
1062	The WWW service encountered a failure configuring the logging properties on the HTTP Control Channel. **Logging Enabled** is %1. **Log File Directory** is %2. **Log Period** is %3. **Log Truncate Size** is %4. The data field contains the error number.
1063	The WWW service encountered a failure requesting metabase change notifications. The data field contains the error number.
1064	During recovery from an unexpected termination of the InetInfo process, the WWW service encountered a failure requesting metabase change notifications. Although the WWW service will continue to run, it is highly probable that it is no longer using current metabase data. Restart the WWW service to correct this condition. The data field contains the error number.
1065	Centralized logging is configured to truncate its log every %1 bytes. Because this value must be at least 1,048,576 bytes (1 megabyte), 1,048,576 bytes will be used.
1066	The WWW service encountered an error attempting to configure centralized logging. It is not configured as expected. The data field contains the error number.

(continued)

Table E.1   WWW Service Events *(continued)*

Event ID	Description
1067	The WWW service property %1 failed range validation. The configured value %2 is outside of the range %3 to %4. The default value, %5, will be used.
1068	The WWW service failed to record the proper state %2 and **Win32Error** %3 of site %1 in the metabase. To correct, start/stop the site, or restart the WWW service. The data field contains the error number.
1069	The WWW service failed to record the proper state %2 and **Win32Error** %3 of application pool %1 in the metabase. To correct, start/stop the application pool, or restart the WWW service. The data field contains the error number.
1070	The WWW service failed to issue recycle requests to all worker processes of application pool %1. The data field contains the error number.
1071	The WWW service failed to enable bandwidth throttling on site %1 because QoS Packet Scheduler is not installed.
1072	The WWW service failed to enable bandwidth throttling on site %1. The data field contains the error number.
1073	The WWW service failed to enable global bandwidth throttling because QoS Packet Scheduler is not installed.
1074	A worker process with process ID of %1 serving application pool %2 has requested a recycle because the worker process reached its allowed processing time limit.
1075	A worker process with process ID of %1 serving application pool %2 has requested a recycle because it reached its allowed request limit.
1076	A worker process with process ID of %1 serving application pool %2 has requested a recycle because it reached its scheduled recycle time.
1077	A worker process with process ID of %1 serving application pool %2 has requested a recycle because it reached its virtual memory limit.
1078	An ISAPI reported an unhealthy condition to its worker process; therefore, the worker process with process ID of %1 serving application pool %2 has requested a recycle.
1079	An administrator has requested a recycle of all worker processes in application pool %1.
1080	The worker processes serving application pool %1 are being recycled, because one or more configuration changes in the properties of the application pool necessitated a restart of the processes.
1081	The worker processes serving application pool %1 are being recycled because of detected problems with the metabase that might make current cached metadata invalid.
1082	A worker process with process ID %2 that serves application pool %1 has been determined to be unhealthy (see previous event log message), but — because a debugger is attached to it — the WWW service will ignore the error.

(continued)

Table E.1   WWW Service Events *(continued)*

Event ID	Description
1083	HTTP.sys provided inconsistent site performance counter data to the WWW service. Therefore, the WWW service will ignore the data provided.
1084	The WWW service's request of HTTP.sys to disable the application pool %1 failed. The data field contains the error number.
1085	The WWW service failed to apply a new configuration for application pool %1. The data field contains the error number.
1086	The WWW service failed to properly configure the load balancer capabilities on application pool %1. The data field contains the error number.
1087	The WWW service failed to properly configure the application pool queue length on application pool %1. The data field contains the error number.
1088	The WWW service failed to properly configure the job object for application pool %1. The data field contains the error number.
1089	The WWW service failed to issue a demand start to HTTP.sys for application pool %1. The data field contains the error number.
1090	The WWW service failed to update the **AutoStart** property for application pool %1. The data field contains the error number.
1091	The WWW service failed to run the auto-stop action for application pool %1. The data field contains the error number.
1092	The WWW service failed to issue a request for the worker process %2 of application pool %1 to supply its performance counters. The data field contains the error number.
1093	The WWW service failed to overlap recycle for application pool %1 worker process %2. The data field contains the error number.
1094	The WWW service failed to disassociate the application %1 from the virtual site %2. The data field contains the error number.
1095	The WWW service failed to delete the configuration group for the application %1 in site %2. The data field contains the error number.
1096	The WWW service failed to remove the URLs for the virtual site %1. The data field contains the error number.
1097	The WWW service failed to set the application pool for the application %1 in site %2. The data field contains the error number.
1098	The WWW service failed to set the maximum connections for the virtual site %1. The data field contains the error number.
1099	The WWW service failed to set the connection time-out for the virtual site %1. The data field contains the error number.

(continued)

Table E.1 WWW Service Events *(continued)*

Event ID	Description
1100	The WWW service failed to create the application %2 in site %1. The data field contains the error number.
1101	The WWW service failed to create application pool %1. The data field contains the error number.
1102	The WWW service failed to create site %1. The data field contains the error number.
1103	The WWW service failed to delete the application %2 in site %1. The data field contains the error number.
1104	The WWW service failed to delete application pool %1. The data field contains the error number.
1105	The WWW service failed to delete site %1. The data field contains the error number.
1106	The WWW service failed to modify the application %2 in site %1. The data field contains the error number.
1107	The WWW service failed to modify application pool %1. The data field contains the error number.
1108	The WWW service failed to modify site %1. The data field contains the error number.
1109	The WWW service failed to set the control channel's filter configuration. The data field contains the error number.
1110	The WWW service failed to write the **AutoStart** property for site %1. The data field contains the error number.
1111	The WWW service failed to delete all IIS-owned Secure Sockets Layer (SSL) configuration data. The data field contains the error number.
1112	The WWW service failed to query SSL configuration data for site %1. The data field contains the error number.
1113	One of the IP/Port combinations for site %1 has already been configured to be used by another site. The other site's SSL configuration will be used.
1114	One of the IP/Port combinations for site %1 has already been configured to be used by another program. The other program's SSL configuration will be used.
1115	The WWW service failed to set SSL configuration data for site %1. The data field contains the error number.
1116	The WWW service failed to delete SSL configuration data for site %1. The data field contains the error number.
1117	A worker process with process ID of %1 serving application pool %2 has requested a recycle because it reached its private-bytes-memory limit.

(continued)

Table E.1   WWW Service Events *(continued)*

Event ID	Description
1118	During recovery from an unexpected termination of the InetInfo process, the WWW service failed to identify the appropriate records requiring deletion from its metadata cache. The data field contains the error number.
1119	During recovery from an unexpected termination of the InetInfo process, the WWW service failed to queue action items necessary to handle the recovery. Restart the WWW service. The data field contains the error number.
1120	The WWW service failed to obtain cache counters from HTTP.sys. The reported performance counters do not include performance counters from HTTP.sys for this gathering. The data field contains the error number.
1121	The WWW service failed to obtain site performance counters from HTTP.sys. The reported performance counters do not include counters from HTTP.sys for this gathering. The data field contains the error number.
1122	The WWW service failed to publish the performance counters it gathered. The data field contains the error number.
1123	The WWW service failed to cancel the performance counter gathering timer. The data field contains the error number.
1124	The WWW service failed to cancel the performance counter timer. The data field contains the error number.
1125	The WWW service failed to start the performance counter gathering timer. The data field contains the error number.
1126	The WWW service failed to copy a change notification for processing. Therefore, the service might not be in sync with the current data in the metabase. The data field contains the error number.
1127	A worker process %2 serving application pool %1 is no longer trusted by the WWW service, based on ill-formed data the worker process sent to the service.
1128	The WWW service was not able to initialize Active Server Pages (ASP) performance counters. The service will, therefore, run without ASP performance counters. Restart the WWW service to start ASP performance-counter gathering. The data field contains the error number.
1129	Cannot register the URL prefix %1 for site %2. Either the network endpoint for the site's IP address could not be created or the IP listen list for HTTP.sys did not contain any usable IP addresses. The site has been deactivated. The data field contains the error number.
1130	Cannot register the URL prefix %1 for site %2. The IP address for the site is not in the HTTP.sys IP listen list. The site has been deactivated. The data field contains the error number.
1131	Cannot register the URL prefix %1 for site %2. Too many listening ports have been configured in HTTP.sys. The site has been deactivated. The data field contains the error number.

WWW Service Worker Process Events

Table E.2 lists the events that the WWW service worker process generates, such as authentication and authorization, application problems, memory monitoring, and so on. These events are listed in the Application log with the source name W3SVC-WP.

Table E.2 Worker Process Events for the WWW Service

Event ID	Description
2201	The HTTP server could not initialize its security. The data is the error.
2203	The HTTP server could not initialize the socket library. The data is the error.
2204	The HTTP server was unable to initialize because of a shortage of available memory. The data is the error.
2206	The HTTP server could not create the main connection socket. The data is the error.
2208	The HTTP server could not create a client connection object for the user at host %1. The connection to this user is terminated. The data is the error.
2214	The HTTP filter DLL %1 failed to load. The data is the error.
2216	The script that was started from the URL %1 with parameters %2 has not responded within the configured time-out period. The HTTP server is terminating the script.
2218	The HTTP server encountered an error processing the server-side include file %1. The error was %2.
2219	The HTTP server encountered an unhandled exception while processing the ISAPI application %1.
2220	The HTTP server was unable to load the ISAPI application %1. The data is the error.
2221	A server-side include file has included itself, or the maximum depth of server-side includes has been exceeded.
2222	An attempt was made to load filter %1 on a server instance, but it requires the SF_NOTIFY_READ_RAW_DATA filter notification so it must be loaded as a global filter.
2223	For compatibility with previous versions of IIS, the filter %1 was loaded as a global filter from the registry. To control the filter with IIS Manager, remove the filter from the registry and add it as a global filter with IIS Manager. Filters in the registry are stored at HKLM\System\CurrentControlSet\Services\W3Svc\Parameters\Filter DLLs.
2226	The server was unable to read the file %1 because of a lack of access permissions.
2227	The server was unable to acquire a license for an SSL connection.
2228	The server stopped serving requests for application %1 because the number of crashes of out-of-process components exceeded a limit.

(continued)

Table E.2   Worker Process Events for the WWW Service *(continued)*

Event ID	Description
2229	The server failed to shut down application %1. The error was %2.
2230	The server was unable to read the file %1. The file does not exist.
2231	The server was unable to read the file %1. The Windows 32 error returned from the attempt is %2.
2232	The server was unable to read the file %1. The file exceeds the maximum allowable size of %2.
2233	The server was unable to allocate a buffer to read the file %1.
2236	The server failed to load application %1. The error was %2.
2237	Out-of-process application %1 terminated unexpectedly.
2238	The job object query failed. The data is the error.
2239	The job object set limit failed. The data is the error.
2240	Schedule a work item for CPU Accounting or Limits failed. The data is the error.
2241	Site %1 hit its CPU Limit. No action was taken.
2242	Site %1 hit its CPU Limit. The priority of all process on that site has been lowered to idle class.
2243	Site %1 hit its CPU Limit. All processes on that site have been terminated.
2244	Site %1 hit its CPU Limit. The site has been paused.
2245	The server certificate for instance %1 has expired or is not yet valid.
2246	The server certificate for instance %1 has been revoked.
2247	The server certificate for instance %1 does not chain up to a trusted root certificate.
2248	One of the certificates in the certificate chain of the server certificate for instance %1 has an invalid signature.
2249	CPU Limits/Accounting failed to queue work item. The data is the error.
2250	The server certificate for instance %1 had invalid metabase data associated with it and could not be retrieved. The error encountered was %2.
2251	A CryptoAPI error was encountered trying to retrieve the server certificate for instance %1. The error encountered was %2.
2252	The server certificate for instance %1 could not be retrieved because it could not be found in a certificate store. The error encountered was %2'.
2253	The server certificate for instance %1 could not be retrieved because of an internal error. The error encountered was %2.
2254	The server Certificate Trust List for instance %1 had invalid metabase data associated with it and could not be retrieved. The error encountered was %2.

(continued)

Table E.2 Worker Process Events for the WWW Service *(continued)*

Event ID	Description
2255	A CryptoAPI error was encountered trying to retrieve the server Certificate Trust List for instance %1. The error encountered was %2.
2256	The server Certificate Trust List for instance %1 could not be retrieved because it could not be found in a certificate store. The error encountered was %2.
2257	The server certificate for instance %1 could not be retrieved because of an internal error. The error number is %2.
2258	The server failed to close client connections to the following URLs during shutdown: %1.
2259	The COM application %1 at %2 failed to activate out of process.
2261	An attempt was made to load filter %1, but it requires the SF_NOTIFY_READ_RAW_DATA filter notification, which is not supported in worker process isolation mode.
2262	ISAPI %1 reported itself as unhealthy for the following reason: %2.
2263	ISAPI %1 reported itself as unhealthy. No reason was given by the ISAPI.
2264	The directory specified for caching compressed content %1 is invalid. Static compression is being disabled.
2265	The registry key for IIS subauthenticator is not configured correctly on the local machine; the anonymous password sync feature is disabled.
2266	The account that the current worker process is running under does not have SeTcbPrivilege privilege; the anonymous password sync feature and the Digest authentication feature are disabled.
2267	A raw ISAPI filter could not be loaded because of a configuration problem. HTTPFilter Service has to be hosted in InetInfo.exe for raw ISAPI filters to work correctly. The most likely reason is that the **IIS5IsolationModeEnabled** setting was changed and HTTPFilter service was not restarted. Restart HTTPFilter for configuration changes to be taken into effect.
2268	Could not load all ISAPI filters for site/service. Therefore, startup was aborted.
2269	The worker process failed to initialize the HTTP.sys communication or the W3svc.exe communication layer and, therefore, could not be started. The data field contains the error number.
2270	IIS client certificate mapping configuration for site %1 failed to be loaded. The data field contains the error number.
2271	Could not initialize the logging module for site %1. The site will, therefore, be nonfunctional.
2272	The registry key for IIS subauthenticator is not configured correctly on the domain controller; the Digest authentication feature is disabled.
2273	The worker process could not access the metabase because a disconnection error occurred. Marking process as unhealthy.

ASP Events and Errors

In Event Viewer, you can open the property pages for each type of log and configure the filter options that generally apply to all events.

IIS increases the degree of control by providing two metabase keys that enable you to specify what is sent to the Windows Events log when ASP events and errors occur: **AspLogErrorRequests** and **AspErrorsToNTLog**.

AspLogErrorRequests

The **AspLogErrorRequests** property controls whether the Web server writes unsuccessful client requests to the Windows event log file. If **AspLogErrorRequests** is set to TRUE, a standard set of ASP error requests are logged.

If **AspLogErrorRequests** is set to TRUE and **AspErrorsToNTLog** is set to FALSE, then the ASP errors are sent to the IIS log. If these errors are serious or logging to the IIS log previously failed, then each error is also sent to the Windows event log.

If **AspLogErrorRequests** is set to FALSE, these errors are sent only to the IIS log and not to the Windows Event Log. If **AspLogErrorRequests** is set to TRUE and **AspErrorsToNTLog** is set to TRUE, then all ASP-related errors go to the Windows event log and the IIS log. For more information about setting the **AspLogErrorRequests** property, see "About Events" in IIS 6.0 Help.

To completely prevent ASP errors from being logged in the IIS log file, you must disable logging altogether. For more information about disabling logging, see "Analyzing Log Files" in this book.

AspErrorsToNTLog

If the **AspErrorsToNTLog** key is set to TRUE, all possible ASP errors are sent to the application event log. If this key is set to FALSE, only a subset of all ASP errors is sent. The subset includes the error numbers 100, 101, 102, 103, 104, 105, 106, 107, 115, 190, 191, 192, 193, 194, 240, 241, and 242. This key cannot be set in IIS Manager. It must be set programmatically, using scripts, for example.

ASP Events

Table E.3 lists the events that the WWW service generates when processing ASP applications that are configured incorrectly or ASP pages that contain errors. These events are listed in the Application log regardless of the value of the **ASPLogErrorRequests** metabase property.

Table E.3   ASP Events

Event ID	Description
0x5	Error: %1.
0x6	Error: %1, %2.
0x7	Error: %1, %2, %3.
0x8	Error: %1, %2, %3, %4.
0x9	Warning: %1.
0x10	Warning: %1, %2.
0x11	Warning: %1, %2, %3.
0x12	Warning: %1, %2, %3, %4.
0x13	Failed to create an ASP session because access was denied when activating COM+ partition %1.
0x14	Failed to create ASP application %1 because of invalid or missing COM+ partition ID.
0x15	Failed to retrieve the anonymous user token for ASP application %1. Global.asa OnEnd routines will not be executed.
0x16	Failed to impersonate the anonymous user for ASP application %1. Global.asa OnEnd routines will not be executed.
0x17	No default script language was specified for application %s. Using default: %s.
0x1f3	Invalid progID.

ASP Errors

Table E.4 lists the errors that the WWW service generates when processing ASP applications that are configured incorrectly or ASP pages that contain errors. These errors are listed in the Application log only if the **ASPLogErrorRequests** metabase property is set to TRUE. If the **ASPErrorsToNTLog** metabase property is also set to TRUE, all the errors get logged to the Windows event application log; otherwise, only a subset is logged. The subset includes the error numbers 100, 101, 102, 103, 104, 105, 106, 107, 115, 190, 191, 192, 193, 194, 240, 241, and 242. These error messages are listed in the Application log with the source name Active Server Pages.

Table E.4 ASP Errors

Error ID	Description
0100	Out of memory. Unable to allocate required memory.
0101	Unexpected error. The function returned |.
0102	Expecting string input. The function expects a string as input.
0103	Expecting numeric input. The function expects a number as input.
0104	Operation not allowed.
0105	Index out of range. An array index is out of range.
0106	Type mismatch. An unhandled data type was encountered.
0107	Data size too large. The size of the data being sent in the request is over the allowed limit.
0108	Create object failed. An error occurred while creating object %s.
0109	Member not found.
0110	Unknown name.
0111	Unknown interface.
0112	Missing parameter.
0113	Script timed out. The maximum amount of time for a script to be executed was exceeded. You can change this limit by specifying a new value for the property **Server.ScriptTimeout** or by changing the value in the IIS administration tools.
0114	Object not free-threaded. The application object accepts only free-threaded objects; object %s is not free-threaded.
0115	Unexpected error. A trappable error (%X) occurred in an external object. The script cannot continue running.
0116	Missing close of script delimiter. The script block lacks the close of the <script> tag (%>).

(continued)

Table E.4   ASP Errors *(continued)*

Error ID	Description
0117	Missing close of <script> tag. The script block lacks the close of the <script> tag (</SCRIPT>) or the close-of-tag symbol (>).
0118	Missing close of <object> tag. The object block lacks the close of the <object> tag (</OBJECT>) or the close-of-tag symbol (>).
0119	Missing **Classid** or **Progid** attribute. The object instance '	' requires a valid **Classid** or **Progid** in the <object> tag.
0120	Invalid **Runat** attribute. The **Runat** attribute of the <script> tag or <object> tag can have only the value 'Server.
0121	Invalid scope in <object> tag. The object instance '	' cannot have Application or Session scope. To create the object instance with Session or Application scope, place the <object> tag in the Global.asa file.
0122	Invalid scope in <object> tag. The object instance '	' must have Application or Session scope. This applies to all objects created in a Global.asa file.
0123	Missing **ID** attribute. The required **ID** attribute of the <object> tag is missing.
0124	Missing **Language** attribute. The required **Language** attribute of the <script> tag is missing.
0125	Missing close of attribute. The value of the '	' attribute has no closing delimiter.
0126	Include file not found. The include file '	' was not found.
0127	Missing close of HTML comment. The HTML comment or server-side include lacks the close tag (-->).
0128	Missing **File** or **Virtual** attribute. The include file name must be specified by using either the **File** or **Virtual** attribute.
0129	Unknown scripting language. The scripting language '	' is not found on the server.
0130	Invalid **File** attribute. **File** attribute '	' cannot start with a forward slash or a backward slash.
0131	Disallowed parent path. The include file '	' cannot contain '..' to indicate the parent directory.
0132	Compilation error. The ASP page '	' could not be processed.
0133	Invalid **ClassID** attribute. The <object> tag has an invalid **ClassID** of '	.
0134	Invalid **ProgID** attribute. The object has an invalid **ProgID** of '	.
0135	Cyclic include. The file '	' is included by itself (perhaps indirectly). Select the **Include files for other include statements** box.
0136	Invalid object instance name. The object instance '	' is attempting to use a reserved name. This name is used by ASP pages intrinsic objects.

(continued)

Table E.4   ASP Errors *(continued)*

Error ID	Description
0137	Invalid global script. Script blocks must be one of the allowed Global.asa procedures. Script directives within <% ... %> are not allowed within the Global.asa file. The allowed procedure names are **Application_OnStart, Application_OnEnd, Session_OnStart,** and **Session_OnEnd.**
0138	Nested script block. A script block cannot be placed inside another script block.
0139	Nested object. An <object> tag cannot be placed inside another <object> tag.
0140	Page command out of order. The @ command must be the first command within the ASP page.
0141	Page command repeated. The @ command can be used only once within the ASP page.
0142	Thread token error. A thread token failed to open.
0143	Invalid application name. A valid application name was not found.
0144	Initialization error. The page-level objects list failed during initialization.
0145	New application failed. The new application could not be added.
0146	New session failed. The new session could not be added.
0147	500 server error.
0148	Server too busy.
0149	Application restarting. The request cannot be processed while the application is being restarted.
0150	Application directory error. The application directory could not be opened.
0151	Change notification error. The change notification event could not be created.
0152	Security error. An error occurred while processing a user's security credentials.
0153	Thread error. A new thread request failed.
0154	Write HTTP header error. The HTTP headers could not be written to the client browser.
0155	Write page content error. The page content could not be written to the client browser.
0156	Header error. The HTTP headers are already written to the client browser. Any HTTP header modifications must be made before writing page content.
0157	Buffering on. Buffering cannot be turned off once it is turned on.
0158	Missing URL. A URL is required.
0159	Buffering off. Buffering must be on.
0160	Logging failure. Failure to write entry to the log.

(continued)

Table E.4   ASP Errors *(continued)*

Error ID	Description
0161	Data type error. The conversion of a **Variant** to a **String** variable failed.
0162	Cannot modify cookie. The cookie 'ASPSessionID' cannot be modified. It is a reserved cookie name.
0163	Invalid comma use. Commas cannot be used within a log entry. Select another delimiter.
0164	Invalid **TimeOut** value. An invalid **TimeOut** value was specified.
0165	**SessionID** error. A **SessionID** string cannot be created.
0166	Uninitialized object. An attempt was made to access an uninitialized object.
0167	Session initialization error. An error occurred while initializing the **Session** object.
0168	Disallowed object use. An intrinsic object cannot be stored within the **Session** object.
0169	Missing object information. An object with missing information cannot be stored in the **Session** object. The threading model information for an object is required.
0170	Delete session error. The session was not deleted properly.
0171	Missing path. The **Path** parameter must be specified for the **MapPath** method.
0172	Invalid path. The **Path** parameter for the **MapPath** method must be a virtual path. A physical path was used.
0173	Invalid path character. An invalid character was specified in the **Path** parameter for the **MapPath** method.
0174	Invalid path characters. An invalid '/' or '\\' was found in the **Path** parameter for the **MapPath** method.
0175	Disallowed path characters. The '..' characters are not allowed in the **Path** parameter for the **MapPath** method.
0176	Path not found. The **Path** parameter for the **MapPath** method did not correspond to a known path.
0177	**Server.CreateObject** failed. %s'
0178	**Server.CreateObject** access error. The call to **Server.CreateObject** failed while checking permissions. Access is denied to this object.
0179	Application initialization error. An error occurred while initializing the **Application** object.
0180	Disallowed object use. An intrinsic object cannot be stored within the **Application** object.
0181	Invalid threading model. An object using the apartment threading model cannot be stored within the **Application** object.
0182	Missing object information. An object with missing information cannot be stored in the **Application** object. The threading model information for the object is required.

(continued)

Table E.4 ASP Errors *(continued)*

Error ID	Description
0183	Empty cookie key. A cookie with an empty key cannot be stored.
0184	Missing cookie name. A name must be specified for a cookie.
0185	Missing default property. A default property was not found for the object.
0186	Error parsing certificate.
0187	Object addition conflict. Could not add object to application. Application was locked down by another request for adding an object.
0188	Disallowed object use. Cannot add objects created by using <object> tags to the session intrinsic.
0189	Disallowed object use. Cannot add objects created by using <object> tags to the application intrinsic.
0190	Unexpected error. A trappable error occurred while releasing an external object.
0191	Unexpected error. A trappable error occurred in the **OnStartPage** method of an external object.
0192	Unexpected error. A trappable error occurred in the **OnEndPage** method of an external object.
0193	**OnStartPage** failed. An error occurred in the **OnStartPage** method of an external object.
0194	**OnEndPage** failed. An error occurred in the **OnEndPage** method of an external object.
0195	Invalid server method call. This method of the **Server** object cannot be called during **Session_OnEnd** and **Application_OnEnd**.
0196	Cannot launch out-of-process component. Only InProc server components should be used. If you want to use LocalServer components, you must set the **AspAllowOutOfProcComponents** metabase setting. Consult the Help file for important considerations.
0197	Disallowed object use. Cannot add object with apartment model behavior to the application intrinsic object.
0198	Server shutting down. Cannot process request.
0199	Disallowed object use. Cannot add **JScript** objects to the session.
0200	Out-of-range **Expires** attribute. The date and time given for the **Expires** attribute is earlier than Jan 1, 1980 or later than Jan 19, 2038, 3:14:07 GMT.
0201	Invalid default script language. The default script language specified for this application is invalid.
0202	Missing code page. The **CodePage** attribute is missing.
0203	Invalid code page. The specified **CodePage** attribute is invalid.

(continued)

Table E.4   ASP Errors *(continued)*

Error ID	Description
0204	Invalid **CodePage** value. An invalid **CodePage** value was specified.
0205	Change notification. Failed to create event for change notification.
0206	Cannot call BinaryRead. Cannot call BinaryRead after using Request.Form collection.
0207	Cannot use Request.Form. Cannot use Request.Form collection after calling BinaryRead.
0208	Cannot use generic Request collection. Cannot use the generic Request collection after calling BinaryRead.
0209	Illegal value for **Transaction** property. The **Transaction** property can only be REQUIRED, REQUIRES_NEW, SUPPORTED, or NOT_SUPPORTED.
0210	Method not implemented. This method has not yet been implemented.
0211	Object out of scope. A built-in ASP object, which is no longer valid, has been referenced.
0212	Cannot clear buffer. Response.Clear is not allowed after a Response.Flush while client debugging is enabled.
0214	Invalid **Path** parameter. The **Path** parameter exceeds the maximum length allowed.
0215	Illegal value for **EnableSessionState** property. The **EnableSessionState** property can be only TRUE or FALSE.
0216	MSDTC Service not running. Transactional Web pages cannot be run if the MSDTC service is not running.
0217	Invalid scope in <object> tag. Object scope must be Page, Session, or Application.
0218	Missing LCID. The LCID attribute is missing.
0219	Invalid LCID. The specified LCID is not available.
0220	Requests for Global.asa not allowed. Requests with the URL pointing to Global.asa are not allowed.
0221	Invalid @ Command directive. The specified '	' option is unknown or invalid.
0222	Invalid TypeLib Specification. The <metadata> tag contains an invalid type library specification.
0223	TypeLib not found. The <metadata> tag contains a type library specification that does not match any registry entry.
0224	Cannot load TypeLib. Cannot load the type library specified in the <metadata> tag.
0225	Cannot wrap TypeLibs. Cannot create a type library wrapper object from the type libraries specified in <metadata> tags.
0226	Cannot modify StaticObjects. StaticObjects collection cannot be modified at run time.
0228	Server.Execute error. The call to Server.Execute failed while loading the page.

(continued)

Table E.4 ASP Errors *(continued)*

Error ID	Description
0229	Server.Transfer failed. The call to Server.Transfer failed
0230	Server.Transfer error. The call to Server.Transfer failed while loading the page.
0231	Server.Execute error. Invalid URL form or fully qualified absolute URL was used. Use relative URLs.
0232	Invalid cookie specification. The <metadata> tag contains an invalid cookie specification.
0233	Cannot load cookie script source. Cannot load cookie script source file specified in the <metadata> tag.
0234	Invalid include directive. Server-side include directives cannot be present in script blocks. Use the **SRC=** attribute of the <script> tag.
0235	Server.Transfer error. Invalid URL form or fully qualified absolute URL was used. Use relative URLs.
0236	Invalid cookie specification. The <metadata> tag contains an invalid or missing **SRC** parameter.
0237	Invalid cookie specification. The <metadata> tag contains an invalid or missing **Name** parameter.
0238	Missing attribute value. No value was specified for the '	' attribute.
0239	Cannot process file. Unicode ASP files are not supported.
0240	Script engine exception. A script engine threw exception %X in %s from %s.
0241	**CreateObject** exception. The **CreateObject** of %s caused exception %X.
0242	Query **OnStartPage** interface exception. Querying the **OnStartPage** or **OnEndPage** methods of object %s caused exception %X.
0243	Invalid <metadata> tag in Global.asa. Only <metadata> TYPE="TypeLib" can be used in Global.asa.
0244	Cannot enable session state. Session state cannot be enabled when it has been disabled in the application.
0245	Mixed usage of code page values. The **@CODEPAGE** value specified differs from that of the including file's code page or the file's saved format.
0246	Too many concurrent users. Try again later.
0247	Bad argument to **BinaryRead**. The argument to **BinaryRead** must be nonnegative.
0248	Script is not transacted. This ASP file must be transacted to use the **ObjectContext** object.
0249	Cannot use IStream on **Request**. Cannot use IStream on **Request** object after using Request.Form collection or Request.BinaryRead.
0250	Invalid default code page. The default code page specified for this application is invalid.
0251	Response buffer limit exceeded. Execution of the ASP page caused the response buffer to exceed its configured limit.

FTP Service Events

Table E.5 lists the events that are generated by the FTP service. The FTP service events are listed in the System log with the source name MSFTPSVC.

Table E.5 FTP Service Events

Event ID	Description
1	FTP server could not initialize its security. The data is the error.
3	FTP server could not initialize the socket library. The data is the error.
4	FTP server was unable to be initialized because of a shortage of available memory. The data is the error.
5	FTP server could not locate the FTP/TCP service. The data is the error.
6	FTP server could not create the main connection socket. The data is the error.
7	FTP server could not create the main connection thread. The data is the error.
8	FTP server could not create a client worker thread for the user at host %1. The connection to this user is terminated. The data is the error.
9	A call to a system service failed unexpectedly. The data is the error.
10	User %1 at host %2 has timed out after %3 seconds of inactivity.
11	An anonymous logon request was received from %1 at host %2.
12	A user logon request was received from %1 at host %2.
13	User %1 failed to log on, could not access the home directory %2.
14	User %1 denied access to the current directory %2 because of a security change.
15	Failed to read metabase property **PassivePortRange** under the FTP service node %1.
16	The FTP service configuration property **PassivePortRange** has the invalid value: %1.

WWW Service Performance Counter Events

Table E.6 lists the events that are generated by the part of the WWW service that monitors and records performance counter data. These events are listed in the Application log with the source name W3Ctrs.

Table E.6   WWW Service Performance Counter Events

Event ID	Description
2000	Unable to query the WWW service performance data. The error code returned by the service is data DWORD 0.
2001	It has taken too long to refresh the WWW service counters; the stale counters are being used instead.
2002	Setting up Web service counters failed; make sure your Web service counters are registered correctly.
2003	It has taken too long to refresh the WWW service counters; the stale counters are being used instead. This is the second message within the past %1 (hours, minutes, seconds). No more stale counter messages will be logged for this client session until the time limit expires. For more information about this message, see the Microsoft Online Support link on the Web Resources page at http://www.microsoft.com/windows/reskits/webresources.

Centralized Binary Log
File Format

Centralized binary log files require a specialized parser to interpret the log data. You can use the file format provided in this appendix to create a custom parser.

In This Appendix

Related Information

- For information about IIS logs, see "Analyzing Log Files" in this book.

Centralized Binary Logging

Centralized binary logging was designed to log as much information as possible while using the least amount of system resources. Therefore, numeric identifiers, which are called *indexes*, are substituted for variable-length strings in key fields. The indexes map the variable-length string to the logged identifier. When centralized binary logging is enabled, every site hosted on a server running Internet Information Services (IIS) sends raw log data to a single file.

File Names

The binary log file has an Internet binary log, or .ibl, file name extension. This file name extension was created so that text utilities that recognize the .log format would not attempt to open the binary log file.

Depending on the recycling option you choose, the binary log file will be named as follows:

- **Date-based recycling**: rayymmddhh.ibl. The time in the name is expressed in Universal Coordinated Time (UTC).

- **Size recycling**: raw#.ibl. IIS assigns a number to each log file, in increments of one. The represents the number of the log file.

Record Order

The typical central binary log file has the records shown in Figure F.1, and they appear in the order shown. However, the exact order depends on the arrival order of cache-hit requests and cache-miss requests.

Figure F.1   Hierarchy of Records in a Central Binary Log File

Header Record (RAW_FILE_HEADER)
Cache Miss Log Record (RAW_FILE_MISS_LOG_DATA)
***
Index Mapping Record (RAW_INDEX_FIELD_DATA)
Cache Hit Log Record (RAW_FILE_HIT_LOG_DATA)
***
Cache Flush Notification Record (RAW_FILE_CACHE_NOTIFICATION)
***

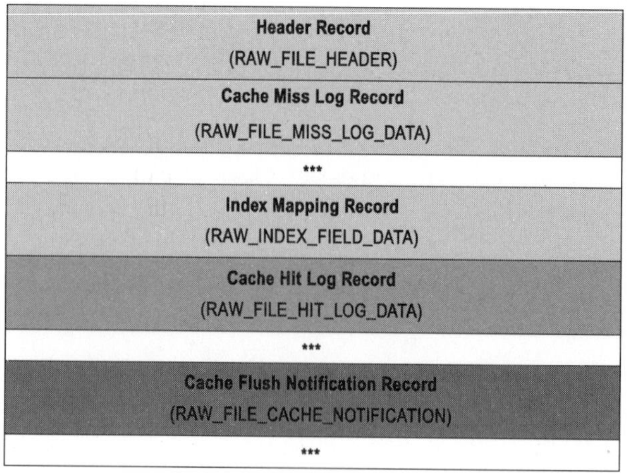

Record Types

All binary log record files have a two-byte **RecordType** field defined as the first element. Parsers should read the **USHORT** field first to determine the record type before parsing the whole record. Table F.1 lists the numbers that represent the binary log file record types.

Table F.1 Record Types

Record Type	Number
#define HTTP_RAW_RECORD_HEADER_TYPE	(0)
#define HTTP_RAW_RECORD_INDEX_DATA_TYPE	(2)
#define HTTP_RAW_RECORD_HIT_LOG_DATA_TYPE	(3)
#define HTTP_RAW_RECORD_MISS_LOG_DATA_TYPE	(4)
#define HTTP_RAW_RECORD_CACHE_NOTIFICATION_DATA_TYPE	(5)

Basic data types, such as **ULONG**, shown in the records in the rest of this appendix are written to the binary log file in host order, unless otherwise specified.

 Note

You must use the Windows.H header file to make most of the following data types available. For more information about the Windows.H header file, search for "Windows.H" on MSDN® Online, which is accessible from the MSDN Online link on the Web Resources page at http://www.microsoft.com/windows/reskits/webresources.

Header Record

The header record is the first log file record. It contains fields that identify which server generated the log file, and the date and time that the file was created. This information enables you to validate the file, see the statement of capabilities, and move the logs from one computer to another for post-processing, all without losing the source of the information.

A header record is always included at the beginning of each log file, and if the server is restarted during the logging period, header records are also written into the middle of each log file. For example, if the server is configured to start a new log file every day and the server is then restarted in the middle of the day, a second header is placed in the middle of that day's log file.

Example F.1 contains a description of the header record with inline comments.

Example F.1 Header Record

```
// Please be aware that Microsoft might change this data format at any time
// and is likely to do so in future Microsoft® Windows® operating system
releases. Developers who use this
// data structure definition will need to alter program logic,
// recompile, and then re-release their applications for future
// releases of Windows (or service packs).
//
#define MAX_COMPUTER_NAME_LEN            (256)

typedef struct _RAW_FILE_HEADER
{
    // Must be RAW_RECORD_HEADER_TYPE, i.e. value is 0
    //
    USHORT          RecordType;

    // Identifies the version of the Internet Binary Log File.
    //
    union {
        struct {
            UCHAR MajorVersion; // MAJOR_RAW_LOG_FILE_VERSION == 1
            UCHAR MinorVersion; // MINOR_RAW_LOG_FILE_VERSION == 0
        };
        USHORT Version;
    };

    // Shows the alignment padding size. sizeof(PVOID). Important for parsers
    // to be able to determine the padding size (depending on the
    // processor architecture of the computer that generated the log field).
    // ie. X86 == 4 bytes ia64 == 8 bytes
    //
    ULONG           AlignmentSize;

// UTC based system timestamp for the raw file creation/opening. (Can be used
// to populate a FILETIME structure.)
    //
    LARGE_INTEGER   DateTime;

    // Name of the server which created/opened the raw file. Maximum computer
// name length is set to 256, and it is null-terminated if the length is not
// exactly 256 characters. This is important to identify the source computer
// for the log. In either case, the parser should skip the remaining bytes
// to reach the next record.
    //
    WCHAR           ComputerName[MAX_COMPUTER_NAME_LEN];

} RAW_FILE_HEADER, *PRAW_FILE_HEADER;
```

File Footers

The binary log file format does not write a footer. You can detect the next file based on the timestamps in the header and the log file records written in the previous log file.

Inline Records

Each request record contains the following inline records:

- The RAWLOGID, which is a unique identifier for URLs.

- An IP address type flag, which tells you whether the IP address is IPv4 or IPv6.

Unique identifier for URLs

Centralized binary logging contains a 64-bit URL identifier. To conserve space, frequent URLs are written once and then given a random identifier called the RAWLOGID. Example F.2 lists a RAWLOGID.

Example F.2   URL Identifier

```
// Please be aware that Microsoft might change this data format at any time
// and is likely to do so in future Windows releases. Developers who use this
// data structure definition will need to alter program logic,
// recompile, and then re-release their applications for future
// releases of Windows (or service packs).
//
typedef struct _RAWLOGID
{
    //
    // The identifier is a 64-bit field and is a random number.
    //

    ULONG    UIDLowPart;
    ULONG    UIDHighPart;

} RAWLOGID, *PRAWLOGID;
```

IP address type

Each request record has either an IPv4 or IPv6 address encoded within it. Additionally, a flag in the first part of the log entry indicates the IP version of the address field. Example F.3 lists an IPv4 address, and Example F.4 lists an IPv6 address.

Example F.3   IPv4 Address

```
// Please be aware that Microsoft might change this data format at any time
// and is likely to do so in future Windows releases. Developers who use this
// data structure definition will need to alter program logic,
// recompile, and then re-release their applications for future
// releases of Windows (or service packs).
//

typedef struct _RAWLOG_IPV4_ADDRESSES {

    // The IPV4 client address or source of the request
    ULONG client;

    // The IPV4 server address or address of the server that received the
    // request
ULONG server;

} RAWLOG_IPV4_ADDRESSES, *PRAWLOG_IPV4_ADDRESSES;
```

Example F.4   IPv6 Address

```
// Please be aware that Microsoft might change this data format at any time
// and is likely to do so in future Windows releases. Developers who use this
// data structure definition will need to alter program logic,
// recompile, and then re-release their applications for future
// releases of Windows (or service packs).
//
typedef struct _RAWLOG_IPV6_ADDRESSES {

    // The IPV6 client address or source of the request
    USHORT client[8];

    // The IPV6 server address or address of the server that received the
request
    USHORT server[8];

} RAWLOG_IPV6_ADDRESSES, *PRAWLOG_IPV6_ADDRESSES;
```

Cache or User-Mode Request

For every HTTP request sent to IIS 6.0, the HTTP protocol stack (HTTP.sys) checks the cache entry for a response that matches the incoming request. If the request matches, then HTTP.sys fulfills the request from the cache. If the request does not match, then requests are sent to the user-mode IIS worker process for further processing. The binary log file contains one record type for cache hits and a different record type for cache misses, which are requests sent to the user-mode IIS worker process.

Centralized binary logging records data for all of the fields that are recorded by default in W3C Extended logging format, except for the User-Agent field. This field is too large to record because the string comes from the client browser, and if an index is used, then it would imply the comparison and hashing of this field for every record that is logged.

Cache-Hit Record

Example F.5 applies to requests that are served directly from the HTTP.sys cache. There is one record per request.

Example F.5 Cache-Hit Record

```
// Please be aware that Microsoft might change this data format at any time
// and is likely to do so in future Windows releases. Developers who use this
// data structure definition will need to alter program logic,
// recompile, and then re-release their applications for future
// releases of Windows (or service packs).
//
typedef struct _RAW_FILE_HIT_LOG_DATA
{
    // Type must be RAW_RECORD_HIT_LOG_DATA_TYPE i.e. value is 3.
    //
    USHORT          RecordType;

    // Optional flags.
    //
    union
    {
        struct
        {
            USHORT IPv6:1;              // Are IPs for this request IPv6 or not?
            USHORT ProtocolVersion:3;  // See protocol version table below.
            USHORT Method:6;           // See HTTP Verb Table below.
            USHORT Reserved:6;
        };
        USHORT Value;
    } Flags;

    // Site ID. Represents which site owns this log record as per the
    // metabase numeric metabase SiteID.
    //
```

(continued)

Example F.5   Cache-Hit Record (continued)

```
    ULONG           SiteID;

    // UTC Timestamp for the Log Hit.
    //
    LARGE_INTEGER   DateTime;

    // The IP Port the request came in on
    //
    USHORT          ServerPort;

    // ProtocolStatus - 200, 404, 503 etc - value should never be
    // greater than 999
    //
    USHORT          ProtocolStatus;

    // Other fields of the response
    //
    ULONG           Win32Status;
    ULONGLONG       TimeTaken;      // in milliseconds
    ULONGLONG       BytesSent;    // in bytes
    ULONGLONG       BytesReceived; // in bytes

    // For cache hits, there will always be at least one Uri Index record
    // written prior to this record. (see _RAW_INDEX_FIELD_DATA record)
    //
    RAWLOGID   UriId;

    // Either IPv4 or IPv6 address structure will follow.
    //
    // _RAWLOG_IPV4_ADDRESSES or
    // _RAWLOG_IPV6_ADDRESSES

} RAW_FILE_HIT_LOG_DATA, *PRAW_FILE_HIT_LOG_DATA;
```

Table F.2 lists the values that correspond to each protocol version.

Table F.2   Protocol Versions

Value	Protocol Version
0	Unknown
1	HTTP 0.9
2	HTTP 1.0
3	HTTP 1.1

Table F.3 lists the HTTP methods used for the binary log file format. The mapping of the method field is essentially the same as the HTTP_VERB type definition in the Http.h HTTP API header file in the Microsoft Platform SDK. For more information about the Http.h header file, search for "HTTP API" on MSDN, which is accessible from the MSDN Online link on the Web Resources page at http://www.microsoft.com/windows/reskits/webresources.

Table F.3   HTTP Methods

Value	HTTP Method
0	Unparsed
1	Unknown (for new verbs)
2	Invalid
3	OPTIONS
4	GET
5	HEAD
6	POST
7	PUT
8	DELETE
9	TRACE
10	CONNECT
11	TRACK
12	MOVE
13	COPY
14	PROPFIND
15	PROPPATCH
16	MKCOL
17	LOCK
18	UNLOCK
19	SEARCH

Cache-Miss Record

Example F.6 applies to requests that are served from the user-mode worker process. There is one record per request.

Example F.6 Cache-Miss Record

```
// Please be aware that Microsoft might change this data format at any time
// and is likely to do so in future Windows releases. Developers who use this
// data structure definition will need to alter program logic,
// recompile, and then re-release their applications for future
// releases of Windows (or service packs).
//
typedef struct _RAW_FILE_MISS_LOG_DATA
{
    // Type must be RAW_RECORD_MISS_LOG_DATA_TYPE i.e. value is 4
    //
    USHORT          RecordType;

    // Optional flags.
    //
    union
    {
        struct
        {
            USHORT IPv6:1;                  // Are IPs for this request IPv6 or not?
            USHORT ProtocolVersion:3;       // See protocol version table above.
            USHORT Method:6;                // See HTTP Verb Table above.
            USHORT Reserved:6;
        };
        USHORT Value;
    } Flags;

    // Site ID. Represents which site owns this log record as per the
    // metabase numeric metabase SiteID.
    //
    ULONG           SiteID;

    // UTC Timestamp for the Log Hit.
    //
    LARGE_INTEGER   DateTime;

    // The IP Port the request came in on.
    //
    USHORT          ServerPort;

    // ProtocolStatus - 200, 404, 503 etc - value should never be
    // greater than 999
    //
    USHORT          ProtocolStatus;
```

(continued)

Example F.6   Cache-Miss Record *(continued)*

```
    // Other fields of the response
    //
    ULONG           Win32Status;
    ULONGLONG       TimeTaken;          // in milliseconds
    ULONGLONG       BytesSent;       // in bytes
    ULONGLONG       BytesReceived;       // in bytes


    // Substatus is only relevant for requests served from user mode.
    // All cache-hit responses will have an implied Substatus of 0.
    //
    USHORT          SubStatus;


    // Variable-length fields follow the structure.
    //
    USHORT          UriStemSize;
    USHORT          UriQuerySize;
    USHORT          UserNameSize;


    // Either IPv4 or IPv6 address structure will follow. The client address
    // appears first, followed by the server address.
    //
    // _RAWLOG_IPV4_ADDRESSES or
    // _RAWLOG_IPV6_ADDRESSES


    // Then the URIStem - UriStemSize bytes
    // Then the URIQuery - UriQuerySize bytes
    // Then the UserName - Align the UserNameSize bytes up to the size of
    // AlignmentSize (in the header record) multiple

} RAW_FILE_MISS_LOG_DATA, *PRAW_FILE_MISS_LOG_DATA;
```

After writing the RAW_FILE_MISS_LOG_DATA record to the file that is already aligned, HTTP.sys appends the variable size strings to the end of the structures. However, if the total length of the bytes written after the structure is not aligned, HTTP.sys provides padding to ensure proper alignment of the next record.

Parsers should be aware of this padding and must skip it after reading the last variable size string that follows the RAW_FILE_MISS_LOG_DATA record.

For example, if a cache-miss record has a URIStem of 8 bytes, URIQuery of 0 bytes, and UserName of 4 bytes, then HTTP.sys adds the following padding:

ALIGN_UP ((8 + 0 + 4), AlignmentSize) - (8 + 0 + 4). This would be 4 bytes for a binary log file generated on an IA64, and 0 bytes for a binary log file generated for I386.

After reading the last variable size string, the parser should skip the padding bytes.

Log File Index Mapping Record

A log file index mapping record maps a specific URL to a RAWLOGID. This record always appears before the RAWLOGID is referenced in a cache-hit record. If a subsequent record for the same URL appears in a log file, then it receives a new RAWLOGID and subsequent cache-hit records refer to the new ID. This occurs because HTTP.sys periodically flushes cached items and recaches after a period of time, and a new RAWLOGID is generated for the recached item. Example F.7 lists the log file index mapping record.

Example F.7 Log File Index Mapping Record

```
// Please be aware that Microsoft might change this data format at any time
// and is likely to do so in future Windows releases. Developers who use this
// data structure definition will need to alter program logic,
// recompile, and then re-release their applications for future
// releases of Windows (or service packs).
//
#define URI_BYTES_INLINED          (4)
#define URI_WCHARS_INLINED         (URI_BYTES_INLINED/sizeof(WCHAR))

typedef struct _RAW_INDEX_FIELD_DATA
{
    // RAW_RECORD_INDEX_DATA_TYPE == i.e. 2
    //
    USHORT          RecordType;

    // Size of the variable size string (in bytes).
    // When reading and writing need to align the DIFF(Size - 4)
    // up to AlignmentSize.
    //
    USHORT          Size;

    // Unique ID for the URI.
    //
    RAWLOGID    Id;

    // Variable size string follows immediately after the structure.
    // Array of 4 bytes is defined to be able to make it PVOID aligned
    // on ia64. Typically URIs will be bigger than 4 bytes.
    //
    WCHAR           Str[URI_WCHARS_INLINED];

} RAW_INDEX_FIELD_DATA, *PRAW_INDEX_FIELD_DATA;
```

Cache Flushes

The HTTP.sys kernel-mode cache sometimes flushes completely. Significant configuration changes, such as changes to bandwidth throttling settings, can trigger a full cache flush. In the rare event that the cache flushes, the binary log file writes a record that indicates that you should dump all unique identifiers in memory and restart the process of recording the URL to new and unique ID mappings.

These records are rare and typically occur on servers that are reconfigured frequently. Example F.8 lists a cache flush record.

Example F.8   Cache Flush Record

```
// Please be aware that Microsoft might change this data format at any time
// and is likely to do so in future Windows releases. Developers who use this
// data structure definition will need to alter program logic,
// recompile, and then re-release their applications for future
// releases of Windows (or service packs).
//
typedef struct _RAW_FILE_CACHE_NOTIFICATION
{
    // Must be RAW_RECORD_CACHE_NOTIFICATION_DATA_TYPE i.e. 5
    //
    USHORT          RecordType;

    // Reserved for alignment
    //
    USHORT          Reserved[3];

} RAW_FILE_CACHE_NOTIFICATION, *PRAW_FILE_CACHE_NOTIFICATION;
```

APPENDIX I

IPv6 and IIS 6.0

Internet Information Services (IIS) 6.0 provides Internet services to clients connecting over the next generation of Internet Protocol (IP) — known as IP version 6 (IPv6). When you use IPv6 with IIS on a server running the Microsoft® Windows® Server 2003 operating system, your sites can respond to both IPv6 requests and Internet Protocol version 4 (IPv4) requests. Although current demand for IPv6 is limited, the adoption of new Internet-connected devices, such as phones and handheld computers, is expected to quickly exhaust the remaining IPv4 address space and speed the transition to IPv6.

In This Appendix

Related Information

- For more information about IIS 6.0 architecture, including HTTP.sys, see "IIS 6.0 Architecture" in this book.

Summary of Protocol Changes from IPv4 to IPv6

In response to concern about the finite number of IPv4 addresses, the Internet Engineering Task Force (IETF) developed a suite of protocols and standards known as Internet Protocol version 6 (IPv6). IPv6 was designed to replace IPv4, which is more than 20 years old. Because IPv6 is expected to become increasingly important as the Internet continues to grow, IPv6 functionality is included in the Microsoft® Windows® XP and the Microsoft® Windows® Server 2003, Standard Edition; Windows® Server 2003, Enterprise Edition; Windows® Server 2003, Datacenter Edition; and Windows® Server 2003, Web Edition operating systems.

The Internet Protocol (IP) is the network-layer protocol used by TCP/IP for addressing and routing packets of data between hosts. The current version of the IP, IPv4, has remained primarily unchanged since RFC 791 was published in 1981. IPv4 is robust, easily implemented, and interoperable, and it scales well. However, continued dramatic growth of the Internet is pushing the limits of IPv4 design. Concerns with IPv4 include the scarcity of public IPv4 addresses for use on the Internet, the size and complexity of its backbone routing tables, and the need for simpler, more automatic configuration.

IPv6, previously named IP Next Generation (IPng), was developed primarily to allow for larger (128-bit) IP addresses. Additional enhancements include the following:

- A more efficient routing infrastructure that allows backbone routers to maintain much smaller routing tables.

- A new header format that reduces header overhead and provides more efficient processing at intermediate routers.

- A simplified host configuration that uses both stateful and stateless address configuration.

- Built-in security provided by Internet Protocol security (IPSec). (In IPv4, IPSec is optional.)

- Better support for Quality of Service (QoS), which is the set of methods or processes that a service-based organization uses to maintain a specific level of quality.

- A way to efficiently manage the interaction of neighboring nodes by using multicast and unicast messaging.

- Extension headers for adding new features to IPv6.

Table G.1 lists pertinent IPv6 RFCs and serves as a useful reference to the source documents.

Table G.1   Summary of Useful Source Documents for Migrating from IPv4 to IPv6

Version	Date	RFC	RFC Title
IPv4	September, 1981	RFC 791	"Internet Protocol" (Protocol specification)
IPv6[1]	January, 1995	RFC 1752	"The Recommendation for the IP Next Generation Protocol" (Standards track for IPv6 General RFCs)
	December, 1995	RFC 1883	"Internet Protocol, Version 6 (IPv6) Specification" (Proposed standard — made obsolete by RFC 2460)
	December, 1995	RFC 1886	"DNS Extensions to support IP version 6" (IPv6 applications RFCs)
	July, 1998	RFC 2373 RFC 3513[2]	"IP Version 6 Addressing Architecture" "Internet Protocol Version 6 (IPv6) Addressing Architecture" (Standards track for IPv6 addressing RFCs)
	December, 1998	RFC 2460	"Internet Protocol, Version 6 (IPv6) Specification" (Standards track for the Network Layer RFCs and Internet drafts)

1. IPv5 was an experimental non-IP real-time stream protocol called ST, which was never widely used.

2. RFC 3513 supercedes RFC 2373; however Windows Server 2003 does not implement its changes with regard to site-local addresses.

In RFC 2460, "Internet Protocol, Version 6 (IPv6) Specification," IPv6 is described as a connectionless, unreliable datagram protocol that is used primarily for addressing packets and routing them between hosts. *Connectionless* means that a session is not established before data exchange begins. *Unreliable* means that delivery is not guaranteed. IPv6, like IPv4, always makes a best-effort attempt to deliver a packet, but an IPv6 packet might be lost, delivered out of sequence, duplicated, or delayed. IPv6 itself does not attempt to recover from these types of errors; the acknowledgment of packet delivery and the recovery of lost packets is done by a higher-layer protocol, such as TCP. TCP performs reliably over both IPv4 and IPv6.

For more information about the design changes needed by IPv4 to accommodate the increasing demands of network traffic, see "Introduction to IPv6" in Help and Support Center for Windows Server 2003. For more information about IPv6, see "IPv6 features" in Help and Support Center for Windows Server 2003.

For more information about RFCs, see the Request For Comments (RFC) link on the Web Resources pageat www.microsoft.com/windows/reskits/webresources.

Comparing IPv4 and IPv6 Addresses

The size of an IPv6 address is 128 bits, which is four times larger than an IPv4 address. In theory, the 32-bit address space that IPv4 uses provides 4,294,967,296 possible addresses; however, previous and current allocation practices limit the number of public IPv4 addresses to a few hundred million. By contrast, the 128-bit address space that IPv6 uses provides 3.4×10^{38} possible addresses.

The size of the IPv6 address allows for subdividing the address into a hierarchical routing structure that reflects the current topology of the Internet. This structure provides great flexibility for hierarchical addressing and routing, which the IPv4-based Internet lacks.

Comparing Address Formats

IPv4 addresses are represented in a *dotted-decimal format*, in which the 32-bit address is divided into four 8-bit sections. Each set of 8 bits is converted into its decimal equivalent and is separated from adjacent 8-bit decimal equivalents by periods. The following is an example of an IPv4 address:

```
131.107.16.200
```

In IPv6, the 128-bit address is divided into eight 16-bit blocks, each of which is converted to a 4-digit hexadecimal number that is separated from adjacent blocks by colons. The resulting representation is called *colon-hexadecimal format*.

The following is an IPv6 address in binary form:

```
0010000111011010000000000110100110000000000000000000010111100111011
0000001010101010000000001111111111111110001010001001110001011010
```

First, the 128-bit address is divided into eight 16-bit blocks, as follows:

```
0010000111011010   0000000011010011   0000000000000000   0010111100111011
0000001010101010   0000000011111111   1111111000101000   1001110001011010
```

Then, each of the eight 16-bit blocks is converted to hexadecimal and delimited with colons. The result is the following:

```
21DA:00D3:0000:2F3B:02AA:00FF:FE28:9C5A
```

An IPv6 address can be further simplified by removing the leading zeros within each 16-bit block. However, each block must have at least a single digit. With leading zero suppression, the address used in this example becomes the following:

```
21DA:D3:0:2F3B:2AA:FF:FE28:9C5A
```

Compressing Zeros in IPv6 Addresses to the Double-Colon Format

IPv6 addressing conventions also allow you to simplify an address that contains long sequences of zeros. If an address contains consecutive groups of 16-bit blocks that are set to 0 in the colon-hexadecimal format, you can compress the consecutive blocks to :: (known as double-colon) to simplify the address. To avoid ambiguity, use zero compression only once within any one address. Otherwise, you cannot determine the number of 0 bits represented by each instance of a double-colon (::).

Table G.2 provides two examples of IP addresses and shows how zero compression changes each address.

Table G.2   Effect of Zero Compression on Sample IP Addresses

Address Before Zero Compression	Address After Zero Compression
FE80:0:0:0:2AA:FF:FE9A:4CA2	FE80::2AA:FF:FE9A:4CA2
FF02:0:0:0:0:0:0:2	FF02::2

To determine how many 0 bits are represented by the double-colon in a compressed address, count the number of blocks in the address, subtract this number from 8, and then multiply the result by 16. For example, the address FF02::2 contains two blocks (the FF02 block and the 2 block). Therefore, the number of bits expressed by the double-colon is 96 (96 = (8 - 2) × 16).

Understanding Prefixes

IPv4 implementations commonly use a dotted-decimal representation of the network prefix length, which is called the subnet mask. IPv6 does not use subnet masks; it supports only prefix length notation.

The *prefix* is the part of an IP address where the bits have fixed values or are the bits of a route or subnet identifier. Prefixes for IPv6 routes and subnet identifiers are expressed in the same way as classless inter-domain routing (CIDR) notation is expressed for IPv4, that is, *address/prefix length*. The *prefix length* specifies the number of left-most bits that make up the subnet prefix. For example, an IPv6 prefix can be represented as follows:

```
3FFE:2900:D005:F28B::/64
```

In this example, the first 64 bits of the global unicast address are the prefix, and the remaining 64 bits (128 - 64 = 64) are the interface ID.

For more information about the architecture of IPv6 addresses, see RFC 2373, "IP Version 6 Addressing Architecture."

Comparing Address Types

If you install IPv6 on a computer that is not connected to a network in which an IPv6 router is present, the computer automatically configures a link-local IPv6 address, which is a type of address that allows you to communicate with computers on your subnet. If you connect your computer to a subnet in which an IPv6 router is present, the router assigns your computer an IPv6 global or site-local address. The *site-local address* allows your computer to communicate within your intranet. The *global address* allows your computer to communicate with computers on the IPv6 Internet.

The left-most bits of an IP address are called the *format prefix* (FP), which indicates the specific type of IPv6 address. IPv6 accommodates many address types, including the following:

- **Unicast addresses**. Provide point-to-point, directed communication between two hosts on a network.

- **Multicast addresses**. Provide a method for sending a single IP packet to multiple hosts in a group. A multicast address is used for one-to-many communication.

- **Anycast addresses**. Provide a method of delivering a packet to the nearest member of a group. Currently, anycast addresses are used only as destination addresses and are assigned only to routers. An anycast address is used for one-to-one-of-many communication.

Table G.3 compares some basic elements of IPv4 and IPv6 addressing.

Table G.3 Comparison of IPv4 and IPv6 Addressing Elements

Address Space Element	IPv4 Address	IPv6 Address
Unspecified address	0.0.0.0	0:0:0:0:0:0:0:0: or ::
Loopback address	127.0.0.1	0:0:0:0:0:0:0:1: or ::1
Address types	Public IPv4 addresses	Global addresses (aggregatable global unicast addresses)

	Private IPv4 addresses, such as:
	    10.0.0.0/8
	    172.16.0.0/12
	    192.168.0.0/16
		Site-local addresses, which always begin with FEC0::/48)

	Automatic Private IP Addressing (APIPA), which uses the 169.254.0.0/16 prefix	Link-local addresses, which always begin with FE80::/64
Text representation	Dotted-decimal format	Colon-hexadecimal format with suppression of leading zeros and zero compression. IPv4-compatible addresses are expressed in dotted-decimal notation.

(continued)

Table G.3   Comparison of IPv4 and IPv6 Addressing Elements *(continued)*

Address Space Element	IPv4 Address	IPv6 Address
Network bits representation	Subnet mask in dotted-decimal format or prefix-length notation	Prefix-length notation only
DNS name resolution	IPv4 host address (A) resource record[1]	IPv6 host address (AAAA) resource record[2]

[1] An A resource record, which is stored on your DNS servers, enables mapping from a host name to an IPv4 32-bit address.

[2] AAAA (quad-A) resource records enable mapping from a host name to an IPv6 128-bit address.

Unicast Addresses

Unicast addresses identify a single interface within the scope of a particular type of unicast address. The scope of an address is the region of the IPv6 network over which the address is unique. With the appropriate unicast routing topology, packets addressed to a unicast address are delivered only to a single interface.

The following are types of unicast IPv6 addresses:

- **Aggregatable global unicast addresses**. Identified by the format prefix (FP) of 001, these addresses are equivalent to public IPv4 addresses.

- **Local-use unicast addresses**. Provide two types of addresses:

  - **Link-local addresses**. Identified by the FP of 1111 1110 10, these addresses are used by nodes when they are communicating with neighboring nodes on the same link.

  - **Site-local addresses**. Identified by the FP of 1111 1110 11, these addresses are equivalent to the IPv4 private address space. Use these addresses between nodes that communicate with other nodes in the same site.

- **Unspecified address**. Used only to indicate the absence of an address; this type of address cannot be assigned to a node. The IPv6 unspecified address, 0:0:0:0:0:0:0:0 or ::, is equivalent to the IPv4 unspecified address of 0.0.0.0.

- **Loopback address**. Used to identify a loopback interface, which enables a node to send packets to itself. The IPv6 loopback address, 0:0:0:0:0:0:0:1 or ::1, is equivalent to the IPv4 loopback address of 127.0.0.1.

- **Transition, or compatibility, addresses**. Provided to help you migrate from IPv4 to IPv6; these addresses allow both types of hosts to coexist on your network.

Types of Transition IPv6 Addresses

To help you transition from IPv4 to IPv6 and to facilitate the coexistence of both types of hosts, IPv6 defines the following transition IPv6 addresses.

IPv4-compatible addresses

IPv4-compatible addresses are used by IPv6/IPv4 nodes that communicate with IPv6 over an IPv4 infrastructure. *IPv6/IPv4 nodes* are nodes that run both the IPv4 and IPv6 protocols. The format for an IPv4-compatible address is 0:0:0:0:0:0:w.x.y.z or ::w.x.y.z (where w.x.y.z is the dotted-decimal representation of a public IPv4 address). The IPv6 protocol for Windows XP and Windows Server 2003 provides support for IPv4-compatible addresses, but support is not enabled by default.

IPv4-mapped addresses

IPv4-mapped addresses are used to represent an IPv4-only node to an IPv6 node. The IPv4-mapped address is never used as a source or destination address for an IPv6 packet. It is used only for internal representation. The format for an IPv4-mapped address is 0:0:0:0:0:FFFF:w.x.y.z or ::FFFF:w.x.y.z. The IPv6 protocol for Windows XP and Windows Server 2003 does not support IPv4-mapped addresses.

6to4 addresses

6to4 addresses are used for communicating between two nodes that are running both IPv4 and IPv6 over the Internet. The 6to4 address is formed by combining the prefix 2002::/16 with the 32 bits of the public IPv4 address of the node or the site of the node, thus forming a 48-bit prefix. For example, for the IPv4 address of 131.107.0.1, the 6to4 address prefix is 2002:836B:1::/48 (where 836B:1 is the colon hexadecimal notation for 131.107.0.1). Support for 6to4 addresses is provided by the IPv6 Helper service (known as the *6to4 service*) that is included with the IPv6 protocol for Windows XP and Windows Server 2003.

Global Addresses

Global addresses, which are identified by an FP of 001, and which are also called aggregatable global unicast addresses, are equivalent to public IPv4 addresses. Global addresses are globally routable and reachable on the IPv6 Internet.

As the name implies, you can aggregate, or summarize, global addresses to produce an efficient routing infrastructure. Unlike the current IPv4-based Internet, which has a mixture of both flat and hierarchical routing, the IPv6-based Internet is designed to support efficient hierarchical addressing and routing. The *scope* of a global address, which is the region of the IPv6 internetwork over which the address is unique, is the entire IPv6 Internet.

Figure G.1 illustrates the structure of an IPv6 global address.

Figure G.1   Structure of an IPv6 Global Address

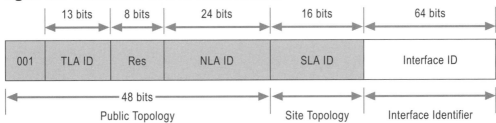

TLA ID field   Indicates the Top Level Aggregation Identifier (TLA ID) for the address. The size of this field is 13 bits. The TLA ID identifies the highest level in the routing hierarchy. TLA IDs are administered by the Internet Assigned Numbers Authority (IANA) and allocated to local Internet registries that, in turn, allocate individual TLA IDs to large, global Internet service providers (ISPs). A 13-bit field allows up to 8,192 different TLA IDs. Routers in the highest level of the IPv6 Internet routing hierarchy (called default-free routers) do not have a default route — only routes with 16-bit prefixes corresponding to the allocated TLA IDs and additional entries for routes based on the TLA ID assigned to the routing region where the router is located.

Res field   Reserves space for future expansion of either the TLA ID or the NLA ID field. The size of this field is 8 bits.

NLA ID field   Indicates the Next Level Aggregation Identifier (NLA ID) for the address. The NLA ID identifies a specific customer site. The size of this field is 24 bits. The NLA ID allows an ISP to create multiple levels of addressing hierarchy to organize addressing and routing and to identify sites. The structure of the ISP's network is not visible to default-free routers.

SLA ID field   Indicates the Site Level Aggregation Identifier (SLA ID) for the address. The SLA ID is used by an individual organization to identify subnets within its site. The size of this field is 16 bits. An organization can use this field to create 65,536 subnets or multiple levels of addressing hierarchy. Being assigned an SLA Id is equivalent to being allocated an IPv4 Class A network ID (assuming that the last octet is used for identifying nodes on subnets). The structure of the customer's network is not visible to the ISP.

Interface ID field   Identifies the interface of a node on a specific subnet. The size of this field is 64 bits.

For more information about IPv6 addressing, see RFC 2373, "IP Version 6 Addressing Architecture." For more information about IETF, including a repository of RFCs, see the Internet Engineering Task Force (IETF) link on the Web Resources page at http://www.microsoft.com/windows/reskits/webresources.

How IIS 6.0 Supports IPv6

Except for the differences in functionality outlined in this section, IIS 6.0 provides the same Web services to clients that connect by using IPv6 as it does for clients that connect by using IPv4.

Differences in IIS Functionality Between IPv4 and IPv6

IIS 6.0 provides the same core functionality for users of IPv6 as it does for users of IPv4. However, only a subset of IIS 6.0 functionality is available for users of IPv6. The following are the most significant differences:

- **The IIS Manager user interface does not support IPv6 addresses**. IIS Manager does not display IPv6 addresses as it does IPv4 addresses; that is, the IIS user interface does not provide a way to work with or manipulate IPv6 addresses. However, manipulating literal hexadecimal IPv6 addresses is usually not recommended, so lack of this functionality is unlikely to prevent you from installing and using IPv6.

- **The IP Address Restrictions feature is not supported**. The IP Address Restrictions feature in IIS 6.0 does not support IPv6 addresses or IPv6 prefixes.

- **Bandwidth throttling is not supported for responses sent over IPv6 addresses**. If you change the **MaxBandwidth** and **MaxGlobalBandwidth** metabase properties, you do not affect IPv6 network traffic. However, connection limits and connection time-outs, which are related IIS 6.0 features, are supported.

- **The ServerBindings and SecureBindings metabase properties do not support IPv6 addresses**. Both properties specify strings that IIS 6.0 uses to determine which network endpoints are used by the server instance. The string format for the **ServerBindings** property is *IPAddress:Port:HostName*. Both the *IPAddress* and *HostName* parameters of the string are optional; however, the *IPAddress* component of the string is limited to storing an IPv4 address. Any unspecified parameters default to an all-inclusive wildcard.

Because of the limitations in IPv6 functionality for these metabase properties, IIS 6.0 functionality for IPv6 is affected as follows:

  - **Site routing is limited to host headers only**. You cannot configure sites to route on an IPv6 address or on a combination of an IPv6 address and host header. This limitation also affects sites that are configured to route based on an IPv4 address. When you install IPv6, sites that are already specifically configured for IPv4 site-based routing do not respond to requests that come in over IPv6.

  - **The number of Secure Sockets Layer (SSL) sites is limited to one**. Due to the IP routing restriction for IPv6, IIS deployments designed for IPv6 addresses are limited to one SSL site per computer.

- **File Transfer Protocol (FTP), Simple Mail Transfer Protocol (SMTP), and Network News Transfer Protocol (NNTP) services are not supported.** IPv6 is supported only for the WWW service. The FTP, SMTP, and NNTP services do not have IPv6 support in IIS 6.0.

- **If you install IPv6 on a computer that is running IIS 6.0, all sites on the computer respond to IPv6 clients.** You cannot configure individual sites or virtual directories to respond to IPv6 traffic while others on the same server respond to IPv4 traffic.

- **Logging tools must support IPv6 address formats in order to function correctly.** IIS writes IPv6 addresses to the log file when IPv6 is enabled and client computers connect to the server by using IPv6 addresses. Log parsing tools that are to be used with log files for IPv6 sites must support IPv6 address formats.

- **The EnableReverseDnsLookup property is not supported.** For IPv4, a value of **true** for the **EnableReverseDnsLookup** metabase property allows reverse DNS lookup to determine the DNS name of the client computer. For IPv6, however, this functionality is not enabled.

Note

Setting the EnableReverseDnsLookup metabase property to true does not cause the REMOTE_HOST server variable to return the DNS name of the client, as it does for IPv4. REMOTE_HOST always contains the IPv6 address, regardless of the EnableReverseDNSLookup property setting.

Using the IPv6-Aware ISAPI Server Variables

When you install IPv6 on a server running IIS 6.0, Internet Server API (ISAPI) server variables provide support for IPv6. The ISAPI framework provides the appropriate local-host and remote-host server variables for IPv6 network addresses: LOCAL_ADDR and REMOTE_ADDR. When clients connect over IPv6, these variables store the IPv6 address.

It is important to note that IPv6 addresses can be longer than IPv4 addresses, so you need to take steps to prevent buffer overruns when you install IPv6.

Important

Buffer overruns are one of the most common causes of security breaches. Preventing buffer overruns helps protect your server from being attacked.

To prevent buffer overruns, you must allocate more space to hold the string representation of IPv6 addresses. For example, the longest possible IPv4 string looks something like "123.123.123.123" (16 characters, including the trailing zero required to express the string in some programming languages), whereas the longest IPv6 string looks like "1111:2222:3333:4444:5555:6666:123.123.123.123%1234567890," which is 57-characters long, including the trailing zero. Therefore, when you allocate buffers, use 16 characters for IPv4 addresses and 57 characters for IPv6 addresses.

Note

The "%1234567890" portion of the string indicates the zone ID, which is an integer that specifies the scope, or zone, of the destination. The zone ID is needed when you are specifying a link-local destination address or a site-local destination address (if you are using multiple sites). For link-local addresses, the zone ID is typically equal to the interface index of the desired sending interface. For site-local addresses, the zone ID is equal to the site number.

Both ISAPI server variables (LOCAL_ADDR and REMOTE_ADDR) use the typical IP address format for the applicable IP version (IPv4 or IPv6). For example, for an IPv6 request, both server variables use an IPv6 IP address in the colon-hexadecimal format; for an IPv4 request, both server variables use an IPv4 IP address in the dotted-decimal format. Note that the IPv6 address is simply a string variable, which can contain the "%" character. For example, fe80::1:1:1:1%4 is an acceptable IPv6 address.

How Installing IPv6 Affects Web Browser Use and Client Connectivity

When you install IPv6 on a computer in your network, two limitations of Internet Explorer 6 (the version provided with Windows Server 2003) can affect the computer's ability to use the Internet Explorer Web browser:

- **Internet Explorer 6 does not connect when literal IPv6 addresses are used in the URL**. Internet Explorer 6 does not support the format for literal IPv6 addresses in URLs that is described in RFC 2732, "Format for Literal IPv6 Addresses in URLs." However, Internet Explorer does support IPv6 by means of DNS name resolution. Therefore, you should create DNS AAAA resource records that resolve Web server names to an IPv6 address and then use Web server names in the URL.

- **Internet Explorer 6 cannot browse IPv6 Web sites by using a proxy server if the proxy server is not IPv6-enabled**. When Internet Explorer is configured to use a proxy server, all name resolution requests for Web sites are forwarded to the proxy server. If the proxy server is not IPv6-enabled, proxy-based requests for local or remote IPv6 Web pages are unsuccessful. For information about how to configure Internet Explorer to operate without the use of a proxy server, see Internet Explorer Help.

Table G.4 shows the network protocol that clients use to connect to different IP configurations.

Table G.4   Client Connectivity Matrix for IPv6

Client IPv6 Awareness	Type of Client Operating System	IIS 6.0 without IPv6 Installed	IIS 6.0 with IPv6 Installed
Client is IPv6 unaware	IPv4-only	Connect over IPv4	Connect over IPv4
	IPv6-only	No connectivity	No connectivity
	IPv4/IPv6	Connect over IPv4	Connect over IPv4
Client is IPv6 aware[1]	IPv4-only	Connect over IPv4	Connect over IPv4
	IPv6-only	No connectivity	Connect over IPv6
	IPv4/IPv6	Connect over IPv4	Connect over IPv6 or IPv4[2]
Client is IPv6-only	IPv4-only	No connectivity	No connectivity
	IPv6-only	No connectivity	Connect over IPv6
	IPv4/IPv6	No connectivity	Connect over IPv6

[1] "IPv6 aware" means that the client can also communicate over IPv4.

[2] When the DNS AAAA server returns the IPv6 and IPv4 addresses to the client, the client uses the connection protocol that applies to the address that is listed first.

Securing IPv6 Networks

Windows Server 2003 currently supports the use of IPv6 only when IPv4 is also installed. Because TCP/IP internetworks are susceptible to a variety of attacks, ranging from passive attacks, such as eavesdropping, to active attacks, such as denial-of-service attacks, be sure to follow best practices for security when using IPv6 on your network. A few general and IPSec-related IPv6 security suggestions follow.

General Recommendations for Securing IPv6 Networks

Be aware of the following known security risks for IPv6, and consider reconfiguring your system to meet the recommendation that is shown for each:

- The installation of an unauthorized router can cause reconfiguration of clients and rerouting of IPv6 traffic.

  To communicate with IPv6 nodes on other network segments, IPv6 must use a default router. A default router is automatically assigned based on the receipt of a router advertisement. Malicious users with physical access to the IPv6-enabled network can install an unauthorized IPv6 router on the network segment, enabling a denial of service attack on IPv6 hosts. The unauthorized IPv6 router can reconfigure IPv6 clients, set itself as the default router, reroute link traffic, and disrupt other network services.

  Recommendation: Ensure that unauthorized individuals do not have physical or wireless access to your network. For more information, see "Best practices for security" in Help and Support Center for Windows Server 2003.

- Internet Connection Firewall (ICF) and Basic Firewall cannot filter or block IPv6 traffic.

    - **ICF**, which is available in the 32-bit versions of Windows Server 2003, Standard Edition, and Windows Server 2003, Enterprise Edition, restricts the traffic that can enter your network from the Internet. Because ICF can filter only IPv4 traffic, IPv6 traffic might get through the firewall and enter your network.

    - **Basic Firewall**, which is a component of Routing and Remote Access, can be enabled for public interfaces. Because Basic Firewall filters only IPv4 traffic, IPv6 traffic might get through the firewall and enter your network.

    Recommendation: If you are running IPv6 on your network, use firewall software or hardware that can filter and block IPv6 traffic.

- On-link computers (computers on a link, or LAN segment) can take control of another IPv6 address, causing on-link devices to create an incorrect entry in their neighbor cache.

    Nodes on an IPv6 link use address resolution to resolve a neighboring node's IPv6 address to its link-layer address in the same way that nodes on an IPv4 link resolve addresses in IPv4. The resolved link-layer IPv6 address becomes an entry in a node's neighbor cache (equivalent to the ARP cache in IPv4). If an attacker causes an IPv6 node to maliciously use another node's address, it can cause other computers on the link to add a false entry to their neighbor cache. All traffic that is intended for the original computer goes instead to the attacker's computer, and the attacker can appear to send traffic from the original computer.

    Recommendation: Ensure that unauthorized individuals do not have physical or wireless access to your network. For more information, see "Best practices for security" in Help and Support Center for Windows Server 2003.

- When native IPv6 connectivity is not present (that is, when an IPv6 router does not exist on the network segment), it is easier to *spoof*, or appear to use, off-link IPv6 source addresses.

    A common defense against IP source address spoofing involves using packet-filtering routers. However, because traffic between hosts on the same link does not cross a router, this protective filtering is not used and spoofing might go undetected.

    Although spoofing can occur in native IPv4 or IPv6 networks, where on-link hosts can spoof off-link addresses in communication with other hosts on the link, the threat is greater outside the native IPv6 network. Outside the native IPv6 network, encapsulation technologies are used. Because the logical link used for packet encapsulation spans a large portion of an IPv4 network (often the entire IPv4 Internet), an attacker can be anywhere on that IPv4 network and still spoof off-link addresses.

    Recommendation: Ensure that an IPv6 router is present on the network segment.

For more information about IPv6 security, see "Security information for IPv6" in Help and Support Center for Windows Server 2003.

Securing with IPSec on IPv6 Networks

The IPv6 protocol for Windows Server 2003 incorporates Internet Protocol security (IPSec), which protects IPv6 data as it is sent over the network. *IPSec* is a set of Internet standards that uses cryptographic security services to provide the following:

- **Confidentiality**. Captured IPSec traffic cannot be deciphered without the appropriate encryption key.

- **Data origin authentication**. IPSec traffic contains a cryptographic checksum that incorporates a shared encryption key so that the receiver can verify that it was actually sent by the apparent sender.

- **Data integrity**. The cryptographic checksum is also used by the receiver to verify that the packet was not modified in transit.

IPSec in IPv6 is separate from, and does not interoperate with, IPSec for TCP/IP. IPSec policies that are configured with the IP Security Policies or Group Policy snap-ins have no effect on IPv6 traffic. You need to manually configure IPSec policies, security associations (SAs), and keys for IPv6. For more information about IPSec for TCP/IP, see "Internet Protocol security (IPSec)" in Help and Support Center for Windows Server 2003. For an example of configuring IPSec for IPv6, see "Using IPSec between two local link hosts" in Help and Support Center for Windows Server 2003.

In addition to the general security recommendations listed in the preceding section, follow these guidelines when you use IPv6 with IPSec:

- **Do not use IPSec for IPv6 in a production environment**. The current implementation of IPSec for IPv6 is not recommended for use in a production environment because it relies on static keying, which means that it has no provisions for updating encryption keys when sequence numbers are reused.

- **Use random numbers to configure SPIs**. When you manually configure IPSec Security Parameters Indexes (SPIs) for IPv6, always use random numbers so that you do not compromise the security of your IPSec for IPv6 policies.

- **Use only supported Encapsulating Security Payload (ESP) (ESP with NULL encryption)**. The IPv6 protocol for Windows Server 2003 does not support the use of IPSec ESP data encryption. However, the use of ESP with NULL encryption is supported. Although NULL encryption uses the ESP header, only data origin authentication and data integrity services are provided.

For more information about IPv6 security features, see "Security features for IPv6" in Help and Support Center for Windows Server 2003.

Installing or Removing IPv6

When you initially install IPv6 on a computer in your network, be sure to install it first in a test environment so that you can configure and test the IPv6 protocol before installing it in your production environment. For more information about setting up a test lab, including typical test lab tasks and a sample infrastructure, see "Setting up an IPv6 test lab" in Help and Support Center for Windows Server 2003.

▶ **To install IPv6**

1. In Control Panel, double-click **Network Connections**.

2. Right-click any local area connection, and then click **Properties**.

3. Click **Install**.

4. In the **Select Network Component Type** dialog box, click **Protocol**, and then click **Add**.

5. In the **Select Network Protocol** dialog box, click **Microsoft TCP/IP version 6**, and then click **OK**.

6. Click **Close** to save changes to your network connection.

After you install the IPv6 protocol, IIS automatically supports IPv6 on your Web server. However, if a Web site is already running when you install IPv6, you must restart IIS before the site begins listening for IPv6 requests. Sites that you create after you enable IPv6 support automatically listen for IPv6.

For more information about how to install the IPv6 network protocol stack, see "IP version 6" in Help and Support Center for Windows Server 2003. For information about restarting IIS, see "Common Administrative Tasks" in this book.

▶ **To remove IPv6**

1. In Control Panel, double-click **Network Connections**.

2. Right-click any local area connection, and then click **Properties**.

3. Click **Microsoft TCP/IP version 6** in the list of installed components, and then click **Uninstall**.

4. In the **Uninstall Microsoft TCP/IP version 6** dialog box, click **Yes**.

5. Click **Close** to save changes to your network connection.

6. Click **Yes** to restart your computer.

   Windows prompts you to restart your computer so that the new settings can take effect.

Additional Resources

These resources contain additional information and tools related to this chapter.

Related Information

- Davies, J. *Understanding IPv6*. Redmond, WA: Microsoft Press, 2003 for information about using IPv6 with Windows Server 2003 and Windows XP.

- Howard, Michael & LeBlanc, David. *Writing Secure Code*. Second Edition. Redmond, WA: Microsoft Press, 2003 for information about buffer overruns.

- Huitema, Christian. *IPv6: The New Internet Protocol*. Second edition. Upper Saddle River, NJ: Prentice Hall PTR, 1998 for information about IPv6.

- The Internet Engineering Task Force (IETF) link on the Web Resources page at http://www.microsoft.com/windows/reskits/webresources for information about IETF, including a repository of RFCs.

- Miller, M. *Implementing IPv6: Supporting the Next Generation of Protocols*. Second edition. Foster City, CA: M&T Books, 2000 for information about using IPv6.

Related Windows Server 2003 Help Topics

For best results in identifying Help topics by title, in Help and Support Center, under the **Search** box, click **Set search options**. Under **Help Topics**, select the **Search in title only** check box.

- "Internet Protocol security (IPSec)" in Help and Support Center for Windows Server 2003.

- "Introduction to IPv6" in Help and Support Center for Windows Server 2003.

- "IP version 6" in Help and Support Center for Windows Server 2003 for information about the IPv6 protocol and how you can use it with Windows Server 2003 and IIS 6.0.

- "IPv6 features" in Help and Support Center for Windows Server 2003.

- "Security information for IPv6" in Help and Support Center for Windows Server 2003.

- "Security features for IPv6" in Help and Support Center for Windows Server 2003.

- "Setting up an IPv6 test lab" in Help and Support Center for Windows Server 2003.

Related Tools

- Ipsec6.exe

  Use the Ipsec6.exe command-line tool to configure IPSec policies and security associations. For more information about Ipsec6.exe, see "IPv6 utilities" in Help and Support Center for Windows Server 2003.

- Netsh.exe

  Use the command-line tool Netsh.exe to configure interfaces, addresses, caches, and routes for IPv6 and to display them on your screen. For more information about Netsh.exe, see Windows Support Tools Help on the Windows Server 2003 operating system CD.

Glossary

Symbols

3DES See definition for Triple DES (3DES).

A

abstract classes Templates used only to derive new Structural classes. Abstract classes cannot be instantiated in the directory.

access control A security mechanism that determines which operations a user, group, service, or computer is authorized to perform on a computer or on a particular object, such as a file, printer, registry subkey, or directory service object. See also group; object; permission; registry.

access control list (ACL) A list of security protections that apply to an entire object, a set of the object's properties, or an individual property of an object. There are two types of access control lists: discretionary and system. See also object.

ACL See definition for access control list (ACL).

Active Directory The Windows-based directory service. Active Directory stores information about objects on a network and makes this information available to users and network administrators. Active Directory gives network users access to permitted resources anywhere on the network using a single logon process. It provides network administrators with an intuitive, hierarchical view of the network and a single point of administration for all network objects. See also directory partition; directory service; domain; forest; object.

Active Directory Service Interfaces (ADSI) A directory service model and a set of Component Object Model (COM) interfaces. ADSI enables Windows applications and Active Directory clients to access several network directory services, including Active Directory. ADSI is supplied as a software development kit (SDK). See also Active Directory; Component Object Model (COM); directory service.

ActiveX A set of technologies that allows software components to interact with one another in a networked environment, regardless of the language in which the components were created.

Address Resolution Protocol (ARP) In TCP/IP, a protocol that uses broadcast traffic on the local network to resolve a logically assigned Internet Protocol version 4 (IPv4) address to its physical hardware or media access control (MAC) layer address.

In asynchronous transfer mode (ATM), ARP is used two different ways. For classical IPv4 over ATM (CLIP), ARP is used to resolve addresses to ATM hardware addresses. For ATM LAN emulation (LANE), ARP is used to resolve Ethernet/802.3 or Token Ring addresses to ATM hardware addresses.

See also asynchronous transfer mode (ATM); Internet Protocol (IP); IP address; packet; Transmission Control Protocol/Internet Protocol (TCP/IP).

administrative credentials Logon information that is used to identify a member of an administrative group. Groups that use administrative credentials include Administrators, Domain Admins, and DNS Admins. Most system-wide or domain-wide tasks require administrative credentials. See also Administrators group; group.

Administrators group On a local computer, a group whose members have the highest level of administrative access to the local computer. Examples of administrative tasks that can be performed by members of this group include installing programs; accessing all files on the computer; auditing access control; and creating, modifying, and deleting local user accounts.

In an Active Directory domain, a group whose members have the highest level of administrative access in the domain. Examples of administrative tasks that can be performed by members of this group include setting domain policy; assigning and resetting domain user account passwords; setting up and managing domain controllers; and creating, modifying, and deleting domain user accounts.

See also access control; Active Directory; auditing; domain; domain controller; group; object.

ADSI See definition for Active Directory Service Interfaces (ADSI).

ADSI provider   COM objects that implement ADSI for a particular namespace (for example, an LDAP namespace such as Active Directory).

agent   An application that runs on a Simple Network Management Protocol (SNMP) managed device. The agent application is the object of management activities. A computer running SNMP agent software is also sometimes referred to as an agent.

aggregation   A composition technique for implementing component objects in which a new object can be built by using one or more existing objects that support some or all of the new object's required interfaces.

American Standard Code for Information Interchange (ASCII)   A standard single-byte character encoding scheme used for text-based data. ASCII uses designated 7-bit or 8-bit number combinations to represent either 128 or 256 possible characters. Standard ASCII uses 7 bits to represent all uppercase and lowercase letters, the numbers 0 through 9, punctuation marks, and special control characters used in U.S. English. Most current x86-based systems support the use of extended (or "high") ASCII. Extended ASCII allows the eighth bit of each character to identify an additional 128 special symbol characters, foreign-language letters, and graphic symbols.

Anonymous access   An authentication mechanism by which users who are able to connect to an Internet site without credentials are assigned to the IUSR_*ComputerName* account and granted the access rights that are assigned to that account. See also access control; Anonymous authentication; authentication.

Anonymous authentication   An authentication mechanism that does not require user accounts and passwords. Anonymous authentication grants remote users the identity IUSR_*ComputerName*. Anonymous authentication is used on the Internet to grant visitors restricted access to predefined public resources. See also Anonymous access; authentication.

Anonymous FTP authentication   A protocol that makes it possible for a user to retrieve documents, files, programs, and other archived data from anywhere on the Internet without having to establish a logon name and password.

apartment-threaded   A threading model in which each method of a component will execute on a thread that is associated with that component. See also multithreaded apartment (MTA); single-threaded apartment (STA).

API   See definition for application programming interface (API).

application   A computer program, such as a word processor or electronic spreadsheet, or a group of Active Server Pages (ASP) scripts and components that perform such tasks.

application isolation   The separation of applications by process boundaries that prevent the applications from affecting one another. Application isolation is configured differently for each of the two Internet Information Services (IIS) isolation modes. See also IIS 5.0 isolation mode; worker process isolation mode.

application pool   A grouping of one or more URLs served by a worker process.

application programming interface (API)   A set of routines that an application uses to request and carry out lower-level services performed by a computer's operating system. These routines usually carry out maintenance tasks such as managing files and displaying information.

application root   The root directory for an application. All directories and files contained within the application root are considered part of the application. Also called an application starting-point directory.

application scope   A way of making data available to all users of an application from all pages of a Web application. A variable or an object instance is given application scope by being stored in the Active Server Pages (ASP) application object. Application scope is useful for global data, such as a global counter.

argument   A constant, variable, or expression that is passed to a procedure.

array   A list of data values—all of the same type—any element of which can be referenced by an expression that consists of the array name followed by an indexing expression. Arrays are part of the fundamentals of data structures, which, in turn, are a major fundamental of computer programming.

ASCII (American Standard Code for Information Interchange)   See definition for American Standard Code for Information Interchange (ASCII).

ASP buffering   Functionality of Active Server Pages (ASP) that temporarily stores all output that is generated by a script until script execution is complete and then sends the output to a client.

association In file name extension mapping, the linking of a file extension, such as .asp, to an application, such as asp.dll. In Windows Management Instrumentation (WMI), an association class represents a relationship between two specific WMI classes. The properties of an association class include pointers, or references, to the two classes or instances.

asymmetric key algorithm See definition for public-key algorithm.

asynchronous transfer mode (ATM) A high-speed, connection-oriented, virtual circuit-based packet switching protocol used to transport many different types of network traffic. ATM packages data in 53-byte, fixed-length cells that can be switched quickly between logical connections on a network. See also protocol.

ATM See definition for asynchronous transfer mode (ATM).

attribute For files, information that indicates whether a file is read-only, hidden, ready for archiving (backing up), compressed, or encrypted, and whether the file contents should be indexed for fast file searching.

In Active Directory, a property of an object. For each object class, the schema defines which attributes an instance of the class must have and which additional attributes it might have.

See also Active Directory; class; object.

auditing The process that tracks the activities of users by recording selected types of events in the security log of a server or a workstation.

authentication The process for verifying that an entity or object is who or what it claims to be. Examples include confirming the source and integrity of information, such as verifying a digital signature or verifying the identity of a user or computer. See also cryptography; Kerberos V5 authentication protocol.

authorization

The process that determines what a user is permitted to do on a computer system or network. See also authentication.

Automation A Component Object Model (COM) based technology that allows for interoperability among ActiveX components, including OLE components. Formerly referred to as *OLE Automation.*

availability A level of service provided by applications, services, or systems. Highly available systems have minimal downtime, whether planned or unplanned. Availability is often expressed as the percentage of time that a service or system is available, for example, 99.9 percent for a service that is down for 8.75 hours a year.

B

bandwidth The data transfer capacity of a transmission medium.

In digital communications, the transfer capacity expressed in bits per second (bps) or megabits per second (Mbps). For example, Ethernet accommodates a bandwidth of 10,000,000 bps or 10 Mbps.

In analog communications, the difference between the highest and lowest frequencies in a specific range. For example, an analog telephone line accommodates a bandwidth of 3,000 hertz (Hz), the difference between the lowest (300 Hz) and highest (3,300 Hz) frequencies that it can carry.

See also bits per second (bps).

bandwidth throttling Setting the maximum portion of total network capacity that a service is allowed to use. An administrator can deliberately limit a server's Internet workload by not allowing it to receive requests at full capacity, thus saving resources for other programs, such as e-mail.

baseline A range of measurements derived from performance monitoring that represents acceptable performance under typical operating conditions.

Basic authentication An authentication mechanism that is supported by most browsers, including Internet Explorer. Basic authentication encodes user name and password data before transmitting it over the network. Note that *encoding* is not the same as *encryption.* Also known as *plaintext authentication.* See also Anonymous authentication; authentication; Digest authentication; encryption.

baud rate   The speed at which a modem communicates. Baud rate refers to the number of times the condition of the line changes. This is equal to bits per second only if each signal corresponds to one bit of transmitted data.

Modems must operate at the same baud rate in order to communicate with each other. If the baud rate of one modem is set higher than that of the other, the faster modem usually alters its baud rate to match that of the slower modem.

See also bits per second (bps); modem (modulator/demodulator).

Berkeley Internet Name Domain (BIND)   An implementation of Domain Name System (DNS) written and ported to most available versions of the UNIX operating system. The Internet Software Consortium maintains the BIND software. See also Domain Name System (DNS).

binary   A base-2 number system in which values are expressed as combinations of two digits, 0 and 1.

BIND   See definition for Berkeley Internet Name Domain (BIND).

binding   A process by which software components and layers are linked together. When a network component is installed, the binding relationships and dependencies for the components are established. Binding allows components to communicate with each other.

bitmask   A value that is used with bit-wise operators (And, Eqv, Imp, Not, Or, Xor) to test the state of individual bits in a particular bit-field value. See also bitmask identifier.

bitmask identifier   For the metabase, a name assigned to a bitmask to help identify its purpose. For example, In IIS 6.0, bitmask 512 is assigned the identifier MD_ACCESS_SCRIPT. See also bitmask.

bits per second (bps)   The number of bits transmitted every second, used as a measure of the speed at which a device, such as a modem, can transfer data. See also modem (modulator/demodulator).

Boolean data type   A data type with only two passable values, True (-1) or False (0). Boolean variables are stored as 16-bit (2-byte) numbers.

both-threaded   A threading model in which the object has the characteristics of an apartment-threaded object as well as a free-threaded object. See also apartment-threaded.

bps   See definition for bits per second (bps).

browser   Software that interprets the markup of files in HTML, formats them into Web pages, and displays them to the end user. Some browsers also permit end users to send and receive e-mail, read newsgroups, and play sound or video files embedded in Web documents.

built-in groups   The default security groups installed with the operating system. Built-in groups have been granted useful collections of rights and built-in abilities.

In most cases, built-in groups provide all the capabilities needed by a particular user. For example, members of the built-in Backup Operators group can back up and restore files and folders. To provide a needed set of capabilities to a user account, assign it to the appropriate built-in group.

See also group.

bulk encryption   A process in which large amounts of data, such as files, e-mail messages, or online communications sessions, are encrypted for confidentiality. It is usually done with a symmetric key algorithm. See also encryption.

C

CA   See definition for certification authority (CA).

cache   A special memory subsystem in which frequently used data values are duplicated for quick access.

call   To transfer program execution to some section of code (usually a subroutine) while saving the necessary information to allow execution to resume at the calling point when the called section has completed execution. When a subroutine call occurs, one or more values (known as arguments or parameters) are often passed to the subroutine, which can then use and sometimes modify these values.

callback function   A function provided by Internet Information Services (IIS) that allows an Internet Server API (ISAPI) extension or filter to access IIS services.

certificate   A digital document that is commonly used for authentication and to secure information on open networks. A certificate securely binds a public key to the entity that holds the corresponding private key. Certificates are digitally signed by the issuing certification authority (CA), and they can be issued for a user, a computer, or a service. See also certification authority (CA); private key; public key.

certificate revocation list (CRL) A document maintained and published by a certification authority that lists certificates that have been revoked. See also certificate; certification authority (CA).

certificate trust list (CTL) A signed list of root certification authority certificates that an administrator considers reputable for designated purposes, such as client authentication or secure e-mail. See also certificate; certification authority (CA).

certificate, client See definition for client certificate.

certification authority (CA) An entity responsible for establishing and vouching for the authenticity of public keys belonging to subjects (usually users or computers) or other certification authorities. Activities of a certification authority can include binding public keys to distinguished names through signed certificates, managing certificate serial numbers, and certificate revocation. See also certificate; public key.

CGI See definition for common gateway interface (CGI).

class A category of objects that share a common set of characteristics. Each object in the directory is an instance of one or more classes in the schema. See also object.

client Any computer or program connecting to, or requesting the services of, another computer or program. Client can also refer to the software that enables the computer or program to establish the connection.

For a local area network (LAN) or the Internet, a computer that uses shared network resources provided by another computer (called a *server*).

See also server.

client certificate A digital certificate that functions in a manner that is similar to a driver's license or passport. Client certificates can contain detailed identification information about the user and organization that issued the certificate.

client tier In the three-tier Web application model, the application or process that requests services from the middle tier, which typically includes a Web server and business processes. See also data source tier; middle tier.

client/server architecture A model of computing in which client applications running on a desktop or personal computer access information on remote servers or host computers. The client portion of the application is typically optimized for user interaction, whereas the server portion provides centralized, multi-user functionality.

cluster In data storage, the smallest amount of disk space that can be allocated to hold a file. All file systems used by Windows organize hard disks based on clusters, which consist of one or more contiguous sectors. The smaller the cluster size, the more efficiently a disk stores information. If no cluster size is specified during formatting, Windows picks defaults based on the size of the volume. These defaults are selected to reduce the amount of space that is lost and the amount of fragmentation on the volume. Also called an *allocation unit*.

In computer networking, a group of independent computers that work together to provide a common set of services and present a single-system image to clients. The use of a cluster enhances the availability of the services and the scalability and manageability of the operating system that provides the services.

See also availability; client; scalability.

code page A means of providing support for character sets and keyboard layouts for different countries or regions. A code page is a table that relates the binary character codes used by a program to keys on the keyboard or to characters on the display.

COM See definition for Component Object Model (COM).

COM+ An extension of the COM (Component Object Model) programming architecture that includes a runtime or execution environment and extensible services, including transaction services, security, load balancing, and automatic memory management. See also Component Object Model (COM).

common gateway interface (CGI) A server-side interface for initiating software services. For example a set of interfaces that describe how a Web server communicates with software on the same computer. Any software can be a CGI program if it handles input and output according to the CGI standard.

Component Object Model (COM) An object-based programming model designed to promote software interoperability; it allows two or more applications or components to easily cooperate with one another, even if they were written by different vendors, at different times, in different programming languages, or if they are running on different computers running different operating systems. OLE technology and ActiveX are both built on top of COM. See also ActiveX.

concrete class In Windows Management Instrumentation (WMI), a class from which you can create an instance because it has a full implementation.

concurrency The appearance of simultaneous execution of processes or transactions by interleaving the execution of multiple pieces of work.

connected user A user who has access to a computer or a resource across the network.

console tree The left pane in Microsoft Management Console (MMC) that displays the items contained in the console. The items in the console tree and their hierarchical organization determine the capabilities of a console. See also details pane.

cookie A block of data that a Web server stores on a client system. When a user returns to the same Web site, the browser sends a copy of the cookie back to the server. Cookies identify users, instruct the server to send a customized version of the requested Web page, and submit account information for the user.

credentials A set of information that includes identification and proof of identification that is used to gain access to local and network resources. Examples of credentials are user names and passwords, smart cards, and certificates. See also certificate.

CRL See definition for certificate revocation list (CRL).

CryptoAPI An application programming interface (API) that is provided as part of Microsoft Windows. CryptoAPI provides a set of functions that allows applications to encrypt or digitally sign data in a flexible manner while providing protection for the user's sensitive private key data. Actual cryptographic operations are performed by independent modules known as *cryptographic service providers (CSPs)*. See also application programming interface (API); cryptographic service provider (CSP); private key.

cryptographic service provider (CSP) The code that performs authentication, encoding, and encryption services that Windows-based applications access through CryptoAPI. A CSP is responsible for creating keys, destroying them, and using them to perform a variety of cryptographic operations. Each CSP provides a different implementation of the CryptoAPI. Some provide stronger cryptographic algorithms, while others use hardware components, such as smart cards. See also authentication; CryptoAPI; encryption.

cryptography The processes, art, and science of keeping messages and data secure. Cryptography is used to enable and ensure confidentiality, data integrity, authentication (entity and data origin), and nonrepudiation. See also authentication.

CSP See definition for cryptographic service provider (CSP).

CTL See definition for certificate trust list (CTL).

custom property A metabase property that is not predefined in the metabase schema (MBSchema.xml) and is created programmatically to meet a specific need. See also schema.

cycle In logging, to close an existing log file and start a new one.

D

daemon A networking program, usually associated with UNIX systems, that runs in the background performing tool functions such as housekeeping or maintenance without user intervention or awareness. Pronounced "demon."

Data Encryption Standard (DES) An encryption algorithm that uses a 56-bit key and maps a 64-bit input block to a 64-bit output block. The key appears to be a 64-bit key, but one bit in each of the eight bytes is used for odd parity, resulting in 56 bits of usable key. See also key.

data source tier A logical layer that represents a computer running a Database Management System (DBMS), such as a SQL Server database. See also client tier; middle tier.

datagram One packet, or unit, of information that includes relevant delivery information, such as the destination address, that is sent through a packet-switching network. See also packet.

DCOM See definition for Distributed Component Object Model (DCOM).

deadlock   A situation in which a thread will not relinquish its exclusive access to a critical section.

debugger   A program designed to aid in detecting, locating, and correcting errors in another program by allowing the programmer to step through the program, examine the data, and monitor conditions such as the values of variables.

decryption   The process of making encrypted data readable again by converting ciphertext to plaintext. See also encryption; plaintext.

default document   The file that is sent by a Web server when it receives a request for a Uniform Resource Locator (URL) that does not specify a file name. This document can be generated automatically by the server, or it can be a custom file that is placed in that directory by the administrator. Sometimes called a default home page.

default gateway   A configuration item for the TCP/IP protocol that is the IP address of a directly reachable IP router. Configuring a default gateway creates a default route in the IP routing table. See also Internet Protocol (IP); IP address; Transmission Control Protocol/Internet Protocol (TCP/IP).

DES   See definition for Data Encryption Standard (DES).

details pane   The right pane in Microsoft Management Console (MMC) that displays details for the selected item in the console tree. The details can be a list of items or they can be administrative properties, services, and events that are acted on by a snap-in. See also console tree; snap-in.

DHCP   See definition for Dynamic Host Configuration Protocol (DHCP).

dial-up connection   The connection to your network if you use a device that uses the telephone network. This includes modems with a standard telephone line, ISDN cards with high-speed ISDN lines, or X.25 networks.

If you are a typical user, you might have one or two dial-up connections, for example, to the Internet and to your corporate network. In a more complex server situation, multiple network modem connections might be used to implement advanced routing.

See also Integrated Services Digital Network (ISDN); modem (modulator/demodulator).

dial-up networking (DUN)   Connecting to a remote network or the Internet through a dial-up connection, such as a modem.

Digest authentication   An authentication mechanism that hashes user name, password, and other data before transmitting it over the network. See also authentication; Basic authentication; encryption; hash.

digital certificate   An electronic certification issued by certification authorities that shows where a program comes from and proves that the installation package has not been altered. Administrators should sign their code with a digital certificate if planning to distribute an Internet Explorer package over the Internet. See also certification authority (CA).

digital signature   The part of a digital certificate that contains an encryption key that uniquely identifies the holder of the certificate. See also certificate; client; key pair.

directory   An information source that contains information about users, computer files, or other objects. In a file system, a directory stores information about files. In a distributed computing environment (such as a Windows domain), the directory stores information about objects such as printers, fax servers, applications, databases, and other users. See also domain; object.

directory browsing   A feature that automatically provides a default Web page of available directories and files to browsers that submit a Uniform Resource Locator (URL) that does not specify a particular file.

directory partition   A contiguous subtree of Active Directory that is replicated as a unit to other domain controllers in the forest that contain a replica of the same subtree. In Active Directory, a single domain controller always holds at least three directory partitions: schema (class and attribute definitions for the directory), configuration (replication topology and related metadata), and domain (subtree that contains the per-domain objects for one domain). Domain controllers running Windows Server 2003 can also store one or more application directory partitions. See also Active Directory; attribute; domain.

directory replication   The copying of a master set of directories from a server (called an export server) to specified servers or workstations (called import computers) in the same or other domains. Replication simplifies the task of maintaining identical sets of directories and files on multiple computers because only a single master copy of the data must be maintained. Files are replicated when they are added to an exported directory and every time a change is saved to the file.

directory service   Both the directory information source and the service that makes the information available and usable. A directory service enables the user to find an object when given any one of its attributes. See also Active Directory; attribute; directory; object.

Distributed Component Object Model (DCOM)   The Microsoft Component Object Model (COM) specification that defines how components communicate over Windows-based networks. Use the DCOM Configuration tool to integrate client/server applications across multiple computers. DCOM can also be used to integrate robust Web browser applications. See also Component Object Model (COM).

distributed processing   A computing environment that contains a client and a server. This structure allows the workload to be divided into parts yet appear as a single process.

DLL   See definition for dynamic-link library (DLL).

DNS   See definition for Domain Name System (DNS).

domain   In Active Directory, a collection of computer, user, and group objects defined by the administrator. These objects share a common directory database, security policies, and security relationships with other domains.

In DNS, any tree or subtree within the DNS namespace. Although the names for DNS domains often correspond to Active Directory domains, DNS domains should not be confused with Active Directory domains.

See also Active Directory; Domain Name System (DNS); object.

domain controller   In an Active Directory forest, a server that contains a writable copy of the Active Directory database, participates in Active Directory replication, and controls access to network resources. Administrators can manage user accounts, network access, shared resources, site topology, and other directory objects from any domain controller in the forest. See also Active Directory; authentication; directory; forest; shared resource.

domain name   The name given by an administrator to a collection of networked computers that share a common directory. Part of the DNS naming structure, domain names consist of a sequence of name labels separated by periods. See also domain; Domain Name System (DNS).

Domain Name System (DNS)   A hierarchical, distributed database that contains mappings of DNS domain names to various types of data, such as IP addresses. DNS enables the location of computers and services by user-friendly names, and it also enables the discovery of other information stored in the database. See also domain name; IP address; ping; Transmission Control Protocol/Internet Protocol (TCP/IP).

DWORD   A data type that is composed of hexadecimal data with a maximum allotted space of 4 bytes.

dynamic binding   Binding (converting symbolic addresses in the program to storage-related addresses) that occurs during program execution. The term often refers to object-oriented applications that determine, during run time, which software routines to call for particular data objects. Also called late binding.

Dynamic Host Configuration Protocol (DHCP)   A TCP/IP service protocol that offers dynamic leased configuration of host IP addresses and distributes other configuration parameters to eligible network clients. DHCP provides safe, reliable, and simple TCP/IP network configuration, prevents address conflicts, and helps conserve the use of client IP addresses on the network.

DHCP uses a client/server model where the DHCP server maintains centralized management of IP addresses that are used on the network. DHCP-supporting clients can then request and obtain lease of an IP address from a DHCP server as part of their network boot process.

See also IP address; Transmission Control Protocol/Internet Protocol (TCP/IP).

Dynamic HTML A collection of features that extends the capabilities of traditional HTML, giving Web authors more flexibility, design options, and creative control over the appearance and behavior of Web pages.

dynamic page A Hypertext Markup Language (HTML) document that contains animated GIFs, Java applets, ActiveX Controls, or dynamic HTML (DHTML). Also, a Web page that is created automatically, based on information that is provided by the user, or that is generated "on the fly" with Active Server Pages (ASP).

dynamic-link library (DLL) An operating system feature that allows executable routines (generally serving a specific function or set of functions) to be stored separately as files with .dll extensions. These routines are loaded only when needed by the program that calls them.

E

early binding Occurs when an object is assigned to a variable that is declared to be of a specific object type. Early bound objects allow the compiler to allocate memory and perform other optimizations before an application executes.

encapsulation The method used to pass data from one protocol over a network within a different protocol. Data from one protocol is wrapped with the header of a different protocol. Encapsulation is described in RFC 1483. See also protocol.

encryption The process of disguising a message or data in such a way as to hide its substance. See also public key encryption; symmetric encryption.

encryption key A bit string that is used in conjunction with an encryption algorithm to encrypt and decrypt data. See also private key; public key.

Ethernet The IEEE 802.3 standard that uses Carrier Sense Multiple Access with Collision Detection (CSMA/CD) as the medium access control. Ethernet supports different mediums, such as coaxial cable, fiber-optic cable, and twisted-pair wiring, and different data rates, such as 10 megabits per second (Mbps).

event Any significant occurrence in the system or an application that requires users to be notified or an entry to be added to a log.

Event Log service A service that records events in the system, security, and application logs. The Event Log service is located in Event Viewer. See also event; event logging; Event Viewer.

event logging The process of recording an audit entry in the audit trail whenever certain events occur, such as services starting and stopping or users logging on and off and accessing resources. See also auditing; event; Event Viewer.

Event Viewer A component you can use to view and manage event logs, gather information about hardware and software problems, and monitor security events. Event Viewer maintains logs about program, security, and system events. See also event; event logging.

extended partition A type of partition that you can create only on basic master boot record (MBR) disks. Extended partitions are useful if you want to create more than four volumes on a basic MBR disk. Unlike primary partitions, you do not format an extended partition with a file system and then assign a drive letter to it. Instead, you create one or more logical drives within the extended partition. After you create a logical drive, you format it and assign it a drive letter. An MBR disk can have up to four primary partitions or three primary partitions, one extended partition, and multiple logical drives. See also logical drive; partition.

Extensible Markup Language (XML) A meta-markup language that provides a format for describing structured data. This facilitates more precise declarations of content and more meaningful search results across multiple platforms. In addition, XML enables a new generation of Web-based data viewing and manipulation applications. See also Hypertext Markup Language (HTML).

extranet A limited subset of computers or users on a public network, typically the Internet, that can access an organization's internal network. For example, the computers or users might belong to a partner organization.

F

failback The process of moving resources, either individually or in a group, back to their preferred node after the node has failed and come back online. See also node.

failover   In server clusters, the process of taking resource groups offline on one node and bringing them online on another node. When failover occurs, all resources within a resource group fail over in a predefined order; resources that depend on other resources are taken offline before, and are brought back online after, the resources on which they depend. See also node; server cluster.

FAT   See definition for file allocation table (FAT).

fat server   In a client/server architecture, a server that performs most of the processing, with the client performing little or no processing.

FAT32   A derivative of the file allocation table (FAT) file system. FAT32 supports smaller cluster sizes and larger volumes than FAT, which results in more efficient space allocation on FAT32 volumes. See also file allocation table (FAT).

fault tolerance   The ability of computer hardware or software to ensure data integrity when hardware failures occur. Fault-tolerant features appear in many server operating systems and include mirrored volumes, RAID-5 volumes, and server clusters. See also cluster.

file allocation table (FAT)   A file system used by MS-DOS and other Windows operating systems to organize and manage files. The file allocation table is a data structure that Windows creates when you format a volume by using FAT or FAT32 file systems. Windows stores information about each file in the file allocation table so that it can retrieve the file later. See also FAT32; NTFS file system.

File Transfer Protocol (FTP)   A member of the TCP/IP suite of protocols, used to copy files between two computers on the Internet. Both computers must support their respective FTP roles: one must be an FTP client and the other an FTP server. See also Transmission Control Protocol/Internet Protocol (TCP/IP).

filter   For Indexing Service, software that extracts content and property values from a document to index them.

For Internet Protocol security (IPSec), a specification of Internet Protocol (IP) traffic that provides the ability to trigger security negotiations for a communication based on the source, destination, and type of IP traffic.

For Internet Information Services (IIS), a feature of Internet Server Application Programming Interface (ISAPI) that allows preprocessing of requests and postprocessing of responses, permitting site-specific handling of Hypertext Transfer Protocol (HTTP) requests and responses.

In IP and Internetwork Packet Exchange (IPX) packet filtering, a definition in a series of definitions that indicates to the router the type of traffic allowed or disallowed on each interface.

See also Internet Information Services (IIS); Internet Protocol (IP); Internet Protocol security (IPSec); Internet Server Application Programming Interface (ISAPI).

firewall   A combination of hardware and software that provides a security system for the flow of network traffic, usually to prevent unauthorized access from outside to an internal network or intranet. Also called a *security-edge gateway*. See also proxy server.

forest   One or more Active Directory domains that share the same class and attribute definitions (schema), site and replication information (configuration), and forest-wide search capabilities (global catalog). Domains in the same forest are linked with two-way, transitive trust relationships. See also Active Directory; domain.

FORTEZZA   A family of security products including PCMCIA-based cards, compatible serial port devices, combination cards (such as FORTEZZA/Modem and FORTEZZA/Ethernet), server boards, and others. FORTEZZA is a registered trademark held by the U.S. National Security Agency.

frame   In synchronous communication, a package of information transmitted as a single unit from one device to another.

FTP   See definition for File Transfer Protocol (FTP).

G

gateway   A dedicated device (or a set of services running on a dedicated computer) that routes network traffic and enables communication between different networking protocols. A gateway is a multiprotocol Internet Protocol (IP) router that translates between different transport protocols or data formats. See also Internet Protocol (IP).

globally unique identifier (GUID) A 16-byte value generated from the unique identifier on a device, the current date and time, and a sequence number. A GUID is used to identify a particular device or component.

graphical user interface (GUI) A display format, like that of Windows, that represents a program's functions with graphic images such as buttons and icons. GUIs enable a user to perform operations and make choices by pointing and clicking with a mouse.

group A collection of users, computers, contacts, and other groups. Groups can be used as security or as e-mail distribution collections. Distribution groups are used only for e-mail. Security groups are used both to grant access to resources and as e-mail distribution lists. See also domain; local group.

group account A collection of user accounts. By making a user account a member of a group, you give the related user all the rights and permissions granted to the group. See also group.

Group Policy The infrastructure within Active Directory directory service that enables directory-based change and configuration management of user and computer settings, including security and user data. You use Group Policy to define configurations for groups of users and computers. With Group Policy, you can specify policy settings for registry-based policies, security, software installation, scripts, folder redirection, remote installation services, and Internet Explorer maintenance. The Group Policy settings that you create are contained in a Group Policy object (GPO). By associating a GPO with selected Active Directory system containers—sites, domains, and organizational units—you can apply the GPO's policy settings to the users and computers in those Active Directory containers. To create an individual GPO, use the Group Policy Object Editor. To manage Group Policy objects across an enterprise, you can use the Group Policy Management console. See also Active Directory.

Guest account A built-in account used to log on to a computer running Windows when a user does not have an account on the computer or domain or in any of the domains trusted by the computer's domain. See also domain.

GUID See definition for globally unique identifier (GUID).

H

hash A fixed-size result that is obtained by applying a one-way mathematical function (sometimes called a *hash algorithm*) to an arbitrary amount of data. If there is a change in the input data, the hash changes. The hash can be used in many operations, including authentication and digital signing. Also called a *message digest*. See also authentication; hash algorithm.

hash algorithm An algorithm that produces a hash value of some piece of data, such as a message or session key. With a good hash algorithm, changes in the input data can change every bit in the resulting hash value; for this reason, hashes are useful in detecting any modification in a data object, such as a message. Furthermore, a good hash algorithm makes it computationally infeasible to construct two independent inputs that have the same hash. Typical hash algorithms include MD2, MD4, MD5, and SHA-1. Also called a *hash function*. See also MD5; Secure Hash Algorithm (SHA-1).

headless server See definition for remotely administered server.

heaps A portion of memory reserved for a program to use for the temporary storage of data structures whose existence or size cannot be determined until the program is running.

Help and Support Center A unified place where a user can access all Help and Support content and services from both Microsoft and the OEM.

hexadecimal A base-16 number system represented by the digits 0 through 9 and the uppercase or lowercase letters A (equivalent to decimal 10) through F (equivalent to decimal 15).

home directory The root directory for a Web site, where the content files are stored. Also called a document root or Web root. In Internet Information Services (IIS), the home directory and all its subdirectories are available to users by default. Also, the root directory for an IIS service. Typically, the home directory for a site contains the home page. See also home page.

home page In the context of Internet Explorer, the home page is the first page users see when they start the browser. "Home page" is also a more general term for the main page of a Web site, which usually contains a main menu or table of contents with links to other pages within the site.

host Any device on a TCP/IP network that has an Internet Protocol (IP) address. Examples of hosts include servers, workstations, network-interface print devices, and routers. Sometimes used to refer to a specific network computer that is running a service used by network or remote clients.

For Network Load Balancing, a cluster consists of multiple hosts connected over a local area network (LAN).

See also client; cluster; local area network (LAN); Network Load Balancing; server; Transmission Control Protocol/Internet Protocol (TCP/IP).

host name The DNS name of a device on a network. These names are used to locate computers on the network. To find another computer, its host name must either appear in the Hosts file or be known by a DNS server. For most Windows-based computers, the host name and the computer name are the same. See also Domain Name System (DNS).

hotfix An update to address an issue identified after a software product has been distributed. Hotfix distribution is limited by its licensing terms.

HTML See definition for Hypertext Markup Language (HTML).

HTTP See definition for Hypertext Transfer Protocol (HTTP).

HTTP header An informational listing at the top of a Hypertext Transfer Protocol (HTTP) request or response.

HTTPS See definition for Secure Hypertext Transfer Protocol.

Hypertext Markup Language (HTML) A simple markup language used to create hypertext documents that are portable from one platform to another. HTML files are simple ASCII text files with codes embedded (indicated by markup tags) to denote formatting and hypertext links. See also American Standard Code for Information Interchange (ASCII).

Hypertext Transfer Protocol (HTTP) The protocol used to transfer information on the World Wide Web. An HTTP address (one kind of Uniform Resource Locator (URL)) takes the following form: http://www.microsoft.com. See also protocol.

I

ICMP See definition for Internet Control Message Protocol (ICMP).

identities, multiple See definition for multiple identities.

identity A person or entity that must be verified by means of authentication, based on criteria such as a password or a certificate. See also authentication; certificate.

IEEE Institute of Electrical and Electronics Engineers, founded in 1963. IEEE is an organization composed of engineers, scientists, and students, best known for developing standards for the computer and electronics industry.

IETF See definition for Internet Engineering Task Force (IETF).

IIS See definition for Internet Information Services (IIS).

IIS 5.0 isolation mode Internet Information Services (IIS) 6.0 isolation mode that simulates the IIS 5.0 Web process model.

IIS Admin Objects A set of methods, provided by Internet Information Services (IIS), that allow applications to access and modify configuration settings in the metabase.

IIS Server Instance resource A server-instance designation used with Internet Information Services (IIS) that supports the WWW and FTP services. IIS server instances are supported as cluster resources by a Resource DLL. IIS Server Instance resources can have dependencies on IP Address resources, Network Name resources, and Physical Disk resources. Access information for server instances does not fail over. See also failover; Internet Information Services (IIS).

impersonation A circumstance that occurs when Windows allows one process to take on the security attributes of another. See also attribute; security.

impersonation token An access token that captures the security information of a client process, allowing a service to "impersonate" the client process in security operations.

in-memory metabase An image of the Internet Information Services (IIS) metabase that has been loaded from disk into the computer's RAM memory and is used while IIS is running. See also metabase.

in-process Internet Server API (ISAPI) extensions that are hosted in the worker process address space. See also Internet Server Application Programming Interface (ISAPI).

in-schema property A metabase property predefined in the metabase schema (MBSchema.xml) file. See also metabase schema.

inheritance In security, a mechanism that allows a specific access control entry (ACE) to be copied from the container where it was applied to all children of the container. Inheritance can be used to manage access to a whole subtree of objects in a single update operation.

In Active Directory, the ability to build new object classes from existing object classes. The new object is defined as a subclass of the original object class. The original object class becomes a superclass of the new object. A subclass inherits the attributes of the superclass, including structure rules and content rules.

In Group Policy, a mechanism that allows policy settings in Group Policy objects (GPOs) that are linked to parent containers to be applied to objects in child containers.

See also Active Directory.

input/output (I/O) port A channel through which data is transferred between a device and the microprocessor. The port appears to the microprocessor as one or more memory addresses that it can use to send or receive data.

Integrated Services Digital Network (ISDN) A digital phone line used to provide higher bandwidth. ISDN in North America is typically available in two forms: Basic Rate Interface (BRI) consists of 2 B-channels at 64 kilobits per second (Kbps) and a D-channel at 16 Kbps; Primary Rate Interface (PRI) consists of 23 B-channels at 64 Kbps and a D-channel at 64 Kbps. An ISDN line must be installed by the phone company at both the calling site and the called site.

Integrated Windows authentication A configuration setting that enables negotiation of authentication protocols in Internet Information Services (IIS). See also Internet Information Services (IIS).

internet *internet*. Two or more network segments connected by routers. Another term for *internetwork*.

Internet. A worldwide network of computers. If you have access to the Internet, you can retrieve information from millions of sources, including schools, governments, businesses, and individuals.

Internet Control Message Protocol (ICMP) A required maintenance protocol in the TCP/IP suite that reports errors and provides simple diagnostic capabilities. ICMP is used by the Ping tool to perform TCP/IP troubleshooting. See also Internet Protocol (IP); protocol; Transmission Control Protocol/Internet Protocol (TCP/IP).

Internet Engineering Task Force (IETF) An open community of network designers, operators, vendors, and researchers concerned with the evolution of Internet architecture and the smooth operation of the Internet. Technical work is performed by working groups organized by topic areas (such as routing, transport, and security) and through mailing lists. Internet standards are developed in IETF Requests for Comments (RFCs), which are a series of notes that discuss many aspects of computing and computer communication, focusing on networking protocols, programs, and concepts.

Internet Information Services (IIS) Software services that support Web site creation, configuration, and management, along with other Internet functions. Internet Information Services include Network News Transfer Protocol (NNTP), File Transfer Protocol (FTP), and Simple Mail Transfer Protocol (SMTP). See also File Transfer Protocol (FTP).

Internet Protocol (IP) A routable protocol in the TCP/IP protocol suite that is responsible for IP addressing, routing, and the fragmentation and reassembly of IP packets. See also packet; Transmission Control Protocol/Internet Protocol (TCP/IP).

Internet Protocol security (IPSec) A set of industry-standard, cryptography-based protection services and protocols. IPSec protects all protocols in the TCP/IP protocol suite except Address Resolution Protocol (ARP). For virtual private network (VPN) connections, IPSec is used in conjunction with Layer Two Tunneling Protocol (L2TP). See also Address Resolution Protocol (ARP); protocol; Transmission Control Protocol/Internet Protocol (TCP/IP).

Internet Server Application Programming Interface (ISAPI) An application programming interface (API) that resides on a server computer for initiating software services tuned for Windows operating systems.

In Microsoft Provisioning System, ISAPI resides on the Web server.

See also application programming interface (API).

Internet service One of any of a number of technologies for making information accessible to users over the Internet. Each Internet service is defined by a protocol, such as Hypertext Transfer Protocol (HTTP), and each is enabled using client/server applications, such as Web browsers and Web servers. Internet protocols are defined in the Request for Comments (RFC) documents that are published by the Internet Engineering Task Force (IETF).

Internet service provider (ISP) A company that provides individuals or companies access to the Internet and the World Wide Web. An ISP provides a telephone number, a user name, a password, and other connection information so users can connect their computers to the ISP's computers. An ISP typically charges a monthly or hourly connection fee.

intranet A network within an organization that uses Internet technologies and protocols, but is available only to certain people, such as employees of a company. Also called a *private network*. See also internet.

IP See definition for Internet Protocol (IP).

IP address For Internet Protocol version 4 (IPv4), a 32-bit address used to identify an interface on a node on an IPv4 internetwork. Each interface on the IP internetwork must be assigned a unique IPv4 address, which is made up of the network ID, plus a unique host ID. This address is typically represented with the decimal value of each octet separated by a period (for example, 192.168.7.27). You can configure the IP address statically or dynamically by using Dynamic Host Configuration Protocol (DHCP).

For Internet Protocol version 6 (IPv6), an identifier that is assigned at the IPv6 layer to an interface or set of interfaces and that can be used as the source or destination of IPv6 packets.

See also Dynamic Host Configuration Protocol (DHCP); Internet Protocol (IP); node; octet.

IPSec See definition for Internet Protocol security (IPSec).

ISAPI See definition for Internet Server Application Programming Interface (ISAPI).**ISDN** See definition for Integrated Services Digital Network (ISDN).

ISP See definition for Internet service provider (ISP).

J

JIT See definition for just-in-time (JIT) activation.

just-in-time (JIT) activation The ability of a Component Object Model (COM) object to be activated only as needed for executing requests from its client. Objects can be deactivated even while clients hold references to them, allowing otherwise idle server resources to be used more productively.

K

Keep-Alive connection A Hypertext Transfer Protocol (HTTP) connection that is not closed after an exchange is completed.

Kerberos V5 authentication protocol An authentication mechanism used to verify user or host identity. The Kerberos V5 authentication protocol is the default authentication service. Internet Protocol security (IPSec) can use the Kerberos protocol for authentication. See also Internet Protocol security (IPSec).

kernel The core of layered architecture that manages the most basic operations of the operating system and the computer's processor. The kernel schedules different blocks of executing code, called threads, for the processor to keep it as busy as possible and coordinates multiple processors to optimize performance. The kernel also synchronizes activities among Executive-level subcomponents, such as I/O Manager and Process Manager, and handles hardware exceptions and other hardware-dependent functions. The kernel works closely with the hardware abstraction layer.

kernel mode A highly privileged mode of operation where program code has direct access to all memory, including the address spaces of all user-mode processes and applications, and to hardware. Also known as *supervisor mode*, *protected mode*, or *Ring 0*.

key In Registry Editor, a folder that appears in the left pane of the Registry Editor window. A key can contain subkeys and entries. For example, Environment is a key of **HKEY_CURRENT_USER**.

In IP security (IPSec), a value used in combination with an algorithm to encrypt or decrypt data. Key settings for IPSec are configurable to provide greater security.

See also Internet Protocol security (IPSec); registry; subkey.

key pair A private key and its related public key. See also private key; public key.

L

late binding See definition for dynamic binding.

LCID See definition for Locale Identifier (LCID).

LDAP See definition for Lightweight Directory Access Protocol (LDAP).

Lightweight Directory Access Protocol (LDAP) The primary access protocol for Active Directory. LDAP is an industry-standard protocol, established by the Internet Engineering Task Force (IETF), that allows users to query and update information in a directory service. Active Directory supports both LDAP version 2 and LDAP version 3. See also Active Directory; directory service; Internet Engineering Task Force (IETF); protocol.

load balancing A technique used by Windows Clustering to scale the performance of a server-based program (such as a Web server) by distributing its client requests across multiple servers within the cluster. Each host can specify the load percentage that it will handle, or the load can be equally distributed across all the hosts. If a host fails, Windows Clustering dynamically redistributes the load among the remaining hosts. See also cluster; host.

local area network (LAN) A communications network connecting a group of computers, printers, and other devices located within a relatively limited area (for example, a building). A LAN enables any connected device to interact with any other on the network.

local group A security group that can be granted rights and permissions on only resources on the computer on which the group is created. Local groups can have any user accounts that are local to the computer as members, as well as users, groups, and computers from a domain to which the computer belongs.

Locale Identifier (LCID) A unique integer that represents a locale for the formatting style of dates, times, currencies and other values, which is different for each geographical location. In Internet Information Services (IIS), the default LCID is the same as the system locale. See also LOCALE_SYSTEM_DEFAULT.

LOCALE_SYSTEM_DEFAULT The default system locale. There is also a default user locale. See also Locale Identifier (LCID).

LocalHost A placeholder for the name of the computer on which a program is running. LocalHost uses the reserved loopback IP address (127.0.0.1 in IPv4 and ::1 in IPv6).

log file A file that stores messages generated by an application, service, or operating system. These messages are used to track the operations performed. For example, Web servers maintain log files listing every request made to the server. Log files are usually plain text (ASCII) files and often have a .log extension.

In Backup, a file that contains a record of the date the tapes were created and the names of files and directories successfully backed up and restored. The Performance Logs and Alerts service also creates log files.

See also American Standard Code for Information Interchange (ASCII).

logical drive A volume that you create within an extended partition on a basic master boot record (MBR) disk. Logical drives are similar to primary partitions, except that you are limited to four primary partitions per disk, whereas you can create an unlimited number of logical drives per disk. A logical drive can be formatted and assigned a drive letter. See also extended partition.

M

Mail or Messaging Application Programming Interface (MAPI) An open and comprehensive messaging interface that is used by developers to create messaging and workgroup applications, such as e-mail, scheduling, calendars, and document management. In a distributed client/server environment, MAPI provides enterprise messaging services within Windows Open Services Architecture (WOSA).

malicious user A person who has legitimate access to a system and poses a security threat to it, such as someone who tries to elevate their user rights to gain access to unauthorized data. See also security; user rights.

Management Information Base (MIB)   Information about aspects of a network that can be managed by using the Simple Network Management Protocol (SNMP). This information is formatted in MIB files that are provided for each service that can be monitored. Most third-party monitors (clients) use SNMP and MIB files to monitor Web, File Transfer Protocol (FTP), and other Windows services. Using SNMP, developers or system administrators can write their own custom monitoring applications.

MAPI   See definition for Mail or Messaging Application Programming Interface (MAPI).

master properties   In Internet Information Services (IIS), properties that are set at the computer level that become default settings for all Web or File Transfer Protocol (FTP) sites on that computer. See also inheritance.

MD5   An industry-standard one-way, 128-bit hashing scheme, developed by RSA Data Security, Inc., and used by various Point-to-Point Protocol (PPP) vendors for encrypted authentication. A hashing scheme is a method for transforming data (for example, a password) in such a way that the result is unique and cannot be changed back to its original form. The Challenge Handshake Authentication Protocol (CHAP) uses challenge-response with one-way MD5 hashing on the response. In this way, you can prove to the server that you know your password without actually sending the password over the network. See also hash algorithm; MD5.

MDAC   See definition for Microsoft Data Access Components (MDAC).

Message Queuing   A message queuing and routing system for Windows that enables distributed applications running at different times to communicate across heterogeneous networks and with computers that may be offline. Message Queuing provides guaranteed message delivery, efficient routing, security, and priority-based messaging. Formerly known as *MSMQ*.

metabase   A hierarchical store of configuration information and schema that is used to configure Internet Information Services (IIS). The metabase performs some of the same functions as the system registry, but it uses less disk space. In physical terms, the metabase is a combination of the MetaBase.xml and MBSchema.xml files and the in-memory metabase.

metabase configuration file   A file that stores Internet Information Services (IIS) configuration settings to disk. This file is named MetaBase.xml by default. When IIS is started or restarted, the configuration settings are read from MetaBase.xml into the IIS cache in memory, which is called the in-memory metabase.

metabase schema   The master configuration file (MBSchema.xml) supplied with Internet Information Services (IIS) that contains all of the predefined properties from which metabase entries are derived.

metadata   Data that is used to describe other data. For example, Indexing Service must maintain data that describes the data in the content index.

method   A procedure (function) that acts on an object.

MIB   See definition for Management Information Base (MIB).

Microsoft Data Access Components (MDAC)   Consists of ActiveX Data Objects (ADO), the Remote Data Service (RDS), Microsoft OLE DB Provider for ODBC, Open Database Connectivity (ODBC), ODBC drivers for Microsoft SQL Server, Microsoft Access and other desktop databases, as well as Oracle databases.

middle tier   The logical layer between a user interface or Web client and the database. This is typically where the Web server resides and where business objects are instantiated. Also known as *application server tier*. See also client tier; data source tier.

modem (modulator/demodulator)   A device that enables computer information to be transmitted and received over a telephone line. The transmitting modem translates digital computer data into analog signals that can be carried over a telephone line. The receiving modem translates the analog signals back to digital form.

MSMQ   See definition for Message Queuing.

MTA   See definition for multithreaded apartment (MTA).

multiple identities   Multiple Web sites that are hosted on one computer. Also called virtual servers.

Multipurpose Internet Mail Extensions mapping (MIME mapping)   A method of configuring browsers to view files that are in multiple formats. An extension of the Internet mail protocol that enables the sending of 8-bit-based e-mail messages, which are used to support extended character sets, voice mail, facsimile images, and so on.

multithreaded apartment (MTA) A form of multithreading that is supported by Component Object Model (COM). In a multithreaded apartment model, all of the threads in the process that have been initialized as free-threaded reside in a single apartment.

multithreading Running several processes in rapid sequence within a single program, regardless of which logical method of multitasking is being used by the operating system. Because the user's sense of time is much slower than the processing speed of a computer, multitasking appears to be simultaneous, even though only one task at a time can use a computer processing cycle.

N

name resolution The process of having software translate between names that are easy for users to work with and numerical IP addresses, which are difficult for users but necessary for TCP/IP communications. Name resolution can be provided by software components such as DNS or WINS. See also Domain Name System (DNS); Transmission Control Protocol/Internet Protocol (TCP/IP); Windows Internet Name Service (WINS).

namespace A naming convention that defines a set of unique names for resources in a network. For DNS, a hierarchical naming structure that identifies each network resource and its place in the hierarchy of the namespace. For WINS, a flat naming structure that identifies each network resource using a single, unique name. See also Domain Name System (DNS); Windows Internet Name Service (WINS).

Network File System (NFS) A service for distributed computing systems that provides a distributed file system, eliminating the need for keeping multiple copies of files on separate computers.

network latency The time it takes for information to be transferred between computers in a network.

Network Load Balancing A Windows network component that uses a distributed algorithm to load-balance Internet Protocol (IP) traffic across a number of hosts, helping to enhance the scalability and availability of mission-critical, IP-based services, such as Terminal Services, Web services, virtual private networking, and streaming media. It also provides high availability by detecting host failures and automatically redistributing traffic to the surviving hosts. See also availability; cluster; host; scalability.

Network News Transfer Protocol (NNTP) A protocol that is used to distribute network news messages to NNTP servers and to NNTP clients (news readers) on the Internet. NNTP provides for the distribution, inquiry, retrieval, and posting of news articles by using a reliable, stream-based transmission of news on the Internet. NNTP is designed in such a way that news articles are stored on a server in a central database, so that users can select specific items to read. Indexing, cross-referencing, and expiration of old messages are also provided. NNTP is defined in RFC 977.

NNTP See definition for Network News Transfer Protocol (NNTP).

node For tree structures, a location on the tree that can have links to one or more items below it.

For local area networks (LANs), a device that is connected to the network and is capable of communicating with other network devices.

For server clusters, a computer system that is an active or inactive member of a cluster.

See also local area network (LAN); server cluster.

NTFS file system An advanced file system that provides performance, security, reliability, and advanced features that are not found in any version of file allocation table (FAT). For example, NTFS guarantees volume consistency by using standard transaction logging and recovery techniques. If a system fails, NTFS uses its log file and checkpoint information to restore the consistency of the file system. NTFS also provides advanced features, such as file and folder permissions, encryption, disk quotas, and compression. See also FAT32; file allocation table (FAT).

O

object An entity, such as a file, folder, shared folder, printer, or Active Directory object, described by a distinct, named set of attributes. For example, the attributes of a File object include its name, location, and size; the attributes of an Active Directory User object might include the user's first name, last name, and e-mail address.

For OLE and ActiveX, an object can also be any piece of information that can be linked to, or embedded into, another object.

See also Active Directory; attribute.

object identifier (OID) An extensible, unique identification number for attributes and classes. Performance counter names have their own object identifiers, which are listed in Management Information Base (MIB) files, to provide performance monitoring applications with access to the counters. See also Management Information Base (MIB); Simple Network Management Protocol (SNMP).

Object Linking and Embedding (OLE) A set of integration standards for transferring and sharing information among client applications. Also, a protocol that enables the creation of compound documents with embedded links to applications, so that a user does not have to switch among applications to make revisions. OLE is based on the Component Object Model (COM), and it enables the development of reusable objects that operate across multiple applications.

Object Linking and Embedding Database (OLE DB) Data-access interfaces that provide consistent access to Structured Query Language (SQL) data sources and non-SQL data sources across an organization and the Internet. See also structured query language (SQL).

object-cache scavenger The code that periodically scans the cache for objects to be discarded. It deletes files that have not been used recently and therefore are unlikely to be used again in the near future.

octet In programming, an octet refers to eight bits or one byte. IP addresses, for example, are typically represented in dotted-decimal notation; that is, with the decimal value of each octet of the address separated by a period.

ODBC See definition for Open Database Connectivity (ODBC).

OID See definition for object identifier (OID).

OLE See definition for Object Linking and Embedding (OLE).

OLE DB See definition for Object Linking and Embedding Database (OLE DB).

Open Database Connectivity (ODBC) An application programming interface (API) that enables applications to access data from a variety of existing data sources. A standard specification for cross-platform database access.

out-of-process For IIS 5.0 isolation mode, ISAPI extensions that are hosted in a surrogate process called DLLHOST.exe, which is managed by COM+. See also IIS 5.0 isolation mode.

out-of-process component A Component Object Model (COM) component that runs in a separate process space from its client. See also process isolation.

out-of-process, pooled See definition for pooled out-of-process.

P-Q

packet An Open Systems Interconnection (OSI) network layer transmission unit that consists of binary information representing both data and a header containing an identification number, source and destination addresses, and error-control data.

page See definition for Web page.

parameter A value that is passed in a function call.

partition A portion of a physical disk that functions as though it were a physically separate disk. After you create a partition, you must format it and assign it a drive letter before you can store data on it.

On basic disks, partitions are known as basic volumes, which include primary partitions and logical drives. On dynamic disks, partitions are known as dynamic volumes, which include simple, striped, spanned, mirrored, and RAID-5 volumes.

See also extended partition.

password authentication See definition for authentication.

path, physical See definition for physical path.

path, relative See definition for relative path.

performance counter In System Monitor, a data item that is associated with a performance object. For each counter selected, System Monitor presents a value corresponding to a particular aspect of the performance that is defined for the performance object.

Perl (Practical Extraction and Report Language) An interpreted language that is based on C and several UNIX utilities. Perl has powerful string-handling features for extracting information from text files. Perl can assemble a string and send it to the shell as a command; therefore, it is often used for system administration tasks. A program in Perl is known as a script. Perl was devised by Larry Wall at the NASA Jet Propulsion Laboratory. See also script.

permission A rule associated with an object to regulate which users can gain access to the object and in what manner. Permissions are assigned or denied by the object's owner. See also object.

physical path A universal naming convention (UNC) directory path. See also relative path.

ping A utility that verifies connections to one or more remote hosts. The ping command uses Internet Control Message Protocol (ICMP) echo request and echo reply packets to determine whether a particular Internet Protocol (IP) system on a network is functional. **Ping** is useful for diagnosing IP network or router failures. See also host; Internet Control Message Protocol (ICMP); Internet Protocol (IP); packet.

plaintext Data that is not encrypted. Sometimes also called *cleartext*. See also encryption.

Point-to-Point Protocol (PPP) A set of industry-standard framing and authentication protocols that are included with Windows to ensure interoperability with other remote access software. PPP negotiates configuration parameters for multiple layers of the Open Systems Interconnection (OSI) model. The Internet standard for serial communications, PPP defines how data packets are exchanged with other Internet-based systems using a modem connection.

Point-to-Point Tunneling Protocol (PPTP) A specification for virtual private networks (VPNs) in which some nodes of a local area network (LAN) are connected through the Internet. PPTP is an open industry standard that supports widely used networking protocols: Internet Protocol (IP), Internetwork Packet Exchange (IPX), and Microsoft NetBIOS Extended User Interface (NetBEUI). Organizations can use PPTP to outsource their remote dial-up needs to an Internet service provider or to other carriers to reduce cost and complexity.

policies Conditions that are set by the system administrator, for example, how quickly account passwords expire and how many unsuccessful logon attempts are allowed before a user is locked out. Policies manage accounts to help prevent exhaustive or random password attacks.

pooled out-of-process For IIS 5.0 isolation mode, a special Web Application Manager (WAM) package that hosts all out-of-process ISAPI extensions that are set to medium isolation within the same DLLHOST.exe process. See also IIS 5.0 isolation mode; out-of-process; Web Application Manager (WAM).

port number A number that identifies a certain Internet application. For example, the default port number for the WWW service is 80.

PPP See definition for Point-to-Point Protocol (PPP).

PPTP See definition for Point-to-Point Tunneling Protocol (PPTP).

private key The secret half of a cryptographic key pair that is used with a public key algorithm. Private keys are typically used to decrypt a symmetric session key, digitally sign data, or decrypt data that has been encrypted with the corresponding public key. See also public key; public key encryption.

process An operating system object that consists of an executable program, a set of virtual memory addresses, and one or more threads. When a program runs, a process is created.

process accounting A feature of Internet Information Services (IIS) that administrators can use to monitor and log resource consumption of Common Gateway Interface (CGI) scripts and out-of-process applications.

process isolation Running an application or component out of process. See also out-of-process component.

property inheritance See definition for inheritance.

protocol A set of rules and conventions for sending information over a network. These rules govern the content, format, timing, sequencing, and error control of messages exchanged among network devices. See also Internet Protocol (IP); Transmission Control Protocol/Internet Protocol (TCP/IP).

provider See definition for WMI provider.

proxy A software program that connects a user to a remote destination through an intermediary gateway.

proxy server A firewall component that manages Internet traffic to and from a local area network (LAN) and that can provide other features, such as document caching and access control. A proxy server can improve performance by supplying frequently requested data, such as a popular Web page, and it can filter and discard requests that the owner does not consider appropriate, such as requests for unauthorized access to proprietary files. See also firewall; local area network (LAN).

public key The nonsecret half of a cryptographic key pair that is used with a public key algorithm. Public keys are typically used when encrypting a session key, verifying a digital signature, or encrypting data that can be decrypted with the corresponding private key. See also key; private key; public key encryption.

public key encryption A method of encryption that uses two encryption keys that are mathematically related. One key is called the *private key* and is kept confidential. The other is called the *public key* and is freely given out to all potential correspondents. In a typical scenario, a sender uses the receiver's public key to encrypt a message. Only the receiver has the related private key to decrypt the message. The complexity of the relationship between the public key and the private key means that, provided the keys are long enough, it is computationally infeasible to determine one from the other. Also called *asymmetric encryption*. See also encryption; private key; public key; symmetric encryption.

public-key algorithm An asymmetric cipher that uses two keys, one for encryption, the public key, and the other for decryption, the private key. See also asymmetric key algorithm; decryption; encryption; private key; public key.

R

RAID See definition for Redundant Array of Independent Disks (RAID).

random access memory (RAM) Memory that can be read from or written to by a computer or other devices. Information stored in RAM is lost when the computer is turned off.

realm A term that is sometimes used for domain, in this case to refer to user domains that are established for security reasons, not Internet domains. For password-protected files, the name of the protected resource or area on the server. If the user tries to access the protected resource while browsing, the name of the realm usually appears in the dialog box that asks for a user name and password.

redirection Redirection can be used to automatically send a user from an outdated Uniform Resource Locator (URL) to a new URL.

Redundant Array of Independent Disks (RAID) A data storage method in which data, along with information used for error correction, such as parity bits, is distributed among two or more hard disk drives to improve performance and reliability. The hard disk array is governed by array management software and a disk controller, which handles the error correction. RAID is generally used on network servers. Several defined levels of RAID offer differing trade-offs among access speed, reliability, and cost. Windows includes three of the RAID levels: Level 0, Level 1, and Level 5.

registry A database repository for information about a computer's configuration. The registry contains information that Windows continually references during operation, such as: profiles for each user; the programs installed on the computer and the types of documents that each can create; property settings for folders and program icons; what hardware exists on the system; and which ports are being used.

The registry is organized hierarchically as a tree, and it is made up of keys and their subkeys, hives, and entries.

See also key; subkey.

relative path A universal naming convention (UNC) directory path with placeholders, or wildcards, at some levels. Also, the physical path that corresponds to a Uniform Resource Locator (URL). See also physical path.

remote procedure call (RPC) In programming, a call by one program to a second program on a remote system. The second program usually performs a task and returns the results of that task to the first program.

remotely administered server A server that you can administer by using a different computer. You typically access this type of server by using a network connection. A remotely administered server can have a local keyboard, mouse, or video card and monitor. If it does not have these peripherals attached, it is also known as a *headless server*. Such servers are often housed in a physically secure location. See also server.

replication The copying from one server node to another of either content or the configuration metabase, or both. This copying can be done either manually or automatically by using replication software. Replication is a necessary function of clustering that ensures fault tolerance. See also fault tolerance.

Request for Comments (RFC) The document series, begun in 1969, that describes the Internet suite of protocols and related experiments. Not all (in fact, very few) RFCs describe Internet standards, but all Internet standards are written up as RFCs. The RFC series of documents is unusual in that the proposed protocols are forwarded by the Internet research and development community, acting on its own behalf, as opposed to the formally reviewed and standardized protocols that are promoted by organizations such as the American National Standards Institute (ANSI).

router An intermediary device on a communications network that expedites message delivery. On a single network linking many computers through a mesh of possible connections, a router receives transmitted messages and forwards them to their correct destinations over the most efficient available route. On an interconnected set of local area networks (LANs) using the same communications protocols, a router serves the somewhat different function of acting as a link between LANs, enabling messages to be sent from one LAN to another.

RPC See definition for remote procedure call (RPC).

RSA A public-key encryption standard for Internet security. This acronym derives from the last names of the inventors of the technology: Rivest, Shamir, and Adleman.

S

scalability A measure of how well a computer, service, or application can grow to meet increasing performance demands. For server clusters, the ability to incrementally add one or more systems to an existing cluster when the overall load of the cluster exceeds its capabilities. See also server cluster.

schema A representation of the structure of something. Classes in Visual Basic and C++ can be said to be schemas of objects, and objects are instances of classes. In Internet Information Services (IIS), the metabase schema represents the structure of the metabase configuration file.

scope In programming, the extent to which an identifier, such as a constant, data type, variable, or routine, can be referenced within a program. Scope can be global or local. Scope can also be affected by the redefinition of identifiers, for example, by giving the same name to both a global variable and a local variable.

script A kind of program that consists of a set of instructions for an application or utility program. A script can be embedded in a Web page. See also ActiveX; common gateway interface (CGI).

scripting engine A program that interprets and executes a script. See also script.

search expression See Other Definition

search interface See Other Definition

search string See Other Definition

Secure Hash Algorithm (SHA-1) An algorithm that generates a 160-bit hash value from an arbitrary amount of input data. SHA-1 is used with the Digital Signature Algorithm (DSA) in the Digital Signature Standard (DSS), among other places. See also hash algorithm.

Secure Hypertext Transfer Protocol A protocol that provides a secure Hypertext Transfer Protocol (HTTP) connection. See also Hypertext Transfer Protocol (HTTP); protocol.

Secure Sockets Layer (SSL) A protocol that supplies secure data communication through data encryption and decryption. SSL uses RSA public-key encryption for specific TCP/IP ports. It is intended for handling commerce payments. An alternative method is Secure-HTTP (S-HTTP), which is used to encrypt specific Web documents, rather than the entire session. SSL is a general-purpose encryption standard. SSL can also be used for Web applications that require a secure link, such as e-commerce applications, or for controlling access to Web-based subscription services.

security On a network, protection of a computer system and its data from harm or loss, implemented especially so that only authorized users can gain access to shared files. See also authorization.

security context The security attributes or rules that are currently in effect. For example, the rules that govern what a user can do to a protected object are determined by security information in the user's access token and in the object's security descriptor. Together, the access token and the security descriptor form a security context for the user's actions on the object. See also object.

Selectable Cryptographic Service Provider See definition for cryptographic service provider (CSP).

server In general, a computer that provides shared resources to network users. See also client; shared resource.

server certificate A unique digital identification that forms the basis of a Web server's Secure Sockets Layer (SSL) security features. Server certificates are obtained from a mutually trusted, third-party organization, and they provide a way for users to authenticate the identity of a Web site.

server cluster A group of computers, known as *nodes*, working together as a single system to ensure that mission-critical applications and resources remain available to clients. A server cluster presents the appearance of a single server to a client. See also cluster; node.

server node An individual computer in a server cluster.

server process A process that hosts Component Object Model (COM) components. A COM component can be loaded into a surrogate server process, either on the client computer (local) or on another computer (remote). It can also be loaded into a client application process (in-process).

server-side include (SSI) A mechanism for including dynamic text in World Wide Web documents. Server-side includes are special command codes that are recognized and interpreted by the server; their output is placed in the document body before the document is sent to the browser. Server-side includes can be used, for example, to include the Date and Time stamp in the text of the file.

session key A digital key that is created by a client, encrypted, and then sent to a server. This key is used to encrypt data that is sent by the client.

shared resource Any device, data, or program that is used by more than one program or one other device. For Windows, *shared resource* refers to any resource that is made available to network users, such as folders, files, printers, and named pipes. *Shared resource* can also refer to a resource on a server that is available to network users. See also server.

Simple Mail Transfer Protocol (SMTP) A TCP/IP protocol for sending messages from one computer to another on a network. This protocol is used on the Internet to route e-mail.

Simple Network Management Protocol (SNMP) The network management protocol of TCP/IP. In SNMP, agents or clients monitor the activity of various devices on the network and report to the network console workstation. The agents or clients can be hardware as well as software. Control information about each device or service is maintained in a structure known as a management information block. One way to access this information is with Performance Counters. See also Management Information Base (MIB).

single-threaded apartment (STA) A form of threading that is supported by Component Object Model (COM). In a single-threaded apartment model, all objects are executed on a single thread and each thread resides within its own apartment.

SMTP See definition for Simple Mail Transfer Protocol (SMTP).

snap-in A type of tool that you can add to a console supported by Microsoft Management Console (MMC). A stand-alone snap-in can be added by itself; an extension snap-in can be added only to extend the function of another snap-in.

sniffer An application or device that can read, monitor, and capture network data exchanges and read network packets. If the packets are not encrypted, a sniffer provides a full view of the data inside the packet. See also packet.

SNMP See definition for Simple Network Management Protocol (SNMP).

socket An identifier for a particular service on a particular node on a network. The socket consists of a node address and a port number, which identifies the service. For example, port 80 on an Internet node indicates a Web server. There are two kinds of sockets: streams (bidirectional) and datagrams. See also datagram; node.

SSI See definition for server-side include (SSI).

SSL See definition for Secure Sockets Layer (SSL).

STA See definition for single-threaded apartment (STA).

stateful object An object that holds private state accumulated from the execution of one or more client calls.

stateless object An object that does not hold private state accumulated from the execution of one or more client calls.

static page A Hypertext Markup Language (HTML) page that is prepared in advance of a request for it and that is sent to the client upon request. This page takes no special action when it is requested. See also dynamic page.

structured query language (SQL) A widely accepted standard database sublanguage used in querying, updating, and managing relational databases.

subkey An element of the registry that contains entries or other subkeys. A tier of the registry that is immediately below a key or a subtree (if the subtree has no keys). See also key; registry.

subnet mask A 32-bit value that enables the recipient of Internet Protocol version 4 (IPv4) packets to distinguish the network ID and host ID portions of the IPv4 address. Typically, subnet masks use the format 255.*x*.*x*.*x*. IPv6 uses network prefix notations rather than subnet masks. See also IP address.

symmetric encryption An encryption algorithm that requires the same secret key to be used for both encryption and decryption. Because of its speed, symmetric encryption is typically used when a message sender needs to encrypt large amounts of data. Also called *secret key encryption*. See also public key encryption.

System Data Source Name (DSN) A name that can be used by any process on the computer. Internet Information Services (IIS) uses system DSNs to access Open Database Connectivity (ODBC) data sources.

systemroot The path and folder name where the Windows system files are located. Typically, this is C:\Windows, although you can designate a different drive or folder when you install Windows. You can use the value %systemroot% to replace the actual location of the folder that contains the Windows system files. To identify your systemroot folder, click **Start**, click **Run**, type **%systemroot%**, and then click **OK**.

Systems Network Architecture (SNA) A communications framework developed by IBM to define network functions and establish standards for enabling computers to share and process data.

T

T1 A U.S. telephone standard for a transmission facility at digital signal level 1 (DS1) with 1.544 megabits per second in North America and 2.048 megabits per second in Europe. The bit rate is with the equivalent bandwidth of approximately twenty-four 56-kilobits-per-second lines. A T1 circuit is capable of serving a minimum of 48 modems at 28.8 kilobits per second or 96 modems at 14.4 kilobits per second. T1 circuits are also used for voice telephone connections. A single T1 line carries 24 telephone connections with 24 telephone numbers. When it is used for voice transmission, a T1 connection must be split into 24 separate circuits.

T3 A U.S. telephone standard for a transmission facility at digital signal level 3 (DS3). T3 is equivalent in bandwidth to 28 T1's, and the bit rate is 44.736 megabits per second. T3 is sometimes called a 45-meg circuit.

TCP/IP See definition for Transmission Control Protocol/Internet Protocol (TCP/IP).

Telnet A protocol that enables an Internet user to log on to and enter commands on a remote computer linked to the Internet, as if the user were using a text-based terminal directly attached to that computer. Telnet is part of the TCP/IP suite of protocols. The term *telnet* also refers to the software (client or server component) that implements this protocol. See also protocol; Transmission Control Protocol/Internet Protocol (TCP/IP).

thread A type of object within a process that runs program instructions. Using multiple threads allows concurrent operations within a process and enables one process to run different parts of its program on different processors simultaneously. A thread has its own set of registers, its own kernel stack, a thread environment block, and a user stack in the address space of its process. See also kernel.

throttling Controlling the maximum amount of bandwidth that is dedicated to Internet traffic on a server. This feature is useful if there are other services (such as e-mail) sharing the server over a busy link.

time-out A setting that automatically cancels an unanswered client request after a certain period of time.

TP   See definition for transaction processing (TP).

transaction processing (TP)   The real-time handling of computerized business transactions as they are received by the system. Also called online transaction processing (OLTP).

Transmission Control Protocol/Internet Protocol (TCP/IP)   A set of networking protocols widely used on the Internet that provides communications across interconnected networks of computers with diverse hardware architectures and various operating systems. TCP/IP includes standards for how computers communicate and conventions for connecting networks and routing traffic. See also Internet Protocol (IP); protocol.

Transport Layer Security (TLS) encryption   A generic security protocol similar to Secure Sockets Layer (SSL), used with Simple Mail Transfer Protocol (SMTP). See also Secure Sockets Layer (SSL).

Triple DES (3DES)   An implementation of Data Encryption Standard (DES) encryption that employs three iterations of cryptographic operations on each segment of data. Each iteration uses a 56-bit key for encryption, which yields 168-bit encryption for the data. Although 3DES is slower than DES because of the additional cryptographic calculations, its protection is far stronger than DES. See also cryptography; Data Encryption Standard (DES); encryption.

two-tier architecture   See definition for client/server architecture.

type library   A binary file that describes a component's methods, properties, and data structure.

U

UNC (Universal Naming Convention) name   The full name of a resource on a network. It conforms to the *\\servername\sharename* syntax, where *servername* is the name of the server and *sharename* is the name of the shared resource. UNC names of directories or files can also include the directory path under the share name, with the following syntax:

\\servername\sharename\directory\filename

Uniform Resource Locator (URL)   A naming convention that uniquely identifies the location of a computer, directory, or file on the Internet. A URL also specifies the appropriate Internet protocol, such as Hypertext Transfer Protocol (HTTP) or File Transfer Protocol (FTP). An example of a URL is http://www.microsoft.com.

Universal Naming Convention (UNC)   A convention for naming files and other resources beginning with two backslashes (\), indicating that the resource exists on a network computer. UNC names conform to the *\\servername\sharename* syntax, where *servername* is the server's name and *sharename* is the name of the shared resource. The UNC name of a directory or file can also include the directory path after the share name, by using the following syntax: *\\servername\sharename\directory\filename.*

upload   In communications, the process of transferring a copy of a file from a local computer to a remote computer by means of a modem or network. With a modem-based communications link, the process generally involves instructing the remote computer to prepare to receive the file on its disk and then wait for the transmission to begin.

URL   See definition for Uniform Resource Locator (URL).

URL directory   See definition for virtual directory.

URL mapping   The process of associating a Uniform Resource Locator (URL) with a physical directory. See also virtual directory.

usage data   Information that an administrator can use to learn how other people access and use a site. By analyzing this data, an administrator can identify a site's most popular (or unpopular) areas and clarify the most common navigational paths through the site.

user rights   Tasks that a user is permitted to perform on a computer system or domain. There are two types of user rights: privileges and logon rights. An example of a privilege is the right to shut down the system. An example of a logon right is the right to log on to a computer locally. Both types are assigned by administrators to individual users or groups as part of the security settings for the computer. See also domain; group.

user type   A DWORD that specifies how data is used. A user type is assigned to an identifier in the metabase.

UTF-8   A method of character encoding that allows for both single and multibyte characters in one string. UTF-8 files take up more space than files that are stored in an American National Standards Institute (ANSI) format. Internet Information Services (IIS) supports Web files that are saved in UTF-8 format or in ANSI format. See also code page.

V

virtual directory A directory name, used in an address, that corresponds to a physical directory on the server. Sometimes called URL mapping.

virtual server A virtual computer that resides on a Hypertext Transfer Protocol (HTTP) server but appears to the user as a separate HTTP server. Several virtual servers can reside on one computer, each capable of running its own programs and each with individualized access to input and peripheral devices. Each virtual server has its own domain name and IP address, and each appears to the user as an individual Web site or File Transfer Protocol (FTP) site. Some Internet service providers (ISPs) use virtual servers for those clients who want to use their own domain names. Also called a Web site.

volatile objects Typically, files that a Web site administrator updates frequently.

W-Z

W3C See definition for World Wide Web Consortium (W3C).

W3SVC See definition for World Wide Web Publishing Service (WWW service).

WAM See definition for Web Application Manager (WAM).

WBEM See definition for Web-Based Enterprise Management (WBEM).

Web application A software program that uses Hypertext Transfer Protocol (HTTP) for its core communication protocol and that delivers Web-based information to the user in the Hypertext Markup Language (HTML) language. Also called a Web-based application.

Web Application Manager (WAM) For IIS 5.0 isolation mode, a COM+ application package that works with DLLHOST.exe to host out-of-process ISAPI extensions. Provides communication between DLLHOST.exe and INETINFO.exe. See also IIS 5.0 isolation mode.

Web Distributed Authoring and Versioning (WebDAV) An extension to the Hypertext Transfer Protocol (HTTP) 1.1 standard that facilitates access to files and directories through an HTTP connection. Remote authors can add, search, delete, or change directories and documents and their properties.

Web farm A Network Load Balancing cluster of IIS servers that support client Web site requests.

Web garden An application pool served by more than one worker process.

Web page A World Wide Web document. A Web page typically consists of a Hypertext Markup Language (HTML) file, with associated files for graphics and scripts, in a particular directory on a particular computer. It is identified by a Uniform Resource Locator (URL).

Web server In general, a computer that is equipped with server software that uses Internet protocols such as Hypertext Transfer Protocol (HTTP) and File Transfer Protocol (FTP) to respond to Web client requests on a TCP/IP network.

Web service extensions ISAPIs and CGIs that extend Internet Information Services (IIS) functionality beyond serving static pages.

Web-Based Enterprise Management (WBEM) An industry initiative to develop a standard technology for accessing management information about systems in an enterprise environment. The Microsoft implementation of Web-based Enterprise Management is Windows Management Instrumentation (WMI).

WebDAV See definition for Web Distributed Authoring and Versioning (WebDAV).

wide area network (WAN) A communications network connecting geographically separated locations that uses long-distance links of third-party telecommunications vendors. See also local area network (LAN).

wildcard character A keyboard character that can be used to represent one or many characters when conducting a query. The question mark (?) represents a single character, and the asterisk (*) represents one or more characters.

Windows Internet Name Service (WINS) A Windows name resolution service for network basic input/output system (NetBIOS) names. WINS is used by hosts running NetBIOS over TCP/IP (NetBT) to register NetBIOS names and to resolve NetBIOS names to Internet Protocol (IP) addresses. See also IP address.

Windows Management Instrumentation (WMI) The Microsoft implementation of Web-Based Enterprise Management (WBEM), which is an industry-wide standard technology for accessing management information about systems in an enterprise environment. WMI uses the Common Information Model (CIM) industry standard to represent managed components in a system. A system developer can develop a WMI interface that allows programmatic access to a system, so that users can write command-line administration scripts and tools. See also Web-Based Enterprise Management (WBEM).

Windows Script Host (WSH) A language-independent scripting host for ActiveX scripting engines on 32-bit Windows platforms.

WMI See definition for Windows Management Instrumentation (WMI).

WMI provider In Windows Management Instrumentation (WMI), a set of interfaces that provide programmatic access to management information in a system. Internet Information Services (IIS) implements a WMI provider in the namespace called MicrosoftIISv2to provide programmatic access to metabase properties and system settings.

worker process The implementation of the core Web server in Internet Information Services (IIS). Worker processes run in W3wp.exe.

worker process isolation mode The new Web process model for Internet Information Services (IIS) 6.0.

worker thread A thread that is created by a component, Internet Server API (ISAPI) extension, or filter to perform asynchronous processing. Using worker threads frees up Internet Information Services (IIS) I/O threads to process additional requests.

working directory The directory in which Web server software is installed.

working set The RAM that is allocated to a process in the Windows operating system.

World Wide Web (WWW) A set of services that run on top of the Internet and provide a cost-effective way of publishing information, supporting collaboration and workflow, and delivering business applications to connected users all over the world. The Web is a collection of Internet host systems that make these services available on the Internet, using the Hypertext Transfer Protocol (HTTP). Web-based information is usually delivered in the form of hypertext and hypermedia, using Hypertext Markup Language (HTML). The most graphical service on the Internet, the Web also has the most sophisticated linking abilities.

World Wide Web Consortium (W3C) An international industry consortium that is jointly hosted by the Massachusetts Institute of Technology Laboratory for Computer Science (MIT/CS) in North America, by the Institut National de Recherche en Informatique et en Automatique (INRIA) in Europe, and by the Keio University Shonan Fujisawa Campus in Asia. W3C was founded in 1994 to develop common standards for the World Wide Web. Initially, the W3C was established in collaboration with CERN, where the Web originated, with support from the Defense Advanced Research Projects Agency (DARPA) and the European Commission.

World Wide Web Publishing Service (WWW service) The service that manages the Internet Information Services (IIS) core components that process HTTP requests and configure and manage Web applications. Formerly known as W3SVC.

WSH See definition for Windows Script Host (WSH).

WWW See definition for World Wide Web (WWW).

WWW Service Administration and Monitoring component A component of the World Wide Web Publishing Service (WWW service) in Internet Information Services (IIS) that is responsible for configuration, by means of the metabase, and for worker process management.

XML See definition for Extensible Markup Language (XML).

Index

Special Characters

A

B

C

I-J

T

X-Z

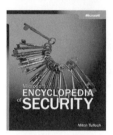
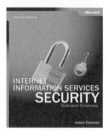

In-depth technical information
for Microsoft Windows Server 2003

Our Windows Server 2003 TECHNICAL REFERENCE series is designed for IT professionals who need in-depth information about specific topics such as TCP/IP protocols and services supported by Windows Server 2003, Internet Information Services security, Active Directory Services, and Virtual Private Networks. Written by leading technical experts, these books include hands-on examples, best practices, and technical tips. Topics are discussed by presenting real-world scenarios and practical how-to information to help IT professionals deploy, support, maintain, optimize, and troubleshoot Microsoft products and technologies. You start with the fundamentals and build comprehension layer by layer until you understand the subject completely.

Microsoft® Windows® Server 2003 TCP/IP Protocols and Services Technical Reference
ISBN: 0-7356-1291-9
U.S.A. $49.99
Canada $76.99

Microsoft Internet Information Services Security Technical Reference
ISBN: 0-7356-1572-1
U.S.A. $49.99
Canada $72.99

Active Directory® Services for Microsoft Windows Server 2003 Technical Reference
ISBN: 0-7356-1577-2
U.S.A. $49.99
Canada $76.99

Deploying Virtual Private Networks with Microsoft Windows Server 2003 Technical Reference
ISBN: 0-7356-1576-4
U.S.A. $49.99
Canada $76.99

To learn more about the full line of Microsoft Press® products for IT professionals, please visit:

microsoft.com/mspress/IT

Minimum System Requirements

To use the Resource Kit tools and other materials, you need:

- PC with 233 MHz or higher processor
- 128 MB of RAM minimum (256 MB of RAM or higher recommended)
- Microsoft Windows Server 2003 or Microsoft Windows XP Professional operating system
- 30 MB of available hard disk space
- Microsoft Internet Explorer 5.01 or higher
- Super VGA (800 x 600) or higher resolution monitor
- CD-ROM or DVD-ROM drive
- Keyboard and Microsoft mouse or compatible pointing device

Note: Although the IIS 6.0 Resource Kit Tools will install on both Windows Server 2003 and Windows XP Professional, not all the tools will function correctly on Windows XP Professional. The tool documentation that is installed with the IIS 6.0 Resource Kit Tools has a System Requirements section for each tool. Please refer to this documentation for more information.

To use Windows Server 2003 Standard Edition Evaluation Software, you need:

- Computer with 550 MHz or higher processor recommended; 133 MHz minimum required; Intel Pentium/Celeron family or AMD K6/Athlon/Duron family or compatible processor.
- 256 MB of RAM or higher recommended; 128 minimum required (maximum 4 GB of RAM).
- 1.5 GB available hard disk space. Actual requirements, including Internet and network access and any related charges, will vary based on your system configuration and the applications and features you choose to install. Additional hard disk space may be required if you are installing over a network.
- CD-ROM or DVD-ROM drive.
- Super VGA (800 x 600) or higher resolution monitor recommended; VGA or hardware that supports console redirection required.
- Keyboard and Microsoft mouse or compatible pointing device, or hardware that supports console redirection.

Uninstall instructions: This time-limited release of Microsoft Windows Server 2003 Standard Edition will expire 180 days after installation. If you decide to discontinue the use of this software, you will need to reinstall your original operating system. You might need to reformat your drive.

Microsoft® Windows® Server 2003
Standard Edition 180-Day Evaluation

The software included in this kit is intended for evaluation and deployment planning purposes only. If you plan to install the software on your primary machine, it is recommended that you back up your existing data prior to installation.

System requirements

To use Microsoft Windows Server 2003 Standard Edition, you need:

- Computer with 550 MHz or higher processor clock speed recommended; 133 MHz minimum required; Intel Pentium/Celeron family, or AMD K6/Athlon/Duron family, or compatible processor (Windows Server 2003 Standard Edition supports up to four CPUs on one server)
- 256 MB of RAM or higher recommended; 128 MB minimum required (maximum 4 GB of RAM)
- 1.25 to 2 GB of available hard-disk space*
- CD-ROM or DVD-ROM drive
- Super VGA (800 × 600) or higher-resolution monitor recommended; VGA or hardware that supports console redirection required
- Keyboard and Microsoft Mouse or compatible pointing device, or hardware that supports console redirection

Additional items or services required to use certain Windows Server 2003 Standard Edition features:

- For Internet access:
  - Some Internet functionality may require Internet access, a Microsoft Passport account, and payment of a separate fee to a service provider; local and/or long-distance telephone toll charges may apply
  - High-speed modem or broadband Internet connection
- For networking:
  - Network adapter appropriate for the type of local-area, wide-area, wireless, or home network to which you wish to connect, and access to an appropriate network infrastructure; access to third-party networks may require additional charges

Note: To ensure that your applications and hardware are Windows Server 2003–ready, be sure to visit **www.microsoft.com/windowsserver2003**.

* Actual requirements will vary based on your system configuration and the applications and features you choose to install. Additional available hard-disk space may be required if you are installing over a network. For more information, please see **www.microsoft.com/windowsserver2003**.

Uninstall instructions

This time-limited release of Microsoft Windows Server 2003 Standard Edition will expire 180 days after installation. If you decide to discontinue the use of this software, you will need to reinstall your original operating system. You may need to reformat your drive.

Get a **Free**
e-mail newsletter, updates,
special offers, links to related books,
and more when you
register online!

Register your Microsoft Press® title on our Web site and you'll get a FREE subscription to our e-mail newsletter, *Microsoft Press Book Connections.* You'll find out about newly released and upcoming books and learning tools, online events, software downloads, special offers and coupons for Microsoft Press customers, and information about major Microsoft® product releases. You can also read useful additional information about all the titles we publish, such as detailed book descriptions, tables of contents and indexes, sample chapters, links to related books and book series, author biographies, and reviews by other customers.

Registration is easy. Just visit this Web page and fill in your information:

http://www.microsoft.com/mspress/register

Microsoft®

Proof of Purchase

Use this page as proof of purchase if participating in a promotion or rebate offer on this title. Proof of purchase must be used in conjunction with other proof(s) of payment such as your dated sales receipt—see offer details.

Internet Information Services (IIS) 6.0 Resource Kit
0-7356-1420-2

CUSTOMER NAME

Microsoft Press, PO Box 97017, Redmond, WA 98073-9830